FROM THE EARTH
How Resources Are Made

HOW OIL IS FORMED

BY KRISTEN RAJCZAK NELSON

 Gareth Stevens
PUBLISHING

Please visit our website, www.garethstevens.com. For a free color catalog of all our high-quality books, call toll free 1-800-542-2595 or fax 1-877-542-2596.

Library of Congress Cataloging-in-Publication Data

Names: Rajczak Nelson, Kristen, author.
Title: How oil is formed / Kristen Rajczak Nelson.
Description: New York : Gareth Stevens Publishing, [2016] | Series:
    From the Earth: how resources are made | Includes bibliographical
    references and index.
Identifiers: LCCN 2016011773 | ISBN 9781482447217 (pbk.) | ISBN 9781482447248 (library bound) | ISBN
9781482447231 (6 pack)
Subjects: LCSH: Petroleum–Geology–Juvenile literature. |
    Petroleum–Juvenile literature. | Petroleum industry and trade–Juvenile
    literature.
Classification: LCC TN870.3 .R35 2016 | DDC 553.2/82–dc23
LC record available at http://lccn.loc.gov/2016011773

Published in 2017 by
Gareth Stevens Publishing
111 East 14th Street, Suite 349
New York, NY 10003

Copyright © 2017 Gareth Stevens Publishing

Designer: Laura Bowen
Editor: Therese Shea

Photo credits: Cover, pp. 1–32 (title bar) Dimec/Shutterstock.com; cover, pp. 1–32 (text box) mattasbestos/
Shutterstock.com; cover, pp. 1–32 (background) Alina G/Shutterstock.com; cover, p. 1 (oil) Ilya Andriyanov/
Shutterstock.com; p. 5 (barrels photo) sakhorn/Shutterstock.com; p. 6 Anan Kaewkhammul/Shutterstock.com;
p. 7 tonton/Shutterstock.com; p. 9 (top left) Biopics/Wikimedia Commons; p. 9 (top right) Jan Hinsch/Science
Photo Library/Getty Images; p. 9 (bottom) De Agostini Picture Library/Getty Images; p. 10 (fern) Anurak
Pongpatimet/Shutterstock.com; p. 10 (coal) Jacek Fulawka/Shutterstock.com; p. 11 (photo) Rich Carey/
Shutterstock.com; p. 11 (cross section) Anil Yanik/Getty Images; p. 12 Edward Kinsman/Getty Images; p. 13
(photo) Monty Rakusen/Getty Images; p. 13 (cross section) Chris Forsey/Getty Images; p. 14 Chubykin Arkady/
Shutterstock.com; p. 15 Lakeview Images/Shutterstock.com; p. 17 Mark A Leman/Getty Images; p. 18 Violet1212/
Wikimedia Commons; p. 19 Oleg Kozlov/Shutterstock.com; p. 20 Matej Kastelic/Shutterstock.com; p. 21
Irene Becker/Moment Mobile/Getty Images; p. 23 Kevork Djansezian/Getty Images News; p. 24 David Sprott/
Shutterstock.com; p. 25 (top) Geo Swan/Wikimedia Commons; p. 25 (turtle and bird) Flickr upload bot/Wikimedia
Commons; p. 27 Justin Sullivan/Getty Images News/Getty Images; p. 28 zhu difeng/Shutterstock.com; p. 29
(photo) TTstudio/Shutterstock.com.

Printed in the United States of America

CPSIA compliance information: Batch #CS16GS: For further information contact Gareth Stevens, New York, New York at 1-800-542-2595.

CONTENTS

Words in the glossary appear in **bold** type the first time they are used in the text.

FUELING OUR LIVES

In most places in the United States, people need cars to get around. So the price of gasoline can have a great effect on how much money people spend each month. What decides the price of gas? Mostly the price of oil does.

Oil is a **natural resource** found deep within Earth. It's a big part of daily life. Most oil is used to make gasoline for cars, but it's also used to make jet fuel, plastic, and chemicals. Before it fuels your car, though, oil goes through a long formation process—one that's millions of years long!

WHAT'S IT CALLED?

Sometimes oil is called petroleum or crude oil. The term "petroleum," however, includes all the liquid, gas, and solid forms of a certain mix of hydrocarbons. Crude oil is the liquid form of petroleum, and that's generally what people mean when they say "oil." Petroleum also includes natural gas and a sticky liquid or solid called bitumen.

PRODUCTS MADE FROM A BARREL OF CRUDE OIL

heavy fuel oil
1 gallon (4 L)

distillates, such as heating oil
1 gallon (4 L)

liquefied petroleum gas
2 gallons (8 L)

jet fuel
4 gallons (15 L)

diesel fuel
12 gallons (45 L)

gasoline
19 gallons (72 L)

other products
7 gallons (27 L)

Crude oil is measured in barrels in the United States. One barrel is equal to 42 gallons (159 L). However, one barrel of oil produces more than 42 gallons of products!

FOSSIL FUELS

Oil, natural gas, and coal are fossil fuels. Fossil fuels are carbon-based matter found beneath Earth's crust that people can use as a source of energy. To tap into the energy of fossil fuels, they need to be heated and mixed with oxygen so that they burn.

Carbon is one of the most common elements in the universe, including on our planet. In fact, it's part of every living thing on Earth. That means your body as well as much of what you eat has carbon in it. Fossil fuels aren't alive, but they form from things that once were!

NUMBER-ONE FOSSIL FUEL?

Because of how much energy is created from oil and how easy it is to transport, it's been the leading fossil fuel used around the world for energy since the mid-1900s. In the United States, coal was the number-one fossil fuel for electricity for a long time. In 2015, natural gas passed it.

crude oil

About 80 percent of all the energy used around the world is created by fossil fuels. Much of it is produced in power plants like this.

7

A LONG, LONG TIME AGO...

Most scientists believe oil began to form millions of years ago, mainly in the Mesozoic era, a time period about 251 to 65.5 million years ago. During this time, dinosaurs roamed Earth, and the oceans were full of plankton. Plankton are tiny plants and animals that float in the oceans and seas. They take in energy from the sun and store it in their bodies as carbon.

In the Mesozoic era, after plankton died, they sunk to the bottom of the oceans. Over time, the remains of these dead plants and animals built up on the ocean floor and were covered with layers of **sediment**.

HYDROCARBONS

Oil is made up of hydrocarbons, which are chemical compounds of carbon and hydrogen atoms. Some hydrocarbons are very simple, but they can also form long chains. Hydrocarbons are found in living trees and plants, including in chemicals called carotenes that make carrots orange and leaves green.

plankton

During the Mesozoic era, which was also the age of the dinosaurs, the bottom of the ocean had little oxygen, which is needed for animal and plant matter to break down. Instead, the matter built up on the ocean floor and was finally covered by sediment.

9

Many sediment layers on top of one another created heat and pressure on the plant and animal remains. Depending on the kind of organic remains, or biomass, and the amount of heat and pressure on an area, either a gas or a liquid was produced. High heat produced oil. But even higher heat or biomass mostly made up of plants produced natural gas. Oil and natural gas are often found near each other.

There's also a **theory** that oil can form naturally, not from organic matter, but from hydrocarbons deep within Earth seeping up into the crust and transforming into the fossil fuel. Many scientists don't believe this is true, however.

HOW COAL FORMS

All the fossil fuels we use formed from some kind of biomass under pressure and heat for millions of years. Oil and natural gas formed from ocean plants and animals. Coal was produced from the remains of plants such as ferns that lived mainly about 360 to 250 million years ago.

fern

coal

HOW OIL FORMS

Tiny ocean plants and animals die.

Remains of ocean plants and animals build up on the bottom of the ocean.

Sediment and more remains pile on top of existing remains.

Heat and pressure build up.

Oil and natural gas form over a long time.

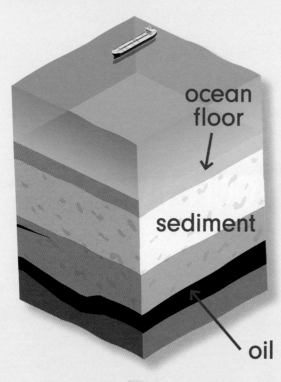

ocean floor

sediment

oil

The formation of oil may seem quick and easy when written out in steps like these, but it takes a lot of time, heat, and pressure!

11

MOVING UNDERGROUND

Once oil forms, it moves through the rock around it by means of tiny holes called pores. It keeps moving until it reaches the surface or until an **impermeable** rock or clay layer stops it. The oil trapped under these layers, called cap rocks, is what companies that extract, or remove, oil are looking for!

Oil **deposits** are called reservoirs. Since natural gas forms in a similar way, it's commonly also found in these reservoirs, as is some water. They separate in layers within the reservoir. Oil is **denser** than natural gas, so it's found in a deeper layer. Water is found below both fossil fuels.

WHAT RESERVOIRS LOOK LIKE

The word "reservoir" is also used to describe a body of water. That's not what an oil reservoir looks like, though! It just looks like rock. The oil is in tiny droplets found in the pores of the rock. There are no puddles of black oil to be found.

oil sandstone

Huge machines like this one are used to extract oil from reservoir rock.

cross section of an oil and gas reservoir

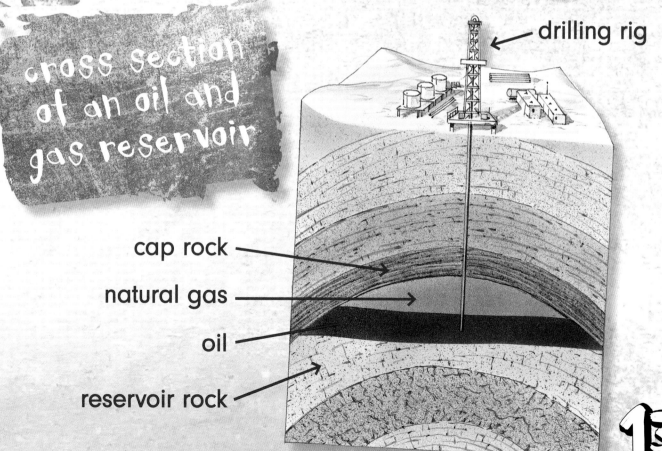

drilling rig

cap rock

natural gas

oil

reservoir rock

13

FINDING OIL

Oil reservoirs can be found hundreds or thousands of feet below Earth's surface, where there were once ancient seas. They may also be below the deepest ocean waters! In order to obtain this valuable natural resource, companies use huge drills to reach the oil reservoirs. But oil companies don't just drill into rock and hope for the best.

With the help of scientists and engineers, oil companies have **technology** that helps locate oil reservoirs. One approach is sending sound waves into rocks at different speeds. By listening to the sound waves and measuring how fast they go through a rock, scientists can find rocks that likely have oil in them.

geophone

INFO UNDERGROUND

Oil-finding technology tells scientists and oil companies more than where oil is found. It can tell the number and size of pores in rock and how fast the tiny oil droplets will move. It also tells drillers where the natural cracks, or fractures, are in the rock so they know where to drill.

Scientists may listen to how the sound waves move through rock on geophones like this one.

15

START THE DRILL

Constructing an oil well to extract oil is a big undertaking. The land around a site must be cleared. Big holes are dug, and rock and mud are removed. The site must be near water, which is needed for extraction, as well as roads, needed for transportation. Sometimes roads must be built.

Do you picture a spurt of oil coming from the ground once a drill goes into an oil reservoir? That's not what happens anymore. There are tools in place that catch oil well "gushers" today. Gushers are part of primary production. This is oil that flows out of the well as pressure on the reservoir is released.

ENVIRONMENTAL IMPACT STUDIES

Before a site is chosen for an oil well, scientists do an environmental impact study. They try to find out how an oil well, and all the machines and people it needs to work, may harm the land and the animals and plants that live there. This study may stop the construction of an oil well if it would be too harmful.

When oil wells are drilled underwater, a support system must be built in the water for the oil rig, which is the technology and tools used for drilling for oil, including the platform.

17

Primary production can go on for days or even years, depending on the reservoir rock. As the pressure underground pushing the oil out is released, the oil flow begins to slow. Drillers may **inject** some of the natural gas found near the oil to create more pressure to push more oil out. After that, oil companies pump water in to extract oil. This is called waterflooding. The water washes the oil droplets from the rock's pores and into the oil well.

Even after using these "secondary recovery" processes, there's still a lot of oil left in most reservoirs!

waterflooding

HOW MUCH IS LEFT?

Oil reservoirs contain different amounts of oil. Imagine a reservoir has 10 barrels of oil in it. After primary production, there may still be six to seven barrels left. Secondary recovery may only extract one-half to one more barrel. That can leave more than half of the oil found in a reservoir behind!

At this oil well in Russia, pumps called "nodding donkeys" work to extract oil.

19

REFINING

At the production site, oil is stored at first in big steel tanks. Then it's moved through pipelines or by tanker trucks, ships, and railcars. Most oil is taken to a refinery, or the place where it will be made ready for use.

Refineries heat the oil to separate the different kinds of hydrocarbons in it. Each kind of hydrocarbon has features that make it good for a certain use. A few kinds are processed further to make gasoline. Others are made into a heavier fuel called diesel, heating oil, and **asphalt**, among other uses.

OIL TRANSPORT

Tanker ships that can hold up to 3 million barrels of oil carry oil from overseas or ocean oil rigs to the United States. While some oil is moved on tanker trucks, pipelines are the number-one way oil and natural gas are moved around the country. The United States has more than 190,000 miles (305,775 km) of underground pipelines through which oil can be transported.

Oil refineries are necessary to making many products. However, some people don't want one built nearby, because they don't think they're pleasant to look at.

21

OIL AND THE ECONOMY

Oil is an important part of the US and global economies. The goods and fuel we use every day are made from or use oil. In addition, transportation of goods and people depends on fuel from oil. So the rise and fall of oil prices can affect the profits of businesses.

Oil prices affect some countries more than others. India, for example, brings in 75 percent of its oil, so low oil prices mean they pay less for it. Countries that sell oil to other countries, such as Venezuela, suffer when prices are low. Some studies say that a drop in oil prices can create a global recession, or a slowdown of economic activity.

OPEC

In 1960, several countries created OPEC, or the Organization of Petroleum Exporting Countries. They state that their purpose is to work together to maintain a stable oil market, keeping those who need petroleum supplied and guaranteeing income for producers and **investors**. Together, these countries have control over about 75 percent of the world's oil supply.

Should production of one natural resource be able to affect so much of the world?

POLLUTION

Most scientists agree that the burning of fossil fuels, including oil, is likely a major contributor to global **climate change**. Earth is slowly getting warmer as the gases given off by burned fossil fuels build up in the atmosphere and don't allow heat to escape.

Oil causes pollution in other ways, too. Big oil leaks, such as the 2010 spill at the Deepwater Horizon oil rig, make the news. But cars dripping motor oil onto asphalt creates pollution, too, when rain sweeps the oil into waterways. Boats and other watercraft can also spill oil. Little spills add up, harming fish, plants, and our water supply.

oil refinery

FRACKING

Hydraulic fracturing—or fracking—is the injection of a mix of water, chemicals, and sand into rocks at a very high pressure in order to extract oil and other fossil fuels. The practice has raised many concerns as polluted water near fracking sites has been linked to animal deaths as well as people's illnesses.

Deepwater Horizon oil spill

Deepwater Horizon was the name of a huge oil rig that operated in the Gulf of Mexico. An explosion on the rig caused millions of barrels of oil to pollute the gulf.

wildlife harmed in the spill

THE FUTURE OF OIL

Right now, much of the world depends on oil for fuel, energy, and the production of many goods. But oil has gotten harder to find. In order to keep up with this demand, scientists and engineers are always looking for new ways to extract more oil from reservoirs.

Chemicals called surfactants have been created to help wash away oil from reservoir rock. They're a little bit like soap! Some oil companies are also sending steam into oil wells to heat the oil and make it move to the surface more easily. Another way to free more oil is by injecting the gas carbon dioxide into the oil well.

BUGS IN THE WELL

Scientists have found that some tiny organisms called microbes might be helpful in extracting oil. They're sent into a well where they eat some of the matter found in the reservoir. They give off gases, building pressure underground that could force more oil to the surface.

There's no way to know how long oil is going to be as valuable as it is because global prices and demand are always changing.

27

YOU DECIDE!

Oil is one of the most important resources on Earth. But does it do more harm than good? Many scientists believe we should be working harder to reduce the amount of oil we use around the world to stop global climate change and pollution. Others are hard at work studying how oil is extracted and trying to make that less harmful to the environment. Still more studies are being done on fuels made from oil that will cause less pollution.

What do you think? Should we depend on oil as much as we do? Maybe you can discover a new fuel source for the world someday!

ALTERNATIVE ENERGY

Sunlight, water, and wind are all being used to create power around the world. So far, the technology isn't available and affordable for everyone to use—but it may be soon! Since the sun is a renewable resource, meaning we won't run out of it, that might be the best way to power our world into the future!

windmills

TOP OIL-PRODUCING COUNTRIES

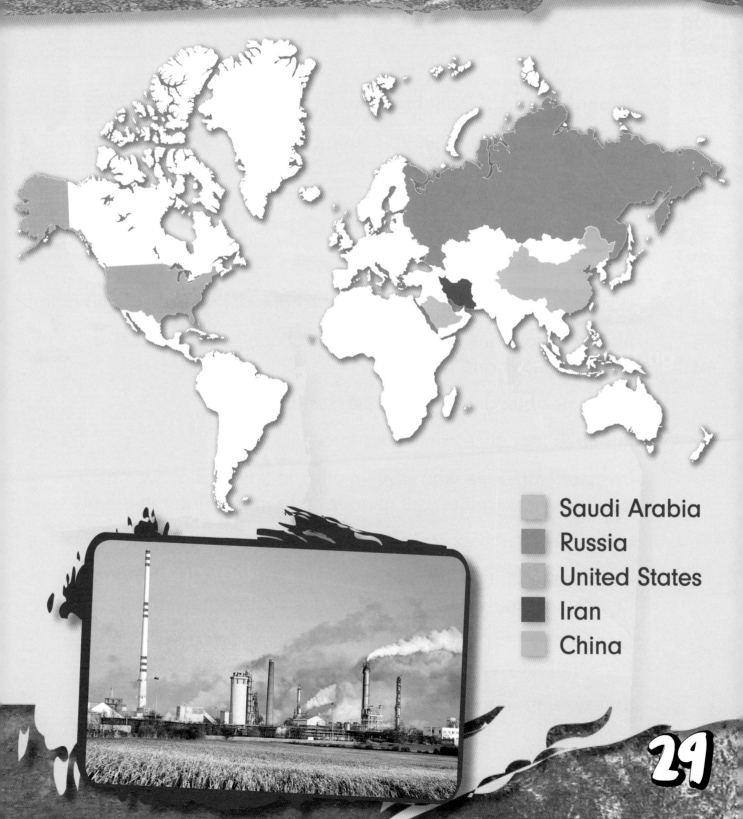

Saudi Arabia
Russia
United States
Iran
China

GLOSSARY

asphalt: a black matter used to make roads

climate change: long-term change in Earth's climate, caused partly by human activities such as burning oil and natural gas

denser: packed more closely together

deposit: an amount of something in the ground that built up over a period of time

distillate: a product that has been changed from a gas into a liquid

hydrocarbon: any of a large group of compounds made up of only carbon and hydrogen

impermeable: unable to be passed through

inject: to introduce something forcefully

investor: someone who gives money to something, such as a business, hoping they will receive more money later in return

natural resource: something in nature that can be used by people

sediment: matter, such as stones and sand, that is carried onto land or into the water by wind, water, or land movement

technology: the way people do something using tools and the tools that they use

theory: a general idea that explains something

FOR MORE INFORMATION

BOOKS

Dickmann, Nancy. *Fracking: Fracturing Rock to Reach Oil and Gas Underground.* New York, NY: Crabtree Publishing Company, 2016.

Hicks, Terry Allan. *The Pros and Cons of Oil.* New York, NY: Cavendish Square Publishing, 2015.

Rice, William B. *Our Resources.* Huntington Beach, CA: Teacher Created Materials, 2016.

WEBSITES

The Story of Fossil Fuels
climatekids.nasa.gov/fossil-fuels-oil/
Read more about the creation of oil and other fossil fuels.

Tiki's Quick Guide to Fracking
tiki.oneworld.org/fracking/fracking.html
Find out more about what fracking is and how it can affect the planet.

INDEX

A FLEXIBLE ORGANIZATION
FOR INSTRUCTORS

Text Learning Objectives

form the framework for organizing your lectures, selecting support materials, and customizing tests for your students.

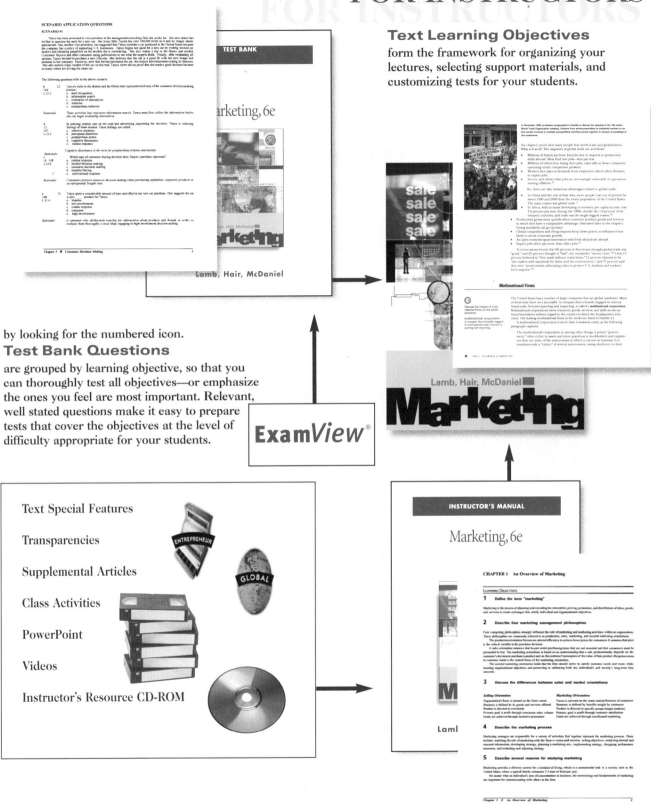

by looking for the numbered icon.

Test Bank Questions

are grouped by learning objective, so that you can thoroughly test all objectives—or emphasize the ones you feel are most important. Relevant, well stated questions make it easy to prepare tests that cover the objectives at the level of difficulty appropriate for your students.

ExamView®

Text Special Features

Transparencies

Supplemental Articles

Class Activities

PowerPoint

Videos

Instructor's Resource CD-ROM

All Lecture Support Materials

come together under their appropriate objectives in the Instructor's Handbook Lecture Outlines, for thorough coverage of all objectives. Annotations tell you the appropriate times to integrate text special features, transparencies, additional examples, supplemental articles and activities, and end-of-chapter pedagogy into your lectures.

marketing
SIXTH EDITION

Charles W. Lamb, Jr.

M.J. Neeley Professor of Marketing
M.J. Neeley School of Business
Texas Christian University

Joseph F. Hair, Jr.

Alvin C. Copeland Endowed Chair of Franchising
and Director, Entrepreneurship Institute
Louisiana State University

Carl McDaniel

Chairman, Department of Marketing
College of Business Administration
University of Texas at Arlington

SOUTH-WESTERN
THOMSON LEARNING

Australia · Canada · Mexico · Singapore · Spain · United Kingdom · United States

Marketing, 6e by Charles W. Lamb, Joseph H. Hair, and Carl McDaniel

Publisher/Team Leader: Dave Shaut
Acquisitions Editor: Pamela M. Person
Developmental Editor: Jamie Gleich-Bryant
Marketing Manager: Marc Callahan
Production Editor: Kelly Keeler
Manufacturing Coordinator: Sandee Milewski
Internal Design: Michael H. Stratton
Cover Design: Michael H. Stratton
Cover Images: PhotoDisc and Digitalvision
Photo Manager: Cary Benbow
Production House: Pre-Press Company, Inc.
Compositor: Pre-Press Company, Inc.
Printer: Transcontinental

Printed in Canada
1 2 3 4 5 04 03 02 01

For more information contact South-Western Publishing, 5101 Madison Road, Cincinnati, Ohio, 45227 or find us on the Internet at http://www.swcollege.com

For permission to use material from this text or product, contact us by
• **telephone:**   **1-800-730-2214**
• **fax:**   **1-800-730-2215**
• **web:**   **http://www.thomsonrights.com**

Library of Congress Cataloging-in-Publication Data

Lamb, Charles W.
    Marketing/Charles W. Lamb, Jr., Joseph F. Hair, Jr., Carl McDaniel.—6th ed.
        p. cm.
    Include bibliographical references and index.
    ISBN 0-324-06861-1 (acid-free paper)
    1. Marketing. 2. Marketing—Management. I. Hair, Joseph F. II. McDaniel, Carl D.
    III. Title.

HF5415 .L2624 2001
658.8—dc21   00-053814

To Julie Baker
—*Charles W. Lamb, Jr.*

To my loving and
supportive wife
Dale and my son
and his wife Joe, III
and Kerrie
—*Joseph F. Hair, Jr.*

To the kids: Raphaël,
Michèle, Sébastien,
Chelley, and Mark
—*Carl McDaniel*

brief contents

contents

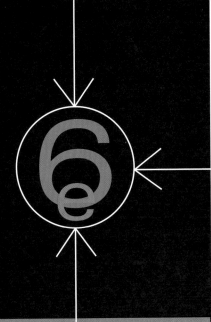

Marketing

You are holding a text that has dramatically increased in number of users and universities with each edition. We are very grateful to the hundreds of professors that selected our text to give college students their very first exposure to the dynamic world of marketing. We are honored that a vast majority of professors stay with our text edition after edition. Our research gives us an indication why this is true. Students find *Marketing,* by Lamb, Hair, and McDaniel, the most exciting, readable, and enjoyable text of their college career.

What Makes Marketing, *6th Edition, so Popular?*

We have done extensive research to provide a comprehensive, up-to-the-minute introduction to the field of marketing. Principles and concepts are illustrated by literally hundreds of new, fresh examples. Our text has been called "lively" and "interesting" many times. You should know that this never means "superficial" or "shallow." The latest concepts and theories are covered in detail in a lucid manner with numerous illustrations. Our responsibility is to continue to build your trust by pursuing excellence not only in the text but in all the ancillaries as well. Our goal is to add value far beyond your expectations in each edition.

Value-Driven Innovations for the 6th Edition

We Have Streamlined the Text.

We have moved most of the material on competitive intelligence (CI) to the CD that accompanies the 6th edition. At your suggestion, we introduce the topic of competitive intelligence in Chapter 8, Decision Support Systems and Marketing Research. Here your students receive a short overview on CI and, for those instructors seeking additional depth, CI material on the CD-ROM can be assigned. We offer you maximum flexibility on treating this hot topic.

We have focused on technology.

E-Marketing Planning Activities

Chapter 2 discusses the purpose and components of a marketing plan. As chapter topics such as market segmentation and consumer behavior are discussed, the corresponding end-of-part exercises direct students to create the related portions of their marketing plan. Students will find activities loaded with on-line resources to help build a marketing plan for either an Internet-only venture or a traditional business. We provide student worksheets on the CD-ROM to accompany the e-marketing planning exercises at the end of each of the seven text parts. Never have your students had access to so many resources for building a marketing plan.

Marketing Builder Express

An "express" version of JIAN's popular MarketingBuilder software, this tool contains everything students need to develop a marketing plan. Students can complete the end-of-part marketing plan activities using the shorter MarketingBuilder Express software templates or using the original Academic Version of MarketingBuilder.

Student CD-ROM

Our CD-ROM provides two new video cases on Enterprise Rent-A-Car and Celestial Seasonings. Each case is followed by a series of questions to challenge your students to think about the marketing strategies of each company and how they can be altered to increase marketing effectiveness. The CD also includes the E-marketing planning activities and worksheets described above. To help your students master the material in *Marketing*, 6th edition, we offer interactive quizzes on each chapter. Wrong answers prompt students to go back to a specific page and reread the material. The CD features PowerPoint™ slides with instructions for making Power Notes. Rather than constantly taking notes, students can listen and absorb your lectures.

Internet Activities and Real-Time Examples

Each chapter contains Internet activities with URLs, tied to organizations mentioned in the text. For example, as students read about how McDonald's segments and target markets, they are directed to real-time examples on McDonald's Web page. Because each activity calls for student production, you can use these mini-exercises as additional homework or quizzing opportunities. In addition, we conclude each chapter with additional Internet activities that relate to chapter content. Students find valuable on-line resources and learn to analyze current Internet marketing strategies. Links to all URLs in the book are located on the text's Internet site at http://lamb.swcollege.com. We have kept the best URLs from the 5th edition and added many new ones to each chapter. Should a URL listed in the book become obsolete, it will be replaced with a new one that still fits the particular context of the activity.

Starbucks

How does Starbucks use its Web site as a loyalty marketing program? Visit the site and see.
http://www.starbucks.com

On Line

On Line

Internet Marketing Chapter

E-commerce changes at the speed of light. We completely rewrite Chapter 19, Internet Marketing, with each edition to explain the dynamic world of e-commerce. The latest marketing innovations, technology shifts, and dot-com success and failures, are covered like no other text. We don't neglect the traditional companies but explain how many of these firms are morphing to "bricks and clicks."

InfoTrac Exercises

The InfoTrac database enables your students to connect with the real world of marketing through academic journals, business and popular magazines and newspapers, and a vast array of government publications. InfoTrac exercises can be found throughout the text to either guide an original research project or provide structured reading exercises.

> the supply and demand curves to customer-determined pricing.
> 12. Go to one of the Internet auction sites listed in this chapter. Report to the class on how the auction process works and the items being auctioned.
> 13. INFOTRAC COLLEGE EDITION How is yield management helping companies achieve competitive advantage? Use InfoTrac to find out (**http://www.infotrac-college.com**). Run a keyword search for "yield management" and read through the headlines to see what industries are profiled most often. Then read the article from the November 15, 1999 issue of *Computerworld* titled "Software Fills Trucks, Maximizes Revenue; Sitton Motor Lines Takes

"Who Wants to Be a Marketer?"

Developed by John Drea of Western Illinois University, this exciting addition to the Sixth Edition of *Marketing* by Lamb, Hair, and McDaniel is a new in-class, computer-based game. "Who Wants to Be a Marketer?" is a fun and exciting way to review terminology and concepts with students. This easy-to-use game only requires Microsoft PowerPoint and a method to display the screen to the entire class (such as a data projector.) "Who Wants to Be a Marketer?" has two rounds of fifty original questions per each chapter, for a total of 1,000 questions! "Who Wants to Be a Marketer?" is only available for adopters of *Marketing* by Lamb, Hair, and McDaniel.

Marketing, 6th Edition Web Site

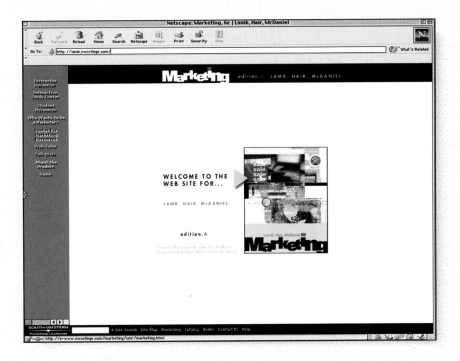

Comprehensive Web Site

Lamb, Hair, McDaniel's Web site contains a wide array of supplementary products for instructors to use in enhancing their course material and presentations, and guiding students down the path to a clear understanding of the concepts presented within the text. It also offers students Web pages dedicated to students' needs and geared toward helping them succeed.

The instructor's site includes: a sample Test Bank and Study Guide chapter, the Instructor's Manual in its entirety, The Fifth and Sixth editions of "Great Ideas in Teaching Marketing", The entire PowerPoint™ presentation available in viewable and printable formats, new to this edition "Who Wants to be a Marketer?", and a features archive of boxes and vignettes from the Fifth Edition.

Student resources include:

✔ Marketing "on-line" segments directly from the new edition

✔ Sample chapters of "Who Wants to be a Marketer"

✔ Ten interactive study guide questions to quiz students' retention of key concepts

✔ Full PowerPoint™ presentation in printable and viewable formats

✔ Career Appendices and a Marketing Resource Center

✔ Marketing Project Plan—a contest which asks students to take the knowledge and understanding they have acquired from the textbook and put it to use in developing a marketing plan for an actual existing company

✔ Study Break with fun links and games

Fresh Content Throughout

We have thoroughly updated and added to our proven features.

We have thoroughly revised the 6th edition with new features
and content throughout the text. You will find:

✔ New content on competitive advantage

✔ An expanded section on poverty of time
and how it influences consumers and marketers

✔ A new section on technological and resource factors
that affect marketing efforts

✔ A new section on fears of globalization and trade

✔ A new section on the impact of the Internet on
global marketing

✔ A new section on e-commerce:

- B2B
- Consumer e-relations tool
- E-commerce is for all sizes of business
- Benefits of e-commerce

✔ An updated section on age segmentation

✔ An updated section on ethnic segmentation

✔ An updated section on perceptual mapping

✔ A new section on secondary information
available on the Internet

✔ Updated lists and descriptions of search engines
and sites of particular interest to marketing researchers

✔ A fully updated section on Internet surveys

✔ A fully updated section and new material on
supply chain management

✔ A fully updated section on technology in
supply chain management

✔ An updated section on global logistics

✔ A fully updated section on on-line retailing

✔ An updated section on the Internet as a
public relations tool

✔ A new section on on line promotions

✔ A new section on the impact of technology on
personal selling

✔ A new section on yield management

✔ A fully updated section on the impact of the
Internet on pricing

✔ A new section on pricing penalties

Cross-Functional Connections

No marketer is an island. Marketing professionals work with every functional area of the company.
Cross-functional connections explore the give and take between marketing and other business functions.
We present cross-functional connections in a thoroughly revised format at the beginning of each section.
Solutions to the topical questions are provided at the end of each section so that students can test their
understanding of how marketing is integrated with the other functions of business.

Entrepreneurship Cases

Entrepreneurship, whether in the newest dot-com or in America's largest corporations, is what has fueled the greatest period of expansion in American history. Our new entrepreneurship cases highlight the challenges facing entrepreneurs in the 21st century. As you might expect, many of these all-new cases focus on Internet companies such as Ebay, Planet Feedback, Napster, Lycos, and Entrypoint.com. But we also recognize that entrepreneurial activities take place across the Fortune 500, so we profile industry giants like W. W. Grainger, which offers over 600,000 maintenance, repair, and operating items, and Ford Motor Company. Both have used a highly entrepreneurial approach in launching their e-commerce programs. Your students will find these cases an exciting and challenging aspect of each chapter.

Use It Now!

Students are often heard to comment, "Yes, I can use this information when I graduate and get into my career but what take-away value can I get right now?" We followed up on this cue by adding a new feature at the end of each chapter entitled, "Use It Now!" This material covers a topic related to the chapter that the student can put to work today. For example, in Chapter 4, Developing a Global Vision, "Use It Now" tells how students can find a job overseas and also offers tips on changing money abroad.

Expanded Coverage
of Integrated Marketing Communications

We listened to your suggestions to add more coverage on integrated marketing communications (IMC). Chapter 14 is now solely devoted to the introduction of IMC. Chapter 15 (new) covers advertising and public relations. Chapter 16 concludes the section with sales promotion and personal selling. The additional chapter gives students more detailed coverage across the spectrum of IMC.

Case entrepreneurship

Encirq: Protecting Privacy on the Web

The rapid development of the Internet and e-commerce in the past couple of years has not come without serious growing pains. This new networking and communication medium created a whole new way for marketers to identify, track, collect information about, and offer targeted messages to consumers. Advertisers can monitor consumers who are surfing for pleasure even if they do not buy anything or divulge any personal information. With just a person's e-mail address and a cookie (an electronic tag that identifies a user's computer with a numeric code), an on-line ad server can easily track users as they click across the Internet landscape. Tracking a consumer's surfing habits enables servers of on-line advertisements to place very targeted ads in front of users. On the surface, this may seem like a benefit to both the advertiser and to the consumer, but there is often an unrealized downside to all of that.

What consumers have been generally unaware of is that these ad serving networks and companies collect and store all of that information on private servers and sell it to other marketing companies and retailers at a handsome profit. Selling on-line profiles seriously compromises a user's privacy, and it almost always happens without that person being aware of it. If Net users are aware of this information brokering, they generally

suit generated mass awareness of the practices of DoubleClick and other similar ad serving networks and fueled public intolerance of such activities. On-line marketers began to suffer from the loss of specific information needed to serve targeted content and advertisements. Most Internet users became extremely guarded about sharing any kind of personal information on-line.

The Encirq Corporation, which at present has the only available solution of its kind, hopes to once and for all resolve the problem that limits marketers and compromises personal privacy. Founded by Mark Vogel and David Posner, Encirq has developed a software application from two unique and perfectly complementary insights. Vogel dreamed of a way for an Internet user's personal information to remain housed on his or her own individual computer. In this way, personal information would be fully protected and controlled by the consumer. Posner had designed a small database that would launch within a user's computer at the exact moment an Internet user connected with a Web server. Driven to solve the privacy problem that analyzing clicking habits on-line created only a thumbnail sketch of buying habits and history—Vogel and Posner devised a product that could be the perfect solution to both.

Use it Now!

Study the Role of a Global Manager

As business becomes more global, chances are that you may become a global manager. Start learning right now what this means and if it's right for you. The life of a global manager can be hectic, as these examples illustrate:

As president of DoubleClick International, a unit of the New York Internet advertising company, Barry Salzman spends about 75 percent of his time traveling. He takes a laptop and four battery packs so he can wade through the 200 e-mail messages he averages daily. Welcome to the world of global management. It's a punishing pace, but it's the only way Mr. Salzman knows how to manage his network of thirteen offices worldwide.

Global managers spend proportionately more of their energy combating the sense of isolation that tends to gnaw at employees in remote offices. Mr. Salzman conducts a conference call every Monday morning for international managers in Canada, Europe, and Asia. Only those who are flying somewhere are excused. "We try to maintain voice contact," he says. "We lose that with computers and e-mail."

Top overseas performers at Secure Computing, a San Jose, California, software de-veloper, are treated to a dinner for two by Christine Hughes, senior vice president of marketing and business development. Ms. Hughes supervises a twenty-four-person staff in North and South America and Asia. One of her missions on trips is to combat the tendency

of foreign-based employees to think the organization is "U.S.-centric," she says. Because they take much longer flights than the typical corporate road warrior, global managers wind up turning airplanes into offices. When she is overseas, Ms. Hughes has her office ship her a package of paperwork overnight, so she can work on the flight home. Mr. Salzman considers flight time some of his most productive; he uses it to answer e-mail and review contracts.

Indeed, a global manager's workday never really ends. Wherever they are, it's still business hours somewhere else. When she's working in Australia, Ms. Hughes usually ends her day in a hotel room, talking with someone at the home office. "I'm on the phone until two in the morning dealing with issues," she says. "You just have to accept that." [70]

One way to see if you might be cut out to be a global manager is to spend some time abroad. The ideal situation is to find a job overseas during the summer months. This experience will help you decide if you want to be a global manager. Also, it will look good on your resume. One source of international jobs information is **http://www.internationaljobs.org/**.

If you can't find a job overseas, save your money and travel abroad. Seeing how others live and work will broaden your horizons and give you a more enlightened view of the world. Even international travel can help you decide what you want to do in the global marketplace.

chapter 5

Item #5 p.61

The Marketing Environment and Marketing Ethics

Ah, the vast Canadian wilderness. If someone could just capture that spirit of the Great White North, package it, and launch a marketing campaign. Someone has: two American guys, Michael Budman and Don Green, transplanted from Detroit, nostalgic for their days at summer camp.

Evoking the rugged imagery of outdoorsy Canada, Roots Canada Ltd. sells such gear as $800 elkskin jackets, leather bags and shoes, casual wear, and even woodsy home furnishings. The company, with annual sales of about $170 million, has grown to 160 stores—including twenty-five in Asia, where Canada's famed wilderness holds considerable allure.

Now, the apparel chain plans a $70 million, five-year expansion drive in the United States and Europe. Having already laid down roots in New York, Aspen, Beverly Hills, and other cities,

and other local comedians. The friendships later helped the company win contracts to supply varsity-style jackets and other merchandise for the cast of *Saturday Night Live* and other television shows.

Roots is hoping its celebrity connections will give it an edge as it expands in the hotly contested U.S. market for casual wear. It is also stocking its U.S. stores with a larger proportion of leather goods, including jackets, bags, and accessories, than its stores in Canada carry. "Club Monaco, Banana Republic, Gap—if you look at stores like that, it's basically all clothing," says Marshall Myles, Roots's executive vice president. "At Roots, it's always been the leather products that people remember."

Competitors are watching. "Their fits are very trendy, very funky, very tapered," says Pashalow Cooper, man-

Opening Vignettes

Each chapter begins with a new, current, real-world story about a marketing decision or situation facing a company. These vignettes have been carefully prepared to stimulate student interest in the topics to come in the chapter and can be used to begin class discussion. A special section before the chapter summary called "Looking Back" answers the teaser questions posed in the opening vignette and helps illustrate how chapter material relates to the real world of marketing. A few of the companies featured in the 6th edition are: LL Bean, Ralston Purina, Target, Williams-Sonoma, and Kinkos.

Boxed Items

Each chapter features two completely new boxes. The "Global Perspectives" feature describes the experiences of real companies doing battle in the global marketplace. This boxed feature is in addition to the myriad of global examples found throughout the text. Every chapter, of course, is written with a global vision. Our second box tackles the often sticky issue of what is right or wrong in marketing. Our "Ethics in Marketing" feature offers provocative examples of how ethics come into play in many marketing decisions. Is it ethical to

Ethics in Marketing

FOR THE RIGHT PRICE, THESE DOCTORS TREAT THEIR PATIENTS AS PRECIOUS

Garrison Bliss and Mitchell Karton, like many doctors, were tired of insurance companies telling them how to care for their patients. Looking for a way around the bureaucracy, the two physicians discovered the price people will pay for peace of mind. Their practice, Seattle Medical Associates, an unusual medical consultancy, where people pay for a doctor's know-how. For a range of fees, patients get unlimited access to a doctor they know who will guide them through the maze of hospitals and medical specialists they may encounter if they do get sick. There are unlimited office visits, an annual physical and X-rays as needed, but no ties to the insurers and health-maintenance organizations that most Americans now en-

counter. SMA doesn't take Medicare or Medicaid either. Instead, it promises the kind of personal, around-the-clock attention that people used to associate with their family doctor.

Many of their longtime patients had to think hard about paying almost $800 more a year on top of other health costs, and a lot of their old patients have left. Others are happy that they stayed. "It's expensive, but this matters," says Julie Blacklow, a fifty-one-year-old freelance television producer who recently called Dr. Karton at 1 A.M. complaining of chest pains that she feared signaled a heart attack. He talked her through her symptoms, then told her—correctly—not to worry. "To give someone access, that may be the best medicine of

all," Ms. Blacklow says. "That's priceless."

Maybe. But such added prices are too high for many Americans and point the way to a multi-tiered medical system in which the quality of care might depend even more than it does today on the thickness of the patient's wallet.[a]

Is there anything you see as unethical about what Bliss and Karton are doing? Would it be unethical if the federal government implemented such a system? When the practice converted to the new pricing system, they lost one-third of their patients. Do the doctors have any obligation to them?

[a] Anita Sharp, "For the Right Price, These Doctors Treat Patients as Precious," *Wall Street*

create huge databases about people's private lives? What about marketing to children? Students will consider these and many other hotly debated ethical questions.

Marketing Miscues

MARKETING MISCUES

DoubleClick's Consumer Tracking Capabilities Backfire

DoubleClick is a global Internet advertising company that delivers more than 5 billion on-line ads per month via its fourteen country networks. Through these sophisticated country networks, advertisers can reach computer users in over eighty countries with one ad purchase. These ads, which include sponsorships, pop-ups, and banners, can target users in any country in their native language. The company's yearly sales revenue was almost $200 million in 1999. However, this was only a small portion of industry on-line ad revenue of $3 billion in 1999—a market that is growing and expected to reach $12 billion by 2003.

DoubleClick, a 1995 entrepreneurial start-up based in New York, does not perform the creative aspects of advertising. Rather, the company sells and manages ads that appear on a network of around 1,500 Web sites that represent nearly 50 percent of all Web traffic.

teeing that personal information wo... other companies. While tracking by "cookies" allow for the monitoring ... on the Internet, user habits are not li... name and address. The potential for ... Abacus to link specific individuals a... habits (site visits, purchases) is enor... lead to DoubleClick having the most ... consumer database in the world.

Consumers as well as consumer... (such as the American Civil Liberties ... for Democracy and Technology, and ... vacy and Information Center) were c... bleClick would even think about inva... Internet users in this manner. The or... and accompanying negative publicit... DoubleClick's stock value. Additiona... partners, Altavista and Kozmo, anno... would either withdraw ads linked to ...

Mistakes can have tough consequences, but they also offer great lessons. This is especially true in marketing. At the end of each part you will find all new cases that describe good and bad ideas that couldn't make it in the rough and tumble marketplace. Often amusing and always interesting, these cases will help your students avoid the same mistakes. A few highlighted firms are: Double Click, IBM, Just for Feet, PETA, and Burger King.

Critical Thinking Cases

Making smart decisions is at the heart of successful marketing. Critical Thinking Cases at the end of each part put your students in the role of decision maker. They will evaluate the marketing plans of well known organizations including the U.S. Military, Disney, Coca Cola, Priceline, and Starbucks.

CRITICAL THINKING CASE

Redefining Prices at Priceline

Founded by forty-six-year-old Jay Walker in 1998, Priceline.com is not a typical dot-com business. From a dot-com selling perspective, the company is the pioneer in the e-commerce system referred to as "demand collection." Basically, Priceline.com matches consumer demand (at a price set by the consumer) with a supplier willing to provide the product or service at the price named by the consumer. It is very unlike bricks and clicks companies that place their catalogs on the Web. From an organizational perspective, company executives are not twenty-somethings wearing jeans and T-shirts. Executives, recruited from companies such as Citigroup and AT&T, often wear suits to work. Additionally, the company is not located in the hotbed of dot-com companies on the West Coast. Rather, company headquarters are on the eastern seaboard of the United States in a suburban office park.

services through affiliated co... and Perfect YardSale.

The purchasing of *travel*... one of the earliest e-commer... as Travelocity.com and Expe... line travel service in the mid-... individual travel providers (e... panies, and hotels) began to ... systems. By 2000, travel was ... gory on the Internet. Of the S... billion in airline reservatio... rooms, and $630 million wer... However, only around 3 perc... ments were made on-line.

It was estimated that 5 m... flown empty each week, with ... 100,000 seats weekly. Pricel... cluded hotels in 1,200 locatio... States. The company's hotel...

Internet Coverage

The Sixth Edition focuses on technology. In addition to all of the innovations described above, we have highlighted Internet coverage throughout the text with the special icon in the margin.

Global Marketing Concepts Throughout the Text

Today most businesses compete not only locally and nationally, but globally as well. Companies that have never given a thought to exporting now face competition from abroad. "Thinking globally" should be a part of every manager's tactical and strategic planning. Accordingly, we address this topic in detail early in Chapter 4. Numerous global examples within the body of the text are identified with the icon shown in the margin.

Global marketing is fully integrated throughout the book, cases, and videos, as well. Our "Global Perspectives" boxes, which appear in nineteen chapters, provide expanded global examples and concepts. Each box concludes with thought-provoking questions carefully prepared to stimulate class discussion. For example, the box in Chapter 7 describes how office supply giant Office Depot fumbled as it tried to establish itself in Japan. Students are asked to identify ways Office Depot could have more effectively segmented the Japanese market.

Global Perspectives

BIG BOY'S ADVENTURES IN THAILAND

With his checkered overalls, cowlick curl, and penchant for double burgers, Big Boy seemed an unlikely fit for Bangkok. "People thought he was a little, well, creepy," says Peter Smythe, the head franchisor for Big Boy restaurants in Thailand. "They kept asking me, 'Is he a Chinese Ronald McDonald?'" Eventually, a few Thai visitors decided Big Boy was a religious icon and laid bowls of rice and incense at his feet.

Now that giants like Burger King and McDonald's have saturated markets around the world, the more obscure fast-food companies are heading overseas. In 1998, the minichains, such as Big Boy and Schlotzkys, opened nearly 800 new restaurants abroad, giving them more than 12,000 units overseas, according to Technomic Inc., a Chicago food-business consultancy. Asia, with more than a billion young consumers, is the prime target.

Still, for the little guys of the business—who don't have the money, supply networks, or global wisdom of a Hamburger University—venturing abroad can be a messy business. Culture clashes, food shortages, and government run-ins are common. Consider the story of Big Boy.

Mr. Smythe, who was living in California at the time, got a call in 1995 from his Thai brother-in-law. They met with a businessman who was looking for an American franchise to bring to Thailand. Smythe found Big Boy, a franchise that seemed a natural for expansion. The first restaurant opened in 1996, but no one came. After interviewing hundreds of customers, Smythe found a number of reasons why people were not coming to his restaurant. Some said the restaurant's "room energy" was bad. Others said the Big Boy statue spooked them. Many explained that they would rather get a sweet satay, noodle bowl, or grilled squid on the street for one-fifth the price of a greasy burger. "It suddenly dawned on me that here I was trying to get a 3,500-year-old culture to eat sixty-four-year-old food," says Smythe.

Big Boy placed a few cheap Thai items on the menu, and customers started trickling in. Today, Smythe owns four Big Boys in Thailand, three in Bangkok, and one in the southern beach town of Pattaya. Sales have doubled since last year, and the larger two are pulling in more than $13,000 a month—about one quarter the average for an American store, but still profitable because of their lower costs.

The menu is a work in progress. Smythe studied the customers who were walking past his restaurants and discovered that they fell into two broad categories: European tourists and Thai young people, including a large number of the young women who work in nearby bars. With help from a Swiss chef, Smythe filled the menu with German specialties like spatzle, beef, and chocolate cake. For the Thais, he added country-style specialties like fried rice and pork omelets. He also added sugar and chili powder to Big Boy's hamburgers to better match the Thai taste buds. The restaurants now make over half their money from Thai food and the rest from European dishes and the occasional milk shake or burger.

"We thought we were bringing American food to the masses," says Smythe. "But now we're bringing Thai and European food to the tourists. It's strange, but you know what? It's working."[a]

Evaluate Big Boy's marketing strategies in Thailand. What lessons can you derive from the Big Boy story?

[a] Robert Frank, "Big Boy's Adventures in Thailand," *Wall Street Journal*, April 12, 2000, pp.

Small Business and Entrepreneurship Are Emphasized in Every Chapter

Many students will either work for a small business or strike out on their own to form an organization. For this reason, a new "Entrepreneurship Case" and an "Application for Entrepreneurs" appear at the end of each chapter. The "Entrepreneurship Cases" apply general marketing concepts to the world of start-ups and small business. The "Applications" are mini-cases designed to illustrate how small business can create strategies using the material in the chapter. In addition, small business examples throughout each chapter are identified by the icon in the margin.

Focus on Ethics

In this edition we continue our emphasis on ethics. The "Ethics in Marketing" boxes, complete with questions focusing on ethical decision making, have been revised in each chapter. Questions and cases designed to highlight ethical issues, such as the Ben and Jerry's and Encirq cases appearing at the end of Chapter 3, give students a sense of the complexity of ethics as the cases lead them to look at the issues from all sides.

Customer Value and Quality are Emphasized in Every Chapter

Delivering superior customer value is now key to success in an increasingly competitive marketplace. We have integrated examples throughout the text that show how issues of value and quality affect marketing decisions at every level. The icon in the margin identifies the placement of these examples.

http://lamb.swcollege.com

Careers in Marketing

The Careers Appendix is still a key feature of the Sixth Edition Web site. It presents information on a variety of marketing careers, with job descriptions and career paths, to familiarize students with employment opportunities in marketing. This appendix also indicates what people in various marketing positions typically earn and how students should go about marketing themselves to prospective employers. A self-assessment questionnaire, a sample résumé and cover letter, and interviewing checklists are only some of the tools we have provided to help your students enter the marketing field.

Popular BusinessLink Video Cases

Twenty videos are available with the Sixth Edition of *Marketing*. Each video is enhanced by text material at the end of appropriate chapters. The companies we feature are ones that both you and your students will recognize: Burton Snowboards, Ben and Jerry's, the Toronto Blue Jays, and many more. Detailed video teaching notes preview each clip and key it to the chapter content for easy integration. Previewing, viewing, and follow-up activities help you present the content through the video, making the marketing experience real for your students.

There you have it!

Proof-positive that *Marketing*, 6th edition offers the freshest material to be found in any textbook.

Value-Driven Pedagogy Holds It Together

Our pedagogy has been developed in response to what you told us delivers value to you and your students. You told us that current examples are important to you, so we have included all-new opening vignettes, new examples throughout the text, and new boxed material in every chapter. You told us that cases that students find relevant are important to you, so we have revised our "Cross-Functional Connections" feature and replaced all of the "Marketing Miscues" and "Critical Thinking Cases" at the end of each part. You said that many of your students planned a career in small business, so we have incorporated numerous new small business examples, updated the entrepreneurship exercises, and added an "Entrepreneurship Case" at the end of each chapter. Finally, you told us that the Integrated Learning System helped your organized your lectures and helped your students study more effectively, so we have retained that important feature.

Fully Integrated Learning System

The text and all major supplements are organized around the learning objectives that appear at the beginning of each chapter to provide you and your students with an easy-to-use Integrated Learning System. A numbered icon like the one shown in the margin identifies each objective in each chapter and appears next to its related material throughout the text, Instructor's Manual, Test Bank, and Study Guide. In other words, every learning objective links the text, Study Guide, Test Bank, and all components of the Instructor's Manual. The system is illustrated on the inside front cover of the text.

Chapter learning objectives are the linchpin of the Integrated Learning System. They provide a structure for your lesson plans—everything you need to assure complete coverage of each objective icon. Do you want to stress more on learning objective 4, Chapter 11, "Explain why services marketing is important to manufacturers?" No problem. Go to the Instructor's Manual, objective 4, Chapter 11, and you'll find supplemental material. Do you want to emphasize the same objective on an exam? Go to the correlation table at the beginning of every chapter in the Test Bank. Here you will find under Chapter 11, learning objective 4, a matrix that lists question types and level of difficulty. Now you can test on objective 4 by type of question and degree of difficulty. This value-driven system for you, the instructor, delivers what it promises—full integration.

The integrated system also delivers value for students as they prepare for exams. The learning objective icons identify all the material in the text and Study Guide that relate to each specific learning objective. Students can easily check their grasp of each objective by reading the text sections, reviewing the corresponding summary section, answering the Study Guide questions for that objective, and returning to the appropriate text sections for further review when they have difficulty with any of the questions. Students can quickly identify all material relating to an objective by simply looking for the learning objective icon. And now every chapter concludes with a detailed study tip to help students master marketing concepts.

Text Pedagogy That Adds Value, Excites Students, and Reinforces Learning

Pedagogical features are meant to reinforce learning, but they need not be boring. We have created teaching tools within the text that will excite student interest as well as teach.

- *Opening Vignettes, Revisited at Chapter Conclusions:* Each chapter begins with a new, current, real-world story about a marketing decision or situation facing a company. A special section before the chapter summary called "Looking Back" answers the teaser questions posed in the opening vignette and helps illustrate how the chapter material relates to the real world of marketing.
- *Key Terms:* Key terms appear in boldface in the text, with definitions in the margins, making it easy for students to check their understanding of key definitions. A complete alphabetical list of key terms appears at the end of each chapter as a study checklist, with page citations for easy reference.
- *Chapter Summaries:* Each chapter ends with a summary that distills the main points of the chapter. Chapter summaries are organized around the learning objectives so that students can use them as a quick check on their achievement of learning goals.
- *Discussion and Writing Questions:* To help students improve their writing skills, we have included writing exercises with the discussion questions at the end of each chapter. These exercises are marked with the icon shown here. The writing questions are designed to be brief so that students can accomplish writing assignments in a short time and grading time is minimized.
- *Team Activities:* The ability to work collaboratively is key to success in today's business world. End-of-chapter team activities, identified by the icon shown here, give students opportunities to learn to work together.
- *Application for Small Business:* These short scenarios prompt students to apply marketing concepts to small business settings. Each scenario ends with provocative questions to aid student analysis.
- *End-of-Chapter Cases:* All chapters conclude with a new Entrepreneurship case and a video case. Marketing concepts are illustrated through the stories of well-known companies and situations.

Innovative Student Supplements

Marketing, 6e, provides an excellent vehicle for learning the fundamentals. However, for students to gain a true understanding of marketing, it's best if they can apply the principles to real-life situations. Included are a variety of supplements that help students apply concepts through the use of hands-on activities.

The GradeMaker Study Guide and Workbook (ISBN 0-324-06863-8) has been updated for the Sixth Edition. The Study guide questions are linked to the learning objectives by numbered icons. Every chapter includes application questions in a variety of formats to help students master the concepts. Study Guide questions are designed to be similar in type and difficulty level to the Test Bank questions. By careful review of the Study Guide, students can dramatically improve their test scores. Each chapter opens with a pre-test, and several review tools are provided throughout the text including chapter outlines with definitions, summarized key points as well as vocabulary practice.

Free Student CD-ROM

An interactive CD is packaged free with every copy of *Marketing*, 6e.

It contains valuable resources such as two all-new video segments on Enterprise Rent-A-Car and Celestial Seasonings. Each segment has an accompanying case. Also on the CD are E-Marketing Planning worksheets to help students with activities at the end of each part, review quizzes for each chapter, PowerPoint slides created specifically for the Sixth Edition as well as a sampling of complimentary extra content to ensure your students' success.

Cadotte: Experience Marketing at the Marketplace

This CD-ROM based exercise will challenge students to make tough marketing-based decisions in a competitive, fast-paced market where the customers are demanding and the competition is working hard to increase market share. Theory comes alive as students learn to manage a new business venture, increase profit, improve customer satisfaction, and capture dominant market share.

Innovative Instructor's Supplements

All components of our comprehensive support package have been developed to help you prepare lectures and tests as quickly and easily as possible. We provide a wealth of information and activities beyond the text to supplement your lectures, as well as teaching aids in a variety of formats to fit your own teaching style.

Instructor Resource CD-ROM

Managing your classroom resources is now easier than ever. The new Instructor Resource CD-ROM (ISBN 0-324-06867-0) contains all key instructor supplements—Instructor's Manual, Test Bank, and PowerPoint.

A Value-Based Instructor's Manual, the Core of Our Integrated Learning System

Each chapter within the Instructor's Manual (ISBN 0-324-06866-2) begins with learning objectives and a summary of key points. The Integrated Learning System then comes together in the chapters' detailed outlines. The outlines correspond with the text and supplements via the learning objectives and refer back to the appropriate support materials for each lecture. Support materials include transparencies with discussion suggestions, additional examples, exhibits, additional articles, activities, boxed materials, and questions. With each edition of *Marketing*, the outlines are always revised and updated to provide the most current information in the field of marketing. In addition to providing complete solutions for text questions and cases, the manual supplies ethical scenarios, summarized articles, and class activities. Our manual is truly "one-stop shopping" for your complete teaching system.

WebTutor Advantage

This product is an enhancement of WebTutor on Blackboard and WebCT; it contains all of the interactive study guide components of the standard WebTutor, with three very valuable content and technology oriented additions. WebTutor Advantage contains video lectures—this valuable student resource combines the robust 500+ PowerPointTM slide presentation with an audio lecture. WebTutor Advantage also contains digitized videos which accompany and add a critical thinking element to the students' learning experience. "Who Wants to be a Marketer?" presented in it's entirety is the third piece of this Advantage product. Also available is our WebTutor standard on Blackboard and WebCT.

Comprehensive Test Bank and Windows Testing Software

To complete the integrated system, our enhanced Test Bank (ISBN 0-324-06870-0), like the other supplements, is organized around the learning objectives. It is available in print and new Windows software formats (ExamView testing software). (ISBN 0-324-006881-6)

You can choose to prepare tests that cover all learning objectives or emphasize those you feel are most important. This updated Test Bank is one of the most comprehensive on the market, with over 3,300 true/false, multiple-choice, and essay questions.

Complete Video Package and Instructor's Manual

This video package (ISBNs 0-324-01703-0, 0-324-01704-9,0-324-01705-7, 0-324-01700-6, 0-324-01701-4, 0-324-02307-3) adds visual impact and current, real-world examples to your lecture presentation. The package includes 20 Video Cases. A detailed Video Instructor's Manual contained within the Instructor's Manual (0-324-06866-2) describes each video and provides outlines for previewing assignments, viewing tips, and follow-up activities.

Other Outstanding Supplements

- *PowerPoint Slides* (ISBN 0-324-06867-0): More than 500 full-color images are provided with *Marketing*, Sixth Edition. Most are creatively prepared visuals that do not repeat the text. Only images that highlight concepts central to the chapter are from the textbook. All you need is Windows to run the PowerPoint viewer and an LCD panel for classroom display.
- *Transparency Acetates* (ISBN 0-324-06882-4): To supplement the PowerPoint presentation, 250 transparency acetates are available. They include figures and ads from the text. Images are tied to the Integrated Learning System through the Instructor's Manual lecture outlines. Transparencies and their discussion prompts appear within the learning objective content where they apply.
- *Handbook for New Instructors* (ISBN 0-324-06868-9): This helpful booklet was specifically designed for instructors preparing to teach their first course in principles of marketing. It provides helpful hints on developing a course outline, lecturing, testing, giving feedback, and assigning projects.
- *New Edition of* **Great Ideas for Teaching Marketing** (ISBN 0-324-06864-6): Edited by the authors of the textbook, *Great Ideas for Teaching Marketing*, Sixth Edition, is a collection of suggestions for improving marketing education by enhancing teaching excellence. The publication includes teaching tips and ideas submitted by marketing educators across the United States and Canada.

Acknowledgements

This book could not have been written and published without the generous expert assistance of many people. First, we wish to thank Julie Baker, The University of Texas at Arlington, for her contributions to several chapters; and Erika Matulich, University of Tampa, for her development of Chapter 2 and e-marketing planning activities. Glenn Voss did an excellent job in updating the Internet chapter. Amelie Storment, once again, provided valuable assistance in the development of several chapters and also created several of the Entrepreneurship cases. We would also like to recognize and thank Vicky Crittenden, Boston College, and Bill Crittenden, Northeastern University, for contributing the Cross-Functional Connections that open each part. Vicky also did an excellent job on the Critical Thinking cases, Marketing Miscues, and several of the Entrepreneurship cases. We must also thank Jeffrey Gleich of Eppointments.com for contributing several Entrepreneurship cases on cutting-edge dot com companies.

We also wish to thank each of the following persons for their work on the best supplement package that is available today. Our gratitude goes out to: Kathryn Dobie, North Carolina A&T State University; Thomas and Betty Pritchett, Kennesaw State University; Davis Folsom, University of South Carolina Beaufort; Deborah Baker, Texas Christian University; John Drea, Western Illinois University; Susan Sartwell; and Susan Carson.

Our secretaries and administrative assistants, Fran Eller at TCU, Susan Sartwell at LSU, and RoseAnn Reddick at UTA, typed the manuscript, provided important quality control, and helped keep the project (and us) on schedule. Their dedication, hard work, and support were exemplary.

Our deepest gratitude goes to the team at Thomson Learning that has made this text a market leader. Jamie Gleich Bryant, our developmental editor, made this text a reality. A special thanks goes to Pamela Person, our acquisitions editor, and Dave Shaut, our Publisher, for their suggestions and support.

Finally, we are particularly indebted to our reviewers:

Barry Ashmen
Bucks County Community College

Thomas S. Bennett
Gaston Community College

P. J. Forrest
Mississippi College

Daniel J. Goebel
University of Southern Mississippi

Mark Green
Simpson College

Richard A. Halberg
Houghton College

Thomas J. Lang
University of Miami

Ronald E. Michaels
University of Central Florida

Monica Perry
University of North Carolina, Charlotte

Dick Rose
University of Phoenix (deceased during the development of the text)

James V. Spiers
Arizona State University

Acknowledgements

Wayne Alexander
Moorhead State University

Linda Anglin
Mankato State University

Thomas S. Bennett
Gaston Community College

James C. Boespflug
Arapahoe Community College

Victoria Bush
University of Mississippi

Joseph E. Cantrell
DeAnza College

G. L. Carr
*University of Alaska
Anchorage*

Deborah Chiviges
Calhoun
*College of Notre Dame of
Maryland*

John Alan Davis
Mohave Community College

William M. Diamond
SUNY–Albany

Jacqueline K. Eastman
Valdosta State University

Kevin M. Elliott
Mankato State University

Karen A. Evans
*Herkimer County Community
College*

Randall S. Hansen
Stetson University

Hari S. Hariharan
*University of Wisconsin–
Madison*

Dorothy R. Harpool
Wichita State University

Timothy S. Hatten
Black Hills State University

James E. Hazeltine
*Northeastern Illinois
University*

Patricia M. Hopkins
California State Polytechnic

Kenneth R. Laird
*Southern Connecticut
State University*

Kenneth D. Lawrence
*New Jersey Institute of
Technology*

J. Gordon Long
Georgia College

Karl Mann
Tennessee Tech University

Cathy L. Martin
*Northeast Louisiana
University*

Irving Mason
*Herkimer County Community
College*

Anil M. Pandya
*Northeastern Illinois
University*

Michael M. Pearson
*Loyola University,
New Orleans*

Constantine G. Petrides
*Borough of Manhattan
Community College*

Peter A. Schneider
Seton Hall University

Donald R. Self
*Auburn University at
Montgomery*

Mark T. Spence
*Southern Connecticut State
College*

James E. Stoddard
University of New Hampshire

Albert J. Taylor
Austin Peay State University

Janice E. Taylor
Miami University of Ohio

Ronald D. Taylor
Mississippi State University

Sandra T. Vernon
*Fayetteville Technical
Community College*

Charles R. Vitaska
Metro State College, Denver

James F. Wenthe
Georgia College

Linda Berns Wright
Mississippi State University

William R. Wynd
*Eastern Washington
University*

Meet the Authors

Charles W. Lamb, Jr.—Texas Christian University

Charles W. Lamb, Jr., is the M. J. Neeley Professor of Marketing, M. J. Neeley School of Business, Texas Christian University. He served as chair of the department of marketing from 1982 to 1988 and again from 1997 to the present. He is currently serving as chairman of the board of governors of the Academy of Marketing Science.

Lamb has authored or co-authored more than a dozen books and anthologies on marketing topics and over 150 articles that have appeared in academic journals and conference proceedings.

In 1997, he was awarded the prestigious Chancellor's Award for Distinguished Research and Creative Activity at TCU. This is the highest honor that the university bestows on its faculty. Other key honors he has received include the M. J. Neeley School of Business Research Award, selection as a Distinguished Fellow of the Academy of Marketing Science and a Fellow of the Southwestern Marketing Association.

Lamb earned an associate degree in business administration from Sinclair Community College, a bachelor's degree from Miami University, an MBA from Wright State University, and a doctorate from Kent State University. He previously served as assistant and associate professor of marketing at Texas A & M University.

Joseph F. Hair, Jr.—Louisiana State University

Joseph Hair is Alvin C. Copeland Endowed Chair of Franchising and Director, Entrepreneurship Institute, Louisiana State University. Previously, Hair held the Phil B. Hardin Chair of Marketing at the University of Mississippi. He has taught graduate and undergraduate marketing and marketing research courses.

Hair has authored 27 books, monographs, and cases and over 60 articles in scholarly journals. He also has participated on many university committees and has chaired numerous departmental task forces. He serves on the editorial review boards of several journals.

He is a member of the American Marketing Association, Academy of Marketing Science, Southern Marketing Association, and Southwestern Marketing Association.

Hair holds a bachelor's degree in economics, a master's degree in marketing, and a doctorate in marketing, all from the University of Florida. He also serves as a marketing consultant to businesses in a variety of industries, ranging from food and retailing to financial services, health care, electronics, and the U.S. Departments of Agriculture and Interior.

Carl McDaniel—University of Texas–Arlington

Carl McDaniel is a professor of marketing at the University of Texas—Arlington, where he has been chairman of the marketing department since 1976. He has been an instructor for more than 20 years and is the recipient of several awards for outstanding teaching. McDaniel has also been a district sales manager for Southwestern Bell Telephone Company. Currently, he serves as a board member of the North Texas Higher Education Authority.

In addition to *Marketing*, McDaniel also has co-authored numerous textbooks in marketing and business. McDaniel's research has appeared in such publications as the *Journal of Marketing Research, Journal of Marketing, Journal of Business Research, Journal of the Academy of Marketing Science,* and *California Management Review.*

McDaniel is a member of the American Marketing Association, Academy of Marketing Science, Southern Marketing Association, Southwestern Marketing Association, and Western Marketing Association.

Besides his academic experience, McDaniel has business experience as the co-owner of a marketing research firm. Recently, McDaniel served as senior consultant to the International Trade Centre (ITC), Geneva, Switzerland. The ITC's mission is to help developing nations increase their exports. He has a bachelor's degree from the University of Arkansas and his master's degree and doctorate from Arizona State University.

part

1

The World of Marketing

CROSS-FUNCTIONAL BUSINESS SYSTEMS: PUTTING THE CUSTOMER AT THE CENTER

As businesses enter the twenty-first century, they are faced with many changes and expectations. Technology has become a driving force in all decisions—whether it is corporate-wide strategic decisions or decisions as to where to place media funds. Businesses are forced to adapt, very quickly, to a new way of doing business via technological innovations. The speed of change in today's business world has led to functional-level management becoming empowered to make decisions that will help give their companies a competitive edge in a rapidly evolving, digitized marketplace.

With strategic decisions being made quickly by functional-level managers, it is imperative that all departments have a customer focus. This focus needs to be reflected in the daily activities of all employees, regardless of the areas in which they work—from accounting, finance, and manufacturing to human resources and marketing. A customer focus that permeates every facet of the organization does not come easily, however, nor has it always been implemented successfully.

Historically, three levels formed a "hierarchy of strategy" within a company: corporate strategy, business strategy, and functional strategy. The corporate and business-level strategies were supported by the individual functional strategies that brought together the various activities necessary to gain the desired competitive advantage. Traditionally, each functional area performs specialized portions of the organization's tasks. For example, the functional-level marketing strategy resolves questions concerning what products deliver customer satisfaction and value, what price to charge, how to distribute products, and what type of marketing communication activities will produce the desired impact. On the other hand, the functional-level manufacturing strategy decides what products should be manufactured and at what production rate, and how to make the products (e.g., labor or capital intensive). Since such functional activities require expertise in only one functional

area, managers have traditionally been trained to manage "vertically."

Such vertical activities have led to the creation of corporate silos in business. An employee working in a silo generally does not understand the importance of his or her processes in providing the final product or service to the customer. Such vertical activities have resulted in departments comprised of functional specialists who have tended to talk only with each other. For example, marketers talk to other marketing folks, operational discussions take place on the shop floor among manufacturing engineers, development team members talk within their R&D groups, and financial analysts and accountants talk with one another.

Individual functional-level strategies resulting from such departmentalization are the center of much intraorganizational conflict. For example, conflict between the marketing group and the production schedule is common. Marketing tends to want output increased or decreased immediately. But the production schedule, once made, is often seen as very inflexible.

The effective formulation and implementation of a customer-focused strategy, however, depends upon functional groups working in partnership with one another. Crossing functional boundaries is referred to as managing "horizontally" and requires a significant level of coordination among business functions. For example, it is imperative that marketing managers take a keen interest in financial issues and that operational managers have a better understanding of the firm's customers.

Today's business environment has put considerable pressure on functional groups to work together more harmoniously. Moving into the twenty-first century, we see a dramatic rush to get products into the marketplace at a much faster rate than ever before. At the same time, customers are much more demanding about what they want in these products. The bottom line is that customers want customized products delivered immediately. Companies such as General Electric, Hewlett-

Packard, and Ford have dedicated considerable time and resources to understanding and implementing high levels of cross-functional integration (often referred to as *internal partnering*).

In General Electric's entry-level Financial Management Program, trainees work in various jobs throughout the world during the first two years of employment. Members of this program change jobs every six months. While each change generally brings a new geographic location, it definitely brings a new cross-functional perspective on GE's businesses. Unfortunately, successful cross-functional interactions in most companies do not come easy and are often mired in conflict. Reasons for conflict between and among functional areas include divergent personalities, physical separation, data differences, and suboptimal reward systems.

Marketing people tend to be extroverted and interact easily with others, while R&D and manufacturing people are frequently introverted and known to work well with individual work processes and output. In addition to being distinct by their personalities, marketers and their product management colleagues in R&D and manufacturing often share the distinction of being housed in different locations. This is surprising when one thinks about the overlap all three groups have on a company's product.

The marketing department is typically located in the company's headquarters—which may be in the heart of a major business district, with sales located strategically close to customers. We often see the company's manufacturing group located in low-wage areas, low-rent districts, and close to suppliers. The manufacturing group may even be located in a different country. It becomes too easy for each department to "do its own thing," particularly if the groups are separated by language differences as well as time zones.

Another major source of conflict between marketing and its R&D and manufacturing counterparts is the type of data collected and used in decision making. Technical specialists in R&D and manufacturing have a difficult time understanding the lack of "hard" data that marketers work with. It is difficult to mesh marketing's attitudinal data with data on cycle times or tensile strength. For example, while marketing's forecasts are rarely 100 percent accurate, manufacturing can usually determine the precise costs associated with production processes.

Not surprisingly, marketing's reward system based on increased sales is often in direct conflict with manufacturing and R&D's reward systems that are driven by cost reduction. Marketing's ability to increase sales may be driven by offering consumers depth in the product line. Unfortunately, increased depth of the line leads to more changeover in the production lines which in turn drives up the cost of production.

A major challenge for marketers has been the development of mechanisms for reducing conflict between the marketing department and other business functions. Because of closer working relationships among human resources and information technology professionals, two major facilitating mechanisms have emerged: cross-functional teams and an information technology infrastructure.

To illustrate this functional integration, we can look at Hewlett-Packard's team approach to all of its product development. From concept to market entry, teams of engineers, marketers, manufacturers, financiers, and accountants bring together traditionally functional-level information into a cohesive program for product introduction at Hewlett-Packard. All information is shared across functional groups, and reports are prepared regularly that include details regarding interactions among functions.

Recognition of the customer's role in the organization and empowering employees are both necessary for success in today's business environment. Rapidly changing technology has made the cross-functional communication process much easier. Teamwork and an information technology infrastructure, in an environment that encourages and rewards better communication among all business functions, will ultimately result in a more satisfied, loyal customer.

Questions for Discussion

1. What is the overlap among marketing, manufacturing, finance, accounting, and human resources? What does each of these functions do that result in this overlap?
2. Why is cross-functional coordination necessary to have a customer-oriented firm?
3. What roles do teamwork and technology play in cross-functional coordination?

Check it Out

For articles and exercises on the material in this part, and for other great study aids, visit the *Marketing* Web site at **http://lamb.swcollege.com**.

chapter 1

Learning Objectives

1 Define the term *marketing*

2 Describe four marketing management philosophies

3 Discuss the differences between sales and market orientations

4 Describe the marketing process

5 Describe several reasons for studying marketing

An Overview of Marketing

Elizabeth Spaulding, Vice President of Customer Satisfaction for L. L. Bean, describes the company's approach to products and customers:

> Our premise is simple: If any product doesn't meet a customer's expectations—whatever they may be—we will replace it, repair it, or refund the customer's money. This policy goes back to 1912, when Leon Leonwood sent out his first one hundred pairs of the Maine Hunting Shoe, promising to refund customers' money if they weren't satisfied. Ninety pairs of those shoes came back because the quality was insufficient—and he sent refunds for all of them. It almost broke him; he had to borrow money from his family to recover. But, he improved the product.
>
> Today, if a customer calls and wants to return a Maine Hunting Shoe, the first thing we do is find out what that customer's expectations were when buying the shoe. Did she expect it to last ten years? If the answer is yes, then there's no question: We'll replace the shoe. If it turns out that she expected it to last only one year, then we'll repair the shoe. The point is that the customer determines the expectation. Not us.
>
> How can we afford to back up that kind of guarantee? It goes back to L. L.'s golden rule, which we have posted in every office: "Sell good merchandise at a reasonable profit. Treat your customers like human beings, and they will always come back for more."
>
> And 99.9 percent of our customers are totally honest. They're just like your neighbors. And when you realize that your customers are just like you, the whole dynamic of your interaction with them changes.[1]

L. L. Bean's philosophy of business has translated into many decades of sales and profits. Describe the company's philosophy of business. Would you want to work for a company such as L. L. Bean?

On Line

L.L. Bean

How does L.L. Bean use its Web site to connect with its market? What indications do you have that this is a customer-oriented company?
http://www.llbean.com

What Is Marketing?

Define the term *marketing*

marketing
The process of planning and executing the conception, pricing, promotion, and distribution of ideas, goods, and services to create exchanges that satisfy individual and organizational goals.

What does the term *marketing* mean to you? Many people think it means the same as personal selling. Others think marketing is the same as personal selling and advertising. Still others believe marketing has something to do with making products available in stores, arranging displays, and maintaining inventories of products for future sales. Actually, marketing includes all of these activities and more.

Marketing has two facets. First, it is a philosophy, an attitude, a perspective, or a management orientation that stresses customer satisfaction. Second, marketing is a set of activities used to implement this philosophy. The American Marketing Association's definition encompasses both perspectives: "**Marketing** is the process of planning and executing the conception, pricing, promotion, and distribution of ideas, goods, and services to create exchanges that satisfy individual and organizational goals."[2]

The Concept of Exchange

exchange
The idea that people give up something to receive something they would rather have.

Exchange is the key term in the definition of marketing. The concept of **exchange** is quite simple. It means that people give up something to receive something they would rather have. Normally we think of money as the medium of exchange. We "give up" money to "get" the goods and services we want. Exchange does not require money, however. Two persons may barter or trade such items as baseball cards or oil paintings.

Five conditions must be satisfied for any kind of exchange to take place:

- There must be at least two parties.
- Each party must have something the other party values.
- Each party must be able to communicate with the other party and deliver the goods or services sought by the other trading party.
- Each party must be free to accept or reject the other's offer.
- Each party must want to deal with the other party.[3]

Exchange will not necessarily take place even if all these conditions exist. They are, however, necessary for exchange to be possible. For example, you may place an advertisement in your local newspaper stating that your used automobile is for sale at a certain price. Several people may call you to ask about the car, some may test-drive it, and one or more may even make you an offer. All five conditions are necessary for an exchange to exist. But unless you reach an agreement with a buyer and actually sell the car, an exchange will not take place. Notice that marketing can occur even if an exchange does not occur. In the example just discussed, you would have engaged in marketing even if no one bought your used automobile.

Marketing Management Philosophies

Describe four marketing management philosophies

Four competing philosophies strongly influence an organization's marketing activities. These philosophies are commonly referred to as production, sales, market, and societal marketing orientations.

Production Orientation

A **production orientation** is a philosophy that focuses on the internal capabilities of the firm rather than on the desires and needs of the marketplace. A production orientation means that management assesses its resources and asks these questions: "What can we do best?" "What can our engineers design?" "What is easy to produce, given our equipment?" In the case of a service organization, managers ask, "What services are most convenient for the firm to offer?" and "Where do our talents lie?" Some have referred to this orientation as a *Field of Dreams* orientation, referring to the movie line, "If we build it, they will come." The $178 billion furniture industry is infamous for its disregard of customers and for its slow cycle times. This has always been a production-oriented industry.[4]

There is nothing wrong with assessing a firm's capabilities; in fact, such assessments are major considerations in strategic marketing planning (see Chapter 2). A production orientation falls short because it does not consider whether the goods and services that the firm produces most efficiently also meet the needs of the marketplace. Sometimes what a firm can best produce is exactly what the market wants. For example, the research and development department of 3M's commercial tape division developed and patented the adhesive component of Post-it Notes a year before a commercial application was identified. In other situations, as when competition is weak or demand exceeds supply, a production-oriented firm can survive and even prosper. More often, however, firms that succeed in competitive markets have a clear understanding that they must first determine what customers want and then produce it, rather than focus on what company management thinks should be produced.

2001 PT CRUISER

CHRYSLER

<div class="sidebar">

production orientation
A philosophy that focuses on the internal capabilities of the firm rather than on the desires and needs of the marketplace.

Chrysler's implementation of the marketing concept has resulted in the wildly successful PT Cruiser automobile. Order lists are so long that the factory is having difficulty keeping up.

</div>

Sales Orientation

A **sales orientation** is based on the ideas that people will buy more goods and services if aggressive sales techniques are used and that high sales result in high profits. Not only are sales to the final buyer emphasized but intermediaries are also encouraged to push manufacturers' products more aggressively. To sales-oriented firms, marketing means selling things and collecting money.

The fundamental problem with a sales orientation, as with a production orientation, is a lack of understanding of the needs and wants of the marketplace. Sales-oriented companies often find that, despite the quality of their sales force, they cannot convince people to buy goods or services that are neither wanted nor needed.

 Research firm Datamonitor says that e-businesses will lose $3.2 billion in sales in 2000 because of inadequate customer service on their Web sites. A Yankelovich survey indicates that 70 percent of all Internet transactions are aborted.[5] Internet businesses that do not make their customers' entire buying experience satisfactory will not be in business very long.

sales orientation
The idea that people will buy more goods and services if aggressive sales techniques are used and that high sales result in high profits.

Market Orientation

The **marketing concept** is a simple and intuitively appealing philosophy. It states that the social and economic justification for an organization's existence is the satisfaction of customer wants and needs while meeting

marketing concept
The idea that the social and economic justification for an organization's existence is the satisfaction of customer wants and needs while meeting organizational objectives.

Adopting a market orientation requires top-management leadership and involvement. Bill Marriott knows this, so each year he travels widely visiting the company's hotels to ensure that every Marriott delivers superior customer value.
© Alex Koester/SYGMA

market orientation
Philosophy that assumes that a sale does not depend on an aggressive sales force but rather on a customer's decision to purchase a product.

organizational objectives. It is based on an understanding that a sale does not depend on an aggressive sales force, but rather on a customer's decision to purchase a product. What a business thinks it produces is not of primary importance to its success. Instead, what customers think they are buying—the perceived value—defines a business. The marketing concept includes the following:

- Focusing on customer wants and needs so the organization can distinguish its product(s) from competitors' offerings
- Integrating all the organization's activities, including production, to satisfy these wants
- Achieving long-term goals for the organization by satisfying customer wants and needs legally and responsibly

The marketing concept recognizes that there is no reason why customers should buy one organization's offerings unless it is in some way better at serving the customers' wants and needs than those offered by competing organizations.

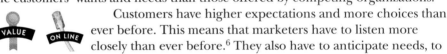

Customers have higher expectations and more choices than ever before. This means that marketers have to listen more closely than ever before.[6] They also have to anticipate needs, to solve problems before they start, to provide service that wows, and to offer responses to mistakes that more than make up for the original error.[7] For example, Netpulse Communications provides Internet connections to health clubs allowing exercisers to surf the Web or check their e-mail while they are working out. Netpulse uses a monitoring system to diagnose problems remotely. So, if a janitor accidentally disconnects a power cord, a service representative can call the club and ask them to plug the machine back in. Nine times out of ten Netpulse reports a problem to the club before anyone there is even aware of it.[8]

Firms that adopt and implement the marketing concept are said to be market oriented. **Market orientation** requires top-management leadership, a customer focus, competitor intelligence, and interfunctional coordination to meet customer wants and needs and deliver superior value. It also entails establishing and maintaining mutually rewarding relationships with customers.

Today, companies of all types are adopting a market orientation. Bill Marriott, Marriott International's CEO, logs an average of 150,000 travel miles each year visiting the company's hotels, inspecting them, and talking to employees at all levels in the organization. According to Marriott, "I want our associates to know that there really is a guy named Marriott who cares about them. . . . I also want to show our team in the field that I value their work enough to take time to check it."[9] Burton Snowboards became the best-known brand in one of the world's fastest-growing sports by identifying its most important customers, figuring out the product that those customers want, and then designing it. Almost every day Burton staffers visit with some of the 300 professional riders worldwide who advise the company. These conversations take place on the slopes and on the phone. If one of them has a suggestion or a problem, a Burton employee calls back within twenty-four hours. Riders help develop virtually every Burton product.[10]

Understanding your competitive arena and competitors' strengths and weaknesses is a critical component of market orientation. This includes assessing what

Western Union

Has Western Union rebounded from its failure to define its competitive arena as telecommunications? Evaluate the company's Web site to find out. Against whom does Western Union seem to be competing in the twenty-first century?

http://www.westernunion.com

On Line

existing or potential competitors might be intending to do tomorrow as well as what they are doing today. Western Union failed to define its competitive arena as telecommunications, concentrating instead on telegraph services, and was eventually outflanked by fax technology. Had Western Union been a market-oriented company, its management might have better understood the changes taking place, seen the competitive threat, and developed strategies to counter the threat.[11]

Market-oriented companies are successful in getting all business functions working together to deliver customer value. Rubbermaid has developed "cross-functional entrepreneurial teams" to overcome the difficulty of getting people from different functional areas to work together in developing new houseware products. These teams are empowered to make decisions and are responsible for results. For example, DaimlerChrysler creates so-called outposts of small cross-functional teams to scout around for new trends and products. A Silicon Valley outpost is doing consumer research on electric cars and is helping designers in the early stages of Net-equipped automobiles.[12]

Societal Marketing Orientation

One reason a market-oriented organization may choose not to deliver the benefits sought by customers is that these benefits may not be good for individuals or society. This philosophy, called a **societal marketing orientation**, states that an organization exists not only to satisfy customer wants and needs and to meet organizational objectives but also to preserve or enhance individuals' and society's long-term best interests. Marketing products and containers that are less toxic than normal, are more durable, contain reusable materials, or are made of recyclable materials is consistent with a societal marketing orientation. Duracell and Eveready battery companies have reduced the levels of mercury in their batteries and will eventually market mercury-free products. Turtle Wax car wash products and detergents are biodegradable and can be "digested" by waste treatment plants. The company's plastic containers are made of recyclable plastic, and its spray products do not use propellants that damage the ozone layer in the earth's upper atmosphere. The "Ethics in Marketing" story in this chapter illustrates a potential conflict between a market orientation and a societal orientation.

When it sees red, it charges.

Introducing the car that changes everything: Prius, the ingenious hybrid vehicle from Toyota. Prius captures the energy produced during normal deceleration and converts it back into power to drive the wheels. When you put on the brakes, Prius charges its own batteries, so it never needs to be plugged in. When you take off, Prius zips away under pure, clean electric power. It saves fuel. It saves gas money. And with up to 90% fewer emissions, it could save so much more.

The new Prius. Starting at $19,995. Destination Charge $485. Total MSRP $20,480.
Visit www.toyota.com/prius or call 800-GO-TOYOTA.

TOYOTA PRIUS | genius

Electric cars have long been considered the environmental solution to automobile emissions. But despite the popularity of the concept, car manufacturers have been unable to deliver performance at the same time. Toyota's Prius hopes to change this.

societal marketing orientation
The idea that an organization exists not only to satisfy customer wants and needs and to meet organizational objectives but also to preserve or enhance individuals' and society's long-term best interests.

Differences Between Sales and Market Orientations

The differences between sales and market orientations are substantial. Exhibit 1.1 compares the two orientations in terms of five characteristics: the organization's focus, the firm's business, those to whom the product is directed, the firm's primary goal, and the tools used to achieve those goals.

Discuss the differences between sales and market orientations

Exhibit **1.1**   Differences Between Sales and Market Orientations

	What is the organization's focus?	What business are you in?	To whom is the product directed?	What is your primary goal?	How do you seek to achieve your goal?
Sales Orientation	Inward, upon the organization's needs	Selling goods and services	Everybody	Profit through maximum sales volume	Primarily through intensive promotion
Market Orientation	Outward, upon the wants and preferences of customers	Satisfying customer wants and needs and delivering superior value	Specific groups of people	Profit through customer satisfaction	Through coordinated marketing and interfunctional activities

The Organization's Focus

Personnel in sales-oriented firms tend to be "inward looking," focusing on selling what the organization makes rather than making what the market wants. Many of the historic sources of competitive advantage—technology, innovation, economies of scale—allowed companies to focus their efforts internally and prosper. Today, many successful firms derive their competitive advantage from an external, market-oriented focus. A market orientation has helped companies such as Boeing, Dell Computer, Hewlett-Packard, and Southwest Airlines outperform their competitors.[13] Today key issues in developing competitive advantage include creating customer value, maintaining customer satisfaction, and building long-term relationships.

customer value
The ratio of benefits to the sacrifice necessary to obtain those benefits.

Customer Value   **Customer value** is the ratio of benefits to the sacrifice necessary to obtain those benefits. The automobile industry illustrates the importance of creating customer value. To penetrate the fiercely competitive luxury automobile market, Lexus adopted a customer-driven approach, with particular emphasis on service. Lexus stresses product quality with a standard of zero defects in manufacturing. The service quality goal is to treat each customer as one would treat a guest in one's home, to pursue the perfect person-to-person relationship, and to strive to improve continually. This pursuit has enabled Lexus to establish a clear quality image and capture a significant share of the luxury car market.

Customer value is not simply a matter of high quality. A high-quality product that is available only at a high price will not be perceived as a good value, nor will bare-bones service or low-quality goods selling for a low price. Instead, customers value goods and services of the quality they expect and that are sold at prices they are willing to pay. Value can be used to sell a Mercedes Benz as well as a $3 Tyson frozen chicken dinner.

Value also stretches beyond quality and price to include customized options and fast delivery. Dell Computer Corporation encourages shoppers to customize products to their liking on their Web sites. The five-day car is a revolutionary concept pioneered by Toyota. They envision customers picking and choosing from a menu of on-screen options, then hitting a button to send the order straight to the factory. Toyota currently equips showrooms in Japan with Internet terminals for option selection and ordering.[14]

Marketers interested in customer value

- *Offer products that perform:* This is the bare minimum requirement. Consumers have lost patience with shoddy merchandise.
- *Give consumers more than they expect:* Dell Computer's mission is "to be the most successful computer company in the world at delivering the best customer experience in markets we

Ethics in Marketing

USING CUSTOMER DATA TO ENCOURAGE MORE FREQUENT GAMBLING

In 1994, Harrah's Entertainment hired a chief marketing officer, Brad Morgan, with experience at Visa and Procter & Gamble, to bring in some outside consumer-marketing savvy. Morgan spoke of sizing up gamblers "psychographically"—rating them according to characteristics such as how much money they are likely to lose, and how frequently they gamble.

Morgan also identified a small group of Harrah's customers who produced most of the company's profits. He says he found that people who lost between $100 and $499 a trip accounted for about 30 percent of gamblers but 80 percent of revenue and, startlingly, nearly 100 percent of the profits. Among themselves, Harrah's officials referred to these customers as "grazers" for their steady casino habits. Publicly, the company settled on another term for its core audience: "avid experienced players." These players became Harrah's target customers.

The company began collecting intimate details on these players when it launched its Total Gold frequent-gambler card in 1997. The electronic cards, inserted in slot machines or handed to casino supervisors, gathered minutiae on gamblers' habits in exchange for letting them know how to attain the free drinks, hotel rooms, show tickets, and other "comps."

In one test, Harrah's chose two similar groups of frequent slot players from Jackson, Mississippi. Members of the control group were offered a typical casino-marketing package worth $125—a free room, two steak meals, and $30 of free chips at the Tunica casino. Members of the test group were offered $60 in chips. The more modest offer generated far more gambling, suggesting that Harrah's had been wasting money giving customers free rooms. Thereafter, profits from the revamped promotion nearly doubled to $60 per person per trip.

In another test, Harrah's focused on a group of monthly gamblers whom the company suspected could be induced to play more frequently because they lived nearby and displayed avid-gambler traits such as hitting slot buttons quickly (playing at "high velocity" in Harrah's parlance). To entice them to make two back-to-back visits, Harrah's sent cash and food offers that expired in consecutive two-week periods. The group's average number of trips per month quickly rose from 1.1 to 1.4.

When a gambler wagers less than usual—by skipping a monthly visit for instance—Harrah's "intervenes" with a letter or a phone call offering a free meal, show ticket, or cash voucher. Telemarketers are trained to get customers to talk about their earlier casino experiences, and then to listen for trigger phrases such as "hotel room" or "steak dinner" to come up with the most alluring offer.

This "Pavlovian marketing," as Richard Mirman, senior vice-president for Harrah's calls it, is a far cry from the traditional methods gambling companies have used to attract customers. Casinos have long depended on the inherent sexiness of their product to reach the low-rolling public. Until Harrah's, they have eschewed the kind of quantitative analysis employed to great effect by other consumer-oriented industries such as airlines and banks. Instead, they have focused on high rollers, doling out VIP perks such as free flights and fine champagne. The masses have been courted with gimmicky contests and, increasingly, with fantastic top-this-one resorts.[a]

Is it ethical for a casino company to use data gathered from and about customers to encourage them to gamble more frequently? How would you feel if you were the subject of what one Harrah's manager called "Pavlovian marketing"? Use this example to illustrate the difference between a market orientation and a societal marketing orientation.

[a] Christina Binkley, "Casino Chain Mines Data on Its Gamblers and Strikes Pay Dirt," *Wall Street Journal,* May 4, 2000, p. A1. Reprinted by permission of the *Wall Street Journal* ©2000 Dow Jones & Co., Inc. All rights reserved worldwide.

serve." What is customer experience? According to Richard Owen, vice president of Dell Online worldwide, "It is the sum total of the interactions that a customer has with a company's products, people, and processes."[15] In other words, Dell gives customers more than they expect.

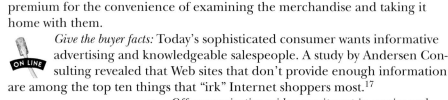
• *Avoid unrealistic pricing:* E-marketers are leveraging Internet technology to redefine how prices are set and negotiated. With lower costs, e-marketers can often offer lower prices than their brick-and-mortar counterparts. The enormous popularity of auction sites such as eBay and Amazon.com and the customer-bid model used by Priceline illustrate that on-line customers are interested in bargain prices.[16] Many are not willing to pay a premium for the convenience of examining the merchandise and taking it home with them.

customer satisfaction
The feeling that a product has met or exceeded the customer's expectations.

• *Give the buyer facts:* Today's sophisticated consumer wants informative advertising and knowledgeable salespeople. A study by Andersen Consulting revealed that Web sites that don't provide enough information are among the top ten things that "irk" Internet shoppers most.[17]

• *Offer organization-wide commitment in service and after-sales support:* People fly Southwest Airlines because the airline offers superior value. Although passengers do not get assigned seats or meals (just peanuts or crackers) when they use the airline, its service is reliable and friendly and costs less than most major airlines. All Southwest employees are involved in the effort to satisfy customers. Pilots tend to the boarding gate when their help is needed and ticket agents help move luggage. One reservation agent flew from Dallas to Tulsa with a frail, elderly woman whose son was afraid she couldn't handle the change of planes by herself on her way to St. Louis.

Customer-intimate companies achieve great success by building longtime relationships with their customers. Home Depot is an industry benchmark in customer satisfaction. Here, employee Juan Cruz loads plywood for a customer preparing her home against an impending hurricane.

Customer Satisfaction **Customer satisfaction** is the feeling that a product has met or exceeded the customer's expectations. Keeping current customers satisfied is just as important as attracting new ones and a lot less expensive. Firms that have a reputation for delivering high levels of customer satisfaction do things differently from their competitors. Top management is obsessed with customer satisfaction and employees throughout the organization understand the link between their job and satisfied customers. The culture of the organization is to focus on delighting customers rather than on selling products.

Staples, the office supply retailer, offers great prices on its paper, pens, fax machines, and other office supplies, but its main strategy is to grow by providing customers with the best solutions to their problems. Their approach is to emulate customer-intimate companies like Home Depot and Airborne Express. These companies do not pursue one-time transactions: They cultivate relationships.

Building Relationships Attracting new customers to a business is only the beginning. The best companies view new customer attraction as the launching point for developing and enhancing a long-term relationship. Companies can expand market share in three ways: attracting new customers, increasing business with existing customers, and retaining current customers. Building relationships with existing customers directly addresses two of the three possibilities and indirectly addresses the other.[18]

Relationship marketing is the name of a strategy that entails forging long-term partnerships with customers. Companies build relationships with customers by offering value and providing customer satisfaction. They are rewarded with repeat sales and referrals that lead to increases in sales, market share, and profits. Costs also fall because serving existing customers is less expensive than attracting new ones. AMR Research reports that it can be ten times more expensive to acquire a new customer than to keep a current one.[19]

The success of Dell Computer Corporation is rooted in relationship marketing. The company sees its customers as individuals, each with a unique need, and Dell's entire marketing program is geared to building relationships with individuals.[20]

The Internet is an effective tool for generating relationships with customers because of its ability to interact with the customer. With the Internet, companies can use e-mail for fast customer service, discussion groups for building a sense of community, and database tracking of buying habits for customizing products.[21]

Customers also benefit from stable relationships with suppliers. Business buyers have found that partnerships with their suppliers are essential to producing high-quality products while cutting costs.[22] Customers remain loyal to firms that provide them greater value and satisfaction than they expect from competing firms.

Most successful relationship marketing strategies depend on customer-oriented personnel, effective training programs, employees with authority to make decisions and solve problems, and teamwork.

Customer-Oriented Personnel   For an organization to be focused on building relationships with customers, employees' attitudes and actions must be customer oriented. An employee may be the only contact a particular customer has with the firm. In that customer's eyes, the employee is the firm. Any person, department, or division that is not customer oriented weakens the positive image of the entire organization. For example, a potential customer who is greeted discourteously may well assume that the employee's attitude represents the whole firm.

The Role of Training   Leading marketers recognize the role of employee training in customer service and relationship building. Of *Fortune's* 100 best companies to work for, fifty-three offer on-site university courses and ninety-one have tuition reimbursement programs.[23] It is no coincidence that the public companies on this list such as Southwest Airlines and Cisco Systems perform much better than other firms in their respective industries. All new employees at Disneyland and Walt Disney World must attend Disney University, a special training program for Disney employees. They must first pass Traditions 1, a day-long course focusing on the Disney philosophy and operational procedures. Then they go on to specialized training. Similarly, McDonald's has Hamburger University. At American Express's Quality University, line employees and managers learn how to treat customers. There is an extra payoff for companies such as Disney and McDonald's that train their employees to be customer oriented. When employees make their customers

relationship marketing
The name of a strategy that entails forging long-term partnerships with customers.

Empowering employees not only boosts job satisfaction, it boosts customer satisfaction. Each FedEx employee has the authority to spend $100 to resolve a customer's complaint on the spot.

empowerment
Delegation of authority to solve customers' problems quickly—usually by the first person that the customer notifies regarding a problem.

teamwork
Collaborative efforts of people to accomplish common objectives.

happy, the employees are more likely to derive satisfaction from their jobs. Having contented workers who are committed to their jobs leads to better customer service and greater employee retention.

Empowerment In addition to training, many marketing-oriented firms are giving employees more authority to solve customer problems on the spot. The term used to describe this delegation of authority is **empowerment**. Employees develop ownership attitudes when they are treated like part-owners of the business and are expected to act the part. These employees manage themselves, are more likely to work hard, account for their own performance and the company's, and take prudent risks to build a stronger business and sustain the company's success.[24] FedEx customer service representatives are trained and empowered to resolve customer problems. Although the average FedEx transaction costs only $16, the customer service representatives are empowered to spend up to $100 to resolve a customer problem.

Empowerment gives customers the feeling that their concerns are being addressed and gives employees the feeling that their expertise matters. The result is greater satisfaction for both customers and employees.

Teamwork Many organizations, such as Southwest Airlines and Walt Disney World, that are frequently noted for delivering superior customer value and providing high levels of customer satisfaction assign employees to teams and teach them team-building skills. **Teamwork** entails collaborative efforts of people to accomplish common objectives. Job performance, company performance, product value, and customer satisfaction all improve when people in the same department or work group begin supporting and assisting each other and emphasize cooperation instead of competition. Performance is also enhanced when people in different areas of responsibility such as production and sales or sales and service practice teamwork, with the ultimate goal of delivering superior customer value and satisfaction.

The Firm's Business

As Exhibit 1.1 illustrates, a sales-oriented firm defines its business (or mission) in terms of goods and services. A market-oriented firm defines its business in terms of the benefits its customers seek. People who spend their money, time, and energy expect to receive benefits, not just goods and services. This distinction has enormous implications.

Because of the limited way it defines its business, a sales-oriented firm often misses opportunities to serve customers whose wants can be met through only a wide range of product offerings instead of specific products. For example, in 1989, 220-year-old Britannica had estimated revenues of $650 million and a worldwide sales force of 7,500. Just five years later, after three consecutive years of losses, the sales force had collapsed to as few as 280 representatives. How did this respected company sink so low? Britannica managers saw that competitors were beginning to use CD-ROM to store huge masses of information but chose to ignore the new computer technology, as well as an offer to team up with Microsoft.

It's not hard to see why parents would rather give their children an encyclopedia on a compact disk instead of a printed one. The CD-ROM versions were either given away or sold by other publishers for under $400. A full thirty-two-volume set of *Encyclopaedia Britannica* weighs about 120 pounds, costs a minimum of $1,500, and takes up four and one half feet of shelf space. If Britannica had defined its business as providing information instead of publishing books, it might not have suffered such a precipitous fall.

Adopting a "better late than never" philosophy, Britannica is making its complete thirty-two-volume set available free on the Internet. The company no longer sells door-to-door and hopes to return to profitability by selling advertising on its Web site.[25]

Answering the question "What is this firm's business?" in terms of the benefits customers seek, instead of goods and services, has at least three important advantages:

- It ensures that the firm keeps focusing on customers and avoids becoming preoccupied with goods, services, or the organization's internal needs.
- It encourages innovation and creativity by reminding people that there are many ways to satisfy customer wants.
- It stimulates an awareness of changes in customer desires and preferences so that product offerings are more likely to remain relevant.

Market orientation and the idea of focusing on customer wants do not mean that customers will always receive everything they want. It is not possible, for example, to profitably manufacture and market automobile tires that will last for 100,000 miles for $25. Furthermore, customers' preferences must be mediated by sound professional judgment as to how to deliver the benefits they seek. As one adage suggests, "People don't know what they want—they only want what they know." Consumers have a limited set of experiences. They are unlikely to request anything beyond those experiences because they are not aware of benefits they may gain from other potential offerings. For example, before the Internet, many people thought that shopping for some products was boring and time consuming, but could not express their need for electronic shopping.

Those to Whom the Product Is Directed

A sales-oriented organization targets its products at "everybody" or "the average customer." A market-oriented organization aims at specific groups of people (see again Exhibit 1.1). The fallacy of developing products directed at the average user is that relatively few average users actually exist. Typically, populations are characterized by diversity. An average is simply a midpoint in some set of characteristics. Because most potential customers are not "average," they are not likely to be attracted to an average product marketed to the average customer. Consider the

market for shampoo as one simple example. There are shampoos for oily hair, dry hair, and dandruff. Some shampoos remove the gray or color hair. Special shampoos are marketed for infants and elderly people. There is even shampoo for people with average or normal hair (whatever that is), but this is a fairly small portion of the total market for shampoo.

A market-oriented organization recognizes that different customer groups and their wants vary. It may therefore need to develop different goods, services, and promotional appeals. A market-oriented organization carefully analyzes the market and divides it into groups of people who are fairly similar in terms of selected characteristics. Then the organization develops marketing programs that will bring about mutually satisfying exchanges with one or more of those groups.

Paying attention to the customer isn't exactly a new concept. Back in the 1920s, General Motors began designing cars for every lifestyle and pocketbook. This was a breakthrough for an industry that had been largely driven by production needs ever since Henry Ford promised any color as long as it was black. Chapter 7 thoroughly explores the topic of analyzing markets and selecting those that appear to be most promising to the firm.

The Firm's Primary Goal

As Exhibit 1.1 illustrates, a sales-oriented organization seeks to achieve profitability through sales volume and tries to convince potential customers to buy, even if the seller knows that the customer and product are mismatched. Sales-oriented organizations place a higher premium on making a sale than on developing a long-term relationship with a customer. In contrast, the ultimate goal of most market-oriented organizations is to make a profit by creating customer value, providing customer satisfaction, and building long-term relationships with customers. The exception is so-called "nonprofit organizations" that exist to achieve goals other than profits. Nonprofit organizations can and should adopt a market orientation. Nonprofit organization marketing is explored further in Chapter 11.

Tools the Organization Uses to Achieve Its Goals

Sales-oriented organizations seek to generate sales volume through intensive promotional activities, mainly personal selling and advertising. In contrast, market-oriented organizations recognize that promotion decisions are only one of four basic marketing mix decisions that have to be made: product decisions, place (or distribution) decisions, promotion decisions, and pricing decisions. A market-oriented organization recognizes each of these four components as important. Furthermore, market-oriented organizations recognize that marketing is not just a responsibility of the marketing department. Interfunctional coordination means that skills and resources throughout the organization are needed to deliver superior customer service and value.[26]

A Word of Caution

This comparison of sales and market orientations is not meant to belittle the role of promotion, especially personal selling, in the marketing mix. Promotion is the means by which organizations communicate with present and prospective customers about the merits and characteristics of their organization and products. Effective promotion is an essential part of effective marketing. Salespeople who work for market-oriented organizations are generally perceived by their customers to be problem solvers and important links to supply sources and new products. Chapter 16 examines the nature of personal selling in more detail.

The Marketing Process

Marketing managers are responsible for a variety of activities that together represent the marketing process. These include the following:

Describe the marketing process

- Understanding the organization's mission and the role marketing plays in fulfilling that mission.
- Setting marketing objectives.
- Gathering, analyzing, and interpreting information about the organization's situation, including its strengths and weaknesses as well as opportunities and threats in the environment.
- Developing a marketing strategy by deciding exactly which wants and whose wants the organization will try to satisfy (target market strategy) and by developing appropriate marketing activities (the marketing mix) to satisfy the desires of selected target markets. The marketing mix combines product, distribution, promotion, and pricing strategies in a way that creates exchanges that satisfy individual and organizational goals. The marketing mix is addressed in the "Global Perspectives" box that follows and is examined in detail in Chapter 2.
- Implementing the marketing strategy.
- Designing performance measures.
- Periodically evaluating marketing efforts, and making changes if needed.

These activities and their relationships form the foundation on which the rest of the book is based. The table of contents at the beginning shows the order in which the activities are described. Exhibit 2.1 in Chapter 2 illustrates their interrelationships.

Why Study Marketing?

Now that you understand the meaning of the term *marketing*, why it is important to adopt a marketing orientation, and how organizations implement this philosophy, you may be asking, "What's in it for me?" or "Why should I study marketing?"

Describe several reasons for studying marketing

CAN AN UNKNOWN CHINESE COMPANY PENETRATE THE U.S. TV MARKET?

Konka is a Chinese government-owned television set maker. It is on a mission to break into the U.S. market and help China become a global power in home electronics, displacing Japan and Korea. Given Konka's obscurity here that may sound like mission impossible, but consider this: Konka, the top TV seller in China, had net income of $60 million in 1999 on sales of $1.6 billion. It is among the biggest TV manufacturers in the world, and expects to churn out 6.5 million sets in 2000. Global leader Matsushita Electric Industrial Company, maker of Panasonic and National brands, expects to make about ten million TVs in 2000.

Konka already has gained a toehold in the U.S. market by selling basic TVs with thirteen- and nineteen-inch screens at cut-rate prices to mom-and-pop dealers. Konka hopes to build on that by introducing bigger-screen models and landing a deal with a national retail chain. Several show interest—including the big kahuna, Wal-Mart Stores Inc.

For the Chinese, landing a Wal-Mart account is about more than just selling TVs. China would like to break its traditional reliance on slow-growth industries such as textiles, take a seat in the World Trade Organization, and gain permanent trade status with the United States.

So Beijing policymakers are aiding the international expansions of Konka and other companies with tax credits, cheap capital, and speedy approvals for moving people and resources.

"We're doing something to change people's thought (that) the label 'Made in China' is cheap and bad," says Wendy Wu, the twenty-nine-year-old marketer dispatched in 1998 to Silicon Valley to lead Konka's U.S. entry. "Whatever the Japanese can do and the Koreans can do, the Chinese can do."

Konka will face some heavy static. The U.S. TV market is jammed, with more than twenty name brands. Konka has already made some costly misjudgments in America, and there's little room for error: The retail chains that sell vast numbers of TVs exert tremendous pressure on manufacturers to keep prices low, making for razor-thin profit margins. And many retailers are simply reluctant to try an unknown brand—one that often gets confused with Tonka and toy trucks.

Wu crafted a sales strategy that relies heavily on price. To give dealers a better profit margin, they sell at ultra low prices—just as Japanese electronics makers did when they first came to the United States. But, to counter perceptions of inferior quality, they offer a one-year guarantee and tout a record of low consumer returns (most TVs typically carry only a ninety-day warranty).

The only child of two professors at Beijing's prestigious Tsinghua University, Wu set off introducing herself to electronics retailers throughout the country. She found mom-and-pop dealers receptive to selling basic TVs with thirteen- and nineteen-inch screens, mainly because they were willing to risk something new to distinguish their stores from big chains.

One of the first buyers, Great Buys Plus Inc. of Evansville, Indiana, decided to sell Konka's nineteen-inch TV in six of its seventeen stores after Wu sent store president Terry Oates a video of Konka's extensive Chinese factories and headquarters. The video convinced Oates that Konka was a reputable manufacturer, and steady sales so far have prompted Great Buys Plus to look at adding bigger Konka TVs. "I think they're making some people sit up and take a look," Oates says.[a]

Describe the end-user that Konka is targeting. Explain Konka's product, distribution, promotion, and pricing strategies for entering the U.S. market.

[a] Evan Ronstad and Karby Leggett, "A Chinese TV Maker Mounts an Invasion of Crowded U.S. Turf," *Wall Street Journal*, May 5, 2000, A1, A6. Reprinted by permission of the *Wall Street Journal* ©2000 Dow Jones & Co., Inc. All rights reserved worldwide.

These are important questions, whether you are majoring in a business field other than marketing (such as accounting, finance, or management information systems) or a nonbusiness field (such as journalism, economics, or agriculture). There are several important reasons to study marketing: Marketing plays an important role in society, marketing is important to businesses, marketing offers outstanding career opportunities, and marketing affects your life every day.

Marketing Plays an Important Role in Society

The total population of the United States exceeds 268 million people. Think about how many transactions are needed each day to feed, clothe, and shelter a population of this size. The number is huge. And yet it all works quite well, partly because the well-developed U.S. economic system efficiently distributes the output of farms and factories. A typical U.S. family, for example, consumes 2.5 tons of food a year. Marketing makes food available when we want it, in desired quantities, at accessible locations, and in sanitary and convenient packages and forms (such as instant and frozen foods).

Marketing Is Important to Businesses

The fundamental objectives of most businesses are survival, profits, and growth. Marketing contributes directly to achieving these objectives. Marketing includes the following activities, which are vital to business organizations: assessing the wants and satisfactions of present and potential customers, designing and managing product offerings, determining prices and pricing policies, developing distribution strategies, and communicating with present and potential customers.

All businesspeople, regardless of specialization or area of responsibility, need to be familiar with the terminology and fundamentals of accounting, finance, management, and marketing. People in all business areas need to be able to communicate with specialists in other areas. Furthermore, marketing is not just a job done by people in a marketing department. Marketing is a part of the job of everyone in the organization. As David Packard of Hewlett-Packard put it: "Marketing is too important to be left to the marketing department."[27] Therefore, a basic understanding of marketing is important to all businesspeople.

Businesses are not the only entities that conduct marketing activities. Not-for-profit organizations like the World Wildlife Fund provide career opportunities in marketing as well.

Marketing Offers Outstanding Career Opportunities

Between a fourth and a third of the entire civilian workforce in the United States performs marketing activities. Marketing offers great career opportunities in such areas as professional selling, marketing research, advertising, retail buying, distribution management, product management, product development, and wholesaling. Marketing career opportunities also exist in a variety of nonbusiness organizations, including hospitals, museums, universities, the armed forces, and various government and social service agencies. (See Chapter 11.)

As the global marketplace becomes more challenging, companies all over the world and of all sizes are going to have to become better marketers. For a comprehensive look at career opportunities in marketing and a variety of other useful information about careers, please visit our Web site at http://lamb.swcollege.com.

Marketing Affects Your Life Every Day

Marketing plays a major role in your everyday life. You participate in the marketing process as a consumer of goods and services. About half of every dollar you spend pays for marketing costs, such as marketing research, product development, packaging, transportation, storage, advertising, and sales expenses. By developing a better understanding of marketing, you will become a better-informed consumer. You will better understand the buying process and be able to negotiate more effectively with sellers. Moreover, you will be better prepared to demand satisfaction when the goods and services you buy do not meet the standards promised by the manufacturer or the marketer.

Looking Ahead

This book is divided into twenty chapters organized into seven major parts. The chapters are written from the marketing manager's perspective. Each chapter begins with a brief list of learning objectives followed by a brief story about a marketing situation faced by a firm or industry. At the end of each of these opening vignettes, thought-provoking questions link the story to the subject addressed in the chapter. Your instructor may wish to begin chapter discussions by asking members of your class to share their views about the questions.

The examples of global marketing highlighted in most chapters will help you understand that marketing takes place all over the world, between buyers and sellers in different countries. These and other global marketing examples throughout the book, marked with the icon shown in the margin, are intended to help you develop a global perspective on marketing.

Marketing ethics is another important topic selected for special treatment throughout the book. Chapters include highlighted stories about firms or industries that have faced ethical dilemmas or have engaged in practices that some consider unethical. Questions are posed to focus your thinking on the key ethical issues raised in each story.

Delivering superior customer value is a key to marketing success in an increasingly competitive environment. Examples of creating or delivering superior customer value are integrated throughout the text and are highlighted with the icon shown in the margin.

Entrepreneurial insights are highlighted with icons. Every chapter also includes an application case related to small business. This material illustrates how entrepreneurs and small businesses can use the principles and concepts discussed in the book.

End-of-chapter materials begin with a final comment on the chapter-opening vignette (Looking Back), followed by a new feature to this edition called "Use It Now!" The purpose of this section is to illustrate how you can apply what you learn in this course right now. Next, a summary of the major topics is provided along with a listing of the key terms introduced in the chapter, and discussion and writing questions (writing questions are identified with the icon in the margin). Specific Internet and team activities appear in the writing and discussion questions. These are identified by appropriate icons. The on-line icon is also placed throughout the text to identify examples relating to technology. Another section, "Application for Entrepreneurs" with discussion questions, is next, followed by a longer entrepreneurship case and a video case with discussion questions.

Marketing 6e is also supported by InfoTrac College Edition. Several chapters throughout the book will give you the opportunity to refine your research skills through exercises specifically designed for InfoTrac. These exercises will be flagged by the icon at the left. All these features are intended to help you develop a more thorough understanding of marketing and enjoy the learning process.

The remaining chapters in Part 1 introduce you to the activities involved in developing a marketing plan, the dynamic environment in which marketing decisions must be made, ethics and social responsibility, and global marketing. Part 2 covers consumer decision making and buyer behavior; business marketing; the concepts of positioning, market segmentation, and targeting; and the nature and uses of marketing research and decision support systems. Parts 3 through 6 examine the elements of the marketing mix—product, distribution, promotion, and pricing. Part 7 contains two chapters. The first examines Internet marketing and the second introduces integrated direct marketing, or one-to-one marketing.

Look back at the story at the beginning of this chapter about L. L. Bean. You should now find the questions at the end of the story to be quite simple and straightforward. L. L. Bean is clearly a market-oriented company. The "satisfaction or your product repaired, replaced or your money back" policy illustrates this orientation. Market-oriented organizations deliver customer value. Review the five bulleted points describing marketers interested in customer value and discuss L. L. Bean in terms of each point.

You also learned in Chapter 1 that employees like to work for companies such as L. L. Bean that are market oriented. You may recall the observation that when employees make their customers happy, the employees are more likely to derive satisfaction from their jobs. Happy customers make employees happy, which leads to better treatment of customers.

Use it Now!

Lisa Imm, 25, an assistant marketing manager at Commtouch, Inc., a global provider of Web-based e-mail, was looking to change fields—from database marketing to Internet marketing. But she had no idea how her current skills would transfer. Bottom line: She needed to network, and fast.

 She didn't hit the party circuit or attend career fairs. Instead, she joined the e-mail list for Silicon Valley Web Grrls (www.webgrrls.com), a networking group for women who work in the technology sector. "I instantly had access to more than 1,000 people without physically having to meet them," Imm says. "The list is my virtual Rolodex."

Imm used the network not only to tap into what jobs were available but also to get valuable advice when she was considering offers: "People wrote back saying, 'I wouldn't work for that company, and this is why.' It was like having 100 personal recruiters and career counselors." A month after gathering information from the Web Grrls community and other sources, Imm landed her job.

What's her advice for others looking to take advantage of the power of a cyber-schmooze? First, be sure to join a group with credentials: "You can refer to the group on your résumé. Many times in an interview people will say, 'Wow! I've used that group too!' It's a great conversation starter." Also, give as generously as you receive. "If you don't respond to people when you've got the advice that they need, then you won't get much out of it."[28]

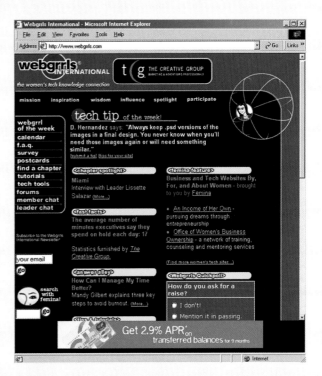

Thinking about a career in marketing isn't something you have to wait to graduate to do. You can begin right now. Check out the Webgrrls site to find out how.

Summary

(1) **Define the term** *marketing.* The ultimate goal of all marketing activity is to facilitate mutually satisfying exchanges between parties. The activities of marketing include the conception, pricing, promotion, and distribution of ideas, goods, and services.

(2) **Describe four marketing management philosophies.** The role of marketing and the character of marketing activities within an organization are strongly influenced by its philosophy and orientation. A production-oriented organization focuses on the internal capabilities of the firm rather than on the desires and needs of the marketplace. A sales orientation is based on the beliefs that people will buy more products if aggressive sales techniques are used and that high sales volumes produce high profits. A market-oriented organization focuses on satisfying customer wants and needs while meeting organizational objectives. A societal marketing orientation goes beyond a market orientation to include the preservation or enhancement of individuals' and society's long-term best interests.

(3) **Discuss the differences between sales and market orientations.** First, sales-oriented firms focus on their own needs; market-oriented firms focus on customers' needs and preferences. Second, sales-oriented companies consider themselves to be deliverers of goods and services, whereas market-oriented companies view themselves as satisfiers of customers. Third, sales-oriented firms direct their products to everyone; market-oriented firms aim at specific segments of the population. Fourth, although the primary goal of both types of firms is profit, sales-oriented businesses pursue maximum sales volume through intensive promotion, whereas market-oriented businesses pursue customer satisfaction through coordinated activities.

(4) **Describe the marketing process.** The marketing process includes understanding the organization's mission and the role marketing plays in fulfilling that mission, setting marketing objectives, scanning the environment, developing a marketing strategy by selecting a target market strategy, developing and implementing a marketing mix, implementing the strategy, designing performance measures, and evaluating marketing efforts and making changes if needed. The marketing mix combines product, distribution (place), promotion, and pricing strategies in a way that creates exchanges satisfying to individual and organizational objectives.

(5) **Describe several reasons for studying marketing.** First, marketing affects the allocation of goods and services that influence a nation's economy and standard of living. Second, an understanding of marketing is crucial to understanding most businesses. Third, career opportunities in marketing are diverse, profitable, and expected to increase significantly during the coming decade. Fourth, understanding marketing makes consumers more informed.

Key Terms

customer satisfaction 12
customer value 10
empowerment 14
exchange 6
marketing 6
marketing concept 7
market orientation 8
production orientation 7
relationship marketing 13
sales orientation 7
societal marketing
    orientation 9
teamwork 14

Discussion and Writing Questions

1. **WRITING** Your company president has decided to restructure the firm and become more market oriented. She is going to announce the changes at an upcoming meeting. She has asked you to prepare a short speech outlining the general reasons for the new company orientation.

2. Donald E. Petersen, chairman of the board of Ford Motor Company, remarked, "If we aren't customer driven, our cars won't be either." Explain how this statement reflects the marketing concept.

3. **WRITING** A friend of yours agrees with the adage "People don't know what they want—they only want what they know." Write your friend a letter expressing the extent to which you think marketers shape consumer wants.

4. Your local supermarket's slogan is "It's your store." However, when you asked one of the stock people to help you find a bag of chips, he told you it was not his job and that you should look a little harder. On your way out, you noticed a sign with an address for complaints. Draft a letter explaining why the supermarket's slogan will never be credible unless their employees carry it out.

5. Give an example of a company that might be successfully following a production orientation. Why might a firm in this industry be successful following such an orientation?

6. Write a letter to a friend or family member explaining why you think that a course in marketing will help you in your career in some field other than marketing.

7. Form a small group of three or four members. Suppose you and your colleagues all work for an up-and-coming gourmet coffee company that has several stores, mostly in large cities across the United States. Your team has been assigned the task of assessing whether or not the company should begin marketing on the Internet.

Each member has been assigned to visit three or four Internet sites for ideas. Some possibilities are

Toys 'R' Us at **http://www.toysrus.com**
Wal-Mart at **http://www.wal-mart.com**
Godiva chocolates at **http://www.godiva.com**
Levi Strauss at **http://www.levi.com**

Use your imagination and look up others. As you can see, many companies are easy to find, as long as you can spell their names. Typically, you would use the following: **http://www.companyname.com**

Has Internet marketing helped the companies whose sites you visited? If so, how? What factors should your company consider before committing to Internet activity? Prepare a three- to five-minute presentation to give to your class.

8. What is the AMA? What does it do? How do its services benefit marketers? **http://www.ama.org/**

9. Logon to InfoTrac at **www.infotrac-college.com** and conduct a keyword search for "marketing." Read a couple of the articles. Based on what you have learned in this chapter, how do these articles describe or relate to marketing?

Application for Entrepreneurs

Lisa King enjoyed working as a camp counselor during the summer. She started about the time she entered high school and continued through college. She even took a job at a camp the summer after graduating from college. She rationalized that this "internship," developing the camp yearbook, would help prepare her for a job in advertising.

As the summer passed by, Lisa spent more time thinking about "what she was going to do when she grew up," as she liked to put it. Her thoughts always seemed to return to camping.

Lisa finally decided that she would like to open a small retail store specializing in camping supplies. The more she thought about it, the better she liked the idea.

She finally got up enough nerve to call her father, Tom, to discuss the idea. Tom's first response was, "Have you prepared a written plan?"

Lisa remembered preparing a marketing plan in her first class in marketing at the University of Miami. She asked her father to FedEx the text to her.

With financial backing from Tom, Lisa and her sister Jill opened Santorini Camping Supply the following fall. They picked the name Santorini because it was their favorite place in the Greek Isles and, as Jill put it, "We just like the name."

On the first day the store was open, a customer asked Lisa if Santorini's guaranteed the products it sold. Lisa proudly replied, "Every product that is purchased from Santorini Camping Supply has a lifetime guarantee. If at any time you are not satisfied with one of our products, you can return it to the store for a full refund or exchange."

Questions

1. What marketing management philosophy is Santorini's expressing? Why have you reached this conclusion?
2. Do you think a lifetime guarantee for this kind of product is too generous? Why or why not?
3. Do you think this policy will contribute to success or to bankruptcy?
4. Suggest other customer service policies that might be appropriate for Santorini's Camping Supply.

Case

entrepreneurship

Entrypoint.com: The Door to Personalized Web Content

When Chris and Greg Hassett formed PED Software in 1992, little did they anticipate such a tumultuous ride for their technology start-up. Their software's key benefit was the ability it offered users to personalize content and data pulled from on-line sources. This capability made Hassett's creation a pioneer in what came to be called "push technology." Eventually launched as PointCast in 1996, the Hassetts' company quickly became an Internet and Wall Street darling. But as fast as its rise was its precipitous fall just one year after launch. Poor performance caused users and investors to become disenchanted with PointCast's technology. Even PointCast's attempts to shift to Web-delivered service were ill-timed and failed to pull the company out of its doldrums.

Enter Bill Gross, the entrepreneur who controls Idealab, a venture capital firm located in Pasadena, California, that invests in a number of prominent Internet companies. In May 1999, one of Idealab's companies, LaunchPad, merged with the beleaguered pioneer of push technology and so raised PointCast from the Internet ash heap. Not three months later, the newly combined company introduced what could become a dominant tool in consumer e-commerce.

As the Internet has exploded, Web sites have proliferated. The number of Web sites where consumers can satisfy their needs is far beyond the number of sites that the average Net surfer will ever stumble across. The first product of the PointCast/LauchPad merger, Entry-Point.com, wants to solve that problem by funneling personalized content to Net users with the goal of reducing the amount of time wasted by surfing through undesired Web pages.

EntryPoint lets users download a toolbar from the Web that sits on the desktop of a user's PC. The toolbar has a variety of menus including News, Sports, Fun, Shop, Finance, Travel, and eWallet, another entrepreneurial venture fueled by Bill Gross. EntryPoint also features a search window, a readout of the Dow Jones Industrial average, and an updated local weather forecast. Users of the toolbar can set it up to select information from a variety of premiere on-line news sources, entertainment providers, financial publications, and travel services. This tailored information scrolls across a window in EntryPoint's toolbar, effectively creating a customized portal on the user's screen that provides instant access to desired information whenever the user is on-line. With eWallet, EntryPoint also gives consumers digital storage for billing information on a variety of their credit cards. When shopping, a user simply has to click on the eWallet icon and select the appropriate credit card icon. The information for that credit card is then automatically transferred to whatever billing template the shopping site provides to the user.

By taking a market-oriented approach to delivering news, entertainment, and valuable shopping services to its customers, EntryPoint clearly wants to facilitate a more valuable exchange between Internet content providers and the end users of that content. It does this by removing many of the obstacles that subtract from the value of using the Internet, such as the sheer number of Web pages, the limited capabilities of search engines, nonstandardized forms, and the time it takes to find wanted material.

Of particular interest is how EntryPoint opens the door to relationship marketing opportunities. For example, clicking on the shopping icon brings up a list of preferred on-line merchants, merchant comparisons, and a list of special offers from those merchants. By matching a user's registration information with their inventory of promotions, merchants can serve up more relevant and attractive offers to their consumers through the EntryPoint toolbar. By presenting these consumers with more valuable offers on the first communication attempt, merchants have a better chance of acquiring customers who will be attentive and receptive to subsequent offers. Once a few transactions have been made between the two parties, a customer is less likely to forge a new relationship with an alternate supplier of the same or similar goods or services. Since customers invest time, effort, and personal information with the merchant, they are unlikely to randomly switch providers and are willing to work with the original provider to build a relationship that will return benefits in addition to the goods and services they buy.

Facilitating purchasing transactions is not the only way EntryPoint creates value for its users. In contrast to traditional portals like Yahoo!, Microsoft Network, Excite, and Lycos, EntryPoint's function is to shrink the amount of information a user accesses to a more manageable level. Traditional portals instead open the doors to the vast expanse of the Web, leaving the customer to sort through an inordinate amount of infor-

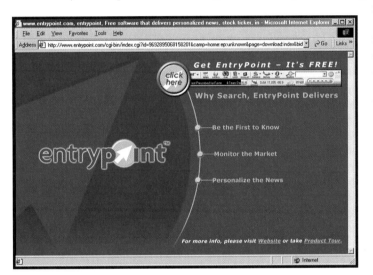

mation. They contribute to what is called the Haystack Effect: When too much information is presented to a decision maker, it actually retards the progress of that person toward the final goal. It is a situation that any Internet user can identify with.

Alternatively, EntryPoint gives users a selection of premiere content providers, allows them to define the specific content they want, and then keeps those requests stored in the memory function of the toolbar. In this way, requests can be accessed in a fraction of the time it would take to search for them through traditional portals. Moreover, users are not subjected to hordes of banner ads running across the toolbar. Ads are only served when users open a window by clicking on a headline that runs across the toolbar or by clicking one of the options on a given menu. EntryPoint must serve ads in order to get some measure of revenue because the only item it receives in exchange from the customer is minor personal information.

EntryPoint has a promising future because it offers a service that gives priority to customer needs. EntryPoint does not provide a Web portal per se. Rather, it is a tool to maximize efficient Web surfing. As consumers increasingly rely on the Internet and suffer from poverty of time, they will continue to demand more efficient Internet functionality. EntryPoint's business model will allow for easy adaptation of its services to the changing needs of the consumer. The direct access to personalized content is completely controlled by the user and is driven more by consumer needs. By trying to be most things to most people instead of all things to all people, EntryPoint is driving inefficiencies out of Internet navigation. As a result, the company formed from two high-profile Internet start-ups is poised to benefit from the inevitable shift in the market that will occur when most users are advanced and knowledgeable enough to preselect content from a menu of the most popular providers.

If EntryPoint plays its cards well, it may over time conceive of even more valuable services to offer its customers. It may even be able to break free of the current model of free content delivery and charge small fees for those services. Initially providing free service is necessary in the Internet market in order to acquire customers, but it is doubtful that major sites will continue to flourish by generating advertising revenue alone. EntryPoint could build a more sustainable business model than the current ad-supported system used by traditional portals if, for example, it beefed up its financial management services, added unique or specialized news services, or provided automatic replenishment of goods and services its customers buy regularly through EntryPoint merchants.

The Internet has become an increasingly valuable tool to those who have access to it and who can utilize it well. Moreover, unlike any previous communication medium, the consumer is driving Internet development more than the providers are. That brings an interesting dynamic to the value exchange between consumers and businesses. More than ever, merchants will have to be extremely sensitive to the demands of consumers and must seek to identify and interpret the consumer's definition of value. EntryPoint is ahead on that learning curve. It understands that as the Internet is more widely adopted and relied upon to manage the daily activities in a person's life, tools that enable its efficient and effective use will enhance the value exchange between businesses and consumers.

Questions

1. Identify the product features and benefits, the pricing system, and the distribution channel that EntryPoint uses.
2. Is EntryPoint a product-oriented, sales-oriented, market-oriented, or societal market-oriented firm? Explain.
3. How would you define EntryPoint's business?
4. Describe the value exchange between EntryPoint and its users. What does each party give up?

Bibliography

http://www.EntryPoint.com

Randall W. Forsyth, "Putting It Together: Bit by Bit, These Sites Gather Investment Data in One Place." *Barron's*, April 3, 2000, p. 56.

Linda Himmelstein and Richard Siklos. "The Rise and Fall of an Internet Star." *Business Week*, April 26, 1999, p. 88.

Andrea Petersen. "LaunchPad Creates EntryPoint, Its First Since Buying PointCast." *Asian Wall Street Journal*, August 9, 1999, p. 7.

Charles Piller and Deborah Vrana. "Idealab Affiliate Ewallet to Buy PointCast Internet." *Los Angeles Times*, May 11, 1999, C-1.

Case

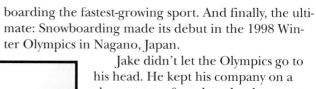

Lord of the Boards

Burton Snowboards, the industry leader, is the brainchild of Jake Burton, an avid rider. Jake's recipe for success is simple: "We always focused on the sport and everything else took care of itself." Burton practically invented the sport in 1977 when he first made crude snowboards in a Vermont workshop. By 1978, he had hit upon a successful formula (horizontally laminated wood) and made 300 boards with an $88 price tag. The next decade saw Jake spending time and money lobbying ski areas to open their slopes to snowboarders. Now they are free to ride just about everywhere. Competitors noted that while they pegged snowboarding as a regional sport, Jake kept his eye on the big picture. He always had a vision. Campaigning tirelessly for snowboarding at resorts led to the creation of the U.S. Open snowboard competition. By 1994, the *Wall Street Journal* spotted the trend and called snow-

boarding the fastest-growing sport. And finally, the ultimate: Snowboarding made its debut in the 1998 Winter Olympics in Nagano, Japan.

Jake didn't let the Olympics go to his head. He kept his company on a clear course of product development, R&D, and lots of riding. The company provides a free season pass to Stowe ski area in Vermont and private lessons for *newbies*, new riders, so excuses for not riding are hard to find. The sport draws mainly the under-thirty crowd, with 88 percent 12 to 24 years old, 83 percent male and 17 percent female. The *Newbie* snowboarding guide gives the basics on the Burton Web site, starting with the idea that equipment and clothing can make or break the ride. First comes the choice of ride (Freestyle, Freeride, or Carving), then three riding options. Next is the choice of board produced in different lengths with different graphics. Boots and bindings are picked next, followed by clothing with the right fit. An on-snow demonstration is considered a must, so Burton posts its travel schedule on the Internet and offers free, local demonstrations and a chance to try on boots, bindings, and the whole setup on the snow. Burton also suggests taking a lesson for maximum fun and safety.

Staying close to the customer is a company hallmark. Burton Snowboards builds on a group of people to get feedback to improve both the company and the sport. Talking to pro riders, sales reps, designers, testers, and Internet users helps the company find out what the riders want. For example, when the company needs new ideas for graphics, designers fly all over the world, sit face to face, and look at what has been developed. The idea is to provide snowboard equipment to *all* people.

To do this, Burton keeps on adding to its product line. Snowboarding performance may be gender blind, but fit is not. That is why Burton manufactures gender-specific clothing and boots that are completely different for men and women in fit but are matched in performance. Years of refining the cut of women's clothing have yielded a line of fully featured gear that really works for snowboarding. Women are the fastest growing segment of riders, and while there are no specific women's boards or bindings, Burton works with their team riders to create board dimensions, flexes, and bindings that work well for smaller, lighter riders. Burton plans to offer functional gear for women, men, and riders of all sizes, abilities, and styles. And as more and more kids aged 6 to 14 get into riding, Burton is stepping up and delivering products that meet the de-mands of these mini-snowboarders. Sometimes kids ride first and the parents follow suit. In the process, snowboarding becomes a family passion.

The Burton strategy has paid off. Annual sales figures are now estimated at well over $150 million, and the company has 500 employees in Vermont and around the world. As the sport of snowboarding matures, many people in the snowboarding community are using the sport to make valuable social contributions that enrich lives. In 1994, Jake Burton started the Chill Program to share snowboarding with poor and at-risk kids. While it is true that heavy industry competition is out there, innovation and love of the sport still make Jake Burton Lord of the Boards.

Questions
1. Describe the exchange process at Burton.
2. How has Jake Burton's entrepreneurial philosophy made his company successful?
3. Does Burton use a sales orientation or a market orientation? Explain.
4. How does Burton Snowboards achieve customer satisfaction?

Bibliography

Reade Bailey. "Jake Burton, King of the Hill." *Ski*, February 1998, pp. 60–67.

Eric Blehm. "The Day of the Locusts." *GQ*, December 1997, pp. 186–187.

Burton Snowboards 1998 Press Kit.

Burton Snowboards Web site: **http://www.burton.com.**

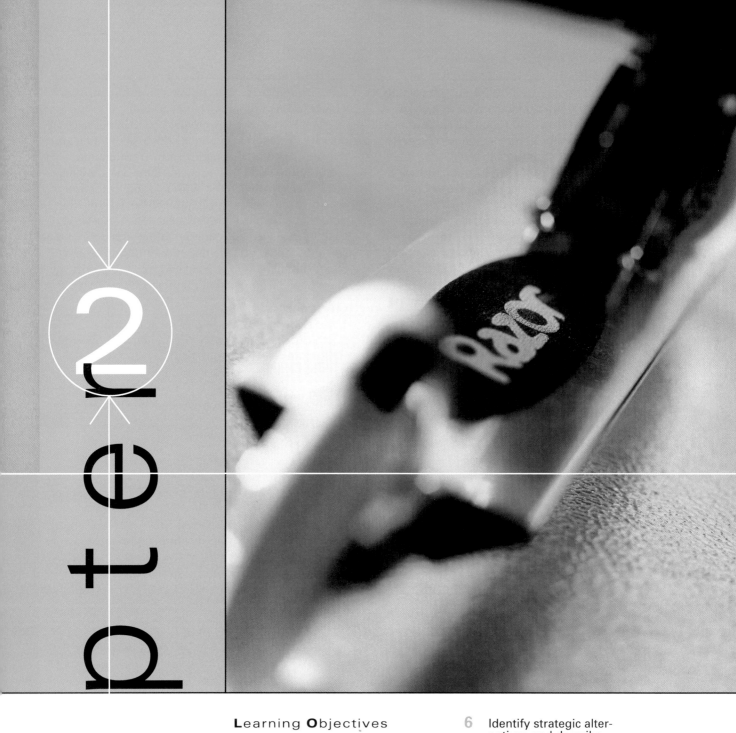

chapter 2

Learning Objectives

1. Understand the importance of strategic marketing and know a basic outline for a marketing plan

2. Develop an appropriate business mission statement

3. Describe the criteria for stating good marketing objectives

4. Explain the components of a situation analysis

5. Identify sources of competitive advantage

6. Identify strategic alternatives and describe tools used to help select alternatives

7. Discuss target market strategies

8. Describe elements of the marketing mix

9. Explain why implementation, evaluation, and control of the marketing plan are necessary

10. Identify several techniques that help make strategic planning effective

Razor Scooters

Back in 1996, Gino Tsai asked his designers to build a small scooter to help him negotiate his sprawling Taiwanese bicycle factory. Tsai got his scooter, and much more, although he never intended to spur a global fad. His staff built what would later be named the Razor, a melding of state-of-the-art technology and trendy aluminum design that has emerged as the hottest wheels since inline skates. This updated classic weighs a mere six pounds and folds up to fit into small spaces.

Scooters had already established themselves in Germany, Japan, and Australia when Richard Thalheimer, the chairman of Sharper Image, saw Razors at a Hong Kong toy show and brought them to his store. The scooter quickly became Sharper Image's number-one selling product.[1] The company's stock price jumped 80 percent following the successful introduction of the Razor.[2]

Interestingly, scooters are attracting consumers from three market segments: kids, college students, and commuters. The kids are hardly surprising, but the adults are taking up an unexpected amount of market share. Wayne Caccamo, director of product marketing for Docent, placed the foot-powered scooters throughout the company's office space in Mountain View, California. Caccamo says it takes employees one minute to walk between the company's lobbies, and scooting takes twenty seconds. He estimates his fifteen scooters are saving Docent $39,840 annually.[3] Scooters are seen as a corporate perk and a stress reduction tool at many firms. At San Francisco's DigitalThink, employees scoot between three buildings on corporate Zappies (electric scooters).[4] One scooter booster is Sarah Jessica Parker, who is often photographed riding her Razor in person and on her television show. Scooters are even catching on among the Amish. Lillian King, an Amish woman from Lancaster, Pennsylvania, says she uses hers for chores that don't require a horse-drawn cart.[5]

Razors, of course, aren't the only scooters out there. Huffy's Micro traces its roots back to a German engineer who craved a no-hassle commute to work. Xooter, a larger, sturdier scooter, is the brainchild of a Silicon Valley professor. Radio Flyer, the famous Chicago-based maker of the Little Red Wagon, was one of the first companies to produce scooters in the 1930s; the company returned scooters to its lineup in 2001.[6] K2 offers several products: the Deuce, which has a larger adult-sized foot deck; the three-wheeled Trifecta, with an adjustable steering mechanism; and the Kickboard, a three-wheeled scooter with active suspension steering.[7] Zapworld's Kick comes with a longer deck and custom colors, and their Zappy offers an electric boost. Nova Cruz offers swanky models of the electric Xooter, including decks made of either birch or carbon-fiber technology.

Despite the intensifying competition, Razor has attained the rarefied status of having its brand name be synonymous with its product, not unlike Rollerblade in the early days of the inline skating category; many people walk into stores and ask for a Razor when they mean they want to see a scooter. Razor holds an estimated 60 percent of the U.S. market, but market share could erode quickly due to rival scooters.[8] Having so many merchandise options to choose from has been a double-edged sword for retailers; stores are worried about item saturation and are wary of bringing in too many scooters. Because Razors can be found virtually anywhere (both online and off), some chains don't sell Razors anymore. Razors were $130 when they were first introduced into the market, but prices have fallen to well under $100. Distribution was uncontrolled until Razor USA was formed late in 2000 to act as the official U.S. Razor distributor and to manage brand development and marketing initiatives.

To further test the scooter product category, safety and legal issues are presenting challenges. As scooter sales soar, so do visits to emergency rooms. The Consumer Product Safety Commission reports that scooter injuries have doubled each month since the scooter's introduction.[9] Not surprisingly, communities are heeding safety concerns and cracking down on scootermania. Many municipalities and schools either mandate safety equipment, or have banned scooters altogether. Montreal-based ZapQuebec.com, maker of the electric Zappy, has found their customers to be predominately commuters in their 40s. There is a significant problem for these grownups: Transport Canada opposes the use of motorized scooters on public roads.[10]

Canton Calvin is the founder of Razor USA. When asked whether he was worried that the Razor was the Rubik's Cube of 2000, Calvin replied, "Maybe the Rubik's Cube of 2003. Obviously when anything explodes this quickly, there's risk of a downturn. But we like to think it's the next Rollerblade."[11] However, retailers are beginning to wonder if the fad will fade.

The Nature of Strategic Planning

Understand the importance of strategic marketing and know a basic outline for a marketing plan

strategic planning
The managerial process of creating and maintaining a fit between the organization's objectives and resources and evolving market opportunities.

Strategic planning is the managerial process of creating and maintaining a fit between the organization's objectives and resources and the evolving market opportunities. The goal of strategic planning is long-run profitability and growth. Thus strategic decisions require long-term commitments of resources.

A strategic error can threaten the firm's survival. On the other hand, a good strategic plan can help protect a firm's resources against competitive onslaughts.[12] For instance, if the March of Dimes had decided to focus on fighting polio, the organization would no longer exist. Most of us view polio as a conquered disease. The March of Dimes survived by making the strategic decision to switch to fighting birth defects.

Strategic marketing management addresses two questions: What is the organization's main activity at a particular time? How will it reach its goals? Here are some examples of strategic decisions:

- The decision of R. J. Reynolds to sell off its Nabisco Group holdings, including popular Oreos, Lifesavers, and Ritz Crackers brands[13]
- The decision of Globalstar and Iridium to declare bankruptcy of their companies' worldwide satellite telephone systems[14]
- ConAgra's purchase of International Home Foods, including Chef Boyardee pasta, Gulden's mustard, and PAM cooking spray[15]
- Smucker's introduction of Uncrustables, a new line of frozen crustless peanut butter and jelly sandwiches, to compete with Kraft Foods' Oscar Mayer Lunchables[16]

All these decisions have affected or will affect each organization's long-run course, its allocation of resources, and ultimately its financial success. In contrast, an operating decision, such as changing the package design for Post's cornflakes or altering the sweetness of a Kraft salad dressing, probably won't have a big impact on the long-run profitability of the company.

How do companies go about strategic marketing planning? How do employees know how to implement the long-term goals of the firm? The answer is a marketing plan.

Strategic planning is critical to business success. Dial rolled out its home dry cleaning kit, Custom Cleaner, after the warm reception of Procter & Gamble's Dryel product.

What Is a Marketing Plan?

planning
The process of anticipating future events and determining strategies to achieve organizational objectives in the future.

marketing planning
Designing activities relating to marketing objectives and the changing marketing environment.

marketing plan
A written document that acts as a guidebook of marketing activities for the marketing manager.

Planning is the process of anticipating future events and determining strategies to achieve organizational objectives in the future. **Marketing planning** involves designing activities relating to marketing objectives and the changing marketing environment. Marketing planning is the basis for all marketing strategies and decisions. Issues such as product lines, distribution channels, marketing communications, and pricing are all delineated in the **marketing plan**. The marketing plan is a written document that acts as a guidebook of marketing activities for the marketing manager. In this chapter, you will learn the importance of writing a marketing plan and the types of information contained in a marketing plan.

Why Write a Marketing Plan?
By specifying objectives and defining the actions required to attain them, a marketing plan provides the basis by which actual and expected performance can be

compared. Marketing can be one of the most expensive and complicated business components but is one of the most important business activities. The written marketing plan provides clearly stated activities that help employees understand and work toward common goals.

Writing a marketing plan allows you to examine the marketing environment in conjunction with the inner workings of the business. Once the marketing plan is written, it serves as a reference point for the success of future activities. Finally, the marketing plan allows the marketing manager to enter the marketplace with an awareness of possibilities and problems.

Marketing Plan Elements

Marketing plans can be presented in many different ways. Most businesses need a written marketing plan because the scope of a marketing plan is large and can be complex. Details about tasks and activity assignments may be lost if communicated orally. Regardless of the way a marketing plan is presented, there are elements common to all marketing plans. These include defining the business mission and objectives, performing a situation analysis, delineating a target market, and establishing components of the marketing mix. Exhibit 2.1 shows these elements, which are also described further below. Other elements that may be included in a plan are budgets, implementation timetables, required marketing research efforts, or elements of advanced strategic planning. An example of a thumbnail marketing plan sketch is contained in Exhibit 2.2.

Writing the Marketing Plan

The creation and implementation of a complete marketing plan will allow the organization to achieve marketing objectives and succeed. However, the marketing plan is only as good as the information it contains and the effort, creativity, and thought that went into its creation. The importance of having a good marketing information system and a wealth of competitive intelligence (covered in Chapter 8) is critical to a thorough and accurate situation analysis. The role of managerial intuition is also important in the creation and selection of marketing strategies. Managers must weigh any information against its accuracy and their own judgment when making a marketing decision.

Note that the overall structure of the marketing plan (Exhibit 2.1) should not be viewed as a series of sequential planning steps. Many of the marketing plan elements are decided on simultaneously and in conjunction with one another. Similarly, the summary sample marketing plan (Exhibit 2.2) does not begin to cover the intricacies and detail of a full marketing plan. Further, the content of every marketing plan is different, depending on the organization, its mission, objectives, targets, and marketing mix components. Visualize how the marketing plan in Exhibit 2.2 would differ if only wireless communication connectivity services (not the physical products) were being offered. How would the plan differ if the target market consisted of Fortune 500 firms with large sales forces instead of executives?

The marketing plan outline in Exhibit 2.8 (pages 52–54) is an expanded set of questions that can guide the formulation of a marketing plan. However, this outline should not be regarded as the only correct format for a marketing plan. Many organizations have their own distinctive format or terminology used for creating a marketing plan. Every marketing plan should be unique to the firm for which it was created. Remember that although the format and order of presentation should be flexible, the same types of questions and topic areas should be covered in any marketing plan.

Exhibit **2.1**

The Marketing Process

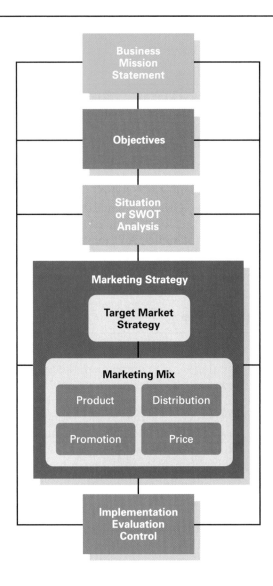

As you can see by the extent of the marketing plan outline in Exhibit 2.8, creating a complete marketing plan is not a simple or quick effort. However, it can be instructive to create summary marketing plans such as the sample summary plan shown in Exhibit 2.2 to get a quick idea of what a firm's marketing strategy is all about.

Defining the Business Mission

Develop an appropriate business mission statement

The foundation of any marketing plan is first answering the question, "What business are we in and where are we going?" The answer is the firm's **mission statement**. Business mission definition profoundly affects long-run resource allocation, profitability, and survival. The mission statement is based on a careful

Exhibit **2.2**

Sample Summary
Marketing Plan

Business Mission	Ultracel is in the business of providing advanced communications technology and communications convenience to mobile users.
Marketing Objective	To achieve 20 percent, in dollar volume, of the wireless telephone market by year-end, 2002.
Situation Analysis	
Strengths	Well-funded organization, highly skilled workforce with low turnover, excellent relationships with suppliers, product differential and sustainable competitive advantage of patented color screen and Internet connectivity.
Weaknesses	Company name not well known, small firm with no manufacturing cost advantages, no long-term contracts with distributors, inexperience in the wireless communications market.
Opportunities	Explosive growth of wireless phone users, worldwide acceptance of cellular technology, newly available digital networks.
Threats	Heavy competition; technology is incompatible with current analog systems; not everyone can afford the systems, potential governmental regulation.
Target Market Selection	Young, mobile executives in North America and Europe, with incomes over $200,000 per year; frequent travelers; computer-dependent individuals.
Marketing Mix	
Product	Personal digital telephone. Brand name: Ultracel-2000. Features: simultaneous voice/data communication, Internet access, operation within buildings, linkups to data subscription and e-mail services, computer data storage, color screen, light weight, 100-hour battery, 3-year unlimited warranty on parts and labor, 24-hour technical support, leather or titanium carrying case.
Place	Available through electronics retailers, upscale computer retailers, or via Web order company direct; products transported via airplane and temperature-controlled motor carrier.
Promotion	Fifty manufacturer's representatives for selling force, with 25 percent commissions; advertising in print media, cable television, and outdoor billboards; sales promotion in the form of introductory product rebates, technology trade shows; public relations efforts to news media and sponsorship of world-championship sporting events; Internet advertising campaign.
Price	Retail price of $299; assuming mild price sensitivity and future price wars. Lease option available; corporate discounts of 20 percent for volume purchases.
Implementation	First quarter: Complete marketing research on price, design promotional campaign, sign contracts with manufacturer's reps. Second quarter: Public relations campaign, product introduction at trade shows, rollout of advertising. Third quarter: Test market international markets.

mission statement
The firm's long-term vision based on a careful analysis of benefits sought by present and potential customers and analysis of existing and anticipated environmental conditions.

marketing myopia
Defining a business in terms of goods and services rather than in terms of the benefits that customers seek.

strategic business unit (SBU)
A subgroup of a single business or collection of related businesses within the larger organization.

analysis of benefits sought by present and potential customers and analysis of existing and anticipated environmental conditions. The firm's long-term vision, embodied in the mission statement, establishes boundaries for all subsequent decisions, objectives, and strategies. The American Marketing Association's mission statement is shown in Exhibit 2.3.

A mission statement should focus on the market or markets the organization is attempting to serve rather than on the good or service offered. Otherwise, a new technology may quickly make the good or service obsolete and the mission statement irrelevant to company functions. Business mission statements that are stated too narrowly suffer from **marketing myopia**—defining a business in terms of goods and services rather than in terms of the benefits that customers seek.[17] In this context, *myopia* means narrow, short-term thinking. For example, Frito-Lay defines its mission as being in the snack-food business rather than in the corn chip business. The mission of sports teams is not just to play games but to serve the interests of the fans. AT&T does not sell telephones or long distance services; it markets communications technology.

Alternatively, business missions may be stated too broadly. "To provide products of superior quality and value that improve the lives of the world's consumers" is probably too broad a mission statement for any firm except Procter & Gamble. Care must be taken when stating what business a firm is in. The mission of Saturn Corporation, a subsidiary of General Motors, is "to design, manufacture, and market vehicles to compete on a global scale, as well as reestablish American technology as the standard for automotive quality."[18] By correctly stating the business mission in terms of the benefits that customers seek, the foundation for the marketing plan is set. Many companies are focusing on designing more appropriate mission statements because these statements are frequently displayed on the World Wide Web.

The organization may need to define a mission statement and objectives for a **strategic business unit (SBU)**, which is a subgroup of a single business or collection of related businesses within the larger organization. A properly defined SBU should have a distinct mission and specific target market, control over its resources, its own competitors, and plans independent of the other SBUs in the organization. Thus, a large firm such as Kraft General Foods may have marketing plans for each of their SBUs, which include breakfast foods, desserts, pet foods, and beverages.

Exhibit **2.3**

American Marketing Association's Mission Statement

The American Marketing Association is an international professional organization for people involved in the practice, study, and teaching of marketing. Our principal roles are:

- To always understand and satisfy the needs of marketers so as to provide them with products and services that will help them be better marketers.
- To empower marketers through information, education, relationships, and resources that will enrich their professional development and careers.
- To advance the thought, application, and ethical practice of marketing.

SOURCE: http://ama.org/about/ama/mission.asp

Setting Marketing Plan Objectives

Before the details of a marketing plan can be developed, goals and objectives for the plan must be stated. Without objectives, there is no basis for measuring the success of marketing plan activities. For example, Exxon's return to shareholders over the last five years has been 135 percent. Sounds great, doesn't it? However, without previously stated objectives, there is no way to know. Actually, Exxon had a goal to be on par with British Petroleum, which returned over 330 percent to shareholders in the same period, so objectives were not met.[19]

A **marketing objective** is a statement of what is to be accomplished through marketing activities. To be useful, stated objectives should meet several criteria. First, objectives should be realistic, measurable, and time specific. It is tempting to state that the objective is "to be the best marketer of ferret food." However, what is "best" for one firm might be sales of one million pounds of ferret food per year, and to another firm, "best" might mean dominant market share. It may also be unrealistic for start-up firms or new products to command dominant market share, given other competitors in the marketplace. Finally, by what time should the goal be met? A more realistic objective would be "To achieve 10 percent dollar market share in the specialty pet food market within twelve months of product introduction."

Second, objectives must also be consistent and indicate the priorities of the organization. Specifically, objectives flow from the business mission statement to the rest of the marketing plan. Exhibit 2.4 shows some well-stated and poorly stated objectives. Notice how well they do or do not meet the above criteria.

Carefully specified objectives serve several functions. First, they communicate marketing management philosophies and provide direction for lower-level marketing managers so that marketing efforts are integrated and pointed in a consistent direction. Objectives also serve as motivators by creating something for employees to strive for. When objectives are attainable and challenging, they motivate those charged with achieving the objectives. Additionally, the process of writing specific

Describe the criteria for stating good marketing objectives

marketing objective
A statement of what is to be accomplished through marketing activities.

Exhibit **2.4**

Examples of Marketing Objectives

Poorly Stated Objectives	Well-Stated Objectives
Our objective is to be a leader in the industry in terms of new product development.	Our objective is to spend 12 percent of sales revenue between 2001 and 2002 on research and development in an effort to introduce at least five new products in 2002.
Our objective is to maximize profits.	Our objective is to achieve a 10 percent return on investment during 2001, with a payback on new investments of no longer than four years.
Our objective is to better serve customers.	Our objective is to obtain customer satisfaction ratings of at least 90 percent on the 2001 annual customer satisfaction survey, and to retain at least 85 percent of our 2001 customers as repeat purchasers in 2002.
Our objective is to be the best that we can be.	Our objective is to increase market share from 30 percent to 40 percent in 2001 by increasing promotional expenditures by 14 percent.

objectives forces executives to clarify their thinking. Finally, objectives form a basis for control; the effectiveness of a plan can be gauged in light of the stated goals.

Conducting a Situation Analysis

Explain the components of a situation analysis

SWOT analysis
Identifying internal strengths (S) and weaknesses (W) and also examining external opportunities (O) and threats (T).

environmental scanning
Collection and interpretation of information about forces, events, and relationships in the external environment that may affect the future of the organization or the implementation of the marketing plan.

Before specific marketing activities can be defined, marketers must understand the current and potential environment that the product or service will be marketed in. A situation analysis is sometimes referred to as a **SWOT analysis;** that is, the firm should identify its internal strengths (S) and weaknesses (W) and also examine external opportunities (O) and threats (T).

When examining internal strengths and weaknesses, the marketing manager should focus on organizational resources such as production costs, marketing skills, financial resources, company or brand image, employee capabilities, and available technology. For example, a potential weakness for AirTrans Airlines (formerly ValuJet) is the age of its airplane fleet, which could indicate an image of danger or low quality. Other weaknesses include high labor turnover rates and limited flights. A potential strength is the low operating costs of the airline, which translate into lower prices for consumers. Another issue to consider in this section of the marketing plan is the historical background of the firm—its sales and profit history.

When examining external opportunities and threats, marketing managers must analyze aspects of the marketing environment. This process is called **environmental scanning**—the collection and interpretation of information about forces, events, and relationships in the external environment that may affect the future of the organization or the implementation of the marketing plan. Environmental scanning helps identify market opportunities and threats and provides guidelines for the design of marketing strategy. The six most often studied macroenvironmental forces are social, demographic, economic, technological, political and legal, and competitive. These forces are examined in detail in Chapter 3. For example, H&R Block, a tax preparation service, benefits from complex changes in tax codes that motivate citizens to have taxes prepared by a professional. Alternatively, tax-simplification or flat-tax plans would allow people to easily prepare their own returns.

Competitive Advantage

Identify sources of competitive advantage

competitive advantage or **differential advantage**
The set of unique features of a company and its products that are perceived by the target market as significant and superior to the competition.

Performing a SWOT analysis allows firms to identify their competitive advantage. A **competitive advantage**, also called a **differential advantage**, is a set of unique features of a company and its products that are perceived by the target market as significant and superior to the competition. It is the factor or factors that cause customers to patronize a firm and not the competition. There are three types of competitive advantages: cost, product/service differentiation, and niche strategies.

Cost Competitive Advantage

Cost leadership can result from obtaining inexpensive raw materials, creating an efficient scale of plant operations, designing products for ease of manufacture, controlling overhead costs, and avoiding marginal customers. DuPont, for example, has an exceptional cost competitive advantage in the production of titanium dioxide. Technicians created a production process using low-cost feedstock, giving DuPont a 20 percent cost advantage over its competitors. The cheaper feedstock technology is complex and can only be accomplished by investing about $100 million and several years of testing time. Having a **cost competitive advantage** means being the low-cost competitor in an industry while maintaining satisfactory profit margins.

A cost competitive advantage enables a firm to deliver superior customer value. Chaparral Steel, for example, is the leading low-cost U.S. steel producer because it uses only scrap iron and steel and a very efficient continuous-casting process to make new steel. In fact, Chaparral is so efficient that it is the only U.S. steel producer that ships to Japan.

cost competitive advantage
Being the low-cost competitor in an industry while maintaining satisfactory profit margins.

Sources of Cost Competitive Advantages

Costs can be reduced in a variety of ways.

- *Experience curves:* **Experience curves** tell us that costs decline at a predictable rate as experience with a product increases. The experience curve effect encompasses a broad range of manufacturing, marketing, and administrative costs. Experience curves reflect learning by doing, technological advances, and economies of scale. Firms like Boeing and Texas Instruments use historical experience curves as a basis for predicting and setting prices. Experience curves allow management to forecast costs and set prices based on anticipated costs as opposed to current costs.

- *Efficient labor:* Labor costs can be an important component of total costs in low-skill, labor-intensive industries such as product assembly and apparel manufacturing. Many U.S. manufacturers such as Nike, Levi Strauss, and Liz Claiborne have gone offshore to achieve cheaper manufacturing costs. Many American companies are also outsourcing activities such as data entry and other labor-intensive jobs.

- *No-frills goods and services:* Marketers can lower costs by removing frills and options from a product or service. Southwest Airlines, for example, offers low fares but no seat assignments or meals. Low prices give Southwest a higher load factor and greater economies of scale, which, in turn, means even lower prices such as Southwest's "Friends Fly Free" promotions.

- *Government subsidies:* Governments may provide assistance to target industries with grants and interest-free loans. Government assistance enabled Japanese semiconductor manufacturers to become global leaders.

- *Product design:* Cutting-edge design technology can help offset high labor costs. BMW is a world leader in designing cars for ease of manufacture and assembly. Reverse engineering—the process of disassembling a product piece by piece to learn its components and clues as to the manufacturing process—can also mean savings. Reverse engineering a low-cost competitor's product can save research and design costs. Japanese engineers have reversed many products such as computer chips, coming out of Silicon Valley.

- *Reengineering:* Reengineering to make firms more efficient often leads to downsizing or layoffs of employees. Reengineering can also mean pruning product lines, closing obsolete factories, and renegotiating contracts with suppliers. General Motors, for example, demanded a 15 percent average price reduction from suppliers during its reengineering.

experience curves
Curves that show costs declining at a predictable rate as experience with a product increases.

Reverse engineering can be an effective way to learn about a competitor's manufacturing process and can potentially mean savings in R&D costs.
© Tom Wagner/SABA

- *Production innovations:* Production innovations such as new technology and simplified production techniques help lower the average cost of production. Technologies such as computer-aided design and computer-aided manufacturing (CAD/CAM) and increasingly sophisticated robots help companies like Boeing, Ford, and General Electric reduce their manufacturing costs.

- *New methods of service delivery:* Medical expenses have been substantially lowered by the use of outpatient surgery and walk-in clinics. Airlines, such as American, are lowering reservation and ticketing costs by encouraging passengers to use the Internet to book flights and by promoting "ticketless travel."

differential competitive advantage
Advantage achieved when a firm provides something that is unique and valuable to buyers beyond simply offering a lower price than the competition.

Differentiation Competitive Advantages

Because cost competitive advantages are subject to continual erosion, differential competitive advantages tend to be longer lasting than cost competitive advantages. The durability of a differential competitive advantage tends to make this strategy more attractive to many top managers. A product/service **differential competitive advantage** exists when a firm provides something unique that is valuable to buyers beyond simply offering a low price. Common differential advantages are brand names (Lexus), a strong dealer network (Caterpillar Tractor for construction work), product reliability (Maytag appliances), image (Neiman Marcus in retailing), or service (FedEx).

Differential competitive advantages can come from two sources:

Having a differential competitive advantage means a product or service offers a unique and valuable benefit other than a low price to consumers. Building on its hallmark of reliability, Maytag has introduced the Accellis, an oven that can cook twice as fast as a conventional oven.

- *Value impressions:* A differential advantage can also be created through **value impressions**. These are features of a product or service that signal value to the customer. A foil package, for example, is often a cue that connotes luxury. The shape of the Joy perfume bottle says "quality" and "exclusivity." Dom Perignon champagne comes in its own special box. Even Wal-Mart's slogan "Everday Low Prices" leaves an impression of value.

- *Augmented products:* An augmented product represents another tool for differentiation. When a company adds features to a good or service not expected by the customer, that good or service is referred to as an **augmented product**. When Oscar Mayer took the commodity items of lunch meat, cheese, and crackers and packaged them as "Lunchables," they created an augmented product.

value impressions
Features of a product or service that signal value to the customer.

augmented product
A product or service developed when a company adds features not expected by the customer.

Sony's efforts to make minicams smaller and more portable result in augmented products. Also, products that offer "less of something" such as calories, fat, sugar, or alcohol content can be augmented products.

Niche Competitive Advantage

A **niche competitive advantage** seeks to target and effectively serve a single segment of the market (see Chapter 7). For small companies with limited resources who potentially face giant competitors, niching may be the only viable option. A market segment that has good growth potential but is not crucial to the success of major competitors is a good candidate for developing a niche strategy.

Many companies using a niche strategy serve only a limited geographic market. Buddy Freddy's is a very successful restaurant chain but is found only in Florida. Migros is the dominant grocery chain in Switzerland. It has no stores outside that small country.

Block Drug Company uses niching by focusing its product line on tooth products. It markets Polident to clean false teeth, Poligrip to hold false teeth, and Sensodyne toothpaste for persons with sensitive teeth. The Orvis Company manufactures and sells everything that a fly fisherman might ever need. Orvis is a very successful nicher.

niche competitive advantage
Advantage achieved when a firm seeks to target and effectively serve a small segment of the market.

Building Tomorrow's Competitive Advantage

The key to having a differential advantage is the ability to sustain that advantage. A **sustainable competitive advantage** is one that cannot be copied by the competition. Top-Flite recently introduced the Strata golf ball. At $3 each, these balls cost three times as much as regular golf balls, but they are flying off the shelf. The Strata has a patented, three-layer construction that improves handling and increases distance. The patent offers a sustainable competitive advantage over Titleist, the number one competitor.[20] Datril was introduced into the pain-reliever market and was touted as being exactly like Tylenol, only cheaper. Tylenol responded by lowering their price, thus destroying Datril's differential advantage and ability to remain on the market. In this case, low price was not a sustainable competitive advantage. Without a differential advantage, target customers don't perceive any reason to patronize an organization instead of its competitors.

sustainable competitive advantage
A differential advantage that cannot be copied by the competition.

The notion of competitive advantage means that a successful firm will stake out a position unique in some manner from its rivals. Imitation of competitors indicates a lack of competitive advantage and almost insures mediocre performance. Moreover, competitors rarely stand still, so it is not surprising that imitation causes managers to feel trapped in a seemingly endless game of catch-up. They are regularly surprised by the new accomplishments of their rivals.

Companies need to build their own competitive advantages rather than copy a competitor. The source of tomorrow's competitive advantages are the skills and assets of the organization. Assets include patents, copyrights, locations, and equipment and technology that are superior to those of the competition. Skills are functions such as customer service and promotion that the firm performs better than its competitors. Travelocity, for example, is known for its ease of online travel reservations. Marketing managers should continually focus the firm's skills and assets on sustaining and creating competitive advantages.

Remember, a sustainable competitive advantage is a function of the speed with which competitors can imitate a leading company's strategy and plans. Imitation requires a competitor to identify the leader's competitive advantage, determine how it is achieved, and then learn how to duplicate it.

Block Drug uses a niche strategy with each of its oral hygiene products. This commercial for Super Polygrip is aimed at denture wearers, but perhaps surprisingly, the woman featured was very young looking. Could this mean that Block is expanding its target market?

The end result of the SWOT analysis and identification of a competitive advantage is to evaluate the strategic direction of the firm. Seeking a strategic window and selecting a strategic alternative are the next steps in marketing planning.

Strategic Windows

strategic window
The limited period during which the "fit" between the key requirements of a market and the particular competencies of a firm are at an optimum.

One technique for identifying opportunities is to seek a **strategic window**—the limited period during which the fit between the key requirements of a market and the particular competencies of a firm are at an optimum. For example, when Celera Genomics Group announced that it had finished sequencing the complete human DNA (over 60,000 genes), biotechnology and drug companies around the world began the race to be the first to find and patent the key disease-related genes. Turning the raw genetic information into practical knowledge for drug discovery and development is challenging, but Exelixis, Inc., and Pharmacia Corporation expect to find genes useful for treating diabetes, Alzheimer's, and cancer within a few years.[21] In France, researchers have developed innovative textiles that allow companies to seize the opportunity to offer specialty clothing. This global strategic window is discussed further in the accompanying Global Perspectives box.

Identify strategic alternatives and describe tools used to help select alternatives

market penetration
A marketing strategy that tries to increase market share among existing customers.

Strategic Alternatives

To discover a marketing opportunity or strategic window, management must know how to identify the alternatives. One method for developing alternatives is the strategic opportunity matrix (see Exhibit 2.5), which matches products with markets. Firms can explore these four options:

- *Market penetration:* A firm using the **market penetration** alternative would try to increase market share among existing customers. If Kraft General Foods started a major campaign for Maxwell House coffee, with aggressive advertising and cents-off coupons to existing customers, it would be following a penetration strategy. McDonald's sold the most Happy Meals in history with a

Global Perspectives

FUTURISTIC FRENCH FABRICS

French researchers are developing a range of innovative textiles, including sheets and pillowcases that kill dust mites on contact, t-shirts woven with tiny ceramic particles that block harmful ultraviolet rays, and special long-term underwear.[a] Neyret, a swank French lingerie manufacturer, will offer panties that are permanently scented with floral fragrance. The perfume is released with a light touch.[b] Francital, a French company

that manufactures clothing for extreme environments, has taken advantage of the new technology and recently debuted a new line of underpants that can go unlaundered for up to thirty days. The cloth allows perspiration to move outward and evaporate, and the specially treated fabric stays odor free. The underwear is being test-driven on a North Pole trek, where explorers will have no chance to wash clothes.

Three pairs of underwear and undershirts have been given to each explorer for the frigid ninety-day trip.[c]

[a] Anne Eisenberg, "New Fabrics Can Keep Wearers Healthy and Smelling Good," *New York Times*, February 3, 2000, p. G7.
[b] "Fabric that Makes No Scents," *New York Times Upfront*, March 27, 2000, p. 6.
[c] Jennifer Harper, "Future Undies," *Insight on the News*, May 1, 2000, p. 27.

promotion that included Ty's Teeny Beanie Babies. Customer databases, discussed in Chapter 8, help managers implement this strategy.

- *Market development:* **Market development** means attracting new customers to existing products. Ideally, new uses for old products stimulate additional sales among existing customers while also bringing in new buyers. McDonald's, for example, has opened restaurants in Russia, China, and Italy and is eagerly expanding into Eastern European countries. Coca-Cola and Pepsi have faster growth in their new foreign markets than at home. In the nonprofit area, the growing emphasis on continuing education and executive development by colleges and universities is a market development strategy.

- *Product development:* A **product development** strategy entails the creation of new products for present markets. The beer industry, for example, is creating "craft brews," which seem like specialty beers brewed in microbreweries. Often, however, such is not the case. Maui Beer Company's Aloha Lager sells its Hawaiian image with a picture of a hula dancer on the label. It is, however, brewed in Portland, Oregon, by giant G. Heileman Brewing Company. Faux-antique labels of Pete's Wicked Ale, one of the nation's hottest craft beers, brag the beer is brewed "one batch at a time. Carefully." That may be, but the batches are four hundred barrels each, and the brewing is done by giant Stroh Brewery Company, maker of Old Milwaukee beer. Icehouse and Red Dog labels identify the maker as Plank Road Brewery. The real brewer: No. 2 beer heavyweight Miller, a unit of Philip Morris Companies, which is using the Plank Road name to get a piece of the craft-brew market.[22]

  Managers following this strategy can rely on their extensive knowledge of the target audience. They usually have a good feel for what customers like and dislike about current products and what existing needs are not being met. In addition, managers can rely on established distribution channels.

- *Diversification:* **Diversification** is a strategy of increasing sales by introducing new products into new markets. For example, LTV Corporation, a steel producer, diversified into the monorail business. Sony practiced a diversification strategy when it acquired Columbia Pictures; although motion pictures are not a new product in the marketplace, it was a new product for Sony. Coca-Cola

The beer industry has used a product development strategy by creating craft brews to penetrate existing markets. Appearing to be specialty beers brewed by microbreweries, these products are all produced by some of the largest breweries in the United States.

market development
Attracting new customers to existing products.

product development
Marketing strategy that entails the creation of marketable new products; process of converting applications for new technologies into marketable products.

diversification
A strategy of increasing sales by introducing new products into new markets.

Exhibit 2.5

Strategic Opportunity Matrix

	Present Product	New Product
Present Market	**Market penetration:** McDonald's sells more Happy Meals with Disney movie promotions.	**Product development:** McDonald's introduces salad shakers and McWater.
New Market	**Market development:** McDonald's opens restaurants in China.	**Diversification:** McDonald's introduces line of children's clothing.

manufactures and markets water-treatment and water-conditioning equipment, which has been a very challenging task for the traditional soft-drink company. A diversification strategy can be risky when a firm is entering unfamiliar markets. On the other hand, it can be very profitable when a firm is entering markets with little or no competition.

Selecting a Strategic Alternative

Selecting which alternative to pursue depends on the overall company philosophy and culture. The choice also depends on the tool used to make the decision. Companies generally have one of two philosophies about when they expect profits. They either pursue profits right away or first seek to increase market share and then pursue profits. In the long run, market share and profitability are compatible goals. Many companies have long followed this credo: Build market share, and profits will surely follow. Michelin, the tire producer, consistently sacrifices short-term profits to achieve market share. But attitudes may be changing. Lou Gerstner, CEO of IBM, has stressed profitability and stock valuation over market share, quality, and customer service since taking over the company. As you can see, the same strategic alternative may be viewed entirely differently by different firms.[23]

A number of tools exist to help managers select a strategic alternative. The most common of these tools are in matrix form. Two of these matrices—portfolio and market attractiveness/company strength—are described in more detail.

Portfolio Matrix Recall that large organizations engaged in strategic planning may create strategic business units. Each SBU has its own rate of return on investment, growth potential, and associated risk. Management must find a balance among the SBUs that yields the overall organization's desired growth and profits with an acceptable level of risk. Some SBUs generate large amounts of cash, and others need cash to foster growth. The challenge is to balance the organization's "portfolio" of SBUs for the best long-term performance.

To determine the future cash contributions and cash requirements expected for each SBU, managers can use the Boston Consulting Group's portfolio matrix. The **portfolio matrix** classifies each SBU by its present or forecasted growth and market share. The underlying assumption is that market share and profitability are strongly linked. The measure of market share used in the portfolio approach is *relative market share,* the ratio between the company's share and the share of the largest competitor. For example, if firm A has a 50 percent share and the competitor has 5 percent, the ratio is 10 to 1. If firm A has a 10 percent market share and the largest competitor has 20 percent, the ratio is 0.5 to 1.

Exhibit 2.6 is a hypothetical portfolio matrix for a large computer manufacturer. The size of the circle in each cell of the matrix represents dollar sales of the SBU relative to dollar sales of the company's other SBUs. The following categories are used in the matrix:

portfolio matrix
Tool for allocating resources among products or strategic business units on the basis of relative market share and market growth rate.

- *Stars:* A **star** is a market leader and growing fast. For example, computer manufacturers have identified the notebook model as a star. Star SBUs usually have large profits but need a lot of cash to finance rapid growth. The best marketing tactic is to protect existing market share by reinvesting earnings in product improvement, better distribution, more promotion, and production efficiency. Management must strive to capture most of the new users as they enter the market.

star
In the portfolio matrix, a business unit that is a fast-growing market leader.

- *Cash cows:* A **cash cow** is an SBU that usually generates more cash than it needs to maintain its market share. It is in a low-growth market, but the product has a dominant market share. Personal computers are categorized as cash cows in Exhibit 2.6. The basic strategy for a cash cow is to maintain market dominance by being the price leader and making technological improvements in the product. Managers should resist pressure to extend the basic line unless they can dramatically increase demand. Instead, they should allocate excess cash to the product categories where growth prospects are the greatest. For instance, Clorox Corporation owns Kingsford Charcoal, Match Charcoal Lighter, and Prime Choice steak sauce. Its cash cow is Clorox bleach, with a 60 percent market share in a low-growth market. Clorox Corporation was highly successful in stretching the Clorox line to include a liquid formula in addition to the original dry bleach. Another example is Heinz, which has two cash cows: ketchup and Weight Watchers frozen dinners.

- *Problem children:* A **problem child**, also called a **question mark**, shows rapid growth but poor profit margins. It has a low market share in a high-growth industry. Problem children need a great deal of cash. Without cash support, they eventually become dogs. The strategy options are to invest heavily to gain

cash cow
In the portfolio matrix, a business unit that usually generates more cash than it needs to maintain its market share.

problem child (question mark)
In the portfolio matrix, a business unit that shows rapid growth but poor profit margins.

Exhibit 2.6

Portfolio Matrix for a Large Computer Manufacturer

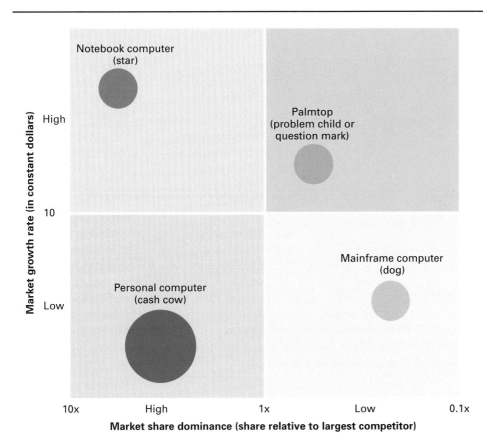

NOTE: The size of the circle represents the dollar sales relative to sales of other SBUs on the matrix—for example, 10× means sales are ten times greater than those of the next largest competitor.

better market share, acquire competitors to get the necessary market share, or drop the SBU. Sometimes a firm can reposition the products of the SBU to move them into the star category.

- *Dogs:* A **dog** has low growth potential and a small market share. Most dogs eventually leave the marketplace. In the computer manufacturer example, the mainframe computer has become a dog. Other examples include Jack-in-the-Box shrimp dinners, Warner-Lambert's Reef mouthwash, and Campbell's Red Kettle soups. Frito-Lay has produced several dogs, including Stuffers cheese-filled snacks, Rumbles granola nuggets, and Toppels cheese-topped crackers— a trio irreverently known as Stumbles, Tumbles, and Twofers. The strategy options for dogs are to harvest or divest.

After classifying the company's SBUs in the matrix, the next step is to allocate future resources for each. The four basic strategies are to

- *Build:* If an organization has an SBU that it believes has the potential to be a star (probably a problem child at present), building would be an appropriate goal. The organization may decide to give up short-term profits and use its financial resources to achieve this goal. Procter & Gamble built Pringles from a money loser to a record profit maker in the 1990s.
- *Hold:* If an SBU is a very successful cash cow, a key goal would surely be to hold or preserve market share so the organization can take advantage of the very positive cash flow. Bisquick has been a prosperous cash cow for General Mills for over two decades.
- *Harvest:* This strategy is appropriate for all SBUs except those classified as stars. The basic goal is to increase the short-term cash return without too much concern for the long-run impact. It is especially worthwhile when more cash is needed from a cash cow with long-run prospects that are unfavorable because of a low market growth rate. For instance, Lever Brothers has been harvesting Lifebuoy soap for a number of years with little promotional backing.
- *Divest:* Getting rid of SBUs with low shares of low-growth markets is often appropriate. Problem children and dogs are most suitable for this strategy. Procter & Gamble dropped Cincaprin, a coated aspirin, because of its low growth potential.

Market Attractiveness/Company Strength Matrix A second model for selecting strategic alternatives, originally developed by General Electric, is known as the **market attractiveness/company strength matrix**. The dimensions used in this matrix—market attractiveness and company strength—are richer and more complete than those used in the portfolio matrix but are much harder to quantify.

Exhibit 2.7 presents a market attractiveness/company strength matrix. The horizontal axis, business position, refers to how well positioned the organization is to take advantage of market opportunities. Does the firm have the technology it needs to effectively penetrate the market? Are its financial resources adequate? Can manufacturing costs be held below those of the competition? Will the firm have bargaining power over suppliers? Can the firm cope with change? The vertical axis measures the attractiveness of a market, which is expressed both quantitatively and qualitatively. Some attributes of an attractive market are high profitability, rapid growth, a lack of government regulation, consumer insensitivity to a price increase, a lack of competition, and availability of technology. The grid is divided into three overall attractiveness zones for each dimension: high, medium, and low.

Those SBUs (or markets) that have low overall attractiveness should be avoided if the organization is not already serving them. If the firm is in these markets, it should either harvest or divest the SBUs. The organization should selec-

Exhibit **2.7**

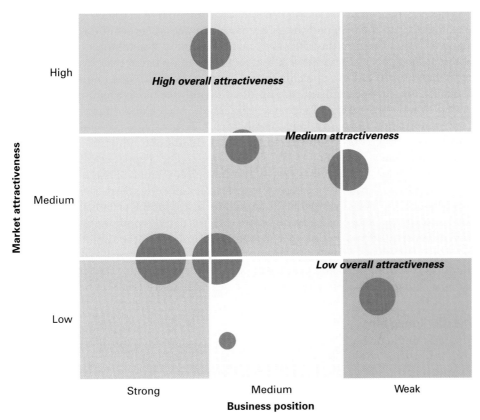

NOTE: Circle size represents dollar sales volume relative to sales of other SBUs on the matrix.

tively maintain markets with medium attractiveness. If attractiveness begins to slip, then the organization should withdraw from the market.

Conditions that are highly attractive—an attractive market plus a strong business position—are the best candidates for investment. For instance, Black & Decker used marketing research to uncover a market for the serious do-it-yourselfer. These people were willing to pay a premium price for quality home tools. For example, research found that this group of consumers wanted a cordless drill that didn't run out of power before the job was complete. Black & Decker responded with a new line called Quantum.

Describing the Marketing Strategy

Marketing strategy involves the activities of selecting and describing one or more target markets and developing and maintaining a marketing mix that will produce mutually satisfying exchanges with target markets.

marketing strategy
The activities of selecting and describing one or more target markets and developing and maintaining a marketing mix that will produce mutually satisfying exchanges with target markets.

Discuss target market strategies

Target Market Strategy
A market segment is a group of individuals or organizations that share one or more characteristics. They therefore may have relatively similar product needs. For example, parents of newborn babies need products such as formula, diapers, and special

foods. The target market strategy identifies the market segment or segments on which to focus. This process begins with a **market opportunity analysis (MOA)**—the description and estimation of the size and sales potential of market segments that are of interest to the firm and the assessment of key competitors in these market segments. After the firm describes the market segments, it may target one or more of them. There are three general strategies for selecting target markets. Target market(s) can be selected by appealing to the entire market with one marketing mix, concentrating on one segment, or appealing to multiple market segments using multiple marketing mixes. The characteristics, advantages, and disadvantages of each strategic option are examined in Chapter 7. Target markets could be smokers who are concerned about white teeth (the target of Topol toothpaste), people concerned about sugar and calories in their soft drinks (Diet Pepsi), or college students needing inexpensive about-town transportation (Yamaha Razz scooter).

Any market segment that is targeted must be fully described. Demographics, psychographics, and buyer behavior should be assessed. Buyer behavior is covered in Chapters 5 and 6. If segments are differentiated by ethnicity, multicultural aspects of the marketing mix should be examined. If the target market is international, it is especially important to describe differences in culture, economic and technological development, and political structure that may impact the marketing plan. Global marketing is covered in more detail in Chapter 4.

The Marketing Mix

The term **marketing mix** refers to a unique blend of product, distribution, promotion, and pricing strategies designed to produce mutually satisfying exchanges with a target market. Distribution is sometimes referred to as place, thus giving us the **four Ps** of the marketing mix: product, place, promotion, and price. The marketing manager can control each component of the marketing mix, but the strategies for all four components must be blended to achieve optimal results. Any marketing mix is only as good as its weakest component. For example, the first pump toothpastes were distributed over cosmetic counters and failed. Not until pump toothpastes were distributed the same way as tube toothpastes did the products succeed. The best promotion and the lowest price cannot save a poor product. Similarly, excellent products with poor distribution, pricing, or promotion will likely fail.

Successful marketing mixes have been carefully designed to satisfy target markets. At first glance, McDonald's and Wendy's may appear to have roughly identical marketing mixes because they are both in the fast-food hamburger business. However, McDonald's has been most successful with targeting parents with young children for lunchtime meals, whereas Wendy's targets the adult crowd for lunches and dinner. McDonald's has playgrounds, Ronald McDonald the clown, and children's Happy Meals. Wendy's has salad bars, carpeted restaurants, and no playgrounds.

Variations in marketing mixes do not occur by chance. Astute marketing managers devise marketing strategies to gain advantages over competitors and best serve the needs and wants of a particular target market segment. By manipulating elements of the marketing mix, marketing managers can fine-tune the customer offering and achieve competitive success.

Product Strategies   Typically, the marketing mix starts with the product "P." The heart of the marketing mix, the starting point, is the product offering and product strategy. It is hard to design a distribution strategy, decide on a promotion campaign, or set a price without knowing the product to be marketed.

The product includes not only the physical unit but also its package, warranty, after-sale service, brand name, company image, value, and many other factors. A Godiva chocolate has many product elements: the chocolate itself, a fancy gold wrapper, a customer satisfaction guarantee, and the prestige of the Godiva brand name. We buy things not only for what they do (benefits) but also for what they mean to us (status, quality, or reputation).

Products can be tangible goods such as computers, ideas like those offered by a consultant, or services such as medical care. Products should also offer customer value. Product decisions are covered in Chapters 9 and 10, and services marketing is detailed in Chapter 11.

Godiva
How does Godiva's Web site communicate its product strategy? What features are you surprised to see on this site?
http://www.godiva.com

On Line

Distribution (Place) Strategies Distribution strategies are concerned with making products available when and where customers want them. Would you rather buy a kiwi fruit at the twenty-four-hour grocery store within walking distance or fly to Australia to pick your own? A part of this place "P" is physical distribution, which involves all the business activities concerned with storing and transporting raw materials or finished products. The goal of distribution is to make sure products arrive in usable condition at designated places when needed. Distribution strategies are covered in Chapters 12 and 13.

Promotion Strategies Promotion includes personal selling, advertising, sales promotion, and public relations. Promotion's role in the marketing mix is to bring about mutually satisfying exchanges with target markets by informing, educating, persuading, and reminding them of the benefits of an organization or a product. A good promotion strategy, like using the Dilbert character in a national promotion strategy for Office Depot, can dramatically increase sales. However, good promotion strategies do not guarantee success. Despite a massive promotional campaign, the movie *Godzilla* had disappointing box-office returns. Each element of the promotion "P" is coordinated and managed with the others to create a promotional blend or mix. These integrated marketing communications activities are described in Chapters 14, 15, and 16. Technology-driven aspects of promotional marketing are covered in Chapters 19 and 20.

Does ad spending really make a difference at the box office? All of the hype surrounding some of 2000's movie releases did little to boost box office revenues. Only about half of the films listed can boast a serious return on their promotional expenditures.

Big Spenders

For the period of January 1 through July 30, here is a list of the 10 films with the highest TV ad budgets, their box-office gross, and their box-office gross rank

	TV Ad Budget	Domestic Box-Office Gross	Rank
Gladiator (DreamWorks)	$29.5	$186.6	2
Chicken Run (DreamWorks)	27.5	106.6	12
The Perfect Storm (Warner Bros.)	25.6	181.4	3
Mission: Impossible 2 (Paramount)	22.7	215.4	1
Rules of Engagement (Paramount)	21.0	61.3	20
Snow Day (Paramount)	20.0	60.0	22
The Patriot (Sony)	19.3	113.3	11
Road Trip (DreamWorks)	19.1	68.5	19
The Road to El Dorado (DreamWorks)	18.3	51.0	29
Mission to Mars (Disney)	18.1	60.9	21

Ad Spending Source: Competitive Media Reporting
Box-Office Source: Exhibitor Relations Co.

SOURCE: Copyright © 2000, Dow Jones & Company, Inc.

Pricing Strategies   Price is what a buyer must give up to obtain a product. It is often the most flexible of the four marketing mix elements—the quickest element to change. Marketers can raise or lower prices more frequently and easily than they can change other marketing mix variables. Price is an important competitive weapon and very important to the organization because price multiplied by the number of units sold equals total revenue for the firm. Pricing decisions are covered in Chapters 17 and 18.

Following Up the Marketing Plan

Explain why implementation, evaluation, and control of the marketing plan are necessary

implementation
The process that turns marketing plans into action assignments and ensures that these assignments are executed in a way that accomplishes the plans' objectives.

evaluation
Gauging the extent to which the marketing objectives have been achieved during the specified time period.

control
Provides the mechanisms for evaluating marketing results in light of the plan's goals and for correcting actions that do not help the organization reach those goals within budget guidelines.

marketing audit
A thorough, systematic, periodic evaluation of the goals, strategies, structure, and performance of the marketing organization.

Implementation
Implementation is the process that turns marketing plans into action assignments and ensures that these assignments are executed in a way that accomplishes the plans' objectives. Implementation activities may involve detailed job assignments, activity descriptions, timelines, budgets, and lots of communication. Although implementation is essentially "doing what you said you were going to do," many organizations repeatedly experience failures in strategy implementation. Brilliant marketing plans are doomed to fail if they are not properly implemented. These detailed communications may or may not be part of the written marketing plan. If they are not part of the plan, they should be specified elsewhere as soon as the plan has been communicated.

Evaluation and Control
After a marketing plan is implemented, it should be evaluated. **Evaluation** entails gauging the extent to which marketing objectives have been achieved during the specified time period. Four common reasons for failing to achieve a marketing objective are unrealistic marketing objectives, inappropriate marketing strategies in the plan, poor implementation, and changes in the environment after the objective was specified and the strategy was implemented.

Once a plan is chosen and implemented, its effectiveness must be monitored. **Control** provides the mechanisms for evaluating marketing results in light of the plan's goals and for correcting actions that do not help the organization reach those goals within budget guidelines. Firms need to establish formal and informal control programs to make the entire operation more efficient.

Perhaps the broadest control device available to marketing managers is the **marketing audit**—a thorough, systematic, periodic evaluation of the goals, strategies, structure, and performance of the marketing organization. A marketing audit helps management allocate marketing resources efficiently. It has four characteristics:

- *Comprehensive:* The marketing audit covers all the major marketing issues facing an organization and not just trouble spots.
- *Systematic:* The marketing audit takes place in an orderly sequence and covers the organization's marketing environment, internal marketing system, and specific marketing activities. The diagnosis is followed by an action plan with both short-run and long-run proposals for improving overall marketing effectiveness.
- *Independent:* The marketing audit is normally conducted by an inside or outside party that is independent enough to have top management's confidence and to be objective.
- *Periodic:* The marketing audit should be carried out on a regular schedule instead of only in a crisis. Whether it seems successful or is in deep trouble, any organization can benefit greatly from such an audit.

Although the main purpose of the marketing audit is to develop a full profile of the organization's marketing effort and to provide a basis for developing and revising the marketing plan, it is also an excellent way to improve communication and raise the level of marketing consciousness within the organization. It is a useful vehicle for selling the philosophy and techniques of strategic marketing to other members of the organization.

Effective Strategic Planning

Effective strategic planning requires continual attention, creativity, and management commitment:

 Identify several techniques that help make strategic planning effective

- Strategic planning is not an annual exercise, in which managers go through the motions and forget about strategic planning until the next year. It should be an ongoing process because the environment is continually changing and the firm's resources and capabilities are continually evolving.
- Sound strategic planning is based on creativity. Managers should challenge assumptions about the firm and the environment and establish new strategies. For example, major oil companies developed the concept of the gasoline service station in an age when cars needed frequent and rather elaborate servicing. They held on to the full-service approach, but independents were quick to respond to new realities and moved to lower-cost self-service and convenience-store operations. The majors took several decades to catch up.
- Perhaps the most critical element in successful strategic planning is top management's support and participation. For example, Michael Anthony, CEO of Brookstone, Inc., racks up hundreds of thousands of frequent flyer miles searching the world for manufacturers and inventors of unique products that can be carried by Brookstone in both retail outlets and catalogs. Anthony has codeveloped some of these products and has also been active in the remodeling efforts of Brookstone's two hundred permanent and seasonal stores. Anthony's participation is paying off with higher revenues and earnings per share.[24]

In the late twentieth century, the Internet constituted a new business strategy. Brookstone responded by opening a Web-based storefront to supplement its retail outlets and catalog operations.

Looking Back

Look back at the story of the Razor scooter. You can see that Razor USA has to engage in a great deal of strategic marketing planning to be a viable player in this competitive market. Additionally, you can see that planning is a continuous process, as Razor's strategies have been modified and added to. For example, just before the 2000 holiday season, Razor USA filed suit against 16 rivals for patent infringement and a Federal judge barred Razor's competitors from making or selling look-alikes. During the legal tangle, Razor hopes to cash in on the six million U.S. scooters sold each year.

Most manufacturers and retailers agree that poorly made knockoffs will go by the wayside and the accessory market of wheels, lights, packs, and safety equipment has strong potential. Industry analysts maintain that scooters are a trend, not a fad, because they are practical. And with Razor planning new models and product improvements each year, the trend is likely to continue.

You should now be able to identify marketing plan elements for Razor USA, including their mission statement, measurable marketing objectives, and components of a SWOT analysis. Does Razor have sustainable competitive advantages? You should be able to identify a target market for Razors and identify the basic marketing mix elements of product, place, promotion, and price. Finally, you can see how Razor has implemented, evaluated, and controlled strategies.

Use it Now!

How do the elements of a marketing plan apply to you personally? Put yourself in the situation of looking for a new job. In this scenario, you are marketing yourself. Let's look at the pieces of a marketing plan to see how to plan on your own marketing.

First, what is your mission? Are you looking only for part-time or temporary experience to enhance your resume, or a career stepping stone, or a full-time, long-term career choice? This mission will help set the stage for the rest of your plan. Next, what are your objectives? Do you need to find a job within the next thirty days, or are you more flexible? Are there specific job activities that you would like to perform? These job activities could be stated in the objectives portion of your resume. Be sure that objectives are very specific; general objectives are of little use to you or an employer.

It's now time for your SWOT analysis. Be very honest in your self-assessment of weakness and strengths, because these issues often come up during job interviews. What about opportunities and threats in the marketplace? Who is your competition? Are there aspects in the external environment that provide strategic windows for your employment? Do you have a competitive advantage? Special leadership skills, international travel, computer experience, team projects, communications efforts, and other attributes should be examined. Any differential advantage you possess should be noted in the cover letter of your resume and your job interview.

What is your target market? Are you only looking for jobs with big, established organizations or small entrepreneurial firms? Companies in a particular industry? Do you have any geographic preferences? When you figure out your target, compile a list of firms that meet your requirements and describe them. The more you know about your target market potential employers, the more prepared you will be in an interview.

You are the product. How can you best present yourself? Think of your own packaging with regard to dress, appearance, mannerisms, and speech. What about place? Are you willing to travel or relocate? Or do you need an employer close to home? How will you travel to the employer? Is telecommuting an option? How will you promote yourself? Careful construction of a cover letter, resume, business card, and personal Web site are all methods that help communicate your skills to a potential employer. Think carefully about pricing issues, including salary, commission, bonuses, overtime, flexible time, insurance, and other benefits. What is a fair price for you? What is a normal price for a company of that size in that industry to offer?

Have you set up an implementation plan for applying to companies? Contacting them for potential interviews? Working on your wardrobe and interviewing skills? Remember to send thank you notes for your interviews as a control measure. When job offers come in, how will you evaluate them? If job offers don't come in, can you find out why and control for those aspects?

As you can see, marketing plan elements can apply to marketing an organization or an individual. And writing down a marketing plan can greatly assist in the search for the perfect strategy or job!

Summary

① **Understand the importance of strategic marketing and know a basic outline for a marketing plan.** Strategic marketing planning is the basis for all marketing strategies and decisions. The marketing plan is a written document that acts as a guidebook of marketing activities for the marketing manager. By specifying objectives and defining the actions required to attain them, a marketing plan provides the basis on which actual and expected performance can be compared.

Although there is no set formula for a marketing plan or a single correct outline, basic factors that should be covered include stating the business mission, setting objectives, performing a situation analysis of internal and external environmental forces, selecting target market(s), delineating a marketing mix (product, place, promotion, and price), and establishing ways to implement, evaluate, and control the plan.

② **Develop an appropriate business mission statement.** The mission statement is based on a careful analysis of benefits sought by present and potential customers and analysis of existing and anticipated environmental conditions. The firm's long-term vision, embodied in the mission statement, establishes boundaries for all subsequent decisions, objectives, and strategies. A mission statement should focus on the market or markets the organization is attempting to serve rather than on the good or service offered.

③ **Describe the criteria for stating good marketing objectives.** Objectives should be realistic, measurable, and time specific. Objectives must also be consistent and indicate the priorities of the organization.

④ **Explain the components of a situation analysis.** In the situation (or SWOT) analysis, the firm should identify its internal strengths (S) and weaknesses (W) and also examine external opportunities (O) and threats (T). When examining external opportunities and threats, marketing managers must analyze aspects of the marketing environment in a process called environmental scanning. The six most often studied macroenvironmental forces are social, demographic, economic, technological, political and legal, and competitive. During the situation analysis, the marketer should try to identify any strategic windows. Additionally, it is crucial that the marketer identify a differential advantage and establish that it is a sustainable competitive advantage.

⑤ **Identify sources of competitive advantage.** A competitive advantage is a set of unique features of a company and its products that are perceived by the target market as significant and superior to the competition. There are three types of competitive advantages: cost, product/service differentiation, and niche strategies. Sources of cost differential advantages include experience curves, efficient labor, no-frills goods and services, government subsidies, product design, reengineering, product innovations, and new methods of service delivery. Differentiation competitive advantages can come from value impressions and augmented products. Niche competitive advantages come from targeting unique segments with specific needs and wants. The goal of all these sources of competitive advantage is to be sustainable.

⑥ **Identify strategic alternatives and describe tools used to help select alternatives.** The strategic opportunity matrix can be used to help management develop strategic alternatives. The four options are market penetration, product development, market development, and diversification. The portfolio matrix is a method of determining the profit potential and investment requirements of a firm's SBUs by classifying them as stars, cash cows, problem children, or dogs and then determining appropriate resource allocations for each. A more detailed alternative to the portfolio matrix is the market attractiveness/company strength matrix, which measures company and market viability.

Exhibit 2.8 Marketing Plan Outline

I. Business Mission

- What is the mission of the firm? What business is it in? How well is its mission understood throughout the organization? Five years from now, what business does it wish to be in?
- Does the firm define its business in terms of benefits its customers want rather than in terms of goods and services?

II. Objectives

- Is the firm's mission statement able to be translated into operational terms regarding the firm's objectives?
- What are the stated objectives of the organization? Are they formally written down? Do they lead logically to clearly stated marketing objectives? Are objectives based on sales, profits, or customers?
- Are the organization's marketing objectives stated in hierarchical order? Are they specific so that progress toward achievement can be measured? Are the objectives reasonable in light of the organization's resources? Are the objectives ambiguous? Do the objectives specify a time frame?
- Is the firm's main goal to maximize customer satisfaction or to get as many customers as possible?

III. Situation Analysis (SWOT Analysis)

- Is there a strategic window that must be taken into account?
- Has one or more differential advantages been identified in the SWOT analysis?
- Are these advantages sustainable against the competition?

A. Internal Strengths and Weaknesses

- What is the history of the firm, including sales, profits, and organizational philosophies?
- What is the nature of the firm and its current situation?
- What resources does the firm have (financial, human, time, experience, asset, skill)?
- What policies inhibit the achievement of the firm's objectives with respect to organization, resource allocation, operations, hiring, training, and so on?

B. External Opportunities and Threats

- *Social:* What major social and lifestyle trends will have an impact on the firm? What action has the firm been taking in response to these trends?
- *Demographics:* What impact will forecasted trends in the size, age, profile, and distribution of population have on the firm? How will the changing nature of the family, the increase in the proportion of women in the workforce, and changes in the ethnic composition of the population affect the firm? What action has the firm taken in response to these developments and trends? Has the firm reevaluated its traditional products and expanded the range of specialized offerings to respond to these changes?

- *Economic:* What major trends in taxation and income sources will have an impact on the firm? What action has the firm taken in response to these trends?
- *Political, Legal, and Financial:* What laws are now being proposed at international, federal, state, and local levels that could affect marketing strategy and tactics? What recent changes in regulations and court decisions affect the firm? What political changes at each government level are taking place? What action has the firm taken in response to these legal and political changes?
- *Competition:* Which organizations are competing with the firm directly by offering a similar product? Which organizations are competing with the firm indirectly by securing its prime prospects' time, money, energy, or commitment? What new competitive trends seem likely to emerge? How effective is the competition? What benefits do competitors offer that the firm does not? Is it appropriate for the firm to compete?
- *Technological:* What major technological changes are occurring that affect the firm?
- *Ecological:* What is the outlook for the cost and availability of natural resources and energy needed by the firm? Are the firm's products, services, and operations environmentally friendly?

IV. Marketing Strategy

A. Target Market Strategy

- Are the members of each market homogeneous or heterogeneous with respect to geographic, sociodemographic, and behavioral characteristics?
- What are the size, growth rate, and national and regional trends in each of the organization's market segments?
- Is the size of each market segment sufficiently large or important to warrant a unique marketing mix?
- Are market segments measurable and accessible to distribution and communication efforts?
- Which are the high- or low-opportunity segments?
- What are the evolving needs and satisfactions being sought by target markets?
- What benefits does the organization offer to each segment? How do these benefits compare with benefits offered by competitors?
- Is the firm positioning itself with a unique product? Is the product needed?
- How much of the firm's business is repeat versus new business? What percentage of the public can be classified as nonusers, light users, or heavy users?
- How do current target markets rate the firm and its competitors with respect to reputation, quality, and price? What is the firm's image with the specific market segments it seeks to serve?

Exhibit 2.8   Marketing Plan Outline *(continued)*

- Does the firm try to direct its products only to specific groups of people or to everybody?
- Who buys the firm's products? How does a potential customer find out about the organization? When and how does a person become a customer?
- What are the major objections given by potential customers as to why they do not buy the firm's products?
- How do customers find out about and decide to purchase the product? When and where?
- Should the firm seek to expand, contract, or change the emphasis of its selected target markets? If so, in which target markets, and how vigorously?
- Could the firm more usefully withdraw from some areas in which there are alternative suppliers and use its resources to serve new, unserved customer groups?
- What publics other than target markets (financial, media, government, citizen, local, general, and internal) represent opportunities or problems for the firm?

B. Marketing Mix

- Does the firm seek to achieve its goal chiefly through coordinated use of marketing activities (product, distribution, promotion, and pricing) or only through intensive promotion?
- Are the objectives and roles of each element of the marketing mix clearly specified?

1. Product

  - What are the major product/service offerings of the firm? Do they complement each other, or is there unnecessary duplication?
  - What are the features and benefits of each product offering?
  - Where is the firm and each major product in its life cycle?
  - What are the pressures among various target markets to increase or decrease the range and quality of products?
  - What are the major weaknesses in each product area? What are the major complaints? What goes wrong most often?
  - Is the product name easy to pronounce? Spell? Recall? Is it descriptive, and does it communicate the benefits the product offers? Does the name distinguish the firm or product from all others?
  - What warranties are offered with the product? Are there other ways to guarantee customer satisfaction?
  - Does the product offer good customer value?
  - How is customer service handled? How is service quality assessed?

2. Place/Distribution

  - Should the firm try to deliver its offerings directly to customers, or can it better deliver selected offerings by involving other organizations? What channel(s) should be used in distributing product offerings?
  - What physical distribution facilities should be used? Where should they be located? What should be their major characteristics?
  - Are members of the target market willing and able to travel some distance to buy the product?

- How good is access to facilities? Can access be improved? Which facilities need priority attention in these areas?
- How are facility locations chosen? Is the site accessible to the target markets? Is it visible to the target markets?
- What is the location and atmosphere of retail establishments? Do these retailers satisfy customers?
- When are products made available to users (season of year, day of week, time of day)? Are these times most appropriate?

3. Promotion

- How does a typical customer find out about the firm's products?
- Does the message the firm delivers gain the attention of the intended target audience? Does it address the wants and needs of the target market, and does it suggest benefits or a means for satisfying these wants? Is the message appropriately positioned?
- Does the promotion effort effectively inform, persuade, educate, and remind customers about the firm's products?
- Does the firm establish budgets and measure effectiveness of promotional efforts?

a. Advertising

  - Which media are currently being used? Has the firm chosen the type of media that will best reach its target markets?
  - Are the types of media used the most cost-effective, and do they contribute positively to the firm's image?
  - Are the dates and times the ads will appear the most appropriate? Has the firm prepared several versions of its advertisements?
  - Does the organization use an outside advertising agency? What functions does the ad agency perform for the organization?
  - What system is used to handle consumer inquiries resulting from advertising and promotions? What follow-up is done?

b. Public Relations

  - Is there a well-conceived public relations and publicity program? Does the program contain the ability to respond to bad publicity?
  - How is public relations normally handled by the firm? By whom? Have those responsible nurtured working relationships with media outlets?
  - Is the firm using all available public relations avenues? Is an effort made to understand each of the publicity outlets' needs and to provide each with story types that will appeal to its audience in readily usable forms?
  - What does the annual report say about the firm and its products? Who is being effectively reached by this vehicle? Does the benefit of publication justify the cost?

continued

Exhibit **2.8** Marketing Plan Outline *(continued)*

c. Personal Selling

- How much of a typical salesperson's time is spent soliciting new customers as compared to serving existing customers?
- How is it determined which prospect will be called on and by whom? How is the frequency of contacts determined?
- How is the sales force compensated? Are there incentives for encouraging more business?
- How is the sales force organized and managed?
- Has the sales force prepared an approach tailored to each prospect?
- Has the firm matched sales personnel with the target market characteristics?
- Is there appropriate follow-up to the initial personal selling effort? Are customers made to feel appreciated?
- Can database or direct marketing be used to replace or supplement the sales force?

d. Sales Promotion

- What is the specific purpose of each sales promotion activity? Why is it offered? What does it try to achieve?
- What categories of sales promotion are being used? Is sales promotion directed to the trade, the final consumer, or both?
- Is the effort directed at all the firm's key publics or restricted to only potential customers?

4. Price

- What levels of pricing and specific prices should be used?
- What mechanisms does the firm have to ensure that the prices charged are acceptable to customers?
- How price sensitive are customers?

- If a price change is put into effect, how will the number of customers change? Will total revenue increase or decrease?
- Which method is used for establishing a price: going rate, demand-oriented, or cost-based?
- What discounts are offered, and with what rationale?
- Has the firm considered the psychological dimensions of price?
- Have price increases kept pace with cost increases, inflation, or competitive levels?
- How are price promotions used?
- Do interested prospects have opportunities to sample products at an introductory price?
- What methods of payment are accepted? Is it in the firm's best interest to use these various payment methods?

V. **Implementation, Evaluation, and Control**

- Is the marketing organization structured appropriately to implement the marketing plan?
- What specific activities must take place? Who is responsible for these activities?
- What is the implementation timetable?
- What other marketing research is necessary?
- What will the financial impact be of this plan on a one-year projected income statement? How does projected income compare with expected revenue if the plan is not implemented?
- What are the performance standards?
- What monitoring procedures (audits) will take place and when?
- Does it seem as though the firm is trying to do too much or not enough?
- Are the core marketing strategies for achieving objectives sound? Are the objectives being met, and are the objectives appropriate?
- Are enough resources (or too many resources) budgeted to accomplish the marketing objectives?

(7) **Discuss target market strategies.** The target market strategy identifies which market segment or segments to focus on. This process begins with a market opportunity analysis (MOA), which describes and estimates the size and sales potential of market segments that are of interest to the firm. In addition, an assessment of key competitors in these market segments is performed. After the market segments are described, one or more may be targeted by the firm. The three strategies for selecting target markets are appealing to the entire market with one marketing mix, concentrating on one segment, or appealing to multiple market segments using multiple marketing mixes.

(8) **Describe elements of the marketing mix.** The marketing mix (or four Ps) is a blend of product, distribution (place), promotion, and pricing strategies designed to produce mutually satisfying exchanges with a target market. The starting point of the marketing mix is the product offering. Products can be tangible goods, ideas, or services. Distribution strategies are concerned with making products available when and where customers want them. Promotion includes personal selling, advertising, sales promotion, and public relations. Price is what a buyer must give up to obtain a product and is often the easiest to change of the four marketing mix elements.

⑨ **Explain why implementation, evaluation, and control of the marketing plan are necessary.** Before a marketing plan can work, it must be implemented; that is, people must perform the actions in the plan. The plan should also be evaluated to see if it has achieved its objectives. Poor implementation can be a major factor in a plan's failure. Control provides the mechanisms for evaluating marketing results in light of the plan's goals and for correcting actions that do not help the organization reach those goals within budget guidelines.

⑩ **Identify several techniques that help make strategic planning effective.** First, management must realize that strategic planning is an ongoing process and not a once-a-year exercise. Second, good strategic planning involves a high level of creativity. The last requirement is top management's support and cooperation.

Discussion and Writing Questions

1. Your cousins want to start their own business, and they are in a hurry. They have decided not to write a marketing plan because they have already gotten funding from your uncle and do not need a formal proposal and because writing such a document would take too long. Explain why it is important for them to write a plan anyway.

2. **ON LINE** How can a new company best define its business mission statement? Can you find examples of good and bad mission statements on the Internet? How could you improve these mission statements?

3. The new marketing manager has stated that the marketing objective of the firm is to do the best job of satisfying the needs and wants of the customer. Explain that although this objective is admirable, it does not meet the criteria for good objectives. What are these criteria? What is a specific example of a better objective?

4. **TEAM** Break into small groups and discuss examples (at least two per person) of the last few products you have purchased. What were the specific strategies used to achieve a differential advantage? Is that differential advantage sustainable against the competition?

5. Perform a mini situation analysis by stating one strength, one weakness, one opportunity, and one threat to your choice of consumer products companies. What are the strategic growth options available for this company, based on your evaluation? Where does your company's product offerings fit on the two strategic matrices discussed in the text?

6. You are given the task of deciding the marketing strategy for a transportation service. How do the elements of the marketing mix change when the target market is (a) corporate international business travelers, (b) low-income workers without personal transportation, or (c) companies with urgent documents or perishable materials to get to customers?

7. **INFOTRAC COLLEGE EDITION** How does the Internet affect the marketing mix? Use Infotrac to find out. Read an article in the July 17, 2000 edition of *Computerworld* magazine titled "Internets's reach even extends to 4P's of marketing" by Don Tapscott. Apply what you learn to question 6.

8. **WRITING** Create a marketing plan to increase enrollment in your school. Write down each step and describe the controls on the plan's implementation.

Application for Entrepreneurs

 Providing security for VIPS—ranging from government officials to movie stars—when they appear in public, typically means deploying protective barriers such as concrete walls or Plexiglas shields. A new product aims to replace those obstructive protection devices. Ibis Technologies, a three-year-old company in Butler, Pennsylvania, has developed an Instantaneous

Key Terms

augmented product 38
cash cow 43
competitive advantage 36
control 48
cost competitive advantage 37
differential advantage 36
differential competitive advantage 38
diversification 41
dog 44
environmental scanning 36
evaluation 48
experience curves 37
four Ps 46
implementation 48
market attractiveness/company strength matrix 44
market development 41
market opportunity analysis (MOA) 46
market penetration 40
marketing audit 48
marketing mix 46
marketing myopia 34
marketing objective 35
marketing plan 30
marketing planning 30
marketing strategy 45
mission statement 34
niche competitive advantage 39
planning 30
portfolio matrix 42
problem child (question mark) 43
product development 41
star 42
strategic business unit (SBU) 34
strategic planning 30
strategic window 40
sustainable competitive advantage 39
SWOT analysis 36
value impressions 38

Personal Protection System (IPPS). The IPPS is a cross between an aircraft ejection seat and a car airbag. In less time than the ear can register the sound of gunfire, the IPPS surrounds the intended victim with a bulletproof shield. This new security device can sit on the floor next to a VIP or terrorist target, or it can be used as a security guard in a busy lobby, disguised as a set of decorative planters.[25]

How does the IPPS work? A radar-senor detects incoming objects (such as bullets or knives) and triggers an inflating airbag. The bulletproof material traps the projectile like a baseball glove folding around a ball. In demonstrations, the shield has deployed quickly enough to survive assaults from .22-caliber through .44-caliber magnum rounds, submachine guns, shotgun blasts at close range, and knife-wielding attackers. Its detection range is about 150 feet. The device can also be fired by radio control.[26] The fully installed system weighs 400 pounds.

The IPPS technology can be extended to other applications, such as protecting vehicles and securing windows on buildings. A key challenge will be the ability to detect electronic signals that might set off the system accidentally, such as cellular phones or aircraft radar. Despite these challenges, Ibis Technology Corporation has been selected as a top technology stock pick by hedge fund manager Jeffrey Puglisi[27] and has been featured prominently as a "company to watch" in *Electronic News* magazine.[28]

Questions

1. What is an appropriate mission statement for Ibis Technologies?
2. What specific objective would you suggest they achieve?
3. What are the strengths, weaknesses, opportunities, and threats in this situation?
4. Does Ibis Technologies have a competitive advantage? Is it sustainable?
5. What strategic growth options can Ibis Technologies pursue?
6. Where does Ibis Technologies and its IPPS fit on strategic matrix tools?
7. What should the target market be? Why?
8. What are the elements of the marketing mix? Describe a brief strategy for each of the four Ps.

Case   intrapreneurship

Ford: Racing to the Internet

When you hear the name Ford Motor Company, probably the last phrase that comes to mind is cutting-edge Net entrepreneurs. Ford has been working quietly, however, to change the perception that it is just another slow reacting Detroit dinosaur. Faced with research that car shoppers are increasingly looking for brand, model, and pricing information on-line, Ford has realized that there are tremendous gains to be had by establishing a presence where its customers are. The company has therefore made a concerted effort to lead the race in building an Internet presence that will return real value to both Ford and its customers. Giving customers more control over and access to the ordering process, building vehicles specifically to customer wants, and delivering them in a timely manner should drive new customers to Ford's dealers. It should also improve retention rates among current customers. All are goals of Ford's Internet strategy, which the multinational car manufacturer hopes will increase its market share and profitability through better penetration of existing markets and development of new ones.

To maximize these strategic opportunities, Ford aims to better define its target, build more desirable products, promote them better through on-line marketing, and improve its distribution system. Using a combination of target marketing and marketing mix strategies, Ford hopes it will do nothing less than revolutionize the way cars are bought, built, and sold. It sank $100 million into its year 2000 on-line marketing initiatives in an effort to do just that.

Investing heavily in marketing on-line provides Ford with luxuries unavailable through the off-line marketing of vehicles. Ford plans to build detailed consumer profiles from information it acquires through Ford.com and through strategic relationships formed with Web sites that have highly targeted audiences. The automotive giant will use new information technology (IT) in conjunction with these profiles to help create a competitive advantage in three ways:

- By building more products to order than its competition
- By developing products suited to the tastes of specific target markets
- By reducing the time it takes to build and deliver a custom-ordered car to a customer

Ford's first step into the on-line world came with development and deployment of its home Web site, Ford.com. When it first went live in 1998, the Web site did exactly what its competitors' sites did—mainly provide increased, up-to-date information on the prices, features, and designs of its models. One year later, Ford.com and its rival sites had little in common. Instead of investing heavily in flashy tricks and graphics-intensive pages, Ford wisely used its on-line marketing budget to aggressively pursue Internet partnerships and build systems that would improve its manufacturing and vehicle delivery processes. In 1999, Ford signed a $5 million agreement with leading women's Web site iVillage.com to sponsor its Women's Auto Center (WAC). In exchange for its $5 million, Ford receives premier advertising placement, access to iVillage.com's data about its consumers' preferences and surfing habits, and top billing in iVillage.com's "Design Your Dream Car" area. Ford also gets to supply automotive articles and general information to the WAC. Ford wants to achieve three goals through the relationship:

- To learn more about what women want in general and from their cars
- To build trust with that target market
- To showcase its many brands

Though Media Metrix ranks Ford consistently in the top fifteen Web properties based on unique monthly visitors, the big-three automaker continued to target even more audiences with promotions and information about its vehicles. Later in 1999, Ford signed another deal with Digital Entertainment Network (DEN), an on-line media company that creates original entertainment programming for Generation Y. Born between 1979 and 1994, Gen Y represents a total market of around sixty million individuals, outranking the baby boomers in numbers. Ford counts on its charter relationship with DEN to yield two key benefits. First, the company wants to introduce Gen Y consumers to Ford cars at an age when they aspire to own their own automobiles. Second, it wants to boost the impulse factor in the car-buying process. Ford hopes that someday a viewer of a DEN program who sees a Ford vehicle in use on the on-line show will be able to click on the car, access information about it, and possibly proceed to order it.

The above two projects should be sufficient to give Ford a lead in leveraging relationships with on-line media partners in an effort to build awareness of its products and better develop the market for those products. The company, however, has announced another alliance that should have an even greater impact on the actual car buying, manufacturing, and delivery systems. The venture is with the official automotive site of the Microsoft Network (MSN), CarPoint.com. CarPoint has specialized in providing car reviews, pricing information, and industry news to its users as well as generating sales leads for dealers. In addition to gaining a competitive advantage by having access to CarPoint's data on consumer preferences, Ford plans to surpass its competition in its ability to react to consumer demand. To do that, it will marry CarPoint's lead-generation capability to a host of new IT systems that together will allow consumers to find specific cars in dealer inventories, in the distribution pipeline, or have them built to their exact preferences. In the event that a car must be built from scratch, Ford's goal is to build the car and deliver it within days. The IT systems will also optimize information flows between Ford and its suppliers so that parts orders are made based on the most up-to-date information on market demand.

Ford hopes its Internet strategy will help to sustain its run as America's most profitable and valuable automotive company. Clearly, it is moving in a direction different and faster than its primary competition, and only time will tell if the investment pays off. If the benefits it achieves for its customers are anything close to what the company anticipates, it is not hard to imagine Ford revolutionizing and digitizing the auto industry for consumers much the way it revolutionized the manufacturing process almost eighty years ago, when Henry Ford introduced the world to the first assembly line.

Questions

1. How has Ford used on-line targeting to attract new customers?
2. Has Ford pursued a market development, market penetration, product development, or diversification strategy, or a combined strategy? Explain and defend your answer.
3. List Ford's differential advantages and explain whether or not they will allow Ford to achieve a sustainable competitive advantage.
4. In your own words, write an effective mission statement for Ford Motor Company.

Bibliography

Roberta Bernstein. "Team Spirit." *Mediaweek,* November 8, 1999; found on-line, no page numbers available.
Bob Wallace and Aaron Ricadela. "Drive to the Web." *Information Week,* Manhasset Publishing. September 27, 1999, pp. 22–24.

Case

video

Marketing Recovery Through Comedy

Been there. Done that. That's what gives stand-up comic Mark Lundholm the edge. His comic routines tell about his experience as an alcoholic, drug addict, drug dealer, tax evader, check forger, and prison inmate. He makes audiences laugh and cry with his personal memories about living in a cardboard box and pointing a loaded gun to his mouth to commit suicide. As for his days of living on the streets of Oakland, California, Lundholm says, "There's a pecking order on the street that is unbelievable. How big you are, how long you've been there, and who you know—those things are the important things. Who you know is more important than who you are on the street."

So why would anybody pay to hear what Lundholm calls "comedy for the chemically challenged"? Drug and alcohol addiction are so widespread today that despite positive efforts like the Just Say No program, alcohol and drug abuse are rising. When Lundholm performs at prisons, treatment centers, and recovery meetings such as Alcoholics Anonymous (AA), audience members can truly identify with Lundholm's stories and so can their friends and families. The population affected by substance abuse cuts across race, age, gender, and social and economic levels.

To those who suffer from addiction, Lundholm shares hope and the joy of fulfillment found in recovery—through the powerful force of laughter. Yet parts of the show are not funny at all. "I'd be lying by omission if I went in and did ninety minutes of comedy," explains Lundholm. He admits freely to audiences that his addiction cost him his wife, his daughter, and his dry cleaning business. His own recovery began in an Oakland drug rehabilitation center in 1988, and the turmoil of his own life serves as material for his three comic shows: "An Evening of 12-Step Humor," "The Insanity Remains," and "I'm Not Judgin', I'm Just Sayin'." Whenever his "close to the bone originality" hits too close to home, Lundholm replies, "I'm not judging, I'm just saying." This catch phrase drew so many laughs that it became the name of a show.

But people in recovery are not the only ones who laugh at Lundholm's routines. He plays the comedy club circuit as well and appeals to "normies," as he calls nonalcoholics. Although the routines revolve around the 12-step program of AA, they embrace enough of life's highs and lows that even "normies" are entertained. Every joke, every story is punctuated with animation—hands waving, feet flying, face contorted into a hundred deviations. Lundholm hits on the trials and tribulations of growing up with parents of the 1950s: "Mark, back away from that TV, you're going to ruin your eyes." Jokes aim at all types of relationships, roles, and human peculiarities.

Now, Lundholm performs at established comedy clubs like Comedy Central, Zanies, and Funny-Bone, but he began his career by opening shows for well-known Russian comic, Yakov Smirnoff. Lundholm's booking agent and personal manager, Jimmy Goings, sells the one-man show directly to comedy venues and also provides entertainment consulting and production services to organizations conducting events. A Web site, videocassettes, tapes, T-shirts, and a book also promote Lundholm as a comedian.

In general, an entertainer's fees grow as name recognition grows, and Lundholm is no exception. As he continues to travel and play the nightclub circuit, higher fees can be negotiated, but he still donates his time to reach people in recovery. Performing forty-six weeks a year nationally and internationally, Lundholm usually includes recovery venues such as the Betty Ford Center, hospitals, halfway houses, and prisons. When performing at a comedy club, he will speak at no charge at a high school in the area about the dangers of drug abuse. Lundholm takes his timely message to teenagers who can really benefit from it.

And this volunteer work has paid off. Solid public relations and much goodwill have come from this commitment to recovery. When writing reviews, the press regularly covers both the nightclub act and the performances at rehabilitation centers and schools. Good public relations, along with good material, have helped Lundholm build his reputation as a comedian and distinguish himself from the multitude of very funny, stand-up comics in the entertainment world. That's how Mark Lundholm markets recovery.

Questions

1. What is Lundholm's mission?
2. What is Lundholm's differential advantage?
3. Who is the target market segment? What is the benefit received?
4. Describe Lundholm's marketing mix.
5. Who is the target market? What is the benefit received?

chapter 3

Learning Objectives

1 Discuss the external environment of marketing, and explain how it affects a firm

2 Describe the social factors that affect marketing

3 Explain the importance to marketing managers of current demographic trends

4 Explain the importance to marketing managers of multiculturalism and growing ethnic markets

5 Identify consumer and marketer reactions to the state of the economy

6 Identify the impact of technology on a firm

7 Discuss the political and legal environment of marketing

8 Explain the basics of foreign and domestic competition

9 Describe the role of ethics and ethical decisions in business

10 Discuss corporate social responsibility

The Marketing Environment and Marketing Ethics

Ah, the vast Canadian wilderness. If someone could just capture that spirit of the Great White North, package it, and launch a marketing campaign. Someone has: two American guys, Michael Budman and Don Green, transplanted from Detroit, nostalgic for their days at summer camp.

Evoking the rugged imagery of outdoorsy Canada, Roots Canada Ltd. sells such gear as $800 elkskin jackets, leather bags and shoes, casual wear, and even woodsy home furnishings. The company, with annual sales of about $170 million, has grown to 160 stores—including twenty-five in Asia, where Canada's famed wilderness holds considerable allure.

Now, the apparel chain plans a $70 million, five-year expansion drive in the United States and Europe. Having already laid down roots in New York, Aspen, Beverly Hills, and other cities, the closely held company initially plans to add some twenty-five outlets at U.S. resorts, including Sun Valley and Vail.

The company struck a chord with Canadians when it adopted the beaver, Canada's national animal, as its logo. Some Roots stores were made to resemble the kind of woodsy lakeside lodge where many Canadians like to vacation.

Roots's founders have long cultivated celebrity connections to help market their products. The late Gilda Radner—who attended summer camp with Messrs. Budman and Green and who used to lend a hand selling shoes in Roots's first store in Toronto—introduced the partners to Dan Aykroyd and other local comedians. The friendships later helped the company win contracts to supply varsity-style jackets and other merchandise for the cast of *Saturday Night Live* and other television shows.

Roots is hoping its celebrity connections will give it an edge as it expands in the hotly contested U.S. market for casual wear. It is also stocking its U.S. stores with a larger proportion of leather goods, including jackets, bags, and accessories, than its stores in Canada carry. "Club Monaco, Banana Republic, Gap—if you look at stores like that, it's basically all clothing," says Marshall Myles, Roots's executive vice president. "At Roots, it's always been the leather products that people remember."

Competitors are watching. "Their fits are very trendy, very funky, very tapered," says Pashadow Cooper, manager of the Eddie Bauer store in New York's trendy Soho district. "We're more outdoorsy," she insists. Still, her store is adding what she calls a new funky line of casual workwear that would compete with Roots.[1]

Competition or a lack of competition represents a threat or opportunity, respectively, to a firm like Roots. Competition is only one of a number of factors in the external environment that can impact a firm. Does the external environment affect the marketing mix of most companies? What other uncontrollable factors in the external environment might impact Roots?

The External Marketing Environment

1

Discuss the external environment of marketing, and explain how it affects a firm

target market
A defined group most likely to buy a firm's product.

As you learned in Chapters 1 and 2, managers create a marketing mix by uniquely combining product, distribution, promotion, and price strategies. The marketing mix is, of course, under the firm's control and is designed to appeal to a specific group of potential buyers. A **target market** is a defined group that managers feel is most likely to buy a firm's product.

Over time, managers must alter the marketing mix because of changes in the environment in which consumers live, work, and make purchasing decisions. Also, as markets mature, some new consumers become part of the target market; others drop out. Those who remain may have different tastes, needs, incomes, lifestyles, and buying habits than the original target consumers.

Although managers can control the marketing mix, they cannot control elements in the external environment that continually mold and reshape the target market. Exhibit 3.1 shows the controllable and uncontrollable variables that affect the target market, whether it consists of consumers or business purchasers. The uncontrollable elements in the center of the diagram continually evolve and create changes in the target market. In contrast, managers can shape and reshape the marketing mix, depicted on the left side of the exhibit, to influence the target market.

Understanding the External Environment

Unless marketing managers understand the external environment, the firm cannot intelligently plan for the future. Thus, many organizations assemble a team of specialists to continually collect and evaluate environmental information, a

Exhibit 3.1 Effect of Uncontrollable Factors in the External Environment on the Marketing Mix

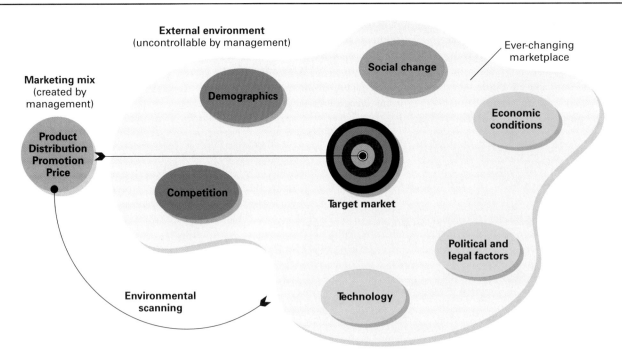

process called environmental scanning. The goal in gathering the environmental data is to identify future market opportunities and threats.

For example, as technology continues to blur the line between personal computers, television, and compact disc players, a company like Sony may find itself competing against a company like Dell. Research shows that children would like to find more games bundled with computer software, while adults are more likely to mention desiring various word-processing and business-related software. Is this information an opportunity or a threat to Dell marketing managers?

Environmental Management

No one business is large or powerful enough to create major change in the external environment. Thus, marketing managers are basically adapters rather than agents of change. For example, despite the huge size of General Motors and Ford, these companies have only recently been able to meet the competitive push by the Japanese for an ever-growing share of the U.S. automobile market. Competition is basically an uncontrollable element in the external environment.

However, a firm is not always completely at the mercy of the external environment. Sometimes a firm can influence external events. For example, extensive lobbying by FedEx enabled it to recently acquire virtually all of the Japanese routes that it has sought. Japan had originally opposed new cargo routes for FedEx. The favorable decision was based on months of lobbying by FedEx at the White House, at several agencies, and in Congress for help in overcoming Japanese resistance. When a company implements strategies that attempt to shape the external environment within which it operates, it is engaging in **environmental management**.

The factors within the external environment that are important to marketing managers can be classified as social, demographic, economic, technological, political and legal, and competitive.

environmental management
When a company implements strategies that attempt to shape the external environment within which it operates.

Social Factors

Social change is perhaps the most difficult external variable for marketing managers to forecast, influence, or integrate into marketing plans. Social factors include our attitudes, values, and lifestyles. Social factors influence the products people buy, the prices paid for products, the effectiveness of specific promotions, and how, where, and when people expect to purchase products.

Describe the social factors that affect marketing

Marketing-Oriented Values of Today

A major change has been taking place in American culture. Labeled *cultural creativity,* it is a comprehensive shift in values, worldviews, and ways of life. It appeals to nearly one-fourth of American adults, or forty-four million people. People who follow this new path are on the leading edge of several kinds of cultural change. They are interested in new kinds of products and services, and they often respond to advertising and marketing in unexpected ways. Cultural creatives are good at synthesizing this information into a "big picture." Their style is to scan an information source efficiently, seize on something they are interested in, and explore that topic in depth.

A second worldview is that of *traditionalism,* the belief system for about 29 percent of Americans (fifty-six million adults), who might also be called *heartlanders.* In America, traditionalism often takes the form of country folks rebelling against big-city slickers. Heartlanders believe in a nostalgic image of small towns and strong churches that defines the Good Old American Ways.[2]

The third worldview is *modernism,* the value set of 47 percent of Americans, or eighty-eight million adults. Modernists include politicians, military leaders, scientists, and intellectuals. Modernists place high value on personal success, consumerism, materialism, and technological rationality. It's valid to say that modernists see the world through the same filters as does *Time* magazine.

Today's shoppers are also environmentalists. Eight in ten U.S. consumers regard themselves as environmentalists, and half of those say they are strong ones.[3] Four out of five shoppers are willing to pay 5 percent more for products packaged with recyclable or biodegradable materials. Many marketers predict that soon it will be very hard to sell a product that isn't environmentally friendly.

poverty of time
A lack of time to do anything but work, commute to work, handle family situations, do housework, shop, sleep, and eat.

The Poverty of Time Today, fewer consumers say that expensive cars, designer clothes, pleasure trips, and "gold" credit cards are necessary components of a happy life. Instead, they put value on nonmaterial accomplishments, such as having control of their lives and being able to take a day off when they want.[4] Dual-career families have a **poverty of time**, with few hours to do anything but work and commute to work, handle family situations, do housework, shop, sleep, and eat. Of the people who say they don't have enough time, only 33 percent said that they were very happy with their lives.[5]

A poverty of time means that people will decrease the amount of time spent doing things they dislike. That means doing less housework and home maintenance, and doing more dining out. It also means paying more attention to brand names—not in search of status, but to make buying decisions quicker and easier. Consumers on a constrained time budget will likely favor small shops over large ones, spend less time comparing prices, use technology to reduce transaction time, and patronize businesses that make life easier.[6]

Time-pressed individuals represent a tremendous marketing opportunity. Kinko's has responded by transforming their copy centers into home offices away from home by adding computer workstations and other resources.

No company has learned this better than Kinko's, the copy-shop empire. A few years ago, Kinko's noticed that busy customers in their stores didn't just want to do their photocopying and head home. They wanted to pop in a store, create a computer document, print it out, staple it, glue it, hole-punch it, and put it in a three-ring binder. In response, Kinko's has added computer workstations to many of its stores, along with sophisticated technical support, and basic supplies that turn each of their copy centers into home offices away from home.

Today, 39 percent of Americans often spend leisure time getting ready for work.[7] It seems that casual Fridays and home offices are further blurring the boundaries between work and leisure. A recent survey noted that the leisure activity done most often was to spend time with the family.[8] There is little doubt that the value employees place on time versus money will continue to shift in favor of time. More employers will offer time off as an incentive. Aladdin Equipment, a Sarasota, Florida, maker of pool and spa replacement parts, achieved a 50 percent reduction in absenteeism and a 10 percent increase in productivity after it launched a 4½-day-a-week production schedule.[9] Perhaps, however, the 7 percent annual growth in home-based self-employment is a backlash against the lack of quality of family time.[10]

The Growth of Component Lifestyles

People in the United States today are piecing together **component lifestyles**. A lifestyle is a mode of living; it is the way people decide to live their lives. In other words, they are choosing products and services that meet diverse needs and interests rather than conforming to traditional stereotypes.

In the past, a person's profession—for instance, banker—defined his or her lifestyle. Today a person can be a banker and also a gourmet, fitness enthusiast, dedicated single parent, and Internet guru. Each of these lifestyles is associated with different goods and services and represents a target audience. For example, for the gourmet, marketers offer cooking utensils, wines, and exotic foods through magazines like *Bon Appetit* and *Gourmet*. The fitness enthusiast buys Adidas equipment and special jogging outfits and reads *Runner* magazine. Component lifestyles increase the complexity of consumers' buying habits. The banker may own a BMW but change the oil himself or herself. He or she may buy fast food for lunch but French wine for dinner, own sophisticated photographic equipment and a low-priced home stereo, and shop for socks at Kmart or Wal-Mart and suits or dresses at Brooks Brothers.

 The unique lifestyles of every consumer can require a different marketing mix. Sometimes blending products for a single target market can result in failure. To the bright young founders of WebTV, it looked like a home run: hook televisions up to the Net and tap into the vast market of couch potatoes curious about the World Wide Web. After burning through an estimated $50 million to advertise the new service, however, WebTV and partners Sony and Philips Electronics counted a disappointing fifty thousand subscribers.

The problem, WebTV now acknowledges, was the wrong marketing message. Couch potatoes want to be better entertained, whereas computer users are content to explore the Internet using small PC screens. A revamped campaign emphasizes entertainment over education.

The Changing Role of Families and Working Women

Component lifestyles have evolved because consumers can choose from a growing number of goods and services, and most have the money to exercise more options. Rising purchasing power has resulted from the growth of dual-income families. Approximately 58 percent of all females between sixteen and sixty-five years old are now in the workforce, and female participation in the labor force is expected to grow to 63 percent by 2005.[11] Today, more than 9 million women-owned businesses in the United States generated $3.6 trillion in revenues.[12] The phenomenon of working women has probably had a greater effect on marketing than has any other social change.

As women's earnings grow, so do their levels of expertise, experience, and authority. Working-age women are not the same group businesses targeted thirty years ago. They expect different things in life—from their jobs, from their spouses, and from the products and services they buy.

The automotive industry has finally begun to realize the power of women in vehicle purchase decisions. Women are the principal buyers for 45 percent of all cars and trucks sold in the United States.[13] Saturn's advertising not only aims to attract women as customers, but also to woo them into the business. In an industry with a woefully small representation of women in sales, 16 percent of Saturn's sales staff are women, compared with 7 percent industry-wide. This has had a visible impact on sales to women. Even though about half of all automotive purchases are made by women, Saturn claims that women buy 64 percent of its cars.[14]

 The growth in the number of working women has meant an increase in dual-career families. Although dual-career families typically have greater household incomes, they have less time for family activities (poverty of time). Their purchasing roles (which define the items traditionally bought by the man or the woman) are changing, as are their purchasing patterns.

Consequently, new opportunities are being created. For example, small businesses are opening daily that cater to dual-career households by offering specialized goods and services. Ice cream and yogurt parlors, cafes, and sports footwear shops have proliferated. With more women than ever working full time, there is a special demand for new household services. Numerous e-commerce companies cater to the busy dual-career family. Among those are Peapod (an Internet supermarket), furniture.com (furniture retailer), Amazon.com (books and a variety of other products), and countless others.

Demographic Factors

Explain the importance to marketing managers of current demographic trends

Another uncontrollable variable in the external environment—also extremely important to marketing managers—is **demography**, the study of people's vital statistics, such as their age, race and ethnicity, and location. Demographics are significant because the basis for any market is people. Demographic characteristics are strongly related to consumer buyer behavior in the marketplace and are good predictors of how the target market will respond to a specific marketing mix. This section describes some marketing trends related to age and location. We will begin by taking a closer look at key age groups.

Generation Y

Those designated by demographics as **Generation Y** were born between 1979 and 1994. They are about sixty million strong, more than three times as large as "Generation X." If this group of consumers does not like the mature brands of the Baby Boomers, or Generation X, then marketers will be in trouble. Why? Simply because of the size of the Gen Y market. For example, baby boomers are into Lexus, Estee Lauder, L. L. Bean, and Coke. Gen Y-ers like Jeep Wrangler, Hard Candy, The North Face, and Mountain Dew.[15]

Gen Y-ers, having grown up in an even more media-saturated, brand-conscious world than their parents, respond to ads differently and prefer to encounter those ads in different places. The marketers that capture Gen Y's attention do so by bringing their messages to the places these kids congregate, whether it's the Internet, a snowboarding tournament, or cable TV. The ads may be funny or disarmingly direct. What they don't do is suggest that the advertiser knows Gen Y better than these savvy consumers know themselves.

Soon a lot of other companies are going to have to learn the nuances of Gen Y marketing. In just a few years, today's teens will be out of college and shopping for their first cars, their first homes, and their first mutual funds. The distinctive buying habits they display today will likely follow them as they enter the high-spending years of adulthood. Companies unable to reach Gen Y will lose out on a vast new market—and could find the doors thrown open to new competitors. "Think of them as this quiet little

The teens of Generation Y constitute a huge market influenced by humor and irony. This ad for the video game Galaga demonstrates both.

group about to change everything," says Edward Winter of the U30 Group, a Knoxville, Tennessee consulting firm.[16]

Generation Y is driving the educational software and snowboard industries and, soon, many others. Hawaiian Tropic, the nation's number three suntan lotion company, has dramatically increased its spring break promotions to Gen Y-ers at Panama City Beach, South Padre Island, and Daytona Beach.[17]

Generation X

Generation X—people born between 1965 and 1978—consists of seventeen million consumers. It is the first generation of latchkey children—products of dual-career households or, in roughly half of the cases, of divorced or separated parents. Generation X began entering the workforce in the era of downsizing and downturn, so its members are likelier than the previous generation to be unemployed, underemployed, and living at home with Mom and Dad. On the other hand, ten million are full-time college students, and fifteen million are married and not living at home.[18] Yet, as a generation that's been bombarded by multiple media since their cradle days, they're savvy and cynical consumers.

The members of Generation X don't mind indulging themselves. Among the young women of Generation X, 38 percent go to the movies in a given month, compared with 19 percent of the women who are now 35 and older. The members of Generation X devote a larger-than-average share of their spending dollars to restaurant meals, alcoholic beverages, clothing, and electronic items such as televisions and stereos.[19] One survey found that the members of Generation X aspire to having a home of their own (87 percent), a lot of money (42 percent), a swimming pool (42 percent), and a vacation home (41 percent).[20] They are more materialistic than past generations but have less hope of achieving their goals.

Travel companies, such as hotels, airlines, and car rental companies who have spent the last thirty years marketing to baby boomers have discovered that Gen X-ers have vastly different preferences and interests from the older generation. To woo them, travel companies are creating unusual perks and unconventional gags in TV commercials. They're taping airfare promos to pizza boxes, teaching kickboxing classes in hotel fitness centers, and replacing buttoned-down restaurants with sweatshirt-casual bistros.

Starwood created an entire hotel chain for those customers, giving it the name W. Each hotel, where rooms go for about $300 a night, features contemporary designs, hip bars and whimsical amenities such as gumball machines with Hot Tamale candies that make them magnets for young travelers, Starwood's Vice President Guy Hensley says. And if they outgrow W's, Starwood hopes they'll switch to its more traditional Sheratons and Westins. "If we catch hold of the Generation X crowd now, they'll stay with us forever," says Hensley.[21]

In 2000 Harley-Davidson/Buell introduced the Buell "Blast" targeted directly to Gen X-ers. This new model is a smaller, lighter, easier-handling, one-cylinder motorcycle, selling for under $4,500, and it is designed specifically for the male or female new rider or novice rider who is not yet ready for the traditionally heavier Harley-Davidson cruising or touring bikes.[22]

Baby Boomers: America's Mass Market

Almost 78 million **baby boomers** were born in the United States between 1946 and 1964, which created a huge market. The oldest are now over fifty, but they cling to

demography
The study of people's vital statistics, such as their age, race and ethnicity, and location.

Generation Y
Consumers born between 1979 and 1994.

Generation X
People born between the years 1965 and 1978.

Although Gen X is not nearly as large as either the baby boomers or Gen Y, it is still a lucrative market. Harley Davidson/Buell designed the styling and the price of the Buell Blast specifically to appeal to the Gen X market.

baby boomers
People born between 1946 and 1964.

their youth. One study found that baby boomers see themselves as continuing to be very active after they turn fifty. They won't even think of themselves as being senior citizens until after they turn sixty (39 percent) or seventy (42 percent).[23]

This group cherishes convenience, which has resulted in a growing demand for home delivery of items like large appliances, furniture, and groceries. In addition, the spreading culture of convenience explains the tremendous appeal of prepared take-out foods and the necessity of VCRs and portable telephones.

Baby boomers' parents raised their children to think for and of themselves. Studies of child-rearing practices show that parents of the 1950s and 1960s consistently ranked "to think for themselves" as the number-one trait they wanted to instill in their children.[24] Postwar affluence also allowed parents to indulge their children as never before. They invested in their children's skills by sending them to college. They encouraged their children to succeed in a job market that rewarded competitive drive more than cooperative spirit and individual skills more than teamwork.

In turn, the sheer size of the generation encouraged businesses to promote the emerging individuality of baby boomers. Even before the oldest baby boomers started earning their own living almost three decades ago, astute businesspeople saw the profits that come from giving millions of young people what they want. Businesses offered individualistic baby boomers a growing array of customized products and services—houses, cars, furniture, appliances, clothes, vacations, jobs, leisure time, and even beliefs.

The importance of individualism among baby boomers led to a **personalized economy**—a system that delivers customized goods and services at a good value on demand. Successful businesses in a personalized economy give customers what they want when they want it. To do this, they must know their customers extremely well. In fact, the intimacy between producer and consumer is exactly what makes an economy personalized.

In the personalized economy, successful products share three characteristics:

- *Customization*: Products are custom designed and marketed to ever-smaller target markets. Today, for example, there are hundreds of cable TV channels from which to choose and millions of Web sites. In 1950, the average grocery store carried about four thousand items; today, that number is closer to sixteen thousand, as manufacturers target increasingly specific needs.[25]
- *Immediacy*: Successful businesses deliver products and services at the convenience of the consumer rather than the producer. Banc One, with locations in the eastern and southern states, for example, opens some of its branches on Saturdays and Sundays. Its twenty-four-hour hot line, staffed by real people, solves problems at the customer's convenience. The immediacy of the personalized economy explains the booming business in one-hour film processing, walk-in medical clinics, and thirty-minute pizzas.
- *Value*: Businesses must price competitively or create innovative products that can command premium prices. Even the most innovative products quickly become commodities in the fast-paced personalized economy, however. Many people now view the PC as a commodity.

As the age of today's average consumer moves toward forty, average consumption patterns are also changing. People in their early forties tend to focus on their families and finances. As this group grows in number, its members will buy more furniture from manufacturers like Lazy Boy, American Martindale, Baker, and Drexel-Heritage to replace the furniture they bought early in their marriages. The demand for family counselors and wellness programs should also increase. Additionally, discount investment brokers like Charles Schwab and E-trade and mutual funds like Fidelity and Dreyfus should profit. Because middle-aged consumers buy more reading materials than any other age group, the market for books and magazines should remain strong throughout the early 2000s. Women ages forty to sixty-four will be the largest age demographic group by the year 2010.[26] Both *Lear* and

personalized economy
Delivering customized goods and services at a good value on demand.

More magazines have been created to target this market. *More* promises features about fashion, beauty, and health, as well as pieces on married life after three decades. And all the models in *More*'s editorial pages are forty-plus.

Right now, baby boomers are concerned with their children and their jobs. These worries will fade as the kids move out of the house and boomers retire. But some things will never change. Baby boomers may always be a little selfish about their leisure time. They may always be a little careless about the way they spend their money. They will probably remain suspicious of the status quo. And they will always love rock and roll.

Older Consumers: Not Just Grandparents

As mentioned above, the oldest baby boomers have already crossed the fifty-plus threshold that many demographers use to define the "mature market." Yet, today's mature consumers are wealthier, healthier, and better educated than those of earlier generations. Although they make up only 26 percent of the population, fifty-plus consumers buy half of all domestic cars, half of all silverware, and nearly half of all home remodeling.[27] Smart marketers are already targeting this growing segment. By 2020, over a third of the population will be fifty years old or older.

Many marketers have yet to tap the full potential of the huge and lucrative senior market because of enduring misconceptions about mature adults, all based on stereotypes. Here are a few:

- *Stereotype:* Older consumers are sick or ailing. *Fact:* A full 85 percent of mature citizens report themselves to be in good or excellent health. Over two-thirds of the elderly have no chronic health problems.[28] People like Mick Jagger are over fifty-five.[29] These people are fit and healthy.
- *Stereotype:* Older consumers are sedentary. *Fact:* Of all travel dollars spent in the United States, 80 percent are spent by people over fifty years old.
- *Stereotype:* Older consumers have a poor retention rate. *Fact:* Senior citizens are readers and much less influenced by TV than are younger consumers.[30] Not only do they retain what they read, but they are willing to read far more copy than younger people are.
- *Stereotype:* Older consumers are interested only in price and are intolerant of change. *Fact:* Although senior citizens are as interested in price as anyone else, they are more interested in value. And a generation that has survived the better part of a century characterized by more technological change than any other in history can hardly be considered resistant to change.[31]

Acceptance of change, however, doesn't mean a lack of brand loyalty. For example, the most critical factor in determining car-owner loyalty is age. The oldest consumers (ages sixty-five and up) are twice as loyal to the make of car as the youngest customers are.[32] The cars most popular with older Americans are Lincoln, Cadillac, and Buick.

Marketers who want to actively pursue the mature market must understand it. Aging consumers create some obvious opportunities. JCPenney's Easy Dressing clothes feature Velcro-fastened clothing for women with arthritis or other ailments who may have difficulty with zippers or buttons. Sales from the first Easy Dressing catalog were three times higher than expected. Chicago-based Cadaco offers a line of games with easy-to-read big print and larger game pieces. The series focuses on nostalgia by including Michigan rummy, hearts, poker, and bingo. Trivia buffs more familiar with Mitch Miller than Guns 'n' Roses can play Parker Brothers'

"The Vintage Years" edition of Trivial Pursuit. The game, aimed at the sixty-plus crowd, poses questions covering the era from Charles Lindbergh to Dwight D. Eisenhower. Even Hollywood is getting in on the act. The summer 2000 blockbuster *Space Cowboys* starred a well-seasoned slate of action heroes: Clint Eastwood (70), James Garner (72), Donald Sutherland (65), and Tommy Lee Jones (54). Consider these other examples, as well, of savvy marketers targeting the mature market:

- To counter diminishing grip strength associated with advancing age, Procter & Gamble offers its Tide laundry detergent with snap-on lids rather than the usual perforated flap.
- Wheaton Medical Technologies markets a pill bottle that has a tiny battery-operated clock that registers the time the container was last opened to take out a pill.
- Knowing that grandparents purchase 25 percent of all toys (about $819 per year spent on their grandkids), F.A.O. Schwarz has added a Grandma's Shop to its two largest stores, complete with older-adult salespeople.
- Mattel, Inc., invited readers of *Modern Maturity* to join its Grandparents Club. For a $10 fee, readers could receive a book of discount coupons; meanwhile, Mattel acquired an invaluable mailing list of potential customers.[33]

Americans on the Move

The average U.S. citizen moves every six years. This trend has implications for marketers. A large influx of new people into an area creates many new marketing opportunities for all types of businesses. Remember, the primary basis of all consumer marketing is people. Conversely, significant out-migration from a city or town may force many of its businesses to move or close down. The cities with the greatest projected population growth from 1995 to 2005 are Houston, Washington, D.C., Atlanta, San Diego, Phoenix, Orlando, and Dallas.[34]

The most populous metro area is Los Angeles–Long Beach with 9,605,904 by 2001. New York follows with 8,723,921 for the same year. New York also has the greatest population density at 7,464 persons per square mile. The lowest population density of the top twenty-four metro areas is Riverside–San Bernardino, California, at 123 people per square mile.[35]

The United States experiences both immigration from other countries and migration within U.S. borders. In the past decade, the six states with the highest levels of immigration from abroad were California, New York, New Jersey, Illinois, Texas, and Massachusetts. The six states with the greatest population increases due to interstate migration were Florida, Georgia, North Carolina, Virginia, Washington, and Arizona.[36]

Immigration raises the cost of public services in areas with large numbers of immigrants, but the influx also benefits the U.S. economy overall. Immigrants add approximately $10 billion to the economy each year with little negative impact on job opportunities for most other residents.[37]

Migration is not just an American phenomenon but also a global one. The movement of people creates new markets and destroys old ones. The "Global Perspectives" box discusses this important trend.

Growing Ethnic Markets

Explain the importance to marketing managers of multiculturalism and growing ethnic markets

The United States is undergoing a new demographic transition: It is becoming a multicultural society. During this decade, the United States will shift further from a society dominated by whites and rooted in Western culture to a society characterized by three large racial and ethnic minorities: African-Americans, U.S. Hispanics, and Asian-Americans. All three minorities will grow in size and in share of

Global Perspectives

A MOVING WORLD

The flow of migrants across borders is large and accelerating, approaching four million people a year. Globally, some 125 million people today live outside their country of birth.

But why? And how will mass migration shape the future? In crassly economic terms, migration involves the poor flowing to the rich. In modern times, that means people go from the sending nations of South Asia, Africa, and Latin America to the receiving nations of Europe and North America.

There's little doubt why migration has reached an all-time high. Income inequality between the richest and poorest nations has been rising for well over a century, at least. The World Bank notes the ratio in average incomes between the richest and poorest countries was about 11 to 1 in 1870, 38 to 1 in 1960, 52 to 1 in 1985, and 49 to 1 in 1998. The richest countries are recording 3 to 5 percent increases in gross domestic product, while some of the poorest actually slide lower—victims of famine, war, social disintegration, inept leadership, and the flight of their best and brightest.

Consider the following four possibilities—drawn from the Millen-

nium Project, a panel organized by the United Nations University—to describe alternative futures for the world between now and 2050.

- *Cybertopia:* Technology creates a better world. China and India become software powerhouses. The gap between rich and poor widens, but telemedicine, tele-education, and telebusiness partnerships spur developing countries' economies. World Trade Organization-sponsored global social safety nets discourage masses of poor from migrating. *Migration level: Low.*
- *The rich get richer:* Population growth slows everywhere but remains higher in Africa and South Asia. The sharp disparity in personal income between the richest and poorest nations widens, from 50 to 1 today to 80 to 1 by 2025. Migration rises, creating tension. By 2025, global corporations step in to develop more skilled workers, offer venture capital, etc. *Migration level: High.*
- *Passive, mean world:* The problem is jobs. Population growth outstrips jobs growth in much of the world. In the rich countries, living standards stagnate. Small

"virtual" companies succeed with transient workforces migrating from country to country. "Drifting and dancing" becomes a way of life. By 2025, trade wars envelope the regional economic blocs. Protectionism spreads in many forms, including nontariff barriers and restrictive immigration policies. *Migration level: High, but resisted strongly.*
- *Trading places:* The once-booming economies of East and Southeast Asia recover and grow, challenging the United States, the European Union, and Japan. The North-South economic gap disappears, a quaint notion from the nineteenth and twentieth centuries. Regions equalize in wealth. *Migration level: Low.*[a]

Do you think immigration is good or bad for the United States? Do you think America should have an "open borders" policy? That is, anyone who wants to come live and work in America can do so? Which of the four scenarios do you believe might come true? Why?

[a] Bernard Wysoki, Jr., "On the Move," *Wall Street Journal*, January 1, 2000, p. R42.

---

the population, while the white majority declines as a percentage of the total. Native Americans and people with roots in Australia, the Middle East, the former Soviet Union, and other parts of the world will further enrich the fabric of U.S. society.

The labor force of the past was dominated by white men who are now retiring. Today's senior workers are equal parts women and men, and still overwhelmingly white. But in the entry-level jobs of 2000, a multicultural labor force emerged. The proportion of workers who are non-Hispanic whites should decrease from 77 percent in 1998 to 74 percent in 2005.

Because so many white men are retiring, the non-Hispanic white labor force will grow only 8 percent between 1994 and 2005. The number of Hispanic workers should grow 36 percent, due to the continued immigration of young adults, higher birth rates, and relatively few retirees. These forces will also boost the number of Asian workers by 39 percent. The number of black workers will increase by

15 percent, a rate slightly slower than the rate of growth of black adults in general (16.5 percent).[38]

Ethnic and Cultural Diversity

Multiculturalism occurs when all major ethnic groups in an area—such as a city, county, or census tract—are roughly equally represented. Because of its current demographic transition, the trend in the United States is toward greater multiculturalism.

San Francisco County is the most diverse county in the nation. The proportions of major ethnic groups are closer to being equal there than anywhere else. People of many ancestries have long been attracted to the area. The least multicultural region is a broad swath stretching from northern New England through the Midwest and into Montana. These areas have few people other than whites. The regions with the lowest level of diversity are found in the agricultural heartland: Nebraska and Iowa.

Marketing Implications of Multiculturalism

The demographic shift and growing multiculturalism create new challenges and opportunities for marketers. The U.S. population grew from 226 million in 1980 to 274 million in 2000, much of that growth taking place in minority markets. Asians are the nation's fastest growing minority group, with a population of eleven million in 2000. The Hispanic population is also growing rapidly, totaling thirty-two million in 2000. African-Americans remain the largest minority group, totaling thirty-five million persons.[39] Today, more than 25 percent of the U.S. population are members of minority groups. There are over 110 different ethnic groups in America.

Demographic shifts will be even more pronounced in the future. Exhibit 3.2 compares the 1999 population mix and the forecasted population mix for 2023. Note that Hispanics will be the fastest growing segment of the population. The diversity of the U.S. population is projected to stabilize around 2023, as the birthrate among minorities levels off.

The marketer's task in a diverse society is more challenging because of differences in educational level and demand for goods and services. What's more, ethnic markets are not homogeneous. There is not an African-American market or a Hispanic market, any more than there is a white market. Instead, there are many niches within ethnic markets that require micromarketing strategies. For example, African Eye, which offers women's designer fashions from Africa, attracted a thousand women to a fashion show at Prince Georges Plaza near Washington, D.C. The show featured the latest creations by Alfadi, a high-fashion Nigerian designer, who also hosted the show. African Eye's dresses and outfits blend African and Western influences and are priced at $50 to $600. Says Mozella Perry Ademiluyi, the president and cofounder of African Eye: "Our customer is professional, 30 to 65, has an income level of $30,000-plus and often is well-traveled. They don't just want to wear something that is African. They want something that is well-tailored, unique, and creative as well."[40]

An alternative to the niche strategy is to maintain a brand's core identity while straddling different languages, cultures, ages, and incomes. Executives with BellSouth Corporation had a message for both Spanish-speaking Hispanic and English-speaking customers throughout the Southeast. Instead of going with two distinct campaigns, they chose Daisy Fuentes, a former MTV personality well known among both audiences. More importantly, she spoke to a third audience: acculturated, bilingual Hispanics. The potential audience included more than 1.422 million Hispanics in 491,000 Hispanic households in Miami-Dade, Broward, and Monroe Counties plus an additional 1 million-plus general market households in the area, according to Strategy Research Corp.[41]

More than just an ad for apparel, Slates is clearly trying to establish itself as the clothier to a youthful, ethnically diverse, on-line population. Publicizing its relationship with Community Connect is a way to demonstrate that the ethnically diverse Slates models are not just for show.

Exhibit 3.2

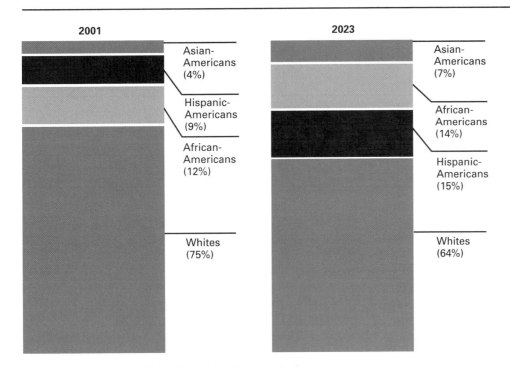

2001

Asian-Americans (4%)

Hispanic-Americans (9%)

African-Americans (12%)

Whites (75%)

2023

Asian-Americans (7%)

African-Americans (14%)

Hispanic-Americans (15%)

Whites (64%)

SOURCE: U.S. Department of Labor, Bureau of the Census projections.

A third strategy for multicultural marketing is to seek common interests, motivations, or needs across ethnic groups. This strategy is sometimes called **stitching niches**, which means combining ethnic, age, income, and lifestyle markets, on some common basis, to form a large market. The result may be a cross-cultural product, such as a frozen pizza-flavored egg roll. Or it may be a product that serves several ethnic markets simultaneously. Ringling Brothers and Barnum and Bailey Circus showcases acts that appeal to many ethnic groups. It broadened its appeal to Asian-Americans by adding the "Mysterious Oriental Art of Hair Hanging." Marguerite Michelle, known as the "ravishing Rapunzel," is suspended in the air on a wire attached to her waist-length hair. When the circus comes to town, the Mexican-born Michelle also goes on Spanish-language radio shows to build recognition for Ringling in the Hispanic market. The circus is promoted as *"El Espectáculo Más Grande del Mundo."*[42]

stitching niches
A strategy for multicultural marketing that combines ethnic, age, income, and lifestyle markets, on some common basis, to form a large market.

The Internet Goes Multicultural Since 1995, non–English-speaking Internet users have gone from less than 10 percent to as high as 50 percent, according to researcher Wired Digital. African-Americans outpace all other segments—including the general market—for on-line adoption, according to Forrester Research.[43]

Today, approximately 40 percent of all African-American households, 43 percent Hispanic-Americans, and 71 percent Asian-Americans are on-line.[44] At the same time, consumers of all ethnic backgrounds are showing a desire to acculturate— or retain distinctly ethnic identities—within the U.S. market. As a result, targeted multicultural Web sites are beginning to proliferate—among them BlackPlanet.com, EverythingBlack.com, and BlackFamilies.com, three popular African-American sites.

Asian-Americans form the most lucrative multicultural market on-line in the United States, based upon Web penetration and household incomes. About 56 percent of Asian-Americans said they were more likely to buy a product advertised in their native language, according to Market Segment Research.[45]

Economic Factors

5

Identify consumer and marketer reactions to the state of the economy

In addition to social and demographic factors, marketing managers must understand and react to the economic environment. The three economic areas of greatest concern to most marketers are the distribution of consumer income, inflation, and recession.

Rising Incomes

As disposable (or after-tax) incomes rise, more families and individuals can afford the "good life." Fortunately, U.S. incomes have continued to rise. After adjustment for inflation, median incomes in the United States rose less than 4 percent between 1980 and 2000.

Today about two-thirds of all U.S. households earn a "middle-class" income. The rough boundaries for a middle-class income are $18,000, above poverty, to about $75,000, just short of wealth. In 1999, almost half the households were in the upper end of the $18,000 to $75,000 range, as opposed to only a quarter in 1980. The percentage of households earning above $75,000 is now over 10 percent.[46] As a result, Americans are buying more goods and services than ever before. For example, in raising a child to age seventeen, a middle-class family will spend over $124,000 in 2000 dollars. This new level of affluence is not limited to professionals or even individuals within specific age or education brackets. Rather, it cuts across all household types, well beyond what businesses traditionally consider to be markets for high-priced goods and services. This rising affluence stems primarily from the increasing number of dual-income families.

During the 2000s, many marketing managers are focusing on families with incomes over $35,000, because this group will have the most discretionary income. The average American household has over $12,000 in discretionary income each year. Some marketers will concentrate their efforts on higher quality, higher priced goods and services. The Lexus automobile and American Airlines' "international class" service for business-class seats on transcontinental flights are examples of this trend.

Inflation

inflation
A general rise in prices without a corresponding increase in wages, which results in decreased purchasing power.

Inflation is a general rise in prices without a corresponding increase in wages, which results in decreased purchasing power. Fortunately, the United States has had a low rate of inflation for over a decade. The late 1990s and early 2000s have been marked by an inflation rate under 4 percent. The low rate of inflation is due to the tremendous productivity of the high-tech sector of the economy and the stability of the price of services. Both education and healthcare costs are rising much more slowly than in the past. The other good news is that the American economy has grown at an annual rate of over 4 percent from 1997 to 2000.[47] These economic conditions benefit marketers, because real wages, and hence purchasing power, go up when inflation stays down. A significant increase in inflation almost always depresses real wages and the ability to buy more goods and services.

In times of low inflation, businesses seeking to increase their profit margins can do so only by increasing their efficiency. If they significantly increase prices, no one will purchase their goods or services.

In more inflationary times, marketers use a number of pricing strategies to cope. (See Chapter 18 for more on these strategies.) But in general, marketers must be aware that inflation causes consumers to either build up or diminish their brand loyalty. In one research session, a consumer panelist noted, "I used to use just Betty Crocker mixes, but now I think of either Betty Crocker or Duncan Hines, depending on which is on sale." Another participant said, "Pennies count now, and so I look at the whole shelf, and I read the ingredients. I don't really understand, but I can tell if it's exactly the same. So now I use this cheaper brand, and honestly, it works just as well." Inflation pressures consumers to make more economical purchases. However, most consumers try hard to maintain their standard of living.

In creating marketing strategies to cope with inflation, managers must realize that, despite what happens to the seller's cost, the buyer is not going to pay more for a product than the subjective value he or she places on it. No matter how compelling the justification might be for a 10 percent price increase, marketers must always examine its impact on demand. Many marketers try to hold prices level as long as is practical.

Recession

A **recession** is a period of economic activity when income, production, and employment tend to fall—all of which reduce demand for goods and services. The problems of inflation and recession go hand in hand, yet recession requires different marketing strategies:

- *Improve existing products and introduce new ones:* The goal is to reduce production hours, waste, and the cost of materials. Recessions increase the demand for goods and services that are economical and efficient, offer value, help organizations streamline practices and procedures, and improve customer service.
- *Maintain and expand customer services:* In a recession, many organizations postpone the purchase of new equipment and materials. Sales of replacement parts and other services may become an important source of income.
- *Emphasize top-of-the-line products and promote product value:* Customers with less to spend will seek demonstrated quality, durability, satisfaction, and capacity to save time and money. High-priced, high-value items consistently fare well during recessions.

recession
A period of economic activity when income, production, and employment tend to fall—all of which reduce demand for goods and services.

Technological and Resource Factors

Sometimes new technology is an effective weapon against inflation and recession. New machines that reduce production costs can be one of a firm's most valuable assets. The power of a personal-computer microchip doubles about every eighteen months. The Pentium Pro, for example, introduced in 1995, contains 5.3 million transistors and performs three hundred million instructions per second (MIPS). The 886 chip, introduced in 2000, will have fifteen million transistors and perform one thousand MIPS. Our ability, as a nation, to maintain and build wealth depends in large part on the speed and effectiveness with which we invent and adopt machines that lift productivity. For example, coal mining is typically thought of as unskilled, backbreaking labor. But visit Cyprus Amax Mineral Company's Twenty-mile Mine near Oak Creek, Colorado, and you will find workers with push-button controls who walk along massive machines that shear thirty-inch slices from an 850-foot coal wall. Laptop computers help miners track equipment breakdowns and water quality.

U.S. companies often have difficulty translating the results of R&D into goods and services. The Japanese are masters at making this transformation. For example, VCRs, flat-panel displays, and compact disc players are based on U.S. research that wasn't exploited at home. The United States excels at **basic research** (or *pure research*), which attempts to expand the frontiers of knowledge but is not aimed at a specific, pragmatic problem. Basic research aims to confirm an existing theory or to learn more about a concept or phenomenon. For example, basic research might focus on high-energy physics. **Applied research**, in contrast, attempts to develop new

Identify the impact of technology on a firm

basic research
Pure research that aims to confirm an existing theory or to learn more about a concept or phenomenon.

applied research
An attempt to develop new or improved products.

or improved products. It is where the United States sometimes falls short, although many U.S. companies do conduct applied research. For example, the United States leads the world in applying basic research to aircraft design and propulsion systems.

The huge investment in information technology has helped America hold down inflation, maintain economic growth, and effectively compete in world markets. Business purchases of information technology have been rising by 25 percent a year since the 1970s. MIT economics professor Erik Brynjolfsson says that hard-to-quantify innovations in the way companies do business are actually far more valuable than the hardware and software they've purchased. "More than $1 trillion in those intangibles has been built up over the past ten years."[48]

The continued growth of e-commerce allows companies to reduce the amount of money they spend on processing an order from $75 to $10 on average, says David Pecaut, co-head of global electronic commerce at Boston Consulting Group.[49] Competition and price transparency will increase as e-commerce spreads, putting downward pressure on profit margins and forcing companies to become more efficient. "This is a safety valve on inflation," Pecaut says. For more examples on how the Internet boosts productivity, see Exhibit 3.3.

Exhibit 3.3

How Companies Are Using the Internet to Boost Productivity Throughout the Organization

Process	Example	Payoff
Innovation	Royal Dutch/Shell's "Game-Changer" teams use the Net to generate new business ideas.	New "Light Touch" oil discovery method found 30 million barrels
Collaboration	Ocean Spray's extranet assesses cranberry quality immediately and helps growers get better prices.	Growers get higher profits; Ocean Spray cuts waste and boosts productivity
Design	Honeywell uses the Net to help fashion a customized prototype of anything from a fan blade to a golf club head.	Design time cut from 6 months to 24 hours
Purchasing	Ford's AutoXchange creates massive on-line trading bazaar for its 30,000 suppliers.	Could save as much as $8 billion in first few years
Manufacturing	BP Amoco, using Net technology from Honeywell, can quickly identify plant inefficiencies.	Stems 2% per day productivity loss in Grange-mouth, Scotland, refinery
Logistics	Cement maker Cemex uses Net-based truck dispatch system to speed deliveries to customers.	Cement delivered within 20 minutes, down from 3 hours
Marketing	Weyerhaeuser uses the Net to weed out its least valuable customers at Marshfield, Wisconsin, door plant.	Boosted the plant's return on net assets from −2% in 1994 to 27% in 1999
Service	GE Power Systems lets customers use the Net to compare the performance of its turbines against other GE turbines in the market.	Turbine productivity expected to rise by 1% to 2% annually

SOURCE: "Working the Web," *Business Week,* February 14, 2000, p. 116.

Political and Legal Factors

Business needs government regulation to protect innovators of new technology, the interests of society in general, one business from another, and consumers. In turn, government needs business, because the marketplace generates taxes that support public efforts to educate our youth, protect our shores, and so on. The private sector also serves as a counterweight to government. The decentralization of power inherent in a private-enterprise system supplies the limitation on government essential for the survival of a democracy.

 Every aspect of the marketing mix is subject to laws and restrictions. It is the duty of marketing managers or their legal assistants to understand these laws and conform to them, because failure to comply with regulations can have major consequences for a firm. Sometimes just sensing trends and taking corrective action before a government agency acts can help avoid regulation. This didn't happen in the case of the tobacco industry. As a result, Joe Camel and the Marlboro Man are fading into the sunset along with other strategies used to promote tobacco products.

However, the challenge is not simply to keep the marketing department out of trouble, but to help it implement creative new programs to accomplish marketing objectives. It is all too easy for a marketing manager or sometimes a lawyer to say no to a marketing innovation that actually entails little risk. For example, an overly cautious lawyer could hold up sales of a desirable new product by warning that the package design could prompt a copyright infringement suit. Thus, it is important to understand thoroughly the laws established by the federal government, state governments, and regulatory agencies to control marketing-related issues.

Federal Legislation

Federal laws that affect marketing fall into several categories. First, the Sherman Act, the Clayton Act, the Federal Trade Commission Act, the Celler-Kefauver Antimerger Act, and the Hart-Scott-Rodino Act were passed to regulate the competitive environment. Second, the Robinson-Patman Act was designed to regulate pricing practices. Third, the Wheeler-Lea Act was created to control false advertising. These key pieces of legislation are summarized in Exhibit 3.4.

State Laws

State legislation that affects marketing varies. Oregon, for example, limits utility advertising to 0.5 percent of the company's net income. California has forced industry to improve consumer products and has also enacted legislation to lower the energy consumption of refrigerators, freezers, and air conditioners. Several states, including New Mexico and Kansas, are considering levying a tax on all in-state commercial advertising.

Regulatory Agencies

Although some state regulatory bodies more actively pursue violations of their marketing statutes, federal regulators generally have the greatest clout. The Consumer Product Safety Commission, the Federal Trade Commission, and the Food and Drug Administration are the three federal agencies most directly and actively involved in marketing affairs. These agencies, plus others, are discussed throughout the book, but a brief introduction is in order at this point.

Discuss the political and legal environment of marketing

The much-publicized Microsoft hearings resulted from charges that the company violated the oldest of U.S. commerce laws—the Sherman Act of 1890. The breakup of Microsoft would cost millions of Americans millions of dollars in reduced pension and mutual fund values but would save the consumer a few dollars on Microsoft products. Is the legal or ethical decision always the best for those involved?

Exhibit 3.4

Primary U.S. Laws That Affect Marketing

Legislation	Impact on Marketing
Sherman Act of 1890	Makes trusts and conspiracies in restraint of trade illegal; makes monopolies and attempts to monopolize a misdemeanor.
Clayton Act of 1914	Outlaws discrimination in prices to different buyers; prohibits tying contracts (which require the buyer of one product to also buy another item in the line); makes illegal the combining of two or more competing corporations by pooling ownership of stock.
Federal Trade Commission Act of 1914	Creates the Federal Trade Commission to deal with antitrust matters; outlaws unfair methods of competition.
Robinson-Patman Act of 1936	Prohibits charging different prices to different buyers of merchandise of like grade and quantity; requires sellers to make any supplementary services or allowances available to all purchasers on a proportionately equal basis.
Wheeler-Lea Amendments to the FTC Act of 1938	Broadens the Federal Trade Commission's power to prohibit practices that might injure the public without affecting competition; outlaws false and deceptive advertising.
Lanham Act of 1946	Establishes protection for trademarks.
Celler-Kefauver Anti-merger Act of 1950	Strengthens the Clayton Act to prevent corporate acquisitions that reduce competition.
Hart-Scott-Rodino Act of 1976	Requires large companies to notify the government of their intent to merge.

Consumer Product Safety Commission (CPSC)
A federal agency established to protect the health and safety of consumers in and around their homes.

The sole purpose of the **Consumer Product Safety Commission (CPSC)** is to protect the health and safety of consumers in and around their homes. The CPSC has the power to set mandatory safety standards for almost all products that consumers use (about fifteen thousand items). The CPSC consists of a five-member committee and about eleven hundred staff members, including technicians, lawyers, and administrative help. The commission can fine offending firms up to $500,000 and sentence their officers to up to a year in prison. It can also ban dangerous products from the marketplace.

Federal Trade Commission (FTC)
A federal agency empowered to prevent persons or corporations from using unfair methods of competition in commerce.

The **Federal Trade Commission (FTC)** also consists of five members, each holding office for seven years. The FTC is empowered to prevent persons or corporations from using unfair methods of competition in commerce. It is authorized to investigate the practices of business combinations and to conduct hearings on antitrust matters and deceptive advertising. The FTC has a vast array of regulatory powers (see Exhibit 3.5). Nevertheless, it is not invincible. For example, the FTC had proposed to ban all advertising to children under age eight, to ban all adver-

tising of the sugared products that are most likely to cause tooth de-
cay to children under age twelve, and to require dental health and
nutritional advertisements to be paid for by industry. Business reacted
by lobbying to reduce the FTC's power. The two-year lobbying effort resulted in
passage of the FTC Improvement Act of 1980. The major provisions of the act
are as follows:

> It bans the use of unfairness as a standard for industrywide rules against ad-
> vertising. All the proposals concerning children's advertising were therefore
> suspended, because they were based almost entirely on the unfairness standard.
> It requires oversight hearings on the FTC every six months. This congressional
> review is designed to keep the commission accountable. Moreover, it keeps
> Congress aware of one of the many regulatory agencies it has created and is
> responsible for monitoring.

Businesses rarely band together to create change in the legal environment as
they did to pass the FTC Improvement Act. Generally, marketing managers only react
to legislation, regulation, and edicts. It is usually less costly to stay attuned to the regulatory environment than to fight the government. If marketers had toned down their
hard-hitting advertisements to children, they might have avoided an FTC inquiry altogether. The FTC also regulates advertising on the Internet as well as Internet abuses
of consumer privacy (discussed in Chapter 8). The **Food and Drug Administration
(FDA)**, another powerful agency, is charged with enforcing regulations against selling

**Food and Drug
Administration (FDA)**
A federal agency charged with enforcing regulations against selling
and distributing adulterated, misbranded, or hazardous food and
drug products.

Exhibit 3.5

Powers of the Federal Trade
Commission

Remedy	Procedure
Cease-and-Desist Order	A final order is issued to cease an illegal practice—and is often challenged in the courts.
Consent Decree	A business consents to stop the questionable practice without admitting its illegality.
Affirmative Disclosure	An advertiser is required to provide additional informa-tion about products in advertisements.
Corrective Advertising	An advertiser is required to correct the past effects of misleading advertising. (For example, 25% of a firm's media budget must be spent on FTC-approved advertise-ments or FTC-specified advertising.)
Restitution	Refunds are required to be given to consumers misled by deceptive advertising. According to a 1975 court-of-appeals decision, this remedy cannot be used except for practices carried out after the issuance of a cease-and-desist order (still on appeal).
Counteradvertising	The FTC proposed that the Federal Communications Commission permit advertisements in broadcast media to counteract advertising claims (also that free time be provided under certain conditions).

and distributing adulterated, misbranded, or hazardous food and drug products. It has recently taken a very aggressive stance against tobacco products.

Competitive Factors

8

Explain the basics of foreign and domestic competition

The competitive environment encompasses the number of competitors a firm must face, the relative size of the competitors, and the degree of interdependence within the industry. Management has little control over the competitive environment confronting a firm.

Competition for Market Share and Profits

As U.S. population growth slows, costs rise, and available resources tighten, firms find that they must work harder to maintain their profits and market share regardless of the form of the competitive market. Take, for example, the competition among airlines. To stop start-up Legend Airlines from starting operations at Dallas's Love Field, American Airlines sued the city of Dallas, the federal government, and the new airline itself. It also lobbied Congress, beseeched its frequent fliers, posted billboards around the city, and secretly paid for radio advertising from a "concerned citizens" group protesting expanded use of Dallas's close-in airport, Love Field. When none of that worked, American's parent, AMR Corporation, leased an asbestos-laden, abandoned terminal at Love Field—an airport it didn't even serve—just as the start-up, Legend Airlines, was negotiating for the same space. AMR said it needed more "office space"—15 miles from its headquarters.

Legend nevertheless prevailed and in March 2000 began flying fifty-six-seat jets to Los Angeles and Washington, offering exclusively first-class seating, gourmet meals, and satellite TV, all for regular coach fare. Not to be outdone, American scrambled for permission to provide similar all-first-class service to major business centers from Love Field, the very kind of long-haul flights it argued so passionately were illegal. As the world's second-largest airline with 700 jets and 70 percent of the traffic at Dallas–Fort Worth International Airport, American is also one of the most aggressive when it comes to battling upstart competitors.[50]

American Airlines is a strong competitor attempting to meet its market share and profit goals. Many old-line market leaders have had difficulty maintaining their competitiveness. For example, in the consumer packaged goods industry (soaps, cleaning products, food items, etc.), market leader Procter & Gamble has gone head-to-head with Unilever for years. Yet these two largest players in the packaged goods industry have lost 10 percent of their market share since 1996.[51] Gains have been made by Bristol-Myers Squibb, Clorox, Colgate-Palmolive, S. C. Johnson, L'Oreal, and Revlon. What happened? According to Gary Stibel, a principle with New England Consulting Group, "These are still two of the finest marketing organizations in the world, but that's their problem. They do what they do so well that they tend to keep doing the same thing over and over again, and it's starting to wear fairly ragged. Their greatest strength, their past success, is turning into their greatest weakness."[52] In other words, they lost their ability to be leaders in innovation.

Sometimes in the heat of competition, tactics can be carried too far. The "Ethics in Marketing" box raises this issue in a discussion of marketers on campus.

Global Competition

American Airlines, Unilever, and Procter & Gamble are savvy international competitors conducting business throughout the world. Many foreign competitors also consider the United States to be a ripe target

Ethics in Marketing

MARKETERS ON CAMPUS: A NEW BAG OF TRICKS

The eighteen men and women huddled in a conference room at a Saturn car dealership on a Saturday afternoon are brainstorming intensely. Winding up a pitch for a new marketing slogan—"We Never Sounded So Good"—Tony Emerson says, "You know what? It's a new company that's getting better and better every year." Christina Vorrises expounds on Saturn's "no-hassle, no haggle thirty-day money-back guarantee." Elizabeth Sadlier exclaims, "I'm ready to promote!"

They sound like pumped-up Saturn marketers. In fact, they are students from Sonoma State University in Rohnert Park, California, in a marketing class funded by the Saturn dealership, and they will be graded on just how well they promote the cars to their peers.

The long arm of corporate marketing has reached onto campuses in many ways, but corporate underwriting of college classes is a new twist. Saturn's parent, General Motors, has funded classes at more than 200 colleges. Others who have paid to have college classes spend a term pitching their products include Time Warner, Wells Fargo, Bristol-Myers Squibb, and Ameritech Advertising Services (now part of SBC Communications).

"One reason we signed on was to get in touch with talented college kids who might like to work with our company," says Ken Godshall, senior vice president of partnership marketing and new business development for Time Consumer Marketing, which underwrote marketing

classes at five schools last semester. Another goal: to sell a total of 375 subscriptions per school.

For schools, the programs typically mean money. It is not uncommon for schools to receive $2,500 for costs related to the marketing project plus a $500 contribution to the faculty project supervisor's department.

"A large number of our 106 colleges are engaged in these kinds of relationships," says Christopher Cabaldon, vice chancellor of the California Community Colleges. "A real-world client for students to work with enhances the quality and practicability" of their classes, he says.

Once the class is set up, students typically use their $2,500 budget to plan a promotional party complete with food, games, prizes, music, and, of course, marketing come-ons. The end result looks like a corporate-sponsored fraternity bash (minus the liquor) and typically attracts hundreds of students.

The underwriting programs outrage critics like Richard Randall, who teaches at North Idaho College. In the spring semester of 1998, when Randall was an instructor in the philosophy department at Washington State University in Pullman, he protested a campus promotion for Chevrolet run by students in a marketing class. He recalls standing for over two hours clutching a picketing sign that read: "Internships OK—but We Are a University, Not a Car Dealership."

"It was the use of a state, tax-payer-supported institution which was very obviously being used to

Jill Fernandez, Tony Emerson, and Allison Young are three of the seventeen Saturn GMMi interns at Sonoma State University in California. They are pictured here after a successful carnival-type event they organized to promote Saturn cars.

sell products," Randall now says. "If this was an academic exercise, then what in the hell were the salespeople doing there?"

The professor of that class at Washington State, David Sprott, is in his third year with the GM program in his marketing class and defends it. "There are never enough funds provided by the state," he says. "Any type of external support that comes without work on our part is a good thing."[a]

Do you agree with Richard Randall? Why or why not? What is your opinion of David's position? Isn't it important for students to gain "real-world" experience?

[a] Ann Marie Chaker, "Pitching Saturns to Your Classmates—For Credit," *Wall Street Journal*, January 31, 2000, pp. B1, B4.

market. Thus, a U.S. marketing manager can no longer worry about only domestic competitors. In automobiles, textiles, watches, televisions, steel, and many other areas, foreign competition has been strong. In the past, foreign firms penetrated U.S. markets by concentrating on price, but today the emphasis has switched to product quality. Nestlé, Sony, Rolls Royce, and Sandoz Pharmaceuticals are noted for quality, not cheap prices.

Global competition is discussed in much more detail in Chapter 4.

Ethical Behavior in Business

Describe the role of ethics and ethical decisions in business

ethics
The moral principles or values that generally govern the conduct of an individual.

morals
The rules people develop as a result of cultural values and norms.

Regardless of the intensity of the competition, firms must compete in an ethical manner. **Ethics** refers to the moral principles or values that generally govern the conduct of an individual or a group. Ethics can also be viewed as the standard of behavior by which conduct is judged. Standards that are legal may not always be ethical, and vice versa. Laws are the values and standards enforceable by the courts. Ethics consists of personal moral principles and values rather than societal prescriptions.

 Defining the boundaries of ethicality and legality can be difficult. Often, judgment is needed to determine whether an action that may be legal is indeed ethical. For example, advertising liquor, tobacco, and X-rated movies in college newspapers is not illegal in many states, but is it ethical?

Morals are the rules people develop as a result of cultural values and norms. Culture is a socializing force that dictates what is right and wrong. Moral standards may also reflect the laws and regulations that affect social and economic behavior. Thus, morals can be considered a foundation of ethical behavior.

Morals are usually characterized as good or bad. "Good" and "bad" have different connotations, including "effective" and "ineffective." A good salesperson makes or exceeds the assigned quota. If the salesperson sells a new stereo or television set to a disadvantaged consumer—knowing full well that the person can't keep up the monthly payments—is the salesperson still a good one? What if the sale enables the salesperson to exceed his or her quota?

Another set of connotations for "good" and "bad" are "conforming" and "deviant" behaviors. A doctor who runs large ads for discounts on open-heart surgery would be considered bad, or unprofessional, in the sense of not conforming to the norms of the medical profession. "Bad" and "good" are also used to express the distinction between criminal and law-abiding behavior. And finally, the terms "good" and "bad" as defined by different religions differ markedly. A Moslem who eats pork would be considered bad, as would a fundamentalist Christian who drinks whiskey.

Morality and Business Ethics

 Today's business ethics actually consists of a subset of major life values learned since birth. The values businesspeople use to make decisions have been acquired through family, educational, and religious institutions.

Ethical values are situation specific and time oriented. Nevertheless, everyone must have an ethical base that applies to conduct in the business world and in personal life. One approach to developing a personal set of ethics is to examine the consequences of a particular act. Who is helped or hurt? How long lasting are the consequences? What actions produce the greatest good for the greatest number of people? A second approach stresses the importance of rules. Rules come in the form of customs, laws, professional standards, and common sense. Consider these examples of rules:

- Always treat others as you would like to be treated.
- Copying copyrighted computer software is against the law.
- It is wrong to lie, bribe, or exploit.

The last approach emphasizes the development of moral character within individuals. Ethical development can be thought of as having three levels:[53]

- *Preconventional morality*, the most basic level, is childlike. It is calculating, self-centered, and even selfish, based on what will be immediately punished or rewarded. Fortunately, most businesspeople have progressed beyond the self-centered and manipulative actions of preconventional morality.
- *Conventional morality* moves from an egocentric viewpoint toward the expectations of society. Loyalty and obedience to the organization (or society) be-

come paramount. At the level of conventional morality, an ethical marketing decision would be concerned only with whether or not it is legal and how it will be viewed by others. This type of morality could be likened to the adage "When in Rome, do as the Romans do."

- *Postconventional morality* represents the morality of the mature adult. At this level, people are less concerned about how others might see them and more concerned about how they see and judge themselves over the long run. A marketing decision maker who has attained a postconventional level of morality might ask, "Even though it is legal and will increase company profits, is it right in the long run? Might it do more harm than good in the end?"

Ethical Decision Making

 How do businesspeople make ethical decisions? There is no cut-and-dried answer. Some of the ethical issues managers face are shown in Exhibit 3.6. Studies show that the following factors tend to influence ethical decision making and judgments:[54]

- *Extent of ethical problems within the organization:* Marketing professionals who perceive fewer ethical problems in their organizations tend to disapprove more strongly of "unethical" or questionable practices than those who perceive more ethical problems. Apparently, the healthier the ethical environment, the greater is the likelihood that marketers will take a strong stand against questionable practices.
- *Top-management actions on ethics:* Top managers can influence the behavior of marketing professionals by encouraging ethical behavior and discouraging unethical behavior.
- *Potential magnitude of the consequences:* The greater the harm done to victims, the more likely it is that marketing professionals will recognize a problem as unethical.
- *Social consensus:* The greater the degree of agreement among managerial peers that an action is harmful, the more likely it is that marketers will recognize a problem as ethical.
- *Probability of a harmful outcome:* The greater the likelihood that an action will result in a harmful outcome, the more likely it is that marketers will recognize a problem as unethical.

Exhibit 3.6

Unethical Practices Marketing Managers May Have to Deal With

- Entertainment and gift giving
- False or misleading advertising
- Misrepresentation of goods, services, and company capabilities
- Lies told customers in order to get the sale
- Manipulation of data (falsifying or misusing statistics or information)
- Misleading product or service warranties
- Unfair manipulation of customers
- Exploitation of children and/or disadvantaged groups

- Invasion of customer privacy
- Sex-oriented advertising appeals
- Product or service deception
- Unsafe products or services
- Price deception
- Price discrimination
- Unfair remarks and inaccurate statements about competitors
- Smaller amounts of product in the same-size packages
- Stereotypical portrayals of women, minority groups, and senior citizens

University of British Columbia Centre for Applied Ethics

Research corporate codes of ethics through the Applied Ethics Resources. Compare the codes of three companies. What common themes do you find?

http://www.ethics.ubc.ca

On Line

- *Length of time between the decision and the onset of consequences:* The shorter the length of time between the action and the onset of negative consequences, the more likely it is that marketers will perceive a problem as unethical.
- *Number of people to be affected:* The greater the number of persons affected by a negative outcome, the more likely it is that marketers will recognize a problem as unethical.

Ethical Guidelines

Many organizations have become more interested in ethical issues. One sign of this interest is the increase in the number of large companies that appoint ethics officers—from virtually none five years ago to almost 25 percent of large corporations now. In addition, many companies of various sizes have developed a **code of ethics** as a guideline to help marketing managers and other employees make better decisions. In fact, in a recent national study, it was found that 60 percent of the companies maintained a code of ethics, 33 percent offered ethics training, and 33 percent employed an ethics officer.[55] Some of the most highly praised codes of ethics are those of Boeing, GTE, Hewlett-Packard, Johnson & Johnson, and Norton Company.

code of ethics
A guideline to help marketing managers and other employees make better decisions.

Creating ethics guidelines has several advantages:

- It helps employees identify what their firm recognizes as acceptable business practices.
- A code of ethics can be an effective internal control on behavior, which is more desirable than external controls like government regulation.
- A written code helps employees avoid confusion when determining whether their decisions are ethical.
- The process of formulating the code of ethics facilitates discussion among employees about what is right and wrong and ultimately creates better decisions.

Businesses, however, must be careful not to make their code of ethics too vague or too detailed. Codes that are too vague give little or no guidance to employees in their day-to-day activities. Codes that are too detailed encourage employees to substitute rules for judgment. For instance, if employees are involved in questionable behavior, they may use the absence of a written rule as a reason to continue behaving that way, even though their conscience may be saying no. The checklist in Exhibit 3.7 is an example of a simple but helpful set of ethical guidelines. Following the checklist will not guarantee the "rightness" of a decision, but it will improve the chances that the decision will be ethical.

Although many companies have issued policies on ethical behavior, marketing managers must still put the policies into effect. They must address the classic "matter of degree" issue. For example, marketing researchers must often resort to deception to obtain unbiased answers to their research questions. Asking for a few minutes of a respondent's time is dishonest if the researcher knows the interview will last forty-five minutes. Should researchers conducting focus groups inform the respondents that there are observers behind a one-way mirror? When respondents know they're being watched, they sometimes are less likely to talk and interact freely. Does a client have an ethical right to obtain questionnaires with the names and addresses of respondents from a market research firm? Many of these con-cerns have been addressed by the Professional Standards Committee of the American Marketing Association. The American Marketing Association's code of ethics is included on its Web site at **http://www.ama.org.**

Exhibit **3.7**

Ethics Checklist

- Does the decision benefit one person or group but hurt or not benefit other individuals or groups? In other words, is my decision fair to all concerned?
- Would individuals or groups, particularly customers, be upset if they knew about my decision?
- Has important information been overlooked because my decision was made without input from other knowledgeable individuals or groups?
- Does my decision presume that my company is an exception to a common practice in this industry and that I therefore have the authority to break a rule?
- Would my decision offend or upset qualified job applicants?
- Will my decision create conflict between individuals or groups within the company?
- Will I have to pull rank or use coercion to implement my decision?
- Would I prefer to avoid the consequences of my decision?
- Did I avoid truthfully answering any of the above questions by telling myself that the risks of getting caught are low or that I could get away with the potentially unethical behavior?

Corporate Social Responsibility

Ethics and social responsibility are closely intertwined. Besides questioning tobacco companies' ethics, one might ask whether they are acting in a socially responsible manner when they promote tobacco. Are companies that produce low-cost handguns socially responsible in light of the fact that these guns are used in the majority of inner-city crimes? **Corporate social responsibility** is a business's concern for society's welfare. This concern is demonstrated by managers who consider both the long-range best interests of the company and the company's relationship to the society within which it operates.

One theorist suggests that total corporate social responsibility has four components: economic, legal, ethical, and philanthropic.[56] The **pyramid of corporate social responsibility**, shown in Exhibit 3.8, portrays economic performance as the foundation for the other three responsibilities. At the same time that it pursues profits (economic responsibility), however, business is expected to obey the law (legal responsibility); to do what is right, just, and fair (ethical responsibilities); and to be a good corporate citizen (philanthropic responsibility). These four components are distinct but together constitute the whole. Still, if the company doesn't make a profit, then the other three responsibilities are moot.

Many companies are already working to make the world a better place to live. Consider these examples:

- Colby Care Nurses, Inc., a home health care service located in Los Angeles County, is offering much needed health care to predominantly black and Hispanic communities that are not often covered by other providers. The company prides itself on giving back to the community by employing its residents and providing role models for its young people.[57]
- Wrigley, the Chicago gum maker, is producing a $10 million commercial campaign aimed at getting African-Americans, Asian-Americans, and Hispanic-Americans to use doctors for regular health maintenance instead of as a last resort.[58]
- Equal Exchange, a $5 million gourmet coffee retailer in Canton, Massachusetts, purchases directly from small cooperatives, owned by farmers themselves, and pledges to pay a fair price—sometimes as much as 50 cents per pound over the market rate.[59]

Discuss corporate social responsibility

corporate social responsibility
Business's concern for society's welfare.

pyramid of corporate social responsibility
A model that suggests corporate social responsibility is composed of economic, legal, ethical, and philanthropic responsibilities and that the firm's economic performance supports the entire structure.

Exhibit **3.8**

Pyramid of Corporate Social Responsibility

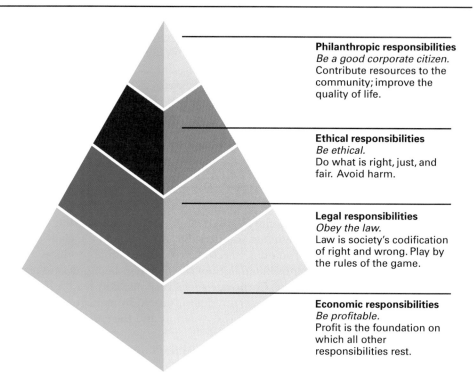

Philanthropic responsibilities
Be a good corporate citizen.
Contribute resources to the community; improve the quality of life.

Ethical responsibilities
Be ethical.
Do what is right, just, and fair. Avoid harm.

Legal responsibilities
Obey the law.
Law is society's codification of right and wrong. Play by the rules of the game.

Economic responsibilities
Be profitable.
Profit is the foundation on which all other responsibilities rest.

- Fetzer Vineyards of California has eliminated 91 percent of its waste since 1991 while sales have doubled. The winery grows grapes organically, relying on natural pest control.[60]
- Ben & Jerry's Ice Cream uses unbleached paper in its cartons and purchases only steroid-free milk.[61]
- The Entrepreneurs' Foundation, in Menlo Park, California, has sixty-one member companies that have each donated roughly $100,000 worth of stock for the purpose of addressing the needs of people in their community.[62]

Looking **B**ack

Look back at the story about Roots Canada Ltd. You should now understand that the external environment affects all firms and their marketing mixes. All of the other external variables, besides competition, can affect Roots. Changing social factors such as a decline of interest in nostalgia-related products would have a strong negative impact on Roots's sales.

Are you at the preconventional, conventional, or postconventional stage of ethical development? If you determine that you are at the preconventional level, you should begin striving for a more mature ethical outlook. This may mean taking an ethics course, reading a book on ethics, or engaging in a lot of introspection about yourself and your values. A person with preconventional ethics will probably have a difficult time succeeding in today's business world.

Ethics: A Part of Everyday Life

Realize that ethics plays a part in our lives every day. We all must answer questions such as these:

How do I balance the time and energy obligations of my work and my family?

How much should I pay my employees?

What should I do with the child of my husband's first marriage who is disrupting our new family?

How am I spending my money?

Should I "borrow" a copy of my friend's software?

If I know my employee is having troubles at home, should I treat her differently?

What should I do if I know a neighbor's child is getting into serious trouble?

How do I react to a sexist or racist joke?

Too many people make decisions about everyday questions without considering the underlying moral and ethical framework of the problems. They are simply swept along by the need to get through the day. Our challenge to you is to always think about the ethical consequences of your actions. Make doing so a habit.

Waiting for dramatic events before consciously tackling ethical considerations is like playing a sport only on the weekend. Just as a weekend warrior often ends up with pulled muscles and poor performance, people who seldom consider the ethical implications of daily activities won't have the coordination to work through the more difficult times in their lives. Don't let this happen to you.

Know Your Ethical Values

 To get a better idea of your own level of ethical development, take an ethics test. Go to **http://www.polley-edu.com/ethics. htm**. Check your responses against those of others and read their comments. This test will give you better insight into yourself.

Work for a Socially Responsible Firm

When you enter the job market, make certain that you are going to work for a socially responsible organization. Ask a prospective employer how the company gives back to society. If you plan to work for a large company, check out *Fortune*'s current list of America's most admired corporations. (It appears around March 1.)

If you plan to work for a multinational firm, examine *Fortune*'s most globally admired corporations, which appears in October. The list is broken down by industry and includes ten to fifteen companies in each industry. Working for an ethical, socially responsible organization will make you proud of the place where you work.

Don't think ethics are a part of your everyday life? Consider the case of Napster. Is it ethical for people to be able to exchange music in this forum without paying royalties to songwriters and performers? Why do you think as you do?

Summary

① Discuss the external environment of marketing and explain how it affects a firm. The external marketing environment consists of social, demographic, economic, technological, political and legal, and competitive variables. Marketers generally cannot control the elements of the external environment. Instead, they must understand how the external environment is changing and the impact of change on the target market. Then marketing managers can create a marketing mix to effectively meet the needs of target customers.

2 **Describe the social factors that affect marketing.** Within the external environment, social factors are perhaps the most difficult for marketers to anticipate. Several major social trends are currently shaping marketing strategies. First, people of all ages have a broader range of interests, defying traditional consumer profiles. Second, changing gender roles are bringing more women into the workforce and increasing the number of men who shop. Third, a greater number of dual-career families has led to a poverty of time, creating a demand for timesaving goods and services.

3 **Explain the importance to marketing managers of current demographic trends.** Today, several basic demographic patterns are influencing marketing mixes. Because the U.S. population is growing at a slower rate, marketers can no longer rely on profits from generally expanding markets. Marketers are also faced with increasingly experienced consumers among the younger generations, many of whom are "turned off" by traditional marketing mixes. And because the population is also growing older, marketers are offering more products that appeal to middle-aged and elderly markets.

4 **Explain the importance to marketing managers of multiculturalism and growing ethnic markets.** Multiculturalism occurs when all major ethnic groups in an area are roughly equally represented. Growing multiculturalism makes the marketer's task more challenging. Niches within ethnic markets may require micromarketing strategies. An alternative to a niche strategy is maintaining a core brand identity while straddling different languages, cultures, ages, and incomes with different promotional campaigns. A third strategy is to seek common interests, motivations, or needs across ethnic groups. E-commerce companies are increasingly targeting America's minority groups.

5 **Identify consumer and marketer reactions to the state of the economy.** Marketers are currently targeting the increasing number of consumers with higher discretionary income by offering higher-quality, higher-priced goods and services. During a time of inflation, marketers generally attempt to maintain level pricing in order to avoid losing customer brand loyalty. During times of recession, many marketers maintain or reduce prices to counter the effects of decreased demand; they also concentrate on increasing production efficiency and improving customer service.

6 **Identify the impact of technology on a firm.** Monitoring new technology is essential to keeping up with competitors in today's marketing environment. For example, in the technologically advanced United States, many companies are losing business to Japanese competitors, who are prospering by concentrating their efforts on developing marketable applications for the latest technological innovations. In the United States, many R&D expenditures go into developing refinements of existing products. U.S. companies must learn to foster and encourage innovation. Without innovation, U.S. companies can't compete in global markets.

7 **Discuss the political and legal environment of marketing.** All marketing activities are subject to state and federal laws and the rulings of regulatory agencies. Marketers are responsible for remaining aware of and abiding by such regulations. Some key federal laws that affect marketing are the Sherman Act, Clayton Act, Federal Trade Commission Act, Robinson-Patman Act, Wheeler-Lea Amendments to the FTC Act, Lanham Act, Celler-Kefauver Antimerger Act, and Hart-Scott-Rodino Act. The Consumer Product Safety Commission, the Federal Trade Commission, and the Food and Drug Administration are the three federal agencies most involved in regulating marketing activities.

8 **Explain the basics of foreign and domestic competition.** The competitive environment encompasses the number of competitors a firm must face, the relative size of the competitors, and the degree of interdependence within the industry. Declining population growth, rising costs, and shortages of resources have heightened domestic competition. Yet with an effective marketing mix, small firms continue to be able to compete with the giants. Meanwhile, dwindling international barriers are bringing in more foreign competitors and offering expanding opportunities for U.S. companies abroad.

9 **Describe the role of ethics and ethical decisions in business.** Business ethics may be viewed as a subset of the values of society as a whole. The ethical conduct of business people is shaped by societal elements, including family, education, religion, and social movements. As members of society, businesspeople are morally obligated to consider the ethical implications of their decisions.

Ethical decision making is approached in three basic ways. The first approach examines the consequences of decisions. The second approach relies on rules and laws to guide decision making. The third approach is based on a theory of moral development that places individuals or groups in one of three developmental stages: preconventional morality, conventional morality, or postconventional morality.

Many companies develop a code of ethics to help their employees make ethical decisions. A code of ethics can help employees identify acceptable business practices, can be an effective internal control on behavior, can help employees avoid confusion when determining the ethicality of decisions, and can facilitate discussion about what is right and wrong.

10 **Discuss corporate social responsibility.** Responsibility in business refers to a firm's concern for the way its decisions affect society. There are several arguments in support of social responsibility. First, many consumers feel business should take responsibility for the social costs of economic growth. A second argument contends that firms act in their own best interest when they help improve the environment within which they operate. Third, firms can avoid restrictive government regulation by responding willingly to societal concerns. Finally, some people argue that because firms have the resources to solve social problems, they are morally obligated to do so.

In contrast, there are critics who argue against corporate social responsibility. According to one argument, the free enterprise system has no way to decide which social programs should have priority. A second argument contends that firms involved in social programs do not generate the profits needed to support the business's activities and earn a fair return for stockholders.

In spite of the arguments against corporate social responsibility, most businesspeople believe they should do more than pursue only profits. Although a company must consider its economic needs first, it must also operate within the law, do what is ethical and fair, and be a good corporate citizen.

Discussion and Writing Questions

1. What is the purpose of environmental scanning? Give an example.
2. Every country has a set of core values and beliefs. These values may vary somewhat from region to region of the nation. Identify five core values for your area of the country. Clip magazine advertisements that reflect these values and bring them to class.
3. Baby boomers in America are aging. Describe how this might affect the marketing mix for the following:
   a. Bally's Health Clubs
   b. McDonald's
   c. Whirlpool Corporation
   d. the State of Florida
   e. Target
4. You have been asked to address a local chamber of commerce on the subject of "Generation Y." Prepare an outline for your talk.

5. Periods of inflation require firms to alter their marketing mix. A recent economic forecast expects inflation to be almost 10 percent during the next 18 months. Your company manufactures hand tools for the home gardener. Write a memo to the company president explaining how the firm may have to alter its marketing mix.

Key Terms

applied research   75
baby boomers   67
basic research   75
code of ethics   84
component lifestyles   65
Consumer Product Safety Commission (CPSC)   78
corporate social responsibility   85
demography   67
environmental management   63
ethics   82
Federal Trade Commission (FTC)   78
Food and Drug Administration (FDA)   79
Generation X   67
Generation Y   67
inflation   74
morals   82
multiculturalism   72
personalized economy   68
poverty of time   64
pyramid of corporate social responsibility   85
recession   75
stitching niches   73
target market   62

6. Give three examples in which technology has benefited marketers. Also, give several examples in which firms have been hurt by not keeping up with technological change.

7. **TEAM** Form six teams and make each one responsible for one of the uncontrollable elements in the marketing environment. Your boss, the company president, has asked each team to provide a one-year and a five-year forecast of what major trends the firm will face. The firm is in the telecommunications equipment industry. It has no plans to become a telecommunications service provider, for example, like MCI and AT&T. Each team should use the library, the Internet, and other data sources to make its forecasts. Each team member should examine a minimum of one data source. The team should then pool its data and prepare its recommendation. A spokesperson for each team should present the findings to the class.

8. Explain how the Internet is impacting multicultural marketing.

9. How should Ford Motor Company market differently to Generation Y, Generation X, and baby boomers?

10. **WRITING** Write a paragraph discussing the ethical dilemma in the following situation and identifying possible solutions: An insurance agent forgets to get the required signature from one of her clients who is buying an automobile insurance policy. The client acknowledges the purchase by giving the agent a signed personal check for the full amount. To avoid embarrassment and inconvenience, the agent forges the client's signature on the insurance application and sends it to the insurance company for processing.

11. **ON LINE** What's the latest news at Web site **http://www.ipo.org**? How can marketers benefit from such information?

12. **ON LINE** What social responsibility concerns could be raised about Web site **http://www.netcasino.com**? For which issues does the Web site seem to exhibit social responsibility?

13. **WRITING** INFOTRAC COLLEGE EDITION Your boss is interested in learning more about marketing ethics and has asked you to prepare a brief memo on the topic. Use InfoTrac (**http://www.infotrac-college.com**) to locate discussions on ethics in the business and popular press. Consult articles in *Ethics Journal* and others as part of your search. Once you have finished your research, write your memo, highlighting what your research says is the hottest issue in ethical marketing.

14. INFOTRAC COLLEGE EDITION Government regulation is a tremendous influence on business behavior. To understand better the current regulatory climate, read a selection of articles from such periodicals as *Occupational Safety and Health Journal, Environmental Law, Health Legislation and Regulation, American Business Law Journal,* and *Policy Review.* List three regulations or situations that you found to be appropriate and three that you considered to be unnecessarily punitive or overly restrictive. Use InfoTrac (**http://www.infotrac-college.com**) to help you with your research.

Application for Entrepreneurs

ENTREPRENEUR Jeanette and Jeff Horowitz just inherited $175,000 from Jeanette's late Polish uncle, David Forski. The couple had always wanted to own a franchise, and after some initial investigation have narrowed their choices down to two. The first is FASTSIGNS, the original retail sign franchise with hundreds of locations and found in virtually every state. Its advantages are business customers, standard business hours, clean, attractive retail environment, national advertising support, and operational and marketing support.

Jeanette and Jeff's other opportunity is a Subway sandwich franchise, a highly rated sandwich system with over 13,000 restaurants. Key advantages are a simple system with no cooking, low initial investment, quality products, and complete training and support.

Questions

1. What are some of the threats in the external environment that Jeanette and Jeff may face?
2. What factors in the external environment may create an opportunity for Jeff and Jeanette?
3. Go to **http://www.subway.com** and **http://www.fastsigns.com** and determine which franchise is most appealing to you. Why?

Case   entrepreneurship

Encirq: Protecting Privacy on the Web

The rapid development of the Internet and e-commerce in the past couple of years has not come without serious growing pains. This new networking and communication medium created a whole new way for marketers to identify, track, collect information about, and offer targeted messages to consumers. Advertisers can monitor consumers who are surfing for pleasure even if they do not buy anything or divulge any personal information. With just a person's e-mail address and a cookie (an electronic tag that identifies a user's computer with a numeric code), an on-line ad server can easily track users as they click across the Internet landscape. Tracking a consumer's surfing habits enables servers of on-line advertisements to place very targeted ads in front of users. On the surface, this may seem like a benefit to both the advertiser and to the consumer, but there is often an unrealized downside to all of that.

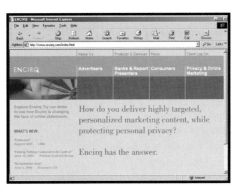

What consumers have been generally unaware of is that these ad serving networks and companies collect and store all of that information on private servers and sell it to other marketing companies and retailers at a handsome profit. Selling on-line profiles seriously compromises a user's privacy, and it almost always happens without that person being aware of it. If Net users are aware of this information brokering, they generally have no idea how this whole system works. In addition, the creation of such information-gathering technologies has far outpaced the implementation of legal and regulatory systems in the Internet space. The result: an extremely gray area where companies can act unethically without fear of serious repercussion.

A 1999 class-action lawsuit was filed against on-line ad server Doubleclick for violating users' privacy. The suit generated mass awareness of the practices of Doubleclick and other similar ad serving networks and fueled public intolerance of such activities. On-line marketers began to suffer from the loss of specific information needed to serve targeted content and advertisements. Most Internet users became extremely guarded about sharing any kind of personal information on-line.

The Encirq Corporation, which at present has the only available solution of its kind, hopes to once and for all resolve the problem that limits marketers and compromises personal privacy. Founded by Mark Vogel and David Posner, Encirq has developed a software application from two unique and perfectly complementary insights. Vogel dreamed of a way for an Internet user's personal information to remain housed on his or her own individual computer. In this way, personal information would be fully protected and controlled by the consumer. Posner had designed a small database that would launch within a user's computer at the exact moment an Internet user connected with a Web server. Driven to solve the privacy problem outlined above—and the marketing problem that analyzing clicking habits on-line created only a thumbnail sketch of buying habits and history—Vogel and Posner devised a product that could be the perfect solution to both.

What they eventually created was Encirq's core product, an enhanced version of an electronic credit card, bank, or similar financial statement called the "Illuminated Statement." Banks and other credit card providers who adopt the Illuminated Statement are able to e-mail cardholders their statements in HTML, the Internet programming language that allows data to be presented in colors, graphics, and links to other Web sites. The Illuminated Statement, therefore, can add several features and functions to the credit card statement that would otherwise be impossible. It can add the logo of a company beside the line item that describes the purchase on a bill, making it easier to read. The logos can also be active links to the original company's Web site and even to the specific department where the purchase was made. Clicking on the purchase amount reveals a detailed history of the transaction—for example, perhaps the entire list of items on a grocery receipt. Empty space between the company logo and the amount of the purchase is available for highly targeted advertising, and it is available without compromising a consumer's privacy.

The mini database that Posner developed resides on a user's computer in the form of a small program that runs every time a consumer opens an Illuminated Statement. The program can analyze the information contained in the statement and build a digital profile of its user that is stored in the mini database. This profile is constantly being refined as Encirq's software program analyzes purchase histories, amounts, and frequencies. Personal information is kept entirely on the user's computer and is therefore inaccessible to on-line ad servers and information collectors as well as to the companies the person bought from. Hence the Internet privacy problem is solved for the consumer.

Although such a product is a boon for consumers, it will never be widely adopted unless marketers of retailers represented on an Illuminated Statement are able to benefit as well. Encirq's solution solves this problem by offering a unique way to match targeted ads with very accurate consumer information. Advertisers and ad servers can still send ads to a user's PC. Those ads, however, will not make it in unless they match favorably with the user's ever-changing digital profile. No personal information that is not already on the Illuminated Statement is needed. The ad servers cannot trace the clicking habits or purchase behavior of individual consumers, and only relevant ads enter a person's statement. E-mail remains unclogged and free for more productive and desired purposes. No amount of information ever leaves the user's PC either. The profile is totally protected, and the information flow is one-way going in.

Encirq believes the software wins on three fronts. First, it fully protects the information of the individual. Second, it ensures that only the most desirable and relevant promotions reach consumers. Third, it turns a simple credit card statement into a mini Web portal. Through the Illuminated Statement, a consumer can access company Web sites, view detailed personal financial information and purchase histories, and take advantage of offers from companies he or she has already done business with. The consumer can even choose to arrange statement information by date, purchase amount, or merchant. Clearly, the idea will gain traction among a consuming public that is increasingly concerned about privacy protection, but it remains to be seen if the companies (like banks and other major merchants) that collect and sell consumers' information will see it as advantageous as the consumers whose rights Encirq seeks to protect.

Questions

1. To people of what marketing-oriented values might Encirq's Illuminated Statement be most appealing? Explain.
2. Explain how Encirq is capitalizing on social and technological changes in the environment.
3. What legal factors will affect the adoption and acceptance of Encirq's Illuminated Statement?
4. Explain why you think Encirq acts or does not act in a socially responsible manner.

Bibliography

Charles E. Rider. "Encirq: Putting Customers in Control," June 15, 2000, published by Patricia Seybold Group. **http://encirq.com**

Susan Kuchinskas. "By Invitation Only," June 13, 2000, *Business 2.0,* pp. 269–278. Imagine Media, **http://imaginemedia.com**

Case

video

Ben & Jerry's: "We Do Good by Doing Good."

Ben & Jerry's tries to make the world a sweeter place. The Vermont manufacturer makes premium ice cream with catchy names like Cherry Garcia—after the Grateful Dead icon—and uses only top quality ingredients. We're all in this together, say the company founders, so let's find innovative ways to show concern for people—

locally, nationally, and around the world. This philosophy is called "caring capitalism." How does it work?

The concept of linked prosperity goes beyond writing a check for charity. Ben & Jerry's actually links itself to others who also wish to improve the quality of life for themselves and others. There are many ways to forge alliances. One way is the PartnerShop, a Ben & Jerry franchise owned and operated by a nonprofit organization. A PartnerShop called Youth Scoops in Ithaca, New York, provides employment and training for youths at risk.

Another way to tie business to values is to buy products from "socially aligned" suppliers, those in agreement with Ben & Jerry's social outlook. The brownies in the Chocolate Fudge Brownie Frozen Yogurt are made by Greyston Bakery in Yonkers, New York, a nonprofit social service network which trains and employs homeless and low-income people for self-sufficiency. Coffee extract is made with beans from Aztec Harvests, a farming company owned by Mexican cooperatives. As part of the minority supplier program, Ben & Jerry's encourages its pecan processor to use the Federation of Southern Co-operatives, a co-op dedicated to supporting African-American family farms. About one-third of 1997 purchases reflects this social mission.

Caring for our planet is still another part of the Ben & Jerry's business philosophy. The company is serious about using and producing environment-friendly products even if it means paying top dollar. The only milk and cream that go into the ice cream come from St. Alban's, a co-op of Vermont family farmers. These dairies do not use rBGH, a growth hormone believed to be bad for cows and bad for the future of small-scale dairy farms. In fact, Ben & Jerry's has started a food fight. The company is challenging laws against national rBGH labeling so consumers can make informed choices when buying dairy products. In 1997, the company won a court case against the state of Illinois, which had taken the position that no rBGH labeling was allowed.

Another bold step was the elimination of bleach in packaging. The pint container, the industry standard, was tested and found to be environmentally poor, so the company invested hundreds of staff hours to analyze chlorine-free packaging sources. Ben & Jerry's will start using its unbleached paper Eco-pint with World's Best Vanilla, eventually expanding its use to all flavors. One dimension of Ben & Jerry's social mission is to create models for change. The company

hopes that its use of unbleached paper will stimulate similar demand by others.

Still, everything at Ben & Jerry's is not peachy. The decision to discontinue purchases of organic fruit and cancel the organic ice cream line caused quite a stir in-house. The high prices paid to dairy farmers were also paid to organic fruit farmers. Once again, the idea was not to create a fully organic line, but to support organic farming and create a model to stimulate demand for organic products. These initiatives would hopefully develop into fully organic products down the line. But organic ingredients proved to be too expensive, and the demand for them too weak. Market research showed that organic ingredient costs exceeded consumer price expectations. And suppliers could only produce 29 percent of Ben & Jerry's total fruit needs. So the project was shelved, but not without some soul searching. Were social mission values being sacrificed for short-term economic considerations? Was Ben & Jerry's selling out?

Maybe yes, maybe no. After all, growing competition and consumer concerns about eating too much fat have caused financial struggles in recent years. Returns to shareholders improved in the late 1990's, but the company was still forced to sell itself to Unilever, the consumer products giant, in April 2000. Balancing a social mission and an economic mission proved to be a bit trickier than expected.

Questions

1. What does values-led mean in tough, competitive times? How can Ben & Jerry's lead with its social mission if there is always an economic argument that can be made to act otherwise?
2. Do you think it's in the shareholders' best interest to select minority and disadvantaged suppliers?
3. Given Ben & Jerry's stance on environmental issues, do you feel that the company has an ethical responsibility (i.e., to do what is right, just, and fair and avoid harm) to use organic fruit and produce an organic ice cream despite the high cost? (Look again at Exhibit 3.8.)
4. What do you think Ben & Jerry's should do to remain competitive?

Bibliography

Ben & Jerry's 1999 Annual Report.

Laura Johannes. "Ben & Jerry's to End Long Relationship with Dreyer's after Takeover Attempt." *Wall Street Journal*, September 1, 1998, p. A3.

chapter 4

Learning Objectives

1 Discuss the importance of global marketing

2 Discuss the impact of multi-national firms on the world economy

3 Describe the external environment facing global marketers

4 Identify the various ways of entering the global marketplace

5 List the basic elements involved in developing a global marketing mix

6 Discover how the Internet is affecting global marketing

Developing a Global Vision

When Wal-Mart opened its first store in Argentina four years ago, it found itself cast in the unaccustomed role of David—against a Goliath of a competitor in Carrefour, the French general merchandise chain. Carrefour has been so readily accepted here since it arrived in 1982 that it is now the country's largest retailer.

So with typical Yankee can-do confidence—some would call it arrogance—Wal-Mart entered the Argentine market with a team of American managers and the same basic store model that worked from Detroit to Dallas. The meat counters featured American cuts like T-bone steaks, not the rib strips and tail rumps that Argentines prefer. Cosmetics counters were filled with bright-colored rouge and lipstick, though Argentine women tend to like a softer, more natural look. And jewelry displays gave prominent placement to emeralds, sapphires, and diamonds, while most women here prefer wearing gold and silver. The first few stores even had hardware departments full of tools and appliances wired for 110-volt electric power; the standard throughout Argentina is 220.

But the miscalculations went beyond the merchandise mix—all the way from the widths of store aisles to the carpeting on the floor. Only by trial and error did Wal-Mart learn that far more Argentine customers than Americans were in the habit of stopping at a store each day. The much greater traffic meant more sales of small items, but also aisles that always seemed overcrowded and floors that always seemed dirty and wore out rapidly. Wal-Mart's current leadership here concedes the point. "Following our blueprint too closely wasn't a good idea," said Donald C. Bland, president and chief executive of Wal-Mart Argentina.

When Wal-Mart came to La Plata in July 1997, it avoided repeating many of its early mistakes. The aisles were made wider than in the first few Buenos Aires stores, and the floor was scuff-resistant tile, not carpet. Metal displays for fish gave way to ceramic tile reminiscent of traditional Argentine fish markets. Wooden wine shelves with overhanging arbors replaced metal racks, a change that bolstered wine sales by 20 percent in other stores.

Tailoring its La Plata store to Argentine tastes meant glazing doughnuts with *dulce de leche,* a caramel-like confection. Clothing racks hold more articles in medium sizes and fewer in large sizes, because Argentines are on average a bit smaller than Americans and like a tighter fit. "Let's call it the tropicalized Wal-Mart way," said Cristian Corsi, an Argentine Wal-Mart district manager, with a smile.[1]

Global marketers often face unique problems in the external environment compared to domestic marketers. Vastly different cultural values and ideas, for example, can present unique challenges as shown above. What are some other variables in the international external environment that can impact global marketers? Is it possible to market products the same way all over the world? Is globalization the wave of the future in international marketing?

On Line

Wal-Mart
Does Wal-Mart publicize its global strategies on either of its Web sites? Visit the sites and explain what you find.
http://www.walmart.com
http://walmartstores.com

Rewards of Global Marketing

Discuss the importance of global marketing

global marketing
Marketing that targets markets throughout the world.

global vision
Recognizing and reacting to international marketing opportunities, being aware of threats from foreign competitors in all markets, and effectively using international distribution networks.

Today, global revolutions are under way in many areas of our lives: management, politics, communications, technology. The word *global* has assumed a new meaning, referring to a boundless mobility and competition in social, business, and intellectual arenas. No longer just an option, **global marketing**—marketing that targets markets throughout the world—has become an imperative for business.

U.S. managers must develop a global vision not only to recognize and react to international marketing opportunities but also to remain competitive at home. Often a U.S. firm's toughest domestic competition comes from foreign companies. Moreover, a global vision enables a manager to understand that customer and distribution networks operate worldwide, blurring geographic and political barriers and making them increasingly irrelevant to business decisions. In summary, having a **global vision** means recognizing and reacting to international marketing opportunities, being aware of threats from foreign competitors in all markets, and effectively using international distribution networks.

Over the past two decades, world trade has climbed from $200 billion a year to over $7 trillion. Countries and companies that were never considered major players in global marketing are now important, some of them showing great skill.

Today, marketers face many challenges to their customary practices. Product development costs are rising, the life of products is getting shorter, and new technology is spreading around the world faster than ever. But marketing winners relish the pace of change instead of fearing it.

A young company with a global vision that has capitalized on new technology is Ashtech in Sunnyvale, California. Ashtech makes equipment to capture and convert satellite signals from the U.S. government's Global Positioning System. Ashtech's chief engineer and his team of ten torture and test everything built by Ashtech—expensive black boxes of chips and circuits that use satellite signals to tell surveyors, farmers, mining machine operators, and others where they are with great accuracy. Over half of Ashtech's output is exported. Its biggest customer is Japan.[2]

Adopting a global vision can be very lucrative for a company. Gillette, for example, gets about two-thirds of its revenue from its international division. About 70 percent of General Motors' profits come from operations outside the United States. While Cheetos and Ruffles haven't done very well in Japan, the potato chip has been quite successful. PepsiCo's (owner of Frito-Lay) overseas snack business brings in more than $3.25 billion annually.[3]

A company with a global vision is Pillsbury. The Pillsbury Doughboy is used in India to sell a product that the company had just about abandoned in America: flour. Pillsbury has many higher-margin products such as microwave pizzas in other parts of the world, but it discovered that in this tradition-bound market, it needed to push the basics.

Even so, selling packaged flour in India has been almost revolutionary, because most Indian housewives still buy raw wheat in bulk, clean it by hand, store it in huge metal hampers, and, every week, carry some to a neighborhood mill, or *chakki*, where it is ground between two stones.

To help reach those housewives, the Doughboy himself has gotten a makeover. In TV advertising, he presses his palms together and bows in the traditional Indian greeting. He speaks six regional languages.

Pillsbury is exploiting a potentially huge business. India consumes about sixty-nine million tons of wheat a year, second only to China. (The United States consumes about twenty-six million tons.) Much of India's wheat ends up as *roti*, a flat bread

Pillsbury is reaping the rewards of having a global marketing strategy in India. Although wheat is still ground by hand at home in the vast majority of cases, Pillsbury is already the market leader in packaged flour.

prepared on a griddle that accompanies almost every meal. In a nation where people traditionally eat with their hands, *roti* is the spoon. The blue Pillsbury flour package, which features the Doughboy hoisting a *roti*, has become the market leader in Bombay.[4]

Global marketing is not a one-way street, whereby only U.S. companies sell their wares and services throughout the world. Foreign competition in the domestic market used to be relatively rare but now is found in almost every industry. In fact, in many industries the United States has lost significant market share to imported products. In electronics, cameras, automobiles, fine china, tractors, leather goods, and a host of other consumer and industrial products, U.S. companies have struggled at home to maintain their market shares against foreign competitors.

For the past two decades, U.S. companies often appeared not to be competitive with foreign rivals. Today, however, America has embarked on a new productivity boom. The United States has the highest productivity among all industrialized countries. The United States is the low-cost producer among industrialized nations, with unit labor costs rising more slowly than in either Japan or Germany. American manufacturers are 10 to 20 percent more productive than German or Japanese manufacturers, and the U.S. service sector is 30 to 50 percent more productive. American business is fully prepared to compete in the global marketplace.

Importance of Global Marketing to the United States

Many countries depend more on international commerce than the United States does. For example, France, Britain, and Germany all derive more than 19 percent of their gross domestic product from world trade, compared to about 12 percent for the United States. Nevertheless, the impact of international business on the U.S. economy is still impressive:

- The United States exports about a fifth of its industrial production and a third of its farm products.[5]
- One of every sixteen jobs in the United States is directly or indirectly supported by exports.
- U.S. businesses export over $500 billion in goods to foreign countries every year, and almost a third of U.S. corporate profits is derived from our international trade and foreign investment.[6]
- In 2000, exports accounted for 20 percent of America's growth in economic activity.[7]
- The United States is the world's leading exporter of grain, selling more than $12 billion of this product a year to foreign countries, or about one-third of all agricultural exports.[8]
- Chemicals, office machinery and computers, automobiles, aircraft, and electrical and industrial machinery make up almost half of all nonagricultural exports.

These statistics might seem to imply that practically every business in the United States is selling its wares throughout the world, but nothing could be further from the truth. About 85 percent of all U.S. exports of manufactured goods are shipped by 250 companies; less than 10 percent of all manufacturing businesses, or around twenty-five thousand companies, export their goods on a regular basis.[9] Most small- and medium-sized firms are essentially nonparticipants in global trade and marketing. Only the very large multinational companies have seriously attempted to compete worldwide. Fortunately, more of the smaller companies are now aggressively pursuing international markets.

The Fear of Trade and Globalization

The 1999 protests in Seattle during the meeting of the World Trade Organization and the 2000 protests in New York during the convocation of the World Bank and the International Monetary Fund (the three organizations are discussed later in

In November 1999, protesters congregated in Seattle to disrupt the opening of the 135-nation World Trade Organization meeting. Factions from environmentalists to industrial workers to on-line youths involved in multiple sociopolitical activities joined together to hamper proceedings at the conference.

the chapter) prove that many people fear world trade and globalization. What is feared? The negatives of global trade are as follows:

- Millions of Americans have lost jobs due to imports or production shifts abroad. Most find new jobs—that pay less.
- Millions of others fear losing their jobs, especially at those companies operating under competitive pressure.
- Workers face pay-cut demands from employers, which often threaten to export jobs.
- Service and white-collar jobs are increasingly vulnerable to operations moving offshore.[10]

Yet, there are also numerous advantages related to global trade:

- In China and the rest of East Asia, more people rose out of poverty between 1990 and 2000 than the entire population of the United States. The main reason was global trade.[11]
- In Africa, with its many developing economies, per capita income rose 3.6 percent per year, during the 1990s, double the 1.8 percent of developed countries, and trade was the single biggest reason.[12]
- Productivity grows more quickly when countries produce goods and services in which they have a comparative advantage (discussed later in the chapter). Living standards can go up faster.
- Global competition and cheap imports keep down prices, so inflation is less likely to arrest economic growth.
- An open economy spurs innovation with fresh ideas from abroad.
- Export jobs often pay more than other jobs.[13]

A recent survey found that 68 percent of Americans thought global trade was "good," and 23 percent thought it "bad"; the remainder "weren't sure."[14] Only 10 percent believed in "free trade without restrictions," 51 percent claimed to be "fair traders with standards for labor and the environment," and 37 percent said they were "protectionist advocating rules to protect U.S. markets and workers from imports."[15]

Multinational Firms

Discuss the impact of multinational firms on the world economy

multinational corporation
A company that is heavily engaged in international trade, beyond exporting and importing.

The United States has a number of large companies that are global marketers. Many of them have been very successful. A company that is heavily engaged in international trade, beyond exporting and importing, is called a **multinational corporation**. Multinational corporations move resources, goods, services, and skills across national boundaries without regard to the country in which the headquarters is located. The leading multinational firms in the world are listed in Exhibit 4.1.

A multinational corporation is more than a business entity, as the following paragraph explains:

The multinational corporation is, among other things, a private "government," often richer in assets and more populous in stockholders and employees than are some of the nation-states in which it carries on business. It is simultaneously a "citizen" of several nation-states, owing obedience to their

Exhibit 4.1

Rank	Company	Country	Revenues ($ Millions)	Employees
1	General Motors	U.S.	176,558.0	388,000
2	Wal-Mart Stores	U.S.	166,809.0	1,140,000
3	Exxon Mobil	U.S.	163,881.0	106,000
4	Ford Motor	U.S.	162,558.0	364,550
5	DaimlerChrysler	Germany	159,985.7	466,938
6	Mitsui	Japan	118,555.2	38,454
7	Mitsubishi	Japan	117,765.6	42,050
8	Toyota Motor	Japan	115,670.9	214,631
9	General Electric	U.S.	111,630.0	340,000
10	Itochu	Japan	109,068.9	5,306
11	Royal Dutch/Shell Group	Brit./Neth.	105,366.0	96,000
12	Sumitomo	Japan	95,701.6	33,057
13	Nippon Telegraph & Telephone	Japan	93,591.7	223,954
14	Marubeni	Japan	91,807.4	32,000
15	Axa	France	87,645.7	92,008
16	International Business Machines	U.S.	87,548.0	307,401
17	BP Amoco	Britain	83,566.0	80,400
18	Citigroup	U.S.	82,005.0	176,900
19	Volkswagen	Germany	80,072.7	306,275
20	Nippon Life Insurance	Japan	78,515.1	71,434
21	Siemens	Germany	75,337.0	443,000
22	Allianz	Germany	74,178.2	113,584
23	Hitachi	Japan	71,858.5	398,348
24	Matsushita Electric Industrial	Japan	65,555.6	290,448
25	Nissho Iwai	Japan	65,393.2	18,446

SOURCE: "The World's Largest Corporations," *Fortune* (July 24, 2000), p. F-1.

laws and paying them taxes, yet having its own objectives and being responsive to a management located in a foreign nation. Small wonder that some critics see in it an irresponsible instrument of private economic power or of economic "imperialism" by its home country. Others view it as an international carrier of advanced management science and technology, an agent for the global transmission of cultures bringing closer the day when a common set of ideals will unite mankind.[16]

Many multinational corporations are enormous. For example, the sales of both Exxon and General Motors are larger than the gross domestic product of all but twenty-two nations in the world. A multinational company may have several worldwide headquarters, depending on where certain markets or technologies are. Britain's APV, a maker of food-processing equipment, has a different headquarters for each of its worldwide businesses. Hewlett-Packard moved the headquarters of its personal computer business from the United States to Grenoble, France. ABB Asea Brown Boveri, the European electrical engineering giant based in Zurich, Switzerland, groups its thousands of products and services into fifty or so business areas. Each is run by a leadership team that crafts global business strategy, sets product development priorities, and decides where to make its products. None of the teams work out of Zurich headquarters; they are scattered around the world. Leadership for power transformers is based in Germany, electric drives in Finland, and process automation in the United States.

Multinational Advantage

Large multinationals have several advantages over other companies. For instance, multinationals can often overcome trade problems. Taiwan and South Korea have long had an embargo against Japanese cars for political reasons and to help domestic carmakers. Yet Honda USA, a Japanese-owned company based in the United States, sends Accords to Taiwan and Korea. Another example is Germany's BASF, a major chemical and drug manufacturer. Its biotechnology research at home is challenged by the environmentally conscious Green movement. So BASF moved its cancer and immune-system research to Cambridge, Massachusetts.

Another advantage for multinationals is their ability to sidestep regulatory problems. U.S. drugmaker SmithKline and Britain's Beecham decided to merge in part so they could avoid licensing and regulatory hassles in their largest markets. The merged company can say it's an insider in both Europe and the United States. "When we go to Brussels, we're a member state [of the European Union]," one executive explains. "And when we go to Washington, we're an American company."[17]

Multinationals can also shift production from one plant to another as market conditions change. When European demand for a certain solvent declined, Dow Chemical instructed its German plant to switch to manufacturing a chemical that had been imported from Louisiana and Texas. Computer models help Dow make decisions like these so it can run its plants more efficiently and keep costs down.

Multinationals can also tap new technology from around the world. Xerox has introduced some eighty different office copiers in the United States that were designed and built by Fuji Xerox, its joint venture with a Japanese company. Versions of the superconcentrated detergent that Procter & Gamble first formulated in Japan in response to a rival's product are now being sold under the Ariel brand name in Europe. Also, consider Otis Elevator's development of the Elevonic 411, an elevator that is programmed to send more cars to floors where demand is high. It was developed by six research centers in five countries. Otis's group in Farmington, Connecticut, handled the systems integration, a Japanese group designed the special motor drives that make the elevators ride smoothly, a French group perfected the door systems, a German group handled the electronics, and a Spanish group took care of the small-geared components. Otis says the international effort saved more than $10 million in design costs and cut the process from four years to two.

Finally, multinationals can often save a lot in labor costs, even in highly unionized countries. For example, Xerox started moving copier-rebuilding work to Mexico, where wages are much lower. Its union in Rochester, New York, objected because it saw that members' jobs were at risk. Eventually the union agreed to change work styles and to improve productivity to keep the jobs at home.

Global Marketing Standardization

Traditionally, marketing-oriented multinational corporations have operated somewhat differently in each country. They use a strategy of providing different product features, packaging, advertising, and so on. However, Ted Levitt, a Harvard professor, described a trend toward what he referred to as "global marketing," with a slightly different meaning.[18] He contended that communication and technology have made the world smaller so that almost everyone everywhere wants all the things they have heard about, seen, or experienced. Thus, he saw the emergence of global markets for standardized consumer products on a huge scale, as opposed to segmented foreign markets with different products. In this book, global marketing is defined as individuals and organizations using a global vision to effectively market goods and services across national boundaries. To make the distinction, we can refer to Levitt's notion as **global marketing standardization**.

Global marketing standardization presumes that the markets throughout the world are becoming more alike. Firms practicing global marketing standardization produce "globally standardized products" to be sold the same way all over the world. Uniform production should enable companies to lower production and marketing costs and increase profits. However, research indicates that superior sales and profits do not necessarily follow from global standardization.[19]

Levitt cited Coca-Cola, Colgate-Palmolive, and McDonald's as successful global marketers. However, Levitt's critics point out that the success of these three companies is really based on variation, not on offering the same product everywhere. McDonald's, for example, changes its salad dressings for French tastes and sells beer and mineral water in its restaurants there. It also offers different products to suit tastes in Germany (where it offers beer) as well as in Japan (where it offers sake). Further, the fact that Coca-Cola and Colgate-Palmolive sell some of their products in more than 160 countries does not signify that they have adopted a high degree of standardization for all their products globally. Only three Coca-Cola brands are standardized, and one of them, Sprite, has a different formulation in Japan. Some Colgate-Palmolive products are marketed in just a few countries. Axion paste dishwashing detergent, for example, was formulated for developing countries, and La Croix Plus detergent was custom made for the French market. Colgate toothpaste is marketed the same way globally, although its advanced Gum Protection Formula is used in only twenty-seven nations.

Nevertheless, some multinational corporations are moving toward a degree of global marketing standardization. Eastman Kodak has launched a world brand of blank tapes for videocassette recorders. Procter & Gamble (P&G) calls its new philosophy "global planning." The idea is to determine which product modifications are necessary from country to country while trying to minimize those modifications. P&G has at least four products that are marketed similarly in most parts of the world: Camay soap, Crest toothpaste, Head and Shoulders shampoo, and Pampers diapers. However, the smell of Camay, the flavor of Crest, and the formula of Head and Shoulders, as well as the advertising, vary from country to country.

global marketing standardization
Production of uniform products that can be sold the same way all over the world.

External Environment Facing Global Marketers

A global marketer or a firm considering global marketing faces problems, often due to the external environment, as many of the same environmental factors that operate in the domestic market also exist internationally. These factors include culture, economic and technological development, political structure and actions, demographic makeup, and natural resources.

Describe the external environment facing global marketers

Culture is a major factor marketers face when marketing products globally. Inca Kola, the largest selling soft drink in Peru, is a symbol of national heritage. Here a firefighter is delivering a case of the beverage to police engaged in a hostage stand-off.

Culture

Central to any society is the common set of values shared by its citizens that determine what is socially acceptable. Culture underlies the family, the educational system, religion, and the social class system. The network of social organizations generates overlapping roles and status positions. These values and roles have a tremendous effect on people's preferences and thus on marketers' options. Inca Kola, a fruity, greenish-yellow carbonated drink, is the largest-selling soft drink in Peru. Despite being compared to "liquid bubble gum," the drink has become a symbol of national pride and heritage. The drink was invented in Peru and contains only fruit indigenous to the country. A local consumer of about a six-pack per day says, "I drink Inca Kola because it makes me feel like a Peruvian." He tells his young daughter, "This is our drink, not something invented overseas. It is named for your ancestors, the great Inca warriors."[20]

Culture may influence product preferences as in Inca Kola or influence the marketing mix in other ways. A U.S. luggage manufacturer found out that culture also affects thinking and perception. The company designed a new Middle East advertising campaign around the image of its luggage being carried on a magic flying carpet. A substantial part of a group in a marketing research study thought they were seeing advertising for Samsonite *carpets*. Green Giant learned that it could not use its Jolly Green Giant in parts of Asia where a green hat worn by a man signifies that he has an unfaithful wife.[21]

Packaging plays a major role in gift giving in Japan. For example, a few pieces of charcoal, purchased at a Japanese department store, to be put in the bath to improve your skin had an elaborate package. The charcoal, with a sticker affixed, was placed in a cup, which was placed in a cloth bag that was tied and then enveloped in shredded paper. The shredded paper was nestled in a small wicker basket. The basket was encased in plastic and then tied with string. A sign explained that the whole ensemble would be wrapped in gift paper, secured with another sticker and a bow, and, of course, placed in a shopping bag. Altogether, about ten layers of wrapping.[22]

Language is another important aspect of culture. Marketers must take care in translating product names, slogans, and promotional messages so as not to convey the wrong meaning. For example, Mitsubishi Motors had to rename its Pajero model in Spanish-speaking countries because the term describes a sexual activity. Toyota Motor's MR2 model dropped the number 2 in France because the combination sounds like a French swearword.[23] The literal translation of Coca-Cola in Chinese characters means "bite the wax tadpole." Marketers must be careful in translating promotions, product instructions, and other materials from one language to another.

When language is combined with a superstition, there can be an amplified effect. In China and Japan, the number four has the same pronunciation as the word that means death. Consequently, a four in your company name or contact information might have a negative connotation. The number eight, however, is considered lucky, and many products are named "88" or "888." Phone numbers with eights denote good fortune, and real estate with eights in the address is likely to sell more quickly—especially if the price ends in "888."[24]

Each country has its own customs and traditions that determine business practices and influence negotiations with foreign customers. In many countries, personal relationships are more important than financial considerations. For instance, skipping social engagements in Mexico may lead to lost sales. Negotiations in Japan often include long evenings of dining, drinking, and entertaining, and only after a close personal relationship has been formed do business negotiations begin. The Japanese go through a very elaborate ritual when exchanging business cards. An American businesswoman had no idea about this important cultural tradition. She came into a meeting and tossed some of her business cards across the table at a group of stunned Japanese executives. One of them turned his back on her and walked out. The deal never went through.[25]

An area in which businesspeople often find it difficult to know what is right in different cultures is the notion of time. There are no overriding rights or wrongs to a particular pace of life. They are simply different. Not understanding a culture's notion of time can sometimes lead to situations that are awkward and embarrassing or, in extreme cases, to a loss of business. Exhibit 4.2 offers six lessons for global marketers about cultural differences on the concept of time.

Fortunately, some habits and customs seem to be the same throughout much of the world. A study of 37,743 consumers from forty different countries found that 95 percent brushed their teeth daily.[26] Other activities that majorities

---

Exhibit 4.2

Six Lessons About the Cultural Notion of Time

- *Lesson 1: Know appropriate arrival time.* Learn to translate appointment times. What is the appropriate time to arrive for an appointment with a professor? With a government official? For a party? When should you expect others to show up, if at all? Should we expect our hosts to be upset if we arrive late—or promptly? Are people expected to assume responsibility for their lateness?
- *Lesson 2: Understand the line between work time and social time.* What is the relationship between work time and down time? Some questions have easy answers: How many hours are there in the workday? Other questions are more difficult to answer. For example, how much of the workday is spent on-task and how much time is spent socializing, chatting, and being pleasant? For Americans in a big city, the typical ratio is in the neighborhood of about 80:20; about 80 percent of work time is spent on-task and about 20 percent is used for fraternizing, chitchatting, and the like. But many countries deviate sharply from this formula. In countries like India and Nepal, for example, be prepared for a balance closer to 50:50. When you are in Japan, the distinction between work and social time can often be meaningless.
- *Lesson 3: Study the rules of the waiting game.* When you arrive in a foreign culture, be sure to inquire about the specifics of their version of the waiting game. Are their rules based on the principle that time is money? Who is expected to wait for whom, under what circumstances, and for how long? Are some players exempt from waiting?
- *Lesson 4: Learn to reinterpret "doing nothing."* How do your hosts treat pauses, silences, or doing nothing at all? Is appearing chronically busy a quality to be admired or pitied? Is doing nothing a waste of time? Is constant activity seen as an even bigger waste of time? What must it be like to live in a country like Brunei, where people begin their day by asking: "What isn't going to happen today?"
- *Lesson 5: Ask about accepted sequences.* Be prepared for what time frames to expect. Each culture sets rules about the sequence of events. Is it work before play or vice versa? Do people take all of their sleep at night or is there a siesta in the midafternoon?
- *Lesson 6: Are people on clock time or event time?* This may be the most slippery lesson of all. A move from clock time to event time requires a complete shift of consciousness. It entails the suspension of industrialized society's temporal golden rule: "Time is money."

SOURCE: From "Re-learning to Tell Time" by Robert Levine, *American Demographics,* January 1998. Reprinted with permission from American Demographics magazine. © 1998 PRIMEDIA Intertec, Stamford, CT.

worldwide engage in include reading a newspaper, listening to the radio, taking a shower, and washing their hair.

Economic and Technological Development

A second major factor in the external environment facing the global marketer is the level of economic development in the countries where it operates. In general, complex and sophisticated industries are found in developed countries, and more basic industries are found in less developed nations. Higher average family incomes are common in the more developed countries compared to the less developed markets. Larger incomes mean greater purchasing power and demand not only for consumer goods and services but also for the machinery and workers required to produce consumer goods.

To appreciate marketing opportunities (or lack of them), it is helpful to examine the five stages of economic growth and technological development: traditional society, preindustrial society, takeoff economy, industrializing society, and fully industrialized society.

traditional society
A society in the earliest stages of economic development, largely agricultural, with a social structure and value system that provide little opportunity for upward mobility.

The Traditional Society   Countries in the traditional stage are in the earliest phase of development. A **traditional society** is largely agricultural, with a social structure and value system that provide little opportunity for upward mobility. The culture may be highly stable, and economic growth may not get started without a powerful disruptive force. Therefore, to introduce single units of technology into such a country is probably wasted effort. In Ghana, for instance, a tollway sixteen miles long and six lanes wide, intended to modernize distribution, does not connect to any city or village or other road.

preindustrial society
A society in the second stage of economic development, involving economic and social change and the emergence of a middle class with an entrepreneurial spirit.

The Preindustrial Society   The second stage of economic development, the **preindustrial society**, involves economic and social change and the emergence of a middle class with an entrepreneurial spirit. Nationalism may begin to rise, along with restrictions on multinational organizations. Countries like Madagascar and Uganda are in this stage. Effective marketing in these countries is very difficult because they lack the modern distribution and communication systems that U.S. marketers often take for granted. Peru, for example, did not establish a television network until 1975.

takeoff economy
A society in the third stage of economic development, involving a period of transition from a developing to a developed nation.

The Takeoff Economy   The **takeoff economy** is the period of transition from a developing to a developed nation. New industries arise and a generally healthy social and political climate emerges. Kenya and Vietnam have entered the takeoff stage. Although politics in Kenya are not considered particularly healthy, there are significant areas of economic growth. Oil exploration is increasing and Kenya is set to become the world's largest exporter of tea. In an effort to develop its economy, Vietnam now offers large tax breaks to foreign investors who promise jobs. Gold Medal Footware, headquartered in Taiwan, now employs five hundred young workers in Danang and hopes to increase the number to twenty-five hundred.

industrializing society
A society in the fourth stage of economic development, when technology spreads from sectors of the economy that powered the takeoff to the rest of the nation.

The Industrializing Society   The fourth phase of economic development is the **industrializing society**. During this era, technology spreads from sectors of the economy that powered the takeoff to the rest of the nation. Mexico, China, India, and Brazil are among the nations in this phase of development.

Countries in the industrializing stage begin to produce capital goods and consumer durable products. These industries also foster economic growth. As a result, a large middle class begins to emerge, and the demand for luxuries and services grows.

One of the fastest growing economies in the world today (about 10 percent per year) is China. This has resulted in per capita incomes quadrupling in only the last decade and a half.[27] A population of 1.2 billion is producing a gross domestic product of over $1.2 trillion a year. This new industrial giant will be the world's largest manufacturing zone, the largest market for such key industries as telecommunications and aerospace, and one of the largest users of capital.

Rapidly growing large markets like China create enormous opportunities for American global marketers. One tempting market, for example, is the twenty-one million babies born in China each year. One-child families are the rule, so parents spare few expenses bringing up the baby. The Walt Disney Company is in department stores in a dozen or so Chinese cities with the Disney Babies line of T-shirts, rattles, and crib linens—all emblazoned with likenesses of baby Mickey Mouses and other characters.

Recently, Michael Dell opened the fourth Dell PC factory in the world in Xiamen, a windswept city halfway between Hong Kong and Shanghai on China's southwestern coast. The point of Dell's push into China seems so obvious as to be a cliché: China is becoming too big a PC market for Dell, or anyone, to ignore. "If we're not in what will soon be the second-biggest PC market in the world," asks John Legere, president of Dell Asia-Pacific, "then how can Dell possibly be a global player?[28]

The Fully Industrialized Society   The **fully industrialized society**, the fifth stage of economic development, is an exporter of manufactured products, many of which are based on advanced technology. Examples include automobiles, computers, airplanes, oil exploration equipment, and telecommunications gear. Britain, Japan, Germany, France, Canada, and the United States fall into this category.

The wealth of the industrialized nations creates tremendous market potential. Therefore, industrialized countries trade extensively. Also, industrialized nations usually ship manufactured goods to developing countries in exchange for raw materials like petroleum, precious metals, and bauxite.

Political Structure and Actions

Political structure is a third important variable facing global marketers. Government policies run the gamut from no private ownership and minimal individual freedom to little central government and maximum personal freedom. As rights of private property increase, government-owned industries and centralized planning tend to decrease. But rarely will a political environment be at one extreme or the other. India, for instance, is a republic with elements of socialism, monopoly capitalism, and competitive capitalism in its political ideology.

Many countries have changed from a centrally planned economy to a market-oriented one. Eastern European nations like Hungary and Poland have also been moving quickly with market reforms. Many of the reforms have increased foreign trade and investment. For example, in Poland, foreigners are now allowed to invest in all areas of industry, including agriculture, manufacturing, and trade. Poland even gives companies that invest in certain sectors some tax advantages.

Changes leading to market-oriented economies are not restricted to Eastern Europe and Russia. Many countries within Latin America are also attempting market reforms. Countries like Brazil, Argentina, and Mexico are reducing government control over many sectors of the economy. They are also selling state-owned companies to foreign and domestic investors and removing trade barriers that have protected their markets against foreign competition. Brazil has now overtaken Italy and Mexico to become the tenth largest automobile manufacturer in the world. India has recently opened up its market of nine hundred million consumers. While India's per capita average income is quite low ($330), an estimated 250 million+ Indians have enough income to be considered middle class.[29]

Actions by governments can either help or hinder foreign competitors. Unfortunately, it is often the latter. In the late 1990s, China decided that price cuts were reducing profits and causing an economic slowdown. It announced price floors (minimums) on autos, steel, sugar, tractors, glass, cashmere, and ostriches.[30] The government's decree virtually eliminated price competition in these industries.

fully industrialized society
A society in the fifth stage of economic development, a system based on the export of manufactured products, many of which are based on advanced technology.

In 1997, a newly elected government of India's wealthiest state cancelled a $2.5 billion power plant project being built by Enron Corporation of Houston.[31] The government claimed that it was too expensive, that bribes had been paid to some politicians, and that it would destroy fish and some famed mango groves. After several years of hard bargaining and concessions by Enron, the project is back on track.

Coca-Cola decided to improve its market share of the soft drink market in France by purchasing Orangina. As the name implies, Orangina is a sweet, orange-flavored French-made concoction. The French government rejected the purchase on antitrust grounds.

Another potential cloud on the horizon for some types of companies doing business abroad is the threat of nationalization, whereby a government takes ownership of certain industries or companies, such as airlines in Italy and Bull Computer in France, to infuse more capital into their development. Industries are also nationalized to allow domestic corporations to sell vital goods below cost. For example, for many years France has been supplying coal to users at a loss.

Legal Considerations Closely related to and often intertwined with the political environment are legal considerations. Nationalistic sentiments of the French led to a 1996 law that requires pop music stations to play at least 40 percent of their songs in French (in spite of the fact that French teenagers love American and English rock and roll).

Many legal structures are designed to either encourage or limit trade. Here are some examples:

- *Tariff: a tax levied on the goods entering a country.* For example, in February 2000 the United States imposed a stiff tariff on steel imports in an effort to protect about five thousand U.S. jobs.[32]
- *Quota: a limit on the amount of a specific product that can enter a country.* The United States has strict quotas for imported textiles, sugar, and many dairy products. Several U.S. companies have sought quotas as a means of protection from foreign competition. For example, Harley-Davidson convinced the U.S. government to place quotas on large motorcycles imported to the United States. These quotas gave the company the opportunity to improve its quality and compete with Japanese motorcycles.
- *Boycott: the exclusion of all products from certain countries or companies.* Governments use boycotts to exclude companies from countries with whom they have a political dispute. Several Arab nations boycotted Coca-Cola because it maintained distributors in Israel.
- *Exchange control: a law compelling a company earning foreign exchange from its exports to sell it to a control agency, usually a central bank.* A company wishing to buy goods abroad must first obtain foreign exchange from the control agency. Generally, exchange controls limit the importation of luxuries. For instance, Avon Products drastically cut back new production lines and products in the Philippines because exchange controls prevented the conversion of pesos to dollars to ship back to the home office. The pesos had to be used in the Philippines. China restricts the amount of foreign currency each Chinese company is allowed to keep from its exports. Therefore, Chinese companies must usually get the government's approval to release funds before they can buy products from foreign companies.
- *Market grouping: also known as a common trade alliance; occurs when several countries agree to work together to form a common trade area that enhances trade opportunities.* The best-known market grouping is the European Community (EC), whose members are Belgium, France, Germany, Italy, Luxembourg, the Netherlands, Denmark, Ireland, Spain, the United Kingdom, Portugal, and Greece. The EC has been evolving for nearly four decades, yet until recently, many trade barriers existed among member nations.

- *Trade agreement: an agreement to stimulate international trade.* Not all government efforts are meant to stifle imports or investment by foreign corporations. The Uruguay Round of trade negotiations is an example of this. Likewise, China's most favored nation (MFN) status is considered a trade agreement. The largest new trade agreement is **Mercosur**, which includes Brazil, Argentina, Chile, Bolivia, Uruguay, and Paraguay. The elimination of most tariffs among the trading partners has resulted in trade revenues currently over $16 billion annually.[38] The economic boom created by Mercosur will undoubtedly cause other nations to seek trade agreements on their own or enter Mercosur. The European Union, discussed on page 108, hopes to have a free-trade pact with Mercosur by 2005.

Mercosur
The largest new trade agreement, which includes Brazil, Argentina, Uruguay, and Paraguay.

Uruguay Round   The **Uruguay Round** is an agreement to dramatically lower trade barriers worldwide. Adopted in 1994, the agreement has been signed by 136 nations.[33] It is the most ambitious global trade agreement ever negotiated. The agreement reduces tariffs by one-third worldwide. This, in turn, should raise global income by $235 billion annually by 2005. Perhaps most notable is the recognition of the new global realities. For the first time there is an agreement covering services, intellectual property rights, and trade-related investment measures such as exchange controls.

Uruguay Round
An agreement to dramatically lower trade barriers worldwide; created the World Trade Organization.

The Uruguay Round makes several major changes in world trading practices:

- *Entertainment, pharmaceuticals, integrated circuits, and software:* New rules will protect patents, copyrights, and trademarks for twenty years. Computer programs receive fifty years' protection and semiconductor chips receive ten years'. But many developing nations will have a decade to phase in patent protection for drugs. France, which limits the number of U.S. movies and TV shows that can be shown, refused to liberalize market access for the U.S. entertainment industry.
- *Financial, legal, and accounting services:* Services come under international trading rules for the first time, potentially creating a vast opportunity for these competitive U.S. industries. Now it will be easier to admit managers and key personnel into a country. Licensing standards for professionals, such as doctors, cannot discriminate against foreign applicants. That is, foreign applicants cannot be held to higher standards than domestic practitioners.
- *Agriculture:* Europe will gradually reduce farm subsidies, opening new opportunities for such U.S. farm exports as wheat and corn. Japan and Korea will begin to import rice. But growers of U.S. sugar, citrus fruit, and peanuts will have their subsidies trimmed.
- *Textiles and apparel:* Strict quotas limiting imports from developing countries will be phased out over ten years, causing further job loss in the U.S. clothing trade. But retailers and consumers will be the big winners, because quotas now add $15 billion a year to clothing prices.
- *A new trade organization:* The new **World Trade Organization (WTO)** replaces the old **General Agreement on Tariffs and Trade (GATT)**, which was created in 1948. The old GATT agreements provided extensive loopholes that enabled countries to avoid the trade-barrier reduction agreements—a situation similar to obeying the law only if you want to! Today, all WTO members must fully comply with all agreements under the Uruguay Round. The WTO also has an effective dispute settlement procedure with strict time limits to resolve disputes.

The new service agreement under the Uruguay Round requires member countries to create adequate penalties against counterfeiting and piracy. China, which is joining the WTO, has done little to control its rampant piracy problems. U.S. producers of records, books, motion pictures, and software lose about $2.5 billion a year to Chinese piracy.[34] This will decline with China's admission to the WTO.

The movies showing at this cinema on the Champs-Élysées, Paris, France, represent a regulated mix of foreign and domestic films. France and more recently Canada have refused to liberalize market access to the U.S. entertainment and publishing industries, respectively.

World Trade Organization (WTO)
A new trade organization that replaces the old General Agreement on Tariffs and Trade (GATT).

General Agreement on Tariffs and Trade (GATT)
Provided loopholes that enabled countries to avoid trade-barrier reduction agreements.

North American Free Trade Agreement (NAFTA)
An agreement between Canada, the United States, and Mexico that created the world's largest free-trade zone.

The trend toward globalization has brought to the fore several specific examples of the influence of political structures and legal considerations: the North American Free Trade Agreement and the European Union.

North American Free Trade Agreement The **North American Free Trade Agreement (NAFTA)** created the world's largest free-trade zone. Ratified by the U.S. Congress in 1993, the agreement includes Canada, the United States, and Mexico, with a combined population of 360 million and economy of $6 trillion.

Canada, the largest U.S. trading partner, entered a free-trade agreement with the United States in 1988. Most of the new long-run opportunities for U.S. business under NAFTA are thus in Mexico, America's third largest trading partner. Tariffs on Mexican exports to the United States averaged just 4 percent before the treaty was signed, and most goods entered the United States duty-free. Therefore, NAFTA opened the Mexican market primarily to U.S. companies. When the treaty went into effect, tariffs on about half the items traded across the Rio Grande disappeared. The pact removed a web of Mexican licensing requirements, quotas, and tariffs that limited transactions in U.S. goods and services. For instance, the pact allows U.S. and Canadian financial-services companies to own subsidiaries in Mexico for the first time in fifty years.

The real test of NAFTA will be whether it delivers rising prosperity on both sides of the Rio Grande. For Mexicans, NAFTA must provide rising wages, better benefits, and an expanding middle class with enough purchasing power to keep buying goods from the United States and Canada. That scenario is plausible in the long run, but not guaranteed. By 2000, employment had risen 10 percent in Canada, 22 percent in Mexico, and 7 percent in the United States since the signing of the treaty.[35] During the same period, American companies invested $11 billion in Mexico and $39 billion in Canada.[36] Also, cross-border trade between the United States and its two neighbors has increased 141 percent since 1994.[37]

NAFTA, to date, has been very successful, displacing some workers but creating far more jobs than have been lost. The intent of U.S. politicians is to ultimately expand NAFTA to South America, Latin America, and Britain. Chile was to be the first new entrant into the organization. Wrangling within the U.S. Congress has blocked NAFTA expansion so far. As a result, countries south of the U.S. border have been forming their own trade agreements. Latin and South American nations are creating a maze of trading arrangements.

Maastricht Treaty
An agreement among twelve countries of the European Community to pursue economic, monetary, and political union.

European Union In 1993, all twelve member countries of the European Community ratified the **Maastricht Treaty**. The treaty, named after the Dutch town where it was developed, proposes to take the EC further toward economic, monetary, and political union. Officially called the Treaty on European Union, the document outlines plans for tightening bonds among the member states and creating a single market. The European Commission, which drafted the treaty, predicts that Maastricht will create over 2 million new jobs by 2002. Also, retail prices in the European Union are expected to fall by a minimum of 6 percent.[39]

Although the heart of the treaty deals with developing a unified European market, Maastricht is also intended to increase integration among the European Union members in areas much closer to the core of national sovereignty. The treaty created a common currency and an independent central bank in 1999. The European Monetary Union (EMU) was launched January 1, 1999, with Germany, France, Spain, Portugal, Austria, the Netherlands, Luxembourg, Ireland, and Finland. Britain, Sweden, and Denmark chose not to join at the outset. Greece was too far from EMU's stringent fiscal requirement to join at the start. A new European Central Bank was also created along with an EMU currency called the euro. The EMU creates a $6.4 trillion economy, the second largest in the world.[40]

Common foreign, security, and defense policies are also goals, as well as European citizenship—whereby any European Union citizen can live, work, vote, and run for office anywhere in the member countries. The treaty standardizes trade rules and coordinates health and safety standards. Duties, customs procedures, and taxes are also standardized. A driver hauling cargo from Amsterdam to Lisbon can now clear four border crossings by showing a single piece of paper. Before the Maastricht Treaty, the same driver would have carried two pounds of paper to cross the same borders. The overall goal is to end the need for a special product for each country—for example, a different Braun electric razor for Italy, Germany, France, and so forth. Goods marked GEC (goods for EC) can be traded freely, without being retested at each border.

Some economists have called the European Union the "United States of Europe." It is an attractive market, with 320 million consumers and purchasing power almost equal to that of the United States. But the European Union will probably never be a United States of Europe. For one thing, even in a united Europe, marketers will not be able to produce a single Europroduct for a generic Euroconsumer. With eleven different languages and individual national customs, Europe will always be far more diverse than the United States. Thus, product differences will continue. It will be a long time, for instance, before the French begin drinking the instant coffee that Britons enjoy. Preferences for washing machines also differ: British homemakers want front-loaders, and the French want top-loaders; Germans like lots of settings and high spin speeds; Italians like lower speeds. Even European companies that think they understand Euroconsumers often have difficulties producing "the right product":

> Atag Holdings NV, a diversified Dutch company whose main business is kitchen appliances, reckoned it was well-placed to expand abroad. Its plant is a mile from the Dutch/German border and near Europe's geographic and population center. And Lidwien Jacobs, a product manager, says she was confident Atag could cater to both the "potato" and "spaghetti" belts—marketers' terms for consumer preferences in northern and southern Europe. But, as Atag quickly discovered, preferences vary much more than that. "To sell in America, you need one or two types of ceramic stove top," Ms. Jacobs says. "In Europe, you need 11."
>
> Belgians, who cook in huge pots, require extra-large burners. Germans like oval pots, and burners to fit. Italians boil large pots of water quickly, for pasta. The French need small burners and very low temperatures for simmering sauces and broths. Such quirks affect every detail. Germans like oven knobs on the front, the French on top. Even clock placement differs. And Atag has had to test market 28 colors. While Continentals prefer black and white, the British demand a vast range, including peach, pigeon blue, and mint green.
>
> "Whatever the product, the British are always different," Ms. Jacobs says with a sigh. Another snag: "Domestic," the name of Atag's basic oven, turns off buyers in Britain, where "domestic" is a synonym for "servant."
>
> Atag's kitchenware unit has lifted foreign sales to 25 percent of its total from 4 percent in the mid-1980s. But it now believes that its range of designs and speed in delivering them, rather than the magic bullet of a Euro-product, will keep it competitive. "People would fight another war, I think, to keep their own cooking habits," Ms. Jacobs jokes.[41]

An entirely different type of problem facing global marketers is the possibility of a protectionist movement by the European Union against outsiders. For example, European automakers have proposed holding Japanese imports at roughly their current 10 percent market share. The Irish, Danes, and Dutch don't make cars and have unrestricted home markets; they would be unhappy about limited imports of Toyotas and Datsuns. But France has a strict quota on Japanese cars to protect Renault and Peugeot. These local carmakers could be hurt if the quota is raised at all.

Interestingly, a number of big U.S. companies are already considered more "European" than many European companies. Coca-Cola and Kellogg's are considered classic European brand names. Ford and General Motors compete for the largest share of auto sales on the continent. IBM and Dell Computer dominate their markets. General Electric, AT&T, and Westinghouse are already strong all over Europe and have invested heavily in new manufacturing facilities throughout the continent.

Although many U.S. firms are well prepared to contend with European competition, the rivalry is perhaps more intense there than anywhere else in the world. In the long run, it is questionable whether Europe has room for eight mass-market automakers, including Ford and GM, when the United States sustains just three. Similarly, an integrated Europe probably doesn't need twelve national airlines.

Demographic Makeup

The three most densely populated nations in the world are China, India, and Indonesia. But that fact alone is not particularly useful to marketers. They also need to know whether the population is mostly urban or rural, because marketers may not have easy access to rural consumers. In Belgium about 90 percent of the population lives in an urban setting, whereas in Kenya almost 80 percent of the population lives in a rural setting. Belgium is thus the more attractive market.

Just as important as population is personal income within a country. The wealthiest countries in the world include Japan, the United States, Switzerland, Sweden, Canada, Germany, and several of the Arab oil-producing nations. At the other extreme are countries like Mali and Bangladesh, with a fraction of the per capita purchasing power of the United States. However, a low per capita income is not in itself enough reason to avoid a country. In countries with low per capita incomes, wealth is not evenly distributed. There are pockets of upper- and middle-class consumers in just about every country of the world. In some countries, such as India, the number of consumers is surprisingly large.

The most significant global economic news of the past decade is the rise of a global middle class. From Shekou, China, to Mexico City and countless cities in between, there are traffic jams, bustling bulldozers, and people hawking tickets to various events. These are all symptoms of a growing middle class. In China, per capita incomes are rising rapidly. Developing countries, excluding Eastern Europe and the former Soviet Union, should grow about 5 percent annually over the next decade.

Growing economies demand professionals. In Asia, accountants, stock analysts, bankers, and even middle managers are in short supply. Rising affluence also creates demand for consumer durables such as refrigerators, VCRs, and automobiles. Companies like Procter & Gamble and Gillette offer an array of products at different price points to attract and keep customers as they move up the income scale. The percentage of the world's population that lives in industrialized nations has been declining since 1960, because industrialized nations have grown slowly and developing nations have grown rapidly. In this decade, more than 90 percent of the world's population growth will occur in developing countries and only 10 percent in the industrialized nations. The United Nations reports that in 2000, 79 percent of the world's population resided in developing countries—for example, Guinea, Bolivia, and Pakistan.

Natural Resources

A final factor in the external environment that has become more evident in the past decade is the shortage of natural resources. For example, petroleum shortages have created huge amounts of wealth for oil-producing countries such as Norway, Saudi Arabia, and the United Arab Emirates. Both consumer and industrial markets have blossomed in these countries. Other countries—such as Indonesia, Mexico, and Venezuela—were able to borrow heavily against oil reserves in order to develop more rapidly. On the other hand, industrial countries like Japan, the United States, and much of Western Europe experienced rampant inflation in the 1970s and an enormous transfer of wealth to the petroleum-rich nations. But during much of the 1980s and 1990s, when the price of oil fell, the petroleum-rich nations suffered. Many were not able to service their foreign debts when their oil revenues were sharply reduced. However, Iraq's invasion of Kuwait in 1990 led to a rapid increase in the price of oil and focused attention on the dependence of industrialized countries on oil imports. The price of oil once again declined following the defeat of Iraq, but the U.S. dependence on foreign oil will likely remain high. In 2000, industrialized nations, once again, felt the pinch of high oil prices. It led to work stoppages and protests in both Britain and France.

Petroleum is not the only natural resource that affects international marketing. Warm climate and lack of water mean that many of Africa's countries will remain importers of foodstuffs. The United States, on the other hand, must rely on Africa for many precious metals. Japan depends heavily on the United States for timber and logs. A Minnesota company manufactures and sells a million pairs of disposable chopsticks to Japan each year. The list could go on, but the point is clear. Vast differences in natural resources create international dependencies, huge shifts of wealth, inflation and recession, export opportunities for countries with abundant resources, and even a stimulus for military intervention.

Global Marketing by the Individual Firm

A company should consider entering the global marketplace only after its management has a solid grasp of the global environment. Some relevant questions are "What are our options in selling abroad?" "How difficult is global marketing?" and "What are the potential risks and returns?" Concrete answers to these questions would probably encourage the many U.S. firms not selling overseas to venture into the international arena. Foreign sales could be an important source of profits.

Companies decide to "go global" for a number of reasons. Perhaps the most stimulating reason is to earn additional profits. Managers may feel that international sales will result in higher profit margins or more added-on profits. A second stimulus is that a firm may have a unique product or technological advantage not available to other international competitors. Such advantages should result in major business successes abroad. In other situations, management may have exclusive market information about foreign customers, marketplaces, or market situations not known to others. While exclusivity can provide an initial motivation for international marketing, managers must realize that competitors can be expected to catch up with the information advantage of the firm. Finally, saturated domestic markets, excess capacity, and potential for economies of scale can also be motivators to "go global." Economies of scale mean that average per-unit production costs fall as output is increased.

Many firms form multinational partnerships—called strategic alliances—to assist them in penetrating global markets; strategic alliances are examined in Chapter 6. Five other methods of entering the global marketplace are, in order of risk, export, licensing, contract manufacturing, the joint venture, and direct investment. (See Exhibit 4.3.)

4

Identify the various ways of entering the global marketplace

Exhibit 4.3

Risk Levels for Five Methods of
Entering the Global Marketplace

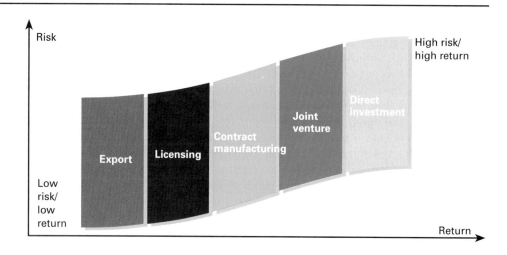

Export

exporting
Selling domestically produced
products to buyers in another
country.

When a company decides to enter the global market, exporting is usually the least complicated and least risky alternative. **Exporting** is selling
domestically produced products to buyers in another country. A company, for example, can sell directly to foreign importers or buyers. Exporting is not
limited to huge corporations such as General Motors or Westinghouse. Indeed,
small companies account for 96 percent of all U.S. exporters, but only 30 percent
of the export volume. The United States is the world's largest exporter.[42] Many
small businesses claim that they lack the money, time, or knowledge of foreign
markets that exporting requires. The U.S. Department of Commerce is trying to
make it increasingly easy for small businesses to enter exporting. The department
has created a pilot program in which it has hired a private company to represent
up to fifty small businesses at specific international trade fairs. For example, FTS,
Incorporated, was hired to represent small firms at a trade show in Italy. The company handed out company brochures and other sales information to interested
prospective Italian clients. Also, after the show was over, FTS gave each participating American company a list of potential Italian distributors for their products.
Each American firm paid only $2,500 to be represented at the trade fair. For com-
panies interested in exporting, the U.S. government stands ready to help in a variety of ways. Some of the federal resources available to companies wanting to enter
exporting are shown in Exhibit 4.4 on pages 114–115.

Instead of selling directly to foreign buyers, a company may decide to sell to
intermediaries located in its domestic market. The most common intermediary is
the export merchant, also known as a **buyer for export**, who is usually treated like
a domestic customer by the domestic manufacturer. The buyer for export assumes
all risks and sells internationally for its own account. The domestic firm is involved
only to the extent that its products are bought in foreign markets.

A second type of intermediary is the **export broker**, who plays the traditional
broker's role by bringing buyer and seller together. The manufacturer still retains
title and assumes all the risks. Export brokers operate primarily in agriculture and
raw materials.

Export agents, a third type of intermediary, are foreign sales agents-distributors
who live in the foreign country and perform the same functions as domestic manufacturers' agents, helping with international financing, shipping, and so on. The
U.S. Department of Commerce has an agent-distributor service that helps about
five thousand U.S. companies a year find an agent or distributor in virtually any
country of the world. A second category of agents resides in the manufacturer's

buyer for export
An intermediary in the global
market who assumes all ownership
risks and sells globally for its own
account.

export broker
An intermediary who plays the
traditional broker's role by bringing buyer and seller together.

export agent
An intermediary who acts like a
manufacturer's agent for the exporter. The export agent lives in
the foreign market.

country but represents foreign buyers. This type of agent acts as a hired purchasing agent for foreign customers operating in the exporter's home market.

Licensing

Another effective way for a firm to move into the global arena with relatively little risk is to sell a license to manufacture its product to someone in a foreign country. **Licensing** is the legal process whereby a licensor allows another firm to use its manufacturing process, trademarks, patents, trade secrets, or other proprietary knowledge. The licensee, in turn, pays the licensor a royalty or fee agreed on by both parties.

Because licensing has many advantages, U.S. companies have eagerly embraced the concept. For instance, Marvel Enterprises granted 4Kids Entertainment international licensing rights for X-Men-the-Movie, X-Men classic, Spider Man classic, the Fantastic Four, Silver Surfer, the Incredible Hulk, Avengers, Captain America, Iron Man, and Daredevil.

4Kids has the rights for Spain, Portugal, United Kingdom, Ireland, France, Italy, Germany, Holland, Belgium, Switzerland, Austria, Israel, Middle East, Greece, and Turkey.[43] Foreign companies are also jumping on the licensing bandwagon. MGI Software Corporation of Canada licensed to Dell Computer the right to install MGI's Video Wave III software. In 2000, Dell shipped twenty million computers with Video Wave III.[44]

A licensor must make sure it can exercise the control over the licensee's activities needed to ensure proper quality, pricing, distribution, and so on. Licensing may also create a new competitor in the long run, if the licensee decides to void the license agreement. International law is often ineffective in stopping such actions. Two common ways of maintaining effective control over licensees are shipping one or more critical components from the United States or locally registering patents and trademarks to the U.S. firm, not to the licensee.

Franchising is one form of licensing that has grown rapidly in recent years. More than 350 U.S. franchisors operate more than thirty-two thousand outlets in foreign countries, bringing in sales of over $6 billion.[45] Over half the international franchises are for fast-food restaurants and business services. As with other forms of licensing, maintaining control over the franchisees is important. For instance, McDonald's was forced to take legal action to buy back its Paris outlets because the franchisee failed to maintain quality standards. McDonald's claimed the Paris franchise was dirty and provided poor service and food.

Contract Manufacturing

Firms that do not want to become involved in licensing or to become heavily involved in global marketing may engage in **contract manufacturing**, which is private-label manufacturing by a foreign company. The foreign company produces a certain volume of products to specification, with the domestic firm's brand name on the goods. The domestic company usually handles the marketing. Thus, the domestic firm can broaden its global marketing base without investing in overseas plant and equipment. After establishing a solid base, the domestic firm may switch to a joint venture or direct investment.

Joint Venture

Joint ventures are similar to licensing agreements. In a **joint venture**, the domestic firm buys part of a foreign company or joins with a foreign company to create a new entity. A joint venture is a quick and relatively inexpensive way to go global

licensing
The legal process whereby a licensor agrees to let another firm use its manufacturing process, trademarks, patents, trade secrets, or other proprietary knowledge.

contract manufacturing
Private-label manufacturing by a foreign company.

joint venture
When a domestic firm buys part of a foreign company or joins with a foreign company to create a new entity.

Exhibit 4.4   Resources to Aid Companies Interested in Exporting

General Trade Information

The U.S. Department of Commerce (DOC) operates a multitude of programs and services designed for people and companies with interest in conducting business abroad:

- **Trade Information Center Fax Retrieval Hotline** is a 24-hour fax information service. Dial (800) USA-TRADE from your Touch-Tone phone, follow the instructions, and the information you request will be automatically faxed to you.
- **Flash Facts** is another 24-hour DOC fax retrieval service for information on specific countries. Here are some of the main numbers to call:

  Eastern Europe Business Information Center:
  (202) 482-5749
  Offices of the Americas (Mexico, Canada, Latin America, and the Caribbean):
  (800) 872-8723
  Asia Business Center (Southeast Asia, Korea, Vietnam, China, Taiwan, Hong Kong, Australia, and New Zealand):
  (202) 482-3875
  Business Information Service for the Newly Independent (former USSR) States:
  (202) 482-3145
  Uruguay Round of the General Agreement on Tariffs and Trade (GATT):
  (800) USA-TRADE
  Business Information Center for Northern Ireland:
  (202) 501-7488

- **National Trade Data Bank (NTDB)** is a one-stop source for export promotion and international trade data, collected by 17 U.S. government agencies.

  The NTDB is available on CD-ROM and by subscription via fax-on-demand and the Internet as part of STAT-USA (http://www.stat-usa.gov). For information on all of NTDBs services and costs, call (202) 482-1986.

Trade and Project Financing

- **Export–Import Bank of the United States (Eximbank)** facilitates the export of U.S. goods and services by providing loans, guarantees, and insurance coverage. Call (800) 565-3946.
- **Overseas Private Investment Corporation (OPIC)** provides investment services, financing, and political risk insurance in more than 130 developing countries. Call (202) 336-8799.
- **Export Credit Guarantee** program of the Foreign Agriculture Service of the Department of Agriculture offers risk protection for U.S. exporters against nonpayment by foreign banks. Call (202) 720-3224.
- **U.S. Small Business Administration** offers a 24-hour electronic bulletin board with professional marketing services and information on trade shows and other promotions overseas. Call (800) 827-5722.
- **World Trade Centers Association**, with a total membership of 400,000 companies worldwide, provides international trade information, including freight forwarders, customs brokers, and international companies. Call (212) 432-2626.

- **United States Council for International Business** is the official U.S. affiliate of the International Chamber of Commerce. Call (212) 354-4480.

Trade Fairs and Exhibitions

- **Certified Trade Fairs**, endorsed by the U.S. Department of Commerce, provide good opportunities to promote exports. For information, call Trade Fair Certification, (202) 482-1609.
- **Matchmaker Trade Delegations** are DOC-recruited and -planned missions designed to introduce businesses to representatives and distributors overseas. For further information, call (202) 482-3119.
- **Certified Trade Missions Program**, sponsored by the International Trade Administration (ITA), provides a flexible format in which to conduct country-specific business overseas. Call (202) 482-4908.

Government Publications

- **Export Yellow Pages** is a free directory of U.S. manufacturers, banks, service organizations, and export trading companies seeking to do business abroad. Contact your local DOC district office.
- **Eastern Europe Looks for Partners**, published bi-monthly by the Central and Eastern Europe Business Information Center, highlights new markets and business opportunities for U.S. firms. Call (202) 482-2645.
- **Destination Japan: A Business Guide for the 90s**, published by the Japan Export Information Center, is a basic guide to doing business with Japan. Call (703) 487-4650 and ask for stock no. PB94164787.
- **Commercial News USA**, published by the ITA, is a 10-time-yearly catalog–magazine to promote U.S. products and services to overseas markets. It is disseminated to 125,000 business readers via U.S. embassies and consulates in 155 countries. For paid listings and advertising rates, call (202) 482-4918.
- **Business America**, published by the ITA, is a monthly compendium of U.S. trade policies and features a calendar of trade shows, exhibitions, fairs, and seminars. Call (202) 512-1800.

Internet Opportunities

- **Country Information**
  Yahoo Index to Countries and Regions
  http://www.yahoo.com/Regional/Countries
  Internet Business Library
  http://www.bschool.ukans.edu/intbuslib/virtual.htm
  Stat-USA
  http://www.stat-usa.gov
  Worldbank
  http://www.worldbank.org
  World Factbook
  http://www.odci.gov/cia/publications
  Japan Information Network
  http://jin.jcic.or.jp/statistics

- **International Commercial Web Sites**
  Malls of Canada International
  http://www.canadamalls.com

Savoy Brands International

Does Empresas-Polar, owner of Savoy Brands International, use Frito-Lay name on the food products page of its Web site? Visit the English version of the site and explain what you find.

http://www.empresas-polar.com/polar

On Line

Exhibit 4.4   *continued*

MexPlaza
http://mexplaza.udg.mx

Virtual Business Plaza (Czech Republic)
http://www.inet.cz

Asia Manufacturing Online
http://asia-mfg.com

Yello Pages of Israel
http://gauss.technion.ac.il

- **Web Sites Fostering International Commerce**

Koblas Currency Converter
http://bin.gnn.com/cgi-bin/gnn

World Index of Chambers of Commerce & Industry
http://www1.usa1.com

U.S. Small Business Administration
http://www.sbaonline.sba.gov/OIT

Open Market
http://www.openmarket.com

U.S. International Trade Administration
http://www.ita.doc.gov

Trade Point Internet Incubator
http://www.wnicc.org/untpdc/training
http://www.unicc.org/untpdc/eto/abouteto.html

Multilingual International Business Directory
http://m-link.com/menu.html

U.S. Council for International Business
http://www.uscib.org

Russian and East European Studies Business and Economic Resources
http://www.pitt.edu/~cjp/rsecon.html

Berkeley Roundtable on International Economy
http://server.berkeley.edu/BRIE

Pacific Region Forum on Business and Management Communication
gopher://hoshi.cic.sfu.ca/11/dlam/business/forum

- **Successful Global Marketing on the WWW**

Virtual Vineyards
http://www.virtualvin.com

International Sony Music Webs
http://www.sonymusic.be

- **Search Engines**

Infoseek Ultra
http://www.ultra.infoseek.com

Metacrawler
http://www.metacrawler.com

There are also country-specific search engines such as the following:
French: Recherche en français
Italian: Ricerca in italiano
German: Suchen Sie deutschsprachigen Webseiten
Spanish: Buscar en español

SOURCE: U.S. Department of Commerce.

and to gain needed expertise. For example, Robert Mondavi Wineries entered into a joint venture with Baron Philippe de Rothschild, owner of Bordeaux's First Growth chateau, Mouton-Rothschild. They created a wine in California called Opus One. It was immediately established as the American vanguard of quality and price. Mondavi has entered other joint ventures with the Frescobaldi family in Tuscany and with Errazuriz in Chile. "We're doing these wines from around the world because they're going to come here anyway," he said. "The industry is going global, so we're going global, too."[46]

Frito-Lay recently formed a joint venture with Savoy Brands International of South America. The joint venture covers nine countries, including Venezuela, Chile, Peru, Ecuador, and parts of Central America. Unlike soft drink or restaurant companies, Frito-Lay doesn't have franchisees who can help cover expansion costs. Also, Frito-Lay must deal with the agricultural sector to ensure an adequate supply of potatoes and corn. And the company needs critical mass so that its manufacturing plants and distribution vehicles can achieve economies of scale. Teaming up with Savoy gives the U.S. snack giant lower costs, better distribution, and increased clout with retailers. Frito-Lay can also push its global brands, such as Doritos, Cheetos, and Lay's, along with Savoy's brands.[47]

Robert Mondavi wineries has a very agressive joint venture strategy. Opus One is the result of pairing with the premier French vintner Mouton-Rothschild. The new brand has been well received by American wine drinkers and hailed for its high quality.

direct foreign investment
Active ownership of a foreign company or of overseas manufacturing or marketing facilities.

After a three-year struggle to wire Europe on its own, America Online, Inc. entered into a series of joint ventures to build a less expensive system more easily.[48]

Joint ventures can be very risky. Many fail; others fall victim to a takeover, in which one partner buys out the other. In a survey of 150 companies involved in joint ventures that ended, three-quarters were found to have been taken over by Japanese partners. Gary Hamel, a professor at the London Business School, regards joint ventures as a race to learn: The partner that learns fastest comes to dominate the relationship and can then rewrite its terms.[49] Thus, a joint venture becomes a new form of competition.

Sometimes joint venture partners simply can't agree on management strategies and policies. For example, Procter & Gamble and its Vietnamese partner can't agree on what to do next in their unprofitable joint venture. Consumer-products giant P&G wants to inject more cash into the business; but because Phuong Dong Soap & Detergent, its state-owned partner, has said it's unable to provide the cash to match it, P&G has offered to buy out the Vietnamese stake. So far Phuong Dong has flatly refused to sell, and Ministry of Planning and Investment officials have described such an option as "impossible."[50]

In a successful joint venture, both parties gain valuable skills from the alliance. In the General Motors–Suzuki joint venture in Canada, for example, both parties have contributed and gained. The alliance, CAMI Automotive, was formed to manufacture low-end cars for the U.S. market. The plant, run by Suzuki management, produces the Geo Metro/Suzuki Swift—the smallest, highest-gas-mileage GM car sold in North America—as well as the Geo Tracker/Suzuki Sidekick sport utility vehicle. Through CAMI, Suzuki has gained access to GM's dealer network and an expanded market for parts and components. GM avoided the cost of developing low-end cars and obtained models it needed to revitalize the lower end of its product line and its average fuel-economy rating. The CAMI factory may be one of the most productive plants in North America. There GM has learned how Japanese carmakers use work teams, run flexible assembly lines, and manage quality control.

Direct Investment

Active ownership of a foreign company or of overseas manufacturing or marketing facilities is **direct foreign investment**. Direct foreign investment by U.S. manufacturers is currently about $50 billion annually.[51] Direct investors have either a controlling interest or a large minority interest in the firm. Thus, they have the greatest potential reward and the greatest potential risk. FedEx lost $1.2 billion in its attempt to build a hub in Europe. It created a huge infrastructure but couldn't generate the package volume to support it. To control losses, the company fired sixty-six hundred international employees and closed offices in over one hundred European cities. FedEx, however, hasn't given up on expansion. It recently invested $400 million to create an Asian hub.[52] Direct investment can often lead to rapid success. MTV has been in the European market only since 1988, yet since 1994 it has had more viewers in Europe than in the United States.[53]

Sometimes firms make direct investments because they can find no suitable local partners. Also, direct investments avoid the communication problems and conflicts of interest that can arise with joint ventures. Other firms simply don't want to share their technology, which they fear may be stolen or ultimately used against them by creating a new competitor. Texas Instruments (TI) has historically been one of the latter companies. "TI was a technology company that hated to share anything," said Akira Ishikawa, senior vice president of TI's semiconductor group. "It wasn't in the culture to share or teach the most advanced semiconductor technologies. It was taboo. If you talked about that, you might be fired immediately."[54] Now TI has changed its attitude and entered into five Asian joint ventures. The reason was primarily to spread its financial risk.

A firm may make a direct foreign investment by acquiring an interest in an existing company or by building new facilities. It might do so because it has trouble transferring some resource to a foreign operation or getting that resource locally. One important resource is personnel, especially managers. If the local labor market is tight, the firm may buy an entire foreign firm and retain all its employees instead of paying higher salaries than competitors.

The United States is a popular place for direct investment by foreign companies. In 2000, the value of foreign-owned businesses in the United States was more than $450 billion.

The Global Marketing Mix

To succeed, firms seeking to enter into foreign trade must still adhere to the principles of the marketing mix. Information gathered on foreign markets through research is the basis for the four Ps of global marketing strategy: product, place (distribution), promotion, and price. Marketing managers who understand the advantages and disadvantages of different ways to enter the global market and the effect of the external environment on the firm's marketing mix have a better chance of reaching their goals.

List the basic elements involved in developing a global marketing mix

The first step in creating a marketing mix is developing a thorough understanding of the global target market. Often this knowledge can be obtained through the same types of marketing research used in the domestic market (see Chapter 8). However, global marketing research is conducted in vastly different environments. Conducting a survey can be difficult in developing countries, where telephone ownership is rare and mail delivery slow or sporadic. Drawing samples based on known population parameters is often difficult because of the lack of data. In some cities in South America, Mexico, and Asia, street maps are unavailable, streets are unidentified, and houses are unnumbered. Moreover, the questions a marketer can ask may differ in other cultures. In some cultures, people tend to be more private than in the United States and do not like to respond to personal questions on surveys. For instance, in France, questions about one's age and income are considered especially rude.

Product and Promotion
With the proper information, a good marketing mix can be developed. One important decision is whether to alter the product or the promotion for the global marketplace. Other options are to radically change the product or to adjust either the promotional message or the product to suit local conditions.

One Product, One Message The strategy of global marketing standardization, which was discussed earlier, means developing a single product for all markets and promoting it the same way all over the world. For instance, Procter & Gamble uses the same product and promotional themes for Head and Shoulders in China as it does in the United States. The advertising draws attention to a person's dandruff problem, which stands out in a nation of black-haired people. Head and Shoulders is now the best-selling shampoo in China despite costing over 300 percent more than local brands. Buoyed by its success with Head and Shoulders, Procter & Gamble is using the same product and same promotion strategy with Tide detergent in China. It also used another common promotion tactic that it has found to be successful in the United States. The company spent half a million dollars to reach agreements with local washing machine manufacturers, which now include a free box of Tide with every new washer.

Metabolife International has devised five herbal medicine products for both the Chinese and American markets. Both markets have a huge demand for herbal products, but their vastly different concepts of medicine have stymied companies that want to unlock both markets with one product. Until now, most dietary-supplement companies in the United States have hawked just one Chinese herb at a time. In China, however, herbs are almost always mixed together in formulas that are sold in a dizzying number of combinations depending on specific symptoms. A typical Chinese pharmacy, for example, offers dozens of herbal cold formulas depending on symptoms.

Metabolife selected five ailments—the common cold, arthritis, headache, premenstrual syndrome, and upset stomach—and asked a team of Chinese doctors to come up with one formula for each. Next, Metabolife researchers analyze the formulas, identify the active ingredients, and put them in pill form. The result is a form of Chinese medicine called Chinac, which offers U.S. consumers a mixture of herbs similar to that found in medicine sold in China but without the variety found in a Chinese pharmacy. For example, the cold pill, called Immune Health Formula, is a mix of herbs aimed at relieving a typical winter flu.

But Metabolife figures Americans and Chinese are becoming more similar in their approach to herbal medicine. For Americans, Chinac offers a quick and easy entrée into what is for most consumers an unfamiliar field of medicine. For Chinese consumers, Metabolife may offer a welcome change to the confusing choices they face in a Chinese pharmacy.[55]

Global media—especially satellite and cable TV networks like Cable News Network International, MTV Networks, and British Sky Broadcasting—make it possible to beam advertising to audiences unreachable a few years ago. "Eighteen-year-olds in Paris have more in common with eighteen-year-olds in New York than with their own parents," says William Roedy, director of MTV Europe. Almost all of MTV's advertisers run unified, English-language campaigns in the twenty-eight nations the firm reaches. The audiences "buy the same products, go to the same movies, listen to the same music, sip the same colas. Global advertising merely works on that premise."[56] Although teens throughout the world prefer movies above all other forms of television programming, they are closely followed by music videos, stand-up comedy, and then sports.

Both Nike and Reebok spend over $100 million a year in promotion outside the United States. Each company practices global marketing standardization to keep its messages clear and its products desirable. Both companies have ex-

Mattel, Scrabble
Hasbro, Monopoly
Visit Mattel's Scrabble site and Hasbro's Monopoly site.
Which game has more of an international presence on
the Internet? Does this surprise you? Why?
http://www.mattelscrabble.com
http://www.monopoly.com

On Line

ploited basketball's surging popularity around the world. Nike sends Charles Barkley to Europe and Asia touting its products. Reebok counters by sending basketball superstar Shaquille O'Neal overseas as its ambassador. One of the main appeals of sneakers is their American style; therefore, the more American an advertising commercial, the better it is. The tag lines—whether in Italy, Germany, Japan, or France—all read the same way in English: "Just do it" and "Planet Reebok."

Even a one-product, one-message strategy may call for some changes to suit local needs, such as variations in the product's measurement units, package sizes, and labeling. Pillsbury, for example, changed the measurement unit for its cake mixes because adding "cups of" has no meaning in many developing countries. Also, in developing countries, packages are often smaller so that consumers with limited incomes can buy them. For instance, cigarettes, chewing gum, and razor blades may be sold individually instead of in packages.

Unchanged products may fail simply because of cultural factors. The game *Trivial Pursuit* failed in Japan. It seems that getting the answers wrong can be seen as a loss of face. Any type of war game tends to do very poorly in Germany, despite the fact that Germany is by far the world's biggest game-playing nation. A successful game in Germany has plenty of details and thick rulebooks. *Monopoly* remains the world's favorite board game; it seems to overcome all cultural barriers. The game is available in twenty-five languages, including Russian, Croatian, and Hebrew.[59]

A "one product, one message" strategy does not work for all products. Parker Brothers' Monopoly, however, uses this strategy very successfully. A French Riviera version of the popular game debuted at the 2000 Cannes film festival. Depicted here is the Russian gameboard.

Product Invention   In the context of global marketing, product invention can be taken to mean either creating a new product for a market or drastically changing an existing product. For the Japanese market, Nabisco had to remove the cream filling from its Oreo cookies because Japanese children thought they were too sweet. Ford thinks it can save billions on its product development costs by developing a single small-car chassis and then altering its styling to suit different countries. Campbell Soup invented a watercress and duck gizzard soup that is now selling well in China. It is also considering a cream of snake soup. Frito-Lay's most popular potato chip in Thailand is shrimp flavored. Dormont Manufacturing Company makes a simple gas hose that hooks up to deep-fat fryers and similar appliances. Sounds like something that could be sold globally, right? Wrong—in Europe differing national standards means that a different hose is required for each country.[57] Minutiae such as the color of the plastic coating or how the end pieces should be attached to the rest of the hose and the couplings themselves create a myriad of design problems for Dormont Manufacturing.

Rather than creating a new product, Coca-Cola simply bought a small but growing soft drink company in India. Now its acquisition, Thums Up cola, outsells Coke by a four-to-one margin in most Indian markets. Donald Short, chief executive at Coca-Cola in India, says in Bombay his business card needs to read CEO of the Thums Up Company, not CEO of Coca-Cola.[58]

Consumers in different countries use products differently. For example, in many countries, clothing is worn much longer between washings than in the United States, so a more durable fabric must be produced and marketed. For Peru, Goodyear developed a tire that contains a higher percentage of natural rubber and has better treads than tires manufactured elsewhere in order to handle the tough Peruvian driving conditions. Rubbermaid has sold millions of open-top wastebaskets in America; Europeans, picky about garbage peeking out of bins, wanted bins with tight lids that snap into place.

Product Adaptation Another alternative for global marketers is to slightly alter a basic product to meet local conditions. Additional pizza toppings offered by Domino's in Japan include corn, curry, squid, and spinach. Japanese housewives couldn't fit American-size bottles of Joy dish soap on their shelves. Procter & Gamble changed the bottle to a compact cylinder that took less space. In areas of France, McDonalds serves duck breast and foie gras instead of beef in the Big Mac. In the Agen region of France the burgers are topped with Roquefort cheese.[59] When Lewis Woolf Griptight, a British manufacturer of infant accessories such as pacifiers, came to the United States, it found subtle differences between United Kingdom and American parents. Elizabeth Lee, marketing manager, noted, "There are subtle differences, but many problems are the same. Whether a cup spills in America or in Madagascar or in the U.K., moms aren't going to like it," she said. "We didn't need to redo all the research to find out that people didn't want cups that spill, but we still had to do research on things like color and packaging."[60] The brand name "Kiddiwinks" is a British word for pacifiers. In the United States, the name was changed to "Binky" because of positive parental reactions in marketing research tests.

Message Adaptation Another global marketing strategy is to maintain the same basic product but alter the promotional strategy. Bicycles are mainly pleasure vehicles in the United States. In many parts of the world, however, they are a family's main mode of transportation. Thus, promotion in these countries should stress durability and efficiency. In contrast, U.S. advertising may emphasize escaping and having fun.

Harley-Davidson decided that its American promotion theme, "One steady constant in an increasingly screwed-up world," wouldn't appeal to the Japanese market. The Japanese ads combine American images with traditional Japanese ones: American riders passing a geisha in a rickshaw, Japanese ponies nibbling at a Harley motorcycle. Waiting lists for Harleys in Japan are now six months long.

In a new effort to increase its international presence, Anheuser-Busch Companies is targeting the fast-growing markets of Argentina, Brazil, and Chile. But breaking with its promotion strategy at home, the brewer is positioning Bud as a trendy drink for affluent youth, peppering the hottest night clubs and bars with giant banners, neon signs, and other promotions. The result: Some rivals jokingly refer to Bud as a North-of-the-Border Corona. The company is handing out red neon signs to upscale discos and restaurants. They're also dispatching young women in tight Bud minidresses to offer free beer at the beach. And they're plastering cities with signs trumpeting Bud as "the most popular beer in the world."

Global marketers find that promotion is a daunting task in some countries. For example, commercial television time is readily available in Canada but severely restricted in Germany. Until recently, marketers in Indonesia had only one subscription TV channel with few viewers (120,000 out of a nation of 180 million people). Because of this limited television audience, several marketers, such as the country's main Toyota dealer, had to develop direct-mail campaigns to reach their target markets.

In America, Optiva Corporation, makers of electric toothbrushes and other dental products, found that the professional dental community would pass along the word about the quality of its products to consumers. European dentists proved to be much less cooperative, necessitating more money being spent on promotion.[61]

Some cultures view a product as having less value if it has to be advertised. In other nations, claims that seem exaggerated by U.S. standards are commonplace. On the other hand, Germany does not permit advertisers to state that their products are "best" or "better" than those of competitors, a description commonly used in U.S. advertising. The hard-sell tactics and sexual themes so common in U.S. advertising are taboo in many countries. Procter & Gamble's advertisements for Cheer detergents were voted least popular in Japan because they used hard-sell testimonials. The negative reaction forced P&G to withdraw Cheer from the Japanese market. In the Middle East, pictures of women in print advertisements have been covered with censor's ink.

Language barriers, translation problems, and cultural differences have generated numerous headaches for international marketing managers. Consider these examples:

- A toothpaste claiming to give users white teeth was especially inappropriate in many areas of Southeast Asia, where the well-to-do chew betel nuts and black teeth are a sign of higher social status.
- Procter & Gamble's Japanese advertising for Camay soap nearly devastated the product. In one commercial, a man meeting a woman for the first time immediately compared her skin to that of a fine porcelain doll. Although the ad had worked in other Asian countries, the man came across as rude and disrespectful in Japan.

Pricing

Once marketing managers have determined a global product and promotion strategy, they can select the remainder of the marketing mix. Pricing presents some unique problems in the global sphere. Exporters must not only cover their production costs but also consider transportation costs, insurance, taxes, and tariffs. When deciding on a final price, marketers must also determine what customers are willing to spend on a particular product. Marketers also need to ensure that their foreign buyers will pay them. Because developing nations lack mass purchasing power, selling to them often poses special pricing problems. Sometimes a product can be simplified in order to lower the price. However, the firm must not assume that low-income countries are willing to accept lower quality. Although the nomads of the Sahara are very poor, they still buy expensive fabrics to make their clothing. Their survival in harsh conditions and extreme temperatures requires this expense. Additionally, certain expensive luxury items can be sold almost anywhere.

Companies must also be careful not to be so enthusiastic about entering a market that they use poor pricing strategies. Sales of Compaq computers have been growing very rapidly in China, but partially because the company has been giving away computers against its will. Recently, a Chinese distributor failed to repay $32 million for computers that Compaq had extended on credit. Analysts say

Compaq is now owed over $100 million by delinquent dealers and distributors in China. Wal-Mart is determined to make significant inroads into Germany but, to date, is losing about $150 million per year. This is primarily due to Wal-Mart's pledge to drop prices 10 percent on 10,000 items in the Asda retail chain, which it purchased.

Dumping   **Dumping** is generally considered to be the sale of an exported product at a price lower than that charged for the same or a like product in the "home" market of the exporter. This practice is thought of as a form of price discrimination that can potentially harm the importing nation's competing industries. Dumping may occur as a result of exporter business strategies that include (1) trying to increase an overseas market share, (2) temporarily distributing products in overseas markets to offset slack demand in the home market, (3) lowering unit costs by exploiting large-scale production, and (4) attempting to maintain stable prices during periods of exchange rate fluctuations.

Historically, the dumping of goods has presented serious problems in international trade. As a result, dumping has led to significant disagreements among countries and diverse views about its harmfulness. Some trade economists view dumping as harmful only when it involves the use of "predatory" practices that intentionally try to eliminate competition and gain monopoly power in a market. They believe that predatory dumping rarely occurs and that antidumping enforcement is a protectionist tool whose cost to consumers and import-using industries exceeds the benefits to the industries receiving protection.

The Uruguay Round rewrites the international law on dumping. The agreement states:

1. Dumping disputes will be resolved by the World Trade Organization.
2. Dumping terms are specifically defined. For example, the "dumped price" must be at least 5 percent below the home market price before it is considered dumping.
3. At least 25 percent of the members of an industry must support its government filing a dumping complaint with the World Trade Organization. In other words, a government can't file a complaint if only one or two firms complain (unless they make up 25 percent of the industry).

Countertrade   Global trade does not always involve cash. Countertrade is a fast-growing way to conduct global business. In **countertrade**, all or part of the payment for goods or services is in the form of other goods or services. Countertrade is thus a form of barter (swapping goods for goods), an age-old practice whose origins have been traced back to cave dwellers. The U.S. Department of Commerce says that roughly 30 percent of all global trade is countertrade.[62] In fact, both India and China have made billion-dollar government purchasing lists, with most of the goods to be paid for by countertrade.

One common type of countertrade is straight barter. For example, PepsiCo sends Pepsi syrup to Russian bottling plants and in payment gets Stolichnaya vodka, which is then marketed in the West. Another form of countertrade is the compensation agreement. Typically, a company provides technology and equipment for a plant in a developing nation and agrees to take full or partial payment in goods produced by that plant. For example, General Tire Company supplied equipment and know-how for a Romanian truck tire plant. In turn, General Tire sold the tires it received from the plant in the United States under the Victoria brand name. Pierre Cardin gives technical advice to China in exchange for silk and cashmere. In these cases, both sides benefit even though they don't use cash.

Atwood Richards is the world's largest company specializing in countertrade. When companies turn over unsold products to Atwood, they receive trade credits. The credits can be used to obtain other products and services Atwood has acquired—

everything from hotel rooms and airline tickets to television advertising time, forklift trucks, carpeting, pulp, envelopes, steel castings, or satellite tracking systems.[63]

Distribution

Solving promotional, price, and product problems does not guarantee global marketing success. The product still has to get adequate distribution. For example, Europeans don't play sports as much as Americans do, so they don't visit sporting-goods stores as often. Realizing this, Reebok started selling its shoes in about eight hundred traditional shoe stores in France. In one year, the company doubled its French sales. Harley-Davidson had to open two company-owned stores in Japan to get distribution for its Harley clothing and clothing accessories.

The Japanese distribution system is considered the most complicated in the world. Imported goods wind their way through layers of agents, wholesalers, and retailers. For example, a bottle of ninety-six aspirins costs about $20 because the bottle passes through at least six wholesalers, each of whom increases the selling price. The result is that the Japanese consumer pays the world's most exorbitant prices. These distribution channels seem to be based on historical and traditional patterns of socially arranged trade-offs, which Japanese officials claim are very hard for the government to change. Today, however, the system seems to be changing because of pressure from the Japanese consumer. Japanese shoppers are now placing low prices ahead of quality in their purchasing decisions. The retailer who can cut distribution costs and therefore the retail price gets the sale. For example, Kojima, a Japanese electronics superstore chain like the U.S. chains Circuit City or Best Buy, had to bypass GE's Japanese distribution partner Toshiba to import its merchandise at a good price. Toshiba's distribution system required refrigerators to pass through too many hands before they reached the retailer. Kojima went directly to GE headquarters in the U.S. and persuaded the company to sell it refrigerators, which were then shipped directly to Kojima. It is now selling GE refrigerators for about $800, which is half the price of a typical Japanese model.

Retail institutions in other countries also may differ from what a company is used to in its domestic market. The terms *department store* and *supermarket* may refer to types of retail outlets that are very different from those found in the United States. Japanese supermarkets, for example, are large multistory buildings that sell not only food but also clothing, furniture, and home appliances. Department stores are even larger outlets, but unlike their U.S. counterparts, they emphasize foodstuffs and operate a restaurant on the premises. For a variety of reasons, U.S.-type retail outlets do not exist or are impractical in developing countries. For instance, consumers may not have the storage space to keep food for several days. Refrigerators, when available, are usually small and do not allow for bulk storage. Attempting to build new retail outlets can be a frustrating battle. In Germany's Ruhr Valley, the discounter All Kauf SB-Warenhaus GmbH has struggled to build a store for fifteen years on land that it owns. Local authorities are blocking construction, however, because they are afraid the store will hurt local retailers.[64]

Europe's freight-rail system is a throwback to another era. No two countries use the same signaling systems or electric current for their trains. Trains in France and Britain run on the left side of dual-track lines, while those in the rest of Europe run on the right. Because France and Spain use two different gauges of track, trains crossing their shared border must stop to let each car be lifted so that its wheels can be changed.[65]

A freight train going from Denmark to France takes twenty-one hours. When it crosses the border into Germany it must change locomotives and drivers. That's because Denmark and Germany use different voltages for electric locomotives and different signaling systems. During the journey it changes drivers and engines several more times. It is also sidetracked to let high-speed passenger trains pass.

Channels of distribution and the physical infrastructure are also inadequate in many developing nations. In China, for example, most goods are carried on poles

Ethics in Marketing

SHOULD NESTLÉ WATER BE SOLD TO THE WORLD'S POOR?

Brushing away flies and fanning herself in the stifling heat, Rukhsana Akhtar sits in a grimy health clinic in Lahore, Pakistan, worrying about how to find clean water for her four children. "We're always sick because the water is so terrible," complains Mrs. Akhtar, a telephone operator who earns just 1,500 rupees ($29) a month. Like many residents, she says the search for safe water is a daily struggle, because the water supply is sporadic and contaminated with sewage. So she scrapes together enough money to buy Nestlé Pure Life, at 18 rupees a bottle. "It's expensive, but the kids need it when they're sick," she explains.

For Nestlé SA, the world's largest food company, consumers like Mrs. Akhtar are fast becoming part of a vast and potentially lucrative new market. Already the global leader in bottled water, with designer labels like Perrier and San Pellegrino, the Swiss food giant is launching Pure Life as an affordable global water brand aimed specifi-

cally at the poor and thirsty in the developing world.

A populist Perrier? Sort of. Along with leveraging its famous name—Pure Life is the first water with the Nestlé name—the company is spending $100 million over a three-year period to roll out Pure Life in as many as twenty countries, hoping to increase volume to one billion liters by 2002.

Peter Brabeck, Nestlé's chief executive, says Pure Life isn't intended to be "a solution" to the world's water problems. He says the idea sprang partly from his experience living in Latin America where "the water tasted terrible." "I said, 'Why not create a product that fulfills basic needs like taste, safety, and high mineral content, but which is made locally to reduce costs?'" he recalls.

Pure Life is hawked at street corners in traffic-clogged Lahore. Middle-class shoppers buy it by the case in supermarkets. On the remote mountain road leading from Islamabad to the hill town of

Murree, Pure Life billboards urge drivers to "drink only Nestlé Pure Life." At small stores along the way, a flurry of banners proclaims: "Pure Safety, Pure Trust. The ideal water. From Nestlé with love."

Pure Life won't reach everyone in Pakistan, where the per capita annual income is roughly $495. "The fact that everybody can't afford Pure Life is unfortunate, but does that mean we shouldn't sell it at all?" asks Hans-Dieter Karlscheuer, director of Paris-based Perrier-Vittel SA, Nestlé's water division. "We can't change the world. We can only try to improve it a little."[a]

Is Nestlé doing a service to people in developing nations? Do you agree with M. Karlscheuer's statement? Why or why not? Is Nestlé simply filling a need in the marketplace? What about simply boiling the water?

[a] Ernest Beck, "Populist Perrier? Nestlé Pitches Bottled Water to World's Poor," *Wall Street Journal*, June 18, 1999, pp. B1, B4.

or human backs, in wheelbarrows and handcarts, or, increasingly (and this is an important advance), on bicycles. Procter & Gamble has resorted to taking traffic maps of the 228 Chinese cities with at least 200,000 citizens and marking them up with locations of small mom-and-pop shops and the big department stores. Divisions of its "ground troops," often wearing white sports shirts with "Winning Team" written on the back, "blitz" each locale and sell and distribute P&G products. Even street-stall owners get a personal pitch.

Sometimes questions are raised about whether a product should be marketed at all in certain countries. Consider the Nestlé story in the "Ethics in Marketing" box.

The Impact of the Internet

6

Discover how the Internet is affecting global marketing

In many respects "going global" is easier than it has ever been before. Opening an e-commerce site on the Internet immediately puts a company in the international marketplace. Sophisticated language translation software can make any site accessible to persons around the world. Global shippers such as UPS, FedEx, and DHL help solve international e-commerce distribution complexities.

The promise of "borderless commerce" and the new "Internet economy" are still being restrained by the old brick-and-mortar rules, regulations, and habits. For example, Americans spend an average of $6,500 per year by credit card whereas Japanese spend less than $2,000. Many Japanese don't even have a credit card. So how does one pay for e-commerce purchases? Seven-Eleven Japan, with over 8,000 convenience stores, has come to the rescue. eS-Books, the Japanese Web site partner of Yahoo! Japan, lets shoppers buy books and videos on the Internet, then specify to which Seven-Eleven the merchandise is to be shipped. The buyer goes to that specific store and pays cash for the e-purchase.[66]

In Germany it is typically cheaper to buy books from Amazon.com in the United Kingdom rather than the local site. Why? Germany, France, and several other European states allow publishing cartels through which groups of book publishers can legally dictate retail prices to booksellers—both on-line and on the ground. *Galileo's Daughter,* a biography by Dava Sobel, for example, sells at the list price of 50.24 marks ($26.99) on Germany's Amazon.de; at Amazon.co.uk, it costs 40 percent less.[67]

The e-commerce site for the American clothing retailer Lands' End in Germany is not allowed to mention its unconditional refund policy because German retailers, which normally do not allow returns after fourteen days, sued and won a court ruling blocking mention of it.

Scandinavians, like the Japanese, are reluctant to use credit cards, the currency of the Internet, and the French have an *horreur* of revealing the private information that Net retailers ask for. French Web sites tend to be decidedly French. For example, FNAC, the largest French video, books, and music retailer, offers a daily "cultural newspaper" at its site.[68]

Europeans have shown themselves interested in saving money through Internet shopping, however. One of the hottest e-commerce sites in Europe, *Letsbuyit.com* in Sweden, is about nothing but bargains.

Buying a piece of steel from a foreign country, or selling a piece of steel abroad, has never been easy. Trade laws, taxes, tariffs, quotas, and the regulations of two governments have to be taken into account. The Internet was supposed to make it easier. Industry observers predicted that MetalSite Inc. and e-Steel Corp., two of the biggest and earliest Internet supply networks, would each create a one-world exchange. After concluding that trade regulations are too complicated to unravel, steel exchanges are backing away from the one-world tax and regulation free concept.

Many businesses in the United States are fighting for a tax-free Internet, while states wrestle with the fact that millions in taxes would be forfeited. If quotas are to be followed, how will steel that is bought and sold many times over the Internet between several countries be tracked to the originating country? Steel slabs can be made in Asia, processed somewhere in Europe, and then sold to Latin America or the United States.

Both MetalSite and e-Steel leave the critical trade-related details to individual buyers and sellers. For instance, once a seller and buyer meet on one of the sites, they have to go off-line and conduct their transaction via phone or fax or in person. At this point, some steel Internet portals do allow companies from every country to see what is available worldwide, and at what price, with just a few clicks of a mouse. And that's at least a giant step toward creating a global steel market.[69]

The Internet is accelerating the breaking down of global commerce barriers. Letsbuyit.com of Sweden is one of the hottest Web sites in Europe. Pages are available in Swedish, French, English, German, Spanish, Finnish, Danish, and Norwegian.

Looking Back

Look back at the story about Wal-Mart in South America. Besides cultural factors, other uncontrollable variables in the global external environment include economic and technological, political, and demographic variables as well as natural resources.

Most products cannot be marketed exactly the same way all over the world. Different cultures, languages, levels of economic development, and distribution channels in global markets usually require either new products or modified products. Pricing, promotion, and distribution strategies must often be altered as well. There is no doubt that international markets will become even more important in the future.

Use it Now!

Study the Role of a Global Manager

As business becomes more global, chances are that you may become a global manager. Start learning right now what this means and if it's right for you. The life of a global manager can be hectic, as these examples illustrate:

As president of DoubleClick International, a unit of the New York Internet advertising company, Barry Salzman spends about 75 percent of his time traveling. He takes a laptop and four battery packs so he can wade through the 200 e-mail messages he averages daily. Welcome to the world of global management. It's a punishing pace, but it's the only way Mr. Salzman knows how to manage his network of thirteen offices worldwide.

Global managers spend proportionately more of their energy combating the sense of isolation that tends to gnaw at employees in remote offices. Mr. Salzman conducts a conference call every Monday morning for international managers in Canada, Europe, and Asia. Only those who are flying somewhere are excused. "We try to maintain voice contact," he says. "We lose that with computers and e-mail."

Top overseas performers at Secure Computing, a San Jose, California, software developer, are treated to a dinner for two by Christine Hughes, senior vice president of marketing and business development. Ms. Hughes supervises a twenty-four-person staff in North and South America and Asia. One of her missions on trips is to combat the tendency of foreign-based employees to think the organization is "U.S.-centric," she says. Because they take much longer flights than the typical corporate road warrior, global managers wind up turning airplanes into offices. When she is overseas, Ms. Hughes has her office ship her a package of paperwork overnight, so she can work on the flight home. Mr. Salzman considers flight time some of his most productive; he uses it to answer e-mail and review contracts.

Indeed, a global manager's workday never really ends. Wherever they are, it's still business hours somewhere else. When she's working in Australia, Ms. Hughes usually ends her day in a hotel room, talking with someone at the home office. "I'm on the phone until two in the morning dealing with issues," she says. "You just have to accept that."[70]

One way to see if you might be cut out to be a global manager is to spend some time abroad. The ideal situation is to find a job overseas during the summer months. This experience will help you decide if you want to be a global manager. Also, it will look good on your resume. One source of international jobs information is **http://www. internationaljobs.org/.**

If you can't find a job overseas, save your money and travel abroad. Seeing how others live and work will broaden your horizons and give you a more enlightened view of the world. Even international travel can help you decide what you want to do in the global marketplace.

Changing Money Abroad

If you travel, work, or study abroad, you are going to need to change U.S. dollars into foreign currency. Making mistakes when changing money can cost you 10 to 20 percent of your bankroll. Here are a few tips about changing money abroad.

1. Know the exchange rate between U.S. dollars and the currencies of the countries you plan to visit before you go. Go to **http://www.cnntn.com/markets/currencies** for the latest quotations. Keep up with the changing rates by reading *USA Today International* or the *International Herald Tribune* every day.
2. Avoid changing money at airports, train stations, and hotels. These places usually have the worst rates. Ask local people where they change money. Locals know where the best rates are.
3. Try to bargain with the clerk. Sometimes you can do better than the posted rate simply by asking.
4. Rather than making several small transactions, make one large exchange. This will often get you a better rate.
5. Don't change more than you will need. You'll pay another fee to change the foreign currency back to U.S. dollars.
6. Use a credit card. Typically, any major credit card will give you a better rate than a change booth or bank. Sometimes the spread is substantial, so minimize cash and use credit.
7. Traveler's checks usually have a worse exchange rate than cash. In other words, a $100 American Express traveler's check will give you less in exchange than a $100 bill. If your traveler's checks are lost or stolen, however, they will be replaced, so the peace of mind is usually worth the added expense.

Summary

① **Discuss the importance of global marketing.** Businesspeople who adopt a global vision are better able to identify global marketing opportunities, understand the nature of global networks, and engage foreign competition in domestic markets.

② **Discuss the impact of multinational firms on the world economy.** Multinational corporations are international traders that regularly operate across national borders. Because of their vast size and financial, technological, and material resources, multinational corporations have a great influence on the world economy. They have the ability to overcome trade problems, save on labor costs, and tap new technology.

③ **Describe the external environment facing global marketers.** Global marketers face the same environmental factors as they do domestically: culture, economic and technological development, political structure and actions, demography, and natural resources. Cultural considerations include societal values, attitudes and beliefs, language, and customary business practices. A country's economic and technological status depends on its stage of industrial development: traditional society, preindustrial society, takeoff economy, industrializing society, or fully industrialized society. The political structure is shaped by political ideology and such policies as tariffs, quotas, boycotts, exchange controls, trade agreements, and market groupings. Demographic variables include population, income distribution, and growth rate.

④ **Identify the various ways of entering the global marketplace.** Firms use the following strategies to enter global markets, in descending order of risk and profit: direct investment, joint venture, contract manufacturing, licensing, and export.

⑤ **List the basic elements involved in developing a global marketing mix.** A firm's major consideration is how much it will adjust the four Ps—product, promotion, place (distribution), and price—within each country. One strategy is to use one product and one promotion message worldwide. A second strategy is to create new products for global markets. A third strategy is to keep the product basically the same but alter the promotional message. A fourth strategy is to slightly alter the product to meet local conditions.

Key Terms

6 **Discover how the Internet is affecting global marketing.** Simply opening a Web site can open the door for international sales. International carriers, like UPS, can help solve logistics problems. Language translation software can help an e-commerce business become multilingual. Yet cultural differences and old-line rules, regulations, and taxes hinder rapid development of e-commerce in many countries.

Discussion and Writing Questions

1. Many marketers now believe that teenagers in the developed countries are becoming "global consumers." That is, they all want and buy the same goods and services. Do you think this is true? If so, what has caused the phenomenon?

2. The sale of cigarettes in many developed countries either has peaked out or is declining. However, the developing markets represent major growth markets. Should U.S. tobacco companies capitalize on this opportunity?

3. Renault and Peugeot dominate the French market but have no presence in the U.S. market. Why do you think that this is true?

4. Candartel, an upscale manufacturer of lamps and lampshades in America, has decided to "go global." Top management is having trouble deciding how to develop the market. What are some market entry options for the firm?

5. Rubbermaid, the U.S. manufacturer of kitchen products and other household items, is considering moving to global marketing standardization. What are the pros and cons of this strategy?

6. **WRITING** Suppose you are marketing manager for a consumer products firm that is about to undertake its first expansion abroad. Write a memo for your staff reminding them of the role culture will play in the new venture. Give examples.

7. What is meant by "having a global vision"? Why is it important?

8. **WRITING** Suppose your state senator has asked you to contribute a brief article to her constituents' newsletter that answers the question, "Will there ever be a 'United States of Europe'?" Write a draft of your article, and include reasons why or why not.

9. **TEAM** Divide into six teams. Each team will be responsible for one of the following industries: entertainment; pharmaceuticals; computers and software; financial, legal, or accounting services; agriculture; and textiles and apparel. Interview one or more executives in each of these industries to determine how the Uruguay Round and NAFTA have affected and will affect their organizations. If a local firm cannot be contacted in your industry, use the library and the Internet to prepare your report.

10. What are the major barriers to international trade? Explain how government policies may be used to either restrict or stimulate global marketing.

11. Explain the impact of the Uruguay Round.

12. Describe how "going global" via the Internet presents opportunities and challenges.

13. **ON LINE** How does the Web site called "The Paris Pages" (**http://www.paris. org**) handle language and translation issues?

14. **ON LINE** What locations does ProNet (**http://www.pronett.com**) serve? Obtain information about at least one arts-and-entertainment venture for three different regions. How does ProNet handle language and translation issues?

15. **ON LINE** What services does the Netzmarkt cyber-mall (**http://www.netzmarkt. de/neu/hinweise.htm**) offer American businesses interested in marketing to Germans?

Application for Entrepreneurs

Larry and Laurie Walther own a shop in Taos, New Mexico, that sells fine rugs crafted by Native Americans. They have expanded their business beyond Taos via direct mail. In fact, they have discovered a growing market in the United Kingdom. It seems that Europeans, particularly the English, French, and Germans, have an ongoing love affair with the Native American culture. Larry and Laurie are now considering a direct mail campaign to Germany. The typical American receives about 350 direct mail pieces per year, whereas a German household gets fewer than seventy. Also, Germany has 40 percent more people than the United Kingdom.

Yet, marketing to Germans by direct mail is different. Most buyers don't use credit cards when purchasing by mail. One German law dictates the size of free samples that can be distributed; another says that advertising mail cannot be camouflaged as a personal letter. Privacy laws restrict the preparation of finely targeted U.S.-style mailing lists. Mail carriers have to obey "no advertising" stickers that many Germans affix to their mailboxes.

Questions

1. Should Larry and Laurie attempt to enter the German market? Why or why not?
2. What can be done to overcome the credit card problem?

Case
entrepreneurship

Lycos: The World's Gateway to the Internet

What started as a stand-alone site with just one URL, Lycos.com, has now blossomed into a vast array of sights with complementary functionalities, goods, information, and services. The Lycos Network, which first earned its name from the group of sites Lycos acquired and partnered with in the United States, now refers to a vast collection of interrelated Web sites and Web ventures formed with prestigious partners from around the world. Lycos understands that Web-based businesses open their doors to customers from any culture, from any country, at any time, and so the company has pursued global marketing tactics to reach customers in every corner of the world. The key has been building partnerships and joint ventures with companies from overseas. Working with Bertelsmann AG in Germany to handle all European properties, Sumitomo Corporation in Japan, Mirae Corporation in Korea to provide to the rest of Asia, and Bell Canada, Lycos has assertively and strategically penetrated international markets and developed a global vision for its Internet services.

Despite its global network of joint ventures, Lycos has avoided a crippling mistake that has felled many other Internet firms: allowing each venture partner to

specify content and user interfaces unique to the country or region in which it operates. This practice could disrupt a user's experience with the portal or confuse site visitors who had seen or experienced different Lycos branding at other Lycos sites. Users probably would lose trust in Lycos's ability to provide a consistent mix of design, usability, culturally relevant content, service, and functionality. Mixed messages could ultimately alienate users from different cultures and countries. To prevent this from happening, Lycos's headquarters in Waltham, Massachusetts, has provided its jointly formed satellite operations with templates and guidelines for Web design so that the branding remains consistent in a global context.

Lycos is aware that the relevance and attractiveness of local content and services are based on the culture (customs, values, education, etc.) and the technological advancement of a given region. This is why the company delegates the responsibility of selecting the appropriate service mix for a given region to the regional office. Each regional headquarters chooses services from the template that are appropriate for the economic and technological development in its region. The marketing and sales offices in the specific countries of the region—such as the one for Europe based in Germany and the one for Asia based in Korea—are charged with local content selection and the translation of content into specific languages. By employing a combination of centralized and decentralized decision making throughout the network, Lycos can keep its branding intact while its marketing strategy and tactics remain highly sensitive to the regional and country-specific tastes and preferences of consumers.

Lycos's German headquarters provides a good example of the company's regional customization strategy. A large number of Europeans depend on wireless Internet applications such as cell phones and wireless Personal Digital Assistants (PDAs) to surf the Net. For this reason the German headquarters opted not to implement Lycos's proprietary e-mail service, MailCity. Instead, it chose to go with a European vendor who has built a short messaging function into its e-mail application. This European technology makes it easy for users of wireless devices to access e-mail via the constrictive screens on their wireless hardware devices. Changing e-mail services has given Lycos deeper penetration into the European market, but this has not been the only benefit. Lycos has gained valuable learning that it can later apply to other markets as the adoption of wireless Internet devices climbs. In a related response to technological and cultural conditions in Europe, Lycos also bundles a free Internet service provider (ISP) with its service package because Europeans generally have easy access to free Internet service. The trade-off for Lycos in bundling the costly service is that the company is likely to acquire more users who will eventually be paying customers of other products and services Lycos has to offer.

Lycos has not, however, put all of its resources into developing partnerships and promoting decentralized decision making in its effort to market globally. To serve the Latin American market, Lycos has hired Latin American talent to run its network of four-teen Latin American sites. With the help of a sophisticated software and consulting package from global marketing specialists at Idiom Inc., Lycos can generate content updates for each country-specific site complete with proper language dialects. The software also tracks language changes over time and ensures timely and relevant content delivery in each country. In short, it makes Lycos more responsive to its market and allows it to more effectively target its content and services to specific markets. A pending merger deal between Lycos and Terra Networks, a Spanish- and Portuguese-language portal and ISP could mean even greater success in Latin America. According to the preliminary terms of the deal, Terra Networks would actually acquire Lycos for $12.5 billion in Terra Network's stock. With combined operations in thirty-seven countries, the merger would give the newly proposed Terra Lycos unprecedented access to Latin American markets and the largest global presence of any Internet company.

Questions

1. Describe the importance of global marketing to Lycos.
2. Identify and explain the entry strategy Lycos has used for entering the global marketplace. Why do you think Lycos has adopted that strategy?
3. How has Lycos standardized its products or services to market effectively on a global scale? What is the benefit of standardizing those products or services?
4. How has Lycos specialized certain products or services in order to better serve markets in different regions of the globe? What is the benefit of customizing those products or services?

Bibliography

Anne Chen and Matt Hicks. "Going Global? Avoid Culture Clashes," *E-commerce Times* (ecommercetimes.com), April 3, 2000.

Anne Chen and Matt Hicks. "Dress for Global Success," *E-commerce Times* (ecommercetimes.com), April 3, 2000.

"Terra to Acquire Lycos for $12.5 Billion in Stock," May 16, 2000. Available in Press Room area of Lycos Web site. **http://www.lycos.com/press**

Case

video

AutoCite: The Ticket to Going Global

"It was a lot easier to sell AutoCite in Australia than in my hometown of Flint, Michigan," says Nick George, Chairman and Chief Financial Officer of Enforcement Technology (ETEC). As one of the pioneers of the hand-held computer industry, ETEC produces AutoCite, a portable, light-weight, hand-held computer used to write parking tickets in a streamlined, user-friendly manner. "American technology is highly respected in other countries, and when you are considered an authority in the field, a leader in parking technology, doors start to open," explains Mr. George.

Because developed countries everywhere have the same parking problems as the United States, they also have the same needs. A multitude of drivers hunting down prime parking places is a familiar scene around the world. ETEC saw this dilemma as a global business opportunity. The company understood that the benefits that appealed to Americans in over 350 agencies in fifty states would also appeal to law enforcement agencies in Australia, New Zealand, Canada, Mexico, and Argentina.

Countries such as Canada and Australia welcomed a product that could do away with ticket books, carbon copies, illegible scribbling, and writer's cramp—the byproducts of the tedious handwritten ticketing process. At the same time, AutoCite promised "payback factors" because the system pays for itself within a year. A city saves money because manually written tickets must be key-punched into data processing equipment and transferred to the main computer. Significant clerical and staff time is then required for shuffling, batching, and tracking citations. Both at home and abroad, the manual process means errors, job dissatisfaction, and unnecessary costs. And mistakes cost money. Foreign buyers saw how automated citations could reduce these errors and fill their city's coffers. They liked the time saved to improved efficiency, which in turn translated into better morale for police and parking departments.

When selling AutoCite in the global marketplace, ETEC relies on two strategies: product standardization and product customization. The hardware for AutoCite is the same everywhere with no modifications—a unique, single-unit construction with a built-in printer for creating parking citations and traffic tickets. There are different models, but they all produce machine-readable characters to issue tickets. Processing parking tickets and collection services are also part and parcel of ETEC's features. Even training is standardized, especially for English-speaking countries like Australia, New Zealand, and Canada.

Rather than design, manufacture, and install hardware and leave the software to somebody else à la Compaq and Microsoft, ETEC produces and maintains both. The company touts its status as a single-source vendor. This gives customers at home and abroad the convenience of one-stop shopping and one company to contact for customer service. Total product support is one of the ETEC's strongest selling points.

This leads to the second part of the global strategy—product customization. AutoCite's software is fully customized to meet each country's needs. For example, in 1994, Australia adopted AutoCite because it had a distinct technological advantage not available in domestic markets. ETEC's engineering division designed and developed a system specifically for the Australian Federal Police, allowing officers to issue traffic tickets, warnings for traffic violations, and parking citations. The codes are different than those used in the United States, and the sequence of information entered into the machine is different (e.g., the Australian AutoCite software prints the ticket number first). In Hispanic countries like Mexico and Argentina, AutoCite is programmed to print the tickets in Spanish.

The adoption of AutoCite by the Australian Federal Police was a world first because ETEC's computers had the capability of performing multiple law enforcement functions. The Australian government was so impressed with this innovation that it awarded its police department the technology and productivity prize. Positive results with the Australian Federal Police pushed ETEC to add more innovations to make its products useful to other Australian and New Zealand agencies, and this has led to increased international sales overall.

Although ETEC and other exporters face currency fluctuations and long-distance transportation issues, George adds quite readily that he spent far less time selling in Canada and other foreign countries than in Michigan. "It was easy to have an appointment with the mayor of Melbourne, Australia, but it took four police chiefs and ten years of effort to write my first order in Flint!"

Questions
1. How does ETEC's product uniqueness and technological advantage help the company do business abroad?
2. Discuss ETEC's global strategies.
3. Harvard professor Ted Levitt sees the emergence of global markets for standardized products as opposed to segmented foreign markets with different products. Do you agree? Explain.
4. What environmental factors might affect ETEC's success abroad?

Bibliography
Press kit for Enforcement Technology.
Telephone interview with Nick George, Chairman and Chief Financial Officer of Enforcement Technology. September 1998.

MARKETING MISCUES

Burger King's International Whopper

International market development is not new to McDonald's and Burger King. These two fast-food pioneers compete head-to-head both nationally and internationally. McDonald's (number one in market share) has continued to stay one step ahead of Burger King (number two market share). Unfortunately for Burger King, the company's international marketing strategy made a "whopper" of a mistake in 1999 when it opened its doors in Ma'ale Adumim, the largest Israeli settlement in the West Bank.

The area, seized by the Israelis in the late 1960s, is at the center of the Middle East conflict. Opening a restaurant in the West Bank was allegedly tantamount to Burger King joining with the Israelis in illegal occupation. As a result, angry Arab and Muslim groups throughout the world threatened a worldwide boycott of Burger King.

Burger King began opening restaurants in Israel in 1993. By 2000, it had forty-six fast food outlets and an Israeli-based supply network. The company also had eighty-four Burger King restaurants in Arab countries.

Country	Number of Restaurants
Kuwait	31
Oman	4
Qatar	3
Saudi Arabia	40
United Arab Emirates	6

The US-based Burger King Corporation, headquartered in Miami, Florida, has over 10,500 outlets in fifty-five countries. Slightly over 90 percent of these fast-food restaurants are owned and operated by independent franchisees. With its largest customer base in the United States, Burger King has begun seeking growth opportunities in Europe, the Middle East, and Africa. A critical mass of customers is clustered in the European markets of Germany, the United Kingdom, and Spain. These markets accounted for around 60 percent of Burger King's European sales in 1999 of $1.3 billion.

One of Burger King's franchisees was blamed for the company's problems in the Middle East. Rikamor Ltd., an independent franchisee in Israel, opened a Burger King food court counter in a new shopping mall in Ma'ale Adumim in early 1999. Ma'ale Adumim is considered to be one of the fastest growing Jewish settlements in the West Bank. Palestinians consider such Jewish settlements to be a key obstacle to peace in the West Bank and Gaza Strip.

In August 1999, Burger King canceled Rikamor's right to operate the site as a Burger King restaurant (which does not mean that the restaurant has to close down, just that the restaurant cannot carry the Burger King name). The company said that Rikamor told Burger King that the food court counter would be in Israel. According to Burger King, the company saw no reason to think otherwise since the two parties had agreed that Rikamor could not open a Burger King in the West Bank until there was a peace accord.

Burger King's international mistake was not so easily resolved, however. Upon cancellation of the use of the Burger King name at the West Bank food counter, Jewish settlers and leaders began calling for an international boycott of all Burger King outlets. Their concern—why should the Arabs and Muslims dictate where they eat?

Questions

1. What major external factors should Burger King (or any multinational corporation) monitor before extending permission to a franchisee to use the company name?
2. What strategies should Burger King implement in attempting to salvage its brand name in the Middle Eastern market as well as to maintain its international market share?
3. How much control should Burger King have over its franchisees to ensure that another Rikamor situation does not develop?

Bibliography

http://www.burgerking.com

"International: A Whopper of a Mistake." *Economist*, September 4, 1999, p. 47.

"Jewish Settlers Call for Boycott of Burger King." *Xinhua News Agency*, August 27, 1999, item number 0827265.

Dana Budeiri. "Burger King Is Now a Mideast Battlefield." *Boston Globe*, August 10, 1999, p. A15.

Carol Casper. "Rapid Change." *Restaurant Business*, February 15, 2000, pp. 62–69.

———. "Uncommon Market." *Restaurant Business*, February 15, 2000, pp. 55–58.

CRITICAL THINKING CASE

Beyond Starbucks: Extending a Brand Name

Starbucks Corporation was facing a major issue: that of ubiquity versus equity. Should the company focus upon growing the business (ubiquity) or growing the brand (equity)? Could the company manage its various growth directions while keeping employees passionate about the brand? With the opening of restaurants, the purchase of a tea company, and the publishing of a cultural literary magazine, was Starbucks at risk of losing sight of its company objective "to establish Starbucks as the most recognized and respected brand in the world?"

The Company

Starbucks began its rapid ascent into consumers' lives with the opening of its first Starbucks Coffee retail shop in Seattle, Washington, in 1971. A mere thirty years later, there are around twenty-five hundred Starbucks locations in thirteen countries. Fueling this rapid growth, Starbucks Coffee International (a wholly owned subsidiary of Starbucks Corporation) opened its first overseas location in Japan in 1996 via a joint venture with Sazaby Inc., a Japanese retailer and restaurateur. Since 1992, the international company has opened stores in Singapore, the Philippines, Taiwan, Thailand, the United Kingdom, New Zealand, Malaysia, China, Kuwait, South Korea, and Lebanon.

Led by Chairman Howard Schultz (who started with Starbucks in 1982 as director of retail operations and marketing), Starbucks thrives on building a rewarding relationship with its customers. The Starbucks brand is delivered by thirty-seven thousand employees to over ten million customers each week, primarily through its company-operated retail stores where the average daily sale is $3.60. Going public in 1992, the company's success is exemplified by its 1999 revenues of $1.7 billion and 1999 profits of over $100 million.

Market Segmentation

Coffee consumption follows a very obvious age segmentation distinction. The typical coffee consumer is over thirty-five years old, with more than three-fourths of the over-thirty-five crowd drinking coffee on a regular basis. This compares with only around one-third of the under-thirty-five group drinking coffee regularly.

A daily habit, coffee is considered to be a morning and/or after-meal drink product. This regimen of coffee drinking flows logically with a benefit segmentation approach to the coffee market. In such instances, the benefit received is tied closely to the caffeine found in coffee. Thus, the market can be segmented by whether or not consumers drink coffee to "wake up" or for the taste enjoyment. As a means to "wake up," coffee consumption becomes a habit, and consumers become accustomed to holding a coffee cup in their hands every morning— to get them going.

Starbucks Retail

The Starbucks brand name has long been associated with its freshly brewed, rich-tasting coffees. This high-quality coffee is sold primarily through company-operated retail stores. Attempting to get its coffee to consumers in various formats, Starbucks introduced a mail-order catalog in 1988. In 1990, the company's specialty sales group began aligning with airline companies to offer Starbucks coffee during flight. In the mid-1990s, Starbucks joined forces with Barnes & Noble and Chapters, a Canadian superstore, and began operating coffee bars within the larger retail establishments. By 2000, Starbucks owned 5 percent of the coffee consumption in America.

Recognizing that many consumers drink coffee for the taste (not just for the caffeine "kick"), Starbucks, in the mid- to late 1990s, began serving low fat, creamy, iced coffee beverages in its retail shops. Quickly following on the heels of this successful product, the company partnered with Pepsi-Cola to begin selling a bottled version of the drink in supermarkets and convenience stores. Starbucks also partnered with Dreyer's Grand Ice Cream to introduce Starbucks coffee-flavored ice cream products in the United States.

Non-Coffee Brand Extensions

In the late 1990s, Starbucks began expanding into non-coffee beverages when it acquired Tazo, an Oregon-based premium tea company. Additionally, the company opened Café Starbucks, a full-service restaurant.

Capitalizing on the company's brand name and an extremely popular in-house music program, Starbucks began selling compact discs in 1995. These compact discs featured such offerings as Chicago blues, rhythm and blues, jazz, and opera. In 1998, the company began offering a Starbucks/Doonesbury line of products (with proceeds directed toward literary nonprofit organizations). Maintaining this connection with the literary world, Starbucks, in partnership with Time Inc., launched *Joe*, a cultural literary magazine in 1999.

In 1998, Starbucks launched its company Web site, www.starbucks.com. It was at this time that Shultz was confronted with the perils of rapid growth and concerns that the company was moving beyond its core competency.

Starbucks on the Net

By late 1999, Starbucks had invested around $4 million on its entry into the Internet world. Starbucks had plans to expand into such product offerings as kitchenware, home furnishings, and gourmet food. The company's grand scheme involved Starbucks becoming a lifestyle portal on the Net.

However, Wall Street was not sold on the idea that Starbucks could extend its brand name so far beyond coffee and related products. The company's share price fell 28 percent in one day, amidst rumors of delayed store openings, lower than expected sales at existing stores, and disappointing supermarket sales of coffee-flavored drink products.

Was Schultz losing his way by not focusing upon the company's core business? Was he attempting to grow the company at the expense of the brand? Should Schultz back away from the Internet expansion?

Questions

1. What is the core business at Starbucks? How did the company build on this core business?
2. What is the risk associated with moving beyond a company's core business?
3. Should Schultz back away from the Internet business? If so, how can he grow the company? If not, how can he extend the Starbucks brand into unrelated offerings while maintaining the company's core business?

Bibliography

http://www.starbucks.com

"Interview with Howard Schultz: Sharing Success." *Executive Excellence,* November 1999, pp. 16–17.

David A. Kaplan. "Trouble Brewing." *Newsweek,* July 19, 1999, pp. 40–41.

Louise Lee. "Now, Starbucks Uses Its Bean." *Business Week,* February 15, 2000, pp. 92–97.

Terry Lefton. "Schultz' Caffeinated Crusade." *Brandweek,* July 5, 1999, pp. 20–25.

David Wellman. "Premium Youth." *Supermarket Business,* November 15, 1999, pp. 48–49.

MARKETING PLANNING ACTIVITIES

The World of Marketing

 In the world of marketing, there are many different types of goods and services offered to many different markets. Throughout this text, you will construct a marketing plan for your chosen company. Writing a marketing plan will give you a full depth of understanding for your company, its customers, and its marketing mix elements. The company you choose should be one that interests you, such as the manufacturer of your favorite product, a local business where you would like to work, or even a business you would like to start yourself to satisfy an unmet need or want. Also refer to Exhibit 2.8 for additional marketing plan subjects.

1. Describe your chosen company. How long has it been in business, or when will it start business? Who are the key players? Is the company small or large? Does it offer a good or service? What are the strengths and weaknesses of this company? What is the orientation and organizational culture?

Marketing*Builder* Exercise

• **Top 20 Questions** template

2. Define the business mission statement for your chosen company (or evaluate and modify an existing mission statement).
3. Set marketing objectives for your chosen company. Make sure the objectives fit the criteria for good objectives.
4. Scan the marketing environment. Identify opportunities and threats to your chosen company in areas such as technology, the economy, the political and legal environment, and competition. Is your competition foreign, domestic, or both? Also identify opportunities and threats based on possible market targets, including social factors, demographic factors, and multicultural issues.

Marketing*Builder* Exercises

• **Industry Analysis** portion of the Market Analysis template
• **Competitive Analysis Matrix** spreadsheet
• **Competition** portion of the **Market Analysis** template
• **Competitive Roundup** portion of the **Market Analysis** template
• **Strengths, Weaknesses, Opportunities,** and **Threats** sections of the **Market Analysis** template

5. Does your chosen business have a differential or competitive advantage? If there is not one, there is no point in marketing the product. Can you create a sustainable advantage with skills, resources, or elements of the marketing mix?
6. Assume your company is or will be marketing globally. How should your company enter the global marketplace? How will international issues affect your firm?
7. Identify any ethical issues that could impact your chosen firm. What steps should be taken to handle these issues?
8. Is there a key factor or assumption that you are using when performing your SWOT analysis? What would happen if this key factor or assumption did not exist?

Marketing*Builder* Exercises

• **Business Risk** portion of the **Market Analysis** template
• **Environmental Risk** portion of the **Market Analysis** template
• **Elements of Risk** table in the **Market Analysis** template

E-MARKETING PLANNING ACTIVITIES

The greatest area of business growth exists in the Internet portion of marketing. For most firms, there are two options for implementing this: to start an Internet business that is wholly operated in the e-marketing world or to create an Internet component of a marketing plan for a traditional, existing business. Both Internet opportunities require careful strategic marketing planning in order for the venture to succeed.

Consider the differences between Amazon (**http://www.amazon.com**), a strictly dot-com business that markets only via the Internet, versus Barnes & Noble (**http://www.barnesandnoble.com**) or Borders (**http://www.borders.com**), both traditional brick-and-mortar retailers that have expanded their offerings to on-line ordering. Alternatively, consider your own business that you would like to start. Will it begin as a dot-com enterprise? Will it later have to expand into a tangible storefront to remain successful? Or would you like to write a strategic marketing plan to help your choice of traditional business expand into the on-line world?

Throughout the rest of this book, these end-of-part e-marketing planning activities will help you build a strategic marketing plan for your choice of firms. If you can't think of your own company, use the examples of the bookstore retailers provided above. For some general help on business plans and marketing plans, visit **http://www.bplans.com** or **http://www.businessplans.org**. Before you begin, you will need to learn about the Internet as a business space. **Looksmart.com** has a category called "Internet Business" that you may find helpful both as a starting point and as you progress through the e-marketing planning activities. Another very useful site is **http://www.emarketer.com**. You should also refer to Exhibit 2.8 for additional marketing plan checklist items (Part I: Business Mission; Part II: Objectives; and Part III: Situation Analysis).

For electronic sources of information, search on the Electric Library at **http://www.elibrary.com** or the Internet Public Library at **http://www.ipl.org**. Another excellent source of information is the Sales and Marketing Executives Marketing Library at **http://www.sell.org**.

The first part of strategic planning deals with the world of marketing, and involves stating your business mission with a marketing orientation, setting objectives, finding a differential advantage, and performing an assessment of strengths, weaknesses, opportunities, and threats. Use the following exercises to guide you through the first part of your strategic marketing plan:

1. List all the ways that your company follows the marketing concept. Can your company satisfy the needs and wants of customers and still be profitable, legal, and socially responsible?

2. What should be the business mission of [...] pany? Write the mission statement, kee[...] the benefits offered to customers rather than the product or service sold. If you are starting the on-line arm of a traditional store, should you make any changes to the company's overall mission statement? For fun, visit the mission statement generator at **http://umweb1.unitedmedia.com/comics/dilbert/career/bin/ms2.cgi**, which may help illustrate how *not* to write your business mission statement.

3. List at least three specific, measurable objectives for your company. Be sure these objectives relate to the mission statement and include a time frame.

4. Begin your SWOT analysis with an analysis of the primary strength by asking, "What is the key differential or competitive advantage of my firm?" Consider what advantages are gained by operating in the Internet space. What are other keys to the potential success of your company? What other strengths can your firm capitalize on?

5. Continue the SWOT analysis by taking an honest look at the weaknesses of your firm. What are the disadvantages to operating in the Internet space? How can you overcome them? You might want to enlist the help of a friend to act as a consultant who can give an unbiased opinion. Are there any ethical problems in the organization?

6. How should your company integrate corporate social responsibility into the plan? Describe how your company will handle privacy concerns. In addition to suggestions for philanthropic responsibilities, write up a brief code of ethics for your firm. To see other codes of ethics, go to **http://csep.iit.edu/codes/**.

7. The last part of the SWOT analysis seeks to identify opportunities and threats in the external marketing environment by performing environmental scanning.
   a. To learn more about demographic, ethnic, and social trends that could impact your firm, investigate data from the U.S. Census Bureau at **http://www.census.gov**.
   b. To learn more about economic factors that could influence the strategies of your firm, visit the United States Economic and Statistics Administration at **http://www.esa.doc.gov** or the Bureau of Economic Analysis at **http://www.bea.doc.gov**.
   c. Be sure to look for computer and Internet usage statistics and think about whether or not they are a positive indicator for the target market you have selected. The resources at **http://cyberatlas.internet.com** and **http://acnielsen.com/products/reports/netwatch** can help. Determine which emerging technologies will impact your company. Are these technological developments opportunities or threats?

d. Understand how political and legal factors may influence your e-marketing decisions at **http://www.lawguru.com**. You may also wish to investigate the Web sites of federal government agencies that regulate your firm and industry. The Federal Trade Commission is at **http://www.ftc.gov**. The Federal Communications Commission is at **http://www.fcc.gov**. The Food and Drug Administration is at http://www.fda.gov. The Consumer Product Safety Commission is at **http://www.cpsc.gov**. The Better Business Bureau is at **http://www.bbb.org**. The Internal Revenue Service is at **http://www.irs.gov**. From here you can download all kinds of required and helpful forms.

e. Identify your key competitors. A simple "yellow pages" (**http://bigbook.com**) listing of firms in the same business category can start your search. For on-line competitors, try **http://huizen.dds.nl/~shopping** or **http://www.bizrate.com**. For more specific information on a competitor, investigate **http://www.companiesonline.com**.

f. Competition often comes from companies that are working on the same exact market as yours. That is especially true in the Internet space. After you search for your direct competition, look for and think about what other companies are positioned to execute a similar business strategy for your target market. Determine if there are any players who might be able to develop technology more quickly or reach your target customers more effectively than you.

g. Because an Internet presence means your product or service is visible to a global community, it is important to assess the international marketplace as well. A listing of international chambers of commerce is at **http://www.worldchambers.com** and the CIA World Factbook is at **http://www.cia.gov/cia/publications/factbook/index.html**.

CROSS-FUNCTIONAL CONNECTIONS SOLUTIONS

Questions

1. What is the overlap among marketing, manufacturing, finance, accounting, and human resources? What does each of these functions do that result in this overlap?

The overlap among all functional areas within a firm lies in providing the final product or service to the consumer. Each functional area contributes in different ways to delivering the desired product to the end customer. Marketing, manufacturing, finance, accounting, and human resources work from the idea that the customer is most important and that the goal is to produce a product that meets the changing needs of consumers. Marketing and manufacturing tend to come into direct contact with the company's customers and products. Finance, accounting, and human resources tend to work on the periphery and may never come into contact with the physical aspects of the product and may never meet the end-user of the product or service. However, working together and utilizing each area's expertise and knowledge results in an integrated production process that aims to satisfy the customer.

2. Why is cross-functional coordination necessary in order to have a customer-oriented firm?

Historically, everyone assumed that the customer belonged to the marketing department. We know now that this is not true. Everyone in the organization must understand the customer's wants and needs in order to satisfy these needs. Without the customer, there would be no need for an organization. For example, no customers would mean no products to develop or manufacture, no accounts receivable, and no need for employees. From the customer's perspective, good or bad products belong to the entire company—not just one particular function. Customers will not keep coming back if the company produces only low-quality merchandise—even if the marketing group has some of the best marketers in the world. Likewise, a high-quality product will not be successful in the marketplace if the product is positioned inaccurately, advertised inappropriately, priced too high or too low, or not available in the right outlets. Therefore, it is imperative that the business functions work together to send the same message to the marketplace.

3. What roles do teamwork and technology play in cross-functional coordination?

Technology has created a digitized marketplace in which business decisions have to be made quickly in order for the firm to remain competitive. Customer demands increase in this fast-paced market, making it necessary for all functional areas to work together to deliver products to a market quickly. In working as a team, functional areas partner in the production/delivery process, sharing relevant information with one another, as well as eliminating wasted time spent when working independently in departments.

Suggested Readings

Bryant Avey. "Building a People-Center Culture in the D-Age." *Chief Executive,* September 1999, p. 10.

Charles H. Noble. "Building the Strategy Implementation Network." *Business Horizons,* November/December 1999, pp. 19–28.

2

part

Analyzing Marketing Opportunities

INFORMATION INTEGRATION TO SATISFY CUSTOMER WANTS AND NEEDS

Understanding customers is at the heart of the information-gathering process. Whether it is determining individual buying behavior, sharpening the company's target marketing skills, or understanding competitive actions, information is the key to success. The traditional perception of information gathering is that it is the "job" of the marketing department. However, many companies have come to realize that the market belongs to the entire company—making it everyone's responsibility to understand the marketplace.

Kellogg USA has focused extensively on improving the focus of its research efforts. The company's strategy involves better cross-functional acquisition and dissemination of market research information. The ultimate goal is to use the information to help move new and improved products into the marketplace much more quickly. In its attempt to increase profits, the company has discarded its traditional product development process that was housed in marketing. Now, the company utilizes cross-functional teams comprised of business functional areas, food technologists, and engineers in its product development efforts. Kellogg's marketers no longer take sole responsibility for the collection and use of information. While these different groups now work in tandem in developing products at Kellogg, the historical debate surrounding type of data continues in many companies.

This information debate between marketing and other functions centers on the qualitative versus quantitative format of functional data. The data collected by marketers is perceived to be qualitative, abstract data when compared to the quantitative data utilized by other functional areas. It has been difficult to get engineers and accountants to understand that marketing data, statistically valid information, is important in making company-wide decisions.

Aside from the need for a general cross-functional sharing of data, there are five major areas in which information gathering and dissemination processes need to be formally integrated across functions:

1. Benchmarking studies
2. Customer teaming
3. Customer satisfaction studies
4. Data-mining
5. Forecasting

Benchmarking is the process of comparing a firm's performance in various activities with the performance of other companies that have completed similar activities. A benchmarking study could focus upon cross-company comparisons of purchasing processes, inventory management, product development cycles, hiring practices, payroll processes, and order fulfillment. Gathering information on a firm's competitors during a benchmarking study involves an extensive amount of secondary research. Recently, cross-functional "shadow teams" have been formed to assist in better benchmarking of competitive activities. These shadow teams integrate internal information with all externally available information on specific competitors.

The Ford Motor Company was an early pioneer of the use of benchmarking. In the early 1980s, the company found itself at a competitive disadvantage when compared to many foreign automobile manufacturers. Ford executives recognized that remaining competitive would demand a steep reduction in costs. One benchmarking study focused upon reducing the number of employees in the accounts payable department. Using information gained in a benchmarking study of its competitors, Ford was able to decrease its accounts payable staff by greater than one-half. The study involved both primary and secondary research—areas in which marketers have extensive training. Similarly, many of the creative aspects (e.g., Six Sigma, Workout) of Jack Welch's tenure at General Electric were the result of benchmarking studies of competing and noncompeting companies.

Many companies are now *teaming* employees with customers in an attempt to bring the customer into the organization. Site visits are one popular way of better understanding needs and/or watching how a finished product is utilized in the business process. These visits involve team members from across various functions. For example, someone from research and development might visit a customer in order to observe in-use practices. Drawing from the on-site visit, the research and development employee could utilize these observations in adapting the product to the customer's needs within the select business framework. Tellabs, a telecommunications company that develops voice and data transmission products, teams its marketers and research and development engineers with customers in an attempt to reduce the risks inherent in new product development.

Additionally, Kodak attempts to gain a better understanding of how customers use its film by sending manufacturing employees to visit with professional users of its film products. Kodak is dependent upon accurate marketplace information in understanding both the customers' buying processes and actual usage of Kodak products.

Customer satisfaction is driven by issues related to the firm's operational functions (for example, inventory management, capital budgeting), the firm's operational capabilities (for example, technology, procedures), as well as the firm's product mix. Therefore, a valid *customer satisfaction study* should gather information that can be shared with manufacturing (regarding satisfaction with speed of delivery), research and development (regarding satisfaction with product quality), human resources (regarding satisfaction with complaint handling), and finance/accounting (regarding satisfaction with credit policies). As such, all of these functional areas need to have input into the design of such studies.

The digital age has led to considerable *data-mining.* E-commerce capabilities have allowed companies to gather and analyze customer information in a matter of minutes, rather than having to wait for results from months-long data gathering processes. This use of technology is where considerable cross-functional interactions must occur. Companies such as DoubleClick, Kozmo, and AltaVista gather and store a wealth of consumer information—information that has to be effectively disseminated to the appropriate individuals.

Forecasting crosses the boundaries of multiple business functions. For example, marketing may offer a discount on a particular price. The impact of this price discount is felt, simultaneously, in many functional areas. A key functional partner in a price discount is manufacturing. The production plan will have to accommodate the expected increase in product sales and the oftentimes below average product sales immediately after the discount period. While price is easy for marketers to change, manufacturing's plans cannot be changed over night. The impact of a price change may be felt in the company's production schedule, the level of finished goods inventory, and the availability of raw materials. Unfortunately, marketing's ability to make price changes quickly has been the cause of much conflict between marketing and manufacturing.

Much of a firm's financial planning is driven by the company's sales forecast. Marketing has historically had a reputation of being too optimistic in its projections. As such, financial planners have been known to take the sales forecast with "a grain of salt," and planning has often evolved around a lower than predicted level of sales. Marketing, then, looks at financial planners as too conservative and as basing their plans on internal data that are not driven by the marketplace.

Predicting worldwide demand has become a forecasting challenge for many companies. With help from a software program, Eastman Chemical Corporation utilizes cross-functional teams to predict demand across its supply chain. Not only is the company now able to make precise forecasts, but the program allows the dissemination of these real-time forecasts over the corporate intranet. This enables the synchronization of production and inventory with customer demand.

Marketplace information is a key driver in all decisions made by a company. Therefore, it is imperative that all functional areas participate in the gathering and dissemination of information. The importance of information is reflected in a new executive position, chief knowledge officer, that is now being staffed in many companies. Without a doubt, success in today's global environment is dependent upon all functional areas understanding the firm's customers and competitors.

Questions for Discussion

1. Why has information historically been perceived as "owned" by the marketing department?
2. What data differences exist across functions?
3. What is the job of a chief knowledge officer?

Check it Out

For articles and exercises on the material in this part, and for other great study aids, visit the *Marketing* Web site at **http://lamb.swcollege.com**

chapter 5

Learning Objectives

1 Explain why marketing managers should understand consumer behavior

2 Analyze the components of the consumer decision-making process

3 Explain the consumer's postpurchase evaluation process

4 Identify the types of consumer buying decisions and discuss the significance of consumer involvement

5 Identify and understand the cultural factors that affect consumer buying decisions

6 Identify and understand the social factors that affect consumer buying decisions

7 Identify and understand the individual factors that affect consumer buying decisions

8 Identify and understand the psychological factors that affect consumer buying decisions

Consumer Decision Making

Forget baby boomers. Today's marketer is more interested in their kids, a group that represents the next big wave of consumers. The buying decisions made by boomers' children will determine the success or failure of products and entire companies in the years to come.

Called Generation Y, they are part of the sixty million plus mass of children born between 1977 and 1994 mostly to baby boomer parents. More than three times the size of Generation X (those born between roughly 1965 and 1976 and comprising a measly seventeen million consumers), they're the biggest thing to hit the American marketing scene since the seventy-two million baby boomers came of age.

Beyond its sheer size, though, Gen Y has little else in common with the baby boomer generation. More racially diverse, Gen Y consumers are even more accepting of diversity than their Gen X counterparts. They are also much more likely to be born into two-income families or single-parent households, are incredibly computer-savvy, and love living in a computer-connected world. And kids today have a lot more disposable income to spend on, well, whatever. This group spends an estimated $140 billion a year, or an average of $90 per week. One in nine teens today has a credit card co-signed by a parent. Not having the burden of car payments or mortgages yet, they spend it on whatever is "cool" at the moment in apparel, footwear, music, entertainment, food and beverages, and hair and makeup products.

So the race is on for marketers to define and capture that elusive cool. Brand names such as Adidas, Tommy Hilfiger, JNCO, FUBU, Abercrombie & Fitch, Vans, Doc Martens, Mudd, and Fila have achieved this honored status—at least for the moment. Fickle Gen Y kids will move on to the next fad as soon as it becomes too mainstream. Therefore, marketers beware; falling off the cool barometer can occur at any moment and without warning. For

instance, trendsetting kids made wide-leg jeans and rave pants their fashion mark. But once the wide-leg look went mainstream, these trendsetters—the most influential fashion customers—abruptly abandoned rave pants in favor of slimmer pants with cargo pickets. Caught by the sudden shift, manufacturers like JNCO and retailers like Gadzooks were left with piles of wide-leg inventory destined for the clearance sale rack.

Mainstream marketers are excited about the coming of Generation Y, but understandably wary. This is the first generation to come along that's big enough to hurt an established brand popular with their parents simply by giving it the cold shoulder. Gen Y is also large enough to launch rival brands with enough heft to threaten the status quo. Nike is one casualty of Gen Y's fickleness. Sales of Nike sneakers bottomed-out after kids decided that white shoes didn't look good with their wide-leg jeans and cargo pants. Image and celebrity advertising that helped build the Nike brand among baby boomers, backfired with Gen Y consumers who respond more to humor, irony, and truth. In its place rose little-known brands like Vans and Airwalk. Similarly, venerable Levi Strauss also lost touch with Gen Y consumers and has seen its market share of jeans erode as more teens have embraced hipper brands. Levi's, they contend, are what their parents wear.

Gen Y consumers are making it clear that companies hoping to win their hearts and wallets will have to learn to think like they do and not like their baby boomer parents. Exposed to media from an early age, Gen Y con-

sumers respond differently to ads and prefer to encounter them in different places. Marketers who succeed are those who bring their messages to the places these kids congregate like the Internet, skateboard parks, or cable television. Gen Y teens also feel they need to identify with older kids and have a certain "look." Abercrombie & Fitch, for instance, understands this segment and how aspirational it is. Aiming for the college student in its advertising and marketing, A&F reaches those in high school, who are dreaming of being at this next stage. Add in a little controversy, as A&F did with its sexually charged catalogs, and teens flock to the brand.

But achieving cool status with today's kids doesn't come easy. To stay in touch with the teen market and remain one of their cool brands, MTV, for instance, conducts hundreds of types of consumer research projects a year addressing kids' behavior. MTV staffers frequent dance clubs and hang out where kids do so they can catch breaking trends early. The cable music station has also learned that when a generation moves on, not to follow it. Instead, MTV focuses on the next group coming up and what their hot buttons are.[1]

What examples can you think of in which a peer influenced your purchase of a product? What effect do you think Gen Y's cultural values, motivations, attitudes, and lifestyles have on their consumer decision-making process? How should marketers respond to teen's ever-changing definition of cool? Questions like these will be answered as you read this chapter on the consumer decision-making process and its influences.

The Importance of Understanding Consumer Behavior

Explain why marketing managers should understand consumer behavior

consumer behavior
Processes a consumer uses to make purchase decisions, as well as to use and dispose of purchased goods or services; also includes factors that influence purchase decisions and the product use.

Consumers' product and service preferences are constantly changing. In order to address this constant state of flux and to create a proper marketing mix for a well-defined market, marketing managers must have a thorough knowledge of consumer behavior. **Consumer behavior** describes how consumers make purchase decisions and how they use and dispose of the purchased goods or services. The study of consumer behavior also includes the analysis of factors that influence purchase decisions and product use.

Understanding how consumers make purchase decisions can help marketing managers in several ways. For example, if a manager knows through research that gas mileage is the most important attribute for a certain target market, the manufacturer can redesign the product to meet that criterion. If the firm cannot change the design in the short run, it can use promotion in an effort to change consumers' decision-making criteria. For example, an automobile manufacturer can advertise a car's maintenance-free features and sporty European style while downplaying gas mileage.

The Consumer Decision-Making Process

Analyze the components of the consumer decision-making process

consumer decision-making process
A five-step process used by consumers when buying goods or services.

When buying products, consumers generally follow the **consumer decision-making process** shown in Exhibit 5.1: (1) need recognition, (2) information search, (3) evaluation of alternatives, (4) purchase, and (5) postpurchase behavior. These five steps represent a general process that moves the consumer from recognition of a product or service need to the evaluation of a purchase. This process is a guideline for studying how consumers make decisions. It is important to note that this guideline does not assume that consumers' decisions will proceed in order through all of the steps of the process. In fact, the consumer may end the process at any time; he or she may not even make a purchase. Explanations as to why a consumer's progression through these steps may vary are offered at the end of the chapter in the section on the types of consumer buying decisions. Before addressing this issue, we will describe each step in the process in greater detail.

Need Recognition

need recognition
Result of an imbalance between actual and desired states.

The first stage in the consumer decision-making process is need recognition. **Need recognition** occurs when consumers are faced with an imbalance between actual and desired states. For example, do you often feel thirsty after strenuous exercise? Has a television commercial for a new sports car ever made you wish you could buy it? Need recognition is triggered when a consumer is exposed to either an internal or an external **stimulus**. Hunger and thirst are *internal stimuli;* the color of an automobile, the design of a package, a brand name mentioned by a friend, an advertisement on television, or cologne worn by a stranger are considered *external stimuli.*

stimulus
Any unit of input affecting one or more of the five senses: sight, smell, taste, touch, hearing.

A marketing manager's objective is to get consumers to recognize an imbalance between their present status and their preferred state. Advertising and sales promotion often provide this stimulus. Surveying buyer preferences provides marketers with consumer wants and needs with which to tailor products and services. Home builder Kaufman & Broad (K&B) Home Corporation in Denver, for instance, annually surveys home buyers to determine which features they actually want in a home. It found that home buyers in Denver could do without fireplaces and basements; buyers in San Francisco wanted fireplaces; buyers everywhere preferred more square footage to vaulted ceilings, and large master bedrooms to formal dining rooms. Now, K&B offers home buyers more custom options instead of building homes first and then hoping for the best.[2]

Exhibit **5.1**

Consumer Decision-Making
Process

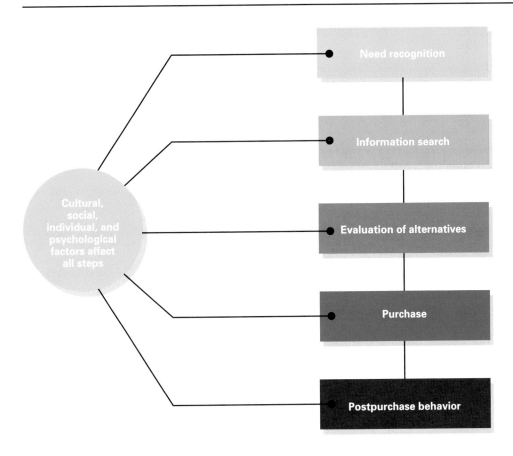

Marketing managers can create wants on the part of the consumer. A **want** exists when someone has an unfulfilled need and has determined that a particular good or service will satisfy it. Young children might want toys, video games, and baseball equipment to meet their innate need to play and learn new skills. Teenagers may want compact discs, fashionable sneakers, and wide-leg jeans to fulfill their need of belonging. A want can be for a specific product or it can be for a certain attribute or feature of a product. For instance, adults may want ready-to-eat meals, drive-through dry cleaning service, and catalog shopping to fulfill their need for convenience. Older consumers may want goods and services that offer convenience, comfort, and security. Remote-controlled appliances, home deliveries, speaker phones, and motorized carts are all designed for comfort and convenience. A personal transmitter that can signal an ambulance or the police in an emergency offers security for older consumers.

Consumers recognize unfulfilled wants in various ways. The two most common occur when a current product isn't performing properly and when the consumer is about to run out of something that is generally kept on hand. Consumers may also recognize unfulfilled wants if they become aware of a product whose features make it seem superior to the one currently used. Such wants are usually created by advertising and other promotional activities. For instance, births of multiples (twins, triplets and even quadruplets) have increased in the last few years due in large part to advances in fertility medicine. As a result, baby products such as strollers and cribs that normally fulfilled the needs of parents of single babies were lacking when it came to multiples. Small marketers have capitalized on these needs by developing innovations like strollers that can accommodate triplets, and quadruplets, L-shaped double cribs for twins, and, in the event of triplets, triangular cribs that fit into the corners of the room to offer parents sight lines to three babies at once.[3]

want
Recognition of an unfulfilled need and a product that will satisfy it.

Marketers selling their products in global markets must carefully observe the needs and wants of consumers in various regions. Unilever hit on an unrecognized need of European consumers when it introduced Persil Tablets, premeasured laundry detergent in tablet form. While the tablets are more expensive than regular laundry detergents, Unilever found that European consumers considered laundry a chore and wanted the process as simple and uncomplicated as possible. Unilever launched the tablets as less messy and more convenient to consumers tackling the pile of dirty clothes on washday. The laundry tablets proved so popular in the United Kingdom that Unilever's Persil brand edged ahead of rival Procter & Gamble's best-selling Ariel powder detergent.[4]

Information Search

After recognizing a need or want, consumers search for information about the various alternatives available to satisfy it. An information search can occur internally, externally, or both. **Internal information search** is the process of recalling information stored in the memory. This stored information stems largely from previous experience with a product. For instance, perhaps while shopping you encounter a brand of cake mix that you tried some time ago. By searching your memory, you can probably remember whether it tasted good, pleased guests, and was easy to prepare.

In contrast, an **external information search** seeks information in the outside environment. There are two basic types of external information sources: nonmarketing-controlled and marketing-controlled. A **nonmarketing-controlled information source** is not associated with marketers promoting a product. A friend might recommend an IBM personal computer because he or she bought one and likes it. Nonmarketing-controlled information sources include personal experience (trying or observing a new product); personal sources (family, friends, acquaintances, and coworkers); and public sources, such as Underwriters Laboratories, *Consumer Reports,* and other rating organizations. For instance, consumers rely heavily on doctor and pharmacist recommendations when buying over-the-counter medications. In a recent survey that studied how consumers choose medicine, more than half started using an OTC drug because a pharmacist recommended it.[5] Similarly, a recent survey on new car purchases by Generation Y found these car buyers were almost twice as likely as older buyers to get information about new cars from friends and relatives. Car manufacturers would therefore be likely to focus their marketing strategy on generating enthusiasm for their models via word of mouth.[6]

On the other hand, a **marketing-controlled information source**, is biased toward a specific product, because it originates with marketers promoting that product. Marketing-controlled information sources include mass-media advertising (radio, newspaper, television, and magazine advertising), sales promotion (contests, displays, premiums, and so forth), salespeople, product labels and packaging, and the Internet. For example, in the same survey on consumers and medicine, 56 percent of those interviewed said information on the label was very important in deciding whether or not to purchase an OTC medication for the first time.[7] Yet, many consumers are wary about the information they receive from marketing-controlled sources, arguing that most marketing campaigns stress the attributes of the product and don't mention the faults. These sentiments tend to be stronger among better-educated and higher-income consumers. For instance, only 13 percent of the consumers interviewed in the medicine study said that advertising is very important in their decision to purchase OTC medications.[8]

The extent to which an individual conducts an external search depends on his or her perceived risk, knowledge, prior experience, and level of interest in the good or service. Generally, as the perceived risk of the purchase increases, the consumer enlarges the search and considers more alternative brands. For instance, assume you want to buy a new car. The decision is a relatively risky one, mainly

internal information search
Process of recalling past information stored in the memory.

external information search
Process of seeking information in the outside environment.

nonmarketing-controlled information source
Product information source that is not associated with advertising or promotion.

marketing-controlled information source
Product information source that originates with marketers promoting the product.

because of cost, so you are motivated to search for information about models, options, gas mileage, durability, and passenger capacity. You may also decide to gather information about more models, because the time expended in finding the data is less than the cost of buying the wrong car. In contrast, you are less likely to expend great effort in searching for the right kind of bath soap. If you make the wrong selection, the cost is minimal and you will have the opportunity to make another selection in a short period of time. A study on the effect of consumers' level of perceived risk found that those who perceive higher risk with a mail-order purchase expend more effort in an external information search and consult a greater number of information sources than do those who perceive lower levels of risk.[9]

A consumer's knowledge about the product or service will also affect the extent of an external information search. If the consumer is knowledgeable and well informed about a potential purchase, he or she is less likely to search for additional information. In addition, the more knowledgeable the consumer is, the more efficiently he or she will conduct the search process, thereby requiring less time to search. Another closely related factor that affects the extent of a consumer's external search is confidence in one's decision-making ability. A confident consumer not only has sufficient stored information about the product but also feels self-assured about making the right decision. People lacking this confidence will continue an information search even when they know a great deal about the product. Consumers with prior experience in buying a certain product will have less perceived risk than inexperienced consumers. Therefore, they will spend less time searching and limit the number of products that they consider.

A third factor influencing the external information search is product experience. Consumers who have had a positive prior experience with a product are more likely to limit their search to only those items related to the positive experience. For example, many consumers are loyal to Honda automobiles, which enjoy low repair rates and consequently high customer satisfaction, and they often own more than one.

Finally, the extent of the search undertaken is positively related to the amount of interest a consumer has in a product. A consumer who is more interested in a product will spend more time searching for information and alternatives. For example, suppose you are a dedicated runner who reads jogging and fitness magazines and catalogs. In searching for a new pair of running shoes, you may enjoy reading about the new brands available and spend more time and effort than other buyers in deciding on the right shoe.

The consumer's information search should yield a group of brands, sometimes called the buyer's **evoked set** (or **consideration set**), which are the consumer's most preferred alternatives. From this set, the buyer will further evaluate the alternatives and make a choice. Consumers do not consider all the brands available in a product category, but they do seriously consider a much smaller set. For example, there are dozens of brands of shampoos and close to two hundred types of automobiles available in the United States, yet most consumers seriously contemplate only about four shampoos and no more than five automobiles when faced with a purchase decision.

evoked set (consideration set)
Group of brands, resulting from an information search, from which a buyer can choose.

Evaluation of Alternatives and Purchase

After getting information and constructing an evoked set of alternative products, the consumer is ready to make a decision. A consumer will use the information stored in memory and obtained from outside sources to develop a set of criteria. These standards help the consumer evaluate and compare alternatives. One way to begin narrowing the number of choices in the evoked set is to pick a product attribute and then exclude all products in the set that don't have that attribute. For instance, assume that John is thinking about buying a new notebook computer to replace his current desktop machine. He is interested in one with a large color active-matrix display, CD-ROM drive, and a processor speed of at least 300 megahertz, so he excludes all notebooks without these features.

Another way to narrow the number of choices is to use cutoffs, or minimum or maximum levels of an attribute that an alternative must pass to be considered. Suppose John still must choose from a wide array of notebook computers that have active-matrix screens, CD-ROM drives, and 300-plus processor speeds. He then names another product attribute: price. Given the amount of money he has set aside for a new computer, John decides he cannot spend more than $2,500. Therefore, he can exclude all notebook computers priced above $2,500. A final way to narrow the choices is to rank the attributes under consideration in order of importance and evaluate the products based on how well they perform on the most important attributes. To reach a final decision, John would pick the most important attributes, such as processor speed and active display, weigh the merits of each, and then evaluate alternative notebook computers on those criteria.

If new brands are added to an evoked set, the consumer's evaluation of the existing brands in that set changes. As a result, certain brands in the original set may become more desirable. Suppose John sees two notebook computers priced at $1,999 and $2,199. At the time, he may judge the $2,199 notebook computer as too expensive and choose not to purchase it. However, if he then adds to his list of alternatives another notebook computer that is priced at $2,499, he may view the $2,199 one as less expensive and decide to purchase it.

The goal of the marketing manager is to determine which attributes are most important in influencing a consumer's choice. Several factors may collectively affect a consumer's evaluation of products. A single attribute, such as price, may not adequately explain how consumers form their evoked set.[10] Moreover, attributes thought to be important to the marketer may not be very important to the consumer. For example, much to the surprise of car sellers, one study found that automobile warranty coverage was the least important factor in a consumer's purchase of a car.[11]

 A brand name can also have a significant impact on a consumer's ultimate choice. In a recent on-line survey, Johnson & Johnson was found to have the best corporate reputation among American companies, benefiting from its heritage as the premier maker of baby powder and shampoo. Respondents uniformly cited the familiarity and comfort they feel in using J&J products on their children. When faced with dozens of products on the drugstore shelf, consumers naturally gravitate toward J&J products. By providing consumers with a certain set of promises, brands in essence simplify the consumer decision-making process so consumers do not have to rethink their options every time they need something.[12]

Following the evaluation of alternatives, the consumer decides which product to buy or decides not to buy a product at all. If he or she decides to make a purchase, the next step in the process is an evaluation of the product after the purchase.

Postpurchase Behavior

When buying products, consumers expect certain outcomes from the purchase. How well these expectations are met determines whether the consumer is satisfied or dissatisfied with the purchase. For example, a person buys a used car with somewhat low expectations for the car's actual performance. Surprisingly, the car turns

3

Explain the consumer's post-purchase evaluation process

out to be one of the best cars she has ever owned. Thus the buyer's satisfaction is high, because her fairly low expectations were exceeded. On the other hand, a consumer who buys a brand-new car would expect it to perform especially well. But if the car turns out to be a lemon, she will be very dissatisfied because her high expectations have not been met. Price often creates high expectations. One study found that higher monthly cable TV bills were associated with greater expectations for cable service. Over time, cable subscribers tended to drop the premium-priced cable channels because their high expectations were not met.[13]

For the marketing manager, one important element of any postpurchase evaluation is reducing any lingering doubts that the decision was sound. When people recognize inconsistency between their values or opinions and their behavior, they tend to feel an inner tension called **cognitive dissonance**. For example, suppose a consumer spends half his monthly salary on a new TV entertainment system. If he stops to think how much he has spent, he will probably feel dissonance. Dissonance occurs because the person knows the purchased product has some disadvantages as well as some advantages. In the case of the entertainment system, the disadvantage of cost battles the advantage of technological superiority.

cognitive dissonance
Inner tension that a consumer experiences after recognizing an inconsistency between behavior and values or opinions.

Consumers try to reduce dissonance by justifying their decision. They might seek new information that reinforces positive ideas about the purchase, avoid information that contradicts their decision, or revoke the original decision by returning the product. People who have just bought a new car often read more advertisements for the newly purchased car than for other cars in order to reduce dissonance. In some instances, people deliberately seek contrary information in order to refute it and reduce dissonance. Dissatisfied customers sometimes rely on word of mouth to reduce cognitive dissonance, by letting friends and family know they are displeased.

Marketing managers can help reduce dissonance through effective communication with purchasers. For example, a customer service manager may slip a note inside the package congratulating the buyer on making a wise decision. Postpurchase letters sent by manufacturers and dissonance-reducing statements in instruction booklets may help customers feel at ease with their purchase. Advertising that displays the product's superiority over competing brands or guarantees can also help relieve the possible dissonance of someone who has already bought the product. Catalog merchant Lands' End, for example, offers consumers a no-questions-asked guarantee: If a product purchased through a Lands' End catalog does not work out, no matter what the reason, the company will provide a prompt, no-hassle refund or exchange. Hyundai Motor Company promotes its "Hyundai Advantage" warranty, which includes ten-year engine and transmission coverage, bumper-to-bumper coverage for five years or 60,000 miles, and five years of unlimited roadside assistance. Hyundai even promises limited reimbursement of lodging expenses incurred as a result of a breakdown.[14]

There's no question that this ad for Isuzu highlights customer value. With a ten-year, 120,000-mile warranty, Isuzu is outpacing its competition and minimizing cognitive dissonance in its customers.

Types of Consumer Buying Decisions and Consumer Involvement

All consumer buying decisions generally fall along a continuum of three broad categories: routine response behavior, limited decision making, and extensive decision making (see Exhibit 5.2). Goods and services in these three categories can best be described in terms of five factors: level of consumer involvement, length of

4

Identify the types of consumer buying decisions and discuss the significance of consumer involvement

Exhibit 5.2

Continuum of Consumer Buying Decisions

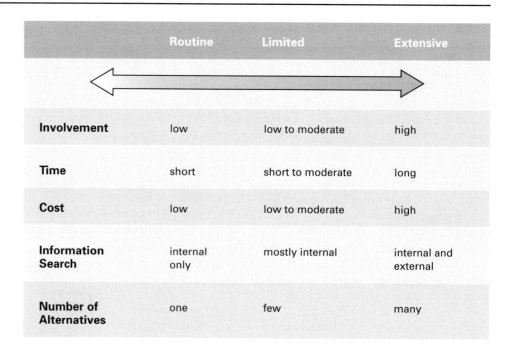

	Routine	Limited	Extensive
Involvement	low	low to moderate	high
Time	short	short to moderate	long
Cost	low	low to moderate	high
Information Search	internal only	mostly internal	internal and external
Number of Alternatives	one	few	many

involvement
Amount of time and effort a buyer invests in the search, evaluation, and decision processes of consumer behavior.

routine response behavior
Type of decision making exhibited by consumers buying frequently purchased, low-cost goods and services; requires little search and decision time.

limited decision making
Type of decision making that requires a moderate amount of time for gathering information and deliberating about an unfamiliar brand in a familiar product category.

extensive decision making
Most complex type of consumer decision making, used when buying an unfamiliar, expensive product or an infrequently bought item; requires use of several criteria for evaluating options and much time for seeking information.

time to make a decision, cost of the good or service, degree of information search, and the number of alternatives considered. The level of consumer involvement is perhaps the most significant determinant in classifying buying decisions. **Involvement** is the amount of time and effort a buyer invests in the search, evaluation, and decision processes of consumer behavior.

Frequently purchased, low-cost goods and services are generally associated with **routine response behavior**. These goods and services can also be called low-involvement products, because consumers spend little time on search and decision before making the purchase. Usually, buyers are familiar with several different brands in the product category but stick with one brand. Consumers engaged in routine response behavior normally don't experience need recognition until they are exposed to advertising or see the product displayed on a store shelf. Consumers buy first and evaluate later, whereas the reverse is true for extensive decision making. A parent, for example, will not stand at the cereal shelf in the grocery store for twenty minutes thinking about which brand of cereal to buy for the children. Instead, he or she will walk by the shelf, find the family's usual brand, and put it into the cart.

Limited decision making typically occurs when a consumer has previous product experience but is unfamiliar with the current brands available. Limited decision making is also associated with lower levels of involvement (although higher than routine decisions) because consumers do expend moderate effort in searching for information or in considering various alternatives. Suppose the children's usual brand of cereal, Kellogg's Corn Flakes, is unavailable in the grocery store. Completely out of cereal at home, the parent now must select another brand. Before making a final selection, he or she may pull from the shelf several brands similar to Kellogg's Corn Flakes, such as Corn Chex and Cheerios, to compare their nutritional value and calories and to decide whether the children will like the new cereal.

Consumers practice **extensive decision making** when buying an unfamiliar, expensive product or an infrequently bought item. This process is the most complex type of consumer buying decision and is associated with high involvement on the part of the consumer. This process resembles the model outlined in Exhibit 5.1.

These consumers want to make the right decision, so they want to know as much as they can about the product category and available brands. People usually experience cognitive dissonance only when buying high-involvement products. Buyers use several criteria for evaluating their options and spend much time seeking information. Buying a home or a car, for example, requires extensive decision making.

The type of decision making that consumers use to purchase a product does not necessarily remain constant. For instance, if a routinely purchased product no longer satisfies, consumers may practice limited or extensive decision making to switch to another brand. And people who first use extensive decision making may then use limited or routine decision making for future purchases. For example, a new mother may first extensively evaluate several brands of disposable diapers before selecting one. Subsequent purchases of diapers will then become routine.

Factors Determining the Level of Consumer Involvement

The level of involvement in the purchase depends on five factors: previous experience, interest, perceived risk, situation, and social visibility.

- *Previous experience:* When consumers have had previous experience with a good or service, the level of involvement typically decreases. After repeated product trials, consumers learn to make quick choices. Because consumers are familiar with the product and know whether it will satisfy their needs, they become less involved in the purchase. For example, consumers with pollen allergies typically buy the sinus medicine that has relieved their symptoms in the past.
- *Interest:* Involvement is directly related to consumer interests, as in cars, music, movies, bicycling, or electronics. Naturally, these areas of interest vary from one individual to another. Although some people have little interest in nursing homes, a person with elderly parents in poor health may be highly interested.
- *Perceived risk of negative consequences:* As the perceived risk in purchasing a product increases, so does a consumer's level of involvement. The types of risks that concern consumers include financial risk, social risk, and psychological risk. First, financial risk is exposure to loss of wealth or purchasing power. Because high risk is associated with high-priced purchases, consumers tend to become extremely involved. Therefore, price and involvement are usually directly related: As price increases, so does the level of involvement. For example, someone who is thinking of buying a home will normally spend much time and effort to find the right one. Second, consumers take social risks when they buy products that can affect people's social opinions of them (for example, driving an old, beat-up car or wearing unstylish clothes). Third, buyers undergo psychological risk if they feel that making the wrong decision might cause some concern or anxiety. For example, should a working parent hire a baby-sitter or enroll the child in a day-care center?
- *Situation:* The circumstances of a purchase may temporarily transform a low-involvement decision into a high-involvement one. High involvement comes into play when the consumer perceives risk in a specific situation. For example, an individual might routinely buy low-priced brands of liquor and wine. However, when the boss visits, the consumer might make a high-involvement decision and buy more prestigious brands.
- *Social visibility:* Involvement also increases as the social visibility of a product increases. Products often on social display include clothing (especially designer labels), jewelry, cars, and furniture. All these items make a statement about the purchaser and, therefore, carry a social risk.

Marketing Implications of Involvement

Marketing strategy varies according to the level of involvement associated with the product. For high-involvement product purchases, marketing managers have several responsibilities. First, promotion to the target market should be extensive and informative. A good ad gives consumers the information they need for making the purchase decision, as well as specifying the benefits and unique advantages of owning the product. For example, manufacturers of high-tech computers and peripheral equipment like scanners, printers, and modems run lengthy ads that detail technical information about such attributes as performance, resolution, and speed. DaimlerChrysler, maker of Mercedes-Benz automobiles, is developing Virtual Vehicle, which uses virtual reality to let customers test different combinations of colors, fabrics, and hubcaps to make the purchase decision easier. A touch screen hung from the ceiling allows customers to walk around a computer-generated image of a car, changing color, fabric, hubcaps, or headlights with a click. Customers can even alter the speaker configuration and hear the result immediately in Dolby stereo sound.[15]

For low-involvement product purchases, consumers may not recognize their wants until they are in the store. Therefore, in-store promotion is an important tool when promoting low-involvement products. Marketing managers have to focus on package design so the product will be eye-catching and easily recognized on the shelf. Examples of products that take this approach are Campbell's soups, Tide detergent, Velveeta cheese, and Heinz ketchup. In-store displays also stimulate sales of low-involvement products. A good display can explain the product's purpose and prompt recognition of a want. Displays of health and beauty aid items in supermarkets have been known to increase sales many times above normal. Coupons, cents-off deals, and two-for-one offers also effectively promote low-involvement items.

Linking a product to a higher-involvement issue is another tactic that marketing managers can use to increase the sales of a low-involvement product. For example, many food products are no longer just nutritious but also low in fat or cholesterol. Although packaged food may normally be a low-involvement product, reference to health issues raises the involvement level. To take advantage of today's interest by aging baby-boomers in healthier foods, H.J. Heinz Company linked its ketchup in a recent advertisement with a growing body of research that suggests lycopene, an antioxidant found in tomatoes, can reduce the risk of prostate and cervical cancer.[16] Similarly, food products, such as Silk soy milk and Gardenburger meatless burgers, both of which contain soy protein, tout their products' health benefits in reducing the risk of coronary heart disease, preventing certain cancers, and reducing the symptoms of menopause. Soy-based products, long-shunned in the United States for their taste, have since seen their sales skyrocket as a result of these health claims.[17]

Factors Influencing Consumer Buying Decisions

The consumer decision-making process does not occur in a vacuum. On the contrary, underlying cultural, social, individual, and psychological factors strongly influence the decision process. They have an effect from the time a consumer perceives a stimulus through postpurchase behavior. Cultural factors, which include culture and values, subculture, and social class, exert the broadest influence over consumer decision making. Social factors sum up the social interactions between a consumer and influential groups of people, such as reference groups, opinion leaders, and family members. Individual factors, which include gender, age, family life-cycle stage, personality, self-concept, and lifestyle, are unique to each individual and play a major role in the type of products and services con-

Exhibit 5.3

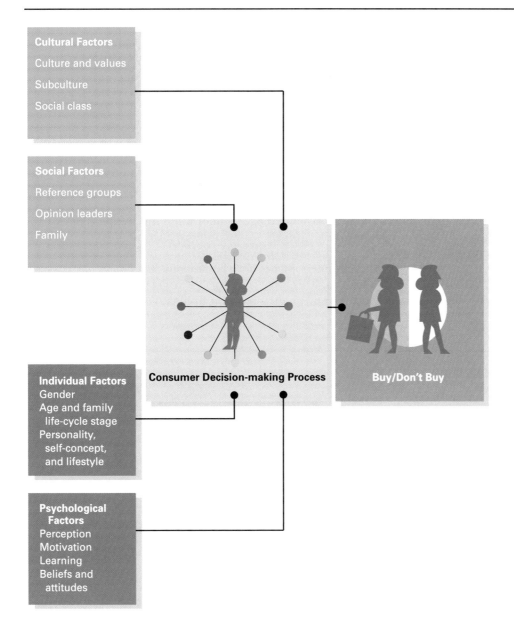

sumers want. Psychological factors determine how consumers perceive and interact with their environments and influence the ultimate decisions consumers make. They include perception, motivation, learning, beliefs, and attitudes. Exhibit 5.3 summarizes these influences.

Cultural Influences on Consumer Buying Decisions

The first major group of factors that influence consumer decision making are cultural factors. Cultural factors exert the broadest and deepest influence over a person's consumer behavior and decision making. Marketers must understand the way a person's culture and its accompanying values, as well as a person's subculture and social class, influence their buying behavior.

Identify and understand the cultural factors that affect consumer buying decisions

culture

Set of values, norms, attitudes, and other meaningful symbols that shape human behavior and the artifacts, or products, of that behavior as they are transmitted from one generation to the next.

Culture and Values

Culture is the essential character of a society that distinguishes it from other cultural groups. The underlying elements of every culture are the values, language, myths, customs, rituals, and laws that shape the behavior of the culture, as well as the material artifacts, or products, of that behavior as they are transmitted from one generation to the next. Exhibit 5.4 lists some defining components of American culture.

Culture is pervasive. Cultural values and influences are the ocean in which individuals swim, and of which most are completely unaware. What people eat, how they dress, what they think and feel, what language they speak are all dimensions of culture. It encompasses all the things consumers do without conscious choice because their culture's values, customs, and rituals are ingrained in their daily habits.

Culture is functional. Human interaction creates values and prescribes acceptable behavior for each culture. By establishing common expectations, culture gives order to society. Sometimes these expectations are coded into laws. For example, drivers in our culture must stop at a red light. Other times these expectations are taken for granted. For example, grocery stores and hospitals are open twenty-four hours whereas bank lobbies are open only during bankers' hours.

Culture is learned. Consumers are not born knowing the values and norms of their society. Instead, they must learn what is acceptable from family and friends. Children learn the values that will govern their behavior from parents, teachers, and

Exhibit 5.4

Components of American Culture

Component	Examples
Values	Success through hard work Emphasis on personal freedom
Language	English as the official language
Myths	Santa Claus delivers presents to good boys and girls on Christmas Eve. Abraham Lincoln walked a mile to return a penny.
Customs	Bathing daily Shaking hands when greeting new people Standard gratuity of 15 percent at restaurants
Rituals	Thanksgiving Day dinner Singing the "Star Spangled Banner" before baseball games Going to church on Sundays
Laws	Child labor laws Sherman Anti-Trust Act guarantees competition.
Material artifacts	Diamond engagement rings Beanie Babies

SOURCE: Adapted from *Consumer Behavior* by William D. Wells and David Prensky. Copyright © 1996 by John Wiley & Sons, Inc. Reprinted by permission of John Wiley & Sons, Inc. All Rights Reserved.

peers. As members of our society, they learn to shake hands when they greet someone, to drive on the right-hand side of the road, and to eat pizza and drink Coca-Cola.

Oprah Winfrey
What kind of role does spirituality play in Oprah Winfrey's show and her other ventures? Visit her Web site and find out.
http://www.oprah.com

On Line

Culture is dynamic. It adapts to changing needs and an evolving environment. The rapid growth of technology in today's world has accelerated the rate of cultural change. Television has changed entertainment patterns and family communication and has heightened public awareness of political and other news events. Automation has increased the amount of leisure time we have and, in some ways, has changed the traditional work ethic. Cultural norms will continue to evolve because of our need for social patterns that solve problems.

The most defining element of a culture is its **values**—the enduring beliefs shared by a society that a specific mode of conduct is personally or socially preferable to another mode of conduct. People's value systems have a great effect on their consumer behavior. Consumers with similar value systems tend to react alike to prices and other marketing-related inducements. Values also correspond to consumption patterns. People who want to protect the environment try to buy only products that don't harm it. Values can also influence consumers' TV viewing habits or the magazines they read. For instance, people who strongly object to violence avoid crime shows and those who oppose pornography do not buy *Hustler*. Core American values, or those values that are considered central to the American way of life, are presented in Exhibit 5.5.

The personal values of target consumers have important implications for marketing managers. When marketers understand the core values that underlie the attitudes that shape the buying patterns of America's consumers and how these values were molded by experiences, they can then target their message more effectively. For example, the personal value systems of matures, baby boomers, and Generation X-ers are quite different. The key to understanding *matures,* or everyone born before 1945, is recognizing the impact of the Great Depression and World War II on their lives. Facing these two immense challenges shaped a generation characterized by discipline, self-denial, financial and social conservatism, and a sense of obligation. Boomers, those individuals nurtured in the bountiful postwar period between 1945 and 1964, believe they are entitled to the wealth and opportunity that seemed endless in their youth. Generation X-ers are very accepting of diversity and individuality. They are also a very entrepreneurial-driven generation, ready to tackle life's challenges for themselves rather than as part of a crowd.[18]

Values represent what is most important in people's lives. Therefore, marketers watch carefully for shifts in consumers' values over time. For example, millions of Americans have acquired a passion for spirituality, as evidenced by the soaring sales of books with religious or spiritual themes and the popularity of CBS's *Touched by an Angel* television show.[19] Many marketers are zeroing in on this spirituality phenomenon among Americans. For instance, after the San Diego Padres baseball team went through a losing streak, lost several key players, and changed ownership, the team needed to rebuild and regain the support of its demoralized fans. So it developed a campaign asking fans to "keep the faith" and resurrected the team's old mascot, a friar, as its new logo. Television ads introduced the "Gospel of Baseball" according to different players to the tunes of gospel music with the refrain "Support the Padres and keep the faith." As a result, attendance doubled and the fans were happy once again.[20]

value
Enduring belief that a specific mode of conduct is personally or socially preferable to another mode of conduct.

Understanding Culture Differences

Underlying core values can vary across cultures. For example, how consumers view and use time is a reflection of the deeply rooted values that each culture shares. The Swiss, for instance, pride themselves on being

Exhibit 5.5

Core American Values

Success	Americans admire hard work, entrepreneurship, achievement, and success. Those achieving success in American society are rewarded with money, status, and prestige. For example, Bill Gates, once a nerdy computer buff, built Microsoft Computers into an internationally known giant. Gates is now one of the richest people in the world today.
Materialism	Americans value owning tangible goods. American society encourages consumption, ownership, and possession. Americans judge others based on their material possessions; for example, the type of car they own, where they live, and what type of clothes they wear.
Freedom	The American culture was founded on the principle of religious and political freedom. The U.S. Constitution and the Bill of Rights assure American citizens the right to life, liberty, and the pursuit of happiness. These freedoms are fundamental to the legal system and the moral fiber of American culture. The Internet, for example, is built on the principle of the right to free speech. Lawmakers who have attempted to limit the material available on the Internet have met with tough free-speech opponents.
Progress	Technological advancements, as well as advances in medicine, science, health, and the quality of products and services, are important to Americans. Each year, for example, more than 25,000 new or improved consumer products are introduced on America's supermarket shelves.*
Youth	Americans are obsessed with youth and spend a good deal of time on products and procedures that make them feel and look younger. Americans spend millions each year on health and beauty aids, health clubs, and healthy foods. Media and advertising encourage the quest for youth by using young, attractive, slim models, such as those in ads from fashion designer Calvin Klein.
Capitalism	Americans believe in a free enterprise system characterized by competition and the chance for monetary success. Capitalism creates choices, quality, and value for Americans. Laws prohibit monopolistic control of a market and regulate free trade. Americans encourage small business success, such as that found by Apple Computer, Wal-Mart, and McDonald's, all of which started as small enterprises with a better idea that toppled the competition.

*Data obtained from the New Products Showcase and Learning Center, Ithaca, New York, Web site at **http://www.showlearn.com**, 1998.
SOURCE: From *Consumer Behavior* by William D. Wells and David Prensky. Copyright © 1996 John Wiley & Sons, Inc. Reprinted by permission of John Wiley & Sons, Inc. All Rights Reserved.

extremely punctual. Brazilians, on the other hand, not only expect a casual lifestyle, but few wear watches and the watches they do wear are often inaccurate. People in France, Germany, and other Western European countries are often referred to as "eating and sleeping cultures" because they spend much more time than Asians or Americans on these two activities. Europeans also work fewer hours per week and enjoy more vacation time. In contrast, people in Japan and the United States spend more time working and take less vacation.[21]

 Without understanding a culture, a firm has little chance of selling products in it. Like people, products have cultural values and rules that influence their perception and use. Culture, therefore, must be understood before the behavior of individuals within the cultural context can be understood.[22] Colors, for example, may have different meanings in global markets than they do at home. In China, white is the color of mourning, and brides wear red; in the United States, black is for mourning, and brides wear white. Pepsi had a dominant market share in Southeast Asia until it changed the color of its coolers and vending equipment from deep regal blue to light ice blue. In that part of the world, light blue is associated with death and mourning. Recall the example from Chapter 4 of Pillsbury selling packaged flour in India. While it is still too early to tell if packaged flour will be a success in India, gains will depend on how quickly Indian housewives embrace convenience and overcome the perception that packaged flour won't taste as good as the flour they grind themselves.[23]

 Language is another important aspect of culture that global marketers must deal with. They must take care in translating product names, slogans, and promotional messages into foreign languages so as not to convey the wrong message. Consider the following examples of blunders made by marketers when delivering their message to Spanish-speaking consumers: General Motors discovered too late that Nova (the name of an economical car) literally means "doesn't go" in Spanish; Coors encouraged its English-speaking customers to "Turn it loose," but the phrase in Spanish means "Suffer from diarrhea"; and when Frank Perdue said, "It takes a tough man to make a tender chicken," Spanish speakers heard "It takes a sexually stimulated man to make a chicken affectionate."

 As more companies expand their operations globally, the need to understand the cultures of foreign countries becomes more important. While marketers expanding into global markets generally adapt their products and business formats to the local culture, some fear that increasing globalization, as well as the proliferation of the Internet, will result in a homogenous world culture of the future. U.S. companies in particular, they fear, are Americanizing the world by exporting bastions of American culture, such as McDonald's fast-food restaurants, Starbucks coffeehouses, Microsoft software, and American movies and entertainment. Read more about this issue in the "Global Perspectives" box.

McDonald's has responded to cultural differences like no other company. Its Web site boasts: "If meeting the demands of local culture means adding to our regular menu, we'll do it." In Japan, the company introduced the Teriyaki McBurger, and in India, McDonald's serves meatless sandwiches.

Subculture

A culture can be divided into subcultures on the basis of demographic characteristics, geographic regions, national and ethnic background, political beliefs, and religious beliefs. A **subculture** is a homogeneous group of people who share elements of the overall culture as well as cultural elements unique to their own group. Within subcultures, people's attitudes, values, and purchase decisions are even more similar than they are within the broader culture. Subcultural differences may result in considerable variation within a culture in what, how, when, and where people buy goods and services.

In the United States alone, countless subcultures can be identified. Many are concentrated geographically. People belonging to the Mormon religion, for

subculture
A homogeneous group of people who share elements of the overall culture as well as unique elements of their own group.

WILL CULTURAL DIFFERENCES SURVIVE A GLOBAL ECONOMY?

Modern industry has established the world market. . . . All old-established national industries . . . are dislodged by new industries whose . . . products are consumed, not only at home, but in every quarter of the globe. In place of old wants . . . we find new wants, requiring for their satisfaction the products of distant lands and climes.

—Karl Marx and Friedrich Engels
The Communist Manifesto

Although Karl Marx and Friedrich Engels wrote these words more than 150 years ago, this passage describes a present-day phenomenon in the world's cultures called *globalization.* Thirty years ago, most Chinese did not own televisions, refrigerators, or washing machines. But as economic reforms allowed more Western companies to offer their goods in China, ordinary people demanded these products. Today, 97 percent of Chinese in cities have televisions and 88 percent have refrigerators and washing machines.

Globalization is not a new concept. Humans have been weaving commercial and cultural connections since the beginning of civilization. Today computers, the Internet, cellular phones, cable television, and cheaper air transportation have accelerated and complicated these connections. Yet, the basic dynamic remains the same: As people cross borders and oceans moving goods and services, their ideas move with them. And cultures change. The difference today is the speed at which these changes take place. Case in point: It took television thirteen years to acquire fifty million users; it took the Internet only five.

Everywhere, it seems, people are experiencing the fusion of cultures. London coffeehouses sell Italian espresso served by Algerian waiters while strains of the Beach Boys singing "I wish they all could be California girls . . ." can be heard in the background. The classic American Barbie doll, once only available as a blond, now comes in some thirty national varieties, including,

most recently, Austrian and Moroccan. At Hollywood High School in Los Angeles, the student body represents thirty-two different languages. Computer games fanatics in the United States play mah-jongg, an ancient Chinese game of strategy and luck, over the Internet against players from all over the world. *Cosmopolitan* magazine, the racy American fashion publication, is read by some 260,000 Chinese women every month. Adventurous diners in the midst of south Louisiana savor authentic Japanese sushi and join in karaoke singing. For about 100 rupees a month—about $2.34—slum-dwelling families in Mumbai (formerly Bombay) can surf more than fifty cable channels including Western imports such as TNT, MTV, CNN, and ESPN. McDonald's now has some 25,000 restaurants worldwide, making the golden arches perhaps the most widely recognized trademark on the globe.

Not everyone is happy about the blending of cultures. Sociologists and anthropologists fear cultural cloning will result from what they regard as the "cultural assault" of ubiquitous Western multinationals such as McDonald's, Coca-Cola, Disney, Nike, MTV, and even the English language itself. Globalization has become a worrisome issue for many cultures. France worries about American films and television elbowing out French entertainment. Indians agonize that American junk food, television, films, blue jeans, pornography, and Christian missionaries will ruin traditional Indian values. Australians, in particular, have been phobically fearful of what they refer to as the remorseless march of American "cultural imperialism." In China, a recent book entitled *China Can Say No* became a bestseller by admonishing Chinese who believe blindly in anything foreign. Critics of globalization are convinced that Western, especially American, influences will pervade every culture, producing, as one observer terms it, one big "McWorld."

But not everyone is paranoid about cultural cloning. Proponents of globalization feel cultural change

is inevitable and part of national evolution. For the most part, they contend, cultures take what they want from other cultures and adapt it to their needs. Tom Freston, CEO of MTV, contends that "kids today, outside of the U.S. in particular, travel with two passports. They have the international passport . . . that plugs them into what is going on with their peers around the world. So when you talk about action movies, sports stars, certain music stars like a Mariah Carey, certain kinds of clothing and styles, there is a homogeneity. But while that trend is going on, they have their other passport that is about their local world, which increasingly is more important to them." Hence, multinationals consistently adapt products and services to meet the needs of peoples in other lands. MTV tailors its music offerings in different countries to include local stars who sing in their own language. McDonald's outlets in India, where there are more than 400 local languages and several very strict religions, serve mutton instead of beef and offer vegetarian menus acceptable to orthodox Hindus. Similarly, Revlon adapted the color palette and composition of its cosmetics to suit the Indian skin and climate.

Cultural change, supporters say, is a reality, not a choice. They believe that cultures won't become more uniform, but instead both old and new tend to transform each other. Globalization won't mean just more television sets or Nike shoes, but rather a common destiny shaped by humanity.[a]

[a] Erla Zwingle, "A World Together," *National Geographic,* August 1999, pp. 10–33; Hillary Mayell, "Death of the Mother Tongue," nationalgeographic.com/NEWS, February 25, 1999; Oliver Burkeman and Emma Brockes, "Trouble Brewing," *The Guardian,* December 3, 1999; "'Americanization' Fears Seem Misplaced," *Canberra Times,* October 24, 1999, p. 19; Swaminathan S Ankleesaria Aiyar, "Does Globalisation Threaten Indian Culture?" *The Economic Times,* December 22, 1999; Naomi Klein, "The Tyranny of Brands," *Australian Financial Review,* February 11, 2000, p. 1; Sally Beatty and Carol Hymowitz, "How MTV Stays Tuned In to Teens," *Wall Street Journal,* March 21, 2000, pp. B1, B4.

Grateful Dead

What kind of marketing program could you design to attract the subculture of Grateful Dead followers? Visit the GD On-line Store to see how marketers are currently doing this. What other elements of the site could help you design a successful program?

http://www.dead.net

On Line

example, are clustered mainly in Utah; Cajuns are located in the bayou regions of southern Louisiana. Hispanics are more predominant in those states that border Mexico, whereas the majority of Chinese, Japanese, and Koreans are found in the Pacific region of the United States.

Other subcultures are geographically dispersed. For example, computer hackers, people who are hearing- or visually-impaired, Harley-Davidson bikers, military families, university professors, and gays may be found throughout the country. Yet they have identifiable attitudes, values, and needs that distinguish them from the larger culture. For instance, Nokia Corporation sells phones that flash or vibrate for people with hearing problems while other companies, such as Nike and Pfizer, have aired commercials featuring people with various disabilities.[24] Similarly, Subaru and Volkswagen have targeted the gay market in ads using subtle symbolism and encrypted messages that speak to gay consumers without offending their mainstream consumers.[25]

If marketers can identify subcultures, they can then design special marketing programs to serve their needs. According to the U.S. Census Bureau, the Hispanic population is the largest and fastest-growing subculture, increasing at a rate of seven times that of the general population. To tap into this large and growing segment, marketers have been spending a larger percentage of their marketing budgets advertising to Hispanics. For instance, Frito-Lay discovered that Hispanics found their products tasted too mild and wanted bolder, spicier flavors. Hispanics were also generally unaware of the company's English-language ads. These discoveries prompted Frito-Lay to develop Doritos Salsa Verde flavored tortilla chips marketed via Spanish-language ads in heavily populated Hispanic areas such as Los Angeles, San Antonio, and Miami.[26] Similarly, computer manufacturer Gateway found that Hispanics were second among U.S. ethnic groups, behind Asian-Americans, in access to the Internet. To reach this lucrative market, Gateway now offers Spanish-language PCs, software, and Internet services.[27]

Identifying subcultures can be a difficult task for a marketing manager. If they can be identified, marketers can design products and services to meet the needs and wants of these specific market segments. The Spanish-language version of *People* magazine is an example of such a product.

PEOPLE en Español is a registered trademark of Time Inc., used with permission.

Social Class

The United States, like other societies, does have a social class system. A **social class** is a group of people who are considered nearly equal in status or community esteem, who regularly socialize among themselves both formally and informally, and who share behavioral norms.

A number of techniques have been used to measure social class, and a number of criteria have been used to define it. One view of contemporary U.S. status structure is shown in Exhibit 5.6 on page 158.

As you can see from Exhibit 5.6, the upper and upper middle classes comprise the small segment of affluent and wealthy Americans. The upper social classes are more likely than other classes to contribute something to society—for example, by volunteer work or active participation in civic affairs. In terms of consumer buying patterns, the affluent are more likely to own their own home and purchase new cars and trucks and are less likely to smoke. The very rich flex their financial

social class
A group of people in a society who are considered nearly equal in status or community esteem, who regularly socialize among themselves both formally and informally, and who share behavioral norms.

Exhibit 5.6

U.S. Social Class

Upper Classes

Capitalist Class	1%	People whose investment decisions shape the national economy; income mostly from assets, earned or inherited; university connections
Upper Middle Class	14%	Upper-level managers, professionals, owners of medium-sized businesses; college-educated; family income nearly twice national average

Middle Classes

Middle Class	33%	Middle-level white-collar, top-level blue-collar; education past high school typical; income somewhat above national average
Working Class	32%	Middle-level blue-collar, lower-level white-collar; income slightly below national average

Lower Classes

Working Poor	11–12%	Low-paid service workers and operatives; some high school education; below mainstream in living standard but above poverty line
Underclass	8–9%	People who are not regularly employed and who depend primarily on the welfare system for sustenance; little schooling; living standard below poverty line

SOURCE: Adapted from Richard P. Coleman, "The Continuing Significance of Social Class to Marketing," *Journal of Consumer Research,* December 1983, p. 267; Dennis Gilbert and Joseph A. Kahl, *The American Class Structure: A Synthesis* (Homewood, IL: Dorsey Press, 1982), ch. 11.

muscles by spending more on owned vacation homes, vacations and cruises, and housekeeping and gardening services. The most affluent consumers are more likely to attend art auctions and galleries, dance performances, operas, the theater, museums, concerts, and sporting events.[28]

The majority of Americans today define themselves as middle class, regardless of their actual income or educational attainment. This phenomenon is most likely due to the fact that working-class Americans tend to aspire to the middle-class lifestyle while some of those who do achieve affluence may downwardly aspire to respectable middle-class status as a matter of principle.[29] Attaining goals and achieving status and prestige are important to middle-class consumers. People falling into the middle class live in the gap between the haves and the have-nots. They aspire to the lifestyle of the more affluent but are constrained by the economic realities and cautious attitudes they share with the working class.

The working class is a distinct subset of the middle class. Interest in organized labor is one of the attributes most common among the working class. This group is more likely to rate job security as the most important reason for taking a job.[30] The working-class person depends heavily on relatives and the community for economic and emotional support. The emphasis on family ties is one sign of the group's intensely local view of the world. They like the local news far more than do middle-class audiences who favor national and world coverage. They are also more likely to vacation closer to home.

Lifestyle distinctions between the social classes are greater than the distinctions within a given class. The most significant separation between the classes is the one between the middle and lower classes. It is here that the major shift in lifestyles appears. Members of the lower class typically fall at or below the poverty level in terms of income. This social class has the highest unemployment rate, and many individuals or families are subsidized through the welfare system. Many are illiterate, with little formal education. Compared to more affluent consumers, lower-class consumers have poorer diets and typically purchase much different types of foods when they shop.

Social class is typically measured as a combination of occupation, income, education, wealth, and other variables. For instance, affluent upper-class consumers are more likely to be executives or self-employed professionals with incomes over $70,000 and at least an undergraduate degree.[31] Working-class and middle-class consumers, on the other hand, are more likely to be service or blue-collar workers, have incomes below $70,000, and have attained only a high school education. Educational attainment, however, seems to be the most reliable indicator of a person's social and economic status (see Exhibit 5.7). Those with college degrees or graduate degrees are more likely to fall into the upper classes, while those people with some college experience but no degree fall closest to traditional concepts of the middle class.

Marketers are interested in social class for two main reasons. First, social class often indicates which medium to use for advertising. Suppose an insurance company seeks to sell its policies to middle-class families. It might advertise during the local evening news because middle-class families tend to watch more television than other classes do. If the company wants to sell more policies to upscale individuals, it might place a print ad in a business publication like the *Wall Street Journal,* or a banner ad on the Internet, which is read by more educated and affluent people.

Second, knowing what products appeal to which social classes can help marketers determine where to best distribute their products. For example, a survey of consumer spending in the Washington, D.C. area reveals a stark contrast between Brie-eaters and Velveeta-eaters. The buyers of Brie, the soft and savory French cheese, are concentrated in the upscale neighborhoods of Northwest D.C. and the western suburbs of Montgomery County, Maryland, and Fairfax County, Virginia, where most residents are executives, white-collar professionals or politicians. Brie fans tend to be college-educated professionals with six-figure incomes and an activist spirit. In contrast, aficionados of Velveeta, processed cheese marketed by Kraft, are concentrated in the middle-class, family-filled suburbs of Prince George's County and the predominantly black D.C. neighborhoods. Velveeta buyers tend to be married with children, high school educated, and employed at modestly paying service and blue-collar jobs.[32]

Exhibit 5.7

Social Class and Education

Percentage of adults in self-identified social classes who have a bachelor's degree or higher, 1994

Social Class	Percent
Lower	8
Working	12
Middle	34
Upper	61

SOURCE: "The New Working Class," *American Demographics,* January 1998, pp. 51–55.

6

Identify and understand the social factors that affect consumer buying decisions

reference group
A group in society that influences an individual's purchasing behavior.

primary membership group
A reference group with which people interact regularly in an informal, face-to-face manner, such as family, friends, or fellow employees.

secondary membership group
A reference group with which people associate less consistently and more formally than a primary membership group, such as a club, professional group, or religious group.

Most consumers are likely to seek out the opinions of others to reduce their search and evaluation effort or uncertainty, especially as the perceived risk of the decision increases. Consumers may also seek out others' opinions for guidance on new products or services, products with image-related attributes, or because attribute information is lacking or uninformative.[33] Specifically, consumers interact socially with reference groups, opinion leaders, and family members to obtain product information and decision approval.

Reference Groups

All the formal and informal groups that influence the buying behavior of an individual are that person's **reference groups**. Consumers may use products or brands to identify with or become a member of a group. They learn from observing how members of their reference groups consume, and they use the same criteria to make their own consumer decisions.

Reference groups can be categorized very broadly as either direct or indirect (see Exhibit 5.8). Direct reference groups are face-to-face membership groups that touch people's lives directly. They can be either primary or secondary. **Primary membership groups** include all groups with which people interact regularly in an informal, face-to-face manner, such as family, friends, and coworkers. In contrast, people associate with **secondary membership groups** less consistently and more formally. These groups might include clubs, professional groups, and religious groups.

Consumers also are influenced by many indirect, nonmembership reference groups that they do not belong to. **Aspirational reference groups** are those that a person would like to join. To join an aspirational group, a person must at least conform to the norms of that group. (**Norms** are the values and attitudes deemed acceptable by the group.) Thus a person who wants to be elected to public office may begin to dress more conservatively, as other politicians do. He or she may go to many of the restaurants and social engagements that city and business leaders attend and try to play a role that is acceptable to voters and other influential peo-

Exhibit **5.8**

Types of Reference Groups

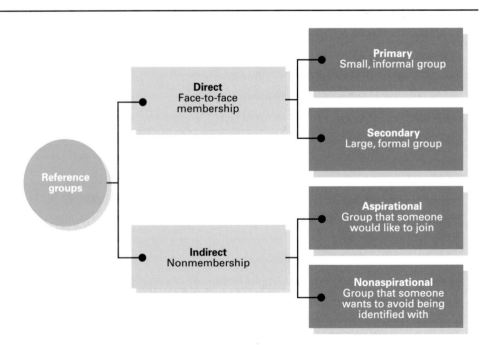

ple. Similarly, a teenager may dye his hair, experiment with body piercing and tattoos, and listen to alternative music to fit in with the "in" group.

Nonaspirational reference groups, or dissociative groups, influence our behavior when we try to maintain distance from them. A consumer may avoid buying some types of clothing or car, going to certain restaurants or stores, or even buying a home in a certain neighborhood in order to avoid being associated with a particular group.

The activities, values, and goals of reference groups directly influence consumer behavior. For marketers, reference groups have three important implications: (1) they serve as information sources and influence perceptions; (2) they affect an individual's aspiration levels; and (3) their norms either constrain or stimulate consumer behavior. For example, Teenage Research Unlimited, an Illinois research firm devoted to uncovering what's cool in the teen market, recently identified four loose groups of today's teens based on their interests in clothes, music, and activities. Tracking these groups reveals how products become cool and how groups influence the adoption of cool products by other groups. According to Teenage Research Unlimited, a trend or fad often starts with "Edge" teens who have the most innovative tastes. These teens are on the cutting edge of fashion and music, and they wear their attitude all over their bodies in the form of tattoos, body piercing, studded jewelry, or colored tresses. Certain fads embraced by Edgers will spark an interest in the small group of teens called "Influencers," who project the look other teens covet. Influencers also create their own trends, like rap music, baggy jeans, and pro sports clothes. Once a fad is embraced and adopted by Influencers, the look becomes cool and desirable. "Conformers" and "Passives" comprise the majority of the teen population, but they will not embrace a fad until it gets its seal of approval from the Influencers.[34]

In Japan, companies have long relied on the nation's high school girls to give them advice during product testing. Fads that catch on among teenage girls often become big trends throughout the country and among Japanese consumers in general. Food manufacturers frequently recruit Tokyo schoolgirls to sample potato chip recipes or chocolate bars. Television networks survey high school girls to fine-tune story lines for higher ratings on prime-time shows. Other companies pay girls to keep diaries of what they buy. Warner-Lambert hired high school girls in 1995 to help choose a new gum flavor. After extensive chewing and comparing, the girls settled on a flavor that became Trickle, now Japan's best-selling bubble gum.[35]

Opinion Leaders

Reference groups frequently include individuals known as group leaders, or **opinion leaders**—those who influence others. Obviously, it is important for marketing managers to persuade such people to purchase their goods or services. Many products and services that are integral parts of Americans' lives today got their initial boost from these influential opinion leaders. For example, VCRs and sport utility vehicles were embraced by opinion leaders well ahead of the general public.

Opinion leaders are often the first to try new products and services out of pure curiosity. They are typically activists in their communities, on the job, and in the marketplace. Opinion leaders tend to be self-indulgent, making them more likely to explore unproven but intriguing products and services. This combination of curiosity, activism, and self-indulgence makes opinion leaders trendsetters in the consumer marketplace.[36] Exhibit 5.9 lists some products and services for which individuals often seek the advice of an opinion leader before purchasing.

Opinion leadership is a casual, face-to-face phenomenon and usually inconspicuous, so locating opinion leaders can be a challenge. Thus marketers often try to create opinion leaders. They may use high school cheerleaders to model new fall fashions or civic leaders to promote insurance, new cars, and other merchandise. Revatex, the makers of JNCO jeans, gives free clothes to trendsetters among teens in

aspirational reference group
A group that someone would like to join.

norm
A value or attitude deemed acceptable by a group.

nonaspirational reference group
A group with which an individual does not want to associate.

opinion leader
An individual who influences the opinions of others.

Exhibit 5.9

Words of Wisdom: Opinion Leaders' Consumer Clout Extends Far Beyond Their Own Purchases

	Average Number of People to Whom Opinion Leaders Recommended Products* in the Past Year	Millions of Recommendations Made, 1995
Restaurant	5.0	70
Vacation destination	5.1	44
TV Show	4.9	45
Car	4.1	29
Retail store	4.7	29
Clothing	4.5	24
Consumer electronics	4.5	16
Office equipment	5.8	12
Stock, mutual fund, CD, etc.	3.4	12

*Among those who recommended the product at all
SOURCE: Roper Starch Worldwide, Inc., New York, NY. Adapted from "Maximizing the Market with Influentials," *American Demographics,* July 1995, p. 42.

the hopes that they will influence the purchase of their brand. Big-name DJs in the rave scene are outfitted by JNCO, as are members of hip, alternative bands favored by the teen crowd. Revatex also sponsors extreme-sports athletes who appeal to the teen market.[37] The National Turkey Federation, a trade group of farmers and turkey processors like Butterball Turkey Company, has seen turkey consumption plateau in recent years. With its small marketing budget, it made more sense for the federation to channel its funds into winning over chefs than attempting to sway individual consumers through mass advertising. After discovering that a growing number of prominent chefs were going on-line to find ideas and inspiration, the federation developed a Web site featuring nationally known chefs demonstrating how to prepare delicious turkey dishes. The site also features interviews with chefs about their careers and the advantages of turkey, and allows people to e-mail them with questions. The federation hopes that if fashionable restaurants begin serving turkey, and serving it in unique ways, more people will want to eat turkey and cook it at home.[38]

On a national level, companies sometimes use movie stars, sports figures, and other celebrities to promote products, hoping they are appropriate opinion leaders. Nike, for example, recently signed golf superstar Tiger Woods as a spokesperson for its products. The company is hoping that consumers will see an affinity between the values that Woods represents and the values that Nike represents— earned success, discipline, hard work, achievement, and integrity. Nike also believes the quality of Tiger Woods playing will be associated with the quality and value of their products.

The effectiveness of celebrity endorsements depends largely on how credible and attractive the spokesperson is and how familiar people are with him or her. Endorsements are most likely to succeed if an association between the spokesperson and the product can be reasonably established. For example, comedian Bill Cosby failed as an endorser for financial products but succeeded with such products as Kodak cameras and Jell-O gelatin. Consumers could not mentally link Bill Cosby with serious investment decisions but could associate him with leisure activities and everyday consumption. Additionally, in the selection of a celebrity endorser, marketers must consider the broader meanings associated with the endorser. Although the endorser may have certain attributes that are desirable for endorsing the product, he or she may also have other attributes that are inappropriate.

A marketing manager can also try to use opinion leaders through group sanctioning or referrals. For example, some companies sell products endorsed by the American Heart Association or the American Cancer Society. McNeil Consumer Products joined forces with the Arthritis Foundation to launch the Arthritis Foundation line of pain relievers that quickly jumped to the number one selling position in the over-the-counter arthritis segment. McNeil and the Arthritis Foundation both saw a unique opportunity to reach the millions of Americans living with the disease.[39] Marketers also seek endorsements from schools, churches, cities, the military, and fraternal organizations as a form of group opinion leadership. Salespeople often ask to use opinion leaders' names as a means of achieving greater personal influence in a sales presentation.

Family

The family is the most important social institution for many consumers, strongly influencing values, attitudes, self-concept—and buying behavior. For example, a family that strongly values good health will have a grocery list distinctly different from that of a family that views every dinner as a gourmet event. Moreover, the family is responsible for the **socialization process**, the passing down of cultural values and norms to children. Children learn by observing their parents' consumption patterns, and so they will tend to shop in a similar pattern.

socialization process
How cultural values and norms are passed down to children.

Decision-making roles among family members tend to vary significantly, depending on the type of item purchased. Family members assume a variety of roles in the purchase process. *Initiators* are the ones who suggest, initiate, or plant the seed for the purchase process. The initiator can be any member of the family. For example, Sister might initiate the product search by asking for a new bicycle as a birthday present. *Influencers* are those members of the family whose opinions are valued. In our example, Mom might function as a price-range watchdog, an influencer whose main role is to veto or approve price ranges. Brother may give his opinion on certain makes of bicycles. The *decision maker* is the member of the family who actually makes the decision to buy or not to buy. For example, Dad or Mom is likely to choose the final brand and model of bicycle to buy after seeking further information from Sister about cosmetic features such as color and imposing additional criteria of his or her own, such as durability and safety. The *purchaser* (probably Dad or Mom) is the one who actually exchanges money for the product. Finally, the *consumer* is the actual user—Sister, in the case of the bicycle.

Marketers should consider family purchase situations along with the distribution of consumer and decision-maker roles among family members. Ordinary marketing views the individual as both decision maker and consumer. Family

Exhibit **5.10**

Relationships Among
Purchasers and Consumers
in the Family

		Purchase Decision Maker		
		Parent(s) Only	Child/Children Only	Some or All Family Members
Consumer	Parent(s)	golf clubs cosmetics wine	Mother's Day card	Christmas gifts minivan
	Child/ Children	diapers breakfast cereal	candy small toys	bicycle
	Some Family Members	videos long-distance phone service	children's movies	computers sports events
	All Family Members	clothing life insurance	fast-food restaurant	swim club membership vacations

SOURCE: From "Pulling The Family's Strings" by Robert Boutillier, *American Demographics,* August 1993. ©1993 PRIMEDIA Intertec, Stamford, CT. Reprinted with permission.

marketing adds several other possibilities: Sometimes more than one family member or all family members are involved in the decision; sometimes only children are involved in the decision; sometimes more than one consumer is involved; and sometimes the decision maker and the consumer are different people. Exhibit 5.10 represents the patterns of family purchasing relationships that are possible.

Children today can have great influence over the purchase decisions of their parents. In many families, with both parents working and short on time, children may be encouraged to participate. In addition, children in single-parent households become more involved in family decision making at an earlier age than children in two-parent households. Children are especially influential in decisions about food, as shown in Exhibit 5.11. Children often help decide where the family goes for fast food and many influence the choice of a full-service restaurant. Kids have input into the kinds of food the family eats at home as well and often influence even the specific brands their parents buy. Finally, children influence purchase decisions for toys, clothes, vacations, recreation, and automobiles, even though they are usually not the actual purchasers of such items. Marketers are aware of the consumer power of children: It is estimated that children twelve and under directly spend $24 billion a year and influence another $300 billion in household spending.[40] Additionally, teens influence the purchase of another $200 billion in goods and services a year for everything from groceries to cars to computers. A poll of parents recently found that children influence 40 percent of parents' purchases while 65 percent of parents explicitly solicit children's opinions about products purchased for the entire household.[41]

Individual Influences on Consumer Buying Decisions

Identify and understand the individual factors that affect consumer buying decisions

A person's buying decisions are also influenced by personal characteristics that are unique to each individual, such as gender; age and life-cycle stage; and personality, self-concept, and lifestyle. Individual characteristics are generally stable over the course of one's life. For instance, most people do not change their gender, and the act of changing personality or lifestyle requires a complete reorientation of

Exhibit 5.11

Aggregate spending in millions of dollars influenced by children aged 4 to 12 on selected items, and per-child spending, 1997

	Aggregate Spending	Per-Child Spending
Food and beverages	$110,320	$3,131
Entertainment	$25,620	$727
Apparel	$17,540	$498
Automobiles	$17,740	$503
Electronics	$6,400	$182
Health and beauty	$3,550	$101

SOURCE: From "Tapping the Three Kids' Markets" by James U. McNeal, *American Demographics,* April 1998. ©1998 PRIMEDIA Intertec, Stamford, CT. Reprinted with permission.

one's life. In the case of age and life-cycle stage, these changes occur gradually over time.

Gender

Physiological differences between men and women result in different needs, such as health and beauty products. Just as important are the distinct cultural, social, and economic roles played by men and women and the effects that these have on their decision-making processes. For instance, when asked what features they would want on their next vehicle, Generation Y men yearn for more gadget and performance-oriented options, such as turbo-diesel or turbo-charged gas engines, run flat tires, and high-intensity headlights. Generation Y women, on the other hand, prefer features that provide organization, practicality, and convenience, such as wet storage area, power rear seats, cargo area dividers, and heated/cooled cupholders.[42]

Developing marketing activities based on gender can be a touchy subject for many companies marketing products to young children. Read about the dangers of gender stereotyping in the "Ethics in Marketing" box that follows on page 166.

Men and women also shop differently. Studies show that men and women share similar motivations in terms of where to shop—that is, seeking reasonable prices, merchandise quality, and a friendly, low-pressure environment—but they don't necessarily feel the same about shopping in general. Most women enjoy shopping; their male counterparts claim to dislike the experience and shop only out of necessity. Further, men desire simple shopping experiences, stores with less variety, and convenience. Stores that are easy to shop in, that are near home or office, or that have knowledgeable personnel appeal more to men than to women.[43] The Internet appeals to men who find its ease of use a more

Marketing along gender lines is legitimate in the adult world, but among children, ethical issues are raised. Mattel has chosen to design computers and software that appeals to either boys or girls. Pictured here is the Barbie version for girls; the company also offers a Hot Wheels version for boys.

TOYS FOR ALL GOOD BOYS AND GIRLS

Consumers got an unexpected lesson in marketing when Toys "R" Us debuted a recent store redesign that separates toys marketed specifically to boys and girls. In "Girl's World" kids can find plenty of dolls, kitchen toys, and makeup stocked on pink shelves. In the red section designated "Boy's World" are trains, action figures, Tonka trucks, and walkie-talkies. Many customers were outraged at the stereotyping of boys and girls.

The new store design was the result of interviews with some 10,000 current and former Toys "R" Us customers. The company identified logical adjacencies, or products likely to be purchased by the same type of consumer, and then placed these next to one another in the store. As a result, Barbies, doll houses, jewelry, and girl's dress-up are found close together, while action figures, sports collectibles, and radio remote-control cars can be found together. After public outcry over the new layout, though, the company has since removed signage that identifies one or the other sections as just for boys or just for girls.

The Toys "R" Us controversy is an example of a marketing practice that has come back in vogue among companies marketing toys, software, and other products to kids: targeting kids based on their gender. For decades companies have adopted a gender-neutral approach when marketing products to kids with the expectation that parents raised in the liberated 1960s and 1970s would resist buying products for their children that reinforced traditional gender roles, especially toys aimed at very young children. Yet, buying patterns and research are proving these expectations wrong. Child development experts point to research that shows boys seem to be starting to act like boys, and girls like girls, sooner than they used to. Boys develop a fascination with battle and competition, while girls gravitate toward play that focuses on creativity and relationships. These differences in male and female play patterns used to emerge around age five or six. But now they are being observed in younger preschoolers. Explanations for this phenomenon include earlier socialization with peers in day care and preschool and earlier exposure to media.

A recent on-line panel of about three hundred kids ages eight to fifteen conducted by Saatchi & Saatchi further outlines the differences between boys and girls in their own words. The research finds today's girls feel empowered to achieve the same things as boys, yet boys and girls still see themselves in traditional gender stereotypes. Girls see themselves as more civilized and gentler, while boys focus their self-image on sports and their peer group. Furthermore, role models for boys and girls are also gender-based. Boys look up to men who are good at what they do, like Tiger Woods and Michael Jordan, while girls are more likely to admire successful women, such as gymnast Elise Ray or singer Brittany Spears.

Many companies are feeling freer these days to acknowledge the differences between boys and girls. Fox Family Channel, for example, has started two new cable networks for boys and girls, ages two to fourteen called the boyzChannel and the girlzChannel. Similarly, software titles conspicuously target girls and boys. Blizzard Entertainment's Starcraft, an outer-space combat game, is marketed with boys in mind while Encore Software's Girls Only! Secret Diary & More and Mattel's Barbie Cool Looks Fashion Designer are marketed exclusively to girls. Mattel also recently developed gender-specific computers for children ages four to twelve. The pink-flowered Barbie computer comes loaded with Barbie software. Its royal-blue Hot Wheels computer for boys includes Hot Wheels software titles and others that appeal to young boys.[a]

What examples of gender marketing have you seen recently? Do you feel that toy marketers should market their products specifically for boys or girls or do you feel their promotion should be gender-neutral? What are the advantages and disadvantages to marketers for each option?

[a] Lisa Bannon, "Why Girls and Boys Get Different Toys," *Wall Street Journal*, February 14, 2000, pp. B1, B4; "Kids Opinions Support New Talk About Gender Marketing," *Selling to Kids*, July 22, 1998; Betsy Hart, "Toy Store Is Newest Battlefield for Feminists," *Chicago Sun-Times*, February 21, 2000, p. 29; Karen Kaplan, "In Software, It's Still a Boy's World," *Los Angeles Times*, June 28, 1999, p. C-1.

---

enjoyable way to shop for clothing and gifts. Many Internet retailers are designing their sites to attract male gift buyers. Banana Republic's Web site prompts customers purchasing gifts to choose a price range. The site then returns five to six different suggestions. Shoppers at eToys on-line store need only know a child's age or interests to find appropriate gifts. To help out its male shoppers, intimate apparel retailer Victoria's Secret lets women create password-protected wish lists and then zap them to their significant others to insure there's no mistaking colors or sizes.[44]

Age and Family Life-Cycle Stage

The age and family life-cycle stage of a consumer can have a significant impact on consumer behavior. How old a consumer is generally indicates what products he or she may be interested in purchasing. Consumer tastes in food, clothing, cars, furniture, and recreation are often age related; for example, the favorite magazines for preteens aged eight to twelve include *Sports Illustrated for Kids*, *Nickelodeon*, and *Ranger Rick*. But as these consumers become teenagers their tastes in magazines diverge in favor of sports titles for boys and fashion/lifestyle titles for girls.[45]

Related to a person's age is his or her place in the family life cycle. As Chapter 7 explains in more detail, the *family life cycle* is an orderly series of stages through which consumers' attitudes and behavioral tendencies evolve through maturity, experience, and changing income and status. Marketers often define their target markets in terms of family life cycle, such as "young singles," "young married with children," and "middle-aged married without children." For instance, young singles spend more than average on alcoholic beverages, education, and entertainment. New parents typically increase their spending on health care, clothing, housing, and food and decrease their spending on alcohol, education, and transportation. Households with older children spend more on food, entertainment, personal care products, and education, as well as cars and gasoline. After their children leave home, spending by older couples on vehicles, women's clothing, health care, and long-distance calls typically increases. For instance, the presence of children in the home is the most significant determinant of the type of vehicle that's driven off the new car lot. Parents are the ultimate need-driven car consumers requiring larger cars and trucks to haul their children and all their belongings. It comes as no surprise then that for all households with children, sport utility vehicles rank either first or second among new-vehicle purchases followed by minivans.[46]

Marketers should also be aware of the many nontraditional life-cycle paths that are common today that provide insights into the needs and wants of such consumers as divorced parents, lifelong singles, and childless couples. Three decades ago, traditional families comprised of married couples with children under eighteen accounted for nearly a majority of U.S. households. Today, traditional family structures make up just 25 percent of all households, while people living alone or with nonfamily members make up more than 30 percent.[47] Furthermore, according to the U.S. Census Bureau, single-father families in which a single father has custody of his children are growing at an annual rate of 10 percent. The shift toward custodial fathers is part of a broader societal change that has put more women on the career track and given men more options at home.[48]

Personality, Self-Concept, and Lifestyle

Each consumer has a unique personality. **Personality** is a broad concept that can be thought of as a way of organizing and grouping how an individual typically reacts to situations. Thus personality combines psychological makeup and environmental forces. It includes people's underlying dispositions, especially their most dominant characteristics. Although personality is one of the least useful concepts in the study of consumer behavior, some marketers believe that personality influences the types and brands of products purchased. For instance, the type of car, clothes, or jewelry a consumer buys may reflect one or more personality traits. Personality traits like those listed in Exhibit 5.12 on page 168 may be used to describe a consumer's personality.

Self-concept, or self-perception, is how consumers perceive themselves. Self-concept includes attitudes, perceptions, beliefs, and self-evaluations. Although self-concept may change, the change is often gradual. Through self-concept, people define their identity, which in turn provides for consistent and coherent behavior.

Self-concept combines the **ideal self-image** (the way an individual would like to be) and the **real self-image** (how an individual actually perceives himself or herself). Generally, we try to raise our real self-image toward our ideal (or at least narrow the gap). Consumers seldom buy products that jeopardize their self-image.

personality
A way of organizing and grouping the consistencies of an individual's reactions to situations.

self-concept
How consumers perceive themselves in terms of attitudes, perceptions, beliefs, and self-evaluations.

ideal self-image
The way an individual would like to be.

real self-image
The way an individual actually perceives himself or herself.

Exhibit 5.12

Some Common
Personality Traits

- Adaptability
- Need for affiliation
- Aggressiveness
- Need for achievement
- Ascendancy
- Autonomy
- Dominance

- Deference
- Defensiveness
- Emotionalism
- Orderliness
- Sociability
- Stability
- Self-confidence

For example, someone who sees herself as a trendsetter wouldn't buy clothing that doesn't project a contemporary image.

Human behavior depends largely on self-concept. Because consumers want to protect their identity as individuals, the products they buy, the stores they patronize, and the credit cards they carry support their self-image. No other product quite reflects a person's self-image than the car he or she drives. In a recent study by J.D. Power and Associates, the number-one reason people switched from mid-size cars to compact sport utility vehicles was exterior and interior styling and appearance. In other words, the car looked more rugged, and that was how SUV drivers wanted to see themselves.[49] Likewise, Mitsubishi found that car buyers did not want to sacrifice a youthful image of themselves just because they have new responsibilities in life. Advertising for the Montero sport utility vehicle and the Eclipse Spyder position these vehicles as "spirited cars for spirited people," encouraging drivers to experience the exhilaration of driving exciting, stylish cars.[50]

By influencing the degree to which consumers perceive a good or service to be self-relevant, marketers can affect consumers' motivation to learn about, shop for, and buy a certain brand. Marketers also consider self-concept important because it helps explain the relationship between individuals' perceptions of themselves and their consumer behavior.

An important component of self-concept is *body image,* the perception of the attractiveness of one's own physical features. For example, individuals who have cosmetic surgery often experience significant improvement in their overall body image and self-concept. Moreover, a person's perception of body image can be a stronger reason for weight loss than either good health or other social factors.[51] With the median age of Americans rising, many companies are introducing products aimed at this group of aging baby boomers who are concerned about their physical appearance. Sales of hair-coloring products for men, for instance, have more than doubled over the last decade while television and print advertisements aimed at getting men to dye the gray out of their hair have tripled. Much of the increase may be due to today's business world's obsession on youth. In the past, looking older and more experienced was a benefit to men in the workplace. But, the rise of fast-paced computer companies and the success of Internet firms are putting younger executives in the workforce, prompting many middle-aged men with natural gray to turn to hair dyes to help them look and feel younger and hipper.[52]

Self-concept plays a key role in consumer behavior. Rogaine ads directed to men—and recently to women—connect with people's desire to appear younger longer.

Personality and self-concept are reflected in lifestyle. A **lifestyle** is a mode of living, as identified by a person's activities, interests, and opinions. *Psychographics* is the analytical technique used to examine consumer lifestyles and to categorize consumers. Unlike personality characteristics, which are hard to describe and measure, lifestyle characteristics are useful in segmenting and targeting consumers. Lifestyle and psychographic analysis explicitly addresses the way consumers outwardly express their inner selves in their social and cultural environment.

Many industries now use psychographics to better understand their market segments. Until recently, many marketers selling products to mothers conveniently assumed that all moms were fairly homogenous and concerned about the same things—the health and well-being of their children—and they could all be reached with the same message. But recent lifestyle research has identified four different types of mothers: (1) the "June Cleaver: The Sequel" moms, who believe in traditional roles of stay-at-home mom and bread-winner dads; (2) the "Tug-of-War" moms, who share some of the same traditional notions of motherhood but are forced to work; (3) the "Strong Shoulders" moms, who are largely single mothers but they have a positive outlook on their lives despite their lower income and little support from their children's dads; and (4) the "Mothers of Invention" moms, who have found creative ways to balance a career with a happy home life. Companies like Procter & Gamble and Pillsbury are now looking at ways of developing more effective marketing strategies to reach these different types of mothers.[53] Psychographics and lifestyle segmentation schemes are discussed in more detail in Chapter 7.

lifestyle
Mode of living as identified by a person's activities, interests, and opinions.

Psychological Influences on Consumer Buying Decisions

An individual's buying decisions are further influenced by psychological factors: perception, motivation, learning, and beliefs and attitudes. These factors are what consumers use to interact with their world. They are the tools consumers use to recognize their feelings, gather and analyze information, formulate thoughts and opinions, and take action. Unlike the other three influences on consumer behavior, psychological influences can be affected by a person's environment because they are applied on specific occasions.[54] For example, you will perceive different stimuli and process these stimuli in different ways depending on whether you are sitting in class concentrating on the instructor, sitting outside of class talking to friends, or sitting in your dorm room watching television.

Identify and understand the psychological factors that affect consumer buying decisions

Perception

The world is full of stimuli. A stimulus is any unit of input affecting one or more of the five senses: sight, smell, taste, touch, hearing. The process by which we select, organize, and interpret these stimuli into a meaningful and coherent picture is called **perception**. In essence, perception is how we see the world around us and how we recognize that we need some help in making a purchasing decision.

People cannot perceive every stimulus in their environment. Therefore, they use **selective exposure** to decide which stimuli to notice and which to ignore. A typical consumer is exposed to more than 250 advertising messages a day but notices only between eleven and twenty.

perception
Process by which people select, organize, and interpret stimuli into a meaningful and coherent picture.

selective exposure
Process whereby a consumer notices certain stimuli and ignores others.

The familiarity of an object, contrast, movement, intensity (such as increased volume), and smell are cues that influence perception. Consumers use these cues to identify and define products and brands. The shape of a product's packaging, such as Coca-Cola's signature contour bottle, for instance, can influence perception. Color is another cue, and it plays a key role in consumers' perceptions. Packaged foods manufacturers use color to trigger unconscious associations for grocery shoppers who typically make their shopping decisions in the blink of an eye. Red, for instance, used on packages of Campbell's soups and SunMaid raisins, is associated with prolonged and increased eating. Green is associated with environmental goodness and healthy, low fat foods. Health Choice entrees and SnackWells cookies use green. Premium products, like Sheba cat food and Ben & Jerry's ice cream, use black and gold on their packaging to convey their use of superior ingredients.[55] The shape and look of product's packaging can also influence perception. Heinz recently reintroduced its classic 24-ounce glass bottle for ketchup, not seen on supermarket shelves since the late 1980s when it was replaced by the plastic squeeze bottle, in an effort to spark nostalgic summer memories. Outdoor ads picture two 1950s-era boys eating hot dogs in a ballpark with the tagline "Heinz was there" alongside a glass bottle of Heinz ketchup.[56]

What is perceived by consumers may also depend on the stimuli's vividness or shock value. Graphic warnings of the hazards associated with a product's use are perceived more readily and remembered more accurately than less vivid warnings or warnings that are written in text. "Sexier" ads excel at attracting the attention of younger consumers. Companies like Calvin Klein and Guess use sensuous ads to "cut through the clutter" of competing ads and other stimuli to capture the attention of the target audience. Similarly, Benetton ads use shock value by portraying taboo social issues, from racism to homosexuality.

selective distortion
A process whereby a consumer changes or distorts information that conflicts with his or her feelings or beliefs.

Two other concepts closely related to selective exposure are selective distortion and selective retention. **Selective distortion** occurs when consumers change or distort information that conflicts with their feelings or beliefs. For example, suppose a consumer buys a Chrysler. After the purchase, if the consumer receives new information about a close alternative brand, such as a Ford, he or she may distort the information to make it more consistent with the prior view that the Chrysler is better than the Ford. Business travelers who fly often may distort or discount information about airline crashes because they must use air travel constantly in their jobs. People who smoke and have no plans to quit may distort information from medical reports and the Surgeon General about the link between cigarettes and lung cancer.

selective retention
A process whereby a consumer remembers only that information that supports his or her personal beliefs.

Selective retention is remembering only information that supports personal feelings or beliefs. The consumer forgets all information that may be inconsistent. After reading a pamphlet that contradicts one's political beliefs, for instance, a person may forget many of the points outlined in it.

Which stimuli will be perceived often depends on the individual. People can be exposed to the same stimuli under identical conditions but perceive them very differently. For example, two people viewing a TV commercial may have different interpretations of the advertising message. One person may be thoroughly engrossed by the message and become highly motivated to buy the product. Thirty seconds after the ad ends, the second person may not be able to recall the content of the message or even the product advertised.

Marketing Implications of Perception   Marketers must recognize the importance of cues, or signals, in consumers' perception of products. Marketing managers first identify the important attributes, such as price or quality, that the targeted consumers want in a product and then design signals to communicate these attributes. For example, consumers will pay more for candy wrapped in expensive-looking foil packages. But shiny labels on wine bottles signify less expensive wines; dull labels indicate more expensive wines. Marketers also often use price as a signal to consumers that the product is of higher quality than competing products. Gibson Guitar Corporation briefly cut prices on many of its guitars to compete with Japanese rivals Yamaha and Ibanez but found instead that it sold more guitars when it charged more for them. Consumers perceived the higher price indicated a better quality instrument.[57]

Of course, brand names send signals to consumers. The brand names of Close-Up toothpaste, DieHard batteries, and Caress moisturizing soap, for example, identify important product qualities. Names chosen for search engines and sites on the Internet, such as Yahoo!, Amazon.com, CDNow, and Excite, are intended to convey excitement, intensity, and vastness. Companies might even change their names to send a message to consumers. As today's electric utility companies increasingly enter into nonregulated markets to sell power, natural gas, and other energy-related products and services, they are finding their old company names may hold some negative perceptions with consumers. Consequently, many are shaking their stodgy "Power & Light & Electric" names in favor of those that let consumers know they are not just about electricity anymore, such as Reliant Energy, Entergy, and Cinergy.

Consumers also perceive quality and reliability with certain brand names. Companies watch their brand identity closely, in large part because a strong link has been established between perceived brand value and customer loyalty. Brand names that consistently enjoy high perceived value from consumers include Kodak, Disney, National Geographic, Mercedes-Benz, and Fisher-Price. Naming a product after a place can also add perceived value by association. Brand names using the words Santa Fe, Dakota, or Texas convey a sense of openness, freedom, and youth, but products named after other locations might conjure up images of pollution and crime.

Marketing managers are also interested in the *threshold level of perception:* the minimum difference in a stimulus that the consumer will notice. This concept is sometimes referred to as the "just-noticeable difference." For example, how much would Sony have to drop the price of a VCR before consumers recognized it as a bargain—$25? $50? or more? One study found that the just-noticeable difference in a stimulus is about a 20 percent change. For example, consumers will likely notice a 20 percent price decrease more quickly than a 15 percent decrease. This marketing principle can be applied to other marketing variables as well, such as package size or loudness of a broadcast advertisement.[58]

Another study showed that the bargain-price threshold for a name brand is lower than that for a store brand. In other words, consumers perceive a bargain more readily when stores offer a small discount on a name-brand item than when they offer the same discount on a store brand; a larger discount is needed to achieve a similar effect for a store brand.[59] Researchers also found that for low-cost grocery items, consumers typically do not see past the second digit in the price. For instance, consumers do not perceive any real difference between two comparable cans of tuna, one priced at $1.52 and the other at $1.59 because they ignore the last digit.[60]

Besides changing such stimuli as price, package size, and volume, marketers can change the product. How many sporty features will General Motors have to add to a basic two-door sedan before consumers begin to perceive the model as a sports car? How many new services will a discount store like Kmart need to add before consumers perceive it as a full-service department store?

Marketing managers who intend to do business in global markets should be aware of how foreign consumers perceive their products. For instance, in Japan, product labels are often written in English or French, even though they may not translate into anything meaningful. But many Japanese associate foreign words on product labels with the exotic, the expensive, and high quality.

Marketers have often been suspected of sending advertising messages subconsciously to consumers in what is known as *subliminal perception*. The controversy began in 1957 when a researcher claimed to have increased popcorn and Coca-Cola sales at a movie theater after flashing "Eat popcorn" and "Drink Coca-Cola" on the screen every five seconds for 1/300th of a second, although the audience did not consciously recognize the messages. Almost immediately consumer protection groups became concerned that advertisers were brainwashing consumers and this practice was pronounced illegal in California and Canada. Although the researcher later admitted to making up the data and scientists have been unable to replicate the study since, consumers are still wary of hidden messages that advertisers may be sending.

Motivation

By studying motivation, marketers can analyze the major forces influencing consumers to buy or not buy products. When you buy a product, you usually do so to fulfill some kind of need. These needs become motives when aroused sufficiently. For instance, suppose this morning you were so hungry before class that you needed to eat something. In response to that need, you stopped at McDonald's for an Egg McMuffin. In other words, you were motivated by hunger to stop at McDonald's. **Motives** are the driving forces that cause a person to take action to satisfy specific needs.

Why are people driven by particular needs at particular times? One popular theory is **Maslow's hierarchy of needs**, shown in Exhibit 5.13, which arranges needs in ascending order of importance: physiological, safety, social, esteem, and self-actualization. As a person fulfills one need, a higher-level need becomes more important.

The most basic human needs are *physiological*—that is the needs for food, water, and shelter. Because they are essential to survival, these needs must be satisfied first. Ads showing a juicy hamburger or a runner gulping down Gatorade after a marathon are examples of appeals to satisfy the physiological needs of hunger and thirst.

motive
A driving force that causes a person to take action to satisfy specific needs.

Maslow's hierarchy of needs
A method of classifying human needs and motivations into five categories in ascending order of importance: physiological, safety, social, esteem, and self-actualization.

Exhibit **5.13**

Maslow's Hierarchy of Needs

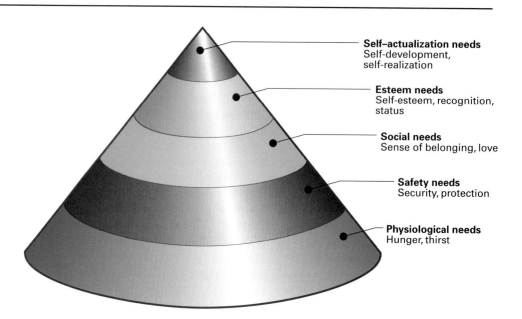

Self–actualization needs
Self-development,
self-realization

Esteem needs
Self-esteem, recognition,
status

Social needs
Sense of belonging, love

Safety needs
Security, protection

Physiological needs
Hunger, thirst

Safety needs include security and freedom from pain and discomfort. Marketers often exploit consumers' fears and anxieties about safety to sell their products. For example, after the Environmental Protection Agency reported that perchloroethylene, a chemical used in dry cleaning, may be a probable human carcinogen, consumers became worried about toxic substances on their dry-cleaned clothes. Dry cleaners using alternative cleaning methods, such as petroleum-based or water-based methods, sprang up to take advantage of these fears, pitching themselves as a safe alternative to traditional dry cleaners using perchloroethylene.[61]

After physiological and safety needs have been fulfilled, *social needs*—especially love and a sense of belonging—become the focus. Love includes acceptance by one's peers, as well as sex and romantic love. Marketing managers probably appeal more to this need than to any other. Ads for clothes, cosmetics, and vacation packages suggest that buying the product can bring love. The need to belong is also a favorite of marketers, especially those marketing products to teens. Shoes and clothing brands such as Nike, adidas, Tommy Hilfiger, Gap, JNCO, and Abercrombie & Fitch score high with teenagers as "cool" brands. Teens who wear these labels feel and look like they belong to the in-crowd.[62]

GLOBAL Love is acceptance without regard to one's contribution. Esteem is acceptance based on one's contribution to the group. *Self-esteem needs* include self-respect and a sense of accomplishment. Esteem needs also include prestige, fame, and recognition of one's accomplishments. Mont Blanc pens, Mercedes-Benz automobiles, and Neiman-Marcus stores all appeal to esteem needs. Asian consumers, in particular, are strongly motivated by status and prestige. Asian individuals are always conscious of their place in a group, institution, or society as a whole. The importance of gaining social recognition turns Asians into probably the most image-conscious consumers in the world. Status-conscious Asians will not hesitate to spend freely on premium brands, such as BMW, Mercedes-Benz, and the best Scotch whiskey and French cognac.[63] This may explain why jewelry sales at Tiffany's in Japan continued to rise even when Japan faced one of its worst economic recessions.[64]

The highest human need is *self-actualization*. It refers to finding self-fulfillment and self-expression, reaching the point in life at which "people are what they feel they should be." Maslow felt that very few people ever attain this level. Even so, advertisements may focus on this type of need. For example, American Express ads convey the message that acquiring its card is one of the highest attainments in life. The U.S. Armed Forces' slogan urges young people to "Be all that you can be."

Even children must satisfy more than just the basic physiological and safety needs. Mattel's Barbie doll, for instance, fulfills a fundamental need that all girls share by playing out what it might be like in the grown-up world. Through Barbie, girls dream of achievement, glamour, romance, adventure, and nurturing. These dreams touch on many timeless needs, ranging from pride and success to belonging and love. Mattel zeros in on these core needs and addresses them with different Barbie products. Over the years, Barbie has been a teacher, a fashion model, a girlfriend, a dentist, an astronaut, a sister, and a veterinarian, to name a few.[65]

Learning

Almost all consumer behavior results from **learning**, which is the process that creates changes in behavior through experience and practice. It is not possible to observe learning directly, but we can infer when it has occurred by a person's actions. For example, suppose you see an advertisement for a new and improved cold medicine. If you go to the store that day and buy that remedy, we infer that you have learned something about the cold medicine.

There are two types of learning: experiential and conceptual. *Experiential learning* occurs when an experience changes your behavior. For example, if you try the new cold medicine when you get home and it does not relieve your symptoms, you may not buy that brand again. *Conceptual learning*, which is not learned through

learning
A process that creates changes in behavior, immediate or expected, through experience and practice.

direct experience, is the second type of learning. Assume, for example, that you are standing at a soft-drink machine and notice a new diet flavor with an artificial sweetener. Because someone has told you that diet beverages leave an aftertaste, you choose a different drink. You have learned that you would not like this new diet drink without ever trying it.

Reinforcement and repetition boost learning. Reinforcement can be positive or negative. If you see a vendor selling frozen yogurt (stimulus), buy it (response), and find the yogurt to be quite refreshing (reward), your behavior has been positively reinforced. On the other hand, if you buy a new flavor of yogurt and it does not taste good (negative reinforcement), you will not buy that flavor of yogurt again (response). Without positive or negative reinforcement, a person will not be motivated to repeat the behavior pattern or to avoid it. Thus if a new brand evokes neutral feelings, some marketing activity, such as a price change or an increase in promotion, may be required to induce further consumption. Learning theory is helpful in reminding marketers that concrete and timely actions are what reinforce desired consumer behavior.

Repetition is a key strategy in promotional campaigns because it can lead to increased learning. Most marketers use repetitious advertising so consumers will learn what their unique advantage is over the competition. Generally, to heighten learning, advertising messages should be spread over time rather than clustered together.

A related learning concept useful to marketing managers is stimulus generalization. In theory, **stimulus generalization** occurs when one response is extended to a second stimulus similar to the first. Marketers often use a successful, well-known brand name for a family of products because it gives consumers familiarity with and knowledge about each product in the family. Such brand-name families spur the introduction of new products and facilitate the sale of existing items. Jell-O frozen pudding pops rely on the familiarity of Jell-O gelatin; Clorox laundry detergent relies on familiarity with Clorox bleach; and Ivory shampoo relies on familiarity with Ivory soap. Starbucks Coffee Company recently introduced four premium flavors of Starbucks ice cream hoping that consumers would transfer their love of Starbucks coffee to ice cream. With only a little publicity and a one-time limited outdoor campaign, quarts of Starbucks coffee ice cream flew off the shelves. The company attributes much of its success with its ice cream brand extension to the strong brand power of Starbucks' fifteen hundred retail coffee stores nationwide.[66] Branding is examined in more detail in Chapter 9.

stimulus generalization
A form of learning that occurs when one response is extended to a second stimulus similar to the first.

GLOBAL
Another form of stimulus generalization occurs when retailers or wholesalers design their packages to resemble well-known manufacturers' brands. Such imitation often confuses consumers, who buy the imitator thinking it's the original. U.S. manufacturers in foreign markets have sometimes found little, if any, brand protection. In South Korea, Procter & Gamble's Ivory soap competes head-on with the Korean brand Bory, which has an almost identical logo on the package. Consumers dissatisfied with Bory may attribute their dissatisfaction to Ivory, never realizing that Bory is an imitator. Counterfeit products are also produced to look exactly like the original. For example, counterfeit Levi's jeans made in China are hot items in Europe, where Levi Strauss has had trouble keeping up with demand. The knockoffs look so much like the real thing that unsuspecting consumers don't know the difference—until after a few washes, when the belt loops fall off and the rivets begin to rust.

The opposite of stimulus generalization is **stimulus discrimination**, which means learning to differentiate among similar products. Consumers usually prefer one product as more rewarding or stimulating. For example, some consumers pre-

Imitation or counterfeit products are designed to confuse consumers, who buy the items thinking they are originals. This problem is common in foreign markets where there is often little brand protection.
© Mark Richards/CONTACT Press Images

fer Coca-Cola and others prefer Pepsi; many insist they can taste a difference between the two brands.

With some types of products—such as aspirin, gasoline, bleach, paper towels—marketers rely on promotion to point out brand differences that consumers would otherwise not recognize. This process, called *product differentiation,* is discussed in more detail in Chapter 7. Usually product differentiation is based on superficial differences. For example, Bayer tells consumers that it's the aspirin "doctors recommend most."

stimulus discrimination
A learned ability to differentiate among similar products.

Beliefs and Attitudes

Beliefs and attitudes are closely linked to values. A **belief** is an organized pattern of knowledge that an individual holds as true about his or her world. A consumer may believe that Sony's camcorder makes the best home videos, tolerates hard use, and is reasonably priced. These beliefs may be based on knowledge, faith, or hearsay. Consumers tend to develop a set of beliefs about a product's attributes and then, through these beliefs, form a *brand image*—a set of beliefs about a particular brand. In turn, the brand image shapes consumers' attitudes toward the product.

belief
An organized pattern of knowledge that an individual holds as true about his or her world.

An **attitude** is a learned tendency to respond consistently toward a given object, such as a brand. Attitudes rest on an individual's value system, which represents personal standards of good and bad, right and wrong, and so forth; therefore, attitudes tend to be more enduring and complex than beliefs.

attitude
A learned tendency to respond consistently toward a given object.

For an example of the nature of attitudes, consider the differing attitudes of consumers around the world toward the habit of purchasing on credit. Americans have long been enthusiastic about charging goods and services and are willing to pay high interest rates for the privilege of postponing payment. To many European consumers, doing what amounts to taking out a loan—even a small one—to pay for anything seems absurd. Germans especially are reluctant to buy on credit. Italy has a sophisticated credit and banking system well suited to handling credit cards, but Italians prefer to carry cash, often huge wads of it. Although most Japanese consumers have credit cards, card purchases amount to less than 1 percent of all consumer transactions. The Japanese have long looked down on credit purchases but acquire cards to use while traveling abroad.[67]

If a good or service is meeting its profit goals, positive attitudes toward the product merely need to be reinforced. However, if the brand is not succeeding, the marketing manager must strive to change target consumers' attitudes toward it. Changes in attitude tend to grow out of an individual's attempt to reconcile long-held values with a constant stream of new information. This change can be accomplished in three ways: changing beliefs about the brand's attributes, changing the relative importance of these beliefs, and adding new beliefs.

Changing Beliefs About Attributes
The first technique is to turn neutral or negative beliefs about product attributes into positive ones. For example, the consumption of eggs has steadily decreased over the years because of consumer belief that eggs contribute to high cholesterol. To counter this belief, the American Egg Board launched a new advertising campaign with "If it ain't eggs, it ain't breakfast" and "the incredible edible egg" theme lines. Accompanying the board's advertising is an extensive public relations campaign that endeavors to give consumers "permission" to eat eggs again with proof of extensive research that shows eggs can be a part of a well-balanced diet.[68] Similarly, Procter & Gamble began a series of television ads to downplay the health worries surrounding the fat substitute olestra, which it manufactures and markets under the brand name Olean, used in Frito-Lay's line of Wow! fat-free chips and salty snacks. The campaign attempts to counter the fact that Olean is made in a laboratory by showing wholesome scenes from an American farm to remind consumers that olestra is made with soybeans.[69]

Changing beliefs about a service can be more difficult because service attributes are intangible. Convincing consumers to switch hairstylists or lawyers or to go to a mall dental clinic can be much more difficult than getting them to change brands of razor blades. Image, which is also largely intangible, significantly determines service patronage. For example, research by the American Bankers Association found that young adults do not have a good understanding of what banks are, and some feel that they don't need banks to invest their money. To counter this image, America's banking industry began a national advertising effort to dispel the belief that banks are just for checking and savings accounts. The association aired several television ads that were based on the stereotype of banks as old-fashioned in the hopes that consumers would see banks as a good place for their investments.[70] Service marketing is explored in detail in Chapter 11.

Changing the Importance of Beliefs   The second approach to modifying attitudes is to change the relative importance of beliefs about an attribute. For years, consumers have known that bran cereals are high in natural fiber. The primary belief associated with this attribute is that the fiber tends to act as a mild, natural laxative. Today, however, cereal marketers promote the high fiber content of bran cereals as a possible factor in preventing certain types of cancer, vastly increasing the importance of this attribute in the minds of consumers.

Marketers can also downplay the importance of some beliefs in favor of others. For example, Chrysler Corporation's Jeep unit strives to maintain the Jeep Grand Cherokee's ruggedness while playing up its luxury features. The newest Grand Cherokees have even more off-road capability, but only 15 percent of owners ever take them off-road. So, its engineers made more room in the back to carry as many as eight bags of golf clubs, developed a climate-control system with infrared beams to track drivers' and passengers' skin temperature to adjust air-conditioning and heating, and designed his-and-her key fobs with buttons that remember settings for the power seats and mirrors and that reprogram the radio stations for different drivers.[71]

Adding New Beliefs   The third approach to transforming attitudes is to add new beliefs. Although changes in consumption patterns often come slowly, cereal marketers are betting that consumers will eventually warm up to the idea of cereal as a snack. A print ad for Ralston Purina's Cookie-Crisp cereal features a boy popping the sugary nuggets into his mouth while he does his homework. Boxes of Kellogg's Cracklin' Oat Bran boast that the cereal tastes like oatmeal cookies and makes "a great snack . . . anytime." Similarly, commercials for Quaker Oats 100% Natural cereal promote eating it straight from the box. James River Corporation, the manufacturer of Dixie paper products, is also attempting to add new beliefs about the uses of its paper plates and cups with an advertising campaign aimed at positioning its product as a "home cleanup replacement." New commercials pitch Dixie paper plates as an alternative to washing dishes after everyday meals.[72]

Adding new beliefs is not easy. For example, when Anheuser-Busch first introduced Bud Dry beer, consumers were confused, because the word "dry" is commonly used to describe wines. Nevertheless, many consumers have since added the new belief that beer too can be described as dry. Volvo faced a similar problem in introducing its sporty C70 convertible and S80 luxury sedan models. For over a quarter of a century, Volvo has successfully crafted an image as the safest car on the road. Yet, with its core target market of baby boomers aging and their children moving out, Volvo also wanted to appeal emotionally to their desire for a fun, powerful, and sexy car while still being safe. Volvo had done such a good job driving home its safety message, however, that consumers had a hard time imagining a Volvo as anything other than a boxy, steel-reinforced tank.[73]

GLOBAL   U.S. companies attempting to market their goods overseas may need to help consumers add new beliefs about a product in general. Coca-Cola and PepsiCo have both found it challenging selling their diet cola brands to consumers in India partly because diet foods of any kind are a new concept there, a country where malnutrition was widespread not too many years ago. Indians also have deep-rooted attitudes that anything labeled "diet" is meant for a sick person, such as a diabetic. As a general rule, most Indians are not diet-conscious, preferring food prepared in the traditional manner that tastes good. Indians are also suspicious of the artificial sweeteners used in diet colas. India's Health Ministry has required warning labels on cans and bottles of Diet Coke and Diet Pepsi saying "Not Recommended for Children."[74]

Looking Back

Returning to the discussion that opened the chapter, you should now be able to see how cultural, social, individual, and psychological factors affect the consumer decision-making process. Purchase decisions by today's teens are influenced by many outside factors, most importantly peer reference groups and opinion leaders. They have unique values and opinions based upon the environment in which they have grown up. Marketers hoping to reach this fickle segment must understand their needs and wants and the influences that shape them. Consumer behavior is a fascinating and often intricate process. An appreciation of consumer behavior and the factors that influence it will help you identify target markets and design effective marketing mixes.

Use it Now!

Find Product Ratings

Consumer Reports Online (**http://www. consumerreports.org**) is your one-stop source for information on hundreds of products you might be interested in purchasing, such as cars and trucks, appliances, electronics, household products, home office equipment, money and investing, health and food products, personal products, and leisure activities. The section on cars and trucks, for instance, offers a wealth of advice for those thinking of buying a new or used car, or seeking safety and maintenance tips. The site includes comparison ratings, reliability reports, negotiation advice, a personal car selector, information on car equipment and accessories, as well as exclusive ratings on auto-buying Web sites. Consumers Union, publisher of *Consumer Reports,* is a nonprofit consumer advocacy group with over sixty years of product testing. The group doesn't accept any outside advertising or support from product manufacturers, so the in-

formation you find is as unbiased as possible, but you have to pay for it as a subscriber.

Find the Best Price

Narrowed down your purchase decision to a single brand or a small set of alternative brands? Now find the best price on the Web with the use of a "shopping bot," a search engine that will systematically search the Web to find the lowest price from on-line retailers and auction sites. Visit CNET Shopper at **http://www.cnet.com** to search for the lowest price on computer systems and accessories, cameras, handheld personal assistants, software, and games. Or visit ShopBest.com (**http://www.shopbest.com**) for a shopping bot that can find the best price for an even broader selection of merchandise. ShopBest.com offers over twenty shopping departments, including apparel, computer hardware and software, art, furniture, music, movies, housewares, and toys.

Summary

1 **Explain why marketing managers should understand consumer behavior.** Consumer behavior describes how consumers make purchase decisions and how they use and dispose of the products they buy. An understanding of consumer behavior reduces marketing managers' uncertainty when they are defining a target market and designing a marketing mix.

2 **Analyze the components of the consumer decision-making process.** The consumer decision-making process begins with need recognition, when stimuli trigger awareness of an unfulfilled want. If additional information is required to make a purchase decision, the consumer may engage in an internal or external information search. The consumer then evaluates the additional information and establishes purchase guidelines. Finally, a purchase decision is made.

3 **Explain the consumer's postpurchase evaluation process.** Consumer postpurchase evaluation is influenced by prepurchase expectations, the prepurchase information search, and the consumer's general level of self-confidence. Cognitive dissonance is the inner tension that a consumer experiences after recognizing a purchased product's disadvantages. When a purchase creates cognitive dissonance, consumers tend to react by seeking positive reinforcement for the purchase decision, avoiding negative information about the purchase decision, or revoking the purchase decision by returning the product.

4 **Identify the types of consumer buying decisions and discuss the significance of consumer involvement.** Consumer decision making falls into three broad categories. First, consumers exhibit routine response behavior for frequently purchased, low-cost items that require very little decision effort; routine response behavior is typically characterized by brand loyalty. Second, consumers engage in limited decision making for occasional purchases or for unfamiliar brands in familiar product categories. Third, consumers practice extensive decision making when making unfamiliar, expensive, or infrequent purchases. High-involvement decisions usually include an extensive information search and a thorough evaluation of alternatives. In contrast, low-involvement decisions are characterized by brand loyalty and a lack of personal identification with the product. The main factors affecting the level of consumer involvement are previous experience, interest, perceived risk of negative consequences (financial, social, and psychological), situation, and social visibility.

5 **Identify and understand the cultural factors that affect consumer buying decisions.** Cultural influences on consumer buying decisions include culture and values, subculture, and social class. Culture is the essential character of a society that distinguishes it from other cultural groups. The underlying elements of every culture are the values, language, myths, customs, rituals, laws, and the artifacts, or products, that are transmitted from one generation to the next. The most defining element of a culture is its values—the enduring beliefs shared by a society that a specific mode of conduct is personally or socially preferable to another mode of conduct. A culture can be divided into subcultures on the basis of demographic characteristics, geographic regions, national and ethnic background, political beliefs, and religious beliefs. Subcultures share elements of the overall culture as well as cultural elements unique to their own group. A social class is a group of people who are considered nearly equal in status or community esteem, who regularly socialize among themselves both formally and informally, and who share behavioral norms.

6 **Identify and understand the social factors that affect consumer buying decisions.** Social factors include such external influences as reference groups, opinion leaders, and family. Consumers seek out others' opinions for guidance on new products or services and products with image-related attributes or because attribute information is lacking or uninformative. Consumers may use products or brands to identify with or become a member of a reference group. Opinion leaders are members of reference groups who influence others' purchase decisions. Family members also influence purchase decisions; children tend to shop in similar patterns as their parents.

7 **Identify and understand the individual factors that affect consumer buying decisions.** Individual factors that affect consumer buying decisions include gender; age and family life-cycle stage; and personality, self-concept, and lifestyle. Beyond obvious physiological differences, men and women differ in their social and economic roles that affect consumer buying decisions. How old a consumer is generally indicates what products he or she may be interested in purchasing. Marketers often define their target markets in terms of consumers' life-cycle stage, following changes in consumers' attitudes and behavioral tendencies as they mature. Finally, certain products and brands reflect consumers' personality, self-concept, and lifestyle.

8 **Identify and understand the psychological factors that affect consumer buying decisions.** Psychological factors include perception, motivation, learning, values, beliefs, and attitudes. These factors allow consumers to interact with the world around them, recognize their feelings, gather and analyze information, formulate thoughts and opinions, and take action. Perception allows consumers to recognize their consumption problems. Motivation is what drives consumers to take action to satisfy specific consumption needs. Almost all consumer behavior results from learning, which is the process that creates changes in behavior through experience. Consumers with similar beliefs and attitudes tend to react alike to marketing-related inducements.

Discussion and Writing Questions

1. Describe the three categories of consumer decision-making behavior. Name typical products for which each type of consumer behavior is used.
2. The type of decision making a consumer uses for a product does not necessarily remain constant. Why? Support your answer with an example from your own experience.
3. How do beliefs and attitudes influence consumer behavior? How can negative attitudes toward a product be changed? How can marketers alter beliefs about a product? Give some examples of how marketers have changed negative attitudes about a product or added or altered beliefs about a product.
4. **WRITING** Recall an occasion when you experienced cognitive dissonance about a purchase. In a letter to a friend, describe the event and explain what you did about it.
5. Family members play many different roles in the buying process: initiator, influencer, decision maker, purchaser, and consumer. In your family, name who might play each of these roles in the purchase of a dinner at Pizza Hut, a summer vacation, Froot Loops breakfast cereal, an Abercrombie & Fitch sweater, golf clubs, an Internet service provider, and a new car.
6. **WRITING** You are a new marketing manager for a firm that produces a line of athletic shoes to be targeted to the college student subculture. In a memo to your boss, list some product attributes that might appeal to this subculture and the steps in your customers' purchase processes, and recommend some marketing strategies that can influence their decision.
7. Assume you are involved in the following consumer decision situations: (a) renting a video to watch with your roommates, (b) choosing a fast-food restaurant to go to with a new friend, (c) buying a popular music compact disc, (d) buying jeans to wear to class. List the factors that would influence your decision in each situation and explain your responses.

8. Visit Carpoint's Web site at **http://carpoint.msn.com/home/New.asp**. How does the site assist consumers in the evaluation stage of choosing a new car? Develop your own hypothetical evoked set of three or four car models and present your comparisons. Which vehicle attributes would be most important in your purchase decision?

9. How can non-marketing periodicals help you understand consumer behavior? Using InfoTrac (**http://www.infotrac-college.com**), research articles from such publications as the *Journal of Psychology, Journal of American Ethnic History, Psychology Today, Race and Class, Working Women, Society*, and others. Select and read three articles that explore different topics (i.e., do not select three articles on psychology). Then, make a list of factors you think could affect consumer purchasing behavior. Include with each factor a way marketers could use this information to their benefit.

Application for Entrepreneurs

Deli Depot is a new franchise opportunity offering cold and hot sandwiches, soup, chili, yogurt, pies, and cookies. It is positioned to compete with Subway and similar sandwich restaurants. Its unique advantages include special sauces on sandwiches, supplementary menu items like soup and pies, and quick delivery within specified zones.

The franchise package offered to franchisees includes information on the factors that typically influence consumers' selection of casual restaurants. These selection factors, in order from most important to least important, include food taste, food variety, value for the money, restaurant reputation, friendliness of employees, and convenience of location.

Robert Powell and a group of investors purchased the right to all franchise locations in the Atlanta metropolitan area. His group estimates that five units can be opened successfully in the first year and that a total of thirty can be opened in the first five years.

Because this is a new franchise, potential customers must first be made aware of Deli Depot and then convinced to try it. Over the long run a loyal customer base must be established to make each Deli Depot a success.

Questions

1. Are Deli Depot's unique advantages strong enough to attract customers from Subway and other sandwich competitors? Why or why not?
2. Are all the important customer selection factors for sandwich restaurants included in the list? Do you agree with the importance rankings? Explain your answers.
3. How can Robert and his group make potential customers aware of the new Deli Depot locations and menu selections?
4. How can Robert and his group convince individuals who try Deli Depot to become regular customers?

Case

entrepreneurship

Verbind: Understanding Consumers in the Internet Space

Since the Internet gained widespread acceptance as a shopping medium in the late 1990s, firms in all product categories have been scrambling to figure out effective ways to market and sell their products and services on-line. Judging from the major customer service failures after the heavy spending during the 1999 holiday shopping season, few have figured out how to do it well. Many e-retailers closed their operations after this season, and the shortcomings of those firms were attributed mostly to poor marketing planning and implementation. One problem was that e-retailers mistakenly saw the Internet as the magic path to bigger profit margins. In addition, although distribution and product costs were equal to those in the off-line world, promotions tended to be more expensive. Combine that with trying to satisfy Internet shoppers' expectations of lower prices when technology and staffing costs often surpassed the costs of maintaining a traditional retail outlet, and you have the recipe for disaster.

An additional factor in many of those on-line business collapses was the inability of marketers to effectively understand consumer behavior in the Internet space. Failure to do so led directly to poorly timed promotions and less than exemplary execution of product and service delivery. Tracking a customer's every move and building standardized customer profiles that were valid proved to be much less useful than originally thought. Internet consumer behavior was tricky. Internet marketers, then, searched for new tools to enable them to improve the relevancy and timing of their promotions, products, and services. What these marketers wanted was the ability to predict a customer's *future* behavior so they could place promotions for their products and services in front of a consumer when they would most likely influence his or her buying decision.

A Boston-based start-up, Verbind, Inc., has developed a product that could be the perfect remedy to the problems facing Internet marketers. The brainchild of Dutch immigrant Huib Geerlings, Verbind's premiere product is an enhanced tracking software called LifeTime. When applied to the transaction data a company receives at its Web site, LifeTime builds a complex behavior map of an individual consumer. When applied in a retailing environment, Verbind's software uses the behavior map to determine a unique "velocity" for each consumer based on what has been bought, as well as how much and how often. LifeTime then performs what is called conjoint analysis, a process which examines what trade-offs, based on product features and price, consumers make during any given buying process.

Most data-mining software stops there, but Life-Time uses the profile it builds to predict the future be-

havior of an individual customer. The benefit of traditional conjoint analysis is that it allows marketers to design products, promotions, and services to address the needs of a particular market. LifeTime, however, is less market-based and more consumer-based. With Verbind's automated tools, on-line marketers can draft their promotions and service offerings and simply sit back while LifeTime predicts an individual consumer's next moves. The software then serves up a highly targeted promotion for a particular product or service. Those offers don't have to come from a fixed pool of promotions, either. Using a set of rules to design promotions based on a combination of the retailers' and consumers' needs, the program can generate offers based almost on a per-consumer basis. The offers, therefore, have the highest possible degree of relevance and appeal. Verbind's Life-Time software goes beyond simple profiling outcomes, like recommending "since you like the Grateful Dead, you might try Pfish." It allows businesses to communicate with each of their customers in an informed way.

Originally designed for Geerling's wine order catalog, LifeTime can be applied in a number of environments to help marketers. For example, Verbind, has already contracted with Reel.com, a reseller of VHS and DVD movies, Fidelity. com, the on-line arm of the major financial institution, and Billserv. com, a provider of electronic billing solutions to firms doing business on-line. Crunching data accumulated by any partner it works with, Verbind uses factors like order timing—its frequency or lack thereof—product preferences, purchase patterns, average purchase amount, and more to predict what kind of buy a consumer may make next. At the on-line movie store Reel.com, Verbind's software might determine that a certain consumer shopping on Saturday is likely to buy a horror movie—only if it is on sale—and two action adventure movies that were released within the last six months. At Fidelity's on-line investment house, LifeTime may detect several spikes in certain investing activities and determine that the time is right to offer a consumer an upgrade in personal services or access to a more exclusive fund. For firms that offer their customers an electronic bill presentment and payment (EBPP) through Billserv.com, the software analyzes the purchase data available on a particular bill, compares the data to the profile on hand for that customer, and ascertains which promotions would be most beneficial to package with the bill.

Verbind's consumer profiling tools do more than allow for the serving of targeted promotions through a Web site or e-mail. LifeTime also tracks a customer's inactivity over time and is capable of notifying marketers when it looks like they are about to lose a customer. For example, if Lifetime detects a customer's bank account is steadily decreasing, Verbind could alert the bank that the customer may be planning to switch institutions. The software also monitors certain behaviors, such as calls to customer service centers, frequently abandoned on-line shopping carts, decreasing visits to a site, or decreased activity while there, and it advises the marketer to engage the consumer on a more personal level through a phone call or a letter. Making personal contact with a consumer, who probably assumes that no one is ever there to listen to them in an on-line environment, can significantly boost a firm's customer retention rates. LifeTime enables its partner firms to connect with their individual customers at the moment their behavior indicates that they are most ready to receive the message.

If the shakeout in the Internet retail sector after the 1999 holiday shopping season revealed anything, it was that stores operating on-line were not truly sensitive to customer wants and demands. Marketers were trying (and in some cases still do try) to force their will upon consumers instead of letting consumers' wants and needs drive the direction of their business. Ignoring the unique behaviors and attitudes of Internet consumers and trying to directly map off-line marketing tactics to the on-line environment has proven to be an ineffective and shortsighted approach. Internet-based firms who want to be market-oriented and want to attract and maintain loyal customers on-line need to be more sensitive to the on-line consumer. And Verbind is poised to help them do just that.

Questions

1. Which component of the consumer decision-making process does Verbind's software influence the most? Explain.
2. Is LifeTime more of a benefit to sellers of low-cost, low-involvement purchase items, or to sellers of more expensive products purchased with less frequency? Explain.
3. Based on the information given, do you think companies who enable e-commerce—like Verbind—are as concerned about the cultural and social factors that affect consumer buying decisions? Explain.
4. Describe the concept of "velocity." How does Verbind use information about a consumer's "velocity" to enhance the marketing efforts directed at that consumer?

Bibliography

Carol Pickering (**http://imaginemedia.com**). "How It Works—They're Watching You." *Business 2.0,* February 2000, pp. 235–236.

"billserv.com, Verbind Inc. Partner to Give Bills and Statements More Marketing Impact," **http://www.verbind.com**, January 5, 2000.

"Verbind and Optus Partner to Pilot 'Smart Billing' Solution for Credit Card Issuers," **http://www.verbind.com**, February 10, 2000.

William Bulkeley. "Verbind Monitors Customers to Predict Their Next Move." *Wall Street Journal,* July 1, 1999, p. B6.

Case

video

Vermont Teddy Bear Co.: Workin' Hard for the Honey

In the tradition of Teddy Roosevelt and the 1902 "Great American Teddy Bear," the Vermont Teddy Bear brand carries on a rich heritage based on the best American values of compassion, generosity, friendship, and a zesty sense of whimsy and fun. Founded in 1981, The Vermont Teddy Bear Co., Inc., is a designer, manufacturer, and marketer of teddy bears and related products that appeal to customers' core values. Because the Vermont Teddy Bear Co. believes that people's value systems have a great effect on what they buy, it has designed bears around popular American themes. Americans admire hard work, entrepreneurship, achievement, and success, so the company has a line of occupational bears. There's Businessman Bear, Doctor Bear, Webster the Computer Bear, and Teacher Bear. Americans also value youth and health, hence the appeal for Fitness Bear. And in this sports-crazed country, official NFL Bears score big points.

The backbone of the Vermont Teddy Bear Co. is the patented and trademarked Bear-Gram. Bear-Grams are personalized teddy bears that are delivered directly to the recipient for special occasions such as birthdays, anniversaries, weddings, and new births, as well as holidays such as Valentine's Day, Christmas, and Mother's Day. Sales are heavily seasonal. The key to the company's sales approach is the concept that buying decisions are based on individual differences. That's why the teddy bears are so highly customized. The company realizes that men and women shop differently, and their cultural, social, and economic roles affect their buying decisions. It has therefore identified its customer profile as being primarily the urban professional male who waits until the last minute to buy a gift but who still wants something special.

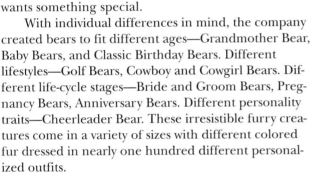

With individual differences in mind, the company created bears to fit different ages—Grandmother Bear, Baby Bears, and Classic Birthday Bears. Different lifestyles—Golf Bears, Cowboy and Cowgirl Bears. Different life-cycle stages—Bride and Groom Bears, Pregnancy Bears, Anniversary Bears. Different personality traits—Cheerleader Bear. These irresistible furry creatures come in a variety of sizes with different colored fur dressed in nearly one hundred different personalized outfits.

Throughout the 1980s, the company wholesaled teddy bears to specialty stores and retailed them through its own outlets. Then in 1990, it introduced radio advertising for the Bear-Gram, positioning it as a novel gift for Valentine's Day and offering listeners a toll-free number to call to order from sales reps, known as Bear Counselors. This test proved so successful that the concept was expanded to other major radio markets. Now, advertising for Valentine's Day has grown to 105 radio stations in eleven different markets, as well as on one syndicated network. Radio ads are frequently tagged with a reference to the company Web site, which in turn provides visual support for the radio advertising. This advertising works well for impulse buyers who hear the radio spot and make the decision to buy.

It is not surprising that annual sales peak at Valentine's Day because the strongest and most endearing

message of the teddy bears is the message of love. Even the company catalog is titled "Red Hot . . . Catalog of Love." Strong psychological influences affect consumer buying decisions, and teddy bears satisfy the important social needs of love and a sense of belonging. Whether it's the Sweetheart Bear or Cupid Bear, these romantic classics deliver the perfect bear hug.

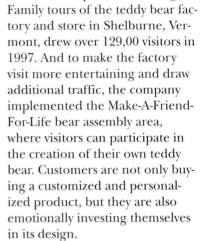

Family tours of the teddy bear factory and store in Shelburne, Vermont, drew over 129,00 visitors in 1997. And to make the factory visit more entertaining and draw additional traffic, the company implemented the Make-A-Friend-For-Life bear assembly area, where visitors can participate in the creation of their own teddy bear. Customers are not only buying a customized and personalized product, but they are also emotionally investing themselves in its design.

Unlike flowers, which only last for a short time, a Vermont Teddy Bear is steadfast and comes with a lifetime guarantee. Designed, cut, and sewn by hand, each bear can be a future heirloom, and if it becomes injured, it can be sent to the Teddy Bear Hospital to be repaired at no charge. All Vermont Teddy Bears arrive at their destinations smiling in a fun gift box with candy and a personalized message.

This complete understanding of its customers and what motivates their buying decisions has paid off. Total company revenues for 1997 reached $16,489,000, showing that these bears are workin' hard for the honey.

Questions
1. Describe the cultural effects on the consumer buying decision for a teddy bear (see Exhibit 5.5).
2. Describe the individual factors that affect the consumer buying decision for a teddy bear.
3. Describe the psychological factors that affect the consumer buying decision for a teddy bear (see Exhibit 5.13).
4. Describe the level of involvement for purchasing a teddy bear (see Exhibit 5.2).

Bibliography
Vermont Teddy Bear Co. catalog
Web site: **http://www.vtbear.com**

chapter 6

Learning Objectives

1 Describe business marketing

2 Describe the role of the Internet in business marketing

3 Discuss the role of relationship marketing and strategic alliances in business marketing

4 Identify the four major categories of business market customers

5 Explain the North American Industry Classification System

6 Explain the major differences between business and consumer markets

7 Describe the seven types of business goods and services

8 Discuss the unique aspects of business buying behavior

In the mid-1990s, American automobile executives complained bitterly that Japan's market for cars and parts was controlled by companies organized into what are called *keiretsus*, and closed to foreign competitors. The United States government demanded that keiretsus be opened to U.S. companies, but Japanese officials refused, arguing that the system made the Japanese economy more efficient.

Since that time, General Motors has dropped its strategy of self-reliance worldwide and adopted the philosophy described by the cliché, "when in Rome, do as the Romans do."

The *Wall Street Journal* reports that GM has quietly pieced together a network of equity alliances with Japanese automakers that, combined, hold the number two–market share position in Japan. Only Toyota holds more market share than GM and its partners Fuji Heavy Industries (maker of Subaru cars), Isuzu Motors, and Suzuki Motor. GM has even established a nonequity alliance with Toyota to develop propulsion technology such as fuel cells, and one with Honda to exchange automobile engines.[1] Both Toyota and Honda have been invited to join the Internet automotive parts exchange created by General Motors, Ford, and Daimler-Chrysler.[2] Japanese executives somewhat jokingly now refer to the new GM keiretsu.

What motivated GM to form strategic alliances in Japan? Do you think these alliances will be successful? What does GM hope to achieve from this strategy?

On Line

Cobalt Group
Covisint

Compare the sites of Covisint and the Cobalt Group. How is the consortium set up by the large auto makers different from the alliances under Cobalt Group and its Motorplace Web site? Is Cobalt Group a keiretsu? If not, how would you describe its relationship to its members?
http://www.cobaltgroup.com
http://www2.motorplace.com
http://www.covisint.com

What Is Business Marketing?

Describe business marketing

business marketing
The marketing of goods and services to individuals and organizations for purposes other than personal consumption.

Business marketing is the marketing of goods and services to individuals and organizations for purposes other than personal consumption. The sale of an overhead projector to your college or university is an example of business marketing. Business products include those that are used to manufacture other products, become part of another product, aid the normal operations of an organization, or are acquired for resale without any substantial change in form. The key characteristic distinguishing business products from consumer products is intended use, not physical characteristics. A product that is purchased for personal or family consumption or as a gift is a consumer good. If that same product, such as a microcomputer or a cellular telephone, is bought for use in a business, it is a business product.

Business Marketing on the Internet

Describe the role of the Internet in business marketing

electronic commerce (e-commerce)
The process of selling goods and services on the Internet.

business e-commerce
Electronic transactions between companies.

consumer e-commerce
Electronic transactions between businesses and individuals that purchase for personal consumption.

In the twenty-first century, information technology industries will drive economic wealth. The innovations developed by the computing, telecommunications, and electronic media industries will affect every business large and small.[3]

The process of selling goods and services on the Internet is called **electronic commerce (e-commerce)** or *electronic business (e-business)*. E-commerce goes beyond selling products through an electronic catalog, however. Among the benefits of the Internet's interactivity are convenience and increased efficiency, better customer service, lower transaction costs, and new relationship-building opportunities.

E-commerce includes two distinct market segments. **Business e-commerce** involves transactions between companies—for example, purchasing raw materials to manufacture products. **Consumer e-commerce**, also called "e-tailing," involves transactions between businesses and individuals that purchase for personal consumption. Although the consumer market has received more media attention, e-commerce between businesses is expected to represent 92 percent of the $4 trillion in e-commerce sales in 2003.[4]

E-commerce—Not Just for Large Corporations
Companies of all sizes are embracing business e-commerce to save hundreds of millions of dollars through lower costs and reduced inventories. Business e-commerce includes all aspects of the supply chain—from product information to order, invoice, fulfillment, payment, and customer service. It's no surprise that high-technology companies were early adopters of e-commerce. Dell Computer sells $1 million worth of computers per day on the Internet. IBM purchases $4 billion of goods and services per year over the Internet, citing significant cost savings and improved connections with customers and business partners as clear benefits.

E-commerce is no longer limited to high-tech companies, however; all types of manufacturing and service companies are becoming active participants. Customers of CSX Corporation, one of the largest freight railroads in the United States, make 400,000 visits to the corporate Web site each month. They consult maps of CSX routes, book shipments, get price quotes, fill out their own bills of lading, calculate freight charges, and track shipments within the firm's 18,000-mile network. CSX's on-line system reduces transaction costs by

E-commerce is quickly spreading into lower-tech areas. CSX, one of the largest freight railroads in the United States, uses a corporate extranet to improve customer service and information distribution.

replacing paper, phone, and fax communications and improving order accuracy. It also reduces staffing requirements. About 60 percent of CSX's shipments are booked electronically, including those sent by General Motors, Home Depot, General Electric, and PepsiCo. In fact, customers like the system so much they check daily to follow the route of railcars carrying their merchandise.[5]

Extranets are becoming a popular business e-commerce tool for such activities as purchasing, inventory management, order fulfillment, information transmission, training, and sales presentations. Like an intranet, an **extranet** is a private network that uses Internet technology and a browser interface. Extranets, however, are accessible only to authorized outsiders with a valid user name and password. Companies can easily designate specific portions of their Web sites to share specific information and processes with suppliers, vendors, partners, customers, and other businesses at remote locations. For example, customers can find account balances and customized catalogs with account-specific pricing.

Extranets are a very efficient format for business e-commerce. Marine Power Europe, a manufacturer of boat parts, saves $1 million a year in order placement and processing costs. Thanks to a special multilingual extranet application, Marine Power's international distributors and dealers can get product information and transact business in their native languages. Multiple users from around the globe can even view the same live document in their native language.[6]

extranet
A private network that uses Internet technology and a browser interface.

Benefits of Business E-Commerce

As many examples in this book demonstrate, companies that use the Internet effectively gain clear advantages. Among the attractions of incorporating e-commerce into business strategies are the following:

1. *Lower prices:* Competition among on-line vendors leads to lower prices for business buyers.
2. *Greater selection of products and vendors:* The Web makes it possible for corporate purchasing agents to find numerous vendors for almost any product.
3. *Access to customer and product sales data:* Companies can develop customer lists and learn their buying characteristics. They can also immediately learn which products are selling best.
4. *Around-the-clock ordering and customer service:* Company Web sites provide extensive product information for prospective customers around the world on a "24/7" basis, thereby expanding markets and facilitating more transactions—without hiring additional personnel. Customers themselves decide how much information they require by clicking on site links. Well-designed sites offer solutions to customer problems and make product suggestions.
5. *Lower costs:* As CSX and its customers learned, cost savings are a major benefit of e-commerce. These can take many forms, from distribution savings to staff reductions and lower costs of purchasing supplies. A report by the Organization for Economic Cooperation and Development (OECD) indicates that companies can reduce customer service costs by 10 to 50 percent and order processing time by 50 to 96 percent, depending on the type of business.[7]
6. *Customized products:* The Internet is revolutionizing product design and manufacturing. No longer do companies have to design and build products well in advance of the sale, basing product decisions on market research. They can use the Internet to take orders for products tailored to customer specifications. Dell Computers was one of the first to allow computer buyers to configure their ideal

computer from menus at Dell's Web site. Even though Dell's build-to-order procedures were remarkably efficient when customers phone in their orders, the Web has increased its efficiency and profitability. Warehouses receive supply orders via Internet messages every two hours instead of daily faxes. Suppliers know about the company's inventory and production plans and get feedback on their performance in meeting shipping deadlines. Inventory on hand is a low eight days, versus competitor Compaq's 26, and revenue is up 55 percent.[8]

The emergence of the Internet has made business markets more competitive than ever before. With the Internet, every business in the world is potentially a local competitor. In 1999, the United States accounted for nearly two-thirds of all business e-commerce transactions. By 2004 its share will be down to 40 percent.[9]

Many business marketers now realize that the Internet is a valuable tool for expanding markets and better serving customers. Exhibit 6.1 identifies eight Internet sites that contain important information for firms interested in competing in foreign markets.

Exhibit 6.1   An Internet Guide to Small-Business Exporting

One of the easiest ways to delve into exporting is to utilize the Internet. Visit these sites, which offer valuable resources as well as links to additional information.

http://www.embpage.org Embassy Web.com is a valuable on-line resource for diplomatic information. This site is a window to hundreds of embassies and consulates around the world.

http://www.exim.gov The Export-Import Bank of the United States was established to aid in financing and to facilitate U.S. exports.

http://www.exporthotline.com Export Hotline contains thousands of market research reports, a trade library, and a variety of other resources focused on all aspects of global trade and investment.

http://www.fita.org Trade associations are invaluable resources on exporting. Visit the Federation of International Trade Associations Web site to take advantage of all of its resources, including a network of three hundred thousand companies belonging to three hundred international trade associations in North America.

http://www.ita.doc.gov The International Trade Administration of the U.S. Department of Commerce is "dedicated to helping U.S. businesses compete in the global marketplace." It offers many resources to encourage, assist, and advocate U.S. exports.

http://www.sba.gov The U.S. Small Business Administration offers a wealth of basic information and resources, including various export support programs. It provides financial, technical, and management assistance to help Americans start, run, and help their businesses grow.

http://www.tradecompass.com Trade Compass offers news, information, and sophisticated database products that help companies and individuals navigate the far reaches of trade, importing, exporting, sales, marketing, logistics, research, and e-business in today's global marketplace.

http://www.tscentral.com TSCentral is an Internet-based provider of information, products, and services for global events. It has global directories offering information on trade shows, seminars, and conferences as well as extensive directories of suppliers, venues, and facilities around the world.

SOURCE: Based on information from Christopher Farrell and Edith Updike, "So You Think the World Is Your Oyster," *Business Week*, June 9, 1997, p. ENT8.

Relationship Marketing and Strategic Alliances

As Chapter 1 explained, relationship marketing is the strategy that entails seeking and establishing ongoing partnerships with customers. Relationship marketing has become an important business marketing strategy as customers have become more demanding and competition has become more intense. Building long-term relationships with customers offers companies a way to build competitive advantage. For example, the FedEx Powership program includes a series of automated shipping, tracking, and invoicing systems that save customers time and money while solidifying their loyalty to FedEx. This produces a win-win situation. FedEx has a satisfied loyal customer, and the customer saves time and money shipping products to their customers.

Discuss the role of relationship marketing and strategic alliances in business marketing

Strategic Alliances

A **strategic alliance**, sometimes called a *strategic partnership*, is a cooperative agreement between business firms. Strategic alliances can take the form of licensing or distribution agreements, joint ventures, research and development consortia, and partnerships. They may be between manufacturers, manufacturers and customers, manufacturers and suppliers, and manufacturers and channel intermediaries. Recall the story at the beginning of this chapter about the strategic alliances that General Motors has established with Japanese manufacturers.

Business marketers form strategic alliances to leverage what they do well by partnering with others who have complementary expertise to achieve the following:[10]

- Access to markets or to technology
- Economies of scale that might be gained by combining manufacturing, R&D, or marketing activities
- Faster entry of new products to markets
- Sharing of risk

GLOBAL For example, General Motors and Isuzu Motors of Japan invested over $300 million in a joint venture to build a new generation of diesel engines for General Motors trucks. Another strategic alliance has united General Motors, Ford, and DaimlerChrysler to create an Internet automobile parts exchange that is expected to be the world's largest Internet company.[11]

UPS has developed strategic alliances with Ford, Nike, and DaimlerChrysler to employ its information-technology expertise to track shipments and handle on-line orders. Ford plans to use UPS to track the more than four million cars and trucks it produces annually. Dealers will be able to log onto an Internet site to find out exactly where the vehicles they have ordered are in the distribution system, much the way customers already can track UPS packages on the Internet using a tracking number.[12]

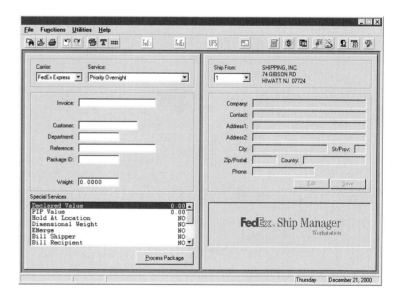

Through its Powership program, FedEx installs computer terminals in its customers' offices.
©1998 Federal Express Corporation. All Rights Reserved.

strategic alliance (strategic partnership)
A cooperative agreement between business firms.

Keiretsu

What can you find out about keiretsu on the Internet? Visit the Web site below. What kind of keiretsu does it support? Does it seem reasonable or just hype? Why do you think so?

http://www.keiretsu.com

On Line

Exhibit **6.2**

Tips for Making Strategic Alliances Successful

- Trust one another (alliances break down when one partner becomes greedy).
- Share a common interest in meeting customer needs.
- Bring different skills to the table.
- Share gains (and have a built-in system for ongoing change).
- Understand which party will have direct contact with the customer.
- Understand that success and profitability are tied to customer satisfaction.

SOURCE: From "Alliance Highlights," *Fortune*, Best Practices Symposium, March 30, 1998. Reprinted by permission.

Some alliances are extremely successful and some are dismal failures. Exhibit 6.2 identifies six tips for making an alliance successful.

Relationships in Other Cultures

Although the terms "relationship marketing" and "strategic alliances" are fairly new, and popularized mostly by American business executives and educators, the concepts have long been familiar in other cultures. Businesses in countries such as Mexico, China, Japan, Korea, and much of Europe rely heavily on personal relationships.

In Japan, for example, the basis of exchange between firms is personal relationships that are developed through what is called *amae*, or indulgent dependency. *Amae* is the feeling of nurturing concern for, and dependence upon, another. Reciprocity and personal relationships contribute to *amae*. Relationships between companies can develop into a **keiretsu**—a network of interlocking corporate affiliates (recall discussion in Chapter 4). Within a keiretsu, executives may sit on the boards of their customers or their suppliers. Members of a keiretsu trade with each other whenever possible and often engage in joint product development, finance, and marketing activity. For example, the Toyota Group *keiretsu* includes fourteen core companies and another 170 that receive preferential treatment. Toyota holds an equity position in many of these 170 member firms and is represented on many of their boards of directors.

Many American firms have found that the best way to compete in Asian countries is to form relationships with Asian firms. For example, Fuji-Xerox markets copiers in Japan and other Asian countries. Ford Motor owns one-third of Mazda Motor Corporation, Japan's fifth largest automaker. Whirlpool has spent $260 million buying controlling interests in four competitors in China and two in India.[13]

keiretsu
A network of interlocking corporate affiliates.

Major Categories of Business Customers

Identify the four major categories of business market customers

The business market consists of four major categories of customers: producers, resellers, governments, and institutions.

Producers

The producer segment of the business market includes profit-oriented individuals and organizations that use purchased goods and services to produce other prod-

The producer segment of the business market includes manufacturing, like this globe production line, as well as construction, finance, transportation, real estate, and others.
© Andy Sacks/Tony Stone Images

ucts, to incorporate into other products, or to facilitate the daily operations of the organization. Examples of producers include construction, manufacturing, transportation, finance, real estate, and food service firms. In the United States there are over thirteen million firms in the producer segment of the business market. Some of these firms are small and others are among the world's largest businesses.

Individual producers often buy large quantities of goods and services. Companies like General Motors spend more than $70 billion annually—more than the gross domestic product of Ireland, Portugal, Turkey, or Greece—on such business products as steel, metal components, and tires. Matsushita Electric Industrial Company featured in the "Global Perspectives" box in this chapter, spends nearly $21 billion on component parts and materials each year.

Resellers

The reseller market includes retail and wholesale businesses that buy finished goods and resell them for a profit. A retailer sells mainly to final consumers; wholesalers sell mostly to retailers and other organizational customers. There

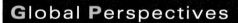

Global Perspectives

MATSUSHITA'S INTERNET BAZAAR

The Matsushita Electric Industrial Company plans to set up a vast Internet bazaar for most of the materials and parts it buys from thousands of suppliers. The Matsushita group, a conglomerate of eleven makers of such products as fax machines, VCRs, and digital camcorders, expects all of its manufacturing-related purchases in Japan to go through the Web-based marketplace. Overseas suppliers will be brought into the system later. Matsushita's initiative is aimed at creating cost savings on the group's procurement budgets (which are valued at 2.2 trillion yen ($20.82 billion) a year in Japan. Given Matsushita's clout, the move could inspire similar steps at

other Japanese companies struggling to restructure but slow to weave the Internet into their manufacturing operations.[a]

Matsushita aims to make sizable savings by turning its fragmented purchasing procedures into a more coherent system on the Internet. More important are the longer-term cost savings Matsushita hopes to generate by standardizing many components used by the group to gain a better bargaining position over suppliers.

Matsushita plans to switch three thousand large-scale suppliers of parts and materials to the Web-based system. Those suppliers account for more than 98 percent of the parts the group buys from seven

thousand suppliers in Japan. The group plans to extend on-line purchasing to overseas operations after the switch in Japan. Matsushita's international purchasing spending is 800 to 900 billion yen annually.

The company isn't planning, at least for now, to invite rival electronics makers into its Internet procurement system—a contrast from GM, Ford, and DaimlerChrysler, three giants who are trying to build the world's largest on-line marketplace to achieve greater economies of scale and are wooing automakers outside their immediate groups.

[a] Norihiko Shirouzu, "Matsushita to Set Up Online Market to Organize Materials Procurement," *Wall Street Journal Interactive Edition,* January 28, 2000, on-line.

are approximately 1.5 million retailers and five hundred thousand wholesalers operating in the United States. Consumer product firms like Procter & Gamble, Kraft General Foods, and Coca-Cola sell directly to large retailers and retail chains and through wholesalers to smaller retail units. Retailing and wholesaling are explored in detail in Chapters 12 and 13.

Business product distributors are wholesalers that buy business products and resell them to business customers. They often carry thousands of items in stock and employ sales forces to call on business customers. Businesses that wish to buy a gross of pencils or 100 pounds of fertilizer typically purchase these items from local distributors rather than directly from manufacturers such as Empire Pencil or Dow Chemical.

Governments

A third major segment of the business market is government. Government organizations include thousands of federal, state, and local buying units. They make up what may be the largest single market for goods and services in the world.

Contracts for government purchases are often put out for bid. Interested vendors submit bids (usually sealed) to provide specified products during a particular time. Sometimes the lowest bidder is awarded the contract. When the lowest bidder is not awarded the contract, strong evidence must be presented to justify the decision. Grounds for rejecting the lowest bid include lack of experience, inadequate financing, or poor past performance. Bidding allows all potential suppliers a fair chance at winning government contracts and helps ensure that public funds are spent wisely.

For doing business with the federal government, there is no better on-line resource than govcon.com. Users can check industry news, consult government databases, and view active contracts.

Federal Government Name just about any good or service and chances are that someone in the federal government uses it. The U.S. federal government is the world's largest customer.

Although much of the federal government's buying is centralized, no single federal agency contracts for all the government's requirements, and no single buyer in any agency purchases all that the agency needs. We can view the federal government as a combination of several large companies with overlapping responsibilities and thousands of small independent units.

 One popular source of information about government procurement is *Commerce Business Daily*. Until recently, businesses hoping to sell to the federal government found the document unorganized, and it often arrived too late to be useful. The new on-line version (**http://www.govcon.com**) is more timely and lets contractors find leads using keyword searches. *Doing Business with the General Services Administration, Selling to the Military,* and *Selling to the U.S. Air Force* are other examples of publications designed to explain how to do business with the federal government.

State, County, and City Government Selling to states, counties, and cities can be less frustrating for both small and large vendors than selling to the federal government. Paperwork is typically simpler and more manageable than it is at the federal level. On the other hand, vendors must decide which of the over eighty-two thousand government units are likely to buy their wares. State and local buying agencies include school districts, highway departments, government-operated hospitals, and housing agencies.

Institutions

The fourth major segment of the business market is institutions that seek to achieve goals other than the standard business goals of profit, market share, and return on investment. This segment includes schools, hospitals, colleges and universities, churches, labor unions, fraternal organizations, civic clubs, foundations, and other so-called nonbusiness organizations.

The North American Industry Classification System

The North American Industry Classification System (NAICS) is an industry classification system introduced in 1997 to replace the standard industrial classification system (SIC). NAICS (pronounced *nakes*) is an all-new system for classifying North American business establishments. The system, developed jointly by the United States, Canada, and Mexico, provides a common industry classification system for the North American Free Trade Association (NAFTA) partners. Goods- or service-producing firms that use identical or similar production processes are grouped together.

NAICS promises to be an extremely valuable tool for business marketers in analyzing, segmenting, and targeting markets. Each classification group should be relatively homogeneous in terms of raw materials required, components used, manufacturing processes employed, and problems faced. The more digits in a code, the more homogenous the group will be. If a supplier understands the needs and requirements of a few firms within a classification, requirements can be projected for all firms in that category. The number, size, and geographic dispersion of firms can also be identified. This information can be converted to market potential estimates, market share estimates, and sales forecasts. It can also be used for identifying potential new customers. NAICS codes can help identify firms that may be prospective users of a supplier's goods and services.

Exhibit 6.3 (on page 194) provides an overview of NAICS. Exhibit 6.4 (on page 195) illustrates the six-digit classification system for two of the twenty NAICS economic sectors: manufacturing and information. The hierarchical structure of NAICS allows industry data to be summarized at several levels of detail. To illustrate:

- The first two digits designate a major economic sector such as agriculture (11) or manufacturing (31–33).
- The third digit designates an economic subsector such as crop production or apparel manufacturing.
- The fourth digit designates an industry group, such as grain and oil seed farming or fiber, yarn, and thread mills.
- The fifth digit designates the NAICS industry, such as wheat farming or broadwoven fabric mills.
- The sixth digit, when used, identifies subdivisions of NAICS industries that accommodate user needs in individual countries.[14]

For a complete listing of all NAICS codes, see **http://www.census.gov/epcd/www/naics.html.**

5

Explain the North American Industry Classification System

The North American Industry Classification System (NAICS)
A detailed numbering system developed by the United States, Canada, and Mexico to classify North American business establishments by their main production processes.

Exhibit 6.3

NAICS Two-Digit Codes and
Corresponding Economic
Sectors

NAICS Codes with Corresponding Economic Sectors	
NAICS Code	**Economic Sector**
11	Agriculture, forestry, and fishing
21	Mining
22	Utilities
23	Construction
31–33	Manufacturing
43	Wholesale trade
44–45	Retail trade
47–48	Transportation
51	Information
52	Finance and insurance
53	Real estate and rental and leasing
56	Professional and technical services
57	Management and support services
61	Education services
62	Health and social assistance
71	Arts, entertainment, and recreation
72	Food services, drinking places, and accommodations
81	Other services, except public administration
93	Public administration
98	Estates and trusts
99	Nonclassifiable

Exhibit **6.4**

NAICS Level	NAICS Code	Example 1 Description	NAICS Code	Example 2 Description
Sector	31–33	Manufacturing	51	Information
Subsector	334	Computer and electronic product manufacturing	513	Broadcasting and telecommunications
Industry Group	3346	Manufacturing and reproduction of magnetic and optical media	5133	Telecommunications
Industry	33461	Manufacturing and reproduction of magnetic and optical media	51332	Wireless telecommunications carriers, except satellite
U.S. Industry	334611	Reproduction of software	513321	Paging

SOURCE: U.S. Census Bureau, "New Code System in NAICS," **http://www.census.gov/pub/epcd/www/ naiscod.htm**.

Business Versus Consumer Markets

The basic philosophy and practice of marketing is the same whether the customer is a business organization or a consumer. Business markets do, however, have characteristics different from consumer markets. Exhibit 6.5 summarizes the main differences between business and consumer markets.

Explain the major differences between business and consumer markets

Demand
Consumer demand for products is quite different from demand in the business market. Unlike consumer demand, business demand is derived, inelastic, joint, and fluctuating.

Derived Demand The demand for business products is called **derived demand** because organizations buy products to be used in producing their customers products. For example, the market for CPUs, hard drives, and CD-ROMs is derived from the demand for personal computers. These items are only valuable as components of computers. Demand for these items rises and falls with the demand for PCs.

Because demand is derived, business marketers must carefully monitor demand patterns and changing preferences in final consumer markets, even though their customers are not in those markets. Moreover, business marketers must carefully monitor their customers' forecasts, because derived demand is based on expectations of future demand for those customers' products.

Some business marketers not only monitor final consumer demand and customer forecasts but also try to influence final consumer demand. Aluminum producers use television and magazine advertisements to point out the convenience and recycling opportunities that aluminum offers to consumers who can choose to purchase soft drinks in either aluminum or plastic containers.

derived demand
The demand for business products.

Exhibit 6.5

Major Characteristics of Business Markets Compared to Consumer Markets

Characteristic	Business Market	Consumer Market
Demand	Organizational	Individual
Purchase volume	Larger	Smaller
Number of customers	Fewer	Many
Location of buyers	Geographically concentrated	Dispersed
Distribution structure	More direct	More indirect
Nature of buying	More professional	More personal
Nature of buying influence	Multiple	Single
Type of negotiations	More complex	Simpler
Use of reciprocity	Yes	No
Use of leasing	Greater	Lesser
Primary promotional method	Personal selling	Advertising

Inelastic Demand The demand for many business products is inelastic with regard to price. *Inelastic demand* means that an increase or decrease in the price of the product will not significantly affect demand for the product. This will be discussed further in Chapter 17.

The price of a product used in the production of or as part of a final product is often a minor portion of the final product's total price. Therefore, demand for the final consumer product is not affected. If the price of automobile paint or spark plugs rose significantly, say 200 percent in one year, do you think the number of new automobiles sold that year would be affected? Probably not.

joint demand
The demand for two or more items used together in a final product.

Joint Demand **Joint demand** occurs when two or more items are used together in a final product. For example, a decline in the availability of memory chips will slow production of microcomputers, which will in turn reduce the demand for disk drives. Many business products, such as hammer heads and hammer handles, also exemplify joint demand.

Fluctuating Demand The demand for business products—particularly new plants and equipment—tends to be more unstable than the demand for consumer products. A small increase or decrease in consumer demand can produce a much larger change in demand for the facilities and equipment needed to make the consumer product. Economists refer to this phenomenon as the **multiplier effect** (or **accelerator principle**).

multiplier effect (accelerator principle)
Phenomenon in which a small increase or decrease in consumer demand can produce a much larger change in demand for the facilities and equipment needed to make the consumer product.

Cummins Engine Company, a producer of heavy-duty diesel engines, uses sophisticated surface grinders to make parts. Suppose Cummins is using twenty surface grinders. Each machine lasts about ten years. Purchases have been timed so two machines will wear out and be replaced annually. If the demand for engine parts does not change, two grinders will be bought this year. If the demand for parts declines slightly, only eighteen grinders may be needed and Cummins won't replace the worn ones. However, suppose in the next year demand returns to previous levels plus a little more. To meet the new level of demand, Cummins will need to replace the two machines that wore out in the first year, the two that wore out in the second year, plus one or more additional machines. The multiplier effect works this way in many industries, producing highly fluctuating demand for business products.

Purchase Volume

Business customers buy in much larger quantities than consumers. Just think how large an order Kellogg typically places for the wheat bran and raisins used to manufacture Raisin Bran. Imagine the number of tires that DaimlerChrysler buys at one time.

Number of Customers

Business marketers usually have far fewer customers than consumer marketers. The advantage is that it is a lot easier to identify prospective buyers, monitor current customers' needs and levels of satisfaction, and personally attend to existing customers. The main disadvantage is that each customer becomes crucial—especially for those manufacturers that have only one customer. In many cases, this customer is the U.S. government.

Location of Buyers

Business customers tend to be much more geographically concentrated than consumers. For instance, more than half the nation's business buyers are located in New York, California, Pennsylvania, Illinois, Ohio, Michigan, and New Jersey. The aircraft and microelectronics industries are concentrated on the West Coast, and many of the firms that supply the automobile manufacturing industry are located in and around Detroit.

Distribution Structure

Many consumer products pass through a distribution system that includes the producer, one or more wholesalers, and a retailer. However, because of many of the characteristics already mentioned, channels of distribution are typically shorter in business marketing. Direct channels, where manufacturers market directly to users, are much more common.

Many businesses that market directly to users are discovering that the Internet offers great potential for reaching new and existing customers domestically and around the world, while reducing costs to both buyers and sellers. Several examples of the expanding potential of the Internet are cited in this chapter.

Nature of Buying

Unlike consumers, business buyers usually approach purchasing rather formally. Businesses use professionally trained purchasing agents or buyers who spend their entire career purchasing a limited number of items. They get to know the items and the sellers well. Some professional purchasers earn the designation of Certified Purchasing Manager (CPM) after participating in a rigorous certification program.

Nature of Buying Influence

Typically, more people are involved in a single business purchase decision than in a consumer purchase. Experts from fields as varied as quality control, marketing, and finance, as well as professional buyers and users, may be grouped in a buying center (discussed later in this chapter).

Type of Negotiations

Consumers are used to negotiating price on automobiles and real estate. In most cases, however, American consumers expect sellers to set the price and other conditions of sale, such as time of delivery and credit terms. In contrast, negotiating is common in business marketing. Buyers and sellers negotiate product specifications, delivery dates, payment terms, and other pricing matters. Sometimes these negotiations occur during many meetings over several months. Final contracts are often very long and detailed.

Use of Reciprocity

reciprocity
A practice where business purchasers choose to buy from their own customers.

Business purchasers often choose to buy from their own customers, a practice known as **reciprocity**. For example, General Motors buys engines for use in its automobiles and trucks from Borg Warner, which in turn buys many of the automobiles and trucks it needs from GM. This practice is neither unethical nor illegal unless one party coerces the other and the result is unfair competition. Reciprocity is generally considered a reasonable business practice. If all possible suppliers sell a similar product for about the same price, doesn't it make sense to buy from those firms that buy from you?

Use of Leasing

Consumers normally buy products rather than lease them. But businesses commonly lease expensive equipment such as computers, construction equipment and vehicles, and automobiles. Leasing allows firms to reduce capital outflow, acquire a seller's latest products, receive better services, and gain tax advantages.

The lessor, the firm providing the product, may be either the manufacturer or an independent firm. The benefits to the lessor include greater total revenue from leasing compared to selling and an opportunity to do business with customers who cannot afford to buy.

Primary Promotional Method

Business marketers tend to emphasize personal selling in their promotion efforts, especially for expensive items, custom-designed products, large-volume purchases, and situations requiring negotiations. The sale of many business products requires a great deal of personal contact. Personal selling is discussed in more detail in Chapter 16.

Types of Business Products

 7

Describe the seven types of business goods and services

major equipment (installations)
Capital goods such as large or expensive machines, mainframe computers, blast furnaces, generators, airplanes, and buildings.

Business products generally fall into one of the following seven categories, depending on their use: major equipment, accessory equipment, raw materials, component parts, processed materials, supplies, and business services.

Major Equipment

Major equipment includes such capital goods as large or expensive machines, mainframe computers, blast furnaces, generators, airplanes, and buildings. (These items are also commonly called **installations**.) Major equipment is depreciated over time rather than charged as an expense in the year it is purchased. In addition, major equipment is often custom-designed for each customer. Personal selling is an important part of the marketing strategy for major equipment because distribution channels are almost always direct from the producer to the business user.

Accessory Equipment

Accessory equipment is generally less expensive and shorter-lived than major equipment. Examples include portable drills, power tools, microcomputers, and fax machines. Accessory equipment is often charged as an expense in the year it is bought rather than depreciated over its useful life. In contrast to major equipment, accessories are more often standardized and are usually bought by more customers. These customers tend to be widely dispersed. For example, all types of businesses buy microcomputers.

Local industrial distributors (wholesalers) play an important role in the marketing of accessory equipment because business buyers often purchase accessories from them. Regardless of where accessories are bought, advertising is a more vital promotional tool for accessory equipment than for major equipment.

Raw Materials

Raw materials are unprocessed extractive or agricultural products—for example, mineral ore, lumber, wheat, corn, fruits, vegetables, and fish. Raw materials become part of finished products. Extensive users, such as steel or lumber mills and food canners, generally buy huge quantities of raw materials. Because there is often a large number of relatively small sellers of raw materials, none can greatly influence price or supply. Thus, the market tends to set the price of raw materials, and individual producers have little pricing flexibility. Promotion is almost always via personal selling, and distribution channels are usually direct from producer to business user.

Component Parts

Component parts are either finished items ready for assembly or products that need very little processing before becoming part of some other product. Examples include spark plugs, tires, and electric motors for automobiles. A special feature of component parts is that they can retain their identity after becoming part of the final product. For example, automobile tires are clearly recognizable as part of a car. Moreover, because component parts often wear out, they may need to be replaced several times during the life of the final product. Thus, there are two important markets for many component parts: the original equipment manufacturer (OEM) market and the replacement market.

Many of the business features listed earlier in Exhibit 6.5 characterize the **OEM** market. The difference between unit costs and selling prices in the OEM market is often small, but profits can be substantial because of volume buying.

The replacement market is composed of organizations and individuals buying component parts to replace worn-out parts. Because components often retain their identity in final products, users may choose to replace a component part with the same brand used by the manufacturer—for example, the same brand of automobile tires or battery. The replacement market operates differently from the OEM market, however. Whether replacement buyers are organizations or individuals, they tend to demonstrate the characteristics of consumer markets that were shown in Exhibit 6.5. Consider, for example, an automobile replacement part. Purchase volume is usually small and there are many customers, geographically dispersed, who typically buy from car dealers or parts stores. Negotiations do not occur, and neither reciprocity nor leasing is usually an issue.

accessory equipment
Goods, such as portable tools and office equipment, that are less expensive and shorter-lived than major equipment.

raw materials
Unprocessed extractive or agricultural products, such as mineral ore, lumber, wheat, corn, fruits, vegetables, and fish.

component parts
Either finished items ready for assembly or products that need very little processing before becoming part of some other product.

Although component parts like tires and spark plugs are easily recognizable, most components are not. This is a selection of parts that can be found in things like hospital beds, motorcycle brakes, and industrial equipment that fills bottles of fabric softener.

OEM
The acronym OEM stands for original equipment manufacturer. OEMs buy business goods that they incorporate into the products that they produce for eventual sale to other producers or to consumers.

processed materials
Products used directly in manufacturing other products.

supplies
Consumable items that do not become part of the final product.

business services
Expense items that do not become part of a final product.

Manufacturers of component parts often direct their advertising toward replacement buyers. Cooper Tire & Rubber, for example, makes and markets component parts—automobile and truck tires—for the replacement market only. General Motors and other car makers compete with independent firms in the market for replacement automobile parts.

Processed Materials
Processed materials are products used directly in manufacturing other products. Unlike raw materials, they have had some processing. Examples include sheet metal, chemicals, specialty steel, lumber, corn syrup, and plastics. Unlike component parts, processed materials do not retain their identity in final products.

Most processed materials are marketed to OEMs or to distributors servicing the OEM market. Processed materials are generally bought according to customer specifications or to some industry standard, as is the case with steel and lumber. Price and service are important factors in choosing a vendor.

Supplies
Supplies are consumable items that do not become part of the final product—for example, lubricants, detergents, paper towels, pencils, and paper. Supplies are normally standardized items that purchasing agents routinely buy. Supplies typically have relatively short lives and are inexpensive compared to other business goods. Because supplies generally fall into one of three categories—maintenance, repair, or operating supplies—this category is often referred to as MRO items.

Competition in the MRO market is intense. Bic and PaperMate, for example, battle for business purchases of inexpensive ballpoint pens.

Business Services
Business services are expense items that do not become part of a final product. Businesses often retain outside providers to perform janitorial, advertising, legal, management consulting, marketing research, maintenance, and other services. Hiring an outside provider makes sense when it costs less than hiring or assigning an employee to perform the task and when an outside provider is needed for particular expertise.

Business Buying Behavior

Discuss the unique aspects of business buying behavior

As you probably have already concluded, business buyers behave differently from consumers. Understanding how purchase decisions are made in organizations is a first step in developing a business selling strategy. There are five important aspects of business buying behavior: buying centers, evaluative criteria, buying situations, purchasing ethics, and customer service.

Buying Centers

buying center
All those persons in an organization who become involved in the purchase decision.

A **buying center** includes all those persons in an organization who become involved in the purchase decision. Membership and influence vary from company to company. For instance, in engineering-dominated firms like Bell Helicopter, the buying center may consist almost entirely of engineers. In marketing-oriented firms like Toyota and IBM, marketing and engineering have almost equal authority. In consumer goods firms like Procter & Gamble, product managers and other marketing decision makers may dominate the buying center. In a small manufacturing company, almost everyone may be a member.

The number of people involved in a buying center varies with the complexity and importance of a purchase decision. The composition of the buying group will usually change from one purchase to another and sometimes even during various stages of the buying process. To make matters more complicated, buying centers do not appear on formal organization charts.

For example, even though a formal committee may have been set up to choose a new plant site, it is only part of the buying center. Other people, like the company president, often play informal yet powerful roles. In a lengthy decision-making process, such as finding a new plant location, some members may drop out of the buying center when they can no longer play a useful role. Others whose talents are needed then become part of the center. No formal announcement of "who is in" and "who is out" is ever made.

Roles in the Buying Center As in family purchasing decisions, several people may play a role in the business purchase process:

- *Initiator:* the person who first suggests making a purchase.
- *Influencers/evaluators:* people who influence the buying decision. They often help define specifications and provide information for evaluating options. Technical personnel are especially important as influencers.
- *Gatekeepers:* group members who regulate the flow of information. Frequently, the purchasing agent views the gatekeeping role as a source of his or her power. A secretary may also act as a gatekeeper by determining which vendors get an appointment with a buyer.
- *Decider:* the person who has the formal or informal power to choose or approve the selection of the supplier or brand. In complex situations, it is often difficult to determine who makes the final decision.
- *Purchaser:* the person who actually negotiates the purchase. It could be anyone from the president of the company to the purchasing agent, depending on the importance of the decision.
- *Users:* members of the organization who will actually use the product. Users often initiate the buying process and help define product specifications.

An example illustrating these basic roles is shown in Exhibit 6.6.

Exhibit 6.6

Buying Center Roles for Computer Purchases

Role	Illustration
Initiator	Division general manager proposes to replace company's computer network.
Influencers/evaluators	Corporate controller's office and vice president of data processing have an important say about which system and vendor the company will deal with.
Gatekeepers	Corporate departments for purchasing and data processing analyze company's needs and recommend likely matches with potential vendors.
Decider	Vice president of administration, with advice from others, selects vendor the company will deal with and system it will buy.
Purchaser	Purchasing agent negotiates terms of sale.
Users	All division employees use the computers.

Implications of Buying Centers for the Marketing Manager   Successful vendors realize the importance of identifying who is in the decision-making unit, each member's relative influence in the buying decision, and each member's evaluative criteria. Successful selling strategies often focus on determining the most important buying influences and tailoring sales presentations to the evaluative criteria most important to these buying-center members.

For example, Loctite Corporation, the manufacturer of Super Glue and industrial adhesives and sealants, found that engineers were the most important influencers and deciders in adhesive and sealant purchase decisions. As a result, Loctite focused its marketing efforts on production and maintenance engineers.

Evaluative Criteria

Business buyers evaluate products and suppliers against three important criteria: quality, service, and price—in that order.

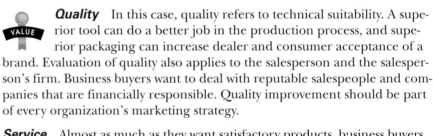

Quality   In this case, quality refers to technical suitability. A superior tool can do a better job in the production process, and superior packaging can increase dealer and consumer acceptance of a brand. Evaluation of quality also applies to the salesperson and the salesperson's firm. Business buyers want to deal with reputable salespeople and companies that are financially responsible. Quality improvement should be part of every organization's marketing strategy.

Service   Almost as much as they want satisfactory products, business buyers want satisfactory service. A purchase offers several opportunities for service. Suppose a vendor is selling heavy equipment. Prepurchase service could include a survey of the buyer's needs. After thorough analysis of the survey findings, the vendor could prepare a report and recommendations in the form of a purchasing proposal. If a purchase results, postpurchase service might consist of installing the equipment and training those who will be using it. Postsale services may also include maintenance and repairs. Another service that business buyers seek is dependability of supply. They must be able to count on delivery of what was ordered when it is scheduled to be delivered. Buyers also welcome services that help them sell their finished products. Services of this sort are especially appropriate when the seller's product is an identifiable part of the buyer's end product.

Businesses require satisfactory postsales service. This may mean installing the equipment or training employees in its use.
© Bob Daemmrich/The Image Works

Price   Business buyers want to buy at low prices—at the lowest prices, under most circumstances. However, a buyer who pressures a supplier to cut prices to a point where the supplier loses money on the sale almost forces shortcuts on quality. The buyer also may, in effect, force the supplier to quit selling to him or her. Then a new source of supply will have to be found.

Buying Situations

Often business firms, especially manufacturers, must decide whether to make something or buy it from an outside supplier. The decision is essentially one of economics. Can an item of similar quality be bought at a lower price elsewhere? If not, is manufacturing it in-house the best use of limited company resources? For example, Briggs & Stratton Corp., a major manufacturer of four-cycle engines, might be able to save $150,000 annually on outside purchases by spending $500,000 on the equipment needed to produce gas throttles internally. Yet Briggs & Stratton could also use that $500,000 to upgrade its carburetor assembly line, which would save

$225,000 annually. If a firm does decide to buy a product instead of making it, the purchase will be a new buy, a modified rebuy, or a straight rebuy.

New Buy A **new buy** is a situation requiring the purchase of a product for the first time. For example, suppose a manufacturing company needs a better way to page managers while they are working on the shop floor. Currently each of the several managers has a distinct ring, for example, two short and one long, that sounds over the plant intercom whenever he or she is being paged by anyone in the factory. The company decides to replace its buzzer system of paging with hand-held wireless radio technology that will allow managers to communicate immediately with the department initiating the page. This situation represents the greatest opportunity for new vendors. No long-term relationship has been established for this product, specifications may be somewhat fluid, and buyers are generally more open to new vendors.

> **new buy**
> A situation requiring the purchase of a product for the first time.

If the new item is a raw material or a critical component part, the buyer cannot afford to run out of supply. The seller must be able to convince the buyer that the seller's firm can consistently deliver a high-quality product on time.

Modified Rebuy A **modified rebuy** is normally less critical and less time-consuming than a new buy. In a modified-rebuy situation, the purchaser wants some change in the original good or service. It may be a new color, greater tensile strength in a component part, more respondents in a marketing research study, or additional services in a janitorial contract.

> **modified rebuy**
> A situation where the purchaser wants some change in the original good or service.

Because the two parties are familiar with each other and credibility has been established, buyer and seller can concentrate on the specifics of the modification. But in some cases, modified rebuys are open to outside bidders. The purchaser uses this strategy to ensure that the new terms are competitive. An example would be the manufacturing company buying radios with a vibrating feature for managers who have trouble hearing the ring over the factory noise. The firm may open the bidding to examine the price/quality offerings of several suppliers.

Straight Rebuy A **straight rebuy** is a situation vendors prefer. The purchaser is not looking for new information or other suppliers. An order is placed and the product is provided as in previous orders. Usually a straight rebuy is routine because the terms of the purchase have been agreed to in earlier negotiations. An example would be the manufacturing company previously cited purchasing additional radios for new managers from the same supplier on a regular basis.

> **straight rebuy**
> A situation in which the purchaser reorders the same goods or services without looking for new information or investigating other suppliers.

One common instrument used in straight-rebuy situations is the purchasing contract. Purchasing contracts are used with products that are bought often and in high volume. In essence, the purchasing contract makes the buyer's decision making routine and promises the salesperson a sure sale. The advantage to the buyer is a quick, confident decision and, to the salesperson, reduced or eliminated competition.

Suppliers must remember not to take straight-rebuy relationships for granted. Retaining existing customers is much easier than attracting new ones.

Purchasing Ethics

The ethics of business buyer and seller relationships are often scrutinized and sometimes criticized by superiors, associates, other prospective suppliers, the general public, and the news media. Lockheed Martin Corporation, mindful of the key problems often faced by professional buyers and sellers, developed the guidelines shown in the "Ethics in Marketing" box.

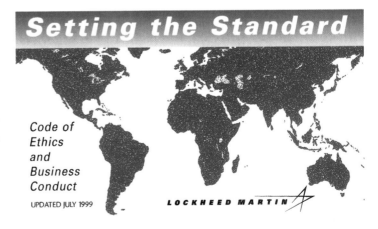

Lockheed Martin's 52-page booklet "Setting the Standard" gives employees a complete set of ethical guidelines the company requires them to follow. The "Quick Quiz" provided toward the end of the booklet is a great checklist in any ethical situation.

THE GIFTS POLICY AT LOCKHEED MARTIN

What policies do firms set on giving gifts to customers and receiving gifts from suppliers? Lockheed Martin Corporation has issued a booklet entitled, "Setting the Standard," which has been adopted by the company's board of directors as its code of ethics and business conduct. It summarizes the virtues and principles that are to guide the business actions of employees as well as Lockheed agents, consultants, contractors, representatives, and suppliers. The following are guidelines regarding gifts and favors.

To Government Personnel: Federal, state, and local government departments and agencies are governed by laws and regulations concerning acceptance by their employees of entertainment, meals, gifts, gratuities, and other things of value from firms and persons with whom those departments and agencies do business or over whom they have regulatory authority. It is the general policy of Lockheed Martin to strictly comply with those laws and regulations. With regard to all federal Executive Branch employees and any other government employees who work for customers or potential customers of the corporation, it is the policy of Lockheed Martin to prohibit its employees from giving them things of value. Permissible exceptions are offering Lockheed Martin advertising or promotional items of *nominal value* such as a coffee mug, calendar, or similar item displaying the company logo, and providing modest refreshments such as soft drinks, coffee, and donuts on an occasional basis in connection with business activities. "Nominal value" is $10.00 or less. (*Note:* Even though this policy may be more restrictive than the U.S.

government's own policy with regard to federal Executive Branch employees, this policy shall govern the conduct of all Lockheed Martin employees.) Legislative, judicial, and state and local government personnel are subject to different restrictions; both the regulations and corporate policies pertaining to them must be consulted before courtesies are offered.

To Nongovernment Personnel: As long as it does not violate the standards of conduct of the recipient's organization, it is an acceptable practice to provide meals, refreshments, and entertainment of reasonable value in conjunction with business discussions with nongovernment personnel. Gifts, other than those of reasonable value ($50.00 or less), to private individuals or companies are prohibited unless specifically approved by the appropriate Ethics Officer or the Corporate Office of Ethics and Business Conduct.

To Foreign Government Personnel and Public Officials: The company may be restricted from giving meals, gifts, gratuities, entertainment, or other things of value to personnel of foreign governments and foreign public officials by the Foreign Corrupt Practices Act and by laws of foreign countries. Employees must discuss such situations with Legal Counsel and consult the Hospitality Guidelines (maintained by the Legal Department) prior to making any gifts or providing any gratuities other than advertising items.

To Lockheed Martin Personnel: Lockheed Martin employees may accept meals, refreshments, or enter-

tainment of *nominal* value in connection with business discussions. While it is difficult to define "nominal" by means of a specific dollar amount, a common sense determination should dictate what would be considered lavish, extravagant, or frequent. It is the personal responsibility of each employee to ensure that his or her acceptance of such meals, refreshments, or entertainment is proper and could not reasonably be construed in any way as an attempt by the offering party to secure favorable treatment.

It Is the Personal Responsibility of Each Employee . . .

Lockheed Martin employees are not permitted to accept funds in any form or amount, or any gift that has a retail or exchange value of $20 or more from individuals, companies, or representatives of companies having or seeking business relationships with Lockheed Martin. If you have any questions about the propriety of a gift, gratuity, or item of value, contact your Ethics Officer or the Corporate Office of Ethics and Business Conduct for guidance.

If you buy goods or services for Lockheed Martin, or are involved in the procurement process, you must treat all suppliers uniformly and fairly. In deciding among competing suppliers, you must objectively and impartially weigh all facts and avoid even the appearance of favoritism. Established routines and procedures should be followed in the procurement of all goods and services.[a]

[a] From "Setting the Standard," *Lockheed Martin Code of Ethics and Business Conduct*, updated August 1997, pp. 1, 6, 7.

Customer Service

Business marketers are increasingly recognizing the benefits of developing a formal system to monitor customer opinions and perceptions of the quality of customer service. Companies like McDonald's, L.L. Bean, and Lexus build their strategies not only around products but also around a few highly developed service skills. Many firms are finding new ways to enhance customer service through technology. Business marketers are leading the way in adoption of new media technologies such as on-line services and CD-ROMs. For example, Honeywell has an on-line store that sells measurement and control instruments directly to corporate buyers. Honeywell's Industrial Store (**http://www. industrialstore.honeywell.com**) carries instruments used by industries ranging from refineries and chemicals to metal, mining, oil, gas, food, and pharmaceuticals. Prospective customers can get quotes and place orders on-line twenty-four hours per day, seven days per week. Orders are quickly filled by the company's order management system.[15] W. W. Grainger (**http://www.grainger.com**) sells about 20 percent of its $9 million per month sales on-line outside of normal business hours. Management believes that its electronic commerce business would grow more if its customer base of plant managers and janitors were more computer literate. Grainger is addressing the problem with workshops for customers.[16]

Looking Back

Look back at the story about General Motors at the beginning of this chapter. You now know that a strategic alliance is a cooperative agreement between business firms. *Keiretsu* is the Japanese term for a network of corporate affiliates. Members of keiretsu trade with each other whenever possible and are often appointed to the boards of directors of other member's organizations.

General Motors was motivated to form strategic alliances in Japan by past failures to expand in Asia on its own. A GM goal is to boost Asian market share from 4 percent in 2000 to 10 percent in 2004.[17] Strategic alliances with Japanese partners are a key component of the growth strategy. GM also hopes that it will benefit from new products and technologies that its partners develop. Some of these are expected to be useful in other parts of the world. GM has already developed small cars with Suzuki for Asia and Europe, and expects to develop several more "Asian value cars" with its affiliates.[18]

How likely are these strategic alliances to be successful? The automobile marketplace is becoming more global each year. Global competitors have to offer a broad range of products and possess technological expertise and sophistication. Automobiles must be designed with local wants and needs in mind. The time is past when all that was needed was an American nameplate to sell automobiles around the world. GM's strategy seems to fit well with the reasons for forming strategic alliances and the tips for making strategic alliances successful that were discussed in this chapter. Overall, the Asian strategic alliance strategy is expected to be successful.

Explore the Possibilities

Starting a business at home is one of the easiest ways to become self-employed. Using the Home Office Association of America (HOAA) Web site (**http://www.hoaa.com**) for ideas, choose a possible business opportunity that interests you and that has business marketing possibilities. Then explore both the HOAA site and the American Association of Home-Based Businesses Web site (**http://www.aahbb.org**) to learn more about how to set up your business.

Learn from an Entrepreneur

What does it really take to become an entrepreneur? Find out by interviewing a local entrepreneur or researching an entrepreneur you've read about in this chapter or in the business press. Get answers to the following questions, as well as any others you'd like to ask:

- How did you develop your vision for the company?
- What are the most important entrepreneurial characteristics that helped you succeed?
- Where did you learn the business skills you needed to run and grow the company?
- How did you research the feasibility of your idea? Prepare your business idea?
- What were the biggest challenges you had to overcome?
- Where did you obtain financing for the company?
- How do you market your products and services to other businesses?
- What are the most important lessons you learned by starting this company?
- What advice do you have for would-be entrepreneurs?

Summary

1 **Describe business marketing.** Business marketing provides goods and services that are bought for use in business rather than for personal consumption. Intended use, not physical characteristics, distinguishes a business product from a consumer product.

2 **Describe the role of the Internet in business marketing.** The rapid expansion and adoption of the Internet has made business markets more competitive than ever before. The number of business buyers and sellers using the Internet is rapidly increasing. Firms are seeking new and better ways to expand markets and sources of supply, increase sales and decrease costs, and better serve customers. With the Internet, every business in the world is potentially a local competitor.

3 **Discuss the role of relationship marketing and strategic alliances in business marketing.** Relationship marketing entails seeking and establishing long-term alliances or partnerships with customers. A strategic alliance is a cooperative agreement between business firms. Firms form alliances to leverage what they do well by partnering with others who have complementary skills.

4 **Identify the four major categories of business market customers.** Producer markets consist of for-profit organizations and individuals that buy products to use in producing other products, as components of other products, or in facilitating business operations. Reseller markets consist of wholesalers and retailers that buy finished products to resell for profit. Government markets include federal, state, county, and city governments that buy goods and services to support their own operations and serve the needs of citizens. Institutional markets consist of very diverse nonbusiness institutions whose main goals do not include profit.

5 **Explain the North American Industry Classification System.** The NAICS provides a way to identify, analyze, segment, and target business and government markets. Organizations can be identified and compared by a numeric code indicating business sector, subsector, industry group, industry, and country industry. NAICS is a valuable tool for analyzing, segmenting, and targeting business markets.

6 Explain the major differences between business and consumer markets. In business markets, demand is derived, price-inelastic, joint, and fluctuating. Purchase volume is much larger than in consumer markets, customers are fewer in number and more geographically concentrated, and distribution channels are more direct. Buying is approached more formally using professional purchasing agents, more people are involved in the buying process, negotiation is more complex, and reciprocity and leasing are more common. And, finally, selling strategy in business markets normally focuses on personal contact rather than on advertising.

7 Describe the seven types of business goods and services. Major equipment includes capital goods, such as heavy machinery. Accessory equipment is typically less expensive and shorter-lived than major equipment. Raw materials are extractive or agricultural products that have not been processed. Component parts are finished or near-finished items to be used as parts of other products. Processed materials are used to manufacture other products. Supplies are consumable and not used as part of a final product. Business services are intangible products that many companies use in their operations.

8 Discuss the unique aspects of business buying behavior. Business buying behavior is distinguished by five fundamental characteristics. First, buying is normally undertaken by a buying center consisting of many people who range widely in authority level. Second, business buyers typically evaluate alternative products and suppliers based on quality, service, and price—in that order. Third, business buying falls into three general categories: new buys, modified rebuys, and straight rebuys. Fourth, the ethics of business buyers and sellers are often scrutinized. Fifth, customer service before, during, and after the sale plays a big role in business purchase decisions.

Discussion and Writing Questions

1. How might derived demand affect the manufacturing of an automobile?
2. Why is relationship or personal selling the best way to promote in business marketing?
3. **WRITING** A colleague of yours has sent you an e-mail seeking your advice as he attempts to sell a new voice-mail system to a local business. Send him a return e-mail describing the various people who might influence the customer's buying decision. Be sure to include suggestions for dealing with the needs of each of these individuals.
4. Intel Corporation supplies microprocessors to Compaq for use in their computers. Describe the buying situation in this relationship, keeping in mind the rapid advancement of technology in this industry.
5. **TEAM** In small groups, brainstorm examples of companies that feature the products in the different business categories. (Avoid examples already listed in the chapter.) Compile a list of ten specific business products including at least one in each category. Then match up with another group. Have each group take turns naming a product and have the other group identify its appropriate category. Try to resolve all discrepancies by discussion. Some identified products might appropriately fit into more than one category.
6. **ON LINE** What business publications, search facilities, sources, and services does the Web site **http://www.demographics.com** offer?
7. **ON LINE** How could you use the Web site **http://www.business2business.on.ca** to help plan a business trip to Toronto? Name three articles featured in the latest issue of *Business To Business Magazine*.
8. **INFOTRAC COLLEGE EDITION** Understanding businesses is key to business marketing. Use Info-Trac (**http://www.infotrac-college.com**) to learn more about a variety of industries. Publications like *Manufacturing Automation, Computer*

Key Terms

accessory equipment   199
business e-commerce   186
business marketing   186
business services   200
buying center   200
component parts   199
consumer e-commerce   186
derived demand   195
electronic commerce
   (e-commerce)   186
extranet   187
joint demand   196
keiretsu   190
major equipment
   (installations)   198
modified rebuy   203
multiplier effect
   (accelerator principle)   196
new buy   203
North American Industry
   Classification System
   (NAICS)   193
OEM   200
processed materials   200
raw materials   199
reciprocity   198
straight rebuy   203
strategic alliance
   (strategic partnership)   189
supplies   200

Weekly, Power Generation Technology & Markets, and *Biotech Equipment Update* can give you insights into many business marketing concepts. Research the industrial publications to find an article on a business marketer that interests you. Write a description of the company using as many concepts from the chapter as possible.

Application for Entrepreneurs

Dan White is an independent video producer whose biggest client is the State of Illinois Agricultural Department. Although this account is big enough to support the entire business, Dan has developed other lines of business to eliminate the risks involved with having only one customer. Dan has also landed a sizable account through a high school friend who is the vice president of Good Hands Insurance. This also happens to be the company that underwrites Dan's life insurance. Additionally, Dan is hired to work on various projects for large production companies. Dan generated this business through long-term relationships built by working on projects for the state of Illinois.

As Dan prepares his business plan for the upcoming year, he is contemplating several strategic changes. Because of the increasing speed at which the video industry is evolving, Dan has observed two important trends. First, he is finding it increasingly difficult to own the latest video equipment that his customers are demanding. Second, Dan's clients are not able to keep up with the recent developments in the industry and would be willing to pay more for his expertise. Dan is looking into a lease for new equipment and he is contemplating increasing the price of his services.

Questions

1. What two-digit NAICS code would you assign to Dan's business?
2. Is Dan's choice to use Good Hands Insurance ethical? Why or why not?
3. How can Dan use the inelasticity of demand to his advantage?
4. Would you advise Dan to lease or buy the new equipment? Why?

Case

intrapreneurship

W. W. Grainger: Moving Maintenance to the Internet Space

For more than seventy years, W. W. Grainger has kept the manufacturing and other labor-intensive industries on their collective feet by supplying the much-needed parts that help keep the machinery and operations running. From tape to electric motors, from chemicals to industrial-strength mops, and from lubricating fluids to lightbulbs, Grainger lists seventy thousand parts in its legendary seven-pound red catalog. In the $220 billion maintenance, repair, and operating supplies (MRO) market, this Chicago-based

company has staked its claim to a $5 billion piece. It has shipped its catalog to purchasing and procurement officers in manufacturing and office-related environments for seventy-two years, and has always enjoyed the reputation of being America's premiere industrial supplier of replacement and supplemental parts. An Old Economy stalwart, Grainger is the kind of company that many would have predicted trouble for with the dawning of widespread adoption of the Internet. Using Net storefronts, Grainger's suppliers would be able to sell directly to its customers, and its New Economy competition would be able to move faster having built completely Internet-focused business models. Grainger, however, has adapted in a way few Old Economy companies have, and its successful entrepreneurship in the Internet space has quieted doubters and reaffirmed its position as the nation's leader in the MRO market.

To battle inefficiencies in its order taking and fulfillment process, Grainger looked to the Internet for a viable solution that would allow it to move quicker, and offer more parts and more value-added services to its customer base. The answer was to launch four distinct Web sites, each with its own unique purpose and functionality, to maintain existing market share and build new business. Grainger.com, the most basic on-line storefront, sells the complete Grainger catalog of parts. Search functions allow customers to drastically reduce the time needed to leaf through the standard catalog for parts. The site also shows real-time inventory status of those parts and greatly simplifies the process of placing large orders. The success of the initiative is reflected in the fact that the average order placed on-line is twice as large as traditional orders, and customers who buy primarily on-line have spent 20 percent more over the course of the year than those ordering through the old red catalog.

Grainger's second Web property, OrderZone.com, is an aggregate marketplace through which Grainger sells its own products and the industrial products of other industrial suppliers like clothing supplier Cintas, VWR Scientific Products, and Lab Safety Products. OrderZone.com extends Grainger's already huge product selection to over 220,000 individual items. FindMRO.com is Grainger's third Web storefront. It stocks and sells specialty items not otherwise found in Grainger's traditional catalog or at Grainger.com—for example, Kevlar gloves or stir-sticks for giant paint vats. Rounding out the group of forward-thinking Web initiatives is GraingerAuction (**http://www.specialbids. com**), a site where Grainger liquidates excess inventory. The site allows users to set up an account and sign up for a special service called Watch List. A buyer can list items that he or she is looking for on an individualized Watch List and Grainger will then notify that person when those items hit the auction block. Grainger has already posted a profit of approximately $100 million on sales made through its Web-based stores, something that the vast majority of the dot.com businesses still only dream about.

Perhaps what has contributed to Grainger's success on the Internet is that its Web sites are well laid out, intuitive to navigate, and void of unwanted clutter like annoying and intrusive banner ads. There is a simplicity in browsing Grainger's on-line catalog, plac-

ing an order, and searching for parts and service information that is not normally found on business-to-consumer Internet retail sites. Grainger knows its buyers are people who know what they want, who are probably repeat customers, and who will buy based on cost or quality alone. Branding and advertising are not likely to sway the industrial purchasing manager whose job it is to find the most cost-effective and reliable parts, regardless of looks, style, or presentation. That is not to say that there is no place for branding in business-to-business marketing. Quite the opposite. Functionality rules in that market, and purchasers are judged on whether they save money or procure reliable parts (not parts that represent any great style).

So instead of differentiating their parts based on style or self-image, business-to-business marketers brand their products to convey images of performance, endurance, or low cost.

Grainger has complemented that no-nonsense marketing approach with a new approach to its off-line promotions efforts. Committing $10 million to its 2000 print advertising campaign for OrderZone.com—a 900 percent increase over the 1999 budget—Grainger has taken a fresh approach to the art of business-to-business messaging. Instead of taking the traditional approach of showing a picture of a product in the center of the page and filling the surrounding space with text heralding the product's superiority, Grainger borrowed a technique generally reserved for business-to-consumer marketers. Ads for OrderZone.com target the individual in charge of making purchasing and procurement decisions within the organization. The ads are meant to appeal to those individuals on an emotional, personal, and professional level, as well as to provoke feelings of aspiration and the desire to succeed.

Occupying two full pages in trade magazines, the ads show the desk space of a purchasing manager who does not use OrderZone.com on one page, and the desk of one who does on the other. The manager who uses OrderZone.com has a clutter-free office and is depicted receiving two tickets to an auto race from a supervisor. In an obvious state of disarray, the other manager is disorganized and haggard and has only managed to build a model truck for show on his desk. The message is clear—use OrderZone.com and you are a savvy purchaser who gains free time and is in good favor with your boss. Waste time ordering parts the old way, and you will be perceived as a laggard with no extra time and no chance to move forward in your job or personal life.

Grainger is not worried about its Web business cannibalizing its existing paper catalog business. In fact, it has made the on-line ordering and fulfillment process so efficient and accurate that it is much more cost effective than filling orders the old way. Don Bielinsky, the Grainger group president, envisions and hopes for a time when over 50 percent of all Grainger orders are placed and filled through the digital medium. Only those who are too slow or too small to conduct business on the Internet would place orders through the paper catalog, and in a world of cheap PC's and available free Internet access, those types of customers are rapidly dwindling.

Questions
1. List the benefits Grainger has enjoyed by moving its business on-line.
2. With whom has Grainger formed strategic partnerships? How has Grainger used those alliances to increase its business and bolster its image on-line?

3. How would you classify the types of business products Grainger sells? To what business market does it sell?
4. How has Grainger adopted consumer-style promotions to improve its business marketing?

Bibliography

Alicia Neumann. "How It Works—A Better Mousetrap Catalog" *Business 2.0,* February 2000, pp. 117–118.

Aaron Baar. "Grainger Targets Purchasers." *Adweek,* May 31, 1999, p. 6.

Peter Girard. "The Spin-off Payoff." *Catalog Age New Canaan,* March 15, 2000, pp. 1, 18–21.

Melanie Warner, Daniel Roth, Erick Schonfeld, and Marc Gunther. "Ten Companies that Get It." *Fortune,* November 8, 1999, pp. 115–117.

Case

video

Burke, Inc.:
Business-to-Business Alliances

As one of the premier international business research and consulting firms in the world, Burke, Inc., provides services to other businesses to help them grow and remain competitive in the marketplace. The successful Cincinnati-based firm has offices and affiliates throughout the United States plus an international division, headquartered in London, which operates in eleven European countries and Japan. To offer solutions to businesses, Burke has four divisions: Burke Marketing Research, Burke Customer Satisfaction Associates, Burke Strategic Consulting Group, and the Training and Development Center.

Burke owes its success to the number and quality of its business relationships. Today's business environment is so complex that companies can no longer operate independently to fulfill their needs, and strategic alliances offer viable solutions. Burke brings more than sixty-five years of industry experience to each business alliance and has joined with companies in a wide variety of industries—agriculture,

communications, financial services, entertainment, publishing, travel, insurance, communications, and health care.

According to Burke's business philosophy, a strategic alliance is particularly strong when both partners bring expertise and different skills to the table. These complementary assets might include access to markets or to technology, economies of scale gained by combining research and development or marketing activities, and sharing of risk. Recently, Burke teamed up with a publisher to produce a national consumer guide to non-prescription drugs. The publisher and author lacked the experience and sophisticated tools needed to gather immediate and accurate information from pharmacists, so they asked Burke Marketing Research to join them. Together, the writer, publisher, and researchers produced a very thorough national consumer's guide. Burke was able to provide the timely information that its partner needed to gain a competitive advantage.

Strategic alliances can be particularly beneficial when companies face stiff competition in the marketplace.

Yet Burke does not take a "cookie cutter" approach that gives different partners solutions based on the same model. Rather, working in teams, researchers customize methods for a specific industry and product or service category. Burke's strong belief in teamwork and specialized service influences every alliance and ultimately strengthens its relationships with its partners. Everyone at Burke understands that business clients operate in different marketing environments and have different business objectives, so each business client works with an account team to see that objectives are met efficiently, economically, and on time. The team analyzes each client's business needs and focuses Burke's broad resources on specific requirements.

Recently, the Burke Strategic Consulting Group formed a partnership with Armstrong Laing, a computer software company, to provide consulting support for businesses that purchase Armstrong Laing's management software. Burke will use the software to assist clients in understanding their true costs and in pinpointing the link between long-term strategies and day-to-day decisions. "This partnership allows us to provide innovative solutions to clients who want better financial results through cost management programs," said Diane Salamon, vice president of Burke, Inc. At the same time, Armstrong Laing describes the partnership as a marriage of management expertise and cutting-edge software that will help customers attain leadership positions in their industries. Teaming up with an outside provider of business services made sense for Armstrong Laing because the company did not have management consulting expertise in-house. And like most business-to-business marketers, Armstrong Laing was selling its products in very large quantities to established organizations like American Express and Blue Cross/Blue Shield and wanted to offer its clients a comprehensive approach of the highest quality.

Still another element of Burke's alliances is relationship marketing—that is, seeking and establishing *ongoing* partnerships. For example, one client was a multinational restaurant company that wished to define its strengths and determine the effect of a change in advertising. To provide this information, Burke built a model to show how market share might be affected by different advertising and made predictions based on this model. But the relationship did not end there. Burke continued to set clear priorities for future communication and operating strategies. This long-term relationship allowed the restaurant company to get maximum ROI (return on image) for its advertising dollars. Long-term relationships like this build trust among partners, especially when they share a common interest in meeting customer needs. In Burke's opinion, far greater customer satisfaction can be achieved through a strategic business alliance.

Questions

1. Why is Burke considered a business marketer?
2. Review Exhibit 6.2. Does Burke follow the tips for making strategic alliances successful?
3. How did Burke's strategic business alliance with Armstrong Laing create a competitive advantage in the marketplace?
4. How does Burke use the principles of relationship marketing?

Bibliography

Burke Marketing Research Press Kit.
Press Releases: *Burke Marketing Research Conducts Survey For National Consumer Guide; Burke Strategic Consulting Group, Armstrong Laing Form Partnership*
Burke Web site: **http://www.burke.com**.

chapter 7

Learning Objectives

1. Describe the characteristics of markets and market segments

2. Explain the importance of market segmentation

3. Discuss criteria for successful market segmentation

4. Describe the bases commonly used to segment consumer markets

5. Describe the bases for segmenting business markets

6. List the steps involved in segmenting markets

7. Discuss alternative strategies for selecting target markets

8. Explain how and why firms implement positioning strategies and how product differentiation plays a role

9. Discuss global market segmentation and targeting issues

Segmenting and Targeting Markets

Liz Claiborne Inc. has remade itself into the Procter & Gamble of fashion, offering a large portfolio of brands including Laundry, Lucky Brand, and Segrets. The company has also become a licensee to make DKNY jeans and a line of Kenneth Cole clothing. Claiborne has even gone downscale, producing cotton sweaters and sportswear sold at Wal-Mart stores. Its goal is to win over a new generation of shoppers with tastes so eclectic that even the trendiest clotheshorses wear a $15 Old Navy top with $300 Prada pants.

Liz Claiborne started dressing career women in 1976. Through the years, the company grew through line extensions, such as Liz Sport, Lizwear, Liz & Co., its large-size Elisabeth label, and Dana Buchman, an upscale spinoff named after one of Ms. Claiborne's top assistants.

Claiborne is helping develop a new template for the fashion industry where the stand-alone fashion house built on a single designer is fast becoming an endangered species. Jones Apparel Group, a Claiborne rival, recently spent $1.3 billion to acquire footwear giant Nine West Group on top of adding labels like Polo Jeans and Todd Oldham.

"We know that women will shop where it is the most convenient to find what they want," explains Paul Charron, Claiborne's chairman and CEO since 1995. Today, 20 percent of Claiborne's sales come from labels other than Liz and the plan is to add even more—but not from the high end. "I want to make money, and you can't do that with couture," he says.

Still, the New York–based company wanted some trendy clothes too, so it bought 7 percent of Kenneth Cole Productions in 1999. It arranged to launch women's wear, featuring sleek sportswear in stretchy fabrics. The collection will be Claiborne's flashiest entry in its twenty-three-year history, and could generate as much as $250 million annually in five years, notes Charron.

Apparel industry consultant David A. Cole offers these observations: "There is a finite limit to the volume you can generate from one brand." By sharing warehouses and back-office operations, big apparel companies like Claiborne and Jones Apparel can "now be seen as brand-management companies that bear little resemblance to the old-line Seventh Avenue even five years ago," said Mr. Cole. Moreover, the fashion game has become more freewheeling—and cutthroat—as discount stores siphon business from department stores and specialty chains. That's why Claiborne took a turn down-market, to bring out an array of labels such as Villager, Crazy Horse, and Russ for chains including JCPenney Co., Sears, and Wal-Mart.

Other big fashion companies have come to the same conclusion. In Europe, Yves Saint Laurent, Fendi, Valentino, Jil Sander, and Helmut Lang are no longer standing alone, having been acquired by luxury-goods powerhouses such as Gucci Group NV and Prada.

Based on this story, how would you define market segmentation and targeting? What type of targeting strategy is Liz Claiborne using? Describe the pros and cons of this targeting strategy for Liz Claiborne.[1] This chapter will help you answer these questions and more.

Market Segmentation

1

Describe the characteristics of markets and market segments

market
People or organizations with needs or wants and the ability and willingness to buy.

market segment
A subgroup of people or organizations sharing one or more characteristics that cause them to have similar product needs.

market segmentation
The process of dividing a market into meaningful, relatively similar, and identifiable segments or groups.

The term *market* means different things to different people. We are all familiar with the supermarket, stock market, labor market, fish market, and flea market. All these types of markets share several characteristics. First, they are composed of people (consumer markets) or organizations (business markets). Second, these people or organizations have wants and needs that can be satisfied by particular product categories. Third, they have the ability to buy the products they seek. Fourth, they are willing to exchange their resources, usually money or credit, for desired products. In sum, a **market** is (1) people or organizations with (2) needs or wants and with (3) the ability and (4) the willingness to buy. A group of people or an organization that lacks any one of these characteristics is not a market.

Within a market, a **market segment** is a subgroup of people or organizations sharing one or more characteristics that cause them to have similar product needs. At one extreme, we can define every person and every organization in the world as a market segment because each is unique. At the other extreme, we can define the entire consumer market as one large market segment and the business market as another large segment. All people have some similar characteristics and needs, as do all organizations.

From a marketing perspective, market segments can be described as somewhere between the two extremes. The process of dividing a market into meaningful, relatively similar, and identifiable segments or groups is called **market segmentation**. The purpose of market segmentation is to enable the marketer to tailor marketing mixes to meet the needs of one or more specific segments.

Exhibit 7.1 illustrates the concept of market segmentation. Each box represents a market consisting of seven persons. This market might vary as follows: one homogeneous market of seven people, a market consisting of seven individual segments, a market composed of two segments based on gender, a market composed of three age segments, or a market composed of five age and gender market segments. Age and gender and many other bases for segmenting markets are examined later in this chapter.

The Importance of Market Segmentation

2

Explain the importance of market segmentation

Until the 1960s, few firms practiced market segmentation. When they did, it was more likely a haphazard effort than a formal marketing strategy. Before 1960, for example, the Coca-Cola Company produced only one beverage and aimed it at the entire soft-drink market. Today, Coca-Cola offers over a dozen different products to market segments based on diverse consumer preferences for flavors and calorie and caffeine content. Coca-Cola offers traditional soft drinks, energy drinks (such as Power Ade), flavored teas, and fruit drinks (Fruitopia).

Market segmentation plays a key role in the marketing strategy of almost all successful organizations and is a powerful marketing tool for several reasons. Most importantly, nearly all markets include groups of people or organizations with different product needs and preferences. Market segmentation helps marketers define customer needs and wants more precisely. Because market segments differ in size and potential, segmentation helps decision makers more accurately define marketing objectives and better allocate resources. In turn, performance can be better evaluated when objectives are more precise.

AnnTaylor Stores Corporation has enjoyed long-term success in the fickle world of women's fashion by focusing on working women in their thirties and for-

Exhibit **7.1**

Concept of Market
Segmentation

No market segmentation

Fully segmented market

Market segmentation
by gender: M,F

Market segmentation
by age group: 1,2,3

Market segmentation
by gender and age group

ties. Women in this segment are pressed for time. At AnnTaylor they could not only find classic styles of clothing, they could also take advantage of the stores' one-stop-wardrobe concept, which allows them to create a wardrobe with just a few purchases. AnnTaylor has developed an unusually loyal base of shoppers and is financially stronger than many of its rivals.[2]

Criteria for Successful Segmentation

Marketers segment markets for three important reasons. First, segmentation enables marketers to identify groups of customers with similar needs and to analyze the characteristics and buying behavior of these groups. Second, segmentation provides marketers with information to help them design marketing mixes specifically matched with the characteristics and desires of one or more segments. Third, segmentation is consistent with the marketing concept of satisfying customer wants and needs while meeting the organization's objectives.

Discuss criteria for successful market segmentation

To be useful, a segmentation scheme must produce segments that meet four basic criteria:

- *Substantiality:* A segment must be large enough to warrant developing and maintaining a special marketing mix. This criterion does not necessarily mean that a segment must have many potential customers. Marketers of custom-designed homes and business buildings, commercial airplanes, and large computer systems typically develop marketing programs tailored to each potential customer's needs. In most cases, however, a market segment needs many potential customers to make commercial sense. In the 1980s, home banking failed because not enough people owned personal computers. Today a larger number of people own computers, and home banking is a growing industry.

- *Identifiability and measurability:* Segments must be identifiable and their size measurable. Data about the population within geographic boundaries, the number of people in various age categories, and other social and demographic characteristics are often easy to get, and they provide fairly concrete measures of segment size. Suppose that a social service agency wants to identify segments by their readiness to participate in a drug and alcohol program or in prenatal care. Unless the agency can measure how many people are willing, indifferent, or unwilling to participate, it will have trouble gauging whether there are enough people to justify setting up the service.

- *Accessibility:* The firm must be able to reach members of targeted segments with customized marketing mixes. Some market segments are hard to reach—for example, senior citizens (especially those with reading or hearing disabilities), individuals who don't speak English, and the illiterate.

- *Responsiveness:* As Exhibit 7.1 illustrates, markets can be segmented using any criteria that seem logical. However, unless one market segment responds to a marketing mix differently from other segments, that segment need not be treated separately. For instance, if all customers are equally price-conscious about a product, there is no need to offer high-, medium-, and low-priced versions to different segments.

Bases for Segmenting Consumer Markets

Describe the bases commonly used to segment consumer markets

segmentation bases (variables)
Characteristics of individuals, groups, or organizations.

Marketers use **segmentation bases,** or **variables,** which are characteristics of individuals, groups, or organizations, to divide a total market into segments. The choice of segmentation bases is crucial because an inappropriate segmentation strategy may lead to lost sales and missed profit opportunities. The key is to identify bases that will produce substantial, measurable, and accessible segments that exhibit different response patterns to marketing mixes.

Markets can be segmented using a single variable, such as age group, or several variables, such as age group, gender, and education. Although it is less precise, single-variable segmentation has the advantage of being simpler and easier to use than multiple-variable segmentation. The disadvantages of multiple-variable segmentation are that it is often harder to use than single-variable segmentation; usable secondary data are less likely to be available; and as the number of segmentation bases increases, the size of individual segments decreases. Nevertheless, the current trend is toward using more rather than fewer variables to segment most markets. Multiple-variable segmentation is clearly more precise than single-variable segmentation.

Consumer goods marketers commonly use one or more of the following characteristics to segment markets: geography, demographics, psychographics, benefits sought, and usage rate.

Geographic Segmentation

geographic segmentation
Segmenting markets by region of the country or world, market size, market density, or climate.

Geographic segmentation refers to segmenting markets by region of the country or world, market size, market density, or climate. Market density means the number of people within a unit of land, such as a census tract. Climate is commonly used for geographic segmentation because of its dramatic impact on residents' needs and purchasing behavior. Snowblowers, water and snow skis, clothing, and air-conditioning and heating systems are products with varying appeal, depending on climate.

Consumer goods companies take a regional approach to marketing for four reasons. First, many firms need to find new ways to generate sales because of sluggish and intensely competitive markets. Second, computerized checkout stations with scanners enable retailers to assess accurately which brands sell best in their region. Third, many packaged-goods manufacturers are introducing new regional brands intended to appeal to local preferences. Fourth, a more regional approach allows consumer-goods companies to react more quickly to competition. For example, Cracker Barrel, a restaurant known in the South for home-style cooking, is altering its menu outside its core Southern market to reflect local tastes. Customers in upstate New York can order Reuben sandwiches, and those in Texas can get eggs with salsa. Miller Lite developed the "Miller Lite True to Texas" marketing program, a statewide campaign targeting Texas beer drinkers. The "Global Perspectives" box provides another example of geographic market segmentation.

Global Perspectives

U.S. SUPERSTORES FIND JAPANESE ARE A HARD SELL

When Office Depot and OfficeMax entered the Japanese market in 1998, Japan's 20,000 small stationery stores shuddered. The stationery industry was archaic, and the stores usually charged full price. The two U.S. companies had plans to open hundreds of office superstores, of a type Japan had never seen, filled with cut-price pens, notebooks, and fax machines.

But the U.S. stores proved to be too big and too American for Japanese consumers. Meanwhile, a nimble local competitor came out of nowhere to trounce the U.S. retailers at their own game. Stumbling, the Americans are changing course, testing store formats that are quite different from their tried and true U.S. formulas.

The U.S. companies ran into a number of problems in trying to translate their formula to appeal to the Japanese. For starters, Japanese office products are very different from those in the United States. For

example, because loose-leaf binders in Japan have two rings instead of three, they had to buy such products from traditional local suppliers. Because they were selling the same products as their Japanese counterparts, they also had to compete extra hard on price. But they did not always get the best sourcing deals, with some suppliers even insisting on going through costly intermediaries for fear of annoying neighborhood stores.

The stores themselves also turned out to be too American. Office Depot opened two U.S.–size stores in Tokyo and Hiroshima. They were more than 20,000 square feet each, and featured wide aisles and signs in English. But with rents in Japan more than twice those in the United States and personnel costs sky-high, the stores were too expensive to run. Japanese were confused by the English-language signs and put off by the warehouse-like atmosphere. Interestingly, when Office De-

pot later reduced the size of one Tokyo store by a third and crammed the merchandise closer together, sales remained the same.

Despite these initial setbacks, Office Depot continues to expand its Japanese operations. Its new stores still have American radio programs playing in the background. But the signs are in Japanese, and the shelves, lining narrow aisles, don't stock as many files or as much copy paper. It is also beefing up its catalogs, to compete with a local discount mail-order stationery company.

Could the American discount office products companies have more effectively segmented their market in Japan, and if so, how? What positioning mistakes did Office Depot and Office Max make in Japan?[a]

[a] Yumiko, Ono, "U.S. Superstores Find Japanese Are a Hard Sell," *Wall Street Journal*, February, 14, 2000, pp. B1, B4.

Demographic Segmentation

Marketers often segment markets on the basis of demographic information because it is widely available and often related to consumers' buying and consuming behavior. Some common bases of **demographic segmentation** are age, gender, income, ethnic background, and family life cycle. The discussion here provides some important information about the main demographic segments.

demographic segmentation
Segmenting markets by age, gender, income, ethnic background, and family life cycle.

Age Segmentation Attracting children is a popular strategy for many companies because they hope to instill brand loyalty early. Furthermore, children influence a great deal of family consumption. There are an estimated twenty-eight million children aged six to twelve in the United States. This generation of kids is computer literate, with 24 percent having on-line access at home, a number that is projected to double by the year 2002. A number of companies offer kid-centered Internet content to appeal to this group, including America Online with its Kids Only service, and a Boston-based children's on-line service called JuniorNet.[3]

"Generation Y" is thirty million strong. They spend $97.3 billion annually, about two-thirds of which goes toward clothing ($33 billion), entertainment ($21 billion), and personal care ($8.3 billion).[4] Some of the biggest companies on the market, such as PepsiCo, Nike, and Levi Strauss have been struggling in their attempts to reach this market. On the other hand, Tommy Hilfiger, a clothing company, found a successful formula for attracting teens. Along with its traditional mass-media ads, it ran unusual promotions, from giving free clothing to teen stars on VH1 and MTV to having teen film stars appearing in Hilfiger ads. In addition, knowing its customers' passion for computer games, it sponsored a Nintendo competition and installed Nintendo terminals in its stores. Generation Y consumers voted Hilfiger jeans their favorite brand in an American Express Company survey.[5]

Age segmentation can clearly define your target, but it can also be restrictive. Volvo has broken out of its older, family image by launching a new ad campaign with ads like the one pictured. The goal is to attract youthful Gen X-ers to a brand most typically associated with family life.

Other age segments are also appealing targets for marketers. The forty-seven million consumers of Generation X have $125 billion in spending power. Volvo, a car that has been targeted to a family-oriented, safety-minded customer, is now also trying to attract members of Generation X. For example, a print ad that showed up in the premier issue of *Talk* magazine reads "Volvo discovers life before babies."[6] The computer-literate Generation X-ers also are a large and viable market for the Internet.

The baby boom generation, born between 1946 and 1964, comprises the largest age segment—about 30 percent of the entire U.S. population. Many in this group are approaching (or past) fifty years of age, and continuing to lead active, fully involved lifestyles. Traditionally, marketers have not explicitly targeted the fifty-plus segment. Gateway, a company that markets personal computers, targets what it calls "aging adventurers," a group defined by an average age of fifty-five, with grown kids and annual incomes ranging from $50,000 to $75,000. Several Gateway TV ads were designed to directly appeal to this group.[7]

Seniors (aged sixty-five and over) are especially attracted to companies that build relationships by taking the time to get to know them and their preferences. As an example, older customers say they prefer catalog shopping to retail outlets because of dissatisfaction with customer service at retail stores. In comparison, a mailing done to target Medicare supplement prospects that included Valentine cards to seniors received a very positive response.[8]

As the senior segment grows, more companies are taking their needs into consideration. The pharmaceutical industry is stepping up its quest to design pill bottles with caps that are easier for seniors to open. For example, in the past two years, Searle has reviewed about two-dozen new bottle and cap prototypes. One design that has promise is the "Friendly and Safe" cap, that can be opened without the fingers having to squeeze the cap at all, and requires less than a quarter turn to open.[9] Seniors also comprise a growing market for the Internet. ThirdAge Media Inc., a San Fransico company, offers a Web site geared toward empty nesters and retirees that includes customized e-mail newsletters that are sent to up to seventy thousand members weekly.[10]

Gender Segmentation   Marketers of products such as clothing, cosmetics, personal care items, magazines, jewelry, and footwear commonly segment markets by gender. Men aged eighteen to forty-nine are the segment most likely to purchase goods on-line. Many Internet companies have advertised to this group to build their brands and get exposure for their sites.[11] However, brands that have traditionally been marketed to men, such as Gillette razors and Rogaine baldness remedy, are increasing their efforts to attract women. Sutherland Golf Inc. makes premium golf balls (which are mostly designed for men) that are designed for women. These balls compress more easily when hit to compensate for the fact that women generally have a slower swing than male golfers.[12] Conversely, "women's" products such as cosmetics, household products, and furniture are also being marketed to men.

Income Segmentation   Income is a popular demographic variable for segmenting markets because income level influences consumers' wants and determines their buying power. Many markets are segmented by income, including the markets for housing, clothing, automobiles, and food. For example, value retailers such as Dollar General are drawing low- and fixed-income customers with easy access, small stores, and rock-bottom pricing.[13] Wal-Mart, on the other hand, is moving away from its traditional rural and middle-income markets by targeting higher-income consumers in upscale areas. The retailer is spending more money on its stores, introducing more high-end merchandise, and upgrading apparel lines.

Ethnic Segmentation   Many companies are segmenting their markets by ethnicity. The three largest ethnic markets are the African-American,

With Internet usage growing among African-Americans, Web sites like Net Noir are attracting thousands of visitors to their highly targeted offerings. Compare NetNoir.com and afronet.com. Which do you think is more appealing? Useful? Why?

Hispanic-American, and Asian-American. These three groups collectively are projected to make up one-third of the country's population by 2010,[14] and have a combined buying power of more than a trillion dollars. Furthermore, minority populations are fast becoming the majority population in major markets.[15] Minority customers may have differences from their white counterparts in their preferences. For example, for 53 percent of Hispanic-Americans and Asian-Americans, and 44 percent of African-Americans, customer service is the most important factor in choosing a phone company, versus 36 percent for whites. Meanwhile, whites are almost twice as likely to buy the lowest-price phone service as nonwhites.[16]

African-Americans African-Americans are the largest minority group in the United States, and their population is expected to grow to more than forty-five million in 2020. Their purchasing power reaches $450 million, and they spend more than whites on luxury items such as cars, clothing, and home furnishings.[17] The Internet is of growing importance as a medium to reach the African-American consumer. While net use among this group lags behind the white population (28 percent of blacks versus 37 percent of whites), African-Americans that are on-line are younger, more affluent, and better educated than African-Americans who do not use the Internet. In addition, nearly 30 percent intend to place orders on-line, compared with 21 percent of the general population.[18] Web sites such as **http://www. netnoir.com** and **http://www.afronet.com** attract thousands of African-Americans with news, information, entertainment, and products of interest to their audiences. Microsoft Corporation developed a CD-ROM entitled "Encarta Africana," which is the first comprehensive encyclopedia of black history and culture.[19]

Hispanic-Americans The U.S. Hispanic population numbers more than thirty million, accounting for more than 11 percent of the total population. By 2050, Hispanic-Americans will comprise almost a quarter of the population. This group also has substantial buying power, reaching $350 billion.[20] Research has shown that the average Hispanic household spent 67 percent more on carbonated soft drinks, 89 percent more on fruit drinks, and 39 percent more on cereal than did the average non-Hispanic household.[21]

The concept of diversity is nowhere more evident than in the Hispanic culture. This segment consists of twenty-one nationalities, each with different cultural, historic, and economic characteristics. Therefore, marketing managers are carefully targeting major segments of this diverse market. One series of Campbells soup ads, for instance, featured a woman cooking, but the individual ads differed in such details as the character's age, the setting, and the music. In the version for Cuban-Americans, a grandmother cooks in a plant-filled kitchen to the sounds of salsa and merengue music. In contrast, the Mexican-American ad showed a young wife preparing food in a brightly colored Southwestern-style kitchen with pop music playing in the background.

A number of companies are directing marketing efforts at Hispanic-Americans. Gateway, the computer manufacturer, launched a marketing program that included TV and radio ads in Spanish, a toll-free number for Spanish-speaking clients, and representatives in sales, customer-service, and tech support who are fluent in the language.[22] General Mills introduced a line of cereals with bilingual packaging.[23] Target, an upscale discount store chain, is remodeling stores in California to appeal to Hispanic-Americans. The company is also refashioning its merchandise mix, developing marketing events and launching a magazine for Hispanics.[24]

Asian-Americans Like Hispanic-Americans, Asian-Americans are a diverse group with thirteen submarkets. The five largest are Chinese, Filipino, Japanese, Asian Indian, and Korean. This population is a fast-growing market of 10.2 million that has an annual purchasing power of $101 million. The Asian-American market is younger and better educated than the general market and has the highest average household income in the United States.[25]

Despite the strong level of purchasing power and affluence in Asian markets, many corporations are reluctant to target this market. Asian marketing experts feel this is due to a lack of solid marketing research data and tracking mechanisms to help companies better understand this segment. The Association of Asian American Advertising Agencies has been established to grow the Asian-American advertising and marketing industry, raise public awareness of the importance of the community, and further the professionalism of the industry.[26]

Some entrepreneurs are building large enclosed malls that cater to Asian consumers. At the Aberdeen Centre near Vancouver, British Columbia, nearly 80 percent of the merchants are Chinese-Canadians, as are 80 percent of the customers. The mall offers fashions made in Hong Kong, a shop for traditional Chinese medicines, and a theater showing Chinese movies. Kung fu martial arts demonstrations and Chinese folk dances are held in the mall on weekends.

Family Life-Cycle Segmentation   The demographic factors of gender, age, and income often do not sufficiently explain why consumer buying behavior varies. Frequently, differences in consumption patterns among people of the same age and gender result from their being in different stages of the family life cycle. The **family life cycle (FLC)** is a series of stages determined by a combination of age, marital status, and the presence or absence of children.

Exhibit 7.2 on page 222 illustrates both traditional and contemporary FLC patterns and shows how families' needs, incomes, resources, and expenditures differ at each stage. The horizontal flow shows the traditional family life cycle. The lower part of the exhibit gives some of the characteristics and purchase patterns of families in each stage of the traditional life cycle. The exhibit also acknowledges that about half of all first marriages end in divorce. When young marrieds move into the young divorced stage, their consumption patterns often revert back to those of the young single stage of the cycle. About four out of five divorced persons remarry by middle age and reenter the traditional life cycle, as indicated by the "recycled flow" in the exhibit.

Psychographic Segmentation
Age, gender, income, ethnicity, family life-cycle stage, and other demographic variables are usually helpful in developing segmentation strategies, but often they don't paint the entire picture. Demographics provides the skeleton, but psychographics adds meat to the bones. **Psychographic segmentation** is market segmentation on the basis of the following variables:

- *Personality:* Personality reflects a person's traits, attitudes, and habits. Porsche Cars North America understood well the demographics of the Porsche owner: a forty-something male college graduate earning over $200,000 per year. However, research discovered that there were five personality types within this general demographic category that more effectively segmented Porsche buyers. Exhibit 7.3 on page 223 describes the five segments. Porsche refined its marketing as a result of the study and, after a previous seven-year slump, the company's U.S. sales rose 48 percent.[27]
- *Motives:* Marketers of baby products and life insurance appeal to consumers' emotional motives— namely, to care for their loved ones. Using appeals to economy, reliability, and dependability, carmakers like Subaru and Suzuki target customers with rational motives. Carmakers like Mercedes-Benz, Jaguar, and Cadillac appeal to customers with status-related motives.
- *Lifestyles:* Lifestyle segmentation divides people into groups according to the way they spend their time, the importance of the things around them, their beliefs, and socioeconomic characteristics such as income and education. For example, Harley-Davidson divides its customers into seven lifestyle segments,

family life cycle (FLC)
A series of stages determined by a combination of age, marital status, and the presence or absence of children.

psychographic segmentation
Market segmentation on the basis of personality, motives, lifestyles, and geodemographics.

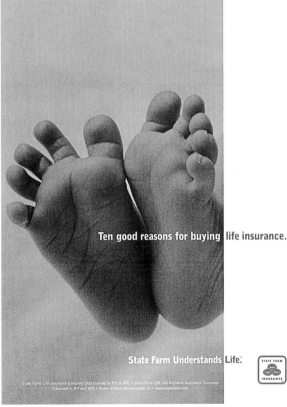

Ten good reasons for buying life insurance.

State Farm Understands Life.

This ad for State Farm clearly appeals to consumers' emotional motives by associating the purchase of life insurance with the caring and responsibility of parenting.
Courtesy State Farm Insurance Companies

Exhibit 7.2 Family Life Cycle

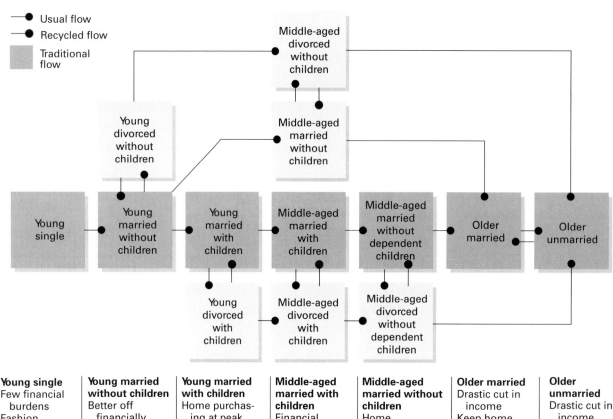

Young single
Few financial burdens
Fashion opinion leaders
Recreation-oriented
Buy: basic kitchen equipment, basic furniture, cars, equipment for mating game, vacations

Young married without children
Better off financially than they will be in near future
Highest purchase rate and highest average purchase of durables
Buy: cars, refrigerators, stoves, sensible and durable furniture, vacations

Young married with children
Home purchasing at peak
Liquid assets low
Dissatisfied with financial position and amount of money saved
Interested in new products
Like advertised products
Buy: washers, dryers, televisions, baby food, chest rubs, cough medicine, vitamins, dolls, wagons, sleds, skates

Middle-aged married with children
Financial position still better
More wives work
Some children get jobs
Hard to influence with advertising
High average purchase of durables
Buy: new and more tasteful furniture, auto travel, unnecessary appliances, boats, dental services, magazines

Middle-aged married without children
Home ownership at peak
Most satisfied with financial position and money saved
Interested in travel, recreation, self-education
Make gifts and contributions
Not interested in new products
Buy: vacations, luxuries, home improvements

Older married
Drastic cut in income
Keep home
Buy: medical appliances, medical care, products that aid health, sleep, and digestion

Older unmarried
Drastic cut in income
Special need for attention, affection, and security
Buy: same medical and product needs as other retired group

from "cocky misfits" who are most likely to be arrogant troublemakers, to "laid-back camper types" committed to cycling and nature, to "classy capitalists" who have wealth and privilege.[28]

- *Geodemographics:* **Geodemographic segmentation** clusters potential customers into neighborhood lifestyle categories. It combines geographic, demographic, and lifestyle segmentations. Geodemographic segmentation

geodemographic segmentation
Segmenting potential customers into neighborhood lifestyle categories.

Exhibit 7.3

Type	% of All Owners	Description
Top Guns	27%	Driven, ambitious types. Power and control matter. They expect to be noticed.
Elitists	24%	Old-money blue bloods. A car is just a car, no matter how expensive. It is not an extension of personality.
Proud Patrons	23%	Ownership is an end in itself. Their car is a trophy earned for hard work, and who cares if anyone sees them in it?
Bon Vivants	17%	Worldly jet setters and thrill seekers. Their car heightens the excitement in their already passionate lives.
Fantasists	9%	Walter Mitty types. Their car is an escape. Not only are they uninterested in impressing others with it, they also feel a little guilty about owning one.

helps marketers develop marketing programs tailored to prospective buyers who live in small geographic regions, such as neighborhoods, or who have very specific lifestyle and demographic characteristics. Kraft General Foods plans to tailor different ads for different neighborhoods in the same region. For example, viewers watching a cable show in a Hispanic neighborhood in Chicago would see different ads during the same commercial breaks than would young, affluent professionals living in a different neighborhood.[29]

Psychographic variables can be used individually to segment markets or can be combined with other variables to provide more detailed descriptions of market segments. One well-known combination approach, offered by SRI International, is called VALS 2 (version 2 of SRI's Values and Lifestyles program). VALS 2 categorizes U.S. consumers by their values, beliefs, and lifestyles rather than by traditional demographic segmentation variables. Many advertising agencies have used VALS segmentation to create effective promotion campaigns.

As Exhibit 7.4 on page 224 shows, the segments in VALS 2 are classified on two dimensions: vertically by their resources and horizontally by their self-orientation. Resources include education, income, self-confidence, health, eagerness to buy, intelligence, and energy level. The resources dimension is a continuum ranging from minimal to abundant. Resources generally increase from adolescence through middle age and decrease with extreme age, depression, financial reverses, and physical or psychological impairment. In contrast, the self-orientation dimension classifies three different ways of buying:

- Beliefs or principles rather than feelings, events, or desire for approval guide principle-oriented consumers in their choices.
- Other people's actions, approval, and opinions strongly influence status-oriented consumers.

Exhibit **7.4**

VALS 2 Dimensions

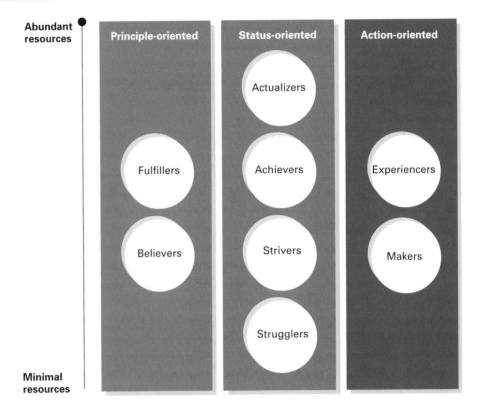

- Action-oriented consumers are prompted by a desire for social or physical activity, variety, and risk.

Exhibit 7.5 describes the eight VALS 2 psychographic segments. Using only the two key dimensions—resources and self-orientation—VALS 2 defines groups of adult consumers who have distinctive attitudes, behavior patterns, and decision-making styles.

Benefit Segmentation

benefit segmentation
The process of grouping customers into market segments according to the benefits they seek from the product.

Benefit segmentation is the process of grouping customers into market segments according to the benefits they seek from the product. Most types of market segmentation are based on the assumption that this variable and customers' needs are related. Benefit segmentation is different because it groups potential customers on the basis of their needs or wants rather than some other characteristic, such as age or gender. The snack-food market, for example, can be divided into six benefit segments, as shown in Exhibit 7.6.

Customer profiles can be developed by examining demographic information associated with people seeking certain benefits. This information can be used to match marketing strategies with selected target

Exhibit **7.5**

- **Actualizers** are successful, sophisticated, active, "take-charge" people with high self-esteem and abundant resources. They are interested in growth and seek to develop, explore, and express themselves in a variety of ways. Their possessions and recreation choices reflect a cultivated taste for the finer things in life.

- **Fulfillers** are mature, satisfied, comfortable, reflective people who value order, knowledge, and responsibility. Most are well educated, well informed about world events, and professionally employed. Fulfillers are conservative, practical consumers; they are concerned about value and durability in the products they buy.

- **Believers** are conservative, conventional people with concrete beliefs and strong attachments to traditional institutions—family, church, community, and nation. As consumers they are conservative and predictable, favoring U.S. products and established brands.

- **Achievers** are successful career- and work-oriented people who like to, and generally do, feel in control of their lives. Achievers live conventional lives, are politically conservative, and respect authority and the status quo. As consumers they favor established goods and services that demonstrate success to peers.

- **Strivers** seek motivation, self-definition, and approval from the world around them. They are easily bored and impulsive. Money defines success for strivers, who lack enough of it. They emulate those who own more impressive possessions, but what they wish to obtain is generally beyond their reach.

- **Experiencers** are young, vital, enthusiastic, and impulsive. They seek variety and excitement and combine an abstract disdain for conformity and authority with an outsider's awe of others' wealth, prestige, and power. Experiencers are avid consumers and spend much of their income on clothing, fast food, music, movies, and video.

- **Makers** are practical people who value self-sufficiency. They live within a traditional context of family, practical work, and physical recreation and have little interest in what lies outside that context. They are unimpressed by material possessions other than those with a practical or functional purpose (for example, tools, pickup trucks, or fishing equipment).

- **Strugglers** have lives that are constricted—chronically poor, ill educated, and low skilled. They lack strong social bonds; they are focused on meeting the urgent needs of the present moment. Aging strugglers are concerned about their health. Strugglers are cautious consumers who represent a very modest demand for most goods and services but are loyal to favorite brands.

markets. Procter & Gamble Company introduced Pampers Rash Guard, a diaper designed to combat diaper rash.[30] To attract time-pressed consumers, Tops Friendly Markets supermarket chain is building stores half the size of some existing ones, and they emphasize efficient shopping with features such as carry-out foods being located near the front of the store.[31]

Usage-Rate Segmentation

Usage-rate segmentation divides a market by the amount of product bought or consumed. Categories vary with the product, but they are likely to include some combination of the following: former users, potential users, first-time users, light or irregular users, medium users, and heavy users. Segmenting by usage rate

usage-rate segmentation
Dividing a market by the amount of product bought or consumed.

Exhibit 7.6 Lifestyle Segmentation of the Snack-Food Market

	Nutritional Snackers	Weight Watchers	Guilty Snackers	Party Snackers	Indiscriminate Snackers	Economical Snackers
% of Snackers	22%	14%	9%	15%	15%	18%
Lifestyle Characteristics	Self-assured, controlled	Outdoorsy, influential, venturesome	Highly anxious, isolated	Sociable	Hedonistic	Self-assured, price-oriented
Benefits Sought	Nutritious, without artificial ingredients, natural	Low in calories, quick energy	Low in calories, good tasting	Good to serve guests, served with pride, go well with beverages	Good tasting, satisfies hunger	Low in price, best value
Consumption Level of Snacks	Light	Light	Heavy	Average	Heavy	Average
Type of Snacks Usually Eaten	Fruits, vegetables, cheese	Yogurt, vegetables	Yogurt, cookies, crackers, candy	Nuts, potato chips, crackers, pretzels	Candy, ice cream, cookies, potato chips, pretzels, popcorn	No specific products
Demographics	Better educated, have younger children	Younger, single	Younger or older, female, lower socio-economic status	Middle-aged, nonurban	Teenager	Have large family, better educated

enables marketers to focus their efforts on heavy users or to develop multiple marketing mixes aimed at different segments. Because heavy users often account for a sizable portion of all product sales, some marketers focus on the heavy-user segment.

The **80/20 principle** holds that 20 percent of all customers generate 80 percent of the demand. Although the percentages are not usually exact, the general idea often holds true. For example, in the fast-food industry, the heavy user accounts for only one of five fast-food patrons, but about 60 percent of all visits to fast-food restaurants. Using this definition, the heavy user (who is most often a single male) accounted for roughly $66 billion of the $110 billion the National Restaurant Association said was spent on fast food in 1999.[32]

Developing customers into heavy users is the goal behind many frequency/loyalty programs like the airlines' frequent flyer programs. Many supermarkets have also designed loyalty programs that reward the heavy-user segment with deals available only to them, such as in-store coupon dispensing systems, loyalty card programs, and special price deals on selected merchandise.

80/20 principle
A principle holding that 20 percent of all customers generate 80 percent of the demand.

Bases for Segmenting Business Markets

The business market consists of four broad segments: producers, resellers, institutions, and government (for a detailed discussion of the characteristics of these segments, see Chapter 6). Whether marketers focus on only one or on all four of these segments, they are likely to find diversity among potential customers. Thus, further market segmentation offers just as many benefits to business marketers as it does to consumer product marketers. Business market segmentation variables can be classified into two major categories: macrosegmentation variables and microsegmentation variables.

Describe the bases for segmenting business markets

Macrosegmentation

Macrosegmentation variables are used to divide business markets into segments according to the following general characteristics:

- *Geographic location:* The demand for some business products varies considerably from one region to another. For instance, many computer hardware and software companies are located in the Silicon Valley region of California. Some markets tend to be regional because buyers prefer to purchase from local suppliers, and distant suppliers often have difficulty competing in terms of price and service. Therefore, firms that sell to geographically concentrated industries benefit by locating operations close to the market.
- *Customer type:* Segmenting by customer type allows business marketers to tailor their marketing mixes to the unique needs of particular types of organizations or industries. Many companies are finding this form of segmentation to be quite effective. For example, The Home Depot, the largest do-it-yourself retail business in the United States, has targeted professional repair and remodeling contractors in addition to consumers.
- *Customer size:* Volume of purchase (heavy, moderate, and light) is a commonly used business-to-business segmentation basis. Another is the buying organization's size, which may affect its purchasing procedures, the types and quantities of products it needs, and its responses to different marketing mixes. Banks frequently offer different services, lines of credit, and overall attention to commercial customers based on their size.
- *Product use:* Many products, especially raw materials like steel, wood, and petroleum, have diverse applications. How customers use a product may influence the amount they buy, their buying criteria, and their selection of vendors. For example, a producer of springs may have customers that use the product in applications as diverse as making machine tools, bicycles, surgical devices, office equipment, telephones, and missile systems.

macrosegmentation
The process of dividing business markets into segments based on general characteristics such as geographic location, customer type, customer size, and product use.

Microsegmentation

Macrosegmentation often produces market segments that are too diverse for targeted marketing strategies. Thus, marketers often find it useful to divide macrosegments based on such variables as customer size or product use into smaller microsegments. **Microsegmentation** is the process of dividing business markets into segments based on the characteristics of decision-making units within a macrosegment. Microsegmentation enables the marketer to more clearly identify market segments and more precisely define target markets. These are some of the typical microsegmentation variables:[33]

- *Key purchasing criteria:* Marketers can segment some business markets by ranking purchasing criteria such as product quality, prompt and reliable delivery, supplier reputation, technical support, and price. For example, Atlas Corporation developed a commanding position in the industrial door market by providing customized products in just four weeks, which is much faster than

microsegmentation
The process of dividing business markets into segments based on the characteristics of decision-making units within a macrosegment.

the industry average of twelve to fifteen weeks. Atlas's primary market is companies with an immediate need for customized doors.

- *Purchasing strategies:* The purchasing strategies of buying organizations can shape microsegments. Two purchasing profiles that have been identified are satisficers and optimizers. **Satisficers** contact familiar suppliers and place the order with the first to satisfy product and delivery requirements. **Optimizers** consider numerous suppliers (both familiar and unfamiliar), solicit bids, and study all proposals carefully before selecting one. Recognizing satisficers and optimizers is quite easy. A few key questions during a sales call, such as "Why do you buy product X from vendor A?," usually produce answers that identify purchaser profiles.

- *Importance of purchase:* Classifying business customers according to the significance they attach to the purchase of a product is especially appropriate when customers use the product differently. This approach is also appropriate when the purchase is considered routine by some customers but very important by others. For instance, a small entrepreneur would consider a laser printer a major capital purchase, but a large office would find it a normal expense.

- *Personal characteristics:* The personal characteristics of purchase decision makers (their demographic characteristics, decision style, tolerance for risk, confidence level, job responsibilities, and so on) influence their buying behavior and thus offer a viable basis for segmenting some business markets. IBM computer buyers, for example, are sometimes characterized as being more risk averse than buyers of less expensive clones that perform essentially the same functions. In advertising, therefore, IBM stresses its reputation for high quality and reliability.

An interesting segmentation strategy that raises ethical questions is described in the "Ethics in Marketing" box.

satisficers
Business customers who place an order with the first familiar supplier to satisfy product and delivery requirements.

optimizers
Business customers who consider numerous suppliers, both familiar and unfamiliar, solicit bids, and study all proposals carefully before selecting one.

Steps in Segmenting a Market

List the steps involved in segmenting markets

The purpose of market segmentation, in both consumer and business markets, is to identify marketing opportunities. Exhibit 7.7 traces the steps below in segmenting a market. Note that steps 5 and 6 are actually marketing activities that follow market segmentation (steps 1 through 4).

1. *Select a market or product category for study:* Define the overall market or product category to be studied. It may be a market in which the firm already competes, a new but related market or product category, or a totally new one. For instance, Anheuser-Busch closely examined the beer market before introducing Michelob Light and Bud Light. Anheuser-Busch also carefully studied the market for salty snacks before introducing the Eagle brand.

Exhibit **7.7**   Steps in Segmenting a Market and Subsequent Activities

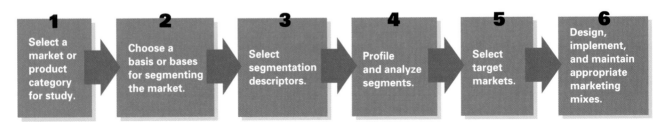

TOBACCO COMPANIES ENLIST THE BAR OWNER TO PUSH THEIR GOODS

With their traditional marketing techniques under siege—tobacco ads have been kicked off billboards and shut out of sports stadiums—cigarette makers are building a new arsenal of selling strategies. Among their hottest prospects: bars that attract young, hip drinkers, and the army of bartenders who interact with them. With vending machines disappearing in many cities, bartenders are now the vital link in selling smokes directly to their customers.

While bar promotions have always been part of the tobacco industry, cigarette makers are now burrowing into urban nightlife like never before. Using large marketing budgets, the biggest U.S. companies are pounding on the doors of bar owners, offering them thousands of dollars in exclusive deals. While RJR Nabisco pays for parties for bartenders and ads, Philip Morris simply cuts a check. In exchange, bar owners promise to use bar supplies plastered with the sponsoring company's brand names. More importantly, the bars often pledge not to sell or promote a rival brand behind their counters.

Once the deal is signed, the companies shower bartenders with perks. Thanks to Philip Morris, for example, Ray Paprocky and his wife spent four days last July at the Crazy Mountain Ranch in Livingston, Montana, biking snow-capped mountains and kayaking down the Yellowstone River. Each night, they would return to their lushly appointed suite to find new binoculars and other gifts on their bed. Philip Morris even gave the Paprocky's $1,500, which they used to pay for the tax consequences of the free trip, valued at over $10,000. Back in Manhattan, Mr. Paprocky tends a yuppie sports bar called Turtle Bay and sells twenty packs of Marlboros—the only cigarette his bar stocks—to the crowd each night. He says, "I do everything I can to push Marlboro and Marlboro Lights. I'm of the school of thought that if you're nice to me, I'm nice to you."

And researchers say bar-goers are particularly receptive to tobacco come-ons. They point to recent evidence of a genetic link between cigarette and alcohol use: Over a third of two-pack-a-day smokers have also suffered from drinking problems. They also point to findings that drinking in social settings tempts ex-smokers to get back into the habit.

To test the effectiveness of its bar program, marketers at British American Tobacco PLC's Brown & Williamson unit polled bar-goers and compared their impressions of its Lucky Strike brand to those who weren't exposed to the bar promotion. "You see an enormous improvement," says Robert Bexon, senior vice president of marketing at Brown & Williamson. He estimates the company spends $30 million a year on its bar program nationwide.

Finally, there is the selling strength of the good old barkeep, whose image as a trusted confidant is firmly burned into cultural consciousness. "People look to the bartender as someone who knows what's hip today and is making an informed choice," says Kevin Berg, whose firm, KBA Marketing, pioneered Reynolds' bar-marketing approach.[a]

Discuss the ethical implications of the tobacco industry's use of bartenders to sell cigarettes to young bar-goers. Do you agree with this form of selling, or not? Defend your answer. What bases for segmenting business markets are the tobacco companies using?

[a] Suein L. Hwang, "Light Brigades: Tobacco Companies Enlist the Bar Owner to Push Their Goods," *Wall Street Journal*, April 21, 1999, pp. A1, A6.

2. *Choose a basis or bases for segmenting the market:* This step requires managerial insight, creativity, and market knowledge. There are no scientific procedures for selecting segmentation variables. However, a successful segmentation scheme must produce segments that meet the four basic criteria discussed earlier in this chapter.

3. *Select segmentation descriptors:* After choosing one or more bases, the marketer must select the segmentation descriptors. Descriptors identify the specific segmentation variables to use. For example, if a company selects demographics as a basis of segmentation, it may use age, occupation, and income as descriptors. A company that selects usage segmentation needs to decide whether to go after heavy users, nonusers, or light users.

4. *Profile and analyze segments:* The profile should include the segments' size, expected growth, purchase frequency, current brand usage, brand loyalty, and long-term sales and profit potential. This information can then be used to rank

potential market segments by profit opportunity, risk, consistency with organizational mission and objectives, and other factors important to the firm.

5. *Select target markets:* Selecting target markets is not a part of but a natural outcome of the segmentation process. It is a major decision that influences and often directly determines the firm's marketing mix. This topic is examined in greater detail later in this chapter.

6. *Design, implement, and maintain appropriate marketing mixes:* The marketing mix has been described as product, distribution, promotion, and pricing strategies intended to bring about mutually satisfying exchange relationships with target markets. Chapters 9 through 18 explore these topics in detail.

Strategies for Selecting Target Markets

Discuss alternative strategies for selecting target markets

target market
A group of people or organizations for which an organization designs, implements, and maintains a marketing mix intended to meet the needs of that group, resulting in mutually satisfying exchanges.

So far this chapter has focused on the market segmentation process, which is only the first step in deciding whom to approach about buying a product. The next task is to choose one or more target markets. A **target market** is a group of people or organizations for which an organization designs, implements, and maintains a marketing mix intended to meet the needs of that group, resulting in mutually satisfying exchanges. The three general strategies for selecting target markets—undifferentiated, concentrated, and multisegment targeting—are illustrated in Exhibit 7.8. Exhibit 7.9 illustrates the advantages and disadvantages of each targeting strategy.

Undifferentiated Targeting
A firm using an **undifferentiated targeting strategy** essentially adopts a mass-market philosophy, viewing the market as one big market with no individual segments. The firm uses one marketing mix for the entire market. A firm that adopts an undifferentiated targeting strategy assumes that individual customers have similar needs that can be met with a common marketing mix.

Exhibit 7.8

Three Strategies for
Selecting Target Markets

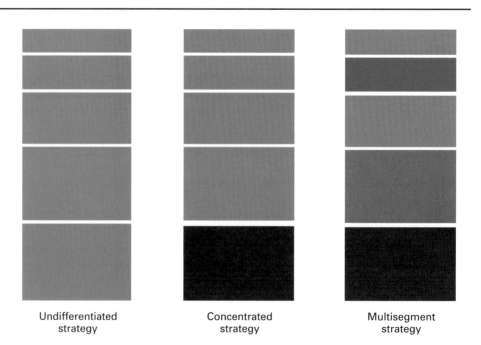

Undifferentiated
strategy

Concentrated
strategy

Multisegment
strategy

Exhibit 7.9

Targeting Strategy	Advantages	Disadvantages
Undifferentiated Targeting	• Potential savings on production/marketing costs • Company more susceptible to competition	• Unimaginative product offerings
Concentrated Targeting	• Concentration of resources • Can better meet the needs of a narrowly defined segment • Allows some small firms to better compete with larger firms • Strong positioning	• Segments too small, or changing • Large competitors may more effectively market to niche segment
Multisegment Targeting	• Greater financial success • Economies of scale in production/marketing	• High costs • Cannibalization

The first firm in an industry sometimes uses an undifferentiated targeting strategy. With no competition, the firm may not need to tailor marketing mixes to the preferences of market segments. Henry Ford's famous quote about the Model T is a classic example of an undifferentiated targeting strategy: "They can have their car in any color they want, as long as it's black." At one time, Coca-Cola used this strategy with a single product and a single size of its familiar green bottle. Marketers of commodity products, such as flour and sugar, are also likely to use an undifferentiated targeting strategy.

One advantage of undifferentiated marketing is the potential for saving on production and marketing. Because only one item is produced, the firm should be able to achieve economies of mass production. Also, marketing costs may be lower when there is only one product to promote and a single channel of distribution. Too often, however, an undifferentiated strategy emerges by default rather than by design, reflecting a failure to consider the advantages of a segmented approach. The result is often sterile, unimaginative product offerings that have little appeal to anyone.

Another problem associated with undifferentiated targeting is that it makes the company more susceptible to competitive inroads. Hershey lost a big share of the candy market to Mars and other candy companies before it changed to a multisegment targeting strategy. Coca-Cola forfeited its position as the leading seller of cola drinks in supermarkets to Pepsi-Cola in the late 1950s, when Pepsi began offering several sizes of containers.

You might think a firm producing a standard product like toilet tissue would adopt an undifferentiated strategy. However, this market has industrial segments and consumer segments. Industrial buyers want an economical, single-ply product sold in boxes of a hundred rolls. The consumer market demands a more versatile product in smaller quantities. Within the consumer market, the product is differentiated with designer print or no print, cushioned or noncushioned, and economy priced or luxury priced. Fort Howard Corporation, the market share leader in industrial toilet paper, does not even sell to the consumer market.

undifferentiated targeting strategy
Marketing approach that views the market as one big market with no individual segments and thus requires a single marketing mix.

Focusing on a concentrated targeting strategy helped Enterprise Rent-A-Car create a new market segment and grow it into a multi-billion dollar business. Today, Enterprise is the largest rental car company in North America and has expanded its operations to include airport service.

Concentrated Targeting

With a **concentrated targeting strategy**, a firm selects a market **niche** (one segment of a market) for targeting its marketing efforts. Because the firm is appealing to a single segment, it can concentrate on understanding the needs, motives, and satisfactions of that segment's members and on developing and maintaining a highly specialized marketing mix. Some firms find that concentrating resources and meeting the needs of a narrowly defined market segment is more profitable than spreading resources over several different segments.

For example, Legend Airlines, which flies out of Love Field in Dallas, uses fifty-six-seat jets and offers exclusively first-class service, gourmet meals, and satellite TV, targeting a profitable niche market—frequent business travelers.[34] Starbuck's became successful by focusing on a group of consumers that wanted gourmet coffee products. Many companies are recognizing that people with disabilities are profitable market segments. Among them is Johnson and Johnson, which launched Independence Technology, a company unit that will produce and market products for people with disabilities. Their first product is the IBOT Transporter, an all-terrain wheelchair.[35] A weekly radio show called "On a Roll: Talk Radio on Life and Disability," hosted by Greg Smith, has attracted sponsors such as Microsoft and BankAmerica.[36]

concentrated targeting strategy
A strategy used to select one segment of a market for targeting marketing efforts.

niche
One segment of a market.

Small firms often adopt a concentrated targeting strategy to compete effectively with much larger firms. For example, Enterprise Rent-A-Car rose to number one in the car rental industry by catering to people with cars in the shop. They have now expanded into the airport rental market.[37]

Some firms, on the other hand, use a concentrated strategy to establish a strong position in a desirable market segment. Porsche, for instance, targets an upscale automobile market through "class appeal, not mass appeal."

Concentrated targeting violates the old adage "Don't put all your eggs in one basket." If the chosen segment is too small or if it shrinks because of environmental changes, the firm may suffer negative consequences. For instance, OshKosh B'Gosh, Inc., was highly successful selling children's wear in the 1980s. It was so successful, however, that the children's line came to define OshKosh's image to the extent that the company could not sell clothes to anyone else. Attempts at marketing older children's clothing, women's casual clothes, and maternity wear were all abandoned. Recognizing it was in the children's-wear business, the company expanded into products such as kids' shoes, children's eyewear, and plush toys.

A concentrated strategy can also be disastrous for a firm that is not successful in its narrowly defined target market. Before Procter & Gamble introduced Head and Shoulders shampoo, several small firms were already selling antidandruff shampoos. Head and Shoulders was introduced with a large promotional campaign, and the new brand captured over half the market immediately. Within a year, several of the firms that had been concentrating on this market segment went out of business.

Multisegment Targeting

A firm that chooses to serve two or more well-defined market segments and develops a distinct marketing mix for each has a **multisegment targeting strategy**. Stouffer's, for example, offers gourmet entrees for one segment of the frozen dinner market and Lean Cuisine for another. Hershey offers premium candies like Golden Almond chocolate bars, packaged in gold foil, that are marketed to an adult audience. Another chocolate bar, called RSVP, is targeted toward consumers who crave the taste of Godiva chocolates at the price of a Hershey bar. Cosmetics companies seek to increase sales and market share by targeting multiple age and ethnic groups. Maybelline and Cover Girl, for example, market different lines to teenage women, young adult women, older women, and African-American women. Mattel targets multiple markets with its Barbie doll. To make Barbie relevant to older girls, the brand has a new logo, new packaging, and an expanded product line of books and trendy apparel. Other new items include an electronic Barbie scrapbook to keep voice-recorded secrets and activity sets for fingernails and make-your-own lip-gloss. To target preteen girls, the company is introducing Barbie dolls with strands of hair studded with rhinestones, street-fashion clothing, and a first ever Barbie bellybutton.[38]

Sometimes organizations use different promotional appeals, rather than completely different marketing mixes, as the basis for a multisegment strategy. Beer marketers such as Adolph Coors and Anheuser-Busch advertise and promote special events targeted toward African-American, Hispanic-American, and Asian-American market segments. The beverages and containers, however, do not differ by ethnic market segment.

Multisegment targeting offers many potential benefits to firms, including greater sales volume, higher profits, larger market share, and economies of scale in manufacturing and marketing. Yet it may also involve greater product design, production, promotion, inventory, marketing research, and management costs. Before deciding to use this strategy, firms should compare the benefits and costs of multisegment targeting to those of undifferentiated and concentrated targeting.

 Another potential cost of multisegment targeting is **cannibalization**, which occurs when sales of a new product cut into sales of a firm's existing products. However, in many cases companies prefer to steal sales from their own brands rather than lose sales to a competitor. Also, in today's fast-paced world of Internet business, some companies are willing to cannibalize existing business to build new business. Bank One launched WingspanBank.com as a freestanding all-Internet bank that would be free to poach Bank One's customers. Likewise, the pet-supply chain Petsmart spun off its on-line venture, Petsmart.com, as a separate company.[39]

multisegment targeting strategy
A strategy that chooses two or more well-defined market segments and develops a distinct marketing mix for each.

cannibalization
Situation that occurs when sales of a new product cut into sales of a firm's existing products.

Positioning

The development of any marketing mix depends on **positioning**, a process that influences potential customers' overall perception of a brand, product line, or organization in general. (**Position** is the place a product, brand, or group of products occupies in consumers' minds relative to competing offerings.) Consumer goods marketers are particularly concerned with positioning. Procter & Gamble, for example, markets eleven different laundry detergents, each with a unique position, as illustrated in Exhibit 7.10 on page 234.

⑧
Explain how and why firms implement positioning strategies and how product differentiation plays a role

Use the Internet to see how the positionings of the detergents listed in Exhibit 7.10 are reflected on their Web sites.

On **L**ine

Exhibit **7.10**

Positioning of Procter & Gamble Detergents

Brand	Positioning	Market Share
Tide	Tough, powerful cleaning	31.1%
Cheer	Tough cleaning and color protection	8.2%
Bold	Detergent plus fabric softener	2.9%
Gain	Sunshine scent and odor-removing formula	2.6%
Era	Stain treatment and stain removal	2.2%
Dash	Value brand	1.8%
Oxydol	Bleach-boosted formula, whitening	1.4%
Solo	Detergent and fabric softener in liquid form	1.2%
Dreft	Outstanding cleaning for baby clothes, safe for tender skin	1.0%
Ivory Snow	Fabric and skin safety on baby clothes and fine washables	0.7%
Ariel	Tough cleaner, aimed at Hispanics	0.1%

SOURCE: Reprinted with permission from the May 3, 1993, issue of *Advertising Age.* Copyright, Crain Communications Inc., 1993.

positioning
Developing a specific marketing mix to influence potential customers' overall perception of a brand, product line, or organization in general.

position
The place a product, brand, or group of products occupies in consumers' minds relative to competing offerings.

Positioning assumes that consumers compare products on the basis of important features. Marketing efforts that emphasize irrelevant features are therefore likely to misfire. For example, Crystal Pepsi and a clear version of Coca-Cola's Tab failed because consumers perceived the "clear" positioning as more of a marketing gimmick than a benefit.

Effective positioning requires assessing the positions occupied by competing products, determining the important dimensions underlying these positions, and choosing a position in the market where the organization's marketing efforts will have the greatest impact. For example, Ford Motor Company is styling the new Taurus models with conventional lines and installing new high-tech protection features. They will position the Taurus as a safe, family sedan, based on marketing research that revealed consumers view safety as a top priority in automobiles.[40]

This Ford print ad reinforces the new positioning of the Taurus as one of the safest cars on the market. Check out the Taurus Web site at http://www.fordvehicles.com/showroom.asp to see if this positioning is extended to the company's on-line channel.

As the previous example illustrates, **product differentiation** is a positioning strategy that many firms use to distinguish their products from those of competitors. The distinctions can be either real or perceived. Tandem Computer designed machines with two central processing units and two memories for computer systems that can never afford to be down or lose their databases (for example, an airline reservation system). In this case, Tandem used product differentiation to create a product with very real advantages for the target market. However, many everyday products, such as bleaches, aspirin, unleaded regular gasoline, and some soaps, are differentiated by such trivial means as brand names, packaging, color, smell, or "secret" additives. The marketer attempts to convince consumers that a particular brand is distinctive and that they should demand it over competing brands.

Some firms, instead of using product differentiation, position their products as being similar to competing products or brands. Artificial sweeteners advertised as tasting like sugar or margarine tasting like butter are two examples.

product differentiation
A positioning strategy that some firms use to distinguish their products from those of competitors.

perceptual mapping
A means of displaying or graphing, in two or more dimensions, the location of products, brands, or groups of products in customers' minds.

Perceptual Mapping

Perceptual mapping is a means of displaying or graphing, in two or more dimensions, the location of products, brands, or groups of products in customers' minds. For example, after several years of decreasing market share and the perception of teenagers that Levi's were not "cool," Levi Strauss has developed a number of youth-oriented fashions, ranging from oddly cut jeans to nylon pants that unzip into shorts. They have also introduced apparel appealing to adults by extending the Dockers and Slates casual-pants brands.[41] The perceptual map in Exhibit 7.11 on page 236 shows Levi's dozens of brands and subbrands, from cheap basics to high-priced fashion.

Positioning Bases

Firms use a variety of bases for positioning, including the following:

- *Attribute:* A product is associated with an attribute, product feature, or customer benefit. Rockport shoes are positioned as an always comfortable brand that is available in a range of styles from working shoes to dress shoes.
- *Price and quality:* This positioning base may stress high price as a signal of quality or emphasize low price as an indication of value. Neiman Marcus uses the high-priced strategy; Kmart has successfully followed the low-price and value strategy. The mass merchandiser Target has developed an interesting position based on price and quality. It is an "upscale discounter," sticking to low prices but offering higher quality and design than most discount chains.[42]
- *Use or application:* AT&T telephone service advertising emphasized communicating with loved ones using the "Reach Out and Touch Someone" campaign.

Exhibit **7.11**

Perceptual Map and Positioning Strategy for Levi-Strauss
Products

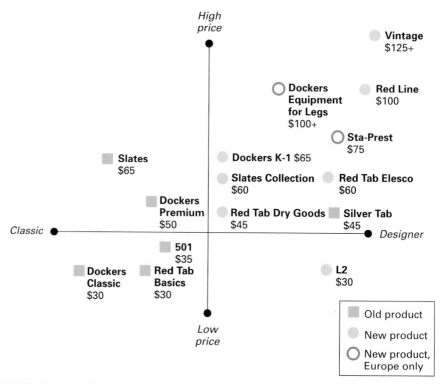

*High
price*

● **Vintage**
$125+

○ **Dockers
Equipment
for Legs**
$100+

● **Red Line**
$100

○ **Sta-Prest**
$75

■ **Slates**
$65

● **Dockers K-1** $65

● **Slates Collection**
$60

● **Red Tab Elesco**
$60

■ **Dockers
Premium**
$50

● **Red Tab Dry Goods**
$45

■ **Silver Tab**
$45

Classic ●————————————————————————● *Designer*

■ **501**
$35

● **L2**
$30

■ **Dockers
Classic**
$30

■ **Red Tab
Basics**
$30

*Low
price*

■ Old product
● New product
○ New product,
Europe only

SOURCE: Nina Munk, "How Levi's Trashed a Great American Brand," *Fortune,* April 12, 1999, p. 84.

Companies often use a mix of positioning bases to reach their target
audience. Mountain Dew is one of
these products. This ad combines
the elements of youth, outdoor fun,
and even irreverence.

Stressing uses or applications can be an effective means of
positioning a product with buyers. Kahlúa liqueur
uses advertising to point out 228 ways to consume the
product.[43]

- *Product user:* This positioning base focuses on a personality
or type of user. Zale Corporation has several jewelry store
concepts, each positioned to a different user. The Zale
stores cater to middle-of-the-road consumers with traditional styles. Their Gordon's stores appeal to a slightly older
clientele with a contemporary look. Guild is positioned for
the more affluent fifty-plus consumer.

- *Product class:* The objective here is to position the product as
being associated with a particular category of products; for
example, positioning a margarine brand with butter.

- *Competitor:* Positioning against competitors is part of any
positioning strategy. The Avis rental car positioning as
number two exemplifies positioning against specific
competitors.

It is not unusual for a marketer to use more than one of these bases. The
AT&T "Reach Out and Touch Someone" campaign that stressed use also emphasized the relatively low cost of long-distance calling. Mountain Dew positioned
its soft drink to the youth market as a thirst-quenching drink that is associated
with teens having fun outdoors.[44]

Repositioning

Sometimes products or companies are repositioned in order to sustain growth in slow markets or to correct positioning mistakes. **Repositioning** is changing consumers' perceptions of a brand in relation to competing brands. To cope with a stagnant liquor industry, a number of companies are attempting to reposition vodka, a spirit without taste, color, or aroma, as a fashion icon with a complex taste. Part of the repositioning effort includes prestige packaging and higher prices.[45] The Kahlúa advertising campaign described above was part of an attempt to reposition the brand by playing up its versatility and shifting its audience from those who thought of it as a dessert type liqueur to those who are choosy, fashionable social drinkers.[46] The National Shooting Sports Foundation, a gun industry trade group, developed new advertising for guns that repositions them as sports equipment, with a focus on safety. The ads discuss the popularity and safety of shooting sports such as hunting and target practice.[47]

repositioning
Changing consumers' perceptions of a brand in relation to competing brands.

Global Issues in Market Segmentation and Targeting

Chapter 4 discussed the trend toward global market standardization, which enables firms like Coca-Cola, Colgate-Palmolive, McDonald's, and Nike to market similar products using similar marketing strategies in many different countries. This chapter has also discussed the trend toward targeting smaller, more precisely defined markets.

The tasks involved in segmenting markets, selecting target markets, and designing, implementing, and maintaining appropriate marketing mixes (described in Exhibit 7.7) are the same whether the marketer has a local perspective or a global vision. The main difference is the segmentation variables commonly used. Countries are commonly grouped using such variables as per capita gross domestic product, geography, religion, culture, or political system.

Some firms have tried to group countries or customer segments around the world using lifestyle or psychographic variables. So-called "Asian yuppies" in places like Singapore, Hong Kong, Japan, and South Korea have substantial spending power and exhibit purchase and consumption behavior similar to that of their better-known counterparts in the United States. In this case, firms may be able to use a global market standardization approach.

 Recall from Chapter 4 that Metabolife International has introduced a line of Chinese herb formulas that were designed to treat five common ailments, such as the common cold and upset stomach. The line, called Chinac, is being marketed to both American and Chinese consumers. For Americans, Chinac offers an easy way to access what is for most consumers an unfamiliar field of medicine. For Chinese, Chinac may offer a welcome change to the numerous and confusing choices they face in a traditional Chinese pharmacy.[48]

9

Discuss global market segmentation and targeting issues

In the story at the beginning of this chapter, market segmentation refers to the process of dividing a market into meaningful, relatively similar, and identifiable segments or groups. Targeting is selecting one or more market segments for which an organization designs, implements, and maintains distinctive marketing mixes. Liz Claiborne has changed from using a concentrated targeting strategy (women's work apparel) to using a multi-segment strategy by offering a number of brands that appeal to different style and price segments

of the women's apparel market. The advantages of this strategy for Liz Claiborne include many opportunities: to grow the company by targeting more than one segment of the market; to capture more sales, profits, and market share; and to realize economies of scale in manufacturing and marketing. The disadvantages are that this strategy may involve more costs for Claiborne, including increased costs for product design, promotion, inventory, and management. There may also be some cannibalization of existing lines.

Use it Now!

Segmenting and targeting markets does not just apply to products you buy. Segmentation principles are also used in all sorts of elections. How often have you heard campaign managers or media reporters use terms like "the female vote," "the black vote," and "the senior vote"?

Even on a university level, students running for elected positions can use targeting strategies to help win the support of blocks of voters. At your

university, there are probably a variety of different types of students, and various student organizations, that could represent market segments that would respond differently to different campaign messages. Some students may not even vote at all.

Apply what you have learned in this chapter in developing a written campaign strategy for yourself or a friend who is running for an elected office on campus.

Summary

1 **Describe the characteristics of markets and market segments.** A market is composed of individuals or organizations with the ability and willingness to make purchases to fulfill their needs or wants. A market segment is a group of individuals or organizations with similar product needs as a result of one or more common characteristics.

2 **Explain the importance of market segmentation.** Before the 1960s, few businesses targeted specific market segments. Today, segmentation is a crucial marketing strategy for nearly all successful organizations. Market segmentation enables marketers to tailor marketing mixes to meet the needs of particular population segments. Segmentation helps marketers identify consumer needs and preferences, areas of declining demand, and new marketing opportunities.

3 **Discuss criteria for successful market segmentation.** Successful market segmentation depends on four basic criteria: (1) a market segment must be substantial and have enough potential customers to be viable; (2) a market segment must be identifiable and measurable; (3) members of a market segment must be accessible to marketing efforts; and (4) a market segment must respond to particular marketing efforts in a way that distinguishes it from other segments.

4 **Describe the bases commonly used to segment consumer markets.** There are five commonly used bases for segmenting consumer markets. Geographic segmentation is based on region, size, density, and climate characteristics. Demographic segmentation consists of age, gender, income level, ethnicity, and family life-cycle characteristics. Psychographic segmentation includes personality, motives, and lifestyle characteristics. Benefits sought is a type of segmentation that identifies customers according to the benefits they seek in a product. Finally, usage segmentation divides a market by the amount of product purchased or consumed.

5 **Describe the bases for segmenting business markets.** Business markets can be segmented on two bases. First, macrosegmentation divides markets according to general characteristics, such as location and customer type. Second, microsegmentation focuses on the decision-making units within macrosegments.

6 **List the steps involved in segmenting markets.** Six steps are involved when segmenting markets: (1) Selecting a market or product category for study; (2) choosing a basis or bases for segmenting the market; (3) selecting segmentation descriptors; (4) profiling and evaluating segments; (5) selecting target markets; and (6) designing, implementing, and maintaining appropriate marketing mixes.

7 **Discuss alternative strategies for selecting target markets.** Marketers select target markets using three different strategies: undifferentiated targeting, concentrated targeting, and multisegment targeting. An undifferentiated targeting strategy assumes that all members of a market have similar needs that can be met with a single marketing mix. A concentrated targeting strategy focuses all marketing efforts on a single market segment. Multisegment targeting is a strategy that uses two or more marketing mixes to target two or more market segments.

8 **Explain how and why firms implement positioning strategies and how product differentiation plays a role.** Positioning is used to influence consumer perceptions of a particular brand, product line, or organization in relation to competitors. The term *position* refers to the place that the offering occupies in consumers' minds. To establish a unique position, many firms use product differentiation, emphasizing the real or perceived differences between competing offerings. Products may be differentiated on the basis of attribute, price and quality, use or application, product user, product class, or competitor.

9 **Discuss global market segmentation and targeting issues.** The key tasks in market segmentation, targeting, and positioning are the same regardless of whether the target market is local, regional, national, or multinational. The main differences are the variables used by marketers in analyzing markets and assessing opportunities and the resources needed to implement strategies.

Key Terms

benefit segmentation 224
cannibalization 233
concentrated targeting strategy 232
demographic segmentation 218
80/20 principle 226
family life cycle (FLC) 221
geodemographic segmentation 222
geographic segmentation 216
macrosegmentation 227
market 214
market segment 214
market segmentation 214
microsegmentation 227
multisegment targeting strategy 233
niche 232
optimizer 228
perceptual mapping 235
position 234
positioning 234
product differentiation 235
psychographic segmentation 221
repositioning 237
satisficers 228
segmentation bases (variables) 216
target market 230
undifferentiated targeting strategy 231
usage-rate segmentation 225

Discussion and Writing Questions

1. Describe market segmentation in terms of the historical evolution of marketing.
2. **WRITING** Choose magazine ads for five different products. For each ad, write a description of the demographic characteristics of the targeted market.
3. **TEAM** Form a team with two other students. Select a product category and brand that are familiar to your team. Using Exhibit 7.9, prepare a market segmentation report and describe a targeting plan.
4. Explain concentrated (niche) targeting. Describe a company not mentioned in the chapter that uses a concentrated targeting strategy.
5. **TEAM** Form a team with two or three other students. Create an idea for a new product. Describe the segment (or segments) you are going to target with the product and develop a positioning strategy for the product.

6. Choose a product category (e.g., blue jeans) and identify at least three different brands and their respective positioning strategies. How is each position communicated to the target audience?

7. Create a perceptual map for the different brands of one of the following products: diet and regular colas, Ford automobiles, fast-food hamburger restaurants, or a product of your choice.

8. Investigate how Delta Airlines (**http://www.delta-air.com**) uses its Web site to cater to its market segments.

9. How are visitors to the following Web site segmented when seeking relevant job openings? Try this search engine and report your results. **http://www.careermag.com**

10. Write a letter to the president of your bank suggesting ideas for increasing profits and enhancing customer service by improving segmentation and targeting strategies. Make your suggestions specific.

Application for Entrepreneurs

Judy Brown has always loved working with animals. She has experience in pet grooming, boarding, and in-home pet sitting. Judy wants to open a full-service business utilizing her skills that is uniquely positioned in relation to the traditional pet grooming/boarding businesses that operate in the town where she lives. Customers that use these current pet services deliver their pets to the firms and later pick them up. Most are open between 9 A.M. and 6 P.M. from Monday through Friday.

Judy lives in a midsize city that is close to a major airport. Many high-tech industries are located in or near her city, so there are a large number of men and women in managerial and information technology positions, and travel is a frequent part of their jobs. A lot of families have pets, so Judy thinks there is a market for pet-related services, despite the current competition.

Questions

1. How should Judy segment the market for pet services?
2. What targeting strategy should Judy use to start her business? Should this strategy change as her business prospers and grows?
3. How should Judy position her pet services business against her competition?

Case

entrepreneurship

**Segmenting the On-line Market:
The Case of eBay**

When Pam Omidyar dreamed of a place where she could meet, talk, and trade with other collectors of Pez candy dispensers, her computer-programming and soon-to-be husband,

Pierre Omidyar, immediately set to work on developing the software that would enable such interaction on-line. Together, in September 1995, they launched eBay.com, and within five short years it was one of the most recognizable brand names on the Internet. From its humble beginnings as a niche Web site, it has become the premier Internet auction showcase. eBay's 4,300 categories include everything from tie-dyed Grateful Dead Beanie Babies to bubblegum cards to nearly new Ferraris and even fine jewelry. Once you find what you're looking for, you can haggle for it in one of the four million daily auctions.

eBay positions itself as a folksy and friendly facilitator of an on-line community that caters to traders with varying tastes and preferences, but the original idea was to service one type of collector in a single geographical area—Pam and Pierre's neighborhood in San Francisco. The Omidyar's customer-focused strategy led to such a high degree of customer satisfaction that awareness of the site quickly spread through the entire Bay area. High customer loyalty, repeat usage, and very strong word-of-mouth advertising (*viral marketing*) fueled eBay's growth. eBay is unique in that it has equal appeal to the occasional Internet surfer, the nostalgic trader, the fanatic trader, the small business in search of used or inexpensive equipment, and those who simply love the thrill of the deal.

In trying to nurture its growing enterprise, eBay's entrepreneurial management team was faced with many marketing challenges that it still grapples with today:

- Attracting users who are accustomed to trading in traditional venues such as auction houses, estate sales, and flea markets
- Convincing Internet users to execute transactions on-line
- Organizing many specific product categories into a much smaller number of broad categories and corresponding market segments
- Developing a marketing mix to reach multiple targets

The first step for eBay was to build a killer product. eBay focuses on delivering a first-class user experience by providing frequent content and auction updates. The sites help areas are customized for either experienced or new users, and detailed collector news and information are available. The second step was developing a pricing schedule to satisfy its broad spectrum of users. Transactions can be executed for as little as twenty-five cents for the seller of a Pez dispenser, but eBay can claim as much as a 5 percent commission on the selling price of an expensive item like a diamond necklace. Under the direction of Senior Vice President of Marketing, Brian Swette, the company rethought its past strategy of restricting online promotions to its own

Web site and has accomplished prolific distribution on the World Wide Web. eBay has struck deals to gain presence on major entry portals like AOL, shopping verticals like MySimon.com, and destination sites like AutoTrader.com.

The final component of the marketing mix, promotion, was the most complex to address. At first glance, eBay has only one product—the on-line auction forum—that it sells to traders and consumers. To that end, eBay has remained faithful to its grassroots marketing effort in the offline world. It has also maintained its presence at trade and collector shows of all kinds in order to evangelize the benefits of auctioning on-line. A closer look at what transpires at the site, however, reveals that eBay is the auction utility of choice for a range of collectors so stratified that on any one day a browser at eBay can encounter auctions for coins, clothes, model airplanes, or more controversial and hence discouraged items like hate-group materials, used underwear, or a human kidney. The challenge for eBay, therefore, is not so much that it has so many different consumers, but that each one of its consumers has very different needs. With that in mind, eBay has chosen to divide markets using a variety of segmentation strategies. It has employed demographic, psychographic, geodemographic, benefit, and usage-rate segmentation techniques to better understand and serve customer needs across a broad range in each.

In order to effectively promote the site to its eclectic audience, eBay developed a complex and comprehensive print advertising campaign aimed at several targets. Working with the advertising agency of Ogilvy & Mather, eBay decided to avoid mass print media and use niche publications. This way, the company could reach an audience that would be more captive at the point of exposure to the advertisement. Unique messaging and advertising copy was developed for campaigns deployed in twelve different vertical markets. Across those twelve markets, eBay selected seventy-five specialty magazines for their highly tailored advertisements. eBay still supports this strategy today. Although segmenting its market into multiple niches was a demanding and complex initiative, it has clearly been a successful tactic.

Currently, over ten million registered users buy and sell one of 450,000 new items posted to the auction site every day. Customers range from infrequent traders to traders who use eBay regularly to generate personal profit streams. eBay has special services such as My eBay and Mister Lister for frequent users and has gone so far as to build a Business Exchange area where it caters to needs of small businesses. Customers can participate in local auctions specific to their geographical region, bid on items whose proceeds go directly to one of many charities, or sign up for eBay magazine. Chat rooms, an on-line library of articles organized by collection category, or eBay's own newsletter all provide information to enhance and empower the customer's trading experience. eBay's success has inspired a proliferation of copycat auction sites, but none enjoys the customer base or widespread brand recognition of the original.

Questions

1. What types of segmentation does eBay use?
2. Does eBay use an undifferentiated, a niche, or a multiple targeting strategy? Discuss the range of tactics eBay uses to reach its target market.

3. Explain the tools eBay has developed for usage-rate segmentation and consider how eBay might use those tools to enhance its profitability.
4. How did eBay tackle the marketing challenges it faced as it grew from an entrepreneurial venture to a multimillion-dollar operation?
5. Describe eBay's target market.

Bibliography

Kipp Cheng. "eBay Best Viral Marketing." *Adweek*, June 28, 1999, p. IQ42.
eBay Web site:
  http://www.ebay.com/community/aboutebay/ overview/index.html
Claire Tristram. "Takin' It to the Street." *MC Technology Marketing Intelligence*, February 1999, pp. 22–28.

Case

video

Labelle Management: Something for Everyone

Sizzling burgers, shakes and fries, pizza, or a thick steak. What's your pleasure? Labelle Management, which owns and operates thirty-one restaurants and hotels, has them all. Headquartered in Mt. Pleasant, Michigan, Labelle has been in the restaurant business since 1948. When McDonald's came to town in the 1970s, Labelle's owners faced stiff competition and decided to add franchises to their holdings. They now own six restaurants located on the main street in town. The key to Labelle's success is its use of benefit segmentation. It groups its customers into market segments according to the benefits they seek from the various restaurant formats. Customers are mainly targeted on the basis of needs and wants. Although Labelle's restaurants compete with one another for customers, they can all coexist because the same people want different benefits at different times.

How does this concept work? Mt. Pleasant is a college town, home to Central Michigan University, an undergraduate campus with seventeen thousand students who choose different restaurants on different occasions. Late at night after studying, the students crave pizza delivered to their dorm, so they call Pixies. This original Labelle, 1950s style, drive-in restaurant offers fast food at low prices, plus rock & roll and lots of nostalgia. Labelle works with sororities, fraternities, athletic groups, and clubs on campus for special events. Students, however, aren't the only ones who are in a hurry. Pixies is the perfect dinner stop for parents on the go, driving the kids to soccer games, piano lessons, or swimming.

For those not interested in fast food but still interested in low prices, Labelle has other options. Ponderosa Steak House is a no-frills franchise offering very good value. For those who are really hungry—students or workers—there are big, juicy steaks, big helpings of potatoes, veggies, and desserts. Customers get a lot of food for the money, and Ponderosa is a natural for groups. The atmosphere is simple, and service is mainly buffet-style.

Labelle's Big Boy Restaurants appeal to families, blue-collar workers, and seniors because of the moderate prices ($3 to $8) for the famous double-decker hamburgers, sandwiches, salads, and dinners. Students also turn out in droves for the $4.99 all-you-can-eat breakfast buffet. Big Boy has been around for a long time, and customers can always count on getting the same good food at the same price. The familiar menu and friendly service account for the high customer loyalty at Big Boy, where managers are selected for their ability to get along with customers of all ages.

On the weekends, students, families, and friends in Mt. Pleasant like to relax and have fun, so ethnic food can be a nice change of pace from everyday meals. The family-priced Italian bistro, Italian Oven, features pasta, salads, and pizza cooked in wood-burning ovens. What makes Italian Oven even more attractive is that it offers entertainment in the form of wandering singers, musicians, and magicians.

It's hard to beat the old Irish pub atmosphere of Bennigan's. Out for a beer, the twenty-somethings like to hang out at this upbeat, upscale bar and grill, although the average tab is at least $10 per person. Part of creating a fun dining experience is creating a daring menu, and new items with trendy names and spicy tastes are standard fare at Bennigan's. Customers expect a high level of service at this Labelle restaurant, which means orders taken promptly and tasty food. College students, businesspeople, and the ladies' lunch crowd like to come to Bennigan's, so the managers and staff have to be attentive, laid-back, and fun in order to meet the needs of such a diverse customer base.

Although Labelle Management casts its nets to attract a wide variety of customers, it adds perks for frequent patrons. Based on the old 80/20 adage that 20 percent of all customers generate 80 percent of demand, Labelle Management tries hard to keep its steady customers happy so they will come back more often. Because 25 percent of Bennigan's sales comes from the bar, Bennigan's offers a beer card; those who drink a hundred or more imported beers get their names on the plaque over the bar. And those who eat six of Pixies' famous Coney Dogs or eight Bitty Burgers have their names written on the wall of fame. Labelle Management knows Mt. Pleasant backwards and forwards and works overtime through diversified restaurant concepts to give community members what they want.

Questions

1. How does LaBelle Management use benefit segmentation to target various market segments?
2. Describe the benefits provided by each restaurant format.
3. How does LaBelle Management use usage-rate segmentation?
4. Explain how service is a benefit that varies with restaurant format.

Bibliography

Labelle Management Web site:
   http://www.labellemgt.com
Video by Learnet Inc.

chapter 8

Learning Objectives

1 Explain the concept and purpose of a marketing decision support system

2 Define marketing research and explain its importance to marketing decision making

3 Describe the steps involved in conducting a marketing research project

4 Discuss the profound impact of the Internet on marketing research

5 Discuss the growing importance of scanner-based research

6 Explain the concept of competitive intelligence

Decision Support Systems and Marketing Research

Juicy Fruit Gum, the oldest brand of the Wm. Wrigley Jr. Company, wasn't chewing up the teen market, gum's top demographic. A few years ago the company found itself under pressure from competitors. Sales and market share were down. How could Wrigley make more young people chew Juicy Fruit? What qualities about Juicy Fruit appeal to teens? From initial marketing research, Wrigley learned that teens chew Juicy Fruit because it's sweet. It refreshes and energizes them. Follow-up research by advertising agency BBDO confirmed what the teens were saying. BBDO asked more than four hundred heavy gum chewers to rate various brands by attributes that best represented them. For Juicy Fruit, respondents picked phrases such as "has the right amount of sweetness" and "is made with natural sweeteners."

Another study by BBDO looked into why teens chew gum. Was it because they're stressed out—or because they forgot to brush their teeth before going to school? Nearly three out of four teenagers said they stick a wad in their mouth when they crave something sweet. And Juicy Fruit was the top brand they chose to fulfill that need (Big Red was a distant second). Clearly the advertising needed to focus on the gum's sweet, satisfying qualities.

BBDO developed four TV commercials with the "Gotta Have Sweet" theme and asked teens to evaluate them. The idea that Juicy Fruit satisfies a craving for something sugary went over well with respondents. "It's sweet. They're trying to hit this into your head," said one participant. An advertising test of two spots also proved that BBDO was on target: Roughly 70 percent of respondents voluntarily recalled the Juicy Fruit name after watching the commercials (the average recall for a brand of sugar gum is 57 percent).

The campaign debuted in late 1998 with an assortment of radio and TV spots geared to twelve- to-twenty-four-year-olds. BBDO also created Juicy Fruit bookcovers to tie into the back-to-school season. One design featured a cheerleader lifting a car to find a pack of Juicy Fruit. Sales of 100-stick boxes of Juicy Fruit rose 5 percent after the start of the ad campaign, versus a 2 percent decline prior to it. Juicy Fruit's market share also increased to 5.3 percent from 4.9 percent, the biggest gain of any established chewing gum brand during the year following the campaign.[1]

Clearly, the series of marketing research studies helped Juicy Fruit raise its market share. What are the various techniques for conducting marketing research? Should managers always do marketing research before they make a decision? How does marketing research relate to decision support systems?

On Line

Wm. Wrigley Jr. Company
Juicy Fruit

See the results of the BBDO campaign on the Juicy Fruit Web site. What about the site tells you it's aimed at teens?
http://www.juicyfruit.com

Marketing Decision Support Systems

Explain the concept and purpose of a marketing decision support system

marketing information
Everyday information about developments in the marketing environment that managers use to prepare and adjust marketing plans.

decision support system (DSS)
An interactive, flexible computerized information system that enables managers to obtain and manipulate information as they are making decisions.

Accurate and timely information is the lifeblood of marketing decision making. Good information can help maximize an organization's sales and efficiently use scarce company resources. To prepare and adjust marketing plans, managers need a system for gathering everyday information about developments in the marketing environment—that is, for gathering **marketing information**. The system most commonly used these days for gathering marketing information is called a *marketing decision support system.*

A marketing **decision support system (DSS)** is an interactive, flexible computerized information system that enables managers to obtain and manipulate information as they are making decisions. A DSS bypasses the information-processing specialist and gives managers access to useful data from their own desks.

These are the characteristics of a true DSS system:

- *Interactive:* Managers give simple instructions and see immediate results. The process is under their direct control; no computer programmer is needed. Managers don't have to wait for scheduled reports.
- *Flexible:* A DSS can sort, regroup, total, average, and manipulate the data in various ways. It will shift gears as the user changes topics, matching information to the problem at hand. For example, the CEO can see highly aggregated figures, and the marketing analyst can view very detailed breakouts.
- *Discovery-oriented:* Managers can probe for trends, isolate problems, and ask "what if" questions.
- *Accessible:* DSS is easy to learn and use by managers who aren't skilled with computers. Novice users should be able to choose a standard, or default, method of using the system. They can bypass optional features so they can work with the basic system right away while gradually learning to apply its advanced features.

A hypothetical example showing how DSS can be used is provided by Renee Smith, vice president and manager of new products for Central Corporation. To evaluate sales of a recently introduced product, Renee can "call up" sales by the week, then by the month, breaking them out at her option by, say, customer segments. As she works at her desktop computer, her inquiries can go in several directions, depending on the decision at hand. If her train of thought raises questions about monthly sales last quarter compared to forecasts, she can use her DSS to analyze problems immediately. Renee might see that her new product's sales were significantly below forecast. Were her forecasts too optimistic? She compares other products' sales to her forecasts and finds that the targets were very accurate. Was something wrong with the product? Is her sales department getting insufficient leads, or is it not putting leads to good use? Thinking a minute about how to examine that question, she checks ratios of leads converted to sales product by product. The results disturb her. Only 5 percent of the new product's leads generated orders, compared to the company's 12 percent all-product average. Why? Renee guesses that the sales force is not supporting the new product vigorously enough. Quantitative information from the DSS perhaps could provide more evidence to back that suspicion. But already having enough quantitative knowledge to satisfy herself, the VP acts on her intuition and experience and decides to have a chat with her sales manager.

database marketing
The creation of a large computerized file of customers' and potential customers' profiles and purchase patterns.

Perhaps the fastest-growing use of DSS is for **database marketing**, which is the creation of a large computerized file of customers' and potential customers' profiles and purchase patterns. It is usually the key tool for successful micromarketing, which relies on very specific information about a market (see Chapter 20).

The Role of Marketing Research

Marketing research is the process of planning, collecting, and analyzing data relevant to a marketing decision. The results of this analysis are then communicated to management. Marketing research plays a key role in the marketing system. It provides decision makers with data on the effectiveness of the current marketing mix and also insights for necessary changes. Furthermore, marketing research is a main data source for both management information systems and DSS.

Marketing research has three roles: descriptive, diagnostic, and predictive. Its *descriptive* role includes gathering and presenting factual statements. For example, what is the historic sales trend in the industry? What are consumers' attitudes toward a product and its advertising? Its *diagnostic* role includes explaining data. For instance, what was the impact on sales of a change in the design of the package? Its *predictive* function is to address "what if" questions. For example, how can the researcher use the descriptive and diagnostic research to predict the results of a planned marketing decision?

Define marketing research and explain its importance to marketing decision making

marketing research
The process of planning, collecting, and analyzing data relevant to a marketing decision.

Management Uses of Marketing Research

Marketing research can help managers in several ways. It improves the quality of decision making and helps managers trace problems. Most important, sound marketing research helps managers focus on the paramount importance of keeping existing customers, aids them to better understand the marketplace, and alerts them to marketplace trends. Marketing research helps managers gauge the perceived value of their goods and services as well as the level of customer satisfaction.

Improving the Quality of Decision Making Managers can sharpen their decision making by using marketing research to explore the desirability of various marketing alternatives. For example, Ford Motor Company has used marketing research to create an aggressive e-commerce marketing strategy. Ford set up the BuyerConnection Web site and joined MSN CarPoint site where consumers can order custom-assembled cars, track their progress, and apply for financing. Ford's Owner-Connection site lets owners get on-line help, manage their warranty service, and check on financing. The company is also teaming up with Yahoo!, TeleTech, CarPoint, iVillage, and bolt.com to conduct research on consumer auto interests and buying patterns of Web-surfing customers.[2] Ford has seen the Internet as an opportunity, not a threat.

Tracing Problems Another way managers use marketing research is to find out why a plan backfires. Was the initial decision incorrect? Did an unforeseen change in the external environment cause the plan to fail? How can the same mistake be avoided in the future?

Keebler introduced Sweet Spots, a shortbread cookie with a huge chocolate drop on it. It has had acceptable sales and is still on the market, but only after using marketing research to overcome several problems. Soon after the cookie's introduction, Keebler increased the box size from 10 ounces at $2.29 to 15 ounces at $3.19. Demand immediately fell. Market research showed that Sweet Spots were now considered more of a luxury than an everyday item. Keebler lowered the price and went back to the 10-ounce box. Even though Sweet Spots originally was aimed at upscale adult females, the company also tried to appeal to kids. In subsequent research, Keebler found that the package graphics appealed to mothers but not to children.[3]

Focusing on the Paramount Importance of Keeping Existing Customers
An inextricable link exists between customer satisfaction and customer loyalty. Long-term relationships simply don't just happen but are grounded in the delivery of service and value by the firm. Customer retention pays big dividends for

organizations. Powered by repeat sales and referrals, revenues and market share grow. Costs fall because firms spend less money and energy attempting to replace defectors. Steady customers are easy to serve because they understand the modus operandi and make fewer demands on employees' time. Increased customer retention also drives job satisfaction and pride, which leads to higher employee retention. In turn, the knowledge employees acquire as they stay longer increases productivity. A Bain & Company study estimates that a decrease in the customer defection rate by 5 percent can boost profits by 25 percent to 95 percent.[4]

When UPS recently began asking broader questions about how it could improve service, it discovered that clients weren't as obsessed with on-time delivery as the company had previously thought. The biggest surprise to UPS management: Customers wanted more interaction with drivers—the only face-to-face contact any of them had with the company. If drivers were less harried and more willing to chat, customers could get some practical advice on shipping. "We've discovered that the highest-rated element we have is our drivers," says Lawrence E. Farrel, UPS's service-quality manager.[5]

In a sharp departure, the company is encouraging its 62,000 delivery drivers to get out of their trucks and visit customers along with salespeople. It also allows drivers an additional thirty minutes a week to spend at their discretion to strengthen ties with customers and perhaps bring in new sales.

Understanding the Ever-Changing Marketplace

Marketing research also helps managers understand what is going on in the marketplace and take advantage of opportunities. Historically, marketing research has been practiced for as long as marketing has existed. The early Phoenicians carried out market demand studies as they traded in the various ports of the Mediterranean Sea. Marco Polo's diary indicates he was performing a marketing research function as he traveled to China. There is even evidence that the Spanish systematically conducted "market surveys" as they explored the New World, and there are examples of marketing research conducted during the Renaissance.

Today, Internet marketing research can help companies quickly and efficiently understand what is happening in the marketplace. For example, Women.com, an on-line community site that offers editorial content and e-commerce services, has surveyed visitors for several years but recently boosted its research efforts. The surveys are designed to discover visitors' demographic and psychographic profiles for the network's internal use, as well as to share with advertisers.

By asking the right questions, UPS discovered that its customers wanted more interaction with drivers. As a result, UPS gave its drivers more time in the week to spend with customers in order to build and strengthen relationships.

Along with collecting basic demographic data, the site also asks visitors about their e-commerce habits (whether they've shopped for or purchased anything online recently, for instance), their feelings about privacy on the Internet, and value and attitudinal questions, such as whether they agree or disagree with statements like "I'm usually the first in my peer group to try something new." Such information provides a picture of the person on the other side of the computer that goes beyond her average age and income, says Regina Lewis, director of research for Women.com Networks, Inc.

Understanding whether visitors are more risk-oriented, family-focused, or career-minded helps Women.com set the right tone when talking to visitors, Lewis says, and has resulted in page redesigns.[6]

Understanding the marketplace is not just a U.S. or industrialized market phenomenon. It is important for managers all over the world to understand the ever-changing marketplace and their customers. The "Global Perspectives" box included here illustrates this point.

Global Perspectives

HEY! GOT FERMENTED MILK?

Foreign companies have discovered Japan's best marketing bellwether: the teenage girl. As Japanese companies have long known, the nation's high-school girls have an uncanny ability to predict which products will be hits with consumers of all age groups. What's more, a select pool of these teens can create a buzz that turns a new product into a nationwide smash.

"A fad that catches on among teenage girls often becomes a big trend throughout the country and among consumers in general," says Etsuko Katsube, a Coca-Cola marketing executive who used teenage girls to market a now-popular soft drink made with fermented milk.

Girl guides are taken very seriously in Japan. Food manufacturers like Calbee Foods Company and Meiji Seika Kaisha Ltd. frequently round up schoolgirls from Tokyo's streets to sample potato-chip recipes or chocolate bars. Asahi Broadcasting Corporation surveys high-school girls to fine-tune story lines for higher ratings on the television network's prime-time dramas.

Other companies pay girls to keep diaries of what they buy.

Boom, one of a group of Tokyo research firms that specialize in teen surveys, offers a portfolio of several thousand Tokyo-area high-school girls that includes, it says, five hundred girls deemed to be "trendsetters." Boom's clients include giants such as 7-Eleven Japan Company and Shiseido Company.

On a recent afternoon, a trio of Tokyo high-school girls sat in a Boom interview room, poking at blobs of fruit gelatin. They were helping Meiji Milk Products Company narrow down a list of six flavors to four that Meiji Milk will sell in 7,300 Japanese convenience stores. Swallowing a spoonful of apple gelatin, fifteen-year-old Kanako Yonemura cocked her head and proclaims, "This is too sweet." The interviewer listened intently. The girl added: "And I'd like to know how many calories it has per serving."

And Shiseido says that by tapping teen insights it unexpectedly hit on a broad market for a low-priced line of nail polishes. The cosmetics maker had named the line Chopi; the girls preferred another name, Neuve. They also persuaded Shiseido to change the container's color from the usual black, white, or silver to beige.

"Just about all the basic ideas for Neuve came from high-school girls," says Masaru Miyagawa, a Shiseido marketing director. The company credits the girls with the fact that a product originally aimed at teens proved appealing to women of all ages. Over the past year, Neuve sales totaled twenty million units. Annual sales of one million units is considered a marketing success in Japan.[a]

Are American teenage women such trendsetters that marketing researchers should focus on them? Is asking teenagers to keep diaries of what they buy really marketing research? Should American food companies purchase research from Boom if they plan to market in Japan?

[a] Norihiko Shirouzu, "Japan's High-School Girls Excel in Art of Setting Trends," *Wall Street Journal,* April 24, 1998, pp. B1, B7.

Steps in a Marketing Research Project

3

Describe the steps involved in conducting a marketing research project

Virtually all firms that have adopted the marketing concept engage in some marketing research because it offers decision makers many benefits. Some companies spend millions on marketing research; others, particularly smaller firms, conduct informal, limited-scale research studies. For example, when Eurasia restaurant, serving Eurasian cuisine, first opened along Chicago's ritzy Michigan Avenue, it drew novelty seekers. But it turned off the important business lunch crowd, and sales began to decline. The owner surveyed several hundred businesspeople working within a mile of the restaurant. He found that they were confused by Eurasia's concept and wanted more traditional Asian fare at lower prices. In response, the restaurant altered its concept; it hired a Thai chef, revamped the menu, and cut prices. The dining room was soon full again.

Whether a research project costs $200 or $2 million, the same general process should be followed. The marketing research process is a scientific approach to decision making that maximizes the chance of getting accurate and meaningful results. Exhibit 8.1 traces the steps: (1) identifying and formulating the problem/opportunity, (2) planning the research design and gathering primary data, (3) specifying the sampling procedures, (4) collecting the data, (5) analyzing the data, (6) preparing and presenting the report, and (7) following up.

The research process begins with the recognition of a marketing problem or opportunity. As changes occur in the firm's external environment, marketing managers are faced with the questions, "Should we change the existing marketing mix?" and, if so, "How?" Marketing research may be used to evaluate product, promotion, distribution, or pricing alternatives. In addition, it is used to find and evaluate new market opportunities.

Exhibit 8.1

The Marketing Research Process

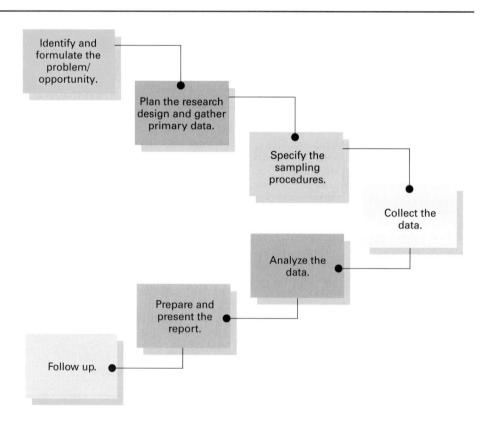

For example, there have been over seventeen million babies born in the United States since 1995. It is the largest generation since the baby boomers. More impressive than their numbers, though, is their wealth. The increase in single-parent and dual-earner households means kids are making shopping decisions once left to mom. Combining allowance, earnings, and gifts, kids fourteen and under will directly spend an estimated $20 billion this year, and they will influence the spending of another $200 billion.[7]

For savvy marketers, these statistics represent opportunity. Marketing research can hone in and clarify where the best opportunities lie. Walt Disney, for example, is launching a twenty-four-hour kids' radio network based on its marketing research. Sometimes research can lead to unexpected results requiring creative uses of the marketing mix. General Motors recently completed an analysis of "backseat consumers," that is, children between five and fifteen years of age. Marketing research discovered that parents often let their children play a tie-breaking role in deciding what car to purchase. Marketing managers, armed with this information, launched several programs. GM purchased the inside cover of *Sports Illustrated for Kids*, a magazine targeted to boys from eight to fourteen years old. The ad featured a brightly colored two-page spread for the Chevy Venture minivan, a vehicle targeted toward young families. GM also sent the minivan into malls and showed Disney movies on a VCR inside the van.

The GM story illustrates an important point about problem/opportunity definition. The **marketing research problem** is information oriented. It involves determining what information is needed and how that information can be obtained efficiently and effectively. The **marketing research objective**, then, is to provide insightful decision-making information. This requires specific pieces of information needed to answer the marketing research problem. Managers must combine this information with their own experience and other information to make a proper decision. In the GM scenario, the marketing research objective was to determine what role, if any, backseat consumers play in a family's decision to purchase an automobile. In contrast, the **management decision problem** is action oriented. Management problems tend to be much broader in scope and far more general, whereas marketing research problems must be more narrowly defined and specific if the research effort is to be successful. Sometimes several research studies must be conducted to solve a broad management problem. Once GM determined that children within this target market played a tie-breaker role, the question became one of what should be done to influence the tie-breakers. GM used marketing research to determine that direct advertising to children in the target market and mall promotions would be the best form of promotion.

Secondary Data

A valuable tool throughout the research process but particularly in the problem/opportunity identification stage is **secondary data**—data previously collected for any purpose other than the one at hand. Secondary information originating within the company includes documents such as annual reports, reports to

GM continues to reap the benefits of its marketing research revealing how important kids are in the family decision-making process. In 2000, the company introduced the Warner Bros. Edition Chevy Venture minivan. This model includes a built-in child's restraining seat, a video player, and an ongoing package called VentureTainment!

secondary data
Data previously collected for any purpose other than the one at hand.

stockholders, product testing results perhaps made available to the news media, and house periodicals composed by the company's personnel for communication to employees, customers, or others. Often this information is incorporated into a company's internal database.

Innumerable outside sources of secondary information also exist, principally in the forms of government (federal, state, and local) departments and agencies that compile and publish summaries of business data. Trade and industry associations also provide published secondary data. Still more data are business periodicals and other news media that regularly publish studies and articles on the economy, specific industries, and even individual companies. The unpublished summarized secondary information from these sources corresponds to internal reports, memos, or special-purpose analyses with limited circulation. Economic considerations or priorities in the organization may preclude publication of these summaries. Most of the sources listed above can be found on the Internet.

Secondary data save time and money if they help solve the researcher's problem. Even if the problem is not solved, secondary data have other advantages. They can aid in formulating the problem statement and suggest research methods and other types of data needed for solving the problem. In addition, secondary data can pinpoint the kinds of people to approach and their locations and serve as a basis of comparison for other data. The disadvantages of secondary data stem mainly from a mismatch between the researcher's unique problem and the purpose for which the secondary data were originally gathered, which are typically different. For example, a major consumer products manufacturer wanted to determine the market potential for a fireplace log made of coal rather than compressed wood byproducts. The researcher found plenty of secondary data about total wood consumed as fuel, quantities consumed in each state, and types of wood burned. Secondary data were also available about consumer attitudes and purchase patterns of wood byproduct fireplace logs. The wealth of secondary data provided the researcher with many insights into the artificial log market. Yet nowhere was there any information that would tell the firm whether consumers would buy artificial logs made of coal.

The quality of secondary data may also pose a problem. Often secondary data sources do not give detailed information that would enable a researcher to assess their quality or relevance. Whenever possible, a researcher needs to address these important questions: Who gathered the data? Why were the data obtained? What methodology was used? How were classifications (such as heavy users versus light users) developed and defined? When was the information gathered?

The New Age of Secondary Information: The Internet

Gathering secondary data, while necessary in almost any research project, has traditionally been a tedious and boring job. The researcher often had to write to government agencies, trade associations, or other secondary data providers and then wait days or weeks for a reply that might never come. Often, one or more trips to the library were required and the researcher might find that needed reports were checked out or missing. In the last few years, the rapid development of the Internet and World Wide Web promise to eliminate the drudgery associated with the collection of secondary data.

Finding Secondary Data on the Internet If you know the address of a particular Web site that contains the secondary data that you are searching for, you can type a description of what you are looking for directly into your Web browser (Netscape Navigator or Microsoft Internet Explorer are the dominant browsers). A Web address or URL (Uniform Resource Locator) is similar to a street address in that it identifies a particular location (Web server and file on that server) on the Web.

Search Engines   Sites such as AltaVista, Excite, and Google have become popular for Web users looking for information on the Web. These organizations offer what are called *search engines* that scan the Web looking for sites on a designated topic. Each search engine uses its own indexing system to locate relevant information. All of them allow users to enter one or more keywords that will initiate a search of the databases of Web sites for all occurrences of those words. They then return listings that allow users to go immediately to the sites described.

Remember that the Internet is a self-publishing medium. Your visits to search engines will yield files with a wide range of quality from a variety of sources. Try out multiple sites when you are investigating a topic.

Directories   In addition to search engines, you can use subject directories on the Web to explore a subject. There are two basic types of directories: (1) academic and professional directories, often created and maintained by subject experts to support the needs of researchers, and (2) commercial portals, which cater to the general public and are competing for traffic. Directories depend upon people to compile their listings.

- *Academic and professional directories* are created by librarians or subject experts and tend to be associated with libraries and academic institutions. These collections are created in order to enhance the research process and help users find high quality sites of interest. A careful selection process is applied, and links to the selected resources are usually annotated. These collections are often created to serve an institution's constituency but may be useful to any researcher. As a rule, these sites do not generate income or carry advertising. INFOMINE, from the University of California, is an example of an academic directory.
- *Commercial portals* are created to generate income and serve the general public. These services link to a wide range of topics and often emphasize entertainment, commerce, hobbies, sports, travel, and other interests not necessarily covered by academic directories. These sites seek to draw traffic in order to support advertising. As a part of this goal, the directory is offered in conjunction with a number of additional customer services. Yahoo! is an example of a commercial portal.

The lines between directories and search engines are blurring. Directories are present at some search engine sites, and sometimes their contents are searched along with content from the general Web. For example, AltaVista offers the Look-Smart directory; Infoseek shares the screen with the directory at the Go Network; Excite has its own directory; and Lycos offers the directory contents from the Netscape Open Directory. Directory results are sometimes placed before search results in order to steer users to the directory's content. This can be a useful way of getting at substantive content relating to your query. Most subject directories offer a search engine mechanism to query the database. A list of popular search engines and directories is shown in Exhibit 8.2 on pages 254 and 255.

Sites of Interest to Marketing Researchers   There are a number of Web sites that are accessed daily by marketing researchers in search of information. These sites offer an incredible variety of information. A list of those used most often is shown in Exhibit 8.3 on pages 256 and 257.

Periodical, Newspaper, and Book Databases   Several excellent periodical, newspaper, and book databases are available to researchers. Some can be directly accessed via the Internet and others through your local library's Web site. A list of these databases is shown in Exhibit 8.4 on page 258.

Exhibit 8.2   Popular Search Engines and Directories

Organization	URL	Description
AOL Search	http://search.aol.com	AOL Search allows its members to search across the Web and AOL's own content from one place. The "external" version, listed above, does not list AOL content. The main listings for categories and Web sites come from the Open Directory (see below). Inktomi (see below) also provides crawler-based results, as backup to the directory information.
AltaVista	http://www.altavista.com	AltaVista is consistently one of the largest search engines on the Web, in terms of pages indexed. Its comprehensive coverage and wide range of power searching commands makes it a particular favorite among researchers. It also offers a number of features designed to appeal to basic users, such as "Ask AltaVista" results, which come from Ask Jeeves (see below), and directory listings primarily from the Open Directory.
Ask Jeeves	http://www.askjeeves.com	Ask Jeeves is a human-powered search service that aims to direct you to the exact page that answers your question. If it fails to find a match within its own database, then it will provide matching Web pages from various search engines.
Direct Hit	http://www.directhit.com	Direct Hit is a company that works with other search engines to refine their results. It does this by monitoring what users click on from the results they see. Sites that get clicked on more than others rise higher in Direct Hit's rankings. Thus, the service dubs itself a "popularity engine." Direct Hit's technology is currently best seen at HotBot. It also refines results at Lycos and is available as an option at LookSmart and MSN Search. The company also crawls the Web and refines this database, which can be viewed via the link listed.
Excite	http://www.excite.com	Excite is one of the most popular search services on the Web. It offers a medium-sized index and integrates non-Web material such as company information and sports scores into its results, when appropriate.
FAST Search	http://www.alltheweb.com	Formerly called All The Web, FAST Search aims to index the entire Web. It was the first search engine to break the 200 million Web page index milestone.
Go / Infoseek	http://www.go.com	Go is a portal site produced by Infoseek and Disney. It offers portal features such as personalization and free e-mail, plus the search capabilities of the former Infoseek search service, which has now been folded into Go. Searchers will find that Go consistently provides quality results in response to many general and broad searches. It also has an impressive human-compiled directory of Web sites.
GoTo	http://www.goto.com	Unlike the other major search engines, GoTo sells its main listings. Companies can pay money to be placed higher in the search results, which GoTo feels improves relevancy. Nonpaid results come from Inktomi.
Google	http://www.google.com	Google is a search engine that makes heavy use of link popularity as a primary way to rank Web sites. This can be especially helpful in finding good sites in response to general searches such as "cars" and "travel," because users across the Web have in essence voted for good sites by linking to them.
HotBot	http://www.hotbot.com	Like AltaVista, HotBot is another favorite among researchers due to its large index of the Web and many power searching features. In most cases, HotBot's first page of results comes from the Direct Hit service (see above), and then secondary results come from the Inktomi search engine, which is also used by other services. It gets its directory information from the Open Directory project (see below).
Inktomi	http://www.inktomi.com	Originally, there was an Inktomi search engine at University of California at Berkeley. The creators then formed their own company with the same name and created a new Inktomi index, which was first used to power HotBot. Now the Inktomi index also powers several other services. All of them tap into the same index, though results may be slightly different. This is because Inktomi provides ways for its partners to use a common index yet distinguish themselves. There is no way to query the Inktomi index directly, as it is only made available through Inktomi's partners with whatever filters and ranking tweaks they may apply.

Exhibit 8.2   *continued*

Organization	URL	Description
iWON	http://www.iwon.com	Backed by U.S. television network CBS, iWon has a directory of Web sites generated automatically by Inktomi, which also provides its more traditional crawler-based results. iWon gives away daily, weekly, and monthly prizes in a marketing model unique among the major services.
LookSmart	http://www.looksmart.com	LookSmart is a human-compiled directory of Web sites. In addition to being a stand-alone service, LookSmart provides directory results to MSN Search, Excite, and many other partners. AltaVista provides LookSmart with search results when a search fails to find a match from among LookSmart's reviews.
Lycos	http://www.lycos.com	Lycos started out as a search engine, depending on listings that came from spidering the Web. In April 1999, it shifted to a directory model similar to Yahoo! Its main listings come from the Open Directory project, and then secondary results come from either Direct Hit or Lycos's own spidering of the Web.
MSN Search	http://search.msn.com	Microsoft's MSN Search service is a LookSmart-powered directory of Web sites, with secondary results that come from AltaVista. RealNames and Direct Hit data are also made available. MSN Search also offers a unique way for Internet Explorer 5 users to save past searches.
Netscape Search	http://search.netscape.com	Netscape Search's results come primarily from the Open Directory and Netscape's own "Smart Browsing" database, which does an excellent job of listing "official" Web sites. Secondary results come from Google. At the Netscape Netcenter portal site, other search engines are also featured.
Northern Light	http://www.northernlight.com	Northern Light is another favorite search engine among researchers. It features one of the largest indexes of the Web, along with the ability to cluster documents by topic. Northern Light also has a set of "special collection" documents that are not readily accessible to search engine spiders. There are documents from thousands of sources, including newswires, magazines, and databases. Searching these documents is free, but there is a charge of up to $4 to view them. There is no charge to view documents on the public Web—only for those within the special collection.
Open Directory	http://dmoz.org	The Open Directory uses volunteer editors to catalog the Web. It was acquired by Netscape in November 1998, and the company pledged that anyone would be able to use information from the directory through an open license arrangement. Netscape itself was the first licensee. Lycos and AOL Search also make heavy use of Open Directory data, while AltaVista and HotBot prominently feature Open Directory categories within their results pages.
RealNames	http://www.realnames.com	The RealNames system is meant to be an easier-to-use alternative to the current Web site addressing system. Those with RealNames-enabled browsers can enter a word like "Nike" to reach the Nike Web site. To date, RealNames has had its biggest success through search engine partnerships. In particular, it is strongly featured in results at AltaVista, Go, and MSN Search.
Snap	http://www.snap.com	Snap is a human-compiled directory of Web sites, supplemented by search results from Inktomi. Like LookSmart, it aims to challenge Yahoo as the champion of categorizing the Web.
WebCrawler	http://www.webcrawler.com	WebCrawler has the smallest index of any major search engine on the Web—think of it as Excite Lite. The small index means WebCrawler is not the place to go when seeking obscure or unusual material. However, some people may feel that by having indexed fewer pages, WebCrawler provides less overwhelming results in response to general searches.
Yahoo!	http://www.yahoo.com	Yahoo! is the Web's most popular search service and has a well-deserved reputation for helping people find information easily. The secret to Yahoo!'s success is human beings. It is the largest human-compiled guide to the Web, employing about 150 editors in an effort to categorize the Web. Yahoo! has over one million sites listed. Yahoo! also supplements its results with those from Inktomi. If a search fails to find a match within Yahoo!'s own listings, then matches from Inktomi are displayed. Inktomi matches also appear after all Yahoo! matches have first been shown. Yahoo! is the oldest major Web site directory, having launched in late 1994.

SOURCE: searchenginewatch.com

Organization	URL	Description
American Demographics/ Marketing Tools	http://www.marketingtools.com	Searches the full text of all of American Demographics and Marketing Tools
American Marketing Association	http://www.ama.org	Searches all of the AMA's publications by using keywords.
BLS Consumer Expenditure Surveys	http://stats.bls.gov/esxprod.htm	Provides information on the buying habits of consumers, including data on their expenditures, income, and consumer credit.
Bureau of Economic Analysis	http://www.bea.doc.gov	Provides a wide range of economic statistics.
Bureau of Transportation Statistics	http://www.bts.gov	Comprehensive source for a wide range of statistics on transportation.
CACI	http://www.demographics.caci.com	On CACI Marketing Systems' site, users can type in their zip codes to get a snapshot of the dominant profile type in their town. Population figures are available for the zips, as are percentages for race and sex. Median household income, average home values, and average rent are also presented.
Centers for Disease Control and Prevention	http://www.cdc.gov/nchswww/ default.html	As the federal government's principal vital and health statistical agency, the National Center for Health Statistics has a lot to offer. The NCHS, a subdivision of the Centers for Disease Control and Prevention, maintains data on vital events, health status, lifestyle and exposure to unhealthy influences, the onset and diagnosis of illness and disability, and the use of health care.
Cyberatlas	http://www.cyberatlas.com	Viewers can browse the latest research compiled from several reputable firms, including Media Metrix, Greenfield Online, Intelliquest, and Inteco. The geography page fills you in on surveys about on-line populations around the world. There's also a generous section on e-commerce that breaks out research in different markets, like advertising, finance, and retail. Peek into the stats toolbox for a mother lode of lists on everything from weekly usage data to the top-ten banner ads.
The Dismal Scientist	http://www.dismal.com	An authoritative site offering timely economic information, with comprehensive data and analysis at the metro, state, and national levels. There's also data and analyses of global issues, including situations facing Asia, South America, and Europe. Visitors can rank states and metro areas on more than 100 economic, socioeconomic, and demographic categories.
Easy Analytic Software	http://www.easidemographics.com	Easy Analytic Software, a New York City–based developer and marketer of demographic data, offers demographic site reports, or three-ring studies, including current estimates for population and households. Each three-ring study offers Census estimates for race, ethnicity, age distribution, income distribution, and weather data. The site also offers one million pages of demographic reports for all zip codes, counties, metropolitan areas, cities, sectional centers, television markets, states, and other geographies.
EconData	http://www.econdata.net	A premier site for researchers interested in economics and demographics. There is a tremendous number of links to government, private, and academic data sources. Check out their top-ten data sources list.

Exhibit **8.3** *continued*

Organization	URL	Description
Economic Research Service, Department of Agriculture	http://www.econ.ag.gov	Provides a wide range of agricultural statistics.
Encyclopedia Britannica	http://www.britannica.com	Entire 32-volume encyclopedia is available free on-line.
Equifax National Decision Systems	http://www.ends.com	Provides access to wide range of secondary data on many topics. Most must be purchased.
Find/SVP	http://www.findsvp.com	Offers consulting and research services. Claims to offer access to the largest private information center in the United States.
Harris Info Service	http://www.harrisinfo.com	Offers business-to-business data on American manufacturers and key decision makers.
Marketing Research Association	http://www.MRA-net.org	Analyzes causes and solutions of "declining respondent cooperation"; links to research suppliers.
Mediamark Research	http://www.mediamark.com/mri/docs/toplinereports.html	Marketers and researchers looking for demographic data on magazines, cable TV, or 53 different product or service categories can find it at Top-Line Reports site. Top-Line Reports breaks down cable TV networks according to viewers' age, sex, median age, and income. Magazines are listed by total audience, circulation, readers per copy, median age, and income.
Nielsen Media Research	http://www.nielsen-netratings.com	Course on Internet audience information. Researchers can find data and Internet growth and user patterns.
Office of Research & Statistics, SSA	http://www.ssa.gov/statistics/ores_home.html	Provides a range of government statistics.
Pcensus for Windows	http://www.tetrad.com	Provides detailed information about the population of metropolitan areas.
Population Reference Bureau	http://www.prb.org/prb	Source of demographic information on population issues.
Service Intelligence	http://www.serviceintelligence.com	The site has an area devoted to customer stories of unpleasant experiences with airlines, banks, restaurants, and other service businesses. It's not all bad news, though—"hero" stories are also included.
Strategic Mapping	http://www.stratmap.com	Offers extensive selection of geographic files, includes detailed geography for entire United States.
U.S. Census Bureau	http://www.census.gov	Very useful source of virtually all census data.
U.S. Demography	http://www.ciesin.org	Excellent source of demographic information concerning the U.S.
USA Data	http://www.usadata.com	Provides access to consumer lifestyle data on a local, regional, or national basis.
World Opinion	http://www.worldopinion.com	Perhaps the premier site for the marketing research industry; thousands of marketing research reports available.

Exhibit 8.4

Full Text Periodical, Newspaper, and Book Databases Used by Marketing Researchers

Source	Description
ABI/Inform Global	Updated monthly; provides bibliographic information and abstracts for approximately 1,000 journals in business and management. Includes full-text entries for approximately 520 journals. Among the major marketing journals now included in full-text format are *Journal of Marketing; JMR: Journal of Marketing Research;* and *Journal of the Academy of Marketing Science.*
Dow Jones Interactive	Includes full-text news and articles from over 3,400 sources including newspapers from around the world, as well as information on companies, industries, stocks, bonds, mutual funds, and foreign exchange rates; updated daily.
Electric Library	Contains over 5 million full-text documents in all subject areas. Content is updated daily and includes an archive of up to twelve years. Covers six separate media types: newspapers and news wires, periodicals, TV and radio program transcripts, literature and reference books, photos, and maps.
Lexis-Nexis	The Lexis-Nexis database contains 2.5 billion searchable documents. Each week, 14.7 million new documents are added. It includes 18,871 news and business sources. Lexis-Nexis is the largest business information service. It offers access to thousands of worldwide newspapers, magazines, trade journals, industry newsletters, tax and accounting information, financial data, public records, legislative data, and company information.
Periodical Abstracts Research II (PAR)	Covers current affairs, business, industry news, cultural events, editorial material, and general interest topics from more than 1,800 general and academic periodicals. Includes full-text articles from more than 600 journals. Full-text coverage began in 1992; updated monthly. Marketing journals are not heavily indexed in this database, but among those that are available full-text are *Direct Marketing; Journal of Consumer Affairs;* and *Sales & Marketing Management.*

Internet Discussion Groups and Special Interest Groups as Sources of Secondary Data A primary means of communicating with other professionals and special interest groups on the Internet is through newsgroups. With an Internet connection and newsreader software, you can visit any newsgroup supported by your service provider. If your service provider does not offer newsgroups or does not carry the group in which you are interested, you can find one of the publicly available newsgroup servers that does carry the group you would like to read.

Newsgroups function much like bulletin boards for a particular topic or interest. A newsgroup is established to focus on a particular topic. Readers stop by that newsgroup to read messages left by other people, post responses to others' questions, and send rebuttals to comments with which they disagree. Generally, there is

newsgroups
Function like bulletin boards. They are established to focus on a particular topic.

some management of the messages to keep discussions within the topic area and to remove offensive material. However, readers of a newsgroup are free to discuss any issue and communicate with anyone in the world that visits that newsgroup. Images and data files can be exchanged in newsgroups, just as they can be exchanged via e-mail.

With over 250,000 newsgroups currently in existence and more being added every day, there is a newsgroup for nearly every hobby, profession, and lifestyle. Both Netscape Navigator and Microsoft Internet Explorer, as well as other browsers, come with newsgroup readers. If you do not already have a newsgroup reader, you can go to one of the search engines and search for one of the freeware or shareware newsgroup readers. These newsgroup readers function much like e-mail programs. Here's how to find a particular newsgroup:

- Connect to the Internet in your usual way.
- Open your newsreader program.
- Search for the topic of interest. Most newsreaders allow you to search the names of the newsgroups for any keywords or topics you are interested in. Some newsreaders, like Microsoft Internet Explorer, also allow you to search the brief descriptions that accompany most newsgroups.
- Select the newsgroup in which you are interested.
- Begin scanning messages. The title of each message generally gives an indication about the subject matter.

Newsgroup messages look like e-mail messages. They contain a subject title, author, and a message body. Unlike normal e-mail messages, newsgroup messages are threaded discussions. This means that any reply to a previous message will appear linked to that message. Therefore, you can follow a discussion between two or more people by starting at the original message and following the links (or threads) to each successive reply. You can send images, sound files, and video clips attached to your message for anyone to download and examine.

Newsgroups can be a valuable source of secondary data if used correctly. Cyberfiber has a group page specifically for business and marketplace topics. Visit the site to see what it's all about.

Planning the Research Design and Gathering Primary Data

Good secondary data can help researchers conduct a thorough situation analysis. With that information, researchers can list their unanswered questions and rank them. Researchers must then decide the exact information required to answer the questions. The **research design** specifies which research questions must be answered, how and when the data will be gathered, and how the data will be analyzed. Typically, the project budget is finalized after the research design has been approved.

Sometimes research questions can be answered by gathering more secondary data; otherwise, primary data may be needed. **Primary data**, or information collected for the first time, can be used for solving the particular problem under investigation. The main advantage of primary data is that they will answer a specific

research design
Specifies which research questions must be answered, how and when the data will be gathered, and how the data will be analyzed.

primary data
Information collected for the first time. Can be used for solving the particular problem under investigation.

research question that secondary data cannot answer. For example, suppose Pillsbury has two new recipes for refrigerated dough for sugar cookies. Which one will consumers like better? Secondary data will not help answer this question. Instead, targeted consumers must try each recipe and evaluate the tastes, textures, and appearances of each cookie. Moreover, primary data are current and researchers know the source. Sometimes researchers gather the data themselves rather than assign projects to outside companies. Researchers also specify the methodology of the research. Secrecy can be maintained because the information is proprietary. In contrast, secondary data are available to all interested parties for relatively small fees.

Gathering primary data is expensive; costs can range from a few thousand dollars for a limited survey to several million for a nationwide study. For instance, a nationwide, fifteen-minute telephone interview with one thousand adult males can cost $50,000 for everything, including a data analysis and report. Because primary data gathering is so expensive, firms commonly cut back on the number of interviews to save money. Larger companies that conduct many research projects use another cost-saving technique. They piggyback studies, or gather data on two different projects using one questionnaire. The drawback is that answering questions about, say, dog food and gourmet coffee may be confusing to respondents. Piggybacking also requires a longer interview (sometimes a half hour or longer), which tires respondents. The quality of the answers typically declines, with people giving curt replies and thinking, "When will this end!" A lengthy interview also makes people less likely to participate in other research surveys.[8]

However, the disadvantages of primary data gathering are usually offset by the advantages. It is often the only way of solving a research problem. And with a variety of techniques available for research—including surveys, observations, and experiments—primary research can address almost any marketing question.

Survey Research   The most popular technique for gathering primary data is **survey research**, in which a researcher interacts with people to obtain facts, opinions, and attitudes. Exhibit 8.5 summarizes the characteristics of traditional forms of research.

In-Home Personal Interviews   Although in-home, personal interviews often provide high-quality information, they tend to be very expensive because of the interviewers' travel time and mileage costs. Therefore, they are rapidly disappearing from the marketing researcher's survey toolbox.

Mall Intercept Interviews   The **mall intercept interview** is conducted in the common areas of shopping malls or in a market research office within the mall. It is the economy version of the door-to-door interview with personal contact between interviewer and respondent, minus the interviewer's travel time and mileage costs. To conduct this type of interview, the research firm rents office space in the mall or pays a significant daily fee. One drawback is that it is hard to get a representative sample of the population.

However, an interviewer can also probe when necessary—a technique used to clarify a person's response. For example, an interviewer might ask, "What did you like best about the salad dressing you just tried?" The respondent might reply, "Taste." This answer doesn't provide a lot of information, so the interviewer could probe by saying, "Can you tell me a little bit more about taste?" The respondent then elaborates: "Yes, it's not too sweet, it has the right amount of pepper, and I love that hint of garlic."

survey research
The most popular technique for gathering primary data in which a researcher interacts with people to obtain facts, opinions, and attitudes.

mall intercept interview
Survey research method that involves interviewing people in the common areas of shopping malls.

Exhibit 8.5   Characteristics of Traditional Forms of Survey Research

Characteristic	In-home Personal Interviews	Mall Intercept Interviews	Central-Location Telephone Interviews	Self-Administered and One-Time Mail Surveys	Mall Panel Surveys	Executive Interviews	Focus Groups
Cost	High	Moderate	Moderate	Low	Moderate	High	Low
Time span	Moderate	Moderate	Fast	Slow	Relatively slow	Moderate	Fast
Use of interviewer probes	Yes	Yes	Yes	No	Yes	Yes	Yes
Ability to show concepts to respondent	Yes (also taste tests)	Yes (also taste tests)	No	Yes	Yes	Yes	Yes
Management control over interviewer	Low	Moderate	High	n/a	n/a	Moderate	High
General data quality	High	Moderate	High to moderate	Moderate to low	Moderate	High	Moderate
Ability to collect large amounts of data	High	Moderate	Moderate to low	Low to moderate	Moderate	Moderate	Moderate
Ability to handle complex questionnaires	High	Moderate	High if computer-aided	Low	Low	High	Low

Mall intercept interviews must be brief. Only the shortest ones are conducted while respondents are standing. Usually researchers invite respondents to their office for interviews, which are still rarely over fifteen minutes long. The researchers often show respondents concepts for new products or a test commercial or have them taste a new food product. The overall quality of mall intercept interviews is about the same as telephone interviews.

Marketing researchers are applying computer technology in mall interviewing. The first technique is **computer-assisted personal interviewing**. The researcher conducts in-person interviews, reads questions to the respondent off a computer screen, and directly keys the respondent's answers into the computer. A second approach is **computer-assisted self-interviewing**. A mall interviewer intercepts and directs willing respondents to nearby computers. Each respondent reads questions off a computer screen and directly keys his or her answers into a computer. The third use of technology is fully automated self-interviewing. Respondents are guided by interviewers or independently approach a centrally located computer station or kiosk, read questions off a screen, and directly key their answers into the station's computer.

Telephone Interviews   Compared to the personal interview, the telephone interview costs less and may provide the best sample of any survey procedure. Although it is often criticized for providing poorer-quality data than the in-home personal interview, studies have shown that this criticism may not be deserved.[9]

Most telephone interviewing is conducted from a specially designed phone room called a **central-location telephone (CLT) facility**. A phone room has many phone lines, individual interviewing stations, sometimes monitoring equipment, and headsets. The research firm typically will interview people nationwide from a single location.

Many CLT facilities offer computer-assisted interviewing. The interviewer reads the questions from a computer screen and enters the respondent's data directly into the computer. The researcher can stop the survey at any point and

computer-assisted personal interviewing
Interviewing method in which the interviewer reads the questions from a computer screen and enters the respondent's data directly into the computer.

computer-assisted self-interviewing
Interviewing method in which a mall interviewer intercepts and directs willing respondents to nearby computers where the respondent reads questions off a computer screen and directly keys his or her answers into a computer.

central-location telephone (CLT) facility
A specially designed phone room used to conduct telephone interviewing.

immediately print out the survey results. Thus, a researcher can get a sense of the project as it unfolds and fine-tune the research design as necessary. An on-line interviewing system can also save time and money because data entry occurs as the response is recorded rather than as a separate process after the interview. Hallmark Cards found that an interviewer administered a printed questionnaire for its Shoebox Greeting cards in twenty-eight minutes. The same questionnaire administered with computer assistance took only eighteen minutes.

Mail Surveys   Mail surveys have several benefits: relatively low cost, elimination of interviewers and field supervisors, centralized control, and actual or promised anonymity for respondents (which may draw more candid responses). Some researchers feel that mail questionnaires give the respondent a chance to reply more thoughtfully and to check records, talk to family members, and so forth. Yet mail questionnaires usually produce low response rates.

Low response rates pose a problem because certain elements of the population tend to respond more than others. The resulting sample may therefore not represent the surveyed population. For example, the sample may have too many retired people and too few working people. In this instance, answers to a question about attitudes toward Social Security might indicate a much more favorable overall view of the system than is actually the case. Another serious problem with mail surveys is that no one probes respondents to clarify or elaborate on their answers.

Mail panels like those operated by Market Facts, National Family Opinion Research, and NPD Research offer an alternative to the one-shot mail survey. A mail panel consists of a sample of households recruited to participate by mail for a given period. Panel members often receive gifts in return for their participation. Essentially, the panel is a sample used several times. In contrast to one-time mail surveys, the response rates from mail panels are high. Rates of 70 percent (of those who agree to participate) are not uncommon.

Executive Interviews   **Executive interviews** are used by marketing researchers to refer to the industrial equivalent of door-to-door interviewing. This type of survey involves interviewing businesspeople, at their offices, concerning industrial products or services. For example, if Hewlett-Packard wanted information regarding user preferences for different features that might be offered in a new line of computer printers, it would need to interview prospective user-purchasers of the printers. It is appropriate to locate and interview these people at their offices.

This type of interviewing is very expensive. First, individuals involved in the purchase decision for the product in question must be identified and located. Sometimes lists can be obtained from various sources, but more frequently screening must be conducted over the telephone. It may be likely that a particular company has individuals of the type being sought. However, locating those people within a large organization can be expensive and time-consuming. Once a qualified person is located, the next step is to get that person to agree to be interviewed and to set a time for the interview. This is not as hard as it might seem because most professionals seem to enjoy talking about topics related to their work.

Finally, an interviewer must go to the particular place at the appointed time. Long waits are frequently encountered; cancellations are not uncommon. This type of survey requires the very best interviewers because they are frequently interviewing on topics that they know very little about. Executive interviewing has essentially the same advantages and disadvantages as in-home interviewing.

Focus Groups   A **focus group** is a type of personal interviewing. Often recruited by random telephone screening, seven to ten people with certain desired characteristics form a focus group. These qualified consumers are usually offered an incentive (typically $30 to $50) to participate in a group discussion. The meeting place (sometimes resembling a living room, sometimes featuring a conference table) has audiotaping and perhaps videotaping equipment. It also likely has a viewing room with a one-way mirror so that clients (manufacturers or retailers) may watch the session. During the session, a moderator, hired by the research company, leads the group discussion.

Focus groups are much more than question-and-answer interviews. The distinction is made between "group dynamics" and "group interviewing." The interaction provided in **group dynamics** is essential to the success of focus-group research; this interaction is the reason for conducting group rather than individual research. One of the essential postulates of group-session usage is the idea that a response from one person may become a stimulus for another, thereby generating an interplay of responses that may yield more than if the same number of people had contributed independently.

Focus groups are occasionally used to brainstorm new product ideas or to screen concepts for new products. Ford Motor Company, for example, asked consumers to drive several automobile prototypes. These "test drivers" were then brought together in focus groups. During the discussions, consumers complained that they were scuffing their shoes because the rear seats lacked foot room. In response, Ford sloped the floor underneath the front seats, widened the space between the seat adjustment tracks, and made the tracks in the Taurus and Sable models out of smooth plastic instead of metal.

A new system by Focus Vision Network allows client companies and advertising agencies to view live focus groups in Chicago, Dallas, Boston, and fifteen other major cities. For example, the private satellite network lets a General Motors researcher observing a San Diego focus group control two cameras in the viewing room. The researcher can get a full-group view or a close-up, zoom, or pan the participants. The researcher can also communicate directly with the moderator using an ear receiver. Ogilvy and Mather (a large New York advertising agency whose clients include StarKist Sea Foods, Seagrams, Mastercard, and Burger King) has installed the system.

The newest development in qualitative research is the on-line or cyber focus group. A number of organizations are currently offering this new means of conducting focus groups. The process is fairly simple.

- The research firm builds a database of respondents via a screening questionnaire on its Web site.
- When a client comes to them with a need for a particular focus group, the firm goes to its database and identifies individuals who appear to qualify. It sends an e-mail message to these individuals, asking them to log on to a particular site at a particular time scheduled for the group. The firm pays them an incentive for their participation.
- The firm develops a discussion guide similar to one for a conventional focus group.
- A moderator runs the group by typing in questions on-line for all to see. The group operates in an environment similar to that of a chat room so that all participants see all questions and all responses.

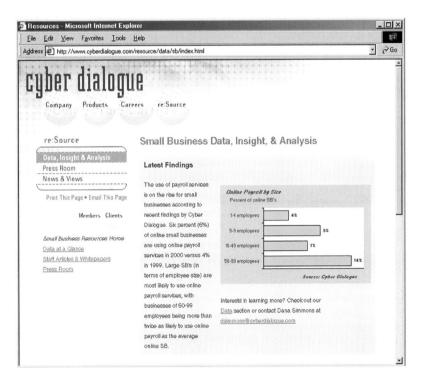

Like many areas, the Internet has revolutionized marketing research. Cyber Dialogue conducts on-line focus groups and also shares its own proprietary research over its Web site, such as the information on payroll services pictured here.

- The firm captures the complete text of the focus group and makes it available for review after the group has finished.

Many advantages are claimed for cyber groups. Cyber Dialogue, a marketing research company specializing in cyber groups, lists the following benefits of on-line focus groups on its Web site:

- *Speed:* Typically, focus groups can be recruited and conducted, with delivery of results, within five days of client approval.
- *Cost effectiveness:* Off-line focus groups incur costs for facility rental, air fare, hotel, and food. None of these costs is incurred with on-line focus groups.
- *Broad geographic scope:* In a given focus group, you can speak to people in Boise, Idaho and Miami, Florida, at the same time.
- *Accessibility:* On-line focus groups give you access to individuals who otherwise might be difficult to recruit (e.g., business travelers, doctors, mothers with infants).
- *Honesty:* From behind their screen names, respondents are anonymous to other respondents and tend to talk more freely about issues that might create inhibitions in a face-to-face group.

Cyber Dialogue prices their focus groups at $3,000. This compares very favorably to a cost in the range of $7,000 without travel costs for conventional focus groups. Unfortunately, no systematic evaluation of on-line focus groups in comparison to conventional focus groups has been done at this time.

Questionnaire Design   All forms of survey research require a questionnaire. Questionnaires ensure that all respondents will be asked the same series of questions. Questionnaires include three basic types of questions: open-ended, closed-ended, and scaled-response (see Exhibit 8.6). An **open-ended question** encourages an answer phrased in the respondent's own words. Researchers get a rich array of information based on the respondent's frame of reference. In contrast, a **closed-ended question** asks the respondent to make a selection from a limited list of responses. Traditionally, marketing researchers separate the two-choice question (called *dichotomous*) from the many-item type (often called *multiple choice*). A **scaled-response question** is a closed-ended question designed to measure the intensity of a respondent's answer.

Closed-ended and scaled-response questions are easier to tabulate than open-ended questions because response choices are fixed. On the other hand, if the researcher is not careful in designing the closed-ended question, an important choice might be omitted. For example, suppose this question were asked on a food study: "What do you normally add to a taco, besides meat, that you have prepared at home?"

open-ended question
An interview question that encourages an answer phrased in the respondent's own words.

closed-ended question
An interview question that asks the respondent to make a selection from a limited list of responses.

scaled-response question
A closed-ended question designed to measure the intensity of a respondent's answer.

Avocado	1
Cheese (Monterey Jack/cheddar)	2
Guacamole	3
Lettuce	4
Mexican hot sauce	5
Olives (black/green)	6
Onions (red/white)	7
Peppers (red/green)	8
Pimento	9
Sour cream	0

Exhibit 8.6 Types of Questions Found on Questionnaires for National Market Research

Open-Ended Questions	Closed-Ended Questions	Scaled-Response Question
1. What advantages, if any, do you think ordering from a mail-order catalog offers compared to shopping at a local retail outlet? (*Probe:* What else?) 2. Why do you have one or more of your rugs or carpets professionally cleaned rather than having you or someone else in the household clean them? 3. What is there about the color of the eye shadow that makes you like it the best?	**Dichotomous** 1. Did you heat the Danish product before serving it? Yes . . . . .1 No . . . . .2 2. The federal government doesn't care what people like me think. Agree . . . . .1 Disagree .2 **Multiple choice** 1. I'd like you to think back to the last footwear of any kind that you bought. I'll read you a list of descriptions and would like for you to tell me which category they fall into. (*Read list and check proper category.*) Dress and/or formal . . . . .1 Casual . . . . .2 Canvas/trainer/gym shoes . . . . . . .3 Specialized athletic shoes . . . . . . .4 Boots . . . . .5 2. In the last three months, have you used Noxzema skin cream . . . (*Check all that apply.*) As a facial wash . . . . .1 For moisturizing the skin . . . . . . .2 For treating blemishes . . . . .3 For cleansing the skin . . . . .4 For treating dry skin . . . . .5 For softening skin . . . . .6 For sunburn . . . . .7 For making the facial skin smooth 8	Now that you have used the rug cleaner, would you say that you . . . (*Check one*) ____Would definitely buy it ____Would probably buy it ____Might or might not buy it ____Probably would not buy it ____Definitely would not buy it

The list seems complete, doesn't it? However, consider the following responses: "I usually add a green, avocado-tasting hot sauce"; "I cut up a mixture of lettuce and spinach"; "I'm a vegetarian; I don't use meat at all. My taco is filled only with guacamole." How would you code these replies? As you can see, the question needs an "other" category.

A good question must also be asked clearly and concisely, and ambiguous language must be avoided. Take, for example, the question "Do you live within ten minutes of here?" The answer depends on the mode of transportation (maybe the person walks), driving speed, perceived time, and other factors. Instead, respondents should see a map with certain areas highlighted and be asked whether they live within one of those areas.

Clarity also implies using reasonable terminology. A questionnaire is not a vocabulary test. Jargon should be avoided, and language should be geared to the target audience. A question such as "What is the level of efficacy of your preponderant dishwasher powder?" would probably be greeted by a lot of blank stares. It would be much simpler to say "Are you (1) very satisfied, (2) somewhat satisfied, or (3) not satisfied with your current brand of dishwasher powder?"

Stating the survey's purpose at the beginning of the interview also improves clarity. The respondents should understand the study's intentions and the interviewer's expectations. Sometimes, of course, to get an unbiased response, the interviewer must disguise the true purpose of the study. If an interviewer says, "We're conducting an image study for American National Bank" and then proceeds to ask a series of questions about the bank, chances are the responses will be biased. Many times respondents will try to provide answers that they believe are "correct" or that the interviewer wants to hear.

Finally, to ensure clarity, the interviewer should avoid asking two questions in one; for example, "How did you like the taste and texture of the Pepperidge Farm coffee cake?" This should be divided into two questions, one concerning taste and the other texture.

A question should not only be clear but also unbiased. A question such as "Have you purchased any quality Black & Decker tools in the past six months?" biases respondents to think of the topic in a certain way (in this case, to link quality and Black & Decker tools). Questions can also be leading: "Weren't you pleased with the good service you received last night at the Holiday Inn?" (The respondent is all but instructed to say yes.) These examples are quite obvious; unfortunately, bias is usually more subtle. Even an interviewer's clothing or gestures can create bias.

Sometimes questions are raised about the ethics of surveying particular groups, such as young children. The "Ethics in Marketing" box provides such an example.

observation research

A research method that relies on three types of observation: people watching people, people watching an activity, and machines watching people.

Observation Research In contrast to survey research, **observation research** depends on watching what people do. Specifically, it can be defined as the systematic process of recording the behavioral patterns of people, objects, and occurrences without questioning or communicating with them. A market researcher using the observation technique witnesses and records information as events occur or compiles evidence from records of past events. Carried a step further, observation may involve watching people or phenomena and may be conducted by human observers or machines. Examples of these various observational situations are shown in Exhibit 8.7 on page 268.

mystery shoppers

Researchers posing as customers who gather observational data about a store.

Two common forms of people-watching-people research are mystery shoppers and one-way mirror observations. **Mystery shoppers** are researchers posing as customers who gather observational data about a store (i.e., are the shelves neatly stocked?) and to collect data about customer/employee interactions. In the latter case, of course, there is communication between the mystery shopper and the employee. The mystery shopper may ask, "How much is this item?" "Do you have this in blue?" or "Can you deliver this by Friday?" The interaction is not an interview, and communication occurs only so the mystery shopper can observe the actions and comments of the employee. Mystery shopping is, therefore, classified as an observational marketing research method even though communication is often involved. Conducted on a continuous basis, mystery shopping can motivate and recognize service performance. Used as a benchmark, mystery shopping can pinpoint strengths and weaknesses for training operations and policy refinements.

Ethics in Marketing

During morning class time recently, sixty elementary school children sat expectantly in the lunchroom of St. Mary's Star of the Sea School in Beverly, Massachusetts, waiting for instructions about what to do with the cups of beverage in front of them. The kids had just completed fifteen minutes of strenuous exercise in the gym and were now ready to dive into the serious business of tasting and evaluating sports drinks.

Following directions given by researchers from Education Market Resources, the children filled in questionnaires measuring how much they enjoyed each of the unnamed drinks. The youngsters loved the process, says their principal, Sister Danielle Sullivan. "I think they felt they were making decisions that mattered," she says.

The beverage marketer loved it, too. That day, the company learned a valuable lesson: Which of its flavors were deemed "yukky" and, more importantly, which varieties kids would push their parents to buy.

Until seven years ago, when Education Market Resources opened, this kind of in-school product testing was almost unheard of. But in the cash-strapped, increasingly free-market world of education, more schools are opening their doors to

companies that want to test which products kids will clamor for.

Is it valuable information? Marketers think so. A leading cereal-maker halted the launch of a campaign to introduce alien figures in one of its brands after test marketing in schools showed kids were ho-hum over the product. "They were going to spend literally millions of dollars to try to increase market share with this whole new concept," said Robert Reynolds, president of Educational Market Resources, "and the kids didn't even like it."

Although marketers may indeed save money, rewards for participating schools are modest. Depending on the complexity of the activity and the number of kids involved, schools earn between $800 to a few thousand dollars for each encounter with Education Market Resources. Gwen Ater, a sixth-grade teacher at Heatherstong Elementary School in Kansas City, Kansas, says she gets $5 per student for surveys such as the one she and her class recently completed for Toys "R" Us. "We're in a district that has good resources, but for things like class trips it's great," Ms. Ater says.

And then there's the argument that kids are wasting valuable learning time "working for peanuts." Ginny Markell, president of the

Ethical questions can obviously be raised regarding the creation of focus groups of school-age children, but what about groups of teenagers? Peter Zollo, pictured here, is moderating a teen focus group for Teen Research Unlimited.

national PTA, says her group opposes product testing during school hours because kids can't afford to give up the instructional time.[a]

Do you think that children should be interviewed in marketing research studies? If so, is school an appropriate place to conduct interviews? Is the money earned worth the learning time sacrificed?

[a] Peggy Farber, "Market Researchers Turn Classrooms Into Test Labs," *Advertising Age* (October 25, 1999), p. 24.

At the Fisher-Price Play Laboratory, children are invited to spend twelve sessions playing with toys. Toy designers watch through one-way mirrors to see how children react to Fisher-Price's and other makers' toys. Fisher-Price, for example, had difficulty designing a toy lawn mower that children would play with. A designer, observing behind the mirror, noticed the children's fascination with soap bubbles. He then created a lawn mower that spewed soap bubbles. It sold over a million units in the first year.

Experiments An **experiment** is a method a researcher can use to gather primary data. The researcher alters one or more variables—price, package design, shelf space, advertising theme, advertising expenditures—while observing the effects of

experiment
A method a researcher uses to gather primary data.

Exhibit **8.7**

Observation Situations

Situation	Example
People watching people	Observers stationed in supermarkets watch consumers select frozen Mexican dinners; the purpose is to see how much comparison shopping people do at the point of purchase.
People watching phenomena	Observer stationed at an intersection counts traffic moving in various directions.
Machines watching people	Movie or videotape cameras record behavior as in the people-watching-people example above.
Machines watching phenomena	Traffic counting machines monitor traffic flow.

Fisher-Price runs a play laboratory in which children are observed through a one-way mirror. Toy designers can see how children react to a variety of toys and get ideas for new creations.
© Michael Greenlar/The Image Works

those alterations on another variable (usually sales). The best experiments are those in which all factors are held constant except the ones being manipulated. The researcher can then observe that changes in sales, for example, result from changes in the amount of money spent on advertising.

Holding all other factors constant in the external environment is a monumental and costly, if not impossible, task. Such factors as competitors' actions, weather, and economic conditions are beyond the researcher's control. Yet market researchers have ways to account for the ever-changing external environment. Mars, the candy company, was losing sales to other candy companies. Traditional surveys showed that the shrinking candy bar was not perceived as a good value. Mars wondered whether a bigger bar sold at the same price would increase sales enough to offset the higher ingredient costs. The company designed an experiment in which the marketing mix stayed the same in different markets but the size of the candy bar varied. The substantial increase in sales of the bigger bar quickly proved that the additional costs would be more than covered by the additional revenue. Mars increased the bar size—and its market share and profits.

Specifying the Sampling Procedures

Once the researchers decide how they will collect primary data, their next step is to select the sampling procedures they will use. A firm can seldom take a census of all possible users of a new product, nor can they all be interviewed. Therefore, a firm must select a sample of the group to be interviewed. A **sample** is a subset from a larger population.

Several questions must be answered before a sampling plan is chosen. First, the population, or **universe**, of interest must be defined. This is the group from which the sample will be drawn. It should include all the people whose opinions, behavior, preferences, attitudes, and so on are of interest to the marketer. For example, in a study whose purpose is to determine the market for a new canned dog food, the universe might be defined to include all current buyers of canned dog food.

After the universe has been defined, the next question is whether the sample must be representative of the population. If the answer is yes, a probability sample is needed. Otherwise, a nonprobability sample might be considered.

Probability Samples   A **probability sample** is a sample in which every element in the population has a known statistical likelihood of being selected. Its most desirable feature is that scientific rules can be used to ensure that the sample represents the population.

One type of probability sample is a **random sample**—a sample arranged in such a way that every element of the population has an equal chance of being selected as part of the sample. For example, suppose a university is interested in getting a cross section of student opinions on a proposed sports complex to be built using student activity fees. If the university can acquire an up-to-date list of all the enrolled students, it can draw a random sample by using random numbers from a table (found in most statistics books) to select students from the list. Common forms of probability and nonprobability samples are shown in Exhibit 8.8 on page 270.

Nonprobability Samples   Any sample in which little or no attempt is made to get a representative cross section of the population can be considered a **nonprobability sample**. A common form of a nonprobability sample is the **convenience sample**, based on using respondents who are convenient or readily accessible to the researcher—for instance, employees, friends, or relatives.

Nonprobability samples are acceptable as long as the researcher understands their nonrepresentative nature. Because of their lower cost, nonprobability samples are the basis of much marketing research.

Types of Errors   Whenever a sample is used in marketing research, two major types of error occur: measurement error and sampling error. **Measurement error** occurs when there is a difference between the information desired by the researcher and the information provided by the measurement process. For example, people may tell an interviewer that they purchase Coors beer when they do not. Measurement error generally tends to be larger than sampling error.

Sampling error occurs when a sample somehow does not represent the target population. Sampling error can be one of several types. Nonresponse error occurs when the sample actually interviewed differs from the sample drawn. This error happens because the original people selected to be interviewed either refused to cooperate or were inaccessible. For example, people who feel embarrassed about their drinking habits may refuse to talk about them.

Frame error, another type of sampling error, arises if the sample drawn from a population differs from the target population. For instance, suppose a telephone survey is conducted to find out Chicago beer drinkers' attitudes toward Coors. If a Chicago telephone directory is used as the *frame* (the device or list from which the respondents are selected), the survey will contain a frame error. Not all Chicago beer drinkers have a phone, and many phone numbers are unlisted. An ideal sample (for example, a sample with no frame error) matches all important characteristics of the target population to be surveyed. Could you find a perfect frame for Chicago beer drinkers?

Random error occurs because the selected sample is an imperfect representation of the overall population. Random error represents how accurately the chosen sample's true average (mean) value reflects the population's true average (mean) value. For example, we might take a random sample of beer drinkers in Chicago and find that 16 percent regularly drink Coors beer. The next day we might repeat the same sampling procedure and discover that 14 percent regularly drink Coors beer. The difference is due to random error.

sample
A subset from a large population.

universe
The population from which a sample will be drawn.

probability sample
A sample in which every element in the population has a known statistical likelihood of being selected.

random sample
A sample arranged in such a way that every element of the population has an equal chance of being selected as part of the sample.

nonprobability sample
Any sample in which little or no attempt is made to get a representative cross section of the population.

convenience sample
A form of nonprobability sample using respondents who are convenient or readily accessible to the researcher—for example, employees, friends, or relatives.

measurement error
An error that occurs when there is a difference between the information desired by the researcher and the information provided by the measurement process.

sampling error
An error that occurs when a sample somehow does not represent the target population.

frame error
An error that occurs when a sample drawn from a population differs from the target population.

random error
An error that occurs because the selected sample is an imperfect representation of the overall population.

Exhibit **8.8**

Probability Samples	
Simple Random Sample	Every member of the population has a known and equal chance of selection.
Stratified Sample	Population is divided into mutually exclusive groups (such as gender or age), then random samples are drawn from *each* group.
Cluster Sample	Population is divided into mutually exclusive groups (such as geographic areas), then a random sample of clusters is selected. The researcher then collects data from all the elements in the selected clusters or from a probability sample of elements within each selected cluster.
Systematic Sample	A list of the population is obtained—i.e., all persons with a checking account at XYZ Bank—and a *skip interval* is obtained by dividing the sample size by the population size. If the sample size is 100 and the bank has 1,000 customers, then the skip interval is 10. The beginning number is randomly chosen within the skip interval. If the beginning number is 8, then the skip pattern would be 8, 18, 28, . . .
Nonprobability Samples	
Convenience Sample	The researcher selects the easiest population members from which to obtain information.
Judgment Sample	The researcher's selection criteria are based on personal judgment that the elements (persons) chosen will likely give accurate information.
Quota Sample	The researcher finds a prescribed number of people in several categories—i.e., owners of large dogs versus owners of small dogs. Respondents are not selected on probability sampling criteria.
Snowball Sample	The selection of additional respondents is made on the basis of referrals from the initial respondents. This is used when a desired type of respondent is hard to find—i.e., persons who have taken round-the-world cruises in the last three years. This technique employs the old adage "Birds of a feather flock together."

Collecting the Data

field service firm
A firm that specializes in interviewing respondents on a subcontracted basis.

Marketing research field service firms collect most primary data. A **field service firm** specializes in interviewing respondents on a subcontracted basis. Many have offices throughout the country. A typical marketing research study involves data collection in several cities, requiring the marketer to work with a comparable number of field service firms. To ensure uniformity among all subcontractors, detailed field instructions should be developed for every job. Nothing should be open to chance; no interpretations of procedures should be left to subcontractors.

Besides conducting interviews, field service firms provide focus group facilities, mall intercept locations, test product storage, and kitchen facilities to prepare test food products. They also conduct retail audits (counting the amount of a product sold off retail shelves). After an in-home interview is completed, field service supervisors validate the survey by recontacting about 15 percent of the respondents. The supervisors verify that certain responses were recorded properly and that the people were actually interviewed.

Analyzing the Data

After collecting the data, the marketing researcher proceeds to the next step in the research process: data analysis. The purpose of this analysis is to interpret and draw conclusions from the mass of collected data. The marketing researcher tries to organize and analyze those data by using one or more techniques common to marketing research: one-way frequency counts, cross-tabulations, and more sophisticated statistical analysis. Of these three techniques, one-way frequency counts are the simplest. One-way frequency tables record the responses to a question. For example, the answers to the question "What brand of microwave popcorn do you buy most often?" would provide a one-way frequency distribution. One-way frequency tables are always done in data analysis, at least as a first step, because they provide the researcher with a general picture of the study's results.

A **cross-tabulation**, or "cross-tab," lets the analyst look at the responses to one question in relation to the responses to one or more other questions. For example, what is the association between gender and the brand of microwave popcorn bought most frequently? Hypothetical answers to this question are shown in Exhibit 8.9. Although the Orville Reddenbacher brand was popular with both males and females, it was more popular with females. Compared with women, men strongly preferred Pop Rite, whereas women were more likely than men to buy Weight Watchers popcorn.

Researchers can use many other more powerful and sophisticated statistical techniques, such as hypothesis testing, measures of association, and regression analysis. A description of these techniques goes beyond the scope of this book but

cross-tabulation
A method of analyzing data that lets the analyst look at the responses to one question in relation to the responses to one or more other questions.

Exhibit 8.9

Hypothetical Cross-Tabulation Between Gender and Brand of Microwave Popcorn Purchased Most Frequently

Brand	Purchase by Gender	
	Male	Female
Orville Reddenbacher	31%	48%
T.V. Time	12	6
Pop Rite	38	4
Act Two	7	23
Weight Watchers	4	18
Other	8	0

can be found in any good marketing research textbook. The use of sophisticated statistical techniques depends on the researchers' objectives and the nature of the data gathered.

Preparing and Presenting the Report

After data analysis has been completed, the researcher must prepare the report and communicate the conclusions and recommendations to management. This is a key step in the process. If the marketing researcher wants managers to carry out the recommendations, he or she must convince them that the results are credible and justified by the data collected.

Researchers are usually required to present both written and oral reports on the project. These reports should be tailored to the audience. They should begin with a clear, concise statement of the research objectives, followed by a complete, but brief and simple, explanation of the research design or methodology employed. A summary of major findings should come next. The conclusion of the report should also present recommendations to management.

Most people who enter marketing will become research users rather than research suppliers. Thus, they must know what to notice in a report. As with many other items we purchase, quality is not always readily apparent. Nor does a high price guarantee superior quality. The basis for measuring the quality of a marketing research report is the research proposal. Did the report meet the objectives established in the proposal? Was the methodology outlined in the proposal followed? Are the conclusions based on logical deductions from the data analysis? Do the recommendations seem prudent, given the conclusions?

Another criterion is the quality of the writing. Is the style crisp and lucid? It has been said that if readers are offered the slightest opportunity to misunderstand, they probably will. The report should also be as concise as possible.

Following Up

The final step in the marketing research process is to follow up. The researcher should determine why management did or did not carry out the recommendations in the report. Was sufficient decision-making information included? What could have been done to make the report more useful to management? A good rapport between the product manager, or whoever authorized the project, and the market researcher is essential. Often they must work together on many studies throughout the year.

The Profound Impact of the Internet on Marketing Research

4

Discuss the profound impact of the Internet on marketing research

In many ways, the Internet has turned the world of marketing research upside-down. Old ways of conducting some types of research may soon seem as quaint as a steam-engine train. New techniques and new ways of conducting traditional marketing research are coming on-line in increasing numbers every day. By 2005, Internet marketing research will account for about 50 percent of all marketing research revenue in the United States.[10]

There are several reasons for the success of Internet marketing research:

- It allows for better and faster decision making through much more rapid access to business intelligence.
- It improves the ability to respond quickly to customer needs and market shifts.
- It makes the conducting of follow-up studies and longitudinal research easier and more fruitful.

On Line

- It slashes labor- and time-intensive research activities (and associated costs), including mailing, telephone solicitation, data entry, data tabulation, and reporting.[11]

Advantages of Internet Surveys

The huge growth in the popularity of Internet surveys is the result of the many advantages offered by the Internet. The specific advantages of Internet surveys are related to many factors:

- *Rapid development, real-time reporting:* Internet surveys can be broadcast to thousands of potential respondents simultaneously. Respondents complete surveys simultaneously, then results are tabulated and posted for corporate clients to view as the returns arrive. The result: survey results can be in a client's hands in significantly less time than would be required for traditional surveys.
- *Dramatically reduced costs:* The Internet can cut costs by 25 to 40 percent and provide results as fast as half the time it takes to do traditional telephone surveys. Data-collection costs account for a large proportion of any traditional market research budget. Telephone surveys are labor-intensive efforts incurring training, telecommunications, and management costs. Electronic methods eliminate these completely. While costs for traditional survey techniques rise proportionally with the number of interviews desired, electronic solicitations can grow in volume with little increase in project costs.
- *Personalized questions and data:* Internet surveys can be highly personalized for greater relevance to each respondent's own situation, thus speeding the response process. Respondents enjoy answering only pertinent questions, being able to pause and resume the survey as needed, having the ability to see previous responses and correct inconsistencies.
- *Improved respondent participation:* Busy respondents may be growing increasingly intolerant of "snail mail" or telephone-based surveys. Internet surveys take half the time to complete than phone interviews do, can be accomplished at the respondent's convenience (after work hours), and are much more stimulating and engaging. Graphics, interactivity, links to incentive sites and real-time summary reports make the interview enjoyable. The result? Much higher response rates.
- *Contact with the hard-to-reach:* Certain groups—doctors, high-income professionals, top management in Global 2000 firms—are among the most surveyed on the planet and the most difficult to reach. Many of these groups are well represented on-line. Internet surveys provide convenient anytime/anywhere access that makes it easy for busy professionals to participate.[12]

The rapid growth of Internet survey research is the result of mushrooming number of Americans on-line—the current estimate being approximately 40 percent. This in turn has meant that researchers are finding on-line and off-line research results are the same. For example, America Online's (AOL) Digital Marketing Services (DMS), an on-line research organization, has done a number of surveys with both on-line and off-line samples. DMS's clients include IBM, Eastman Kodak, and Procter & Gamble. In well over 100 side-by-side comparisons of on-line and off-line studies, both techniques led clients to the same business decisions.[13] The guidance one gets from both sets of data was the same.

Internet Samples Internet samples may be classified as unrestricted, screened, and recruited.[14] In an **unrestricted Internet sample**, anyone who desires can complete the questionnaire. It is fully self-selecting and probably representative of nothing except Web surfers. The problem is exacerbated if the same Internet user can access the questionnaire repeatedly. For example, *InfoWorld*, a computer user magazine, decided to conduct its Readers Choice survey for the first time on the Internet. The results were so skewed by repeat voting for one product that the

unrestricted Internet sample
A survey in which anyone with a computer and modem can fill out the questionnaire.

screened Internet sample
An Internet sample with quotas based on desired sample characteristics.

entire survey was publicly abandoned and the editor asked for readers' help to avoid the problem again. A simple solution to repeat respondents is to lock respondents out of the site after they have filled out the questionnaire.

Screened Internet samples adjust for the unrepresentativeness of the self-selected respondents by imposing quotas based on some desired sample characteristics. These are often demographic characteristics such as gender, income, and geographic region, or product-related criteria such as past purchase behavior, job responsibilities, or current product use. The applications for screened samples are generally similar to those for unrestricted samples.

Screened sample questionnaires typically use a branching or skip pattern for asking screening questions to determine whether or not the full questionnaire should be presented to a respondent. Some Web survey systems can make immediate market segment calculations that assign a respondent to a particular segment based on screening questions, then select the appropriate questionnaire to match the respondent's segment.

Alternatively, some Internet research providers maintain a "panel house" that recruits respondents who fill out a preliminary classification questionnaire. This information is used to classify respondents into demographic segments. Clients specify the desired segments, and the respondents who match the desired demographics are permitted to fill out the questionnaires of all clients who specify that segment.

recruited Internet sample
A sample in which respondents are prerecruited and must qualify to participate. They are then e-mailed a questionnaire or directed to a secure Web site.

Recruited Internet samples are used for targeted populations in surveys that require more control over the makeup of the sample. Respondents are recruited by telephone, mail, e-mail, or in person. After qualification, they are sent the questionnaire by e-mail or are directed to a Web site that contains a link to the questionnaire. At Web sites, passwords are normally used to restrict access to the questionnaire to the recruited sample members. Since the makeup of the sample is known, completions can be monitored, and follow-up messages can be sent to those who do not complete the questionnaire, in order to improve the participation rate.

Recruited samples are ideal in applications that already have a database from which to recruit the sample. For example, a good application would be a survey that used a customer database to recruit respondents for a purchaser satisfaction study.

Other Uses of the Internet by Marketing Researchers

Conducting surveys is not all of the Internet revolution in marketing research. The management of the research process and the dissemination of information have also been greatly enhanced by the Internet. Several key areas have been impacted by the Internet:

- *The distribution of requests for proposals (RFPs) and proposals:* Companies can now quickly and efficiently send RFPs to a select e-mail list of research suppliers. In turn, research suppliers can develop proposals and e-mail them back to clients. A process that used to take days using snail mail now occurs in a matter of hours.
- *Collaboration between the client and the research supplier in the management of a research project:* A researcher and client might both be looking at a proposal, RFP, report, or some type of statistical analysis at the same time on their computer screens while discussing it over the telephone. This is very powerful and efficient. Changes in the sample size, quotas, and other aspects of the research plan can be discussed and made immediately.
- *Data management and on-line analysis:* Clients can access their survey via the research supplier's secure Web site and monitor the data gathering in real time. The client can use sophisticated tools to actually do data analysis as the survey develops. This real time analysis may result in changes in the questionnaire,

IRI
BehaviorScan

Find out more about IRI's scanner technology at the BehaviorScan Web site. Based on what you see on the site, how popular is scanner research?
http://www.behaviorscan.com

On Line

sample size, or the types of respondents being interviewed. The research supplier and the client become partners in "just-in-time" marketing research.

- *Publication and distribution of reports:* Reports can be published to the Web directly from programs such as PowerPoint and all the latest versions of leading word processing, spreadsheet, and presentation software packages. This means that results are available to appropriate managers worldwide on an almost instantaneous basis. Reports can be searched for content of interest using the same Web browser used to view the report.
- *Viewing of oral presentations of marketing research surveys by widely scattered audiences:* By placing oral presentations on password protected Web sites, managers throughout the world can see and hear the actual client presentation. This saves time and money by avoiding the need for the managers to travel to a central meeting site.[15]

scanner-based research
A system for gathering information from a single group of respondents by continuously monitoring the advertising, promotion, and pricing they are exposed to and the things they buy.

BehaviorScan
A scanner-based research program that tracks the purchases of 3,000 households through store scanners.

InfoScan
A scanner-based sales-tracking service for the consumer packaged-goods industry.

Scanner-Based Research

Scanner-based research is a system for gathering information from a single group of respondents by continuously monitoring the advertising, promotion, and pricing they are exposed to and the things they buy. The variables measured are advertising campaigns, coupons, displays, and product prices. The result is a huge database of marketing efforts and consumer behavior. Scanner-based research is bringing ever closer the Holy Grail of marketing research: an accurate, objective picture of the direct causal relationship between different kinds of marketing efforts and actual sales.

Discuss the growing importance of scanner-based research

The two major scanner-based suppliers are Information Resources Incorporated (IRI) and the A.C. Nielsen Company. Each has about half the market. However, IRI is the founder of scanner-based research.

IRI's first product is called **BehaviorScan**. A household panel (a group of three thousand long-term participants in the research project) has been recruited and maintained in each BehaviorScan town. Panel members shop with an ID card, which is presented at the checkout in scanner-equipped grocery stores and drugstores, allowing IRI to track electronically each household's purchases, item by item, over time. It uses microcomputers to measure TV viewing in each panel household and can send special commercials to panel member television sets. With such a measure of household purchasing, it is possible to manipulate marketing variables, such as TV advertising or consumer promotions, or to introduce a new product and analyze real changes in consumer buying behavior.

IRI's most successful product is **InfoScan**—a scanner-based sales-tracking service for the consumer packaged-goods industry. Retail sales, detailed consumer purchasing information (including measurement of store loyalty and total grocery basket expenditures), and promotional activity by manufacturers and retailers are monitored and evaluated for all bar-coded products. Data are collected weekly from more than 31,000 supermarkets, drug stores, and mass merchandisers.[16]

IRI's BehaviorScan product allows IRI to track individual household purchases over time. Participants in the household panel present an ID card at the checkout of a scanner-equipped grocery store.

When Should Marketing Research Be Conducted?

When managers have several possible solutions to a problem, they should not instinctively call for marketing research. In fact, the first decision to make is whether to conduct marketing research at all.

Some companies have been conducting research in certain markets for many years. Such firms understand the characteristics of target customers and their likes and dislikes about existing products. Under these circumstances, further research would be repetitive and waste money. Procter & Gamble, for example, has extensive knowledge of the coffee market. After it conducted initial taste tests with Folgers Instant Coffee, P&G went into national distribution without further research. Consolidated Foods Kitchen of Sara Lee followed the same strategy with its frozen croissants, as did Quaker Oats with Chewy Granola Bars. This tactic, however, does not always work. P&G marketers thought they understood the pain reliever market thoroughly, so they bypassed market research for Encaprin aspirin in capsules. Because it lacked a distinct competitive advantage over existing products, however, the product failed and was withdrawn from the market.

Managers rarely have such great trust in their judgment that they would refuse more information if it were available and free. But they might have enough confidence that they would be unwilling to pay very much for the information or to wait a long time to receive it. The willingness to acquire additional decision-making information depends on managers' perceptions of its quality, price, and timing. Of course, if perfect information were available—that is, the data conclusively showed which alternative to choose—decision makers would be willing to pay more for it than for information that still left uncertainty. In summary, research should be undertaken only when the expected value of the information is greater than the cost of obtaining it.

Competitive Intelligence

Explain the concept of competitive intelligence

competitive intelligence (CI)
An intelligence system that helps managers assess their competition and vendors in order to become more efficient and effective competitors.

Derived from military intelligence, competitive intelligence is an important tool for helping a firm overcome a competitor's advantage. Specifically, competitive intelligence can help identify the advantage, play a major role in determining how the advantage was achieved, and then provide insights on how it was achieved.

Competitive intelligence (CI) is the creation of a system that helps managers assess their competitors and their vendors in order to become a more efficient and effective competitor. Intelligence is analyzed information. It becomes decision-making intelligence when it has implications for the organization. For example, a primary competitor may have plans to introduce a product with performance standards equal to ours but with a 15 percent cost advantage. The new product will reach the market in eight months. This intelligence has important decision-making and policy consequences for management. Competitive intelligence and environmental scanning (where management gathers data about the external environment—see Chapter 2) combine to create marketing intelligence. Marketing intelligence is then used as input into a marketing decision support system.

Advantages of Competitive Intelligence
CI is one of the hottest areas in marketing today. Firms like General Motors, Ford, GTW, P&G Industries, AT&T, Motorola, and many others have large, well-established CI units. Aided by CI, the Ford Taurus came about after Ford engineers examined competitors' cars and incorporated the best features into one auto.[17]

CI helps managers assess their competition and their vendors, which, in turn, means fewer surprises. Competitive intelligence allows managers to predict changes in business relationships, identify marketplace opportunities, guard against threats, forecast a competitor's strategy, discover new or potential competitors, learn from the success or failure of others, learn about new technologies that can affect the company, and learn about the impact of government regulations on the competition. In summary, CI promotes effective and efficient decision making, which should lead to greater profitability. Sheena Sharp, Principal, Sharp Information Research, says: "CI gives the company the competitive advantage of foresight and allows it to learn today what will be discovered by others tomorrow."[18]

Several years ago NutraSweet's patent on the artificial sweetener *aspartame* was expiring and the company faced potential disaster. Management was afraid that chemical and food companies would move into the market. NutraSweet analyzed competitors' prices, customer relations, expansion plans, and advertising campaigns. The company used the information to cut costs, improve service, and preserve most of its market. "We maintained over 80 percent of our market," said NutraSweet Company's Robert E. Flynn. He said that competitive intelligence practices are worth $50 million a year to his company.

Sources of Competitive Intelligence

The Internet and its databases are a great source of competitive intelligence. A CI researcher can use Internet databases to answer these and other questions:

- What articles were written about this market?
- What companies are associated with this product group?
- What patents have been filed for this technology?
- What are the major magazines or texts in this industry?
- What are the chances that I will find something in print on the target company?
- How many companies are in the same industry as the target company?
- Who are the reporters studying this industry?
- How can I be updated on industry and company events without having to constantly request the information?
- How can I compile a list of the leading experts in the industry and the key institutions they are associated with?

Non–computer-based sources of competitive intelligence can be found in a variety of areas:

- Company's salespeople, who can directly observe and ask questions about the competition.
- Experts with in-depth knowledge of a subject or activity.
- CI Consultants, who can use their knowledge and experience to gather needed information quickly and efficiently.
- Government Agencies, a valuable source of all types of data.
- Uniform Commercial Code Filings (UCC), a system that identifies goods that are leased or pledged as collateral. An excellent source for learning about a company's latest additions to plant assets.
- Suppliers, a group that may offer information on products shipped to a competitor.
- Periodicals, a good source for timely articles on successes, failures, opportunities, and threats.
- Yellow Pages, which often provide data on number of competitors, trading areas, and special offerings.
- Trade shows, official gatherings where competitors display their latest offerings.

This list is not exhaustive but it does provide an idea of how CI can be gathered.

Read more about competitive intelligence in the extra module on your *Marketing* CD-ROM.

Look back at the story about Juicy Fruit gum at the beginning of this chapter. A company can use survey research, observations, or experiments to conduct marketing research.

Unless a company has extensive knowledge of the problem at hand, which is based on research, it should probably conduct marketing research. Yet, managers should also be reasonably sure that the cost of gathering the information will be less than the value of the data gathered.

Key marketing data often come from a company's own decision support system, which continually gathers data from a variety of sources and funnels it to decision makers. It then manipulates the data to make better decisions. DSS data are often supplemented by marketing research information.

Use it Now!

As a consumer, you participate in shaping consumer products by the choices you make and the products and services you buy. You can become a better consumer by actively participating in marketing surveys and learning more about the products you buy.

Participate in Marketing Research Surveys

All of us get tired of telephone solicitations where people try to sell us everything from new carpet to chimney cleaning. Recognize that marketing research surveys are different. A true marketing research survey will *never* involve a sales pitch nor will the research firm sell your name to a database marketer. The purpose of marketing research is to build better goods and services for you and me. If you help out such researchers, you ultimately help yourself. The Council for Marketing and Opinion Research (CMOR) is an organization of hundreds of marketing research professionals that is dedicated to preserving the integrity of the research industry. If you receive a call from someone who tries to sell you something under the guise of marketing research, get the name and address of the organization. Call CMOR at 1 (800) 887-CMOR and report the abuse.

Summary

① Explain the concept and purpose of a marketing decision support system. Decision support systems make data instantly available to marketing managers and allow them to manipulate the data themselves to make marketing decisions. Four characteristics of decision support systems make them especially useful to marketing managers: They are interactive, flexible, discovery oriented, and accessible. Decision support systems give managers access to information immediately and without outside assistance. They allow users to manipulate data in a variety of ways and to answer "what if" questions. And, finally, they are accessible to novice computer users.

② Define marketing research and explain its importance to marketing decision making. Marketing research is a process of collecting and analyzing data for the purpose of solving specific marketing problems. Marketers use marketing research to explore the profitability of marketing strategies. They can examine why particular strategies failed and analyze characteristics of specific market segments. Managers can use research findings to help keep current customers. Moreover, marketing research allows management to behave proactively rather than reactively by identifying newly emerging patterns in society and the economy.

③ Describe the steps involved in conducting a marketing research project. The marketing research process involves several basic steps. First, the researcher and the decision maker must agree on a problem statement or set of research objectives. The researcher then creates an overall research design to specify how primary data will be gathered and analyzed. Before collecting data, the researcher decides whether the group to be interviewed will be a probability or nonprobability sample. Field service firms are often hired to carry out data collection. Once data have been collected, the researcher analyzes them using statistical analysis. The researcher then prepares and presents oral and written reports, with conclusions and recommendations, to management. As a final step, the researcher determines whether the recommendations were implemented and what could have been done to make the project more successful.

4 **Discuss the profound impact of the Internet on marketing research.** The Internet has vastly simplified the secondary data search process, placing more sources of information in front of researchers than ever before. Internet survey research is surging in popularity. Internet surveys can be created rapidly and reported in real time. They are also relatively inexpensive and can be easily personalized. Often researchers can contact respondents who are difficult to reach via the Internet. The Internet can also be used to distribute research proposals and reports and to facilitate collaboration between the client and the research supplier. Clients can access real-time data and analyze it as the collection process continues.

5 **Discuss the growing importance of scanner-based research.** A scanner-based research system enables marketers to monitor a market panel's exposure and reaction to such variables as advertising, coupons, store displays, packaging, and price. By analyzing these variables in relation to the panel's subsequent buying behavior, marketers gain useful insight into sales and marketing strategies.

6 **Explain the concept of competitive intelligence.** Competitive intelligence (CI) is the creation of an intelligence system that helps managers assess their competition and their vendors in order to become more efficient and effective competitors. Intelligence is analyzed information, and it becomes decision-making intelligence when it has implications for the organization.

CI helps managers assess their competition and vendors. It leads to fewer surprises. CI allows managers to predict changes in business relationships, guard against threats, forecast a competitor's strategy, and develop a successful marketing plan.

The Internet and databases accessed by the Internet offer excellent sources of CI. Company personnel, particularly sales and service representatives, are usually good sources of CI. Many companies require their salespersons to routinely fill out CI reports. Other external sources of competitive intelligence include experts, CI consultants, government agencies, UCC filings, suppliers, newspapers and other publications, Yellow Pages, and trade shows.

Discussion and Writing Questions

1. The task of marketing is to create exchanges. What role might marketing research play in the facilitation of the exchange process?
2. Marketing research has traditionally been associated with manufacturers of consumer goods. Today, we are experiencing an increasing number of organizations, both profit and nonprofit, using marketing research. Why do you think this trend exists? Give some examples.
3. **WRITING** Write a reply to the following statement: "I own a restaurant in the downtown area. I see customers every day whom I know on a first-name basis. I understand their likes and dislikes. If I put something on the menu and it doesn't sell, I know that they didn't like it. I also read the magazine *Modern Restaurants*, so I know what the trends are in the industry. This is all of the marketing research I need to do."
4. Give an example of (a) the descriptive role of marketing research, (b) the diagnostic role, and (c) the predictive function of marketing research.

5. Critique the following methodologies and suggest more appropriate alternatives:
   a. A supermarket was interested in determining its image. It dropped a short questionnaire into the grocery bag of each customer before putting in the groceries.
   b. To assess the extent of its trade area, a shopping mall stationed interviewers in the parking lot every Monday and Friday evening. Interviewers walked up to persons after they had parked their cars and asked them for their zip codes.
   c. To assess the popularity of a new movie, a major studio invited people to call a 900 number and vote yes, they would see it again, or no, they would not. Each caller was billed a $2 charge.

6. **WRITING** You have been charged with determining how to attract more business majors to your school. Write an outline of the steps you would take, including the sampling procedures, to accomplish the task.

7. Why is secondary data sometimes preferred to primary data?

8. In the absence of company problems, is there any reason to develop a marketing decision support system?

9. Discuss when focus groups should and should not be used.

10. **TEAM** Divide the class into teams of eight persons. Each group will conduct a focus group on the quality and number of services that your college is providing to its students. One person from each group should be chosen to act as moderator. Remember, it is the moderator's job to facilitate discussion, not to lead the discussion. These groups should last approximately forty-five minutes. If possible, the groups should be videotaped or recorded. Upon completion, each group should write a brief report of its results. Consider offering to meet with the dean of students to share the results of your research.

11. Why do you think that CI is so hot in today's environment?

12. **WRITING** Prepare a memo to your boss at United Airlines and outline why the organization needs a CI unit.

13. **TEAM** Form a team with three other students. Each team must choose a firm in the PC manufacturing industry and then go to the Web site of the firm and acquire as much competitive intelligence as possible. Each team will then prepare a five-minute oral presentation on its findings.

14. **ON LINE** Use the Internet and a Web browser, such as Lycos or Yahoo!, and type "marketing research." You will then have thousands of options. Pick a Web site that you find interesting and report on its content to the class.

15. **ON LINE** Why has the Internet been of such great value to researchers seeking secondary data?

16. **ON LINE** Go to **http://www.yankelovich.com**. Explain to the class the nature and scope of the Yankelovich MONITOR. How can marketing researchers use the data from this research?

17. **ON LINE** Go to **http://www.icpsr.umich.edu/gss**. What is the General Social Survey? Compare and contrast its usefulness to marketing researchers with the Yankelovich MONITOR.

18. **ON LINE** You are interested in home-building trends in the United States because your company (Whirlpool) is a major supplier of kitchen appliances. Go to **http://www.nahb.com** and describe what types of information at this site might be of interest to Whirlpool.

19. **ON LINE** What are the advantages and disadvantages of conducting surveys on the Internet?

20.  Explain the three types of Internet samples and discuss why a researcher might choose one over the other.

21. Go to **http://www.raosoft.com/raosoft** and explain how the company's software lets you distribute questionnaires over the Internet.

22. Go to **http://acop.com/** and tell the class about the site and what type of Internet sample is being drawn. Also, describe the types of surveys being taken.

23. Go to **http://www.autonomy.com/** and explain what type of marketing research resources are offered at the site.

24. Go to **http://www.acnielsen.com** and **http://www.infores.com** and determine what A.C. Nielsen and IRI are saying on the Web about their latest scanner-based technology.

25. Participate in a survey at one of the following URLs and report your experience to the class:

- GVU Semiannual Survey on Web Usage
  http://www.cc.gatech.edu/gvu/user_surveys/
- Personality test
  http://www.users.interport.net/~zang/personality.html
- Emotional intelligence test
  http://www.utne.com/lens/bms/9bmseq.html
- Values and Lifestyles (VALS) test
  http://future.sri.com/vals/valshome.html
- On-line transactions and privacy survey
  http://www.hermes.bus.umich.edu/cgi-gin/spsurvey/questi.pl
- Various on-line surveys on topics like politics and consumer trends
  http://www.survey.net/
- Prudential Securities Investment Personality Quiz
  http://www.prusec.com/quiz.htm
- Various surveys
  http://www.dssresearch.com/mainsite/surveys.htm

26. Go to **http://emporium.turnpike.net/** and explain how this site can yield competitive intelligence.

Application for Entrepreneurs

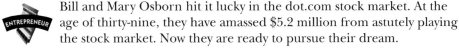 Bill and Mary Osborn hit it lucky in the dot.com stock market. At the age of thirty-nine, they have amassed $5.2 million from astutely playing the stock market. Now they are ready to pursue their dream.

The Osborns have always wanted to live in Colorado and have dreamed of owning a small hotel. Mary hit upon the idea of doing both—that is, building a hotel in Colorado that they could manage. Initial research uncovered the following information.

When asked which two or three things are most important in choosing a hotel for a vacation, Americans put nonsmoking rooms first (40 percent). Twenty-four-hour access to food (36 percent), quality in-room amenities such as coffeemakers and hair dryers (34 percent), athletic facilities (31 percent), and "good evening facilities" (26 percent) are next. They rank supervised activities for children much higher than business travelers (10 percent versus 3 percent).

Overnight business travelers, who traveled in the past year, in contrast, focus on things that will make their trip more productive. Like vacationers, they rate nonsmoking rooms tops (46 percent). But they put quality in-room amenities (39 percent) and transportation to the airport (32 percent) next. And, while they cite many of the same things as vacationers as also being important, they put a much higher priority on some things, particularly in-room connections for computer, fax, and on-line access (21 percent, seventeen points higher than vacationers), being able to earn airline miles (15 percent, up 8), and frequent guest programs (14 percent, up 5).

Questions

Use the Internet to help determine the following:
1. What price range should be offered?
2. Where in Colorado should the hotel be built?
3. Should the hotel cater primarily to business or vacation travelers?
4. What amenities and features should the hotel offer?
5. Should Mary and Bill consider becoming a franchisee?

Case

entrepreneurship

PlanetFeedback.com
The Voice of One. The Power of Many.

The security of a large, world-renowned company was not enough to satisfy interactive marketing specialist Pete Blackshaw, who left Procter & Gamble in October 1999 to start his own business, PlanetFeedback.com. As a service provider, PlanetFeedback offers consumers a streamlined connection to companies where they can voice complaints, offer praise, or just reach the right person quickly.

Market research found that while many have the desire only one in twenty-five consumers actually provide positive or negative feedback to companies. Basically, the barriers—not being able to find a company address and the time involved in preparing a letter—are too high. To counteract these barriers, PlanetFeedback's dynamic letter generator helps users by providing an e-mail letter template, ensuring that the e-mail gets to the right person (via the company's database

of companies), and copying other involved parties as well as the appropriate government and consumer agencies. To this end, the company's slogan is "The voice of one. The power of many."

PlanetFeedback will not make money from consumers using the service, nor will it accept advertising on its Web site. The company plans to make money by selling the consumer information it collects to company marketers. This information will include reports on how consumers view competitors in a particular product market. For example, American Airlines can buy information about consumers' views of all service providers in the airline industry.

Blackshaw feels that the real power of PlanetFeedback lies in its ability to identify and track influential consumers. The company will monitor the type of feedback (positive or negative) a person sends to a company, as well as the type of people copied on the correspondence (e.g., relative, friend, government agency). From this information, the company will develop a "viral index" that will identify influential consumers for particular product categories. PlanetFeedback will be able to provide businesses with virtual groups of their most influential consumers—the consumers who tend to tell others what they think about products or services. Corporations can then target information to these consumers who can then spread positive word-of-mouth about the product or service, or the company could use these influencers to test new product concepts. Longer term, the company plans to form the Viral Consumer Consortium, a group of business leaders, senior managers, and academics from marketing and consumer research who will study the phenomenon of word-of-mouth referral and influence in the Internet world.

In December 1999 Blackshaw secured an initial $16 million in venture financing. Institutional investors in the start-up included Flatiron Partners, Lycos Ventures, Allen & Company, and Blue Chip Venture Company. By June 2000, the company had netted an additional $25 million in its second round of institutional funding. Financiers in this second round included many existing investors as well as General Atlantic Partners (leading the deal with $14.4 million), Protos LLC, and N.J. Nicholas (former CEO at Time Warner).

As is typical with start-ups, PlanetFeedback is not yet making money. To do this, the company will have to establish itself as a premier destination for consumer complaints and praises. It has to do this amidst competition from other Internet start-ups such as Feedback Direct, uGripe, eComplaints, speakout, and Epinions. What is unique about PlanetFeedback.com that will drive consumers to their Web site and thus provide the company with the ability to collect and sell market research?

Questions

1. What is PlanetFeedback.com—a customer service provider or a market research provider?
2. Why would venture capitalists invest in a company such as PlanetFeedback?
3. What is unique about PlanetFeedback that will drive consumers to its Web site?
4. What is PlanetFeedback offering businesses that traditional market research firms cannot offer?

Bibliography

Anonymous. "PlanetFeedback.com Launches New Web Channel for Consumer Power." *Business Wire*, February 17, 2000. On-line.

Anonymous. "PlanetFeedback.com Spearheads New Viral Consumer Consortium." *Business Wire*, May 9, 2000. On-line.

Jeff Neff. "PlanetFeedback Wants Consumers' Comments: Dot-com Appraisals, Supplies Marketers Data." *Advertising Age*, December 13, 1999. On-line, Crain Communications.

Dan Primack. "VCs Land on PlanetFeedback.com," *Private Equity Week.* June 5, 2000. On-line, Securities Data Publishing.

Case

video

Burke Marketing Research: The Right Way to Make the Right Decision

Accurate and timely information is the lifeblood of marketing decision making. With good information, a company can increase sales and use its resources wisely. At Burke Marketing Research, planning, collecting, and analyzing data is an integral part of helping clients make key decisions by answering important questions. What is the historic sales trend in the industry? What was the impact of a change in package design on sales? What if we change flavors? To answer questions like these, Burke has developed several research methods that examine and diagnose common marketing problems. The methods result from years of experience dealing with recurrent marketing problems across many industry and product categories. Some of these methods include PricePoint, STAGES, and ICE, or Integrated Concept Evaluation System.

PricePoint is a research method designed for use within the communications and technology industry. It is ideal for new products or services that are so original that buyers cannot compare them with other products on the market. As part of the PricePoint research, Burke interviews potential buyers and describes and demonstrates the new product or service idea. After that, researchers ask key questions to measure perceptions about price and willingness to pay. These results are used in a model that can estimate demand for the new product at various price levels. In the face of brutal competition, Burke's clients receive the edge they need to make decisions about a new product based on possible demand. With tools like this, companies can then set solid pricing strategies.

Another useful research method Burke offers its clients is STAGES. This model was developed to learn how attitudes affect each of the five stages of the buying process: awareness, consideration, trial, adoption, and customer loyalty. STAGES can answer several important questions: How does awareness become a willingness to buy? Why do some buyers reject products? Why do others become loyal customers? At Burke, researchers picture the purchase decision process as a funnel, where customers are lost at each stage. This loss occurs because customers lack awareness, have misperceptions, or do not have needs that match the product messages. The goal of STAGES is to help Burke's clients reduce the number of customers lost at each step in the buying process.

With STAGES, Burke can also respond to research findings that show that customers continuously evaluate products and services throughout the buying process but use different criteria at each stage. For example, a product must meet one set of requirements to get considered and another set for purchase on a trial basis. Once tried, there may be different requirements for a product to be adopted or bought repeatedly. Burke's customized STAGES model can identify the key attributes that drive each stage of a purchase, simulate these changes in attributes, and predict the overall effect on purchase decisions.

PricePoint and STAGES are not, however, always used alone. Burke researchers can combine them to produce a more detailed analysis for a client. An integrated approach helps a company understand the ever-changing dynamics of the market so it can seize the best business opportunity. One integrated approach employed by Burke is called ICE, or Integrated Concept Evaluation system. This model combines several research methods to help clients select which product idea would best meet the customer's need. One of Burke's clients was a major communications company that wanted to explore consumer interest in several new product ideas. These concepts were so innovative that there was no framework in place for comparing them to each other or to existing products, or for determining what price consumers would be willing to pay. The client needed information about the potential demand for each product concept under various pricing plans. In addition, the client wanted to be able to evaluate the specific benefits associated with each product. This information would be helpful in providing direction for future communications campaigns. The ICE research model used a combination of methods, including PricePoint and another method to evaluate benefits called Benefit Deficiency Analysis, to help the communications company map out a product development strategy.

To support all its customized models, Burke uses proven data collection methods such as focus groups, mail and telephone surveys, and mall intercepts. The completed research leads to results that, once interpreted, serve as the basis for the research analysis. This analysis is communicated clearly and concisely to the client in the research report, which in turn helps the company make better decisions and develop better products and services to satisfy customers. In every business relationship, Burke picks the right research method to help clients make the right decisions.

Questions

1. Does Burke fulfill the roles of marketing research as described in the chapter? Explain.
2. What are the ways that Burke benefits a client?
3. How does Burke improve the quality of decision making for its clients?
4. How does Burke keep its clients competitive?

Quiz yourself using this exciting marketing game where the questions on all topics start easy and get progressively harder. This is Marketing!

who wants to be a marketer?

click here!

So you want to be a marketer? Put your knowledge to the test.

Closing 2

MARKETING MISCUES

Taking the Haughty Out of Haute Links

Why would a Californian (or anyone for that matter) prefer a fast-food burger or hot dog, fries, and diet soda to a healthy, gourmet sausage sandwich accompanied by a premium microbrew? Unfortunately, Haute Links, located in Lake Forest, California, has been experiencing flat sales in a market in which it is the only hot dog restaurant. How did this small business owner get himself into such a pickle?

Lake Forest, California, boasts slightly over a hundred restaurants with a wide range of fare—from specialty foreign cuisine (Chinese, French, Italian, Japanese, Mexican, Mongolian, Persian, Peruvian, Thai, Vietnamese) to fast food from McDonald's, Burger King, and Wendy's. The city has around twelve sandwich shops that specialize in sandwiches and/or subs. Of all of these restaurants in Lake Forest, Haute Links is the only "real" hot dog shop.

Hot dog shops are rather popular in southern California. The hot dog restaurant business is dominated by Wienerschnitzel, the largest hot dog fast-food chain in the world. The company sells over 70 million hot dogs a year in its 300 plus restaurants, with over 200 of these shops located in California. In addition, Dodger Stadium in Los Angeles, California, is the national top seller of hot dogs during the baseball season. Of the almost 27 million hot dogs eaten during baseball games, Dodger fans consume around 1.3 million "Dodger Dogs." Even with this large volume, hot dogs command less than 5 percent of annual food court sales and only around 10 percent of annual retail store sales.

Sales of Haute Links' sausages were flat at $250,000 in 1999. With "health" as a main selling point, the restaurant's marketing program focuses on the nutritional benefits of the shop's private-label links. In a product market where there are around 100 varieties of sausages, the links (ground turkey, chicken, spices, and cheese) at Haute Links have less fat (even when loaded with toppings) than most burgers, burritos, or subs. As such, the owner posted these health benefits on the restaurant's walls, menus, and windows. Initial advertising consisted of discounts in the local shopper and coupons in mass mailings.

As a small business, however, the shop cannot survive on flat and lower than expected annual sales. An evaluation of Haute Link's marketing strategy revealed the following:

- The shop was wasting dollars on people who would never try the product—no matter how low fat or high quality.
- The owner had forgotten that a sausage sandwich is a want—not a need.
- The owner had failed to focus upon the product's main selling point—taste.

An informal survey of Haute Links' customers found that 80 percent of the customer base was men. The shop's initial marketing strategy had focused upon the idea that anyone could be converted to a sausage eater if the sausage was healthy. Therefore, the taste of the sandwich was not receiving its due attention in a market with plenty of alternative product offerings.

To rectify past mistakes, the owner has been advised to stop trying to convince all consumers that sausage is good for them. In doing this, the shop has been reminded that it is really only selling sausage—not a prestigious product in the grand scheme of restaurant foods. The new marketing communications will focus upon "guy advertising" with a lighthearted tone. Suggested tag lines include: "Guys love us. Spare tires hate us" and "Sausage that's probably healthier than you are."

Questions for Discussion

1. Describe the market segment Haute Links was targeting in its initial marketing program. How does this segment compare to the "new" market segment?
2. How does relationship marketing fit into the marketing strategy at Haute Links?

Bibliography

Janet Riley and James Ratchford. "Americans Expected to Enjoy 26.5 Million Hot Dogs During 2000 Baseball Season." Online: **http://www.hot-dog.org**.
http://www.wienerschnitzel.com
Cyndia Zwahlen. "Small Business: Sandwich Shop Seeks Elusive Link to Success." *Los Angeles Times*, March 15, 2000, p. C6.

CRITICAL THINKING CASE

Redefining Prices at Priceline

Founded by forty-six-year-old Jay Walker in 1998, Price-line.com is not a typical dot-com business. From a dot-com selling perspective, the company is the pioneer in the e-commerce system referred to as "demand collection." Basically, Priceline.com matches consumer demand (at a price set by the consumer) with a supplier willing to provide the product or service at the price named by the consumer. It is very unlike bricks and clicks companies that place their catalogs on the Web. From an organizational perspective, company executives are not twenty-somethings wearing jeans and T-shirts. Executives, recruited from companies such as Citigroup and AT&T, often wear suits to work. Additionally, the company is not located in the hotbed of dot-com companies on the West Coast. Rather, company headquarters are on the eastern seaboard of the United States in a suburban office park.

Success at Priceline.com is atypical as well. Using the "name your own price" tag line, the company has proved to be very successful in the consumer market. With more than two million customers in the consumer market, revenue growth for the company was predicted to be 130 percent in 2000. Priceline.com is planning, however, for a portion of this 130 percent revenue growth to come from its entry into the business-to-business (B2B) market.

Priceline's Demand Collection System

Fulfilling its mission to connect all of its customers to the things they need on their own terms, Priceline.com's demand collection system allows consumers to use the Internet to save money on various products and services. Priceline's system relies upon sellers that have excess supply—with the proposition that selling the excess at the price the consumer is willing to pay generates incremental revenue.

Purchasing on Priceline.com requires the consumer to request a product or service at a particular price. The offer is guaranteed by the buyer's credit card and held open for a specified period of time so that Priceline can work with its suppliers. Priceline communicates the individual's request to participating sellers in its network. If the request is satisfied—the product or service can be provided at the requested price—the order is fulfilled with no cancellation options.

Product Lines

By mid-2000, Priceline.com provided buying and selling consumer market opportunities across four product cat-egories: travel, home finance, automotive, and telecommunications. Additionally, the company offered two services through affiliated companies, WebHouse Club and Perfect YardSale.

The purchasing of *travel services* on the Web was one of the earliest e-commerce entries. Companies such as Travelocity.com and Expedia.com began providing on-line travel service in the mid- to late-1990s. Additionally, individual travel providers (e.g., airlines, car rental companies, and hotels) began to offer on-line reservations systems. By 2000, travel was the single largest retail category on the Internet. Of the $7 billion booked on-line, $5 billion were airline reservations, $1 billion were hotel rooms, and $630 million were car rental reservations. However, only around 3 percent of all travel arrangements were made on-line.

It was estimated that 5 million airline seats were flown empty each week, with Priceline.com selling about 100,000 seats weekly. Priceline.com's hotel service included hotels in 1,200 locations throughout the United States. The company's hotel service was booking around 20,000 hotel rooms a week in 2000.

The company's *home finance service* linked consumers with providers of mortgages, home equity loans, and refinancing. Through the Priceline mortgage offering, Priceline.com could connect customers with financial service providers who would guarantee/lock-in the interest rate and closing costs within one hour of the customer's offer.

By the middle of 2000, Priceline's *automotive service* allowed consumers in twenty-six states to select a car and name a price for the car. Priceline.com would then attempt to find the car for the consumer at the requested price. The consumer did not have to do anything beyond making the on-line request.

In early 2000, Priceline.com began offering a *telecommunications service.* The long-distance calling service could save consumers up to 40 percent on most standard base rates on monthly U.S. and international long-distance calls.

Through its WebHouse Club affiliate, consumers could name their own price for groceries. After naming the price on-line, consumers would pick up the groceries at their local supermarket. While savings could climb to 40 percent of the grocery bill, Priceline abandoned this service before the national rollout because the company was underwriting the millions of dollars saved itself.

From the Consumer Market to the B2B Market

Less than two years after the start of company operations, Priceline.com made plans to begin serving the business-to-business marketplace in the telecommunications field. The initial product offering was "name-your-own price" long-distance phone service.

Within months of this initial B2B offering, Priceline.com and American Express formed a marketing alliance. The purpose of this alliance was for American Express to market Priceline's B2B portal to its two million small business customers. These customers would then receive a 5 percent discount on all purchases on Priceline.com. In turn, Priceline.com would promote American Express small business cards to its customers, who could apply for an AMEX card while on-line at Priceline.com. All new accounts generated via Priceline.com would have a $25 credit on Priceline.com purchases.

Future B2B market entries were expected to include media buying, freight and cargo, and office equipment.

Questions for Discussion

1. Describe the consumer buying process at Priceline.com.
2. Will this buying process differ in the B2B market?
3. What are similarities/differences between Priceline's consumer market customer base and the new B2B customer base?

Bibliography

Karin Price Mueller. "Priceline.com Has Little to Fear from Competition." *Boston Herald,* March 23, 2000, p. 37.

Allen Myerson. "Behind 'Name Your Own Price' Lies a Mesh of Partners." *New York Times,* March 29, 2000, p. H24.

Anne Newman. "Priceline Piles into B2B Services." *Business Week,* March 20, 2000, p. 50.

http://www.priceline.com

MARKETING PLANNING ACTIVITIES

Analyzing Marketing Opportunities

The next step in preparing a marketing plan for the company you have already chosen is to get a thorough understanding of the marketing opportunities in terms of marketing to customers. The following activities will help you better understand the marketplace, which will increase your chances of success in developing an appropriate marketing mix. Also refer to Exhibit 2.8 for additional marketing plan subjects.

1. Identify the NAIC code for your chosen company's industry. Perform a brief industry analysis (from U.S. *Industrial Outlook,* for example) of your firm's industry, based on the NAIC code.
2. To whom does your company market (consumer, industrial, government, not-for-profit, or a combination of targets)? Within each market, are there specific segments or niches that your company can concentrate on? If so, which one(s) would you focus on and why? What are the factors used to create these segments?

Marketing*Builder* Exercise
- **Market Segment** portion of the **Market Analysis** template

3. Describe your company's target market segment(s). Use demographics, pyschographics, geographics, economic factors, size, growth rates, trends, SIC codes, and any other appropriate descriptors.

Marketing*Builder* Exercise
- **Customer Profile** portion of the **Market Analysis** template

4. Describe the decision-making process that customers go through when purchasing your company's product or service. What are the critical factors that influence this purchase-behavior process?
5. Choose four characteristics of your firm's product offering. Using these factors for axes, draw two positioning grids and fill in the quadrants with competitor's offerings as well as your own. Are there any "holes" of needs and wants that are not being filled?

Marketing*Builder* Exercise
- **Positioning** portion of the **Marketing Communications** template

6. Are there critical issues that must be explored with primary marketing research before you can implement your marketing plan? These might include items such as customer demand, purchase intentions, customer perceptions of product quality, price perceptions, and reaction to critical promotion.

Marketing*Builder* Exercises
- **Product Launch Chart** spreadsheet
- **Operating Budget** spreadsheet
- **Sales Forecast and Analysis** spreadsheet

E-MARKETING PLANNING ACTIVITIES

In the first part of your strategic e-marketing plan, you stated your business mission and objectives, and performed a detailed situation analysis, including internal company strengths and weaknesses and external environmental opportunities and threats. Recall that you are either doing a strategic marketing plan for an existing bookstore retailer with a new on-line presence, or a dot-com bookstore retailer, or a company of your own choosing.

For continued general assistance on business plans and marketing plans, visit **http://www.bplans.com** or **http://www.businessplans.org**. For electronic sources of information, search on the Electric Library at **http://wwws.elibrary.com** or the Internet Public Library at **http://www.ipl.org**. Another excellent source of information is the Sales and Marketing Executives Marketing Library at **http://www.sell.org**. You should also refer to Exhibit 2.8 for additional marketing plan checklist items (Part IV.A.: Target Market Strategy).

The next stage of the strategic planning process involves further investigation of Internet opportunities, with a special focus on potential customers. Try to understand both consumer and business decision making because Internet businesses can be built to serve either market. In fact, most experts predict the business-to-business sector of the Internet to be several times larger than the business-to-consumer sector. Knowing how to perform marketing research to find out more about both customers and competitors is key for any strategic marketing plan.

Use the following exercises to guide you through the second part of your strategic e-marketing plan:

1. To analyze market opportunities within your industry, first find the NAIC or SIC code of your company. You can find SIC codes at **http://www.wave.net/upg/immigration/sic_index.html**. These codes will help you perform further research. For example, register with the free site **http://www.zapdata.com** and get market analyses and profiles for your firm and industry. The Statistical Data Locators site (**http://www.ntu.edu.sg/library/stat/statdata.htm**) is another good collection of statistical and economic sources from countries and regions outside the United States.
2. List all the markets (either consumer or business-to-business) that are potential customers of your organization. Try to identify segments within each of these markets. What are the Internet capabilities in those markets? Does the fact that you are trying to encourage those segments to access your product or service via the Internet change which segments are most important to your business? How? What are the factors used to create these segments? Which segments should your company focus on and why? A resource indicating segment-specific resources is available at **http://www.awool.com/awool**. Additionally, the U.S. Census has a number of databases you can access with statistics for different marketing segments at **http://tier2.census.gov/dbappweb.htm**. You can also look at the unique challenges of business-to-business e-marketing at **http://www.biz2biz.com**.
3. Describe your company's selected target market segment(s). Use demographics, geographics, psychographics, size, growth, and any other appropriate descriptors. What role does the Internet play in your target market's life? How is the target market for your Internet business different from that of a traditional business in your market? Then describe the likely decision-making processes that customers go through when purchasing your firm's offering. How will this decision-making affect your e-marketing focus and your market offering? If you have a brick-and-mortar presence, will you encourage any existing customers to shop on-line? Why?
4. Using the list of key differential advantages described in the first part of your e-marketing plan, create a series of positioning grids, using two factors each as dimensions (see Exhibit 7.11 for an example). Then plot the list of key competitors identified earlier onto these positioning grids. Is your company too close to a key competitor? Are there spaces where consumer needs and wants are unsatisfied? Check out the concepts and models used by Positioning Strategies at **http://www.positioning.com** to increase your understanding of positioning strategies. Consider how the Internet changes what factors are important to your success in your market space. Is technology the most important factor for your firm, or are there other ways for you to differentiate from and beat your competition?
5. What types of primary marketing research will you need to collect to support the assumptions and objectives in your e-marketing plan? Often, marketing research is a key requirement before implementation. List some critical research questions and decide which form of research you would use. Design a brief Internet customer satisfaction survey that you could place on your Web site. Use the "Survey Wiz" to help you with your questionnaire at **http://psych.fullerton.edu/mbirnbaum/programs/surveyWiz.HTM**. Also check out Insight Express at **http://www.insightexpress.com**.

6. What type of competitive intelligence will you need to gather in order to monitor your market space? How can analyzing the job offerings, mission or "about us" statement, products and services descriptions, or other general information on your competitors' Web sites help you figure out their strategic direction? What areas of a Web site could you scan to gather competitive information? Perhaps you will need to select a clipping service. Go to **http://www. looksmart.com** and search for "News Clipping Services." For an excellent compilation of competitive intelligence tools, go to **http://www.fuld.com/ i3/index.html**.

CROSS-FUNCTIONAL CONNECTIONS SOLUTIONS

Questions

1. Why has information historically been perceived as "owned" by the marketing department?

   There are probably a few general answers to this question. One, because the information is referred to as "marketing research" rather than "market" or "marketplace," it automatically denotes that it is part of the marketing department. Also, the research has traditionally been conducted by the marketing department—reinforcing the notion that the marketing department owns it. Additionally, prior to the 1990s, the marketing department was the only formal link between the company and customer. Because a primary focus of marketing research is the customer, it was always owned by the marketing department.

2. What data differences exist across functions?

   The historical data debate between marketing and other business functions centers on the qualitative versus quantitative format of the data. The data collected by marketers are perceived to be "touchy-feely" data when compared to the "hard" data utilized by other functional areas. In addition to unit sales and competitive offerings, marketing data looks at customers' perceptions—something very "soft" when compared to other functional data. For example, manufacturing can cite exact production output, cost, and cycle data, and R&D has precise specifications for tensile strength, electrical usage, and battery power. Add accounting data with its general accounting standards to the "hard" data side of the picture, and it's not surprising that data differences cause cross-functional conflict within a firm.

3. What is the job of a chief knowledge officer?

   The chief knowledge officer is a company executive who manages institutional learning. CKO's are responsible for integrating internal and external knowledge into their companies. In addition to monitoring this information, the CKO creates and propagates new knowledge based on industry observations, best practices, and benchmarking studies. The CKO shares the collected knowledge with all members of firm, thereby providing them with consistently important and relevant information.

Suggested Readings

James A. Cook. "Web Browser Brings Product Demand into Focus." *Logistics Management and Distribution,* May 1999, pp. 67–70.

Alex Taylor III. "Kellogg Cranks Up Its Idea Machine." *Fortune,* July 5, 1999, pp. 181–182.

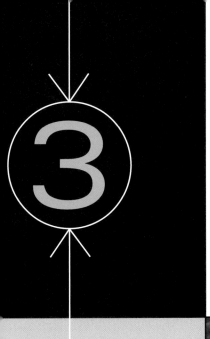

3

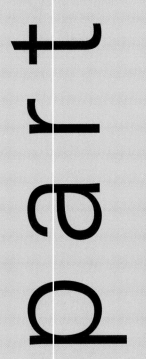

part

Product Decisions

BLURRING FUNCTIONAL LINES IN SPEED-TO-MARKET INITIATIVES

Marketing focuses upon a company's products/services from a *demand-side* perspective. Via marketing research methods, marketers determine current and future wants and needs. Once these wants and needs are determined, marketing then expects the research and development group to develop a device that will satisfy customer demands. When developed, the expectation is that the manufacturing group will produce the device. The device becomes a true product with the development of a marketing program that adds value to customers.

Manufacturing and research and development typically view products from a *supply-side* perspective; in this framework, however, new product conception is the job of the research and development group for design, with the device then produced by the manufacturing group. The supply-side role of marketing is getting the marketplace to want the product. From this perspective, marketing is the functional group that tells the marketplace about the product's performance but has no input as to what actually goes into the product.

Many business people have suggested that whether a company or product is driven by a demand-side or a supply-side focus is dependent upon the nature of the product. For example, highly technological products such as component parts of a computer would be based more on supply-side thinking. Prior to the development of products such as Intel components (which make computers function better) or PCMCIA cards by SystemSoft Corporation (which allow computers to communicate via a modem), consumers probably did not have sufficient knowledge to ask for such component parts. Consumer products (such as snack foods or personal care products), however, appear to be better examples of demand-side concepts.

The demand-side versus supply-side thinking has resulted in three major areas of conflict between marketing and research and development/manufacturing: managing variety, managing availability, and managing reliability. Generally, marketing wants a large variety of high-quality products for customers to choose from and will promise the shortest delivery time necessary to get the order. On the flip side, research and development and manufacturing prefer fewer models so that they can devote attention to a smaller number of projects—resulting in high quality, without holding too many products in inventory.

Research and development and manufacturing functional groups have become quite efficient at working together—using processes referred to as "design-factory fit," "concurrent engineering," "design for manufacturability and assembly," and "early manufacturing involvement." Basically, all of these concepts refer to advance linkage between a product's design and its manufacturing needs so that the manufacturing group will be ready to make the product once it has been designed. Companies have been quite successful at implementing these concepts. Ryobi Group, a Japanese manufacturer of products such as power tools and power equipment, utilized design for manufacturability and assembly in the development of a new engine for hand-held power equipment. The company successfully included its marketing group in the new product development process by receiving input with respect to customers' desired product features.

The efficient coordinating processes developed on the technical side of business have been meshed with customers' demands for high quality, highly customized products that can be delivered immediately. Such expectations are in direct contrast to traditional thinking. Traditionally, companies made standardized products available immediately, with customers understanding that customization would result in delays in delivery. Today's marketplace is increasingly demanding that companies compete on both time and customization.

The key to providing customized products quickly is a multidisciplinary approach to business. Marketplace demands of immediacy and customization have focused attention on marketing, research and development, and manufacturing. Traditionally, products were conceptualized by one function, given to another function to produce, and then handed over to another function to sell. However, competing on time in the new product development process does away with linear product development. Now, the expectation is that the final product is high quality and has moved through the company's functional processes in at least half the time of the traditional linear process.

Xerox has become a leader in utilizing cross-functional teams to both improve product quality and speed new products to market. Harley-Davidson uses cross-functional teams from concept to market. Implementing the cross-functional team approach helped save the company from possible demise in the latter half of the twentieth century. The general idea is that a company can design a product that satisfies customers' demands while simultaneously designing a product that is quicker and easier to assemble. This type of design and assembly requires a high level of coordination among marketing, research and development, and manufacturing.

Boeing refers to this type of coordination as "paperless design." The design of the Boeing 777 utilized teams of research and development, manufacturing, marketing, customers, and finance—with all team members interacting to assemble an airplane on a computer system that allowed them to model the airplane and iron out bugs long before the major expense of building a prototype.

Manufacturers also have focused on meeting customization and speed to market demands with "modularization." With modular components, some of a product's component parts fit in all, or most, of the company's products. Many of the power tools made by Black & Decker are made with modular components. The modularity reduces the number of individual parts, allowing the firm to quickly customize the product beyond its core architecture. However, modularization does increase the time and cost of (re)designing products. As such, marketing, manufacturing, and finance have to work closely with research and development to demonstrate the long-term payoff of modularization.

The finance and accounting areas have also been particularly thorny areas concerning both new and existing products. Financial managers often complain that marketers are not held to the same financial standards as the rest of the company, particularly when rolling out a new product. In turn, marketers feel the need to justify each expenditure—even though the payback on market-

ing allocations, such as advertising, is not immediate and/or always easily discernible. This type of friction, referred to as "creative friction" at Harley-Davidson, between marketing and finance/accounting can slow the development cycle and be in direct conflict to the speed-to-market initiatives the company may be taking. The product innovator 3M has been at the forefront of using management accounting tools to integrate customer value and shareholder value.

Typically we think of new products in terms of tangible items. However, cross-functional coordination is particularly important in the introduction and delivery of a new or existing service. Since the production and marketing of a service happen simultaneously, it is imperative that these two functions are closely integrated. The 1990s focus on customer service, which will no doubt be an even greater issue in the twenty-first century, has added another function to this marketing-production coupling—human resources.

Employees are at the heart of customer service. The front-line employee plays a pivotal role in delivering high-quality service. A service provider's profitability and growth objectives are driven by customer loyalty, which is in turn driven by customer satisfaction, which is the direct result of human interaction with the service provider.

Whether it is developing a new product/service or managing the existing product line or service offerings, cross-functional teamwork is necessary for company-wide success. Successful interaction between marketing and all other business functions is imperative for competitive advantage in today's rapidly changing marketplace.

Questions for Discussion

1. What is the difference between the demand-side perspective and the supply-side perspective to doing business? Is either perspective more appropriate?
2. What are some of the popular business terms used to describe cross-functional integration?
3. Why are employees (whether in marketing or not) at the heart of customer service?

Check it Out

For articles and exercises on the material in this part, and for other great study aids, visit the *Marketing* Web site at **http://lamb.swcollege.com**

chapter 9

Learning Objectives

1 Define the term *product*

2 Classify consumer products

3 Define the terms *product item, product line,* and *product mix*

4 Describe marketing uses of branding

5 Describe marketing uses of packaging and labeling

6 Discuss global issues in branding and packaging

7 Describe how and why product warranties are important marketing tools

Product Concepts

McDonald's Corporation is developing or expanding several lines of McDonald's-brand consumer goods. Germans are buying McDonald's-brand ketchup, and for some time American parents have been finding McKids clothing and shoes at Wal-Mart stores. Under consideration now are McDonald's-brand snacks and other packaged goods, as well as a line of McDonald's books and videos.

Jack Greenberg, McDonald's chief executive, says placing the McDonald's brand on new products and services is one of three prongs in his growth strategy, along with improving burger sales and buying other kinds of restaurants. "We have an obligation to explore ways to leverage our brand," he says.

The brand extension strategy could involve new products both inside and outside McDonald's restaurants. Inside, the company is experimenting in Austria, Australia, and the United Kingdom with in-between-meal products. This involves a separate section called McCafe that serves gourmet coffee and snacks. If successful, that operation could also create a market for McDonald's snacks, such as ice cream bars and baked goods, in grocery stores and elsewhere.

As for the clothes business, McDonald's has been at it for some time.

More than a decade ago, it had an unsuccessful joint venture with Sears Roebuck to sell McDonald's apparel at Sears stores and at forty-seven McKids specialty stores. The effort was hurt by slow sales overall and a shift in business strategy at Sears.

In the past few years, though, McDonald's has been reviving its McKids line of apparel, shoes, and bedding, pushing them with Wal-Mart Stores, Inc. The clothing doesn't feature Ronald McDonald, and the golden arches themselves are understated, appearing only on tags. Sales of the clothing have grown 20 percent a year, Wal-Mart says.

Because McDonald's is a company obsessed with image and control, new products and services could introduce new risks. It won't be easy to produce Ronald McDonald videos that are reverent but still relevant to today's knowing children. Can McDonald's impose the same rigorous standards on an apparel maker that it does on its franchisees? What if McDonald's-brand clothes wind up in a heap on a clearance table?[1]

What do you think "leveraging our brand" means? Do you think McDonald's brand-extension strategy is sound? Evaluate the McCafe concept.

What Is a Product?

Define the term *product*

product
Everything, both favorable and unfavorable, that a person receives in an exchange.

The product offering, the heart of an organization's marketing program, is usually the starting point in creating a marketing mix. A marketing manager cannot determine a price, design a promotion strategy, or create a distribution channel until the firm has a product to sell. Moreover, an excellent distribution channel, a persuasive promotion campaign, and a fair price have no value with a poor or inadequate product offering.

A **product** may be defined as everything, both favorable and unfavorable, that a person receives in an exchange. A product may be a tangible good like a pair of shoes, a service like a haircut, an idea like "don't litter," or any combination of these three. Packaging, style, color, options, and size are some typical product features. Just as important are intangibles such as service, the seller's image, the manufacturer's reputation, and the way consumers believe others will view the product.

To most people, the term "product" means a tangible good. However, services and ideas are also products. (Chapter 11 focuses specifically on the unique aspects of marketing services.) The marketing process identified in Chapter 1 is the same whether the product marketed is a good, a service, an idea, or some combination of these.

Types of Consumer Products

Classify consumer products

business product (industrial product)
A product used to manufacture other goods or services, to facilitate an organization's operations, or to resell to other customers.

consumer product
Product bought to satisfy an individual's personal wants.

Products can be classified as either business (industrial) or consumer products, depending on the buyer's intentions. The key distinction between the two types of products is their intended use. If the intended use is a business purpose, the product is classified as a business or industrial product. As explained in Chapter 6, a **business product** is used to manufacture other goods or services, to facilitate an organization's operations, or to resell to other customers. A **consumer product** is bought to satisfy an individual's personal wants. Sometimes the same item can be classified as either a business or a consumer product, depending on its intended use. Examples include lightbulbs, pencils and paper, and microcomputers.

We need to know about product classifications because business and consumer products are marketed differently. They are marketed to different target markets and tend to use different distribution, promotion, and pricing strategies.

Chapter 6 examined seven categories of business products: major equipment, accessory equipment, component parts, processed materials, raw materials, supplies, and services. The current chapter examines an effective way of categorizing consumer products. Although there are several ways to classify them, the most popular approach includes these four types: convenience products, shopping products, specialty products, and unsought products. (See Exhibit 9.1.) This approach classifies products according to how much effort is normally used to shop for them.

Convenience Products

convenience product
A relatively inexpensive item that merits little shopping effort.

A **convenience product** is a relatively inexpensive item that merits little shopping effort—that is, a consumer is unwilling to shop extensively for such an item. Candy, soft drinks, combs, aspirin, small hardware items, dry cleaning, and car washes fall into the convenience product category.

Consumers buy convenience products regularly, usually without much planning. Nevertheless, consumers do know the brand names of popular convenience products, such as Coca-Cola, Bayer aspirin, and Right Guard deodorant. Convenience products normally require wide distribution in order to sell sufficient quantities to meet profit goals.

Exhibit **9.1**

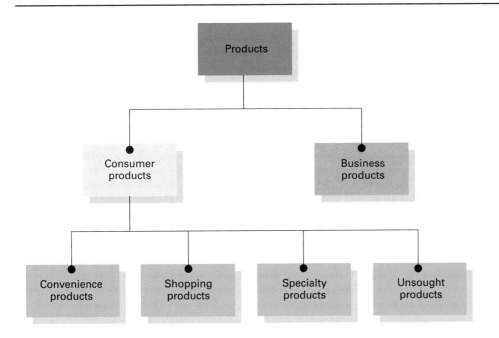

Shopping Products

A **shopping product** is usually more expensive than a convenience product and is found in fewer stores. Consumers usually buy a shopping product only after comparing several brands or stores on style, practicality, price, and lifestyle compatibility. They are willing to invest some effort into this process to get the desired benefits.

There are two types of shopping products: homogeneous and heterogeneous. Consumers perceive *homogeneous* shopping products as basically similar—for example, washers, dryers, refrigerators, and televisions. With homogeneous shopping products, consumers typically look for the lowest-priced brand that has the desired features.

In contrast, consumers perceive *heterogeneous* shopping products as essentially different—for example, furniture, clothing, housing, and universities. Consumers often have trouble comparing heterogeneous shopping products because the prices, quality, and features vary so much. The benefit of comparing heterogeneous shopping products is "finding the best product or brand for me"; this decision is often highly individual.

shopping product
A product that requires comparison shopping, because it is usually more expensive than a convenience product and found in fewer stores.

With homogenous products such as washers and dryers, consumers typically buy the lowest-priced brand that has the desired features.
© Jeff Greenberg

Specialty Products

When consumers search extensively for a particular item and are very reluctant to accept substitutes, that item is a **specialty product**. Fine watches, Rolls Royce automobiles, expensive stereo equipment, gourmet restaurants, and highly specialized forms of medical care are generally considered specialty products.

specialty product
A particular item that consumers search extensively for and are very reluctant to accept substitutes.

Marketers of specialty products often use selective, status-conscious advertising to maintain their product's exclusive image. Distribution is often limited to one or a very few outlets in a geographic area. Brand names and quality of service are often very important.

Unsought Products

unsought product
A product unknown to the potential buyer or a known product that the buyer does not actively seek.

A product unknown to the potential buyer or a known product that the buyer does not actively seek is referred to as an **unsought product**. New products fall into this category until advertising and distribution increase consumer awareness of them.

Some goods are always marketed as unsought items, especially needed products we do not like to think about or care to spend money on. Insurance, burial plots, encyclopedias, and similar items require aggressive personal selling and highly persuasive advertising. Salespeople actively seek leads to potential buyers. Because consumers usually do not seek out this type of product, the company must go directly to them through a salesperson, direct mail, or direct-response advertising.

Product Items, Lines, and Mixes

Define the terms *product item, product line,* and *product mix*

product item
A specific version of a product that can be designated as a distinct offering among an organization's products.

Rarely does a company sell a single product. More often, it sells a variety of things. A **product item** is a specific version of a product that can be designated as a distinct offering among an organization's products. Gillette's MACH 3 razor is an example of a product item. (See Exhibit 9.2.)

A group of closely related product items is a **product line**. For example, the column in Exhibit 9.2 titled "Blades and Razors" represents one of Gillette's product lines. Different container sizes and shapes also distinguish items in a product line. Diet Coke, for example, is available in cans and various plastic containers. Each size and each container are separate product items.

Exhibit 9.2

Gillette's Product
Lines and Product Mix

	Width of the Product Mix			
	Blades and Razors	Toiletries	Writing Instruments	Lighters
Depth of the Product Lines	MACH 3	Series	Paper Mate	Cricket
	Sensor	Adorn	Flair	S.T. Dupont
	Trac II	Toni		
	Atra	Right Guard		
	Swivel	Silkience		
	Double-Edge	Soft and Dri		
	Lady Gillette	Foamy		
	Super Speed	Dry Look		
	Twin Injector	Dry Idea		
	Techmatic	Brush Plus		

Marriott

Does Marriott use its product lines to organize its Web site? How so? Compare the sites for the different hotels listed on the site. What conclusions can you draw about Marriott's product mix based on what you see at the various sites?

http://www.marriott.com

On Line

An organization's **product mix** includes all the products it sells. All Gillette's products—blades and razors, toiletries, writing instruments, and lighters—constitute its product mix. Each product item in the product mix may require a separate marketing strategy. In some cases, however, product lines and even entire product mixes share some marketing strategy components. Nike promoted all of its product items and lines with the theme "Just Do It."

Organizations derive several benefits from organizing related items into product lines, including the following:

- *Advertising economies:* Product lines provide economies of scale in advertising. Several products can be advertised under the umbrella of the line. Campbell's can talk about its soup being "m-m-good" and promote the entire line.
- *Package uniformity:* A product line can benefit from package uniformity. All packages in the line may have a common look and still keep their individual identities. Again, Campbell's soup is a good example.
- *Standardized components:* Product lines allow firms to standardize components, thus reducing manufacturing and inventory costs. For example, many of the components Samsonite uses in its folding tables and chairs are also used in its patio furniture. General Motors uses the same parts on many automobile makes and models.
- *Efficient sales and distribution:* A product line enables sales personnel for companies like Procter & Gamble to provide a full range of choices to customers. Distributors and retailers are often more inclined to stock the company's products if it offers a full line. Transportation and warehousing costs are likely to be lower for a product line than for a collection of individual items.
- *Equivalent quality:* Purchasers usually expect and believe that all products in a line are about equal in quality. Consumers expect that all Campbell's soups and all Mary Kay cosmetics will be of similar quality.

Product mix width (or breadth) refers to the number of product lines an organization offers. In Exhibit 9.2, for example, the width of Gillette's product mix is four product lines. **Product line depth** is the number of product items in a product line. As shown in Exhibit 9.2, the blades and razors product line consists of ten product items; the toiletries product line includes ten product items.

Firms increase the *width* of their product mix to diversify risk. To generate sales and boost profits, firms spread risk across many product lines rather than depend on only one or two. Firms also widen their product mix to capitalize on established reputations. By introducing new product lines, Kodak capitalized on its image as a leader in photographic products. Kodak's product lines now include film, processing, still cameras, movie cameras, paper, and chemicals. Limited Inc., a company that mostly comprises women's apparel stores (Limited, Limited Too, Victoria's Secret) developed a line of make-up under the Victoria's Secret brand.

Firms increase the *depth* of product lines to attract buyers with different preferences, to increase sales and profits by further segmenting the market, to capitalize on economies of scale in production and marketing, and to even out seasonal sales patterns. Marriott International has fourteen different lodging brands that are divided into three groups. The full service group includes flagship Marriott, upscale Renaissance Hotels and Resorts, and Marriott Conference Centers. The select service group includes Courtyard, Spring Hill Suites, and Fairfield Inn. The extended stay group includes Residence Inn and Execu Stay.[2]

product line
A group of closely related product items.

product mix
All products that an organization sells.

product mix width
The number of product lines an organization offers.

product line depth
The number of product items in a product line.

Adjustments to Product Items, Lines, and Mixes

Over time, firms change product items, lines, and mixes to take advantage of new technical or product developments or to respond to changes in the environment. They may adjust by modifying products, repositioning products, or extending or contracting product lines.

Product Modification

product modification
Changing one or more of a product's characteristics.

Marketing managers must decide if and when to modify existing products. **Product modification** changes one or more of a product's characteristics:

- *Quality modification:* change in a product's dependability or durability. Reducing a product's quality may let the manufacturer lower the price and appeal to target markets unable to afford the original product. On the other hand, increasing quality can help the firm compete with rival firms. Increasing quality can also result in increased brand loyalty, greater ability to raise prices, or new opportunities for market segmentation. Inexpensive ink-jet printers have improved in quality to the point that they produce photo-quality images. These printers are now competing with camera film.[3] In order to appeal to a more upscale market, Robert Mondavi Winery is introducing a high-end wine called Twin Oaks to prestige restaurants and hotels. The company is trying to differentiate this wine from the one they sell in supermarkets.[4]

- *Functional modification:* change in a product's versatility, effectiveness, convenience, or safety. Hostess introduced a line of fruit and grain cereal bars to extend its equity in the snack market beyond the dessert-type products they have traditionally offered. These bars are targeted to higher-income females who want a tastier version of a low-fat, vitamin-fortified breakfast alternative.[5] Lea & Perrins is offering its steak sauce in a value-priced squeeze bottle with a "no mess, stay clean" cap.[6]

planned obsolescence
The practice of modifying products so those that have already been sold become obsolete before they actually need replacement.

- *Style modification:* aesthetic product change, rather than a quality or functional change. Clothing manufacturers commonly use style modifications to motivate customers to replace products before they are worn out. **Planned obsolescence** is a term commonly used to describe the practice of modifying products so those that have already been sold become obsolete before they actually need replacement. Some argue that planned obsolescence is wasteful; some claim it is unethical. Marketers respond that consumers favor style modifications because they like changes in the appearance of goods like clothing and cars. Marketers also contend that consumers, not manufacturers and marketers, decide when styles are obsolete.

Repositioning

Repositioning, as Chapter 7 explained, is changing consumers' perceptions of a brand. For example, Procter & Gamble has dropped the word "oil" from its Oil of Olay product line. The company hopes that the simpler name "Olay" will make the line of skin-care products and cosmetics more appealing to younger women, who do not like the idea of oil.[7]

Changing demographics, declining sales, or changes in the social environment often motivate firms to reposition established brands. Gum is a product that has become boring for a lot of today's teens, who have gravitated to a number of non-gum products such as mints like Altoids and TicTacs. Wrigley's is trying to

Can you think of a scenario where a pair of Levi's jeans, like those being made at this factory in Capetown, South Africa, would be obsolete? How has Levi's extended its product line to combat any potential obsolescence of its blue jeans?
© Louise Gubb/The Image Works

Unilever

Can Unilever delete anything from its product lines? Visit the company's product category pages on its "Brands" Web page to see the number of existing products and new products planned. Write a proposal for contracting one of Unilever's product lines.

http://www.unilever.com

On Line

boost gum sales partly by revamping old standbys like Juicy Fruit and Big Red with youth-oriented ads and Internet tie-ins.[8]

Product Line Extensions

A **product line extension** occurs when a company's management decides to add products to an existing product line in order to compete more broadly in the industry. Minute Maid has added two calcium-fortified juices—Premium Home-Squeezed Style orange juice and Ruby Red Grapefruit Blend—to attract health-conscious baby boomers.[9] Procter & Gamble is extending its shampoo brand Pantene with its first anti-dandruff product—Pro V Anti-Dandruff—positioned distinctly for women.[10]

product line extension
Adding additional products to an existing product line in order to compete more broadly in the industry.

Product Line Contraction

Does the world really need thirty-one varieties of Head & Shoulders shampoo? Or fifty-two versions of Crest? Black & Decker has decided the answer is no. The company has deleted a number of household products—Dustbusters, SnakeLight flashlights, and toaster ovens—and is concentrating on power tools.[11] Symptoms of product line overextension include the following:

- Some products in the line do not contribute to profits because of low sales or cannibalize sales of other items in the line.
- Manufacturing or marketing resources are disproportionately allocated to slow-moving products.
- Some items in the line are obsolete because of new product entries in the line or new products offered by competitors.

Three major benefits are likely when a firm contracts overextended product lines. First, resources become concentrated on the most important products. Second, managers no longer waste resources trying to improve the sales and profits of poorly performing products. Third, new product items have a greater chance of being successful because more financial and human resources are available to manage them.

Branding

The success of any business or consumer product depends in part on the target market's ability to distinguish one product from another. Branding is the main tool marketers use to distinguish their products from the competition's.

A **brand** is a name, term, symbol, design, or combination thereof that identifies a seller's products and differentiates them from competitors' products. A **brand name** is that part of a brand that can be spoken, including letters (GM, YMCA), words (Chevrolet), and numbers (WD-40, 7-Eleven). The elements of a brand that cannot be spoken are called the **brand mark**—for example, the well-known Mercedes-Benz and Delta Airlines symbols.

Benefits of Branding

Branding has three main purposes: product identification, repeat sales, and new-product sales. The most important purpose is *product identification*. Branding allows marketers to distinguish their products from all others. Many brand names are familiar to consumers and indicate quality.

Describe marketing uses of branding

brand
A name, term, symbol, design, or combination thereof that identifies a seller's products and differentiates them from competitors' products.

brand name
That part of a brand that can be spoken, including letters, words, and numbers.

brand mark
The elements of a brand that cannot be spoken.

The term **brand equity** refers to the value of company and brand names. A brand that has high awareness, perceived quality, and brand loyalty among customers has high brand equity. A brand with strong brand equity is a valuable asset.

The term **master brand** has been used to refer to a brand so dominant in consumers' minds that they think of it immediately when a product category, use, attribute, or customer benefit is mentioned.[12] Exhibit 9.3 lists the master brands in several product categories. How many other brands can you name in these eleven categories? Can you name any other product categories in which the master brands listed in Exhibit 9.3 compete? Probably not many. Campbell's means soup to consumers; it doesn't mean high-quality food products.

What constitutes a good brand name? Most effective brand names have several of the following features:

- Is easy to pronounce (by both domestic and foreign buyers)
- Is easy to recognize
- Is easy to remember
- Is short
- Is distinctive, unique
- Describes the product
- Describes product use
- Describes product benefits
- Has a positive connotation

Exhibit 9.3

Master Brands in
Selected Product Categories

Product Category	Master Brand
Baking soda	Arm & Hammer
Adhesive bandages	Band-Aid
Rum	Bacardi
Antacids	Alka-Seltzer
Gelatin	Jell-O
Soup	Campbell's
Salt	Morton
Toy Trains	Lionel
Cream cheese	Philadelphia
Crayons	Crayola
Petroleum jelly	Vaseline

SOURCE: From "Strategies for Leveraging Master Brands" by Peter H. Farquhar et al., *Marketing Research*, September 1992, pp. 32–43. Reprinted by permission of the American Marketing Association.

- Reinforces the desired product image
- Is legally protectable in home and foreign markets of interest

Obviously no brand exhibits all of these characteristics. The most important issue is that the brand can be protected for exclusive use by its owner.

U.S. brands command substantial premiums in many places around the world. For example, Gillette disposable razors sell for twice the price of local brands in India. However, other countries have produced brands that are also leaders in some industries, as the "Global Perspectives" example illustrates.

The best generator of *repeat sales* is satisfied customers. Branding helps consumers identify products they wish to buy again and avoid those they do not. **Brand loyalty**, a consistent preference for one brand over all others, is quite high in some product categories. Over half the users in product categories such as cigarettes, mayonnaise, toothpaste, coffee, headache remedies, photographic film, bath soap, and catsup are loyal to one brand. Brand identity is essential to developing brand loyalty.

The third main purpose of branding is to *facilitate new-product sales.* Company and brand names like those listed in Exhibit 9.3 are extremely useful when introducing new products.

brand loyalty
A consistent preference for one brand over all others.

Global Perspectives

TAKING THE DRILL AND THE PAIN OUT OF DENTISTRY

Swedish dentists Rolf Bornstein and Dan Ericson have spent the past thirteen years on a quest to take the drill, and the pain, out of dentistry. The product they have developed is Carisolv, a gel that eats away decayed tooth material, which is then replaced with a conventional filling. The amino acid-based gel is formulated to leave gums and healthy tooth material intact. Carisolv is sold in Europe and is awaiting U.S. government approval.

But the product and its makers will have a tough time convincing dentists, who have spent their careers drilling, to start gelling. "When I go out lecturing to dentists in Europe and other parts of the world, I always ask them, 'How many of you like to drill?' and of course all of them do," Dr. Bornstein says. "Then I ask, 'How many of you like to be drilled on?' and so far I haven't got one hand up," he laughs. He hasn't won many converts, however.

The reluctance of dentists is only part of the problem. In some European countries, such as Den-

mark and Holland, additional costs of Carisolv aren't covered by the public dental-insurance system.

New ideas in dentistry aren't new in Sweden. In 1948, Sweden's Astra AB (now AstraZeneca PLC) launched xylocaine, a local anesthesia now used world-wide by dentists and surgeons. The first truly effective fluoride toothpaste followed in the early 1960s. In 1965 the Swedish doctor Per-Ingvar Branemark invented dental implants, which replace dentures by imbedding false teeth into the gums with titanium screws. In the early 1970s Per Axelsson and Jan Lindhe discovered the importance of plaque control in preventing cavities.

The Carisolv concept is based on an earlier U.S. product, an acid-based solution called Caridex marketed in the 1980s. The solution took too long to remove a cavity, and it required a large machine to pump the acid solution into the tooth. The product went nowhere. But Dr. Bornstein was intrigued and alerted Dr. Ericson, one of the world's ex-

perts on cavities. "We already knew then that we could do it so much better, and we saw that the future of dentistry would be based on minimally invasive techniques," recalls Dr. Bornstein. After many trials, the Carisolv gel was born.

Medi Team, the small company that makes Carisolv, lacks the resources for a major advertising campaign. Instead, it is pinning its hopes on the next generation of dentists by encouraging dental schools to teach the Carisolv method. So far, Carisolv has made it on to the syllabus at fifteen European dental schools.[a]

Evaluate the name Carisolv using the characteristics of effective brand names described on pages 302–303. Can you think of any brand extensions of this product that might be appropriate in the future?

[a] Alfred Kueppers, "Gel From Sweden Dissolves Cavity Pain," *Wall Street Journal*, May 15, 2000, p. B11A.

On Line

where's the one place all our brands hang out together?

introducing the **PG.com** network

The new pg.com lets you **do more**,
learn more and **get more** from
P&G and our brands than ever before...

Discover the surprising number of online resources our brands have to offer.

Try and buy products before they're available in stores.

Share your ideas for improving our products and creating new ones.

and coming soon... Take advantage of new tools to help manage your P&G shareholders account.

www.pg.com

Procter & Gamble has an extensive Web presence to support its complete slate of brands. In 2000, the company launched the pg.com network, touting it as "the one place where all our brands hang out together."

generic product
A no-frills, no-brand-name, low-cost product that is simply identified by its product category.

The Internet provides firms a new alternative for generating brand awareness, promoting a desired brand image, stimulating new and repeat brand sales, and enhancing brand loyalty and building brand equity. A number of packaged goods firms, such as Procter & Gamble, Campbell's Soup, and Gerber, have a presence on-line. Unilever's Lipton Recipe Secrets has launched a Web site that will be a part of an interactive test in which the company plans to measure brand awareness, attitudes, and product usage as a result of consumers' exposure to the site.[13]

Branding Strategies

Firms face complex branding decisions. As Exhibit 9.4 illustrates, the first decision is whether to brand at all. Some firms actually use the lack of a brand name as a selling point. These unbranded products are called generic products. Firms that decide to brand their products may choose to follow a policy of using manufacturers' brands, private (distributor) brands, or both. In either case, they must then decide among a policy of individual branding (different brands for different products), family branding (common names for different products), or a combination of individual branding and family branding.

Generic Products Versus Branded Products

A **generic product** is typically a no-frills, no-brand-name, low-cost product that is simply identified by its product category. (Note that a generic product and a brand name that becomes generic, such as cellophane, are not the same thing.) Generic products have captured significant market shares in some product categories, such as canned fruits, canned vegetables, and paper products. These unbranded products are frequently identified only by black stenciled lettering on white packages.

The main appeal of generics is their low price. Generic grocery products are usually 30 to 40 percent less expensive than manufacturers' brands in the same product category and 20 to 25 percent less expensive than retailer-owned brands.

Pharmaceuticals make up another product category where generics have made inroads. When patents on successful pharmaceutical products expire, low-cost generics rapidly appear on the market. For example, when the patent on Merck's popular antiarthritis drug Clinoril expired, sales declined by 50 percent almost immediately.

Exhibit 9.4 Major Branding Decisions

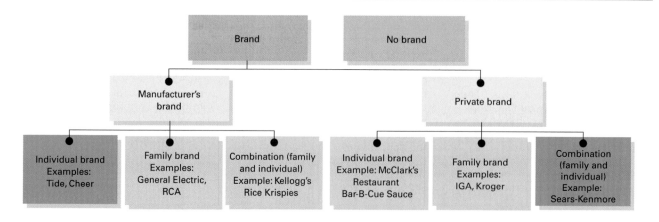

Manufacturers' Brands Versus Private Brands

The brand name of a manufacturer—such as Kodak, Lazy Boy, and Fruit of the Loom—is called a **manufacturer's brand**. Sometimes the term "national brand" is used as a synonym for "manufacturer's brand." This term is not always accurate, however, because many manufacturers serve only regional markets. The term manufacturer's brand more precisely defines the brand's owner.

A **private brand** is a brand name owned by a wholesaler or a retailer. Hunt Club (a JCPenney brand), Sam's American Choice (Wal-Mart), and IGA (Independent Grocers' Association) are all private brands. Private brands now account for over 20 percent of sales at all U.S. mass merchandisers, drugstores, and supermarkets. At some stores, the penetration is much higher: At Target, for example, more than 50 percent of the merchandise is exclusive to the store. And across the board, the growth of store brands is greater than that of national brands.[14] Marketing experts predict private labels to make up as much as 30 percent of grocery sales within five years—particularly as the consolidation continues among big supermarkets.[15]

Exhibit 9.5 illustrates key issues that wholesalers and retailers should consider in deciding whether to sell manufacturers' brands or private brands. Many firms, such as JCPenney, Kmart, and Safeway, offer a combination of both. In fact, JCPenney and Sears have turned their low-priced, private-label jeans into some of the most popular brands around, thanks to hip marketing campaigns that feature rock bands, Web sites, and imagery targeted at teens.[16]

manufacturer's brand
The brand name of a manufacturer.

private brand
A brand name owned by a wholesaler or a retailer.

Exhibit 9.5

Comparing Manufacturers' and Private Brands from the Reseller's Perspective

Key Advantages of Carrying Manufacturers' Brands	Key Advantages of Carrying Private Brands
• Heavy advertising to the consumer by manufacturers like Procter & Gamble helps develop strong consumer loyalties.	• A wholesaler or retailer can usually earn higher profits on its own brand. In addition, because the private brand is exclusive, there is less pressure to mark the price down to meet competition.
• Well-known manufacturers' brands, such as Kodak and Fisher-Price, can attract new customers and enhance the dealer's (wholesaler's or retailer's) prestige.	• A manufacturer can decide to drop a brand or a reseller at any time or even to become a direct competitor to its dealers.
• Many manufacturers offer rapid delivery, enabling the dealer to carry less inventory.	• A private brand ties the customer to the wholesaler or retailer. A person who wants a Die-Hard battery must go to Sears.
• If a dealer happens to sell a manufacturer's brand of poor quality, the customer may simply switch brands but remain loyal to the dealer.	• Wholesalers and retailers have no control over the intensity of distribution of manufacturers' brands. Wal-Mart store managers don't have to worry about competing with other sellers of Sam's American Choice products or Ol' Roy dog food. They know that these brands are sold only in Wal-Mart and Sam's Wholesale Club stores.

Individual Brands Versus Family Brands

individual branding
Using different brand names for different products.

Many companies use different brand names for different products, a practice referred to as **individual branding**. Companies use individual brands when their products vary greatly in use or performance. For instance, it would not make sense to use the same brand name for a pair of dress socks and a baseball bat. Procter & Gamble targets different segments of the laundry detergent market with Bold, Cheer, Dash, Dreft, Era, Gain, Ivory Snow, Oxydol, Solo, and Tide. Marriott International also targets different market segments with Courtyard by Marriott, Residence Inn, and Fairfield Inn.

family brand
Marketing several different products under the same brand name.

On the other hand, a company that markets several different products under the same brand name is using a **family brand**. Sony's family brand includes radios, television sets, stereos, and other electronic products. A brand name can only be stretched so far, however. Do you know the differences among Holiday Inn, Holiday Inn Express, Holiday Inn Select, Holiday Inn Sunspree Resort, Holiday Inn Garden Court, and Holiday Inn Hotel & Suites? Neither do most travelers.

Cobranding

cobranding
Placing two or more brand names on a product or its package.

Cobranding entails placing two or more brand names on a product or its package. There are three types of cobranding. *Ingredient branding* identifies the brand of a part that makes up the product. Examples of ingredient branding are Intel (a microprocessor) in a personal computer, such as Compaq, or a premium leather interior (Coach) in an automobile (Lincoln). *Cooperative branding* is where two brands receiving equal treatment borrow on each other's brand equity, such as Citibank and American Airlines, or American Express and Sheraton. Finally, there is *complementary branding*, where products are advertised or marketed together to suggest usage, such as a spirits brand (Seagram's) and a compatible mixer (7-Up).[17]

Cobranding is a useful strategy when a combination of brand names enhances the prestige or perceived value of a product or when it benefits brand owners and users. Toyota Motor's luxury division introduced a Platinum version of its Lexus brand. For a premium of as much as 10 percent above the base sticker prices, buyers will get upgraded paint, leathers and accessories, and a free two-year subscription to the $300-a-year American Express Platinum Card. Both companies say that the Platinum Series models will reinforce their brands while delivering added value.[18]

Cobranding may also be used when two or more organizations wish to collaborate to offer a product. Beacon Sweets of Mooresville, North Carolina, bought the rights to Baskin-Robbins Ice Cream and launched Hard Candy Creations featuring five Baskin-Robbins ice cream flavors. The Baskin-Robbins name gave Beacon's candy instant brand recognition.[19] Nabisco and Kraft Foods' Post cereal have teamed up to offer Oreo O's cereal.[20]

Cobranding can be a useful strategy, particularly when the brands involved convey quality and prestige. This strategy is perhaps most recognized in food products, like Oreo's cereal or cookies-and-cream ice cream with Oreo's.

GLOBAL European firms have been slower to adopt cobranding than U.S. firms have. One reason is that European customers seem to be more skeptical than U.S. customers in trying new brands. European retailers also typically have less shelf space than their U.S. counterparts and are less willing to give new brands a try.

Trademarks

A **trademark** is the exclusive right to use a brand or part of a brand. Others are prohibited from using the brand without permission. A **service mark** performs the same function for services, such as H&R Block and Weight Watchers. Parts of a brand or other product identification may qualify for trademark protection. Some examples are

- Shapes, such as the Jeep front grille and the Coca-Cola bottle
- Ornamental color or design, such as the decoration on Nike tennis shoes, the black-and-copper color combination of a Duracell battery, Levi's small tag on the left side of the rear pocket of its jeans, or the cutoff black cone on the top of Cross pens
- Catchy phrases, such as Prudential's "Own a piece of the rock," Merrill Lynch's "We're bullish on America," and Budweiser's "This Bud's for you"
- Abbreviations, such as Bud, Coke, or The Met

A New York property company that purchased the Chrysler Building in Manhattan has even sought trademark registration for the building's elaborate exterior, its lobby's ceiling, and even its elevator doors. Its distinctive pinnacle is already trademarked.[21] In 1977, General Electric Broadcasting Company was one of the first companies to register a sound (the sound that a ship's bell clock makes) as a service mark.

The Trademark Revision Act of 1988 allows organizations to register trademarks based on a bona fide intention to use them (normally, within six months following the issuance of the trademark) for ten years. To renew the trademark, the company must prove it is using it. Rights to a trademark last as long as the mark is used. Normally, if the firm does not use it for two years, the trademark is considered abandoned, and a new user can claim exclusive ownership of the mark.

ON LINE In November 1999, legislation went into effect that changes trademark law to explicitly apply to the on-line world. This law includes financial penalties for those who violate trademarked products or those who register an otherwise trademarked term as a domain name.[22]

Companies that fail to protect their trademarks face the problem of their product names becoming generic. A **generic product name** identifies a product by class or type and cannot be trademarked. Former brand names that were not sufficiently protected by their owners and were subsequently declared to be generic product names in U.S. courts include aspirin, cellophane, linoleum, thermos, kerosene, monopoly, cola, and shredded wheat.

Companies like Rolls Royce, Cross, Xerox, Levi Strauss, Frigidaire, and McDonald's aggressively enforce their trademarks. Rolls Royce, Coca-Cola, and Xerox even run newspaper and magazine ads stating that their names are trademarks and should not be used as descriptive or generic terms. Some ads threaten lawsuits against competitors that violate trademarks.

Despite severe penalties for trademark violations, trademark infringement lawsuits are not uncommon. One of the major battles is over brand names that closely resemble another brand name. Donna Karan filed a lawsuit against Donnkenny Inc., whose Nasdaq trading symbol—DNKY—was too close to Karan's DKNY trademark.

Companies must also contend with fake or unauthorized brands, such as fake Levi's jeans, Microsoft software, Rolex watches, Reebok and Nike footwear, and Louis Vuitton handbags. Copycat golf clubs, such as Big Bursa, a knockoff of Callaway's popular Big Bertha, are growing in sales.

GLOBAL In Europe, you can sue counterfeiters only if your brand, logo, or trademark is formally registered. Until recently, formal registration was required in each country in which a company sought protection. A company can now register its trademark in all European Union (EU) member countries with one application.

trademark
The exclusive right to use a brand or part of a brand.

service mark
Trademark for a service.

generic product name
Identifies a product by class or type and cannot be trademarked.

Packaging

Describe marketing uses of packaging and labeling

Packages have always served a practical function—that is, they hold contents together and protect goods as they move through the distribution channel. Today, however, packaging is also a container for promoting the product and making it easier and safer to use.

Packaging Functions

The three most important functions of packaging are to contain and protect products, promote products, and facilitate the storage, use, and convenience of products. A fourth function of packaging that is becoming increasingly important is to facilitate recycling and reduce environmental damage.

Containing and Protecting Products   The most obvious function of packaging is to contain products that are liquid, granular, or otherwise divisible. Packaging also enables manufacturers, wholesalers, and retailers to market products in specific quantities, such as ounces.

Physical protection is another obvious function of packaging. Most products are handled several times between the time they are manufactured, harvested, or otherwise produced and the time they are consumed or used. Many products are shipped, stored, and inspected several times between production and consumption. Some, like milk, need to be refrigerated. Others, like beer, are sensitive to light. Still others, like medicines and bandages, need to be kept sterile. Packages protect products from breakage, evaporation, spillage, spoilage, light, heat, cold, infestation, and many other conditions.

Promoting Products   Packaging does more than identify the brand, list the ingredients, specify features, and give directions. A package differentiates a product from competing products and may associate a new product with a family of other products from the same manufacturer. Welch's repackaged its line of grape juice–based jams, jellies, and juices to unify the line and get more impact on the shelf.

Packages use designs, colors, shapes, and materials to try to influence consumers' perceptions and buying behavior. For example, marketing research shows that health-conscious consumers are likely to think that any food is probably good for them as long as it comes in green packaging. Two top brands of low-fat foods—Snackwell's and Healthy Choice—use green packaging.[23] Sunsweet Growers, appealing to baby boomers' interest in health foods, used the theme "Be good to yourself" on new packages for its line of prune products.[24]

Packaging has a measurable effect on sales. Quaker Oats revised the package for Rice-a-Roni without making any other changes in marketing strategy and experienced a 44 percent increase in sales in one year.

Repackaging has sometimes been used to promote new uses for products in a way that may raise questions, as the "Ethics in Marketing" example illustrates.

Facilitating Storage, Use, and Convenience   Wholesalers and retailers prefer packages that are easy to ship, store, and stock on shelves. They also like packages that protect products, prevent spoilage or breakage, and extend the product's shelf life.

Consumers' requirements for convenience cover many dimensions. Consumers are constantly seeking items that are easy to handle, open, and reclose, although some consumers want packages that are tamperproof or childproof. Consumers also want reusable and disposable packages. Surveys conducted by

Hungry Jack introduced its microwaveable syrup bottle in 1999. This packaging innovation makes it much easier to use the product.

THOSE NEW MEDICINES THAT FIGHT MIGRAINES LOOK AWFULLY FAMILIAR

Ads from Motrin Migraine tout the drug for "people who don't fool around with pain." Motrin Migraine, the ads promise, "kicks butt." This may sound like welcome news to the country's estimated twenty-eight million migraine sufferers. But Motrin Migraine is actually a marketing, not a medical, breakthrough. Motrin Migraine, along with Advil Migraine and Excedrin Migraine, the other new over-the-counter migraine drugs, are exactly the same pill as the original versions, with the same ingredients in the same dose. They are simply in a different package.

Motrin Migraine contains 200 milligrams of ibuprofen, just like regular Motrin. Advil Migraine also contains 200 milligrams of ibuprofen, just like regular Advil. And Excedrin Migraine contains the same combination of aspirin, acetaminophen, and caffeine found in extra-strength Excedrin. The only difference is that the Food and Drug Administration (FDA) now allows the three pain relievers to claim they ease the pain of migraine headache, in addition to other aches and pains.

For years, the FDA wouldn't allow makers of over-the-counter pain relievers to claim the drugs could treat migraines. But after Bristol-Myers Squibb presented the FDA with its own migraine studies, the FDA in 1998 approved Excedrin for that purpose. The agency, however, decided migraine sufferers needed different information about symptoms, dosing, and when to see a doctor than people with regular headaches. As a result, the FDA asked Bristol Meyers to create a second package for Excedrin Migraine.

Drug marketers have found that repackaging pills under different names can translate into big sales. At a time when overall sales of pain relievers in the United States rose just 4 percent, Excedrin Migraine sales in 1999 surged 40 percent to $67 million. Tylenol Arthritis, a repackaged version of Tylenol Extended Relief, jumped more than sixfold to $67 million, according to Information Resources of Chicago. A Bristol Meyers spokeswoman says that while Excedrin Migraine has taken some sales away from regular Excedrin, most of the growth is from new customers.

Joseph Codispoti, senior director of clinical development for McNeil Consumer Health Care, the Johnson & Johnson unit that makes both Motrin and Tylenol, says the repackaging of pain relievers for specific health problems helps the consumer better understand the medicine's benefits. Because many migraine sufferers don't seek medical treatment, the repackaging of regular pain relievers as migraine medicine gives consumers who are self-medicating with over-the-counter drugs some needed information, he says.

Bristol Meyers initially took out newspaper and television ads explaining that the pills in extra-strength Excedrin and Excedrin Migraine were the same. The FDA objected, saying consumers might use regular Excedrin to treat migraines, which, even though it was the same pill, didn't carry the same warning information.[a]

Do you think the repackaging strategy of pain relievers is an ethical practice? Explain your answer.

[a] Tara Parker-Pope, "Those New Medicines That Fight Migraines Look Awfully Familiar," *Wall Street Journal*, May 5, 2000, p. B1.

Sales & Marketing Management magazine revealed that consumers dislike—and avoid buying—leaky ice cream boxes, overly heavy or fat vinegar bottles, immovable pry-up lids on glass bottles, key-opener sardine cans, and hard-to-pour cereal boxes. Such packaging innovations as zipper tear strips, hinged lids, tab slots, screw-on tops, and pour spouts were introduced to solve these and other problems. C&H Sugar designed a new four-pound carton with an easy-to-pour, reclosable top.[25]

Some firms use packaging to segment markets. For example, the C&H carton is targeted to consumers who don't do a lot of baking and are willing to pay at least twenty cents more for the package. Different-size packages appeal to heavy, moderate, and light users. Salt is sold in package sizes ranging from single serving to picnic size to giant economy size. Campbell's soup is packaged in single-serving cans aimed at the elderly and singles market segments. Beer and soft drinks are similarly marketed in various package sizes and types. Packaging convenience can increase a product's utility and, therefore, its market share and profits. Guinness Bass Import is testing a packaged-draft system that allows consumers to drink nitrogenated Guinness Stout right out of the bottle. This package could win converts among consumers who prefer to drink beer straight from the bottle and in nightclubs that only offer beer in bottles rather than in a glass or on draft.[26]

Facilitating Recycling and Reducing Environmental Damage One of the most important packaging issues in the 1990s is compatibility with the environment.

Some firms use their packaging to target environmentally concerned market segments. Brocato International markets shampoo and hair conditioner in bottles that are biodegradable in landfills. Procter & Gamble markets Sure Pro and Old Spice in "eco-friendly" pump-spray packages that do not rely on aerosol propellants. Other firms that have introduced pump sprays include S.C. Johnson (Pledge furniture polish), Reckitt & Coleman Household Products (Woolite rug cleaner), Rollout L.P. (Take 5 cleanser), and Richardson-Vicks (Vidal Sassoon hair spray).

Labeling

persuasive labeling
A type of package labeling that focuses on a promotional theme or logo and consumer information is secondary.

An integral part of any package is its label. Labeling generally takes one of two forms: persuasive or informational. **Persuasive labeling** focuses on a promotional theme or logo, and consumer information is secondary. Price Pfister developed a new, persuasive label—featuring a picture of a faucet, the brand name, and the logo—with the goal of strengthening brand identity and becoming known as a brand instead of as a manufacturer. Note that the standard promotional claims— such as "new," "improved," and "super"—are no longer very persuasive. Consumers have been saturated with "newness" and thus discount these claims.

informational labeling
A type of package labeling designed to help consumers make proper product selections and lower their cognitive dissonance after the purchase.

Informational labeling, in contrast, is designed to help consumers make proper product selections and lower their cognitive dissonance after the purchase. Sears attaches a "label of confidence" to all its floor coverings. This label gives such product information as durability, color, features, cleanability, care instructions, and construction standards. Most major furniture manufacturers affix labels to their wares that explain the products' construction features, such as type of frame, number of coils, and fabric characteristics. The Nutritional Labeling and Education Act of 1990 mandated detailed nutritional information on most food packages and standards for health claims on food packaging. An important outcome of this legislation is guidelines from the Food and Drug Administration for using terms like *low fat, light, reduced cholesterol, low sodium, low calorie, and fresh.*

Universal Product Codes

universal product codes (UPCs)
A series of thick and thin vertical lines (bar codes), readable by computerized optical scanners, that represent numbers used to track products.

The **universal product codes (UPCs)** that appear on most items in supermarkets and other high-volume outlets were first introduced in 1974. Because the numerical codes appear as a series of thick and thin vertical lines, they are often called *bar codes.* The lines are read by computerized optical scanners that match codes with brand names, package sizes, and prices. They also print information on cash register tapes and help retailers rapidly and accurately prepare records of customer purchases, control inventories, and track sales. The UPC system and scanners are also used in single-source research (see Chapter 8).

Global Issues in Branding and Packaging

Discuss global issues in branding and packaging

International marketers must address several concerns regarding branding and packaging.

Branding

When planning to enter a foreign market with an existing product, a firm has three options for handling the brand name:

- *One brand name everywhere:* This strategy is useful when the company markets mainly one product and the brand name does not have negative connotations in any local market. The Coca-Cola Company uses a one-brand-name strategy in 195 countries around the world. The advantages of a one-brand-name strategy are greater identification of the product from market to market and ease of coordinating promotion from market to market.
- *Adaptations and modifications:* A one-brand-name strategy is not possible when the name cannot be pronounced in the local language, when the brand name is owned by someone else, or when the brand name has a negative or vulgar connotation in the local language. The Iranian detergent "Barf," for example, might encounter some problems in the U.S. market.[27]
- *Different brand names in different markets:* Local brand names are often used when translation or pronunciation problems occur, when the marketer wants the brand to appear to be a local brand, or when regulations require localization. Gillette's Silkience hair conditioner is called Soyance in France and Sientel in Italy. The adaptations were deemed to be more appealing in the local markets. Coca-Cola's Sprite brand had to be renamed Kin in Korea to satisfy a government prohibition on the unnecessary use of foreign words. Snuggle fabric softener is called FaFa in Japan, Cajoline in France, and other cuddly names elsewhere in the world.

Packaging

Three aspects of packaging that are especially important in international marketing are labeling, aesthetics, and climate considerations. The major *labeling* concern is properly translating ingredient, promotional, and instructional information on labels. In Eastern Europe, packages of Ariel detergent are printed in fourteen languages, from Latvian to Lithuanian. Care must also be employed in meeting all local labeling requirements. Several years ago, an Italian judge ordered that all bottles of Coca-Cola be removed from retail shelves because the ingredients were not properly labeled. Labeling is also harder in countries like Belgium and Finland, which require it to be bilingual.

Package *aesthetics* may also require some attention. The key is to stay attuned to cultural traits in host countries. For example, colors may have different connotations. Red is associated with witchcraft in some countries, green may be a sign of danger, and white may be symbolic of death. Aesthetics also influence package size. Soft drinks are not sold in six-packs in countries that lack refrigeration. In some countries, products like detergent may be bought only in small quantities because of a lack of storage space. Other products, like cigarettes, may be bought in small quantities, and even single units, because of the low purchasing power of buyers.

Coca-Cola uses a one-brand-name strategy in 195 countries around the world. Its product and positive image are recognizable almost everywhere.
© Jeff Greenberg

On the other hand, simple visual elements of the brand, such as a symbol or logo, can be a standardizing element across products and countries. For example, when Scott Paper wanted to establish a global brand identity for its product line, it used a single brand mark for all product lines that had the flexibility to accommodate such variables as country-specific product names.

Extreme *climates* and long-distance shipping necessitate sturdier and more durable packages for goods sold overseas. Spillage, spoilage, and breakage are all more important concerns when products are shipped long distances or frequently handled during shipping and storage. Packages may also have to ensure a longer product life if the time between production and consumption lengthens significantly.

Product Warranties

Describe how and why product warranties are important marketing tools

warranty
A confirmation of the quality or performance of a good or service.

express warranty
A written guarantee.

implied warranty
An unwritten guarantee that the good or service is fit for the purpose for which it was sold.

Just as a package is designed to protect the product, a **warranty** protects the buyer and gives essential information about the product. A warranty confirms the quality or performance of a good or service. An **express warranty** is a written guarantee. Express warranties range from simple statements—such as "100 percent cotton" (a guarantee of quality) and "complete satisfaction guaranteed" (a statement of performance)—to extensive documents written in technical language. In contrast, an **implied warranty** is an unwritten guarantee that the good or service is fit for the purpose for which it was sold. All sales have an implied warranty under the Uniform Commercial Code.

Congress passed the Magnuson-Moss Warranty–Federal Trade Commission Improvement Act in 1975 to help consumers understand warranties and get action from manufacturers and dealers. A manufacturer that promises a full warranty must meet certain minimum standards, including repair "within a reasonable time and without charge" of any defects and replacement of the merchandise or a full refund if the product does not work "after a reasonable number of attempts" at repair. Any warranty that does not live up to this tough prescription must be "conspicuously" promoted as a limited warranty.

Looking Back

Look back at the story that opens the chapter about McDonald's-brand extension strategies. "Leveraging our brand" means that McDonald's hopes to use the positive perceptions, or image, that consumers have of the McDonald's name to help the company successfully market other types of products. McDonald's strategy may be sound, depending on the product category and execution of the marketing strategy. For example, they could be successful at marketing children's videos and books if they can offer good quality products that children like and their parents approve of. The McCafe idea may be straying too far from McDonald's positioning strategy. Gourmet coffee and snacks may not fit with McDonald's fast-food image. These new products will also not appeal to the McDonald's main target market—kids.

Evaluate Your School

Have you ever thought of your university as a product? Maybe not, but the concepts of product line, product mix, and branding can be applied to universities just as they are to products. How would you describe your university along these lines to a prospective student from your town? From a larger city? From abroad? Using the concepts in this chapter, write a brief description of your university designed to familiarize prospective students with its offerings and compare it with the official materials found at the Admis-

sions Office. How does your description stack up?

VALUE Are you a prospective student yourself? If you are thinking about transferring or about graduate school, you are. You can use the concepts in this chapter to help you compare the various schools you are considering. Thinking about universities as products or brands can help you make your decision and identify the pros and cons of each institution. It can also help you determine value: Is the tuition charged worth the product you will receive?

Summary

1 **Define the term** *product.* A product is anything, desired or not, that a person or organization receives in an exchange. The basic goal of purchasing decisions is to receive the tangible and intangible benefits associated with a product. Tangible aspects include packaging, style, color, size, and features. Intangible qualities include service, the retailer's image, the manufacturer's reputation, and the social status associated with a product. An organization's product offering is the crucial element in any marketing mix.

2 **Classify consumer products.** Consumer products are classified into four categories: convenience products, shopping products, specialty products, and unsought products. Convenience products are relatively inexpensive and require limited shopping effort. Shopping products are of two types: homogeneous and heterogeneous. Because of the similarity of homogeneous products, they are differentiated mainly by price and features. In contrast, heterogeneous products appeal to consumers because of their distinct characteristics. Specialty products possess unique benefits that are highly desirable to certain customers. Finally, unsought products are either new products or products that require aggressive selling because they are generally avoided or overlooked by consumers.

3 **Define the terms** *product item,* *product line,* **and** *product mix.* A product item is a specific version of a product that can be designated as a distinct offering among an organization's products. A product line is a group of closely related products offered by an organization. An organization's product mix includes all the products it sells. Product mix width refers to the number of product lines an organization offers. Product line depth is the number of product items in a product line. Firms modify existing products by changing their quality, functional characteristics, or style. Product line extension occurs when a firm adds new products to existing product lines.

4 **Describe marketing uses of branding.** A brand is a name, term, or symbol that identifies and differentiates a firm's products. Established brands encourage customer loyalty and help new products succeed. Branding strategies require decisions about individual, family, manufacturers', and private brands.

5 **Describe marketing uses of packaging and labeling.** Packaging has four functions: containing and protecting products; promoting products; facilitating product storage, use, and convenience; and facilitating recycling and reducing

Key Terms

environmental damage. As a tool for promotion, packaging identifies the brand and its features. It also serves the critical function of differentiating a product from competing products and linking it with related products from the same manufacturer. The label is an integral part of the package, with persuasive and informational functions. In essence, the package is the marketer's last chance to influence buyers before they make a purchase decision.

6 **Discuss global issues in branding and packaging.** In addition to brand piracy, international marketers must address a variety of concerns regarding branding and packaging, including choosing a brand name policy, translating labels and meeting host-country labeling requirements, making packages aesthetically compatible with host-country cultures, and offering the sizes of packages preferred in host countries.

7 **Describe how and why product warranties are important marketing tools.** Product warranties are important tools because they offer consumers protection and help them gauge product quality.

Discussion and Writing Questions

1. **TEAM** Break into groups of four or five. From the following list of products, have the members of the group classify each product into the category (convenience, shopping, specialty, unsought) that they think fits best from their perspective as consumers (i.e., if they were buying the product): Coca-Cola (brand), car stereo, winter coat, pair of shoes, life insurance, blue jeans, hamburgers, shampoo, canned vegetables, frozen pizza.

2. **WRITING** A local civic organization has asked you to give a luncheon presentation about planned obsolescence. Rather than pursuing a negative approach by talking about how businesses exploit customers through planned obsolescence, you have decided to talk about the benefits of producing products that do not last forever. Prepare a one-page outline of your presentation.

3. **WRITING** A local supermarket would like to introduce their own brand of paper goods (e.g., paper towels, facial tissue, etc.) to sell alongside their current inventory. The company has hired you to generate a report outlining the advantages and disadvantages of doing so. Write the report.

4. Identify five outstanding brand names, and explain why each is included in your list.

5. **WRITING** Find a product at home that has a distinctive package. Write a paragraph evaluating that package based on the four functions of packaging discussed in the chapter.

6. How have several snack food companies modified their product to serve the emerging needs of their customers?

7. **ON LINE** What is the product mix offered at Web site **http://www.marriott.com**?

8. **ON LINE** **GLOBAL** List the countries to which Levi Strauss & Co. markets through Web site **http://www.levi.com**. How do the product offerings differ between the United States and European selections?

9. **INFOTRAC COLLEGE EDITION** Learn more about how product warranties are handled worldwide. Using InfoTrac (**http://www.infotrac-college.com**) run a keyword search for "warranty" or "guarantee" and a country of interest to you. For example, search for "warranty" and "Germany" or "guarantee" and "Mexico." Write a paragraph on what you discover.

Application for Entrepreneurs

The Baker family owns one of the largest catfish farms in central Texas, known for raising the sweetest catfish in the area. After graduating from college with a degree in marketing, Frank Baker returned to the farm with a mind full of new ways to cash in on the farm's reputation. At the time, the family allowed the butcher at the local supermarket to use the Baker name on their catfish. In central Texas, eating Baker Farms catfish was a sign of status. Frank, eager to put his degree to work, convinced his family that they could make money off their name by selling their catfish products already packaged to supermarkets. After hearing the idea, the family quickly met to formulate a plan to begin selling Baker Farms catfish.

Questions

1. What type of product is the Baker family selling? List your reasons.
2. What type of branding is the Baker family using? List your reasons.
3. How should Baker Farms catfish be packaged?
4. Assuming that the Baker family wishes to reposition their catfish products, what would be an optimal strategy?

Case entrepreneurship

Maps à la Carte

A love of maps combined with some computer savvy may have translated into a viable business for two Massachusetts entrepreneurs. Ed McNierney and Bill Everett, both former executives at Kodak Company's software subsidiary in Billerica, Massachusetts, launched Maps à la Carte's Topozone.com Web site in November 1999. Founded in 1999, Maps à la Carte is a Digital Cartographic Business Partner with the U.S. Geological Survey.

Topographic maps are used extensively by hikers, surveyors, and geologists. They contain information such as elevation, positioning, and landmarks and are produced by the U.S. Geological Survey. Unfortunately, these 60,000 different maps do not fit together when users try to move from map to map. For example, some of the maps are curved at the edges, some are rectangles, and they may even come in different scales. McNierney and Everett were able to solve such problems with Topozone.com.

Targeting the more than fifty million outdoor recreation enthusiasts (both McNierney and Everett are avid outdoorsmen), the Topozone.com site is the first interactive, seamless U.S. topographic map site on the Web.

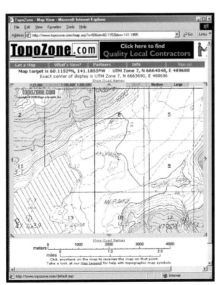

Prior to this on-line capability, outdoor recreation enthusiasts had to use paper and CD-ROM topographic maps to plan their outdoor adventures. Map giant DeLorme Publishing Company offers topographic maps on CD-ROMs and Maptech Inc. includes topographic maps on its site. However, DeLorme's CD-ROMs sell for around $100, and Maptech, with its emphasis on nautical areas, has tended to target boaters rather than hikers. As such, U.S. Geological Survey and industry experts suggest that Topozone.com, with its high quality and extensive site search tools, is the map industry leader.

Within six months of launch, the Topozone.com site was averaging around 150,000 visitors a month. In addition to outdoor enthusiasts, the site was reaching beyond the intended target market. Visitors included genealogists, hobbyists, and cemetery associations. Additionally, the site won About.com's "1999 Best of the Net" award and was designated as the number one on-line geography site, replacing MapQuest.

While Maps à la Carte's new product offering appeared to be a huge success, company executives were not experiencing overnight wealth. With a good product service idea that was lauded by many, the company was not charging consumers to print out screen maps. By June 2000, the company had only made $50,000 in revenue from advertising and licensing fees. Maps à la Carte licensed its Topozone.com topographic map content to leading Web sites such as MapQuest.com, Trails.com, GreatLodge.com, ALLOUTDOORS.com, and PointsBeyond.com, and the company was offering banner advertising opportunities.

To make money on this new product venture, McNierney and Everett developed a business model wherein they would give away the topographic map data and sell consumers the software that allowed users to make full use of the better quality maps available at Topozone.com. To work within this new product development business model, Maps à la Carte sold almost 20 percent of the company to Navitrak, a Canadian mapping company, in June 2000 for approximately $1 million. Navitrak is a wireless navigation technology company specializing in the development and manufacture of personal navigation devices. Along with this 20 percent acquisition, the companies will work together to further develop topographic mapping systems for the outdoor recreation market.

As entrepreneurs, McNierney and Everett developed and introduced a product that satisfied a need of outdoor enthusiasts and others. With a major investment by Navitrak, the two must focus upon extending the product concept into new markets and/or product extensions. With the fast pace of change and development in Internet-related offerings and a slew of potential competitors, McNierney and Everett have to move quickly.

Questions

1. What type of product does Topozone.com offer?
2. Should Maps à la Carte consider a branding strategy?
3. Should Maps à la Carte combine with Navitrak in a cobranding strategy? What would be the benefits of cobranding?

Bibliography

Stephanie Stoughton. "Path to Success." *Boston Globe*, June 17, 2000, pp. C1–C2.

"Topozone Launches Interactive Topographic Map Size, Revolutionizes Topographic Map Industry." *PR Newswire*, November 30, 1999. On-line.

http://www.topozone.com

Case

video

Ben & Jerry's: Taste and Innovation

What's in a name? Everything, at Ben & Jerry's, makers of mouth-watering ice cream in smooth and chunky flavors. Produced in Vermont from local dairy products and spring water, Ben & Jerry's strong brand image is one of high quality, innovative flavors, and barrel-of-laughs names. Products like Chunky Monkey, Vanilla Like It Oughta Be, Chubby Hubby, and Chocolate Chip Cookie Dough delight the palette and underscore the whimsical image of the company. To honor Grateful Dead icon, Jerry Garcia, and to appeal to youthful audiences, the company created Cherry Garcia ice cream in 1987. And today their newest flavor is Dilbert: Totally Nuts, named for the hapless comic strip hero of today's workaday world.

But the names aren't only funny. They carry a lot of weight supporting the company's brand equity. They have also created value based on customer recognition of the brand and loyalty among customers who like both the ice cream and the company mandate to improve society and the environment. Actually, Ben & Jerry's social philosophy plays a major role in making the company name well known. For example, Phish Food, chocolate ice cream with fish-shaped chocolate chunks, is named for the Vermont-based rock band Phish. On each pint container of Phish Food, the band pledges, "Our share of the proceeds from this pint goes to environmental efforts in the Lake Champlain Region of Vermont, so enjoy the good taste and karma." In 1997, sales of Phish Food generated royalties of $159,000.

Also in 1997, royalties in the amount of $55,000 were paid on the sale of Doonesberry Sorbet. Pints of Doonesberry include the following message, signed by the cartoon strip's character Mike Doonesbury: "P.S. All creator royalties go to charity, so your purchase represents an orderly transfer of wealth you can feel proud of." Royalty funds from Doonesberry Sorbet go to education, AIDS treatment and prevention, reducing poverty, and human rights.

Though premium ice cream is still the company favorite, Ben & Jerry's expanded the product mix because the original product was high in fat, and today's consumers wanted low-fat, healthier products with more nutritional value. So, product lines now include low-fat ice cream, low-fat and nonfat frozen yogurts, and fat-free sorbet. The idea is "to blend flavor that tastes very fattening into ice cream that isn't." All the product lines share the same marketing strategy, complete with offbeat humor and catchy names. For Ben & Jerry's twentieth birthday, new low-fat flavors were introduced—Coconut Cream Pie Low Fat, S'Mores, and Blackberry Cobbler. Within each product line, some flavors have become so well known that they constitute brands unto themselves. For example, Cherry Garcia is available in both the premium and frozen yogurt categories.

Catchy names and expanded product lines are not the only marketing strategies followed at Ben & Jerry's, where even the packaging is considered a promotional element. That's why all product lines are packaged in similarly designed and illustrated pint containers. Because consumers often believe that different product lines made by the same manufacturer are equal in quality, those who love the ice cream may try the yogurt, especially because their packaging looks alike.

To celebrate the company's twentieth birthday, the pint package was redesigned to be fun and colorful and to have an appetizing look. Packaging at Ben & Jerry's, however, also conveys important messages regarding the ingredients. In addition to the information on charitable contributions, the labels on pint cartons state, "We oppose rBGH, Recombinant Bovine Growth Hormone. The family farmers who supply our milk and cream pledge not to treat their cows with

rBGH. . . ." The company's overarching belief in social responsibility—whether it be the consumers' right to know what they are eating or the corporate call to social giving—is reflected and advertised in its package designs.

Packaging materials themselves have become a test case of the company's pledge to improve the environment. One goal is to make the transition to totally chlorine-free paper for pint containers because the bleaching process releases pollutants into the air. Although these kinds of measures seem on the surface to be great marketing hooks, still the public does not always favor company initiatives. Packaging for Peace Pops ice cream bars was redesigned and this message added: "We package our Peace Pops in bags, not individual boxes, because it puts less trash in the landfill." But sales declined as a result because customers wanted the packaging of their premium ice cream to reflect its high quality and high price. Reluctantly, the company changed packaging back to boxes. As a compromise, the new Peanut Butter & Jelly bar is in a plastic bag inside a chlorine-free box.

Questions

1. What are the tangible and intangible dimensions of Ben & Jerry's products?
2. Why did Ben & Jerry's develop several product lines?
3. Describe Ben & Jerry's brand equity.
4. What is the advantage of Ben & Jerry's using one marketing strategy for the entire product mix?

Bibliography
Ben & Jerry's annual report
Ben & Jerry's Web site: **http://www.benjerry.com**

chapter 10

Learning Objectives

1 Explain the importance of developing new products and describe the six categories of new products

2 Explain the steps in the new-product development process

3 Explain why some products succeed and others fail

4 Discuss global issues in new-product development

5 Explain the diffusion process through which new products are adopted

6 Explain the concept of product life cycles

Developing and Managing Products

By day, Ronald A. Lewis II toiled in his lab at Ralston Purina Company, sharing the results of his research with almost no one. By night, twenty-eight-year-old Lewis went into his laundry room in the basement of his suburban condominium and conducted further experiments on his pets, a miniature schnauzer named Bruce Wayne and a miniature dachshund named Selina Kyle.

When friends visited, Lewis warned them not to go in the basement. Neighbors wondered why the dogs were so seldom seen outside. When anyone asked what he was doing at work, Lewis politely declined to answer.

Now, at last, the secret can be revealed. Lewis and Ralston Purina have been working on a product that could fundamentally change the nature of pet ownership: dog litter.

For more than three years, Ralston Purina researchers have been studying what they refer to as canine elimination behavior. They have come away convinced that dogs can and should be taught to behave a little more like cats. And they believe that humans will spend heavily to have house-trained canines and the freedom that comes with that.

The company's new product, called *Secondnature*, is aimed primarily at small dogs in big cities. Ralston Purina hopes Secondnature will prove as popular as cat litter, a $900 million a year industry with fat profit margins.

Ralston executives imagine a world without pooper-scoopers, a world in which dogs wouldn't have to be walked in foul weather, where elderly people in high-rise apartments could have canine companionship even if they can't get out for walks, where single working people would no longer have to rely on professional dog walkers.

If dog litter really caught on, the dog population might grow by millions. Animal shelters say trouble with house-training is the biggest reason dog owners abandon their pets. A boom in the dog population would translate into a boom in dog food sales, too. Pet food accounts for 53 percent of Ralston's $4.7 billion in sales, compared with about 5 percent for cat litter. The rest comes largely from a battery division Ralston is spinning off.[1]

How would you go about testing this new product before introducing it? How would you introduce it to prospective customers? Do you think it will succeed or fail?

The Importance of New Products

Explain the importance of developing new products and describe the six categories of new products

New products are important to sustain growth and profits and to replace obsolete items. 3M Corp. introduces about 500 new products each year. Johnson & Johnson and Gillette expect products launched in the past five years to account for 36 and 50 percent of annual revenue, respectively.[2]

The number of new product introductions continues to rise. Marketing Intelligence, Ltd., identified less than 14,000 new product introductions in 1989 and over 25,000 in 1998. Less than 6 percent of the new products introduced in most years appear to be truly innovative.[3]

Categories of New Products

new product
A product new to the world, the market, the producer, the seller, or some combination of these.

The term **new product** is somewhat confusing, because its meaning varies widely. Actually, there are several "correct" definitions of the term. A product can be new to the world, to the market, to the producer or seller, or to some combination of these. There are six categories of new products:

- *New-to-the-world products* (also called *discontinuous innovations*): These products create an entirely new market. The telephone, television, computer, and facsimile machine are commonly cited examples of new-to-the-world products.
- *New product lines:* These products, which the firm has not previously offered, allow it to enter an established market. Heinz Frozen Foods recently introduced a new product line called Boston Market Home Style following a ten-year licensing deal with Boston Chicken, Inc. The new line will anchor the premium end of three Heinz lines that include Budget Gourmet (a value product line) and Smart Ones (a nutritionally oriented product line).[4]
- *Additions to existing product lines:* This category includes new products that supplement a firm's established line. As Exhibit 9.2 in Chapter 9 illustrated, Gillette's MACH 3 is an addition to the company's blades and razors product line.
- *Improvements or revisions of existing products:* The "new and improved" product may be significantly or slightly changed. For example, Breyers Soft 'n Creamy! ice cream "scoops right out without bending the spoon." Anyone who has ever sat around for fifteen minutes waiting for a half-gallon of ice cream to thaw would certainly agree that this is a product improvement. Most new products fit into this category.

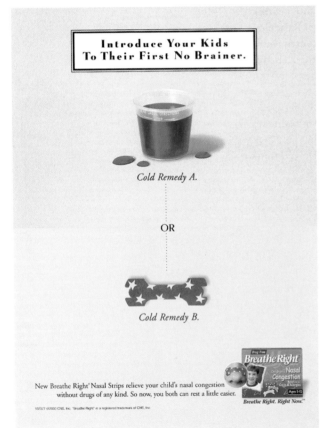

Introduce Your Kids To Their First No Brainer.

Cold Remedy A.

OR

Cold Remedy B.

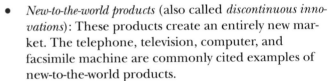

New Breathe Right® Nasal Strips relieve your child's nasal congestion without drugs of any kind. So now, you both can rest a little easier.

Into what category of new products do you think the Breathe Right Nasal Strip falls? It could possibly fall into more than one: additions to existing product lines and repositioned products. How?

- *Repositioned products:* These are existing products targeted at new markets or market segments. Following a 2 to 3 percent annual sales decline for ten years, Cutty Sark Scots Whiskey is no longer trying to compete head-on with super premium brands like Glenfiddich and blended scotch brands such as Chivas Regal and Dewars. The new target is twenty-something blue-collar males.[5]

- *Lower-priced products:* This category refers to products that provide performance similar to competing brands at a lower price. Hewlett-Packard Laser Jet 3100 is a scanner, copier, printer, and fax machine combined. This new product is priced lower than many conventional color copiers and much lower than the combined price of the four items purchased separately.[6]

The New-Product Development Process

The management and technology consulting firm Booz, Allen, and Hamilton has studied the new-product development process for over thirty years. Analyzing five major studies undertaken during this period, the firm has concluded that the companies most likely to succeed in developing and introducing new products are those that take the following actions:

Explain the steps in the new-product development process

- Make the long-term commitment needed to support innovation and new product development
- Use a company-specific approach, driven by corporate objectives and strategies, with a well-defined new-product strategy at its core
- Capitalize on experience to achieve and maintain competitive advantage
- Establish an environment—a management style, organizational structure, and degree of top-management support—conducive to achieving company-specific new-product and corporate objectives

Most companies follow a formal new-product development process, usually starting with a new-product strategy. Exhibit 10.1 traces the seven-step process,

Exhibit **10.1**

New-Product Development Process

New-product strategy

Idea generation

Idea screening

Business analysis

Development

Test marketing

Commercialization

New product

which is discussed in detail in this section. The exhibit is funnel-shaped to highlight the fact that each stage acts as a screen. The purpose is to filter out unworkable ideas.

New-Product Strategy

new-product strategy
A plan that links the new-product development process with the objectives of the marketing department, the business unit, and the corporation.

A **new-product strategy** links the new-product development process with the objectives of the marketing department, the business unit, and the corporation. A new-product strategy must be compatible with these objectives, and in turn, all three objectives must be consistent with one another.

A new-product strategy is part of the organization's overall marketing strategy. It sharpens the focus and provides general guidelines for generating, screening, and evaluating new-product ideas. The new-product strategy specifies the roles that new products must play in the organization's overall plan and describes the characteristics of products the organization wants to offer and the markets it wants to serve.

Idea Generation

New-product ideas come from many sources, such as customers, employees, distributors, competitors, research and development, and consultants.

Going direct to the customer to learn about people's cookout needs is what helped the Thermos work team create a new type of outdoor grill. Tapping customers can be a very effective method of generating new product ideas.
© James Schnepf/Liaison International

- *Customers:* The marketing concept suggests that customers' wants and needs should be the springboard for developing new products. Thermos, the vacuum bottle manufacturer, provides an interesting example of how companies tap customers for ideas. The company's first step in developing an innovative home barbecue grill was to send ten members of its interdisciplinary new-product team into the field for about a month. Their assignment was to learn all about people's cookout needs and to invent a product to meet them. In cities that included Boston, Los Angeles, and Columbus, Ohio, the team conducted focus groups, visited people's homes, and even videotaped barbecues.

- *Employees:* Marketing personnel—advertising and marketing research employees, as well as salespeople—often create new-product ideas, because they analyze and are involved in the marketplace. Firms such as Procter & Gamble reward employees who submit winning new product ideas with stock options.[7] The very successful introduction of Post-it Notes started with an employee's idea. In 1974, the research and development department of 3M's commercial tape division developed and patented the adhesive component of Post-it Notes. However, it was a year before an employee of the commercial tape division, who sang in a church choir, identified a use for the adhesive. He had been using paper clips and slips of paper to mark places in hymn books. But the paper clips damaged his books, and the slips of paper fell out. The solution, as we now all know, was to apply the adhesive to small pieces of paper and sell them in packages.

- *Distributors:* A well-trained sales force routinely asks distributors about needs that are not being met. Because they are closer to end users, distributors are often more aware of customer needs than are manufacturers. The inspiration for Rubbermaid's litter-free lunch box, named Sidekick, came from a distributor. The distributor suggested that Rubbermaid place some of its plastic containers inside a lunch box and sell the box as an alternative to plastic wrap and paper bags.

- *Competitors:* No firms rely solely on internally generated ideas for new products. A big part of any organization's marketing intelligence system should be monitoring the performance of competitors' products. One purpose of competitive monitoring is to determine which, if any, of the competitors' products should be copied.

There is plenty of information about competitors on the World Wide Web. For example, AltaVista (**http://www.altavista.digital.com**) is a powerful index tool that can be used to locate information about products and companies. Fuld & Co.'s competitive intelligence guide provides links to a variety of market intelligence sites.

- *Research and development (R&D):* R&D is carried out in four distinct ways. Basic research is scientific research aimed at discovering new technologies. Applied research takes these new technologies and tries to find useful applications for them. **Product development** goes one step further by converting applications into marketable products. *Product modification* makes cosmetic or functional changes in existing products. Many new-product breakthroughs come from R&D activities. Pert Plus, Procter & Gamble's combination shampoo and conditioner, was invented in the laboratory.
- *Consultants:* Outside consultants are always available to examine a business and recommend product ideas. Examples include the Weston Group; Booz, Allen, and Hamilton; and Management Decisions. Traditionally, consultants determine whether a company has a balanced portfolio of products and, if not, what new-product ideas are needed to offset the imbalance. For instance, an outside consultant conceived Airwick's highly successful Carpet Fresh carpet cleaner.

product development
Marketing strategy that entails the creation of marketable new products; process of converting applications for new technologies into marketable products.

Creativity is the wellspring of new-product ideas, regardless of who comes up with them. A variety of approaches and techniques have been developed to stimulate creative thinking. The two considered most useful for generating new-product ideas are brainstorming and focus group exercises. The goal of **brainstorming** is to get a group to think of unlimited ways to vary a product or solve a problem. Group members avoid criticism of an idea, no matter how ridiculous it may seem. Objective evaluation is postponed. The sheer quantity of ideas is what matters. As noted in Chapter 8, an objective of focus group interviews is to stimulate insightful comments through group interaction. Focus groups usually consist of seven to ten people. Sometimes consumer focus groups generate excellent new-product ideas—for example, Cycle dog food, Stick-Up room deodorizers, Dustbuster vacuum cleaners, and Wendy's salad bar. In the industrial market, machine tools, keyboard designs, aircraft interiors, and backhoe accessories have evolved from focus groups.

brainstorming
The process of getting a group to think of unlimited ways to vary a product or solve a problem.

Idea Screening

After new ideas have been generated, they pass through the first filter in the product development process. This stage, called **screening**, eliminates ideas that are inconsistent with the organization's new-product strategy or are obviously inappropriate for some other reason. The new-product committee, the new-product department, or some other formally appointed group performs the screening review. At Royal Dutch/Shell, small groups known as "GameChangers" meet weekly online to evaluate new products and process ideas submitted by employees.[8] In 1999, these review teams evaluated 320 ideas submitted by employees. Of Shell's five top business initiatives since that time, four emerged from GameChanger teams.[9] Most new-product ideas are rejected at the screening stage.

screening
The first filter in the product development process, which eliminates ideas that are inconsistent with the organization's new-product strategy or are obviously inappropriate for some other reason.

Concept tests are often used at the screening stage to rate concept (or product) alternatives. A **concept test** evaluates a new-product idea, usually before any prototype has been created. Typically, researchers get consumer reactions to descriptions and visual representations of a proposed product.

Concept tests are considered fairly good predictors of success for line extensions. They have also been relatively precise predictors of success for new products that are not copycat items, are not easily classified into existing product categories, and do not require major changes in consumer behavior—such as Betty Crocker Tuna Helper, Cycle dog food, and Libby Fruit Float. However, concept tests are usually inaccurate in predicting the success of new products that create new consumption patterns and require major changes in consumer behavior—such as microwave ovens, videocassette recorders, computers, and word processors.

Business Analysis

New-product ideas that survive the initial screening process move to the **business analysis** stage, where preliminary figures for demand, cost, sales, and profitability are calculated. For the first time, costs and revenues are estimated and compared. Depending on the nature of the product and the company, this process may be simple or complex.

The newness of the product, the size of the market, and the nature of competition all affect the accuracy of revenue projections. In an established market like soft drinks, industry estimates of total market size are available. Forecasting market share for a new entry is a bigger challenge.

Analyzing overall economic trends and their impact on estimated sales is especially important in product categories that are sensitive to fluctuations in the business cycle. If consumers view the economy as uncertain and risky, they will put off buying durable goods like major home appliances, automobiles, and homes. Likewise, business buyers postpone major equipment purchases if they expect a recession.

These questions are commonly asked during the business analysis stage:

- What is the likely demand for the product?
- What impact would the new product probably have on total sales, profits, market share, and return on investment?
- How would the introduction of the product affect existing products? Would the new product cannibalize existing products?
- Would current customers benefit from the product?
- Would the product enhance the image of the company's overall product mix?
- Would the new product affect current employees in any way? Would it lead to hiring more people or reducing the size of the workforce?
- What new facilities, if any, would be needed?
- How might competitors respond?
- What is the risk of failure? Is the company willing to take the risk?

Answering these and related questions may require studies of markets, competition, costs, and technical capabilities. But at the end of this stage, management should have a good understanding of the product's market potential. This full understanding is important, because costs increase dramatically once a product idea enters the development stage.

Development

In the early stage of **development**, the R&D department or engineering department may develop a prototype of the product. During this stage, the firm should start sketching a marketing strategy. The marketing department should decide on the product's packaging, branding, labeling, and so forth. In addition, it should map out preliminary promotion, price, and distribution strategies. The technical feasibility of manufacturing the product at an acceptable cost should also be thoroughly examined.

The development stage can last a long time and thus be very expensive. Crest toothpaste was in the development stage for ten years. It took eighteen years to develop Minute Rice, fifteen years to develop the Polaroid Colorpack camera, fifteen years to develop the Xerox copy machine, and fifty-five years to develop television. Gillette spent six years and more than $750 million developing the MACH 3 razor.[10] Preliminary efforts to develop a three-bladed razor began 28 years before the 1998 launch of MACH 3.[11]

ON LINE The development process works best when all the involved areas (R&D, marketing, engineering, production, and even suppliers) work together rather than sequentially, a process called **simultaneous product development.** This approach allows firms to shorten the development process and reduce costs. With simultaneous product development, all relevant functional areas and outside suppliers participate in all stages of the development process. Rather than proceeding through highly structured stages, the cross-functional team operates in unison. Involving key suppliers early in the process capitalizes on their specialized knowledge and enables them to design and develop critical component parts.

simultaneous product development
A new team-oriented approach to new-product development.

ON LINE The Internet is a useful tool for implementing simultaneous product development. On the Net, multiple partners from a variety of locations can meet regularly to assess new product ideas, analyze markets and demographics, and review cost information. Ideas judged to be feasible can quickly be converted into new products. For example, Procter & Gamble has created an autonomous idea laboratory called Corporate New Ventures. Its mission is to encourage ideas for products and put the best ideas into speedy production. Corporate New Ventures has $250 million in seed money and reports directly to top management. DaimlerChrysler and Nortel have similar on-line groups whose primary goal is to drive innovation at a rate never before experienced by these companies.[12]

Laboratory tests are often conducted on prototype models during the development stage. User safety is an important aspect of laboratory testing, which actually subjects products to much more severe treatment than is expected by end users. The Consumer Product Safety Act of 1972 requires manufacturers to conduct a "reasonable testing program" to ensure that their products conform to established safety standards.

Many products that test well in the laboratory are also tried out in homes or businesses. Examples of product categories well suited for such use tests include human and pet food products, household cleaning products, and industrial chemicals and supplies. These products are all relatively inexpensive, and their performance characteristics are apparent to users. For example, at the W. K. Kellogg Institute for Food and Nutrition Research, cross-functional teams of employees spend their days cooking, eating, and comparing notes. Management believes that creativity comes from diversity, so researchers with unusual backgrounds are recruited. One engineer studied music in college. The Institute employs people from twenty-two different countries. The company is quite pleased with the results produced by the Institute. In one recent month, researchers generated sixty-five new product ideas and ninety-four new packaging ideas.[13]

Most products require some refinement based on the results of laboratory and use tests. A second stage of development often takes place before test marketing.

Despite the high costs, Kellogg's is committed to test marketing its products. Cross-functional research teams are comprised of diverse individuals and have yielded wonderful results for the company.

What can you find out on the Internet about current test marketing? Use the AltaVista search engine and type in "Test Marketing."
http://www.altavista.com

On Line

test marketing
The limited introduction of a product and a marketing program to determine the reactions of potential customers in a market situation.

Test Marketing

After products and marketing programs have been developed, they are usually tested in the marketplace. **Test marketing** is the limited introduction of a product and a marketing program to determine the reactions of potential customers in a market situation. Test marketing allows management to evaluate alternative strategies and to assess how well the various aspects of the marketing mix fit together. Anheuser-Busch test-marketed its Tequiza brand beer in Albuquerque, Houston, and Pomona, California, before introducing it nationwide.[14]

The cities chosen as test sites should reflect market conditions in the new product's projected market area. Yet no "magic city" exists that can universally represent market conditions, and a product's success in one city doesn't guarantee

Exhibit 10.2

Checklist for Selecting Test Markets

In choosing a test market, many criteria need to be considered, especially the following:
Similarity to planned distribution outlets
Relative isolation from other cities
Availability of advertising media that will cooperate
Diversified cross section of ages, religions, cultural-societal preferences, etc.
No atypical purchasing habits
Representative population size
Typical per capita income
Good record as a test city, but not overly used
Not easily "jammed" by competitors
Stability of year-round sales
No dominant television station; multiple newspapers, magazines, and radio stations
Availability of retailers that will cooperate
Availability of research and audit services
Freedom from unusual influences, such as one industry's dominance or heavy tourism

that it will be a nationwide hit. When selecting test market cities, researchers should therefore find locations where the demographics and purchasing habits mirror the overall market. The company should also have good distribution in test cities. Moreover, test locations should be isolated from the media. If the TV stations in a particular market reach a very large area outside that market, the advertising used for the test product may pull in many consumers from outside the market. The product may then appear more successful than it really is. Exhibit 10.2 provides a useful checklist of criteria for selecting test markets.

The High Costs of Test Marketing

Test marketing frequently takes one year or longer and costs can exceed $1 million. Some products remain in test markets even longer. McDonald's spent twelve years developing and testing salads before introducing them. Despite the cost, many firms believe it is a lot better to fail in a test market than in a national introduction.

Because test marketing is so expensive, some companies do not test line extensions of well-known brands. For example, because the Folger's brand is well known, Procter & Gamble faced little risk in distributing its instant decaffeinated version nationally. Consolidated Foods Kitchen of Sara Lee followed the same approach with its frozen croissants. Other products introduced without being test marketed include General Foods' International Coffees, Quaker Oats' Chewy Granola Bars and Granola Dipps, and Pillsbury's Milk Break Bars.

The high cost of test marketing is not purely financial. One unavoidable problem is that test marketing exposes the new product and its marketing mix to competitors before its introduction. Thus, the element of surprise is lost. Several years ago, for example, Procter & Gamble began testing a ready-to-spread Duncan Hines frosting. General Mills took note and rushed to market with its own Betty Crocker brand, which now is the best-selling brand of ready-to-spread frosting. Competitors can also sabotage or "jam" a testing program by introducing their own sales promotion, pricing, or advertising campaign. The purpose is to hide or distort the normal conditions that the testing firm might expect in the market. When Coca-Cola tested its contour can (a curvy can inspired by Coke's trademark bottle) in 1997 at a premium price, PepsiCo counterattacked furiously by offering discounts on its cola products.[15]

Alternatives to Test Marketing

Many firms are looking for cheaper, faster, safer alternatives to traditional test marketing. In the early 1980s, Information Resources Incorporated pioneered one alternative: single-source research using supermarket scanner data (discussed in Chapter 8). A typical supermarket scanner test costs about $300,000. Another alternative to traditional test marketing is **simulated (laboratory) market testing**. Advertising and other promotional materials for several products, including the test product, are shown to members of the product's target market. These people are then taken to shop at a mock or real store, where their purchases are recorded. Shopper behavior, including repeat purchasing, is monitored to assess the product's likely performance under true market conditions. Research firms offer simulated market tests for $25,000 to $100,000, compared to $1 million or more for full-scale test marketing.

simulated (laboratory) market testing
Presentation of advertising and other promotion materials for several products, including a test product, to members of the product's target market.

Despite these alternatives, most firms still consider test marketing essential for most new products. The high price of failure simply prohibits the widespread introduction of most new products without testing. Sometimes, however, when risks of failure are estimated to be low, it is better to skip test marketing and move directly from development to commercialization.

Test marketing is also frequently bypassed for product line extensions. The "Ethics in Marketing" box illustrates a seemingly low-risk product introduction.

Ethics in Marketing

WHAT'S IN A NAME?

AT&T Corporation, the largest telecommunications company in the United States, launched the Lucky Dog Telephone Company brand to help the parent company compete against "dial-around" phone carriers. The upstart dial-arounds have grabbed business from AT&T by encouraging customers to dial a special code—in the case of MCI World-Com 10-10-321—as a way to bypass their home carrier.

Advertising for Lucky Dog doesn't reveal that it is a subsidiary of AT&T. The downscale ads are a far cry from "Reach out and touch someone." Featuring talking dogs, a prize-giveaway, and voice-overs by actor Larry Hagman and cast members from the old sitcom *The Jeffersons*, the spots promote Lucky Dog's low rates and its own dial-

around code, 10-10-345. The ads are quite a change from previous AT&T campaigns that criticized MCI's dial-around service for misleading customers about savings.

Dial-arounds are an attractive option to some consumers because there is usually no monthly fee, and rates are comparable to some of MCI and AT&T's heavily advertised regular discounts. But sometimes dial-around customers don't save much and might spend more. For example, Lucky Dog has a 10-cent hookup fee for every call, which can add up for customers who make many calls per month.

With its new effort, AT&T risks channeling its own high-paying customers into a lower-priced option. Even worse, there is the potential for cheapening AT&T's name. Ads

featuring talking animals wearing human clothes seem more suited to a kid's drink than a blue-chip corporate icon. According to one former AT&T executive, "If it looks like a dog and barks like a dog, it's probably really a dog—and it doesn't matter if it is named Lucky."[a]

Is Lucky Dog a new product? If so, what category of new products does it fit into? Describe and evaluate AT&T's strategy. Is it ethical for a firm such as AT&T to introduce a fighting brand without disclosing the brand's owner? Discuss.

[a] Stephanie W. Mehta, "Dog Teaches New Trick to AT&T," *Wall Street Journal*, October 7, 1998, pp. B1, B4. Reprinted by permission of the *Wall Street Journal*. © 1998 Dow Jones & Company, Inc. All Rights Reserved Worldwide.

Commercialization

commercialization
The decision to market a product.

The final stage in the new-product development process is **commercialization**, the decision to market a product. The decision to commercialize the product sets several tasks in motion: ordering production materials and equipment, starting production, building inventories, shipping the product to field distribution points, training the sales force, announcing the new product to the trade, and advertising to potential customers.

The time from the initial commercialization decision to the product's actual introduction varies. It can range from a few weeks for simple products that use existing equipment to several years for technical products that require custom manufacturing equipment.

The total cost of development and initial introduction can be staggering. Gillette spent $750 million developing MACH 3 and the first-year marketing budget for the new three-bladed razor was $300 million.[16]

 For some products, a well-planned Internet campaign can provide new-product information for people who are looking for the solutions that a particular new product offers. Attempting to reach customers at the point in time when they need a product is much more cost-effective and efficient than communicating with a target market that may eventually have a need for the product.

Despite the high cost of developing and testing new products, 85 percent of all new-product introductions fail.[17] Products fail for a number of reasons. One com-

Explain why some products succeed and others fail

mon reason is that they simply do not offer any discernible benefit compared to existing products. Another commonly cited factor in new-product failures is a poor match between product features and customer desires. For example, there are telephone systems on the market with over seven hundred different functions, although the average user is happy with just ten functions. Other reasons for failure include overestimation of market size, incorrect positioning, a price too high or too low, inadequate distribution, poor promotion, or simply an inferior product compared to those of competitors.

Failure can be a matter of degree. Absolute failure occurs when a company cannot recoup its development, marketing, and production costs. The product actually loses money for the company. A relative product failure results when the product returns a profit but fails to achieve sales, profit, or market share goals.

High costs and other risks of developing and testing new products do not stop many companies, such as Rubbermaid, Colgate-Palmolive, Campbell's Soup, 3M Corp., and Procter & Gamble, from aggressively developing and introducing new products.

The most important factor in successful new-product introduction is a good match between the product and market needs—as the marketing concept would predict. Successful new products deliver a meaningful and perceivable benefit to a sizable number of people or organizations and are different in some meaningful way from their intended substitutes. Firms that routinely experience success in new-product introductions tend to share the following characteristics:

- A history of carefully listening to customers
- An obsession with producing the best product possible
- A vision of what the market will be like in the future
- Strong leadership
- A commitment to new-product development
- A project-based team approach to new-product development
- Getting every aspect of the product development process right.[18]

Global Issues in New-Product Development

Increasing globalization of markets and of competition provides a reason for multinational firms to consider new-product development from a worldwide perspective. A firm that starts with a global strategy is better able to develop products that are marketable worldwide. In many multinational corporations, every product is developed for potential worldwide distribution, and unique market requirements are built in whenever possible. Procter & Gamble introduced Pampers Phases into global markets within one month of introducing the product in the United States. P&G's goal was to have the product on the shelf in ninety countries within one year. The objective was to establish brand loyalty among dealers and consumers before foreign competitors could react.

We often hear about how popular American products are in foreign countries. Recently, U.S. companies such as Levi Strauss & Co., Coca-Cola Co., RJR Nabisco, Inc., and Nike, Inc. have been finding that products popular in foreign markets can become hits in the United States "All of our

4

Discuss global issues in new-product development

Insights for new products are coming increasingly from around the world. An Argentine success, Häagen-Dazs's dulce de leche, is gaining popularity in the United States where in-store displays promote the new flavor.

products used to be driven almost 100 percent by consumers in the United States," says Juliet Moran, Nike's Director of International Marketing. "But, we're now finding we're getting insights from around the world."[19]

An example is Häagen-Dazs new ice cream flavor *dulce de leche* originally introduced in Buenos Aires in 1997. The brand is named after a caramelized milk drink that is popular in Argentina. *Dulce de leche* became an instant success in Argentina. The brand has since been introduced in the United States, and sales are increasing at over 25 percent per month.

Another example is Altoids, the popular breath mint. Altoids is a 200-year-old British product originally used to calm upset stomachs. It currently holds over 15 percent of the U.S. breath mint market.[20]

Levi's has told its U.S. managers that looking abroad for product ideas is part of their job. "Three or four years ago, that would have been inconceivable in this company," says Robert Holloway, Levi Strauss's vice-president for business development. "People had a much narrower view."[21]

Some global marketers design their products to meet regulations and other key requirements in their major markets and then, if necessary, meet smaller markets' requirements country by country. Nissan develops lead-country car models that can, with minor changes, be sold in most markets. For the remaining markets, Nissan provides other models that can readily be adapted. With this approach, Nissan has been able to reduce the number of its basic models from forty-eight to eighteen. There are, however, exceptions to this approach.

The Spread of New Products

adopter
A consumer who was happy enough with his or her trial experience with a product to use it again.

Explain the diffusion process through which new products are adopted

innovation
A product perceived as new by a potential adopter.

diffusion
The process by which the adoption of an innovation spreads.

Managers have a better chance of successfully marketing products if they understand how consumers learn about and adopt products. A person who buys a new product never before tried may ultimately become an **adopter**, a consumer who was happy enough with his or her trial experience with a product to use it again.

Diffusion of Innovation

An **innovation** is a product perceived as new by a potential adopter. It really doesn't matter whether the product is "new to the world" or some other category of new product. If it is new to a potential adopter, it is an innovation in this context. **Diffusion** is the process by which the adoption of an innovation spreads.

Five categories of adopters participate in the diffusion process:

- *Innovators:* the first 2.5 percent of all those who adopt the product. Innovators are eager to try new ideas and products, almost as an obsession. In addition to having higher incomes, they are more worldly and more active outside their community than noninnovators. They rely less on group norms and are more self-confident. Because they are well educated, they are more likely to get their information from scientific sources and experts. Innovators are characterized as being venturesome.
- *Early adopters:* the next 13.5 percent to adopt the product. Although early adopters are not the very first, they do adopt early in the product's life cycle. Compared to innovators, they rely much more on group norms and values. They are also more oriented to the local community, in contrast to the innova-

tor's worldly outlook. Early adopters are more likely than innovators to be opinion leaders because of their closer affiliation with groups. The respect of others is a dominant characteristic of early adopters.

- *Early majority:* the next 34 percent to adopt. The early majority weighs the pros and cons before adopting a new product. They are likely to collect more information and evaluate more brands than early adopters, therefore extending the adoption process. They rely on the group for information but are unlikely to be opinion leaders themselves. Instead, they tend to be opinion leaders' friends and neighbors. The early majority is an important link in the process of diffusing new ideas, because they are positioned between earlier and later adopters. A dominant characteristic of the early majority is deliberateness.

- *Late majority:* the next 34 percent to adopt. The late majority adopts a new product because most of their friends have already adopted it. Because they also rely on group norms, their adoption stems from pressure to conform. This group tends to be older and below average in income and education. They depend mainly on word-of-mouth communication rather than on the mass media. The dominant characteristic of the late majority is skepticism.

- *Laggards:* the final 16 percent to adopt. Like innovators, laggards do not rely on group norms. Their independence is rooted in their ties to tradition. Thus, the past heavily influences their decisions. By the time laggards adopt an innovation, it has probably been outmoded and replaced by something else. For example, they may have bought their first black-and-white TV set after color television was already widely diffused. Laggards have the longest adoption time and the lowest socioeconomic status. They tend to be suspicious of new products and alienated from a rapidly advancing society. The dominant value of laggards is tradition. Marketers typically ignore laggards, who do not seem to be motivated by advertising or personal selling.

Exhibit 10.3 on p. 332 illustrates the diffusion of several familiar products throughout the United States. Virtually every household is equipped with electricity, a range, a refrigerator, and a radio. Interestingly, a larger portion of U.S. households are now equipped with color televisions than with telephones. Note that some of these product categories may never be adopted by 100 percent of the population. The adopter categories refer to all of those who will eventually adopt a product, not the entire population.

Product Characteristics and the Rate of Adoption

Five product characteristics can be used to predict and explain the rate of acceptance and diffusion of a new product:

- *Complexity:* the degree of difficulty involved in understanding and using a new product. The more complex the product, the slower is its diffusion. For instance, before many of their functions were automated, 35mm cameras were used primarily by hobbyists and professionals. They were just too complex for most people to learn to operate.

- *Compatibility:* the degree to which the new product is consistent with existing values and product knowledge, past experiences, and current needs. Incompatible products diffuse more slowly than compatible products. For example, the introduction of contraceptives is incompatible in countries where religious beliefs discourage the use of birth control techniques.

- *Relative advantage:* the degree to which a product is perceived as superior to existing substitutes. For example, because it reduces cooking time, the microwave oven has a clear relative advantage over a conventional oven.

- *Observability:* the degree to which the benefits or other results of using the product can be observed by others and communicated to target customers.

Exhibit **10.3** Characteristics of the Elements in the Promotional Mix

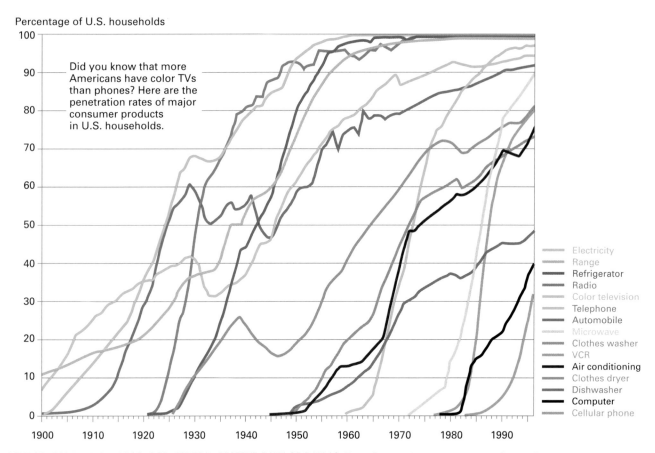

Percentage of U.S. households

Did you know that more Americans have color TVs than phones? Here are the penetration rates of major consumer products in U.S. households.

Electricity
Range
Refrigerator
Radio
Color television
Telephone
Automobile
Microwave
Clothes washer
VCR
Air conditioning
Clothes dryer
Dishwasher
Computer
Cellular phone

SOURCE: FORTUNE CHART/SOURCE: FEDERAL RESERVE BANK OF DALLAS. From *Fortune,* June 8, 1998, p. 64. © 1998 Time Inc. All rights reserved. Reprinted by permission.

For instance, fashion items and automobiles are highly visible and more observable than personal care items.

- *"Trialability":* the degree to which a product can be tried on a limited basis. It is much easier to try a new toothpaste or breakfast cereal than a new automobile or microcomputer. Demonstrations in showrooms and test drives are different from in-home trial use. To stimulate trials, marketers use free-sampling programs, tasting displays, and small package sizes.

Marketing Implications of the Adoption Process

Two types of communication aid the diffusion process: *word-of-mouth communication* among consumers and communication from marketers to consumers. Word-of-mouth communication within and across groups speeds diffusion. Opinion leaders discuss new products with their followers and with other opinion leaders. Marketers must therefore ensure that opinion leaders have the types of information desired in the media that they use. Suppliers of some products, such as professional and healthcare services, rely almost solely on word-of-mouth communication for new business.

The second type of communication aiding the diffusion process is *communication directly from the marketer to potential adopters.* Messages directed toward early adopters should normally use different appeals than messages directed toward the early majority, the late majority, or the laggards. Early adopters are more important than innovators because they make up a larger group, are more socially active, and are usually opinion leaders.

As the focus of a promotional campaign shifts from early adopters to the early majority and the late majority, marketers should study the dominant characteristics, buying behavior, and media characteristics of these target markets. Then they should revise messages and media strategy to fit. The diffusion model helps guide marketers in developing and implementing promotion strategy.

Product Life Cycles

The **product life cycle (PLC)** is one of the most familiar concepts in marketing. Few other general concepts have been so widely discussed. Although some researchers have challenged the theoretical basis and managerial value of the PLC, most believe it has great potential as a marketing management tool.

The product life cycle is a concept that provides a way to trace the stages of a product's acceptance, from its introduction (birth) to its decline (death). As Exhibit 10.4 shows, a product progresses through four major stages: introduction, growth, maturity, and decline. Note that the product life cycle illustrated does not refer to any one brand; rather, it refers to the life cycle for a product category or product class. A **product category** includes all brands that satisfy a particular type of need. Product categories include passenger cars, cigarettes, soft drinks, and coffee.

The time a product spends in any one stage of the life cycle may vary dramatically. Some products, such as fad items, move through the entire cycle in weeks. Others, such as electric clothes washers and dryers, stay in the maturity stage for decades. Exhibit 10.4 illustrates the typical life cycle for a consumer durable good, such as a washer or dryer. In contrast, Exhibit 10.5 illustrates typical life cycles for styles (such as formal, business, or casual clothing), fashions (such as miniskirts or stirrup pants), and fads (such as leopard-print clothing). Changes in a product, its uses, its image, or its positioning can extend that product's life cycle.

The product life cycle concept does not tell managers the length of a product's life cycle or its duration in any stage. It does not dictate marketing strategy. It is simply a tool to help marketers forecast future events and suggest appropriate strategies.

Explain the concept of product life cycles

product life cycle (PLC)
A concept that provides a way to trace the stages of a product's acceptance, from its introduction (birth) to its decline (death).

product category
All brands that satisfy a particular type of need.

Exhibit **10.4**

Four Stages of the
Product Life Cycle

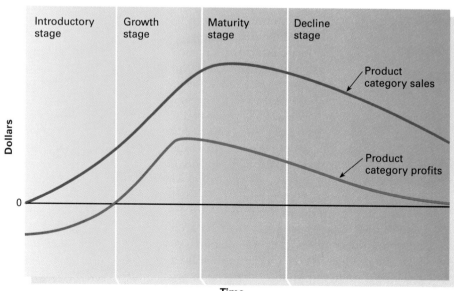

Exhibit **10.5**

Product Life Cycles for Styles,
Fashions, and Fads

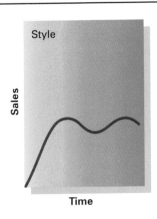

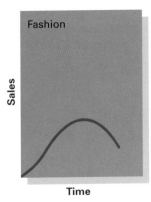

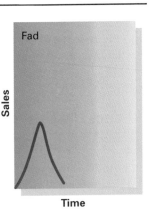

Introductory Stage

introductory stage
The full-scale launch of a new
product into the marketplace.

The **introductory stage** of the product life cycle represents the full-scale launch of a new product into the marketplace. Computer databases for personal use, room-deodorizing air-conditioning filters, and wind-powered home electric generators are all product categories that have recently entered the product life cycle. A high failure rate, little competition, frequent product modification, and limited distribution typify the introduction stage of the PLC.

Marketing costs in the introductory stage are normally high for several reasons. High dealer margins are often needed to obtain adequate distribution, and incentives are needed to get consumers to try the new product. Advertising expenses are high because of the need to educate consumers about the new product's benefits. Production costs are also often high in this stage, as product and manufacturing flaws are identified and corrected and efforts are undertaken to develop mass-production economies.

As Exhibit 10.4 illustrates, sales normally increase slowly during the introductory stage. Moreover, profits are usually negative because of research and development costs, factory tooling, and high introduction costs. The length of the introductory phase is largely determined by product characteristics, such as the product's advantages over substitute products, the educational effort required to make the product known, and management's commitment of resources to the new item. A short introductory period is usually preferred to help reduce the impact of negative earnings and cash flows. As soon as the product gets off the ground, the financial burden should begin to diminish. Also, a short introduction helps dispel some of the uncertainty regarding whether or not the new product will be successful.

Styles, fashions, and fads tend to
follow different product life cycles.
Based on what you see in Exhibits
10.4 and 10.5, what do you think
the life cycle is for Pokemon car-
toons and movies? For Pokemon
toys and other products?

Promotion strategy in the introductory stage focuses on developing product awareness and informing consumers about the product category's potential benefits. At this stage, the communication challenge is to stimulate primary demand—demand for the product in general rather than for a specific brand. Intensive personal selling is often required to gain acceptance for the product among wholesalers and retailers. Promotion of convenience products often requires

Wendy's

Follow Wendy's advertisements from the first network commercials to present-day ads. How has Wendy's developed and promoted new products to successfully compete in the maturity stage?

http://www.wendys.com/the_ads/ads_frame.html

On Line

heavy consumer sampling and couponing. Shopping and specialty products demand educational advertising and personal selling to the final consumer.

Growth Stage

If a product category survives the introductory stage, it advances to the **growth stage** of the life cycle. In this stage, sales typically grow at an increasing rate, many competitors enter the market, and large companies may start to acquire small pioneering firms. Profits rise rapidly in the growth stage, reach their peak, and begin declining as competition intensifies. Emphasis switches from primary demand promotion (for example, promoting personal digital assistants (pdas)) to aggressive brand advertising and communication of the differences between brands (for example, promoting Casio versus Palm and Visor).

Distribution becomes a major key to success during the growth stage, as well as in later stages. Manufacturers scramble to sign up dealers and distributors and to build long-term relationships. Without adequate distribution, it is impossible to establish a strong market position.

growth stage
The second stage of the product life cycle when sales typically grow at an increasing rate, many competitors enter the market, large companies may start acquiring small pioneering firms, and profits are healthy.

Maturity Stage

A period during which sales increase at a decreasing rate signals the beginning of the **maturity stage** of the life cycle. New users cannot be added indefinitely, and sooner or later the market approaches saturation. Normally, this is the longest stage of the product life cycle. As you saw in Exhibit 10.3, many major household appliances are in the maturity stage of their life cycles.

For shopping products and many specialty products, annual models begin to appear during the maturity stage. Product lines are lengthened to appeal to additional market segments. Service and repair assume more important roles as manufacturers strive to distinguish their products from others. Product design changes tend to become stylistic (How can the product be made different?) rather than functional (How can the product be made better?).

maturity stage
A period during which sales increase at a decreasing rate.

As prices and profits continue to fall, marginal competitors start dropping out of the market. Dealer margins also shrink, resulting in less shelf space for mature items, lower dealer inventories, and a general reluctance to promote the product. Thus promotion to dealers often intensifies during this stage, in order to retain loyalty.

Heavy consumer promotion by the manufacturer is also required to maintain market share. Consider these well-known examples of competition in the maturity stage: the so-called "cola war" featuring Coke and Pepsi, the "beer war" featuring Anheuser-Busch's Budweiser brands and Philip Morris's Miller brands, and the "burger wars" pitting leader McDonald's against challengers Burger King and Wendy's.

Another characteristic of the maturity stage is the emergence of so-called "niche marketers" that target narrow, well-defined, underserved segments of a market. Starbucks Coffee targets its gourmet line at the only segment of the coffee market that is growing: new, younger, more affluent coffee drinkers.

Coffee is an example of a product in the maturity stage where niche marketers have emerged. Starbucks, for example, targets its gourmet products at newer, younger, more affluent coffee drinkers.
© Vincent Dewitt/Stock Boston Inc./PNI

Decline Stage

A long-run drop in sales signals the beginning of the **decline stage**. The rate of decline is governed by how rapidly consumer tastes change or substitute products are adopted. Many convenience products and fad items lose their market overnight, leaving large inventories of unsold items, such as designer jeans. Others die more slowly, like citizen band (CB) radios, black-and-white console television sets, and nonelectronic wristwatches.

Some firms have developed successful strategies for marketing products in the decline stage of the product life cycle. They eliminate all nonessential marketing expenses and let sales decline as more and more customers discontinue purchasing the products. Eventually, the product is withdrawn from the market.

Implications for Marketing Management

The product life cycle concept encourages marketing managers to plan so they can take the initiative instead of reacting to past events. The product life cycle is especially useful as a predicting or forecasting tool. Because products pass through distinctive stages, it is often possible to estimate a product's location on the curve using historical data. Profits, like sales, tend to follow a predictable path over a product's life cycle.

Exhibit 10.6 briefly summarizes some typical marketing strategies during each stage of the product life cycle. Exhibit 10.7 shows the relationship between the adopter categories and stages of the product life cycle. Note that the various categories of adopters first buy products in different stages of the product life cycle. Almost all sales in the maturity and decline stages represent repeat purchasing.

Exhibit 10.6 Typical Marketing Strategies During the Product Life Cycle

Marketing Mix Strategy	Product Life Cycle Stage			
	Introduction	**Growth**	**Maturity**	**Decline**
Product Strategy	Limited number of models; frequent product modifications	Expanded number of models; frequent product modifications	Large number of models	Elimination of unprofitable models and brands
Distribution Strategy	Distribution usually limited, depending on product; intensive efforts and high margins often needed to attract wholesalers and retailers	Expanded number of dealers; intensive efforts to establish long-term relationships with wholesalers and retailers	Extensive number of dealers; margins declining; intensive efforts to retain distributors and shelf space	Unprofitable outlets phased out
Promotion Strategy	Develop product awareness; stimulate primary demand; use intensive personal selling to distributors; use sampling and couponing for consumers	Stimulate selective demand; advertise brand aggressively	Stimulate selective demand; advertise brand aggressively; promote heavily to retain dealers and customers	Phase out all promotion
Pricing Strategy	Prices are usually high to recover development costs (see Chapter 17)	Prices begin to fall toward end of growth stage as result of competitive pressure	Prices continue to fall	Prices stabilize at relatively low level; small price rises are possible if competition is negligible

Exhibit **10.7**

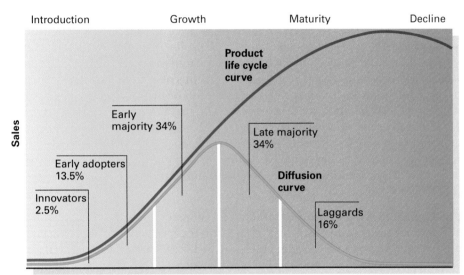

Diffusion curve: Percentage of total adoptions by category
Product life cycle curve: Time

Looking Back

Look back at the story at the beginning of this chapter about Ralston Purina developing a dog litter called *Secondnature*. Ralston tested its new product by giving free puppies and free litter systems to employees with no background in animal training and solicited feedback from them.[22]

Prior to introducing the new product, Ralston studied the strategies of selected other firms. They concluded that a strategy of involving influential experts would be more persuasive than most forms of promotion. They decided to market Secondnature through dog trainers, veterinarians, and breeders rather than other types of outlets such as grocery stores. They also decided not to use national television advertising, but rather to rely on their distributors to introduce and promote Secondnature to potential customers.[23]

Will Secondnature succeed or fail? We learned in this chapter that 85 percent of all new product introductions fail. This one sounds like a good idea—if it works!

Use it Now!

Stay Informed

To keep current with the changing trends and new products in the financial services industry, arm yourself with information. A banking Web site that will help you make informed decisions is **http://www.bankrate.com**. It has a How-to section that teaches the basics of banking and helps you calculate your payment on loans. The site's collection of interest rate information covers everything from car loans to money market accounts and enables you to compare rates from financial institutions in all fifty states. You can also check the fees different banks charge for their services and compare them to on-line banking service charges.

Locate Lenders

More and more financial institutions are expanding their lending to entrepreneurs and small business owners. The following Web sites help start-ups and small businesses find financing:

- **http://www.cashfinder.com** Ten financial institutions participate in this program, which offers lines of credit, loans, credit cards, and leasing. You can download free software that lets you complete a loan application form and print it before faxing or mailing it to the lenders.
- **http://cgi.pathfinder.com** This site lists the top commercial lenders to small business. It provides links to national and regional bank holding companies, such as Wells Fargo, that make loans under $250,000.
- **http://www.ibaa.org** The Web site of the Independent Bankers Association of America provides leads to all U.S. community banks.

Summary

1 **Explain the importance of developing new products and describe the six categories of new products.** New products are important to sustain growth and profits and to replace obsolete items. New products can be classified as new-to-the-world products (discontinuous innovations), new product lines, additions to existing product lines, improvements or revisions of existing products, repositioned products, or lower-cost products. To sustain or increase profits, a firm must introduce at least one new successful product before a previous product advances to the maturity stage and profit levels begin to drop. Several factors make it more important than ever for firms to consistently introduce new products: shortened product life cycles, rapidly changing technology and consumer priorities, the high rate of new-product failures, and the length of time needed to implement new-product ideas.

2 **Explain the steps in the new-product development process.** First, a firm forms a new-product strategy by outlining the characteristics and roles of future products. Then new-product ideas are generated by customers, employees, distributors, competitors, and internal research and development personnel. Once a product idea has survived initial screening by an appointed screening group, it undergoes business analysis to determine its potential profitability. If a product concept seems viable, it progresses into the development phase, in which the technical and economic feasibility of the manufacturing process is evaluated. The development phase also includes laboratory and use testing of a product for performance and safety. Following initial testing and refinement, most products are introduced in a test market to evaluate consumer response and marketing strategies. Finally, test market successes are propelled into full commercialization. The commercialization process means starting up production, building inventories, shipping to distributors, training a sales force, announcing the product to the trade, and advertising to consumers.

3 **Explain why some products succeed and others fail.** The most important factor in determining the success of a new product is the extent to which the product matches the needs of the market. Good matches are frequently successful. Poor matches are not.

4 **Discuss global issues in new-product development.** A marketer with global vision seeks to develop products that can easily be adapted to suit local needs. The goal is not simply to develop a standard product that can be sold worldwide. Smart global marketers also look for good product ideas worldwide, not just in their home country.

5 **Explain the diffusion process through which new products are adopted.** The diffusion process is the spread of a new product from its producer to ultimate adopters. Adopters in the diffusion process belong to five categories: innovators, early adopters, the early majority, the late majority, and laggards. Product characteristics that affect the rate of adoption include product complexity, compatibility with existing social values, relative advantage over existing substitutes, visibility, and "trialability." The diffusion process is facilitated by word-of-mouth communication and communication from marketers to consumers.

6 **Explain the concept of product life cycles.** All product categories undergo a life cycle with four stages: introduction, growth, maturity, and decline. The rate at which products move through these stages varies dramatically. Marketing managers use the product life cycle concept as an analytical tool to forecast a product's future and devise effective marketing strategies.

Key Terms

Discussion and Writing Questions

1. List the advantages of simultaneous product development.
2. **TEAM** In small groups, brainstorm ideas for a new wet-weather clothing line. What type of product would potential customers want and need? Prepare and deliver a brief presentation to your class.
3. **WRITING** You are a marketing manager for Nike. Your department has come up with the idea of manufacturing a baseball bat for use in colleges around the nation. Assuming you are in the business analysis stage, write a brief analysis based on the questions in the "Business Analysis" section of the chapter.
4. What are the major disadvantages to test marketing and how might they be avoided?
5. Describe some products whose adoption rates have been affected by complexity, compatibility, relative advantage, observability, and/or "trialability."
6. What type of adopter behavior do you typically follow? Explain.
7. **INFOTRAC COLLEGE EDITION** Place the personal computer on the product life cycle curve, and give reasons for placing it where you did. Use Info Trac (**www.infotrac-college.com**) to consult publications like *Technology Review, Computer World,* and *Computer Weekly* to help support your position.
8. **ON LINE** How could information from customer orders at **http://www.pizzahut.com** help the company's marketers plan new-product developments?
9. How is customer input affecting the development of Baked Lay's potato chips? Go to **http://www.fritolay.com** to find out.

Application for Entrepreneurs

ENTREPRENEUR Joyce Strand went to the oven to remove the newest batch of beef jerky that she would later sell to the Frontenac Central Store. To her surprise, she had turned the oven up too high, and the beef jerky had dried to a crisp. Although the texture was much different, the jerky still had its unmistakable taste. Joyce decided to take it to the Central Store anyway and let the customers decide. The new snack became a huge success in the snack food section of the store. Because of her recent success, Joyce began experimenting with different tastes and textures of snack foods that she sells at the Central Store. Realizing that innovation can be very profitable, Joyce now actively looks for new ways to please her customers.

Questions

1. How might Joyce ensure that proper attention is paid to developing new products?
2. What factors should she be aware of that might lead to product failure?

Case entrepreneurship

A New Direction for NetTV

ON LINE When it was launched in California in February 1996, NetTV had a clear focus: to enter the infotainment market by delivering the highest quality digital entertainment. With four members of the management team, product development and marketing for NetTV were managed internally, with production outsourced to two ISO/9000 certified multinational corporations. Prior to founding NetTV, all members of the management team were working in technology-related businesses in the United States. CEO Ron Perkes was a founder of Tangent Computer; CFO Peter Ohtaki was an investment banker advising technology clients at Unterberg Towbin and Morgan Stanley; Director of Sales Brent Vorous worked in sales at Computer Sciences Corporation, Data General, and Tangent Computer; and Director of Marketing Michael Carrier worked in multimedia communications for Emery Worldwide, the San Jose News' Mercury Center.com Web site, and various television stations in California and Washington, DC.

Soon after the company's incorporation, these entrepreneurs introduced WorldVision, a new product having several notable features:

- Stereo TV/monitor that worked both as a computer monitor and a stand-alone TV monitor, with twice the resolution of conventional televisions
- Screen sizes of 29 inches, 33 inches, or 37 inches
- Separate video and computer inputs
- Audio output jacks that allowed connection to a home stereo system
- Multimedia features that included CD-ROM player, cable-ready TV tuner, video capture, video snapshots, 3D stereo, and an arcade-style game controller
- 100–166 MHz Intel Pentium processor
- 8–16 MB of RAM
- 1–1.6 GB hard drive
- Built-in video scaler
- 28.8 bps fax/modem
- Wireless keyboard with built-in trackball

After nearly $5 million in development and marketing expenses, WorldVision was introduced into the $80 billion consumer electronics marketplace in 1996 at a price of $2,995. The product was distributed through computer and home electronics stores.

Although NetTV was one of the first companies to enter the infotainment market and offer a PC/TV product, competition was strong. Major competitors who entered the infotainment market around the same time as NetTV were Gateway 2000 with its Destination, priced around $4,000; ELLi Computer, with ELLiVision Gamma, also around $4,000; and Toshiba's Infinia, priced at $3,000.

First year sales of WorldVision were projected to be in the tens of thousands, with revenue around $30 million. Unfortunately, shipments were only around 1,200 sets in the first fifteen months of business. NetTV was not alone in its failure—the expected synergy of the personal computer and television was not happening quickly. For example, sales of the Destination by Gateway 2000 were not as high as anticipated.

In true entrepreneurial spirit, however, Ron Perkes and his management team have not given up. NetTV now targets the U.S. education market. Using the same digital entertainment technology, NetTV builds digital data monitors and DVD multimedia computers for the classroom. While currently focusing upon the education market, managers at NetTV still see hope in the home market. They expect a growing need to connect a variety of devices (digital television, digital videodisks, high-definition television) to fuel interest in their all-purpose WorldVision product. However, does WorldVision offer discernible benefits that will make it desirable to electronic-savvy consumers who now have alternatives such as WebTV, cable modems, and digital phone service from telephone companies?

Questions

1. What type of new product is WorldVision?
2. Where are products for the infotainment market on the product life cycle?
3. How do the characteristics of WorldVision relate to its rate of adoption?
4. Is there hope for NetTV's WorldVision?

Bibliography

Bruce Brown. "Couch Potato PCs." *PC Magazine Online,* May 6, 1997. On-line.

Lee Gomes. "It Sounded So Good . . . : The History of Consumer Electronics Is Littered with Failure." *Wall Street Journal,* June 15, 1998, p. R22.

"NetTV Revolutionizes Home Entertainment and Learning," *Business Wire,* April 2, 1996. On-line.

http://www.net-tv.net

Still Shaky? Here's a tip

The main diagrams in this chapter are Exhibits 10.1, 10.4, 10.5, and 10.7. On a separate sheet, write the titles of these exhibits. Then, with your book closed, try to reproduce the diagrams exactly as they are in the book. Write a short description of what the diagram depicts, and open your book to check your work.

Case

AutoCite: Traffic Ticket and Parking Citation System

For decades, the writing of a traffic ticket was only the first step in a long manual process. An officer dropped off the ticket at the station, and from there it went to the records department for sorting and batching. It was then transmitted to the judicial system and data processing. The handwritten information was keypunched into the mainframe and then returned for filing. At each step, tickets were flagged for errors, but mistakes regularly surfaced, resulting in an inefficient process.

This situation prompted companies such as Epson, Grid, Husky, Symbol, and Telxon to market general purpose, hand-held computers to police departments. But these devices required officers to wear a clumsy printer on their belts or strapped over their shoulders, and such computer configurations were not designed for citation management.

Enforcement Technology, Inc. (ETEC) recognized an unsatisfied need and set out to develop a new product that would deal the final blow to the bulky, inefficient computers. ETEC focused on developing a product so unique that once introduced, it would outdate the competition. The new product, called AutoCite, is a portable, lightweight, hand-held computer with a built-in printer, specialized for issuing traffic tickets and parking citations.

ETEC's new product strategy was to carve out a market niche through specialization. Competitors sold general purpose computers—hardware only, requiring customers to purchase obligatory software from other companies. To distinguish AutoCite from other brands, ETEC produced a complete package of hardware *and* software. In addition, ETEC provided product training and totally maintained AutoCite at every level. Customers found it highly convenient to look to a single supplier for both sales and service.

AutoCite's success encouraged ETEC to analyze other needs in the citation process and develop the technology to meet them. The result is a fully automated system of products that work in harmony. AutoCite is now updated to include a magnetic stripe and bar code reading capability so that information is entered automatically from the magnetic stripe on the back of a driver's license. Using a prestored "hotsheet," AutoCite alerts the officer with "Wants or Warrants" keyed to the driver's license number. AutoPROCESS handles citations through on-line court and hearing scheduling. AutoALARM is a false alarm management system, which includes citation issuance computers, window decal distribution, alarm permit updates and payments, and billing statements.

The AutoCite Patrol Car System is an AutoCite unit that adapts to the notebook (laptop) computer in a patrol car to issue traffic tickets; it is particularly useful for issuing moving citations and preparing interviews and crime, accident, and arrest reports.

This product line is fully supported by ETEC's cash management and delinquent collection services. The company has parking enforcement centers to process in- and out-of-state tickets for their customers and has implemented a follow-up service to collect delinquent citations. But these services are only part of the benefits.

Cities, universities, and agencies are saving money in processing costs and recovery of delinquent fines. In one year, ETEC collected $600,000 for the city of San Diego by taking a backlog of sixty thousand citations and going back as far as two years for collections. Now ETEC processes about three thousand delinquent out-of-state parking citations each month for roughly $50,000 in new revenue. With results like this, AutoCite can pay for itself within a year.

Revenue generation is complemented by an additional benefit: The use of AutoCite has been shown to reduce the indirect costs associated with low staff productivity. Data entry, which used to eat into staff and clerical time, is now a memory in departments and agencies. And the error rate is smaller. There's also an intangible benefit— better employee morale. In Long Beach, California, officers have been pleased with ETEC's reliable computers and high-quality customer service. Their increased efficiency has led to greater job satisfaction, which in turn has positively affected morale on the entire police force.

By creating a fully automated citation management process, ETEC has police departments and agencies in the United States and abroad singing its praises. Adopted by over three hundred agencies in the United States, over fifty colleges and universities, and agencies in eight foreign countries, the AutoCite full-service solution for citation management is well positioned to build on its resounding success.

Questions
1. Describe the product development process for AutoCite.
2. Why has AutoCite been successful?
3. How did ETEC develop the product line?
4. What strategy should ETEC follow in introducing new products for law enforcement?

Bibliography
Press Kit: Enforcement Technology, Inc.

chapter 11

At a time when polls suggest service in America is hitting all-time lows, Commerce Bancorp is showing that good service can be good business. Most banks say the average customers don't make them much money, so they slap them with complicated fees or push them to those irksome automated phone centers. Commerce has a different approach that borrows more from McDonald's than from Banking 101: Rather than squeeze customers, it looks for volume.

Commerce offers free checking and free money orders. Their teller service is open from 7:30 in the morning to 8 at night. And branches are staffed with real tellers on weekends and holidays—even a few hours on Sundays. Commerce takes the basic service and branding concepts found at the fast-food giants—right down to the big red "C" in front of each branch evoking the golden arches—and applied them to its branches. It keeps long hours, and it moves teller lines by reducing many teller functions to one-touch keystrokes, making deposit receipts almost as easy as supersizing an Extra Value Meal. It even has bathrooms in each branch.

Besides the big red "C" signs on the front of the bank, each branch has the same, open, glass-heavy architecture, the same red-black-and-gray design, the same carpet, desks, and blinds. Vernon W. Hill II, the founder, president, and chairman of Commerce, believes this sends a message of consistent, dependable service.

Bank officers often pose as customers and pull up to a branch's drive-through window. During the transaction, they may ask a question, such as "Do you have savings-bond applications?" and rate the teller on the response using the scale poor, fair, good, or wow. Branches that consistently "Wow the Customer!" win awards. "We treat service almost like a cult," says Dennis DiFlorio, executive vice-president.

Earnings at Commerce are growing by 16 percent, compared with about 9 percent for the industry. Total deposits have doubled in the past five years, reflecting a sharp increase in branch openings in the past two years—to 120 from 88—but Hill notes that he usually opens a new branch only after the existing ones hit capacity. Commerce wants to be a growth retailer such as a Nordstrom or Starbucks. It will open thirty branches in 2000, bringing its total to about 150, and no other bank comes close to that rate of openings.

For Commerce, the challenge now is to maintain service while growing. The company spends about $100,000 on marketing each new branch opening to create a hometown feeling, and the event is a flashback to another banking era. On a recent Saturday in the Philadelphia suburb of Flourtown, the neighborhood is slowly turning out to pick up free Commerce cups and pens. A magician is twisting balloons, a disk jockey is spinning oldies. There's a raffle and free soft drinks and hot dogs. Wayne Gomes, a Philadelphia Phillies relief pitcher, is signing photos for kids in Little League uniforms.

Commerce is pouring money into brick and mortar as financial services are going increasingly on-line. Some say that leaves Hill exposed, but he is betting customers will still want branch service. His on-line clients, he notes, also visit his branches on average five times a month—and unlike other banks, his doesn't slap fees on them when they do. The result? Commerce has 21 percent of its customers banking on-line—a Web penetration rate that is higher than that of any other U.S. bank with an active Web strategy.[1]

How does a service, like banking, differ from goods—for example, soft drinks, blue jeans, or cars? What kind of service does Commerce Bancorp offer its customers? What will be the challenges as Commerce continues to grow?

The Importance of Services

Discuss the importance of services to the economy

service
The result of applying human or mechanical efforts to people or objects.

A **service** is the result of applying human or mechanical efforts to people or objects. Services involve a deed, a performance, or an effort that cannot be physically possessed. Today, the service sector substantially influences the U.S. economy. The service sector accounts for 76 percent of the U.S. gross domestic product and 79 percent of employment.[2] The demand for services is expected to continue. According to the Bureau of Labor Statistics, service occupations will be responsible for all net job growth through the year 2005, as can be seen in Exhibit 11.1. Much of this demand results from demographics. An aging population will need nurses, home health care, physical therapists, and social workers. Two-earner families need child care, housecleaning, and lawn care services. Also increasing will be the demand for information managers, such as computer engineers and systems analysts. There is also a growing market for service companies worldwide.

The marketing process described in Chapter 1 is the same for all types of products, whether they are goods or services. Many ideas and strategies discussed throughout this book have been illustrated with service examples. In many ways, marketing is marketing, regardless of the product's characteristics. However, services have some unique characteristics that distinguish them from goods, and marketing strategies need to be adjusted for these characteristics.

How Services Differ from Goods

Discuss the differences between services and goods

intangibility
Services that cannot be touched, seen, tasted, heard, or felt in the same manner in which goods can be sensed.

Services have four unique characteristics that distinguish them from goods: intangibility, inseparability, heterogeneity, and perishability.

Intangibility
The basic difference between services and goods is that services are intangible. Because of their **intangibility**, they cannot be touched, seen, tasted, heard, or felt in

Exhibit 11.1   Service-Producing Industries and Job Growth

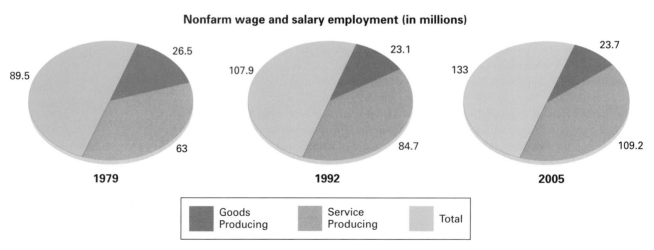

Nonfarm wage and salary employment (in millions)

1979 — 89.5, 26.5, 63
1992 — 107.9, 23.1, 84.7
2005 — 133, 23.7, 109.2

Goods Producing • Service Producing • Total

SOURCE: *Arlington Star Telegram,* September 2, 1996, p. B9.

the same manner in which goods can be sensed. Services cannot be stored and are often easy to duplicate.

Evaluating the quality of services before or even after making a purchase is harder than evaluating the quality of goods because, compared to goods, services tend to exhibit fewer search qualities. A **search quality** is a characteristic that can be easily assessed before purchase—for instance, the color of an appliance or automobile. At the same time, services tend to exhibit more experience and credence qualities. An **experience quality** is a characteristic that can be assessed only after use, such as the quality of a meal in a restaurant or the actual experience of a vacation. A **credence quality** is a characteristic that consumers may have difficulty assessing even after purchase because they do not have the necessary knowledge or experience. Medical and consulting services are examples of services that exhibit credence qualities.

These characteristics also make it harder for marketers to communicate the benefits of an intangible service than to communicate the benefits of tangible goods. Thus, marketers often rely on tangible cues to communicate a service's nature and quality. For example, Traveler's Insurance Company's use of the umbrella symbol helps make tangible the benefit of protection that insurance provides.

The facilities that customers visit, or from which services are delivered, are a critical tangible part of the total service offering. Messages about the organization are communicated to customers through such elements as the decor, the clutter or neatness of service areas, and the staff's manners and dress. The Sheraton Hotel chain is replacing its outdated shag carpeting and flowered bedspreads with pin stripes and sleigh beds. Their goal is to restore a reputation for reliability and comfort, and to avoid scaring off travelers with tacky accommodations. The new design will feature clubby library-like furnishings and practical amenities like ergonomic desk chairs and two-line phones. The remodeling is also a part of the strategy followed by Sheraton's parent company, Starwood Hotels & Resorts Worldwide, to differentiate the company's hotel brands aesthetically. For example, it wants its Sheratons to attract conservative business travelers, while its Westin Hotels are targeting younger, hipper, and somewhat richer overnighters.[3]

search quality
A characteristic that can be easily assessed before purchase.

experience quality
A characteristic that can be assessed only after use.

credence quality
A characteristic that consumers may have difficulty assessing even after purchase because they do not have the necessary knowledge or experience.

Inseparability

Goods are produced, sold, and then consumed. In contrast, services are often sold, produced, and consumed at the same time. In other words, their production and consumption are inseparable activities. **Inseparability** means that, because consumers must be present during the production of services like haircuts or surgery, they are actually involved in the production of the services they buy. For example, McDonald's is planning to install self-serve odering devices in its stores, to augment its human order takers.[4] That type of consumer involvement is rare in goods manufacturing.

Inseparability also means that services cannot normally be produced in a centralized location and consumed in decentralized locations, as goods typically are. Services are also inseparable from the perspective of the service provider. Thus,

Because KFC uses standardized preparation procedures, the meal you could order at its restaurant in the Itae Won shopping area of Seoul, South Korea, would be consistent with what you would get at the KFC in the smallest of American towns.

Enterprise Rent-A-Car

How does Enterprise Rent-A-Car use its Web site to combat perishability?

http://www.enterprise.com

On Line

the quality of service that firms are able to deliver depends on the quality of their employees.

Heterogeneity

inseparability
A characteristic of services that allows them to be produced and consumed simultaneously.

heterogeneity
A characteristic of services that makes them less standardized and uniform than goods.

One great strength of McDonald's is consistency. Whether customers order a Big Mac and french fries in Fort Worth, Tokyo, or Moscow, they know exactly what they are going to get. This is not the case with many service providers. **Heterogeneity** means that services tend to be less standardized and uniform than goods. For example, physicians in a group practice or barbers in a barber shop differ within each group in their technical and interpersonal skills. A given physician's or barber's performance may even vary depending on time of day, physical health, or some other factor. Because services tend to be labor intensive and production and consumption are inseparable, consistency and quality control can be hard to achieve.

Standardization and training help increase consistency and reliability. Limited-menu restaurants like Pizza Hut and KFC offer customers high consistency from one visit to the next because of standardized preparation procedures. Another way to increase consistency is to mechanize the process. Banks have reduced the inconsistency of teller services by providing automated teller machines. Airport x-ray surveillance equipment has replaced manual searching of baggage. Automatic coin receptacles on toll roads have replaced human collectors.

Perishability

perishability
A characteristic of services that prevents them from being stored, warehoused, or inventoried.

All services are subject to **perishability**, which means that they cannot be stored, warehoused, or inventoried. An empty hotel room or airplane seat produces no revenue that day. The revenue is lost. Yet service organizations are often forced to turn away full-price customers during peak periods.

One of the most important challenges in many service industries is finding ways to synchronize supply and demand. The philosophy that some revenue is better than none has prompted many hotels to offer deep discounts on weekends and during the off-season and has prompted airlines to adopt similar pricing strategies during off-peak hours. Car rental agencies, movie theaters, and restaurants also use discounts to encourage demand during nonpeak periods.

Service Quality

3

Describe the components of service quality and the gap model of service quality

Because of the four unique characteristics of services, service quality is more difficult to define and measure than is quality of tangible goods. Business executives rank the improvement of service quality as one of the most critical challenges facing them today.

Research has shown that customers evaluate service quality by the following five components:[5]

reliability
The ability to perform a service dependably, accurately, and consistently.

- *Reliability:* the ability to perform the service dependably, accurately, and consistently. Reliability is performing the service right the first time. This component has been found to be the one most important to consumers.

responsiveness
The ability to provide prompt service.

- *Responsiveness:* the ability to provide prompt service. Examples of responsiveness include calling the customer back quickly, serving lunch fast to someone who is in a hurry, or mailing a transaction slip immediately.

- *Assurance:* the knowledge and courtesy of employees and their ability to convey trust. Skilled employees who treat customers with respect and make customers feel that they can trust the firm exemplify assurance.
- *Empathy:* caring, individualized attention to customers. Firms whose employees recognize customers, call them by name, and learn their customers' specific requirements are providing empathy. Union Square Hospitality Group, owner of several popular New York City restaurants, will return items customers have left behind by messenger or FedEx so the customers do not have to return to retrieve their belongings.[6]
- *Tangibles:* the physical evidence of the service. The tangible parts of a service include the physical facilities, tools, and equipment used to provide the service, such as a doctor's office or an ATM, and the appearance of personnel.

Overall service quality is measured by combining customers' evaluations for all five components.

The Gap Model of Service Quality

 A model of service quality called the **gap model** identifies five gaps that can cause problems in service delivery and influence customer evaluations of service quality.[7] These gaps are illustrated in Exhibit 11.2:

- *Gap 1:* the gap between what customers want and what management thinks customers want. This gap results from a lack of understanding or

assurance
The knowledge and courtesy of employees and their ability to convey trust.

empathy
Caring, individualized attention to customers.

tangibles
The physical evidence of a service, including the physical facilities, tools, and equipment used to provide the service.

gap model
A model identifying five gaps that can cause problems in service delivery and influence customer evaluations of service quality.

Exhibit 11.2

Gap Model of Service Quality

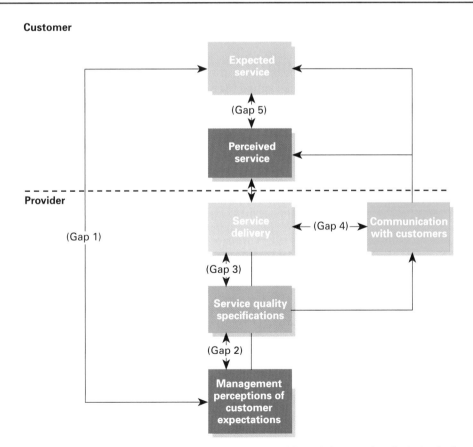

Evaluate your last Internet purchase according to Gaps 4 and 5. How could the company better bridge those gaps?

    ◀ ▶   On Line

a misinterpretation of the customers' needs, wants, or desires. A firm that does little or no customer satisfaction research is likely to experience this gap. An important step in closing gap 1 is to keep in touch with what customers want by doing research on customer needs and customer satisfaction. Every year, Susquehanna Health System, recipient of the 1999 Global Best Practices Awards in the category of Exceeding Customer Expectations, looks at their own as well as national surveys of patient statisfaction to determine what patients really want.[8]

- *Gap 2:* the gap between what management thinks customers want and the quality specifications that management develops to provide the service. Essentially, this gap is the result of management's inability to translate customers' needs into delivery systems within the firm. For example, Kentucky Fried Chicken once rated its managers' success according to "chicken efficiency," or how much chicken they threw away at the end of the night. Consumers who came in late at night would either have to wait for chicken to be cooked or settle for chicken several hours old. The "chicken efficiency" measurement did not take customers into account, and financial performance suffered.[9]

- *Gap 3:* the gap between the service quality specifications and the service that is actually provided. If both gaps 1 and 2 have been closed, then gap 3 is due to the inability of management and employees to do what should be done. Poorly trained or poorly motivated workers can cause this gap. Management needs to ensure that employees have the skills and the proper tools to perform their jobs. Other techniques that help to close gap 3 are training employees so they know what management expects and encouraging teamwork.

- *Gap 4:* the gap between what the company provides and what the customer is told it provides. This is clearly a communication gap. It may include misleading or deceptive advertising campaigns promising more than the firm can deliver or doing "whatever it takes" to get the business. To close this gap, companies need to create realistic customer expectations through honest, accurate communication about what the firms can provide.

- *Gap 5:* the gap between the service that customers receive and the service they want. This gap can be positive or negative. For example, if a patient expects to wait twenty minutes in the physician's office before seeing the physician but waits only ten minutes, the patient's evaluation of service quality will be high. However, a forty-minute wait would result in a lower evaluation.

When any one or more of these gaps are large, service quality is perceived as low. As the gaps shrink, service quality improves.

Services Marketing in Manufacturing

4

Explain why services marketing is important to manufacturers

A comparison of goods and services marketing is beneficial, but in reality it is hard to distinguish clearly between manufacturing and service firms. Indeed, many manufacturing firms can point to service as a major factor in their success. For example, maintenance and repair services are important to buyers of copy machines.

One reason that goods manufacturers stress service is that it might give them a strong competitive advantage, especially in industries in which products are perceived as similar. In the auto-

Historically, IBM has been a manufacturer of goods, but Big Blue has recently shifted its focus from selling goods to selling services. The company uses its Web site ibm.com to market its e-business solutions and its consulting activities.

mobile industry, for example, few quality differences between car brands are perceived by consumers. Knowing that, General Motors has developed new guidelines for sales techniques and quality customer service and will link dealer incentive payments to how well the guidelines are followed. IBM has changed its focus from computer hardware to services that offer data-processing "solutions." These services include planning, installing, and running their computer systems; connecting remote offices; managing Lotus Notes installations; and bringing clients up to speed in e-business.[10]

Marketing Mixes for Services

Services' unique characteristics—intangibility, inseparability, heterogeneity, and perishability—make marketing more challenging. Elements of the marketing mix (product, distribution, promotion, and pricing) need to be adjusted to meet the special needs created by these characteristics.

Develop marketing mixes for services

Product (Service) Strategy

The development of "product" strategy in services marketing requires planning focused on the service process.[11] Three types of processing occur:

- *People processing* takes place when the service is directed at a customer. Examples are transportation services, hairstyling, health clubs, and dental and health care.
- *Possession processing* occurs when the service is directed at something a customer owns. Examples are lawn care, car repair, dry cleaning, and veterinary services.
- *Information processing* involves the use of technology (for example, computers) or brainpower. Examples are accounting, education, and legal and financial services.

Because customers' experiences and involvement differ for each of these types of services, marketing strategies may also differ. For example, people-processing services require more customer participation than do possession-processing services, which means marketing strategies for the former will need to focus more on inseparability and heterogeneity issues.

Core and Supplementary Services

The service offering can be viewed as a bundle of activities that includes the **core service**, which is the most basic benefit the customer is buying, and a group of **supplementary services** that support or enhance the core service. Exhibit 11.3 illustrates these concepts for FedEx. The core service is overnight transportation and delivery of packages, which involves possession processing. The supplementary services, some of which involve information processing, include problem solving, advice and information, billing statements, and order taking.

core service
The most basic benefit the consumer is buying.

supplementary services
A group of services that support or enhance the core service.

Exhibit 11.3

Core and Supplementary
Services for FedEx

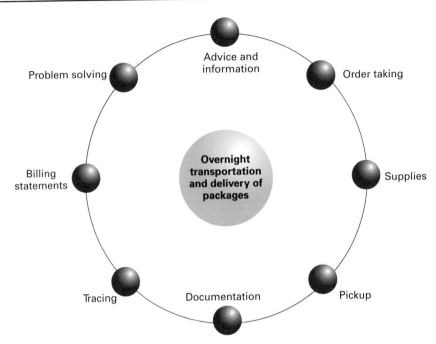

SOURCE: From *Services Marketing*, 3rd ed., by Christopher H. Lovelock, © 1996. Reprinted by permission of Prentice-Hall, Inc., Upper Saddle River, NJ.

In many service industries, the core service becomes a commodity as competition increases. Thus, firms usually emphasize supplementary services to create a competitive advantage. Virgin Atlantic, Malaysia Airlines, and Japan Airlines provide complimentary limo service to and from the airport. Virgin's chauffeurs check in passengers en route. In some cities, United Airlines delivers passengers' luggage to their hotels so they can go straight to business meetings.[12] On the other hand, some firms are positioning themselves in the marketplace by greatly reducing supplementary services. For example, Microtel Inn is an amenity-free hotel concept known as "fast lodging." These low-cost hotels have one- and two-bedroom accommodations and a swimming pool, but no meeting rooms or other services.

Mass Customization

An important issue in developing the service offering is whether to customize or standardize it. Customized services are more flexible and respond to individual customers' needs. They also usually command a higher price. The traditional law firm, which treats each case differently according to the client's situation, offers customized services. Standardized services are more efficient and cost less. Unlike the traditional law firm, for example, Hyatt Legal Services offers low-cost, standardized service "packages" for those with uncomplicated legal needs, such as drawing up a will or mediating an uncontested divorce.

Instead of choosing to either standardize or customize a service, a firm may incorporate elements of both by adopting an emerging strategy called **mass customization**. Mass customization uses technology to deliver customized services on a mass basis, which results in giving each customer whatever she or he asks for.

For example, a feature on the Lands' End Web site allows women to define their figures on-line, receive advice on what swimsuits will flatter their shapes, and mix and match more than 216 combinations of colors

mass customization
A strategy that uses technology to deliver customized services on a mass basis.

and styles. Several airlines are designing services to cater to travelers' individual needs and preferences. Some will serve dinner to passengers when they want to eat it, rather than when the airline wants to serve it. More airlines are offering video-on-demand systems, which let passengers start or stop their movie anytime they want. British Airlines predicts that there will be airline seats that will read passengers' shapes and program their seat-position preferences into smart cards.[13]

The Service Mix

Most service organizations market more than one service. For example, ChemLawn offers lawn care, shrub care, carpet cleaning, and industrial lawn services. Each organization's service mix represents a set of opportunities, risks, and challenges. Each part of the service mix should make a different contribution in achieving the firm's goals. To succeed, each service may also need a different level of financial support.

Making services more personalized is the goal of mass customization. On-demand video systems in airplanes are an example of this.

 Designing a service strategy therefore means deciding what new services to introduce to which target market, what existing services to maintain, and what services to eliminate. For example, in order to increase membership, AAA added financial services, credit cards, and travel perks. Organic, a San Francisco-based company that designs Web sites for clients, has set up two new service divisions: Organic Communications, a full-service public relations department; and Organic Logistics, which helps clients to figure out how to get products ordered on-line into customers' hands.[14]

Distribution Strategy

Distribution strategies for service organizations must focus on such issues as convenience, number of outlets, direct versus indirect distribution, location, and scheduling. A key factor influencing the selection of a service provider is convenience. Therefore, service firms must offer convenience. American Airlines, for example, invested millions of dollars developing the SABRE reservation system to make the reservation process more convenient for independent travel agents. This system is one of the most widely used reservation systems in the industry.

An important distribution objective for many service firms is the *number of outlets* to use or the number of outlets to open during a certain time. Generally, the intensity of distribution should meet, but not exceed, the target market's needs and preferences. Having too few outlets may inconvenience customers; having too many outlets may boost costs unnecessarily. Intensity of distribution may also depend on the image desired. Having only a few outlets may make the service seem more exclusive or selective.

 The next service distribution decision is whether to distribute services to end users *directly* or *indirectly* through other firms. Because of the intangible nature of services, many service firms have to use direct distribution or franchising. Examples include legal, medical, accounting, and personal care services. The newest form of direct distribution is the Internet. Most of the major airlines are now using on-line services to sell tickets directly to consumers, which results in lower distribution costs for the airline companies. Merrill Lynch offers Merrill Lynch OnLine, an Internet-based service that connects clients with company representatives. Other firms with standardized service packages have developed indirect channels using independent intermediaries. For example, NationsBank is offering teller services and loan services to customers in small satellite facilities located in Albertson's grocery stores in Texas. An important issue for service companies that distribute their offerings over the Internet is customer privacy, as the "Ethics in Marketing" box illustrates.

NEW QUESTIONS ABOUT MEDICAL PRIVACY

Cancer patients navigating the Internet in search of information and support have found a lifeline in nonprofit sites such as the University of Pennsylvania's Oncolink, the National Institutes of Health's Medline, and the Association of Cancer Online Resources. Now, growing demand has prompted the emergence of several commercial Web sites.

Among the newcomers are Oncology.com, cancerpage.com, CancerSource.com, and cancer-facts.com Their pitch to consumers is that their for-profit sites can offer far more sophisticated services than the nonprofits can afford. But to offer them for free, they must run ads and enter partnerships with sponsors.

More importantly, in exchange for access to sophisticated medical data and expert advice, the companies are asking patients to give personal data that, in turn, will be sold to advertisers and business partners and used by the Web sites to create products to sell back to pa-

tients. Medical privacy, already a hot-button issue on the Internet, is especially relevant for cancer patients, who may face discrimination in everything from employment and insurance to social situations.

Some experts worry about for-profit motives when it comes to a catastrophic disease like cancer. "It raises some real concerns about confidentiality," says Martin J, Murphy, editor of a leading peer-reviewed cancer journal, the *Oncologist*. "There should be the seal of the confessional when it comes to anonymity, and no information about the patient should even be kept [by the Web site], let alone passed along" to advertisers and marketers.

Dr. Murphy, a cancer survivor, doesn't object to pharmaceutical companies supporting sites with unrestricted grants, or displaying banners for their drugs. "But when a site is for-profit, I worry that there is potential for really exploiting people who are at their most vulnerable."

All the cancer-related Web sites typically promise to treat health-related information confidentially but say that anything patients transmit or post to the sites can be used for any purpose. Oncology.com warns that failure to provide all the information it asks for will "limit access and functionality" within the Web site. The cancer sites make clear they will share demographic data with pharmaceutical companies, and use information about member patients for market research.

One thing patients can look for on a Web site is the pledge to abide by the HONcode principles, including confidentiality, of the nonprofit Health in the Net Foundation. But the group doesn't police sites.[a]

Do you think the for-profit cancer-related Web sites are ethical? Explain your answer.

SOURCE: Laura Landro, "Cancer Support Sites Are Raising Questions About Medical Privacy," *Wall Street Journal*, April 28, 2000, p. B1.

The *location* of a service most clearly reveals the relationship between its target market strategy and distribution strategy. Reportedly, Conrad Hilton claimed that the three most important factors in determining a hotel's success are "location, location, and location." Several banks deliver their services in roving bank offices. NationsBank sends a portable ATM around Florida to dispense cash at parades and provide bank services during emergencies such as hurricanes. First Chicago drives its mobile bank into inner-city neighborhoods to reach the poorer customers who are often given little attention by banks—and to help fulfill its legally mandated community-investment commitments without building costly new branches.[15]

For time-dependent service providers like airlines, physicians, and dentists, scheduling is often a more important factor. Scheduling is sometimes the most important factor in a customer's choice of airline.

Promotion Strategy

Consumers and business users have more trouble evaluating services than goods, because services are less tangible. In turn, marketers have more trouble promoting intangible services than tangible goods. Here are four promotion strategies they can try:

- *Stressing tangible cues:* A tangible cue is a concrete symbol of the service offering. To make their intangible services more tangible, hotels turn down the bedcovers and put mints on the pillows. Insurance companies use symbols like rocks, blankets, umbrellas, and hands to help make their intangible services appear tangible. Merrill Lynch uses a bull to help give its services substance.
- *Using personal information sources:* A personal information source is someone consumers are familiar with (such as a celebrity) or someone they know or can relate to personally. Celebrity endorsements are sometimes used to reduce customers' perceived risk in choosing a service. Service firms may also seek to simulate positive word-of-mouth communication among present and prospective customers by using real customers in their ads.
- *Creating a strong organizational image:* One way to create an image is to manage the evidence, including the physical environment of the service facility, the appearance of the service employees, and the tangible items associated with a service (like stationery, bills, and business cards). For example, McDonald's has created a strong organizational image with its Golden Arches, relatively standardized interiors, and employee uniforms. Another way to create an image is through branding. MCI Communications has grown by creating and promoting brands in the commodity business of common-carrier long-distance service. Examples of MCI brands are Friends and Family and 1-800-COLLECT.
- *Engaging in postpurchase communication:* Postpurchase communication refers to the follow-up activities that a service firm might engage in after a customer transaction. Postcard surveys, telephone calls, brochures, and various other types of follow-up show customers that their feedback matters and their patronage is appreciated.

To communicate the benefits of intangible services, marketers often rely on concrete symbols. The umbrella symbol used by Traveler's Insurance signifies protection. This helps give the company's service substance.
Courtesy Travelers Life & Annuity

Price Strategy

Considerations in pricing a service are similar to the pricing considerations to be discussed in Chapters 17 and 18. However, the unique characteristics of services present two special pricing challenges.[16]

First, in order to price a service, it is important to define the unit of service consumption. For example, should pricing be based on completing a specific service task (cutting a customer's hair), or should it be time based (how long it takes to cut a customer's hair)? Some services include the consumption of goods, such as food and beverages. Restaurants charge customers for food and drink rather than the use of a table and chairs. Some transportation firms charge by distance; others charge a flat rate.

Second, for services that are composed of multiple elements, the issue is whether pricing should be based on a "bundle" of elements or whether each element should be priced separately. A bundled price may be preferable when consumers dislike having to pay "extra" for every part of the service (for example, paying extra for baggage or food on an airplane), and it is simpler for the firm to administer. For instance, MCI offered a basic communications package that cost $4.95 a month. The package included thirty minutes of telephone time, five hours of Internet access, a personal number that could route calls to several locations, and a calling card. Alternatively, customers may not want to pay for service elements they do not use. Many furniture stores now have "unbundled" delivery charges from the price of the furniture. Customers who wish to can pick up the furniture at the store, saving on the delivery fee.

Marketers should set performance objectives when pricing each service. Three categories of pricing objectives have been suggested:

- *Revenue-oriented pricing* focuses on maximizing the surplus of income over costs. A limitation of this approach is that determining costs can be difficult for many services.
- *Operations-oriented pricing* seeks to match supply and demand by varying prices. For example, matching hotel demand to the number of available rooms can be achieved by raising prices at peak times and decreasing them during slow times.
- *Patronage-oriented pricing* tries to maximize the number of customers using the service. Thus, prices vary with different market segments' ability to pay, and methods of payment (such as credit) are offered that increase the likelihood of a purchase.

A firm may need to use more than one type of pricing objective. In fact, all three objectives probably need to be included to some degree in pricing strategy, although the importance of each type may vary depending on the type of service provided, the prices that competitors are charging, the differing ability of various customer segments to pay, or the opportunity to negotiate price. For customized services (for example, legal services and construction services), customers may also have the ability to negotiate a price.

Relationship Marketing in Services

6

Discuss relationship marketing in services

Many services involve ongoing interaction between the service organization and the customer. Thus, they can benefit from relationship marketing, the strategy described in Chapter 1, as a means of attracting, developing, and retaining customer relationships. The idea is to develop strong loyalty by creating satisfied customers who will buy additional services from the firm and are unlikely to switch to a competitor. Satisfied customers are also likely to engage in positive word-of-mouth communication, thereby helping to bring in new customers.

Many businesses have found that it is more cost effective to hang on to the customers they have than only to try to attract new ones. A bank executive, for example, found that increasing customer retention by 2 percent can have the same effect on profits as reducing costs by 10 percent.

It has been suggested that relationship marketing can be practiced at three levels (see Exhibit 11.4):[17]

- *Level 1:* The firm uses pricing incentives to encourage customers to continue doing business with it. Examples include the frequent flyer programs offered by many airlines and the free or discounted travel services given to frequent hotel guests. This level of relationship marketing is the least effective in the long term because its price-based advantage is easily imitated by other firms.

Exhibit 11.4

Level	Type of Bond	Degree of Service Customization	Main Element of Marketing Mix	Potential for Long-Term Advantage Over Competitors
1	Financial	Low	Price	Low
2	Financial, social	Medium	Personal communication	Medium
3	Financial, social, structural	Medium to high	Service delivery	High

SOURCE: Reprinted with the permission of the Free Press, a division of Simon & Schuster, Inc. from *Marketing Services: Competing Through Quality* by Leonard L. Berry and A. Parasuraman. Copyright © 1991 by the Free Press.

- *Level 2:* This level of relationship marketing also uses pricing incentives but seeks to build social bonds with customers. The firm stays in touch with customers, learns about their needs, and designs services to meet those needs. 1-800-FLOWERS, for example, developed an on-line Gift Reminder Program. Customers who reach the company via their Web site can register unlimited birthdays, anniversaries, or other special occasions. Five days before each occasion and at their request, 1-800-FLOWERS sends them an e-mail reminder.[18] Level 2 relationship marketing has a higher potential for keeping the firm ahead of the competition than does level 1 relationship marketing.
- *Level 3:* At this level, the firm again uses financial and social bonds but adds structural bonds to the formula. Structural bonds are developed by offering value-added services that are not readily available from other firms. Hertz's #1 Club Gold program allows members to call and reserve a car, board a courtesy bus at the airport, tell the driver their name, and get dropped off in front of their car. Hertz also starts up the car and turns on the air conditioning or heat, depending on the temperature. Marketing programs like this one have the strongest potential for sustaining long-term relationships with customers.

Internal Marketing in Service Firms

Services are performances, so the quality of a firm's employees is an important part of building long-term relationships with customers. Employees who like their jobs and are satisfied with the firm they work for are more likely to deliver superior service to customers. In other words, a firm that makes its employees happy has a better chance of keeping its customers coming back. Studies show that replacing an employee costs roughly 1.5 times a year's pay. Also, companies with highly committed employees have been found to post sharply higher shareholder returns.[19] Thus, it is critical that service firms practice **internal marketing**, which means treating employees as customers and developing systems and benefits that satisfy their needs. These are the activities involved in internal marketing: competing for talent, offering a vision, training employees, stressing teamwork, giving

7

Explain internal marketing in services

internal marketing
Treating employees as customers and developing systems and benefits that satisfy their needs.

employees more freedom to make decisions, measuring and rewarding good service performance, and knowing employees' needs.[20]

Companies have instituted a wide variety of programs designed to satisfy employees. Some companies are offering their employees concierges that run errands to help ease the lives of time-strapped, stressed-out workers and retain happy employees.[21] Marriott International set up a twenty-four-hour hotline to answer questions from employees having personal and family problems.[22] These examples illustrate how service firms can invest in their most important resource—their employees.

A concierge service for employees is one program designed to keep employees satisfied. By helping to reduce the stress level of the employees, companies can retain a happier, more productive staff.

Global Issues in Services Marketing

Discuss global issues in services marketing

The international marketing of services is a major part of global business, and the United States has become the world's largest exporter of services. Competition in international services is increasing rapidly, however.

To be successful in the global marketplace, service firms must first determine the nature of their core product. Then the marketing mix elements (additional services, pricing, promotion, distribution) should be designed to take into account each country's cultural, technological, and political environment.

Because of their competitive advantages, many U.S. service industries have been able to enter the global marketplace. U.S. banks, for example, have advantages in customer service and collections management. The field of construction and engineering services offers great global potential; U.S. companies have vast experience in this industry, so economies of scale are possible for machinery and materials, human resource management, and project management. The U.S. insurance industry has substantial knowledge about underwriting, risk evaluation, and insurance operations that it can export to other countries. American restaurant chains also have great potential for globalization, as the "Global Perspectives" box on the next page illustrates.

Nonprofit Organization Marketing

Describe nonprofit organization marketing

nonprofit organization
An organization that exists to achieve some goal other than the usual business goals of profit, market share, or return on investment.

A **nonprofit organization** is an organization that exists to achieve some goal other than the usual business goals of profit, market share, or return on investment. Nonprofit organizations share important characteristics with private-sector service firms. Both market intangible products. Both often require the customer to be present during the production process. Both for-profit and nonprofit services vary greatly from producer to producer and from day to day, even from the same producer. Neither for-profit nor nonprofit services can be stored in the way that tangible goods can be produced, saved, and sold at a later date.

Few people realize that nonprofit organizations account for over 20 percent of the economic activity in the United States. The cost of government, the predominant form of nonprofit organization, has become the biggest single item in the American family budget—more than housing, food, or health care. Together, fed-

BIG BOY'S ADVENTURES IN THAILAND

With his checkered overalls, cowlick curl, and penchant for double burgers, Big Boy seemed an unlikely fit for Bangkok. "People thought he was a little, well, creepy," says Peter Smythe, the head franchisor for Big Boy restaurants in Thailand. "They kept asking me, 'Is he a Chinese Ronald McDonald?'" Eventually, a few Thai visitors decided Big Boy was a religious icon and laid bowls of rice and incense at his feet.

Now that giants like Burger King and McDonald's have saturated markets around the world, the more obscure fast-food companies are heading overseas. In 1998, the minichains, such as Big Boy and Schlotzkys, opened nearly 800 new restaurants abroad, giving them more than 12,000 units overseas, according to Technomic Inc., a Chicago food-business consultancy. Asia, with more than a billion young consumers, is the prime target.

Still, for the little guys of the business—who don't have the money, supply networks, or global wisdom of a Hamburger University—venturing abroad can be a messy business. Culture clashes, food shortages, and government run-ins are common. Consider the story of Big Boy.

Mr. Smythe, who was living in California at the time, got a call in 1995 from his Thai brother-in-law. They met with a businessman who was looking for an American franchise to bring to Thailand. Smythe found Big Boy, a franchise that seemed a natural for expansion. The first restaurant opened in 1996, but no one came. After interviewing hundreds of customers, Smythe found a number of reasons why people were not coming to his restaurant. Some said the restaurant's "room energy" was bad. Others said the Big Boy statue spooked them. Many explained that they would rather get a sweet satay, noodle bowl, or grilled squid on the street for one-fifth the price of a greasy burger. "It suddenly dawned on me that here I was trying to get a 3,500-year-old culture to eat sixty-four-year-old food," says Smythe.

Big Boy placed a few cheap Thai items on the menu, and customers started trickling in. Today, Smythe owns four Big Boys in Thailand, three in Bangkok, and one in the southern beach town of Pattaya. Sales have doubled since last year, and the larger two are pulling in more than $13,000 a month—about one quarter the average for an American store, but still profitable because of their lower costs.

The menu is a work in progress. Smythe studied the customers who were walking past his restaurants and discovered that they fell into two broad categories: European tourists and Thai young people, including a large number of the young women who work in nearby bars. With help from a Swiss chef, Smythe filled the menu with German specialties like spatzle, beef, and chocolate cake. For the Thais, he added country-style specialties like fried rice and pork omelets. He also added sugar and chili powder to Big Boy's hamburgers to better match the Thai taste buds. The restaurants now make over half their money from Thai food and the rest from European dishes and the occasional milk shake or burger.

"We thought we were bringing American food to the masses," says Smythe. "But now we're bringing Thai and European food to the tourists. It's strange, but you know what? It's working."[a]

Evaluate Big Boy's marketing strategies in Thailand. What lessons can you derive from the Big Boy story?

[a] Robert Frank, "Big Boy's Adventures in Thailand," *Wall Street Journal*, April 12, 2000, pp. B1, B4.

---

eral, state, and local governments collect revenues that amount to more than a third of the U.S. gross domestic product. Moreover, they employ nearly one of every five nonagricultural civilian workers. In addition to government entities, nonprofit organizations include hundreds of thousands of private museums, theaters, schools, and churches.

What Is Nonprofit Organization Marketing?

Nonprofit organization marketing is the effort by nonprofit organizations to bring about mutually satisfying exchanges with target markets. Although these organizations vary substantially in size and purpose and operate in different environments, most perform the following marketing activities:

- Identify the customers they wish to serve or attract (although they usually use another term, such as *clients, patients, members,* or *sponsors)*

nonprofit organization marketing
The effort by nonprofit organizations to bring about mutually satisfying exchanges with target markets.

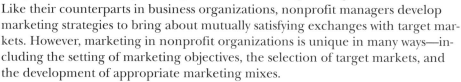

On Line

Explain the unique aspects of nonprofit organization marketing

- Explicitly or implicitly specify objectives
- Develop, manage, and eliminate programs and services
- Decide on prices to charge (although they use other terms, such as *fees, donations, tuition, fares, fines,* or *rates*)
- Schedule events or programs, and determine where they will be held or where services will be offered
- Communicate their availability through brochures, signs, public service announcements, or advertisements

Often, the nonprofit organizations that carry out these functions do not realize they are engaged in marketing.

Unique Aspects of Nonprofit Organization Marketing Strategies

Like their counterparts in business organizations, nonprofit managers develop marketing strategies to bring about mutually satisfying exchanges with target markets. However, marketing in nonprofit organizations is unique in many ways—including the setting of marketing objectives, the selection of target markets, and the development of appropriate marketing mixes.

Objectives In the private sector, the profit motive is both an objective for guiding decisions and a criterion for evaluating results. Nonprofit organizations do not seek to make a profit for redistribution to owners or shareholders. Rather, their focus is often on generating enough funds to cover expenses. The Methodist Church does not gauge its success by the amount of money left in offering plates. The Museum of Science and Industry does not base its performance evaluations on the dollar value of tokens put into the turnstile.

Most nonprofit organizations are expected to provide equitable, effective, and efficient services that respond to the wants and preferences of multiple constituencies. These include users, payers, donors, politicians, appointed officials, the media, and the general public. Nonprofit organizations cannot measure their success or failure in strictly financial terms.

The lack of a financial "bottom line" and the existence of multiple, diverse, intangible, and sometimes vague or conflicting objectives make prioritizing objectives, making decisions, and evaluating performance hard for nonprofit managers. They must often use approaches different from the ones commonly used in the private sector. For example, Planned Parenthood has devised a system for basing salary increases on how employees perform in relation to the objectives they set each year.

Target Markets Three issues relating to target markets are unique to nonprofit organizations:

- *Apathetic or strongly opposed targets:* Private-sector organizations usually give priority to developing those market segments that are most likely to respond to particular offerings. In contrast, nonprofit organizations must often target those who are apathetic about or strongly opposed to receiving their services, such as vaccinations, family-planning guidance, help for problems of drug or alcohol abuse, and psychological counseling.
- *Pressure to adopt undifferentiated segmentation strategies:* Nonprofit organizations often adopt undifferentiated strategies (see Chapter 7) by default. Sometimes they fail to recognize the advantages of targeting, or an undifferentiated approach may appear to offer economies of scale and low per capita costs. In other in-

stances, nonprofit organizations are pressured or required to serve the maximum number of people by targeting the average user. The problem with developing services targeted at the average user is that there are few "average" users. Therefore, such strategies typically fail to fully satisfy any market segment.

- *Complementary positioning:* The main role of many nonprofit organizations is to provide services, with available resources, to those who are not adequately served by private-sector organizations. As a result, the nonprofit organization must often complement rather than compete with the efforts of others. The positioning task is to identify underserved market segments and to develop marketing programs that match their needs rather than to target the niches that may be most profitable. For example, a university library may see itself as complementing the services of the public library, rather than as competing with it.

Product Decisions   There are three product-related distinctions between business and nonprofit organizations:

- *Benefit complexity:* Rather than simple product concepts, like "Fly the friendly skies" or "We earn money the old-fashioned way," nonprofit organizations often market complex behaviors or ideas. Examples include the need to exercise or eat right, not to drink and drive, and not to smoke tobacco. The benefits that a person receives are complex, long term, and intangible, and therefore are more difficult to communicate to consumers.

- *Benefit strength:* The benefit strength of many nonprofit offerings is quite weak or indirect. What are the direct, personal benefits to you of driving fifty-five miles per hour, donating blood, or asking your neighbors to contribute money to a charity? In contrast, most private-sector service organizations can offer customers direct, personal benefits in an exchange relationship.

- *Involvement:* Many nonprofit organizations market products that elicit very low involvement ("Prevent forest fires" or "Don't litter") or very high involvement ("Join the military" or "Stop smoking"). The typical range for private-sector goods is much narrower. Traditional promotional tools may be inadequate to motivate adoption of either low- or high-involvement products.

Distribution Decisions   A nonprofit organization's capacity for distributing its service offerings to potential customer groups when and where they want them is typically a key variable in determining the success of those service offerings. For example, most state land-grant universities offer extension programs throughout their state to reach the general public. Many large universities have one or more satellite campus locations to provide easier access for students in other areas. Some educational institutions also offer classes to students at off-campus locations via interactive video technology.

The extent to which a service depends on fixed facilities has important implications for distribution decisions. Obviously, services like rail transit and lake fishing can be delivered only at specific points. Many nonprofit services, however, do not depend on special facilities. Counseling, for example, need not take place in agency offices; it may occur wherever counselors and clients can meet. Probation services, outreach youth programs, and educational courses taught on commuter trains are other examples of deliverable services.

Promotion Decisions   Many nonprofit organizations are explicitly or implicitly prohibited from advertising, thus limiting their promotion options. Most federal agencies fall into this category. Other nonprofit organizations simply do not have the resources to retain advertising agencies, promotion consultants, or marketing staff. However, nonprofit organizations have a few special promotion resources to call on:

- *Professional volunteers:* Nonprofit organizations often seek out marketing, sales, and advertising professionals to help them develop and implement

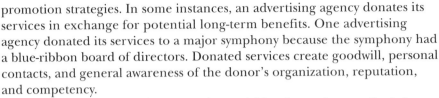
promotion strategies. In some instances, an advertising agency donates its services in exchange for potential long-term benefits. One advertising agency donated its services to a major symphony because the symphony had a blue-ribbon board of directors. Donated services create goodwill, personal contacts, and general awareness of the donor's organization, reputation, and competency.

- *Sales promotion activities:* Sales promotion activities that make use of existing services or other resources are increasingly being used to draw attention to the offerings of nonprofit organizations. Campus Crusade for Christ recently gave more than a dozen prospective donors tickets to the Super Bowl.[23]

public service advertisement (PSA)

An announcement that promotes a program of a federal, state, or local government or of a nonprofit organization.

- *Public service advertising:* A **public service advertisement (PSA)** is an announcement that promotes a program of a federal, state, or local government or of a nonprofit organization. Unlike a commercial advertiser, the sponsor of the PSA does not pay for the time or space. Instead, it is donated by the medium. The Advertising Council has developed PSAs that are some of the most memorable advertisements of all time. For example, Smokey the Bear reminded everyone to be careful not to start forest fires. The Internet will soon be used for PSAs as the nonprofit Advertising Council expands its ability to disseminate banners across the Web.[24]

- *Licensing:* Some nonprofit organizations have found that licensing their names and/or images is an effective way to communicate to a large audience. For example, the Vatican is trying to raise money and spread the word about the Catholic Church through a licensing program. This program puts images from the Vatican library's art collection, architecture, frescoes, and manuscripts on T-shirts, glassware, candles, and ornaments.

Nonprofit organizations must often be creative in how they promote and market their services. To spread the word about the Catholic Church, the Vatican has chosen to license images from its library's art collection for use on salable merchandise.

© Corbis/Massimo Listri

Pricing Decisions   Five key characteristics distinguish the pricing decisions of nonprofit organizations from those of the profit sector:

- *Pricing objectives:* Revenue is the main pricing objective in the profit sector or, more specifically, profit maximization, sales maximization, or target return on sales or investment. Many nonprofit organizations must also be concerned about revenue. However, nonprofit organizations often seek to either partially or fully defray costs rather than achieve a profit for distribution to stockholders. Nonprofit organizations also seek to redistribute income—for instance, through taxation and sliding-scale fees. Moreover, they strive to allocate resources fairly among individuals or households or across geographic or political boundaries.

- *Nonfinancial prices:* In many nonprofit situations, consumers are not charged a monetary price but instead must absorb nonmonetary costs. The importance of those costs is illustrated by the large number of eligible citizens who do not take advantage of so-called free services for the poverty stricken. In many public assistance programs, about half the people who are eligible don't participate. Nonmonetary costs consist of the opportunity cost of time, embarrassment costs, and effort costs.

- *Indirect payment:* Indirect payment through taxes is common to marketers of "free" services, such as libraries, fire protection, and police protection. Indirect payment is not a common practice in the profit sector.
- *Separation between payers and users:* By design, the services of many charitable organizations are provided for those who are relatively poor and largely paid for by those who have better finances. Although examples of separation between payers and users can be found in the profit sector (such as insurance claims), the practice is much less prevalent.
- *Below-cost pricing:* An example of below-cost pricing is university tuition. Virtually all private and public colleges and universities price their services below full cost.

Looking Back

Look back at the story about Commerce Bancorp at the beginning of this chapter. After reading the chapter, you should know the answers to the questions posed at the end of the story. A service, like banking, differs from goods on four characteristics: intangibility, inseparability, heterogeneity, and perishability. Commerce offers numerous financial services to its customers. The challenges facing Commerce as it grows include how to continue offering the same level of personalized service to customers, how to balance its on-line and brick-and-mortar operations, and how to maintain an internal culture that is service-driven.

Use it Now!

Consider all the services you use in a week. Do they always meet your expectations? A new Internet company called Planetfeedback.com can help you complain or compliment companies more effectively. Planetfeedback.com offers a letter template and a database full of corporate addresses to help you send a product or service complaint—or compliment—to the appropriate person in an organization.

Think of a service you used recently that did not deliver all it promised or all you expected. Use http://www.planetfeedback.com to compose and send an e-mail letter to the company. Recount your experience and suggest ways the company can improve its service quality.

Or you may want to compliment a service provider on a job well done. Use Planetfeedback .com or send a snail-mail letter to the company, thanking them for the great service.

For more information on Planetfeedback.com, reread the Entrepreneurship case at the end of Chapter 8.

Summary

1 **Discuss the importance of services to the economy.** The service sector plays a crucial role in the U.S. economy, employing about three-quarters of the work-force and accounting for more than 60 percent of the gross domestic product.

2 **Discuss the differences between services and goods.** Services are distinguished by four characteristics: intangibility, inseparability, heterogeneity, and perishability. Services are intangible in that they lack clearly identifiable physical characteristics, making it difficult for marketers to communicate their specific benefits to potential customers. The production and consumption of services are typically inseparable. Services are heterogeneous because their quality depends on such variables as the service provider, individual consumer, location, and so on.

Finally, services are perishable in the sense that they cannot be stored or saved. As a result, synchronizing supply with demand is particularly challenging in the service industry.

(3) **Describe the components of service quality and the gap model of service quality.** There are five components of service quality: reliability (ability to perform the service dependably, accurately, and consistently), responsiveness (providing prompt service), assurance (knowledge and courtesy of employees and their ability to convey trust), empathy (caring, individualized attention), and tangibles (physical evidence of the service).

The gap model identifies five key discrepancies that can influence customer evaluations of service quality. When the gaps are large, service quality is low. As the gaps shrink, service quality improves. Gap 1 is found between customer expectations and management's perceptions of those expectations. Gap 2 is found between management's perception of what the customer wants and specifications for service quality. Gap 3 is found between service quality specifications and delivery of the service. Gap 4 is found between service delivery and what the company promises to the customer through external communication. Gap 5 is found between customers' service expectations and their perceptions of service performance.

(4) **Explain why services marketing is important to manufacturers.** Although manufacturers are marketing mainly goods, the related services they provide often give them a competitive advantage—especially when competing goods are quite similar.

(5) **Develop marketing mixes for services.** "Product" (service) strategy issues include what is being processed (people, possessions, information), core and supplementary services, customization versus standardization, and the service mix or portfolio. Distribution decisions involve convenience, number of outlets, direct versus indirect distribution, and scheduling. Stressing tangible cues, using personal sources of information, creating strong organizational images, and engaging in postpurchase communication are effective promotion strategies. Pricing objectives for services can be revenue oriented, operations oriented, patronage oriented, or any combination of the three.

(6) **Discuss relationship marketing in services.** Relationship marketing in services involves attracting, developing, and retaining customer relationships. There are three levels of relationship marketing: Level 1 focuses on pricing incentives; level 2 uses pricing incentives and social bonds with customers; and level 3 uses pricing, social bonds, and structural bonds to build long-term relationships.

(7) **Explain internal marketing in services.** Internal marketing means treating employees as customers and developing systems and benefits that satisfy their needs. Employees who like their jobs and are happy with the firm they work for are more likely to deliver good service. Internal marketing activities include competing for talent, offering a vision, training employees, stressing teamwork, giving employees freedom to make decisions, measuring and rewarding good service performance, and knowing employees' needs.

(8) **Discuss global issues in services marketing.** The United States has become the world's largest exporter of services. Although competition is keen, the United States has a competitive advantage because of its vast experience in many service industries. To be successful globally, service firms must adjust their marketing mix for the environment of each target country.

(9) **Describe nonprofit organization marketing.** Nonprofit organizations pursue goals other than profit, market share, and return on investment. Nonprofit organization marketing facilitates mutually satisfying exchanges between nonprofit organizations and their target markets.

10 **Explain the unique aspects of nonprofit organization marketing.** Several unique characteristics distinguish nonbusiness marketing strategy, including a concern with services and social behaviors rather than manufactured goods and profit; a difficult, undifferentiated, and in some ways marginal target market; a complex product that may have only indirect benefits and elicit very low involvement; a short, direct, immediate distribution channel; a relative lack of resources for promotion; and prices only indirectly related to the exchange between the producer and the consumer of services.

Discussion and Writing Questions

1. Explain what the search, experience, and credence qualities are for medical services.

2. **WRITING** Assume that you are the manager of a restaurant. Write a list of implications of inseparability for your firm.

3. Analyze a recent experience that you have had with a service business (for example, hairdresser, movie theater, car repair, restaurant) in terms of your expectations and perceptions about each of the five components of service quality.

4. **WRITING** Apply what you have learned about service quality to your university food service, and write a memo to the food service manager making recommendations for change, if needed.

5. **TEAM** Form a team with at least two other classmates, and come up with an idea for a new service. Develop a marketing mix strategy for the new service.

6. **TEAM** For the service developed in Question 5, have the members of the team discuss how they would design a relationship marketing strategy.

7. **WRITING** Write a list of some of the issues you would have to consider in taking your new service (from Question 5) global. How would you change your marketing mix to address those issues?

8. **TEAM** Form a team with two or three classmates. Using the promotion strategies discussed in the chapter, design a promotion strategy for your college or university.

9. Your nonprofit community theater is having problems attracting new patrons. Most of its current patrons are fifty years old and older. What other target markets might be viable? For each target market you choose, identify what promotion activities you would use to attract it.

10. **ON LINE** What services does the Web site **http://www.travelweb.com** offer? How do visitors use the Special Offer List?

11. **ON LINE** How can marketers benefit from the service offered at Web site **http://www.liszt.com**? Select a subcategory under "Business" that has more than one entry, and describe the mailing lists you find.

Application for Entrepreneurs

ENTREPRENEUR Amanda Baker has decided she wants to start a marketing consulting business. She has been able to generate solid financial backing for her venture because she already has developed an outstanding reputation as a creative and successful marketer, so start-up resources are not a large problem. Amanda will target small companies with her services. Her business will be located in a medium-sized community not far from a large city.

Questions

1. How can Amanda tangibilize her service for potential clients?
2. What can Amanda do to ensure she will offer a quality service to her clients?
3. What marketing strategies can Amanda use to help her develop long-term relationships with her clients?

Case

entrepreneurship

Closing the Digital Divide in the Inner City

Entering the new millennium, there were more than 350,000 unfilled technology jobs. In the Chicago area alone, there were 18,000 technology positions to be filled. To satisfy this demand for technology professionals, Leslie Beller resigned from Jobs for Youth in 1999 and founded the Inner City Computer Stars Foundation. Start-up funds came from two investors at the Chicago Mercantile Exchange ($15,000) and a December 1999 fundraiser ($50,000). Largely known as i.c.stars, the Chicago-based not-for-profit organization is focused upon closing the so-called "digital divide."

Closing the digital divide is about making sure information is available to everyone, not just a few select groups. Disenfranchised groups in the technology revolution include minorities, females, the poor, and the disabled. Beller's organization, i.c.stars, is a technology-training program that focuses upon inner-city, primarily African-American and Latino youth. The goal is to prepare eighteen to twenty-four-year-olds for the technology, telecommunications, and Internet industry workplace.

As a nonprofit organization, Beller has two very different target markets: (1) inner-city youth who will participate in the technology training program and (2) the investment community who will provide funding for the program (and eventually jobs for the trained youth).

The technology training program is an intensive three-month program that includes a cost-of-living stipend for the participant. The first month focuses upon topics such as HTML, Java, and project management. During the second month, participants develop and execute their own Web sites, which are hosted at the **http://www.icstars.org** portal. In the third month, the participants work with paying clients on Web-related projects. The objective, at the end of the third month, is to place program participants in webmaster or IT professional positions. The first program began in June 2000 with ten inner-city youth from the south and west sides of Chicago and from uptown Chicago.

Targeting the Chicago-investment community, i.c.stars hopes to raise $1 million to keep the organization operational through September 2001. The organization plans to accomplish this via a not-for-profit road show where various aspects of i.c.stars are presented and described. Unlike traditional not-for-profit fundraising efforts that target foundations, the road show targets angel investors, venture capital groups, and corporations with a real-time presentation of the organization. The road show allows i.c.stars to operate as a dot.com company in its fundraising. Investors can sign up to participate in the organization's activities at the road show Web site, **http://www.iccapital.com**. The key selling point in the road show is the opportunity to gain social equity in the future of the Chicago community.

Business Plan

i.c.stars' five-year business plan calls for the organization to eventually generate revenue through placement fees and production contracts. To be financially stable within five years, i.c.stars has the following timetable:

- Years 1 and 2: Perfect the three-month training program model
- Years 2 and 3: Serve the Chicago community and technology market
- Years 3 and 4: Create an i.c.stars consulting service around the organization's core competencies of assessment, diversity/workplace culture training, IT leadership training, and project management
- Year 5: Financial stability through training programs

Continued Success

By mid-2000, i.c.stars had lined up an impressive group of corporate sponsors. Groups such as William Blair & Company, closerlook.com, Lante Corporation, Blue-Meteor, Arthur Andersen, and Expedior, as well as many angel investors, have contributed to i.c.stars' success to date. Beller, however, has to continue developing such sponsorship relationships if she wants to accomplish her five-year plan and achieve the long-term goal of not only financial stability but the crossing of the digital divide between technology and minority groups.

Questions

1. What is i.c.stars' product?
2. What is unique about the i.c.stars' marketing strategy?
3. Does i.c.stars face any pricing issues?
4. What does Beller need to do to continue building sponsorship relationships?

Bibliography

"Chicago-Based 'Dot-Org' i.c.stars Adapts Web Approaches to Not-for-Profit Initiative." *PR Newswire*, May 23, 2000. On-line.

"i.c.stars Addresses Digital Divide and Creates a New Business Model for Not-for-Profits." *PR Newswire*, May 16, 2000. On-line.

Darcy Evon. "Crossing Electronic Lines." *Chicago Software News*, March 2000. On-line.

Howard Wolinsky. "Tech Leaders Push to Close Digital Divide." *Chicago Sun-Times*, April 18, 2000. On-line.

http://www.iccapital.com

http://www.icstars.org

Case

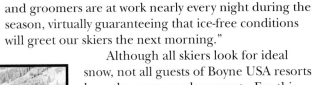

Boyne USA: At Your Service . . .

Vacations don't last forever, and nothing is more disappointing to the ski buff than to drive or fly all the way to the mountain on that one weekend off only to find snow that is icy or slushy. By choosing the right destination, this kind of vacation fiasco can be avoided, or at least it can if your choice is a Boyne USA resort. Excellent snow is just one of the ways that Boyne USA's resorts pamper their guests, where skiers can always count on well-packed powder, well-groomed slopes, and lots of glistening cross-country trails. The readers of *Ski Magazine* rated Boyne Mountain No. 1 in snowmaking in the United States, and Boyne Highlands was ranked No. 4. Boyne USA's founder, Everett Kircher, credits this to skillful snowmaking: ". . . we make snow many nights during the winter whenever temperatures are right. Not because we don't have enough base on the slopes. We make extra snow to provide top-quality skiing for the next day. Our state-of-the-art tillers

and groomers are at work nearly every night during the season, virtually guaranteeing that ice-free conditions will greet our skiers the next morning."

Although all skiers look for ideal snow, not all guests of Boyne USA resorts have the same needs or wants. For this reason the Boyne resort network offers a variety of facilities, locations, and promotions. At each resort, guests can stay at the lodge, with or without meals included, or rent condominiums where a group of friends can stay together. The serious vacationer can buy a house or condo as an investment; and for company retreats, complete convention and meeting facilities are available for mixing business with pleasure. The Boyne Highlands Resort, the flagship of Boyne USA, is nestled in the hills and valleys of northwest lower Michigan. This Bavarian-style resort offers world-class golf and skiing on seven thousand acres of scenic countryside, and the main lodge is a rambling ivy-covered structure reminiscent of alpine country houses but fitted with 165 rooms.

In addition to the main lodge at Boyne Highlands, there is a condo-hotel, Heather Highlands, with 126 spacious suites featuring fireplaces and fully equipped kitchens. Another hotel, the Inn, features saunas and a heated, indoor jet pool that connects to an outdoor pool and patio area. Since business travelers have different needs from those of vacationers, Boyne Highlands prides itself on offering meeting planners a wide choice of tastefully decorated facilities, from large slope-side exhibit halls to small, plush boardrooms. Boyne can handle conferences for six to six hundred people with style and efficiency thanks to its well-seasoned convention staff. In addition, Boyne offers tennis courts, sauna and health club, breathtaking forests and hills for hiking and mountain biking, ski and golf lessons, pro shops, and day trips to Traverse City and Mackinac, two of Michigan's most popular destinations.

If Michigan is too far, that's no problem because Boyne USA has six resorts located from coast to coast—in Washington, Utah, Montana, and Florida. Several diverse locations make it convenient for people in most areas of the country to come to a Boyne resort and spend time on the links, on the slopes, or at the fishing hole, not in the airport or on the road. Because Boyne USA has resorts in both warm and cold climates, it can serve many different types of vacationers. Boyne USA also makes it easy to plan a vacation at any one of its resorts. In addition to booking through a travel agent, Boyne USA allows travelers to make their own reservations by calling its toll-free number and through its Web site. Vacationers can also get information about upcoming events and specials, like *Ski with the Greats, Instructional Weekends,* or *Take Your Daughter to the Slopes Day.* Excellent computer graphics show the weather conditions on the slopes and golf courses at each resort twenty-four hours a day.

Another way Boyne USA attracts vacationers is by offering a variety of ski and golf packages that appeal to different budgets and different time schedules. By taking advantage of off-peak times, people on tight budgets can really save money on lodging and have enough for clothing and equipment. The resorts offer lower prices during the week and off-season as well as special packages that include lift tickets, lessons, and sleighride dinners. The Big Sky resort in Montana offers Ski-In, Ski-Out Lodging at 50 percent off. The Super Saver Weeks Packages include lift tickets, lodging, and a deluxe breakfast daily for half off normal rates. For a four night/three day stay from November 25 to December 11, the cost per person is $213, based on double occupancy. These special promotions make skiing vacations affordable for many, and they help the resorts accommodate the high volume of full-price customers during weekends and holiday periods without having to turn people away. Shifting customers to weekdays and off-peak times minimizes overcrowding and never compromises Boyne USA's pledge to provide first-rate customer service at all times. With its attentive service and such a wide variety of facilities, locations, events, activities, promotions, and scenery, Boyne USA is truly a service expert.

Questions

1. Services are intangible, inseparable from the provider, perishable, and heterogeneous. How do these characteristics apply to Boyne USA's services?
2. Using Exhibit 11.3, explain the core and supplementary services offered at Boyne resorts.
3. Discuss Boyne USA's distribution of services.
4. How does Boyne synchronize supply and demand at the resorts?

Bibliography

Boyne USA Resorts, *Lifestyle Magazine,* Winter 1997–98; Spring/Summer 1998

Boyne USA Web site: **http://www.boyne.com**

MARKETING MISCUES

A Bumpy Ride for Saturn

The Saturn Corporation, a wholly owned subsidiary of General Motors, was formed in January 1985 as GM's attempt to design and manufacture small cars in the United States. Known worldwide for its large automobiles, GM was looking for a way to expand its image in order to compete effectively against foreign automobile manufacturers. While owned by General Motors, a separate company would prevent consumers from easily linking their long-established perceptions of General Motors' cars (large, stodgy, family cars) to the newer, small cars.

Saturn Corporation was created around a no-hassle, no-haggle approach to selling. That is, the sticker price on the car was the price that the consumer would pay for the car. Saturn ultimately became the champion at nurturing an automotive brand name. In a survey conducted by A.T. Kearney, Saturn was acknowledged as the best example of brand management, ahead of such luxury auto makers as BMW, Mercedes-Benz, and Lexus.

Despite this brand name superiority, the 1999 J.D. Power & Associates' sales-satisfaction index did not rank Saturn at the top—the first time in years that the company had not received the highest ranking. Instead, consumers ranked the car manufacturer sixth in customer satisfaction. While small-car sales have risen 7 percent in the past few years, Saturn sales have declined 20 percent since its peak of 286,000 cars in 1994. One can easily see that the company has been having problems getting consumers interested in its cars.

After such phenomenal success in sales and recognition, where did the company go wrong? Reports suggest that Saturn Corporation did not err in understanding its market. Quantitative and qualitative research on Saturn customers as well as import owners in the midsize market found that shoppers looked at price, dependability, styling, and safety in making buying decisions. Based upon these findings, the company designed its new L-Series ("L" for larger) midsize car in 1999. The Saturn L-Series was to be the car that Saturn's customers would purchase as they and their young families began to outgrow the Saturn's introductory line of autos, the S-Series.

Unfortunately, the L-Series did not turn out to be the savior that Saturn Corporation had hoped for.

Although initial marketing research was solid, the L-Series' product development process was bumpy. Attempting to reduce development and production costs, GM required Saturn to design the L-Series to share the basic chassis undercarriage with the Vectra, a model sold by GM's Opel group in Europe. Unfortunately, shortcomings in adapting the European design to the U.S. market slowed the L-Series production processes. The delayed introduction hit the U.S. market at the slowest time for car buying—which means the L-Series was introduced while competitors were running incentive "deals" (e.g., rebates, credit terms). Saturn's no haggling policy meant that Saturn dealers were not able to compete with such deals. To further complicate matters, Saturn's introductory advertising, "Next Big Thing," failed to convey the message that the L-Series was larger than the S-Series.

With weak demand for the L-Series, Saturn was forced to temporarily shut down one of its assembly lines in March 2000. The production slowdown was an attempt to clear automobile retail lots of a forty-day surplus of cars. (A retail lot typically has a sixty-day supply of cars; Saturn dealers were experiencing a 100-day supply.)

Questions for Discussion

1. How could the complexities of the global launch (i.e., design and production spanning multiple continents) of the L-Series have been avoided by Saturn?
2. Is the advertising to blame for the slow launch of the L-Series?
3. What can marketers do to resurrect the L-Series and lead the Saturn Corporation back to success?

Bibliography

Warren Brown. "Saturn to Reduce Mid-Size Car Output." *Washington Post,* March 24, 2000, p. E-2.

Mary Connelly. "As Brand, Saturn Runs Rings 'Round the Competition." *Advertising Age,* April 6, 1998, pp. S4+.

Kendra Parker. "The Next Big Thing." *American Demographics,* January 2000, pp. 38–39.

David Welch. "Running Rings Around Saturn." *Business Week,* February 21, 2000, pp. 114–118.

http://www.gm.com.

http://www.saturn.com.

MARKETING MISCUES

Crest-fallen: Procter & Gamble Trips Over Its String of New Products

With core brands like Tide laundry detergent, Downy fabric softener, Crest toothpaste, Charmin toilet paper, Bounty paper towels, and Pampers diapers, how can a company go wrong? That's just what management, shareholders, and Wall Street were asking in March 2000 when Procter & Gamble, the world's largest consumer products company, missed its earnings target and saw its stock go into a tailspin.

The 163-year-old corporate giant has more leading brands than any other consumer products company in the world. Built around cornerstone brands like Tide, Ivory, Folgers, and many others (see Exhibit A), P&G has not historically been a fast-moving, nimble organization. In 1998, newly named CEO Durk Jager sought to reinvent P&G in a new economy image by focusing on new products, reducing fastidious attention to cost-cutting, and allowing budgets to be loosely shifted between brands. Under his eighteen-month tenure, P&G's blistering stream of new products included several new

Exhibit A   P&G at a Glance

Global Business Unit	Product Lines	Brands
Baby Care, Feminine Care, and Tissues & Towels	Baby diapers and baby wipes	Dodot, Luvs, Pampers
	Feminine protection pads, pantiliners, and tampons	Always, Lines, Whisper, Tampax
	Paper towels, toilet tissue, and facial tissue	Bounty, Charmin, Puffs
Beauty Care	Cosmetics, fragrances, hair care, antiperspirants, and skin/beauty care	Cover Girl, Max Factor, Hugo Boss, Head & Shoulders, Pantene Pro-V, Pert Plus, Physique, Rejoice, Vidal Sassoon, Secret Olay Skin Care Bars, Safeguard, Zest, Olay Cosmetics, SK-II
Fabric & Home Care	Bleach and prewash additives, care for special fabrics, dish care, fabric conditioners, fruit and vegetable wash, household cleaner, and laundry	Ace Bleach and Prewash Additives, Dryel, Febreze, Cascade, Dawn, Fairy Dish, Joy, Bounce, Downy, Lenor Fabric Conditioner, Fit, Swiffer, Ace Detergent, Ariel Bold, Cheer, Dash, Gain, Tide
Food & Beverage	Shortening and oil, beverages, peanut butter, and snacks	Crisco, Folgers, Millstone, Sunny Delight, Jif, Pringles
Health Care & Corporate New Ventures	Prescription drugs, health/oral care, pet health and nutrition	Actonel, Asacol, NyQuil/DayQuil, PUR, Vicks VapoRub, Crest, Eukanuba, IAMS

SOURCE: Procter & Gamble 2000 Annual Report.

Exhibit B

P&G's Billion-Dollar Brands

- Always
- Ariel
- Bounty
- Charmin
- Downy

- Folgers
- Pantene
- Pringles
- Tide
- Vidal Sassoon

to the world products and many improvements of existing products, P&G's hallmark. The Dryel home dry cleaning kit, Febreze odor neutralizing spray, Swiffer wipes and broom, and Fit vegetable wash numbered among the most successful. Dryel and Swiffer in particular were developed and expanded in record time and had high revenue expectations.

And these products are only a small sampling of what is in the company's R&D pipeline. With more than 8,000 scientists and researchers on its payroll, P&G applies for roughly 3,000 patents each year. Currently, the company holds over 27,000 patents and is one of the top ten patent-producing companies in the world. P&G introduced more new brands in 1999 and 2000 than ever before in its long history, but it also acquired such popular brands as IAMS and Eukanuba pet foods and Millstone coffee.

Despite these impressive figures, not all new products and brand acquisitions met with great success in the marketplace. For example, Pampers' focus on a higher quality diaper at a premium price resulted in the much-hailed Rash Guard product. Unfortunately, this new diaper technology failed to help Pampers recapture market share lost to competitor Kimberly Clark's Huggies brand, whose goal is to increase breathability without increasing cost. Some question the focus of Pampers on premium quality diapers. Robert Izmirlian, an analyst with Standard and Poor's Equity Group, has summed it up best: "There comes a point where people just aren't going to spend a ridiculous sum of money on a special diaper."[a] In addition, Jager was unable to successfully expand P&G's prescription drug lines through acquisitions of first Warner-Lambert and then American Home Products. After having been rebuffed for his overtures to Gillette, investors severely punished Jager's botched takeovers, so much so that Jager abandoned the high-risk acquisitions.

During the 1999–2000 period of rollout fever, many of P&G's core brands were neglected—even those on its billion-dollar roster (see Exhibits B and C). Stars like Pampers, Bounty, and Folgers all suffered. Pampers failed to grow at a rate equal to its category; Bounty consumption in units fell over 8 percent; and Folgers, unable to overcome the hurdles of a declining category, lost on all fronts. Only Tide, by far P&G's largest brand, managed to grow substantially within a declining category.

Violating the cardinal rule of each brand keeping its own budget, Jager allowed marketing resources for these and other mainstay brands, perhaps seen as invincible, to be shunted to new product promotions. Compounding P&G's woes were a budgetary revision that compensated managers for rolling out brands rather than generating profits, and an accounting revision that allowed for spending based on target sales. On the surface these changes seemed to be achieving their intended goal: P&G was rolling out new products faster and in greater number than ever before. In fact, however, business overspending meant that costs rose faster than sales, and earnings declined by around 11 percent. It was this severe swing that caused money managers to unload large blocks of P&G stock in early 2000.

Faced with stock values 50 percent off their peak and two successive quarters of earnings warnings, P&G replaced Durk Jager in June 2000 with A. G. Lafley, a long-time Procter executive. Many believed that Jager's strategy was prudent and that he was simply not given enough time to prove it viable, let alone profitable. Lafley himself announced that P&G's growth strategy would keep the same key building blocks:

1. Building established and profitable brands
2. Introducing new brands and entering new categories
3. Acquiring brands that strengthen existing business or entering new markets
4. Improving the mix of the brand portfolio with more premium-performance, higher-priced brands[b]

Although Lafley is sticking to the four-point growth strategy mapped out by Jager, he has also clearly said that P&G is "focusing sharply on *building our biggest, strongest global brands* [sic], the core of our business." He also has tightened down innovation by stating that the company is "*making tougher choices about investing in new products and new businesses* [sic]."[c]

[a] Frazier, p. 14.

[b] Procter & Gamble 2000 Annual Report, p. 5.
[c] Procter & Gamble 2000 Annual Report, p. 5.

Exhibit C

Stuck in the Slow Aisle

P&G Brands	Tide	Charmin	Folgers	Pampers	Bounty
Sales (billions)*	$1,821	$1,221	$1,088	$1,053	$1,046
% change	3.4	9.2	−2	3.4	3.9
Unit sales (millions)	249	351	247	79.8	444
% change	−4	0.1	−3.1	−2.4	−8.3
Category dollar growth**	−3.7%	7.6%	−2.4%	5.7%	3.7%

SOURCE: Cincinnati Business Courier, Information Resources, Inc., and ACNielsen.
*Figures are for 52 weeks ending June 18, 2000.
**Dollar volume change for the year ending May 20, 2000 compared to same period previous year.

The breakneck speed of innovation may slow, but don't expect it to come screeching to a halt. Tide counted at least six improvements and/or additions by the end of 2000, including Tide Deep Clean and Tide Rapid Action Tablets. Crest will introduce a new home teeth bleaching product with Crest Whitestrips. Downy Wrinkle Reducer will seek to replace ironing. Pampers will allow consumers to purchase diaper gift certificates on-line. Even the recently launched Febreze will roll out an addition: Clean Wash odor eliminator that is added to the wash cycle along with detergent. So much for resting on your brands.

Questions for Discussion

1. Categorize the brands discussed in this case according to Lafley's four-point growth strategy. What can you conclude from your tally? Note that some brands may fall into more than one category.
2. Jager's drive to increase numbers and kinds of new products came at a cost to what?
3. For a company known for new product development, why did rolling out unprecedented numbers of new products prove detrimental to P&G?

Bibliography

Mya Frazier. "P&G's Core Brands Lost Out During Jager Reign." *Cincinnati Business Courier*, July 28, 2000, pp. 1, 14.

Emily Nelson and Nikhil Deogun. "Lafley Takes on Gamble: New P&G Chief Faces Challenge in Balancing Firm's Old, New Brands." *Wall Street Journal*, June 12, 2000, p. C1.

———. "Course Correction: Reformer Jager Was Too Much for P&G; So What Will Work?" *Wall Street Journal*, June 9, 2000, p. A1.

Procter & Gamble 2000 Annual Report.

CRITICAL THINKING CASE

Coke: Leveraging the Brand

Douglas Daft, CEO of Coca-Cola, may have to tackle what could be one of the biggest questions surrounding his company's core product. Is the Coke brand still as special in the new millennium as it was back at the start of the twentieth century?

John S. Pemberton, a pharmacist in Atlanta, made his first batch of Coca-Cola syrup in 1886. Today, the Coca-Cola Company has become a major multinational company, with more than sixteen million consumers worldwide and 31,000 employees. Headquartered in Atlanta, the company consists of five geographic groups: (1) North America, (2) Latin America, (3) Greater Europe, (4) Africa and Middle East, and (5) Asia Pacific. Additionally, Coca-Cola owns the Houston-based Minute Maid Company, the world's leading marketer of juices and juice drinks.

Coca-Cola's corporate mission is to maximize shareowner value over time by increasing volume, expanding sales worldwide, maximizing long-term cash flows, and improving economic profit. The company attempts to execute its strategy through its six key beliefs:

- Consumer demand drives the company's decision making.
- The Coca-Cola brand is the core product.
- The company offers a broad selection of nonalcoholic ready-to-drink beverages.
- Coca-Cola will be the best marketer in the world.
- The company thinks and acts locally.
- The company will serve as a model for what a corporate citizen should represent.

Coca-Cola's Brands

Two factors have contributed strongly to Coca-Cola's success: (1) its direct marketing approach (often referred to as "from the TV set to the store shelf") and (2) the company's distribution system of independent local franchisees. However, it has been the company's core brands that have actually touched the lives of consumers around the world. These core brands include Coca-Cola (developed in 1886), Fanta (revived as we now know it in 1955), Sprite (debuted in 1961), and Diet Coke (introduced in 1982). Additionally, there are over 500 flavor combinations marketed worldwide, including such products as coffee, tea, bottled water, and fruit drinks.

The "Soft" Drink Market

Unfortunately for soft drink producers, 1999 was not a good year for the beverage industry. The U.S. soft drink volume experienced growth of only 0.6 percent over 1998, with per capita consumption down for the first time in thirty years. Consumption of orange juice was on the rise in the late 1990s into 2000. At the same time, the bottled water market grew from a $200 million market in the 1970s to a $5 billion growth industry in 2000. This growth has been attributed to three major factors: (1) health concerns, (2) the convenience/portability of small bottles, and (3) the opportunity to try something different.

Who would have thought that drinking water would be seen as "trying something different"? Interestingly, however, taste is defining the market. There are juice-flavored waters, sweet waters, waters that taste strong and chalky, as well as waters with no taste at all. Add to this the waters enhanced with herbal preparations (e.g., St. John's wort, echinacea, ginseng) and nutrients (calcium) and one finds a market that appears to be offering a healthy alternative to carbonated drinks! With Perrier, Poland Spring, and Zephyr Hills leading the U.S. bottled-water industry, Douglas Daft is set for battle and thinks Coca-Cola can become a product leader in this alternative beverage segment.

Daft's interest in the alternative beverage market is fueled by a mass exodus from the soda market. Consumers are worried about the harmful effects of ingredients such as caffeine and aspartame. However, Coca-Cola has never focused major attention on its noncarbonated offerings. Rather, the company has allowed these noncarbonated products to follow "me-too" strategies—developing products and entering markets after other companies have shown the success of such diverse product offerings. Becoming a leader in the beverage market, rather than the soft-drink leader, has some observers questioning the strength of Coke's brand equity.

Coca-Cola's Brand Equity

Coca-Cola has built its brand equity on a limited number of core brands. The strength of the Coke brand, however, has not left room for any trial and error in experimenting with new products. Many consumers still remember the company's unsuccessful attempt in the early 1980s to change the taste of its original Coke product. Rather than possibly dilute its brand equity with product mistakes, Coca-Cola has not put the Coke name on its me-too products. The company has utilized a global branding strategy only for its major brand—basically assuming that there is worldwide desire for a single product.

With consumer preferences changing the nature of the beverage marketplace, Daft's tenure at Coca-Cola may be remembered by whether he allows the Coke brand name to be put on all Coca-Cola products (e.g., water, mango juice in Latin America, rice drinks in Asia) in an attempt to be all things to all people. If the results are positive, Daft will have allowed the company and its shareholders to reap the benefits of brand equity. If the results are less than favorable, Daft risks being blamed for diluting the company's brand equity.

Questions

1. What does the term "brand equity" mean in relation to the Coca-Cola Company?
2. Describe Coca-Cola's branding strategy.
3. Why might the company's move into alternative beverages dilute its core brand?
4. Where are Coca-Cola's core brands on the product life cycle?
5. Should Coca-Cola put the Coke brand on alternative beverages?

Bibliography

Carol L. Bowers. "Bottled Water Business Take Off." *Utility Business,* March 2000, pp. 36–37.

Dean Foust and Debora Rubin. "Now, Coke Is No Longer 'It'." *Business Week,* February 28, 2000, pp. 148–151.

Kate MacArthur. "Coke Crisis: Equity Erodes as Brand Troubles Mount." *Advertising Age,* April 24, 2000, p. 3.

Greg W. Prince. "The Year of Living Dangerously." *Beverage World,* March 15, 2000, pp. 34–51.

Rupert Wright. "Coca-Cola: Ice-Cold Times for an Icon." *The Independent—London,* January 30, 2000, p. 27.

http://www.thecolacompany.com.

MARKETING PLANNING ACTIVITIES

Product Decisions

The next part of the marketing plan is a description of the elements of the marketing mix, starting with the product or service offering. Be sure that your product plans match the needs and wants of the target market identified and described in the previous section. Also, refer to Exhibit 2.8 for additional marketing plan subjects.

1. What type(s) of consumer or business-to-business product is your chosen firm offering?
2. Place your company's offerings into a product portfolio. Consider the broader impact of marketing a product item within a line or mix. Factors to consider are those such as price, image, complementary products, distribution relationship, and so on.
3. Does your chosen company have a brand name and brand mark? If not, design both. If so, evaluate the ability of the brand name and mark to communicate effectively to the target market.
4. How is your firm's product packaged and labeled? Is the packaging strategy appropriate for the target market(s)? Does the package "fit" with distribution, promotion, and price elements?
5. Evaluate the warranties or guarantees offered by your firm, including product return policies.

Marketing*Builder* Exercise

- **Returns and Adjustments Policy** portion of the **Sales Plan** template

6. Place your company's product in the appropriate stage of the product life cycle. What are the implications of being in this stage? What should your firm prepare for in the future?

Marketing*Builder* Exercise

- **Product Life Cycles** portion of the **Market Analysis** template

7. What categories of adopters are likely to buy your company's products? Is the product diffusing slowly or quickly throughout the marketplace? Why?
8. What service aspects are provided with the product? How is customer service handled? What elements of service quality can your firm focus on?

Marketing*Builder* Exercise

- **Customer Service** portion of the **Sales Plan** template

9. With whom should your chosen company practice relationship marketing?
10. Does the product offer good customer value?

Marketing*Builder* Exercise

- **Product Launch Budget** in the **Marketing Budget** spreadsheet

E-MARKETING PLANNING ACTIVITIES

In the first part of your strategic e-marketing plan, you stated your business mission and objectives, and performed a detailed SWOT analysis. In the second part of the plan you identified and described target market segments and described their buying behaviors and decision-making processes. In addition, you identified sources of competitive intelligence and the need for any further marketing research before the e-marketing plan could be implemented. Recall that you are either doing a strategic marketing plan for an existing bookstore retailer with a new on-line presence, or a dot-com bookstore retailer, or an e-company of your own choosing.

For continued general assistance on business plans and marketing plans, visit **http://www.bplans.com** or **http://www.businessplans.org**. For electronic sources of information, search on the Electric Library at **http://wwws.elibrary.com/** or the Internet Public Library at **http://www.ipl.org/**. Another excellent source of information is the Sales and Marketing Executives Marketing Library at **http://www.sell.org/**. You should also refer to Exhibit 2.8 for additional marketing plan checklist items (Part IV.B.1.: Marketing Mix—Product).

The next stage of the strategic planning process involves defining the elements of the marketing mix: product, place, promotion, and pricing strategies. This third part of the e-planning process will focus on product and service components. A key issue is to make sure that the strategies recommended here match the needs and wants of the target audience(s) identified earlier.

Use the following exercises to guide you through the third part of your strategic marketing plan:

1. How would you classify the offering to your customers? Is it a consumer product? A business-to-business product? A good or a service? Both? How does this classification change the focus of your e-marketing plan? Is your product unique enough to be patented? Check with the U.S. Patent and Trademark Office at **http://www.uspto.gov**.

2. How does this offering fit within a product portfolio? Is it a single item offering, or does it have to be consistent or complementary with other offerings or lines? Are there any special product features that selling on the Internet would allow you to add or force you to take away?

3. Design or evaluate the brand name and brand logo. Is strong branding more or less important in an Internet environment? Why? What makes branding so important? If your firm needs to hire a professional branding company, look for "Naming and Branding Marketing Firms" on **http://www.looksmart.com**. Of particular importance are firms that can translate your brand name into other languages and check for negative implications. Try translations yourself at **http://www.iTools.com/research-it/research-it.html**. You can also try to generate brand names made up of random syllables or test a brand name's meaning at **http://www.nomina.net/**.

4. What will your company Internet address be? To check and see what URLs are available, go to **http://www.companyname.com** and try some out. Should your URL be the same as your company name? Why or why not? What happens if a customer mistypes your name? Should you register under alternative spellings?

5. Is the product packaged and labeled? How should it be packaged and why? Does the package and label design match other communications tools? How is this an opportunity to communicate with your customers?

6. How will customers return products they purchased from the Web site? Design the parameters for warranties and return policies. Should your return policy be stricter on-line than off-line? Why or why not?

7. Where does the offering fit into the product life cycle? What implications does the PLC stage have for product and service strategies? Is the PLC lengthened, shortened, or not affected by selling it on-line? Will selling your offering on the Internet make it seem earlier on the PLC to your customers? Why?

8. What elements of the diffusion process can you control to make sure your offering diffuses more quickly throughout the adopter categories and marketplace in general? Will positive word-of-mouth be easier or harder to generate on-line?

9. List specific examples of how you can incorporate all five elements of service quality into your e-marketing offering. What tactics can you define that would minimize any potential service quality gaps? What impact will selling on the Internet have on your customer service operation?

10. E-marketing is particularly vulnerable to breakdowns in client relationships. Which sorts of bonds should be stressed in the relationship marketing strategy? How can your company "touch" its customers differently on-line than off-line? Are there advantages to on-line customer service? Disadvantages?

CROSS-FUNCTIONAL CONNECTIONS SOLUTIONS

Functional Lines Blur in Speed to Market

Questions

1. What is the difference between the demand-side perspective and the supply-side perspective to doing business? Is either perspective more appropriate?

   The demand-side perspective focuses upon determining, via marketing research, the customer's wants and needs. Products/services are then developed that satisfy these wants and needs. Once developed, marketing adds the finishing touches by positioning the products/services in such a manner that the customers recognize that the products/services will fulfill their demands. Demand-side starts with the customer and ends with the customer, with marketing and the other business functions working in the middle.

   The supply-side perspective takes the position that engineers should develop and manufacture leading-edge products. Once developed and manufactured, marketing then introduces the product to the customer by telling the customer about the product's performance. Supply-side tends to start with the research and development group, then it moves to the manufacturing group and then to marketing, after which it eventually ends with the customer.

   As marketers, we believe that the demand-side perspective is the best approach to doing business. However, some argue that the supply-side perspective is more appropriate for high-technology products—that if we waited for the customer, we would not yet have call-waiting, microwave ovens, or video games.

2. What are some of the popular business terms used to describe cross-functional integration?

   design-factory fit
   concurrent engineering
   design for manufacturability and assembly
   early manufacturing involvement
   paperless design
   modularization

3. Why are all employees (whether involved in marketing or not) at the heart of customer service?

   A customer does not generally work directly with the marketing department when purchasing a product or service. Instead, the customer may be asking questions of someone on the store floor who was hired to stock shelves, work the cash register, or sweep the floor. The responses that customers receive from these employees tend to represent the customer's image of the company. Also, when a customer calls to check on the status of a repair, the customer is speaking with someone who may have been hired to answer the telephone. However, this receptionist is the customer's first contact within the organization and provides a lasting impression of the way the company treats its customers. The way all employees treat the customer becomes intermingled with the product's quality and can drive the customer's perception of quality either up or down.

Suggested Readings

Donald Gerwin. "Team Empowerment in New Product Development." *Business Horizons,* July/August 1999, pp. 29–36.

Avan R. Jassawalla and Hemant C. Sashittal. "Cross-Functional Dynamics in New Product Development." *Research Technology Management,* January/February 2000, pp. 46–49.

part **4**

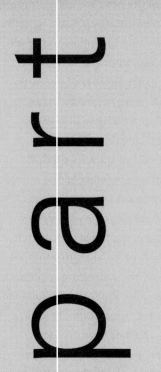

Distribution Decisions

CROSS-FUNCTIONAL COLLABORATION IN MANAGING DISTRIBUTION

Achieving customer satisfaction means that the company must have the right product at the right place at the right time (and at the right price). The need for cross-functional coordination in developing and producing a high-quality product is clear. Getting the product to the consumer at the right place and time is also a result of considerable interaction among marketing and its internal and external partners. Once designed, developed, and produced, marketing and its partners must get the product from the factory to the end-user using the best methods. The giant retailer Wal-Mart has based much of its competitive success on its ability to get the right product in the right stores at the right time—products that are then sold to customers via the company's helpful, friendly sales staff.

There are considerable costs associated with getting a high-quality product out the door, and manufacturing has been a key marketing partner in making the delivery process successful. Advanced manufacturing systems (AMS) have been developed that not only reduce costs (ultimately affecting the price charged to the customer) but also allow faster product delivery. Two popular advanced manufacturing systems are just-in-time (JIT) and electronic data interchange (EDI).

A just-in-time manufacturing system allows the production of a product as needed, instead of producing for stock. The effect that such a manufacturing system has on a channel intermediary is to ultimately change the channel structure. Customers may be able to receive products directly from the manufacturer rather than having to receive the product via a distribution channel. The absence of a channel intermediary not only makes products available quickly, but it also results in fewer channel members and, in turn, decreased costs—the ultimate in efficiency of operations. However, marketing must make sure that the change in the channel structure is not only more efficient but also more effective. That is, marketing has to determine if the channel intermediary provides a service that will otherwise be unavailable if the product is shipped directly to the customer from the manufacturer.

The use of electronic data interchange can significantly increase the efficiency of operations between the shop floor and distribution of the product. EDI permits the exchange of information electronically—using data collected at the point-of-sale and transmitted automatically to the manufacturing department. This allows manufacturing to know the exact number of available units at any point in time, allowing the manufacturing group to time its production and delivery to meet the customer's specific needs. Eli Lilly Canada is a healthcare company that must be able to trace its product movements from the time of manufacture to the point of customer delivery. The company uses a wireless data communication process to track this movement. Its radio frequency based warehouse management system was implemented by a cross-functional team comprised of manufacturing, technology, and marketing experts.

In some instances, retail sales data transmitted electronically to the manufacturing group starts the machines on the shop floor. Such quick response to channel needs can dramatically reduce the time from order entry to delivery. Benetton, the Italian clothing company, uses its retail data to actually schedule specific factories that make its clothes. Such enterprise-wide integrated systems are revolutionizing the retail industry. Retailers are now able to electronically assimilate and transmit inventory data for individual stores, as well as information as to what products are selling at what price in what market.

Many companies have seen the cycle time from order entry to delivery cut in half due to direct (and immediate) interactions between channel members and the manufacturing function in a firm. This reduction in cycle time also allows retailers to limit the amount of inventory they need to warehouse, which in turn lowers cost and, ultimately, price. British Airways Engineering has focused on the maintenance and repair side of its organization in order to provide better turnaround times for its customers. The company's Sonic Project has allowed the organization to provide greater customer satisfaction through a better understanding of the fleet repair cycle. Historically, items for repair would slowly pass through all stages of the repair process—a process that could take as long as fifty to sixty days. Today, the average cycle time, much to customers' delight, is down to fourteen days.

As seen from these examples, operational efficiencies in linking marketing's distribution to manufacturing's production processes are the result of well thought out cross-functional plans. Such plans have to be developed in conjunction with both marketing and manufacturing functional groups. Benefits to consumers appear in both dollar savings and improved customer service.

One important aspect of the channel of distribution is the actual delivery of the company's products. The equipment used to make deliveries is an important factor. Decisions regarding the type of transportation equipment—from aircraft to rail cars—receive considerable input from both the marketing and finance/accounting groups. For example, marketing might prefer that its perishable product be delivered by air to avoid any spoilage. From a cost-effectiveness viewpoint, however, the financial group might determine that the product should be shipped by truck—that the costs associated with any spoiled product would be offset by the savings from shipping by truck instead of air. The two functional groups have to balance customer demands with the relative costs of shipment. The manufacturing group must be involved as well, to ensure that appropriate and cost-effective packaging is used for the transportation method ultimately selected.

FedEx exemplifies the type of company that has been able to balance external market considerations with internal cost effectiveness. The company has experienced great marketplace success with its guaranteed overnight delivery. At the heart of its overnight delivery system is a company-owned fleet of airplanes that operates out of the company's hub in Memphis, Tennessee. Additionally, the company's delivery vans are equipped with computers so that individual shipments can be traced throughout the distribution process. This extensive network of distribution required input from marketing as to what it would take to become an industry

leader and from finance/accounting as to the costs associated with owning a fleet of airplanes and installing computers in delivery vans.

A functional department that cannot be overlooked in a company's distribution process is the human resources department. This is particularly important for a service provider (such as FedEx or a hospital emergency room) since the people are the ones who actually make the logistical process work appropriately. An interesting aspect of a service provider is that production and delivery of the company's product (service) takes place simultaneously. Therefore, functional integration has to occur at the point of delivery. The customer's perception of quality delivery is determined by the actual tasks performed as well as by the way employees talk, look, and act. This makes it imperative that marketing and human resources work together to hire and train the right people.

Coordination between marketing and other business functions is necessary to get a high-quality, competitively priced product or service to the end user in a timely manner. Companies such as UPS and FedEx that compete for the same customers have become experts at developing channel systems that utilize all functional components of the organization in getting the right product/service to the right customer at just the right time.

Technology is a powerful force behind improvements in distribution. In the future, more and more companies will be combining cross-functional skills with information technology infrastructures to better serve customers.

Questions for Discussion

1. What are some of the popular advanced manufacturing systems and how do they interact with marketing?

2. What is an enterprise-wide integrated distribution system? What is marketing's role in such a system?

3. How do production and delivery happen simultaneously in the service sector? What other functional areas are important partners in the service arena?

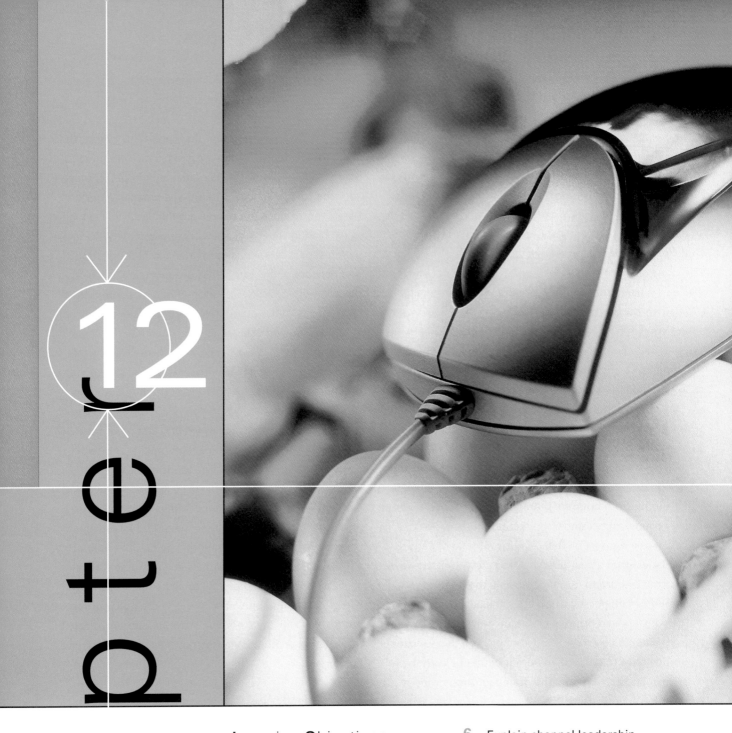

chapter 12

Learning Objectives

1 Explain what a marketing channel is and why inter-mediaries are needed

2 Define the types of channel intermediaries and describe their functions and activities

3 Describe the channel structures for consumer and business-to-business products and discuss alternative channel arrangements

4 Define supply chain management and discuss its benefits

5 Discuss the issues that influence channel strategy

6 Explain channel leadership, conflict, and partnering

7 Describe the logistical components of the supply chain

8 Discuss the concept of balancing logistics service and cost

9 Discuss new technology and emerging trends in supply chain management

10 Discuss channels and distribution decisions in global markets

11 Identify the special problems and opportunities associated with distribution in service organizations

Marketing Channels and Supply Chain Management

Webvan's debut as an on-line retailer of groceries is a huge wake-up call for the nation's $468 billion supermarket industry as direct delivery of groceries sidesteps the traditional retail channel of food distribution. Operating in the large metropolitan areas of San Francisco, Atlanta, Seattle, Washington, and several other U.S. cities, Webvan functions as a full-service on-line grocer and drugstore, providing free delivery, customer convenience, and low prices. Customers can shop on-line twenty-four hours a day, seven days a week from Webvan's Web site, selecting a 30-minute delivery window at the time most convenient to them. Orders are then hand-delivered to the customer's desired location on the same day or up to seven days later. On-line shoppers can purchase grocery staples along with fresh produce, meats and seafood, baked goods and desserts from local bakeries, prepared meals, best-selling books, fresh-cut flowers, wine, pet supplies, as well as home products such as batteries, film, and lightbulbs. The Web site, which combines features such as personalized lists and personal "aisles" that save its customers time and help them make food decisions, was recently ranked the number one on-line grocer.

Behind Webvan's promise of quick delivery and low prices is a state-of-the-art inventory management system, automated distribution centers, and a fleet of trucks and custom delivery vans allowing the company to reduce traditional retail costs, passing the savings on to the customers while providing greater convenience. Each market is fashioned into a hub-and-spoke system which consists of a highly automated distribution center feeding ten to twelve substations located within a fifty-mile radius. Rather than use traditional

shippers, Webvan owns its entire distribution network including hundreds of trucks and vans.

The distribution centers at the hub of each system are no ordinary warehouses. Webvan's 336,000 square-foot distribution center in Oakland, California, serves the San Francisco metropolitan area. The warehouse stores some 50,000 different products, or the equivalent of eighteen traditional supermarkets. As national and local suppliers drop off goods at the distribution center, they are stocked on rotating carousels, rather than shelves in rows. When an order is placed, color-coded bins, called totes, wind their way around a five-mile network of conveyor belts to the different areas where packaged goods, freezer items, produce, meats, and other products are stored. As each tote approaches these areas, Webvan workers pick the items from the rotating carousels that bring the products directly to the pickers. Carousels, which hold about 8,900 grocery items, save time that pickers would otherwise waste walking up and down countless rows to fill orders. Webvan claims its carousel system lets workers pick roughly two-and-a-half times more items per hour than they could with other systems. In a single hour, Webvan workers can pack 450 grocery items for shoppers—nearly ten times the productivity of a traditional "shopper" used by other on-line grocers who wheel a cart through a store or warehouse.

Once orders are picked and packed, they're loaded onto refrigerated trucks and taken to a substation, where the load is broken down into individual routes. Route-planning software then assigns each driver a feasible schedule with deliveries planned for every ten to thirty minutes. Webvan's

drivers then shuttle orders to the customers' homes where they are unpacked. Each working day, Webvan drivers deliver groceries and other goods to the homes of anywhere from twelve to twenty-five on-line shoppers. In the San Francisco area, Webvan counts over 20,000 active customers and its drivers have achieved a 99 percent on-time delivery record. Webvan plans expansion into over twenty-five major U.S. cities by 2003.[1]

What advantages does Webvan receive from selling in marketing channels directly to the customer, thus bypassing traditional retailing intermediaries? Traditional grocers, like Albertson's and Kroger, have taken notice of Webvan's e-commerce efforts and have begun experimenting with on-line grocery ordering and direct delivery. What areas of distribution, such as inventory, materials handling, or transportation, could be streamlined to help these traditional retailers compete more effectively in today's wired world? Similar questions will be addressed throughout the chapter discussion on marketing channels and supply chain management.

Marketing Channels

Explain what a marketing channel is and why intermediaries are needed

marketing channel (channel of distribution)
A set of interdependent organizations that ease the transfer of ownership as products move from producer to business user or consumer.

channel members
All parties in the marketing channel that negotiate with one another, buy and sell products, and facilitate the change of ownership between buyer and seller in the course of moving the product from the manufacturer into the hands of the final consumer.

supply chain
The connected chain of all of the business entities, both internal and external to the company, that perform or support the logistics function.

The term *channel* is derived from the Latin word *canalis*, that means canal. A marketing channel can be viewed as a large canal or pipeline through which products, their ownership, communication, financing and payment, and accompanying risk flow to the consumer. Formally, a **marketing channel** (also called a **channel of distribution**) is a business structure of interdependent organizations that reach from the point of product origin to the consumer with the purpose of moving products to their final consumption destination. Marketing channels facilitate the physical movement of goods through the supply chain, representing "place" in the marketing mix (product, price, promotion, and place) and encompassing the processes involved in getting the right product to the right place at the right time.

Many different types of organizations participate in marketing channels. **Channel members** (also called *intermediaries, resellers,* and *middlemen*) negotiate with one another, buy and sell products, and facilitate the change of ownership between buyer and seller in the course of moving the product from the manufacturer into the hands of the final consumer. An important aspect of marketing channels is the joint effort of all channel members to create a continuous and seamless supply chain. The **supply chain** is the connected chain of all of the business entities, both internal and external to the company, that perform or support the marketing channel functions. As products move through the supply chain, channel members facilitate the distribution process by providing specialization and division of labor, overcoming discrepancies, and providing contact efficiency.

Providing Specialization and Division of Labor
According to the concept of specialization and division of labor, breaking down a complex task into smaller, simpler ones and allocating them to specialists will create greater efficiency and lower average production costs. Manufacturers achieve economies of scale through the use of efficient equipment capable of producing large quantities of a single product.

Marketing channels can also attain economies of scale through specialization and division of labor by aiding producers who lack the motivation, financing, or expertise to market directly to end users or consumers. In some cases, as with most consumer convenience goods, such as soft drinks, the cost of marketing directly to millions of consumers—taking and shipping individual orders—is prohibitive. For this reason, producers hire channel members, such as wholesalers and retailers, to do what the producers are not equipped to do or what channel members are better prepared to do. Channel members can do some things more efficiently than producers because they have built good relationships with their customers. Therefore, their specialized expertise enhances the overall performance of the channel.

Overcoming Discrepancies
Marketing channels also aid in overcoming discrepancies of quantity, assortment, time, and space created by economies of scale in production. For example, assume that Pillsbury can efficiently produce its Hungry Jack instant pancake mix only at a rate of 5,000 units in a typical day. Not even the most ardent pancake fan could consume that amount in a year, much less in a day. The quantity produced to achieve low unit costs has created a **discrepancy of quantity**, which is the difference between the amount of product produced and the amount an end user wants to buy. By storing the product and distributing it in the appropriate amounts, marketing channels overcome quantity discrepancies by making products available in the quantities that consumers desire.

Mass production creates not only discrepancies of quantity but also discrepancies of assortment. A **discrepancy of assortment** occurs when a consumer does not have all of the items needed to receive full satisfaction from a product. For pancakes to have maximum satisfaction, several other products are required to complete the

discrepancy of quantity
The difference between the amount of product produced and the amount an end user wants to buy.

discrepancy of assortment
The lack of all the items a customer needs to receive full satisfaction from a product or products.

assortment. At the very least, most people want a knife, fork, plate, butter, and syrup. Others might add orange juice, coffee, cream, sugar, eggs, and bacon or sausage. Even though Pillsbury is a large consumer products company, it does not come close to providing the optimal assortment to go with its Hungry Jack pancakes. To overcome discrepancies of assortment, marketing channels assemble in one place many of the products necessary to complete a consumer's needed assortment.

A **temporal discrepancy** is created when a product is produced but a consumer is not ready to buy it. Marketing channels overcome temporal discrepancies by maintaining inventories in anticipation of demand. For example, manufacturers of seasonal merchandise, such as Christmas decorations, are in operation all year even though consumer demand is concentrated during certain months of the year.

Furthermore, because mass production requires many potential buyers, markets are usually scattered over large geographic regions, creating a **spatial discrepancy**. Often global, or at least nationwide, markets are needed to absorb the outputs of mass producers. Marketing channels overcome spatial discrepancies by making products available in locations convenient to consumers. For example, automobile manufacturers overcome spatial discrepancies by franchising dealerships close to consumers.

temporal discrepancy
A situation that occurs when a product is produced but a customer is not ready to buy it.

spatial discrepancy
The difference between the location of a producer and the location of widely scattered markets.

Providing Contact Efficiency

The third need fulfilled by marketing channels is a way to provide contact efficiency. Consider your extra costs if supermarkets, department stores, and shopping centers or malls did not exist. Suppose you had to buy your milk at a dairy and your meat at a stockyard. Imagine buying your eggs and chicken at a hatchery and your fruits and vegetables at various farms. You would spend a great deal of time, money, and energy just shopping for a few groceries. Supply chains simplify distribution by cutting the number of transactions required to get products from manufacturers to consumers and making an assortment of goods available in one location.

Consider the example illustrated in Exhibit 12.1. Four consumers each want to buy a television set. Without a retail intermediary like Circuit City, television

Exhibit 12.1 How Marketing Channels Reduce the Number of Required Transactions

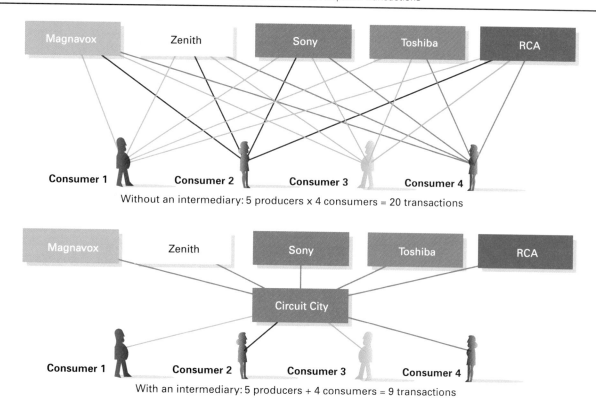

Without an intermediary: 5 producers x 4 consumers = 20 transactions

With an intermediary: 5 producers + 4 consumers = 9 transactions

manufacturers Magnavox, Zenith, Sony, Toshiba, and RCA would each have to make four contacts to reach the four buyers who are in the target market, totaling twenty transactions. However, when Circuit City acts as an intermediary between the producer and consumers, each producer only has to make one contact, reducing the number of transactions to nine. Each producer sells to one retailer rather than to four consumers. In turn, consumers buy from one retailer instead of from five producers.

Channel Intermediaries and Their Functions

Define the types of channel intermediaries and describe their functions and activities

retailer
A channel intermediary that sells mainly to consumers.

merchant wholesaler
An institution that buys goods from manufacturers and resells them to businesses, government agencies, and other wholesalers or retailers and that receives and takes title to goods, stores them in its own warehouses, and later ships them.

agents and brokers
Wholesaling intermediaries who facilitate the sale of a product from producer to end user by representing retailers, wholesalers, or manufacturers and do not take title to the product.

Intermediaries in a channel negotiate with one another, facilitate the change of ownership between buyers and sellers, and physically move products from the manufacturer to the final consumer. The most prominent difference separating intermediaries is whether or not they take title to the product. *Taking title* means they own the merchandise and control the terms of the sale—for example, price and delivery date. Retailers and merchant wholesalers are examples of intermediaries who take title to products in the marketing channel and resell them. **Retailers** are firms that sell mainly to consumers. Retailers will be discussed in more detail in Chapter 13.

Merchant wholesalers are those organizations that facilitate the movement of products and services from the manufacturer to producers, resellers, governments, institutions, and retailers. All merchant wholesalers take title to the goods they sell, and most of them operate one or more warehouses in which they receive goods, store them, and later reship them. Customers are mostly small- or moderate-sized retailers, but merchant wholesalers also market to manufacturers and institutional clients.

Other intermediaries do not take title to goods and services they market but do facilitate the exchange of ownership between sellers and buyers. **Agents and brokers** simply facilitate the sale of a product from producer to end user by representing retailers, wholesalers, or manufacturers. Title reflects ownership, and ownership usually implies control. Unlike wholesalers, agents or brokers only facilitate sales and generally have little input into the terms of the sale. They do, however, get a fee or commission based on sales volume.

Variations in channel structures are due in large part to variations in the numbers and types of wholesaling intermediaries. Generally, product characteristics, buyer considerations, and market conditions determine that type of intermediary the manufacturer should use. Product characteristics which may dictate a certain type of wholesaling intermediary include whether the product is standardized or customized, the complexity of the product, and the gross margin of the product. Buyer considerations affecting wholesaler choice include how often the product is purchased and how long the buyer is willing to wait to receive the product. Market characteristics determining wholesaler type include how many buyers are in the market and whether they are concentrated in a general location or are widely dispersed. Exhibit 12.2 shows these determining factors. For example, a manufacturer that produces only a few engines a year for space rockets will probably use an agent or broker to sell its product. In addition, the handful of customers that need the product are most likely concentrated near rocket launching sites, again making an agent or broker more practical. On the other hand, a book publisher who prints thousands of books and has many widely dispersed customers with year-round demand for its product will probably use a merchant wholesaler.

Channel Functions Performed by Intermediaries
Retailing and wholesaling intermediaries in marketing channels perform several essential functions that make the flow of goods between producer and buyer

Exhibit **12.2**

Factor	Merchant Wholesalers	Agents or Brokers
Nature of Product	Standard	Nonstandard, custom
Technicality of Product	Complex	Simple
Product's Gross Margin	High	Low
Frequency of Ordering	Frequent	Infrequent
Time Between Order and Receipt of Shipment	Buyer desires shorter lead time	Buyer satisfied with long lead time
Number of Customers	Many	Few
Concentration of Customers	Dispersed	Concentrated

SOURCE: Reprinted by permission of the publisher. From Donald M. Jackson and Michael F. D'Amico, "Products and Markets Served by Distributors and Agents," pp. 27–33 in *Industrial Marketing Management*. Copyright 1989 by Elsevier Science Inc.

possible. The three basic functions that intermediaries perform are summarized in Exhibit 12.3.

Transactional functions involve contacting and communicating with prospective buyers to make them aware of existing products and explain their features, advantages, and benefits. Intermediaries in the supply chain also provide *logistical* functions. **Logistics** is a term borrowed from the military that describes the process of strategically managing the efficient flow and storage of raw materials, in-process inventory, and finished goods from point of origin to point of consumption. Logistical functions include transporting, storing, sorting out, accumulating, allocating, and assorting products into either homogeneous or heterogeneous collections. For example, grading agricultural products typifies the sorting-out process while consolidation of many lots of grade A eggs from different sources into one lot illustrates the accumulation process. Supermarkets or other retailers perform the assorting function by assembling thousands of different items that match their customers' desires.

The third basic channel function, *facilitating*, includes research and financing. Research provides information about channel members and consumers by getting answers to key questions: Who are the buyers? Where are they located? Why do they buy? Financing ensures that channel members have the money to keep products moving through the channel to the ultimate consumer.

A single company may provide one, two, or all three functions. Consider Kramer Beverage Company, a Coors beer distributor. As a beer distributor, Kramer provides transactional, logistical, and facilitating channel functions. Sales representatives contact local bars and restaurants to negotiate the terms of the sale, possibly giving the customer a discount for large purchases, and make arrangements for when the beer will be delivered. At the same time, Kramer also provides a facilitating function by extending credit to the customer. Kramer merchandising representatives, meanwhile, assist in promoting the beer on a local level by hanging

logistics
The process of strategically managing the efficient flow and storage of raw materials, in-process inventory, and finished goods from point of origin to point of consumption.

Exhibit 12.3

Marketing Channel Functions
Performed by Intermediaries

Type of Function	Description
Transactional Functions	**Contacting and promoting:** Contacting potential customers, promoting products, and soliciting orders **Negotiating:** Determining how many goods or services to buy and sell, type of transportation to use, when to deliver, and method and timing of payment **Risk-taking:** Assuming the risk of owning inventory

Logistical Functions	**Physically distributing:** Transporting and sorting goods to overcome temporal and spatial discrepancies
	
	Storing: Maintaining inventories and protecting goods
	
	Sorting: Overcoming discrepancies of quantity and assortment by
	    Sorting out: Breaking down a heterogeneous supply into separate homogeneous stocks
	    Accumulation: Combining similar stocks into a larger homogeneous supply
	    Allocation: Breaking a homogeneous supply into smaller and smaller lots ("breaking bulk")
	    Assortment: Combining products into collections or assortments that buyers want available at one place

Facilitating Function	**Researching:** Gathering information about other channel members and consumers **Financing:** Extending credit and other financial services to facilitate the flow of goods through the channel to the final consumer

Coors beer signs and posters. Kramer also provides logistical functions by accumulating the many types of Coors beer from the Coors manufacturing plant in Golden, Colorado, and storing them in its refrigerated warehouse. When an order needs to be filled, Kramer then sorts the beer into heterogeneous collections for each particular customer. For example, the local Chili's Grill & Bar may need two kegs of Coors, three kegs of Coors Light, and two cases of Killian's Red in bottles. The beer will then be loaded onto a refrigerated truck and transported to the restaurant. Upon arrival, the Kramer delivery person will transport the kegs and cases of beer into the restaurant's refrigerator and may also restock the coolers behind the bar.

Although individual members can be added to or deleted from a channel, someone must still perform these essential functions. They can be performed by producers, end users, or consumers, channel intermediaries such as wholesalers and retailers, and sometimes nonmember channel participants. For example, if a manufacturer decides to eliminate its private fleet of trucks, it must still have a way to move the goods to the wholesaler. This task may be accomplished by the wholesaler, which may have its own fleet of trucks, or by a nonmember channel participant, such as an independent trucking firm. Nonmembers also provide many other essential functions that may have at one time been provided by a channel member. For example, research firms may perform the research function; advertising agencies, the promotion function; transportation and storage firms the physical distribution function; and banks, the financing function.

What kind of marketing channel functions can be performed over the Internet? Why do you think so?

On Line

Channel Structures

There are many routes a product can take to reach its final consumer. Marketers search for the most efficient channel from the many alternatives available. Marketing a consumer convenience good like gum or candy differs from marketing a specialty good like a Mercedes-Benz. The two products require much different distribution channels. Likewise, the appropriate channel for a major equipment supplier like Boeing Aircraft would be unsuitable for an accessory equipment producer like Black & Decker. In order to illustrate the differences in typical marketing channels for consumer and business-to-business products like these, the next sections discuss the structures of marketing channels for each product type. Alternative channel structures are also discussed.

3

Describe the channel structures for consumer and business-to-business products and discuss alternative channel arrangements

Channels for Consumer Products

Exhibit 12.4 illustrates the four ways manufacturers can route products to consumers. Producers use the **direct channel** to sell directly to consumers. Direct marketing activities—including telemarketing, mail-order and catalog shopping, and forms of electronic retailing like on-line shopping and shop-at-home television networks—are a good example of this type of channel structure. For example, home computer users can purchase Dell computers directly over the telephone or directly from Dell's Internet Web site. There are no intermediaries. Producer-owned stores and factory outlet stores—like Sherwin-Williams, Polo/Ralph Lauren, Oneida, and West Point Pepperel—are other examples of direct channels. Farmers' markets are also direct channels. Direct marketing and factory outlets are discussed in more detail in Chapter 13.

direct channel
A distribution channel in which producers sell directly to consumers.

Exhibit 12.4   Marketing Channels for Consumer Products

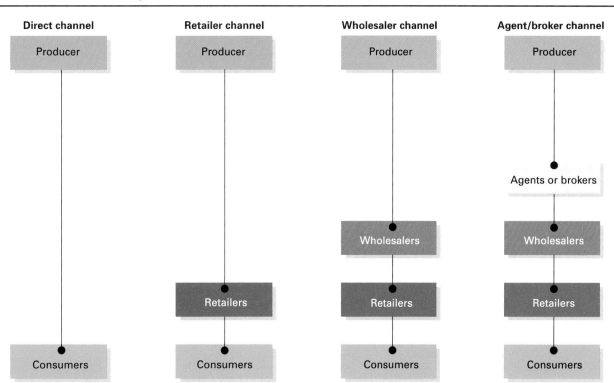

At the other end of the spectrum, an *agent/broker channel* involves a fairly complicated process. Agent/broker channels are typically used in markets with many small manufacturers and many retailers that lack the resources to find each other. Agents or brokers bring manufacturers and wholesalers together for negotiations, but they do not take title to merchandise. Ownership passes directly to one or more wholesalers and then to retailers. Finally, retailers sell to the ultimate consumer of the product. For example, a food broker represents buyers and sellers of grocery products. The broker acts on behalf of many different producers and negotiates the sale of their products to wholesalers that specialize in foodstuffs. These wholesalers in turn sell to grocers and convenience stores.

Most consumer products are sold through distribution channels similar to the other two alternatives: the retailer channel and the wholesaler channel. A *retailer channel* is most common when the retailer is large and can buy in large quantities directly from the manufacturer. Wal-Mart, Sears, and car dealers are examples of retailers that often bypass a wholesaler. A *wholesaler channel* is frequently used for low-cost items that are frequently purchased, such as candy, cigarettes, and magazines. For example, M&M/Mars sells candies and chocolates to wholesalers in large quantities. The wholesalers then break these quantities into smaller quantities to satisfy individual retailer orders.

Channels for Business-to-Business and Industrial Products

As Exhibit 12.5 illustrates, five channel structures are common in business-to-business and industrial markets. First, direct channels are typical in business-to-business and industrial markets. For example, manufacturers buy large quantities of raw materials, major equipment, processed materials, and supplies directly from other manufacturers. Manufacturers that require suppliers to meet detailed technical specifications often prefer direct channels. The direct communication required between Chrysler and its suppliers, for example, along with the tremendous size of the orders, makes anything but a direct channel impractical. The

Exhibit 12.5   Channels for Business-to-Business and Industrial Products

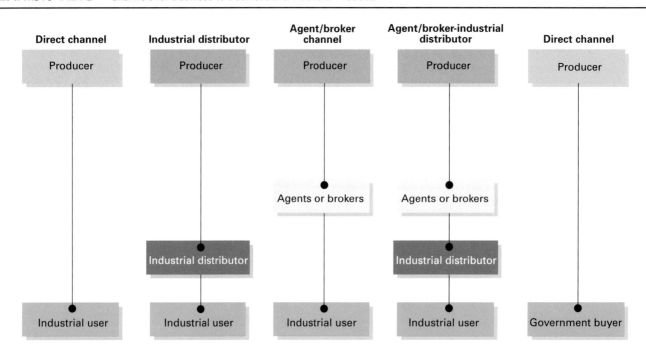

channel from producer to government buyers is also a direct channel. Since much of government buying is done through bidding, a direct channel is attractive. Dell Computer Corporation, for example, is the top seller of desktop computers to federal, state, and local government agencies in the United States, which it sells through direct channels.[2]

Companies selling standardized items of moderate or low value often rely on *industrial distributors.* In many ways, an industrial distributor is like a supermarket for organizations. Industrial distributors are wholesalers and channel members that buy and take title to products. Moreover, they usually keep inventories of their products and sell and service them. Often small manufacturers cannot afford to employ their own sales force. Instead, they rely on manufacturers' representatives or selling agents to sell to either industrial distributors or users.

The Internet is increasingly being used in business-to-business channels as a more direct and efficient means of purchasing and selling supplies and raw materials. Internet experts expect on-line business-to-business commerce to reach $1.3 trillion by 2003, far surpassing their expectations for consumer Internet purchases.[3] Until recently, many hospitals and physicians needing to purchase medical supplies and equipment were required to search through paper catalogs published by each manufacturer to find what they wanted. With an urgent need to cut costs without jeopardizing patient care, on-line buying from medical-supply companies streamline orders through the use of searchable databases and electronic ordering.[4] Other industries are creating supplier networks on the Internet to speed up ordering and keep costs low. Both General Motors and Ford are creating separate on-line trading communities for their suppliers, each encompassing thousands of vendors. For GM, on-line trading will replace the current process of issuing paper purchase orders for the $87 billion a year it spends on raw materials and supplies purchased from over 30,000 different suppliers.[5]

Alternative Channel Arrangements

Rarely does a producer use just one type of channel to move its product. It usually employs several different or alternative channels, which include multiple channels, nontraditional channels, and strategic channel alliances.

Multiple Channels When a producer selects two or more channels to distribute the same product to target markets, this arrangement is called **dual distribution** (or **multiple distribution**). For example, Whirlpool sells its washers, dryers, and refrigerators directly to home and apartment builders and contractors, but it also sells these same appliances to retail stores that sell to consumers. J. Crew, which has traditionally used direct-mail channels, has now opened retail and outlet stores as well as an Internet site equipped for electronic shopping. Similarly, computer maker Gateway, which sells personal computers to home consumers using the telephone and Internet, has forged new dealer channels to reach the business market through a program called Gateway Partners. The company has also opened over 200 Gateway Country Stores in the United States and forty abroad where Gateway customers can configure and purchase new computers, bring in malfunctioning equipment, or learn how to surf the Web.[6] Multiple channels may also be employed by producers with unique second brands. For example, the Walt Disney Company routinely releases first-run animated films to movie theaters and then releases a sequel directly to the home-video market. Such

dual distribution (multiple distribution)
The use of two or more channels to distribute the same product to target markets.

J. Crew sells its clothes through its catalog, its Web site, and its stores, like this one in Santa Monica, California. Multiple distribution enables the company to reach its customers wherever they are.

sequels as *Aladdin and the King of Thieves* and *Beauty and the Beast: The Enchanted Christmas* follow up its theater blockbusters.

Nontraditional Channels Often nontraditional channel arrangements help differentiate a firm's product from the competition. For example, manufacturers may decide to use nontraditional channels such as the Internet, mail-order channels or infomercials, to sell its products instead of going through traditional retailer channels. Although nontraditional channels may limit a brand's coverage, they can give a producer serving a niche market a way to gain market access and customer attention without having to establish channel intermediaries. Nontraditional channels can also provide another avenue of sales for larger firms. For example, Campbell Soup Company is testing a soup-dispensing machine that works like a soda fountain to sell hot soup in convenience stores.[7] As you recall from the opening story at the beginning of this chapter, the rise in the popularity of the Internet for consumer purchases has also created nontraditional channels for many goods, such as groceries. Many consumers can now purchase grocery items by clicking a mouse rather than going to a supermarket. Groceries ordered on-line are instead delivered right to a customer's doorstep. Streamline. com, based in Massachusetts, even installs a refrigerator in their customers' garages so they don't have to be home for deliveries.[8]

strategic channel alliance
A cooperative agreement between business firms to use the other's already established distribution channel.

Strategic Channel Alliances Producers often form **strategic channel alliances**, which use another manufacturer's already-established channel. Alliances are used most often when the creation of marketing channel relationships may be too expensive and time-consuming. Starbucks and Kraft Foods have a long-term licensing arrangement to stock Starbucks coffee on supermarket shelves nationwide. Under the arrangement, Seattle-based Starbucks will roast and package the coffee, and Kraft will market and distribute it in supermarkets, first in the United States and eventually around the world. By forming a strategic channel alliance with Kraft, Starbucks' brand of coffee will be sold by Kraft's 3,500 salespeople, one of the largest direct-selling teams in the food industry. The alliance will allow Starbucks to distribute its coffee through grocery stores nationwide much quicker than it would have been able to do alone.[9]

Strategic channel alliances are also common for selling in global markets where cultural differences, distance, or other barriers can inhibit channel establishment. U.S. software giant Oracle has a strategic alliance with Japanese computer giant Fujitsu in the Asian-Pacific region. Under the alliance, Fujitsu distributes and markets Oracle's information management software on Fujitsu servers in Australia, China, Hong Kong, Thailand, and Vietnam.[10]

Supply Chain Management

Define supply chain management and discuss its benefits

supply chain management
A management system that coordinates and integrates all of the activities performed by supply chain members into a seamless process, from the source to the point of consumption, resulting in enhanced customer and economic value.

Supply chain management coordinates and integrates all of the activities performed by supply chain members into a seamless process, from the source to the point of consumption. Continuously evolving, supply chain management is a philosophy that seeks to unify the competencies and resources of business functions both within the firm and outside in the firm's allied channel partners. The result is a highly competitive, customer-satisfying supply system focused on developing innovative solutions and synchronizing the flow of goods, services, and information to create enhanced customer value.[11]

An important element of supply chain management is that it is completely customer driven. In the mass-production era, manufacturers produced standardized products that were "pushed" down through the supply channel to the consumer. In contrast, in today's marketplace, products are being driven by customers, who expect to receive product configurations and services matched to their unique needs.[12] For example, Dell only builds computers according to its customers' precise specifications, such as the amount of RAM memory, type of monitor, modem, or CD drive, amount of hard disk space, and so on. The company is a leader in supply chain management as it works with its suppliers to provide the right components for its customers' needs. Today, supply chain management is viewed as a key means of differentiation for a firm and a critical component in marketing and corporate strategy. The focus is on pulling products into the marketplace and partnering with members of the supply chain to work together and share information with the goal of enhancing customer value.

This reversal of the flow of demand from a "push" to a "pull" has resulted in a radical reformulation of both market expectations and traditional marketing, production, and distribution functions. Through the channel partnership of suppliers, manufacturers, wholesalers, and retailers along the entire supply chain who work together toward the common goal of creating customer value, supply chain management allows companies to respond with the unique product configuration and mix of services demanded by the customer. Today, supply chain management plays a dual role: first, as a *communicator* of customer demand that extends from the point of sale all the way back to the supplier, and second, as a *physical flow process* that engineers the timely and cost-effective movement of goods through the entire supply pipeline.[13]

Accordingly, supply chain managers are responsible for making channel strategy decisions, coordinating the sourcing and procurement of raw materials, scheduling production, processing orders, managing inventory, transporting and storing supplies and finished goods, and coordinating customer service activities. Supply chain managers are also responsible for the management of information that flows through the supply chain. Coordinating the relationships between the company and its external partners, such as vendors, carriers, and third-party companies is also a critical function of supply chain management.[14] Specifically, supply chain management includes these activities:

- Determining the channel strategy and level of distribution intensity required for the successful distribution of the product through the supply chain
- Managing relationships in the supply chain with the ultimate goal of cultivating and coordinating strategic partnerships with supply chain members to meet the unique needs of the customer and create customer value
- Managing the logistical components of the supply chain, which include the following:

    The movement of information and customer requirements up and down the supply chain

    The planning of production and inventory levels in response to consumer demand

    The movement and storage of raw materials and parts from their sources to the production site

    The movement of raw materials, semimanufactured products, and finished products within and among plants, warehouses, and distribution centers

    The movement of finished goods to intermediaries and final buyers
- Balancing the costs of the supply chain with the level of service demanded by the customer

In summary, supply chain managers are responsible for directing raw materials and parts to the production department and the finished or semifinished product through warehouses and eventually to the intermediary

or end user. Above all, supply chain management begins and ends with the customer. Instead of forcing into the market a product that may or may not sell quickly, supply chain managers react to actual customer demand. By doing so, the flow of raw materials, finished product, and packaging materials is minimized at every point in the supply chain, resulting in lower costs and increased customer value. Exhibit 12.6 depicts the supply chain process.

Benefits of Supply Chain Management

The benefits of supply chain management are many. A study by the Center for Transportation Studies at the Massachusetts Institute of Technology found that the most commonly reported bottom-line benefits center on reduced costs in inventory management, transportation, warehousing, and packaging; improved service through techniques like time-based delivery and make-to-order; and enhanced revenues, which result from such supply chain-related achievements as higher product availability and more customized products.[15] Research has shown a clear relationship between supply chain performance and profitability. Leaders in supply chain practices spent 5 to 6 percent less on supply chain management as a percentage of sales than the average performers. For a

Exhibit 12.6   The Supply Chain Process

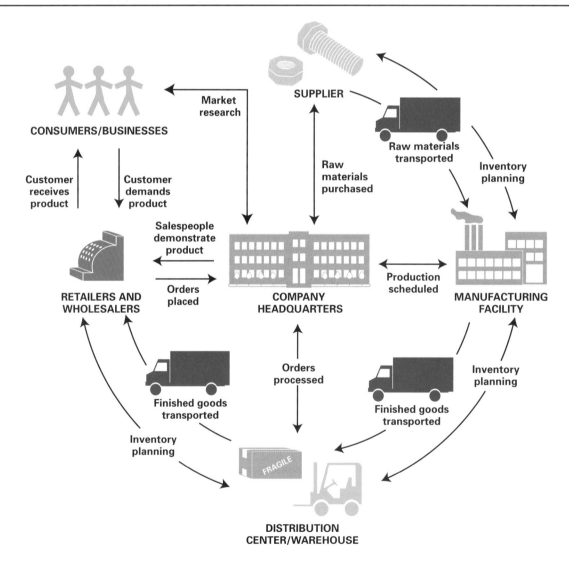

company with $500 million in sales, this translates to a $25 million to $30 million cost advantage annually.[16]

Another study by A.T. Kearney looked at supply chain management from a different angle—specifically, the costs of not paying careful attention to the supply chain process. The Kearney consultants found that supply chain inefficiencies, such as late deliveries, stagnant inventories, and the higher costs they produce, could waste as much as 25 percent of a company's operating costs. Assuming even a relatively low profit margin of 3 to 4 percent, a 5 percent reduction in supply chain waste could double a company's profitability.[17]

Making Channel Strategy Decisions

Devising a marketing channel strategy requires several critical decisions. Supply chain managers must decide what role distribution will play in the overall marketing strategy. In addition, they must be sure that the channel strategy chosen is consistent with product, promotion, and pricing strategies. In making these decisions, marketing managers must analyze what factors will influence the choice of channel and what level of distribution intensity will be appropriate.

Factors Affecting Channel Choice

Supply chain managers must answer many questions before choosing a marketing channel. The final choice depends on the analysis of several factors, which often interact. These factors can be grouped as market factors, product factors, and producer factors.

Market Factors Among the most important market factors affecting the choice of distribution channel are target customer considerations. Specifically, supply chain managers should answer the following questions: Who are the potential customers? What do they buy? Where do they buy? When do they buy? How do they buy? Additionally, the choice of channel depends on whether the producer is selling to consumers or to industrial customers. Industrial customers' buying habits are very different from those of consumers. Industrial customers tend to buy in larger quantities and require more customer service. Consumers usually buy in very small quantities and sometimes do not mind if they get no service at all, as in a discount store.

Geographic location and size of the market are also important to channel selection. As a rule, if the target market is concentrated in one or more specific areas, then direct selling through a sales force is appropriate. When markets are more widely dispersed, intermediaries would be less expensive. The size of the market also influences channel choice. Generally, a very large market requires more intermediaries. For instance, Procter & Gamble has to reach millions of consumers with its many brands of household goods. It needs many intermediaries, including wholesalers and retailers.

Product Factors Products that are more complex, customized, and expensive tend to benefit from shorter and more direct marketing channels. These types of products sell better through a direct sales force. Examples include pharmaceuticals, scientific instruments, airplanes, and mainframe computer systems. On the other hand, the more standardized a product is, the longer its distribution channel can be and the greater the number of intermediaries that can be involved. For example, the formula for chewing gum is about the same from producer to producer, with the exception of flavor and shape. Chewing gum is also very inexpensive. As a result, the distribution channel for gum tends to involve many wholesalers and retailers.

The product's life cycle is also an important factor in choosing a marketing channel. In fact, the choice of channel may change over the life of the product. For example, when photocopiers were first available, they were typically sold by a direct sales force. Now, however, photocopiers can be found in several places, including warehouse clubs, electronics superstores, and mail-order catalogs. As products become more common and less intimidating to potential users, producers tend to look for alternative channels. Gatorade was originally sold to sports teams, gyms, and fitness clubs. As the drink became more popular, mainstream supermarket channels were added, followed by convenience stores and drugstores. Now Gatorade can be found in vending machines and even in some fast-food restaurants.

Originally developed as a sports drink, Gatorade fast became a popular beverage for a variety of situations. As such, the company expanded its distribution network to include such channels as vending machines.

Another factor is the delicacy of the product. Perishable products like vegetables and milk have a relatively short life span. Fragile products like china and crystal require a minimum amount of handling. Therefore, both require fairly short marketing channels.

Producer Factors   Several factors pertaining to the producer itself are important to the selection of a marketing channel. In general, producers with large financial, managerial, and marketing resources are better able to use more direct channels. These producers have the ability to hire and train their own sales force, warehouse their own goods, and extend credit to their customers. Smaller or weaker firms, on the other hand, must rely on intermediaries to provide these services for them. Compared to producers with only one or two product lines, producers that sell several products in a related area are able to choose channels that are more direct. Sales expenses then can be spread over more products.

A producer's desire to control pricing, positioning, brand image, and customer support also tends to influence channel selection. For instance, firms that sell products with exclusive brand images, such as designer perfumes and clothing, usually avoid channels in which discount retailers are present. Manufacturers of upscale products, such as Gucci (handbags) and Godiva (chocolates), may sell their wares only in expensive stores in order to maintain an image of exclusivity. Many producers have opted to risk their image, however, and test sales in discount channels. Levi Strauss expanded its distribution to include JCPenney and Sears. JCPenney is now Levi Strauss's biggest customer.

Levels of Distribution Intensity

Organizations have three options for intensity of distribution: intensive distribution, selective distribution, or exclusive distribution (see Exhibit 12.7).

intensive distribution
A form of distribution aimed at having a product available in every outlet where target customers might want to buy it.

Intensive Distribution   **Intensive distribution** is a form of distribution aimed at maximum market coverage. The manufacturer tries to have the product available in every outlet where potential customers might want to buy it. If buyers are unwilling to search for a product (as is true of convenience goods and operating supplies), the product must be very accessible to buyers. A low-value product that is purchased frequently may require a lengthy channel. For example, candy is found in almost every type of retail store imaginable. It is typically sold to retailers in small quantities by a food or candy wholesaler. The Wrigley Company could not afford to sell its gum directly to every service station, drugstore, supermarket, and discount store. The cost would be too high.

Most manufacturers pursuing an intensive distribution strategy sell to a large percentage of the wholesalers willing to stock their products. Retailers' willingness (or unwillingness) to handle items tends to control the manufacturer's ability to

Exhibit 12.7

Intensity Level	Distribution Intensity Objective	Number of Intermediaries in Each Market	Examples
Intensive	Achieve mass market selling; popular with health and beauty aids and convenience goods that must be available everywhere	Many	Pepsi-Cola, Frito-Lay potato chips, Huggies diapers, Alpo dog food, Crayola crayons
Selective	Work closely with selected intermediaries who meet certain criteria; typically used for shopping goods and some specialty goods	Several	Donna Karan clothing, Hewlett-Packard printers, Burton snowboards, Aveda aromatherapy products
Exclusive	Work with a single intermediary for products that require special resources or positioning; typically used for specialty goods and major industrial equipment	One	BMW cars, Rolex watches, Subway franchise

achieve intensive distribution. For example, a retailer already carrying ten brands of gum may show little enthusiasm for one more brand.

Selective Distribution   **Selective distribution** is achieved by screening dealers and retailers to eliminate all but a few in any single area. Because only a few are chosen, the consumer must seek out the product. Maytag, for instance, uses a selective distribution system by choosing a select handful of appliance retailers in a geographic area to sell its line of washers and dryers and other appliances. Maytag may use several screening criteria to find the right dealers, such as ability to service its appliances, the ability to handle a large volume of merchandise, or their image as a reputable retailer.

Selective distribution strategies often hinge on a manufacturer's desire to maintain a superior product image to be able to charge a premium price. DKNY clothing, for instance, is sold only in select retail outlets, mainly full-price department stores. Likewise, premium pet-food brands such as Hill's Pet Nutrition and Ralston-Purina's ProPlan are distributed chiefly through specialty petfood stores and veterinarians, rather than mass retailers like Wal-Mart, so that a premium price can be charged. Procter & Gamble, which purchased rival premium petfood brand Iams, recently expanded Iams's selective distribution strategy to include mass retailer Target. The strategy could jeopardize Iams's high price strategy and disenfranchise the breeders and veterinarians who have been the brand's primary source of strength over the years.[18]

Exclusive Distribution   The most restrictive form of market coverage is **exclusive distribution**, which entails only one or a few dealers within a given area. Because buyers may have to search or travel extensively to buy the product, exclusive

selective distribution
A form of distribution achieved by screening dealers to eliminate all but a few in any single area.

exclusive distribution
A form of distribution that establishes one or a few dealers within a given area.

On Line

distribution is usually confined to consumer specialty goods, a few shopping goods, and major industrial equipment. Products such as Rolls Royce automobiles, Chris-Craft power boats, and Pettibone tower cranes are distributed under exclusive arrangements. Sometimes exclusive territories are granted by new companies (such as franchisers) to obtain market coverage in a particular area. Limited distribution may also serve to project an exclusive image for the product.

Retailers and wholesalers may be unwilling to commit the time and money necessary to promote and service a product unless the manufacturer guarantees them an exclusive territory. This arrangement shields the dealer from direct competition and enables it to be the main beneficiary of the manufacturer's promotion efforts in that geographic area. With exclusive distribution, channels of communication are usually well established, because the manufacturer works with a limited number of dealers rather than many accounts.

Exclusive distribution has been part of retailing for years. Toy makers often make toys exclusively for certain retailers that can't be found elsewhere. Exclusive distribution might also take place within a retailer's store rather than a geographical area—for example, when a retailer agrees not to sell a manufacturer's competing brands. Radio Shack, for instance, has prospered in recent years by offering electronics manufacturers exclusivity within its stores. When Sprint Corporation was looking for a retail base in the mid-1990s from which to sell its new wireless phone network, Radio Shack offered to make Sprint its exclusive national wireless provider. The agreement has helped Sprint become the leader in digital personal communications services, selling more wireless phones than rivals Best Buy, Circuit City, and Sears. Radio Shack has cut similar exclusive distribution deals with Compaq Computers, broadband Internet service provider Northpoint Communications, and RCA for audio and video equipment.[19]

Managing Channel Relationships

Explain channel leadership, conflict, and partnering

channel power
The capacity of a particular marketing channel member to control or influence the behavior of other channel members.

channel control
A situation that occurs when one marketing channel member intentionally affects another member's behavior.

channel leader (channel captain)
A member of a marketing channel that exercises authority and power over the activities of other channel members.

A marketing channel is more than a set of institutions linked by economic ties. Social relationships play an important role in building unity among channel members. A critical aspect of supply chain management, therefore, is managing the social relationships among channel members to achieve synergy. The basic social dimensions of channels are power, control, leadership, conflict, and partnering.

Channel Power, Control, and Leadership

Channel power is a channel member's capacity to control or influence the behavior of other channel members. **Channel control** occurs when one channel member affects another member's behavior. To achieve control, a channel member assumes channel leadership and exercises authority and power. This member is termed the **channel leader**, or **channel captain**. In one marketing channel, a manufacturer may be the leader because it controls new product designs and product availability. In another, a retailer may be the channel leader because it wields power and control over the retail price, inventory levels, and postsale service.

The exercise of channel power is a routine element of many business activities in which the outcome is often more efficient operations and cost savings. For years, distributing magazines was a simple, inefficient business. Most cities had one wholesaler who purchased magazine titles from publishers for 60 percent of the magazine's cover price. The wholesaler delivered new issues to retail stores, who purchased the magazines from the wholesaler at 80 percent of the magazine's cover price. The retailer, the wholesaler, and the publisher each got a cut from every magazine sold. The wholesalers sent unsold magazines back to the publisher. Then supermarket giant Safeway, in an effort to control costs, decided to reduce the number of single-city magazine wholesalers it traditionally dealt with by opening up several large regions to competitive bidding. Other big retailers, such as Wal-Mart, Albertson's, Kroger, and Walgreen, soon followed suit. In order to win contracts for larger regions, wholesalers were forced to offer better terms and expand their operations or go out of business. Now, retailers typically pay just 70 to 75 percent of a magazine's cover price and the number of wholesalers it deals with have been drastically reduced. Wal-Mart, for instance, now deals with just three distributors nationwide, down from over 300. In turn, many wholesalers are exerting their own power onto magazine publishers in an effort to remain profitable. One wholesaler recently required that for new titles publishers must provide it a "minimum discount" from the cover price of 44 percent (meaning it would pay no more than 56 percent, compared with the current 60 percent norm) in an effort to reduce returns, an expensive and unprofitable part of the business. Other wholesalers are demanding new fees from publishers for magazines deemed unprofitable.[20]

Channel Conflict

Inequitable channel relationships often lead to **channel conflict**, which is a clash of goals and methods among the members of a distribution channel. In a broad context, conflict may not be bad. Often it arises because staid, traditional channel members refuse to keep pace with the times. Removing an outdated intermediary may result in reduced costs for the entire supply chain.

Sources of conflicts among channel members can be due to many different situations and factors. Oftentimes, conflict arises because channel members have conflicting goals. For instance, athletic footwear retailers want to sell as many shoes as possible in order to maximize profits, regardless of whether the shoe is manufactured by Nike, adidas, or Saucony. But the Nike manufacturer wants a certain sales volume and market share in each market.

Conflict can also arise when channel members fail to fulfill expectations of other channel members—for example, when a franchisee does not follow the rules set down by the franchiser, or when communications channels break down between channel members. For example, if a manufacturer reduces the length of warranty coverage and fails to communicate this change to dealers, then conflict may occur when dealers make repairs with the expectation that they will be reimbursed by the manufacturer. Further, ideological differences and different perceptions of reality can also cause conflict among channel members. For example, retailers may believe "the customer is always right" and offer a very liberal return policy. Wholesalers and manufacturers may feel that people "try to get something for nothing" or don't follow product instructions carefully. Their differing views of allowable returns will undoubtably conflict with those of retailers.

Conflict within a channel can be either horizontal or vertical. **Horizontal conflict** occurs among channel members on the same level, such as two or more different wholesalers or two or more different retailers, that handle the same manufacturer's brands. This type of channel conflict is found most often when manufacturers practice dual or multiple distribution strategies. For instance, there was considerable channel conflict after computer manufacturers began distributing their computers beyond the

channel conflict
A clash of goals and methods between distribution channel members.

horizontal conflict
A channel conflict that occurs among channel members on the same level.

traditional computer resellers and to discount stores, department stores, warehouse clubs, and giant electronic superstores, such as Circuit City and CompUSA. Horizontal conflict can also occur when channel members on the same level feel they are being treated unfairly by the manufacturer. For example, the American Booksellers Association, a group representing small independent booksellers, recently filed a lawsuit against bookstore giants Barnes & Noble and Borders, claiming they violated antitrust laws by using their buying power to demand "illegal and secret" discounts from publishers. These deals, the association contends, put independent booksellers at a serious competitive disadvantage.[21]

Many regard horizontal conflict as healthy competition. Much more serious is **vertical conflict**, which occurs between different levels in a marketing channel, most typically between the manufacturer and wholesaler and the manufacturer and retailer. Producer-versus-wholesaler conflict occurs when the producer chooses to bypass the wholesaler to deal directly with the consumer or retailer. For example, conflict arose when several producers agreed to Wal-Mart's request to deal with it directly, bypassing middlemen altogether.

Dual distribution strategies can also cause vertical conflict in the channel. For example, wireless telephone carriers, such as AT&T and Bell Atlantic, traditionally sold cellular phone service through local dealers, usually small electronic stores. Faced with increased competition from upstarts, carriers now are opening their own stores and mall kiosks, as well as offering special prices and telemarketing to reach potential customers in their homes. Local dealers, who helped build the cellphone market in the early 1980s, say the carriers are trying to squeeze them out of business.[22] Similarly, manufacturers who are experimenting with selling to customers directly over the Internet are also creating conflict with their traditional retailing intermediaries. For example, high-end furniture maker and retailer Ethan Allen was met with considerable resistance from the independent licensees who own and manage three-quarters of the company's 300-plus brick-and-mortar stores when it decided to open its own Web site for e-commerce. To counter its dealers' opposition to the plan, Ethan Allen promised its dealers a cut of the Internet revenue if they agreed to deliver much of the merchandise, accept returns and handle the minor repairs often needed when furniture comes out of the crate.[23]

Producers and retailers may also disagree over the terms of the sale or other aspects of the business relationship. When Procter & Gamble introduced "everyday low pricing" to its retail channel members, a strategy designed to standardize wholesale prices and eliminate most trade promotions, many retailers retaliated. Some cut the variety of P&G sizes they carried or eliminated marginal brands. Others moved P&G brands from prime shelf space to less visible shelves.

vertical conflict
A channel conflict that occurs between different levels in a marketing channel, most typically between the manufacturer and wholesaler or between the manufacturer and retailer.

When Ethan Allen began to sell direct through its Web site, its independent licensees strongly resisted. This vertical conflict was resolved when the company recruited dealers to deliver merchandise and handle returns, and gave them a percentage of the revenue generated by on-line sales.

Channel Partnering

Regardless of the locus of power, channel members rely heavily on one another. Even the most powerful manufacturers depend on dealers to sell their products; even the most powerful retailers require the products provided by suppliers. In sharp contrast to the adversarial relationships of the past between buyers and sellers, contemporary management thought emphasizes the development of close working partnerships among channel members. **Channel partnering**, or **channel cooperation**, is the joint effort of all channel members to create a supply chain that serves customers and creates a competitive advantage. Channel partnering is vital if each member is to gain something from other members. By cooperating, retailers, wholesalers, manufacturers, and suppliers can speed up inventory replenishment, improve customer service, and reduce the total costs of the marketing channel.

Channel alliances and partnerships can be directly traced, in part, to attempts by firms to leverage the intellectual, material, and marketing resources of their business partners worldwide to make entry into far-flung markets easier and more cost-effective. The growth of channel partnering is also due to the growth of an information infrastructure that fosters cooperation and sharing of information in national as well as global markets.[24] A comparison between companies that approach the marketplace unilaterally and those that engage in channel cooperation and form partnerships is detailed in Exhibit 12.8.

Collaborating channel partners meet the needs of consumers more effectively by ensuring the right products reach shelves at the right time and at a lower cost, boosting sales and profits. Forced to become more efficient in a highly competitive environment, retailers and their vendors, for instance, have turned many formerly adversarial relationships into partnerships. Wal-Mart's Retail Link technology, for example, gives some 3,200 vendors access to its point-of-sale data to replenish inventory at its more than three thousand stores. Based on sales data, vendors customized Wal-Mart's workwear clothing inventory at each store according to demographics, regional tastes, and weather patterns. As a result of vendor partnerships, Wal-Mart's overall inventory was reduced by 25 percent while sales rose 15 percent.[25]

channel partnering (channel cooperation)
The joint effort of all channel members to create a supply chain that serves customers and creates a competitive advantage.

Exhibit 12.8 Transaction- Versus Partnership-Based Firms

	Transaction-Based	Partnership-Based
Relationships between manufacturer and supplier	• Short-term • Adversarial • Independent • Price more important	• Long-term • Cooperative • Dependent • Value-added services more important
Number of suppliers	Many	Few
Level of information sharing	Minimal	High
Investment required	Minimal	High

SOURCE: David Frederick Ross, *Competing Through Supply Chain Management: Creating Market-Winning Strategies Through Supply Chain Partnerships* (New York: Chapman & Hall, 1998), p. 61.

7

Describe the logistical components of the supply chain

logistics information system
Information technology that integrates and links all of the logistics functions of the supply chain.

supply chain team
An entire group of individuals who orchestrate the movement of goods, services, and information from the source to the consumer.

Now that you are familiar with the structure and strategy of marketing channels and the role of supply chain management, it is important to also understand the physical means through which products move through the supply chain. As mentioned earlier, supply chain management coordinates and integrates all of the activities performed by supply chain members into a seamless process. The supply chain consists of several interrelated and integrated logistical components: (1) sourcing and procurement of raw materials and supplies; (2) production scheduling; (3) order processing; (4) inventory control; (5) warehousing and materials-handling; and (6) transportation. These components are shown in Exhibit 12.9.

Integrating and linking all of the logistics components of the supply chain is the **logistics information system**. Today's supply chain logisticians are at the forefront of information technology, which is not just a functional affiliate of supply chain management. Rather it is the enabler, the facilitator, the linkage that connects the various components and partners of the supply chain into an integrated whole. Electronic data interchange, on-board computers, satellite and cellular communications systems, materials-handling and warehouse-management software, enterprise-wide systems solutions, and the Internet are among the information enablers of successful supply chain management.[26]

The **supply chain team**, in concert with the logistics information system, orchestrates the movement of goods, services, and information from the source to the consumer. Supply chain teams typically cut across organizational boundaries, embracing all parties who participate in moving product to market. The best supply chain teams also move beyond the organization to include the external participants in the chain, such as suppliers, transportation carriers, and third-party logistics suppliers. Members of the supply chain communicate, coordinate, and cooperate extensively.[27]

Exhibit 12.9

Integrated Logistical Components of the Supply Chain

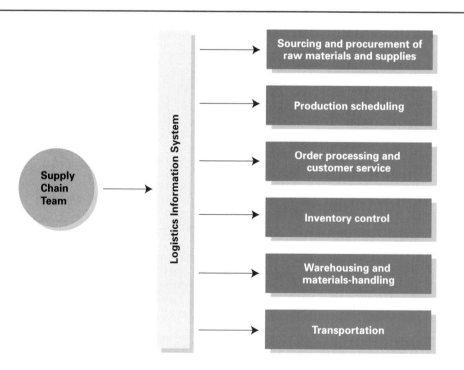

Sourcing and Procurement

One of the most important links in the supply chain is that between the manufacturer and the supplier. Purchasing professionals are on the front lines of supply chain management. Purchasing departments plan purchasing strategies, develop specifications, select suppliers, and negotiate price and service levels.

The goal of most sourcing and procurement activities is to reduce the costs of raw materials and supplies. Purchasing professionals have traditionally relied on tough negotiations to get the lowest price possible from suppliers of raw materials, supplies, and components. However, the traditional approach of simply negotiating the lowest price doesn't always fit well with the philosophy of supply chain management. In its position at the top of the supply chain, the purchasing function is crucial to the success of the manufacturer's relationship with its customers down the line. Yet, purchasing efforts rarely look toward the bottom of the chain.[28]

Perhaps the biggest contribution purchasing can make to supply chain management is in the area of vendor relations. Companies can use the purchasing function to strategically manage suppliers in order to reduce the total cost of materials and services. Through enhanced vendor relations, buyers and sellers can develop cooperative relationships that reduce costs and improve efficiency with the aim of lowering prices and enhancing profits.[29] By integrating suppliers into their companies' businesses, purchasing managers have become better able to streamline purchasing processes, manage inventory levels, and reduce overall costs of the sourcing and procurement operations.[30]

Production Scheduling

In traditional mass-market manufacturing, production begins when forecasts call for additional products to be made or inventory control systems signal low inventory levels. The firm then makes a product, and transports it to their own warehouses or those of intermediaries, where it waits to be ordered from retailers or customers. Production scheduling based on pushing a product down to the consumer obviously has its disadvantages, the most notable being that companies risk making products that may become obsolete or that consumers don't want in the first place.

In a customer "pull" manufacturing environment, which is growing in popularity, production of goods or services is not scheduled until an order is placed by the customer specifying the desired configuration. For instance, at Gateway Computers a personal computer is not built until a customer selects the desired configuration and places an order over the telephone or on the Internet. This process, known as **mass customization**, or **build-to-order**, uniquely tailors mass-market goods and services to the needs of the individuals who buy them. Companies as diverse as BMW, Dell Computers, Levi Strauss, Mattel, and a slew of Web-based businesses are adopting mass customization to maintain or obtain a competitive edge.

As more companies move toward mass customization versus the mass marketing of goods, continuous dialogue with the customer becomes ever more important. For example, Levi Strauss has made measure-to-fit women's jeans for several years. With the help of a sales associate, customers create the jeans they want by picking from six colors, three basic models, five different leg openings, and two types of fly. Each customer is measured for a correct fit. Then their order is entered into a Web-based terminal linked to the stitching machines in

mass customization (build-to-order)
A production method whereby products are not made until an order is placed by the customer; products are made according to customer specifications.

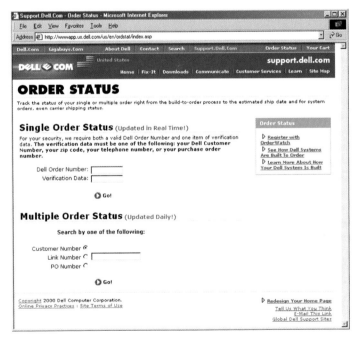

Build-to-order computers are more than commonplace today, thanks to the direct selling model of Dell Computer. The company allows customers to track their orders throughout manufacturing and shipping.

the factory. Two to three weeks later the jeans arrive in the mail. A bar-code tag sealed to the pocket lining stores the measurements for simple reordering.[31]

Just-in-Time Manufacturing An important manufacturing process common today among manufacturers is just-in-time manufacturing. Borrowed from the Japanese, **just-in-time production** (**JIT**), sometimes called *lean production*, requires manufacturers to work closely with suppliers and transportation providers to get required items to the assembly line or factory floor at the precise time they are needed for production. For the manufacturer, JIT means that raw materials arrive at the assembly line in guaranteed working order "just in time" to be installed, and finished products are generally shipped to the customer immediately after completion. For the supplier, JIT means supplying customers with products in just a few days, or even a few hours, rather than weeks. For the ultimate consumer, JIT means lower costs, shorter lead times, and products that more closely meet their needs.

just-in-time production (JIT)
A process that redefines and simplifies manufacturing by reducing inventory levels and delivering raw materials just when they are needed on the production line.

JIT benefits manufacturers most by reducing their raw materials inventories. For example, at Dell Computer Corporation's Texas plant, computer components are often delivered just minutes before they are needed. Chips, boards, and drives are kept in trucks backed up into bays located fifty feet from the beginning of the production line. On average, the time it takes Dell to buy parts and sell them as a finished product is only eight days.[32] Similarly, Customized Transportation Inc., which is based in Jacksonville, Florida, provides General Motors' plant in Kansas City with automobile interior door-panel modules at the exact moment they are needed on the production line. Although GM selects the door supplier, CTI issues the purchase orders and buys the material from those vendors. CTI then assembles the door-panel modules, places them in racks and delivers them to the production line. CTI is linked to GM's real-time production system, so it knows where specific autos are in the production process. As soon as CTI is notified electronically that a car is out of the paint shop, it starts to build the panels for that specific vehicle to be delivered in four hours. This arrangement helps GM reduce inventory levels as well as manage its assets more wisely.[33]

Additionally, JIT shortens lead times—the time it takes to get parts from a supplier after an order has been placed. Manufacturers also enjoy better relationships with suppliers and can decrease their production and storeroom costs. Because there is little safety stock, and therefore no margin for error, the manufacturer cannot afford to make a mistake. As a result, a manufacturer using JIT must be sure it receives high-quality parts from all vendors and must be confident that the supplier will meet all delivery commitments. Finally, JIT tends to reduce the amount of paperwork.

Order Processing

The order is often the catalyst that brings the supply chain in motion, especially in the build-to-order environments of leading computer manufacturers such as Dell and Gateway. The **order processing system** processes the requirements of the customer and sends the information into the supply chain via the logistics information system. The order goes to the manufacturer's warehouse. If the order is in stock, the order is filled and arrangements are made to ship it. If the order is not in stock, it triggers a replenishment request that finds its way to the factory floor.

order processing system
A system whereby orders are entered into the supply chain and filled.

The role of proper order processing in providing good service cannot be overemphasized. As an order enters the system, management must monitor two flows: the flow of goods and the flow of information. Often the best-laid plans of marketers can get entangled in the order processing system. Obviously, good communication among sales representatives, office personnel, and warehouse and shipping personnel is essential to correct order processing. Shipping incorrect merchandise or partially filled orders can create just as much dissatisfaction as stockouts or slow deliveries. The flow of goods and information must be continually monitored so mistakes can be corrected before an invoice is prepared and the merchandise shipped.

On Line

Order processing is becoming more automated through the use of computer technology known as **electronic data interchange (EDI)**. The basic idea behind EDI is to replace the paper documents that usually accompany business transactions, such as purchase orders and invoices, with electronic transmission of the needed information. Companies that use EDI can reduce inventory levels, improve cash flow, streamline operations, and increase the speed and accuracy of information transmission. EDI is also believed to create a closer relationship between buyers and sellers.

It should not be surprising that retailers have become major users of EDI. For Wal-Mart, Target, Kmart, and the like, logistics speed and accuracy are crucial competitive tools in an overcrowded retail environment. Many big retailers are helping their suppliers acquire EDI technology so that they can be linked into the system. EDI works hand in hand with retailers' *efficient consumer response* programs, which are designed to have the right products on the shelf, in the right styles and colors, through improved inventory, ordering, and distribution techniques. (See Chapter 13 for more discussion of retailers' use of EDI techniques.)

Inventory Control

Closely interrelated to the procurement, manufacturing, and ordering processes is the **inventory control system**—a method that develops and maintains an adequate assortment of materials or products to meet a manufacturer's or a customer's demands.

Inventory decisions, for both raw materials and finished goods, have a big impact on supply chain costs and the level of service provided. If too many products are kept in inventory, costs increase—as do risks of obsolescence, theft, and damage. If too few products are kept on hand, then the company risks product shortages and angry customers, and ultimately lost sales. A study by Procter & Gamble found that out-of-stock products reduced consumer purchases by more than 3 percent per shopping trip, and 48 percent of P&G's products were out of stock at least once a month, costing the company valuable sales and customer satisfaction.[34] The goal of inventory management, therefore, is to keep inventory levels as low as possible while maintaining an adequate supply of goods to meet customer demand.

Managing inventory from the supplier to the manufacturer is called **materials requirement planning** (**MRP**), or **materials management**. This system also encompasses the sourcing and procurement operations, signaling purchasing when more raw materials, supplies, or components will need to be replenished for the production of more goods. Systems that manage the finished goods inventory from manufacturer to end user is commonly referred to as **distribution resource planning** (**DRP**). Both inventory systems use various inputs, such as sales forecasts, available inventory, outstanding orders, lead times, and mode of transportation to be used, to determine what actions must be taken to replenish goods at all points in the supply chain. Demand in the system is collected at each level in the supply chain, from the retailer back up the chain to the manufacturer. With the use of electronic data interchange, the transmission speed of the information can be greatly accelerated, thereby enhancing the quick-response needs of today's competitive marketplace.[35] Exhibit 12.10 provides an example of inventory replenishment using distribution resource planning from the retailer to the manufacturer.

Enhanced versions of DRP have emerged, especially in the retailing and supermarket industries, under the names of *continuous replenishment* (CR), *efficient consumer response* (ECR), and *vendor managed inventory* (VMI). Although these systems are beyond the scope of this discussion, all are designed to increase the

electronic data interchange (EDI)
Information technology that replaces the paper documents that usually accompany business transactions, such as purchase orders and invoices, with electronic transmission of the needed information to reduce inventory levels, improve cash flow, streamline operations, and increase the speed and accuracy of information transmission.

inventory control system
A method of developing and maintaining an adequate assortment of materials or products to meet a manufacturer's or a customer's demand.

materials requirement planning (MRP) (materials management)
An inventory control system that manages the replenishment of raw materials, supplies, and components from the supplier to the manufacturer.

distribution resource planning (DRP)
An inventory control system that manages the replenishment of goods from the manufacturer to the final consumer.

Exhibit 12.10

Inventory Replenishment Example

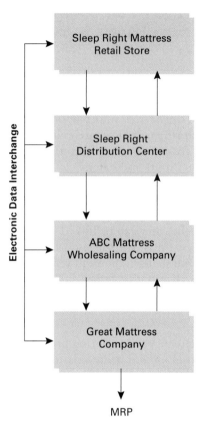

Sleep Right is planning a promotion on the Great Mattress Company's Gentle Rest mattress. Sales forecast is for fifty units to be sold. Sleep Right has ten open Gentle Rest orders with its distribution center. New mattresses must be delivered in two weeks in time for the promotion.

Sleep Right's Distribution Center is electronically notified of the order of fifty new Gentle Rest mattresses. It currently has twenty Gentle Rest mattresses in inventory and begins putting together the transportation plans to deliver these to the Sleep Right Store. Delivery takes one day. It orders forty new mattresses from its mattress wholesaler to make up the difference.

ABC Mattress Wholesaling Company is electronically notified of Sleep Right DC's order of forty new Gentle Rest mattresses. It currently does not have any of these in stock but electronically orders forty from the Great Mattress Company's factory. Once it receives the new mattresses, it can have them delivered to the Sleep Right DC in two days.

The Great Mattress Company electronically receives ABC's order and forwards it to the factory floor. Production of a new mattress takes twenty minutes. The total order of forty mattresses can be ready to be shipped to ABC in two days. Delivery takes one day. Raw material supplies for this order are electronically requested from Great Mattress's supply partners, who deliver the needed materials just-in-time to its stitching machines.

speed by which inventory needs can be communicated throughout the supply chain by utilizing information technology to migrate from pushing product down the supply chain to pulling inventory onto retailers' shelves driven by actual customer demand. The mechanics of CR, ECR, and VMI focus on increasing the flow and sharing of sensitive information across the distribution pipeline, which, in turn, accelerates the flow of product from the manufacturer to the point of sale. Procter & Gamble, for instance, estimates it has saved its retail partners, such as retail giant Wal-Mart, more than $65 million through more efficient logistics management resulting from such inventory control methods.[36]

Just-in-time manufacturing processes have had a significant impact on reducing inventory levels. Since JIT requires supplies to be delivered at the time they are needed on the factory floor, little inventory is needed. With JIT the purchasing firm can reduce the amount of raw materials and parts it keeps on hand by ordering more often and in smaller amounts. And lower inventory levels due to JIT can give firms a competitive edge through the flexibility to halt production of existing products in favor of those gaining popularity with consumers. Savings also come from less capital tied up in inventory and from the reduced need for storage facilities.[37]

Warehousing and Materials-Handling

Supply chain logisticians oversee the constant flow of raw materials from suppliers to manufacturer and finished goods from the manufacturer to the ultimate consumer. While just-in-time manufacturing processes may eliminate the need to warehouse many raw materials, manufacturers may often keep some safety stock on hand in the event of an emergency, such as a strike at a supplier's plant or a catastrophic event that temporarily stops the flow of raw materials to the production line. Likewise, the final user may not need or want the goods at the same time the manufacturer produces and wants to sell them. Products like grain and corn are produced seasonally, but consumers demand them year-round. Other products, such as Christmas ornaments and turkeys, are produced year-round, but consumers do not want them until autumn or winter. Therefore, management must have a storage system to hold these products until they are shipped.

Storage is what helps manufacturers manage supply and demand, or production and consumption. It provides time utility to buyers and sellers, which means that the seller stores the product until the buyer wants or needs it. Even when products are used regularly, not seasonally, many manufacturers store excess products in case the demand surpasses the amount produced at a given time. Storing additional product does have disadvantages, however, including the costs of insurance on the stored product, taxes, obsolescence or spoilage, theft, and warehouse operating costs. Another drawback is opportunity costs—that is, the lost opportunities of using for something else the money that is tied up in stored product.

A **materials-handling system** moves inventory into, within, and out of the warehouse. Materials handling includes these functions:

- Receiving goods into the warehouse or distribution center
- Identifying, sorting, and labeling the goods
- Dispatching the goods to a temporary storage area
- Recalling, selecting, or picking the goods for shipment (may include packaging the product in a protective container for shipping)

The goal of the materials-handling system is to move items quickly with minimal handling. With a manual, nonautomated materials-handling system, a product may be handled more than a dozen times. Each time it is handled, the cost and risk of damage increase; each lifting of a product stresses its package. Consequently, most manufacturers today have moved to automated systems. Scanners quickly identify goods entering and leaving a warehouse through bar-coded labels affixed to the packaging. Automatic storage and retrieval systems automatically store and pick goods in the warehouse or distribution center. Automated materials-handling systems decrease product handling and ensure accurate placement of product, as well as improve the accuracy of order picking and the rates of on-time shipment.

Fingerhut Companies, for example, operates warehouses and fills orders for the Web sites of Wal-Mart, eToys, Fingerhut, and other on-line merchants. Inside its sprawling St. Cloud, Minnesota, warehouse, every aspect of moving goods in and out is computerized down to the minutest detail. Every item's location in the warehouse is precisely charted. Computers scan each customer's order as it arrives, checking the dimensions of every item on the list to calculate the smallest possible box that can be used for shipping. Hundreds of employees whiz through the aisles on forklifts and cargo haulers, snatching goods off thousands of shelves and delivering them to packers who box the orders and drop them on conveyor belts. Every item has a special code indicating such things as weight (a heavy item is shipped by itself) or cost (a valuable item is shipped in disguise) to speed up packing. Red lasers then scan each package as it speeds past on the conveyor belt to make sure the packaging matches the product specifications. Packages that pass inspection are then routed to one of three dozen shipping bays, where trucks await to haul the goods for mailing points all over America. Fingerhut's high-tech warehouse operation has become one of the Internet's most efficient distribution centers, processing as many as 30,000 items in an hour.[38]

materials-handling system
A method of moving inventory into, within, and out of the warehouse.

Transportation

Transportation typically accounts for between 5 to 10 percent of the price of goods.[39] Supply chain logisticians must decide which mode of transportation to use to move products from supplier to producer and from producer to buyer.

These decision are, of course, related to all other logistics decisions. The five major modes of transportation are railroads, motor carriers, pipelines, water transportation, and airways. Supply chain managers generally choose a mode of transportation on the basis of several criteria:

- *Cost:* The total amount a specific carrier charges to move the product from the point of origin to the destination
- *Transit time:* The total time a carrier has possession of goods, including the time required for pickup and delivery, handling, and movement between the point of origin and the destination
- *Reliability:* The consistency with which the carrier delivers goods on time and in acceptable condition
- *Capability:* The ability of the carrier to provide the appropriate equipment and conditions for moving specific kinds of goods, such as those that must be transported in a controlled environment (for example, under refrigeration)
- *Accessibility:* A carrier's ability to move goods over a specific route or network
- *Traceability:* The relative ease with which a shipment can be located and transferred

The mode of transportation used depends on the needs of the shipper, as they relate to the six criteria described above. Exhibit 12.11 compares the basic modes of transportation on these criteria.

In many cases, especially in a just-in-time manufacturing environment, the transportation network replaces the warehouse or eliminates the expense of storing inventories as goods are timed to arrive the moment they're needed on the assembly line or for shipment to customers. Cisco Systems recently partnered with FedEx to coordinate all of Cisco's shipping and gradually eliminate virtually all of the company's warehousing needs by reducing inventory levels. Cisco traditionally inventoried finished goods from its factories in the United States, Mexico, Britain, and Asia so that the whole order could be shipped to the customer at once. But with Cisco's sales booming, the company did not want to continue building new warehouses, paying for reshipping, and owning tens of millions of dollars of inventory while it awaited shipment to the customer. FedEx helped Cisco formulate a plan to merge orders in transit. As many as a hundred different boxes destined for a single customer can now be shipped

Exhibit 12.11

Criteria for Ranking Modes of Transportation

	Highest				Lowest
Relative cost	Air	Truck	Rail	Pipe	Water
Transit time	Water	Rail	Pipe	Truck	Air
Reliability	Pipe	Truck	Rail	Air	Water
Capability	Water	Rail	Truck	Air	Pipe
Accessibility	Truck	Rail	Air	Water	Pipe
Traceability	Air	Truck	Rail	Water	Pipe

independently as soon as they are manufactured and assembled as they reach the customer's door.[40]

Balancing Logistics Service and Cost

Logistics service is the package of activities performed by a supply chain member to ensure that the right product is in the right place at the right time. Customers are rarely interested in the activities themselves; instead, they are interested in the results or the benefits they receive from those activities—namely, efficient distribution. At the most basic level, customers demand availability, timeliness, and quality. Specifically, customers expect product availability at the time of order, minimal effort required to place the order, prompt and consistent delivery, and undamaged goods when they are finally received.

Most supply chain managers try to set their service level at a point that maximizes service yet minimizes cost. To do so, they must examine the total cost of all parts of the supply chain—sourcing and procurement of raw materials, warehousing and materials handling, inventory control, order processing, and transportation—using the *total cost approach*. The basic idea of the total cost approach is to examine the relationship of factors such as cost of raw materials, number of warehouses, size of finished-goods inventory, and transportation expenses. Of course, the cost of any single element should also be examined in relation to the level of customer service. Thus, the supply chain is viewed as a whole, not as a series of unrelated activities.

Ideally, the supply chain manager would like to optimize overall logistics performance so that costs are minimized while the desired level of supply chain service is maintained. Consequently, implementing the total cost approach requires trade-offs. For example, a supplier that wants to provide next-day delivery to its customers and also to minimize transportation costs must make a trade-off between the desired level of service (expensive next-day delivery) and the transportation goal (minimal costs).

Often the high cost of air transportation can be justified under the total cost approach. Rapid delivery may drastically reduce the number of warehouses required at distant locations. Therefore, the higher cost of using air freight may be more than justified by the savings in inventory and warehouse expenses, as shown in Exhibit 12.12. The Limited uses a quick-response logistics infrastructure to respond to market information collected from actual point-of-sale data that tracks real-time consumer preferences. Premium air transportation is used for time-sensitive fashions to ensure immediate market availability, while basic articles of clothing are shipped by less costly means. The savings from reduced inventory levels make this a cost-effective solution.[41]

A new breed of supply chain managers, however, is decreasing the emphasis on reducing logistics costs to the lowest possible level. Instead, these managers are favoring the exploitation of logistics capabilities to increase customer satisfaction and maintain customer demand. According to the Global Logistics Research Team at Michigan State University, many firms are using their logistics capabilities to achieve business success. These firms are developing competencies that are "superior to competition in terms of satisfying customer expectations and requirements." They define world-class logistical competencies to include the following:

- Devising logistics service strategies to meet the specific requirements of customers as a way to position and differentiate themselves from the competition
- Integrating all members of the supply chain to achieve internal logistical operating excellence and development of external supply chain relationships
- Determining and responding quickly to changing logistical requirements

Discuss the concept of balancing logistics service and cost

logistics service
Interrelated activities performed by a member of the supply chain to ensure that the right product is in the right place at the right time.

Exhibit **12.12**

How Using Air Freight Lowers
Logistics Cost Under the Total
Cost Approach

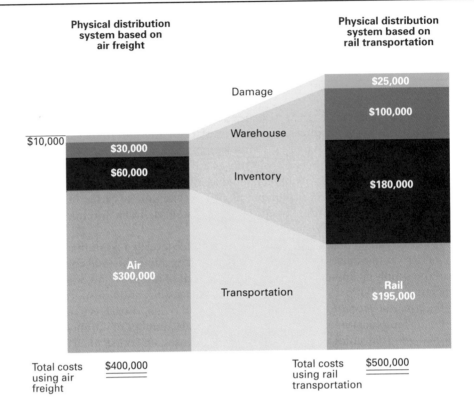

**Physical distribution
system based on
air freight**

**Physical distribution
system based on
rail transportation**

$25,000

Damage

$10,000

$100,000

$30,000

Warehouse

$60,000

Inventory

$180,000

Air
$300,000

Transportation

Rail
$195,000

Total costs
using air
freight $400,000

Total costs
using rail
transportation $500,000

- Constant monitoring of all internal and external aspects of the supply chain to ensure the right product is in the right place at the right time[42]

For example, warehousing facilities are increasingly providing value-added services that go well beyond mere storage. In the past, overnight delivery was considered an extra service for a warehouse to provide. Today, warehouses are more likely to engage in product-transformation services, such as custom palletization, kitting, repackaging, or even final assembly of a product.[43] A recent study by KPMG Management Consulting found that there is a growing belief among executives that the supply chain can contribute as much or more to corporate success than branding. Specifically, these companies believe that an efficiently managed supply chain can result in service excellence and this, ultimately, may mean more to customers than branding.[44]

Trends in Supply Chain Management

9

Discuss new technology and
emerging trends in supply
chain management

Several technological advances and business trends affect the job of the supply chain manager today. Three of the most outstanding trends are advanced computer technology, outsourcing of logistics functions, and electronic distribution.

Advanced Computer Technology

Advanced computer technology has boosted the efficiency of logistics dramatically with tools such as automatic identification systems (auto ID) using bar coding and radio-frequency technology, communications technology, and supply chain software systems that help synchronize the flow of goods and

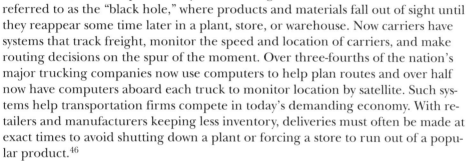

Matt Spangler and others are pictured here picking orders from the media cage at Amazon.com's Seattle distribution center. Amazon's command of the supply chain has translated into increased sales and customer satisfaction, but the company is still struggling to turn a profit.

information with customer demand. Amazon.com's state-of-the-art distribution centers, for instance, use sophisticated order picking systems that utilize computer terminals to guide workers through the picking and packing process. Radio-frequency technology, which uses radio signals that work with scanned bar codes identifying products, directs Amazon's workers to the exact locations in the warehouse where the product is stored. Warehouse management software examines pick rates, location, and picking and storage patterns, and builds combinations of customer orders for shipping. After installing these supply chain technology tools, Amazon saw a 70 percent improvement in operational efficiency.[45]

One of the major goals of technology is to bring up-to-date information to the supply chain manager's desk. For instance, the transportation system has long been referred to as the "black hole," where products and materials fall out of sight until they reappear some time later in a plant, store, or warehouse. Now carriers have systems that track freight, monitor the speed and location of carriers, and make routing decisions on the spur of the moment. Over three-fourths of the nation's major trucking companies now use computers to help plan routes and over half now have computers aboard each truck to monitor location by satellite. Such systems help transportation firms compete in today's demanding economy. With retailers and manufacturers keeping less inventory, deliveries must often be made at exact times to avoid shutting down a plant or forcing a store to run out of a popular product.[46]

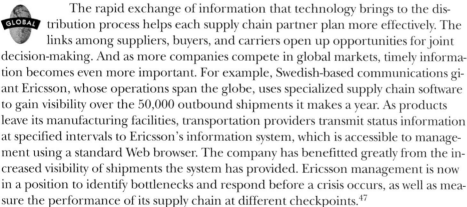 The rapid exchange of information that technology brings to the distribution process helps each supply chain partner plan more effectively. The links among suppliers, buyers, and carriers open up opportunities for joint decision-making. And as more companies compete in global markets, timely information becomes even more important. For example, Swedish-based communications giant Ericsson, whose operations span the globe, uses specialized supply chain software to gain visibility over the 50,000 outbound shipments it makes a year. As products leave its manufacturing facilities, transportation providers transmit status information at specified intervals to Ericsson's information system, which is accessible to management using a standard Web browser. The company has benefitted greatly from the increased visibility of shipments the system has provided. Ericsson management is now in a position to identify bottlenecks and respond before a crisis occurs, as well as measure the performance of its supply chain at different checkpoints.[47]

Outsourcing Logistics Functions

External partners are becoming increasingly important in the efficient deployment of supply chain management. **Outsourcing**, or **contract logistics**, is a rapidly growing segment of the distribution industry in which a manufacturer or supplier turns over the entire function of buying and managing transportation or another function of the supply chain, such as warehousing, to an independent third party. Many manufacturers are turning to outside partners for their logistics expertise in an effort to focus on the core competencies that they do best. Partners create and manage entire solutions for getting products where they need to be, when it needs to be there. Logistics partners offer staff, an infrastructure, and services that reach consumers virtually anywhere in the world. Because a logistics provider is focused, clients receive service in a timely efficient manner, thereby increasing customers'

outsourcing (contract logistics)
A manufacturer's or supplier's use of an independent third party to manage an entire function of the logistics system, such as transportation, warehousing, or order processing.

Peter Dobrow, president of Concept Blue, Inc., displays examples of envelopes with on-line postage and standard postage. Although Concept Blue regularly uses Stamps.com, the nascent industry of electronic stamp distribution is struggling to convince consumers to pay a premium for the convenience.

level of satisfaction and boosting their perception of added value to a company's offerings.[48] A recent study found that nearly 75 percent of U.S. manufacturers and suppliers are either using or considering using a third-party logistics service.[49]

Third-party contract logistics allows companies to cut inventories, locate stock at fewer plants and distribution centers, and still provide the same service level or even better. The companies then can refocus investment on their core business. Ford Motor Company decided to use third-party logistics provider UPS Worldwide Logistics Group to manage the delivery of Ford, Lincoln, and Mercury cars and trucks in the United States, Canada, and Mexico. The companies say they expect the alliance will reduce the time it takes to move vehicles from Ford's plants to dealers and customers by up to 40 percent. The alliance will also provide Web-based information systems that allow Ford and its dealers to track individual vehicle status from production through final delivery.[50]

Many firms are taking outsourcing one step further by allowing business partners to take over the final assembly of their product or its packaging in an effort to reduce inventory costs, speed up delivery, or meet customer requirements better. Ryder assembles and packages twenty-two different combinations of shrink-wrapped boxes that contain the ice trays, drawers, shelves, doors, and other accessories for the various refrigerator models Whirlpool sells. Before, Whirlpool would install the accessories in the refrigerators at the plant—a source of considerable factory-floor confusion.[51] IBM, for example, allows some of its distributors to do more of the final product assembly. Today, about 31 percent of its U.S. desktop personal computers are assembled by eleven business partners, many of whom may install non-IBM components. One reseller actually assembles some of its IBM orders in a warehouse right next to IBM's factory in North Carolina, saving on distribution costs.[52] For Nike's new athletic-equipment division, contract logistics provider Menlo Logistics inflates basketballs, soccer balls, and footballs, which come in half-inflated because they take up less room. The logistics company also puts the balls in colorful packages and sticks on price tags for some sports retailers.[53]

Electronic Distribution

Electronic distribution is the most recent development in the logistics arena. Broadly defined, **electronic distribution** includes any kind of product or service that can be distributed electronically, whether over traditional forms such as fiber optic cable or through satellite transmission of electronic signals. For instance, instead of buying and installing software from stores, computer users increasingly can purchase software over the Internet and download it electronically to their personal computers or rent the same software from Internet services that have the program available for use on their servers. For example, Intuit Inc. allows people to fill out their tax returns on its Web site rather than buying its TurboTax software.[54] Postage stamps can now be purchased on-line through E-Stamp, which uses a silver-dollar size "vault" attached to the purchaser's computer to keep track of postage purchases.[55] Similarly, on-line ticket companies and movie theaters have recently developed the technology to sell tickets to sporting events, concerts, and movies via the Internet, which consumers can print at home on a standard computer printer.[56] Digital technology is also revolutionizing the way music is distributed. Consumers can now download digital music files that can be played on their computer or portable players, often without paying for the music. This controversial form of electronic distribution is discussed in the "Ethics in Marketing" box.

electronic distribution
A distribution technique that includes any kind of product or service that can be distributed electronically, whether over traditional forms such as fiber optic cable or through satellite transmission of electronic signals.

MP3: ILLEGAL DISTRIBUTION OR FAIR USE?

Fueled by music fans around the world, the Internet is changing the distribution model of yet another industry, promising radical changes in the way consumers buy music and hear about new artists through the use of digital MP3 file technology.

MP3, an acronym for MPEG Audio Layer 3, is software that lets the music from a CD be transferred to a personal computer, where it can be played through speakers or shared with others over the Internet. The software compresses music into digital audio files that can then be played by hundreds of software programs as well as portable MP3 players. The MP3 format is very efficient—at its highest quality setting the music is nearly indistinguishable from a CD. An advantage to MP3 technology is that MP3 players play music files that are stored from its rewriteable memory rather than a compact disc. As a result, the devices never skip, making them a good option for listeners on the move. And MP3 players are smaller and weigh less than most cellular phones. One of the best things about MP3 players, however, is their customization capability. Users can create a personalized selection of songs by just dragging and dropping icons in a window. Songs can be deleted and arranged on a computer, after which they are transferred to the player through a parallel port connector or speedy USB port.

Finding tunes to fill the MP3 player's memory, however, is the controversial part of MP3's story. Hundreds of thousands of MP3 files are posted all over the Internet, thanks to music fans with a personal computer. Unsigned artists also distribute their music in MP3 format to increase their exposure. Using the shareware MP3 utility, thousands of users are connected over the Internet forming a communal library of freely shared music. Internet sites such as MP3.com, audiogalaxy, filequest, and scour.net have powerful search engines that comb the Web

searching for and categorizing MP3 files. Other sites, like Napster, allow users to download its free software, which indexes MP3 music files on the user's hard drive and makes them visible to other Napster users when connected to the Internet. From there, all it takes is a simple title or artist search to find other users from whom to download MP3 files, without paying for them. Downloading MP3 files takes a few minutes with a regular modem and only a few seconds with a high-speed Internet connection, like DSL or cable modems.

By 2003, industry experts predict that almost 6 million households will be digitally downloading music from the Internet. In fact, Napster has become such a sensation that it has been charged with clogging college computer networks with students who swap tunes relentlessly. Recently, Limp Bizkit's "I Know Why You Hate Me," the title track for *Mission: Impossible 2*, appeared on the Napster network days before Paramount released it on the movie's official Web site.

Not surprisingly, the MP3 explosion is driving the recording industry nuts since many of the MP3 files on the Web are pirated in violation of copyright law. Recording companies have a lot to lose from MP3 technology. Most importantly, it threatens to reduce the middleman role of the traditional record labels. Since their profits come from controlling the distribution of music from signed artists and receiving royalties for every CD purchased, record labels view the Internet and MP3 as facilitating the piracy of recorded music. In January 2000, the Recording Industry Association of America filed a lawsuit against Napster and MP3.com, claiming copyright infringement. Four months later, a federal judge ruled that MP3.com had indeed infringed on the copyrights of five big record companies with its My.MP3.com service that acts as a "virtual

locker," allowing people to listen to music they already own from MP3.com's database of more than 80,000 CDs.

Despite record label fears of piracy, a growing number of artists are eager to distribute their music in digital MP3 shareware format, believing it will create more opportunities for fledgling artists and may eventually lead to self-representation and generate higher royalties. Others feel that the Internet will help launch new artists who will then seek record contracts with the major labels. Proponents of MP3 argue that as with many other business models that have been turned upside down due to the Internet, the recording industry needs to rethink how it will distribute music in the wake of the Internet explosion.[a]

Should consumers be allowed "fair use" of music content on the Web without having to pay? What are the advantages of MP3 technology to artists? What are some advantages to recording companies? Predict what the future of music distribution will be like five years from now.

[a]Dana Blankenhorn, "MP3 Chorus Grows Louder," *Advertising Age*, March 20, 2000, p. s22; Lee Gomes, "Laying New Tracks: MP3 Is Transforming the Way Bands Build a Following; And the Way Record Companies Find Talent," *Wall Street Journal*, March 20, 2000, p. R14; Kraig Kujawa, "Music for the New Millennium; Portable MP3 Digital Music Players Are Already Making CDs Look Like 8-Track Tapes," *Chicago Tribune*, April 20, 2000, p. 5; Ken Yamada, "Shop Talk: Wake Up, Music Industry," On-line (**http://www.redherring.com**) May 2, 2000; Mike Snider, "Making Waves with an E-Music Strategy," *USA Today*, March 2, 2000, p. 3D; Lee Gomes, "Free Tunes for Everyone!" *Wall Street Journal*, June 15, 1999, pp. B1, B4; Jim Heid, "MP3 Fans Get New Players, Services—Will Squabbles Stop the Music?" *PC World Online*, May 1, 2000, p. 1; Martin Peers, "MP3.com Has Infringed on Copyrights of Five Record Firms, Judge Decides," *Wall Street Journal*, May 1, 2000, p. A3; Anna Wilde Mathews, "Web Music Isn't Just for Kids." *Wall Street Journal*, September 26, 2000, B1.

Channels and Distribution Decisions for Global Markets

Discuss channels and distribution decisions in global markets

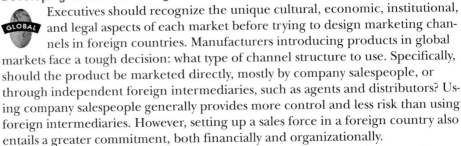

The world is indeed becoming a friendlier place for marketers. The surging popularity of free-market economics, such as the European Community and the North American Free Trade Agreement, over the past decade or so has swept away many barriers. As a result, businesses are finding that the world market is more appealing than ever. Thus, global marketing channels and management of the supply chain are important to U.S. corporations that export their products or manufacture abroad.

Developing Global Marketing Channels

Executives should recognize the unique cultural, economic, institutional, and legal aspects of each market before trying to design marketing channels in foreign countries. Manufacturers introducing products in global markets face a tough decision: what type of channel structure to use. Specifically, should the product be marketed directly, mostly by company salespeople, or through independent foreign intermediaries, such as agents and distributors? Using company salespeople generally provides more control and less risk than using foreign intermediaries. However, setting up a sales force in a foreign country also entails a greater commitment, both financially and organizationally.

Marketers should be aware that the channel structure abroad may not be very similar to channels in the United States. For instance, U.S. firms wishing to sell goods in Japan frequently must go through three layers of wholesalers and sub-wholesalers: the national or primary wholesalers, the secondary or regional wholesalers, and the local wholesalers. Amway succeeded in Japan by circumventing Japan's inefficient and expensive retail distribution system by offering alternative ways to shop via mail order catalogs and home visits by Amway distributors. Through its savvy distribution system, Amway Japan is one of that country's most profitable companies.[57]

The channel types available in foreign countries usually differ as well. The more highly developed a nation is economically, the more specialized its channel types. Therefore, a marketer wishing to sell in Germany or Japan will have several channel types to choose from. Conversely, developing countries like India, Ethiopia, and Venezuela have limited channel types available; there are typically few mail-order channels, vending machines, or specialized retailers and wholesalers.

Marketers must also be aware of "gray" marketing channels in many foreign countries, in which products are distributed through unauthorized channel intermediaries. For example, bootleg videocassette disk copies of the new *Star Wars* movie *Episode 1: The Phantom Menace* poured onto the streets of Hong Kong, Singapore, Kuala Lumpur, and Jakarta just days after its release in U.S. theaters. Most of the low-quality video disks were shot in U.S. theaters with hand-held video cameras, some even showing audience members getting up and down. With advances in technology and a continued thirst for U.S. films abroad, pirate video-making has become big business. According to the Motion Picture Association, film makers suffer over $550 million in lost sales each year. In 1998 alone, officials seized 42 million illegal video copies, up nearly tenfold from the previous year. It's unclear exactly how the smugglers got the disks on the market so fast, but new production methods have made video pirating easier and cheaper than ever before. Videocassette disks can be stamped out in three seconds and simple manufacturing lines can crank out hundreds of thousands of disks a day for less than 15 cents each. The disks are then distributed by air courier, truck, van, and even bicycle to Asian street retailers. Officials suspect that most of the pirated copies were produced in Malaysia where lax law enforcement, low labor costs, and its central location in Asia makes it a hub for the gray market movie industry.[58]

The Internet has also proved to be a way for pirates to circumvent authorized distribution channels, especially in the case of popular prescription drugs. The U.S. Customs Service reports that its seizures of prescription drugs have skyrocketed in recent years due mostly to consumers ordering drugs from foreign Internet sites. In 1999, custom officials seized 1.9 million pills improperly brought into the United States, some because they hadn't been approved for use in the United States, others because they didn't comply with U.S. labeling laws.[59] Of the 500 or so on-line drug sites, most offer just a handful of the most popular drugs, like Viagra and the diet drug Xenical, which consumers can get following approval by a doctor who is affiliated with the site and who never sees the patient. The drugs find their way to on-line drug companies when drug manufacturers sell their drugs to wholesalers, who in turn sell to nontraditional pharmacies.[60]

Global Logistics and Supply Chain Management

As global trade becomes a more decisive factor in success or failure for firms of all sizes, a well-thought-out global logistics strategy becomes ever more important. Uncertainty regarding shipping usually tops the list of reasons why companies, especially smaller ones, resist international markets. Even companies that have scored overseas successes often are vulnerable to logistical problems. Large companies have the capital to create global logistics systems, but smaller companies often must rely on the services of carriers and freight forwarders to get their products to overseas markets. The Internet, however, is making it easier for many companies to deal with global supply chain management issues. Some companies are using Web-based applications to communicate more easily with their global partners, as is shown in the "Global Perspectives" box.

One of the most critical global logistical issues for importers of any size is coping with the legalities of trade in other countries. Shippers and distributors must be aware of the permits, licenses, and registrations they may need to acquire and, depending on the type of product they are importing, the tariffs, quotas, and other regulations that apply in each country. Another important factor to consider is the transportation infrastructure in a country. For example, Russia has limited transportation infrastructure outside the major cities, such as roads that can withstand heavy freight trucks, and few reliable transportation companies of any type. In China, post offices aren't equipped for bulk mailings and they don't deliver parcels to residential addresses. So Germany's Bertelsmann Book Club created its own crew of seventy bicycle-riding deliverymen in Shanghai to deliver books to book club members.[61] Recall the freight train example from Chapter 4. In Europe, shipping freight by rail can be an excruciating experience for supply chain managers since no two European countries use the same signaling systems or electric current for their trains. Freight trains crossing borders must often stop to change locomotives and drivers before resuming their journeys. Trains in France and Britain run on the left side of dual-track lines, while those in the rest of Europe run on the right. And because France and Spain use two different gauges of track, trains crossing their shared border must stop to let each car be lifted so the wheels can be changed.[62]

Other emerging countries have similar situations. In Nigeria, for example, a crumbling road system, aging trucks, and safety concerns forced Nestlé to rethink its traditional distribution methods. Instead of operating a central warehouse, the company built small warehouses across the country. For safety reasons, trucks carrying Nestlé goods are allowed to travel only during daylight hours, frequently

THE INTERNET BRINGS GLOBAL LOGISTICS CLOSER TOGETHER

 Internet technologies are making it easier for global supply chain managers to ship products around the world, helping companies large and small manage their increasingly complex global fulfillment strategies. More and more, global logistics strategies will intertwine traditional distribution methods with the real-time capabilities of the Internet, allowing global supply chain managers to more efficiently move products around the world. Two such Internet technologies that are causing a stir in the world of global supply chain management are Web-enabled supply chain management systems and global transportation exchanges.

While large companies still rely heavily on electronic data interchange (EDI) to transmit and receive order requests along the supply chain, small and midsize manufacturers in the far reaches of Asia, Latin America, and the Caribbean are relatively low-tech companies and don't possess the financial means or the technological sophistication to handle EDI. Internet technologies, such as Java and the Extensible Markup Language (XML), are playing a larger role in developing systems to exchange information among global companies and their partners in the far-flung reaches of the world. Home Depot, the $38.4 billion Atlanta-based home-improvement retailer, for instance, partners with some three hundred overseas manufacturers. The retailer uses a payment system accessible from the Internet that caters to its small suppliers who don't have the capability to use EDI. Another example is Lexington,

Massachusetts–based Stride Rite Corporation, the $573 million retailer of children's athletic and casual footwear. The shoe company buys nearly all of its shoes from overseas manufacturers, mostly independently owned footwear makers in China. Its on-line order management system allows Stride Rite service reps to track specific orders for their customers from the time the shipment leaves the Far East until it arrives at the warehouse doors.

Cisco recently realized the need to streamline its supply chain between the company's San Jose, California, plant and its European customers with an Internet solution. Cisco's European customers previously had been responsible for handling freight movement from the San Jose shipping dock to their final destinations in Europe. This system, however, meant that Cisco's shipping area suffered from intense congestion as more than 150 customers crowded the dock to pick up shipments. Cisco partnered with UPS Worldwide Logistics to help unclog the congestion by coordinating deliveries to UPS's European distribution center where customer fulfillment now occurs. UPS integrates Cisco shipment information into its own Logistics Management System, which is accessible from the Internet. Cisco employees can now go to the UPS Web site at any time to review and update the status of orders.

Global transportation exchanges are another recent phenomenon credited to today's increasingly connected world. With the explosion of worldwide trade, due in large part to the explosion of Internet-based companies, organizations that exist primarily or entirely

on the Internet, supply chain managers more than ever need the information necessary to determine the most cost-effective shipping method. By leveraging the near-universal reach of the Internet, transportation exchanges seek to match carriers and their available space to manufacturers and distributors looking to keep goods flowing seamlessly through the supply chain. On the Celarix.com transportation exchange, for instance, more than seventy shippers and ten ocean carriers actively post real-time cargo and available space. Kitchenware retailer Williams-Sonoma, which ships its products to fifty-two different countries, uses the exchange to help reduce the time spent negotiating transportation contracts with foreign carriers. The flexibility allows Williams-Sonoma to better respond to the natural peaks and valleys inherent to retailing.[a]

What other global supply chain components could be streamlined using Internet applications? What are the benefits of an Internet exchange that brings shippers and transportation carriers around the world together? What might be some disadvantages?

[a]Eric Chabrow, "Supply Chains Go Global—The Internet Levels the Geographic Playing Field and Lets Companies Reach Into the Farthest Corners of the Planet for Partners and Customers," *Information Week*, April 3, 2000, p. 50; John Day, "They Do More Than Carry the Load—Third-Party Logistics Providers Evolve into Supply-Chain Partners," *Electronic Buyers' News*, January 10, 2000, p. 57; Rick Gurin, "Global Communities Seek Even Tighter Bonds: The Internet Is Playing a Key Role as Companies Seek to Adjust Worldwide Fulfillment Strategies," *Automatic I.D. News*, November 1999, p. 51.

under armed guard.[63] Similarly, a wave of coffee heists from trucks and warehouses in Brazil prompted coffee exporters to develop new safety systems in the supply chain. Most Brazilian coffee exporters now send their coffee on the road in convoys of at least three trucks, do not allow travel at night, and have equipped drivers with cellular phones. They are even prepared to send a security car with the convoy if necessary.[64]

Channels and Distribution Decisions for Services

The fastest-growing part of our economy is the service sector. Although distribution in the service sector is difficult to visualize, the same skills, techniques, and strategies used to manage inventory can also be used to manage service inventory—for instance, hospital beds, bank accounts, or airline seats. The quality of the planning and execution of distribution can have a major impact on costs and customer satisfaction.

Identify the special problems and opportunities associated with distribution in service organizations

One thing that sets service distribution apart from traditional manufacturing distribution is that, in a service environment, production and consumption are simultaneous. In manufacturing, a production setback can often be remedied by using safety stock or a faster mode of transportation. Such substitution is not possible with a service. The benefits of a service are also relatively intangible—that is, you can't normally see the benefits of a service, such as a doctor's physical exam. But a consumer can normally see the benefits provided by a product—for example, a vacuum cleaner removing dirt from the carpet.

Because service industries are so customer-oriented, customer service is a priority. Service distribution focuses on three main areas:

- *Minimizing wait times:* Minimizing the amount of time customers wait in line to deposit a check, wait for their food at a restaurant, or wait in a doctor's office for an appointment is a key factor in maintaining the quality of service. People tend to overestimate the amount of time they spend waiting in line, researchers report, and unexplained waiting seems longer than explained waits. To reduce anxiety among waiting customers, some restaurants give patrons pagers that allow them to roam around or go to the bar. Banks sometimes install electronic boards displaying stock quotes or sports scores. Car rental companies reward repeat customers by eliminating their waits altogether.[65] Airports have designed comfortable sitting areas with televisions and children's play areas for those waiting to board planes. Some service companies are using sophisticated technology to further ease their customers' waiting time. A quarter of Alaska Airline's thirteen million customers, for instance, now check in for flights from their own personal computers or at computerized airport kiosks that ask the required security questions, determine seat preferences, and print boarding passes. In Anchorage, the carrier has also introduced a related technology device that allows its passengers to tag and check their own luggage so they don't have to stand in line waiting for a clerk.[66] Similarly, many hotels are experimenting with electronic check-in kiosks. Travelers can insert their credit

Gas stations have recently hit upon a great way to reduce the time a customer spends at the pump. Mobile Speed Pass allows the user to electronically and automatically pay at the pump by waving a coded key fob near the reader on the gas pump. Reduced time paying for gas means that stations can sell gasoline almost as fast as customers can pump.

cards to check in upon arrival to receive their room key, get directions and print maps to area restaurants and attractions, and print out their hotel bills.[67]

- *Managing service capacity:* For product manufacturers, inventory acts as a buffer, enabling them to provide the product during periods of peak demand without extraordinary efforts. Service firms don't have this luxury. If they don't have the capacity to meet demand, they must either turn down some prospective customers, let service levels slip, or expand capacity. For instance, at tax time a tax preparation firm may have so many customers desiring its services that it has to either turn business away or add temporary offices or preparers. Popular restaurants risk losing business when seating is unavailable or the wait is too long.

- *Improving delivery through new distribution channels:* Like manufacturers, service firms are now experimenting with different distribution channels for their services. These new channels can increase the time that services are available (such as using the Internet to disseminate information and services twenty-four hours) or add to customer convenience (like pizza delivery, walk-in medical clinics, or a dry cleaner located in the supermarket). For example, many banks are experimenting with mobile bank branches. The South Side Bank & Trust Company in Peoria, Illinois, sends a mobile bank branch to retirement homes in the area. These scheduled weekly stops assist senior citizens who may not have reliable transportation. The modified motor home is equipped with wireless communication, bank security, ATM, safe, check protector, laser printer, and fax.[68]

The Internet is fast becoming an alternative channel through which to deliver services. Consumers can now purchase plane tickets, plan a vacation cruise, reserve a hotel room, pay bills, purchase mutual funds, and receive electronic newspapers in cyberspace. Insurance giant Allstate, for instance, now sells car and home insurance directly to consumers in some states through the Internet in addition to its traditional network of agents. The effort reduces costs so that Allstate can stay competitive with rival insurance companies Progressive and Geico that already target customers directly.[69] Similarly, airlines are steering more of their customers to their Web sites to purchase tickets to keep down distribution costs. Compared to traditional ticket sales that involve high labor expenses, it costs airlines little to sell tickets on-line. Additionally, there are no travel agent commissions or computer reservation system fees. These sites also provide travelers with information on prices, flight availability, and frequent-flier accounts.[70]

Looking Back

As you complete this chapter, you should be able to see how marketing channels operate and how supply chain management is necessary to move goods from the manufacturer to the final consumer. Companies can choose from several different marketing channels to sell their products. For example, as the opening story discussed, Webvan is turning the traditional grocery industry upside down as it revolutionizes selling groceries and other goods through the Internet. Shoppers can now surf Webvan's Web site to purchase milk and bread instead of traveling to their nearest grocery or convenience store, thus eliminating traditional retailing intermediaries.

Buy Your Textbooks Through a Direct Marketing Channel

Save money and valuable loafing or study time by buying your textbooks from on-line textbook sellers, such as Big Words (**bigwords.com**), **ecampus. com**, or **VarsityBooks.com**. These sites provide students with the right textbooks, at the right price, right in time for classes to begin. And, instead of having to wait in line at the bookstore with your course curriculum, you can zap your book list to any of the cyber-bookstores that work with your school and then have them delivered directly to your dorm room. Since approximately nine out of ten of the fifteen million students enrolled in higher-education institutions use the Internet, buying textbooks on-line is a natural fit.

Have a Product You Want to Sell on the Web?

Specialized Web sites can help you set up an e-commerce site with minimal effort and cost. Sites such as **BizLand.com**, **Bigstep.com**, and **Go2Net** help small business owners create e-commerce Web sites where purchases can be accepted on-line with a credit card. BizLand's site, for instance, provides free on-line storefronts and shopping carts, custom domain names, e-mail, business promotional tools, site monitoring, plus lots more. Easy-to-use software helps merchants build and maintain catalogs of products and services to sell over the Internet. The sites are becoming very popular; Bizland's membership swelled to over 500,000 small business owners from all fifty states plus 150 countries in just one year.

Summary

① **Explain what a marketing channel is and why intermediaries are needed.** A marketing channel is a business structure of interdependent organizations that reach from the point of product origin to the consumer with the purpose of physically moving products to their final consumption destination, representing "place" in the marketing mix and encompassing the processes involved in getting the right product to the right place at the right time. Members of a marketing channel create a continuous and seamless supply chain that performs or supports the marketing channel functions. Channel members provide economies to the distribution process in the form of specialization and division of labor, overcoming discrepancies in quantity, assortment, time, and space, and providing contact efficiency.

② **Define the types of channel intermediaries and describe their functions and activities.** The most prominent difference separating intermediaries is whether or not they take title to the product, such as retailers and merchant wholesalers. Retailers are firms that sell mainly to consumers. Merchant wholesalers are those organizations that facilitate the movement of products and services from the manufacturer to producers, resellers, governments, institutions, and retailers. Agents and brokers, on the other hand, do not take title to goods and services they market but do facilitate the exchange of ownership between sellers and buyers. Channel intermediaries perform three basic types of functions. Transactional functions include contacting and promoting, negotiating, and risk taking. Logistical functions performed by channel members include physical distribution, storing, and sorting functions. Finally, channel members may perform facilitating functions, such as researching and financing.

③ **Describe the channel structures for consumer and business-to-business products and discuss alternative channel arrangements.** Marketing channels for consumer and business-to-business products vary in degree of complexity. The simplest consumer product channel involves direct selling from producers to consumers. Businesses may sell directly to business or government buyers. Marketing channels grow more complex as intermediaries become involved. Consumer product channel intermediaries include agents, brokers, wholesalers, and retailers.

Business product channel intermediaries include agents, brokers, and industrial distributors. Marketers often use alternative channel arrangements to move their products to the consumer. With dual distribution or multiple distribution, they choose two or more different channels to distribute the same product. Nontraditional channels help differentiate a firm's product from the competitor's or provide a manufacturer with another avenue for sales. Finally, strategic channel alliances are arrangements that use another manufacturer's already established channel.

4 **Define supply chain management and discuss its benefits.** Supply chain management coordinates and integrates all of the activities performed by supply chain members into a seamless process from the source to the point of consumption. The responsibilities of a supply chain manager include developing channel design strategies, managing the relationships of supply chain members, sourcing and procurement of raw materials, scheduling production, processing orders, managing inventory and storing product, and selecting transportation modes. The supply chain manager is also responsible for managing customer service and the information that flows through the supply chain. The benefits of supply chain management include reduced costs in inventory management, transportation, warehousing, and packaging; improved service through techniques like time-based delivery and make-to-order; and enhanced revenues, which result from such supply chain–related achievements as higher product availability and more customized products

5 **Discuss the issues that influence channel strategy.** When determining marketing channel strategy, the supply chain manager must determine what market, product, and producer factors will influence the choice of channel. The manager must also determine the appropriate level of distribution intensity. Intensive distribution is distribution aimed at maximum market coverage. Selective distribution is achieved by screening dealers to eliminate all but a few in any single area. The most restrictive form of market coverage is exclusive distribution, which entails only one or a few dealers within a given area.

6 **Explain channel leadership, conflict, and partnering.** Power, control, leadership, conflict, and partnering are the main social dimensions of marketing channel relationships. Channel power refers to the capacity of one channel member to control or influence other channel members. Channel control occurs when one channel member intentionally affects another member's behavior. Channel leadership is the exercise of authority and power. Channel conflict occurs when there is a clash of goals and methods among the members of a distribution channel. Channel conflict can be either horizontal, among channel members at the same level, or vertical, among channel members at different levels of the channel. Channel partnering is the joint effort of all channel members to create a supply chain that serves customers and creates a competitive advantage. Collaborating channel partners meet the needs of consumers more effectively by ensuring the right products reach shelves at the right time and at a lower cost, boosting sales and profits.

7 **Describe the logistical components of the supply chain.** The logistics supply chain consists of several interrelated and integrated logistical components: (1) sourcing and procurement of raw materials and supplies; (2) production scheduling; (3) order processing; (4) inventory control; (5) warehousing and materials-handling; and (6) transportation. Integrating and linking all of the logistics functions of the supply chain is the logistics information system. Information technology connects the various components and partners of the supply chain into an integrated whole. The supply chain team, in concert with the logistics information system, orchestrates the movement of goods, services, and information from the source to the consumer. Supply chain teams typically cut across organizational boundaries, embracing all parties who participate in moving product to market. Procurement deals with the purchase of raw materials, supplies, and components according to production scheduling. Order processing monitors the flow of goods and information (order entry and order handling). Inventory control systems regulate when and how much to buy (order timing and order quantity) Warehousing provides storage of goods until needed by the customer while the materials-handling system moves inventory into, within, and out of the warehouse. Finally, the major modes of transportation include railroads, motor carriers, pipelines, waterways, and airways.

8 **Discuss the concept of balancing logistics service and cost.** Today, logistics service is recognized as an area in which a firm can distinguish itself from the competition. Many supply chain managers strive to achieve an optimal balance of customer service and total distribution cost. Important aspects of service are availability of product, timeliness of deliveries, and quality (accuracy and condition) of shipments. In evaluating costs, supply chain managers examine all parts of the supply chain using the total cost approach. Many supply chain managers are decreasing their emphasis on reducing logistics costs to the lowest possible level in favor of exploiting logistics capabilities to increase customer satisfaction and maintain customer demand.

9 **Discuss new technology and emerging trends in supply chain management.** Several trends are emerging that affect the job of today's supply chain manager. Technology and automation are bringing up-to-date distribution information to the decision maker's desk. Technology is also linking suppliers, buyers, and carriers for joint decision making, and it has created a new electronic distribution channel. Many companies are saving money and time by outsourcing third-party carriers to handle some or all aspects of the distribution process.

10 **Discuss channels and distribution decisions in global markets.** Global marketing channels are becoming more important to U.S. companies seeking growth abroad. Manufacturers introducing products in foreign countries must decide what type of channel structure to use—in particular, whether the product should be marketed through direct channels or through foreign intermediaries. Marketers should be aware that channel structures in foreign markets may be very different from those they are accustomed to in the United States. Global distribution expertise is also emerging as an important skill for supply chain managers as many countries are removing trade barriers.

11 **Identify the special problems and opportunities associated with distribution in service organizations.** Managers in service industries use the same skills, techniques, and strategies to manage logistics functions as managers in goods-producing industries. The distribution of services focuses on three main areas: minimizing wait times, managing service capacity, and improving delivery through new distribution channels.

Discussion and Writing Questions

1. Describe the most likely marketing channel structure for each of these consumer products: candy bars, Tupperware products, nonfiction books, new automobiles, farmer's market produce, and stereo equipment. Now, construct alternative channels for these same products.

2. Discuss the reasons intermediaries are important to the distribution of most goods. What important functions do they provide?

3. INFOTRAC COLLEGE EDITION Dell Computers successfully uses a direct channel to sell computers and equipment it manufactures to consumers over the telephone and Internet. How has Dell affected traditional computer retailers with brick-and-mortar buildings? How have other computer manufacturers,

Key Terms

agents and brokers 382
channel conflict 395
channel control 394
channel leader (channel captain) 394
channel members 380
channel partnering (channel cooperation) 397
channel power 394
direct channel 385
discrepancy of assortment 380
discrepancy of quantity 380
distribution resource planning (DRP) 401
dual distribution (multiple distribution) 387
electronic data interchange (EDI) 401
electronic distribution 408
exclusive distribution 393
horizontal conflict 395
intensive distribution 392
inventory control system 401
just-in-time production (JIT) 400
logistics 383
logistics information system 398
logistics service 405
marketing channel (channel of distribution) 380
mass customization (build-to-order) 399
materials-handling system 403
materials requirement planning (MRP) (materials management) 401
merchant wholesaler 382
order processing system 400
outsourcing (contract logistics) 407
retailer 382
selective distribution 393
spatial discrepancy 381
strategic channel alliance 388
supply chain 380
supply chain management 388
supply chain team 398
temporal discrepancy 381
vertical conflict 396

such as Compaq and IBM, countered Dell's competitive advantage in its direct channel? Use Infotrac (**http://www.infotrac-college.com**) to search for articles on this topic. You may also need to consult your campus library's databases on companies and articles to search for this information.

4. Decide which distribution intensity level—intensive, selective, or exclusive— are used for the following products, and why: Rolex watches, Land Rover sport utility vehicles, M&Ms, special edition Barbie dolls, Crest toothpaste.

5. **WRITING** You have been hired to design an alternative marketing channel for a firm specializing in the manufacturing and marketing of novelties for college student organizations. In a memo to the president of the firm, describe how the channel operates.

6. Discuss the benefits of supply chain management. How does the implementation of supply chain management result in enhanced customer value?

7. Discuss the trade-offs between logistics service and cost. How can the high cost of expensive air transportation to enhance service be offset? How does logistics service impact customer satisfaction?

8. Discuss the impact of just-in-time production on the entire supply chain. Specifically, how does JIT affect suppliers, procurement planning, inventory levels, mode of transportation selected, and warehousing? What are the benefits of JIT to the end consumer?

9. Assume that you are the supply chain manager for a producer of expensive, high-tech computer components. Identify the most suitable method(s) of transporting your product in terms of cost, transit time, reliability, capability, accessibility, and traceability. Now, assume you are the supply chain manager for a producer of milk. How does this change your choice of transportation?

10. **WRITING** Assume that you are the marketing manager of a hospital. Write a report indicating the distribution functions that concern you. Discuss the similarities and dissimilarities of distribution for services and for goods.

11. **ON LINE** Visit the Web site of Menlo Logistics at **http://www.menlolog.com**. What logistics functions can this third-party logistics supplier provide? How does its mission fit in with the supply chain management philosophy?

12. **INFOTRAC COLLEGE EDITION** **WRITING** Use InfoTrac (**http://www.infotrac-college.com**) to locate the following article in the June 12, 2000 issue of *Computerworld* magazine: "Filling Orders a Hot E-Business: Companies Race to Offer Logistics Services" by Julia King. Read the article and write a summary of the implications of Internet commerce on U.S. transportation and logistics industries.

13. **INFOTRAC COLLEGE EDITION** How are transportation and logistics issues handled around the world? To find out, consult the *Transportation Journal* using InfoTrac (**http://www.infotrac-college.com**). Create a grid comparing at least two countries according to standard procedures, particular challenges faced, and creative solutions to problems they have encountered.

Application for Entrepreneurs

ENTREPRENEUR Boudreaux has owned and operated a small spice-manufacturing business in south Louisiana for about ten years. Boudreaux has also experimented with preparing and selling several sauces, mostly for meats and salads. For the most part, the firm has sold its products locally. But on occasion, distributors have signed contracts to sell Boudreaux's products regionally. Boudreaux's most recent product—a spicy Cajun mayonnaise—has been a huge success locally, and several inquiries have come from large distributors about the possibilities of selling the mayonnaise regionally and perhaps nationally. No research has been conducted to determine the level or scope of demand for the mayonnaise. Also, it has been packaged and sold in only a twelve-ounce bottle. The red-and-white label just says "Boudreaux's Cajun Mayonnaise" and lists the major ingredients.

Questions

1. What should Boudreaux do to help the firm decide how best to market the new Cajun mayonnaise?
2. Should Boudreaux sign a contract with one of the distributors to sell the Cajun mayonnaise, or should his firm try to sell the product directly to one or more of the major supermarket chains?

Case

entrepreneurship

CarsDirect.com: Driving Car Buyers to the Internet

CarsDirect.com is heating up the new car industry. The country's first direct broker of cars on the Internet has sent auto makers, on-line-buying services, and dealer groups scrambling to control the growing number of customers going on-line to shortcut the traditional process of shopping for new and used vehicles. The Internet startup has sparked a flurry of copycat Web sites dedicated to the direct-to-consumer purchase of cars, like CarOrder.com, DriveOff.com, Carpoint.com, and Greenlight.com.

Backed by Michael Dell's personal investment firm, CarsDirect.com was conceived by Bill Gross, chairman of Idealab, a venture incubator that has also launched other Internet successes, such as eToys, Tickets.com, and Cooking.com. After becoming frustrated with his own efforts at buying an auto on-line, Gross realized that current Internet options for car buying were not only inadequate but did nothing to leverage available technology on behalf of the consumer. At the time of his search, on-line car sites functioned only as lead generators for local dealers, requiring him to close the sale of his car the old-fashioned way: haggling at the dealership with the untrustworthiest of people—a car salesman.

His vision, CarsDirect.com, sells cars entirely through the Internet, allowing consumers to bypass traditional car dealers in their negotiations. As a car broker, CarsDirect.com offers Web buyers a car at a fixed price based on recent average selling prices. Then, CarsDirect.com works through its network of existing dealers to get the car at that price. Since CarsDirect.com doesn't hold franchise agreements with any car manufacturers, consumers enjoy an impartial and unbiased shopping experience as well as an unrivaled selection. In contrast, buying cars the old-fashioned way makes consumers travel from car dealer to car dealer looking for the models they are interested in or the best price.

Car buyers visiting CarsDirect.com can research a car by searching the site's extensive database, which provides objective information on price, performance, and options for more than 2,500 different makes and models—virtually every production vehicle available in the United States. CarsDirect.com's research tools let buyers compare the features of vehicles and see in seconds the manufacturer's suggested retail price, the invoice, and, most importantly, the price CarsDirect.com can get for them. If a consumer wants to buy, payment is arranged completely on-line to close the deal. Financing options are provided through CarsDirect.com's financial partner Bank One, the nation's fifth-largest bank and a major automotive lender. Then, the buyer

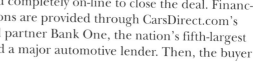

Still Shaky? Here's a tip

In the margin next to each paragraph or section in the chapter, write the question that the section answers. For example, "What discrepancies do marketing channels aid in overcoming?" could go on page 380. Once you have questions throughout the chapter, you can quiz yourself by using a blank piece of paper to cover the content. To check yourself, reveal each paragraph after you have answered the corresponding question.

can arrange for delivery of the vehicle at home or the office or pick it up from a local automotive retailer.

With on-line auto sales expected to reach about 5 percent of total sales by 2000, there are still big hurdles ahead for car brokers like CarsDirect.com. General Motors, for instance, recently warned its 7,700 dealers to cease and desist from using on-line car-buying sites like CarsDirect.com. The largest obstacle, however, is the myriad of state franchise laws that protect car dealers and restrict direct sales of automobiles. Car brokers have found that no two states' franchise laws are the same, and many include rules that are arcane or impractical. Texas, the nation's second biggest automotive market, has the most restrictive dealer-protection laws in the country. There, only state-licensed dealers can sell cars. Brokering of cars to consumers by anyone other than a dealer is strictly prohibited. As a result, car brokers have had to redesign their direct-sales model around Texas laws. CarsDirect.com, for instance, currently does not offer cars to residents of Texas. Often, instead of trying to bypass dealers, Internet car brokers are forming alliances with dealers or reworking their strategies to become more dealer-friendly to comply with state law.

Questions

1. Explain how CarsDirect.com fits into the channel structure for car retailing to consumers.
2. How has CarsDirect.com's selling model caused channel conflict?
3. Visit CarsDirect.com's Web site at **http://www.carsdirect.com**. Give examples of how its Web site simplifies the car-buying process for consumers.

Bibliography

CarsDirect.com Web site at **http://www.carsdirect.com**.

Robert Elder Jr. and Jonathan Weil. "To Sell Cars in Texas, Online Firms Are Forced to Enter the Real World." *Wall Street Journal*, January 26, 2000, pp. T1, T4.

Maynard M. Gordon. "Battle Lines Forming in the Wild World of the Automotive Web Sites." *Ward's Dealer Business*, June 1, 2000, p. 12.

Chris Knap. "Online Car Sales Will Rise, Analysts Say." *KRTBN Knight-Ridder Tribune Business News: The Orange County Register—California*, September 19, 1999.

Jennifer Montgomery. "Texas State Law Bars Residents from Buying Cars Online," *KRTBN Knight-Ridder Tribune Business News: Houston Chronicle—Texas*, March 19, 2000.

Fara Warner. "Racing for Slice of a $350 Billion Pie, Online Auto-Sales Sites Retool." *Wall Street Journal*, January 24, 2000, pp. B1, B6.

———. "New Tactics Shake Up Online Auto Retailing." *Wall Street Journal*, October 18, 1999, p. B1.

———. "CarsDirect.com Bets on One-Stop, Desktop Showroom." *Wall Street Journal*, May 17, 1999, p. B4.

Scott Woolley. "A Car Dealer by Any Other Name." *Forbes*, November 29, 1999, pp. 113–116.

Case

video

Burton Snowboards: Going Global

Burton Snowboards is a designer and manufacturer of premier snowboarding equipment, and since its somewhat humble start in 1977, the company has grown from a single workshop in Vermont into an international retailer. Higher sales require a more involved distribution system, so in 1992, Burton relocated its offices to Burlington, Vermont. Because Burlington offered easy access to an international airport, a larger workforce, and more business services, Burton expected to achieve better distribution of its products from its new headquarters. In conjunction with smaller offices in Austria and Japan, the Burlington office links Burton to retailers and consumers in the United States and abroad. Although Burton does all its manufacturing in Vermont, it has warehouses in Vermont, New York, Europe, and Asia.

In order to reach the maximum number of customers, Burton uses dual distribution. This means that it sells the same products to snowboarders through direct and indirect marketing channels. One outlet in its direct marketing strategy is its headquarters in Burlington, where Burton sells to roughly one hundred customers a day. The headquarters houses the manufacturing facility, offices, and a factory showroom, whose retail store sells everything Burton makes, from hard goods to soft goods. The hard-good line includes snowboards, bindings, boots, board and travel bags, and back packs, and the soft goods are five categories of specially designed clothing made from highly breathable and highly waterproof insulated fabrics. Direct marketing of products is also handled through mail order, catalog shopping, and on-line Internet retailing. The latest addition to the company's direct marketing efforts, the Burton Web site gives a detailed description of all the products and explains the many different kinds of snowboards and gear available each season. Internet users can then order the catalog from the American, European, or Japanese offices.

The Internet and Burton's dual distribution strategy have made it easy for customers around the world to buy Burton products, but this has not always been so. Prior to 1985, Burton was sending snowboards to Europe based on individual requests, but the company finally realized that it could simplify distribution by cutting the number of transactions required to get products from the factory to the rider. In response to this need, the Burton Snowboard company decided to develop a marketing channel using intermediaries, dealers, and distributors who buy and resell the products.

Burton intermediaries provide the specialized expertise necessary for efficient product education and distribution. Distributors and dealers communicate with new and repeat customers to create awareness of Burton's product features, advantages, and benefits. Perhaps more importantly, however, intermediaries ensure that the right quantities, proportions, and assortments of products are available at one location so that riders have the right number and kind of items they need when they need them. After all, having a great snowboard doesn't mean much unless you have the bindings to go with it. Burton's supply chain connects all the business entities that move company products to the right place at the right time, and this chain allows Burton to avoid discrepancies that could reduce customer satisfaction, cost the company repeat business, or compromise its reputation. To support its extensive distribution network, Burton uses a supply chain information system to track every piece of inventory throughout the world and to monitor ordering, delivery, and bill payment.

When the company first decided to use intermediaries, Jake Burton, the company founder and owner, had to choose a marketing channel strategy that took the particulars of the market, his company, and its products into consideration. He had to ask the question, "Where are the potential snowboarders?" The answer to that primary question has been constantly evolving since it was first asked. When the company started, it advertised in major publications and filled orders as they came in directly to the Vermont office. As the popularity of snowboarding increased to the point of being accepted at most American ski resorts, national distribution began to make more sense. When Burton saw the untapped potential of the European market, he opened up shop in Austria. By the late

1990s, Burton Snowboards was doing business in twenty-seven countries.

Product factors also influenced the company channel decisions. Burton snowboards are highly customized, varying in length, type of ride (freestyle, freeride, or carving), and graphic design. For such specialized products, a shorter, more direct marketing channel is preferable. Channel selection is also influenced by the type of manufacturer. Jake Burton's investment in Burton Snowboards is reflected in the distribution strategy the company has pursued. Because he personally spent years developing the sport of snowboarding and the products that go with it, Burton wanted to control his company's pricing, positioning, brand image, and customer support initiatives.

Another issue affecting Burton's channel strategy was the level of distribution intensity—that is, the number of outlets available to customers for buying snowboards and other Burton products. Jake Burton chose selective distribution, screening dealers to eliminate all but a few retailers in any single area and having the company's outside sales force and internal distribution management staff work closely with this focused group of American retailers. In Europe, the challenge of screening prospective distributors was more difficult, so Jake Burton carefully selected only dealers who were dedicated to the sport of snowboarding.

Burton Snowboards has risen to be the industry leader in its market, and its multipronged distribution strategy that uses both direct and indirect channels is what allows the company to provide top-of-the-line snowboards, bindings, boots, and clothing to snowboarders worldwide.

Questions

1. Describe Burton Snowboards' dual distribution.
2. What advantages does Burton gain from using a channel of distribution?
3. How do marketing channels help Burton overcome discrepancies?
4. Using Exhibit 12.7, explain the intensity of distribution levels. Why did Burton choose selective distribution?

Bibliography

Reade Bailey. "Jake Burton, King of the Hill." *Ski*, February 1998, pp. 67–68.
Burton Snowboards Press Kit.
Burton Web site: **http://www.burton.com**.

chapter 13

Learning Objectives

1 Discuss the importance of retailing in the U.S. economy

2 Explain the dimensions by which retailers can be classified

3 Describe the major types of retail operations

4 Discuss nonstore retailing techniques

5 Define franchising and describe its two basic forms

6 List the major tasks involved in developing a retail marketing strategy

7 Discuss the challenges of expanding retailing operations into global markets

8 Describe future trends in retailing

Target, it seems, is right on target.

Target Stores, the jewel of retail conglomerate Target Corporation—which also owns Dayton's, Hudson's, Mervyn's, and Marshall Field's department stores—has successfully carved a unique niche for itself as an upscale discounter, a term that may seem like an oxymoron. The chain's retailing strategy is prominently displayed on its Web site: to be the best place to buy high-quality merchandise at low prices in surroundings that make shopping fun. Although Target typically stocks the usual discount store merchandise—casual apparel and home furnishings and accessories such as sheets, towels, small appliances, and housewares—the ambience and product assortment are more upscale and trendy than that of other discounters. Its Pro Spirit line of activewear, for instance, is made of 80/20 cotton/polyester, while private-label activewear found at other mass merchants has a 50/50 cotton/polyester content. Many of its home product lines are designed by well-known designers such as Michael Graves, Phillippe Starck, Liuginio Cozzi, and Franco Olivo.

With its upscale merchandise assortment, Target seeks an affluent clientele, one that is more white collar than the blue collar crowd attracted by other discounters, like Wal-Mart and Kmart. Target customers' median household income is $43,000 and more than 75 percent have attended or completed college. At Kmart and Wal-Mart, in contrast, customers' median income is in the $25,000-and-below range. Consequently, Target has wedged itself in between several retail formats so that they essentially don't have a direct competitor. Retail experts say that Target no longer views Wal-Mart as its prime competitor as it expands across the country. Rather, the chain has its sights set on shoppers who frequent JC Penny and Sears to fuel future growth. The image Target is projecting reflects its mission statement: "to be a department store alternative."

With sales of $23 billion annually and over nine hundred stores in forty-four states, the chain has strongly relied on its department store roots in the development of its retailing philosophy. Over the years, Target has nurtured a very strong relationship with fashion goods and fashion trends. Consequently, Target rarely misses a trend. By keeping a close tab on the pulse of its core target market, Target can offer the consumer a lower-priced alternative to hot products with its own private-label brands such as Xhiliration, Merona, Pro Spirit, and Cherokee. For instance, when cargo pants became a hot fashion item at major retailers like the Gap, Target was right there with it offering its own private brand of cargo pants.

In Target's favor is the fact that discount stores have gained stature with shoppers over the past decade. The stigma once attached to shopping at a discount store has virtually disappeared as more and more consumers look for quality and value. With its designer looks and low prices, the store has become a favorite with trendsetters, who have fondly nicknamed it "Tar-zhay," as the French might pronounce it. Affirming its popularity, a recent *USA Today* poll found that Target is "in" among fashion trendsetters. The chain has also profited from the recent popularity of "cheapskate chic," or the pairing of designer duds with discount merchandise. Shoppers have no problem these days pairing a $200 blouse purchased at a high-end retailer with a $20 pair of pants from Target, and boasting about it.

While the retailer has mastered the art of bringing fashion to discounted sportswear, towels, and teapots, it plans to do the same in terms of food. With the ambitious goal of becoming the first national upscale grocer, Target is now venturing into the supercenter retail format with SuperTarget, a combination discount store and grocery store under one roof. But while supercenter competitors Wal-Mart and Kmart stock only best-selling national brands and their own private labels, Target is taking a more gourmet approach. SuperTargets stock preseasoned roasts and seafood, a wide range of prepared meals-to-go and gourmet brands of pastas and sauces alongside its own Archer Farms private label. Chefs adorned in white hats and coats prepare specialty sandwiches and desserts in full view of customers. Carrying upscale brands, such as a line of cooking oils by Dean & Deluca, which owns a handful of gourmet eateries in such trendy places as Manhattan, SuperTarget aims to bring fashion to food. SuperTarget also includes an aisle of natural foods, the likes of which might be found at specialty chains such as Whole Foods Markets. Additionally, each location features a Starbuck's coffee outlet. Target plans to open 200 to 300 SuperTargets within the next ten years.[1]

Growing sales in an increasingly crowded retail market is a major concern for today's retailers. How does a retailer's target market determine its merchandise selection? How important is location to the success of a store? What factors are included in developing a store's atmosphere? This chapter seeks to answer these questions and many more by discussing retailers' important role in moving products and services to the ultimate consumer. We begin with a discussion of the role of retailing and the ways in which retail operations can be classified followed by a description of the decisions involved in developing a retail marketing strategy.

The Role of Retailing

1

Discuss the importance of retailing in the U.S. economy

retailing
All the activities directly related to the sale of goods and services to the ultimate consumer for personal, nonbusiness use.

Retailing—all the activities directly related to the sale of goods and services to the ultimate consumer for personal, nonbusiness use—has enhanced the quality of our daily lives. When we shop for groceries, hair styling, clothes, books, and many other products and services, we are involved in retailing. The millions of goods and services provided by retailers mirror the needs and styles of U.S. society.

Retailing affects all of us directly or indirectly. The retailing industry is one of the largest employers; over 1.6 million U.S. retailers employ more than twenty million people, or nearly one out of every five workers. At the store level, retailing is still considered a mom-and-pop business. Almost nine out of ten retail companies employ fewer than twenty employees and, according to the National Retail Federation, 95 percent of all retailers operate just one store.[2]

The U.S. economy is heavily dependent on retailing. Retailers ring up over $2.7 trillion in sales annually, almost a third of the gross domestic product (GDP).[3] Although most retailers are quite small, a few giant organizations dominate the industry, most notably Wal-Mart, whose annual U.S. sales alone account for about 5 percent of all retail sales. Who are these giants? Exhibit 13.1 lists the ten largest U.S. retailers.

Classification of Retail Operations

2

Explain the dimensions by which retailers can be classified

A retail establishment can be classified according to its ownership, level of service, product assortment, and price. Specifically, retailers use the latter three variables to position themselves in the competitive marketplace. (As noted in Chapter 7, positioning is the strategy used to influence how consumers perceive one product in relation to all competing products.) These three variables can be combined in several ways to create distinctly different retail operations. Exhibit 13.2 lists the major types of retail stores discussed in this chapter and classifies them by level of service, product assortment, price, and gross margin.

Ownership

Retailers can be broadly classified by form of ownership: independent, part of a chain, or franchise outlet. Retailers owned by a single person or partnership and not operated as part of a larger retail institution are **independent retailers**. Around the world, most retailers are independent, operating one or a few stores in their community. Local florists, shoe stores, and ethnic food markets typically fit this classification.

independent retailers
Retailers owned by a single person or partnership and not operated as part of a larger retail institution.

chain stores
Stores owned and operated as a group by a single organization.

franchise
The right to operate a business or to sell a product.

Chain stores are owned and operated as a group by a single organization. Under this form of ownership, many administrative tasks are handled by the home office for the entire chain. The home office also buys most of the merchandise sold in the stores.

Franchises are owned and operated by individuals but are licensed by a larger supporting organization. Franchising combines the advantages of independent ownership with those of the chain store organization. Franchising is discussed in more detail later in the chapter.

Level of Service

The level of service that retailers provide can be classified along a continuum, from full service to self-service. Some retailers, such as exclusive clothing stores, offer high levels of service. They provide alterations, credit, delivery, consulting,

Exhibit **13.1**

1998 Rank	Company	Retailing Formats	1998 Revenues (in billions)	1998 Number of Stores
1	**Wal-Mart** Bentonville, Arkansas	Discount stores, super-centers, and warehouse clubs	$137.6	3,519
2	**Sears, Roebuck** Hoffman Estates, Illinois	Department stores, catalogs, home centers, and specialty	$41.3	3,145
3	**Kmart** Troy, Michigan	Discount stores and supercenters	$33.7	2,161
4	**Target Corporation*** Minneapolis, Minnesota	Discount stores and department stores	$31.0	1,182
5	**JCPenney** Plano, Texas	Department stores, catalogs, and drug stores	$30.7	3,904
6	**The Home Depot** Atlanta, Georgia	Home centers	$30.2	761
7	**Kroger** Cincinnati, Ohio	Supermarkets and convenience stores	$28.2	2,187
8	**Safeway** Pleasanton, California	Supermarkets	$24.5	1,497
9	**Costco** Issaquah, Washington	Warehouse clubs	$24.3	278
10	**American Stores Company** Salt Lake City, Utah	Supermarkets and drug stores	$19.9	1,580

* Renamed Target Corporation in January 2000; formerly was Dayton Hudson Corporation.
SOURCE: National Retail Federation; David P. Schultz, "The Nation's Biggest Retail Companies," *Stores*, July 1999, **http://www.stores.org**. Sales figures include international sales.

liberal return policies, layaway, gift wrapping, and personal shopping. Discount stores usually offer fewer services. Retailers like factory outlets and warehouse clubs offer virtually no services.

Product Assortment

The third basis for positioning or classifying stores is by the breadth and depth of their product line. Specialty stores—for example, Hallmark card stores, Lady Foot Locker, and TCBY yogurt shops—are the most concentrated in their product assortment, usually carrying single or narrow product lines but in considerable

Exhibit 13.2

Types of Stores and
Their Characteristics

Type of Retailer	Level of Service	Product Assortment	Price	Gross Margin
Department store	Moderately high to high	Broad	Moderate to high	Moderately high
Specialty store	High	Narrow	Moderate to high	High
Supermarket	Low	Broad	Moderate	Low
Convenience store	Low	Medium to narrow	Moderately high	Moderately high
Drugstore	Low to moderate	Medium	Moderate	Low
Full-line discount store	Moderate to low	Medium to broad	Moderately low	Moderately low
Discount specialty store	Moderate to low	Medium to broad	Moderately low to low	Moderately low
Warehouse clubs	Low	Broad	Low to very low	Low
Off-price retailer	Low	Medium to narrow	Low	Low
Restaurant	Low to high	Narrow	Low to high	Low to high

depth. On the other end of the spectrum, full-line discounters typically carry broad assortments of merchandise with limited depth. For example, Target carries automotive supplies, household cleaning products, and pet food. However, Target may carry only four or five brands of canned dog food; a supermarket may carry as many as twenty.

Other retailers, such as factory outlet stores, may carry only part of a single line. Liz Claiborne, a major manufacturer of women's clothing, sells only certain items of its own brand in its many outlet stores. Discount specialty stores like Home Depot or Toys "R" Us carry a broad assortment in concentrated product lines, such as building and home supplies or toys.

Price

Price is a fourth way to position retail stores. Traditional department stores and specialty stores typically charge the full "suggested retail price." In contrast, discounters, factory outlets, and offprice retailers use low prices as a major lure for shoppers.

gross margin
The amount of money the retailer makes as a percentage of sales after the cost of goods sold is subtracted.

The last column in Exhibit 13.2 shows the typical **gross margin**—how much the retailer makes as a percentage of sales after the cost of goods sold is subtracted. The level of gross margin and the price level generally match. For example, a traditional jewelry store has high prices and high gross margins. A factory outlet has low prices and low gross margins. Markdowns on merchandise during sale periods and price wars among competitors, in which stores lower prices on certain items in an effort to win customers, cause gross margins to decline. When Wal-Mart entered the grocery business in a small Arkansas community, a fierce price war ensued. By the time the price war was in full swing, the price of a quart of milk had plummeted by more than 50 percent (below the price of a pint) and a loaf of bread sold for only 9¢, prices at which no retailer could make a profit.

Major Types of Retail Operations

There are several types of retail stores. Each offers a different product assortment, type of service, and price level, according to its customers' shopping preferences.

Department Stores

Housing several departments under one roof, a **department store** carries a wide variety of shopping and specialty goods, including apparel, cosmetics, housewares, electronics, and sometimes furniture. Purchases are generally made within each department rather than at one central check-out area. Each department is treated as a separate buying center to achieve economies in promotion, buying, service, and control. Each department is usually headed by a **buyer**, a department head who not only selects the merchandise for his or her department but may also be responsible for promotion and for personnel. For a consistent, uniform store image, central management sets broad policies about the types of merchandise carried and price ranges. Central management is also responsible for the overall advertising program, credit policies, store expansion, customer service, and so on.

Large independent department stores are rare today. Most are owned by national chains. Among the largest U.S. department store chains are Sears, Target Corporation, JCPenney, Federated Department Stores, and May Department Stores. All operate more than one chain of retail stores, from discount chains to upscale clothiers. Two up-and-coming department store chains are Dillard's, based in Little Rock, Arkansas, and Nordstrom, with corporate headquarters in Seattle. Dillard's is known for its distribution expertise; Nordstrom offers innovative customer service. In the past few years, much attention has been centered on these two growing chains, and both have a very promising future.

In recent years, consumers have become more cost conscious and value oriented. Specialty retailers like The Gap, discounters, catalog outlets, and even on-line Internet shopping alternatives are offering superior merchandise selection and presentation, sharper pricing, and greater convenience to take sales away from department stores. They have also been quicker to adopt new technology and invest in labor-saving strategies. In addition, their leaner cost structure translates into lower prices for the customer. Meanwhile, manufacturers like Liz Claiborne, Bass, Calvin Klein, and Polo/Ralph Lauren have opened outlet stores of their own and more discount stores such as Wal-Mart and Target have upgraded their apparel assortments, taking more sales away from department stores.

Department store managers are using several strategies to preserve their market share. One is to reposition department stores as specialty outlets. They are

Describe the major types of retail operations

department store
A store housing several departments under one roof.

buyer
A department head who selects the merchandise for his or her department and may also be responsible for promotion and personnel.

Liz Claiborne designs often are placed in a specialty boutique area like this one in Lord & Taylor's New York City store. Subdividing larger fashion departments helps large stores create the feel of specialty outlets.

dividing departments into miniboutiques, each featuring a distinct fashion taste, as specialty stores do. For example, many upscale department stores feature Donna Karan and Liz Claiborne boutiques within their stores. Department stores are also enhancing customer service to shift the focus away from price. Services include complimentary alterations, longer store hours, personalized attention, after-sale follow-up, and personal wardrobe planning. Finally, department stores are expanding, remodeling, and revitalizing to show off new merchandising directions and to reflect the growth in their marketing areas.

Specialty Stores

specialty store
A retail store specializing in a given type of merchandise.

Specialty store formats allow retailers to refine their segmentation strategies and tailor their merchandise to specific target markets. A **specialty store** is not only a type of store but also a method of retail operations—namely, specializing in a given type of merchandise. Examples include children's clothing, men's clothing, candy, baked goods, gourmet coffee, sporting goods, and pet supplies. A typical specialty store carries a deeper but narrower assortment of specialty merchandise than does a department store. Generally, specialty stores' knowledgeable sales clerks offer more attentive customer service. The format has become very powerful in the apparel market and other areas. Waldenbooks, Victoria's Secret, The Body Shop, Foot Locker, and Crate & Barrel are several successful chain specialty retailers.

Consumers in specialty outlets usually consider price to be secondary. Instead, the distinctive merchandise, the store's physical appearance, and the caliber of the staff determine its popularity. Independent specialty toy stores, for instance, often shun the mass-produced toys that typically sell in Kmart or Toys "R" Us in favor of more educational toys or toys that are hard to find, such as Brio's wooden train sets. Because they cannot compete on price with the big toy stores, independent toy retailers offer enhanced service such as personal shopping and free gift wrapping.[4] Manufacturers often favor introducing new products in small specialty stores before moving on to larger retail and department stores.

Small specialty stores also provide a low-risk testing ground for many new product concepts. Nike, for instance, often uses athletic footwear retailer Foot Locker as its venue for new shoe introductions. Nike recently introduced its $130 Tuned Air running shoe exclusively at Foot Locker shoe outlets. While the arrangement protects Foot Locker from price competition from other retailers, allowing it to charge full retail price, it also creates an image of exclusivity for Nike.[5]

Supermarkets

supermarket
A large, departmentalized, self-service retailer that specializes in food and some nonfood items.

U.S. consumers spend about a tenth of their disposable income in **supermarkets**—large, departmentalized, self-service retailers that specialize in food and some nonfood items.

A decade ago, industry experts predicted the decline of the supermarket industry, whose slim profit margins of just 1 to 2 percent of sales left it vulnerable. These experts originally felt that supermarkets would merely need an ever-growing customer base to sustain volume and compensate for low margins. Although the annual population growth averaged less than 1 percent a year, supermarkets still experienced declining sales. As a result, experts were forced to examine not only population trends but also demographic and lifestyle changes of consumers. They discovered several trends affecting the supermarket industry.

For example, as dual-income and single-parent families increase, consumers are eating out more or are too busy to prepare meals at home. According to the U.S. Department of Agriculture, Americans spent only about two-thirds of their food money in retail grocery stores, compared with a third spent for food away from home. In comparison, Americans spent over three-fourths of their food money in grocery stores in 1950.[6] The growth in the away-from-home food market has been driven by the entry of more women into the workforce and their need for convenience and time-saving products. Working couples need one-stop shopping, and the increasing number of affluent customers are willing to pay for specialty and prepared foods.

As stores seek to meet consumer demand for one-stop shopping, conventional supermarkets are being replaced by bigger *superstores*, which are usually twice the size of supermarkets. Superstores meet the needs of today's customers for convenience, variety, and service. Superstores offer one-stop shopping for many food and nonfood needs, as well as many services—including pharmacies, flower shops, salad bars, in-store bakeries, takeout food sections, sit-down restaurants, health food sections, video rentals, dry-cleaning services, shoe repair, photo processing, and banking. Some even offer family dentistry or optical shops. This tendency to offer a wide variety of nontraditional goods and services under one roof is called **scrambled merchandising**. Canada's largest supermarket chain Loblaw exemplifies this trend: along with dry cleaning, a liquor store, a coffee shop, pharmacy, and banking center it also offers video-game and cell-phone sales outlets, leases space to a clothing chain and a fitness club complete with a sauna, tanning beds, and daycare center. Loblaw's ancillary services aim to attract today's time-strapped customers by providing one-stop shopping.[7]

Another demographic trend affecting supermarkets is expanding ethnicity. Over the next fifty years, nonwhite ethnic groups will constitute the fastest-growing segments of the American population. According to the U.S. Census Bureau, the most pronounced population growth will be seen among Hispanics, Asian-Americans, and African-Americans. If current trends in shopping patterns among ethnic groups continue, these demographic changes promise to have a vast impact on supermarket retailers. For example, both African-American and Hispanic households now outspend white American households on weekly grocery shopping. In terms of shopping habits, African-Americans and Hispanics tend to be conservative, looking for products and brands they know and trust and patronizing stores that reliably meet their needs. It will also be increasingly important for supermarkets to tailor their stores' product mix to reflect the demographics of the population they serve.[8]

Many supermarket chains are tailoring marketing strategies to appeal to specific consumer segments to help them stand out in an increasingly competitive marketplace. Most notably is the shift toward *loyalty marketing programs* that reward loyal customers carrying frequent-shopper cards with discounts or gifts. Once scanned at the checkout, frequent-shopper cards help supermarket retailers electronically track shopper's buying habits. Sixty percent of customers who shop at the 110 stores operated by South Carolina-based Piggly Wiggly, for instance, carry the Pig's Favorite loyalty card. Customers use their card each time they shop to get special discounts on items. Piggly Wiggly also uses consumer purchase data stored in its database to determine customer preferences. If management sees that a customer buys flowers regularly, then they send that customer a coupon redeemable in its floral department.[9]

Drugstores

Drugstores stock pharmacy-related products and services as their main draw. Consumers are most often attracted to a drugstore by its pharmacy or pharmacist, its convenience, or because it honors their third-party prescription drug plan. Drugstores also carry an extensive selection of over-the-counter (OTC) medications, cosmetics, health and beauty aids, seasonal merchandise, specialty items such as greeting cards and a limited selection of toys, and some nonrefrigerated convenience foods.[10] As competition has increased from

scrambled merchandising
The tendency to offer a wide variety of nontraditional goods and services under one roof.

drugstore
A retail store that stocks pharmacy-related products and services as its main draw.

mass merchandisers and supermarkets with their own pharmacies, as well as from direct-mail prescription services, drugstores have been adding value-added services such as twenty-four-hour operations and drive-through pharmacies. Even more competition is expected as Wal-Mart rolls out its newest retailing concept, the Wal-Mart Neighborhood Market, a smaller store format featuring general grocery items, health and beauty aids, and a drive-through pharmacy. Its pharmacy business has done exceptionally well in test markets with the drive-through pharmacy window proving very popular. Already, about 20 to 25 percent of total pharmacy sales at Neighborhood Market stores come from the drive-through.[11]

Demographic trends in the United States look favorable for the drugstore industry. As the baby boom population continues to age, they will spend an increasing percentage of their disposable income on health care and wellness. This is good news for the drugstore industry, as the average sixty-year-old purchases fifteen prescriptions per year, nearly twice as many as the average thirty-year-old. Because baby boomers are attentive to their health and keenly sensitive about their looks, the increased traffic at the pharmacy counter in the future should also spur sales in other traditionally strong drugstore merchandise categories, most notably over-the-counter drugs, vitamins, and health and beauty aids.[12]

Convenience Stores

A **convenience store** can be defined as a miniature supermarket, carrying only a limited line of high-turnover convenience goods. These self-service stores are typically located near residential areas and are open twenty-four hours, seven days a week. Convenience stores offer exactly what their name implies: convenient location, long hours, fast service. However, prices are almost always higher at a convenience store than at a supermarket. Thus the customer pays for the convenience.

From the mid-1970s to the mid-1980s, hundreds of new convenience stores opened, many with self-service gas pumps. Full-service gas stations fought back by closing service bays and opening miniature stores of their own, selling convenience items like cigarettes, sodas, and snacks. Supermarkets and discount stores also wooed customers with one-stop shopping and quick checkout. To combat the gas stations' and supermarkets' competition, convenience store operators have changed their strategy. They have expanded their offerings of nonfood items with video rentals, health and beauty aids, upscale sandwich and salad lines, and more fresh produce. Some convenience stores are even selling Pizza Hut and Taco Bell products prepared in the store.

Discount Stores

A **discount store** is a retailer that competes on the basis of low prices, high turnover, and high volume. Discounters can be classified into four major categories: full-line discount stores, discount specialty stores, warehouse clubs, and off-price discount retailers.

Full-Line Discount Stores   Compared to traditional department stores, **full-line discount stores** offer consumers very limited service and carry a much broader assortment of well-known, nationally branded "hard goods," including housewares, toys, automotive parts, hardware, sporting goods, and garden items, as well as clothing, bedding, and linens. Some even carry limited nonperishable food items, such as soft drinks, canned goods, and potato chips. As with department stores, national chains dominate the discounters. Full-line discounters are often called mass merchandisers. **Mass merchandising** is the retailing strategy whereby retailers use moderate to low prices on large quantities of merchandise and lower service to stimulate high turnover of products.

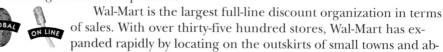
Wal-Mart is the largest full-line discount organization in terms of sales. With over thirty-five hundred stores, Wal-Mart has expanded rapidly by locating on the outskirts of small towns and ab-

Margin glossary

convenience store
A miniature supermarket, carrying only a limited line of high-turnover convenience goods.

discount store
A retailer that competes on the basis of low prices, high turnover, and high volume.

full-line discount stores
A retailer that offers consumers very limited service and carries a broad assortment of well-known, nationally branded "hard goods."

mass merchandising
Retailing strategy using moderate to low prices on large quantities of merchandise and lower service to stimulate high turnover of products.

sorbing business for miles around. Much of Wal-Mart's success has been attributed to its merchandising foresight, cost consciousness, efficient communication and distribution systems, and involved, motivated employees. Wal-Mart is credited with pioneering the retail strategy of "every-day low pricing," a strategy now widely copied by retailers the world over. Besides expanding throughout all fifty states and Puerto Rico, Wal-Mart has expanded globally into Mexico, Canada, Brazil, Argentina, China, Indonesia, Germany, Korea, and, most recently, the United Kingdom with its purchase of Asda, Britain's third-largest supermarket chain, with 229 stores.[13] Wal-Mart has also become a formidable retailing giant in on-line shopping, concentrating on toys and electronics. With tie-ins to its stores across the country, Wal-Mart is expected to introduce millions of customers to on-line shopping with in-store kiosks linking to the site and the ability to handle returns and exchanges from Internet sales at its physical stores.[14]

A hybrid of the full-line discounter is the hypermarket, a concept adapted from the Europeans. The flashy **hypermarket** format combines a supermarket and full-line discount store in a space ranging from 200,000 to 300,000 square feet. Although they have enjoyed widespread success in Europe, where consumers have fewer retailing choices, hypermarkets have been much less successful in the United States. Most Europeans still need to visit several small stores just for their food needs, which makes hypermarkets a good alternative. Americans, on the other hand, can easily pick among a host of stores that offer large selections of merchandise. According to retailing executives and analysts, American customers have found hypermarkets to be too big. Both Wal-Mart's Hypermart USA and Kmart's American Fare hypermarket formats never got beyond the experimental stage.

hypermarket
A retail store that combines a supermarket and full-line discount store in a space ranging from 200,000 to 300,000 square feet.

Similar to a hypermarket, but only half the size, is the **supercenter**, which combines groceries and general merchandise goods with a wide range of services including pharmacy, dry cleaning, portrait studios, photo finishing, hair salons, optical shops, and restaurants—all in one location. For supercenter operators like Wal-mart, food is a customer magnet that sharply increases the store's overall volume, while taking customers away from traditional supermarkets.[15] Wal-Mart now operates over 600 SuperCenters and plans to replace many older Wal-Marts with this format. Along with Kmart, which is opening similar Big Kmart supercenters of its own, the two retailers pose a significant threat to traditional supermarkets and drugstores. Recall from the opening story that Target is pursuing a similar strategy as well.

supercenter
Retail store that combines groceries and general merchandise goods with a wide range of services.

Supercenters are also threatening to push Europe's traditional small and medium-sized food stores into extinction. Old-fashioned corner stores and family businesses are giving way to larger chains that offer food, drugs, services, and general merchandise all in one place. Many European countries are passing legislation to make it more difficult for supercenters to open. In France, for example, laws were passed that banned authorizations for new supercenters over 1,000 square meters (10,800 square feet). Belgium and Portugal have passed similar bans. In Britain and the Netherlands, areas outside towns and cities are off limits to superstores. By imposing planning and building restrictions for large stores, these countries are trying to accommodate environmental concerns, movements to revive city centers, and the worries of small shopkeepers.

An increasingly popular variation of off-price retailing at full-line discount stores is *extreme-value retailing*, the most notable examples being Dollar General and Family Dollar. Extreme-value retailers have grown in popularity as major discounters continue to shift toward the supercenter format, broadening their customer base and increasing their offerings of higher-priced goods aimed at higher-income consumers. This has created an opening for extreme-value retailers to entice shoppers from the low-income segment. Low- and fixed-income customers are drawn to extreme-value retailers, whose stores are located within their communities. Extreme-value retailers also build smaller stores (a typical store is about the size of one department in a Wal-Mart superstore) with a narrower selection of merchandise emphasizing day-to-day necessities. Rock-bottom prices are also key to their success. With the average transaction under $10, extreme value retailers have found low price to be far more critical to building traffic and loyalty than any other retailing format.[16]

Specialty Discount Stores

Another discount niche includes the single-line **specialty discount stores**—for example, stores selling sporting goods, electronics, auto parts, office supplies, and toys. These stores offer a nearly complete selection of single-line merchandise and use self-service, discount prices, high volume, and high turnover to their advantage. Specialty discount stores are often termed **category killers** because they so heavily dominate their narrow merchandise segment. Examples include Toys "R" Us in toys, Circuit City and BestBuy in electronics, Staples and Office Depot in office supplies, Home Depot in home improvement supplies, IKEA in home furnishings, and Bed, Bath & Beyond in kitchen and bath accessories.

Toys "R" Us was the first category killer, offering a giant selection of toys, usually over fifteen thousand different items per store, at prices usually 10 to 15 percent less than competitors'. When Toys "R" Us came on the retail scene, department stores were generally limiting their toy assortments to the Christmas season. Toys "R" Us offered a broad assortment of inventory all year long. Additionally, the playing field was scattered with many small toy chains or mom-and-pop stores. With its bright warehouse-style stores, Toys "R" Us gobbled up market share, and many small toy stores failed and department stores eliminated their toy departments. The Toys "R" Us chain—currently an $11.9 billion company with over 1,500 stores worldwide—now commands about a quarter of the U.S. retail toy business. Toys "R" Us first went international in 1984 with stores in Canada and Singapore. Since then, the company has opened over 450 stores in over two dozen foreign countries. Toys "R" Us expanded its category-killer retailing concept to include over 200 Kids "R" Us children's clothing stores and 130 Babies "R" Us baby products stores. In addition, Toys "R" Us has ventured into on-line retailing at its Web site, **http://www.toysrus.com**, which garnered $49 million in sales in 1999. There, customers can choose toys, games, and play equipment to be shipped directly to their homes, use the site's gift selection service, or search for hard-to-find toys.[17]

Other specialty segments have followed the lead of Toys "R" Us, hoping to build similar retailing empires in highly fragmented mom-and-pop markets. For instance, the home improvement industry was once dominated by professional builders and small hardware stores that offered a basic staple of products. Similarly, prior to the creation of PETsMart and Petco pet supplies chains, the pet industry was dominated by thousands of independent neighborhood pet stores. Another industry that was very fragmented was the office products industry. As more people began to work from home, replacing their typewriters with personal computers and purchasing fax machines, the local stationery store, with its limited selection of paper and writing materials, quickly became obsolete. The industry is now dominated by Office Depot, Staples, and OfficeMax, each stocking some five to seven thousand different types of products. Category-dominant retailers like these serve their customers by offering an unequaled selection of merchandise, stores that make shopping easy, and low prices every day, which eliminates the need for time-consuming comparison shopping.[18]

Warehouse Membership Clubs   **Warehouse membership clubs** sell a limited selection of brand-name appliances, household items, and groceries. These are usually sold in bulk from warehouse outlets on a cash-and-carry basis to members only. Individual members of warehouse clubs are charged low or no membership fees.

Warehouse clubs have had a major impact on supermarkets. With 90,000 square feet or more, warehouse clubs offer 60 to 70 percent general merchandise and health and beauty care products, with grocery-related items making up the difference.[19] Warehouse club members tend to be more educated and more affluent and have a larger household than regular supermarket shoppers. These core customers use warehouse clubs to stock up on staples; then they go to specialty outlets or food stores for perishables.

Fierce competition is commonplace in the warehouse club industry. Common practices include price slashing, selling below cost, locating outlets to compete directly with each other, and sometimes hiring away rivals' employees to get an edge in local markets. Currently, the stores primarily comprising the warehouse club category are Wal-Mart's Sam's Club, Costco, and BJ's Wholesale Club.

Off-Price Retailers   An **off-price retailer** sells at prices 25 percent or more below traditional department store prices because it pays cash for its stock and usually doesn't ask for return privileges. Off-price retailers buy manufacturers' overruns at cost or even less. They also absorb goods from bankrupt stores, irregular merchandise, and unsold end-of-season output. Nevertheless, much off-price retailer merchandise is first-quality, current goods. Because buyers for off-price retailers purchase only what is available or what they can get a good deal on, merchandise styles and brands often change monthly. Today there are hundreds of off-price retailers, the best known being T. J. Maxx, Ross Stores, Marshall's, Home Goods, and Tuesday Morning.

Factory outlets are an interesting variation on the off-price concept. A **factory outlet** is an off-price retailer that is owned and operated by a manufacturer. Thus it carries one line of merchandise—its own. Each season, from 5 to 10 percent of a manufacturer's output does not sell through regular distribution channels because it consists of close-outs (merchandise being discontinued), factory seconds, and canceled orders. With factory outlets, manufacturers can regulate where their surplus is sold, and they can realize higher profit margins than they would by disposing of the goods through independent wholesalers and retailers. Factory outlet malls typically locate in out-of-the-way rural areas or near vacation destinations. Most are situated at least thirty miles from urban or suburban shopping areas so manufacturers don't alienate their department store accounts by selling the same goods virtually next door at a discount.

Several manufacturers reaping the benefits of outlet mall popularity include Liz Claiborne, J. Crew, and Calvin Klein clothiers; West Point Pepperel textiles; Oneida silversmiths; and Dansk kitchenwares. Top-drawer department stores—including Saks Fifth Avenue and Neiman Marcus—have also opened outlet stores to sell hard-to-move merchandise. Dillard Department Stores has opened a series of clearance centers to make final attempts to move merchandise that failed to sell in the department store. In order to move their clearance items, Nordstrom's operates Nordstrom Rack and Boston's Filene's has Filene's Basement.

As outlet malls have gained in popularity, however, they are beginning to act less and less like traditional outlets in which manufacturers sold surplus or damaged goods. For instance, some manufacturers such as The Gap, Brooks Brothers, Ann Taylor, and Donna Karan now make lower-quality lines specifically for their outlet stores.[20] Further, outlet centers in many locations are competing head-on with regional malls by incorporating entertainment to draw customers. Sawgrass Mills located outside of Ft. Lauderdale, Florida, boasts an eighteen-screen theater,

warehouse membership clubs
A limited-service merchant wholesaler that sells a limited selection of brand-name appliances, household items, and groceries on a cash-and-carry basis to members, usually small businesses and groups.

off-price retailer
A retailer that sells at prices 25 percent or more below traditional department store prices because it pays cash for its stock and usually doesn't ask for return privileges.

factory outlet
An off-price retailer that is owned and operated by a manufacturer.

forty restaurants, and a Sega GameWorks, featuring high-tech games in a night-club atmosphere. The center is now Florida's second-largest tourist attraction after Disney World.[21] Outlet store centers are also cropping up closer and closer to major metropolitan centers. Manufacturers are decreasing their sensitivity toward department stores that carry their brands at full retail price and choosing to locate closer to the customer to be more accessible. Prime Outlets Hagerstown (Maryland), for instance, is only a short distance away from two major urban centers, Baltimore and Washington, D.C., and it is loudly advertising some of the manufacturer names in the center.[22]

Restaurants

Restaurants straddle the line between a retailing establishment and a service establishment. Restaurants do sell tangible products, food and drink, but they also provide a valuable service for consumers in the form of food preparation and food service. Most restaurants could even fall into the definition of a specialty retailer given that most concentrate their menu offerings on a distinctive type of cuisine—for example, Olive Garden Italian restaurants, Starbucks coffeehouses, Popeye's Fried Chicken, and Pizza Hut pizza restaurants.

As a retailing institution, restaurants must deal with many of the same issues as a more traditional retailer, such as personnel, distribution, inventory management, promotion, pricing, and location. Restaurants and food service retailers run the spectrum from those offering limited service and inexpensive food, such as fast-food chains or the local snack bar or coffee house, to those that offer sit-down service and moderate to high prices, such as the likes of the Outback Steakhouse & Saloon chain or a local trendy Italian bistro.

Eating out is an important part of America's daily activities and is growing in strength. According to the National Restaurant Association, Americans consume an average of 4.1 commercially prepared meals per week. Moreover, food away from home accounts for anywhere from 25 percent of the household food budget for low-income families to nearly 50 percent for those with high incomes. The trend in eating out has been fueled in large part by the increase in working mothers and dual-income families who have more money to eat out but less time to spend preparing meals at home.[23] Although consumers are eating out more, food service companies have generally overexpanded in terms of the number of retail locations. In the fast-food segment, for instance, the number of restaurants has increased from one outlet per 1,672 people in the United States to one for every 1,343 persons.[24]

Still, the restaurant industry remains one of the most entrepreneurial of businesses and one of the most competitive. Because barriers to entering the restaurant industry are low, the opportunity appeals to many people. The risks, however, are great. About 50 percent of all new restaurants fail within the first year of operation. Restaurants face competition not only from other restaurants but also from the consumer who can easily choose to cook at home. Competition has fostered innovation in the restaurant industry, such as Pizza Hut's introduction of The Edge pizza, to the ever-changing menus at fast-food restaurants. Seeking out and targeting underserved distribution niches is another way restaurants are competing with one another to reach consumers. Fast-food operators are increasingly looking to provide service at locations such as hospitals, airports, schools, and highway rest stops.[25] Some Mobil stations feature Dunkin' Donuts shops, and Churchs Chicken shares space with some Texaco convenience store franchises. These pairings save money on property leases, lure more customers, and foster innovation.[26]

More restaurants are now competing directly with supermarkets by offering take-out and delivery in an effort to capture more of the home meal replacement market. Eatzi's Market & Bakery, for instance, is a cross between a gourmet grocery store and an upscale delicatessen where chefs behind counters cook, bake, and prepare meals. Eatzi's now has markets open in Dallas, Houston, Atlanta, and Rockville, Maryland, where their chefs create over 100 ready-to-go entrees, 75 cheeses, 50 breads, and 125 desserts, and even fresh sushi. Consumers can even purchase wine, flowers, and cigars to complement their prepared meal.[27]

Nonstore Retailing

The retailing methods discussed so far have been at the origin in-store methods, in which customers must physically shop at stores. In contrast, **nonstore retailing** is shopping without visiting a store. Because consumers demand convenience, nonstore retailing is currently growing faster than in-store retailing. The major forms of nonstore retailing are automatic vending, direct retailing, direct marketing, and electronic retailing.

Automatic Vending

A low-profile yet important form of retailing is **automatic vending**, the use of machines to offer goods for sale—for example, the cola, candy, or snack vending machines found in college cafeterias and office buildings. Vending is the most pervasive retail business, with about six million vending machines in the United States selling $30 billion annually. Food and beverage account for about 85 percent of all sales from vending machines. Due to their convenience, consumers are willing to pay higher prices for products from a vending machine than for the same products in traditional retail settings.[28]

Retailers are constantly seeking new opportunities to sell via vending. For example, in an attempt to expand its distribution beyond supermarkets, convenience stores, and delicatessens, Snapple has developed a glass-front vending machine capable of offering fifty-four different flavors simultaneously. Many vending machines today also sell nontraditional kinds of merchandise, such as videos, toys, stickers, and sports cards. Vending machines in college libraries sell computer diskettes, pens and highlighters, and other office-type supplies. Kodak cameras and film can now be purchased from vending machines in sports stadiums, on beaches, and on mountains. Moviegoers still humming the tunes from the movie they just viewed can purchase the soundtrack for $15 by inserting their credit card into vending machines set up in theater lobbies. Department store shoppers can purchase Joe Boxer boxer shorts from its Underwear to Go vending machines. Marketers are also experimenting with fresh foods in vending machines. Canteen Vending Services, the nation's largest vendor operator, has been stocking fresh sandwiches in its food machines from nationally known restaurants such as Hardee's, Blimpie, and Nathan's.[29]

Nick Graham, CEO of Joe Boxer, stands next to his Undo Vendo machine at the company's San Francisco headquarters. The vending machine dispenses boxer shorts in a pop-top can.

Direct Retailing

In **direct retailing**, representatives sell products door-to-door, office-to-office, or at home sales parties. Companies like Avon, Mary Kay Cosmetics, The Pampered Chef, Usbourne Books, and World Book Encyclopedia depend on these techniques. Even personal computers are now being sold through direct retailing

4

Discuss nonstore retailing techniques

nonstore retailing
Shopping without visiting a store.

automatic vending
The use of machines to offer goods for sale.

direct retailing
The selling of products by representatives who work door-to-door, office-to-office, or at home parties.

methods. Hand Technologies, based in Austin, Texas, sells computers using a team of consultants to sell computer products via demonstrations in the home and local seminars for schools and families. The company targets new users of technology who need more support with the purchase, setup, and learning of computers and the Internet. The company now has over a thousand part-time consultants to sell personal computers directly to the customer.[30]

Most direct retailers seem to favor party plans these days in lieu of door-to-door canvassing. Party plans call for one person, the host, to gather as many prospective buyers as possible. Most parties are a combination social affair and sales demonstration. For instance, d.terrell, an Atlanta-based direct-sales apparel manufacturer, sells its fashionable women's clothes through wardrobe consultants who several times a year transform their homes into makeshift boutiques. Friends and acquaintances can select a full season's wardrobe in a friendly environment while bypassing the inconveniences and unknowledgeable salespeople at the mall.[31]

 The sales of direct retailers have suffered as women have entered the workforce. Working women are not home during the day and have little time to attend selling parties. Although most direct sellers like Avon and Tupperware still advocate the party plan method, the realities of the marketplace have forced them to be more creative in reaching their target customer. Direct sales representatives now hold parties in offices, parks, and even parking lots. Others hold informal gatherings in which shoppers can just drop in at their convenience or offer self-improvement classes. Many direct retailers are also turning to direct mail, telephone, or more traditional retailing venues to find new avenues to their customers and increase sales. Avon, for instance, has begun opening cosmetic kiosk counters, called Avon Beauty Centers, in malls and strip centers. Direct retailers are also experimenting with the Internet to reach more buyers and increase sales. Amway recently launched an entirely new on-line spin-off, called Quixtar.com. Customers access the site using referral numbers unique to each of the Amway reps, which ensures the reps earn commissions. Avon, Tupperware, and Mary Kay have followed Amway's lead by setting up Internet retail sites. At Avon's site, individual reps have created home pages that link from Avon's home page so that the sale will still go through them.[32]

In response to the decline in U.S. sales, many direct retailers are exploring opportunities in other countries. Amway, the direct seller of shampoo, detergent, toothpaste, and other household products, is one company that has benefited from overseas expansion. Bypassing the joint ventures and lavish advertising campaigns most consumer companies must use to expand overseas, Amway instead mobilized its ethnically diverse sales force to return to their home countries and spread the word, missionary-like, to friends and families. This strategy has helped turn the company into a multinational juggernaut with a sales force of 2.5 million and $68 billion in sales. Today, Amway peddles its products in forty-three countries from Hungary to Malaysia to Brazil. Amway's goal is to have overseas markets account for 80 percent of its sales during the next decade.[33]

Direct Marketing

direct marketing (direct-response marketing)
Techniques used to get consumers to make a purchase from their home, office, or other nonretail setting.

Direct marketing, sometimes called **direct-response marketing**, refers to the techniques used to get consumers to make a purchase from their home, office, or other nonretail setting. Those techniques include direct mail, catalogs and mail order, telemarketing, and electronic retailing. Shoppers using these methods are less bound by traditional shopping situations. Time-strapped consumers and those who live in rural or suburban areas are most likely to be direct-response shoppers, because they value the convenience and flexibility that direct marketing provides.

Direct Mail   Direct mail can be the most efficient or the least efficient retailing method, depending on the quality of the mailing list and the effectiveness of the mailing piece. With direct mail, marketers can precisely target their customers according to demographics, geographics, and even psychographics. Good mailing lists come from an internal database or are available from list brokers for about $35 to $150 per thousand names. For example, a Los Angeles computer software manufacturer selling programs for managing medical records may buy a list of all the physicians in the area. The software manufacturer may then design a direct-mail piece explaining the benefits of its system and send the piece to each physician. Today, direct mailers are even using videocassettes in place of letters and brochures to deliver their sales message to consumers.

Direct mailers are becoming more sophisticated in their targeting of the "right" customers. Using statistical methods to analyze census data, lifestyle and financial information, and past-purchase and credit history, direct mailers can pick out those most likely to buy their products. For example, a direct marketer like Dell Computers might use this technique to target 500,000 people with the right spending patterns, demographics, and preferences. Without it, Dell could easily mail millions of solicitations annually. Some solicitations could be targeted to only 10,000 of the best prospects, however, saving the company millions in postage while still preserving sales.

Catalogs and Mail Order   Consumers can now buy just about anything through the mail, from the mundane like books, music, and polo shirts to the outlandish, such as the $5 million diamond-and-ruby-studded bra available through the Victoria's Secret catalog. Although women make up the bulk of catalog shoppers, the percentage of male catalog shoppers has soared in recent years. As changing demographics has shifted more of the shopping responsibility onto men, shopping via catalog or mail order is seen as a more sensible solution to men than a trek to a mall.[34]

Successful catalogs are usually created and designed for highly segmented markets. Sears, whose catalog sales had dropped off, replaced its "big book" with a collection of more successful specialty catalogs targeted to specific market segments. Certain types of retailers are also using mail order to good effect. For example, computer manufacturers have discovered that mail order is a lucrative way to sell computers to home and small-business users, evidenced by the huge successes of Dell Computers and Gateway. Through its direct business model, Dell Computers is now a $25 billion company and the leading supplier of personal computers to business customers, government agencies, educational institutions, and consumers in the United States. Dell migrated its sales to the Internet in 1997 with astonishing results. The company now sells $40 million worth of computers and computer equipment on-line every day.[35]

Improved customer service and quick delivery policies have boosted consumer confidence in mail order. L.L. Bean and Lands' End are two catalog companies known for their excellent customer service. Shoppers may order twenty-four hours a day and return any merchandise for any reason for a full refund. Other successful mail-order catalogs—including Spiegel, J. Crew, Victoria's Secret, and Lillian Vernon—target hard-working, home-oriented baby boomers who don't have time to visit or would rather not visit a retail store. To remain competitive and save time for customers, catalog companies are building computer databases containing customer information so they do not have to repeatedly give their addresses, credit card information, and so on. They also are working with overnight shippers such as UPS and FedEx to speed up deliveries. Indeed, some products can be ordered as late at 12:30 A.M. and still arrive the same day by 10:30 A.M.

Telemarketing   **Telemarketing** is the use of the telephone to sell directly to consumers. It consists of outbound sales calls, usually unsolicited, and inbound calls—that is, orders through toll-free 800 numbers or fee-based 900 numbers.

Outbound telemarketing is an attractive direct-marketing technique because of rising postage rates and decreasing long-distance phone rates. Skyrocketing field sales costs also have put pressure on marketing managers to use outbound telemarketing. Searching for ways to keep costs under control, marketing managers are discovering how to pinpoint prospects quickly, zero in on serious buyers, and keep in close touch with regular customers. Meanwhile, they are reserving expensive, time-consuming, in-person calls for closing sales.

Inbound telemarketing programs, which use 800 and 900 numbers, are mainly used to take orders, generate leads, and provide customer service. Inbound 800 telemarketing has successfully supplemented direct-response TV, radio, and print advertising for more than twenty-five years. The more recently introduced 900 numbers, which customers pay to call, are gaining popularity as a cost-effective way for companies to target customers. One of the major benefits of 900 numbers is that they allow marketers to generate qualified responses. Although the charge may reduce the total volume of calls, the calls that do come through are from customers who have a true interest in the product.

Electronic Retailing

Electronic retailing includes the twenty-four-hour, shop-at-home television networks and on-line retailing.

Shop-at-Home Networks   The shop-at-home television networks are specialized forms of direct-response marketing. These shows display merchandise, with the retail price, to home viewers. Viewers can phone in their orders directly on a toll-free line and shop with a credit card. The shop-at-home industry has quickly grown into a billion-dollar business with a loyal customer following. Shop-at-home networks have the capability of reaching nearly every home that has a television set.

The best-known shop-at-home networks are the Home Shopping Network and the QVC (Quality, Value, Convenience) Network. Home shopping networks are now branching out with new products to appeal to more affluent audiences—the age and income profile of a typical home-shopping viewer is 31+ with household earnings of more than $60,000. Food marketers like Hershey Foods, Campbell Soup, and Kellogg's are the latest companies to test the potential of shop-at-home networks, especially with new product introductions. Hershey introduced its Pot of Gold boxed candy line on QVC, selling sixteen hundred boxes of candy in four minutes. Campbell plans a full hour on the QVC network to sell reproductions of the first Campbell Kid dolls. Campbell will also showcase historical advertising and videos related to the merchandise being sold. Similarly, Kellogg's introduced Cocoa Frosted Flakes on home shopping channels rather than using traditional channels.[36]

On-line Retailing   For years, shopping at home meant looking through catalogs and then placing an order over the telephone. For many people today, however, it now means turning on a computer, surfing retail Web sites, and selecting and ordering products on-line with the click of a mouse. **On-line retailing**, or *e-tailing*, is a type of shopping available to consumers with personal computers and access to the Internet. Roughly four out of every ten homes today has a personal computer, with about a quarter of those connected to the Internet.[37]

On-line retailing has exploded in the last several years as consumers have found this type of shopping convenient and, in many instances, less costly. Consumers can shop without leaving home, choose from a wide selection of merchants, use shopping comparison services to search the Web for the best price, and then have the items delivered to their doorsteps. As a result, on-line shopping is growing at an incredibly rapid pace. Exact figures are difficult to pinpoint, but industry experts estimate that on-line retail sales will reach about $36 billion in 2000, two-and-a-half times 1999 on-line sales estimates of roughly $15 billion.[38]

Original Web-based retailers, like Amazon.com and CDNow, pioneered on-line retailing, selling merchandise more cheaply and conveniently than their brick-and-mortar competition. Amazon.com has become one of the nation's biggest booksellers via the Internet. On-line shoppers can search Amazon's database of over one million titles, read on-line reviews and receive e-mail alerts about their favorite subjects and authors. CDNow's Internet site offers more than 166,000 music CD titles and buyers can receive their orders within twenty-four hours. Consumers in some metropolitan areas can even purchase groceries over the Internet from Web retailers such as Webvan, HomeGrocer.com, and Peapod, giving traditional supermarkets a run for their money. As these grocery services expand into new markets, on-line grocery sales are projected to exceed $10 billion in the next few years.[39]

Most traditional retailers have now jumped on the Internet bandwagon, allowing shoppers to purchase the same merchandise found in their stores from their Web site. On-line retailing also fits well with traditional catalog companies, such as Lands' End and Eddie Bauer who already have established distribution networks. In a drastic turnabout in its retail strategy, computer software retailer Egghead recently closed all of its brick-and-mortar stores moving its entire business onto the Web, adding ".com" to the end of its name. Software purchased at the company's site, **http://www.egghead.com**, can be downloaded directly to the purchaser's computer.

As the popularity of on-line retailing grows and more consumers become computer savvy, retailers are experimenting with ways to make their physical stores, their Internet sites, and catalogs all work together. Retailer and cataloger Williams-Sonoma, for example, recently linked its store gift-registry to its Web site, allowing brides to see who has bought what in real time. Banana Republic stores in New York and Santa Monica, California, have Web stations where customers can order items that aren't on the shelves.[40] At Le Printemps department store in Paris, rollerblading salespeople equipped with ultra-lightweight laptop computers, wireless networking gear, and video cameras skate around the store broadcasting live onto the company's Web site. As they roll around the aisles, they can chat on-line with shoppers making merchandise requests.[41]

A relatively new phenomenon in on-line retailing is the success of auctions run by Internet companies like eBay and Amazon.com. With close to two million items for sale each day, ranging from antique clocks to car stereos, eBay leads the trend in cyberspace auctions. Internet auction services, like eBay, run the Web service and collect a token listing fee, plus a commission of 1 to 5 percent when a sale is completed.[42] Amazon's auction site has even teamed up with high-end art auction house Sotheby's to offer thousands of rare coins, sports collectibles, postwar books, jewelry, and furniture. Each item carries a stamp of authenticity from Sotheby's or one of the 2,800 art and antiques dealers worldwide who have signed exclusive agreements to supply items to Sotheby's on-line auction site.[43] On-line

Le Printemps department store in Paris takes on-line retailing to an extreme. The in-store Web-camera puts you right in the heart of the store by broadcasting live to the company's Web site and by interacting with on-line customers in real-time.

auctions are expected to account for sales of $8.1 billion by 2001 and their popularity is attracting new entrants to the field. Dell Computers, for example, recently established its own on-line auction site that couples sales of outlet-store goods and refurbished Dell computers with customers' used equipment.[44]

Franchising

5

Define franchising and describe its two basic forms

franchiser
The originator of a trade name, product, methods of operation, and so on, that grants operating rights to another party to sell its product.

franchisee
An individual or business that is granted the right to sell another party's product.

A *franchise* is a continuing relationship in which a franchiser grants to a franchisee the business rights to operate or to sell a product. The **franchiser** originates the trade name, product, methods of operation, and so on. The **franchisee**, in return, pays the franchiser for the right to use its name, product, or business methods. A franchise agreement between the two parties usually lasts for ten to twenty years, at which time the franchisee can renew the agreement with the franchiser if both parties are agreeable.

To be granted the rights to a franchise, a franchisee usually pays an initial, one-time franchise fee. The amount of this fee depends solely on the individual franchiser, but it generally ranges from $5,000 to $150,000. In addition to this initial franchise fee, the franchisee is expected to pay weekly, biweekly, or monthly royalty fees, usually in the range of 3 to 7 percent of gross revenues. The franchisee may also be expected to pay advertising fees, which usually cover the cost of promotional materials and, if the franchise organization is large enough, regional or national advertising. A McDonald's franchise, for example, costs an initial $45,000 per store plus a monthly fee based upon the restaurant's sales performance and base rent. In addition, a new McDonald's franchisee can expect start-up costs for equipment and pre-opening expenses to range from $433,000 to $715,000. The size of the restaurant facility, area of the country, inventory, selection of kitchen equipment, signage, and style of decor and landscaping affect new restaurant costs.[45] While the dollar amount will vary depending on the type of franchise format, fees such as these are typical for all major franchisers, including Burger King, Jani-King, Athlete's Foot, and Subway.

Franchising is not new. General Motors has used this approach since 1898, and Rexall drugstores, since 1901. Today there are over half a million franchised establishments in the United States, with combined sales approaching $1 trillion, or about 40 percent of all retail trade. While franchised restaurants attract most of those dollars, hundreds of retail and service franchises, such as Alphagraphics Printshops, Mail Boxes, Etc., and Sylvan Learning Systems, are also thriving. It's estimated that a new franchise opens in the United States every six and a half minutes.[46] Exhibit 13.3 lists some facts about some of the largest and more well-known U.S. companies in franchising.

There are two basic forms of franchises today: product and trade name franchising and business format franchising. In *product and trade name franchising*, a dealer agrees to sell certain products provided by a manufacturer or a wholesaler. This approach has been used most widely in the auto and truck, soft-drink bottling, tire, and gasoline service industries. For example, a local tire retailer may hold a franchise to sell Michelin tires. Likewise, the Coca-Cola bottler in a particular area is a product and trade name franchisee licensed to bottle and sell Coca-Cola's soft drinks.

Business format franchising is an ongoing business relationship between a franchiser and a franchisee. Typically, a franchiser "sells" a franchisee the rights to use the franchiser's format or approach to doing business. This form of franchising has rapidly expanded since the 1950s through retailing, restaurant, food-service, hotel and motel, printing, and real estate franchises. Fast-food restaurants like McDonald's, Wendy's, and Burger King use this kind of franchising, as well as other companies such as Hyatt Corporation, Unocal Corporation, and Mobil Corpora-

Exhibit **13.3** Largest U.S. Franchisers

Franchiser	Type of Business	Total Units	Initial Investment
McDonald's Corporation Oak Brook, Illinois	Fast food	Franchised units: 18,361 Company-owned units: 5,262	$408,600–$647,000
Southland Corporation (7-Eleven) Dallas, Texas	Convenience stores	Franchised units: 15,572 Company-owned units: 2,666	Not available
Subway Sandwiches & Salads Milford, Connecticut	Fast food	Franchised units: 13,537 Company-owned units: 2	$66,200–$175,000
Burger King Corporation Miami, Florida	Fast food	Franchised units: 7,495 Company-owned units: 758	$73,000–$511,000
KFC Corporation Louisville, Kentucky	Fast food	Franchised units: 3,255 Company-owned units: 1,759	Not available
Pizza Hut, Inc. Dallas, Texas	Pizza	Franchised units: 4,200 Company-owned units: 2,800	Not available
Tandy Corporation Fort Worth, Texas	Consumer electronics	Franchised units: 6,779 Company-owned units: 1,890	$60,000+
Jani-King International Dallas, Texas	Janitorial, cleaning services	Franchised units: 7,700 Company-owned units: 35	$5,500–$80,000
Taco Bell Corporation Dallas, Texas	Fast food	Franchised units: 4,600 Company-owned units: 3,044	$200,000+
International Dairy Queen Minneapolis, Minnesota	Ice cream, fast food	Franchised units: 5,347 Company-owned units: NA	Not available

SOURCE: Franchise Opportunities Guide Online, International Franchise Association, Washington, D.C., **http://www.franchise.org**.

tion. Prospective McDonald's franchisees must be willing to train at least a year and work in restaurants without pay before they are granted a franchise to operate. Months of training teaches franchisees how to adhere to the detailed business system that made McDonald's famous for consistency around the world.[47]

Like other retailers, franchisers are seeking new growth abroad. Hundreds of U.S. franchisers have begun international expansion, actively looking for foreign franchisees to open new locations. Wendy's International, for instance, will soon open its first franchise in Panama. The hamburger chain has 4,750 franchised units in the United States and 650 overseas in thirty-four different countries, including one hundred in Japan, twenty-four in Venezuela, twenty-six in Argentina, and one outlet in Bali. Countries in Asia and Central Europe that are recovering from difficult economic times have produced a new crop of potential franchisees—well-educated men and women who are out of work but have a wide range of experience in business to offer. The International Franchise Association now lists over fifty national franchise organizations in countries from Argentina to Zimbabwe.[48]

Franchisers sometimes allow franchisees to alter their business format slightly in foreign markets. For example, McDonald's franchisees in Japan offer food items that appeal to Japanese tastes, such as steamed dumplings, curry with rice, and roast pork cutlet burgers with melted cheese. McDonald's franchisees in India serve mutton instead of beef because most Indians are Hindu, a religion whose followers believe cows to be a sacred symbol of the source of life. The menu also features rice-based Vegetable Burgers made with peas, carrots, red pepper, beans, and Indian spices as well as Vegetable McNuggets.

Retail Marketing Strategy

List the major tasks involved in developing a retail marketing strategy

Retailers must develop marketing strategies based on overall goals and strategic plans. Retailing goals might include more traffic, higher sales of a specific item, a more upscale image, or heightened public awareness of the retail operation. The strategies that retailers use to obtain their goals might include a sale, an updated decor, or a new advertisement. The key tasks in strategic retailing are defining and selecting a target market and developing the "six Ps" of the retailing mix to successfully meet the needs of the chosen target market: the traditional four Ps plus personnel and presentation, as discussed below.

Defining a Target Market

The first and foremost task in developing a retail strategy is to define the target market. This process begins with market segmentation, the topic of Chapter 7. Successful retailing has always been based on knowing the customer. Sometimes retailing chains have floundered because management loses sight of the customers the stores should be serving. For example, The Limited experienced phenomenal growth in the 1980s selling trendy apparel to young women. As their customer base matured, however, The Limited missed the opportunity to provide them with fashion options that better reflected the sensibilities of an older consumer. Furthermore, The Limited moved into careerwear, an unsuccessful strategy that only confused its remaining customers and forced the company to close some units.

Target markets in retailing are often defined by demographics, geographics, and psychographics. Claire's Stores, for instance, targets twelve- to fourteen-year-old girls who may get most of their wardrobe at The Gap but spend their allowances accessorizing at Claire's. To keep up with the fashion trends of its target market, Claire's executives read teen magazines, watch teen-oriented shows like *Friends* and *Beverly Hills 90210*, and listen to a lot of music.[49]

Determining a target market is a prerequisite to creating the retailing mix. For example, Target's merchandising approach for sporting goods is to match its product assortment to the demographics of the local store and region. The amount of space devoted to sporting goods, as well as in-store promotions, also varies according to each store's target market. Similarly, Ann Taylor caters to working women in their thirties and forties—a group of customers notoriously pressed for time. Consequently, its stores offer a one-stop wardrobe solution with color-coordinated blouses, sweaters, skirts, and trousers that make it easy to create a wardrobe with just a few purchases.[50]

Choosing the Retailing Mix

retailing mix
A combination of the six Ps—product, place, promotion, price, presentation, and personnel—to sell goods and services to the ultimate consumer.

Retailers combine the elements of the retailing mix to come up with a single retailing method to attract the target market. The **retailing mix** consists of six Ps: the four Ps of the marketing mix (product, place, promotion, and price) plus presentation and personnel. (See Exhibit 13.4.)

Exhibit **13.4**

The Retailing Mix

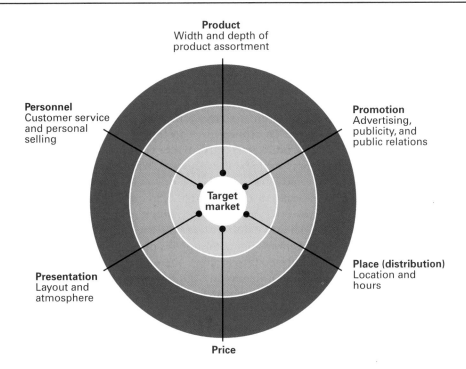

Product
Width and depth of
product assortment

Personnel
Customer service
and personal
selling

Promotion
Advertising,
publicity, and
public relations

**Target
market**

Presentation
Layout and
atmosphere

Place (distribution)
Location and
hours

Price

The combination of the six Ps projects a store's image, which influences consumers' perceptions. Using these impressions of stores, shoppers position one store against another. A retail marketing manager must make sure that the store's positioning is compatible with the target customers' expectations. As discussed at the beginning of the chapter, retail stores can be positioned on three broad dimensions: service provided by store personnel, product assortment, and price. Management should use everything else—place, presentation, and promotion— to fine-tune the basic positioning of the store.

The Product Offering   The first element in the retailing mix is the **product offering**, also called the *product assortment* or *merchandise mix*. Retailers decide what to sell on the basis of what their target market wants to buy. They can base their decision on market research, past sales, fashion trends, customer requests, and other sources. For example, Ames Department Store's core customer base is made up of households with $30,000 to $45,000 in annual income. Through target market research, the company found a significant correlation between lower income and heavier weight. As a result, Ames offers $8.99 acrylic sweaters and $5.99 sweatpants, along with "husky" merchandise for kids and few, if any, petite sizes for model-thin women.[51]

Developing a product offering is essentially a question of width and depth of the product assortment. *Width* refers to the assortment of products offered; *depth* refers to the number of different brands offered within each assortment. Price, store design, displays, and service are important to consumers in determining where to shop, but the most critical factor is merchandise selection. This reasoning also holds true for on-line retailers. Amazon.com, for instance, has ambitious plans to build the world's biggest on-line department store so shoppers can get whatever they want with one click on their Web browsers. As with a traditional department store or mass merchandiser, Amazon offers considerable width in its product assortment with millions of different items, including

product offering
The mix of products offered to the consumer by the retailer; also called the *product assortment* or *merchandise mix.*

ON LINE

books, music, toys, videos, tools and hardware, health and beauty aids, electronics, and software. Recently, Amazon invited thousands of small merchants to do business in a new section on its Web site, called zShops. Conversely, on-line specialty retailers, such as eToys, Garden.com, CDNow, and Blockbuster's Reel.com, focus on a single category of merchandise, hoping to attract loyal customers with a larger depth of products at lower prices and better customer service.[52] Many on-line retailers purposely focus on single product line niches that could never garner enough foot traffic to support a traditional brick-and-mortar store. Mustardstore.com, for instance, offers 660 different gourmet mustards, while Fridgedoor.com sells 1,500 different types of refrigerator magnets to collectors.[53]

After determining what products will satisfy target customers' desires, retailers must find sources of supply and evaluate the products. When the right products are found, the retail buyer negotiates a purchase contract. The buying function can either be performed in-house or be delegated to an outside firm. The goods must then be moved from the seller to the retailer, which means shipping, storing, and stocking the inventory. The trick is to manage the inventory by cutting prices to move slow goods and by keeping adequate supplies of hot-selling items in stock. As in all good systems, the final step is to evaluate the entire process to seek more efficient methods and eliminate problems and bottlenecks.

One of the more efficient new methods of managing inventory and streamlining the way products are moved from supplier to distributor to retailer is called *efficient consumer response* (**ECR**). At the heart of ECR is *electronic data interchange* (**EDI**), the computer-to-computer exchange of information, including automatic shipping notifications, invoices, inventory data, and forecasts. In a full implementation of ECR, products are scanned at the retail store when purchased, which updates the store's inventory lists. Headquarters then polls the stores to retrieve the data needed to produce an order. The vendor confirms the order, shipping date, and delivery time, then ships the order and transmits the invoice electronically. The item is received at the warehouse, scanned into inventory, and then sent to the store. The invoice and receiving data are reconciled, and payment via an electronic transfer of funds completes the process.

Many retailers are experimenting with or have successfully implemented ECR and EDI. Calendar Club, a mall-based kiosk retailer of calendars, uses ECR and EDI to get the right products at each kiosk, which only operate about 120 days of the year, as quickly as possible. With virtually zero storage space in its kiosks, Calendar Club has to keep close tabs on what is selling in each kiosk. During the hectic holiday season, some kiosks sell more than one thousand calendars a day. Therefore, replenishment has to be fast enough to take advantage of the brief sales window. To do that, Calendar Club developed an ECR replenishment solution in which point-of-sale data from each kiosk are electronically communicated to company headquarters every night. Once received, the information is analyzed, and unique replenishment orders for each kiosk are generated and sent to the distribution center for picking, packing, and shipping.[54]

Advances in computer technology have also helped retailers spot new opportunities, such as the latest fashions. These styles can be recreated on a computer, and the designs can be transmitted electronically to manufacturers for production. New merchandise can be produced and put on store shelves in weeks rather than months. This speed gives retailers like Dillard's a competitive advantage over other fashion retailers.

As margins drop and competition intensifies, retailers are becoming ever more aware of the advantages of **private-label brands**, or those brands that are designed and developed using the retailer's name. Because the cost of goods typically makes up between 70 and 85 percent of a retailer's expenses, eliminating middlemen can shave costs. As a result, prices of private-label goods are typically lower than for national brands, giving customers greater value. Private-label branding is

private-label brands
Brands that are designed and developed using the retailer's name.

not new. For decades, Sears has fashioned its Kenmore, Craftsman, and DieHard brands into household names. Lately, Wal-Mart has begun rolling out its own private-label brands, such as White Cloud paper products, Spring Valley nutritional supplements, Sam's American Choice laundry detergent, EverActive alkaline batteries, and EverStart auto batteries, with much success. Its Ol' Roy dog food and Sam's American Choice garden fertilizer are now the best-selling brands in their categories. As the nation's largest retailer, Wal-Mart's foray into private-labels worries many brand marketers, such as Procter & Gamble, which manufactures Tide laundry detergent. Whereas Wal-Mart was once its biggest customer, the giant retailer is transforming itself into its biggest competitor with the introduction of Sam's American Choice laundry soap that sells for 25 to 30 percent lower. And while Wal-Mart's private labels might not steal significant sales away from popular brands like Tide, in the long run smaller second- and third-tier brands that don't bring consumers to the shelves may have a difficult time surviving.[55]

Promotion Strategy Retail promotion strategy includes advertising, public relations and publicity, and sales promotion. The goal is to help position the store in consumers' minds. Retailers design intriguing ads, stage special events, and develop promotions aimed at their target markets. For example, today's grand openings are a carefully orchestrated blend of advertising, merchandising, goodwill, and glitter. All the elements of an opening—press coverage, special events, media advertising, and store displays—are carefully planned.

Retailers' advertising is carried out mostly at the local level, although retail giants like Sears and JCPenney can advertise nationally. Local advertising by retailers is more specific communication about their stores, such as location, merchandise, hours, prices, and special sales. On the other hand, national advertising by retailers generally focuses on image. The "Softer Side of Sears" national advertising campaign, for example, was used to help reposition Sears as a low-priced but fashion-conscious apparel retailer. An accompanying campaign, "Come See the Many Sides of Sears," was used to promote the retailer's nonapparel merchandise, such as tools, paint, and car parts.

Often large retailers and well-known clothing designers or manufacturers of exclusive specialty products share the spotlight in an advertisement. For example, ads linking Ralph Lauren and Foley's, a department store chain, let everyone know that Foley's sells the latest fashions. In turn, they enhance Ralph Lauren's prestige by associating it with a successful, distinguished fashion retailer. Although this type of arrangement, called *cooperative advertising*, is prevalent in the apparel industry, it has only recently become more common between packaged goods companies and retailers. Traditionally, marketers would just pay retailers to feature products in store mailers or a marketer would develop a TV campaign and simply tack on several retailers' names at the end of a product commercial or at the bottom of a print ad. However, now cooperative advertising has become more collaborative, with clear dual objectives. For example, a Pepsi advertisement might invite viewers to visit their nearest Kroger store for twelve-packs of their favorite soft drink at a competitive price.

Many retailers are forgoing media advertising these days in favor of direct mail or frequent shopper programs. Direct mail and catalog programs are luring many

Sears has built its private label Craftsman brand into a tool powerhouse. The king of home remodeling, Bob Villa, formerly of This Old House, is even spokesman for the line of successful products.

retailers in the hope they will prove a cost-effective means of increasing brand loyalty and spending by core customers. Nordstrom, for example, mails catalogs featuring brand-name and private-brand clothing, shoes, and accessories to target the shop-at-home crowd. Home repair outlets such as Lowe's and Home Depot have also used direct mail, often around holidays when people have time off to complete needed repairs. Restaurants and small retailers have successfully used frequent diner or frequent shopper programs for years. Now many big retailers, like mass merchandiser Sears and Neiman Marcus and Federated department store chains, are offering frequent shopper programs or loyalty programs that shower top shoppers with perks ranging from advance notice of sales and free gift wrapping to store discounts based on spending. The InCircle loyalty program at Neiman Marcus, for example, rewards loyal customers who charge more than $3,000 annually on their Neiman Marcus credit card. Customers earn one point for each dollar charged that can be redeemed at different levels for everything from bottles of Dom Perignon champagne to new, fully loaded Jaguars, or Caribbean cruises for two.[56]

The Proper Location   Another element in the retailing mix is place, or site location. Selecting a proper site is a critical decision. First, it is a large, long-term commitment of resources that can reduce a retailer's future flexibility. Whether the retailer leases or purchases, the location decision implies some degree of permanence. Second, the location will affect future growth. The chosen area should be growing economically so it can sustain the original store and any future stores. Last, the local environment may change over time. If the location's value deteriorates, the store may have to be relocated or closed.

Site location begins by choosing a community. This decision depends largely on economic growth potential and stability, the competition, political climate, and so on. Some of the savviest location experts in recent years have been T. J. Maxx and Toys "R" Us. Both retailers put the majority of their new locations in rapidly growing areas where the population closely matches their customer base.

Sometimes it is not the economic profile or political climate that makes a community a good location but rather its geographic location. Locating its stores in over two hundred small towns and cities has made the Buckle, a retailer of designer apparel aimed at teens, quite a success. Big-name designer retailers have traditionally shunned rural America, harboring the illusion that rural youths don't know or care about fashion. However, the Buckle, which stocks such well-known fashion names as Tommy Hilfiger, Nautica, Polo by Ralph Lauren, and JNCO, is a hit with rural teens who possess the means and willingness to pay full price for fashion.[57] Office-supply superstores have also found small towns to be more attractive than larger cities. The Staples store located in Lebanon, New Hampshire, a town of 12,600 people, produces twice the annual sales of the average Staples store.[58]

After settling on a geographic region or community, retailers must choose a specific site. In addition to growth potential, the important factors are neighborhood socioeconomic characteristics, traffic flows, land costs, zoning regulations, and public transportation. Retailers should also consider where competitors are located as well as their own stores. A particular site's visibility, parking, entrance and exit locations, accessibility, and safety and security issues are other variables contributing to site selection success. Additionally, *retail synergy*, or how well a store's format meshes with the surrounding retail environment, is also important.[59] Retail decision makers probably would not locate a Dollar General store next door to a Neiman-Marcus department store.

"Location, location, location" has long been the retailing axiom emphasizing the importance of site selection in making a store profitable. Wal-Mart became the largest retailer in the country by locating in underserved small towns. Offering such services as hair salons, mail centers, optometrists, travel agencies, pharmacies, and food outlets, a discounter like Wal-Mart has every retail destination that the average small town has, translated to a single site. Similarly, Saks Fifth Avenue has been slowly branching out beyond malls by locating smaller Saks stores, called Saks Main Street, in the heart of affluent suburbia. At about forty-six thousand square feet, about a third of the size or less than the full-line Saks Fifth Avenue store, Main Street stores can locate where its core customers already live and shop: the main shopping streets of affluent suburbs and towns. Saks' research told them that more and more of their customers did not want to leave their communities to go shopping in huge regional malls, so Saks made it more convenient by opening Main Street stores where they live. Main Street stores are already proving to be more productive than its full-line versions, averaging $400 to $500 per square foot compared to $300 to $350 for full-line stores. Also, people who live close to a Main Street store shop as much as eight times a month; regional mall locations are more likely to be shopped only twice a month.[60]

One final decision about location faces retailers: whether to have a freestanding unit or to become a shopping center or mall tenant.

Freestanding Stores   An isolated, freestanding location can be used by large retailers like Wal-Mart, Kmart, or Target and sellers of shopping goods like furniture and cars, because they are "destination" stores, or those stores consumers will purposely plan to visit. In other words, customers will seek them out. An isolated store location may have the advantages of low site cost or rent and no nearby competitors. On the other hand, it may be hard to attract customers to a freestanding location, and no other retailers are around to share costs.

Freestanding units are increasing in popularity by retailers as they strive to make their stores more convenient to access, more enticing to shop, and more profitable. Freestanding site location now accounts for more than half of the millions of square feet of retail construction starts in the United States as more and more retailers are deciding not to locate in pedestrian malls. Perhaps the greatest reason for developing a freestanding site is greater visibility. Retailers often feel they get lost in huge centers and malls, but freestanding units can help stores develop an identity with shoppers. The ability to grow at faster rates through freestanding buildings has also propelled the surge toward stand-alone units. Retailers like The Sports Authority, Linens & Things, and Bed, Bath & Beyond choose to be freestanding in order to achieve their expansion objectives. Waiting for shopping centers to be built can be counterproductive to an aggressive expansion plan.[61] Drugstore chains have been aggressively relocating their existing mall and shopping center stores to freestanding sites, especially street corner sites for drive-through accessibility, much to the dismay of urban preservationists. Read about this dilemma in the "Ethics in Marketing" box.

Shopping Centers   The tremendous boom in shopping centers began after World War II, as the U.S. population started migrating to the suburbs. The first shopping centers were *strip centers*, typically located along a busy street. They usually included a supermarket, a variety store, and perhaps a few specialty stores. Essentially unplanned business districts, these strip centers remain popular.

Next, the small *community shopping centers* emerged, with one or two small department store branches, more specialty shops, one or two restaurants, and several apparel stores. These centers offer a broader variety of shopping, specialty, and convenience goods, provide large off-street parking lots, and usually span 75,000 to 300,000 square feet of retail space.

Finally, along came the huge *regional malls*. Regional malls are either entirely enclosed or roofed to allow shopping in any weather. Many are landscaped with trees, fountains, sculptures, and the like to enhance the shopping environment. They have acres of free parking. The *anchor stores* or *generator stores* (JCPenney,

PRESERVATIONISTS PROTEST AS DRUGSTORES FUEL EXPANSION PLANS

Fueled by the increased demand for prescription drugs by America's aging population and lower drug co-payments, drugstore chains are expanding like wildfire across the country. The chains, most notably CVS, Walgreens, and Rite Aid, target high-visibility, easy-access corners to build or relocate freestanding stores. In some cases, they build right across the street from their competitor. Opening plenty of big new stores with drive-through pharmacies and ample parking is one of the best ways to deal with the needs of aging, time-pressed customers, the chains say.

But to local preservationists, these stores are a blight—out-of-character, cookie-cutter boxes that overwhelm neighboring buildings. The drugstore chains have a tendency to target prominent downtown corners in commercial districts, or Main Streets, as they are often called, much to the dismay of community activists and preservationists. In many cases, historic buildings, they say, are bulldozed to make room for the chains and their expansive parking lots. In Richmond, Indiana, for instance, the First Friends Meeting house, one of the oldest Quaker meeting-houses in the state, dating to 1878, was razed to make way for a CVS unit and parking lot. In DeKalb, Illinois, a 1906 white limestone and marble domed-roof post office was replaced with a Walgreens.

Sentiment against drugstore expansion has reached a national

fervor. Recently, the National Trust for Historic Preservation singled out chain drugstores as threats to "Main and Main," the mythical prime intersections of America's downtowns. The group is particularly concerned about drugstore locations in established downtowns, rather than those in suburbs that have few historic buildings. This presents a particular dilemma: The long decline of these downtown commercial districts has itself been a serious threat to historic buildings. Yet, chain drugstores are often among the first businesses to try moving back into a downtown.

The drugstore chains claim they are bringing convenient, affordable stores closer to where people live, and often to areas struggling for economic development. A spokesman for Walgreen Company, the nation's largest chain, defends their expansion decisions by saying that they do not target specific buildings for sites but rather intersections or locations. Existing buildings, they contend, often don't meet the company's needs for adequate parking or drive-through service. The chains also insist that they don't destroy buildings that are genuinely historic. Most of the buildings in question are simply old and in many cases vacant and dilapidated.

But preservationists say developers often ignore local concerns. Often preservationists don't want to block the drugstores but simply want them to consider the architectural and historic significance of the

buildings and neighborhoods instead of demolishing them. Community preservation groups often suggest alternative sites or request that the chains develop stores that fit into the character of the neighborhood.

As a result of protest, the chains have begun to convert many old buildings into drugstores instead of razing them. In Washington, D.C., for instance, the darkened MacArthur Theater was renovated into a CVS store, leaving the marquee intact, Other stores have been constructed so that they come up to the sidewalk, have windows at street level, use bricks like their neighbors, and keep their parking in the back. A new Rite Aid in Camden, Maine, for example, looks like three classic New England buildings side by side.[a]

Do you feel drugstore expansion helps or hinders downtowns? What can these chains do to mesh more with existing structures? How else could drugstore chains cater to consumers' increasing need for convenience rather than adding drive-through service?

[a] Laura Johannes. "As Drugstores Pop Up Everywhere, Towns Cry Foul," *Wall Street Journal*, June 11, 1999. pp. B1, B4; Maryann Haggerty. "A Prescription for Blight? Historic Preservationists Cite Chain Drugstores as a Threat," *Washington Post*, June 14, 1999. p. F10; George McLaren. "Drug Stores' Development Angers Preservationist Around Nation," *Indianapolis Star and News*, November 11, 1998; Geneva Overholser. "The Box Stops Here," *Washington Post*, October 31, 1999. p. B07.

Sears, or major department stores) are usually located at opposite ends of the mall to create heavy foot traffic. The newly opened superregional Coral Ridge Mall located in Coralville, Iowa, for instance, occupies 1.2 million square feet of space and is conveniently located next to Iowa City, a state university campus, and major interstates and highways. An Iowa State University study found that Iowa City lacked a number of the retail facilities common to similar-sized metropolitan areas and that residents frequently traveled to Cedar Rapids, about thirty minutes away, for items they could not find at the local malls or the downtown shopping district. This lack of retail presence made Coral Ridge an immediate success in its market.[62]

Locating in a community shopping center or regional mall offers several advantages. First, the facilities are designed to attract shoppers. Second, the shopping environment, anchor stores, and "village square" activities draw customers. Third, ample parking is available. Fourth, the center or mall projects a unified image. Fifth, tenants also share the expenses of the mall's common area and promotions for the whole mall. Finally, malls can target different demographic groups. Some malls are considered upscale; others are aimed at people shopping for bargains.

Locating in a shopping center or mall does have disadvantages. These include expensive leases, the chance that common promotion efforts will not attract customers to a particular store, lease restrictions on merchandise carried and hours of operation, the anchor stores' domination of the tenants' association, and the possibility of having direct competitors within the same facility. Consumers have also become more pressed for time in recent years and have decreased the number of visits and the time they spend in malls in favor of more convenient stand-alone stores and neighborhood centers. Faced with this trend, mall developers have improved the layout of many malls to make it more convenient for customers to shop. For instance, the RiverTown Crossings center in Grandville, Michigan, clusters competing stores, like Abercrombie Kids, GapKids, Gymboree, and other kid's clothing stores in one section of the mall to accommodate time-strapped parents.[63]

Retail Prices

Another important element in the retailing mix is price. It is important to understand that retailing's ultimate goal is to sell products to consumers and that the right price is critical in ensuring sales. Because retail prices are usually based on the cost of the merchandise, an essential part of pricing is efficient and timely buying.

Price is also a key element in a retail store's positioning strategy and classification. Higher prices often indicate a level of quality and help reinforce the prestigious image of retailers, as they do for Lord & Taylor, Saks Fifth Avenue, Gucci, Cartier, and Neiman Marcus. On the other hand, discounters and off-price retailers, such as Target and T. J. Maxx, offer a good value for the money. There are even stores, such as Dollar Tree, where everything costs shoppers one dollar. Dollar Tree's single-price-point strategy is aimed at getting higher-income customers to make impulse purchases through what analysts call the "wow factor"—the excitement of discovering an item costs only a dollar.[64]

A pricing trend among American retailers that seems to be here to stay is *everyday low pricing*, or EDLP. Introduced to the retail industry by Wal-Mart, EDLP offers consumers a low price all the time rather than holding periodic sales on merchandise. Even large retail giants, like Federated Department Stores, parent of Macy's and Bloomingdales, have phased out deep discounts and sales in favor of lower prices every day. Similarly, The Gap reduced prices on denim jeans, denim shirts, socks, and other items to protect and broaden the company's share of the casual clothes market. Supermarkets such as Albertson's and Winn Dixie have also found success in EDLP.

Presentation of the Retail Store

The presentation of a retail store helps determine the store's image and positions the retail store in consumers' minds. For instance, a retailer that wants to position itself as an upscale store would use a lavish or sophisticated presentation.

The main element of a store's presentation is its **atmosphere**, the overall impression conveyed by a store's physical layout, decor, and surroundings. The atmosphere might create a relaxed or busy feeling, a sense of luxury or of efficiency, a friendly or cold attitude, a sense of organization or of clutter, or a fun or serious mood. For example, the look at Express stores is designed to make suburban shoppers feel as though they have just strolled into a Parisian boutique. Signage is often

atmosphere
The overall impression conveyed by a store's physical layout, decor, and surroundings.

How can a company create an atmosphere on its Web site? Visit the pages of some of your favorite retailers to see if they have been able to recreate the store atmosphere on the Internet.

On Line

in French, and the background music has a European flair. Likewise, retail stores based on the colorful, quirky world of Nickelodeon television feature cabinets covered with green slime, garbage cans at the end of aisles, tilted walls, purple ceilings, and bright hues and bold patterns. Nickelodeon stores include plenty of interactive features, making the space a fun place for children of all ages.[65]

More often these days retailers are adding an element of entertainment to their store atmosphere. The Nike Town store in Chicago looks more like a museum than like a traditional retail store. The three-story space displays products amid life-size Michael Jordan statues and glassed-in relics like baseball legend Nolan Ryan's shoes. A History of Air exhibit explains the pockets of air on the bottom of some Nike shoes. A video theater plays Nike commercials and short films featuring Nike gear.

The layout of retail stores is a key factor in their success. Layout is planned so that all space in the store is used effectively, including aisles, fixtures, merchandise displays, and nonselling areas. Effective store layout ensures the customer's shopping ease and convenience, but it has a powerful influence on customer traffic patterns and purchasing behavior. Best Buy recently rolled out a new store format that put higher-priced digital goods in the center aisles, along with salespeople, and moved electronic standbys, like cables and headphones, to self-service sections. Most of its tall, warehouse-style product shelves have been cut down to give customers a better view of the whole store and sales reps a better view of customers. Sales reps are assigned to the "full serve" product zone located in the middle of the store and move into the self-service areas only if a customer needs help. Best Buy hopes the changes in layout will improve sales and profits by better utilizing its sales staff to push more lucrative items.[66]

Layout also includes where products are placed in the store. Many technologically advanced retailers are using a technique called *market-basket analysis* to analyze the huge amounts of data collected through their point-of-purchase scanning equipment. The analysis looks for products that are commonly purchased together to help retailers remerchandise their stores to place products in the right places.[67] Wal-Mart uses market-basket analysis to determine where in the store to stock products for customer convenience. Bananas are placed not only in the produce section but also in the cereal aisle. Kleenex tissues are in the paper-goods aisle and also mixed in with the cold medicines. Measuring spoons are in the housewares and also hanging next to Crisco shortening. During October, flashlights are not only in the hardware aisle but also with the Halloween costumes.[68]

These are the most influential factors in creating a store's atmosphere:

- *Employee type and density:* Employee type refers to an employee's general characteristics—for instance, neat, friendly, knowledgeable, or service oriented. Density is the number of employees per thousand square feet of selling space. A discounter like Kmart has a low employee density that creates a "do-it-yourself," casual atmosphere. In contrast, Neiman Marcus's density is much higher, denoting readiness to serve the customer's every whim. Too many employees and not enough customers, however, can convey an air of desperation and intimidate customers.
- *Merchandise type and density:* The type of merchandise carried and how it is displayed add to the atmosphere the retailer is trying to create. A prestigious retailer like Saks or Marshall Field's carries the best brand names and displays them in a neat, uncluttered arrangement. Discounters and off-price retailers may sell some well-known brands, but many carry seconds or out-of-season goods. Their merchandise may be stacked so high that it falls into the aisles, helping create the impression that "We've got so much stuff, we're practically giving it away."
- *Fixture type and density:* Fixtures can be elegant (rich woods), trendy (chrome and smoked glass), or consist of old, beat-up tables, such as in an antique

store. The fixtures should be consistent with the general atmosphere the store is trying to create. The Gap creates a relaxed and uncluttered atmosphere by displaying its merchandise on tables and shelves rather than on traditional pipe rack, allowing customers to see and touch the merchandise more easily. Adding technology as a fixture is a recent successful trend in coffee shops and lounges. The most popular examples include adding PCs to provide Internet access to customers and ultimately get them to remain in the store longer.

- *Sound:* Sound can be pleasant or unpleasant for a customer. Classical music at a nice Italian restaurant helps create ambience, just as country-and-western music does at a truck stop. Kmart recently installed wireless telephone service in all of its Super Kmarts to help create a more peaceful environment for customers who were irritated by overhead paging.[69] Music can also entice customers to stay in the store longer and buy more or eat quickly and leave a table for others. For instance, researchers have found that rapid music tends to make people eat more, chew less, and take bigger bites whereas slow music prompts people to dine more leisurely and eat less.[70] Retailers can tailor their musical atmosphere to their shoppers' demographics and the merchandise they're selling. Music can control the pace of the store traffic, create an image, and attract or direct the shopper's attention. For example, Harrods in London features music by live harpists, pianists, and marching bagpipers to create different atmospheres in different departments. Coffee shops are also getting into the music business as are theme restaurants like Hard Rock Cafe, Planet Hollywood, Harley Davidson Cafe, and Rainforest Café, which turn eating a hamburger and fries into an experience. Au Bon Pain, Starbucks, and Victoria's Secret have all sold copies of their background music, hoping that the music will remind consumers of the feeling of being in their stores.

- *Odors:* Smell can either stimulate or detract from sales. The wonderful smell of pastries and breads entices bakery customers. Conversely, customers can be repulsed by bad odors such as cigarette smoke, musty smells, antiseptic odors, and overly powerful room deodorizers. If a grocery store pumps in the smell of baked goods, sales in that department increase threefold. Department stores have pumped in fragrances that are pleasing to their target market, and the response has been favorable. Not surprisingly, retailers are increasingly using fragrance as a key design element, as important as layout, lighting, and background music. Research suggests that people evaluate merchandise more positively, spend more time shopping, and are generally in a better mood when an agreeable odor is present. Retailers use fragrances as an extension of their retail strategy. The Rainforest Cafe, for instance, pumps fresh-flower extracts into its retail sections. Similarly, the Christmas Store at Disney World, which is open year-round, is infused with the scents of evergreen and spiced apple cider. Jordan's Furniture in Massachusetts and New Hampshire uses the scent of pine in its country-style sections to make the environment more interesting and make customers linger longer.[71]

This enormous frog sculpture crowns the entrance to the Rainforest Café in Chicago, Illinois. Coupled with the giant toadstools that flank the doors, the sculptures that decorate the outside of the restaurant create an impression of fun and whimsy.

- *Visual factors:* Colors can create a mood or focus attention and therefore are an important factor in atmosphere. Red, yellow, and orange are considered warm colors and are used when a feeling of warmth and closeness is desired. Cool colors like blue, green, and violet are used to open up closed-in places and create an air of elegance and cleanliness. Some colors are better for display. For instance, diamonds appear most striking against black or dark blue velvet. The lighting can also have an important effect on store atmosphere. Jewelry is best displayed under high-intensity spotlights and cosmetics under more natural lighting. Many retailers have found that natural lighting, either from windows or skylights, can lead to increased sales. Outdoor lighting can also impact consumer patronage. Consumers often are afraid to shop after dark in many areas and prefer strong lighting for safety. The outdoor facade of the store also adds to its ambience and helps create favorable first impressions by shoppers. For example, on the top of the roof over the door at Cup o' Joe specialty coffee shop in Lennox Town Square, Columbus, Ohio, sits a twelve-foot wide by six-foot tall coffee mug. The coffee shop's designers used the exaggerated storefront to call attention to its site, which would have otherwise gotten lost amid its big-box neighbors Old Navy, Target, and an AMC Theater.[72]

Personnel and Customer Service   People are a unique aspect of retailing. Most retail sales involve a customer–salesperson relationship, if only briefly. When customers shop at a grocery store, the cashiers check and bag their groceries. When customers shop at a prestigious clothier, the sales clerks may help select the styles, sizes, and colors. They may also assist in the fitting process, offer alteration services, wrap purchases, and even offer a glass of champagne. Sales personnel provide their customers with the amount of service prescribed in the retail strategy of the store.

A recent study found that 35 percent of consumers have had negative shopping experiences, with nearly one in ten switching retailers afterwards.[73] Good service, therefore, is even more important in a slow-growth economy, when companies survive by keeping the customers they have. Studies show that customer retention results in above-average profits and superior growth. Home Depot is one company that has embraced that philosophy and provides its customers with excellent service. Home Depot salespeople, often recruited from the ranks of carpenters and electricians, are encouraged to spend all the time needed with customers, even if it's hours. On-line retailers also benefit from good customer service. A recent survey of on-line shoppers revealed that 75 percent of shoppers said they are more likely to return to e-commerce sites when they've received good customer service. Exemplary customer service is especially important to on-line shoppers contemplating big-ticket purchases, such as airplane tickets, computers, and consumer electronics.[74]

Retail salespeople serve another important selling function: They persuade shoppers to buy. They must therefore be able to persuade customers that what they are selling is what the customer needs. Salespeople are trained in two common selling techniques: trading up and suggestion selling. Trading up means persuading customers to buy a higher-priced item than they originally intended to buy. However, to avoid selling customers something they do not need or want, salespeople should take care when practicing trading-up techniques. Suggestion selling, a common practice among most retailers, seeks to broaden customers' original purchases with related items. For example, McDonald's cashiers may ask customers whether they would like a hot apple pie with their hamburger and fries. Suggestion selling and trading up should always help shoppers recognize true needs rather than sell them unwanted merchandise.

Global Retailing

7
Discuss the challenges of expanding retailing operations into global markets

It is no accident that U.S. retailers are now testing their store concepts on a global basis. With the battle for market share among domestic retailers showing no sign of abating and growth prospects dismal, mature retailers are looking for growth opportunities in the growing consumer economies of other countries. American retailers have made quite an impact on the global market, as Exhibit 13.5 displays. Four of the top ten global retailers are from the United States, with Wal-Mart holding the top spot with sales about three times that of its nearest competitors.

Several events have made expansion across national borders more feasible. First, the spread of communication networks and mass media has homogenized tastes and product preferences to some extent around the world. As a result, the casual American lifestyle and the products that symbolize it, such as Levi's jeans and Nike sportswear, have become more appealing. Second, the lowering of trade barriers and tariffs, such as with the North American Free Trade Agreement (NAFTA) and the formation of the European Union (EU), has facilitated the expansion of American retailers to Mexico, Canada, and Europe.[75] Last, high growth potential in underserved markets is also luring U.S. retailers abroad into Latin America, South America, and Asia. China contains a quarter of the world's population and only recently opened its markets to outside concerns. Although the majority of China's population still lacks adequate consumer spending power, projections call for the country's economy to eclipse all others in the next twenty-five years.[76]

Before taking the plunge into the international retailing arena, the soundest advice retailers can heed is to do their homework. (See Exhibit 13.6.) Analysts

Exhibit 13.5

The United States and Germany Dominate Global Retailing

Rank	Retailer	Country of Origin	Formats	1998 Sales ($ million)*
1	Wal-Mart Stores	United States	Discount/ warehouse club	137,634
2	Metro AG	Germany	Diversified	52,131
3	Sears, Roebuck	United States	Department store/ general merchandise	36,704
4	Rewe Gruppe	Germany	Diversified	36,212
5	Kmart	United States	Discount/specialty	33,674
6	Edeka Gruppe (include. AVA)	Germany	Diversified	32,573
7	Aldi Gruppe	Germany	Food/discount	32,403
8	Dayton Hudson	United States	Discount/ department store	30,951
9	Carrefour	France	Hypermarket	30,4890
10	Tengelmann	Germany	Diversified	30,243

*All amounts are in millions of U.S. dollars, using average 1998 exchange rates. All data are corporate level for retail-diversified companies, excluding VAT and nonretailing revenue when available.
SOURCE: Reported in "Global Retailing in the Connected Economy," *Chain Store Age*, December 1999; Goldman, Sachs & Company.

Exhibit **13.6**

Factors Used to Analyze
Global Retail Markets

- **Market size and economics:** Analyzing factors such as population and demographic trends, economics (including gross domestic product and consumer spending), and political trends that could make or break the success of a retailer in a foreign country. For instance, in China the central government has been urging middle-income Chinese to buy their own housing. For retailers, this means plenty of new apartments and homes to fill with more electronics, bigger refrigerators and kitchens for edibles, and roomier closets.

- **Infrastructure and distribution:** Building global supply chains and securing qualified labor can be particularly challenging in emerging markets. Expansion to Canada and Mexico is simpler logistically for U.S. retailers than transporting their stores across oceans. In many developing countries such as China, underdeveloped transportation infrastructures as well as few logistics providers pose daunting distribution challenges to retailers trying to stock products in stores.

- **Competition:** Assessing the current competitive landscape and how the retailer could bring innovations to the market. Compared to the United States, Mexico, for instance, is considered grossly understored; the country has less than 550 square feet of food and apparel stores per thousand people, compared to 20,000 square feet per thousand people in the United States. Similarly, Europe has a higher percentage of independent, mom-and-pop operations. The highly fragmented European market appears ripe for well-capitalized U.S. big-box retailers.

- **Operations:** Assessing how operational concerns, such as real estate, labor and inventory, will affect the success of an overseas unit. For instance, labor laws vary drastically from country to country. Cultural differences also affect holidays, number of vacation days for employees, and hours of operation. U.S. retail stores are open an average of seventy hours a week whereas retail stores in Greece are only open about forty-six hours a week.

- **Financial and tax reporting:** Addressing issues such as currency fluctuations, the hedging of risks, and how a region's tax regime and incentives would fit in to a retailer's overall tax strategy. A lot of retailers are entering Argentina, Brazil, and Chile because their markets are open and their business economies and financial systems are more "Western-like."

- **Merchandise acceptability:** Conducting research to understand local consumer needs, preferences, and buying habits, and then reinventing the assortment to match the culture of the region. For instance, back-to-school sales occur in April in Japan, and August in Europe is a traditionally slow retailing month because most Europeans are on vacation. When IKEA came to the United States, it learned that it needed to offer larger beds, furniture with larger drawers, and different assortments of kitchen utensils.

- **Partnering capability:** Considering the availability of suitable partners in a desired country or region. Starbucks Coffee typically picks distribution and supply partners before it decides on a country or region because poor strategic alliances or logistics partnering can make or break a retail operation.

SOURCE: From "Global Retailing '97," Ernst & Young special report for *Chain Store Age*, December 1997. Reprinted by permission from Chain Store Age. Copyright Lebhar-Friedman, Inc., 425 Park Avenue, NY, NY 10022.

from consulting firm Ernst & Young count among the prerequisites for going global a secure and profitable position domestically, a long-term perspective as many foreign operations take longer to set up and longer to turn a profit, and a global strategy that meshes with the retailer's overall corporate strategy. Retailers should first determine what their core competency is, whether it be low prices, a distinctive fashion look, or excellent customer service, and determine whether this differentiation is what the local market wants. For instance, The Gap's international success is attributable to its allegiance to the "American casual" formula that made it so successful in its home market, including The Gap name. Similarly, wherever shoppers travel, they can reasonably expect to experience Wal-Mart's friendliness, the quality, service, and cleanliness of McDonald's, or the brand statements of Marks & Spencer, The Body Shop, and IKEA.[77]

However, in addition to keeping their core strengths when going global, retailers also need to skillfully make adjustments. Therefore, a major part of a retailer's advance "homework" is to understand what products will sell in foreign locales. Color preferences, taste preferences, service expectations, the preferred cut of a garment, and shopper's physiques vary worldwide, as does customer acceptance of foreign brands or private-label merchandise. Differences also dictate the placement of goods within a retail store. In some cultures, for instance, men's and women's clothing should not be merchandised adjacent to each other. Latin Americans want fruits and vegetables located at the front of a store. In the United States it's standard practice to place lower-priced private-label merchandise to the right of name brands because "natural" eye flow will cause a shopper to comparison shop to the right. That merchandising approach doesn't necessarily hold true, however, in countries where people read up and down or right to left.[78]

Read about how some global retailers adapt their product mix and marketing to appeal to local customers in the "Global Perspectives" box.

Trends in Retailing

Predicting the future is always risky, but the use of entertainment to lure customers, a shift toward providing greater convenience to receive the patronage of today's precision shoppers, and the emergence of customer management programs to foster loyalty and enhance communications with a retailer's best customers are three of the more important trends for retailing's future.

Describe future trends in retailing

Entertainment

Adding entertainment to the retail environment is one of the most popular strategies in retailing in recent years. Small retailers as well as national chains are using entertainment to set themselves apart from the competition.

Entertainment is not limited to music, videos, fashion shows, or guest appearances by soap opera stars or book authors. Entertainment includes anything that makes shoppers have a good time, that stimulates their senses or emotions, and that gets them into a store, keeps them there, and encourages them to buy and to keep coming back. The quiet, comfortable couches and cafes of bookstores and combination book and music retailers such as Barnes & Noble, Books-a-Million, Borders, and Media Play are entertaining just as are the Gershwin tunes coming from the piano in a Nordstrom's atrium. Catching the attention of many younger consumers, however, involves the flash and glitz of video screens on walls in clothing stores, hair salons, and theme restaurants. For example, the Virgin Megastore located in Lake Buena Vista, Florida, next door to Walt Disney World's Pleasure Island, features a platform over the entrance that can be lowered for live-music performances. Inside, the atmosphere is electrified by the ever-changing backdrop

WHEN IN ROME, THINK LIKE THE ROMANS

It's a dangerous temptation for big retailers that routinely open dozens of new stores each year to open international stores using a cookie-cutter approach. However well a retailer fares in its own country, it doesn't mean they will have the same success by just using the same formula in another country. To succeed in international markets, retailers often must adapt to the needs and desires of consumers of diverse culture. This often means developing a merchandise assortment and designing a store atmosphere that appeal to local tastes.

Recall from Chapter 7 how big box office supply retailer Office Depot stumbled badly in Japan after opening its behemoth stores there. The stores proved to be too big and too American for Japanese consumers and their merchandise mix was not adapted to meet Japanese needs. Loose-leaf binders in Japan, for instance, have two rings instead of three. Additionally, Office Depot stores featured wide aisles and signs in English. Consequently, Japanese consumers were confused by the English-language signs and put off by the warehouse-like atmosphere. When Office Depot later reduced the size of one of its stores in Tokyo by a third and placed the merchandise closer together, sales remained the same. Office Depot has since learned from its mistakes in Japan. It recently opened stores that

are about a fifth of the size of its American stores, signs are in Japanese, aisles are narrower, and their merchandise more reflects Japanese needs.

Wal-Mart has also struggled in foreign markets, especially in Mexico, Brazil, and some other South American markets, because its merchandise often reflected U.S. tastes, rather than local ones. As Wal-Mart expands across Europe, it is using lessons learned from its stores in Mexico and South America to adapt some products to local tastes. For instance, in Germany the image of Sam Walton's English setter on packages of its private-label dog food, Ol' Roy, was replaced with a terrier. The terrier breed is popular in Germany, whereas setters aren't familiar. Wal-Mart's diaper supplier, Drypers, changed its design, too, after focus groups indicated that Germans weren't interested in the fancy touches—such as aloe vera or cute cartoon designs—that Americans want.

Having three decades of experience operating outside their home markets has been a formidable weapon for French retailers Promodes and Carrefour, which recently merged. At the Continent hypermarket chain in Turkey, owned by the conglomerate, research revealed that many shoppers found the cavernous, brightly lit hypermarket too open and orderly. Turkish

shoppers are more accustomed to the chaos of traditional street bazaars, where merchants gut fish on the ground and sidewalk peddlers sell everything from phones to children's toys. Shoppers felt uncomfortable in antiseptic surroundings. The French retailer borrowed some merchandising techniques from a Turkish chain and redesigned the store with large metal baskets and cutaway cardboard boxes in aisles and filled them with inexpensive items. By French standards, the store looks cluttered, but customers like the ability to rummage through the bins and handle the merchandise as they can in the traditional market.[a]

What factors should retailers consider when expanding into a new international market? What sources of information would be helpful to a retailer in a new country? Do you know of any other examples in which a retailer adapted its merchandise or store atmosphere to local customs?

[a] Yumiko Ono. "U.S. Superstores Find Japanese Are a Hard Sell," *Wall Street Journal*, February 14, 2000. pp. B1, B4; Ernest Beck and Emily Nelson. "Differences of Style: As Wal-Mart Invades Europe, Rivals Rush to Match Its Formula," *Wall Street Journal*, October 6, 1999. pp. A1, A6; David Woodruff. "For French Retailers, a Weapon Against Wal-Mart." *Wall Street Journal*, September 27, 1999. pp. B1, B4.

of music, video images, banners, and lighting. A live disc jockey spins tunes high above the crowd from a metal and glass booth. Customers can sample music at one of the more than three hundred listening stations that line the first floor perimeter. On the second floor, customers can sip coffee in the cafe, use demo games and software, view videos, or surf the Web.[79]

Convenience and Efficiency

Today's consumer is increasingly looking for ways to shop more quickly and efficiently. With 75 percent of women working full- or part-time, consumers no longer

Entertainment in the retail environment is at its pinnacle in the Donna Karan New York boutique. Customers sit at a coffee bar while a grid of televisions provides the single screen for a fashion show broadcast.

have the time to devote to shopping as they once did. A recent study found the number of trips that consumers take to the mall, for instance, has declined by more than 50 percent since the early 1990s. On top of that, the number of stores that they visit when they get there is down by two-thirds.[80] Consumers are also spending less time when they do visit a mall. Today, the average mall visit lasts just an hour, down from ninety minutes in 1982.[81]

The declines not only reflect the increase in working women but can also be attributed to all consumers being more stretched for time. As consumers have become more focused on entertainment and leisure activities, they have become "precision shoppers." Consumers are more purposeful in their shopping, reducing the number of stores they visit and the time they spend shopping. The precision shopper is also less likely to buy on impulse.[82]

As a result, retailers must learn to better manage the patronage experience. Consumers are no longer satisfied because a store merely met their expectations. They desire delightful experiences brought about by retailers who anticipate consumers' expectations and go the extra mile to exceed them on a regular basis. Dimensions in which retailers can far exceed expectations include shopping assistance, the buying process, delivery and installation of the product, service after the sale, and disposal and renewal of the product.

Examples of ways this can be done include offering services such as pick-up for shoppers who do not want to fight traffic, baby-sitting services, free drinks and refreshments during shopping, and preferred shopper parking spaces. For example, IGA supermarkets in Ohio offer parents a child-care center where they can leave their kids while buying groceries. The play area includes computers, puzzles and crayons, a two-level maze, and a thirty-two-inch television. Video monitors throughout the stores allow parents to check in on their kids.[83] Supermarkets and drugstores are adding conveniences such as drive-through windows to pick up prescriptions and are offering additional services such as flu shots, cholesterol screenings, and even in-store health clinics.[84] In addition, retailers who maintain records of consumers' preferences in product features will be able to offer individualized attention to consumers during product selection. Sales associates can preselect items that are most likely to be preferred by the customer. For example, the store's records may indicate that a consumer prefers a particular style of suit, leading the sales associate to show the consumer the new suits for the season in that style.[85]

ON LINE

Experts predict that in the future retailers, especially supermarkets, will become true marketers rather than marketers that act as distribution centers. For instance, packaged goods and staples won't be sold in supermarkets. Instead, they will be delivered directly to consumers at home, within fifteen minutes of an order's placement, freeing shoppers to visit stores for things they enjoy buying—fresh produce, meats, and the fixings for a dinner party. Consumers who need staples would use hand scanners to record products' bar codes and update electronic shopping lists. Magazine ads would also carry bar codes so consumers could scan pages to put new products on their lists. Already, Frigidaire has produced a concept model refrigerator that comes complete with a video screen and bar-code scanner, with which consumers can reorder products by scanning their used-up container across the door. The scanner picks up the UPC and automatically reorders a fresh supply. The video screen also connects to the Internet, allowing consumers to check e-mail, pay bills, check their bank account, and shop on-line.[86]

Customer Management

Today, prime locations and unique merchandise are not the primary indicators of success they once were in the retail environment.[87] Instead, retailers are recognizing that customer equity is one of the only ways to sustain true competitive advantage. Through customer management strategies, leading retailers are intensifying their efforts to identify, satisfy, retain, and maximize the value of their best customers. Enabled by database technology, these forward-focused retailers are employing strategies designed to capture customers' share of mind, wallet, and time. Using database technology to manage customer relationships, called *one-to-one marketing*, is the topic of Chapter 20.

Three emerging customer management strategies retailers are embracing include customer relationship marketing, loyalty programs, and clienteling. Regardless of the strategy used, the intent is the same—to foster loyalty and develop an ongoing dialogue with a retailer's best customers. *Customer relationship marketing* (CRM) originated out of the need to more accurately target a fragmented customer base that was becoming increasingly more difficult to reach with mass advertising vehicles like television and newspapers. True CRM links customer information to transaction data collected through point-of-sale scanning systems to glean knowledge about customer purchase histories, shopping preferences, motivations, and triggers and leverages that knowledge throughout the organization to make customer-centric business decisions. After Camelot Music analyzed the data it keeps on customers, it discovered that a large number of seniors were purchasing rap and alternative music as gifts for younger relatives. In response, Camelot targeted a mailing to those seniors identifying music selections and genres that would appeal to the youngsters on their holiday shopping lists. Camelot received a 17 percent response rate to the mailer, which accounted for a sales increase of 37 percent more than for a control group that did not receive the mailer. The seniors came in and bought merchandise, thanking Camelot for making their gift-buying decisions easy for them.[88]

Armed with richer customer databases and the technology to gather and analyze customer and sales data, retailers are now taking active measures to develop loyalty programs that identify and reward their best customers. Sears' KidVantage program, for example, provides savings to members with young children. Similarly, specialty retailer Loehmann's, which offers women's designer apparel at discounted prices, uses data from its Insider Club to understand what customers are purchasing, when they are purchasing, and the type of events they prefer. In addition to periodic coupon and members-only savings, Insider Club members, currently 1.6 million strong, are notified of items and sales events. Loehmann's also launched a cobranded Insider Club Platinum Visa Card that provides a rebate on purchases.

Another approach to managing and building long-term relationships with best customers is *clienteling*. Saks Fifth Avenue, for example, strongly emphasizes personal contact on the part of managers and sales associates with customers. Associates collect and maintain detailed electronic client profiles that can be used to provide enhanced service. Sales associates are also encouraged to service clients across all departments so that the associates, already familiar with size and style preferences, can address clients' complete wardrobe needs as opposed to merely selling merchandise from their assigned department.

Think back now to the opening story about Target's phenomenal success as an upscale discounter. With sales growing exponentially, the chain's retailing strategy of providing quality, fashionable products at a low price in a fun atmosphere has proved to be a big hit with its core target market. Every element in Target's retailing mix, from merchandise assortment to price levels, service levels, atmosphere, and location, must be carefully considered to provide its customers with the products and shopping experience they are looking for. This is no easy feat for retailers, but finding the right combination can mean the difference between success and failure. And Target has indeed found success.

Use it Now!

Study Franchise Opportunities
Franchising offers an alternative to starting a business on your own. But which franchise is a good match for your interests and skills? Narrow the field of the thousands of different franchise opportunities by visiting the Franchise Handbook Online at **http://www.franchise1.com**. There you will find articles with checklists to help you thoroughly research a franchise and its industry, as well as a directory of franchise opportunities. Armed with this information, you can develop a questionnaire to evaluate a prospective franchise. Also visit the International Franchise Association, a Washington D.C. trade group, at **http://www.franchise.org** for more information about franchising and if it's right for you.

Stop Junk Mail
If you are upset about junk mail, contact the Direct Marketing Association and have your name removed from mailing lists. The e-mail address is **http://www.the-dma.org**. You can also join an umbrella organization dedicated to stopping the flood of junk e-mail, intrusive telemarketing calls, and junk mail. One such organization is Zero Junk Mail, found at **http://www.zerojunkmail.com**.

Summary

1 **Discuss the importance of retailing in the U.S. economy.** Retailing plays a vital role in the U.S. economy for two main reasons. First, retail businesses contribute to our high standard of living by providing a vast number and diversity of goods and services. Second, retailing employs a large part of the U.S. working population—over 20 million people.

2 **Explain the dimensions by which retailers can be classified.** Many different kinds of retailers exist. A retail establishment can be classified according to its ownership, level of service, product assortment, and price. On the basis of ownership, retailers can be broadly differentiated as independent retailers, chain stores, or franchise outlets. The level of service retailers provide can be classified along a continuum of high to low. Retailers also classify themselves by the breadth and depth of their product assortment; some retailers have concentrated product assortments whereas others have extensive product assortments. Last, general price levels also classify a store, from discounters offering low prices to exclusive specialty stores where high prices are the norm. Retailers use these latter three variables to position themselves in the marketplace.

3 **Describe the major types of retail operations.** The major types of retail stores are department stores, specialty retailers, supermarkets, drugstores, convenience stores, discount stores, and restaurants. Department stores carry a wide assortment of shopping and specialty goods, are organized into relatively independent departments, and offset higher prices by emphasizing customer service and decor. Specialty retailers typically carry a narrower but deeper assortment of merchandise, emphasizing distinctive products and a high level of customer service. Supermarkets are large self-service retailers that offer a wide variety of food products and some nonfood items. Drugstores are retail formats that sell mostly prescription and over-the-counter medications, health and beauty aids, cosmetics, and specialty items. Convenience stores carry a limited line of high-turnover convenience goods. Discount stores offer low-priced general merchandise and consist of four types: full-line discounters, discount specialty retailers, warehouse clubs, and off-price retailers. Finally, restaurants straddle the line between the retailing and services industries; whereas restaurants sell a product, food and drink, to final consumers, they also can be considered service marketers because they provide consumers with the service of preparing food and providing table service.

4 Discuss nonstore retailing techniques. Nonstore retailing, which is shopping outside a store setting, has three major categories. Automatic vending uses machines to offer products for sale. In direct retailing, the sales transaction occurs in a home setting, typically through door-to-door sales or party plan selling. Direct marketing refers to the techniques used to get consumers to buy from their homes or place of business. Those techniques include direct mail, catalogs and mail order, telemarketing, and electronic retailing, such as home shopping channels and on-line retailing using the Internet.

5 Define franchising and describe its two basic forms. Franchising is a continuing relationship in which a franchiser grants to a franchisee the business rights to operate or to sell a product. Modern franchising takes two basic forms. In product and trade name franchising, a dealer agrees to buy or sell certain products or product lines from a particular manufacturer or wholesaler. Business format franchising is an ongoing business relationship in which a franchisee uses a franchiser's name, format, or method of business in return for several types of fees.

6 List the major tasks involved in developing a retail marketing strategy. Retail management begins with defining the target market, typically on the basis of demographic, geographic, or psychographic characteristics. After determining the target market, retail managers must develop the six variables of the retailing mix: product, promotion, place, price, presentation, and personnel.

7 Discuss the challenges of expanding retailing operations into global markets. With increased competition and slow domestic growth, mature retailers are looking for growth opportunities in the developing consumer economies of other countries. The homogenization of tastes and product preferences around the world, the lowering of trade barriers, and the emergence of underserved markets have made the prospects of expanding across national borders more feasible for many retailers. Retailers wanting to expand globally should first determine what their core competency is and determine whether this differentiation is what the local market wants. Retailers also need to skillfully make adjustments in product mix to meet local demands.

8 Describe future trends in retailing. Three major trends are evident in retailing today. First, adding entertainment to the retail environment is one of the most popular strategies in retailing in recent years. Small retailers as well as national chains are using entertainment to set themselves apart from the competition. Second, retailers of the future will offer more convenience and efficiency to

Key Terms

consumers as consumers become more precise on their shopping trips. Staples won't be sold in stores but instead will be delivered directly to the consumer, freeing shoppers to visit stores for products they enjoy buying. Advances in technology will make it easier for consumers to obtain the products they want. Last, more and more retailers are using the information they collect about their customers at the point of sale to develop customer management programs, including customer relationship marketing, loyalty programs, and clienteling.

Discussion and Writing Questions

1. Discuss the possible marketing implications of the recent trend toward supercenters, which combine a supermarket and a full-line discount store.

2. Explain the function of warehouse clubs. Why are they classified as both wholesalers and retailers?

3. Identify a successful retail business in your community. What marketing strategies have led to its success?

4. **WRITING** You want to convince your boss, the owner of a retail store, of the importance of store atmosphere. Write a memo citing specific examples of how store atmosphere affects your own shopping behavior.

5. What advantages does franchising provide to franchisers as well as franchisees?

6. **WRITING** **INFOTRAC COLLEGE EDITION** You have been asked to write a brief article about the way consumer demand for convenience and efficiency is influencing the future of retailing. Write the outline for your article. Once you have written your outline, locate the article in the June 1998 issue of *Business Credit* magazine titled, "Electronic Retailing: A Threat to Brick and Mortar Retailers?" by Keith Ackerman. How does your article differ? Is Ackerman's article still relevant this many years later?

7. Your retail clothing company is considering expanding into Mexico. What information about the country and its customs should you collect before opening a store in Mexico?

8. **TEAM** **WRITING** Form a team of three classmates to identify different retail stores in your city where pet supplies are sold. Include non-store forms of retailing as well, such as catalogs, the Internet, or the local veterinarian. Team members should divide up and visit all the different retailing outlets for pet supplies. Prepare a report describing the differences in brands and products sold at each of the retailing formats and the differences in store characteristics and service levels. For example, which brands are sold via mass merchandiser, independent specialty store, or other venue. Suggest why different products and brands are distributed through different types of stores.

9. **ON LINE** Go to the Gift Shop at on-line wine retailer Wine.com's Web site at **http://www.wine.com/**. How does this site help shoppers select gifts?

10. **ON LINE** How much does the most powerful computer with the fastest modem, most memory, largest monitor, biggest hard drive, and all the available peripherals cost at **http://www.dell.com**? Then visit a store like Best Buy or Circuit City and price a comparable computer. How can you explain any price differences between the two retail operations? Explain any differences in features that you encountered. What conclusions can you draw from your research?

11. **ON LINE** Why should retailers market their printed catalogs on-line? Look at Web site **http://www.catalogsite.com**.

Application for Entrepreneurs

Ron Johnson is developing a retail strategy to open up his new athletic shoe and sports equipment store. He has decided to carry Nike and Converse as his two lines of athletic shoes. This will give him top-of-the-line merchandise (Nike) and a lower-priced, high-quality alternative (Converse). He obtained permission from one of his former professors to hold brainstorming sessions in a couple of his classes. From these sessions, he identified the following evaluative criteria customers might use in selecting a particular athletic shoe to purchase: (1) attractiveness/style/color, (2) brand name, (3) comfort, (4) price, (5) endorsement, and (6) quality. He also determined that location, a friend's recommendation, brands carried, and store atmosphere are important in selecting a place to purchase athletic shoes.

Questions

1. What type of retailing strategy should Ron use?
2. Which elements of the retailing mix are relatively more important?

Case

entrepreneurship

Delia's Retails to Teens: You Go, gURL

Stephen Kahn knew he had a good idea for a new direct retailing business: sell funky clothes and accessories targeted to Sabrina-wannabe girls between the ages of ten and twenty-four. The problem was convincing financial backers that his idea was more than good—it was very lucrative. When he first presented his idea to venture capitalists, they scoffed at his business plan and refused to lend him money. Teens, they said, are an elusive group with limited financial resources and no access to credit cards. Moreover, teens are fickle and the pace in teen fashion trends is often too fast for retailers to keep up.

Convinced that this overlooked niche had potential, Kahn, a former leveraged-buyout specialist and recent Yale grad, put up $100,000 of his own money and turned to family and friends for the other $1 million startup capital he needed to print and mass mail his first catalog, called Delia's. Launched from a Brooklyn garage in 1993, Delia's startled Wall Street with its success, quickly becoming the nation's leading direct retailer of teen fashion.

Kahn's hunch about preteen and teenage girls, it turns out, was right on target. According to Teenage Research Unlimited, a consulting firm specializing in the teen market, young adults between the ages of twelve and nineteen spent an estimated $153 billion in 1999, or roughly $90 a week. Parents provide over half of their teens' incomes on an as-needed basis, with the rest coming from odd jobs, gifts, and allowances. Further, teens increasingly have access to their parents' credit cards, and, in a growing number of cases, are acquiring their own credit cards with an adult sponsor. Parents are also setting up "digital on-line credit accounts" for their teens' on-line spending funded by their own credit cards. Not obligated to pay rent or other household expenses, most teens are free to spend their money on whatever they choose—accessories, CDs, and, most importantly, apparel. Additionally, buying decisions in teen apparel are being made at increasingly younger ages.

One of the most significant reasons for Delia's phenomenal success is the fact that it makes funky fashion accessible and affordable to preteen and teenage girls all across the nation. For young girls in rural and remote areas that lack options to buy cool clothes, Delia's serves as an equalizer of teen fashion. Now, teens in small midwestern or southern towns have the same fashion choices as their counterparts living in Los Angeles or New York. In schools all across the country, critiquing the latest Delia's catalog has become a lunchtime ritual.

After some fairly harrowing experiences with several suppliers early on, Kahn and partner Christopher Edgar, his ex-Yale University roommate, developed more of their own private-label merchandise in order to offer Delia's target market more unique clothing and accessories. More recent catalogs also attempt to target a slightly older demographic, aiming to be aspirational to preteens while not turning off older girls. The duo also weeded out suppliers that couldn't make consistent product and on-time shipments and opened their own warehousing facility to better control the fulfillment process and improve quality. These measures paid off for Delia's: Revenue in 2000 hit $215 million and its mailing list numbers more than 11 million. Not bad for a company that had sales of $150,000 just five years earlier.

Delia's has taken a multichannel approach to retailing. In addition to its successful direct mail catalog, the company has opened some two dozen retail stores, operates several e-commerce sites, and has expanded into other teen niches, such as teenage boys and older girls. Before venturing into Internet commerce, Kahn laid a strong foundation by buying **http://www.gURL.com**, a Web site dedicated to teenage girls online. The site features entertaining content, chat rooms, home page hosting, and e-mail services. Kahn then established several sites on the Web, each targeting a different teen customer, including a Delia's online boutique (**http://www.delias.com**), a teenage boys' apparel store (**http://www.droog.com**), and a home-furnishings store for kids (**http://www.contentsonline.com**). Kahn also engineered a deal with Yahoo to open an on-line store (**http://www.yahoo.com/stores**) on its Yahoo Shopping service. With virtually no advertising, the on-line stores have attracted over 100,000 on-line buyers and more than 5,000 catalog requests each day.

Questions

1. What type of retailer is Delia's?
2. Describe Delia's retailing strategy as best as you can in terms of product, price, place, promotion, people, and presentation.
3. Visit Delia's Web site at **http://www.delias.com**. How does it entertain and involve young girls in its brand? What is the focal point of the Web site?

Bibliography

Soozhana Choi. "Funky Fashions for Teen-Age Girls." *Gannett News Service*, March 16, 1999.

Becky Ebenkamp. "Stephen Kahn." *Brandweek*, November 8, 1999, p. 32.

Laura Keating. "The In Crowd: Retail Rushes to Keep Pace with Generation Y." *Shopping Center World*, May 30, 2000.

Melanie Kletter. "Catalogs Lose Teen Appeal." *WWD*, March 2, 2000, p. 11.

Paul Miller. "Apparel: Trends Analysis." *Catalog Age*, March 15, 2000, pp. 65–69.

David S. Murphy. "Delia's Next Big Step." *Fortune*, February 15, 1999, pp. 192[C]–192[H].

Vicki M. Young. "Playing the Junior Game." *WWD*, October 27, 1999, p. 20.

———. "Teen Shopping Heats Up Online." *WWD*, February 3, 2000, p. 26B.

Case

video

Hudson's: Shopping Euphoria at the Somerset Collection

The Somerset Collection is an upscale shopping mall outside of Detroit, complete with a glass dome that encloses the center and casts natural light throughout. Somerset features elegant specialty stores and department stores such as Neiman Marcus and Saks Fifth Avenue. In 1995, Somerset planned for major expansion, with two new anchor department stores—Nordstrom and Hudson's—to open in late 1996. The simultaneous opening of these stores would pit Hudson's against the legendary customer service of Nordstrom. The challenge for Hudson's was to build a store to compete head-to-head with Nordstrom on all levels, especially customer service.

In order to successfully meet this challenge, Hudson's had to develop a sound retailing strategy to carry them past the grand opening and into the future. The first task was to define the target market; this decision would influence all subsequent planning and was a prerequisite to creating the right retailing mix. Since Hudson's stores typically target middle-income shoppers, not the high-end buyers of Somerset, the management team had to completely rethink its target market. The new store would have to appeal to the upscale shopper, and the product assortment had to match the demographics of *this* local store and region—not those of Hudson's other locations.

Hudson's combined and built upon the elements of the retailing mix to arrive at a retailing method tailored to Somerset's target market. Hudson's retailing mix consisted of the four Ps of the marketing mix (product, place, promotion, and price) plus personnel and presentation. Managers realized that the right combination of the six Ps would project Hudson's image into the higher echelons of retailing and influence customer perception. Based on their general impression of the Somerset stores, shoppers would position Hudson's against Saks, Neiman's, and the new Nordstrom on three broad dimensions: product assortment, price, and service by store personnel.

Managers at Hudson's saw Somerset as a golden opportunity to showcase their store's strengths: assortment and service. Unlike the other anchor stores at Somerset, Hudson's offered a broad assortment of products and services, including a spa and a home division. Hudson's merchandise provided *width*, the assortment of products offered, as well as *depth*, the number of different brands offered within each assortment. Hudson's had the full power of the Dayton Hudson Company behind it, giving it access to many sources of supply for the very best merchandise, from high fashion to upscale bed and bath items. Price was also a key element in Hudson's positioning strategy because higher prices indicate a certain level of quality and help reinforce the prestigious image of a retailer.

A critical piece of Hudson's new upscale strategy was creating the right atmosphere through the physical layout, decor, and surroundings. The presentation of the store needed to make a great first and lasting impression. Hudson's market research had shown that customers wanted an appealing shopping environment with wide aisles and fitting rooms with seats. The new Hudson's store fit the bill, conveying a sense of luxury. It was designed with elegant lighting, ten-foot-wide aisles, real wood flooring and paneling, and rugs designed by the firm that had carpeted the Oval Office. Elegant displays accented the decor and added visual appeal to the merchandise.

Entertainment was another element of Hudson's strategy. Rather than limit themselves to a pianist playing a baby grand piano, the Hudson's marketers wanted music that would mirror both their shoppers' demographics and the merchandise throughout the store. For these reasons, they elected to vary music selection by department: classical music for the evening wear department, pop music in sportswear. By playing with the music selection throughout the store, Hudson's managers felt they could control the pace of store traffic, create an image, and attract or direct a shopper's attention to specific merchandise and services. Pleasant odors, like the smell of fragrances, were incorporated to further enhance the store's atmosphere and to stimulate shoppers' senses or emotions. All of these elements, along with visual factors such as colors, were strategically combined to create the desired store presentation that would favorably influence buying decisions and win repeat customers.

Excellent customer service was another key part of Hudson's plan at the Somerset Collection. Always looking closely at service, Hudson's kept raising the benchmark. The managers added a dedicated trainer to hire and train employees at the Somerset store alone. Instead of making prior retail experience a requirement for employment, Hudson's managers preferred to build a staff of amiable individuals with good interpersonal skills. When customers come to Hudson's at Somerset, sales personnel perform the ritual tasks of helping them select styles, sizes, and colors, but the sales staff also assists in the fitting process, offers alteration services, wraps purchases, and offers refreshments.

Successfully implementing its detailed retail strategy has led Hudson's to adopt programs that foster more personal contact between managers, sales associates, and customers. Both their experience and research indicate that customer retention leads to above-average profits and superior growth. By identifying, satisfying, retaining, and maximizing the value of its best customers, the Hudson's store at Somerset has competed effectively against not only customer service giant Nordstrom but also the other anchor stores. A well-planned retail strategy, combined with strong assortment and service, has allowed Hudson's Somerset Collection store to prosper.

Questions

1. Why was target marketing so important to Hudson's retail strategy?
2. Why did Hudson's feel that its product assortment was a competitive strength?
3. Identify the elements of the store presentation. Why is presentation important?
4. How does Hudson's service make the store competitive?

Bibliography

Video by Learnet: A Case Study in Retail Strategy: Hudson's Somerset Collection

MARKETING MISCUES

Just for Feet Stopped in Its Tracks

By mid-1998, Just for Feet Inc. was the fastest-growing athletic shoe retailer in the United States. Despite an industry drop in athletic shoe sales, the chain store retailer had almost 300 stores and had earned almost $500 million in 1997. What happened to the stores' distribution strategy to force the retailer into Chapter 11 bankruptcy two years later?

Founded in 1977, Just for Feet quickly became the number-two retail chain, behind Foot Locker, in the athletic shoe industry. Headquartered in Birmingham, Alabama, the chain's success was due in part to its retail entertainment strategy, which combined selection, service, and excitement. In addition to a creative display of a wide selection of athletic shoes and apparel, superstore locations often housed a functional, full-length basketball court. The company's Web site, **http://www. feet.com**, also attempted to reflect the brick-and-mortar entertainment concept via Web promotions such as product giveaways, digital gift certificates, and contests. By the beginning of 1999, the chain operated 132 superstores in twenty-seven states and Puerto Rico.

In addition to rapid growth via its Just for Feet retail stores, the company also expanded its retail acquisitions. In 1997, the company acquired Florida-based Athletic Attic and Michigan-based Imperial Sports. The company continued its rapid acquisition strategy in 1998 when it purchased the New Jersey-based Sneaker Stadium.

Unfortunately, after twenty consecutive quarters of same-store sales growth, the chain's success began to unravel in late 1999. While the sporting goods industry was hitting a decline, Just for Feet was acquiring an abundance of retail space dedicated to athletic apparel. These acquisitions left Just for Feet with heavy debt and excess inventory. Adding fuel to inventory and debt problems was a January 1999 Super Bowl Just for Feet commercial that generated considerable negative publicity for the company. Labeled as racist, the ad pictured a Kenyan runner who had been drugged and fitted with athletic shoes.

Initially, Just for Feet attempted to reduce costs by closing some of its Athletic Attic locations. All the while, the company was attempting to find ways to reduce its huge inventory problem. Failing to overcome its financial problems, Just for Feet filed for Chapter 11 bankruptcy protection in late 1999—a mere one year after sporting goods industry observers predicted that the chain would hit $1 billion in sales.

In early 2000, New Jersey-based Footstar Inc. acquired the Just for Feet superstores, its specialty stores, the name, and the Internet business for around $70 million. With this acquisition, Footstar became the second largest athletic footwear and apparel retailer in the United States. Just for Feet will complement Footstar's current athletic footwear businesses, Footaction (branded athletic footwear) and Meldisco (discount footwear distributed primarily through Kmart). Footstar's marketing strategy in acquiring Just for Feet is to reach out to the less fashion-driven and more value-driven consumer through the superstore format in the suburbs.

Questions for Discussion

1. Is the demise of Just for Feet a benefit to the athletic retailing industry? Why or why not?
2. How can a retail chain know when to stop, or at least slow, expansion?
3. What went wrong with the distribution strategy at Just for Feet?

Bibliography

"Adidas' Perfect Marketing Pitch." *Footwear News*, August 2, 1999, p. 8.

"Footstar Purchases a Number of Just for Feet Stores." *Sporting Goods Business*, March 1, 2000, p. 12.

Dean Foust. "Chapter 11 Never Looked So Good." *Business Week*, March 20, 2000, p. 44.

Nicole Harris. "Just for Feet IS Making Tracks: Its "Big-Box" Shoe Stores Have Walked All Over Rivals." *Business Week*, July 20, 1998, p. 70.

Don Milazzo. "Footwear Retailers Chase Just for Feet." *Orlando Business Journal*, December 24, 1999, p. 5.

"The Other Shoe Drops at Just for Feet." *Sporting Goods Business*, February 14, 2000, p. 10.

Tim Schooley. "Athletic Attic Parent Plans to Close 85 Stores." *Pittsburgh Business Times*, November 5, 1999, p. 9.

CRITICAL THINKING CASE

Disney Consumer Products

Competition Stealing the Magic of Disney

Today's Walt Disney Company is a multimedia conglomerate that has come a long way from the production and delivery of classic animated films. The Disney Consumer Products division headquartered in Burbank, California, offers Disney characters in more than eighty countries. Operations within Disney Consumer Products include the Disney Store, merchandise licensing, book and magazine publishing, the Web site, and ESPN the Store. In addition to consumer products, the Walt Disney Company owns television networks and is famous for its theme parks and resorts. Annual revenue for all of Disney's businesses approached $25 billion by the year 2000.

While the Walt Disney Company, overall, was experiencing strong earnings in the first half of 2000, the Disney Consumer Products group was struggling with relatively flat earnings. The strategy for turning around the group's profit involved investing $500 million in the conglomerate's twenty-year-old retail store concept, the Disney Store.

There are over 700 Disney Stores in eleven countries throughout the world. These stores have helped set the standard for the entertainment retail genre. Retail as entertainment attempts to involve consumers not only in a store's products but also to engage the consumer in the entire shopping experience. For example, sales employees at the Disney Store wear Disney theme clothing and Disney videos play on a wall in the store. Essentially, the store attempts to connect with consumers on a level that goes beyond the tangible store products. However, there are concerns as to whether the retail as entertainment environment is capable of pulling Disney Consumer Products out of the doldrums. The battle for consumers' minds (and dollars) has taken on a new perspective as more and more companies attack Disney's entertainment retail turf.

Retail as Entertainment

Even with slim margins and erratic monthly sales, many entertainment companies are beginning to enter the retail entertainment marketplace. While Disney and Warner Brothers (with its WB Studio Stores) have long owned the retail entertainment sector, companies such as Discovery Communications and Nickelodeon are launching their own entries in this retail sector. Discovery Communications is grounding its store concept in the world of dinosaurs, aviation, world cultures, and the future. On the flip side, Nickelodeon's concept appears grounded in the more artistic mode of presentation.

Lava lamps, wild-colored walls and ceilings, and the famous Nickelodeon sliminess are attempts to set Nickelodeon stores apart from retail entertainment competitors.

Rebounding from Weak Sales: Disney Store On-line

Stiff competition in the retail entertainment sector has resulted in weaker sales for Disney. In early 2000, Michael Eisner, CEO of the Walt Disney Company, assured company shareholders that Disney Consumer Products was set to rebound from its weak sales postings. A key player in this turnaround strategy is the recently appointed president of Disney Consumer Products, Andrew Mooney. Prior to his appointment, Mooney spent twenty years at Nike Inc., most recently serving as chief marketing officer. Foremost in Mooney's turnaround strategy are initiatives involving the Disney Store.

As the new person brought in to spearhead the turnaround of Disney's merchandising division, Mooney is placing considerable importance on the distribution of Disney memorabilia. Part of his initiatives include redesigning the existing 715 brick-and-mortar stores and making them more interactive and spacious. Disney Consumer Products has also taken the store into the virtual world via the Disney Store on-line (**http://www. disneystore.com**), which brings Disney theme products into consumers' homes. For interested consumers, Disney's new, refurbished brick-and-mortar stores will be linked to the on-line store via computer kiosks located in the Disney store.

Disney on-line has thus far been a success. It is estimated that 50 percent of site users purchase on-line. With the site seeing a doubling of traffic soon after its debut, its revenue is five times greater than the company's traditional stores, and average orders are double those of store purchases. A key variable in Disney's on-line success has been its speed of delivery. Through the use of technology, packages can be shipped within hours of a customer's order placement—almost as fast as Mary Poppins can clean up the nursery.

Questions for Discussion

1. Describe the retail environment in which the Disney Store operates.
2. Who is the customer for the Disney Store? What is the link between the store's environment and this customer base?
3. Could the on-line shopping experience be driving the decline in sales at the brick-and-mortar stores? Has the company risked cannibalization by having multiple methods of distribution?
4. Who is the customer shopping Disney on-line?

Bibliography

Tom Bawden. "Disney Stores in L300m Overhaul." *Marketing Week*, November 18, 1999, p. 5.

Becky Ebenkamp. "The Show Must Go on . . . the Shelves." *Brandweek*, March 16, 1998, pp. 26+.

John Evan Frook. "Disney Tempts Web Visitors to Buy." *Internetweek*, March 23, 1998, p. 19.

Jill Goldsmith. "ABC Heyday Offsets Disney Studio Dip." *Daily Variety*, May 4, 2000, p. 1.

Ann Keeton. "Disney CEO Explains 'Mickey Mouse' Strategy to Investors." *Dow Jones News Service*, February 2, 2000.

http://www.disney.com

MARKETING PLANNING ACTIVITIES

Distribution Decisions

The next part of the marketing mix to be described for the marketing plan is the "place" portion, or distribution. Be sure that your distribution plans match the

 needs and wants of the target market identified and described earlier and are compatible with the product and service issues discussed in the previous section. Also refer to Exhibit 2.8 for additional marketing plan subjects.

1. Discuss the implications of dual/multiple distribution. If your firm sells through a major department store and its own catalog and then decides to have an on-line World Wide Web site and open its own store in a factory outlet, what will happen to channel relationships? To the final price offered to consumers? To promotional vehicles?

Marketing*Builder* Exercise

- **Distribution Channels** portion of the **Sales Plan** template

2. Decide what channel(s) your chosen company should be using. Describe the intermediaries involved and their likely behavior. What are the implications of these channels?

Marketing*Builder* Exercise

- **Alliances** portion of the **Sales Source Analysis** spreadsheet

3. Which distribution intensity level would be best for your company's product? Justify your decision.

4. What type of physical distribution facilities will be necessary to distribute the product? Where should they be located? How should the product be distributed? Justify your selection of transportation mode(s).

5. What types of retail establishments might be used for your firm's product? Are they in locations convenient to the target customers? What is the atmosphere of the facility for each type?

E-MARKETING PLANNING ACTIVITIES

In the first part of your strategic e-marketing plan, you stated your business mission and objectives and performed a detailed SWOT analysis. In the second part of the plan you identified and described target market segments and identified sources of CI and the need for further marketing research. Next, you began the process of defining the marketing mix, starting with the first component: product. Recall that you are either writing a strategic marketing plan for an existing bookstore retailer with a new on-line presence, or a dot-com bookstore retailer, or an e-company of your own choosing.

For continued general assistance on business plans and marketing plans, visit **http://www.bplans.com** or **http://www.businessplans.org**. For electronic sources

of information, search the Electric Library at **http://www.elibrary.com** or the Internet Public Library at **http://www.ipl.org**. Another excellent source of information is the Sales and Marketing Executives Marketing Library at **http://www.sell.org**. You should also refer to Exhibit 2.8 for additional marketing plan checklist items (Part IV.B.2.: Marketing Mix—Place/Distribution).

The next stage of the strategic planning process continues defining the elements of the marketing mix, and this section focuses on place, or distribution. Distribution is a key component of an e-business that seems "invisible" to the consumer, because the consumer may not care where your firm is located but wants product delivery quickly and inexpensively. Creating a worldwide distribution system is an additional challenge to the e-marketer.

Use the following exercises to guide you through the distribution part of your strategic marketing plan:

1. Most e-marketers assume that a direct distribution channel, with no intermediaries, is the most efficient and least costly method for getting product offerings to customers. However, if you decide on a direct distribution channel, you will also have to identify warehouses, fulfillment services, transportation firms, packing companies, and many other facilitating agencies. Does your firm have the capabilities to handle this, or should your firm invest in channel members to take over these tasks and functions? Check out the code of Internet Commerce Standards at **http://www.gii.com/standard/index.html**.

2. Describe the conflict that might arise from having both an e-marketing offering as well as a brick-and-mortar offering. If distribution costs are different, will your firm set the same or different prices for end customers?

3. Which level of distribution intensity will your firm be best able to handle? Why?

4. What physical distribution facilities will be needed to complete delivery of products and services to the buyer? Where should these facilities be located? Check out the Warehouse Location Simulation at **http://www.orie.cornell.edu/~jackson/whsloc.html**.

5. What other types of channel facilitators will you require for getting your product offering to your customers? Search under **http://www.looksmart.com** for either "Full Service Direct Marketing Firms" or "E-commerce Transaction Management Products."

6. How can you get the atmosphere of the brick-and-mortar offering to match the offering of your Web site?

7. If you have developed a service, to what other Web sites might you "distribute" your Internet-based service? How will working with these other Web sites help you reach your target audience? Are there other Web sites from which you might accept distribution deals from in order to make your product or service offering stronger? Explain how strategic distribution with other Web sites or services can give you a competitive advantage.

CROSS-FUNCTIONAL CONNECTIONS SOLUTIONS

Questions

1. What are some of the popular advanced manufacturing systems and how do they interact with marketing?

   Advanced manufacturing systems—which include just-in-time (JIT), manufacturing resources planning (MRP), and electronic data interchange (EDI)—allow a firm to compete on both time and quality. The systems allow for a quicker response to customers' demands as well as a shortening of the new-product production cycle. The systems allow firms to produce a large variety of high-quality products in a reduced cycle time. Consequently, such systems result in more timely deliveries.

2. What is an enterprise-wide integrated distribution system? What is marketing's role in such a system?

   Simply put, an enterprise-wide integrated distribution system brings together all aspects of the business in order to get products to customers in a timely manner. Such a system generally relies heavily upon automated exchanges among various channel parties. The marketing function's role in such a system is varied and may include channel selection strategies, automatic customer data transmission to the shop floor, wireless tracking of a customer's order, and/or customer satisfaction measures.

3. How do production and delivery happen simultaneously in the service sector? What other functional areas are important partners in the service arena?

   A unique characteristic of a service is its inseparability; that is, services are generally sold, produced, and consumed at the same time. Consumers must be present during the production and delivery of a service. For example, a consumer receives a haircut at the same time as the haircut is being produced. This inseparability means that the service cannot be produced in one location and delivered at another location. Thus, the quality of the service depends upon the quality of the employee—making human resources a very important cross-functional partner.

Suggested Readings

Alexander E. Ellinger. "Improving Marketing/Logistics Cross-Functional Collaborations in the Supply Chain." *Industrial Marketing Management*, January 2000, pp. 85–96.

Perry A. Trunick. "New Demands for Tomorrow's Manager." *Transportation & Distribution*, December 1998, pp. 18–19.

5

part

Promotion Decisions

UNDERSTANDING MARKETING COMMUNICATIONS'
CONTRIBUTION TO FIRM VALUE

When purchasing a product or service, a customer does not think in terms of advertising, sales promotion, public relations, and personal selling, nor does he or she think in terms of marketing, manufacturing, accounting, finance, research and development, and human resources. Rather, the product or service received by the customer is the sum of all of the internal processes, just as the communications message is the sum of all of the communications vehicles available to the firm. It is the company's responsibility to make certain that the product/service received by the customer is consistent with the message that the customer has received via the firm's integrated marketing communications. For example, advertising for Priceline.com touts its ease of use. Therefore, when a potential customer attempts to buy something using Priceline.com, there should not be complicating features that make it difficult for the customer to buy products on-line.

Product quality is an issue that touches at the heart of a firm's operational processes. Marketers love to tout a product's superior quality when communicating with potential customers. When a company's communications strategy focuses upon promoting quality features, pressure is placed on research and development, manufacturing, and human resources to deliver on quality. Unfortunately, issues that mean quality to a scientist or an engineer in a manufacturing or research and development department may not readily translate to perceptions of quality by the customer.

If a firm's communications program entices the consumer to try a product or service, the product or service must then be consistent with the consumer's expectations of the quality. Too frequently, marketers have developed award-winning communications campaigns for a new product, only to see the product fail in the market due to inconsistency between what the communications program is conveying and what is delivered in the product.

The need for interaction between marketing and manufacturing does not stop with the product introduction campaign, however. At any point in a product's life cycle, marketing may decide to promote the product. For example, Colgate-Palmolive may decide to offer a price discount over a two- or three-week period, to advertise heavily, and/or to offer coupons in a freestanding insert for one of its bar soaps. From marketing's perspective, the hope is that a consumer will try the soap due to the heavy marketing communications effort (and keep using the product even after the communications effort has stopped).

Marketing at Colgate-Palmolive would need to work closely with manufacturing when planning such an extensive product promotion. Otherwise manufacturing will be producing the product at its traditional level, which will be inconsistent with marketing's promotional sales plan. An integrated marketing communications program that generates high demand for a product is only as good as the product's availability. That is, a well-orchestrated marketing campaign can create a powerful purchasing stimulus. But when manufacturing cannot meet demand, consumers consider competitive brands in order to satisfy the product want or need stimulated by the marketing communications program.

Advertising and promotional efforts tend to be a source of friction between marketing and financial managers. Oddly, advertising and promotional expenditures are generally viewed as cost elements rather than investments in the product or brand. Marketers view these expenditures as investments in building the business, much like companies invest in personnel in order to have a well-managed organization. Customer satisfaction and repeat business depend upon constant maintenance by the marketing department. In contrast, accountants often view advertising and promotional expenses as variable costs. Unfortunately, viewed as variable costs, advertising expenses are tied directly to sales increases and decreases, and marketing budgets are often cut when they are needed most.

Personal selling is a component of integrated marketing communications where considerable interaction among functions has been occurring and where expenses tend to be viewed as investments since human capital is involved. It is no longer sufficient for a salesperson to have good personal interaction skills to be successful. Now, salespeople have to possess intimate knowledge of the products they present to potential consumers. For example, a sales representative for South-Western College Publishing has to understand the topics covered in a particular textbook in order to talk knowledgeably to professors in the area. At Kele & Associates, a business-to-business supplier of building automation peripherals, sales and accounting collaborate to better understand national account profitability. The company understands that nurturing a current account is less expensive than identifying and developing new accounts.

At the same time, it is no longer sufficient for research and development engineers or manufacturing specialists to work only within their limited domains. Many firms are now insisting that research and development and manufacturing talk directly with customers. Not surprisingly, such an external emphasis is in direct contrast with the technical orientation of research and development and manufacturing employees. Additionally, it is often assumed that salespeople are more extroverted than research and development and manufacturing employees, who are considered to be inherently introverted. Firms such as Motorola and Intuit expect that their engineers will go on sales calls. These engineers may visit customers with a marketing person as part of a sales call or separately in order to watch the customer use the product. There seems to be no better way of developing and manufacturing innovative, cutting-edge products than to have the people who work directly with the product also working closely with the end user.

On the flip side of this, companies could consider including salespeople on cross-functional new-product development teams. Salespeople are the ones out in the field who see how customers use the company's products on a daily basis and hear what customers are saying as far as preferences. They can bring the voice of the customer into the firm. Additionally, salespeople are great sources of competitive intelligence as they are often the first to hear (from a customer) about a competitor's new product.

The sales area is also beginning to work closely with the finance, accounting, and human resource groups with regard to compensation systems. Firms are beginning to move from sales objectives (volume and/or revenue) to financial objectives (profit). By linking sales commissions to profit-related objectives, firms stress the importance of understanding the firm's margin versus focusing solely upon product revenue. Computer giants such as IBM and Hewlett-Packard follow a variable commission strategy that links a salesperson's commission to a product's profit margin.

While finance and accounting will generally be focused upon the profit aspect of the salesperson's objectives, human resources will have to work closely with the salesperson in order to develop the most appropriate compensation system for the types of accounts in the salesperson's territory. Additionally, the human resources staff is trained in methods to help the salesperson clarify individual goals, regarding responsibilities and desired accomplishments, that will be consistent with company-wide strategic goals. In today's business environment of teamwork and cross selling, the human resources department may also be called upon to help interview and train potential sales personnel.

The clear linkage among finance, accounting, human resources, and marketing with regard to a firm's selling strategy is exemplified in IBM's focus on profits and customer satisfaction. As mentioned earlier, IBM follows a variable commission strategy that ties a salesperson's commission to margins on the company's products. Sixty percent of the commission is tied to profit margin. Interestingly, the other 40 percent of the commission is linked to customer satisfaction. Customer satisfaction is measured according to the customer's perception of how well its IBM sales team has helped it achieve its own company objectives.

A successful integrated marketing communications program is dependent upon marketing working closely with research and development and manufacturing with regard to quality and availability. Simultaneously, marketing has to interact closely with finance, accounting, and human resources in order to establish appropriate goals and objectives for its marketing communications programs. It is the sum of the external messages and internal operations that produces a satisfied customer.

Questions for Discussion

1. Why is the company's marketing communications of particular concern to research and development and manufacturing?
2. Why do financial managers view advertising and promotional expenditures as costs?
3. How has personal selling become functionally integrated?

chapter 14

Learning Objectives

1 Discuss the role of promotion in the marketing mix

2 Discuss the elements of the promotional mix

3 Describe the communication process

4 Explain the goals and tasks of promotion

5 Discuss the AIDA concept and its relationship to the promotional mix

6 Describe the factors that affect the promotional mix

7 Discuss the concept of integrated marketing communications

In just fifteen years, America Online has gone from being nothing to being the largest Internet-access provider in the United States, serving twenty-one million subscribers and ringing up $2 billion in revenue. A relative baby compared to long-standing traditional marketers like Coca-Cola and Pillsbury, AOL serves about 42 percent of U.S. on-line households and is on the brink of becoming the number one media company with its takeover of Time Warner. And the company is just getting started.

Central to AOL's impressive track record has been its integrated promotional strategy of aggressive ubiquity. In other words, AOL is just about anywhere there is a customer interested in getting on-line. AOL links all aspects of its promotional strategy to send one clear, consistent message across all media and all forms of promotion.

The cornerstone of AOL's success has been the mailing of millions of trial-membership CDs to allow prospective users to sample its service risk-free. These CDs also appear on the checkout counters in computer stores, grocery stores, and video stores, free to anyone who is interested in giving the company a try. While giving out disks is more expensive than other promotional methods, AOL's marketing director knew that if she could just get people to put the disk in their computers, they would see what AOL's potential was. The plan is definitely working. In 1999, AOL attracted six million new subscribers, more than any other Internet service provider has in total membership.

Additionally, AOL spends about $50 million each year on media advertising. Cable television receives the lion's share of their advertising budget, followed by magazine and network television advertisements. Unlike the irreverent ads many dot-coms are known for, AOL's advertising is surprisingly straightforward and simple. Ads briefly outline the company's services and show testimonials of satisfied users. Since its main target market consists of consumers new to the Web, this promotional strategy works very well. Some radio and TV spots even direct customers to a toll-free number to call to sign up for AOL service.

Publicity garnered from a major motion picture—*You've Got Mail,* a romantic comedy starring Meg Ryan and Tom Hanks—also hasn't hurt the growing company. The actors play rival bookstore owners who fall in love via e-mail on AOL. The movie, which gets its name from the audio message that AOL users hear when they have mail in their electronic message box, helped identify the company as part of popular culture where e-mail addresses are as common as telephone numbers.

A main factor accounting for AOL's phenomenal success is the collaboration its salespeople have with the rest of the company. AOL's 120 salespeople are responsible for bringing in nonsubscription business, mainly from advertising sales, e-commerce, and marketing partnerships. Reps are organized by industry, such as health care, consumer packaged goods, and real estate, and are trained to look at every marketing partner's business as if it were their own. AOL salespeople look at their clients' current marketing systems and show them how the Internet can benefit them. The company's aggressive sales force has signed big advertising and marketing deals with Office Depot, Coca-Cola, and Kinko's.[1]

As you can see, America Online places considerable emphasis on promotion in its marketing mix. What types of promotional tools are available to companies and what factors influence the choice of tool? Why is a consistent, integrated marketing message important to a promotional plan? These questions, and others, will be answered as you read the chapter.

On Line

America Online

How does AOL use its Web site as a piece of its integrated marketing communications strategy? Are there references to any outside advertising or promotions activities?
http://www.aol.com

The Role of Promotion in the Marketing Mix

Discuss the role of promotion in the marketing mix

promotion
Communication by marketers that informs, persuades, and reminds potential buyers of a product in order to influence an opinion or elicit a response.

promotional strategy
A plan for the optimal use of the elements of promotion: advertising, public relations, personal selling, and sales promotion.

differential advantage
One or more unique aspects of an organization that cause target consumers to patronize that firm rather than competitors.

Few goods or services, no matter how well developed, priced, or distributed, can survive in the marketplace without effective **promotion**—communication by marketers that informs, persuades, and reminds potential buyers of a product in order to influence their opinion or elicit a response.

Promotional strategy is a plan for the optimal use of the elements of promotion: advertising, public relations, personal selling, and sales promotion. As Exhibit 14.1 shows, the marketing manager determines the goals of the company's promotional strategy in light of the firm's overall goals for the marketing mix—product, place (distribution), promotion, and price. Using these overall goals, marketers combine the elements of the promotional strategy (the promotional mix) into a coordinated plan. The promotion plan then becomes an integral part of the marketing strategy for reaching the target market.

The main function of a marketer's promotional strategy is to convince target customers that the goods and services offered provide a differential advantage over the competition. A **differential advantage** is the set of unique features of a company and its products that are perceived by the target market as significant and superior to the competition. Such features can include high product quality, rapid delivery, low prices, excellent service, or a feature not offered by the compe-

Exhibit 14.1

Role of Promotion in the Marketing Mix

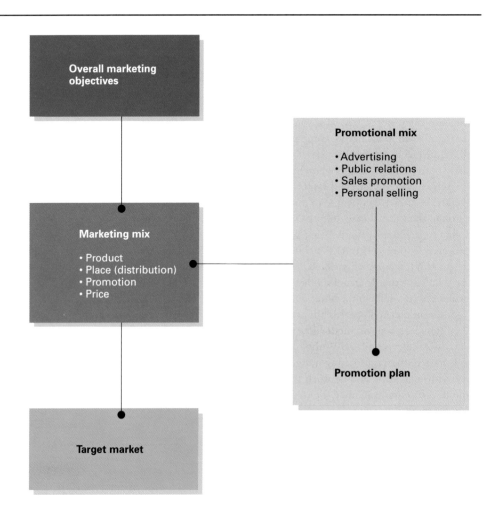

Revlon ColorStay Lipcolor promises unsmeared lipstick all day long. By effectively communicating this differential advantage through advertising, Revlon can stimulate demand for its smudge-free line of make-up.
Courtesy Revlon

tition. For example, Revlon ColorStay Lipcolor promises unsmeared lipstick all day long. By effectively communicating this differential advantage through advertising featuring model Cindy Crawford, Revlon can stimulate demand for its smudge-free line of makeup. Promotion is therefore a vital part of the marketing mix, informing consumers of a product's benefits and thus positioning the product in the marketplace.

The Promotional Mix

Most promotional strategies use several ingredients—which may include advertising, public relations, sales promotion, and personal selling—to reach a target market. That combination is called the **promotional mix**. The proper promotional mix is the one that management believes will meet the needs of the target market and fulfill the organization's overall goals. The more funds allocated to each promotional ingredient and the more managerial emphasis placed on each technique, the more important that element is thought to be in the overall mix.

Advertising

Almost all companies selling a good or a service use some form of advertising, whether it be in the form of a multimillion-dollar campaign or a simple classified ad in a newspaper. **Advertising** is any form of paid communication in which the sponsor or company is identified. Traditional media—such as television, radio, newspapers, magazines, books, direct mail, billboards, and transit cards (advertisements on buses and taxis and at bus stops)—are most commonly used to transmit advertisements to consumers. With the increasing fragmentation of traditional media choices, marketers are finding many new and innovative ways to send their advertisements to consumers, such as with interactive video technology located in department stores and supermarkets and through Internet Web sites and electronic mail.

One of the primary benefits of advertising is its ability to communicate to a large number of people at one time. Cost per contact, therefore, is typically very low. Advertising has the advantage of being able to reach the masses (for instance, through national television networks), but it can also be microtargeted to small groups of potential customers, such as television ads on a targeted cable network or through print advertising in a trade magazine.

Although the cost per contact in advertising is very low, the total cost to advertise is typically very high. This hurdle tends to restrict advertising on a national basis to only those companies that are financially able to do so. For instance, to introduce the women's version of its hit Mach 3 razor, Gillette spent more than $40 million in media advertising, such as network television and print advertisements.[2] Few small companies can match this level of spending for a national campaign. Chapter 15 examines advertising in greater detail.

Public Relations

Concerned about how they are perceived by their target markets, organizations often spend large sums to build a positive public image. **Public relations** is the marketing function that evaluates public attitudes, identifies areas within the organization that

Discuss the elements of the promotional mix

promotional mix
Combination of promotion tools—including advertising, public relations, personal selling, and sales promotion—used to reach the target market and fulfill the organization's overall goals.

advertising
Impersonal, one-way mass communication about a product or organization that is paid for by a marketer.

public relations
The marketing function that evaluates public attitudes, identifies areas within the organization that the public may be interested in, and executes a program of action to earn public understanding and acceptance.

the public may be interested in, and executes a program of action to earn public understanding and acceptance. Public relations helps an organization communicate with its customers, suppliers, stockholders, government officials, employees, and the community in which it operates. Marketers use public relations not only to maintain a positive image but also to educate the public about the company's goals and objectives, introduce new products, and help support the sales effort. Random House turned NBC anchor Tom Brokaw's nonfiction book *The Greatest Generation*, a tribute to the generation that came of age during World War II, into a national bestseller through a savvy public relations and publicity plan. The likable and trusted Mr. Brokaw toured the country promoting *The Greatest Generation* at bookstores, often accompanied by several of the extraordinary people profiled in the book. The newscaster also appeared on more than twenty-five television and radio shows to promote his book, including *Late Show with David Letterman* and *Live with Regis and Kathie Lee*. Excerpts of the book appeared in *Good Housekeeping;* readers were invited to write accounts of their own personal or family war experiences, the winner being awarded with a lunch with Brokaw. *The Greatest Generation* went on to become the fastest-selling nonfiction book in Random House's history and one of the greatest publishing successes of all time.[3]

World War II U.S. Navy veteran John DeTucci has his copy of *The Greatest Generation* signed by the author, Tom Brokaw, after a special high school diploma ceremony for Cambridge, Massachusetts veterans. This was but one of a string of stops Mr. Brokaw made to promote his book.

publicity
Public information about a company, good, or service appearing in the mass media as a news item.

A solid public relations program can generate favorable **publicity**—public information about a company, good, or service appearing in the mass media as a news item. The organization is not generally identified as the source of the information. The soy industry received favorable publicity and an increase in sales after the Food and Drug Administration approved a health claim for food labeling suggesting a link between soy protein and the reduced risk of coronary heart disease.[4] This incident underscores a peculiar reality of marketing: No matter how many millions are spent on advertising, nothing sells a product better than free publicity.

Although an organization does not pay for this kind of mass media exposure, publicity should not be viewed as free. Preparing news releases, staging special events, and persuading media personnel to print or broadcast them costs money. During the year-and-a-half it took the FDA to approve the soy claim, meatless burger marketer Gardenburger was busy capitalizing on the pre-approval buzz on soy and readying a public relations plan to put its brand at the forefront should the FDA approve the claim. While the FDA was mulling its final decision, Gardenburger used interim packaging touting its soy burgers as "great-tasting and packed with soy protein" to spark interest among those who were hearing about soy's health attributes in the press. Gardenburger also provided footage of its factory lines to major media outlets. These tactics proved quite beneficial for the soy marketer: Seventy-five newspapers and one hundred television stations used Gardenburger's packaging and production line footage in their coverage of the soy story, reaching some thirty-five million consumers. Two months after the FDA's approval, Gardenburger's sales had risen 25 percent.[5] Public relations and publicity are examined further in Chapter 15.

Sales Promotion

sales promotion
Marketing activities—other than personal selling, advertising, and public relations—that stimulate consumer buying and dealer effectiveness.

Sales promotion consists of all marketing activities—other than personal selling, advertising, and public relations—that stimulate consumer purchasing and dealer effectiveness. Sales promotion is generally a short-run tool used to stimulate immediate increases in demand. Sales promotion can be aimed at end consumers, trade customers, or a company's employees. Sales promotions include free samples, contests, premiums, trade shows, vacation giveaways, and coupons. A major promotional campaign might use several of these sales promotion tools. For example, a joint marketing program by two milk producer interest groups, Dairy Management and the National Fluid Milk Processors, developed an under-the-cap "Milk Mustache Fame Game" sweepstakes. The winner would get the opportunity to become a "Milk Mustache" celebrity on 200 million gallons of milk. The joint promotional effort also included free-with-purchase giveaways, such as "Milk Mustache" celebrity calendars as well as tie-ins for in-store promotional displays with Warner Brothers' DC Comics superheros and stars from the WB Network.[6]

Often marketers use sales promotion to improve the effectiveness of other ingredients in the promotional mix, especially advertising and personal selling. Research shows that sales promotion complements advertising by yielding faster sales responses. Freschetta Foods, a division of Tony's Pizza Service, for example, hit the roads to take on competitors in the frozen pizza marketing wars by creating twelve vehicles equipped with mobile kitchens. Each mobile unit offered free samples of Freschetta pizza to demonstrate the product's taste at fairs and festivals across the country. Equipped with a fifteen-foot inflatable Freschetta's pizza box and a sound system, the traveling pizzeria was able to create an "instant event" at any location. All told, the mobile kitchens traveled 80,000 miles and passed out more than 500,000 samples. The sampling was critical to Freschetta's goal of driving product trial and getting consumers to switch brands of frozen pizza.[7] Sales promotion is discussed in more detail in Chapter 16.

Personal Selling

Personal selling is a purchase situation in which two people communicate in an attempt to influence each other. In this dyad, both the buyer and seller have specific objectives they wish to accomplish. The buyer may need to minimize cost or assure a quality product, for instance, while the salesperson may need to maximize revenue and profits.[8]

Traditional methods of personal selling include a planned presentation to one or more prospective buyers for the purpose of making a sale. Whether it takes place face-to-face or over the phone, personal selling attempts to persuade the buyer to accept a point of view or convince the buyer to take some action. For example, a car salesperson may try to persuade a car buyer that a particular model is superior to a competing model in certain features, such as gas mileage, roominess, and interior styling. Once the buyer is somewhat convinced, then the salesperson may attempt to elicit some action from the buyer, such as a test drive or a purchase. Frequently, in this traditional view of personal selling, the objectives of the salesperson are at the expense of the buyer, creating a win-lose outcome.

More current notions on the subject of personal selling emphasize the relationship that develops between a salesperson and a buyer. This concept is more typical with business- and industrial-type goods, such as heavy machinery or computer systems, than with consumer goods. Relationship selling emphasizes a win-win outcome and the accomplishment of mutual objectives that benefits both buyer and salesperson in the long term. Relationship selling does not seek either a quick sale or a temporary increase in sales—rather, it attempts to create involvement and loyalty by building a lasting bond with the customer.[9] Personal selling and relationship selling are discussed in Chapter 16.

personal selling
Planned presentation to one or more prospective buyers for the purpose of making a sale.

PT Cruiser

How is DaimlerChrysler using its Web site to communicate its marketing message to its youthful audience? Does the site seem geared to the demographic DaimlerChrysler is seeking to attract? Check out the PT Collection link. Based on what you see at these sites, do you think DaimlerChrysler will be successful with its target audience?

http://www.chryslercars.com/pt_cruiser
http://www.moparcollection.com/home_ptcruiser.htm

 On Line

Marketing Communication

Describe the communication process

communication
The process by which we exchange or share meanings through a common set of symbols.

Promotional strategy is closely related to the process of communication. As humans, we assign meaning to feelings, ideas, facts, attitudes, and emotions. **Communication** is the process by which we exchange or share meanings through a common set of symbols. When a company develops a new product, changes an old one, or simply tries to increase sales of an existing good or service, it must communicate its selling message to potential customers. Marketers communicate information about the firm and its products to the target market and various publics through its promotion programs. Pepsi commercials, for example, send messages to their target audience of kids through the use of sports figures such as basketball star Shaquille O'Neal. Read Shaq's own words about the power of marketing and advertising in Exhibit 14.2.

Communication can be divided into two major categories: interpersonal communication and mass communication. **Interpersonal communication** is direct, face-to-face communication between two or more people. When communicating face to face, people see the other person's reaction and can respond almost immediately. A salesperson speaking directly with a client is an example of marketing communication that is interpersonal.

interpersonal communication
Direct, fact-to-face communication between two or more people.

mass communication
The communication of a concept or message to large audiences.

Mass communication refers to communicating a concept or message to large audiences. A great deal of marketing communication is directed to consumers as a whole, usually through a mass medium such as television or newspapers. When a company advertises, it generally does not personally know the people with whom it is trying to communicate. Furthermore, the company is unable to respond immediately to consumers' reactions to its message. Instead, the marketing manager must wait to see whether people are reacting positively or negatively to the mass-communicated promotion. Any clutter from competitors' messages or other distractions in the environment can reduce the effectiveness of the mass communication effort.

The Communication Process

Marketers are both senders and receivers of messages. As *senders*, marketers attempt to inform, persuade, and remind the target market to adopt courses of action compatible with the need to promote the purchase of goods and services. As *receivers*, marketers attune themselves to the target market in order to develop the appropriate messages, adapt existing messages, and spot new communication opportunities. In this way, marketing communication is a two-way, rather than one-way, process.[10] The two-way nature of the communication process is shown in Exhibit 14.3.

The Sender and Encoding

sender
Originator of the message in the communication process.

The **sender** is the originator of the message in the communication process. In an interpersonal conversation, the sender may be a parent, a friend, or a salesperson. For an advertisement or press release, the sender is the company itself. Daimler-Chrysler, for example, is the sender of a message introducing and promoting its novel PT Cruiser. The car, aimed at young Generation Y and X consumers, combines elements of a minivan, an SUV, a London cab, and a '38 Chevy Tudor sedan.

encoding
The conversion of a sender's ideas and thoughts into a message, usually in the form of words or signs.

Encoding is the conversion of the sender's ideas and thoughts into a message, usually in the form of words or signs. DaimlerChrysler might encode its PT Cruiser

Exhibit 14.2

While on the outside looking in, I did not realize that marketing was so complicated. I never knew that a person, such as an athlete, could have such a powerful effect on peoples' thought processes and purchasing behavior. The use of a well-known athlete in marketing a product or service can have a great impact on the sales of that product or service. Look at Michael Jordan. Almost overnight most every kid either was wearing or wanted to wear Air Jordan shoes.

Why does this happen? Is it the appeal of a great athlete or is it great marketing? The answer is "none of the above." It's both. In my years as a professional basketball player, I have seen first-hand the dramatic appeal that athletes have for the fans and public in general. Top-name athletes are like E.F. Hutton—when they talk, people listen. But why do they listen? I believe they listen to us, the athletes, because we have credibility. The effectiveness of celebrity endorsements depends largely on how credible and attractive the spokesperson is and how familiar people are with him or her. Companies sometimes use sports figures and other celebrities to promote products hoping they are appropriate opinion leaders.

Because of an athlete's fame and fortune, or attraction, the athlete can often have the right credibility to be a successful spokesperson. The best definition of credibility that I could find was by James Gordon in his book, *Rhetoric of Western Thought*. He said that attraction "can come from a person's observable talents, achievements, occupational position or status, personality and appearance, and style."* That may be why a famous athlete's personality and position can help him or her communicate more effectively than a not-so-famous athlete.

Credibility is a positive force in the persuasive promotion used predominantly by cola marketers like Pepsi because of what I like to call "dreamful attraction." For example, when I was young, I dreamed that I was like Dr. J., the famous basketball player for the Philadelphia 76ers. I would take his head off a poster and put my head on it. I wanted to be Dr. J. That is dreamful attraction. The youth of today are no different. Just the other day a kid stopped me and told me that he wanted to be like me. He had a dreamful attraction. This dreamful attraction can help sell products. In my case, Pepsi, Spalding, Kenner, and Reebok are hoping that they are able to package properly and market whatever dreamful attraction I might have for their target audience—kids.

There are many ways to communicate to my target audience. I find that the most effective way for me is through television commercials. This avenue gives me a chance to express myself and show my real feelings about a message we are trying to communicate—either visually or vocally. I feel that I have what Clint Eastwood has—"Sudden Impaq." My impact is revealed through my sense of humor and my nonverbal communication. Take a look at the videos that come with this text and you will hear more about my role in developing TV commercials.

Why does Shaq sell? Communication. Although the verbal communication in many of my commercials is slim, the impact is still there. This makes me believe even more in the quote that who you are can almost be as important as what you say. But if you can blend the two together—who you are and what you have to say—then imagine how much more successful the communication message can be in the marketing process. Andre Agassi's favorite quote from his Canon commercial is "Image is everything." If it is not everything, it is almost everything. If you have the right image, match it with the right product, and market it properly, then success should follow.

I have been involved in commercials and the marketing of products for only a short time, but I have learned a great deal. If there is one formula for success in selling products, it would be this: Marketing plus credibility and image plus effective communications equals increase in sales—hopefully.

Now, you can call me Dr. Shaq, M.E. (Marketing Expert).

*James Gordon, *Rhetoric of Western Thought,* Dubuque, Iowa: Kendall-Hunt Publishing Co., 1976, p. 207.

message into an advertisement, or a Chrysler salesperson might encode the promotional message as a sales presentation to a prospective car buyer taking a test drive.

A basic principle of encoding is that what matters is not what the source says but what the receiver hears. One way of conveying a message that the receiver will hear properly is to use concrete words and pictures. For example, detailed print advertising for the PT Cruiser shows off its distinctive appearance and explains its

Exhibit 14.3 Communication Process

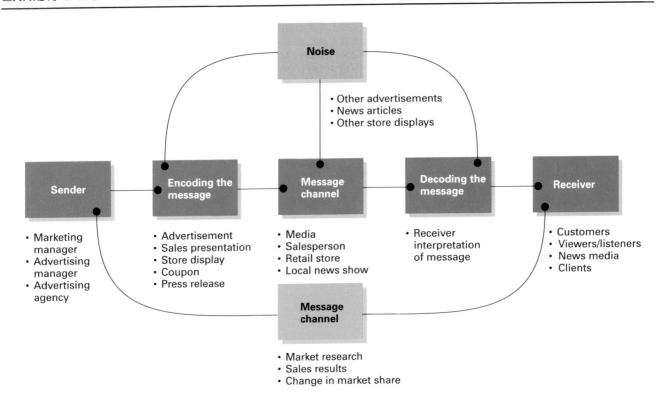

channel
A medium of communication—such as a voice, radio, or newspaper—for transmitting a message.

noise
Anything that interferes with, distorts, or slows down the transmission of information.

receiver
Person who decodes a message.

decoding
Interpretation of the language and symbols sent by the source through a channel.

unique features. Television advertising demonstrates the versatility and practicality of its interior, comparing its design and ease of use to a Swiss Army knife.

Message Transmission Transmission of a message requires a **channel**—a voice, radio, newspaper, or other communication medium. A facial expression or gesture can also serve as a channel.

Reception occurs when the message is detected by the receiver and enters his or her frame of reference. In a two-way conversation such as a sales pitch given by a sales representative to a potential client, reception is normally high. In contrast, the desired receivers may or may not detect the message when it is mass communicated, because most media are cluttered by **noise**—anything that interferes with, distorts, or slows down the transmission of information. In some media over-crowded with advertisers, such as newspapers and television, the noise level is high and the reception level is low. For example, reception of the PT Cruiser's ads may be hampered by competing car-related ads, other advertisements, or by stories in a magazine or newspaper. Transmission can also be hindered by situational factors such as physical surroundings like light, sound, location, and weather; the presence of other people; or the temporary moods consumers might bring to the situation. Mass communication may not even reach all the right consumers. Some members of the target audience may be watching television when the PT Cruiser is advertised, but others may not be.

The Receiver and Decoding Marketers communicate their message through a channel to customers, or **receivers**, who will decode the message. **Decoding** is the interpretation of the language and symbols sent by the source through a channel. Common understanding between two communicators, or a common frame of reference, is required for effective communication. Therefore, marketing managers must ensure a proper match between the message to be conveyed and the target market's attitudes and ideas.

Even though a message has been received, it will not necessarily be properly decoded—or even seen, viewed, or heard—because of selective exposure, distortion, and retention (refer to Chapter 5).[11] Even when people receive a message, they tend to manipulate, alter, and modify it to reflect their own biases, needs, knowledge, and culture. Factors that can lead to miscommunication are differences in age, social class, education, culture, and ethnicity. Further, because people don't always listen or read carefully, they can easily misinterpret what is said or written. In fact, researchers have found that a large proportion of both printed and televised communications are misunderstood by consumers. Bright colors and bold graphics have been shown to increase consumers' comprehension of marketing communication. However, even these techniques are not foolproof. A classic example of miscommunication occurred when Lever Brothers mailed out samples of its then new dishwashing liquid, Sunlight, which contains real lemon juice. The package clearly stated that Sunlight was a household cleaning product. However, many people saw the word sunlight, the large picture of lemons, and the phrase "with real lemon juice" and thought the product was lemon juice.

Marketers targeting consumers in foreign countries must also worry about the translation and possible miscommunication of their promotional messages by other cultures. An important issue for global marketers is whether to standardize or customize the message for each global culture marketed to. For instance, when advertising the PT Cruiser in foreign markets, DaimlerChrysler might choose to use the same commercials and selling points as it does in the United States, or it might choose to develop unique ads for each country or culture. Explore this issue more in the "Global Perspectives" box.

Feedback In interpersonal communication, the receiver's response to a message is direct **feedback** to the source. Feedback may be verbal, as in saying "I agree," or nonverbal, as in nodding, smiling, frowning, or gesturing.

feedback
Receiver's response to a message.

Because mass communicators like DaimlerChrysler are often cut off from direct feedback, they must rely on market research or analysis of sales trends, such as the number of PT Cruisers sold, for indirect feedback. DaimlerChrysler might use such measurements as the percentage of television viewers or magazine readers who recognize, recall, or state they have been exposed to the PT Cruiser message. Indirect feedback enables mass communicators to decide whether to continue, modify, or drop a message.

The Communication Process and the Promotional Mix

The four elements of the promotional mix differ in their ability to affect the target audience. For instance, promotional mix elements may communicate with the consumer directly or indirectly. The message may flow one way or two ways. Feedback may be fast or slow, a little or a lot. Likewise, the communicator may have varying degrees of control over message delivery, content, and flexibility. Exhibit 14.4 on page 483 outlines differences among the promotional mix elements with respect to mode of communication, marketer's control over the communication process, amount and speed of feedback, direction of message flow, marketer's control over the message, identification of the sender, speed in reaching large audiences, and message flexibility.

From Exhibit 14.4, you can see that most elements of the promotional mix are indirect and impersonal when used to communicate with a target market, providing only one direction of message flow. For example, advertising, public relations, and sales promotion are generally impersonal, one-way means of mass communication. Because they provide no opportunity for direct feedback, they cannot adapt easily to consumers' changing preferences, individual differences, and personal goals.

Personal selling, on the other hand, is personal, two-way communication. The salesperson is able to receive immediate feedback from the consumer and adjust

On Line

Global Perspectives

ONE MESSAGE OR MANY MESSAGES?

One of the hottest debates for global marketing professionals today is whether to customize or standardize promotional messages. On one side of the fence are those who believe the message should be tailored to each country or region to be most effective. Since different cultures perceive and react to promotional messages differently, this school of thought advocates the marketer must know something about the intended audiences' culture in order to communicate effectively. Kodak, for instance, favors a customized approach to advertising in China because consumer tastes and values vary between mainland China and the more progressive Taiwan and Hong Kong areas. In Taiwan and Hong Kong, which are quickly catching up to the United States and Europe in film sales volume, Kodak targets a young, innovative audience. In mainland China, which is comparatively far behind technologically except in a few urban centers, the approach is more lifestyle-oriented.

Some would disagree, however, advocating a single message for all countries. Following this standardized approach, a marketer would develop and deliver one message, translated into the language of each country, to all target markets. Supporters of this approach insist that consumers everywhere have the same basic needs and desires and can therefore be persuaded by universal communication. Furthermore, they say, standardized messages create unified brand images worldwide and the marketer eliminates the inefficiencies of trying to reinvent the meaning of its brand in every country. For example, through research Heinz concluded that teens around the world are really more alike in their use of ketchup than they are dissimilar. Its $50 million teen-oriented global advertising campaign

rolled out to seventy-five countries with only minor creative tweaks in the food the teens were pouring the ketchup over. Similarly, Procter & Gamble's new Dryel home dry-cleaning kit was launched in the United States, Europe, and parts of Asia and Latin America using the same packaging, brand name, and advertising reflecting universal cleaning needs.

Possibly the best answer to this dilemma is to use a mixture of standardization and customization—that is, standardizing the message while paying attention to local differences in the execution of the message. For example, Coca-Cola uses a standardized appeal when promoting its cola, but tailors the message to regional and international markets. All ads incorporate the tagline "Coca-Cola. Enjoy," but the campaign's "Enjoy" melody has nineteen different versions created along genres as varied as reggae, techno, hip-hop, and country depending on demographic and regional preferences. While this mixture of standardization and customization seems to be successful for many global marketers, it only works as long as the message truly plays to a worldwide audience. For example, IBM was successful with its "Solutions for a small planet" campaign since people all over the world have similar information and computing needs. The global imagery of the campaign is achieved through the use of the same footage in each country. The difference is the use of local subtitles to translate the "foreign" language of the commercial.

While efficiencies can be achieved by producing a single promotional message for worldwide use, the approach only makes sense if it does not run counter to social mores, ethnic issues, or religious taboos. For example, an ad for Levi's jeans shows a young man buying condoms from

a pharmacist and hiding them in the small side pocket of his jeans. When he goes to pick up his date, he discovers that her father is the pharmacist he met earlier. While the commercial was a hit in the United Kingdom, it would not play well in a strongly Catholic country, like Spain or Italy, where joking about contraception and premarital sex would raise difficult cultural issues.[a]

While some of the marketers discussed here have been successful using a global approach to promotion, not every product or service is suited for a unified message. What types of products do you think would benefit from a standardized approach to promotion? What types would fare better using a tailored approach?

[a] Audrey Snee, "Kodak Divides Up China in Order to Conquer It," *Ad Age International*, January 1998, p. 20; Juliana Koranteng, "Reebok Finds Its Second Wind as It Pursues Global Presence," *Ad Age International*, January 1998, p. 18; Stephanie Thompson, "Coca-Cola Taps Local Pleasures to Push Clasic," *Advertising Age*, January 17, 2000, p. 53; Jack Neff, "Test It in Paris, France, Launch It in Paris, Texas," *Advertising Age*, May 31, 1999, p. 28; Tara Parker-Pope, "P&G Cleaning Products Get on Fast Track," *Wall Street Journal*, May 18, 1999, p. B6; Sarah Ellison, "Sex-Themed Ads Often Don't Travel Well," *Wall Street Journal*, March 31, 2000, p. B7; James Caporimo, "Worldwide Advertising Has Benefits, But One Size Doesn't Always Fit All," *Brandweek*, July 17, 1995, p. 16; Ali Kanso, "International Advertising Strategies: Global Commitment to Local Vision," *Journal of Advertising Research*, January–February 1992, pp. 10–14; Wayne M. McCullough, "Global Advertising Which Acts Locally: The IBM Subtitles Campaign," *Journal of Advertising Research*, May–June 1996, pp. 11–15; Martin S. Roth, "Effects of Global Market Conditions on Brand Image Customization and Brand Performance," *Journal of Advertising*, Winter 1995, p. 55(21). See also Carolyn A. Lin, "Cultural Differences in Message Strategies: A Comparison Between American and Japanese Television Commercials," *Journal of Advertising Research*, July–August, 1993, pp. 40–47; Fred Zandpour et al., "Global Reach and Local Touch: Achieving Cultural Fitness in TV Advertising," *Journal of Advertising Research*, September–October, 1994, pp. 35–63.

	Advertising	Public Relations	Sales Promotion	Personal Selling
Mode of Communication	Indirect and nonpersonal	Usually indirect and nonpersonal	Usually indirect and nonpersonal	Direct and face-to-face
Communicator Control over Situation	Low	Moderate to low	Moderate to low	High
Amount of Feedback	Little	Little	Little to moderate	Much
Speed of Feedback	Delayed	Delayed	Varies	Immediate
Direction of Message Flow	One-way	One-way	Mostly one-way	Two-way
Control over Message Content	Yes	No	Yes	Yes
Identification of Sponsor	Yes	No	Yes	Yes
Speed in Reaching Large Audience	Fast	Usually fast	Fast	Slow
Message Flexibility	Same message to all audiences	Usually no direct control over message	Same message to varied target audiences	Tailored to prospective buyer

the message in response. Personal selling, however, is very slow in dispersing the marketer's message to large audiences. Because a salesperson can only communicate to one person or a small group of persons at one time, it is a poor choice if the marketer wants to send a message to many potential buyers.

The Goals and Tasks of Promotion

People communicate with one another for many reasons. They seek amusement, ask for help, give assistance or instructions, provide information, and express ideas and thoughts. Promotion, on the other hand, seeks to modify behavior and thoughts in some way. For example, promoters may try to persuade consumers to eat at Burger King rather than at McDonald's. Promotion also strives to reinforce existing behavior—for instance, getting consumers to continue to dine at Burger King once they have switched. The source (the seller) hopes to project a favorable image or to motivate purchase of the company's goods and services.

Promotion can perform one or more of three tasks: *inform* the target audience, *persuade* the target audience, or *remind* the target audience. Often a marketer will

Explain the goals and tasks of promotion

try to accomplish two or more of these tasks at the same time. Exhibit 14.5 lists the three tasks of promotion and some examples of each.

Informing

Informative promotion may seek to convert an existing need into a want or to stimulate interest in a new product. It is generally more prevalent during the early stages of the product life cycle. People typically will not buy a product service or support a nonprofit organization until they know its purpose and its benefits to them. Informative messages are important for promoting complex and technical products such as automobiles, computers, and investment services. Informative promotion is also important for a "new" brand being introduced into an "old" product class—for example, a new brand of detergent entering the well-established laundry detergent product category dominated by well-known brands such as Tide and Cheer. The new product cannot establish itself against more mature products unless potential buyers are aware of it, understand its benefits, and understand its positioning in the marketplace.

Persuading

Persuasive promotion is designed to stimulate a purchase or an action—for example, to drink more Coca-Cola or to use H&R Block tax services. Persuasion normally becomes the main promotion goal when the product enters the growth stage of its life cycle. By this time, the target market should have general product awareness and some knowledge of how the product can fulfill their wants. Therefore, the promotional task switches from informing consumers about the product category to persuading them to buy the company's brand rather than the competitor's. At this time, the promotional message emphasizes the product's real and perceived differential advantages, often appealing to emotional needs such as love, belonging, self-esteem, and ego satisfaction.

Persuasion can also be an important goal for very competitive mature product categories such as many household items, soft drinks, beer, and banking services.

Exhibit 14.5

Promotion Tasks and Examples

- **Informative promotion**
  Increasing the awareness of a new brand, product class, or product attribute
  Explaining how the product works
  Suggesting new uses for a product
  Building a company image

- **Persuasive promotion**
  Encouraging brand switching
  Changing customers' perceptions of product attributes
  Influencing customers to buy now
  Persuading customers to call

- **Reminder promotion**
  Reminding consumers that the product may be needed in the near future
  Reminding consumers where to buy the product
  Maintaining consumer awareness

In a marketplace characterized by many competitors, the promotional message often encourages brand switching and aims to convert some buyers into loyal users. For example, to persuade new customers to switch their checking accounts, a bank's marketing manager may offer a year's worth of free checks with no fees.

Critics believe that some promotional messages and techniques can be too persuasive, causing consumers to buy products and services they really don't need. Read about this issue in the "Ethics in Marketing" box.

Reminding

Reminder promotion is used to keep the product and brand name in the public's mind. This type of promotion prevails during the maturity stage of the life cycle. It assumes that the target market has already been persuaded of the good's or service's merits. Its purpose is simply to trigger a memory. Crest toothpaste, Tide laundry detergent, Miller beer, and many other consumer products often use reminder promotion.

Ethics in Marketing

BEWARE THE PERSUASIVENESS OF PROMOTIONS

Kirby Company likes to compare its vacuum cleaners to a Porsche. Rather than the plastic parts found in cheaper vacuum cleaners, Kirby cleaners feature die-cast aluminum bases and handles and wooden rollers. The motors are so powerful they can suck up a bucket of dirt dumped on a thick shag rug and not leave a speck behind. Available attachments can convert the Kirby vacuum into a leaf blower and even a spray painter.

But with a price tag of about $1,500, the Kirby model costs more than four times that of other top-of-the-line vacuums. Distributors sell Kirby vacuums exclusively door-to-door using aggressive selling techniques, often to people who can least afford to purchase such an expensive appliance. One elderly couple, who lived in a trailer park in Florida, were approached by two Kirby salesmen who persisted that they needed a new vacuum, even though their old one worked fine and they had only one room with carpet in their mobile home. The purchase far exceeded their monthly

income and the finance plan the salesmen set up for the couple would have brought the total payments to more than $2,500. After trying to cancel the deal, the couple was told the sale was final. Only after enlisting the help of an attorney were they able to rescind the transaction. This incident, as well as over 600 other complaints filed against Kirby with consumer protection agencies in fifteen states, has led to an investigation of the company's aggressive promotional tactics.

Kirby is hardly alone. In Canada, door-to-door salesmen for gas broker Priority Gas Marketing say field managers employed by a company hired by the broker told them to use misleading tactics to convince homeowners to sign five-year natural gas-supply contracts. While salespeople were trained in ethical sales tactics during training sessions in the office, once they hit the road in the company van, workers say the field managers told them to discard what they had learned and use another misleading pitch. Salespeople were also told to talk fast so cus-

tomers didn't have a chance to object. Deregulation of utilities in the United Kingdom has led to similar stories of unethical door-to-door selling tactics. There, customers tell of being threatened or tricked into signing gas or electricity contracts. Customers told of answering and signing "customer satisfaction surveys" only to find out later that the survey was actually a contract to take over their gas supply.[a]

Telemarketers and other direct marketers have also been known to use some very persuasive pitches to get customers to purchase something. Even salespeople in stores can often talk you into purchasing something you don't need. What can you do to protect yourself from high-pressure sales tactics?

[a] Joseph B. Cahill, "Here's the Pitch: How Kirby Persuades Uncertain Consumers to Buy $1,500 Vacuum," *Wall Street Journal*, October 4, 1999, pp. A1, A10; Valerie Lawton, "Sales Reps Rap Gas Broker's Marketing Practices," *Toronto Star*, March 24, 1998, p. D1; Tom Robbins, "Hard-Sell Gas Salesmen Draw New Anger," *Sunday Times—London News International*, January 23, 2000, p. 12.

Promotional Goals and the AIDA Concept

5

Discuss the AIDA concept and its relationship to the promotional mix

AIDA concept
Model that outlines the process for achieving promotional goals in terms of stages of consumer involvement with the message; the acronym stands for *attention, interest, desire,* and *action.*

The ultimate goal of any promotion is to get someone to buy a good or service or, in the case of nonprofit organizations, to take some action (for instance, donate blood). A classic model for reaching promotional goals is called the **AIDA concept**.[12] The acronym stands for *attention, interest, desire,* and *action*—the stages of consumer involvement with a promotional message.

This model proposes that consumers respond to marketing messages in a cognitive (thinking), affective (feeling), and conative (doing) sequence. First, the promotion manager attracts a person's *attention* by (in personal selling) a greeting and approach or (in advertising and sales promotion) loud volume, unusual contrasts, bold headlines, movement, bright colors, and so on. Next, a good sales presentation, demonstration, or advertisement creates *interest* in the product and then, by illustrating how the product's features will satisfy the consumer's needs, *desire.* Finally, a special offer or a strong closing sales pitch may be used to obtain purchase *action.*

The AIDA concept assumes that promotion propels consumers along the following four steps in the purchase-decision process:

1. *Attention:* The advertiser must first gain the attention of the target market. A firm cannot sell something if the market does not know that the good or service exists. Imagine that Acme Company, a pet food manufacturer, is introducing a new brand of cat food called Stripes, specially formulated for finicky cats. To increase the general awareness of its new brand, Acme heavily publicizes the introduction and places several ads on TV and in consumer magazines.

2. *Interest:* Simple awareness of a brand seldom leads to a sale. The next step is to create interest in the product. A print ad or TV commercial can't actually tell pet owners whether their cats will like Stripes. Thus, Acme might send samples of the new cat food to cat owners to create interest in the new brand.

3. *Desire:* Even though owners (and their cats) may like Stripes, they may not see any advantage over competing brands, especially if owners are brand loyal. Therefore, Acme must create brand preference by explaining the product's differential advantage over the competition. Specifically, Acme has to show that cats want to eat nothing else. Advertising at this stage claims that Stripes will satisfy "even the pickiest of the litter." Although pet owners may come to prefer Stripes to other brands, they still may not have developed the desire to buy the new brand. At this stage Acme might offer the consumer additional reasons to buy Stripes, such as easy-to-open, zip-lock packaging that keeps the product fresh; additional vitamins and minerals that healthy cats need; or feline taste-test results.

4. *Action:* Some members of the target market may now be convinced to buy Stripes but have yet to make the purchase. Displays in grocery stores, coupons, premiums, and trial-size packages can often push the complacent shopper into purchase.

Most buyers involved in high-involvement purchase situations pass through the four stages of the AIDA model on the way to making a purchase. The promoter's task is to determine where on the purchase ladder most of the target consumers are located and design a promotion plan to meet their needs. For instance, if Acme has determined that about half its buyers are in the preference or convic-

Exhibit 14.6

	Attention	Interest	Desire	Action
Advertising	Very effective	Very effective	Somewhat effective	Not effective
Public Relations	Very effective	Very effective	Very effective	Not effective
Sales Promotion	Somewhat effective	Somewhat effective	Very effective	Very effective
Personal Selling	Somewhat effective	Very effective	Very effective	Somewhat effective

When the Elements of Promotion Are Most Useful

tion stage but have not bought Stripes cat food for some reason, the company may mail cents-off coupons to cat owners to prompt them to buy.

The AIDA concept does not explain how all promotions influence purchase decisions. The model suggests that promotional effectiveness can be measured in terms of consumers progressing from one stage to the next. However, the order of stages in the model as well as whether consumers go through all steps has been much debated. For example, purchase can occur without interest or desire, perhaps when a low-involvement product is bought on impulse. Regardless of the order of the stages or consumers' progression through these stages, the AIDA concept helps marketers by suggesting which promotional strategy will be most effective.[13]

AIDA and the Promotional Mix

Exhibit 14.6 depicts the relationship between the promotional mix and the AIDA model. It shows that, although advertising does have an impact in the later stages, it is most useful in gaining attention for goods or services. In contrast, personal selling reaches fewer people at first. Salespeople are more effective at creating customer interest for merchandise or a service and at creating desire. For example, advertising may help a potential computer purchaser gain knowledge and information about competing brands, but the salesperson in an electronics store may be the one who actually encourages the buyer to decide a particular brand is the best choice. The salesperson also has the advantage of having the computer physically there to demonstrate its capabilities to the buyer.

Public relations has its greatest impact in gaining attention for a company, good, or service. Many companies can attract attention and build goodwill by sponsoring community events that benefit a worthy cause such as antidrug and antigang programs. Such sponsorships project a positive image of the firm and its products into the minds of consumers and potential consumers. Good publicity can also help develop consumer desire for a product. Book publishers push to get their titles listed on the best-seller lists of major publications, such as *Publishers Weekly* or the *New York Times*. Book authors also make appearances on talk-shows and at book stores to personally sign books and speak to fans. Similarly, movie marketers use prerelease publicity to raise the profile of their movies

This cosmetics saleswoman at Bloomingdales can create desire for her line of products by showing her potential customer how wonderful she looks after using them. Salespeople are very effective at creating desire, particularly in this type of situation.

and to increase initial box office sales. For example, most major motion picture studios have their own Web sites with multimedia clips and publicity photos of their current movies to attract viewers. Furthermore, movie promoters will include publicity gained from reviewers' quotes and Academy Award nominations in their advertising.

Sales promotion's greatest strength is in creating strong desire and purchase intent. Coupons and other price-off promotions are techniques used to persuade customers to buy new products. Frequent-buyer sales promotion programs, popular among retailers, allow consumers to accumulate points or dollars that can later be redeemed for goods. Frequent-buyer programs tend to increase purchase intent and loyalty and encourage repeat purchases. Randall's food stores in Texas, for example, annually reward loyal shoppers with "turkey bucks" during the weeks prior to Thanksgiving. Turkey bucks can then be redeemed for free turkeys.

Factors Affecting the Promotional Mix

Describe the factors that affect the promotional mix

Promotional mixes vary a great deal from one product and one industry to the next. Normally, advertising and personal selling are used to promote goods and services, supported and supplemented by sales promotion. Public relations helps develop a positive image for the organization and the product line. However, a firm may choose not to use all four promotional elements in its promotional mix, or it may choose to use them in varying degrees. The particular promotional mix chosen by a firm for a product or service depends on several factors: nature of the product, stage in the product life cycle, target market characteristics, type of buying decision, available funds for promotion, and use of either a push or a pull strategy.

Nature of the Product

Characteristics of the product itself can influence the promotional mix. For instance, a product can be classified as either a business product or a consumer product (refer to Chapter 9). As business products are often custom-tailored to the buyer's exact specifications, they are often not well suited to mass promotion. Therefore, producers of most business goods, such as computer systems or industrial machinery, rely more heavily on personal selling than on advertising. Informative personal selling is common for industrial installations, accessories, and component parts and materials. Advertising, however, still serves a purpose in promoting business goods. Advertisements in trade media may be used to create general buyer awareness and interest. Moreover, advertising can help locate potential customers for the sales force. For example, print media advertising often includes coupons soliciting the potential customer to "fill this out for more detailed information."

On the other hand, because consumer products generally are not custom-made, they do not require the selling efforts of a company representative who can tailor them to the user's needs. Thus consumer goods are promoted mainly through advertising to create brand familiarity. Broadcast advertising, newspapers, and consumer-oriented magazines are used extensively to promote consumer goods, especially nondurables. Sales promotion, the brand name, and the product's packaging are about twice as important for consumer goods as for business products. Persuasive personal selling is important at the retail level for shopping goods such as automobiles and appliances.

The costs and risks associated with a product also influence the promotional mix. As a general rule, when the costs or risks of using a product increase, personal selling becomes more important. Items that are a small part of a firm's budget (supply items) or of a consumer's budget (convenience products) do not require a salesperson to close the sale. In fact, inexpensive items cannot support the cost of a salesperson's time and effort unless the potential volume is high. On the other hand, expensive and complex machinery, new buildings, cars, and new homes represent a considerable investment. A salesperson must assure buyers that they are spending their money wisely and not taking an undue financial risk.

Social risk is an issue as well. Many consumer goods are not products of great social importance because they do not reflect social position. People do not experience much social risk in buying a loaf of bread or a candy bar. However, buying some shopping products and many specialty products such as jewelry and clothing does involve a social risk. Many consumers depend on sales personnel for guidance and advice in making the "proper" choice.

Stage in the Product Life Cycle

The product's stage in its life cycle is a big factor in designing a promotional mix (see Exhibit 14.7). During the *introduction stage*, the basic goal of promotion is to inform the target audience that the product is available. Initially, the emphasis is on the general product class—for example, personal computer systems. This emphasis gradually changes to awareness of specific brands, such as IBM, Apple, and Compaq. Typically, both extensive advertising and public relations inform the target audience of the product class or brand and heighten awareness levels. Sales promotion encourages early trial of the product, and personal selling gets retailers to carry the product.

When the product reaches the *growth stage* of the life cycle, the promotion blend may shift. Often a change is necessary because different types of potential buyers are targeted. Although advertising and public relations continue to be major elements of the promotional mix, sales promotion can be reduced, because consumers need fewer incentives to purchase. The promotional strategy is to emphasize the product's differential advantage over the competition. Persuasive promotion is used to build and maintain brand loyalty to support the product during the growth stage. By this stage, personal selling has usually succeeded in getting adequate distribution for the product.

Exhibit 14.7   Product Life Cycle and the Promotional Mix

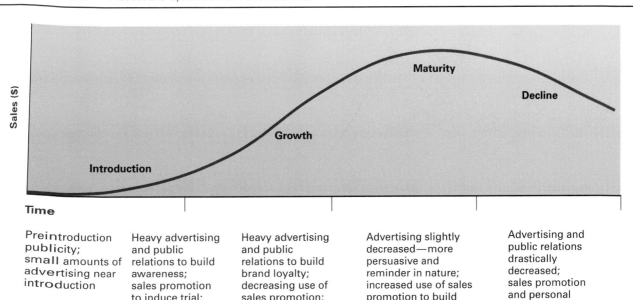

As the product reaches the *maturity stage* of its life cycle, competition becomes fiercer, and thus persuasive and reminder advertising are more strongly emphasized. Sales promotion comes back into focus as product sellers try to increase their market share.

All promotion, especially advertising, is reduced as the product enters the *decline stage*. Nevertheless, personal selling and sales promotion efforts may be maintained, particularly at the retail level.

Target Market Characteristics

A target market characterized by widely scattered potential customers, highly informed buyers, and brand-loyal repeat purchasers generally requires a promotional mix with more advertising and sales promotion and less personal selling. Sometimes, however, personal selling is required even when buyers are well informed and geographically dispersed. Although industrial installations and component parts may be sold to extremely competent people with extensive education and work experience, salespeople must still be present to explain the product and work out the details of the purchase agreement.

Often firms sell goods and services in markets where potential customers are hard to locate. Print advertising can be used to find them. The reader is invited to call for more information or to mail in a reply card for a detailed brochure. As the calls or cards are received, salespeople are sent to visit the potential customers.

Type of Buying Decision

The promotional mix also depends on the type of buying decision—for example, a routine decision or a complex decision. For routine consumer decisions like buying toothpaste or soft drinks, the most effective promotion calls attention to the brand or reminds the consumer about the brand. Advertising and, especially, sales promotion are the most productive promotion tools to use for routine decisions.

If the decision is neither routine nor complex, advertising and public relations help establish awareness for the good or service. Suppose a man is looking for a bottle of wine to serve to his dinner guests. As a beer drinker, he is not familiar with wines, yet he has seen advertising for Sutter Home wine and has also read an article in a popular magazine about the Sutter Home winery. He may be more likely to buy this brand because he is already aware of it.

In contrast, consumers making complex buying decisions are more extensively involved. They rely on large amounts of information to help them reach a purchase decision. Personal selling is most effective in helping these consumers decide. For example, consumers thinking about buying a car usually depend on a salesperson to provide the information they need to reach a decision. Print advertising may also be used for high-involvement purchase decisions because it can often provide a large amount of information to the consumer.

Consumers making complex buying decisions often depend on the salesperson to provide important product information. Purchasing a car is one such example. Can you think of others?
© Christopher Bissell/Tony Stone Images

Available Funds

Money, or the lack of it, may easily be the most important factor in determining the promotional mix. A small, undercapitalized manufacturer may rely heavily on free publicity if its product is unique. If the situation warrants a sales force, a financially strained firm may turn to manufacturers' agents, who work on a commission basis with no advances or expense accounts. Even well-capitalized organizations may not be able to afford the advertising rates of publications like *Better Homes and Gardens*, *Reader's Digest*, and the *Wall Street Journal*. The price of a high-profile advertisement in these media could support a salesperson for a year.

When funds are available to permit a mix of promotional elements, a firm will generally try to optimize its return on promotion dollars while minimizing the *cost per contact*, or the cost of reaching one member of the target market. In general, the cost per contact is very high for personal selling, public relations, and sales promotions like sampling and demonstrations. On the other hand, for the number of people national advertising reaches, it has a very low cost per contact.

Usually there is a trade-off among the funds available, the number of people in the target market, the quality of communication needed, and the relative costs of the promotional elements. A company may have to forgo a full-page, color advertisement in *People* magazine in order to pay for a personal selling effort. Although the magazine ad will reach more people than personal selling, the high cost of the magazine space is a problem.

Push and Pull Strategies

The last factor that affects the promotional mix is whether a push or a pull promotional strategy will be used. Manufacturers may use aggressive personal selling and trade advertising to convince a wholesaler or a retailer to carry and sell their merchandise. This approach is known as a **push strategy** (see Exhibit 14.8). The wholesaler, in turn, must often push the merchandise forward by persuading the retailer to handle the goods. The retailer then uses advertising, displays, and other forms of promotion to convince the consumer to buy the "pushed" products. This concept also applies to services. For example, the Jamaican Tourism Board targets promotions to travel agencies, which in turn tell their customers about the benefits of vacationing in Jamaica.

At the other extreme is a **pull strategy**, which stimulates consumer demand to obtain product distribution. Rather than trying to sell to the wholesaler, the manufacturer using a pull strategy focuses its promotional efforts on end consumers or opinion leaders. For example, Colgate-Palmolive sent thirty million samples of its new Colgate Total toothpaste to dental practitioners nationwide to create demand.[14] As consumers begin demanding the product, the retailer orders the merchandise from the wholesaler. The wholesaler, confronted with rising demand, then places an

push strategy
A marketing strategy that uses aggressive personal selling and trade advertising to convince a wholesaler or a retailer to carry and sell particular merchandise.

pull strategy
A marketing strategy that stimulates consumer demand to obtain product distribution.

Exhibit 14.8 Push Strategy Versus Pull Strategy

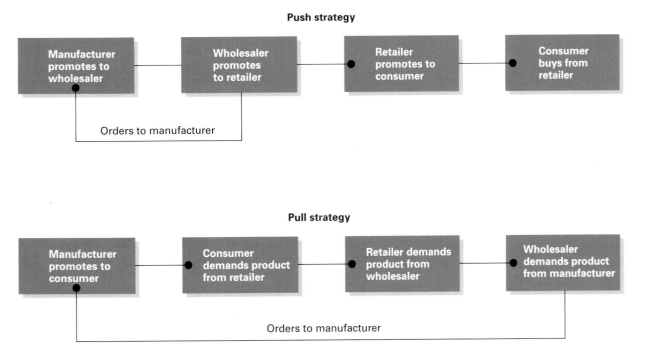

order for the "pulled" merchandise from the manufacturer. Consumer demand pulls the product through the channel of distribution (see Exhibit 14.8). Heavy sampling, introductory consumer advertising, cents-off campaigns, and couponing are part of a pull strategy. Using a pull strategy, the Jamaican Tourism Board may entice travelers to visit by advertising heavily in consumer magazines or offering discounts on hotels or airfare.

Rarely does a company use a pull or a push strategy exclusively. Instead, the mix will emphasize one of these strategies. For example, pharmaceutical companies generally use a push strategy, through personal selling and trade advertising, to promote their drugs and therapies to physicians. Sales presentations and advertisements in medical journals give physicians the detailed information they need to prescribe medication to their patients. Most pharmaceutical companies supplement their push promotional strategy with a pull strategy targeted directly to potential patients through advertisements in consumer magazines and on television.

Integrated Marketing Communications

Discuss the concept of integrated marketing communications

Ideally, marketing communications from each promotional mix element (personal selling, advertising, sales promotion, and public relations) should be integrated—that is, the message reaching the consumer should be the same regardless of whether it is from an advertisement, a salesperson in the field, a magazine article, or a coupon in a newspaper insert.

From the consumer's standpoint, a company's communications are already integrated. Consumers do not think in terms of the four elements of promotion: advertising, sales promotion, public relations, and personal selling. Instead, everything is an "ad." The only people who can disintegrate these communications elements are the marketers themselves. Unfortunately, many marketers neglect this fact when planning promotional messages and fail to integrate their communication efforts from one element to the next. The most common rift typically occurs between personal selling and the other elements of the promotional mix.

integrated marketing communications (IMC)
A method of carefully coordinating all promotional activities to produce a consistent, unified message that is customer focused.

This unintegrated, disjointed approach to promotion has propelled more companies to adopt the concept of **integrated marketing communications (IMC)**. IMC is the method of carefully coordinating all promotional activities—media advertising, sales promotion, personal selling, public relations, as well as direct marketing, packaging, and other forms of communication—to produce a consistent, unified message that is customer focused.[15] Following the concept of IMC, marketing managers carefully work out the roles that various promotional elements will play in the marketing mix. Timing of promotional activities is coordinated and the results of each campaign are carefully monitored to improve future use of the promotional mix tools. Typically, a marketing communications director is appointed who has overall responsibility for integrating the company's marketing communications.

Movie marketing campaigns benefit greatly from an integrated marketing communications approach. Those campaigns that are most integrated generally have more impact and make a deeper impression on potential moviegoers, leading to higher box-office sales. An integrated marketing approach, for instance, was used for the summer 1998 release of *Godzilla* by TriStar Pictures and Sony Pictures Entertainment. To heighten the anticipation for the film and its monster star, the movie's producers kept *Godzilla* under wraps until the day the film opened. Consumers only saw the film's signature green and the line "Size does matter." The first previews for the movie arrived a full year in advance, proclaiming Memorial Day 1998 as the day *Godzilla* would be revealed. Outdoor advertising compared the yet-to-be-seen monster's twenty-three-story size to famous urban landmarks such as Yankee Stadium in New York. Sales promotional support for the movie included

This ad for Carnation evaporated milk appears in the November 2000 Spanish-language edition of *People* magazine. Note the English translations and the recipe for the apple-raisin bread. Find out if the English-language version featured a different recipe.

Dreyer's Grand Ice Cream, which created a special flavor, Godzilla Vanilla, with vanilla chunks in the shape of the monster; a sweepstakes sponsored by Duracell that gave the winner a swimming pool shaped like Godzilla's foot; a Kodak television spot that blended movie footage to dramatize a young man's efforts to photograph Godzilla with a disposable camera; and Taco Bell, which paired Godzilla with its talking chihuahua. Commemorative tickets were also issued to those who bought seats at the first screening of the film on opening day, autographed by the film's makers and accompanied by Taco Bell coupons.[16]

The concept of integrated marketing communications has been growing in popularity for several reasons. First, the proliferation of thousands of media choices beyond traditional television has made promotion a more complicated task. Instead of promoting a product just through mass media options, like television and magazines, promotional messages today can appear in many varied sources. Further, the mass market has also fragmented—more selectively segmented markets and an increase in niche marketing have replaced the traditional broad market groups that marketers promoted to in years past. For instance, many popular magazines now have Spanish-language editions targeted toward America's growing Hispanic population. Finally, marketers have slashed their advertising spending in favor of promotional techniques that generate immediate sales responses and those that are more easily measured, such as direct marketing. Thus, the interest in integrated marketing communications is largely a reaction to the scrutiny that marketing communications has come under, and particularly to suggestions that uncoordinated promotional activity leads to a strategy that is wasteful and inefficient.[17]

Looking Back

America Online does not just use one element of the promotional mix to promote its Internet service to on-line users. Rather, it uses a mix of promotional elements: advertising, public relations and publicity, sales promotion, and personal selling. AOL's integrated promotional plan conveys a consistent and clear message of the company and its services and has proved crucial to the company's domination of the Internet and its success at recruiting new subscribers. As you read the next two chapters, keep in mind that marketers try to choose the mix of promotional elements that will best promote their good or service. Rarely will a marketer rely on just one method of promotion.

Use it Now!

Learn a New Form of Communication

Learn American Sign Language and communicate through your hands, gestures, and body movements. Visit the Deaf World Web site at **http://www.deafworldweb.org** to learn how to sign letters and words. Also visit HandSpeak at **http://www.handspeak.com** for a practical visual dictionary of sign language for everyday life.

Become a Marketing Guerilla

Entrepreneurs and small businesses don't always have big promotional budgets. For hundreds of low-cost promotional ideas, turn to the Guerilla Marketing Web page at **http://www.gmarketing.com**. Find out how to promote effectively for a fraction of what the big guys spend.

Summary

1 **Discuss the role of promotion in the marketing mix.** Promotion is communication by marketers that informs, persuades, and reminds potential buyers
of a product in order to influence an opinion or elicit a response. Promotional
strategy is the plan for using the elements of promotion—advertising, public relations, sales promotion, and personal selling—to meet the firm's overall objectives
and marketing goals. Based on these objectives, the elements of the promotional
strategy become a coordinated promotion plan. The promotion plan then becomes an integral part of the total marketing strategy for reaching the target
market along with product, distribution, and price.

2 **Discuss the elements of the promotional mix.** The elements of the promotional mix include advertising, public relations, sales promotion, and personal selling. Advertising is a form of impersonal, one-way mass communication
paid for by the source. Public relations is the function of promotion concerned
with a firm's public image. Firms can't buy good publicity, but they can take steps
to create a positive company image. Sales promotion is typically used to back up
other components of the promotional mix by stimulating immediate demand. Finally, personal selling typically involves direct communication, in person or by telephone; the seller tries to initiate a purchase by informing and persuading one or
more potential buyers.

3 **Describe the communication process.** The communication process has several steps. When an individual or organization has a message it wishes to
convey to a target audience, it encodes that message using language and symbols
familiar to the intended receiver and sends the message through a channel of
communication. Noise in the transmission channel distorts the source's intended
message. Reception occurs if the message falls within the receiver's frame of reference. The receiver decodes the message and usually provides feedback to the
source. Normally, feedback is direct for interpersonal communication and indirect for mass communication.

4 **Explain the goals and tasks of promotion.** The fundamental goals of promotion are to induce, modify, or reinforce behavior by informing, persuading, and reminding. Informative promotion explains a good's or service's
purpose and benefits. Promotion that informs the consumer is typically used to
increase demand for a general product category or to introduce a new good or
service. Persuasive promotion is designed to stimulate a purchase or an action.
Promotion that persuades the consumer to buy is essential during the growth
stage of the product life cycle, when competition becomes fierce. Reminder promotion is used to keep the product and brand name in the public's mind. Promotions that remind are generally used during the maturity stage of the product
life cycle.

5 **Discuss the AIDA concept and its relationship to the promotional mix.** The
AIDA model outlines the four basic stages in the purchase decision-making
process, which are initiated and propelled by promotional activities: (1) attention,
(2) interest, (3) desire, and (4) action. The components of the promotional mix
have varying levels of influence at each stage of the AIDA model. Advertising is
a good tool for increasing awareness and knowledge of a good or service. Sales
promotion is effective when consumers are at the purchase stage of the decision-
making process. Personal selling is most effective in developing customer interest
and desire.

6 **Describe the factors that affect the promotional mix.** Promotion managers
consider many factors when creating promotional mixes. These factors include the nature of the product, product life cycle stage, target market characteris-

tics, the type of buying decision involved, availability of funds, and feasibility of push or pull strategies. Because most business products tend to be custom-tailored to the buyer's exact specifications, the marketing manager may choose a promotional mix that relies more heavily on personal selling. On the other hand, consumer products are generally mass produced and lend themselves more to mass promotional efforts such as advertising and sales promotion. As products move through different stages of the product life cycle, marketers will choose to use different promotional elements. For example, advertising is emphasized more in the introductory stage of the product life cycle than in the decline stage. Characteristics of the target market, such as geographic location of potential buyers and brand loyalty, influence the promotional mix as does whether the buying decision is complex or routine. The amount of funds a firm has to allocate to promotion may also help determine the promotional mix. Small firms with limited funds may rely more heavily on public relations, whereas larger firms may be able to afford broadcast or print advertising. Last, if a firm uses a push strategy to promote the product or service, the marketing manager may choose to use aggressive advertising and personal selling to wholesalers and retailers. If a pull strategy is chosen, then the manager often relies on aggressive mass promotion, such as advertising and sales promotion, to stimulate consumer demand.

7 **Discuss the concept of integrated marketing communications.** Integrated marketing communications is the method of carefully coordinating all promotional activities—advertising, sales promotion, personal selling, public relations, as well as direct marketing, packaging, and other forms of communication—to produce a consistent, unified, customer-focused message. Marketing managers carefully coordinate all promotional activities to ensure that consumers see and hear one message. Integrated marketing communications has received more attention in recent years due to the proliferation of media choices, the fragmentation of mass markets into more segmented niches, and the decrease in advertising spending in favor of promotional techniques that generate an immediate sales response.

Key Terms

advertising 475
AIDA concept 486
channel 480
communication 478
decoding 480
differential advantage 474
encoding 478
feedback 481
integrated marketing communications (IMC) 492
interpersonal communication 478
mass communication 478
noise 480
personal selling 477
promotion 474
promotional mix 475
promotional strategy 474
publicity 476
public relations 475
pull strategy 491
push strategy 491
receiver 480
sales promotion 476
sender 478

Discussion and Writing Questions

1. What is a promotional strategy? Explain the concept of a differential advantage in relation to promotional strategy.
2. Why is understanding the target market a crucial aspect of the communication process?
3. Discuss the importance of integrated marketing communications. Give some current examples of companies that are and are not practicing integrated marketing communications.
4. Why might a marketing manager choose to promote his or her product using persuasion? Give some current examples of persuasive promotion.
5. Explain the difference between a "pull" and a "push" promotional strategy. Under what conditions should each strategy be used?
6. Discuss the AIDA concept. How do these different stages of consumer involvement affect the promotional mix?
7. **WRITING** As the promotional manager for a new line of cosmetics targeted to preteen girls, you have been assigned the task of deciding which promotional mix elements—advertising, public relations, sales promotion, and personal selling—should be used in promoting it. Your budget for promoting the preteen cosmetics line is limited. Write a promotional plan explaining your choice of promotional mix elements given the nature of the product, the stage in the product life cycle, target market characteristics, type of buying decision, available funds, and pull or push strategy.

8. Choose two companies, one a consumer products company and the other an on-line retailer. Conduct some research on these two companies in terms of their promotional practices by observation (such as looking in magazines, the newspaper, television, Web site, etc.) and searching at your campus library. You may also use Infotrac (**http://www.infotrac-college.com**) to locate any articles written on the promotional activities of the companies you select. Describe some of the types of promotions that these companies have engaged in during the last year—for example, ran television ads, sponsored an event, held a sweepstakes, or expanded sales force. To the best of your abilities, determine the objective of each promotion in relation to the AIDA model. For example, the objective of a magazine ad might be to create awareness or interest, while the objective of a coupon might be to stimulate the action of purchase. Also note if the companies' promotions are integrated or not.

9. Choose a partner from class and go together to interview the owners or managers of several small businesses in your city. Ask them what their promotional objectives are and why. Are they trying to inform, persuade, or remind customers to do business with them? Also determine whether they believe they have an awareness problem or whether they need to persuade customers to come to them instead of to competitors. Ask them to list the characteristics of their primary market, the strengths and weaknesses of their direct competitors, and how they are positioning their store to compete. Prepare a report to present in class summarizing your findings.

10. Visit **http://www.teenresearch.com**. What research can this company offer about the size and growth of the teen market, the buying power of teenagers, and their buying habits? Why might these statistics be important to a company targeting teenagers in terms of marketing communications and promotion strategy?

Application for Entrepreneurs

Be Safe is a small, independent business that markets child-proofing services to parents with small children and to day care centers and home day care providers. For a small fee, Jill Sherman, the owner, will visit the customer's home or facility and point out areas that might be dangerous to the safety of small children, such as exposed electrical outlets, poisonous products and plants, or falling hazards. Jill also sells and installs safety items in homes and facilities to make them safer for children. Currently, most of her business comes through referrals or the Yellow Pages, but she would like to increase her business through some form of promotion, although her budget to do so will be small. She has noticed that many of her clients, especially new parents, don't know much about child safety in the home or about the products that can help deter child injuries. Other clients, especially day care centers, know about child safety but often install the wrong products or don't maintain a safe environment at all times, exposing children to danger.

Questions

1. What goals should Be Safe's promotional efforts try to achieve? How will these goals differ by target market?
2. How might the type of buying decision and the nature of this service influence the promotional mix?
3. Given Be Safe's small budget, what types of promotional methods would you suggest?

Nantucket Nectars: Blending Marketing Methods for a Juicy Success

After graduating from Brown University in the spring of 1989, college friends Tom First and Tom Scott moved to Nantucket Island, Massachusetts, determined to make it on their own and avoid the inevitable coat-and-tie corporate life. There, the two friends opened a boat-based delivery business in Nantucket Harbor to service the visiting yachts that came to the remote island in the warmer months. Having the summer of their lives, the pair delivered coffee, muffins, laundry, and other necessities to well-to-do island visitors and worked other odd jobs to earn money, such as shelling scallops, washing dogs, and pumping sewage. Then Nantucket's ferocious winter kicked in, and their business slowed to a crawl.

One night during their first winter, the Toms started mixing fruit in a blender, trying to recreate a peach nectar that First had tasted during his travels to Spain. Stumbling on some flavorful concoctions, their entrepreneurial spirits took over and First and Scott decided to hand-bottle their juices in recycled wine bottles and sell them off their boat when the yachts returned with the warmer weather. They called their juices Nantucket Nectars and sold 2,000 bottles at $1 apiece the next summer. Encouraged by their initial sales, First and Scott decided to go into the juice business.

In the beginning, the pair targeted New England colleges close to Nantucket Island and Boston and the young adults there that would most likely be receptive to their antiestablishment and underdog image. They pitched a big purple tent at football games and other college events, handing out juice and T-shirts with the distinct Nantucket Nectars' logo. Their low-cost, grass roots marketing early on helped position Nantucket Nectars as the youthful, natural, and independent alternative to larger juice and beverage companies.

They also stumbled upon an effective radio advertising campaign. After booking a recording session, the Toms never got around to actually writing a script for their ad. Instead, they persuaded the radio producer to just record them talking. First and Scott "shot the breeze" for a couple of hours, reminiscing about their early days as "Juice Guys," and then edited the conversation for a radio spot. What resulted was an off-the-cuff, down-to-earth radio ad that ended up winning an award for excellence in radio advertising.

Nantucket Nectars still prefers such homespun techniques to promote its many juice flavors. The company uses "mobile marketing squads" that drive purple Winnebagos to outdoor events frequented by the company's coveted consumers—eighteen- to thirty-five-year-olds. Members of the company's high-energy, purple-shirted juice squad hand out free samples of the company's flavorful juices to sports fans, marathoners, and concertgoers. Mobile squads will also swap any competitor's product for a new cold bottle of Nantucket Nectars.

To introduce its latest Squeezed Nectars line of juice teas and lemonades packaged in distinctive wide-mouthed glass canning jars, the company relied heavily on sampling and promotions to create a buzz. In addition, the Toms decided to invite their grandmothers to promote the new line. In radio spots, the grandmothers chat with Scott and First about a wide range of topics, but mostly about how lemonade was made long ago, reinforcing the idea that Nantucket Nectars' lemonades taste just like grandma's.

From its humble beginnings, Nantucket Nectars has grown to be a major player in the premium juice drink category with a loyal following. While "Juice Guys" First and Scott have had their share of bumps along the way, their once tiny company now employs over one hundred people, and revenues top $80 million. Their evolving juice lineup—fifty different flavors in all—are sold in about forty states and in Britain, France, Korea, the Caribbean, South and Central America, and Canada. The Toms still consider themselves the underdog in the premium juice industry. But no matter how much Nantucket Nectars grows, Scott says, he will always be looking for ways to change since the only way to succeed in this competitive environment is to be entrepreneurial.

Questions

1. What elements of the promotional mix does Nantucket Nectars utilize to promote its juice line?

Still **S**haky? Here's a tip

Use the learning objectives list on page 472 as a study tool. After reading the whole chapter, return to the beginning and write the summary for each objective. Check your work by reading the actual summary points on pages 494 and 495.

2. Where would you place Nantucket Nectars in the product life cycle? How does this affect the company's choice of promotional mix elements?

3. Visit the company's Web site at **http://www.juiceguys. com**. Give examples of how its Web site conveys its folksy, down-to-earth image.

Bibliography

Katrina Burger. "A Drink With an Attitude." *Forbes*, February 10, 1997.

Joel Kurtzman. "Advertising for All the Little Guys." *Fortune*, April 12, 2000, p. 162.

Greg Masters. "All Juiced Up," *Discount Merchandiser*, July 1999, p. 107.

Gwen Moran. "Go, Granny, Go." *Entrepreneur Magazine*, March 2000.

Nantucket Nectars Web site at **http://www.juiceguys.com**.

"Nantucket Nectars Will Tie Up in Denver." *Denver Rocky Mountain News*, February 14, 1999.

Nancy Coltun Webster. "Squeezed Nectars: Chris Testa." *Advertising Age*, June 26, 2000, p. s4.

"What Have You Become?" *Entrepreneur Magazine*, May 2000.

Case

video

Boyne USA Resorts' *Lifestyles* Magazine: Promoting the Ultimate Playground

Boyne USA Resorts' *Lifestyles* magazine has a circulation of five hundred thousand. Through direct mail, newsstand distribution, and trade show exposure, the magazine reaches an audience from Montana to Michigan and from Washington to Utah. Boyne USA Resorts is the largest privately owned resort corporation in the country and has a very diverse audience. In many ways, *Lifestyles* epitomizes Boyne's integrated approach to communication about available services. All promotional activities—media advertising, sales promotion, personal selling, public relations, as well as direct marketing—have a consistent, unified message. This integrated approach to promotion can be seen in every issue of *Lifestyles*, which informs the target audience of skiers and golfers, persuades them to come to a Boyne resort, and reminds them of special events and sales promotions.

Lifestyles articles advertise all the amenities of the resorts: the inns, condominiums, and vacation homes; the superb quality of the slopes, cross-country skiing trails, and manicured golf courses; other activities such as hiking, biking, and fishing; and the gourmet restaurants. The section entitled "Distinctive Resort Properties for Sale" lists available real estate for sale and invites readers to contact a Boyne real estate professional who will work one-to-one with prospective buyers. Also highlighted in *Lifestyles* is the Boyne team of convention planners, who offer companies a wide choice of tastefully decorated facilities and conferences for six to six hundred people.

Lifestyles also describes Boyne's special events, which are carefully orchestrated to build good public relations nationwide. By identifying areas of public interest and offering programs to generate public awareness, Boyne USA maintains a positive image and educates the public about its goal to be a premier ski and golf resort. The company's special events calendar at the Michigan resorts is full. Ski with the Greats is a popular event with celebrities on hand to hold clinics, a challenge race, and award prizes at the après-ski party. At the Hawaiian Tropic, contestants from around the state come to Boyne Mountain to compete in an evening gown and swimsuit competition, a fashion show, a limbo dance, and a Mr. Boyne contest, all of which culminate in a party with live entertainment. Dannon Winterfest, put on in conjunction with the Dannon Company, has tents and inflatables set up around Boyne Mountain with product sampling, a dance contest, an après-ski party, and merchandise giveaways. And the World Pro Snowboard Tour features international racers who compete for $250,000 in prize money. These events give the resorts lots of publicity, and regardless of how much advertising is done, nothing generates more excitement about Boyne USA than extensive media coverage.

In addition to informing readers about the resorts, *Lifestyles* persuades them to visit. "Want your ten-year-olds to spend more time outside? Get them a **FREE** Gold Season Pass to Boyne USA Resorts!" This promotion offers a complimentary pass that entitles ten-year-olds to unlimited skiing and snowboarding at Boyne Mountain and Boyne Highlands. Another powerful way to draw skiers to the resorts is to make skiing affordable. As the *Lifestyles* article explains, "No longer will non-skiers be able to use the expense of skiing or snowboarding as an excuse to remain couch potatoes this winter. For just $29, beginners will get a 90-minute lesson, equipment, and a beginner area lift ticket." The promotions information in *Lifestyles* is regularly updated on the Boyne Web site to remind vacationers about special events, skiing and golfing packages, and clothing or equipment.

A key element in the promotional mix for Boyne USA resorts is *Lifestyles* magazine's pull strategy to stimulate consumer demand. The scenic photos of the slopes and golf courses, lovely inns, and sumptuous dining entice readers to learn more about the resorts, and such deep discounts on weekday packages encourage readers to call travel agencies, use the toll-free number, or e-mail for information. Once visitors arrive at the resorts, this pull strategy is supported by a push strategy through the personal selling of real estate, clothing and equipment, and conventions. At Boyne, the push strategy is more about relationships and trust, so sales people are viewed as consultants who help the resort connect with its guests. For example, meeting planners work diligently with key accounts to develop long-term relationships, and carefully planned family events, such as Take Your Daughter to the Slopes Day or Ski Free with Lodging, make skiing affordable and so build customer loyalty.

Lifestyles is just the beginning of Boyne USA's well-coordinated promotion strategy, a strategy that is customer focused to bring vacationers back to the ultimate playground year after year.

Questions
1. Using Exhibit 14.1, what is the role of promotion in Boyne USA's marketing mix?
2. How does *Lifestyle* magazine encompass all of Boyne's promotional activities?
3. Using Exhibit 14.5, explain the three tasks of promotion at Boyne USA resorts.
4. How do push and pull strategies affect Boyne's promotional mix?

Bibliography
Boyne USA Resorts, *Lifestyles* magazine: Winter 1997–98; Spring/Summer 1998.
Boyne USA Web site: **http://www.boyneusa.com**

chapter 15

Learning Objectives

1 Discuss the effect of advertising on market share and consumers

2 Identify the major types of advertising

3 Discuss the creative decisions in developing an advertising campaign

4 Describe media evaluation and selection techniques

5 Discuss the role of public relations in the promotional mix

Advertising and Public Relations

At midnight on Friday, July 8, 2000, lines of sleepy-eyed children and their parents at New York City's Lincoln Center Barnes & Noble bookstore stretched two city blocks, baffling late-night strollers. In San Francisco, staffers at a tiny bookstore named Cover to Cover dressed themselves in pajamas to greet 400 kids waiting for the store to open at midnight. In Coral Gables, Florida, Books & Books threw a party with magic tricks and a fortune-teller for hundreds of children. Selected stores in the Borders chain opened their doors at the witching hour with magic shows, costume parties, and live owls. Television crews and print reporters swarmed around these kids and their parents waiting in line, looking for a few good stories.

What were all these bookstores up to? And why were all these children up way past their bedtimes? For the new "Harry Potter" book, of course. Booksellers large and small witnessed the marketing magic of Harry Potter as the much-anticipated fourth book in the children's series, *Harry Potter and the Goblet of Fire,* appeared at midnight on July 8—and then flew off the shelves. Kept under a cloak of secrecy for months, the novel broke book-selling records worldwide, with a first-print run by the book's British and U.S. publishers totaling a staggering 5.3 million copies.

At the more than 430 Barnes & Noble bookstores that staged special midnight events to kick off sales, more than 114,000 copies of J. K. Rowling's latest children's fantasy were sold in one hour. Over 93,000 copies were sold from Barnes&Noble.com's Web site on Friday night in addition to the 360,000 copies preordered. Amazon.com received 350,020 preorders as of 12:01 EST Saturday.

These fantastic sales records were the result of a carefully crafted advertising and public relations plan by book publisher Scholastic and the author. Employing military-style secrecy, Ms. Rowling and Scholastic kept most of the details about the new book, the fourth in the series about the orphaned boy with wizard powers, under wraps for months before its release. Printers and binders were sworn to secrecy. Antsy readers didn't even know the plot or the title, for that matter, until it leaked out in the British press. Booksellers were forbidden to open any cartons of the books until the appointed hour on Friday night, adding to the frenzy. Scholastic even required bookstores to sign affidavits ensuring the novel would not be sold before midnight.

The parties continued well into Saturday at bookstores around the world. Many opened their doors early on Saturday, serving breakfast to kids and their parents who began lining up in the predawn hours. That same day, planes gliding over beaches on Long Island, the Jersey shore, Los Angeles, Chicago, and Hilton Head, South Carolina, displayed banners reading, "*Harry Potter and the Goblet of Fire.* Read it now!" And a giant screen in New York's Times Square heralded the new book to the throngs of people walking the streets.[1]

How do marketers like Scholastic decide what type of advertising message should be conveyed to prospective buyers? How do marketers decide which media to use? How does public relations and publicity benefit a marketer's promotional plan? Answers to these questions and many more will be found as you read through this chapter.

The Effects of Advertising

Discuss the effects of advertising on market share and consumers

Advertising is defined in Chapter 14 as any form of impersonal, paid communication in which the sponsor or company is identified. It is a popular form of promotion, especially for consumer packaged goods and services. Advertising spending increases annually, with estimated U.S. advertising expenditures now exceeding $215 billion per year.[2]

Although total advertising expenditures seem large, the industry itself is very small. Only about 272,000 people are employed in the advertising departments of manufacturers, wholesalers, and retailers and in the five thousand or so U.S. advertising agencies.[3] This figure also includes people working in media services, such as radio and television, magazines and newspapers, and direct-mail firms.

The amount of money budgeted for advertising by some firms is staggering (see Exhibit 15.1.) General Motors, Procter & Gamble, and Philip Morris each spend over $2 billion annually on national advertising alone. That's over $6 million a day by each company. If sales promotion and public relations are included, this figure rises even higher. Over ninety additional companies spend over $200 million each.

Exhibit 15.1

Top Ten Leaders by U.S. Advertising Spending: 1999

Rank	Advertiser	Total U.S. Ad Spending in 1999 (in millions)	Average Ad Spending per Day in 1999
1	**General Motors,** Detroit	$4,040.4	$11,069,590
2	**Procter & Gamble,** Cincinnati	$2,611.8	$7,155,620
3	**Philip Morris,** New York	$2,201.6	$6,031,780
4	**Pfizer,** New York	$2,142.4	$5,869,590
5	**AT&T Corporation,** Basking Ridge, NJ	$1,950.9	$5,344,930
6	**DaimlerChrysler,** Auburn Hills, Michigan/Stuttgart, Germany	$1,804.1	$4,942,740
7	**Ford Motor,** Dearborn, Michigan	$1,639.8	$4,492,600
8	**Sears, Roebuck & Company,** Chicago	$1,505.2	$4,123,840
9	**PepsiCo,** Purchase, New York	$1,315.7	$3,604,660
10	**Verizon Communications,** New York	$1,312.7	$3,596,440

SOURCE: Computed from data obtained from "100 Leaders by U.S. Advertising Spending," *Advertising Age,* September 25, 2000, p. s2.

Spending on advertising varies by industry. For example, the game and toy industry has one of the highest ratios of advertising dollars to sales. For every dollar of merchandise sold in the toy industry, for example, about twelve to fifteen cents is spent on advertising the toy to consumers. Book publishers spend roughly twenty-seven cents on advertising for every dollar of book revenue. Other consumer goods manufacturers that spend heavily on advertising in relation to total sales include sugar and confectionary products manufacturers, watchmakers, perfume and cosmetic manufacturers, detergent makers, and wine and liquor companies.[4]

Advertising and Market Share

Today's most successful brands of consumer goods, like Ivory soap and Coca-Cola, were built by heavy advertising and marketing investments long ago. Today's advertising dollars are spent on maintaining brand awareness and market share.

New brands with a small market share tend to spend proportionately more for advertising and sales promotion than those with a large market share, typically for two reasons. First, beyond a certain level of spending for advertising and sales promotion, diminishing returns set in. That is, sales or market share begins to decrease no matter how much is spent on advertising and sales promotion. This phenomenon is called the **advertising response function**. Understanding of the advertising response function helps marketers use budgets wisely. A market leader like Ruffles potato chips may spend proportionately less on advertising than newcomer Frito-Lay's Baked Lay's brand. Frito-Lay spends more on its brand in an attempt to increase awareness and market share. Ruffles, on the other hand, spends only as much as needed to maintain market share; anything more would reap diminishing benefits. Because Ruffles has already captured the attention of the majority of the target market, it needs only to remind customers of its product.

The second reason that new brands tend to require higher spending for advertising and sales promotion is that a certain minimum level of exposure is needed to measurably affect purchase habits. If Frito-Lay advertised Baked Lay's chips in only one or two publications and bought only one or two television spots, it certainly would not achieve the exposure needed to penetrate consumers' perceptual defenses, obtain awareness and comprehension, and ultimately affect their purchase intentions. Instead, Baked Lay's was introduced through advertising in many different media for a sustained period of time.

The Effects of Advertising on Consumers

Advertising affects consumers' daily lives, informing them about products and services and influencing their attitudes, beliefs, and ultimately their purchases. The average U.S. citizen is exposed to hundreds of advertisements a day from all types of advertising media. In just the television media alone, researchers estimate that the average person spends over four hours a day watching TV.[5] With network television airing an average of almost twenty-one minutes of commercials during each hour of daytime programming, consumers are surely affected in some way by advertising.[6] Advertising affects the TV programs people watch, the content of the newspapers they read, the politicians they elect, the medicines they take, and the toys their children play with. Consequently, the influence of advertising on the U.S. socioeconomic system has been the subject of extensive debate among economists, marketers, sociologists, psychologists, politicians, consumerists, and many others.

While advertising cannot change consumers' deeply rooted values and attitudes, advertising may succeed in transforming a person's negative attitude toward a product into a positive one. For instance, serious or dramatic advertisements are more effective at changing consumers' negative attitudes. Humorous ads, on the other hand, have been shown to be more effective at shaping attitudes when consumers already have a positive image of the advertised brand.[7] For this reason, beer marketers often use humorous ads to communicate with their core market of young adults.

advertising response function
A phenomenon in which spending for advertising and sales promotion increases sales or market share up to a certain level but then produces diminishing returns.

Advertising also reinforces positive attitudes toward brands. When consumers have a neutral or favorable frame of reference toward a product or brand, advertising often positively influences them. When consumers are already highly loyal to a brand, they may buy more of it when advertising and promotion for that brand increase.[8] This is why market leaders like General Motors and Procter & Gamble spend billions of dollars annually to reinforce and remind their loyal customers about the benefits of their cars and household products.

Further, advertising can affect the way consumers rank a brand's attributes, such as color, taste, smell, and texture. For example, in years past, car ads emphasized such brand attributes as roominess, speed, and low maintenance. Today, however, car marketers have added safety to the list. Safety features like antilock brakes, power door locks, and air bags are now a standard part of the message in many carmakers' ads.

Major Types of Advertising

Identify the major types of advertising

institutional advertising
A form of advertising designed to enhance a company's image rather than promote a particular product.

The firm's promotional objectives determine the type of advertising it uses. If the goal of the promotion plan is to build up the image of the company or the industry, **institutional advertising** may be used. In contrast, if the advertiser wants to enhance the sales of a specific good or service, **product advertising** is used.

Institutional Advertising

Advertising in the United States has historically been product oriented. However, modern corporations market multiple products and need a different type of advertising. Institutional advertising, or corporate advertising, promotes the corporation as a whole and is designed to establish, change, or maintain the corporation's identity. It usually does not ask the audience to do anything but maintain a favorable attitude toward the advertiser and its goods and services. American Honda Motor Company recently embarked on a corporate campaign to promote the Honda brand as a whole rather than one specific model or product category. While Honda is well known for its cars and motorcycles, few consumers know it also builds lawnmowers, power equipment, marine engines, and jet engines. The campaign focuses on product diversity, environmentalism, and innovation. The diversity spot, for instance, shows the full array of Honda-brand products in an attempt to carry over the good feeling consumers have about their Honda vehicles toward other Honda products.[9]

HARMONY

*A workplace that works
creates an almost audible hum,
a buzz that means people are
inspired, confident and passionate
about what they do.*

At DaimlerChrysler we bring together all kinds of people with their richly varied origins, perspectives and life experiences. And then, they perform, drawing on their diversity to enrich and enhance the finished products.

Together, they create the harmony of our workplace.

DAIMLERCHRYSLER
Expect the extraordinary
www.daimlerchrysler.com

Institutional advertising can help DaimlerChrysler present a more consolidated image after the high profile merger. Rather than tout any of the company's cars, this ad focuses on what DaimlerChrysler offers as a company and a workplace.

A form of institutional advertising called **advocacy advertising** is typically used to safeguard against negative consumer attitudes and to enhance the company's credibility among consumers who already favor its position.[10] Often, corporations use advocacy advertising to express their views on controversial issues. At other times, firms' advocacy campaigns react to criticism or blame, some in direct response to criticism by the media. Other advocacy campaigns may try to ward off increased regulation, damaging legislation, or the outcome of a lawsuit. Dow Chemical ran a series of ads in the New Orleans market that played up its corporate citizenship in the weeks preceding a silicone breast implant trial there. Other spots running at the same time, courtesy of a nonprofit group of which Dow is a member, highlighted the benefits of silicone products. The spot featured a little girl with a life-saving silicone device called a shunt in her brain, and her mother railing against greedy personal-injury lawyers.[11]

Product Advertising

Unlike institutional advertising, product advertising promotes the benefits of a specific good or service. The product's stage in its life cycle often determines which type of product advertising is used: pioneering advertising, competitive advertising, or comparative advertising.

Archer Daniels & Midland
BASF

ADM is a business marketer, but recently it has begun to pay for TV advertising. How does its Web site reflect this new consumer orientation? Compare ADM's site to that of BASF, another business marketer that in the past has advertised in primarily consumer venues. Which company's site demonstrates an attempt to connect with the end-user of its products? Why is this?
http://www.admworld.com
http://www.basf.com

On Line

Pioneering Advertising **Pioneering advertising** is intended to stimulate primary demand for a new product or product category. Heavily used during the introductory stage of the product life cycle, pioneering advertising offers consumers in-depth information about the benefits of the product class. Pioneering advertising also seeks to create interest. Saturn Corporation used pioneering advertising to introduce its new line of larger L-series sedans and station wagons. After a month of "teaser" ads touting "The next big thing from Saturn," the company launched sixty- and ninety-second national television spots showing the new car models. The L-series launch was vital to Saturn's desire to freshen its product lineup and grow beyond a small-car brand. The goal of its pioneering ad campaign was to convince Saturn owners to trade up to the larger Saturn L-series vehicles as they grew older and increased their family size, rather than purchase midsize imports like the Toyota Camry and the Honda Accord.[12]

Competitive Advertising Firms use competitive or brand advertising when a product enters the growth phase of the product life cycle and other companies begin to enter the marketplace. Instead of building demand for the product category, the goal of **competitive advertising** is to influence demand for a specific brand. Often promotion becomes less informative and appeals more to emotions during this phase. Advertisements may begin to stress subtle differences between brands, with heavy emphasis on building recall of a brand name and creating a favorable attitude toward the brand. Automobile advertising has long used very competitive messages, drawing distinctions based on such factors as quality, performance, and image.

Comparative Advertising **Comparative advertising** directly or indirectly compares two or more competing brands on one or more specific attributes. Some advertisers even use comparative advertising against their own brands. Products experiencing sluggish growth or those entering the marketplace against strong competitors are more likely to employ comparative claims in their advertising. For instance, comparative ads from pizza maker Papa Johns claims its pizza beat Pizza Hut pizza in a blind taste test. The comparative television spot contrasts its sauce—using a glamour shot of vine-ripened tomatoes—with Pizza Hut's, depicted as thick red goo scooped from a plastic bag.[13] Another comparative spot depicts a sculptor creating statues out of tomato paste used by rivals. The spot then shows tomato sauce easily flowing from a Papa Johns' can.[14]

Before the 1970s, comparative advertising was allowed only if the competing brand was veiled and unidentified. In 1971, however, the Federal Trade Commission (FTC) fostered the growth of comparative advertising by saying that it provided information to the customer and that advertisers were more skillful than the government in communicating this information. Federal rulings prohibit advertisers from falsely describing competitors' products and allow competitors to sue if ads show their products or mention their brand names in an incorrect or false manner. A federal judge recently ruled Papa Johns must stop using the slogan "Better Ingredients, Better Pizza" in its ads and on pizza boxes following a lawsuit brought against it by rival Pizza Hut as a result of its comparative advertising.[15]

advocacy advertising
A form of advertising in which an organization expresses its views on controversial issues or responds to media attacks.

product advertising
A form of advertising that touts the benefits of a specific good or service.

pioneering advertising
A form of advertising designed to stimulate primary demand for a new product or product category.

competitive advertising
A form of advertising designed to influence demand for a specific brand.

comparative advertising
A form of advertising that compares two or more specifically named or shown competing brands on one or more specific attributes.

FTC rules also apply to advertisers making false claims about their own products. The FTC recently ordered Novartis Corporation, maker of Doan's Pills, to implement an $8 million ad campaign to correct prior advertising that fostered the misbelief that Doan's Pills are better than other over-the-counter analgesics for treating back pain. The commission determined that Doan's ads from 1987 to 1996 falsely presented the brand as better for back pain than other remedies. Novartis was ordered to run ads saying, "Although Doan's is an effective pain reliever, there is no evidence that it is more effective than other pain relievers for back pain." Those words also must appear on packaging for one year.[16]

Comparative advertising in other nations is often exaggerated by U.S. standards. In Mexico, for instance, comparative ads between Procter & Gamble's Pringles chips and Frito-Lay's Sabritas potato chips have escalated into a potato chip war. Recent advertising compares the ingredients of a Sabritas label with a Pringles label. The label shows that the Pringles chips are made with dehydrated potatoes while potatoes used in Sabritas chips are "naturally grown Mexican potatoes." P&G counterpunched with advertising that asks "100% Mexican Potatoes?" showing a Sabritas chip bag under a magnifying glass that carries the information "Made in the U.S.A."[17] More often, however, the hard-sell tactics found in comparative ads are taboo in other cultures. Until the 1980s, Japanese regulations all but prohibited comparative ads; ads that failed to compare objectively were considered slanderous. Nevertheless, although the Japanese have traditionally favored a soft-sell advertising approach, consumers are witnessing a trend toward comparative ads. Germany, Italy, Belgium, and France, for example, do not permit advertisers to claim that their products are best or better than competitors' products, which are common claims in U.S. advertising. In the Netherlands, car advertisers cannot make claims in their advertising about fuel consumption or environmental aspects of the car. Similarly, Lands' End has run afoul of a German law prohibiting lifetime guarantee claims, which happens to be one of Lands' End's guiding principles. Germany's law is making it difficult for the direct retailer to sell its clothes and advertise its lifetime guarantee through the Internet and direct mail.[18]

Creative Decisions in Advertising

Discuss the creative decisions in developing an advertising campaign

advertising campaign
A series of related advertisements focusing on a common theme, slogan, and set of advertising appeals.

advertising objective
A specific communication task that a campaign should accomplish for a specified target audience during a specified period.

Advertisements that are seen on television, in magazines, and on the Internet are typically the result of an **advertising campaign**—a series of related advertisements focusing on a common theme, slogan, and set of advertising appeals. It is a specific advertising effort for a particular product that extends for a defined period of time. For example, on-line grocer Webvan developed an advertising campaign around an anti-grocery store theme with the tagline, "Same groceries, no store. Webvan: You may never go to the store again." The campaign is part of a positioning effort to sell the on-line grocer as the most convenient way to get groceries delivered to consumers' homes. The television ads focus on things people hate about shopping at a store, such as over-touched produce and slow checkouts. As its on-line service becomes available in different markets across the country, Webvan runs this campaign to introduce the concept to area consumers.[19]

Before any creative work can begin on an advertising campaign, it is important to determine what goals or objectives the advertising should achieve. An **advertising objective** identifies the specific communication task that a campaign should accomplish for a specified target audience during a specified period. The objectives of a specific advertising campaign often depend on the overall corporate objectives and the product being advertised. For instance, the objective of Internet computer software and hardware retailer Outpost.com's recent outrageously humorous campaign was to increase awareness of the Outpost.com name. Ads depicted gerbils being blown out of a cannon at an Outpost.com sign and ravenous wolves attacking a marching band busy spelling out the company's name on a football field. While the ads did not mention what type of products Outpost sold, the campaign's sole objective was to capture the viewers' attention and help them remember its name and Web address.[20]

The DAGMAR approach (Defining Advertising Goals for Measured Advertising Results) is one method of setting objectives. According to this method, all advertising objectives should precisely define the target audience, the desired percentage change in some specified measure of effectiveness, and the time frame in which that change is to occur. For example, the objectives of an advertising campaign for Gillette's MACH3 shaving system might be achieving a 50 percent product trial rate within the first six months of introduction as a result of its advertising campaign.

Once objectives are defined, creative work can begin on the advertising campaign. Advertising campaigns often follow the AIDA model, which was discussed in Chapter 14. Depending on where consumers are in the AIDA process, the creative development of an advertising campaign might focus on creating attention, arousing interest, stimulating desire, or ultimately leading to the action of buying the product. Specifically, creative decisions include identifying product benefits, developing and evaluating advertising appeals, executing the message, and evaluating the effectiveness of the campaign.

Identifying Product Benefits

A well-known rule of thumb in the advertising industry is "Sell the sizzle, not the steak"—that is, in advertising the goal is to sell the benefits of the product, not its attributes. An attribute is simply a feature of the product such as its easy-open package or special formulation. A benefit is what consumers will receive or achieve by using the product. A benefit should answer the consumer's question "What's in it for me?" Benefits might be such things as convenience, pleasure, savings, or relief. A quick test to determine whether you are offering attributes or benefits in your advertising is to ask "So?" Consider this example:

> *Attribute:* "The Gillette MACH3 shaving system has three blades aligned progressively nearer to the face, each coated with a microscopic layer of carbon, mounted on a forward-pivoting shaver to automatically adjust to the curves and contours of a man's face." "So . . . ?"
> *Benefit:* "So, you'll get a closer, smoother, and safer shave than ever before with fewer strokes and less irritation."[21]

Marketing research and intuition are usually used to unearth the perceived benefits of a product and to rank consumers' preferences for these benefits. Gillette's rival Schick is advertising its razors on the basis of safety. Schick's research shows that safety is among the top three attributes men look for in a razor. As a result, its advertising campaign touts the benefits of a safe shave rather than a close shave.[22]

Developing and Evaluating Advertising Appeals

An **advertising appeal** identifies a reason for a person to buy a product. Developing advertising appeals, a challenging task, is typically the responsibility of the creative people in the advertising agency. Advertising appeals typically play off of consumers' emotions, such as fear or love, or address some need or want the consumer has, such as a need for convenience or the desire to save money.

Advertising campaigns can focus on one or more advertising appeals. Often the appeals are quite general, thus allowing the firm to develop a number of subthemes

advertising appeal
Reason for a person to buy a product.

Exhibit **15.2**

Common Advertising
Appeals

Profit	Lets consumers know whether the product will save them money, make them money, or keep them from losing money
Health	Appeals to those who are body-conscious or who want to be healthy
Love or Romance	Is used often in selling cosmetics and perfumes
Fear	Can center around social embarrassment, growing old, or losing one's health; because of its power, requires advertiser to exercise care in execution
Admiration	Is the reason that celebrity spokespeople are used so often in advertising
Convenience	Is often used for fast-food restaurants and microwave foods
Fun and Pleasure	Are the key to advertising vacations, beer, amusement parks, and more
Vanity and Egotism	Are used most often for expensive or conspicuous items such as cars and clothing
Environmental Consciousness	Centers around protecting the environment and being considerate of others in the community

The Clio-award winning Got Milk? advertising campaign typically relies on the admiration appeal with celebrities–even the Simpsons–sporting the now famous milk mustache. The use of Terrell Davis in the campaign, however, reinforces the fundamental health appeals of strength and fitness.

or minicampaigns using both advertising and sales promotion. Several possible advertising appeals are listed in Exhibit 15.2.

Choosing the best appeal from those developed normally requires market research. Criteria for evaluation include desirability, exclusiveness, and believability. The appeal first must make a positive impression on and be desirable to the target market. It must also be exclusive or unique; consumers must be able to distinguish the advertiser's message from competitors' messages. Most important, the appeal should be believable. An appeal that makes extravagant claims not only wastes promotional dollars but also creates ill will for the advertiser.

The advertising appeal selected for the campaign becomes what advertisers call its **unique selling proposition**. The unique selling proposition usually becomes the campaign's slogan. Gillette's MACH3 advertising campaign aimed at men carries the slogan "Three blades, fewer strokes, less irritation." This is also MACH3's unique selling proposition, implying that its razor's high-tech features are important and can help reduce discomfort caused by shaving.[23]

Effective slogans often become so ingrained that consumers can immediately conjure up images of the product just by hearing the slogan. For example, most consumers can easily name the companies and products behind these memorable slogans or even hum the jingle that goes along with some of them: "Have it your way," "Tastes great, less filling," "Ring around the collar," and "Tum te Tum Tum." Advertisers often revive old slogans or jingles in the hope that the nostalgia will create good feelings with consumers. Pillsbury Company recently brought back its Jolly Green Giant spokescharacter and his familiar "Ho Ho Ho" tagline to celebrate the giant's seventy-fifth anniversary.[24] Similarly, Clorox Company recently recycled the slogan "Don't get mad—get Glad," for its Gladware disposable food storage containers while Coca-Cola revived the "Enjoy" tagline to draw on past marketing success using the word to describe the pleasurable experience of drinking Coca-Cola Classic.[25]

unique selling proposition
Desirable, exclusive, and believable advertising appeal selected as the theme for a campaign.

Executing the Message

Message execution is the way an advertisement portrays its information. In general, the AIDA (see Chapter 14) plan is a good blueprint for executing an advertising message. Any ad should immediately draw the reader's, viewer's, or listener's attention. The advertiser must then use the message to hold consumers' interest, create desire for the good or service, and ultimately motivate action: a purchase.

The style in which the message is executed is one of the most creative elements of an advertisement. Exhibit 15.3 lists some examples of executional styles used by advertisers. Executional styles often dictate what type of media is to be employed to convey the message. Scientific executional styles lend themselves well to print advertising where more information can be conveyed. On the other hand, demonstration and musical styles are more likely found in broadcast advertising.

Injecting humor into an advertisement is a popular and effective executional style. Humorous executional styles are more often used in radio and television advertising than in print or magazine advertising where humor is less easily communicated. Humorous ads are typically used for lower risk, routine purchases such as candy, cigarettes and soft drinks than for higher risk purchases or those that are expensive, durable, or flamboyant.[26] Bud Light's consistent humorous approach in its advertising maintains the brand's relevancy with its twenty-one- to twenty-seven-year-old target market. Humorous spots, such as the one showing two young Gen-Xers trying to decide between beer and toilet paper at the cash register, have helped Bud Light increase sales by 11 percent in recent years.[27]

Executional styles for foreign advertising are often quite different from those we are accustomed to in the United States. Sometimes they are sexually oriented or aesthetically imaginative. For example, European advertising avoids the direct-sell approaches common in United States ads and instead is more indirect, more symbolic, and above all more visual. Nike, known in the United States for "in-your-face" advertising and irreverent slogans such as "Just Do It," discovered that its brash advertising did not appeal to Europeans. A television commercial of Satan and his demons playing soccer against a team of Nike endorsers was a hit in America. However, many European stations refused to run it, saying it was too scary and offensive to show in prime time, when kids were watching.[28]

Japanese advertising is known for relying on fantasy and mood to sell products. Ads in Japan notoriously lack the emphatic selling demonstrations found in U.S. advertising, limit the exposure of unique product features, and avoid direct comparisons to competitors' products. Japanese ads often feature cartoon characters or place the actors in irrelevant situations. For example, one advertisement promotes an insect spray while showing the actor having teeth extracted at the dentist's office. One explanation of Japan's preference for

Advertising in Japan takes a softsell approach because Japanese consumers are naturally suspicious of companies that need to emphasize the virtues of a product.
© Tom Wagner/SABA

Exhibit **15.3**

Slice-of-Life	Depicts people in normal settings, such as at the dinner table or in their car. McDonald's often uses slice-of-life styles showing youngsters munching french fries and Happy Meals on family outings.
Lifestyle	Shows how well the product will fit in with the consumer's lifestyle. As their Volkswagen Jetta moves through the streets of the French Quarter, the Gen X drivers plug in a techno music CD and marvel at how the rhythms of the world mimic the ambient vibe inside their vehicle.
Spokesperson/ Testimonial	Can feature a celebrity, company official, or typical consumer making a testimonial or endorsing a product. Sarah Michelle Gellar, star of *Buffy the Vampire Slayer,* endorses Maybelline cosmetics while country singer Shania Twain introduced Revlon's ColorStay Liquid Lip. Dell Computers founder Michael Dell touts his vision of the customer experience via Dell in television ads.
Fantasy	Creates a fantasy for the viewer built around use of the product. Carmakers often use this style to let viewers fantasize about how they would feel to be speeding around tight corners or down long country roads in their cars.
Humorous	Advertisers often use humor in their ads, such as Snicker's "Not Going Anywhere for a While" campaign featuring hundreds of souls waiting, sometimes impatiently, to get into heaven.
Real/Animated Product Symbols	Creates a character that represents the product in advertisements, such as the Energizer bunny, Starkist's Charlie the Tuna, or General Mills' longtime icon, Betty Crocker, redesigned for the new millennium.
Mood or Image	Builds a mood or image around the product, such as peace, love, or beauty. DeBeers ads depicting shadowy silhouettes wearing diamond engagement rings and diamond necklaces portray passion and intimacy while extolling that a "diamond is forever."
Demonstration	Shows consumers the expected benefit. Many consumer products use this technique. Laundry detergent spots are famous for demonstrating how their product will clean clothes whiter and brighter. Fort James Corporation recently demonstrated in television commercials how its Dixie Rinse & ReUse disposable stoneware product line can stand up to the heat of a blow torch and survive a cycle in a clothes washer.
Musical	Conveys the message of the advertisement through song. For example, Nike's recent ads depicting a marathoner's tortured feet, skier Pikabo Street's surgery scarred knee, and a surfer's thigh scarred by a shark attack while strains of Joe Cocker's "You Are So Beautiful" are heard in the background.
Scientific	Uses research or scientific evidence to give a brand superiority over competitors. Pain relievers like Advil, Bayer, and Excedrin use scientific evidence in their ads.

soft-sell advertising is cultural: Japanese consumers are naturally suspicious of someone who needs to extol the virtues of a product. Additionally, unlike advertising agencies in the United States, which consider working for competing companies to be unethical, Japan's larger ad agencies customarily maintain business relationships with competing advertisers. Ads are less hard-hitting so as not to offend other clients.[29]

Post-Campaign Evaluation

Evaluating an advertising campaign can be the most demanding task facing advertisers. How do advertisers know whether the campaign led to an increase in sales or market share or elevated awareness of the product? Most advertising campaigns aim to create an image for the good or service instead of asking for action, so their real effect is unknown. So many variables shape the effectiveness of an ad that, in many cases, advertisers must guess whether their money has been well spent. Despite this gray area, marketers spend a considerable amount of time studying advertising effectiveness and its probable impact on sales, market share, or awareness.

Testing ad effectiveness can be done either before or after the campaign. Before a campaign is released, marketing managers use pretests to determine the best advertising appeal, layout, and media vehicle. After advertisers implement a campaign, they often conduct tests to measure its effectiveness. Several monitoring techniques can be used to determine whether the campaign has met its original goals. Even if a campaign has been highly successful, advertisers still typically do a postcampaign analysis. They assess how the campaign might have been more efficient and what factors contributed to its success.

Media Decisions in Advertising

A major decision for advertisers is the choice of **medium**—the channel used to convey a message to a target market. **Media planning**, therefore, is the series of decisions advertisers make regarding the selection and use of media, allowing the marketer to optimally and cost-effectively communicate the message to the target audience.[30] Specifically, advertisers must determine which types of media will best communicate the benefits of their product or service to the target audience and when and for how long the advertisement will run.

Promotional objectives and the appeal and executional style of the advertising strongly affect the selection of media. It is important to understand that both creative and media decisions are made at the same time. Creative work cannot be completed without knowing which medium will be used to convey the message to the target market. For instance, creative planning will likely differ for an ad to be displayed on an outdoor billboard versus that placed in a print medium, such as a newspaper or magazine. In many cases, the advertising objectives dictate the medium and the creative approach to be used. For example, if the objective is to demonstrate how fast a product operates, a TV commercial that shows this action may be the best choice.

As mentioned at the beginning of the chapter, U.S. advertisers spend over $215 billion on media advertising annually. Where does all this money go? About 48 percent, or $102 billion, is spent in media monitored by national reporting services—newspapers, magazines, Yellow Pages, Internet, radio, television, and outdoor media. The remaining 52 percent, or $113 billion, is spent in unmonitored media, such as direct mail, trade exhibits, cooperative advertising, brochures,

Describe media evaluation and selection techniques

medium
The channel used to convey a message to a target market.

media planning
The series of decisions advertisers make regarding the selection and use of media, allowing the marketer to optimally and cost-effectively communicate the message to the target audience.

Exhibit 15.4

Domestic Advertising Spending
in Measured Media for 1999

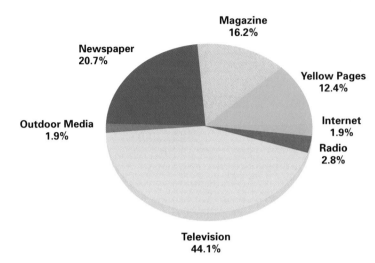

Newspaper
20.7%

Magazine
16.2%

Yellow Pages
12.4%

Outdoor Media
1.9%

Internet
1.9%

Radio
2.8%

Television
44.1%

SOURCE: "Domestic Advertising Spending by Media," *Advertising Age*, September 25, 2000, p. s4.

couponing, catalogs, and special events. Exhibit 15.4 breaks down the $102 billion spent in monitored advertising by media type. As you can see, nearly half of every dollar spent in measured media goes toward purchasing time for TV ads. The nation's largest advertisers, such as those listed earlier in Exhibit 15.1, spend even more on television advertising—about 63 cents of every dollar spent in measured media.[31]

Media Types

Advertising media are channels that advertisers use in mass communication. The seven major advertising media are newspapers, magazines, radio, television, outdoor media, Yellow Pages, and the Internet. Exhibit 15.5 summarizes the advantages and disadvantages of these major channels. In recent years, however, alternative media vehicles have emerged that give advertisers innovative ways to reach their target audience and avoid advertising clutter.

Newspapers   The advantages of newspaper advertising include geographic flexibility and timeliness. Because copywriters can usually prepare newspaper ads quickly and at a reasonable cost, local merchants can reach their target market almost daily. However, because newspapers are generally a mass-market medium, they may not be the best vehicle for marketers trying to reach a very narrow market. For example, local newspapers are not the best media vehicles for reaching purchasers of specialty steel products or even tropical fish. These target consumers make up very small, specialized markets. Newspaper advertising also encounters a lot of distractions from competing ads and news stories; thus one company's ad may not be particularly visible.

The largest source of newspaper ad revenue is local retailers, classified ads, and cooperative advertising. In **cooperative advertising**, the manufacturer and the retailer split the costs of advertising the manufacturer's brand. One reason manufacturers use cooperative advertising is the impracticality of listing all their dealers in national advertising. Also, co-op advertising encourages retailers to devote more effort to the manufacturer's lines.

Magazines   Compared to the cost of other media, the cost per contact in magazine advertising is usually high. However, the cost per potential customer may be

cooperative advertising
An arrangement in which the manufacturer and the retailer split the costs of advertising the manufacturer's brand.

Exhibit 15.5

Advantages and
Disadvantages of Major
Advertising Media

Medium	Advantages	Disadvantages
Newspapers	Geographic selectivity and flexibility; short-term advertiser commitments; news value and immediacy; year-round readership; high individual market coverage; co-op and local tie-in availability; short lead time	Little demographic selectivity; limited color capabilities; low pass-along rate; may be expensive
Magazines	Good reproduction, especially for color; demographic selectivity; regional selectivity; local market selectivity; relatively long advertising life; high pass-along rate	Long-term advertiser commitments; slow audience buildup; limited demonstration capabilities; lack of urgency; long lead time
Radio	Low cost; immediacy of message; can be scheduled on short notice; relatively no seasonal change in audience; highly portable; short-term advertiser commitments; entertainment carryover	No visual treatment; short advertising life of message; high frequency required to generate comprehension and retention; distractions from background sound; commercial clutter
Television	Ability to reach a wide, diverse audience; low cost per thousand; creative opportunities for demonstration; immediacy of messages; entertainment carryover; demographic selectivity with cable stations	Short life of message; some consumer skepticism about claims; high campaign cost; little demographic selectivity with network stations; long-term advertiser commitments; long lead times required for production; commercial clutter
Outdoor media	Repetition; moderate cost; flexibility; geographic selectivity	Short message; lack of demographic selectivity; high "noise" level distracting audience
Internet	Fastest growing medium; ability to reach a narrow target audience; relatively short lead time required for creating Web-based advertising; moderate cost	Difficult to measure ad effectiveness and return on investment; ad exposure relies on "click-through" from banner ads; not all consumers have access to the Internet

much lower, because magazines are often targeted to specialized audiences and thus reach more potential customers. The most frequent types of products advertised in magazines include automobiles, apparel, computers, and cigarettes.

One of the main advantages of magazine advertising is its market selectivity. Magazines are published for virtually every market segment. For instance, *PC Week* is a leading computer magazine; *Working Mother* targets one of the fastest growing consumer segments; *Sports Illustrated* is a successful all-around sporting publication; *Marketing News* is a trade magazine for the marketing professional; *The Source* is a niche publication geared to young urbanites with a passion for hip-hop music.

Radio   Radio has several strengths as an advertising medium: selectivity and audience segmentation, a large out-of-home audience, low unit and production costs, timeliness, and geographic flexibility. Local advertisers are the most frequent users of radio advertising contributing over three-quarters of all radio ad revenues. Like newspapers, radio also lends itself well to cooperative advertising.

Long merely an afterthought to many advertisers, radio advertising is enjoying a resurgence in popularity. As Americans become more mobile and pressed for time, other media such as network television and newspapers struggle to retain viewers and readers. Radio listening, however, has grown in step with population increases mainly because its immediate, portable nature meshes so well with a fast-paced lifestyle. The ability to target specific demographic groups is also a major selling point for radio stations, attracting advertisers who are pursuing narrowly defined audiences that are more likely to respond to certain kinds of ads and products. Moreover, radio listeners tend to listen habitually and at predictable times, with the most popular radio listening hours during "drive time," when commuters form a vast captive audience.[32]

Television   Because television is an audiovisual medium, it provides advertisers with many creative opportunities. Television broadcasters include network television, independent stations, cable television, and a relative newcomer, direct broadcast satellite television. ABC, CBS, NBC, and the Fox Network dominate network television, which reaches a wide and diverse market. Conversely, cable television and direct broadcast satellite systems, such as DirecTV and PrimeStar, offer consumers a multitude of channels devoted exclusively to particular audiences—for example, women, children, African-Americans, nature lovers, senior citizens, Christians, Hispanics, sports fans, fitness enthusiasts. Because of its targeted channels, cable television is often characterized as "narrowcasting" by media buyers. One recent study found that viewers watching cable television programming paid more attention to commercials than those watching broadcast television programming.[33]

Advertising time on television can be very expensive, especially for network stations and popular cable stations. A thirty-second spot during *The Oprah Winfrey Show* goes for $60,000, for instance, while the same length spot would cost $105,000 during *Entertainment Tonight* and about $140,000 during a *Friends* rerun.[34] Rates are even more expensive during first-run prime time shows or special television events. Advertisers spend about $545,000 for thirty-second spots during NBC's *ER*, for example, and about $380,000 for spots during ABC's *Monday Night Football*.[35] One thirty-second spot during the 2000 Super Bowl telecast cost advertisers an average of $2.2 million.[36]

infomercial
A thirty-minute or longer advertisement that looks more like a TV talk show than a sales pitch.

A relatively new form of television advertising is the **infomercial**, a thirty-minute or longer advertisement. Infomercials are an attractive advertising vehicle for many marketers because of the cheap air time and the relatively small production cost. Advertisers say the infomercial is an ideal way to present complicated information to potential customers, which other advertising vehicles typically don't allow time to do. The U.S. Navy, for instance, recently aired a thirty-minute infomercial to explain the benefits of military service in order to buoy sagging enlistments. The Navy developed the longer format after realizing that thirty- and sixty-second advertisements were not able to provide the amount of information potential recruits needed to make the decision to enlist. The infomercial, aimed at the eighteen- to-twenty-five-year-old market, included interviews and comments from Navy recruits, Navy Seals, radar operators, and photographers.[37] One of the best success stories of infomercial effectiveness belongs to the marketers of the Tae-Bo fitness video. Since the kickboxing regime was first aired via TV infomercials, the video has rocketed up the video charts and, at times, has even bested heavy-selling Walt Disney children's movies.[38]

Looksmart
Yahoo!

How easy is it to find out advertising options on the Internet? Go to Looksmart's and Yahoo's advertiser pages. What kind of information do they require from you? Send an e-mail requesting information and compare what you receive.
http://www.looksmart.com/aboutus/media
http://www.yahoo.com/info/advertising

On Line

Outdoor Media   Outdoor or out-of-home advertising is a flexible, low-cost medium that may take a variety of forms. Examples include billboards, skywriting, giant inflatables, minibillboards in malls and on bus stop shelters, signs in sports arenas, lighted moving signs in bus terminals and airports, and ads painted on the sides of cars, trucks, buses, or even water towers. Marketers have even begun utilizing the plywood scaffolding that often rings downtown construction sites. Manhattan's Times Square, with an estimated 1.5 million daily pedestrians and recent construction projects, for example, has been a popular area for outdoor advertising using scaffolding.[39]

Outdoor advertising reaches a broad and diverse market and is, therefore, ideal for promoting convenience products and services as well as directing consumers to local businesses. One of outdoor's main advantages over other media is that its exposure frequency is very high, yet the amount of clutter from competing ads is very low. Outdoor advertising also has the ability to be customized to local marketing needs. For these reasons, local business establishments, such as local services and amusements, hotels and motels, and local retail stores and restaurants, are the leading outdoor advertisers.[40]

Despite the loss of tobacco advertising (tobacco companies agreed to stop advertising in outdoor media as part of a 1998 settlement with states that had sued to recover money spent on treatment of smokers), outdoor advertising has been growing in recent years. This growth has been mainly due to the fragmentation of other media, more exposure as people spend more time commuting, and improved billboard quality through the use of computers.[41] Additionally, Internet companies have found outdoor advertising an ideal medium to build awareness of their Web sites. When Internet portal Quepasa.com wanted to build awareness of its Spanish-language Internet site quickly, it advertised on 2,500 billboards in twenty-three high-density Hispanic communities around the country.[42]

Outdoor advertising is also becoming more innovative. For example, when Delta Air Lines wanted to make a big splash to launch its new business class service, it kicked off the effort by creating a "living" billboard overlooking Manhattan's Times Square. Live humans could be seen lounging in a replica of its redesigned airline seats high above the street below.[43]

The Internet   The World Wide Web and the Internet have undoubtedly shaken up the advertising world. With ad revenues approaching $6 billion in 2000, the Internet has established itself as a solid advertising medium. On-line advertising has made significant gains since the early 1990s, making up an ever-larger portion of companies' total advertising budgets. By 2004, Internet advertising is expected to increase to $21 billion and represent close to 8 percent of total media spending.[44] Popular Internet sites and search engines, such as Netscape and Yahoo!, as well as on-line service providers like America Online, generally sell advertising space, called "banners," to marketers to promote their goods and

Outdoor advertising is becoming increasingly innovative and three-dimensional. Delta's living billboard is an example of how far you can go with outdoor media.

On Line

services. Internet surfers click on these banners that link them to more information about the advertised product or service.

Advertising executives and academicians have hotly debated the effectiveness of banner ads. Some research suggests that on-line banners work as well at boosting brand and advertising awareness as their TV counterpart.[45] Other industry observers feel that banner ads have been largely ineffective, with low click-through rates and recall. Estimates of click-through rates on banner ads have steadily dropped to a dismal 0.5 percent of the time, due in part to ad clutter on the Web and less interest by consumers surfing on-line.[46] Another study found that consumers are less likely to trust the information contained in Web ads than other more traditional media.[47] New forms of Web advertising, however, are beginning to transcend the static company logo and message found in banner ads in favor of *broadband advertising*, which features interactivity, electronic commerce, sound, and animation. In a recent study, broadband ads were found to be more memorable, more effective at shifting users' understanding of a brand, and better able to capture users' attention for longer periods of time.[48]

Web advertisers are also becoming more targeted with their approach to advertising by studying clickstream data. On-line ad broker DoubleClick, for instance, tracks and collects information about Web users' behavior on-line, such as what sites they have visited in the past, information supplied when registering at various on-line sites, or their computer's Internet (IP) address. DoubleClick then analyzes these pieces of information, creating an anonymous profile of the on-line customer. According to parameters created by the advertiser, DoubleClick delivers a targeted message to the Web page popping up on a user's screen. This kind of ad targeting makes Web advertising potentially much more attractive than traditional advertising media. Whereas television and print advertising shoot for swaths of the population, targeted Web advertising offers advertisers the potential to deliver an ad to exactly the kind of person they want to reach.[49] For example, a Web surfer who visits golf sites and purchases plane tickets on-line might be a good candidate to receive advertising about golf or leisure travel packages.

Marketing on the Internet and World Wide Web is discussed in more detail in Chapter 19.

Alternative Media To cut through the clutter of traditional advertising media, advertisers are creating new media vehicles to advertise their products, some ordinary and others quite innovative. Alternative media vehicles can include shopping carts in grocery stores, computer screen savers, CD-ROMs, interactive kiosks in department stores, and advertisements run before movies at the cinema and on rented videocassettes. In fact, just about anything can become a vehicle for displaying advertising. For instance, bistros and cafes in France are turning their tabletops into billboards for companies like United Airlines, Swatch watches, and an assortment of other goods and services, with the idea being that while patrons sip espresso, they can also read an advertiser's message in a relaxed atmosphere.[50] Otis Elevator Company recently unveiled plans to put video screens in elevators to display news, information and advertising to capture the attention of affluent workers in large office buildings.[51] And some airports are even placing advertisements on their baggage carousels noting that travelers often wait fifteen to twenty minutes for bags, enough time to see an ad roll by at least eight times.[52]

Some critics, however, feel that today's ever-expanding media choices are leading to "ad creep" in which there is no safe haven for consumers who are fed-up with the constant bombardment of advertising messages. Read more about this issue in the "Ethics in Marketing" box.

Lunch hour elevator passengers follow the stock market through the wireless Internet device installed by the elevator door. Otis Elevator, Captivate, and eBillboards are entering this alternative media space and bringing weather, news, sports, and stock market data to elevator riders in many of the largest cities in the United States.

PUSHING THE LIMITS OF ADVERTISING

Ads for a new movie are flashed on automatic teller machine screens. The images of soft drink bottles are rolled into the sand on New Jersey beaches from the boardwalk to the water's edge. Posters pitch everything from skin cream to condoms from the inner door of a bathroom stall. Even New York City's public transportation system now sells the space on the back of its electronic fare cards to advertisers like Sprint, Virgin Megastore, and the Fox News Channel.

Advertising, it seems, is everywhere and for many consumers it's getting harder and harder to find refuge from its reach. Often called "ad creep," the growing intrusiveness of advertising and marketing messages reflects an escalating race between marketers and consumers. As advertisers find it more difficult to be noticed in cluttered and fragmented traditional media choices, they are broadening their imaginations to assault consumers with their messages in unexpected places. Advertising in traditional media is also becoming prohibitively expensive. Prime-time television commercials can cost up to $500,000 for one thirty-second spot even though cable networks, videos, and the Internet have been drawing viewers away from broadcast networks for years. And technology is allowing marketers to reach consumers in places never before available.

New media choices seem boundless—advertising space is being sold on video cases, parking lot tickets, golf scorecards, delivery trucks, gas pumps, even garbage cans. Ordinary cars are being transformed into roving billboards by wrapping them with digitally printed adhesive vinyl wrap commonly used on municipal buses. Car owners are

paid to drive a certain number of miles or on specified highways and some cars come equipped with global positioning systems that track their movements. Wrap technology is also being used to display advertisers' messages on sailboats that cruise up and down New York and San Francisco waterways.

Advertisers are also invading consumers in more personal spaces. AT&T Corporation is testing prerecorded advertisements for AT&T services before connecting long-distance telephone calls. Advertising is also being tested on cell phones that offer Internet access, even though there's not much room on the phones' tiny screens. A Finnish on-line brokerage firm, eQ Online, recently became the first advertiser to run a campaign on Web-enabled wireless phones. When users of the phones clicked on the Web address for a popular Finnish business-news site, up popped an ad for eQ. Users either clicked on the ad, which gave them real-time stock quotes, or continued to the news site.

Even outer space is not safe anymore from advertising's reach. Pizza Hut recently created a thirty-foot-high version of the company's new logo on an unmanned Russian Proton rocket. The company settled on the rocket advertisement only after efforts to project the chain's updated logo on the moon via laser beam failed. Similarly, a group of investors recently purchased the aging Russian Mir space station with the hopes of one day turning it into a profit-making ad vehicle and entertainment site.

Technology is pushing the limits of advertising, promising a future of little escape for consumers. Already marketers have developed billboards that speak to consumers as

they walk by. Another marketer is developing a peripheral device that attaches to computers and releases scents, such as the smell of a new-car interior, fresh doughnuts, or a charbroiled hamburger. The creator envisions a world in which technology begins to replicate touch and other senses with such authenticity that marketers place consumers in "full immersion, simulating reality at more and more powerful levels." As technology advances, futurists imagine a world in which advertisers will "narrowcast" messages directly into consumers' brains, eliciting emotional responses that impel them to buy their products.[a]

Will consumers eventually say enough is enough? Or will they learn to tune out intrusive ad messages? How might this phenomenon eventually influence the effectiveness of advertising in traditional media?

[a] Skip Wollenberg, "Ads Launch Space Invasion; Selling of Products Is Far-Flung," *Burlington Free Press*, May 30, 1999, pp. E7–8; Charles Pappas, "Ad Nauseam," *Advertising Age*, July 10, 2000, pp. 16–18; Jonathan Kaufman, "The Omnipresent Persuaders," *Wall Street Journal*, January 1, 2000, p. R26; Leslie Chang, "Read Me, Recharge Me, Put Me in Your Wallet," *American Demographics*, January 1999; Rodney Ho, "Several Start-Ups Are Wrapping Cars in Advertisements," *Wall Street Journal*, June 6, 2000, p. B2; Amanda Beeler, "Billboards Set Sail with Ads on Yachts," *Advertising Age*, April 24, 2000, p. 22; Stephanie N. Mehta, "AT&T Takes Risky New Road, Playing Ad Messages to Long-Distance Callers," *Wall Street Journal*, December 7, 1999, p. B8; Jennifer Rewick, "Online Ads Turn to Hand-Held Devices," *Wall Street Journal*, February 4, 2000, p. B6; Richard Gibson, "For Pizza Hut, a New Pie-in-the-Sky Ad Strategy," *Wall Street Journal*, September 30, 1999, pp. B1, B6; Neal Boudette, "Star Struck: U.S. Space Buffs See Otherworldly Profit in Russia's Rickety Mir," *Wall Street Journal*, June 16, 2000, pp. A1, A8.

Media Selection Considerations

An important element in any advertising campaign is the **media mix**, the combination of media to be used. Media mix decisions are typically based on several factors: cost per contact, reach, frequency, target audience considerations, flexibility of the medium, noise level, and the life span of the medium.

Cost per contact is the cost of reaching one member of the target market. Naturally, as the size of the audience increases, so does the total cost. Cost per contact enables an advertiser to compare media vehicles, such as television versus radio or magazine versus newspaper, or more specifically *Newsweek* versus *Time*. An advertiser debating whether to spend local advertising dollars for TV spots or radio spots could consider the cost per contact of each. The advertiser might then pick the vehicle with the lowest cost per contact to maximize advertising punch for the money spent.

Reach is the number of different target consumers who are exposed to a commercial at least once during a specific period, usually four weeks. The media plans for product introductions and attempts at increasing brand awareness usually emphasize reach. For example, an advertiser might try to reach 70 percent of the target audience during the first three months of the campaign. Reach is related to a medium's ratings, generally referred to in the industry as *gross ratings points*, or GRP. A television program with a higher GRP means that more people are tuning in to the show and the reach is higher. Accordingly, as GRP increases for a particular medium, so does cost per contact.

Because the typical ad is short-lived and because often only a small portion of an ad may be perceived at one time, advertisers repeat their ads so consumers will remember the message. **Frequency** is the number of times an individual is exposed to a message during a specific period. Advertisers use average frequency to measure the intensity of a specific medium's coverage. For example, Gillette might want an average exposure frequency of three for its MACH3 television ads; that is, among all the television viewers who saw the ad, they each saw it an average of three times. Exhibit 15.6 provides a glimpse at exposure and frequency rates for some of today's top brands.

Media selection is also a matter of matching the advertising medium with the product's target market. If marketers are trying to reach teenage females, they might select *Seventeen* magazine. If they are trying to reach consumers over fifty years old, they may choose *Modern Maturity* magazine. A medium's ability to reach a precisely defined market is its **audience selectivity**. Some media vehicles, like general newspapers and network television, appeal to a wide cross section of the population. Others—such as *Bride's, Popular Mechanics, Architectural Digest*, MTV, ESPN, and Christian radio stations—appeal to very specific groups. Viewer profiles for a sampling of popular cable networks are presented in Exhibit 15.7.

The *flexibility* of a medium can be extremely important to an advertiser. In the past, because of printing timetables, pasteup requirements, and so on, some magazines required final ad copy several months before publication. Therefore, magazine advertising traditionally could not adapt as rapidly to changing market conditions. While this is fast changing due to computer technology that creates electronic ad images and layouts, the lead-time for magazine advertising is still considerably longer. Radio and Internet advertising, on the other hand, provide maximum flexibility. Usually, the advertiser can change a radio ad on the day it is aired, if necessary. Similarly, advertisements on the Internet can be changed in minutes with the click of a few buttons.

Noise level is the level of distraction to the target audience in a medium. For example, to understand a televised promotional message, viewers must watch and listen carefully. But they often watch television with others, who may well provide distractions. Noise can also be created by competing ads, as when a street is lined with billboards or when a television program is cluttered with competing ads.

---

media mix
The combination of media to be used for a promotional campaign.

cost per contact
The cost of reaching one member of the target market.

reach
The number of target consumers exposed to a commercial at least once during a specific period, usually four weeks.

frequency
The number of times an individual is exposed to a given message during a specific period.

audience selectivity
The ability of an advertising medium to reach a precisely defined market.

Exhibit **15.6**

Exposure and Frequency of
Top TV Advertisers* *Week of
May 25–31, 1998*

Advertised Brand	Household Exposures (in millions)**	Number of Times Ad Aired
Burger King	285.8	57
JCPenney	181.6	31
Pontiac Grand Am	173.3	25
Boston Market	166.1	27
Ford autos and trucks	162.5	21
Honda Accord	152.4	23
Nissan Altima	150.7	14
AT&T	143.4	22
Wendy's	137.0	26
Miller Lite	131.8	12

*Advertisers getting the most exposure during prime-time TV on ABC, CBS, NBC, Fox, UPN, and WB networks
**One household might be exposed to several ads each day.
SOURCES: "Nielsen's Top TV Advertisers," *USA Today*, June 15, 1998, p. 8B; Nielsen Media Research, Monitor Plus Service.

Exhibit **15.7**

Selected Cable Television
Network Viewer Profiles

BET	Targeted to African-Americans ages 18 to 49.
CNBC	*Business Day* viewers have a median household net worth of over $1 million; 98% are college educated; 80% use their computer daily; 69% connect to the Internet daily.
Discovery Channel	Appeals to adults 25 to 54 with household incomes over $75,000.
ESPN Classic	Delivers a higher concentration of men aged 18 to 49 than the ten most widely distributed cable networks.
House & Garden Television (HGTV)	Appeals strongly to men and women who own their own homes with incomes of $75,000 or more; most likely to be in professional or managerial position.
Lifetime Network	Top cable network aimed at working women.
MTV	Number one rated cable network for 12- to 24-year-olds; Watched by over 305 million households in 87 territories around the globe.

SOURCE: "2000 Cable Programming Guide," *Advertising Age*, June 5, 2000.

About two-thirds of a newspaper's pages are now filled with advertising. In a recent Sunday issue of the *Los Angeles Times* there were over 1,000 ads, not counting the small classifieds. Even more space is dedicated to ads in magazines. For example, 85 percent of the space in the February/March issue of *Brides* magazine was devoted to advertisements. In contrast, direct mail is a private medium with a low noise level. Typically, no other advertising media or news stories compete for direct-mail readers' attention.

Media have either a short or long life span. *Life span* means that messages can either quickly fade or persist as tangible copy to be carefully studied. For example, a radio commercial may last less than a minute. Listeners can't replay the commercial unless they have recorded the program. One way advertisers overcome this problem is by repeating radio ads often. In contrast, a magazine has a relatively long life span. A person may read several articles, put the magazine down, and pick it up a week later to continue reading. In addition, magazines often have a high pass-along rate. That is, one person will read the publication and then give it to someone else to read.

Media planners have traditionally relied upon the above factors for selecting an effective media mix, with reach, frequency, and cost often the overriding criteria. Some recent studies, however, question the reliance media planners have traditionally placed on reach and frequency. For instance, one recent study suggests that well-established brands with familiar messages may need fewer exposures to be effective, while newer brands or brands with unfamiliar messages may need more exposures to become familiar.[53]

Additionally, media planners today have hundreds more media options now than forty years ago when network television reigned. For instance, there are over 1,600 television stations across the country. In the Los Angeles market alone, there are now seventy-nine radio stations, seven offering an "adult contemporary" format. The number of unique magazine titles has more than doubled over the last decade, with publications now targeting every target market possible. Satellite television can now bring hundreds of channels into viewers' homes. The Internet provides media planners with even more targeted choices in which to send their messages. And alternative media choices are popping up in some very unlikely places. *Media fragmentation* is forcing media planners to pay as much attention to where they place their advertising, as to how often the advertisement is repeated. New research suggests evaluating reach along with frequency in assessing the effectiveness of advertising. That is, it may be more important to reach as many consumers in as many media vehicles as possible than to achieve a certain number of exposures in any one particular medium.[54] In evaluating reach versus frequency, therefore, the media planner ultimately must select an approach that is most likely to result in the ad being understood and remembered when a purchase decision is being made.

Advertising researchers are also discussing the qualitative factors that should be present during media selection. These qualitative factors include such things as attention to the commercial and the program, involvement, program liking, lack of distractions, and other audience behaviors that affect the likelihood that a commercial message is being seen and, hopefully, absorbed. While advertisers can advertise their product in as many media as possible and repeat the ad as many times as they like, the ad still may not be effective if the audience is not paying attention.[55] Recent research into audience attentiveness for television, for example, shows that the longer viewers stay tuned to a particular program, the more memorable they find the commercials. The study suggests that "holding power," not ratings (the number of people tuning in to any part of the program), is more important when selecting media vehicles, challenging long-held assumptions that the higher the rating of program, the higher the cost to advertise during them. For instance, television program *ER*, the top-rated show among twenty-five- to

media schedule
Designation of the media, the specific publications or programs, and the insertion dates of advertising.

continuous media schedule
A media scheduling strategy used for products in the latter stages of the product life cycle, in which advertising is run steadily throughout the advertising period.

fifty-four-year-olds, which costs close to $500,000 for a thirty-second spot, measures relatively lower for holding power than the low-rated program, *Candid Camera*, which ranks high in holding power, but costs only $55,000 for a thirty-second spot.[56]

Media Scheduling

After choosing the media for the advertising campaign, advertisers must schedule the ads. A **media schedule** designates the medium or media to be used (such as magazines, television, or radio), the specific vehicles (such as *People* magazine, *Friends* TV show, or Howard Stern's national radio program), and the insertion dates of the advertising.

There are three basic types of media schedules:

- Products in the latter stages of the product life cycle, which are advertised on a reminder basis, use a **continuous media schedule**. A continuous schedule allows the advertising to run steadily throughout the advertising period. Examples include Ivory soap, Coca-Cola, and Marlboro cigarettes.
- With a **flighted media schedule**, the advertiser may schedule the ads heavily every other month or every two weeks to achieve a greater impact with an increased frequency and reach at those times. Movie studios might schedule television advertising on Wednesday and Thursday nights, when moviegoers are deciding which films to see that weekend. A variation is the **pulsing media schedule**, which combines continuous scheduling with flighting. Continuous advertising is simply heavier during the best sale periods. A retail department store may advertise on a year-round basis but place more advertising during certain sale periods such as Thanksgiving, Christmas, and back-to-school.
- Certain times of the year call for a **seasonal media schedule**. Products like Contac cold tablets and Coppertone suntan lotion, which are used more during certain times of the year, tend to follow a seasonal strategy. Advertising for champagne is concentrated during the weeks of Christmas and New Year's, whereas health clubs concentrate their advertising in January to take advantage of New Year's resolutions.

New research comparing continuous media schedules versus flighted ones finds that continuous schedules for television advertisements are more effective than flighting in driving sales. The research suggests that it may be more important to get exposure as close as possible to the time when someone is going to make a purchase. For example, if a consumer shops on a weekly basis, the best time to reach that person is right before he or she shops. Therefore, the advertiser should maintain a continuous schedule over as long a period of time as possible.[57] Often called *recency planning*, this new theory of scheduling is now commonly used for scheduling television advertising for frequently purchased products, such as Coca-Cola or Tide detergent. Recency planning's main premise is that advertising works by influencing the brand choice of people who are ready to buy.[58]

flighted media schedule
A media scheduling strategy in which ads are run heavily every other month or every two weeks, to achieve a greater impact with an increased frequency and reach at those times.

pulsing media schedule
A media scheduling strategy that uses continuous scheduling throughout the year coupled with a flighted schedule during the best sales periods.

seasonal media schedule
A media scheduling strategy that runs advertising only during times of the year when the product is most likely to be used.

This ad for Butterball turkeys is an example of a seasonal advertising strategy. Besides Thanksgiving, what other times of year do you think Butterball would benefit from concentrated advertising? How could these be a part of an IMC?
Courtesy The Butterball Turkey Company

Public Relations

5

Discuss the role of public relations in the promotional mix

Public relations is the element in the promotional mix that evaluates public attitudes, identifies issues that may elicit public concern, and executes programs to gain public understanding and acceptance. Like advertising and sales promotion, public relations is a vital link in a progressive company's marketing communication mix. Marketing managers plan solid public relations campaigns that fit into overall marketing plans and focus on targeted audiences. These campaigns strive to maintain a positive image of the corporation in the eyes of the public. Before launching public relations programs, managers evaluate public attitudes and company actions. Then they create programs to capitalize on the factors that enhance the firm's image and minimize the factors that could generate a negative image.

Many people associate public relations with publicity. *Publicity* is the effort to capture media attention—for example, through articles or editorials in publications or through human-interest stories on radio or television programs. Corporations usually initiate publicity through a press release that furthers their public relations plans. A company about to introduce a new product or open a new store may send press releases to the media in the hope that the story will be published or broadcast. Savvy publicity can often create overnight sensations. Artisan Entertainment hoped its independent film, *The Blair Witch Project,* would be its summer 1999 hit, but couldn't spend big-studio advertising dollars to advertise it. So Artisan turned to a public relations strategy to build excitement and curiosity about the film. The cornerstone of its strategy proved to be the film's Web site, which showed outtakes from unused footage, faked official documents, and interviews that suggested a police cover-up to build the legend of the Blair Witch. At the height of the campaign, the site was getting three million hits a day. Artisan also used "street" teams to distribute missing person fliers and stick figures. It also held film screenings on forty college campuses across the country. When the film finally opened after weeks of built-up suspense, it quickly became a hit, breaking attendance records and topping opening weekend numbers for such heavyweights as *Star Wars: The Phantom Menace.*[59]

Donating products or services to worthy causes also creates favorable publicity. When the Iowa septuplets were born, consumer-products companies showered the babies and their parents with free goods. Gerber Products Company made an all-they-can-eat offer of baby and toddler food; Sony Electronics donated a camcorder to help the family capture the memories of the newborns; Toys "R" Us outfitted the family with cribs, changing tables, car seats, and strollers; Cadbury Schweppes PLC's Motts unit donated sixteen years' worth of apple sauce and juice; Procter & Gamble Company became the official diaper sponsor with a "lifetime" supply offer (about two years worth of diapers); and Maytag Corporation offered to design a new kitchen, complete with at least two of every appliance, in the new home being built to replace the family's modest two-bedroom dwelling.[60]

Public relations departments may perform any or all of the following functions:

- *Press relations:* placing positive, newsworthy information in the news media to attract attention to a product, a service, or a person associated with the firm or institution
- *Product publicity:* publicizing specific products or services
- *Corporate communication:* creating internal and external messages to promote a positive image of the firm or institution
- *Public affairs:* building and maintaining national or local community relations
- *Lobbying:* influencing legislators and government officials to promote or defeat legislation and regulation

- *Employee and investor relations:* maintaining positive relationships with employees, shareholders, and others in the financial community
- *Crisis management:* responding to unfavorable publicity or a negative event

Major Public Relations Tools

Several tools are commonly used by public relations professionals, including new product publicity, product placement, consumer education, event sponsorship, and issue sponsorship. A relatively new tool public relations professionals are using in increasing numbers is a Web site on the Internet. Although many of these tools require an active role on the part of the public relations professional, such as writing press releases and engaging in proactive media relations, many of these techniques create their own publicity.

New-Product Publicity   Publicity is instrumental in introducing new products and services. Publicity can help advertisers explain what's different about their new product by prompting free news stories or positive word of mouth about it. During the introductory period, an especially innovative new product often needs more exposure than conventional, paid advertising affords. Public relations professionals write press releases or develop videos in an effort to generate news about their new product. They also jockey for exposure of their product or service at major events, on popular television and news shows, or in the hands of influential people. When the Krispy Kreme doughnut chain opened an outlet in Phoenix, company officials arranged for the store's first customer to be Arizona's Maricopa County Sheriff Joe Arpaio, billed as "the toughest sheriff in America" who makes his prisoners wear pink underwear. Before television cameras, the famous sheriff ate his doughnut and declared, "These doughnuts are so good they should be illegal."[61]

Product Placement   Marketers can also garner publicity by making sure their products appear at special events or in movies or television shows. Krispy Kreme doughnuts, for example, have had cameo roles in the movie *Primary Colors* and on such television shows as *Ally McBeal* and *NYPD Blue.* On *The Tonight Show,* host Jay Leno recently joked about policemen and their supposed weakness for doughnuts while gleefully displaying a picture of a police officer biting into a Krispy Kreme.[62] Similarly, in the TNN action series *18 Wheels of Justice,* Kenworth Truck Company lent out its rigs to the show's producers in exchange for multiple shots of the truck, mention of the company name in the closing credits, and a guarantee of six minutes of exposure per episode.[63] Product placement is also catching on in other countries. Read the "Global Perspectives" box to find out how marketers are placing their products in Chinese soap operas.

Companies reap invaluable product exposure through product placement, usually at a fraction of the cost of paid-for advertising. Often, the fee for exposure is in merchandise. Fashion designer Georgio Armani, for example, uses celebrities to burnish his brand in the eyes of the public. Former Los Angeles Lakers basketball coach Pat Riley was outfitted for games in customized Armani suits. Whenever the Lakers played, the courtside cameras captured Mr. Riley pacing up and down dressed in Armani. Soon, every coach and player in the NBA started filling his closets with Armani suits. Armani also provides free gowns and tuxedos to select Hollywood stars to

Consumer education can not only influence the buying decision but can result in better, more loyal customers. BMW's instructional driving tour is a way to show off its car's capabilities to prospective purchasers and current owners without mounting expensive advertising campaigns.

Global Perspectives

PRODUCT PLACEMENT IN CHINESE SOAP OPERA

To the delight of marketers, soap is suddenly showing up on the set of China's popular soap opera *Love Talks*, one of the first television series in China engineered by advertisers. Set in a fictitious Shanghai ad agency, the soap opera features the budding romance between a veteran male account director and a novice account executive. The unique aspect of this show is the obvious placement of brand-name products visible throughout the show. For example, one scene shows the soap's star Qu Ying, rushing to work, leaving an important folder at home. The camera zooms in on the forgotten folder, which just happens to be sitting next to a big tube of Pond's Vaseline Intensive Care lotion. The scene then cuts to Ms. Qu in a cab where she is applying Maybelline lipstick, when she notices the missing folder—oh no! Quickly, she borrows a Motorola mobile phone from a handsome stranger in another car.

Marketers, such as Unilever, Motorola, Maybelline, Duracell, and General Electric, have already signed up as sponsors of *Love Talks*. Other brands, such as Braun and Nike, have also cashed in on sponsorships, promotion, and product placement opportunities with the Chinese soap opera. Show sponsorships cost $240,000 to $360,000. Television in China is still under strict government control, but shows such as *Love Talks* are demonstrating new opportunities for advertisers.

While paying to have a product appear in movies or television shows is old hat in the United States and other countries, the concept is revolutionary in China. Most commercials on Chinese state-run television are run in back-to-back, ten-minute-long "bricks," or segments. Due to the large number of commercials that run during each brick, it's difficult for any one advertiser to attract viewers' attention with just a thirty-second ad. Product placement, therefore, provides an innovative way for a product to get noticed. Advertisers are also at-tracted to the drama since its viewers represent a burgeoning middle class in the world's most populous country.

Love Talks, produced by United Media, now airs on 128 of China's 800 television stations. The show has been so popular with viewers that the production company has begun developing two more series—one about an architect's family life, called *Home*, and another about a modeling agency, called *Model*. The original *Love Talks* series has also been syndicated to broadcasters in Taiwan, Hong Kong, Thailand, Malaysia, and Singapore.[a]

Can you recall any name-brand products that you saw in a television series or a motion picture? How did this affect your perception of the brand?

[a] Peter Wonacott, "Chinese TV Discovers Product Placement," *Wall Street Journal*, January 26, 2000, p. B12; Normandy Madden, "Sponsors Follow Twists of Chinese Soap Operas," *Advertising Age International*, January 1, 2000, p. 9.

---

wear on Oscar night. For special celebrity clients, like Jodie Foster, Armani furnishes a wardrobe during movie promotional tours.[64]

Consumer Education Some major firms believe that educated consumers are better, more loyal customers. Financial planning firms often sponsor free educational seminars on money management, retirement planning, and investing in the hope that the consumer will choose its organization for its future financial needs. Likewise, computer hardware and software firms, realizing that many consumers feel intimidated by new technology and recognizing the strong relationship between learning and purchasing patterns, sponsor computer seminars and free in-store demonstrations. BMW of North America, for example, recently sponsored an instructional driving school for teenagers in thirteen major cities across the United States. Teens received a special four-hour training session that included driving techniques, accident avoidance skills, and traction aid tricks with the help of a professional driver.[65]

Event Sponsorship   Public relations managers can sponsor events or community activities that are sufficiently newsworthy to achieve press coverage; at the same time, these events also reinforce brand identification. Sporting, music, and arts events remain the most popular choices of event sponsors, although many are now turning to more specialized events such as tie-ins with schools, charities, and other community service organizations. For example, NBC, Emap Petersen, Mountain Dew, Doritos, Toyota, Hasbro Interactive, the U.S. Marines, Ultimate Speed Stick, and Unionbay sponsored the Gravity Games extreme sporting event that competes with ESPN's highly successful X Games. Some 200,000 spectators, a large majority of them young males between the ages of twelve and twenty-four, descended on Providence, Rhode Island, for the eight-day festival. Sponsors gave away free samples, hosted extreme athlete autograph sessions and sports demonstrations, and organized alternative music concerts.[66]

Marketers can also create their own events tied around their product. The state of Hawaii recently organized its own mall touring event, titled "Experience Aloha: Hawaii on Tour," to promote the islands as a tourist destination. The tour traveled to twenty-two U.S. cities for weekend mall visits that included hula dancers, chefs cooking Hawaiian cuisine, lei-making demonstrations, and a virtual reality film simulating a helicopter ride over Hawaii's islands.[67]

Issue Sponsorship   Corporations can build public awareness and loyalty by supporting their customers' favorite issues. Education, health care, and social programs get the largest share of corporate funding. Firms often donate a percentage of sales or profits to a worthy cause that their target market is likely to favor. For example, BMW's "Ultimate Driving Experience" test-driving events support the Susan G. Komen Breast Cancer Foundation by donating one dollar for every mile consumers test-drive cars through local dealerships.[68]

"Green marketing" has also become an important way for companies to build awareness and loyalty by promoting a popular issue. By positioning their brands as ecologically sound, marketers can convey concern for the environment and society as a whole. Burger King and McDonald's no longer use styrofoam cartons to package their burgers in an effort to decrease waste in landfills. In a similar effort, Wal-Mart has opened environmentally friendly stores to appeal to consumers' desire to save the environment. The stores' air conditioning systems use a non-ozone-depleting refrigerant, rainwater is collected from parking lots and roofs for watering the landscape, skylights allow natural light into the store, cart corrals are made of recycled plastic, and parking lots are recycled asphalt.

Internet Web Sites   Public relations professionals are increasingly using their Internet Web sites as a vehicle to post news releases on products, product enhancements, strategic relationships, and financial earnings. Corporate press releases, technical papers and articles, and product news help inform the press, customers, prospects, industry analysts, stockholders, and others of the firm's products and services and their applications. The Web site can also be an open forum for new product ideas, product improvements, and customer feedback. On-line reviews from opinion leaders also help marketers sway shopping decisions in their favor. Amazon.com, for instance, features reviews from well-known music and book critics to help shoppers select CDs and novels. Additionally, Amazon's site includes over two million reviews posted by customers themselves.[69]

Several marketers are also using the Internet as a way to create word-of-mouth buzz. When executives at RCA Records embarked upon turning teen pop singer Christina Aguilera's debut album into a hit, the Internet played a crucial role. The company hired a team of young cybersurfers to swarm the Web and start chatting about Ms. Aguilera on popular teen sites such as **www.alloy.com**, **www.bolt.com**, and **www.gurl.com**. The team casually posted information in chatrooms and on bulletin boards about her upcoming single, as well as lobbied big sites like America Online to run features on the teen singer. As Aguilera's single "Genie in a Bottle" got more radio airplay, the team fed fans more information about her via the Web and encouraged them to request the song on radio stations and MTV. The effort helped drive "Genie" to the top of the singles chart and her album debuted at No. 1, reaching double platinum status in record time.[70]

Managing Unfavorable Publicity

Although the majority of marketers try to avoid unpleasant situations, crises do happen. Intel faced this reality after consumers became aware of an obscure flaw in its Pentium chip. In our free-press environment, publicity is not easily controlled, especially in a crisis. **Crisis management** is the coordinated effort to handle the effects of unfavorable publicity, ensuring fast and accurate communication in times of emergency.

A good public relations staff is perhaps more important in bad times than in good. Companies must have a communication policy firmly in hand before a disaster occurs, because timing is uncontrollable. Following the January 2000 crash of Alaska Airlines Flight 261, the Seattle carrier was reeling not only from the crash but also from three separate federal investigations, aggressive media coverage by Seattle newspapers, lawsuits brought by crash victims' families, and a letter from its own maintenance employees claiming they were pressured into cutting corners on safety. Company chairman and chief executive John F. Kelly quickly went public with plans to hire a team of outside experts to conduct a comprehensive audit of the airline and interview the mechanics who raised the safety concerns. He also established a telephone hotline to his office for employees having safety concerns and created a new position, vice president of safety, to help restore the airline's credibility with its employees and customers.[71]

A good public relations and crisis management plan helped steer the Walt Disney Company out of a public relations mess after it was twice forced to postpone the maiden voyage of its new cruise ship, *Disney Magic*, due to production delays. Forty cruises originally scheduled to begin sailing in March 1998 were canceled, forcing approximately ninety-six thousand potential travelers to change their plans. Because travelers who booked early are Disney's most enthusiastic fans, the company had a virtual public relations nightmare. To begin fixing the damage, Disney overnighted apologies to disappointed travelers offering 50 percent discounts to those who had been inconvenienced twice, and 25 percent discounts to those bumped once. Disney also offered full refunds to those who didn't rebook and covered any lost commissions for travel agents.[72] Similarly, Internet auctioneer eBay used effective crisis management to climb its way out of a public relations mess after a computer crash halted its bidding operations for twenty-two hours. The outage left nearly 2.3 million auctions stranded in the middle of bids, infuriating customers and sellers. To sooth users' frustrations, eBay sent messages apologizing for the disruption and promising to aggressively hire more computer-network experts. The company also refunded users' listing fees totaling close to $5 million.[73]

crisis management
A coordinated effort to handle the effects of unfavorable publicity or of another unexpected, unfavorable event.

As you finish reading this chapter, think back to the opening story about the wildly successful release of *Harry Potter and the Goblet of Fire*. For the novel's launch date, Scholastic's promotional team went through the same creative steps as other marketers when advertising their products—from determining what appeal to use to choosing the appropriate executional style. Great effort was also expended in deciding which medium would best reach the desired target market of preteen children. Public relations and publicity also played a significant role in the book's release. Secrecy surrounding the highly anticipated book escalated interest by kids and their parents.

Use it Now!

Becoming a Media Expert

Find the perfect magazine to advertise your product or service. Visit the MediaFinder Web site at **http://www.mediafinder.com**. The site has a searchable database of thousands of magazines. Or visit Channel Seven at **http://www.channelseven.com** to find news and views on hot new advertising mediums.

Ticked Off About That Ad?

File a complaint with the Better Business Bureau. See which companies get the most complaints about their advertising at the Better Business Bureau's Web site at **http://www.bbb.org/advertising/index.html**. Want to avoid legal problems with your advertising campaign? Find detailed information about advertising law and Federal Trade Commission regulations at **http://www.advertisinglaw.com**.

How to Write a Press Release

Visit **http://www.press-release-writing.com** to learn the right way to get publicity for your product or service. This Web site offers sample press releases, templates, formatting suggestions, and basic information that should always be included. The service also helps you distribute your press release to thousands of different media outlets.

Summary

1 Discuss the effect of advertising on market share and consumers. Advertising helps marketers increase or maintain brand awareness and, subsequently, market share. Typically, more is spent to advertise new brands with a small market share than to advertise older brands. Brands with a large market share use advertising mainly to maintain their share of the market. Advertising affects consumers' daily lives as well as their purchases. Although advertising can seldom change strongly held consumer attitudes and values, it may transform a consumer's negative attitude toward a product into a positive one. Additionally, when consumers are highly loyal to a brand, they may buy more of that brand when advertising is increased. Last, advertising can also change the importance of a brand's attributes to consumers. By emphasizing different brand attributes, advertisers can change their appeal in response to consumers' changing needs or try to achieve an advantage over competing brands.

2 Identify the major types of advertising. Advertising is any form of nonpersonal, paid communication in which the sponsor or company is identified. The two major types of advertising are institutional advertising and product advertising. Institutional advertising is not product oriented; rather, its purpose is to foster a positive company image among the general public, investment community, customers, and employees. Product advertising is designed mainly to promote goods and services, and it is classified into three main categories: pioneering, competitive, and comparative. A product's place in the product life cycle is a major determinant of the type of advertising used to promote it.

③ Discuss the creative decisions in developing an advertising campaign. Before any creative work can begin on an advertising campaign, it is important to determine what goals or objectives the advertising should achieve. The objectives of a specific advertising campaign often depend on the overall corporate objectives and the product being advertised. Once objectives are defined, creative work can begin on the advertising campaign. Creative decisions include identifying the product's benefits, developing possible advertising appeals, evaluating and selecting the advertising appeals, executing the advertising message, and evaluating the effectiveness of the campaign.

④ Describe media evaluation and selection techniques. Media evaluation and selection make up a crucial step in the advertising campaign process. Major types of advertising media include newspapers, magazines, radio, television, outdoor advertising such as billboards and bus panels, and the Internet. Recent trends in advertising media include fax, video shopping carts, computer screen savers, and cinema and video advertising. Promotion managers choose the advertising campaign's media mix on the basis of the following variables: cost per contact, reach, frequency, characteristics of the target audience, flexibility of the medium, noise level, and the life span of the medium. After choosing the media mix, a media schedule designates when the advertisement will appear and the specific vehicles it will appear in.

⑤ Discuss the role of public relations in the promotional mix. Public relations is a vital part of a firm's promotional mix. A company fosters good publicity to enhance its image and promote its products. Popular public relations tools include new product publicity, product placement, consumer education, event sponsorship, issue sponsorship, and Internet Web sites. An equally important aspect of public relations is managing unfavorable publicity in a way that is least damaging to a firm's image.

Discussion and Writing Questions

1. How can advertising and publicity work together? Give an example.
2. Discuss the reasons why new brands with a smaller market share spend proportionately more on advertising than brands with a larger market share.
3. At what stage in a product's life cycle are pioneering, competitive, and comparative advertising most likely to occur? Give a current example of each type of advertising.
4. What is an advertising appeal? Give some examples of advertising appeals you have observed recently in the media.
5. What are the advantages of radio advertising? Why is radio expanding as an advertising medium?
6. **WRITING** You are the advertising manager of a sailing magazine, and one of your biggest potential advertisers has questioned your rates. Write the firm a letter explaining why you believe your audience selectivity is worth the extra expense for advertisers.
7. **WRITING** As the new public relations director for a sportswear company, you have been asked to set public relations objectives for a new line of athletic shoes to be introduced to the teen market. Draft a memo outlining the objectives you propose for the shoe's introduction and your reasons for them.
8. **WRITING** Reports have just surfaced that your company, a fast-food chain, sold contaminated food products that have made several people seriously ill. As your company's public relations manager, devise a plan to handle the crisis.

9. Identify an appropriate media mix for the following products:
   a. Chewing tobacco
   b. *People* magazine
   c. Weed-Eaters
   d. Foot odor killers
   e. "Drink responsibly" campaigns by beer brewers

10. **WRITING** Design a full-page magazine advertisement for a new brand of soft drink. The name of the new drink, as well as package design, is at the discretion of the student. On a separate sheet, specify the benefits stressed or appeals made in the advertisement.

11. **TEAM** Form a three-person team. Divide the responsibility for getting newspaper advertisements and menus for several local restaurants. While you are at the restaurants to obtain copies of their menus, observe the atmosphere and interview the manager to determine what he or she believes are the primary reasons people choose to dine with them. Pool your information and develop a table comparing the restaurants in terms of convenience of location, value for the money, food variety and quality, atmosphere, and so on. Rank the restaurants in terms of their appeal to college students. Explain the basis of your rankings. What other market segment would be attracted to the restaurants and why? Do the newspaper advertisements emphasize the most effective appeal for a particular restaurant? Explain.

12. **WRITING** **INFOTRAC COLLEGE EDITION** The Ford/Firestone tire recall of 2000 was one of the biggest public relations nightmares of recent memory. How well did the companies handle the situation? Use InfoTrac (**http://www.infotrac-college.com**) to run a keyword search on "Ford public relations." Read a selection of the articles, then write an analysis of CEO Jac Nasser's performance in the face of this crisis. What did he do well? What could he have done better? Evaluate his solution to the problem.

Application for Entrepreneurs

ENTREPRENEUR Quality of service is increasingly the basis for deciding where to do business. Customers are five times more likely to return to a particular business if they perceive that it is providing higher quality service than the competition.

The Student Copy Center is a local business competing with Kinko's and a couple of other national franchise copy centers. Its owner, Mack Bayles, just attended a Small Business Administration workshop on customer service. He learned that when people say they expect good customer service, they most often mean they want prompt and accurate service from friendly, knowledgeable, and courteous employees. The presenter also emphasized that all market segments, even the most price conscious, expect good customer service. Mack wants to use this knowledge to develop an effective advertising campaign.

Mack has no idea what his customers think about either his copy business or that of his competitors. He decides, therefore, to ask his customers to complete a brief survey while in his store. From his survey he learns that Student Copy Center is considered friendlier and more courteous than the major competitors but is rated lower on speed of service.

Questions

1. What should Mack do before developing his advertising campaign?
2. Should Mack use comparative ads?
3. What advertising appeal would be most effective for Mack? Why?

The Move from TV to TiVo

In the late 1990s, Silicon Graphics Inc. employees Mike Ramsay and Jim Barton were working together on the *Full-Service Network Project* in Orlando, Florida, a joint venture between Time Warner and Silicon Graphics to create the first large-scale interactive television system, when they hit upon an idea. They could build the same type of system that would give viewers control over their television programming and their time, but with far greater intelligence and ease-of-use, at a price the average customer could afford.

Their idea was the genesis of TiVo, a revolutionary new service that puts viewers in control of their television-viewing experience in a way never before possible. TiVo's service uses an electronic device called a personal video recorder (PVR) that can digitally save up to thirty hours of television programs. But instead of punching in times and channels one at a time to record a show on a video cassette tape, like with a VCR, the PVR uses a phone line to download television program schedules through a pop-up window on the television screen. TiVo subscribers then click on any shows they want to select and digitally record them.

With TiVo, viewers get more control than ever over what they want to watch on television. Subscribers can digitally record their favorite shows, organizing their own schedules of shows to watch when they want, not bound by the timetable of any network schedule. With some television networks that TiVo has partnered with, subscribers can even select shows as they are advertised in televised promotions. For instance, if a subscriber sees a promo for an upcoming show to be aired on Showtime, she can click on a small icon in the corner of her television screen during the promo to automatically record it when the program is run. No more having to remember when the desired show will come on to catch it. TiVo can also automatically record subscribers' favorite shows every week or suggest other shows that they might want to catch based on their interests.

The digital recorders, manufactured for TiVo by Philips Consumer Electronics and SONY Corporation and costing about $400, provide several features that are superior to a conventional VCR and its limited recording capabilities. During live programs, for example, viewers can pause during a broadcast while the PVR keeps recording. PVRs can also provide instant replay so avid sports fans will never miss a play again. Additionally, PVRs include a skip button so that viewers can bypass television commercials or catch up with live programming that they have paused.

Based in Sunnyvale, California, TiVo currently has over 35,000 subscribers to its service with projections of continued growth. While analysts expect PVRs to take several years to reach the market penetration of the ubiquitous VCR, projections are that PVRs will be in fourteen million homes by 2005, possibly making PVRs the fastest-growing consumer electronic product in history. If this prediction pans out, the impact on television from PVRs and TiVo-like services could be enormous. For instance, since TiVo subscribers can create their own programming schedule, prime time would become increasingly irrelevant as more shows get recorded for later viewing. Additionally, viewers armed with the ability to fast-forward through commercials would see less of them; analysts are estimating that the viewing of commercials will decrease by 50 percent by 2009 with increased market penetration of PVRs.

Not surprisingly, TiVo and PVRs have most advertising and television executives watching carefully to see how the technology emerges. TiVo believes its technology is actually an opportunity for advertisers to target their audiences more directly. By knowing what shows consumers are interested in or the demographics of the household, commercials could be tailored accordingly. For instance, General Motors is working with TiVo to deliver customized advertising through PVRs. If, for example, the household is a family of five, it could play a commercial for a GM van in the spot during a recorded show. But if the home is occupied by a single man, GM might instead play a Corvette ad.

For now, many in the entertainment industry have decided it's better to join than oppose personal video recording services. Entertainment giants like America Online, DIRECTV, Discovery Communications, NBC, Walt Disney Company, Blockbuster, Cox Communications, Showtime Networks, Home Box Office, and others have partnered with TiVo to develop programming and advertising solutions. Blockbuster, for instance, is working with TiVo to develop a video on demand service that will eventually allow TiVo subscribers to obtain movies directly through their TiVo recorders. Similarly, Internet film site iFilm is delivering unique film content, previously available only on the Web, to TiVo customers via the television.

Questions

1. If the majority of TiVo viewers fast-forward through commercials, advertisers will be essentially wasting the millions of dollars they spend on them. What solutions might you suggest to advertisers as TiVo gains in popularity?

2. How might TiVo and PVRs affect traditional television networks that rely on advertising revenue to support original programming?

3. How might the popularity of TiVo's service affect traditional media selection criteria like reach and frequency?

Bibliography

Bill Carter. "Will This Machine Change Television?" *New York Times*, July 5, 1999, p. 1.

Jim Cooper. "Inside the Box." *Brandweek*, May 8, 2000, p. C32.

Marla Matzer Rose. "TV Advertisers Worry About Growth of New PVRs." *Chicago Tribune*, April 14, 2000, p. 4.

Erin Strout. "The End of TV Advertising?" *Sales & Marketing Management*. January 2000, p. 15.

TiVo Web site at **http://www.tivo.com**

"TiVo Signs Showtime." *Advertising Age*. May 16, 2000.

Case

Red Roof Inns: Ads to Charm, Disarm, and Deliver

During the seventies and eighties, when economy lodging was far less competitive than it is today, billboards broadcasting "Sleep Cheap" grabbed the attention of road-weary business travelers and brought them to the nearest Red Roof Inn. In addition to saying "low cost," however, "Sleep Cheap" also said "low level," and occupancy rates at Red Roof Inns started to decline nationwide. Hired to reverse this image was the W. B. Doner advertising agency, whose philosophy was best articulated by its founder, Brod Doner: "Ads are created to charm, disarm, and deliver." For the Red Roof account, Brod wanted creativity that would persuade, motivate, and make something happen.

The Doner Agency realized that advertising copy cannot change consumers' deeply rooted values and attitudes, but it could succeed in transforming a person's negative attitude about Red Roof's economy lodging into a positive one. Advertising could affect the way consumers ranked Red Roof's primary attribute—prices lower than the competition for the same economy hotel room—and thus motivate them to try spending the night at a Red Roof Inn.

As part of a comprehensive promotion plan, an advertising campaign was set in motion to transmit the sales message to the target market. The Doner agency, in conjunction with Red Roof Inns executives, decided that the advertising campaign would target the business travelers on a limited expense account who most likely arrive late at night and leave early the next morning. The specific communication in the advertising campaign mirrored Red Roof's corporate objective to increase market share in the economy lodging market. The whole point of the advertising was to convey the idea that a hotel room doesn't have to be expensive to be good. After all, "Why pay $70 when you can have the same good night's sleep for $30 less at Red Roof Inn?" the commercials asked.

The advertising campaign then moved into the creative and media decision phase. The Doner team stuck to its core philosophy: Although highly creative ads win accolades from peers in the advertising business, the bottom line is to sell products and services to the client. And the results have to be measurable. "Sleep Cheap" was replaced by "Hit the Roof," which

was featured primarily in television spots. In addition to television, Doner's integrated marketing approach used radio, billboards, direct mail, print, and the Internet to drive home the same message of value.

The initial creative effort came alive in a television commercial centered around one simple concept—spending $70 for a night's stay in a hotel room is throwing money away. To make the concept visual, a business traveler stood at the top of Hoover Dam while a celebrity spokesperson literally threw the traveler's wallet from the dam into the raging waters below. Such an outrageous act provoked humor *and* underscored a well-known adage in advertising—sell the benefit. The message here was clear: What the consumer receives by staying at Red Roof Inns is money in his or her pocket. Put another way, a stay at Red Roof Inns keeps a customer from wasting hard-earned cash. Red Roof Inns was trying to differentiate itself on price, but more importantly on value.

Making claims of better value was not enough to universally boost business, so another TV spot was designed to increase occupancy rates at Red Roof during the slow period of January through March. The same celebrity, now well associated with Red Roof Inns, handed a telephone to a business customer and urged him to call and compare Red Roof's rates with those offered by other economy lodging chains like Hampton Inn. The competitors' rates were consistently $5 to $10 a night higher. The same tag line, "Hit the Roof," continued to reinforce the same unified message of value. Building on the success of prior campaigns, the Doner agency again selected humor as the creative style to execute the message. The commercial generated awareness by challenging viewers to call and compare rates. It sparked viewer interest in learning about room rates; it peaked viewer desire to save money; and, it is hoped, it resulted in a stay at Red Roof.

The Doner agency has handled the Red Roof Inns account for twelve years, and the advertising appeal has remained consistent the whole time. The appeal plays on the customer's desire for thrift, convenience, and a nice place to stay. Both the initial and subsequent ad campaigns produced measurable results. When the ad campaigns were evaluated, market share was shown to have increased despite heavy competition, and occupancy rates during slack periods had improved. Brod Doner's advertising mantra—ads that charm, disarm, and deliver—has certainly made today's business travelers "Hit the Roof."

Questions

1. Using Exhibit 15.2, describe the advertising campaign decision process for Red Roof Inns.
2. Why did the Doner Agency identify the benefits of Red Roof Inns in the TV commercial?
3. Describe the advertising appeal used in the campaign.
4. How does Red Roof's advertising campaign follow AIDA as depicted in Exhibit 14.5?

Bibliography

John DeCerchio. "Osmosis, Fiat Passed Doner Philosophy," *Advertising Age.* March 3, 1997, C6-7.

John McDonough. "W. B. Doner, 60th Anniversary," *Advertising Age.* March 3, 1997, C1-2.

Video by Learnet Inc.: A Case Study in Advertising Strategy: Red Roof Inn

Web site: **http://www.redroof.com**

chapter 16

Learning Objectives

1 Define and state the objectives of sales promotion

2 Discuss the most common forms of consumer sales promotion

3 List the most common forms of trade sales promotion

4 Describe personal selling

5 Discuss the key differences between relationship selling and traditional selling

6 List the steps in the selling process

7 Describe the functions of sales management

Sales Promotion and Personal Selling

From a sleepy chain of twenty-four-hour copy shops for college kids and business travelers, Kinko's has transformed itself into a major provider of services for the business-to-business market. While its retail stores have always done well, the company identified real opportunities for increasing revenues from big corporate customers. Trouble was, the sales force as it existed was happy simply being order takers and signing small corporate deals, not worrying about repeat business or building customer relationships.

So in 1999, Kinko's began a reorganization of its field sales force into one strong organization with a single mission: create long-term profitable relationships with big companies that want to outsource their printing and copy needs. This was a tall order for a company that had no established sales process, no common compensation plan with goals, no training, and no common marketing collateral. But with input from the salespeople and their managers, Kinko's reorganization team revamped the sales force by developing a common vision and go-to-market strategy along with new compensation plans, training programs, and sales materials.

An important step in its reorganization plan was to create a sales process for its salespeople to follow. Salespeople used to sell any way they wanted, creating a jumbled perception of Kinko's in the marketplace. So Kinko's developed a new sales process that it calls the Customer Relationship Cycle. Every Kinko's salesperson, and the support organization that works out of Kinko's retail branches, adheres to this seven-step process: assess customer needs, plan how Kinko's can help them, offer a solution, close the deal, fulfill the project, support an ongoing relationship, and expand the relationship to bring in more business from the customer. The creation of a common sales process has helped Kinko's salespeople create more fulfilling and substantive relationships with their customers.

Instituting a new sales process alone can't change salespeople overnight. Kinko's needed to give its salespeople the tools to sell with and the training to help them sell better. For a company that was in the business of creating high-quality documents, the salespeople themselves had no quality marketing collateral to use during sales presentations. Within ninety days of the reorganization, Kinko's executives issued kits to salespeople that contained slick one-page documents on each of the products and services that Kinko's provides. Kinko's sales force also went through a two-day training course focused on the seven-step customer relationship cycle and how to succeed at each step.

Kinko's also had to revamp the way it paid its reps. The company's compensation plan as it was did little to motivate the sales force, and salespeople were compensated in different ways with various goals. It was obvious that the reason overall sales goals had not been met for the past several years was due to a lack of clear business objectives. Ultimately, Kinko's created a new pay plan that rewarded everyone based on the same business objectives. Salespeople are now compensated based on how well they meet the company's overall business goals, such as increasing incremental revenue, creating long-term customer relationships, and providing good customer service.

Within six months of instituting these changes, Kinko's salespeople have achieved nearly 110 percent of the company's stated objectives, showing that results happen when the sales organization is focused on goals and motivated to achieve them.[1]

What is a sales process and why is it important to personal selling? What role does training play in a successful sales organization? What other ways beside compensation can sales managers motivate their salespeople? These questions and others about personal selling and sales management will be answered in the second part of this chapter after discussing the topic of sales promotion.

Sales Promotion

Define and state the objectives of sales promotion

In addition to using advertising, public relations, and personal selling, marketing managers can use sales promotion to increase the effectiveness of their promotional efforts. *Sales promotion* is marketing communication activities, other than advertising, personal selling, and public relations, in which a short-term incentive motivates consumers or members of the distribution channel to purchase a good or service immediately, either by lowering the price or by adding value.

Advertising offers the consumer a reason to buy; sales promotion offers an incentive to buy. Both are important, but sales promotion is usually cheaper than advertising and easier to measure. A major national TV advertising campaign may cost over $2 million to create, produce, and place. In contrast, a newspaper coupon campaign or promotional contest may cost only about half as much. It is hard to figure exactly how many people buy a product as a result of seeing a TV ad. However, with sales promotion, marketers know the precise number of coupons redeemed or the number of contest entries.

Sales promotion is usually targeted toward either of two distinctly different markets. **Consumer sales promotion** is targeted to the ultimate consumer market. **Trade sales promotion** is directed to members of the marketing channel, such as wholesalers and retailers. Sales promotion has become an important element in a marketer's integrated marketing communications program (see Chapter 14). Sales promotion expenditures have been steadily increasing over the last several years as a result of increased competition, the ever-expanding array of available media choices, consumers and retailers demanding more deals from manufacturers, and the continued reliance on accountable and measurable marketing strategies. In addition, product and service marketers who have traditionally ignored sales promotion activities, such as power companies and restaurants, have discovered the marketing power of sales promotion. In fact, PROMO Magazine estimates that marketers spend some $20 billion a year on advertisements in which their sales promotions were either the star or costar.[2]

consumer sales promotion
Sales promotion activities targeting the ultimate consumer.

trade sales promotion
Sales promotion activities targeting a channel member, such as a wholesaler or retailer.

The Objectives of Sales Promotion

Sales promotion usually works best in affecting behavior rather than attitudes. Immediate purchase is the goal of sales promotion, regardless of the form it takes. Therefore, it seems to make more sense when planning a sales promotion campaign to target customers according to their general behavior. For instance, is the consumer loyal to your product or to your competitor's? Does the consumer switch brands readily in favor of the best deal? Does the consumer buy only the least expensive product, no matter what? Does the consumer buy any products in your category at all?

The objectives of a promotion depend on the general behavior of target consumers (see Exhibit 16.1). For example, marketers who are targeting loyal users of their product actually don't want to change behavior. Instead, they need to reinforce existing behavior or increase product usage. An effective tool for strengthening brand loyalty is the *frequent buyer program* that rewards consumers for repeat purchases. Other types of promotions are more effective with customers prone to brand switching or with those who are loyal to a competitor's product. The cents-off coupon, free sample, or eye-catching display in a store will often entice shoppers to try a different brand. Consumers who do not use the product may be enticed to try it through the distribution of free samples.

Once marketers understand the dynamics occurring within their product category and have determined the particular consumers and consumer behaviors they want to influence, they can then go about selecting promotional tools to achieve these goals.

Exhibit 16.1 Types of Consumers and Sales Promotion Goals

Type of Buyer	Desired Results	Sales Promotion Examples
Loyal customers People who buy your product most or all of the time	Reinforce behavior, increase consumption, change purchase timing	• Loyalty marketing programs, such as frequent buyer cards or frequent shopper clubs • Bonus packs that give loyal consumers an incentive to stock up or premiums offered in return for proofs of purchase
Competitor's customers People who buy a competitor's product most or all of the time	Break loyalty, persuade to switch to your brand	• Sampling to introduce your product's superior qualities compared to their brand • Sweepstakes, contests, or premiums that create interest in the product
Brand switchers People who buy a variety of products in the category	Persuade to buy your brand more often	• Any promotion that lowers the price of the product, such as coupons, price-off packages, and bonus packs • Trade deals that help make the product more readily available than competing products
Price buyers People who consistently buy the least expensive brand	Appeal with low prices or supply added value that makes price less important	• Coupons, price-off packages, refunds, or trade deals that reduce the price of the brand to match that of the brand that would have been purchased

SOURCE: From *Sales Promotion Essentials*, 2nd ed., by Don E. Schultz, William A. Robinson, and Lisa A. Petrison. Reprinted by permission of NTC Publishing Group, 4255 Touhy Ave., Lincolnwood, IL 60048.

Tools for Consumer Sales Promotion

Marketing managers must decide which consumer sales promotion devices to use in a specific campaign. The methods chosen must suit the objectives to ensure success of the overall promotion plan. Popular tools for consumer sales promotion are coupons and rebates, premiums, loyalty marketing programs, contests and sweepstakes, sampling, and point-of-purchase promotion. Consumer sales promotion tools have also been easily transferred to on-line versions to entice Internet users to visit sites, purchase products, or use services on the Web.

Discuss the most common forms of consumer sales promotion

Coupons and Rebates   A **coupon** is a certificate that entitles consumers to an immediate price reduction when they buy the product. Coupons are a particularly good way to encourage product trial and repurchase. They are also likely to increase the amount of a product bought.

coupon
A certificate that entitles consumers to an immediate price reduction when they buy the product.

Coupon distribution has been steadily declining in recent years as packaged-goods marketers attempt to wean consumers off coupon clipping. Although approximately 250 billion coupons are distributed each year, only about 2 percent, or about 5 billion, are actually redeemed by consumers.[3] Part of the problem is that coupons are often wasted on consumers who have no interest in the product, such as pet food or feminine products coupons that reach the petless or men. This is due mainly to the typical distribution of coupons in mass media newspaper Sunday inserts. Additionally, coupons are more likely to encourage repeat purchase by regular users, customers who would have purchased the product regardless, than stimulate product trial by nonusers.

Coolsavings.com

Describe the special deals you can find advertised on Coolsavings.com. Are there any coupons that you would print and use? What seems to be the target market for this site? Are there any premiums being currently offered?

http://www1.coolsavings.com

On Line

Because of their high cost and disappointing redemption rates, many marketers are reevaluating their use of coupons. By shortening the time the coupon can be redeemed, some marketers have increased redemption rates by creating a greater sense of urgency to redeem the coupon. Other marketers are deemphasizing their use of coupons in favor of everyday low pricing, while others are distributing single, all-purpose coupons that can be redeemed for several brands. In-store coupons are becoming more popular as they have proved more likely to affect customer buying decisions.

Instant coupons on product packages, coupons distributed from on-shelf coupon-dispensing machines, and electronic coupons issued at the checkout counter are achieving much higher redemption rates. Redemption of instant coupons, for example, are about seventeen times that of traditional newspaper coupons, suggesting that consumers are making more in-store purchase decisions.[4]

Rebates are similar to coupons in that they offer the purchaser a price reduction; however, because the purchaser must mail in a rebate form and usually some proof of purchase, the reward is not as immediate. Traditionally used by food and cigarette manufacturers, rebates now appear on all types of products, from computers and software to film and baby seats. Consumers purchasing Earth's Best baby foods, for example, received a $2 rebate when they also bought the children's music CD "More Songs from Pooh Corner" by singer Kenny Loggins. In exchange, Earth's Best got to place its own coupons inside the Sony CD package.[5]

Manufacturers prefer rebates for several reasons. Rebates allow manufacturers to offer price cuts to consumers directly. Manufacturers have more control over rebate promotions because they can be rolled out and shut off quickly. Further, because buyers must fill out forms with their names, addresses, and other data, manufacturers use rebate programs to build customer databases. Perhaps the best reason of all to offer rebates is that although rebates are particularly good at enticing purchase, most consumers never bother to redeem them. Redemption rates for rebates run between 5 and 10 percent.[6]

Although coupons are a high-cost promotion alternative, they are still holding their own. Instant coupons are one way promoters can fight lackluster redemption rates.

rebate
A cash refund given for the purchase of a product during a specific period.

premium
An extra item offered to the consumer, usually in exchange for some proof of purchase of the promoted product.

Premiums   A **premium** is an extra item offered to the consumer, usually in exchange for some proof that the promoted product has been purchased. Premiums reinforce the consumer's purchase decision, increase consumption, and persuade nonusers to switch brands. Premiums like telephones, tote bags, and umbrellas are available when consumers buy cosmetics, magazines, bank services, rental cars, and so on. Probably the best example of the use of premiums is the McDonald's Happy Meal that rewards children with a small toy in the meal. The fast-food marketer's lucrative pacts with Ty Inc., marketer of Beanie Babies, and Disney have placed their Happy Meals in high demand with children. Teenie Beanie Babies premiums and combo meals including toys are linked to popular Disney movies like *Tarzan* and *Dinosaurs*.

Premiums can also include more product for the regular price, such as two-for-the-price-of-one bonus packs or packages that include more of the product. Kellogg's, for instance, added two more pastries and waffles to its Pop Tarts and Eggo packages without increasing the price in an effort to boost market share lost to private-label brands and new competitors. The promotion was so successful the company decided to keep the additional product in its regular packaging.

Loyalty Marketing Programs **Loyalty marketing programs**, or **frequent buyer programs**, reward loyal consumers for making multiple purchases. Popularized by the airline industry in the mid-1980s through frequent flyer programs, loyalty marketing enables companies to strategically invest sales promotion dollars in activities designed to capture greater profits from customers already loyal to the product or company.[7] One study concluded that if a company retains an additional 5 percent of its customers each year, profits will increase by at least 25 percent. What's more, improving customer retention by a mere 2 percent can decrease costs by as much as 10 percent.[8] R. J. Reynolds Tobacco Company's loyalty program for its Doral brand of cigarettes, for example, has helped the company boost market share of the brand over 6 percent at a time when most cigarette sales were flat.[9]

The objective of loyalty marketing programs is to build long-term, mutually beneficial relationships between a company and its key customers. Frequent-shopper card programs offered by many supermarkets and other retailers have become so popular that about 46 percent of all American households now belong to one, holding an average of 3.2 cards.[10] Through membership, shoppers might receive discounts, recipes, alerts about new products, and other enticing offers. In exchange, retailers are able to build customer databases that help them understand customer preferences.

loyalty marketing program
A promotional program designed to build long-term, mutually beneficial relationships between a company and its key customers.

frequent buyer program
A loyalty program in which loyal consumers are rewarded for making multiple purchases of a particular good or service.

Contests and Sweepstakes Contests and sweepstakes are generally designed to create interest in a good or service, often to encourage brand switching. *Contests* are promotions in which participants use some skill or ability to compete for prizes. A consumer contest usually requires entrants to answer questions, complete sentences, or write a paragraph about the product and submit proof of purchase. Winning a *sweepstakes*, on the other hand, depends on chance or luck, and participation is free. Sweepstakes usually draw about ten times more entries than contests do.

While contests and sweepstakes may draw considerable interest and publicity, generally they are not effective tools for generating long-term sales. To increase their effectiveness, sales promotion managers must make certain that the award will appeal to the target market.[11] For example, Home & Garden Television Network's annual "Dream Home Giveaway" sweepstakes awards one lucky viewer with a fully furnished, custom-built home. The promotion is cosponsored by Sears, which stocks the home with Kenmore appliances, a Craftsman workshop, home fashions, lawn and garden equipment, and home electronics, and General Motors Corporation, which fills the garage with a new sport utility vehicle. The annual sweepstakes typically draws over 4 million entries.[12] Additionally, offering several smaller prizes to many winners instead of one huge prize awarded to just one person will increase the effectiveness of the promotion. To ensure that most people don't go away empty-handed, McDonald's hugely successful Monopoly game awards multiple prizes, including electronics, trips, cars, cash, and thousands of free food prizes, to several people, rather than a single grand prize.

Sweepstakes have been under increased scrutiny by the federal government after several high-profile class action suits charged the industry with unscrupulous promotional practices. Read about this issue in the "Ethics in Marketing" box.

Contests are a long-standing way to attract attention to a product. Guinness beer's essay contest received a response far greater than the company had anticipated and was more successful than any previous promotional campaign.
© John Welzenbach/The Stock Market

NEW SWEEPSTAKES LAW PROTECTS CONSUMERS

Magazine publishers have long relied on sweepstakes promotions through companies like American Family Publishers and Publishers Clearing House to bring in new subscribers. Traditionally, about 25 percent of magazine subscriptions for the top 125 titles come from sweepstakes promotions. Some titles get as much as 50 percent of their new subscriptions from sweepstakes.

Magazine sweepstakes companies often rely on hard-sell pitches to attract sweepstakes entrants and increase magazine subscriptions. For instance, American Family Publishers often used the line "It's down to a two-person race for $11,000,000. You and one other person . . ." on sweepstakes envelopes. The companies sometimes used official-looking documents in their offers that some consumers confused as being official letters notifying them that they had actually won. Ubiquitous pitchman Ed McMahon became synonymous with magazine subscription sweepstakes, lending his credibility to attract thousands of entrants. All in all, the sweepstakes companies' hard-sell tactics and promises of million-dollar prizes spurred thousands of consumers to enter in the hopes that they would be the next winner. Many of these consumers were under the assumption that purchasing magazines increased their chances of winning.

This all changed, however, after two Georgetown University law professors sued American Family Publishers in 1998 over its sweepstakes practices. Florida later became the first state to sue, alleging the company used "unethical, oppressive, unscrupulous" tactics to sell magazine subscriptions. Florida's suit ensued after about 20 sweepstakes contestants flew to Tampa to claim an $11 million jackpot they mistakenly believed they had won. Other suits brought by individuals claim that they sunk hundreds of dollars into magazine subscriptions believing a purchase would increase their chances of winning. Others believed that they had to purchase a magazine just to enter.

As a result, Congress passed the Deceptive Mail Prevention & Enforcement Act to protect consumers against misleading pitches and promises in sweepstakes promotions. The act includes these provisions:

- *Disclosure:* Sweepstakes mailers must say "no purchase is necessary to win" and "a purchase will not improve an individual's chance of winning" three times, on the sweepstakes letter, the order form, and again under a listing of rules. These disclosure statements must be prominently located so they are "clear and conspicuous."
- *Misleading statements:* Statements that imply an individual has already won or could be disqualified from receiving future mailings for not ordering are barred.
- *List purges:* Sweepstakes marketers must list both a toll-free number and an address for consumers to get taken off sweepstakes lists, and then remove anyone calling or writing within thirty-five days.
- *Enforcement:* The U.S. Postal Service has the authority to halt mailings nationally and under some conditions can dispose of mailings that violate the rules. Marketers can be fined up to $2 million for violations.

Industry observers worry that the new legislation will severely hurt magazine subscriptions. Already many magazine titles have seen their sales decline as a result of the negative publicity surrounding the sweepstakes. Softer sales tactics and disclosures will likely decrease the number of people entering the sweepstakes and magazine publishers will have to devise other promotional tools to increase subscriptions. Publishers Clearing House, however, feels that increased disclosure will be positive for the industry by increasing consumer confidence with sweepstakes promotions.[a]

Have you ever entered a sweepstakes? What was your reasoning for doing so? Were you under the impression that purchasing the product would increase your chances of winning?

[a] Erin White, "Sweepstakes Concern Seeks Creditor Shield," *Wall Street Journal*, November 1,1999, p. B8; Ira Teinowitz, "Congress Nears Accord on Sweepstakes Limits," *Advertising Age*, August 9,1999, p. 33; Ira Teinowitz, "Marketers Yield to Sweepstakes Curbs," *Advertising Age*, May 24, 2000, p. 61; "Sweepstakes Legislation Now Law," *Advertising Age*, December 15, 1999.

---

sampling
A promotional program that allows the consumer the opportunity to try a product or service for free.

Sampling Consumers generally perceive a certain amount of risk in trying new products. Many are afraid of trying something they will not like (such as a new food item) or spending too much money and getting little reward. **Sampling** allows the customer to try a product risk-free. Recent research on sampling effectiveness indicates that among those consumers who had never before purchased the product, 71 percent indicated that the free sample would encourage them to try a product. Additionally, 67 percent said they have switched brands because they were satisfied with a free sample.[13]

Sampling can be accomplished by directly mailing the sample to the customer, delivering the sample door to door, packaging the sample with another product, or demonstrating or sampling the product at a retail store. To help position Dunkin' Donuts as more than just a doughnut chain, the company gave away six million free doughnuts for one day to celebrate the retiring of its well-known Fred the Baker spokesman. The offer lured in new and lapsed customers to see how the chain, with some thirty-three hundred U.S. outlets, has evolved from its doughnut roots to a place for bagels, pastries, and specialty coffee drinks.[14]

Sampling at special events is a popular, effective, and high-profile distribution method that permits marketers to piggyback onto fun-based consumer activities—including sporting events, college fests, fairs and festivals, beach events, and chili cook-offs. To help demonstrate Sprint PCS wireless telecommunications products to young adults in Los Angeles, one of the nation's most competitive wireless zones, Sprint hired members of a local high school track team to run alongside Los Angeles Marathon competitors. Runners were able to use a Sprint PCS phone to call friends and family for free at mile 19 of the twenty-six-mile event. Sprint even supplied moviegoers waiting in line at an L.A. theater with free phones to make a call.[15]

Distributing samples to specific location types where consumers regularly meet for a common objective or interest, such as health clubs, churches or doctors' offices, is one of the most efficient methods of sampling. If someone visits a health club regularly, chances are he or she is a good prospect for a health-food product or vitamin supplement. Likewise, patients of doctors who specialize in diabetes management are excellent candidates for trial samples of sugar-free snacks, diagnostic kits, or other diabetes-related products. Additionally, the credibility of their being distributed at the health club or the doctor's office implies a powerful third-party endorsement.[16]

Point-of-Purchase Promotion

Point-of-purchase promotion includes any promotional display set up at the retailer's location to build traffic, advertise the product, or induce impulse buying. Point-of-purchase promotions include shelf "talkers" (signs attached to store shelves), shelf extenders (attachments that extend shelves so products stand out), ads on grocery carts and bags, end-aisle and floor-stand displays, television monitors at supermarket checkout counters, in-store audio messages, and audiovisual displays. One big advantage of point-of-purchase promotion is that it offers manufacturers a captive audience in retail stores. Up to 70 percent of all purchase decisions are made in the store, according to research conducted by the Point-of-Purchase Advertising Institute, with 88 percent of food purchase decisions made in-store.[17] Therefore, point-of-purchase works better for impulse products—those products bought without prior decision by the consumer—than for planned purchases. Fifty-two percent of soft drink sales and 31 percent of chip and snack sales are attributable to in-store point-of-purchase promotions.[18]

> **point-of-purchase display**
> Promotional display set up at the retailer's location to build traffic, advertise the product, or induce impulse buying.

On-line Sales Promotion

On-line sales promotions have been booming in recent years due to the overwhelming popularity of the Internet. Marketers funneled some $926 million into on-line sales promotions in 1999 and expected to spend close to $2 billion in 2000. Sales promotion on the Internet has proved to be more effective and cost-efficient, generating response rates that are three to five times higher than their off-line counterparts.[19] According to a recent survey of marketers, the most effective types of on-line sales promotions are free merchandise, sweepstakes, free shipping with purchases, and coupons.[20]

Eager to boost traffic, Internet retailers have been busy giving away free services or equipment, such as personal computers, to lure consumers not only to

On Line

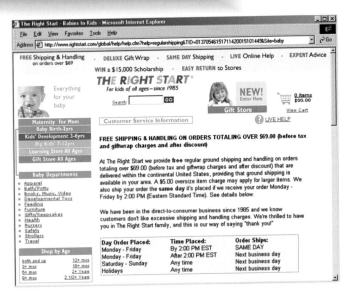

Waiving shipping charges can give Internet retailers an edge over catalogs (which charge shipping) and brick-and-mortar stores (which charge tax). RightStart.com has a very specific free shipping policy. Do you think it motivates consumers to buy from RightStart?

List the most common forms of trade sales promotion

trade allowance
A price reduction offered by manufacturers to intermediaries, such as wholesalers and retailers.

push money
Money offered to channel intermediaries to encourage them to "push" products—that is, to encourage other members of the channel to sell the products.

their own Web site but to the Internet in general. For example, on-line toy retailer RightStart.com waives shipping charges for orders over a certain amount. Wine.com routinely sends e-mail offering discounts on wine purchases to customers on its mailing list. Sega Enterprises gave away free Dreamcast video-game consoles, which list for $199, to customers who subscribed to its new Sega Web service for two years at $21.95 a month. The company is betting the giveaway will spur sales of its game software and help it tap into the expanding community of Internet game players. Sega also hopes to steal customers from market leaders Sony Corporation, which markets the PlayStation 2, and Nintendo.[21]

After several years of declining coupon distribution due to high cost and low redemption rates, many marketers have begun experimenting with distributing coupons on-line. SuperMarkets Online, for instance, operates a Web site where shoppers can print coupons for consumer goods from their home printer. The company has found higher redemption rates of on-line coupons compared to traditional coupons.

On-line versions of loyalty programs are also popping up. At CBS SportsLine's Web site, sports fans are rewarded merely for stopping by. Surfers get points for each page they view which can later be redeemed for sports merchandise, private e-mail messages from sports celebrities, concert and event tickets, and more. Members of its loyalty program, which now total more than 200,000, view twice as many pages on SportsLine's Web site than non-members.[22] Sampling is also available on the Web with sites that allow consumers to register to receive free samples of products in exchange for their feedback.

Tools for Trade Sales Promotion

Whereas consumer promotions *pull* a product through the channel by creating demand, trade promotions *push* a product through the distribution channel (see Chapter 12). When selling to members of the distribution channel, manufacturers use many of the same sales promotion tools used in consumer promotions—such as sales contests, premiums, and point-of-purchase displays. Several tools, however, are unique to manufacturers and intermediaries:

- *Trade allowances:* A **trade allowance** is a price reduction offered by manufacturers to intermediaries such as wholesalers and retailers. The price reduction or rebate is given in exchange for doing something specific, such as allocating space for a new product or buying something during special periods. For example, a local dealer could receive a special discount for running its own promotion on GE telephones.
- *Push money:* Intermediaries receive **push money** as a bonus for pushing the manufacturer's brand through the distribution channel. Often the push money is directed toward a retailer's salespeople. Through its Retail Masters incentive program, cigarette marketer Philip Morris rewards participating retailers with cash payouts based on sales and display of Philip Morris cigarette brands. Retailers earn extra money by restricting displays of competing cigarette brands and offering a free Philip Morris cigarette to smokers of other brands to promote brand switching.[23]
- *Training:* Sometimes a manufacturer will train an intermediary's personnel if the product is rather complex—as frequently occurs in the computer and telecommunication industries. For example, if a large department store pur-

chases an NCR computerized cash register system, NCR may provide free training so the salespeople can learn how to use the new system.

- *Free merchandise:* Often a manufacturer offers retailers free merchandise in lieu of quantity discounts. For example, a breakfast cereal manufacturer may throw in one case of free cereal for every twenty cases ordered by the retailer. Occasionally, free merchandise is used as payment for trade allowances normally provided through other sales promotions. Instead of giving a retailer a price reduction for buying a certain quantity of merchandise, the manufacturer may throw in extra merchandise "free" (that is, at a cost that would equal the price reduction).

- *Store demonstrations:* Manufacturers can also arrange with retailers to perform an in-store demonstration. Food manufacturers often send representatives to grocery stores and supermarkets to let customers sample a product while shopping. Cosmetic companies also send their representatives to department stores to promote their beauty aids by performing facials and makeovers for customers.

- *Business meetings, conventions, and trade shows:* Trade association meetings, conferences, and conventions are an important aspect of sales promotion and a growing, multibillion-dollar market. At these shows, manufacturers, distributors, and other vendors have the chance to display their goods or describe their services to customers and potential customers. The cost per potential customer contacted at a show is estimated to be only 25 to 35 percent that of a personal sales call. Trade shows have been uniquely effective in introducing new products; they can establish products in the marketplace more quickly than can advertising, direct marketing, or sales calls. Companies participate in trade shows to attract and identify new prospects, serve current customers, introduce new products, enhance corporate image, test the market response to new products, enhance corporate morale, and gather competitive product information.

Trade promotions are popular among manufacturers for many reasons. Trade sales promotion tools help manufacturers gain new distributors for their products, obtain wholesaler and retailer support for consumer sales promotions, build or reduce dealer inventories, and improve trade relations. Car manufacturers annually sponsor dozens of auto shows for consumers. Many of the displays feature interactive computer stations where consumers enter vehicle specifications and get a printout of prices and local dealer names. In return, the local car dealers get the names of good prospects. The shows attract millions of consumers, providing dealers with increased store traffic as well as good leads.

Personal Selling

As mentioned in Chapter 15, *personal selling* is direct communication between a sales representative and one or more prospective buyers in an attempt to influence each other in a purchase situation.

In a sense, all businesspeople are salespeople. An individual may become a plant manager, a chemist, an engineer, or a member of any profession and yet still have to sell. During a job search, applicants must "sell" themselves to prospective employers in an interview. To reach the top in most organizations, individuals need to sell ideas to peers, superiors, and subordinates. Most important, people must sell themselves and their ideas to just about everyone with whom they have

Describe personal selling

a continuing relationship and to many other people they see only once or twice. Chances are that students majoring in business or marketing will start their professional careers in sales. Even students in nonbusiness majors may pursue a sales career. Personal selling offers several advantages over other forms of promotion:

- Personal selling provides a detailed explanation or demonstration of the product. This capability is especially needed for complex or new goods and services.
- The sales message can be varied according to the motivations and interests of each prospective customer. Moreover, when the prospect has questions or raises objections, the salesperson is there to provide explanations. In contrast, advertising and sales promotion can only respond to the objections the copywriter thinks are important to customers.
- Personal selling can be directed only to qualified prospects. Other forms of promotion include some unavoidable waste because many people in the audience are not prospective customers.
- Personal selling costs can be controlled by adjusting the size of the sales force (and resulting expenses) in one-person increments. On the other hand, advertising and sales promotion must often be purchased in fairly large amounts.
- Perhaps the most important advantage is that personal selling is considerably more effective than other forms of promotion in obtaining a sale and gaining a satisfied customer.

Personal selling might work better than other forms of promotion given certain customer and product characteristics. Generally speaking, personal selling becomes more important as the number of potential customers decreases, as the complexity of the product increases, and as the value of the product grows (see Exhibit 16.2). When there are relatively few potential customers and the value of the good or service is relatively sufficient, the time and travel costs of personally visiting each prospect are justifiable. For highly complex goods, such as business jets or private communication systems, a salesperson is needed to determine the prospective customer's needs, explain the product's basic advantages, and propose the exact features and accessories that will meet the client's needs.

Relationship Selling

Discuss the key differences between relationship selling and traditional selling

Until recently, marketing theory and practice concerning personal selling focused almost entirely on a planned presentation to prospective customers for the sole purpose of making the sale. Marketers were most concerned with making a one-time sale and then moving on to the next prospect. Whether it took place face-to-face during a personal sales call or by selling over the telephone (telemarketing), traditional personal selling methods attempted to persuade the buyer to accept a point of view or convince the buyer to take some action. Once the customer was

Exhibit 16.2

Comparison of Personal Selling and Advertising/Sales Promotion

Personal selling is more important if . . .	Advertising and sales promotion are more important if . . .
The product has a high value.	The product has a low value.
It is a custom-made product.	It is a standardized product.
There are few customers.	There are many customers.
The product is technically complex.	The product is simple to understand.
Customers are concentrated.	Customers are geographically dispersed.
Examples: insurance policies, custom windows, airplane engines	**Examples:** soap, magazine subscriptions, cotton T-shirts

somewhat convinced, then the sales-person used a variety of techniques in an attempt to elicit a purchase. Frequently, the objectives of the salesperson were at the expense of the buyer, creating a win-lose outcome.[24] Although this type of sales approach has not disappeared entirely, it is being used less and less often by professional salespeople.

In contrast, modern views of personal selling emphasize the relationship that develops between a salesperson and a buyer. **Relationship selling**, or **consultative selling**, is a multistage process that emphasizes personalization and empathy as key ingredients in identifying prospects and developing them as long-term, satisfied customers. The focus is on building mutual trust between the buyer and seller with the delivery of anticipated, long-term, value-added benefits to the buyer.[25] Relationship or consultative salespeople, therefore, become consultants, partners, and problem solvers for their customers. They strive to build long-term relationships with key accounts by developing trust over time. The focus shifts from a one-time sale to a long-term relationship in which the salesperson works with the customer to develop solutions for enhancing the customer's bottom line. Thus, relationship selling emphasizes a win-win outcome.[26]

The end result of relationship selling tends to be loyal customers who purchase from the company time after time. A relationship selling strategy focused on retaining customers costs a company less than if it were constantly prospecting and selling to new customers. One consulting firm estimates that if a small to midsize company were to increase its customer retention rate by just 5 percent, its profits would double in about ten years. Further, the average Fortune 500 company could instantly double its revenue growth with that same 5 percent boost in retention.[27]

Relationship selling is more typical with selling situations for industrial-type goods, such as heavy machinery or computer systems, and services, such as airlines and insurance, than for consumer goods. For example, Kinko's built a long-term business relationship with PeopleSoft. The software maker now gives much of its training and education materials printing jobs to Kinko's a deal worth close to $5 million in revenues. Through the close relationship it has forged with the company, Kinko's representatives are even invited to sit in on internal planning meetings in PeopleSoft's human resources department at the company's headquarters.[28]

Exhibit 16.3 lists the key differences between traditional personal selling and relationship or consultative selling. These differences will become more apparent as we explore the personal selling process later in the chapter.

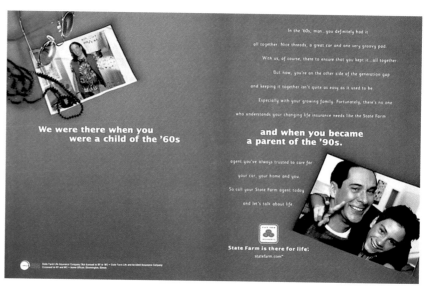

Relationship selling emphasizes personalization and empathy in the process of developing long-term customers. This ad for State Farm showcases the commitment of the company to its customers throughout their various life stages.

relationship selling (consultative selling)
A sales practice that involves building, maintaining, and enhancing interactions with customers in order to develop long-term satisfaction through mutually beneficial partnerships.

Steps in the Selling Process

Although personal selling may sound like a relatively simple task, completing a sale actually requires several steps. The **sales process**, or **sales cycle**, is simply the set of steps a salesperson goes through to sell a particular product or service. The sales process or cycle can be unique for each product or service, depending on the features of the product or service, characteristics of customer segments, and internal processes in place within the firm, such as how leads are gathered.

List the steps in the selling process

sales process (sales cycle)
The set of steps a salesperson goes through in a particular organization to sell a particular product or service.

Exhibit 16.3

Key Differences Between Traditional Selling and Relationship Selling

Traditional Personal Selling	Relationship or Consultative Selling
Sell products (goods and services)	Sell advice, assistance, and counsel
Focus on closing sales	Focus on improving the customer's bottom line
Limited sales planning	Consider sales planning as top priority
Spend most contact time telling customers about product	Spend most contact time attempting to build a problem-solving environment with the customer
Conduct "product-specific" needs assessment	Conduct discovery in the full scope of the customer's operations
"Lone wolf" approach to the account	Team approach to the account
Proposals and presentations based on pricing and product features	Proposals and presentations based on profit-impact and strategic benefits to the customer
Sales follow-up is short term, focused on product delivery	Sales follow-up is long term, focused on long-term relationship enhancement

SOURCE: Robert M. Peterson, Patrick L. Schul, and George H. Lucas, Jr., "Consultative Selling: Walking the Walk in the New Selling Environment," National Conference on Sales Management, *Proceedings*, March 1996.

Some sales take only a few minutes, but others may take months or years to complete, especially when selling customized goods or services. The typical sale for Eastman Kodak's line of high-speed motion analysis cameras takes anywhere from nine to eighteen months to close.[29] On the other end of the spectrum, sales of its more basic cameras to retailers are generally more routine and may take only a few days. Whether a salesperson spends a few minutes or a few years on a sale, these are the seven basic steps in the personal selling process:

1. Generating leads
2. Qualifying leads
3. Approaching the customer and probing needs
4. Developing and proposing solutions
5. Handling objections
6. Closing the sale
7. Following up

Like other forms of promotion, these steps of selling follow the AIDA concept discussed in Chapter 14. Once a salesperson has located a prospect with the authority to buy, he or she tries to get the prospect's attention. A thorough needs assessment turned into an effective sales proposal and presentation should generate interest. After developing the customer's initial desire (preferably during the presentation of the sales proposal), the salesperson seeks action in the close by trying to get an agreement to buy. Follow-up after the sale, the final step in the selling process, not only lowers cognitive dissonance (refer to Chapter 5) but also may open up opportunities to discuss future sales. Effective follow-up will also lead to repeat business in which the process may start all over again at the needs assessment step.

Traditional selling and relationship selling follow the same basic steps. What is different between the two selling methods is the relative importance placed on key steps in the process (see Exhibit 16.4). Traditional selling efforts are transaction oriented, focusing on generating as many leads as possible, making as many presentations as possible, and closing as many sales as possible. Minimal effort is placed on asking questions to identify customer needs and wants or matching these needs and wants to the benefits of the product or service. In contrast, the salesperson practicing relationship selling emphasizes an up-front investment in the time and effort needed to uncover each customer's specific needs and wants and matching to them, as closely as possible, the product or service offering. By doing the homework up front, the salesperson creates the conditions necessary for a relatively straightforward close.[30] Let's look at each step of the selling process individually.

Generating Leads

Initial groundwork must precede communication between the potential buyer and the salesperson. **Lead generation**, or **prospecting**, is the identification of those firms and people most likely to buy the seller's offerings. These firms or people become "sales leads" or "prospects."

Sales leads can be secured in several different ways, most notably through advertising, trade shows and conventions, or direct-mail and telemarketing programs. Favorable publicity also helps to create leads. Company records of past client purchases are another excellent source of leads. Many sales professionals are also securing valuable leads from their firm's Internet Web site. Sales managers predict that over half of all sales leads will come from the Internet in the future.[31]

lead generation (prospecting)
Identification of those firms and people most likely to buy the seller's offerings.

Exhibit 16.4

Relative Amount of Time Spent in Key Steps of the Selling Process

Key Selling Steps	Traditional Selling	Relationship/Consultative Selling
Generating leads	High	Low
Qualifying leads	Low	High
Approaching the customer and probing needs	Low	High
Developing and proposing solutions	Low	High
Handling objections	High	Low
Closing the sale	High	Low
Following up	Low	High

referral
A recommendation to a salesperson from a customer or business associate.

networking
A process of finding out about potential clients from friends, business contacts, coworkers, acquaintances, and fellow members in professional and civic organizations.

cold calling
A form of lead generation in which the salesperson approaches potential buyers without any prior knowledge of the prospects' needs or financial status.

lead qualification
Determination of a sales prospect's (1) recognized need, (2) buying power, and (3) receptivity and accessibility.

Another way to gather a lead is through a **referral**—a recommendation from a customer or business associate. The advantages of referrals over other forms of prospecting include highly qualified leads, higher closing rates, larger initial transactions, and shorter sales cycles. Simply put, the salesperson and the company can earn more money in less time when prospecting using referrals. To increase the number of referrals they receive, some companies even pay or send small gifts to customers or suppliers who provide referrals. Research has suggested that one referral is as valuable as up to twelve cold calls. However, although 80 percent of clients would be willing to give referrals, only 20 percent are ever asked.[32]

Networking is the related method of using friends, business contacts, coworkers, acquaintances, and fellow members in professional and civic organizations to find out about potential clients. Salespeople for BKM Total Office, an office furniture supplier in San Diego, regularly visit with local architects and designers who build new office space in the area. They also network with people in other industries, such as telecommunications. If a company is buying a new phone system for a facility, for example, it's likely they may need office furniture as well.[33]

Before the advent of more sophisticated methods of lead generation, such as direct mail and telemarketing, most prospecting was done through **cold calling**—a form of lead generation in which the salesperson approaches potential buyers without any prior knowledge of the prospects' needs or financial status. Although this method is still used, many sales managers have realized the inefficiencies of having their top salespeople use their valuable selling time searching for the proverbial "needle in a haystack." Passing the job of cold calling to a lower-cost employee, such as a sales support person, allows salespeople to spend more of their time and use their relationship-building skills on prospects that have already been identified.[34]

Qualifying Leads

When a prospect shows interest in learning more about a product, the salesperson has the opportunity to follow up, or qualify, the lead. Personally visiting unqualified prospects wastes valuable salesperson time and company resources. Often many leads go unanswered because salespeople are given no indication as to how qualified the leads are in terms of interest and ability to purchase. One study that surveyed 400 marketers whose companies advertise in trade publications found that almost 40 percent of the leads generated went completely unanswered, most likely due to the fact that they were unqualified.[35]

Lead qualification consists of determining whether the prospect has three things:[36]

- *A recognized need:* The most basic criterion for determining whether or not someone is a prospect for a product is a need that is not being satisfied. The salesperson should first consider prospects who are aware of a need but should not discount prospects who have not yet recognized that they have one. With a little more information about the product, they may decide they do have a need for it. Preliminary interviews and questioning can often provide the salesperson with enough information to determine whether there is a need.
- *Buying power:* Buying power involves both authority to make the purchase decision and access to funds to pay for it. To avoid wasting time and money, the salesperson needs to identify the purchasing authority and the ability to pay before making a presentation. Organizational charts and information about a firm's credit standing can provide valuable clues.

- *Receptivity and accessibility:* The prospect must be willing to see the salesperson and be accessible to the salesperson. Some prospects simply refuse to see salespeople. Others, because of their stature in their organization, will only see a salesperson or sales manager with similar stature.

Often the task of lead qualification is handled by a telemarketing group or a sales support person who *prequalifies* the lead for the salesperson. Prequalification systems free sales representatives from the time-consuming task of following up on leads to determine need, buying power, and receptiveness. Prequalification systems may even set up initial appointments with the prospect for the salesperson. The result is more time for the sales force to spend in front of interested customers. Macromedia, a San Francisco-based software company, recently implemented a comprehensive, automated lead-management system that allows it to track leads from inception to close. Leads gathered are qualified by phone, fax, or on the Internet. Based on this information, the system assigns each lead a grade and priority status and then directs it to the appropriate salesperson. The system continues to track the leads in order to create sales and manufacturing forecasts. And when a sale is closed it allows management to evaluate return on investment for its different lead-generation programs.[37]

With more and more companies setting up Web sites on the Internet, qualifying on-line leads has also received some attention. The object of a company's Web site should be to get visitors to register, indicate what products they are interested in, and offer up some information on their time frame and resources. Leads from the Internet can then be prioritized (those indicating a short time frame, for instance, given a higher priority) and then transferred to salespeople. Often Web site visitors can be enticed to answer questions with offers of free merchandise or information. Enticing visitors to register also allows companies to customize future electronic interactions—for example, by giving prospects who visit the Web site their choice from a menu of products tailored specifically to their needs.[38]

Approaching the Customer and Probing Needs

Prior to approaching the customer, the salesperson should learn as much as possible about the prospect's organization and its buyers. This process, called the **preapproach**, describes the "homework" that must be done by the salesperson before contacting the prospect. This may include consulting standard reference sources, such as Moody's, Standard & Poor's, or Dun & Bradstreet, or contacting acquaintances or others who may have information about the prospect. Another preapproach task is to determine whether the actual approach should be a personal visit, a phone call, a letter, or some other form of communication.

During the sales approach, the salesperson either talks to the prospect or secures an appointment for a future time in which to probe the prospect further as to his or her needs. Relationship selling theorists suggest that salespeople should begin developing mutual trust with their prospect during the approach. Salespeople should use the approach as a way of introducing themselves and their company and products. They must sell themselves before they can sell the product. Small talk that introduces sincerity and some suggestion of friendship is encouraged to build rapport with the prospect, but remarks that could be construed as insincere should be avoided.[39]

It can be a challenge to cull information from Web site visitors, but Levenger.com has quite a detailed registration page. Visit the site to determine if you would be willing to provide all of the information requested.

preapproach
A process that describes the "homework" that must be done by a salesperson before he or she contacts a prospect.

needs assessment
A determination of the customer's specific needs and wants and the range of options a customer has for satisfying them.

The salesperson's ultimate goal during the approach is to conduct a **needs assessment** to find out as much as possible about the prospect's situation. This involves interviewing the customer to determine his or her specific needs and wants and the range of options the customer has for satisfying them. The salesperson should be determining how to maximize the fit between what he or she can offer and what the prospective customer wants. As part of the needs assessment, the consultative salesperson must know everything there is to know about the following:[40]

- *The product or service:* Product knowledge is the cornerstone for conducting a successful needs analysis. The consultative salesperson must be an expert on his or her product or service, including technical specifications, the product's features and benefits, pricing and billing procedures, warranty and service support, performance comparisons with the competition, other customers' experiences with the product, and current advertising and promotional campaign messages.
- *Customers and their needs:* The salesperson should know more about customers than they know about themselves. That's the secret to relationship and consultative selling, where the salesperson acts not only as a supplier of products and services but also as a trusted consultant and advisor. The professional sales-person doesn't just sell products. He or she brings to each client business-building ideas and solutions to problems. For the customer, consulting a professional salesperson is like having another vital person on the team at no cost.
- *The competition:* The salesperson must know as much about the competitor's company and products as he or she knows about his or her own company. *Competitive intelligence* includes many factors: who the competitors are and what is known about them; how their products and services compare; advantages and disadvantages; and strengths and weaknesses.
- *The industry:* Knowing the industry involves active research on the part of the salesperson. This means attending industry and trade association meetings, reading articles published in industry and trade journals, keeping track of legislation and regulation that affect the industry, awareness of product alternatives and innovations from domestic and foreign competition, and having a feel for economic and financial conditions that may impact the industry.

Creating a *customer profile* during the approach helps salespeople optimize their time and resources. This profile is then used to help develop an intelligent analysis of the prospect's needs in preparation for the next step, developing and proposing solutions. Customer profile information is typically stored and manipulated using sales force automation software packages designed for use on laptop computers. Sales force automation software provides sales reps with a computerized and efficient method of collecting customer information for use during the entire sales process. Further, customer and sales data stored in a computer database can be easily shared among sales team members. The information can also be appended with industry statistics, sales or meeting notes, billing data, and other information that may be pertinent to the prospect or the prospect's company. The more salespeople know about their prospects, the better they can meet their needs.

Salespeople should wrap up their sales approach and need-probing mission by summarizing the prospect's need, problem, and interest. The salesperson should also get a commitment from the customer to some kind of action, whether it's reading promotional material or agreeing to a demonstration. This commitment helps qualify the prospect further and justify additional time invested by the salesperson. The salesperson should reiterate the action he or she promises to take, such as sending information or calling back to provide answers to questions. The date and time of the next call should be set at the conclusion of the sales approach as well as an agenda for the next call in terms of what the salesperson hopes to accomplish, such as providing a demonstration or presenting a solution.[41]

Developing and Proposing Solutions

Once the salesperson has gathered the appropriate information about the client's needs and wants, the next step is to determine whether his or her company's products or services match the needs of the prospective customer. The salesperson then develops a solution, or possibly several solutions, in which the salesperson's product or service solves the client's problems or meets a specific need.

These solutions are typically presented to the client in the form of a sales proposal presented at a sales presentation. A **sales proposal** is a written document or professional presentation that outlines how the company's product or service will meet or exceed the client's needs. The **sales presentation** is the formal meeting in which the salesperson has the opportunity to present the sales proposal. The presentation should be explicitly tied to the prospect's expressed needs. Further, the prospect should be involved in the presentation by being encouraged to participate in demonstrations or by exposure to computer exercises, slides, video or audio, flipcharts, photographs, and so on.[42]

Technology has become an important part of presenting solutions for many salespeople. Salespeople for Dell Computer Corporation, for example, don't just tell potential clients how much money they will save if they buy Dell PCs, they prove it. Through a sophisticated software program called Product Expert, Dell's corporate account reps show clients how much it will cost to buy, deploy, and maintain a Dell PC over its lifetime. The software, which reps download onto their laptop PCs before going on a sales call, allows the client to plug in variables specific to their business, such as how many employees use PCs, how many desktop units are purchased annually, what their integration needs are, and how much technical support is required. After manipulating and tallying the data, clients can then print out an executive summary. Because the savings information is presented to clients in a tangible format, the software is now an integral part of Dell's sales proposals.[43]

Because the salesperson often has only one opportunity to present solutions, the quality of both the sales proposal and presentation can make or break the sale. Salespeople must be able to present the proposal and handle any customer objections confidently and professionally. For a powerful presentation, salespeople should be well prepared, rehearse what they are going to say, use direct eye contact, ask open-ended questions, and be poised. Nothing dies faster than a boring presentation. Salespeople should add energy to the presentation through gestures, voice inflection, and speaking forcefully.[44] If the salesperson doesn't have a convincing and confident manner, then the prospect will very often forget the information. Prospects take in body language, voice patterns, dress, and body type. Often customers are more likely to remember how salespeople present themselves than what salespeople say.

Handling Objections

Rarely does a prospect say "I'll buy it" right after a presentation. Often there are objections raised or perhaps questions about the proposal and the product. The potential buyer may insist that the price is too high, that he or she does not have enough information to make a decision, or that the good or service will not satisfy the present need. The buyer may also lack confidence in the seller's organization or product.

One of the first lessons that every salesperson learns is that objections to the product should not be taken personally as confrontations or insults. Rather, a salesperson should view objections as requests for information. A good salesperson considers objections a legitimate part of the purchase decision. To handle objections effectively, the salesperson should anticipate specific objections such as concerns about price, fully investigate the objection with the customer, be wary of what the competition is offering, and, above all, stay calm. Before a crucial sales presentation with an important prospect, for example, Dell Computer salespeople

sales proposal
A formal written document or professional presentation that outlines how the salesperson's product or service will meet or exceed the prospect's needs.

sales presentation
A formal meeting in which the salesperson presents a sales proposal to a prospective buyer.

anticipated that the customer would have doubts that Dell's direct selling model would provide them with the same level of service and dedication they could get from a reseller. Being prepared helped Dell win the contract.[45]

Often, the salesperson can use the objection to close the sale. If the customer tries to pit suppliers against each other to drive down the price, the salesperson should be prepared to point out weaknesses in the competitor's offer and stand by the quality in his or her own proposal.[46]

Closing the Sale

At the end of the presentation, the salesperson should ask the customer how he or she would like to proceed. If the customer exhibits signs that he or she is ready to purchase and all questions have been answered and objections have been met, then the salesperson can try to close the sale. Customers often give signals during or after the presentation that they are ready to buy or are not interested. Examples include changes in facial expressions, gestures, and questions asked. The salesperson should look for these signals and respond appropriately.

Closing requires courage and skill. Naturally, the salesperson wants to avoid rejection, and asking for a sale carries with it the risk of a negative answer. A salesperson should keep an open mind when asking for the sale and be prepared for either a yes or a no. Rarely is a sale closed on the first call. In fact, the typical salesperson averages about 765 sales calls a year, many of which are repeat calls to the same client in an attempt to make the sale.[47] Some salespeople may negotiate with large accounts for several years before closing a sale. As you can see, building a good relationship with the customer is very important. Often, if the salesperson has developed a strong relationship with the customer, only minimal efforts are needed to close a sale.

negotiation
The process during which both the salesperson and the prospect offer special concessions in an attempt to arrive at a sales agreement.

Negotiation often plays a key role in the closing of the sale. **Negotiation** is the process during which both the salesperson and the prospect offer special concessions in an attempt to arrive at a sales agreement. For example, the salesperson may offer a price cut, free installation, free service, or a trial order. Effective negotiators, however, avoid using price as a negotiation tool because cutting price directly affects a company's profitability. Because companies spend millions on advertising and product development to create value, when salespeople give in to price negotiations too quickly, it decreases the value of the product. Instead, effective salespeople should emphasize value to the customer, rendering price a nonissue. Salespeople should also be prepared to ask for trade-offs and try to avoid giving unilateral concessions. If the customer asks for a 5 percent discount, the salesperson should be ready with what to ask for in return, such as more volume or flexibility with a delivery schedule.[48]

More and more U.S. companies are expanding their marketing and selling efforts into global markets. Salespeople selling in foreign markets should tailor their presentation and closing styles to each market. Different personalities and skills will be successful in some countries and absolute failures in others. For instance, if a salesperson is an excellent closer and always focused on the next sale, doing business in Latin America might be difficult. The reason is that in Latin America people want to take a long time building a personal relationship with their suppliers.[49] Read about other global dos and don'ts of selling in the "Global Perspectives" box.

Following Up

follow-up
The final step of the selling process, in which the salesperson ensures that delivery schedules are met, that the goods or services perform as promised, and that the buyers' employees are properly trained to use the products.

Unfortunately, many salespeople hold the attitude that making the sale is all that's important. Once the sale is made, they can forget about their customers. They are wrong. Salespeople's responsibilities do not end with making the sales and placing the orders. One of the most important aspects of their jobs is **follow-up**—the final step in the delivery process, in which they must ensure that delivery schedules are met, that the goods or services perform as promised, and that the buyers' employees are properly trained to use the products.

GLOBAL DOS AND DON'TS IN SELLING

Most large companies with operations on foreign soil are employing locals to sell their products—international buyers are often cold to Americans trying to peddle their wares. So the Americans who find themselves trying to sell internationally had better be prepared.

Most selling skills that are successful in America also will work overseas. However, knowing how to act in certain cultures can be the difference between closing the deal and losing a customer. There are certain things Americans take for granted that could easily cost them a deal overseas. A simple thumbs-up sign that we give everyday could offend a customer in another country. Here, from many international business experts, are some things to watch out for in certain countries and regions around the world.

- **Arab Countries:** Don't use your left hand to hold, offer, or receive materials because Arabs use their left hand to touch toilet paper. If you must use your left hand to write, apologize for doing so. Handshakes in Arab countries are a bit limp and last longer than typical American handshakes.
- **China:** Never talk business on the first meeting—it's disrespectful. Don't refuse tea during a business discussion. Always drink it, even if you're offered a dozen cups a day. Never begin to eat or drink before your host does. Also, printed materials presented to Chinese business leaders should be in black and white, because colors have great significance for the Chinese. The Chinese tend to be extremely meticulous, looking to create long-term relationships with a supplier before agreeing to buy anything. Chinese are more intradependent and tend to include more people in on a deal. Most deals in

China are finalized in a social setting, either over drinks or dinner. Additionally, getting to know the businessperson's family will personalize and strengthen the relationship.
- **European Countries:** Western and Eastern Europeans reshake hands whenever they're apart for even a short period of time, for example, lunch.
- **France:** Don't schedule a breakfast meeting—the French tend not to meet until after 10 A.M. Since the French knowledge of wine is far greater than that of most Americans, avoid giving wine or wine-related gifts to French clients. The French also prefer gifts that are of French origin.
- **Germany:** Don't address a business associate by his or her first name, even if you've known each other for years. Always wait for an invitation to do so. Also, breakfast meetings are unheard of here, too. Salespeople should expect a sober, rigid business climate and negotiations that lack flexibility and compromise.
- **Central and South America:** People here don't take the clock too seriously—scheduling more than two appointments in one day can prove disastrous. Latin Americans also tend to use a lighter, lingering handshake. Negotiations with Central and South American customers typically include a great deal of bargaining. Personal relationships are also important in Central and South America, so salespeople should make face-to-face contact with their clients during meetings and presentations.
- **Japan:** Don't bring up business on the golf course—always wait for your host to take the initiative. Don't cross your legs in Japan—showing the bottom of the foot is insulting. Japanese businesspeople shake hands

with one firm gesture combined with a slight bow, which should be returned. Japanese prefer gifts from well-known American stores, such as Tiffany's or Saks Fifth Avenue. Also, the higher the position of the recipient, the more elaborately wrapped the gift should be.
- **Mexico:** Don't send a bouquet of red or yellow flowers as a gift—Mexicans associate those colors with evil spirits and death. Instead, send a box of premium chocolates. Including a small gift for the client's children creates a positive impression.
- **Vietnam:** When meeting a Vietnamese woman, wait for her to extend a hand first—she may simply nod or bow slightly, the most common form of greeting in Vietnam. Vietnamese do not like to be touched or patted on the back or shoulders in social situations.
- **Miscellaneous:** The thumbs-up gesture is considered offensive in the Middle East, rude in Australia, and a sign of "OK" in France. It's rude to cross your arms while facing someone in Turkey. In the Middle East don't ask, "How's the family?"—it's considered too personal. In most Asian countries, staring directly into a person's eyes is considered discourteous.[a]

[a] Andy Cohen, "Global Dos and Don'ts," *Sales & Marketing Management*, June 1996, p. 72; Esmond D. Smith, Jr., and Cuong Pham, "Doing Business in Vietnam: A Cultural Guide," *Business Horizons*, May–June 1996, pp. 47–51; "Five Tips for International Handshaking," *Sales & Marketing Management*, July 1997, p. 90, from Dorothea Johnson, director of The Protocol School of Washington; Tricia Campbell, "What to Give Overseas," *Sales & Marketing Management*, September 1997, p. 85; "Negotiating: Getting to Yes, Chinese-Style," *Sales & Marketing Management*, July 1996, pp. 44–45; Michelle Marchetti, "Selling in China? Go Slowly," *Sales & Marketing Management*, January 1997, pp. 35–36; Sergey Frank, "Global Negotiating: Vive Les Différences!" *Sales & Marketing Management*, May 1992, pp. 64–69.

Whereas the traditional sales approach's extent of follow-up with the customer is generally limited to successful product delivery and performance, a basic goal of relationship selling is to motivate customers to come back, again and again, by developing and nurturing long-term relationships. Most businesses depend on repeat sales, and repeat sales depend on thorough and continued follow-up by the salesperson. Finding a new customer is far more expensive than retaining an existing customer. When customers feel abandoned, cognitive dissonance arises and repeat sales decline. Today this issue is more pertinent than ever, because customers are far less loyal to brands and vendors. Buyers are more inclined to look for the best deal, especially in the case of poor after-the-sale follow-up. More and more buyers favor building a relationship with sellers.

 Dell Computer Corporation is one company that is committed to enhancing its customers' satisfaction through effective follow-up and customer support. Dell developed an extensive extranet system, called Premier Pages, that is designed to give Dell's contract customers product, pricing, and service information at the touch of a mouse. Each Dell customer gets its own password-protected Premier Page found at an unlisted URL on the Web. Access includes product information, pricing structures, an employee-purchase plan (which gives customers' employees discounts on Dell products bought for personal use), on-line product ordering, and up-to-date purchase-history reports. The costs to Dell have been justified in customer satisfaction alone. One customer estimated saving $2 million on technical support costs thanks to Premier Pages. Another customer reported that it redeployed most of its procurement people and uses the remaining ones more efficiently.[50]

Sales Management

⑦

Describe the functions of sales management

There is an old adage in business that nothing happens until a sale is made. Without sales there is no need for accountants, production workers, or even a company president. Sales provide the fuel that keeps the corporate engines humming. Companies like Cisco Systems, International Paper, and Johnson Controls, and several thousand other manufacturers would cease to exist without successful salespeople. Even companies like Procter & Gamble and Kraft General Foods that mainly sell consumer goods and use extensive advertising campaigns still rely on salespeople to move products through the channel of distribution. Thus sales management is one of marketing's most critical specialties. Effective sales management stems from a highly success oriented sales force that accomplishes its mission economically and efficiently. Poor sales management can lead to unmet profit objectives or even to the downfall of the corporation.

Just as selling is a personal relationship, so is sales management. Although the sales manager's basic job is to maximize sales at a reasonable cost while also maximizing profits, he or she also has many other important responsibilities and decisions:

1. Defining sales goals and the sales process
2. Determining the sales force structure
3. Recruiting and training the sales force
4. Compensating and motivating the sales force
5. Evaluating the sales force

Defining Sales Goals and the Sales Process

Effective sales management begins with a determination of sales goals. Without goals to achieve, salesperson performance would be mediocre at best, and the company would likely fail. Like any marketing objective, sales goals should be stated in clear, precise, and measurable terms and should always specify a time frame for their fulfillment. Overall sales force goals are usually stated in terms of desired dollar sales volume, market share, or profit level. For example, a life insurance company may have a goal to sell $50 million in life insurance policies annually, to attain a 12 percent market share, or to achieve $1 million in profits. Individual salespeople are also assigned goals in the form of quotas. A **quota** is simply a statement of the salesperson's sales goals, usually based on sales volume alone but sometimes including key accounts (those with greatest potential), new accounts, repeat sales, and specific products.

Great sales managers focus not only on sales goals but also on the entire process that drives their sales organizations to reach those goals. Without a keen understanding of the sales process, a manager will never be successful—no matter how defined the sales goals or how great the sales reps. An important responsibility of the sales manager, therefore, is to determine the most effective and efficient sales process to follow in selling each different product and service. Although the basic steps of the sales process are the same as discussed earlier in the chapter (i.e., lead generation and qualification, approach and needs assessment, proposal creation and presentation, handling objections, closing, and follow-up), a manager must formally define the specific procedures salespeople go through to do their jobs—for example, where leads are generated, how they are qualified, what the best way is to approach potential clients, and what terms can be negotiated during closing. Like Kinko's, discussed in the chapter's opening story, Enron Energy Services, a division of energy giant Enron Corporation, is one company that has developed an effective sales process for its sales organizations. With a sales cycle that often stretches out to a year, Enron's reps need a process to follow so they remain constantly focused on their high-level accounts. The first step in Enron's sales process begins even before a salesperson calls on a prospective customer for its energy services. Salespeople must first qualify prospects according to several criteria, such as whether a company has centralized decision-making and whether they use enough energy to need Enron as a supplier. When an Enron rep finally calls on customers, he or she already knows a good deal about them.[51]

Determining the Sales Force Structure

Because personal selling is so costly, no sales department can afford to be disorganized. Proper design helps the sales manager organize and delegate sales duties and provide direction for salespeople. Sales departments are most commonly organized by geographic regions, by product line, by marketing function performed (such as account development or account maintenance), by market or industry, or by individual client or account. The sales force for IBM could be organized into sales territories covering New England, the Midwest, the South, and the West Coast or could be organized into distinct groups selling personal computer systems and mainframe computer systems. IBM salespeople may also be assigned to a specific industry or market, for example, the telecommunications industry, or to key clients such as AT&T and MCI.

Market- or industry-based structures and key account structures are gaining popularity in today's competitive selling environment, especially with the emphasis on relationship selling. Being familiar with one industry or market allows sales reps to become experts in their fields and thereby offer better solutions and service. Further, by organizing the sales force around specific customers, many companies hope to improve customer service, encourage collaboration with other arms of the company, and unite salespeople in customer-focused sales teams. Internet advertising solutions company DoubleClick, for example, realigned its 175 salespeople into six vertical industry channels: automotive, business, entertainment and youth, technology, women and health, and travel. Previously, DoubleClick salespeople sold Internet ad space in a variety of different categories. Now salespeople can focus on one category, get a better understanding of the sites

quota
A statement of the individual salesperson's sales objectives, usually based on sales volume alone but sometimes including key accounts (those with greatest potential), new accounts, repeat sales, and specific products.

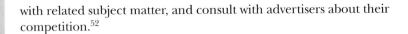
with related subject matter, and consult with advertisers about their competition.[52]

Recruiting and Training the Sales Force

Sales force recruitment should be based on an accurate, detailed description of the sales task as defined by the sales manager. Aside from the usual characteristics such as level of experience or education, what traits should sales managers look for in applicants? One of the most important traits of top performers is ego strength, or having a strong, healthy self-esteem and the ability to bounce back from rejection. Great salespeople also have a sense of urgency and competitiveness that pushes their sales to completion. Moreover, they have a desire to persuade people and close the sale. Effective salespeople are also assertive; they have the ability to be firm in one-to-one negotiations, to lead the sales process, and to get their point across confidently, without being overbearing or aggressive. They are sociable, willing to take risks, and capable of understanding complex concepts and ideas. Additionally, great salespeople are creative in developing client solutions, and they possess empathy—the ability to place oneself in someone else's shoes. Not surprisingly, in a recent study of top salespeople, almost 95 percent claim their sales style is relationship-oriented rather than transaction-oriented.[53]

Ongoing training is the key to a successful sales force. Training helps to refresh old skills and to hone interpersonal and communication skills.

After the sales recruit has been hired and given a brief orientation, training begins. A new salesperson generally receives instruction in company policies and practices, selling techniques, product knowledge, industry and customer characteristics, and nonselling duties such as filling out sales and market information reports or using a sales automation computer program. Firms that sell complex products generally offer the most extensive training programs. Pharmaceutical giant Merck, for example, takes a highly scientific approach to its market and trains its reps to understand the science of the medicine it sells so that they can maintain a peer-to-peer discussion with the physicians they call upon.[54]

Most successful sales organizations have learned that training is not just for newly hired salespeople. Instead, training is offered to all salespeople in an ongoing effort to hone selling skills and relationship building. In pursuit of solid salesperson-client relationships, training programs now seek to improve salespeople's consultative selling and listening skills and to broaden their product and customer knowledge. In addition, training programs stress the interpersonal skills needed to become the contact person for customers. Because negotiation is increasingly important in closing a sale, salespeople are also trained to negotiate effectively without risking profits. Financial services firm Charles Schwab, for instance, developed an ongoing education program, called LEAP (Learning for Excellence in Advice and Professionalism), which includes a curriculum of Web and classroom courses and a series of off-site workshops for salespeople at different stages of their professional development. Because its salespeople offer customers financial advice, the company wants to make sure that its entire sales force is educated to give their clients unbiased information.[55]

Compensating and Motivating the Sales Force

Compensation planning is one of the sales manager's toughest jobs. Only good planning will ensure that compensation attracts, motivates, and retains good salespeople. Generally, companies and industries with lower levels of compensation suffer higher turnover rates, which increases costs and decreases effectiveness.

Therefore, compensation needs to be competitive enough to attract and motivate the best salespeople. Firms sometimes take profit into account when developing their compensation plans. Instead of paying salespeople on overall volume, they pay according to the profitability achieved from selling each product. Still other companies tie a part of the salesperson's total compensation to customer satisfaction assessed through periodic customer surveys.

The three basic compensation methods for salespeople are commission, salary, and combination plans. A typical commission plan gives salespeople a specified percentage of their sales revenue. A **straight commission** system compensates the salesperson only when a sale is made. On the other end of the spectrum, a **straight salary** system compensates a salesperson with a stated salary regardless of sales productivity. Most companies, however, offer a compromise between straight commission and straight salary plans. A *combination system* offers a base salary plus an incentive—usually a commission or a bonus. Combination systems have benefits for both the sales manager and the salesperson. The salary portion of the plan helps the manager control the sales force; the incentive provides motivation. For the salesperson, a combination plan offers an incentive to excel while minimizing the extremely wide swings in earnings that may occur when the economy surges or contracts too much.

As the emphasis on relationship selling increases, many sales managers feel that tying a portion of a salesperson's compensation to a client's satisfaction with the salesperson and the company encourages relationship building. To determine this, sales managers can survey clients on a salesperson's ability to create realistic expectations and how responsive the person is to customer needs.[56] At GE Aircraft Engines, a portion of its salespeople's total compensation plan is tied to customer service and satisfaction measured through surveys. Therefore, making sure that the customer is satisfied leads to a bigger paycheck for the salesperson.[57]

Although the compensation plan motivates a salesperson to sell, sometimes it is not enough to produce the volume of sales or the profit margin required by sales management. Sales managers, therefore, often offer rewards or incentives, such as recognition at ceremonies, plaques, vacations, merchandise, and pay raises or cash bonuses. The most popular incentives are cash rewards, used by over 60 percent of sales organizations.[58] Rewards may help increase overall sales volume, add new accounts, improve morale and goodwill, move slow items, and bolster slow sales. They can be used to achieve long-term or short-term objectives, such as unloading overstocked inventory and meeting a monthly or quarterly sales goal.

Motivation also takes the form of effective sales leadership on the part of the sales manager. An effective sales manager is inspirational to his or her salespeople, encouraging them to achieve their goals through clear and enthusiastic communications. He or she has a clear vision and commitment to the mission of the organization and the ability to instill pride and earn the respect of employees. Effective sales leaders continuously increase their knowledge and skill base while also encouraging others to do so. In a recent study that assessed the attributes of sales leaders, the best sales leaders share a number of key personality traits (see Exhibit 16.5), such as a sense of urgency, openness to new ideas, and a desire to take risks. These traits separate motivational sales leaders from mere sales managers.

Evaluating the Sales Force

The final task of sales managers is evaluating the effectiveness and performance of the sales force. To evaluate the sales force, the sales manager needs feedback—that is, regular information from salespeople. Typical performance measures include sales volume, contribution to profit, calls per order, sales or profits per call, or percentage of calls achieving specific goals such as sales of products that the firm is heavily promoting.

Performance information helps the sales manager monitor a salesperson's progress through the sales cycle and pinpoint where breakdowns may be occurring.

straight commission
A method of compensation in which the salesperson is paid some percentage when a sale is made.

straight salary
A method of compensation in which the salesperson receives a salary regardless of sales productivity.

Exhibit 16.5

Seven Key Leadership Traits
of Effective Sales Leaders

Effective sales leaders . . .	
Are assertive	Assertive sales leaders know when and how to get tough and how to assert their authority.
Possess ego drive	Sales leaders with ego drive have the desire and ability to persuade their reps to take action.
Possess ego strength	Sales leaders with ego strength are able to not only make sure they bounce back from rejection but also make sure their reps rebound, too.
Take risks	Risk-taking sales leaders are willing to go out on a limb in an effort to make a sale or enhance a relationship.
Are innovative	Innovative sales leaders stay open to new ideas and new ways of conducting business.
Have a sense of urgency	Urgent sales leaders understand that getting things done now is critical to winning and keeping business.
Are empathetic	Empathetic sales leaders help their reps grow by listening and understanding.

SOURCE: Table adapted from "The 7 Traits of Great Sales Leaders" by Geoffrey Brewer, *Sales & Marketing Management*, July 1997, pp. 38–46. Reprinted with permission.

For example, by knowing the number of prospects an individual salesperson has in each step of the sales cycle process and determining where prospects are falling out of the sales cycle, a manager can determine how effective a salesperson may be at lead generation, needs assessment, proposal generation, presenting, closing, and follow-up stages. This information can then tell a manager what sales skills may need to be reassessed or retrained. For example, if a sales manager notices a sales rep seems to be letting too many prospects slip away after presenting proposals, it may mean he or she needs help with developing proposals, handling objections, or closing sales.

The Impact of Technology on Personal Selling

Automation of the sales force is constantly changing the landscape of personal selling. Today's salesperson is linked via laptop computer to headquarters, streamlining the process of placing orders and getting information. Mobile telephones, pagers, personal data assistants, and e-mail allow salespeople to be more accessible to their company and clients. Furthermore, the Internet provides salespeople with a vast resource of information on clients, competitors, and their industry. When implemented correctly, sales force automation can streamline a company's entire selling process, saving salespeople time and allowing them to focus on customer solutions, as well as providing information when they need it at the point of sale.[59]

E-business, or buying, selling, marketing, collaborating with partners, and servicing customers electronically using the Internet, is also having a significant impact on personal selling. Forrester Research, a technology research firm, predicts that by 2002, 98 percent of large companies, 85 percent of medium-sized companies, and 47 percent of small companies will be engaged in e-commerce.[60] Additionally, 85 percent of business respondents regard e-business as vital to their company's success.[61] For customers, the Web has become a powerful tool to get accurate and up-to-date information on products, pricing, and order status. The Internet also cost-effectively processes orders and services requests. While on the surface the Internet might look like a threat to the job security of salespeople. The Web is actually freeing up sales reps from tedious administrative tasks, like shipping catalogs, placing routine orders, or tracking orders. This leaves them more time to focus on the needs of their clients. At Carlson Wagonlit Travel, for instance, shifting sales of routine products to the Web like short-haul shuttle flights is freeing up travel agents to do more outbound selling to high-potential customers.[62]

Looking Back

As you think back to the opening story, recall how Kinko's successfully reorganized its sales organization. The sales force now has clear objectives, a proven sales process that focuses on building customer relationships, marketing materials and training to support the sales process, and a com-pensation plan that motivates and rewards. Kinko's sales force went from one of mere order takers to one consisting of true consultative sellers focused on providing its clients with the best solutions and service possible.

Use it Now!

Get Free Product Samples On-line
Receive free samples of consumer products by registering on-line at **http://www.FreeSamples. com** and **http://www.StartSampling.com**. There you can choose from a variety of free products, such as beauty aids, pet food, and new food products. In exchange, you provide marketers with feedback on what you liked and didn't like about the product.

Sell Yourself
Go to Amazon.com and under the search engine type "selling yourself." Order one or more books available to improve your selling skills. Also, con-sider a Dale Carnegie training course. For more information, go to **http://www.dale-carnegie.com/**.

Looking for a Sales Job?
Find job leads in the *Sales and Marketing Management* magazine careers section at **http://www. salesandmarketing.com/smmnew/resources/ careers.asp**. Or visit popular employment site Monster.com (**http://www.monster.com**) and use their searchable database to search for sales opportunities in a specific geographic area. You can also post your resume at these and a number of other employment sites.

Summary

1 **Define and state the objectives of sales promotion.** Sales promotion compromises those marketing communication activities, other than advertising, personal selling, and public relations, in which a short-term incentive motivates consumers or members of the distribution channel to purchase a good or service immediately, either by lowering the price or by adding value. The main objectives of sales promotion are to increase trial purchases, consumer inventories, and repeat purchases. Sales promotion is also used to encourage brand switching and to build brand loyalty. Sales promotion supports advertising activities.

2 **Discuss the most common forms of consumer sales promotion.** Consumer forms of sales promotion include coupons and rebates, premiums, loyalty marketing programs, contests and sweepstakes, sampling, and point-of-purchase displays. Coupons are certificates entitling consumers to an immediate price reduction when they purchase a product or service. Coupons are a particularly good way to encourage product trial and brand switching. Similar to coupons, rebates provide purchasers with a price reduction, although it is not immediate. To receive a rebate, consumers must generally mail in a rebate form with a proof of purchase. Premiums offer an extra item or incentive to the consumer for buying a product or service. Premiums reinforce the consumer's purchase decision, increase consumption, and persuade nonusers to switch brands. Rewarding loyal customers is the basis of loyalty marketing programs. Loyalty programs are extremely effective at building long-term, mutually beneficial relationships between a company and its key customers. Contests and sweepstakes are generally designed to create interest, often to encourage brand switching. Because consumers perceive risk in trying new products, sampling is an effective method for gaining new customers. Finally, point-of-purchase displays set up at the retailer's location build traffic, advertise the product, and induce impulse buying.

3 **List the most common forms of trade sales promotion.** Manufacturers use many of the same sales promotion tools used in consumer promotions, such as sales contests, premiums, and point-of-purchase displays. In addition, manufacturers and channel intermediaries use several unique promotional strategies: trade allowances, push money, training programs, free merchandise, store demonstrations, and meetings, conventions, and trade shows.

4 **Describe personal selling.** Personal selling is direct communication between a sales representative and one or more prospective buyers in an attempt to influence each other in a purchase situation. Broadly speaking, all businesspeople use personal selling to promote themselves and their ideas. Personal selling offers several advantages over other forms of promotion. Personal selling allows salespeople to thoroughly explain and demonstrate a product. Salespeople have the flexibility to tailor a sales proposal to the needs and preferences of individual customers. Personal selling is more efficient than other forms of promotion because salespeople target qualified prospects and avoid wasting efforts on unlikely buyers. Personal selling affords greater managerial control over promotion costs. Finally, personal selling is the most effective method of closing a sale and producing satisfied customers.

5 **Discuss the key differences between relationship selling and traditional selling.** Relationship selling is the practice of building, maintaining, and enhancing interactions with customers in order to develop long-term satisfaction through mutually beneficial partnerships. Traditional selling, on the other hand, is transaction focused. That is, the salesperson is most concerned with making one-time sales and moving on to the next prospect. Salespeople practicing relationship selling spend more time understanding a prospect's needs and developing solutions to meet those needs.

6 **List the steps in the selling process.** The selling process is composed of seven basic steps: (1) generating leads, (2) qualifying leads, (3) assessing approach and needs, (4) developing and proposing solutions, (5) handling objections, (6) closing the sale, and (7) following up.

7 **Describe the functions of sales management.** Sales management is a critical area of marketing that performs several important functions. Sales managers set overall company sales goals and define the sales process most effective for achieving those goals. They determine sales force structure based on geographic, product, functional, or customer variables. Managers develop the sales force through recruiting and training. Sales management motivates the sales force through compensation planning, motivational tools, and effective sales leadership. Finally, sales managers evaluate the sales force through salesperson feedback and other methods of determining their performance.

Discussion and Writing Questions

1. Discuss how different forms of sales promotion can erode or build brand loyalty. If a company's objective were to enhance customer loyalty to its products, what sales promotion techniques would be most appropriate?
2. What forms of consumer sales promotion might induce impulse purchases? What forms of sales promotion are more effective at persuading consumers to switch brands?
3. How is trade sales promotion different from consumer sales promotion? How is it the same?
4. **WRITING** You have recently been assigned the task of developing promotional techniques to introduce your company's new product, a Cajun chicken sandwich. Advertising spending is limited, so the introduction will only include some low-budget sales promotion techniques. Write a sales promotion plan that will increase awareness of your new sandwich and allow your customer base to try it risk-free.
5. Discuss the role of personal selling in promoting products. What advantages does personal selling offer over other forms of promotion?
6. What are the key differences between relationship selling and traditional methods of selling? What types of products or services do you think would be conducive to relationship selling?
7. **WRITING** You are a new salesperson for a well-known medical software company, and one of your clients is a large group of physicians. You have just arranged an initial meeting with the office manager. Develop a list of questions you might ask at this meeting to uncover the group's specific needs.
8. What does sales follow-up entail? Why is it an essential step in the selling process, particularly from the perspective of relationship selling? How does it relate to cognitive dissonance?
9. **TEAM** Form a three-person team. Go to the local grocery store and write down all of the forms of sales promotion you see, including company name, product being promoted, form of promotion, and objective. Also, make a note of the sales promotion's message or offer, such as "two-for-one" or "cents off." Create a table that lists this information, then rate the effectiveness of each one, in your opinion, on a scale from 1 to 5 where 1 is "poor" and 5 is "excellent." Present a summary of your findings to the class. What kind of conclusions can you draw about product type and promotion?
10. **ON LINE** Visit the site **http://www.netcentives.com**. How does this company help on-line businesses conduct loyalty marketing programs. Present some examples.
11. **INFOTRAC COLLEGE EDITION** **ON LINE** Managing a sales force in today's e-business environment can be difficult, especially with the Internet perceived as a threat to job security. Use InfoTrac (**http://www.infotrac-college.com**) to locate an article in the August 2000 issue of *Electronic News* titled, "Creating a Web-Savvy Sales Force" by Wally York. Read the article and list York's key elements. How does this tie in with what you read in the chapter?
12. **TEAM** With two classmates, select a company or business near campus that has a sales force. Using York's article (from Question 11) as a starting point, list all the things the company would need to do to create an e-savvy sales force.

13. **INFOTRAC COLLEGE EDITION** Without revenue, a company cannot survive, and sales is the means to that end. How important is the effectiveness of a company's sales force? Use InfoTrac (**http://www.infotrac-college.com**) to run a keyword search for "sales force" or "sales force automation." Skim six to ten articles and write down all the automation tools (software and hardware) that you discover.

Application for Entrepreneurs

Morgan's is a retail clothing store offering high-quality, reasonably priced merchandise. Its target markets include students at the local university and working individuals, primarily in the age range eighteen to thirty-five. The location is about three miles from the campus in an upscale strip center next to a small, local mall. For several years the owner has been using several student interns as part-time salespersons and assistant managers. He has been able to find good workers, but turnover is high and training new employees takes a lot of time. Also, his sales training has consisted mostly of asking new student interns to review the internship reports of former student employees. To reduce these problems he has considered hiring a college graduate full-time and fewer part-time interns. The full-time employee should reduce turnover and the need for repeated training and be able to help him develop a better sales training approach. He pays the interns between $7.00 and $10.00 per hour, depending on their experience. College graduates would have to be paid between $27,000 and $30,000 per year plus benefits.

Questions

1. What factors must be considered in making this decision?
2. Should he hire a college graduate as a full-time employee? Why?

Case   entrepreneurship

Varsity Group: The Campus Bookstore Alternative

U.S. college students spend more than $3 billion each year purchasing the roughly seventy million textbooks needed for their classes. As each new semester or quarter begins, students all across the country dread the long waits in line at the local college bookstore to purchase the books they need, often at exorbitant prices. Internet start-up Varsity Group, however, promises an end to the inconvenience and horrendous lines. And students can save money, too.

Founded in 1997 as VarsityBooks.com, the company is helping revolutionize the college textbook industry by

selling textbooks on-line. Today, only about 1 percent of college textbooks are sold via the Web. But with close to 100 percent of college students using the Internet and over 70 percent logging on daily, the potential for Varsity Group and other on-line textbook retailers to make it big is enormous. On-line textbook retailers can offer all the conveniences of Internet shopping, such as round-the-clock service and a wider selection than the local college bookstore's shelf space allows. And because Varsity Group has no brick-and-mortar storefront and few storage costs, it can sell some textbooks for as much as 40 percent less than traditional textbook sellers.

If Varsity Group does succeed in the on-line textbook market, a big reason will be its most unusual promotional tactics. Instead of putting its entire promotional budget into buying ads in the campus newspaper or on local radio stations, Varsity Group recruits college students to help promote its Web site on college campuses and to persuade their classmates to purchase their textbooks from the company's Web site instead of at inconvenient campus bookstores where prices are higher. Close to three thousand students on six hundred U.S. campuses have signed on to become representatives for Varsity Group. Campus reps receive hourly and commission-based wages and the freedom to execute their own campaigns. Lead campus reps enjoy business cards, stock options, a PalmPilot, and a flexible budget. Reps also attend biannual training programs to listen to speakers on marketing best practices, case studies, codes of conduct, and team management skills.

Student reps employ a number of grassroots promotional and sales techniques to promote VarsityBooks.com. Reps sponsor parties, dress local bands in VarsityBooks.com t-shirts, and send e-mails to student organizations and professors. They hand out candy bars, granola bars, and lollipops with VarsityBooks.com coupons. At Florida State University, campus reps used sidewalk chalk to pen messages such as "Smashing Savings" on sidewalks around campus. At Stanford University, Varsity reps passed out coupons at a nearby movie theater. Other reps distribute price comparison flyers for particular courses at classroom doorways. The most effective ploy for Varsity reps, however, has been getting professors to plug the Web site or to let them speak to students during classes.

Seeing the potential of its network of college reps, Varsity Group recently leveraged its network to promote products from other companies, spinning off a marketing services division called College Impact. For the fall of 2000, the company developed "Varsity Bags," a back-to-school program that uses branded book bags containing products, coupons, and promotional materials from some of the nation's top companies. Varsity Bags were distributed directly into the hands of over 500,000 college students as they began the new school year by its network of campus representatives. Additionally, the first 200,000 students who made purchases from VarsityBooks.com also received a Varsity Bag with the shipment of their books. Companies that participated in the Varsity Bag promotion included AT&T Wireless, adidas, Compaq, Staples.com, Bolt, Clinique, GTE Credit Services, eBags, iFuse, StockBack, REI, Riffage, Teach for America, Pogo.com, and Magazine Line. The company has also partnered with companies such as Ben & Jerry's Homemade Ice Cream and Papa Johns to reach the lucrative college market through its network of campus representatives.

Questions

1. How does Varsity Group's network of campus representatives resemble a sales force?
2. What sales promotional techniques does Varsity Group employ?
3. Visit Varsity Group's Web site at **http://www. varsitybooks.com** and click on the page that provides information about being a campus rep. What qualifications and experiences do you think Varsity Group looks for in a student's application?

Bibliography

Jeff Gottlieb. "Internet Vendors Test College Textbook Market." *Los Angeles Times*, June 25, 2000, p. B-1.

Ann M. Mack. "Textbook Case." *Brandweek*, August 7, 2000, p. IQ30.

Karen Solomon. "College Bound." *Business 2.0*, April 1999.

Jeffrey A. Tannenbaum. "Marketers on Campus: A New Bag of Tricks," *Wall Street Journal*, January 31, 2000, pp. B1, B8.

http://www.varsitybooks.com; press releases found at Varsity Group Web site at **http://www.varsity-group.com**.

Steven M. Zeitchik. "Capitalism on Campus." *Business 2.0*, May 2000.

Case

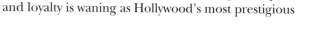

GFI Entertainment:
Get Rid of That Agent? No Way!

"Get rid of that agent of yours" was the hallmark pitch of Sue Mengers, Hollywood superagent in the 1960s and 1970s. More often than not, that was all it took to lure the targeted star to Mengers' roster. In today's Hollywood, not much has changed. Poaching is rampant and loyalty is waning as Hollywood's most prestigious talent agencies battle for the rights to represent the entertainment industry's biggest earners. The stakes are excruciatingly high, and not helping the situation are stars like Kevin Costner and Sharon Stone who are shunning agents and managers altogether, choosing to negotiate on their own and use their personal attorneys to close deals.

After forty years in the talent business, San Francisco-based GFI Entertainment knows these risks. That's why its principal, Jimmy Goings, focuses his talent management business on building relationships. Goings represents dozens of performers, from comedians to musicians. As their manager, he is responsible for scheduling his clients at various venues, from clubs to conferences to colleges. One of the most successful of Goings' clients is Mark Lundholm, a comedian whose routine finds the humor in recovery from addiction (see Chapter 2). Since Goings takes care of the business details of all Lundholm's performances, Lundholm can focus on the creative aspects of his craft. According to Lundholm, Goings can promote him better than he could himself by initiating word-of-mouth marketing with lines like, "You have GOT to see this guy. He's great!" Goings also makes sure that Lundholm gets seen at the right places at the right time.

The key to successful talent promotion is relationship selling. Goings must build and maintain strong relationships with the buyers of entertainment services, such as corporations, conference planners, recovery groups, and club owners. This is especially important in the case of clubs where Lundholm has not previously performed. Comedians are not as rare as they once were, and competition for bookings is fierce. A decreasing number of comedy clubs means fewer venues for up-and-coming performers to get experience. Add to this the decreasing number of television shows and segments dedicated to stand-up comedy routines, and the overall result is limited opportunities for exposure.

Jimmy Goings and Mark Lundholm know this, so Goings employs many personal selling strategies in his promotional activities. He spends most of his time on the phone, pitching his clients' acts and arranging performances. Goings likes to ask what his customers are looking for right away. That way he can match customer needs with the various talent on GFI's roster. Goings supports his sales pitch with high quality acts. Once the artist performs, the door is open for future business and long-term relationships, but not unless

Goings follows up well. The post-show follow-up is perhaps the most important sales strategy Goings uses. Regular follow-up allows GFI to find out how the audience responded to the show, how much revenue was generated, and how long the show is expected to run. In the case of Lundholm, the Funny Bone in South Bend, Indiana is a regular venue, and Goings has developed a strong relationship with its owner.

But building relationships is not reserved for buyers of entertainment alone—Goings and his performers also enjoy strong partnerships. For example, Mark Lundholm likens their relationship to a marriage in that a lot of hard work goes into it. Lundholm even admits that Goings' suggestions—like taking acting lessons—are not always initially well received. Goings, however, usually manages to sell Lundholm on his ideas, and Lundholm is open to anything that will improve his show. This kind of honest communication is the foundation of their relationship and their professional success. Through dialogue, they can explore areas to expand their offerings and ways to increase their sales. After all, Goings is paid a commission on his artists' total revenue.

Since career breaks no longer come on the heels of a five-minute bit on *The Late Show With David Letterman*, Goings must provide a solid sales plan for each of his clients. And the strong relationships he builds with both talent and buyers means that his artists are less likely to jump ship at the first offer from a talent-hungry agent professing, "You'd be better off with me."

Questions

1. Why is having a manager a valuable promotional tool for an artist?
2. What kind of relationship is important to talent managers?
3. What personal selling strategies does Goings employ as part of his promotional activities?

Bibliography

Christopher Grove. "Where Is the Love? As Live Platforms Dry Up, Comics Struggle to Be Seen." *Variety.* July 17, 2000, p. 37.

John Hiscock, "Sharks Infest Hollywood's Talent Pool: The Talk of the Town Is a New War Between the Top Talent Agents." *The Daily Telegraph.* August 12, 2000. Retrieved from Dow Jones Publication Library at **http://nrstg1p.djnr.com**

Learnet video on GFI Entertainment

http://www.gfientertainment.com

http://www.marklundholm.com

MARKETING MISCUES

Got Beer?—Ad Campaign Crashes

In October 1993, the milk industry took charge of its own destiny and aired the first "Got Milk?" advertisement. Originating in California, these ads almost single-handedly stopped the national decline in milk consumption. Additionally, the ads have been credited with changing the world of advertising. The Got Milk? campaign proved that creative advertising could resurrect an ancient product like milk. The success of the campaign has led to many knockoff ads. The most recent one, which was lambasted by many, was the "Got Beer?" promotional campaign launched by People for the Ethical Treatment of Animals (PETA).

PETA is an international nonprofit organization based in Norfolk, Virginia. The organization operates under the principle that "animals are not ours to eat, wear, experiment on, or use for entertainment." With over 600,000 members worldwide, PETA is the largest animal rights organization in the world.

Targeted toward college students, the campaign was launched just in time for the 2000 spring break (a time renowned for excess alcohol consumption). PETA's campaign urged students to "wipe off those milk mustaches and replace them with foam from brew, not moo." With the Got Milk? ads as a guide, PETA's advertisements depicted students with foamy beer mustaches. PETA insisted that the ads were not an attempt to heighten alcohol use among college students. Rather, the organization says that the ads were designed to raise awareness of animal cruelty. Surprising to many is PETA's suggestion that beer is a healthier drink than milk. The group's Web site goes so far as to claim that dairy products are linked to allergies, constipation, obesity, cancer, heart disease, and osteoporosis.

A mere two weeks after the ad hit the airwaves, PETA pulled the campaign amidst protests made by the Mothers Against Drunk Driving organization (MADD), which said that the ad was irresponsible and would encourage college students to drink. PETA appeared to be valuing the lives of cows over people. Otherwise, how could it be exhibiting no concern for human lives lost at the hands of drunk drivers?

The renamed campaign, "Dump Dairy," continues to target college students. Switching to the Internet to promote its cause against milk, the http://www. milksucks.com Web site allowed students to obtain a free bottle opener with the slogan, "Save a cow's life. Drink responsibly. Don't drink milk." The Web site must have been successful. It received over 40,000 hits in thirty-six hours, and PETA claimed that 1,500 new students joined the group's College Activist Network.

One has to wonder if being forced to drop the Got Beer? campaign depicted a marketing mistake on the part of PETA or whether all of the publicity received by the campaign was beneficial to the organization.

Questions for Discussion

1. Should a not-for-profit tax-exempt organization be allowed to target underage drinkers with ads such as Got Beer?
2. Are there any similarities between PETA's beer-drinking campaign and campaigns for controversial groups such as tobacco companies? Would an alcohol producer be allowed to run ads such as PETA's?
3. Was the Got Beer? campaign a success or failure? Explain.

Bibliography

Linda Wilson Fuoco. "PETA's 'Got Beer?' Spoof Upsets MADD." *Pittsburgh Post-Gazette*, April 1, 2000, p. W-8.

Beverly Kelley. "Anti-Milk Campaign Backfires on Animal Rights Group PETA." *Ventura County Star*, March 27, 2000, p. B07.

Courtner Lower. "'Got Beer' Campaign Comes Under Fire, Ditched by Activists." *Montana Kaimin via U-Wire*, March 29, 2000, On-line.

Jeff Manning. *Got Milk? The Book.* Rocklin, CA: Prima Publishing, 1999.

http://www.milksucks.com

http://www.peta-online.org

CRITICAL THINKING: THE U.S. MILITARY

Crisis on the Homefront

With unemployment in the United States at a thirty-year low and more young people attending college directly out of high school, the U.S. military is having a very difficult time recruiting new soldiers. The proportion of the target group, eighteen- to twenty-four-year-old men and women, who enlist in the U.S. military has declined 7 percent in the ten-year period between 1990 and 2000. Interestingly, the shortfall of new recruits comes at a time when the military is 30 percent smaller than it was in 1990.

All of the services operating within the confines of the U.S. armed forces are facing severe shortages. Recruiting goals in 1999 were not met by the Army, Navy, or Air Force. The Army needed 74,500 new soldiers, the Navy needed 53,234 new recruits, and the Air Force needed 33,800 men and women. The only wing of the armed forces to meet its 1999 recruiting goal of 35,000 recruits was the Marines.

The military draft ended in 1973 under President Richard Nixon, at a time when the public's perception of the armed forces was extremely negative due to the national disillusionment with the Vietnam War. Today, the current shortfall in military recruiting has led some to question the long-term survival of an all-volunteer armed services.

Target Market

The military's target market encompasses young men and women with high school diplomas, a group born after 1978 and dubbed Generation Y. Recruiting in this age group has been complicated by both generational and demographic shifts.

From a generational perspective, most high school and college students are not intimately familiar with the military. Fewer than 6 percent of the under sixty-five age group in the United States served in the military. A potential recruit may only know about military experiences from a grandparent. Due to the mobility of the American population, however, many military experiences are not even handed down to grandchildren since the interaction between grandparents and grandchildren is often restricted to only one or two family visits a year. Added to this generational concern is the fact that the proportion of military veterans has dropped to barely one-third of the U.S. population (as compared to two-thirds historically).

Demographic shifts have led to a lack of interest and/or knowledge about military life. Members of the Generation Y market segment have numerous career options. With financial aid relatively easy to attain in the early 2000s, the expectation has become one of moving from high school to college. For those opting out of college, unemployment is at an all-time low and dot-com companies are not as concerned about college degrees as they are about creativity and computer skills.

Combined with these generational and demographic shifts is the fact that members of this target market have essentially grown up without the threat of war. Rather than hearing about the merits and prestige of being in the U.S. military, the target market knows more about the negatives of the military—sexual harassment and gay-bashing.

Alternative Strategies for Increasing the Number of Recruits

Two major alternatives exist for increasing the number of military recruits: lowering the standards for recruits or promoting the merits of military service.

The first alternative has met strong opposition. Currently, 10 percent of recruits can be non–high school graduates. One suggested program is to recruit 2,000 high school dropouts who have general equivalency diplomas (GEDs). However, holders of GEDs have typically not performed as well as high school graduates. Another option is to accept some Category IV enlistees—a group that encompasses those with below-average IQs who score in the tenth to thirtieth percentile on the military's entrance exam.

The second alternative involves a massive investment in promotional and advertising initiatives. This alternative would require nearly a threefold increase in advertising expenditures. All four areas of the armed services are concerned with raising awareness about military life. The ads would need to depict both the opportunities and experiences available in the military as well as day-to-day adventures of military living. In tune with the focus upon advertising, possible promotional efforts include the recruiting of "stars" to appear in ads (e.g., Tom Cruise, Harrison Ford, Spike Lee), high-tech road shows that would visit high schools and shopping malls, and event sponsorships. Web sites for each of the four services and advertising banners on Web sites frequented by the target market have already proved successful for the military. Estimates are that the Internet attracted 1,000 new Navy recruits in 1999 and that the Marine site generates one recruit per twenty leads.

There is no doubt in the minds of officials at the U.S. Pentagon that something has to be done to attract the 200,000 recruits needed to maintain quality armed services. Can the U.S. military utilize the tools of corporate marketers to create a new image for the service and increase its number of recruits?

Questions for Discussion

1. Profile the target market of the U.S. military.
2. What are the pros and cons of utilizing advertising and promotion in this government sector?
3. Should the U.S. military standardize advertising across all four services, or should each service customize its own ads?

Bibliography

Alicia K. Borlik. "Recruitment Ads: New Strategies, New Messages." *The Voice News*, American Forces Press Services, 1999. On-line.

Diane Brady. "Uncle Sam Wants You . . . To Have Fun!" *Business Week*, February 21, 2000, pp. 98–101.

Joseph L. Galloway. "Not in the Army Now." *U.S. News Online,* March 1, 1999.

Richard J. Newman. "Dumbing Down the Military." *U.S. News Online*, November 23, 1998.

Michael D. Towle. "Pentagon Seeking Ways to Increase Enlistments." *Star-Telegram Washington Bureau*, September 13, 1999. On-line.

http://www.goarmy.com, http://www.navy.com, http://www.airforce.com, http://www.marines.com.

MARKETING PLANNING ACTIVITIES

Integrated Marketing Communications

The next part of the marketing mix to be described for the marketing plan is the promotion element, which covers areas such as advertising, public relations, sales promotion, personal selling, and Internet marketing.

 Be sure that your promotion plans match the needs and wants of the target market identified and described earlier and are compatible with the product, service, and distribution issues discussed in the previous sections. Also refer to Exhibit 2.8 for additional marketing plan subjects.

1. Evaluate your firm's promotion objectives. Remember that promotions cannot be directly tied with sales because there are too many other factors (competition, environment, price, distribution, product, customer service, company reputation, and so on) that affect sales. State specific objectives that can be tied directly to the result of promotional activities—for example, number of people redeeming a coupon, share of audience during a commercial, percent attitude change before and after a telemarketing campaign, or number of people calling a toll-free information hotline.

Marketing*Builder* Exercises
- **Marketing Strategy** portion of **Marketing Communications** template
- **Marketing Budget** spreadsheet
- **Operating Budget** spreadsheet
- **Source Code Master List** spreadsheet
- **Agency Selection Matrix** spreadsheet

2. What is your chosen company's promotional message? Does this message inform, remind, persuade, or educate the target market?

Marketing*Builder* Exercise
- **Advertising and Promotion** portion of the **Marketing Communications** template

3. Investigate different media placement rates (such as for a school newspaper, local newspaper, national newspaper, local radio station, local TV station, general or specialty interest magazine, local billboard, transit advertising, or the Internet). You can either call local media or consult *Standard Rate and Data Services (SRDS)*. Which media should your firm use? Which media can your firm afford? When should media be used?

Marketing*Builder* Exercises
- **Advertising Schedule** template
- **Preliminary Media Schedule** portion of the **Marketing Communications** template

4. List the public relations activities that your chosen company should pursue. How should bad publicity be handled?

Marketing*Builder* Exercise
- **Public Relations** portion of the **Marketing Communications** template

5. Evaluate or create printed materials for your chosen company (such as data sheets, brochures, stationery, or rate cards). Does the literature sufficiently answer questions? Provide enough information for further contact? Effectively promote product features and customer service? Note a differential or competitive advantage.

Marketing*Builder* Exercises
- **Collateral Planning Matrix** spreadsheet
- **Direct Mail Analysis** spreadsheet

- **Sales Support Collateral Materials** section of the **Marketing Communications** template
- **Corporate Capabilities Brochure** section of the **Marketing Communications** template

6. What trade shows could your firm attend? Search the *Eventline* database for trade shows appropriate to your firm. Order media kits and explore the feasibility and costs of attending those trade shows.

Marketing*Builder* Exercises

- **Trade Show** portion of the **Marketing Communications** template
- **Trade Show Checklist** and **Schedule** template

7. What other sales promotion tools could your firm use? What are the costs? What is the impact of using these methods on pricing?
8. Identify and justify the best type (internal or external) and structure (product, customer, geographic, etc.) for your firm's sales force.

Marketing*Builder* Exercises

- **Current Selling Methods** portion of the **Sales Plan** template
- **Marketing Responsibilities** portion of the **Sales Plan** template
- **Sales Strategy** portion of the **Sales Plan** template
- **Sales Source Analysis** spreadsheet

9. How should your firm hire, motivate, and compensate its sales force?

Marketing*Builder* Exercise

- **Commission Sales Forecast & Tracker** spreadsheet

10. Design a sales approach for your company's sales force to use.

Marketing*Builder* Exercise

- **Next Steps** portion of the **Sales Plan** template

11. Explore the World Wide Web/Internet to research your company, its competition, and the industry in general. How is advertising and promotion being handled in this medium?

E-MARKETING PLANNING ACTIVITIES

You began your strategic e-marketing plan by stating your business mission and objectives and detailing a SWOT analysis. In the second part of the plan you identified and described target market segments and identified sources of competitive intelligence and the need for further marketing research. Next, you began the process of defining the marketing mix, starting with the components of product and distribution. Recall that you are either writing a strategic marketing plan for an existing pet store retailer with a new on-line presence, a dot-com pet store retailer, or an e-company of your own choosing.

For continued general assistance on business plans and marketing plans, visit **http://www.bplans.com** or **http://www.businessplans.org**. For electronic sources of information, search on the Electric Library at **http://wwws.elibrary.com** or the Internet Public Library at **http://www.ipl.org**. Another excellent source of information is the Sales and Marketing Executives Marketing Library at **http://www.sell.org**. You should also refer to Exhibit 2.8 for additional marketing plan checklist items (Part IV.B.3: Marketing Mix—Promotion).

The next stage of the strategic planning process continues defining the elements of the marketing mix, and this section focuses on promotions. Integrating promotional communications seamlessly with an electronic offering presents unique challenges for the marketer be-

cause Web-based strategies are so different from traditional media. Even so, it is important to consider all parts of the promotion mix, including advertising, public relations, sales promotion, and personal selling. An excellent on-line resource with many links to promotion sites is **http://advertising.utexas.edu/world**.

Use the following exercises to guide you through the promotions part of your strategic marketing plan:

1. Define your promotional objectives. What specific results do you hope to accomplish, and which promotional tools will be responsible? How will you use promotions to differentiate yourself from your competition? Remember *not to* tie promotions activities directly to sales results. Other communications and activity objectives are more appropriate. Remember to have off-line promotions drive on-line traffic.
2. Design a promotional message or theme. Make sure this message will work across both traditional and electronic media. How is your promotional message consistent with your branding? Is this message or slogan unique and important enough to be copyrighted? Check with the U.S. Copyright Office at **http://lcweb.loc.gov/copyright**.
3. Will you be designing and producing all your promotion tools in house, or do you need to find an agency? What are the advantages of designing pro-

motional tools in-house? Disadvantages? Try **http://www.agencyfinder.com** to assist in your decision or investigate **http://pwr.com/creative** to find additional creative talent to enhance your own work.

4. To request on-line media kits from both traditional and electronic media sources, go to the Kit Director at **http://www.mediadirector.com**. Additionally, you can register to get free advertising and rate information from **http://www.adratecard.com**, which includes information about radio, newspaper, magazine, television, outdoor, and Internet media rates and buying.

5. Are there different advertising concerns for the Internet-only firm than for the firm with an established brick-and-mortar presence? If so, what are they? Design the advertising for each medium selected in question 4. Do all advertising pieces carry a uniform theme and style? Is there sufficient information about benefits offered to consumers? Do customers have an option for obtaining further information?

6. List the public relations activities that your company should do. Be sure to make them consistent with your branding and other promotions. In addition, write a plan for handling bad publicity. Bad publicity travels at lightspeed over the Internet and is much more of a challenge to an e-marketer. Check out **http://urbanlegends.about.com** to see how misinformation can travel the Internet and cause public relations nightmares for companies. Think about using a news clipping service for your company (such as one you hired to gather competitive intelligence earlier). For further public relations resources, visit **http://www.webcom.com/impulse/prlist.html**. For a list of media that accept on-line submissions, go to **http://www.islandnet.com/~deathnet/media_email.html**.

7. Think about ways your promotions could turn a first-time customer or deal-hunter into a repeat, loyal customer. Which sales promotion tools should your company use? For a listing of tradeshows, go to **http://www.exhibitornet.com** and look for the directory of shows, or the Trade Show News Network at **http://www.tsnn.com/sbs**. What about on-line coupons? There are dozens of on-line coupon sites that you can find with any search engine. What about promotional products? Try **http://www.promotionalproducts.com** for help.

8. Will you need a sales force? If so, what type, structure, organization, and compensation method would you use? You may find that in e-marketing, a sales force is more of a customer service and customer relations management tool. True selling activities may be limited to selling and buying on-line media space and links. In many circumstances, forming strategic partnerships and distribution deals have replaced traditional sales in the Internet space. What types of alliances and partnerships will you pursue? Will you work with other on-line firms, off-line firms, or both?

CROSS-FUNCTIONAL CONNECTIONS SOLUTIONS

Understanding Marketing Communications' Contribution to Firm Value

Questions

1. Why is a company's marketing communications of particular concern to research and development and manufacturing?

Marketers have a tendency to refer to product quality in their communications with potential customers. However, it is not the marketing department that has its hands in the development and production of the actual product. The R&D and manufacturing groups provide the physical product that marketing presents to customers. If a customer is dissatisfied with the product's quality, then it is typically the "hands-on" groups who are blamed for the low-quality product.

2. Why do financial managers view advertising and promotional expenditures as costs?

Financial managers believe there is a direct correlation between advertising and promotional expenditures and sales. In recognizing this relationship, financial managers view these expenditures as variable costs, thinking that one directly affects the other. Financial analysts are result oriented and ultimately will base their allocation of funds on whether or not the product is selling; they view an increase in sales as "money well spent." Unfortunately, viewing this relationship as such can be detrimental to the product; advertising budgets may be cut, based on low sales numbers, when they are needed most. These expenditures should be viewed as fixed costs, unrelated to sales increases or decreases.

3. How has personal selling become functionally integrated?

There are many areas in which personal selling has become functionally integrated. One major change in the salesperson's skill set has become the need to possess intimate knowledge of the products being presented to a customer. It is no longer sufficient to have great personal interacting skills—the salesperson has to clearly understand the products he or she is presenting. Another major area of integration has been the involvement of R&D and manufacturing in customer visits. Finance, accounting, and human resources are taking a much stronger role in the sales process with regard to compensation systems, cross selling, and teamwork.

Suggested Readings

Bob Donath. "Tell Bean Counters Your Variable is Fixed." *Marketing News*, June 19, 2000, p. 14.

Erin Strout. "Planning to Profit from National Accounts." *Sales and Marketing Management*, October 1999, p. 107.

6

part

Pricing Decisions

PRICING TO SATISFY BOTH INTERNAL AND EXTERNAL DEMANDS

Pricing is the one element of the marketing mix that is "owned" by multiple groups within a company. As such, there is considerable cross-functional input into the pricing decision process. Unfortunately, there is usually little agreement across functions as to the best price to give a particular product.

Marketing is interested in pricing to provide value to the customer, while meeting competitors' prices. Since costs determine the floor on prices, the accounting group has traditionally identified with a cost-plus pricing approach. Naturally, finance has a keen interest in the pricing process in relation to its targets for return on investment. The relationship between price and demand has downstream effects on the manufacturing process, bringing production capabilities into the pricing decisions—particularly in relation to the company's ability to produce the number of units needed to break even. Research and development pays close attention to the introductory price of the product since this is considered to be the point at which development costs are recouped. With all of these interested parties, it is hard to say if any one particular functional group is actually in charge of the final pricing decision!

The pricing decision must be viewed as an interactive process. There is a strong need for cross-functional interaction. For example, if marketing identifies an initial price as too high to capture customer interest, research and development and manufacturing must be consulted to see if product features, product materials, or assembly processes can be modified to decrease costs. Finance and accounting must be involved in reevaluating appropriate margins.

Probably one of the major breakthroughs in the cross-functional ownership of the pricing process has been activity-based costing (ABC). Just as marketing and manufacturing have long focused upon product customization, activity-based costing provides the capability to customize price. The method requires input from marketing, accounting, and manufacturing. Essentially, activity-based costing uses cost drivers to assign

costs. The process requires a clear market segmentation approach based on customer needs. Activity-based costing allows the company to determine what will have to be done to satisfy customers' needs and assign a cost to each of these activities. In this way, firms can distinguish between the truly profitable customers and those who may purchase in volume but require so much work (activities) that they are actually unprofitable customers.

Recognizing the importance of accounting information in the pricing process is something marketers have long considered. Tactically, marketers have long recognized that accurate cost data is needed to make good pricing decisions, but traditional accounting methods were faulted for being too production oriented. However, it is this cost information that points to the lowest possible price that can be charged for a product without losing money on a per item basis (considering traditional accounting methods).

The activity-based system, however, goes beyond the cost of manufacturing and looks at how much it costs to maintain individual customer accounts. Ultimately, activity-based costing allow marketers to price products/services to individual consumers based upon the total cost to provide the product or service. From a marketer's perspective, for example, travel time to visit with a customer would be included as a cost and could be reflected in the price charged to that particular customer.

The conflict caused by pricing is especially evident in the sale of automobiles in the European Union. Due to government pricing regulations, it is often cheaper for customers to buy their cars from a dealer in another country. For example, an English consumer will spend considerably less money for a car when buying it in another country and then registering the car in England. However, a right-hand drive car may not be immediately available in the other country. The non-English dealer has to order a right-hand drive car where most delivered cars are left-hand drive. In this situation implementing activity-based costing might show that doing business with noncountry buyers is more expensive than dealers had realized.

Products such as CDs, software, and prescription medications do not fall easily within a traditional pricing process. The pricing of such products extends the pricing initiative into functional departments that include engineers and the legal department. It is very difficult to determine the actual costs involved in developing these types of products. Burning a new CD, making duplicates of software, or making one additional pill on the machine is unlikely to correlate with the price of the product. Rather, it is the human investment, time, and legal maneuvering that transpire in the development of these types of products that have to be considered. Production costs do not accurately reflect the firm's investment expenses.

Additionally, some products fall in the category of "better than, but not as good as" competitive products. Computer products and computer peripherals fall in this category. Such new products have to be priced higher than the "better than" competitive products and lower than the "not as good as" competitive products. Listening solely to accountants and their pure cost data might price a product too close to the high-end competitor (with better capabilities) or too close to the low-end competitor (therefore not conveying the value added of the new product offering).

The marketing function is generally the driver in day-to-day price decisions. The speed at which price can change in response to competitive pressure is somewhat astounding. Price per gallon of gasoline at the local Mobil station may be $1.57 on Monday, $1.59 on Tuesday, and $1.53 on Wednesday. Such price changes can have an effect on the company's demand. Thus, pricing decisions must be coordinated with supply decisions. In the case of the Mobil station, there could also be an impact on the number of workers needed to service customers on any given day. Although marketers try to think about the overall organizational impact of their daily pricing decisions, minor changes can have a ripple effect in the organization. Price promotions are an example of the downstream effects of day-to-day pricing decisions.

A major objective of a price promotion campaign is stimulating increased demand for the firm's product. Studies show that the sales rate changes during and immediately after the campaign. Such fluctuating sales have a dual effect upon the manufacturer. For example, a Kroger store will increase the quantity ordered of liter bottles of Coca-Cola so it will have inventory on hand during a promotional period. But the store may order more than it expects to sell during the promotional period so that it can sell the discounted bottles at the regular price (i.e., greater margin) after the promotional period. This reduces normal delivery after the promotion and puts the Kroger store in the comfortable position of waiting until the next deal to repurchase.

This sort of buying behavior disrupts the production and delivery cycle and may mean having to ask employees to work extra shifts (thus increasing manufacturing costs due to overtime pay) to help meet demand. Decreased purchasing after the price promotion period has the opposite effect. Manufacturing may need to build excess inventory in order to maintain a stable production flow, thus driving up inventory costs.

The relative importance of marketing's internal partners in the pricing process relates closely to the product life cycle. Accounting, finance, and research and development have particular interests that appear to be addressed during the introductory stage of the life cycle. Manufacturing's interest in the pricing process seems more prevalent during the growth stage when the production facility is attempting to reach economies of scale. Once the product reaches maturity, all competitive manufacturers are operating with similar cost structures, and pricing is most clearly driven by the external environment. However, overall monitoring of product revenue is important throughout a product's life cycle.

Too many variables are at play in the pricing decision to say that the decision is the responsibility of any particular function. Rather, all functions have a need for functional-level input. However, it is safe to say that marketing has the broadest perspective on pricing since it is the function that looks at both internal cost issues as well as external demand pressures.

Questions for Discussion

1. Should marketing play the lead role in coordinating the pricing decision? Explain why or why not.
2. How is activity-based costing more market oriented than traditional accounting methods?
3. What kinds of internal problems are caused by price promotions?

chapter 17

Learning Objectives

1 Discuss the importance of pricing decisions to the economy and to the individual firm

2 List and explain a variety of pricing objectives

3 Explain the role of demand in price determination

4 Understand the concept of yield management systems

5 Describe cost-oriented pricing strategies

6 Demonstrate how the product life cycle, competition, distribution and promotion strategies, customer demands, the Internet and extranets, and perceptions of quality can affect price

Pricing Concepts

Mid-year 2000 should have been turbulent times for airlines. Jet-fuel prices had doubled over a twelve-month period, labor costs were up sharply, and passenger revenue weakened as the big carriers added planes to the skies faster than demand warranted.

In similar though rougher weather in 1992, major airlines tallied $4.8 billion in losses. In mid-2000, they reported almost record profits. Why? Airlines, those heavy-metal symbols of old-line industry, have become one of the biggest beneficiaries of the new economy. An industry that forecasters predicted would be hurt by new technologies such as video-conferencing has instead turned technology to its advantage, blunting the impact of economic jolts such as the fuel-price rise. "Technology has made all the difference in the world between airlines making money and airlines losing money," says Gregory D. Brenneman, president of Continental Airlines. "We used to go bankrupt when oil prices got this high and supply and demand got out of whack."

In the past, airline cost-cutting was rather crude and obvious: cramming seats closer together, for example, or removing olives from salads, then removing salads altogether. Technological improvements were mostly limited to behind-the-scenes operations such as crew scheduling and cockpit duties.

On Continental's old mainframes, a question such as "What happens if prices are raised 5 percent" typically took three weeks to calculate. Now, pricing guru Bill Brunger sits in his glass-walled office in downtown Houston zapping through hundreds of scenarios on a personal computer. Spotting a slow-selling market, he asks the computer to use past experience to estimate the result of opening more seats to frequent-flier rewards, or posting the market as an Internet special. As a result, seats in one market get filled without having to offer an across-the-board fare sale that could erode profits in many markets. "We can be a lot smarter," Brunger says. "Revenue management is all of our profit, and more."

Rather than running calculations flight-by-flight, the latest generation of yield-management systems evaluates thousands of possible connections for each flight. Continental, for example, offers about 30,000 possible routings with its 2,200 daily departures. It now evaluates whether a seat on an Austin-Houston flight should be sold to a local customer for $100 or to a customer paying $1,000 to connect from Austin to New York through Houston. Sometimes, it's better to take the local $100 Austin-Houston passenger if the airline can fill the Houston-to-New York seat with a higher-paying Houston–New York customer, or maybe an even higher paying Mexico City–New York customer making a connection in Houston.

If it works, airlines fill as many seats as possible with leisure passengers who buy tickets weeks in advance while leaving just enough for their best customers: last-minute, high-fare business travelers. The new system has yielded an additional 0.5 to 0.7 percent in revenue, or about $50 million, for Continental.

The same system evaluates the consequences of canceling or delaying a flight. A cancellation may mean a plane doesn't get required overnight maintenance work, or it could mean losing high-fare business travelers. The system, which can show instantly the amount of revenue on each flight, even makes suggestions, such as holding a flight five minutes because several high-fare passengers are trying to connect. Flights with VIPs onboard are flagged for special treatment.

Even the quality of meals is sometimes adjusted based on passenger load: hot lunches for flights with lots of business travelers, but snack sacks for a planeload of cheap-ticket vacationers.[1]

What is the relationship between costs, revenues, and profits? Airlines are now using the Internet to sell tickets. Will the Internet have a major impact on pricing? What role are yield management systems, such as the one used by Continental, playing in increased profitability? Can price influence the perceived quality of a product?

The Importance of Price

Discuss the importance of pricing decisions to the economy and to the individual firm

price
That which is given up in an exchange to acquire a good or service.

Price means one thing to the consumer and something else to the seller. To the consumer, it is the cost of something. To the seller, price is revenue, the primary source of profits. In the broadest sense, price allocates resources in a free-market economy. With so many ways of looking at price, it's no wonder that marketing managers find the task of setting prices a challenge.

What Is Price?

Price is that which is given up in an exchange to acquire a good or service. Price is typically the money exchanged for the good or service. It may also be time lost while waiting to acquire the good or service. For example, many people waited all day at Southwest Airlines's ticket counters during the company's twenty-fifth anniversary sale. Even then, some people didn't get the deeply discounted tickets that they had been hoping for. Price also might include "lost dignity" for an individual who loses his job and must rely on charity to obtain food and clothing.

Consumers are interested in obtaining a "reasonable price." "Reasonable price" really means "perceived reasonable value" at the time of the transaction. One of the authors of this textbook bought a fancy European-designed toaster for about $45. The toaster's wide mouth made it possible to toast a bagel, warm a muffin, and, with a special $15 attachment, make a grilled sandwich. The author felt that a toaster with all these features surely must be worth the total price of $60. But after three months of using the device, toast burned around the edges and raw in the middle lost its appeal. The disappointed buyer put the toaster in the attic. Why didn't he return it to the retailer? Because the boutique had gone out of business, and no other local retailer carried the brand. Also, there was no U.S. service center. Remember, the price paid is based on the satisfaction consumers *expect* to receive from a product and not necessarily the satisfaction they *actually* receive.

Price can relate to anything with perceived value, not just money. When goods and services are exchanged, the trade is called *barter*. For example, if you exchange this book for a chemistry book at the end of the term, you have engaged in barter. The price you paid for the chemistry book was this textbook.

Target combines upscale and discount in its trendy ads, which feature the affordable prices of cleverly combined items: blindspot mirrors for $1.99 and a beaded handbag for $14.99.

revenue
The price charged to customers multiplied by the number of units sold.

profit
Revenue minus expenses.

The Importance of Price to Marketing Managers

Prices are the key to revenues, which in turn are the key to profits for an organization. **Revenue** is the price charged to customers multiplied by the number of units sold. Revenue is what pays for every activity of the company: production, finance, sales, distribution, and so on. What's left over (if anything) is **profit**. Managers usually strive to charge a price that will earn a fair profit.

To earn a profit, managers must choose a price that is not too high or too low, a price that equals the perceived value to target consumers. If a price is set too high in consumers' minds, the perceived value will be less than the cost, and sales opportunities will be lost. Many mainstream purchasers of cars, sporting goods, CDs, tools, wedding gowns, and computers are buying "used or preowned" items to get a better deal. Pricing a new product too high may give an incentive to some shoppers to go to a "preowned" or consignment retailer.[2]

Lost sales mean lost revenue. Conversely, if a price is too low, it may be perceived as a great value for the consumer, but the firm loses revenue it could have earned. Setting prices too low may not even attract as many buyers as managers might think. One study surveyed over two thousand shoppers at national chains around the country and found that over 60 percent intended to buy full-price items only.[3] Retailers that place too much emphasis on discounts may not be able to meet the expectations of full-price customers.

Trying to set the right price is one of the most stressful and pressure-filled tasks of the marketing manager, as trends in the consumer market attest:

- Confronting a flood of new products, potential buyers carefully evaluate the price of each one against the value of existing products.
- The increased availability of bargain-priced private and generic brands has put downward pressure on overall prices.
- Many firms are trying to maintain or regain their market share by cutting prices. For example, IBM has regained some PC market share by aggressively cutting prices.[4]

 In the organizational market, where customers include both governments and businesses, buyers are also becoming more price sensitive and better informed. In the consumer market, consumers are using the Internet to make wiser purchasing decisions. Computerized information systems enable the organizational buyer to compare price and performance with great ease and accuracy. Improved communication and the increased use of telemarketing and computer-aided selling have also opened up many markets to new competitors. Finally, competition in general is increasing, so some installations, accessories, and component parts are being marketed like indistinguishable commodities.

Pricing Objectives

To survive in today's highly competitive marketplace, companies need pricing objectives that are specific, attainable, and measurable. Realistic pricing goals then require periodic monitoring to determine the effectiveness of the company's strategy. For convenience, pricing objectives can be divided into three categories: profit oriented, sales oriented, and status quo.

Profit-Oriented Pricing Objectives

Profit-oriented objectives include profit maximization, satisfactory profits, and target return on investment. A brief discussion of each of these objectives follows.

Profit Maximization *Profit maximization* means setting prices so that total revenue is as large as possible relative to total costs. (A more theoretically precise definition and explanation of profit maximization appears later in the chapter.) Profit maximization does not always signify unreasonably high prices, however. Both price and profits depend on the type of competitive environment a firm faces, such as being in a monopoly position (being the only seller) or selling in a much more competitive situation. Also, remember that a firm cannot charge a price higher than the product's perceived value. Many firms do not have the accounting data they need for maximizing profits. It sounds simple to say that a company should keep producing and selling goods or services as long as revenues exceed costs. Yet it is often hard to set up an accurate accounting system to determine the point of profit maximization.

Sometimes managers say that their company is trying to maximize profits—in other words, trying to make as much money as possible. Although this goal may sound impressive to stockholders, it is not good enough for planning. The statement "We want to make all the money we can" is vague and lacks focus. It gives management license to do just about anything it wants to do.

2

List and explain a variety of pricing objectives

Satisfactory Profits Satisfactory profits are a reasonable level of profits. Rather than maximizing profits, many organizations strive for profits that are satisfactory to the stockholders and management—in other words, a level of profits consistent with the level of risk an organization faces. In a risky industry, a satisfactory profit may be 35 percent. In a low-risk industry, it might be 7 percent. To maximize profits, a small-business owner might have to keep his or her store open seven days a week. However, the owner might not want to work that hard and might be satisfied with less profit.

return on investment (ROI)
Net profit after taxes divided by total assets.

Target Return on Investment The most common profit objective is a target **return on investment (ROI)**, sometimes called the firm's return on total assets. ROI measures the overall effectiveness of management in generating profits with its available assets. The higher the firm's return on investment, the better off the firm is. Many companies—including Du Pont, General Motors, Navistar, Exxon, and Union Carbide—use target return on investment as their main pricing goal.

Return on investment is calculated as follows:

$$\text{Return on investment} = \frac{\text{Net profits after taxes}}{\text{Total assets}}$$

Assume that in 2002 Johnson Controls had assets of $4.5 million, net profits of $550,000, and a target ROI of 10 percent. This was the actual ROI:

$$\text{ROI} = \frac{550,000}{4,500,000}$$

$$= 12.2 \text{ percent}$$

As you can see, the ROI for Johnson Controls exceeded its target, which indicates that the company prospered in 2002.

Comparing the 12.2 percent ROI with the industry average provides a more meaningful picture, however. Any ROI needs to be evaluated in terms of the competitive environment, risks in the industry, and economic conditions. Generally speaking, firms seek ROIs in the 10 to 30 percent range. For example, General Electric seeks a 25 percent ROI, whereas Alcoa, Rubbermaid, and most major pharmaceutical companies strive for a 20 percent ROI. However, in some industries such as the grocery industry a return of under 5 percent is common and acceptable.

A company with a target ROI can predetermine its desired level of profitability. The marketing manager can use the standard, such as 10 percent ROI, to determine whether a particular price and marketing mix are feasible. In addition, however, the manager must weigh the risk of a given strategy even if the return is in the acceptable range.

Sales-Oriented Pricing Objectives

Sales-oriented pricing objectives are based either on market share or on dollar or unit sales. The effective marketing manager should be familiar with these pricing objectives.

market share
A company's product sales as a percentage of total sales for that industry.

Market Share **Market share** is a company's product sales as a percentage of total sales for that industry. Sales can be reported in dollars or in units of product. It is very important to know whether market share is expressed in revenue or units, because the results may be different. Consider four companies competing in an industry with 2,000 total unit sales and total industry revenue of $4 million (see Exhibit 17.1). Company A has the largest unit market share at 50 percent, but it has only 25 percent of the revenue market share. In contrast, company D has only a 15 percent unit share but the largest revenue share: 30 percent. Usually, market share is expressed in terms of revenue and not units.

Many companies believe that maintaining or increasing market share is an indicator of the effectiveness of their marketing mix. Larger market shares have

Exhibit **17.1**

Two Ways to Measure Market Share (Units and Revenue)

Company	Units Sold	Unit Price	Total Revenue	Unit Market Share	Revenue Market Share
A	1,000	$1.00	$1,000,000	50%	25%
B	200	4.00	800,000	10	20
C	500	2.00	1,000,000	25	25
D	300	4.00	1,200,000	15	30
Total	2,000		$4,000,000		

indeed often meant higher profits, thanks to greater economies of scale, market power, and ability to compensate top-quality management. Conventional wisdom also says that market share and return on investment are strongly related. For the most part they are; however, many companies with low market share survive and even prosper. To succeed with a low market share, companies need to compete in industries with slow growth and few product changes—for instance, industrial component parts and supplies. Otherwise, they must vie in an industry that makes frequently bought items, such as consumer convenience goods.

The 1990s proved that the conventional wisdom about market share and profitability isn't always reliable. Because of extreme competition in some industries, many market share leaders either did not reach their target ROI or actually lost money. The airline, personal computer, and food industries had this problem. Procter & Gamble switched from market share to ROI objectives after realizing that profits don't automatically follow from a large market share. PepsiCo says its new Pepsi challenge is to be No. 1 in share of industry profit, not in share of sales volume.

Still, the struggle for market share can be all-consuming for some companies. For over a decade, Maxwell House and Folgers, the biggest U.S. coffee brands, have been locked in a struggle to dominate the market. Their weapons have been advertising, perpetual rounds of price cutting, and millions upon millions of cents-off coupons. At this point, Maxwell House, a unit of Kraft General Foods, has regained a few drops of market share that it had lost to Folgers, a unit of Procter & Gamble, earlier in the war. Maxwell House's strategy has been to advertise heavily (spending over $100 million a year) and to introduce new products that lure consumers with taste rather than price. Examples include ready-made coffee in refrigerator cartons and coffee syrup, both designed for consumers to pour and microwave as needed. Nevertheless, Folgers is still the nation's best-selling coffee, although the Kraft General Foods brands, which include Yuban and Sanka, account for a 35 percent market share. P&G has 32 percent of the U.S. coffee market.

Research organizations like A. C. Nielsen and Information Resources Inc. provide excellent market share reports for many different industries. These

Meat is not as expensive as it has been historically, but some premium cuts can still be pricey. As prices for cuts like veal and filet fall, more people are inclined to take advantage of a rare bargain, and so more is sold at lower prices.

reports enable companies to track their performance in various product categories over time.

Sales Maximization   Rather than strive for market share, sometimes companies try to maximize sales. The objective of maximizing sales ignores profits, competition, and the marketing environment as long as sales are rising.

If a company is strapped for funds or faces an uncertain future, it may try to generate a maximum amount of cash in the short run. Management's task when using this objective is to calculate which price–quantity relationship generates the greatest cash revenue. Sales maximization can also be effectively used on a temporary basis to sell off excess inventory. It is not uncommon to find Christmas cards, ornaments, and so on discounted at 50 to 70 percent off retail prices after the holiday season. In addition, management can use sales maximization for year-end sales to clear out old models before introducing the new ones.

Maximization of cash should never be a long-run objective, because cash maximization may mean little or no profitability. Without profits, a company cannot survive.

Status Quo Pricing Objectives

status quo pricing
A pricing objective that maintains existing prices or meets the competition's prices.

Status quo pricing seeks to maintain existing prices or to meet the competition's prices. This third category of pricing objectives has the major advantage of requiring little planning. It is essentially a passive policy.

Often, firms competing in an industry with an established price leader simply meet the competition's prices. These industries typically have fewer price wars than those with direct price competition. In other cases, managers regularly shop competitors' stores to ensure that their prices are comparable. Target's middle managers must visit competing Kmart stores weekly to compare prices and then make adjustments. In response to MCI Worldcom's claims that its long-distance service is overpriced, AT&T struck back with advertisements showing that its rates are essentially equal to competitors'. AT&T was attempting to convince target consumers that it follows a status quo pricing strategy.

The Demand Determinant of Price

Explain the role of demand in price determination

After marketing managers establish pricing goals, they must set specific prices to reach those goals. The price they set for each product depends mostly on two factors: the demand for the good or service and the cost to the seller for that good or service. When pricing goals are mainly sales oriented, demand considerations usually dominate. Other factors, such as distribution and promotion strategies, perceived quality, demands of large customers, the Internet, and stage of the product life cycle, can also influence price.

The Nature of Demand

demand
The quantity of a product that will be sold in the market at various prices for a specified period.

Demand is the quantity of a product that will be sold in the market at various prices for a specified period. The quantity of a product that people will buy depends on its price. The higher the price, the fewer goods or services consumers will demand. Conversely, the lower the price, the more goods or services they will demand.

Exhibit **17.2**

(a) Demand curve

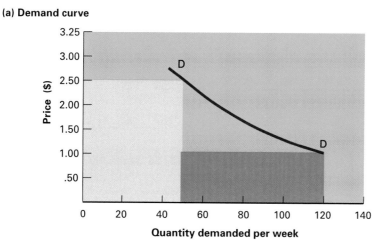

(b) Demand schedule

Price per package of gourmet popcorn ($)	Packages of gourmet popcorn demanded per week
3.00	35
2.50	50
2.00	65
1.50	85
1.00	120

This trend is illustrated in Exhibit 17.2(a), which graphs the demand per week for gourmet popcorn at a local retailer at various prices. This graph is called a *demand curve*. The vertical axis of the graph shows different prices of gourmet popcorn, measured in dollars per package. The horizontal axis measures the quantity of gourmet popcorn that will be demanded per week at each price. For example, at a price of $2.50, 50 packages will be sold per week; at $1.00, consumers will demand 120 packages—as the *demand schedule* in Exhibit 17.2(b) shows.

The demand curve in Exhibit 17.2 slopes downward and to the right, which indicates that more gourmet popcorn is demanded as the price is lowered. In other words, if popcorn manufacturers put a greater quantity on the market, then their hope of selling all of it will be realized only by selling it at a lower price.

One reason why more is sold at lower prices than at higher prices is that lower prices bring in new buyers. This fact might not be so obvious with gourmet popcorn, but consider the example of steak. As the price of steak drops lower and lower, some people who have not been eating steak will probably start buying it rather than hamburger. With each reduction in price, existing customers may buy extra amounts. Similarly, if the price of gourmet popcorn falls low enough, some people will buy more than they have bought in the past.

Supply is the quantity of a product that will be offered to the market by a supplier or suppliers at various prices for a specified period. Exhibit 17.3(a) illustrates the resulting *supply curve* for gourmet popcorn. Unlike the falling demand curve, the supply curve for gourmet popcorn slopes upward and to the right. At higher prices, gourmet popcorn manufacturers will obtain more resources (popcorn, flavorings, salt) and produce more gourmet popcorn. If the price consumers are willing to pay for gourmet popcorn increases, producers can afford to buy more ingredients.

Output tends to increase at higher prices because manufacturers can sell more packages of gourmet popcorn and earn greater profits. The *supply schedule* in Exhibit 17.3(b) shows that at $2 suppliers are willing to place 110 packages of gourmet popcorn on the market, but that they will offer 140 packages at a price of $3.

supply
The quantity of a product that will be offered to the market by a supplier at various prices for a specified period.

Exhibit 17.3

Supply Curve and Supply
Schedule for Gourmet
Popcorn

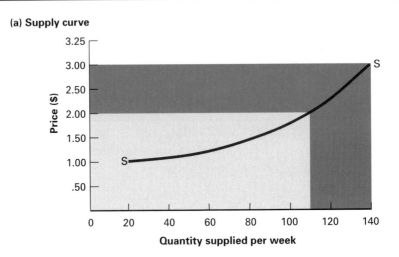

(a) Supply curve

(b) Supply schedule

Price per package of gourmet popcorn ($)	Packages of gourmet popcorn supplied per week
3.00	140
2.50	130
2.00	110
1.50	85
1.00	25

How Demand and Supply Establish Prices   At this point, let's combine the concepts of demand and supply to see how competitive market prices are determined. So far, the premise is that if the price is X, then consumers will purchase Y amount of gourmet popcorn. How high or low will prices actually go? How many packages of gourmet popcorn will be produced? How many packages will be consumed? The demand curve cannot predict consumption, nor can the supply curve alone forecast production. Instead, we need to look at what happens when supply and demand interact—as shown in Exhibit 17.4.

Exhibit 17.4

Equilibrium Price for Gourmet
Popcorn

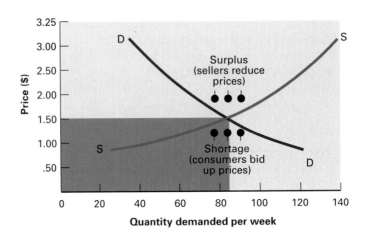

At a price of $3, the public would demand only 35 packages of gourmet popcorn. However, suppliers stand ready to place 140 packages on the market at this price (data from the demand and supply schedules). If they do, they would create a surplus of 105 packages of gourmet popcorn. How does a merchant eliminate a surplus? It lowers the price.

At a price of $1, 120 packages would be demanded, but only 25 would be placed on the market. A shortage of 95 units would be created. If a product is in short supply and consumers want it, how do they entice the dealer to part with one unit? They offer more money—that is, pay a higher price.

Now let's examine a price of $1.50. At this price, 85 packages are demanded and 85 are supplied. When demand and supply are equal, a state called **price equilibrium** is achieved. A temporary price below equilibrium—say $1.00—results in a shortage, because at that price the demand for gourmet popcorn is greater than the available supply. Shortages put upward pressure on price. As long as demand and supply remain the same, however, temporary price increases or decreases tend to return to equilibrium. At equilibrium, there is no inclination for prices to rise or fall.

An equilibrium price may not be reached all at once. Prices may fluctuate during a trial-and-error period as the market for a good or service moves toward equilibrium. Sooner or later, however, demand and supply will settle into proper balance.

price equilibrium
The price at which demand and supply are equal.

Elasticity of Demand

To appreciate demand analysis, you should understand the concept of elasticity. **Elasticity of demand** refers to consumers' responsiveness or sensitivity to changes in price. **Elastic demand** occurs when consumers buy more or less of a product when the price changes. Conversely, **inelastic demand** means that an increase or a decrease in price will not significantly affect demand for the product.

Elasticity over the range of a demand curve can be measured by using this formula:

$$\text{Elasticity } (E) = \frac{\text{Percentage change in quantity demanded of good A}}{\text{Percentage change in price of good A}}$$

If E is greater than 1, demand is elastic.
If E is less than 1, demand is inelastic.
If E is equal to 1, demand is unitary.

Unitary elasticity means that an increase in sales exactly offsets a decrease in prices so that total revenue remains the same.

Elasticity can be measured by observing these changes in total revenue:

If price goes down and revenue goes up, demand is elastic.
If price goes down and revenue goes down, demand is inelastic.
If price goes up and revenue goes up, demand is inelastic.
If price goes up and revenue goes down, demand is elastic.
If price goes up or down and revenue stays the same, elasticity is unitary.

Exhibit 17.5(a) shows a very elastic demand curve. Decreasing the price of a Sony VCR from $300 to $200 increases sales from 18,000 units to 59,000 units. Revenue increases from $5.4 million ($300 × 18,000) to $11.8 million ($200 × 59,000). The price decrease results in a large increase in sales and revenue.

Exhibit 17.5(b) shows a completely inelastic demand curve. The state of Nevada dropped its used-car vehicle inspection fee from $20 to $10. The state continued to inspect about 400,000 used cars annually. Decreasing the price (inspection fee) 50 percent did not cause people to buy more used cars. Demand is

elasticity of demand
Consumers' responsiveness or sensitivity to changes in price.

elastic demand
A situation in which consumer demand is sensitive to changes in price.

inelastic demand
A situation in which an increase or a decrease in price will not significantly affect demand for the product.

unitary elasticity
A situation in which total revenue remains the same when prices change.

Exhibit **17.5**

Elasticity of Demand for Sony
VCRs and Auto Inspection
Stickers

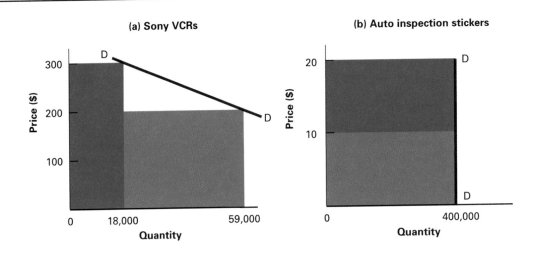

completely inelastic for inspection fees, which are required by law. Thus, it also
follows that Nevada could double the original fee to $40 and double the state's in-
spection revenues. People won't quit buying used cars if the inspection fee increases—within a reasonable range.

Exhibit 17.6 presents the demand curve and demand schedule for three-
ounce bottles of Spring Break suntan lotion. Let's follow the demand curve from
the highest price to the lowest and examine what happens to elasticity as the price
decreases.

Inelastic Demand   The initial decrease in the price of Spring Break suntan lotion,
from $5.00 to $2.25, results in a decrease in total revenue of $969 ($5,075 – $4,106).
When price and total revenue fall, demand is inelastic. The decrease in price is
much greater than the increase in suntan lotion sales (810 bottles). Demand is
therefore not very flexible in the price range $5.00 to $2.25.

When demand is inelastic, sellers can raise prices and increase total revenue.
Often, items that are relatively inexpensive but convenient tend to have inelastic
demand.

Elastic Demand   In the example of Spring Break suntan lotion, shown in Exhibit 17.6, when the price is dropped from $2.25 to $1.00, total revenue increases
by $679 ($4,785 − $4,106). An increase in total revenue when price falls indicates
that demand is elastic. Let's measure Spring Break's elasticity of demand when the
price drops from $2.25 to $1.00 by applying the earlier-mentioned formula:

$$E = \frac{\text{Change in quantity} / (\text{Sum of quantities} /2)}{\text{Change in price} / (\text{Sum of prices} /2)}$$

$$= \frac{(4,785 - 1,825) / [(1,825 + 4,785) / 2]}{(2.25) - 1 / [(2.25 + 1.00) / 2]}$$

$$= \frac{2,960 / 3,305}{1.25 / 1.63}$$

$$= \frac{.896}{.767}$$

$$= 1.17$$

Because *E* is greater than 1, demand is elastic.

Factors That Affect Elasticity   Several factors affect elasticity of demand, including the following:

Exhibit **17.6**

(a) Demand curve

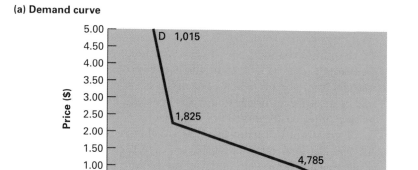

(b) Demand schedule

Price ($)	Quantity demanded	Total revenue (price x quantity)	Elasticity
5.00	1,015	$5,075 ●	⎫ Inelastic
2.25	1,825	4,106 ●	⎭
1.00	4,785	4,785 ●	Elastic
0.25	6,380	4,785 ●	Unitary

- *Availability of substitutes:* When many substitute products are available, the consumer can easily switch from one product to another, making demand elastic. The same is true in reverse: A person with complete renal failure will pay whatever is charged for a kidney transplant because there is no substitute.
- *Price relative to purchasing power:* If a price is so low that it is an inconsequential part of an individual's budget, demand will be inelastic. For example, if the price of salt doubles, consumers will not stop putting salt and pepper on their eggs, because salt is cheap anyway.
- *Product durability:* Consumers often have the option of repairing durable products rather than replacing them, thus prolonging their useful life. If a person had planned to buy a new car and the prices suddenly began to rise, he or she might elect to fix the old car and drive it for another year. In other words, people are sensitive to the price increase, and demand is elastic.
- *A product's other uses:* The greater the number of different uses for a product, the more elastic demand tends to be. If a product has only one use, as may be true of a new medicine, the quantity purchased probably will not vary as price varies. A person will consume only the prescribed quantity, regardless of price. On the other hand, a product like steel has many possible applications. As its price falls, steel becomes more economically feasible in a wider variety of applications, thereby making demand relatively elastic.

The Power of Yield Management Systems

When competitive pressures are high, a company must know when it can raise prices to maximize its revenues. More and more companies are turning to yield management systems to help adjust prices. First developed in the airline industry, **yield management systems** (**YMS**) use complex mathematical software to profitably fill unused capacity. The software employs techniques such as discounting early purchases, limiting early sales at these discounted prices, and overbooking capacity. YMS now are appearing in other services such as lodging, other transportation forms, rental firms, and even hospitals.[5]

Understand the concept of yield management systems

yield management systems (YMS)
A technique for adjusting prices that uses complex mathematical software to profitably fill unused capacity by discounting early purchases, limiting early sales at these discounted prices, and overbooking capacity.

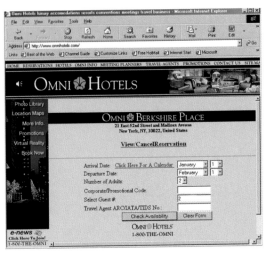

Although yield management is being implemented across diverse and multiple industries, it is the hallmark of the travel industry. Often hotels like Omni offer different weekend specials each week in order to encourage the kind of spontaneous travel that will maximize company revenues.

Yield management systems are spreading beyond service industries as their popularity increases. The lessons of airlines and hotels aren't entirely applicable to other industries because plane seats and hotel beds are perishable—if they go empty, the revenue opportunity is lost forever. So it makes sense to slash prices to move toward capacity if it's possible to do so without reducing the prices that other customers pay. Cars and steel aren't so perishable. Still, the capacity to make these goods is perishable. An underused factory or mill is a lost revenue opportunity. So it makes sense to cut prices to use up capacity if it's possible to do so while getting other customers to pay full price.

Ford Motor Company used YMS to change the mix of vehicles it sells. In 1999, Ford earned $7.2 billion, a record for any auto maker in history, while actually losing market share. But behind those numbers was a 420,000-unit decrease in sales of low-margin vehicles, such as Escorts and Aspires, and a 600,000-unit increase in sales of high-margin vehicles, such as Crown Victorias and Explorers. Ford cut prices on its most profitable vehicles enough to spur demand but not so much that they ceased to have attractive margins. "This is probably the biggest driver of Ford's profitability," says Lloyd E. Hansen, Ford's controller for North America and global marketing.[6]

Some companies, such as American Airlines and Omni Hotels, are creating their own YMS software. Omni Charm (Centralized Hotel Automated Revenue Management), created by Omni Hotels, predicts demand and indicates when to discount rooms and when to charge the maximum. Marriott, with a similar system, earns an additional estimated $400 million per year.[7]

The Cost Determinant of Price

Describe cost-oriented pricing strategies

variable cost
A cost that varies with changes in the level of output.

fixed cost
A cost that does not change as output is increased or decreased.

average variable cost (AVC)
Total variable costs divided by quantity of output.

average total cost (ATC)
Total costs divided by quantity of output.

marginal cost (MC)
The change in total costs associated with a one-unit change in output.

Sometimes companies minimize or ignore the importance of demand and decide to price their products largely or solely on the basis of costs. Prices determined strictly on the basis of costs may be too high for the target market, thereby reducing or eliminating sales. On the other hand, cost-based prices may be too low, causing the firm to earn a lower return than it should. However, costs should generally be part of any price determination, if only as a floor below which a good or service must not be priced in the long run.

The idea of cost may seem simple, but it is actually a multifaceted concept, especially for producers of goods and services. A **variable cost** is a cost that deviates with changes in the level of output; an example of a variable cost is the cost of materials. In contrast, a **fixed cost** does not change as output is increased or decreased. Examples include rent and executives' salaries.

In order to compare the cost of production to the selling price of a product, it is helpful to calculate costs per unit, or average costs. **Average variable cost (AVC)** equals total variable costs divided by quantity of output. **Average total cost (ATC)** equals total costs divided by output. As plotted on the graph in Exhibit 17.7(a), AVC and ATC are basically U-shaped curves. In contrast, average fixed costs (AFC) decline continually as output increases, because total fixed costs are constant.

Marginal cost (MC) is the change in total costs associated with a one-unit change in output. Exhibit 17.7(b) shows that when output rises from seven to eight units, the change in total cost is from $640 to $750; therefore, marginal cost is $110.

All the curves illustrated in Exhibit 17.7(a) have definite relationships:

- AVC plus AFC equals ATC.
- MC falls for a while and then turns upward, in this case with the fourth unit. At that point diminishing returns set in, meaning that less output is produced for every additional dollar spent on variable input.

Exhibit 17.7

(a) Cost curves

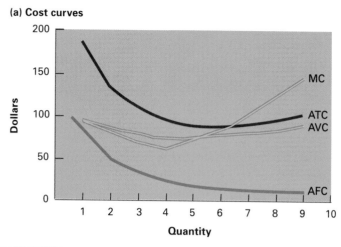

(b) Cost schedule

(1) Total product (Q)	(2) Total fixed cost (TFC)	(3) Total variable cost (TVC)	(4) Total cost (TC)	(5) Average fixed cost (AFC)	(6) Average variable cost (AVC)	(7) Average total cost (ATC)	(8) Marginal cost (MC)
			TC = TFC + TVC	AFC = $\frac{TFC}{Q}$	AVC = $\frac{TVC}{Q}$	ATC = $\frac{TC}{Q}$	(MC) = $\frac{\text{change in TC}}{\text{change in Q}}$
0	$100	$ 0	$ 100	—	—	—	—
1	100	90	190	$100.00	$90.00	$190.00	$ 90
2	100	170	270	50.00	85.00	135.00	80
3	100	240	340	33.33	80.00	113.33	70
4	100	300	400	25.00	75.00	100.00	60
5	100	370	470	20.00	74.00	94.00	70
6	100	450	550	16.67	75.00	91.67	80
7	100	540	640	14.29	77.14	91.43	90
8	100	650	750	12.50	81.25	93.75	110
9	100	780	880	11.11	86.67	97.78	130
10	100	930	1030	10.00	93.00	103.00	150

- MC intersects both AVC and ATC at their lowest possible points.
- When MC is less than AVC or ATC, the incremental cost will continue to pull the averages down. Conversely, when MC is greater than AVC or ATC, it pulls the averages up, and ATC and AVC begin to rise.
- The minimum point on the ATC curve is the least cost point for a fixed-capacity firm, although it is not necessarily the most profitable point.

Costs can be used to set prices in a variety of ways. The first two methods discussed here, markup pricing and formula pricing, are relatively simple. The other three—profit maximization pricing, break-even pricing, and target-return pricing—make use of the more complicated concepts of cost.

markup pricing
The cost of buying the product from the producer plus amounts for profit and for expenses not otherwise accounted for.

keystoning
The practice of marking up prices by 100 percent, or doubling the cost.

Markup Pricing

Markup pricing, the most popular method used by wholesalers and retailers to establish a selling price, does not directly analyze the costs of production. Instead, **markup pricing** is the cost of buying the product from the producer, plus amounts for profit and for expenses not otherwise accounted for. The total determines the selling price.

A retailer, for example, adds a certain percentage to the cost of the merchandise received to arrive at the retail price. An item that costs the retailer $1.80 and is sold for $2.20 carries a markup of 40¢, which is a markup of 22 percent of the cost (40¢ ÷ $1.80). Retailers tend to discuss markup in terms of its percentage of the retail price—in this example, 18 percent (40¢ ÷ $2.20). The difference between the retailer's cost and the selling price (40¢) is the gross margin, as Chapter 13 explained.

Markups are often based on experience. For example, many small retailers mark up merchandise 100 percent over cost. (In other words, they double the cost.) This tactic is called **keystoning**. Some other factors that influence markups are the merchandise's appeal to customers, past response to the markup (an implicit demand consideration), the item's promotional value, the seasonality of the goods, their fashion appeal, the product's traditional selling price, and competition. Most retailers avoid any set markup because of such considerations as promotional value and seasonality.

The biggest advantage of markup pricing is its simplicity. The primary disadvantage is that it ignores demand and may result in overpricing or underpricing the merchandise.

High markups can sometimes raise ethical questions. This notion is related to the unusual medical practice discussed in the "Ethics in Marketing" box.

Ethics in Marketing

FOR THE RIGHT PRICE, THESE DOCTORS TREAT THEIR PATIENTS AS PRECIOUS

Garrison Bliss and Mitchell Karton, like many doctors, were tired of insurance companies telling them how to care for their patients. Looking for a way around the bureaucracy, the two physicians discovered the price people will pay for peace of mind.

Their practice, Seattle Medical Associates, is an unusual medical consultancy, where people pay for a doctor's know-how. For a range of fees, patients get unlimited access to a doctor they know who will guide them through the maze of hospitals and medical specialists they may encounter if they do get sick. There are unlimited office visits, an annual physical, and X-rays as needed, but no ties to the insurers and health-maintenance organizations that most Americans now encounter.

SMA doesn't take Medicare or Medicaid either. Instead, it promises the kind of personal, around-the-clock attention that people used to associate with their family doctor.

Many of their longtime patients had to think hard about paying almost $800 more a year on top of other health costs, and a lot of their old patients have left. Others are happy that they stayed. "It's expensive, but this matters," says Julie Blacklow, a fifty-one-year-old freelance television producer who recently called Dr. Karton at 1 A.M. complaining of chest pains that she feared signaled a heart attack. He talked her through her symptoms, then told her—correctly—not to worry. "To give someone access, that may be the best medicine of

all," Ms. Blacklow says. "That's priceless."

Maybe. But such added prices are too high for many Americans and point the way to a multitiered medical system in which the quality of care might depend even more than it does today on the thickness of the patient's wallet.[a]

Is there anything you see as unethical about what Bliss and Karton are doing? Would it be unethical if the federal government implemented such a system? When the practice converted to the new pricing system, they lost one-third of their patients. Do the doctors have any obligation to them?

[a] Anita Sharp. "For the Right Price, These Doctors Treat Patients as Precious," *Wall Street Journal*, August 12, 1998, pp. A1, A6.

Profit Maximization Pricing

Producers tend to use more complicated methods of setting prices than distributors use. One is **profit maximization**, which occurs when marginal revenue equals marginal cost. You learned earlier that marginal cost is the change in total costs associated with a one-unit change in output. Similarly, **marginal revenue (MR)** is the extra revenue associated with selling an extra unit of output. As long as the revenue of the last unit produced and sold is greater than the cost of the last unit produced and sold, the firm should continue manufacturing and selling the product.

Exhibit 17.8 shows the marginal revenues and marginal costs for a hypothetical firm, using the cost data from Exhibit 17.7(b). The profit-maximizing quantity, where MR = MC, is six units. You might say, "If profit is zero, why produce the sixth unit? Why not stop at five?" In fact, you would be right. The firm, however, would not know that the fifth unit would produce zero profits until it determined that profits were no longer increasing. Economists suggest producing up to the point where MR = MC. If marginal revenue is just one penny greater than marginal costs, it will still increase total profits.

profit maximization
A method of setting prices that occurs when marginal revenue equals marginal cost.

marginal revenue (MR)
The extra revenue associated with selling an extra unit of output or the change in total revenue with a one-unit change in output.

Break-Even Pricing

Now let's take a closer look at the relationship between sales and cost. **Break-even analysis** determines what sales volume must be reached before the company breaks even (its total costs equal total revenue) and no profits are earned.

break-even analysis
A method of determining what sales volume must be reached before total revenue equals total costs.

Exhibit 17.8

Point of Profit Maximization

Quantity	Marginal Revenue (MR)	Marginal Cost (MC)	Cumulative Total Profit
0	—	—	—
1	140	90	50
2	130	80	100
3	105	70	135
4	95	60	170
5	85	70	185
*6	80	80	185
7	75	90	170
8	60	110	120
9	50	130	40
10	40	150	(70)

*Profit maximization

The typical break-even model assumes a given fixed cost and a constant average variable cost. Suppose that Universal Sportswear, a hypothetical firm, has fixed costs of $2,000 and that the cost of labor and materials for each unit produced is 50¢. Assume that it can sell up to 6,000 units of its product at $1 without having to lower its price.

Exhibit 17.9(a) illustrates Universal Sportswear's break-even point. As Exhibit 17.9(b) indicates, Universal Sportswear's total variable costs increase by 50¢ every time a new unit is produced, and total fixed costs remain constant at $2,000 regardless of the level of output. Therefore, 4,000 units of output give Universal Sportswear $2,000 in fixed costs and $2,000 in total variable costs (4,000 units × 50¢), or $4,000 in total costs.

Revenue is also $4,000 (4,000 units × $1), giving a net profit of zero dollars at the break-even point of 4,000 units. Notice that once the firm gets past the break-even point, the gap between total revenue and total cost gets wider and wider, because both functions are assumed to be linear.

Exhibit 17.9

Costs, Revenues, and Break-Even Point for Universal Sportswear

(a) Break-even point

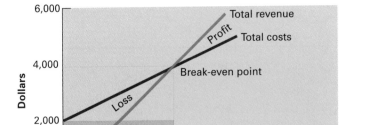

(b) Costs and revenues

Output	Total fixed costs	Average variable costs	Total variable costs	Average total costs	Average revenue (price)	Total revenue	Total costs	Profit or loss
500	$2,000	$0.50	$ 250	$4.50	$1.00	$ 500	$2,250	($1,750)
1,000	2,000	0.50	500	2.50	1.00	1,000	2,500	(1,500)
1,500	2,000	0.50	750	1.83	1.00	1,500	2,750	(1,250)
2,000	2,000	0.50	1,000	1.50	1.00	2,000	3,000	(1,000)
2,500	2,000	0.50	1,250	1.30	1.00	2,500	3,250	(750)
3,000	2,000	0.50	1,500	1.17	1.00	3,000	3,500	(500)
3,500	2,000	0.50	1,750	1.07	1.00	3,500	3,750	(250)
*4,000	2,000	0.50	2,000	1.00	1.00	4,000	4,000	(0)
4,500	2,000	0.50	2,250	.94	1.00	4,500	4,250	250
5,000	2,000	0.50	2,500	.90	1.00	5,000	4,500	500
5,500	2,000	0.50	2,750	.86	1.00	5,500	4,750	750
6,000	2,000	0.50	3,000	.83	1.00	6,000	5,000	1,000

*Break-even point

The formula for calculating break-even quantities is simple:

$$\text{Break-even quantity} = \frac{\text{Total fixed costs}}{\text{Fixed cost contribution}}$$

Fixed cost contribution is the price minus the average variable cost. Therefore, for Universal Sportswear,

$$\text{Break-even quantity} = \frac{\$2,000}{(\$1.00 - 50¢)} = \frac{\$2,000}{50¢}$$
$$= 4,000 \text{ units}$$

The advantage of break-even analysis is that it provides a quick estimate of how much the firm must sell to break even and how much profit can be earned if a higher sales volume is obtained. If a firm is operating close to the break-even point, it may want to see what can be done to reduce costs or increase sales. Moreover, in a simple break-even analysis, it is not necessary to compute marginal costs and marginal revenues, because price and average cost per unit are assumed to be constant. Also, because accounting data for marginal cost and revenue are frequently unavailable, it is convenient not to have to depend on that information.

Break-even analysis is not without several important limitations. Sometimes it is hard to know whether a cost is fixed or variable. If labor wins a tough guaranteed-employment contract, are the resulting expenses a fixed cost? Are middle-level executives' salaries fixed costs? More important than cost determination is the fact that simple break-even analysis ignores demand. How does Universal Sportswear know it can sell 4,000 units at $1? Could it sell the same 4,000 units at $2 or even $5? Obviously, this information would profoundly affect the firm's pricing decisions.

Other Determinants of Price

Other factors besides demand and costs can influence price. For example, the stages in the product life cycle, the competition, and the product distribution strategy, promotion strategy, and perceived quality can all affect pricing.

Stages in the Product Life Cycle

As a product moves through its life cycle (see Chapter 9), the demand for the product and the competitive conditions tend to change:

- *Introductory stage:* Management usually sets prices high during the introductory stage. One reason is that it hopes to recover its development costs quickly. In addition, demand originates in the core of the market (the customers whose needs ideally match the product's attributes) and thus is relatively inelastic. On the other hand, if the target market is highly price sensitive, management often finds it better to price the product at the market level or lower. For example, when Kraft General Foods brought out Country Time lemonade, it was priced like similar products in the highly competitive beverage market because the market was price sensitive.

- *Growth stage:* Prices generally begin to stabilize as the product enters the growth stage. There are several reasons. First, competitors have entered the market, increasing the available supply. Second, the product has begun to appeal to a broader market, often lower income groups. Finally, economies of scale are lowering costs, and the savings can be passed on to the consumer in the form of lower prices.

- *Maturity stage:* Maturity usually brings further price decreases as competition increases and inefficient, high-cost firms are eliminated. Distribution channels

Demonstrate how the product life cycle, competition, distribution and promotion strategies, customer demands, the Internet and extranets, and perceptions of quality can affect price

become a significant cost factor, however, because of the need to offer wide product lines for highly segmented markets, extensive service requirements, and the sheer number of dealers necessary to absorb high-volume production. The manufacturers that remain in the market toward the end of the maturity stage typically offer similar prices. Usually only the most efficient remain, and they have comparable costs. At this stage, price increases are usually cost initiated, not demand initiated. Nor do price reductions in the late phase of maturity stimulate much demand. Because demand is limited and producers have similar cost structures, the remaining competitors will probably match price reductions.

- *Decline stage:* The final stage of the life cycle may see further price decreases as the few remaining competitors try to salvage the last vestiges of demand. When only one firm is left in the market, prices begin to stabilize. In fact, prices may eventually rise dramatically if the product survives and moves into the specialty goods category, as horse-drawn carriages and vinyl records have.

The Competition

Competition varies during the product life cycle, of course, and so at times it may strongly affect pricing decisions. Although a firm may not have any competition at first, the high prices it charges may eventually induce another firm to enter the market. Several Internet auto sellers, such as Autobytel.com, have sprung up in response to the perceived high profit margins earned by car dealers.

Competition may strongly impact price. On-line auto brokers have emerged as significant competitors to traditional dealers. The perceived high profit margins—and corresponding high price—earned by car dealers has created an opening where lower price competition can flourish.

On the other hand, intense competition can sometimes lead to price wars. What pulls companies into such self-defeating price wars? Often, they make the mistake of measuring their success by market share rather than by profitability—but something more is at play. Michael Marn, a partner at McKinsey, the worldwide management consulting company, who heads its pricing practice worldwide, says that price wars are often caused by companies misreading or misunderstanding competitors. Marn tells of one McKinsey client, a company that dominated the market for adhesive labels nationwide. After a small competitor built a tiny factory in southern Florida with no prospects for further expansion, the company reacted with a nationwide price cut of 15 to 20 percent and, says Marn, "gave away profitability for two years." Typically, concludes Marn, price wars are "overreactions to threats that either aren't there at all or are not as big as they seem."[8]

One company recently took action to avoid a calamitous price war by outsmarting its competition. A company (call it Acme) heard that its competitor was trying to steal some business by offering a low price to one of its best customers. Instead of immediately cutting its prices, Acme visited three of its competitor's best clients and said they figured the client was paying x, the same price that the competitor had quoted to Acme's own customer. Within days, Acme's competitor had retracted its low-price offer to its client. Presumably, the competitor had received calls from three angry clients asking for the same special deal.

Distribution Strategy

An effective distribution network can often overcome other minor flaws in the marketing mix. For example, although consumers may perceive a price as being slightly higher than normal, they may buy the product anyway if it is being sold at a convenient retail outlet.

Adequate distribution for a new product can often be attained by offering a larger-than-usual profit margin to distributors. A variation on this strategy is to give dealers a large trade allowance to help offset the costs of promotion and further stimulate demand at the retail level.

Manufacturers have gradually been losing control within the distribution channel to wholesalers and retailers, which often adopt pricing strategies that serve their own purposes. For instance, some distributors are **selling against the brand**: They place well-known brands on the shelves at high prices while offering other brands—typically, their private-label brands, such as Craftsman tools, Kroger pears, or Cost Cutter paper towels—at lower prices. Of course, sales of the higher priced brands decline.

Wholesalers and retailers may also go outside traditional distribution channels to buy gray-market goods. As explained previously, distributors obtain the goods through unauthorized channels for less than they would normally pay so they can sell the goods with a bigger-than-normal markup or at a reduced price. Imports seem to be particularly susceptible to gray marketing. Porsches, JVC stereos, and Seiko watches are among the brand-name products that have experienced this problem. Although consumers may pay less for gray-market goods, they often find that the manufacturer won't honor the warranty.

Manufacturers can regain some control over price by using an exclusive distribution system, by franchising, or by avoiding doing business with price-cutting discounters. Manufacturers can also package merchandise with the selling price marked on it or place goods on consignment. The best way for manufacturers to control prices, however, is to develop brand loyalty in consumers by delivering quality and value.

Sometimes governments will intervene to try and influence prices in a distribution channel. The "Global Perspectives" box describes a unique attempt to change prices by passing a rather unusual law.

Global Perspectives

CAN A NEW FRENCH LAW INFLUENCE CONSUMERS TO PUSH FOR HIGHER PRICES PAID TO FARMERS?

Sometimes the French really do seem to think differently. In the country that Descartes imprinted with Cartesian logic, people side with transit workers when bus, rail, and subway strikes make it impossible to get to work on time. And logically, at the height of the summer fruit and vegetable season, prices should be lower. But by a logic perhaps only the French can understand, fruit and vegetable producers are hoping that a new government regulation requiring retail stores to post the wholesale prices they paid for the produce alongside the retail price—which is always much higher—will pressure wholesalers to pay the producers more.

By Gallic logic, French consumers seeing the wholesale and retail prices on the shelves will side with underdog farmers, just as they

do with underdog railway workers, and show their solidarity by pressuring wholesale distributors to be fairer to producers, explained one farmer, Guy Savanier, from his apricot orchard and vineyard near Nîmes.

"The consumer will know that every product with two prices listed is a product in difficulty," Mr. Savanier said. "We hope they will buy more, which will increase demand and raise prices." That sounded like economic logic, but Savanier hoped there would be something more. "We also expect a civic attitude by distributors, in the sense that they will accept a more equitable sharing of profit margins," he said. Ergo, French supermarkets, the villains in Savanier's eyes, will pay producers more for French fruits and vegetables but not raise supermarket retail

prices. "We don't want consumers to pay more," he said.

Michel-Édouard Leclerc, the head of a chain of supermarkets that bears his name, called the new regulation "a political solution responding to a demand by agricultural unions that won't make prices rise."[a]

You have just found out that your supermarket paid 70 cents a pound wholesale for the apricots that they are selling to you for $1.48. Would you ask the supermarket to pay more to the wholesaler or reduce the retail price? Would this French law work in America? What is it that the French government doesn't seem to understand about pricing?

[a] Craig Whitney. "Solidarity and the Price of Apricots," *New York Times*, August 21, 1999, p. A4.

The Impact of the Internet and Extranets

The Internet, corporate networks, and wireless setups are linking people, machines, and companies around the globe—and connecting sellers and buyers as never before. This link is enabling buyers to quickly and easily compare products and prices, putting them in a better bargaining position. At the same time, the technology allows sellers to collect detailed data about customers' buying habits, preferences, even spending limits, so they can tailor their products and prices—all of which raises hopes of a more efficient marketplace.

Prices are already coming down as a result of the Internet. Although e-commerce is still only a small part of total retail sales, the Web is a haven for people looking for a bargain. The percentage difference from ordinary retail outlets, including shipping costs from e-retailers are prescription drugs (−28%), apparel (−38%), alcohol and cigarettes (−28%), and home electronics (−4%).[9]

In some ways, pricing strategies have become more difficult for retailers. Early Web retailers used deep discounts to attract pioneering Internet consumers and keep them coming back. Since then, however, e-commerce has been changing fast. Many more customers are now on-line, roaming from one site to the next, calling up price-comparison sites, and banding together to buy in bulk. At the same time, more companies with brick-and-mortar operations have set up shop on-line.

Should a merchant, for instance, slash prices and try to compete with the lowest of the lowball discounters out there—those clearly willing to take a loss on sales to build a base in advertising revenue? What if a "click-and-mortar" retailer is branching onto the Web from a chain of real-world stores? Can it undercut the prices in its regular stores?

The pricing revolution, though, goes beyond the Net. Companies also are creating private networks, or **extranets**, that link them with their suppliers and customers. These systems make it possible to get a precise handle on inventory, costs, and demand at any given moment—and adjust prices instantly. In the past, there was a significant cost associated with changing prices, known as the "menu cost." For a company with a large product line, it could take months for price adjustments to filter down to distributors, retailers, and salespeople. Streamlined networks reduce menu cost and time to near zero.[10]

Two trailblazers in Net commerce are Southern California Gas Company and Priceline. Deregulation of the energy industry means that customers can shop for an energy supplier just like a long distance company. Southern California Gas saw this as an opportunity and created the Energy Marketplace. This is a Web-based exchange that lets customers shop for the best gas prices. Small and mid-size gas providers list their prices on the exchange. That lowers their marketing costs and gives them access to a broader market—putting them on equal footing with big energy suppliers. Customers, mostly businesses, save money by shopping for the best price or locking in long-term deals when prices are low. Southern California Gas, as a distributor, increases its volume of business and collects a subscription fee from gas providers that use the exchange.

Priceline.com started because of a vendor problem. That is, how to sell 500,000 airline seats that go unsold daily. Most businesses with excess inventory cut their prices over time. Airlines can't because they hope to sell high-price tickets to last-minute business travelers. The other problem is that many of the empty seats are on early or late flights that nobody wants to take. Priceline.com lets consumers "name their own price" for those empty seats. If an airline is willing to accept the bid, the consumer gets a cheap ticket.

Priceline.com agreed to impose heavy restrictions on whatever discount tickets the airlines made available. For example, customers submitting bids must guarantee their offer up-front with a credit card. They have to agree to accept a departure any-

extranet
A private electronic network that links a company with its suppliers and customers.

On Line

time between 6 A.M. and 10 P.M. They can't specify an airline. They can't get frequent-flier miles, switch flights, or get refunds. And in most cases they have to change planes or make at least one stop.

Here is how Priceline.com really works: Priceline negotiates with participating carriers for access to unsold seats at special prices. Those prices, which the airlines may revise as often as several times a day, are entered into Priceline's private computer database before any bid arrives. When one does come in, computers check whether a match is available; the bidder is then notified by e-mail. In other words, a bid is filled only if it meets (or exceeds) a price previously named by one of Priceline's airlines. Sure, consumers can "name" prices at Priceline, but it remains the airlines that set them. Indeed, because Priceline keeps the prices of its available tickets secret, the company offers consumers what is truly a revolutionary opportunity: the chance to pay more than the asking price.[11]

Today, Priceline.com has moved into rental cars, hotel rooms, telephone minutes, and other services. In the future, the Internet company hopes to offer auto and life insurance and electronics. However, Priceline would soon face stiff competition from its own suppliers. Hyatt, Hilton, Marriott, Starwood Hotels & Resorts, and Cendant—most of which sell excess hotel rooms through Priceline—are having "serious" discussions about starting their own company to distribute over the Internet.[12] A consortium of twelve major airlines including Continental, United, and American are planning to create their own company to sell discounted airlines seats over the Internet.

Internet Auctions   The Internet auction business is huge. EBay alone has ten million customers and a market value of $21 billion. Now, business is picking up the electronic gavel. The auto-parts auctioneer planned by General Motors, Ford, and DaimlerChrysler is expected to handle $250 billion in transactions a year.[13] Bidders can indeed save money at e-auctions. One study compared prices in 473 on-line auctions with prices of identical goods bought from on-line catalogs. The average auction discount was 25 percent for goods bought from a retailer with both an auction and a catalog site.[14] Part of the lure of buying on-line is that shoppers don't have to go to a flea market or use up a coveted weekend day or worry about the weather. Plus, bidding itself can be fun and exciting. Already, over 35 percent of on-line buyers have purchased something through an on-line auction.[15] A few of the most popular auction sites are the following

The Internet has had a most significant impact on pricing in numerous industries. Priceline.com has flourished serving as a combination yield-manager and auction block for open airline tickets, hotel rooms, and rental cars. It remains to be seen if its move into such areas as long distance will prove to be as successful.

- **http://www.auctions.amazon.com:** Link to Sotheby's for qualified sellers of high-end items.
- **http://www.ebay.com:** Most popular auction site.
- **http://www.fairmarket.com:** Network of one hundred sites that share listings.
- **http://www.auctions.yahoo.com:** Free listings and numerous selling categories.

Promotion Strategy

Price is often used as a promotional tool to increase consumer interest. The weekly flyers sent out by grocery stores in the Sunday newspaper, for instance, advertise many products with special low prices. Crested Butte Ski Resort in Colorado tried a unique twist on price promotions. It made the unusual offer of free skiing between Thanksgiving and Christmas. Its only revenues were voluntary contributions from lodging and restaurant owners who benefited from the droves of skiers taking advantage of the promotion. Lodging during the slack period is now booked solid, and on the busiest days nine thousand skiers jam slopes designed for about sixty-five hundred. Crested Butte Resort no longer loses money during this time of the year.

Pricing can be a tool for trade promotions as well. For example, Levi's Dockers (casual men's pants) are very popular with white-collar men ages twenty-five to forty-five, a growing and lucrative market. Sensing an opportunity, rival pants-maker Bugle Boy began offering similar pants at cheaper wholesale prices, which gave retailers a bigger gross margin than they were getting with Dockers. Levi Strauss & Co. had to either lower prices or risk its $400 million annual Docker sales. Although Levi Strauss intended its cheapest Dockers to retail for $35, it started selling Dockers to retailers for $18 a pair. Retailers could then advertise Dockers at a very attractive retail price of $25.

Demands of Large Customers

Large customers of manufacturers such as Wal-Mart, JCPenney, and other department stores often make specific pricing demands that the suppliers must agree to. Department stores are making greater-than-ever demands from their suppliers to cover the heavy discounts and markdowns on their own selling floors. They want suppliers to guarantee their stores' profit margins, and they insist on cash rebates if the guarantee isn't met. They are also exacting fines for violations of ticketing, packing, and shipping rules. Cumulatively, the demands are nearly wiping out profits for all but the very biggest suppliers, according to fashion designers and garment makers.

Few stores ask for stiffer margin guarantees than May's Lord & Taylor chain.[16] Makers of moderate-priced dresses say Lord & Taylor is the entry point for vendors hoping to do business with other May department store chains like Hecht's and Foley's. May sets the profitability bar high, insisting on a guaranteed profit margin in some cases as high as 48 percent, according to Beau Baker, former chief executive officer of Beau David Inc., a small dress company.

In the past when a garment maker sold to a store, the two parties would agree on a retail price and at the end of the season the supplier would rebate some of the cost of markdowns. Discounts and markdowns were far rarer then than they are today: Department stores could afford plenty of sales help to push products. However, as stores cut labor costs, they came to rely on promotional markdowns and sales to move goods—with suppliers covering profit-margin shortfalls.

The Relationship of Price to Quality

Consumers tend to rely on a high price as a predictor of good quality when there is great uncertainty involved in the purchase decision. Reliance on price as an indicator of quality seems to exist for all products, but it reveals itself more strongly for some items than for others.[17] Among the products that benefit from this phenomenon are coffee, stockings, aspirin, salt, floor wax, shampoo, clothing, furniture, perfume, whiskey, and many services. If the consumer obtains additional information—for instance, about the brand or the store—then reliance on price as an indicator of quality decreases.[18] In the absence of other information, people typically assume that prices are higher because the products contain better materials, because they are made more carefully, or, in the case of professional services, because the provider has more expertise. In other words, consumers assume that "You get what you pay for." One study has shown that some people believe "You get what you pay for" much more strongly than others; that is, some consumers tend to rely much more heavily on price as a quality indicator than others do.[19] In general, consumers tend to be more accurate in their price-quality assessments for nondurable goods (such as ice cream, frozen pizza, or oven cleaner) than for durable goods (such as coffeemakers, gas grills, or ten-speed bikes).[20] Knowledgeable merchants take these consumer attitudes into account when devising their pricing strategies. **Prestige pricing** is charging a high

prestige pricing
Charging a high price to help promote a high-quality image.

price to help promote a high-quality image. A successful prestige pricing strategy requires a retail price that is reasonably consistent with consumers' expectations. No one goes shopping at a Gucci's shop in New York and expects to pay $9.95 for a pair of loafers. In fact, demand would fall drastically at such a low price. Bayer aspirin would probably lose market share over the long run if it lowered its prices. A new mustard packaged in a crockery jar was not successful until its price was doubled.

Consumers also expect private or store brands to be cheaper than national brands. However, if the price difference between a private brand and a nationally distributed manufacturer's brand is *too* great, consumers tend to believe that the private brand is inferior. On the other hand, if the savings aren't big enough, there is little incentive to buy the private brand. One study of scanner data found that if the price difference between the national brand and the private brand was less than 10 percent, people tended not to buy the private brand. If the price difference was greater than 20 percent, consumers perceived the private brand to be inferior.[21]

In sum, the most recent research has shown that a well-known brand name is used by people in many countries as their primary indicator of quality. If the product does not have this feature, then price, followed by the physical appearance of the item, is used to judge quality. After a well-known brand name, price, and physical appearance, the reputation of the retailer is used by consumers as an indicator of quality.[22]

Looking Back

Look back at the story at the beginning of this chapter on how the airlines are now making money. The relationships between costs, revenues, and profit are direct. Revenue minus costs equals profits. Profits can be increased by increasing revenues, lowering costs, or both. The Internet is already having a major impact on pricing. Consumers are finding better deals and making better decisions by comparing prices. Old-line manufacturers face the dilemma of competing directly with their channel members if the manufacturer sells through its own Web site.

Yield management systems will help boost revenues of not only services businesses but old-line manufacturers as well. This in turn will mean increased profits for the organization.

Price can have an impact on perceived quality, depending on a number of issues, such as the type of product, advertising, and the consumer's personality. A well-known brand is usually more important than price in consumers' quality perceptions.

Use it Now!

If you want to save money on airline tickets or hotel rooms, give Priceline.com a try. No, you won't get an airline ticket from New York to Los Angeles for $100. But if you can be flexible, you should save some money. Priceline sells many of its tickets for about the same price as the twenty-one-day advance fare even when the flight is booked only two days prior to departure.

If you like checking out airlines' last-minute on-line travel deals but hate sifting through all those weekly e-mails, here's a solution: Smarter Living (**http://www.smarterliving.com**) is a service that sorts through the special deals of twenty major airlines and sends them out weekly in a single electronic newsletter. Sign up free at its Web site.

For good values on airline seats, also check out **http://www.cheaptickets.com**; for hotel rooms try **http://www.hoteldiscounters.com**.

Summary

① **Discuss the importance of pricing decisions to the economy and to the individual firm.** Pricing plays an integral role in the U.S. economy by allocating goods and services among consumers, governments, and businesses. Pricing is essential in business because it creates revenue, which is the basis of all business activity. In setting prices, marketing managers strive to find a level high enough to produce a satisfactory profit.

② **List and explain a variety of pricing objectives.** Establishing realistic and measurable pricing objectives is a critical part of any firm's marketing strategy. Pricing objectives are commonly classified into three categories: profit oriented, sales oriented, and status quo. Profit-oriented pricing is based on profit maximization, a satisfactory level of profit, or a target return on investment. The goal of profit maximization is to generate as much revenue as possible in relation to cost. Often, a more practical approach than profit maximization is setting prices to produce profits that will satisfy management and stockholders. The most common profit-oriented strategy is pricing for a specific return on investment relative to a firm's assets. The second type of pricing objective is sales oriented, and it focuses on either maintaining a percentage share of the market or maximizing dollar or unit sales. The third type of pricing objective aims to maintain the status quo by matching competitors' prices.

③ **Explain the role of demand in price determination.** Demand is a key determinant of price. When establishing prices, a firm must first determine demand for its product. A typical demand schedule shows an inverse relationship between quantity demanded and price: When price is lowered, sales increase; and when price is increased, the quantity demanded falls. However, for prestige products, there may be a direct relationship between demand and price: The quantity demanded will increase as price increases.

Marketing managers must also consider demand elasticity when setting prices. Elasticity of demand is the degree to which the quantity demanded fluctuates with changes in price. If consumers are sensitive to changes in price, demand is elastic; if they are insensitive to price changes, demand is inelastic. Thus, an increase in price will result in lower sales for an elastic product and little or no loss in sales for an inelastic product.

④ **Understand the concept of yield management systems.** Yield management systems use complex mathematical software to profitably fill unused capacity. The software uses techniques such as discounting early purchases, limiting early sales at these discounted prices, and overbooking capacity. These systems are primarily used in services businesses and are substantially raising revenues.

⑤ **Describe cost-oriented pricing strategies.** The other major determinant of price is cost. Marketers use several cost-oriented pricing strategies. To cover their own expenses and obtain a profit, wholesalers and retailers commonly use markup pricing: They tack an extra amount onto the manufacturer's original price. Another pricing technique is to maximize profits by setting price where marginal revenue equals marginal cost. Still another pricing strategy determines how much a firm must sell to break even and uses this amount as a reference point for adjusting price.

⑥ **Demonstrate how the product life cycle, competition, distribution and promotion strategies, customer demands, the Internet and extranets, and perceptions of quality can affect price.** The price of a product normally changes as it moves through the life cycle and as demand for the product and competitive conditions change. Management often sets a high price at the introductory stage, and the high price tends to attract competition. The competition usually drives prices down, because individual competitors lower prices to gain market share.

Adequate distribution for a new product can sometimes be obtained by offering a larger-than-usual profit margin to wholesalers and retailers. The Internet enables consumers to compare products and prices quickly and efficiently. Extranets help control costs and lower prices. Price is also used as a promotional tool to attract customers. Special low prices often attract new customers and entice existing customers to buy more. Demands of large customers can squeeze the profit margins of suppliers.

Perceptions of quality also can influence pricing strategies. A firm trying to project a prestigious image often charges a premium price for a product. Consumers tend to equate high prices with high quality.

Discussion and Writing Questions

1. Why is pricing so important to the marketing manager?
2. Explain the role of supply and demand in determining price.
3. If a firm can increase its total revenue by raising its price, shouldn't it do so?
4. Explain the concepts of elastic and inelastic demand. Why should managers understand these concepts?
5. **WRITING** Your firm has based its pricing strictly on cost in the past. As the newly hired marketing manager, you believe this policy should change. Write the president a memo explaining your reasons.
6. Why is it important for managers to understand the concept of break-even points? Are there any drawbacks?
7. Give an example of each major type of pricing objective.
8. Why are so many companies adopting yield management systems?
9. **TEAM** Divide the class into teams of five. Each team will be assigned a different grocery store from a different chain. (An independent is fine.) Appoint a group leader. The group leaders should meet as a group and pick fifteen nationally branded grocery items. Each item should be specifically described as to brand name and size of the package. Each team will then proceed to its assigned store and collect price data on the fifteen items. The team should also gather price data on fifteen similar store brands and fifteen generics, if possible.

    Each team should present its results to the class and discuss why there are price variations between stores, national brands, store brands, and generics.

    As a next step, go back to your assigned store and share the overall results with the store manager. Bring back the manager's comments and share them with the class.
10. How does the stage of a product's life cycle affect price? Give some examples.
11. **ON LINE** Go back to **Priceline.com**. Can you research a ticket's price before purchasing it? What products and services are available for purchasing? How comfortable are you with naming your own price? Relate the supply and demand curves to customer-determined pricing.
12. **ON LINE** Go to one of the Internet auction sites listed in this chapter. Report to the class on how the auction process works and the items being auctioned.
13. **INFOTRAC COLLEGE EDITION** How is yield management helping companies achieve competitive advantage? Use InfoTrac to find out (**http://www.infotrac-college.com**). Run a keyword search for "yield management" and read through the headlines to see what industries are profiled most often. Then read the article from the November 15, 1999 issue of *Computerworld* titled "Software Fills Trucks, Maximizes Revenue; Sitton Motor Lines Takes

Lead in Applying Analysis Tool Outside the Travel Industry" by Matthew Schwartz. Answer the following questions:

- How is Sitton Motor Lines using yield management principles and software?
- Describe the implementation of the new software.
- What other industries are cited as good candidates for yield management?

14. *INFOTRAC COLLEGE EDITION* How important is pricing when a company is entering new markets? The article in the July 2000 issue of *Across the Board* titled "Is the Price Right?" by Peter Meyer can tell you. Print out the article using InfoTrac (**http://www.infotrac-college.com**) and then underline all of the chapter concepts that it discusses. What issues does the article address that the chapter does not? What issues does the chapter address that are not included in the article?

Application for Entrepreneurs

Bernie Opinal has decided to wash windows in his neighborhood during spring break instead of heading to Daytona Beach with his buddies. Bernie lives with his parents in a neighborhood with homes typically in the 3,000- to 3,500-square-foot range. Bernie plans to hire his little brother Butch to help him. His plan is to clean every window inside and out, plus replace any missing caulking or weatherstripping at no extra charge. His estimated demand and associated costs are as follows:

Output	P	AR	MR	MC	AVC	ATC
0				—	—	—
1	$140.00			$31.00	$31.00	$54.00
2	130.00			28.00	29.50	41.00
3	120.00			31.00	30.00	37.67
4	110.00			34.00	31.00	36.75
5	100.00			37.00	32.20	36.80
6	90.00			40.00	33.50	37.33
7	80.00			43.00	34.86	38.14
8	70.00			46.00	36.25	39.13
9	60.00			49.00	37.67	40.22
10	50.00			52.00	39.10	41.40

Questions

1. What is the marginal and average revenue at each price?
2. How many houses should Bernie contract with to maximize profits?
3. What is the total profit at profit maximization?

Napster: Rocking & Rolling the Music Industry

It was in May 1999 that eighteen-year-old Shawn Fanning launched Napster, the world's leading file-sharing community. Functioning as a digital matchmaker, the Napster software allows users to search each other's on-line Napster directories for songs of interest. Music is not stored on Napster's server. Rather, Napster matches the IP addresses of music downloaders and downloadees. Basically, Napster users visit each other's computers to listen to and download music. With thirty employees, the company secured $15 million in venture capital funding in 2000.

Not surprisingly, many in the music industry are unhappy with Napster. Often referred to as the world's largest bootleg record collection, Napster is faced with copyright infringement battles with several groups. The music companies' trade group, the Recording Industry Association of America (RIAA) has filed suit against Napster; Ron Stone, manager for Bonnie Raitt and Tracy Chapman, says that Napster is aiding and abetting theft of music; one of the most popular heavy metal bands, Metallica, and the rapper, Dr. Dre, are suing on copyright issues. As though having the music industry up in arms over the business is not enough, network administrators at over one hundred universities have banned student use of Napster, which was slowing down, and in some instances shutting down, university computer systems.

With all of the hoopla surrounding Napster and its copyright infringement lawsuits, a key marketing issue at Napster is often overlooked. That is, how does a company like Napster make money? Fanning (who christened his start-up company with a version of his own nickname, Nappy), a dropout of Northeastern University in Boston, has become a paper millionaire. However, he and his management contingent need to turn the company into a moneymaking site if it is to remain solvent (assuming the company survives its legal problems). The question then becomes whether or not consumers will pay for the capability to download music off the Internet, and, if so, how Napster will charge for such downloading.

Several pricing models exist for Napster to consider. A popular model is for Napster to have advertising as its main source of revenue, with music downloads remaining free to users. Another pricing model that is under consideration by music companies such as BMG, Sony, Warner, and EMusic is to sell digital files of music as entire albums or individual tracks. Napster would charge the user for each individual download. Napster would then become similar to a music retailer by paying royalties for each download sale. A variation of this pricing model would be for Napster to charge its users a fixed monthly service charge. The revenue from such fees could be divided among the artists whose music was downloaded.

As an entrepreneurial start-up, Napster is leading the pack in changing the way companies distribute music over the Web. However, like many such ventures, Napster has become a common household name but has yet to generate revenue. Legal issues aside, Shawn Fanning and crew need to determine how to price their company's product for e-commerce success. Even if Napster is shut down by the RIAA and musicians, entrepreneur Fanning will probably continue to develop and introduce software products such as Napster. To go beyond his status as a paper millionaire entrepreneur, Fanning has to make money on the software products he introduces. Not giving them away will be the key to his financial success.

Questions

1. What pricing objectives should be part of Napster's pricing model?
2. What variables should Fanning and others at Napster consider in the pricing equation?
3. As a service provider, how is Napster's distribution of music tied to its pricing strategy?

Bibliography

Spencer Ante. "Shawn Fanning." *Business Week*, May 15, 2000, p. EB54.

Don Clark and Martin Peers. "Will Consumers Pay for Music Downloads?" *Wall Street Journal*, June 20, 2000. On-line.

Warren Cohen. "Napster Is Rocking the Music Industry." *U.S. News & World Report*, March 6, 2000. On-line.

Lee Gomes. "Napster Says Sharing Music Files Through the Internet Is Legal." *Wall Street Journal,* June 14, 2000. On-line.

Karl Taro Greenfield. "The Free Juke Box." *Time.com,* March 27, 2000. On-line.

Matt Richtel and Neil Strauss. "Metallica to Try to Prevent Fans from Downloading Recordings." *New York Times*, May 3, 2000, p. C1.

http://www.napster.com.

Case

video

Toronto Blue Jays: Ballpark Pricing

The opening pitch of 1999 marks the start of the Toronto Blue Jays' twenty-third season in the American League for a 162-game schedule. In 1998, the Jays scored 88 wins against 74 losses and 1 tie, and brought in their first winning season since 1993. For home games, the Jays play in the world's most-advanced retractable-roof stadium, with seating for 50,516. It is luxuriously called the Sky Dome, and the ball club invested $5 million in it for preferred supplier status and a Sky Box.

With a winning record like this and a state-of-the-art ballpark, the Jays feel their tickets are a great value because of the satisfaction fans can expect to receive from the ball game. Their pricing structure is based on the perceived value of a game, the entertainment, the love of baseball, and the action—not just the money. Every season the Blue Jays have to balance two key economic factors when determining their ticket prices: the demand for seats by baseball fans and the sky-rocketing costs of running a major league baseball club.

Despite this balancing act, the front office does not expect consumers to be really sensitive to fluctuations in price. This was particularly true of the 1999 season, when the fans were expected to turn out in great numbers in spite of rising ticket prices. This inelastic demand for Blue Jays tickets can be attributed in large part to the fact that the team played so well in 1998, but also to the fact that loyal Blue Jays fans could never stay away. They are simply willing to pay the price to support their team.

Another reason for the inelastic demand for Blue Jays tickets is that there is no locally available substitute.

Sports fans can support any number of sports (baseball to tennis) or watch amateurs play; but for major league baseball in Toronto, the Blue Jays are the only game in town. The purchasing power of Torontonians is also an important factor in the inelastic demand for Blue Jays tickets. The Blue Jays front office provides a wide range of ticket options (preferred or general seating, a season's subscription or a single ticket), so that even if their prices were to increase, most residents in the Toronto area could still easily afford the same category of ticket, or a lower category ticket, and so would not miss a game.

For the Blue Jays, pricing strategies are not just a financial necessity, they are also a promotional tool used to increase fan attendance. At all Saturday home games and nonholiday weekday games, senior citizens and young people up to fourteen years old can purchase tickets (except the most expensive ones) for half price. Season ticket holders receive special benefits: the same seats for every game, guaranteed tickets for postseason games played at home, a complimentary Toronto Blue Jays media guide and calendar, and the convenience of entering the Sky Dome on game day without having to wait in line at the ticket window. Group ticket sales also receive special treatment: preferred seating; personal services from the group sales staff; and promotional posters, pocket schedules, and stickers. These perks help persuade large groups (five hundred or more) to use a game as a social event; a fund-raiser; or a way to promote a business, a social group, or a sports organization.

Ticket sales provide a large portion of the Blue Jays' revenue, but merchandising is also responsible for a significant percentage. A wide selection of Blue Jays souvenirs and gifts is sold at the ballpark, at Blue Jays Bullpen Souvenir Stores, and at finer department stores across Canada. In addition to these retail outlets, free catalogs are available by calling a toll-free number, and the complete line of Jays merchandise is available on-line from a wholly owned Jays subsidiary. Caps, jerseys, and jackets, like those worn on the field by the players, and accessories, novelties, and collectibles are all available for sale.

The Blue Jays merchandising machine uses a prestige pricing strategy; charging high prices helps promote the Jays' high-quality image. Although jackets range from $39.59 to $197.99 and jerseys range from $29.69 to $155.09, consumers are willing to pay a high price for official, authentic merchandise that has been approved by the Blue Jays and by Major League Baseball.

Inelastic ticket demand and the prestige pricing of merchandise are fueled by the success of the ball team. Because the Toronto Blue Jays are a winning team, their loyal fans are willing to pay the price to see them play ball.

Questions

1. What considerations are included in the Jays ticket pricing structure?
2. Why is demand for Blue Jays tickets inelastic?
3. How do the Jays use price as a promotional tool?
4. What pricing strategy is used for Blue Jays merchandise?

Bibliography

Toronto Blue Jays Web site: **http://www.bluejays.ca/**

chapter 18

Learning Objectives

1 Describe the procedure for setting the right price

2 Identify the legal and ethical constraints on pricing decisions

3 Explain how discounts, geographic pricing, and other special pricing tactics can be used to fine-tune the base price

4 Discuss product line pricing

5 Describe the role of pricing during periods of inflation and recession

Setting the Right Price

Dining in the fall at Quilty's, a stylish New York restaurant, Jaime Wolf knew something about his $23.50 pork chop was bothering him. When he looked at his plate, he realized what it was: The price. "The food was good, but it didn't seem good enough to match the price," recalls Mr. Wolf, a lawyer. So how much did his meal cost the eatery? About $6.25.

So it goes with entrée economics. As any diner can't help but notice, it isn't just the quality of the cuisine that is rising in these booming economic times. The tab is, too. Indeed, the average menu price rose 13 percent from 1995 to 2000—edging out inflation and far outpacing the rise in wholesale food prices. In some hot spots such as New York, Los Angeles, and San Francisco, even the once-untouchable $50-a-plate barrier has finally been shattered.

What do restaurants really pay for the stuff on our plates? The *Wall Street Journal—Weekend Journal* decided to dine out—and find out. They talked to food consultants, restaurateurs, and chefs, and deconstructed the prices on dozens of dishes, from the persimmon salad at Pinot Bistro in Studio City, California, to the filet mignon at Charlie Palmer Steak in Las Vegas.

Some of what they discovered was a bit hard to swallow. For one thing, the conventional wisdom has always been that restaurants get you on the liquor—and indeed, they typically charge five times more for whiskey and wine than they pay for them. But certain kinds of foods have even more staggering markups. Mussels turn out to be one of the biggest cash crops—with markups of as much as 650 percent—and if you are a vegetarian, the price multiples on your entrees are so high you basically are subsidizing the carnivores around you.

But the biggest sticker shock of all may be on a big pink fish. Farm-raised salmon—referred to in the trade as "the chicken of the sea"—could well be the food industry's best-kept secret. It costs just $2.50 a pound wholesale and is often priced at a whopping 900 percent markup or more. "People think it's an elegant dish," says Brian Buckley, director of management studies at Peter Kump's New York Cooking School. "They don't think about it being farm-raised. They see the bears swiping at it as it goes upstream on a National Geographic special."

At the popular New York eatery Docks, a ten-ounce portion of grilled salmon with coleslaw and potatoes is $19.50. Actual cost of the ingredients? $1.90, the restaurant says.

To be fair, focusing on the cost of a restaurant meal's raw ingredients is like calculating the value of a Picasso based on the cost of the paint. When we eat out, we also are paying for labor, atmosphere, and overhead. Restaurants need to make a profit just like any other business. "We are not the Red Cross," says Eric Ripert, the chef and co-owner of Le Bernardin, a high-end seafood restaurant in New York. "What's the point if we're not making money?"

Boiled down, there's a simple rule of restaurant finances that explains all this—and can help you eat more for your dining dollar. Call it the 300 percent solution. Many independently owned restaurants, from the fanciest *boite* in Boston to a barbecue joint in Dallas, aim for an overall food markup of 300 percent—or four times—the cost of the raw ingredients. But some ingredients—especially prime cuts of beef and gourmet seafood such as day-boat scallops—cost the restaurant so much that diners wouldn't tolerate such a high markup on them.

So, since restaurants can't ratchet up the rates enough on those items, they have to make it up on the cheap stuff, such as salmon, lettuce, and pasta.

Consider the Charlie Palmer Steak in Las Vegas. The restaurant charges $27 for an 11-ounce filet, for which it pays $9.50—a relatively skimpy markup of less than 200 percent. But it makes a bundle on vegetables and side orders such as the $7 steak fries (which cost the restaurant 65 cents a portion—or a 977 percent markup). "The steakhouse mentality is that a steak is a steak," says chef-owner Charlie Palmer. "You want sauce on the side? That's $8. You want a potato? That's $5. And no one says a word." In fact, before he opened the restaurant, Palmer estimated the average tab per diner would be $56; instead, because the side dishes are so popular, it is $73.[1]

What are the advantages and disadvantages of restaurants charging premium prices? How can restaurants alter the base prices for, say, a steak? What kinds of discounts could restaurants offer?

Describe the procedure for setting the right price

Setting the right price on a product is a four-step process (see Exhibit 18.1):

1. Establish pricing goals.
2. Estimate demand, costs, and profits.
3. Choose a price strategy to help determine a base price.
4. Fine tune the base price with pricing tactics.

The first three steps are discussed next; the fourth step is discussed later in the chapter.

Establish Pricing Goals

The first step in setting the right price is to establish pricing goals. Recall from Chapter 17 that pricing objectives fall into three categories: profit oriented, sales oriented, and status quo. These goals are derived from the firm's overall objectives.

A good understanding of the marketplace and of the consumer can sometimes tell a manager very quickly whether a goal is realistic. For example, if firm A's objective of a 20 percent target return on investment (ROI), and its product development and implementation costs are $5 million, the market must be rather large or must support the price required to earn a 20 percent ROI. Assume that company B has a pricing objective that all new products must reach at least 15 percent market share within three years after their introduction. A thorough study of the environment may convince the marketing manager that the competition is too strong and the market share goal can't be met.

All pricing objectives have trade-offs that managers must weigh. A profit maximization objective may require a bigger initial investment than the firm can com-

Exhibit 18.1

Steps in Setting the Right Price on a Product

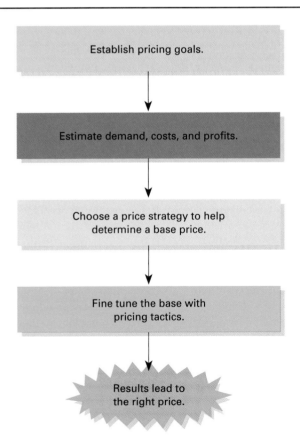

mit or wants to commit. Reaching the desired market share often means sacrificing short-term profit, because without careful management, long-term profit goals may not be met. Meeting the competition is the easiest pricing goal to implement. However, can managers really afford to ignore demand and costs, the life cycle stage, and other considerations? When creating pricing objectives, managers must consider these trade-offs in light of the target customer and the environment.

Estimate Demand, Costs, and Profits

Chapter 17 explained that total revenue is a function of price and quantity demanded and that quantity demanded depends on elasticity. After establishing pricing goals, managers should estimate total revenue at a variety of prices. Next, they should determine corresponding costs for each price. They are then ready to estimate how much profit, if any, and how much market share can be earned at each possible price. These data become the heart of the developing price policy. Managers can study the options in light of revenues, costs, and profits. In turn, this information can help determine which price can best meet the firm's pricing goals.

Choose a Price Strategy

The basic, long-term pricing framework for a good or service should be a logical extension of the pricing objectives. The marketing manager's chosen **price strategy** defines the initial price and gives direction for price movements over the product life cycle.

The price strategy sets a competitive price in a specific market segment, based on a well-defined positioning strategy. Changing a price level from premium to superpremium may require a change in the product itself, the target customers served, the promotional strategy, or the distribution channels. Thus, changing a price strategy can require dramatic alterations in the marketing mix. A carmaker cannot successfully compete in the superpremium category if the car looks and drives like an economy car.

A company's freedom in pricing a new product and devising a price strategy depends on the market conditions and the other elements of the marketing mix. If a firm launches a new item resembling several others already on the market, its pricing freedom will be restricted. To succeed, the company will probably have to charge a price close to the average market price. In contrast, a firm that introduces a totally new product with no close substitutes will have considerable pricing freedom.

The three basic strategies for setting a price on a good or service are price skimming, penetration pricing, and status quo pricing. A discussion of each type follows.

SEND THE KIDS TO YOUR ROOM!

Introducing Ceiva. The digital picture frame that lets you share photos over the internet. It's easy to set up. Easy to use. You don't even need a computer to receive photos. And anyone you want can send photos to your Ceiva frame from just about anywhere. Set your sights on one. And get one for your parents. So you can send the kids to their house whenever you want. SHARE photos EVERYDAY

ceiva.com

New products with no close substitutes are less restricted in the pricing strategies they can pursue. How do you think Ceiva will price this Internet-connected digital picture frame? Keep in mind that other factors besides novelty may affect the pricing strategy.

Price Skimming Price skimming is sometimes called a "market-plus" approach to pricing, because it denotes a high price relative to the prices of competing products. Radius Corporation produces unique oval-headed toothbrushes made of black neoprene that look like a scuba-diving accessory. Radius uses a skimming policy, pricing the toothbrushes at $9.95, compared to around $2.00 for a regular toothbrush.[2]

The term **price skimming** is derived from the phrase "skimming the cream off the top." Companies often use this strategy for new products when the product is perceived by the target market as having unique advantages. For example, Caterpillar sets premium prices on its construction equipment to support and capture its high perceived value. Genzyme Corporation introduced Ceredase as the first effective treatment for Gaucher's disease. The pill allows patients to avoid years of painful physical deterioration and lead normal lives. A year's supply for one patient can exceed $300,000.

price skimming
A pricing policy whereby a firm charges a high introductory price, often coupled with heavy promotion.

As a product progresses through its life cycle, the firm may lower its price to successfully reach larger market segments. Economists have described this type of pricing as "sliding down the demand curve." Not all companies slide down the curve. Genentech's TPA, a drug that clears blood clots, was still priced at $2,200 a dose four years after its introduction, despite competition from a much lower priced competitor.

Price skimming works best when the market is willing to buy the product even though it carries an above-average price. If, for example, some purchasing agents feel that Caterpillar equipment is far superior to competitors' products, then Caterpillar can charge premium prices successfully. Firms can also effectively use price skimming when a product is well protected legally, when it represents a technological breakthrough, or when it has in some other way blocked entry to competitors. Managers may follow a skimming strategy when production cannot be expanded rapidly because of technological difficulties, shortages, or constraints imposed by the skill and time required to produce a product. As long as demand is greater than supply, skimming is an attainable strategy.

A successful skimming strategy enables management to recover its product development or "educational" costs quickly. (Often, consumers must be "taught" the advantages of a radically new item, such as high-definition TV.) Even if the market perceives an introductory price as too high, managers can easily correct the problem by lowering the price. Firms often feel it is better to test the market at a high price and then lower the price if sales are too slow. They are tacitly saying, "If there are any premium-price buyers in the market, let's reach them first and maximize our revenue per unit." Successful skimming strategies are not limited to products. Well-known athletes, entertainers, lawyers, and hairstylists are experts at price skimming.[3] Naturally, a skimming strategy will encourage competitors to enter the market.

penetration pricing
A pricing policy whereby a firm charges a relatively low price for a product initially as a way to reach the mass market.

Penetration Pricing Penetration pricing is at the end of the spectrum, opposite skimming. **Penetration pricing** means charging a relatively low price for a product as a way to reach the mass market. The low price is designed to capture a large share of a substantial market, resulting in lower production costs. If a marketing manager has made obtaining a large market share the firm's pricing objective, penetration pricing is a logical choice.

Penetration pricing does mean lower profit per unit, however. Therefore, to reach the break-even point, it requires higher volume sales than would a skimming policy. If reaching a high volume of sales takes a long time, then the recovery of product development costs will also be slow. As you might expect, penetration pricing tends to discourage competition.

A penetration strategy tends to be effective in a price-sensitive market. Price should decline more rapidly when demand is elastic, because the market can be expanded through a lower price. Also, price sensitivity and greater competitive pressure should lead to a lower initial price and a relatively slow decline in the price later. Southwest Airlines' success is based on penetration pricing. By flying only the Boeing 737, it realizes efficiencies in stocking parts and training pilots and mechanics. It also saves by avoiding a costly computer reservation system, such as Apollo or SABRE, and by not serving meals. Southwest has a cost per seat mile of 7.0¢—the lowest in the industry. Costs per seat mile for other major carriers are USAir, 10.8¢; United, 9.6¢; Delta, 9.4¢; Northwest, 9.1¢; and American, 8.9¢.

If a firm has a fixed cost structure and each sale provides a large contribution to those fixed costs, penetration pricing can boost sales and provide large increases to profits—but only if the market size grows or if competitors choose not to respond. Low prices can draw additional buyers to enter the market. The increased sales can justify production expansion or the adoption of new technologies, both of which can reduce costs. And, if firms have excess capacity, even low-priced business can provide incremental dollars toward fixed costs.

Penetration pricing can also be effective if a large experience curve will cause costs per unit to drop significantly. The experience curve proposes that per-unit costs will go down as a firm's production experience increases. On average, for each doubling of production, a firm can expect per-unit costs to decline by roughly 20 percent. Cost declines can be significant in the early stages of production. Manufacturers who fail to take advantage of these effects will find themselves at a competitive cost disadvantage relative to others who are further along the curve.

The big advantage of penetration pricing is that it typically discourages or blocks competition from entering a market. The disadvantage is that penetration means gearing up for mass production to sell a large volume at a low price. What if the volume fails to materialize? The company is faced with huge losses from building or converting a factory to the failed product. Skimming, in contrast, lets a firm "stick its toe in the water" and see if the limited demand exists at the high price. If not, the firm can simply lower the price. Skimming lets a company start out with a small production facility and expand it gradually as price falls and demand increases.

Another problem with penetration pricing is when a prestige brand moves to penetration pricing to gain market share and fails. When Omega watches—once a brand more prestigious than Rolex—was trying to improve market share, it adopted a penetration pricing strategy that succeeded in destroying the watch's brand image by flooding the market with lower-priced products. Omega never gained sufficient share on the lower price/lower image competitors to justify destroying its brand image and high-priced position with upscale buyers. Similar outcomes were experienced by the Cadillac Cimarron and Lacoste clothing.[4]

Sometimes marketers use unusual pricing schemes to reach their pricing goals. One of the most bizarre is discussed in the "Global Perspectives" box.

Global Perspectives

JUST PICK A PRICE—ANY PRICE

When the upscale restaurant Just Around the Corner opened in London, it was described as "lunatic" and "economically irresponsible." The reason: Menus don't carry prices, and the restaurant lets customers decide how much they should pay for their meal. But twelve years and a recession later, critics have had to eat their words. Just Around the Corner has developed a large and loyal following, and weekend tables have to be booked weeks in advance.

Most of the patrons aren't bargain hunters either. "I make more money from this restaurant than from any of my other establishments," says Michael Vasos, who owns four other London eateries. Rather than underpaying, the well-heeled patrons generally overpay—on average spending 20 percent more than the price of the same meal at one of Mr. Vasos's other restaurants. "Fixing the price is disconcerting. But it's a welcome change from being overcharged," says Adam Macqueen, whose party left £80 ($133) plus tip to cover a meal for four with wine. (Mr. Vasos says £20 a head was about right.)

Vasos got the idea from watching how customers at his other restaurants tipped. "If you please people, they leave more money," he says. "I just thought, why not leave the whole lot up to them?" Vasos does concede that some customers seriously underpay. In such cases, the server politely returns the payment. "We say thank you very much, you had a nice meal here and we don't want to spoil it," Vasos says, adding, "They go red, they go out, and they never come back."

On other occasions, customers have wildly overestimated their bills. Vasos cites four American businessmen who left £600 for a three-course meal worth about £25 a head. "They asked if it was OK. I said, 'Of course.' If that's what they thought it was worth, then fine!"[a]

Other London restaurants have not followed Just Around the Corner's lead. Why do you think that this is true? Would such a scheme work in the United States? Could this idea work for other types of businesses? If yes, give an example.

[a] Imogen Wall. "It May Be a Dog-Eat-Dog World, But Dining Here Won't Prove It," *Wall Street Journal*, December 11, 1998, p. B1.

Status Quo Pricing The third basic price strategy a firm may choose is status quo pricing, or meeting the competition. (See also Chapter 17.) It means charging a price identical to or very close to the competition's price. Montgomery Ward, for example, makes sure it is charging comparable prices by sending representatives to shop at Sears stores.

Although status quo pricing has the advantage of simplicity, its disadvantage is that the strategy may ignore demand or cost or both. However, meeting the competition may be the safest route to long-term survival if the firm is comparatively small.

The Legality and Ethics of Price Strategy

Identify the legal and ethical constraints on pricing decisions

As we mentioned in Chapter 3, some pricing decisions are subject to government regulation. Before marketing managers establish any price strategy, they should know the laws that limit their decision making. Among the issues that fall into this category are unfair trade practices, price fixing, price discrimination, and predatory pricing.

Unfair Trade Practices

unfair trade practice acts
Laws that prohibit wholesalers and retailers from selling below cost.

price fixing
An agreement between two or more firms on the price they will charge for a product.

In over half the states, **unfair trade practice acts** put a floor under wholesale and retail prices. Selling below cost in these states is illegal. Wholesalers and retailers must usually take a certain minimum percentage markup on their combined merchandise cost and transportation cost. The most common markup figures are 6 percent at the retail level and 2 percent at the wholesale level. If a specific wholesaler or retailer can provide "conclusive proof" that operating costs are lower than the minimum required figure, lower prices may be allowed.

The intent of unfair trade practice acts is to protect small local firms from giants like Wal-Mart and Target, which operate very efficiently on razor-thin profit margins. However, state enforcement of unfair trade practice laws has generally been lax, partly because low prices benefit local consumers.

Archer Daniels Midland Co. executive, Michael Andreas, center, leaves the federal courthouse with members of his family after being sentenced in a price-fixing scheme in 1999. Andreas and fellow ADM executive Terrance Wilson were each sentenced to two years in federal prison and fined $350,000. The charges stemmed from the price-fixing of lysine, a soybean-based feed additive that promotes the growth of hogs and poultry.

Price Fixing

Price fixing is an agreement between two or more firms on the price they will charge for a product. Suppose two or more executives from competing firms meet to decide how much to charge for a product or to decide which of them will submit the lowest bid on a certain contract. Such practices are illegal under the Sherman Act and the Federal Trade Commission Act. Offenders have received fines and sometimes prison terms. Price fixing is one area where the law is quite clear, and the Justice Department's enforcement is vigorous.

In the past several years, the Justice Department has vigorously pursued price fixing. For example, a jury found three Archer-Daniels-Midland Company executives guilty of fixing the price of lysine, a livestock feed additive. Two of the executives spent two years in prison and the company paid $197 million in fines.[5]

Two companies have pleaded guilty to fixing prices and allocating market shares worldwide for graphite electrodes, used in steel minimills. UCAR International paid a $110 million fine, the largest in antitrust history. A judge recently rejected a $29 million fine against Showa Denko Carbon, a U.S. unit of a Japanese company, as too low.

Dutch, Belgian, and U.S. companies paid more than $65 million in criminal fines for rigging bids for marine services in the North Sea and Gulf of Mexico. Under one agreement for heavy-lift barges, conspirators agreed to divide customers, pool revenues, and split profits—and they put it all in writing.

BayerAG, the huge German multinational corporation (makers of Bayer aspirin), recently agreed to pay $46 million to settle a price-fixing lawsuit accusing it of conspiring with Archer-Daniels-Midland to fix citric acid prices. ADM also pleaded guilty to one criminal charge of price fixing.[6]

Price Discrimination

The Robinson-Patman Act of 1936 prohibits any firm from selling to two or more different buyers, within a reasonably short time, commodities (not services) of like grade and quality at different prices where the result would be to substantially lessen competition. The act also makes it illegal for a seller to offer two buyers different supplementary services and for buyers to use their purchasing power to force sellers into granting discriminatory prices or services.

Six elements are therefore needed for a violation of the Robinson-Patman Act to occur:

- There must be price discrimination; that is, the seller must charge different prices to different customers for the same product.
- The transaction must occur in interstate commerce.
- The seller must discriminate by price among two or more purchasers; that is, the seller must make two or more actual sales within a reasonably short time.
- The products sold must be commodities or other tangible goods.
- The products sold must be of like grade and quality, not necessarily identical. If the goods are truly interchangeable and substitutable, then they are of like grade and quality.
- There must be significant competitive injury.

The Robinson-Patman Act provides three defenses for the seller charged with price discrimination (in each case the burden is on the defendant to prove the defense):

- *Cost:* A firm can charge different prices to different customers if the prices represent manufacturing or quantity discount savings.
- *Market conditions:* Price variations are justified if designed to meet fluid product or market conditions. Examples include the deterioration of perishable goods, the obsolescence of seasonal products, a distress sale under court order, and a legitimate going-out-of-business sale.
- *Competition:* A reduction in price may be necessary to stay even with the competition. Specifically, if a competitor undercuts the price quoted by a seller to a buyer, the law authorizes the seller to lower the price charged to the buyer for the product in question

Predatory Pricing

Predatory pricing is the practice of charging a very low price for a product with the intent of driving competitors out of business or out of a market. Once competitors have been driven out, the firm raises its prices. This practice is illegal under the Sherman Act and the Federal Trade Commission Act. Proving the use of the practice is difficult and expensive, however. A defendant must show that the predator, the destructive company, explicitly tried to ruin a competitor and that the predatory price was below the defendant's average cost.[7]

predatory pricing
The practice of charging a very low price for a product with the intent of driving competitors out of business or out of a market.

Tactics for Fine-Tuning the Base Price

Explain how discounts, geographic pricing, and other special pricing tactics can be used to fine-tune the base price

base price
The general price level at which the company expects to sell the good or service.

After managers understand both the legal and the marketing consequences of price strategies, they should set a **base price**, the general price level at which the company expects to sell the good or service. The general price level is correlated with the pricing policy: above the market (price skimming), at the market (status quo pricing), or below the market (penetration pricing). The final step, then, is to fine-tune the base price.

Fine-tuning techniques are short-run approaches that do not change the general price level. They do, however, result in changes within a general price level. These pricing tactics allow the firm to adjust for competition in certain markets, meet ever-changing government regulations, take advantage of unique demand situations, and meet promotional and positioning goals. Fine-tuning pricing tactics include various sorts of discounts, geographic pricing, and special pricing tactics.

Discounts, Allowances, Rebates, and Value Pricing

A base price can be lowered through the use of discounts and the related tactics of allowances, rebates, and value pricing. Managers use the various forms of discounts to encourage customers to do what they would not ordinarily do, such as paying cash rather than using credit, taking delivery out of season, or performing certain functions within a distribution channel. A summary of the most common tactics is as follows:

quantity discount
A price reduction offered to buyers buying in multiple units or above a specified dollar amount.

cumulative quantity discount
A deduction from list price that applies to the buyer's total purchases made during a specific period.

noncumulative quantity discount
A deduction from list price that applies to a single order rather than to the total volume of orders placed during a certain period.

cash discount
A price reduction offered to a consumer, an industrial user, or a marketing intermediary in return for prompt payment of a bill.

functional discount (trade discount)
A discount to wholesalers and retailers for performing channel functions.

seasonal discount
A price reduction for buying merchandise out of season.

promotional allowance (trade allowance)
A payment to a dealer for promoting the manufacturer's products.

- *Quantity discounts:* When buyers get a lower price for buying in multiple units or above a specified dollar amount, they are receiving a **quantity discount**. A **cumulative quantity discount** is a deduction from list price that applies to the buyer's total purchases made during a specific period; it is intended to encourage customer loyalty. In contrast, a **noncumulative quantity discount** is a deduction from list price that applies to a single order rather than to the total volume of orders placed during a certain period. It is intended to encourage orders in large quantities.
- *Cash discounts:* A **cash discount** is a price reduction offered to a consumer, an industrial user, or a marketing intermediary in return for prompt payment of a bill. Prompt payment saves the seller carrying charges and billing expenses and allows the seller to avoid bad debt.
- *Functional discounts:* When distribution channel intermediaries, such as wholesalers or retailers, perform a service or function for the manufacturer, they must be compensated. This compensation, typically a percentage discount from the base price, is called a **functional discount** (or **trade discount**). Functional discounts vary greatly from channel to channel, depending on the tasks performed by the intermediary.
- *Seasonal discounts:* A **seasonal discount** is a price reduction for buying merchandise out of season. It shifts the storage function to the purchaser. Seasonal discounts also enable manufacturers to maintain a steady production schedule year-round.
- *Promotional allowances:* A **promotional allowance** (also known as a **trade allowance**) is a payment to a dealer for promoting the manufacturer's products. It is both a pricing tool and a promotional device. As a pricing tool, a promotional allowance is like a functional discount. If, for example, a retailer runs an ad for a manufacturer's product, the manufacturer may pay half the cost. If a retailer sets up a special display, the manufacturer may include a certain quantity of free goods in the retailer's next order.

- *Rebates:* A **rebate** is a cash refund given for the purchase of a product during a specific period. The advantage of a rebate over a simple price reduction for stimulating demand is that a rebate is a temporary inducement that can be taken away without altering the basic price structure. A manufacturer that uses a simple price reduction for a short time may meet resistance when trying to restore the price to its original, higher level.

rebate
A cash refund given for the purchase of a product during a specific period.

Value-Based Pricing

Value-based pricing is a pricing strategy that has grown out of the quality movement. Instead of figuring prices based on costs or competitors' prices, it starts with the customer, considers the competition, and then determines the appropriate price. The basic assumption is that the firm is customer driven, seeking to understand the attributes customers want in the goods and services they buy and the value of that bundle of attributes to customers. Because very few firms operate in a pure monopoly, however, a marketer using value-based pricing must also determine the value of competitive offerings to customers. Customers determine the value of a product (not just its price) relative to the value of alternatives. In value-based pricing, therefore, the price of the product is set at a level that seems to the customer to be a good price compared with the prices of other options.

value-based pricing
The price is set at a level that seems to the customer to be a good price compared to the prices of other options.

An important type of value pricing is everyday low prices, which has evolved because of trade loading. **Trade loading** occurs when a manufacturer temporarily lowers the price to induce wholesalers and retailers to buy more goods than can be sold in a reasonable time. Say that Procter & Gamble offers Super Valu an additional thirty cents off the normal price for a bottle of Prell. The Super Valu buyer jumps at the bargain and buys a three-month supply of Prell. Typically, Super Valu would pass along the discount to customers for about a month, but then return to the original price for the last two months, thereby reaping some extra profit.

trade loading
The practice of temporarily lowering the price to induce wholesalers and retailers to buy more goods than can be sold in a reasonable time.

Trade discounts like these have more than tripled in the past decade, to around $38 billion. The practice is most common in the consumer packaged-goods industry. An estimated $100 billion in grocery products, mostly nonperishables, sit at any one time on trucks and railcars or stacked inside distribution centers, caught in gridlock because of trade loading. This idle inventory is estimated to add about $20 billion a year to the nation's $400 billion grocery bill.[8]

However, it is estimated that such practices generate about 70 percent of wholesalers' profits and 40 percent of supermarkets' profits.[9] Wholesalers and retailers have understandably become addicted to trade-loading deals.

Unfortunately, trade loading ultimately costs consumers (and manufacturers) money, as shown in Exhibit 18.2. It "whipsaws" production and distribution and increases the manufacturer's costs. The largest U.S. packaged-goods manufacturer, Procter & Gamble, estimates that it has created over $1 billion worth of unproductive inventory, which has sat in P&G's distribution pipeline. Moreover, P&G's former chairman, Edward Arzt, notes:

Trade loading has caused the erosion of consumer loyalty. As retailers and wholesalers buy on deals and discounts, they pass wide price swings to consumers in an unpredictable pattern, and these shoppers, no dummies, increasingly "forward buy" themselves. People have reached

Cash rebates can be a definite incentive to purchase a product. By offering a $4.00 rebate, Jobst is hoping to generate sales for its line of support knee socks.

Exhibit 18.2

Costs of Trade Loading

With trade loading

The manufacturer stockpiles ingredients and packaging supplies to meet peak production levels.

Plants prepare huge runs. Scheduling is chaotic, with more overtime and temporary workers.

Freight companies charge premium rates for the manufacturer's periodic blow-out shipments.

Distributors overstock as they binge on short-term discounts. Cartons sit for weeks inside warehouses.

At distribution centers, the goods get overhandled. Damaged items go back to the manufacturer.

Twelve weeks after the items leave the production line, they may not be fresh for the consumer.

Without trade loading

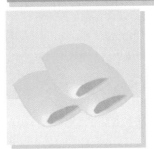

No more panic purchases are necessary. The company cuts down on inventories, freeing up cash.

Factories run on normal shifts. The company cuts down on overtime pay and supplemental workers.

The manufacturer eliminates peak-and-valley distribution. That helps it save 5 percent in shipping costs.

Wholesalers' inventories get cut in half. That means storage and handling costs decline 17 percent.

Retailers receive undamaged products. The perception of the manufacturer's quality improves.

The consumer gets the goods 25 days earlier, and—even better news— at a 6 percent lower price.

SOURCE: "The Dumbest Marketing Ploy," by Patricia Sellers. *Fortune*, October 3, 1992, pp. 88–89. © 1992 Time, Inc. All rights reserved. Original art by Jim McManus. Adapted by permission.

the point where they won't buy unless a product is on sale. Shopping store to store for the best deal, they bulk up on whichever item—P&G's Crest or Colgate-Palmolive's Colgate, P&G's Tide or Lever Brothers' Wish—is on promotion that week.[10]

P&G has decided to attack the trade-loading problem with **everyday low prices (EDLP)**, the tactic of offering lower prices (often 10 to 25 percent lower) and maintaining those prices while eliminating functional discounts that result in trade loading. Instead of selling, say, a case of cake mix for $10.00 most of the time and then for $7.00 to load the trade, P&G will sell the case for $8.50 all the time. Since 1994, P&G has reduced its list prices by 12 percent to 24 percent on all of its U.S. brands.[11] EDLP has worked, as profits are at a twenty-one-year high for the company.

Geographic Pricing

Because many sellers ship their wares to a nationwide or even a worldwide market, the cost of freight can greatly affect the total cost of a product. Sellers may use several different geographic pricing tactics to moderate the impact of freight costs on distant customers. The following methods of geographic pricing are the most common:

- *FOB origin pricing:* **FOB origin pricing**, also called FOB factory or FOB shipping point, is a price tactic that requires the buyer to absorb the freight costs from the shipping point ("free on board"). The farther buyers are from sellers, the more they pay, because transportation costs generally increase with the distance merchandise is shipped.

- *Uniform delivered pricing:* If the marketing manager wants total costs, including freight, to be equal for all purchasers of identical products, the firm will adopt uniform delivered pricing, or "postage stamp" pricing. With **uniform delivered pricing**, the seller pays the actual freight charges and bills every purchaser an identical, flat freight charge.

- *Zone pricing:* A marketing manager who wants to equalize total costs among buyers within large geographic areas—but not necessarily all of the seller's market area—may modify the base price with a zone-pricing tactic. **Zone pricing** is a modification of uniform delivered pricing. Rather than placing the entire United States (or its total market) under a uniform freight rate, the firm divides it into segments or zones and charges a flat freight rate to all customers in a given zone. The U.S. Postal Service's parcel post rate structure is probably the best known zone-pricing system in the country.

- *Freight absorption pricing:* In **freight absorption pricing**, the seller pays all or part of the actual freight charges and does not pass them on to the buyer. The manager may use this tactic in intensely competitive areas or as a way to break into new market areas.

- *Basing-point pricing:* With **basing-point pricing**, the seller designates a location as a basing point and charges all buyers the freight cost from that point, regardless of the city from which the goods are shipped. Thanks to several adverse court rulings, basing-point pricing has waned in popularity. Freight fees charged when none were actually incurred, called *phantom freight*, have been declared illegal.

everyday low prices (EDLP)
A price tactic of permanently reducing prices 10 to 25 percent below the traditional levels while eliminating trade discounts that create trade loading.

FOB origin pricing
A price tactic that requires the buyer to absorb the freight costs from the shipping point ("free on board").

uniform delivered pricing
A price tactic in which the seller pays the actual freight charges and bills every purchaser an identical, flat freight charge.

zone pricing
A modification of uniform delivered pricing that divides the United States (or the total market) into segments or zones and charges a flat freight rate to all customers in a given zone.

Zone pricing allows a marketing manager to equalize total costs among buyers in a large geographic area. How successful do you think the United States Postal Service would be in implementing a zone pricing system for letters as it does for parcels? Explain your answer.
© Corbis/Eye Ubiquitous

freight absorption pricing
A price tactic in which the seller pays all or part of the actual freight charges and does not pass them on to the buyer.

basing-point pricing
A price tactic that charges freight from a given (basing) point, regardless of the city from which the goods are shipped.

single-price tactic
A price tactic that offers all goods and services at the same price (or perhaps two or three prices).

flexible pricing (variable pricing)
A price tactic in which different customers pay different prices for essentially the same merchandise bought in equal quantities.

Special Pricing Tactics

Unlike geographic pricing, special pricing tactics are unique and defy neat categorization. Managers use these tactics for various reasons—for example, to stimulate demand for specific products, to increase store patronage, and to offer a wider variety of merchandise at a specific price point. Special pricing tactics include a single-price tactic, flexible pricing, professional services pricing, price lining, leader pricing, bait pricing, odd–even pricing, price bundling, and two-part pricing. A brief overview of each of these tactics follows, along with a manager's reasons for using that tactic or a combination of tactics to change the base price.

Single-Price Tactic   A merchant using a **single-price tactic** offers all goods and services at the same price (or perhaps two or three prices). Retailers using this tactic include One Price Clothing Stores, Dre$$ to the Nine$, Your $10 Store, and Fashions $9.99. One Price Clothing Stores, for example, tend to be small, about three thousand square feet. Their goal is to offer merchandise that would sell for at least $15 to $18 in other stores. The stores carry pants, shirts, blouses, sweaters, and shorts for juniors, misses, and large-sized women. The stores do not feature any seconds or irregular items, and everything is sold for $6.

Single-price selling removes price comparisons from the buyer's decision-making process. The consumer just looks for suitability and the highest perceived quality. The retailer enjoys the benefits of a simplified pricing system and minimal clerical errors. However, continually rising costs are a headache for retailers following this strategy. In times of inflation, they must frequently raise the selling price.

Flexible Pricing   **Flexible pricing** (or **variable pricing**) means that different customers pay different prices for essentially the same merchandise bought in equal quantities. This tactic is often found in the sale of shopping goods, specialty merchandise, and most industrial goods except supply items. Car dealers, many appliance retailers, and manufacturers of industrial installations, accessories, and component parts commonly follow the practice. It allows the seller to adjust for competition by meeting another seller's price. Thus, a marketing manager with a status quo pricing objective might readily adopt the tactic. Flexible pricing also enables the seller to close a sale with price-conscious consumers. If buyers show promise of becoming large-volume shoppers, flexible pricing can be used to lure their business.

The obvious disadvantages of flexible pricing are the lack of consistent profit margins, the potential ill will of high-paying purchasers, the tendency for salespeople to automatically lower the price to make a sale, and the possibility of a price war among sellers. The disadvantages of flexible pricing have led the automobile industry to experiment with one price for all buyers. General Motors uses a one-price tactic for some of its models, including the Saturn and the Buick Regal.

Professional Services Pricing   Professional services pricing is used by people with lengthy experience, training, and often certification by a licensing board—for example, lawyers, physicians, and family counselors. Professionals sometimes charge customers at an hourly rate, but sometimes fees are based on the solution of a problem or performance of an act (such as an eye examination) rather than on the actual time involved. A surgeon may perform a heart operation and charge a flat fee of $5,000. The operation itself may require only four hours, resulting in a hefty $1,250 hourly rate. The physician justifies the fee because of the lengthy education and internship required to learn the complex procedures of a heart operation. Lawyers also sometimes use flat-rate pricing, such as $500 for completing a divorce and $50 for handling a traffic ticket.

Those who use professional pricing have an ethical responsibility not to overcharge a customer. Because demand is sometimes highly inelastic, such as when a person requires heart surgery or a daily insulin shot to survive, there may be a temptation to charge "all the traffic will bear."

New, costly drugs and vaccines can create ethical concerns on who should receive treatment and how much the government should pay. These topics are discussed in the "Ethics in Marketing" box.

Price Lining   When a seller establishes a series of prices for a type of merchandise, it creates a price line. **Price lining** is the practice of offering a product line with several items at specific price points. For example, Hon, an office furniture manufacturer, may offer its four-drawer file cabinets at $125, $250, and $400. The Limited may offer women's dresses at $40, $70, and $100, with no merchandise marked at prices between those figures. Instead of a normal demand curve running from $40 to $100, The Limited has three demand points (prices). Theoretically, the "curve" exists only because people would buy goods at the in-between prices if it were possible to do so. For example, a number of dresses could be sold at $60, but no sales will occur at that price because $60 is not part of the price line.

Price lining reduces confusion for both the salesperson and the consumer. The buyer may be offered a wider variety of merchandise at each established price. Price lines may also enable a seller to reach several market segments. For buyers, the question of price may be quite simple: All they have to do is find a suitable product at the predetermined price. Moreover, price lining is a valuable tactic for the marketing manager, because the firm may be able to carry a smaller total

price lining
The practice of offering a product line with several items at specific price points.

Ethics in Marketing

VACCINE'S PRICE PRESENTS A DILEMMA ABOUT ITS USE

Should the government scale back the use of a major new childhood vaccine simply because of its unusually high price? Hopes are still high that the vaccine, called Prevenar, will prevent scores of deaths and millions of illnesses in the United States from meningitis, pneumonia, blood poisoning, and ear infections. But at $232 for a four-dose series, Prevenar will cost as much as all other approved childhood vaccinations combined.

That price is just too high, say some doctors advising the government. So instead of giving the vaccine to all children up to age five, the Centers for Disease Control and Prevention's Advisory Committee on Immunization Practices recommended that Prevenar be given just to the children at highest risk: those under the age of two.

For decades, research has proved that vaccines save more money than they cost by preventing expensive and deadly illnesses. As most new vaccines came along, government panels readily recom-

mended that all American children get them. And the government has picked up much of the tab, paying for half of all childhood immunizations in the United States.

But as manufacturers increasingly target less-severe illnesses with pricey medications, government experts will be forced to begin debating if the cure is worth the cost. This same debate has for years roiled adult medical care—and has emerged as central in discussions over the future of Medicare—but it is only now making its way into childhood vaccines.

No one is disputing Prevenar's medical value. The vaccine targets pneumococcal bacteria that cause about 3,000 cases of meningitis, thousands more cases of blood poisoning, 100,000 to 135,000 hospitalizations for pneumonia and millions of infant ear infections every year in the United States.

A narrower age range would be a disappointment to American Home Products Corporation, which manufactures Prevenar. The vaccine

has been under development since 1986, and it has seven different types of the pneumococcal bacteria. "That costs a lot of money," says Dr. Paradiso, Vice President of the Syeth-Ayerst Laboratories division of American Home. He also notes that immunizing older kids is more cost-effective than immunizing infants, because children two and older need just one shot, not four. Each shot costs $58.

However, experts concerned about the overall cost of a vaccination program argue that vaccinating kids ages two and older—who aren't as susceptible to illness—isn't nearly as beneficial.[a]

Should price be a factor in determining who receives vaccinations? Do you think in this case it should be given only to children under the age of two? Who should make this decision?

[a] "Vaccine's Price Drives a Debate About Its Use," *Wall Street Journal*, February 16, 2000, pp. B1, B4.

inventory than it could without price lines. The results may include fewer markdowns, simplified purchasing, and lower inventory carrying charges.

Price lines also present drawbacks, especially if costs are continually rising. Sellers can offset rising costs in three ways. First, they can begin stocking lower quality merchandise at each price point. Second, sellers can change the prices, although frequent price line changes confuse buyers. Third, sellers can accept lower profit margins and hold quality and prices constant. This third alternative has short-run benefits, but its long-run handicaps may drive sellers out of business.

leader pricing (loss-leader pricing)
A price tactic in which a product is sold near or even below cost in the hope that shoppers will buy other items once they are in the store.

Leader Pricing   **Leader pricing** (or **loss-leader pricing**) is an attempt by the marketing manager to attract customers by selling a product near or even below cost, hoping that shoppers will buy other items once they are in the store. This type of pricing appears weekly in the newspaper advertising of supermarkets, specialty stores, and department stores. Leader pricing is normally used on well-known items that consumers can easily recognize as bargains at the special price. The goal is not necessarily to sell large quantities of leader items, but to try to appeal to customers who might shop elsewhere.

Leader pricing is not limited to products. Health clubs offer a one-month free trial as a loss leader. Lawyers give a free initial consultation. And restaurants distribute two-for-one coupons and "welcome to the neighborhood" free meal coupons.[12]

bait pricing
A price tactic that tries to get consumers into a store through false or misleading price advertising and then uses high-pressure selling to persuade consumers to buy more expensive merchandise.

Bait Pricing   In contrast to leader pricing, which is a genuine attempt to give the consumer a reduced price, bait pricing is deceptive. **Bait pricing** tries to get the consumer into a store through false or misleading price advertising and then uses high-pressure selling to persuade the consumer to buy more expensive merchandise. You may have seen this ad or a similar one:

> REPOSSESSED . . . Singer slant-needle sewing machine . . . take over 8 payments of $5.10 per month . . . ABC Sewing Center.

This is bait. When a customer goes in to see the machine, a salesperson says that it has just been sold or else shows the prospective buyer a piece of junk no one would buy. Then the salesperson says, "But I've got a really good deal on this fine new model." This is the switch that may cause a susceptible consumer to walk out with a $400 machine. The Federal Trade Commission considers bait pricing a deceptive act and has banned its use in interstate commerce. Most states also ban bait pricing, but sometimes enforcement is lax.

odd–even pricing (psychological pricing)
A price tactic that uses odd-numbered prices to connote bargains and even-numbered prices to imply quality.

Odd–Even Pricing   **Odd–even pricing** (or **psychological pricing**) means pricing at odd-numbered prices to connote a bargain and pricing at even-numbered prices to imply quality. For years, many retailers have used this tactic to price their products in odd numbers—for example, $99.95 or $49.95—in order to make consumers feel that they are paying a lower price for the product.

Some retailers favor odd-numbered prices because they believe that $9.99 sounds much less imposing to customers than $10.00. Other retailers believe that the use of an odd-numbered price signals to consumers that the price is at the lowest level possible, thereby encouraging them to buy more units. Neither theory has ever been conclusively proved, although one study found that consumers perceive odd-priced products as being on sale.[13] The most recent research shows that consumers do purchase more at odd prices.[14]

Even-numbered pricing is sometimes used to denote quality. Examples include a fine perfume at $100 a bottle, a good watch at $500, or a mink coat at $3,000. The demand curve for such items would also be sawtoothed, except that the outside edges would represent even-numbered prices and, therefore, elastic demand.

price bundling
Marketing two or more products in a single package for a special price.

Price Bundling   **Price bundling** is marketing two or more products in a single package for a special price. Examples include the sale of maintenance contracts with computer hardware and other office equipment, packages of stereo equipment, packages of options on cars, weekend hotel packages that include a room and several meals, and airline vacation packages. Microsoft now offers "suites" of software that bundle spreadsheets, word processing, graphics, electronic mail, Internet access, and groupware for networks of microcomputers. Price bundling can stimulate demand for the bundled items if the target market perceives the price as a good value.[15]

Services like hotels and airlines sell a perishable commodity (hotel rooms and airline seats) with relatively constant fixed costs. Bundling can be an important income stream for these businesses because the variable cost tends to be low—for instance, the cost of cleaning a hotel room or putting one more passenger on an airplane. Therefore, most of the revenue can help cover fixed costs and generate profits.[16]

The automobile industry has a different motive for bundling. People buy cars only every three to five years. Thus, selling options is a somewhat rare opportunity for the car dealer. Price bundling can help the dealer sell a maximum number of options.

A related price tactic is **unbundling**, or reducing the bundle of services that comes with the basic product. Rather than raise the price of hotel rooms, some hotel chains have started charging registered guests for parking. To help hold the line on costs, some stores require customers to pay for gift wrapping.

Two-Part Pricing **Two-part pricing** means establishing two separate charges to consume a single good or service. Tennis clubs and health clubs charge a membership fee and a flat fee each time a person uses certain equipment or facilities. In other cases they charge a base rate for a certain level of usage, such as ten racquetball games per month, and a surcharge for anything over that amount.[17]

Consumers sometimes prefer two-part pricing because they are uncertain about the number and the types of activities they might use at places like an amusement park. Also, the people who use a service most often pay a higher total price. Two-part pricing can increase a seller's revenue by attracting consumers who would not pay a high fee even for unlimited use. For example, a health club might be able to sell only 100 memberships at $700 annually with unlimited use of facilities, for total revenue of $70,000. However, perhaps it could sell 900 memberships at $200 with a guarantee of using the racquetball courts ten times a month. Every use over ten would require the member to pay a $5 fee. Thus, membership revenue would provide a base of $180,000, with some additional usage fees coming in throughout the year.

Consumer Penalties

More and more businesses are adopting **consumer penalties**—extra fees paid by consumers for violating the terms of a purchase agreement (see Exhibit 18.3).

Businesses impose consumer penalties for two reasons: They will allegedly (1) suffer an irrevocable revenue loss and/or (2) incur significant additional transaction costs should customers be unable or unwilling to complete their purchase obligations. For the company, these customer payments are part of doing business in a highly competitive marketplace. With profit margins in many companies increasingly coming under pressure, organizations are looking to stem losses resulting

Club Med

Imagine a paradise where kids play all day and parents can relax. At Club Med Family Villages, you'll enjoy a fun-filled vacation where one price includes it all. With Children's Clubs available for kids from 4 months and up, they can enjoy exciting activities such as circus school, in-line skating, soccer camp, and more. Of course, you can stop by and see your kids any time you want, but chances are, they'll be having too much fun to even notice. Which gives you time for something you rarely get a chance to do. Kick back and relax.

one week all-inclusive from $899
1-800-CLUB MED
OR CALL YOUR TRAVEL AGENT
clubmed.com

Re-new

Club Med advertises an all-inclusive vacation for one from $899 in this humorous ad. Included in the price are the room, airfare, meals, sports, and children's clubs. However, there are also several contingencies placed on this bundled vacation and listed in the ad's fine print.

unbundling
Reducing the bundle of services that comes with the basic product.

two-part pricing
A price tactic that charges two separate amounts to consume a single good or service.

consumer penalty
An extra fee paid by the consumer for violating the terms of the purchase agreement.

Exhibit 18.3   Common Consumer Penalties

1. Airlines

- The penalty for changing reservations on discount tickets has recently been raised to $75.00 for most airlines.
- Lost ticket can result in traveler paying full price for a new ticket, with possible refund later, but usually with an administration penalty fee added.
- In 1996, some travel agents started charging an additional $10 to $20 penalty for canceled tickets with values under $200.

2. Automobiles

- Early terminations of car leases have penalties associated with them. In some cases, deposits on canceled leases can be subject to penalties.
- Car owners in England pay penalties, administration fees, and commission if they cancel an insurance policy early.

3. Banks

- Penalties are often associated with early withdrawal of a certificate of deposit.
- Some banks charge penalties for too many withdrawals in a month.
- Some have monthly penalties of $5 to $10 if a client's balance falls below a minimum level.
- Banks can charge late fees, in addition to interest, for tardy payments.
- The Senate Banking Committee is examining legislation to prohibit banks with ATM machines from charging penalty fees to users who are customers of another bank.

4. Car Rentals

- Rental companies often have $25 to $100 penalties for no-shows for specialty vehicles. Budget, National, and Dollar/Thrifty are experimenting with no-show fees on all rentals.

5. Child Day-care

- Many day-care centers charge a penalty of up to $5 a minute when parents are late in picking up their children.

6. Cellular phones

- Companies have cancellation penalties, often in the small print on the back of a contract, that can run as high as $525.

7. Credit and Debit Cards

- Some vendors now charge late fees (beyond normal interest). Lenders collect about $2 billion in late charges each year.
- GE Rewards Mastercard recently began charging $25 a year for those who pay their bill each year, in full, on time. Advanta credit card company may charge $25 for six-month inactivity on an account and $25 to close an account.

8. Cruises

- If a cruise is sailing, even if there are hurricane warnings, some cruise lines will assess penalties if a passenger cancels.
- Even trip cancellation insurance will not ensure a refund if the traveler has embarked on the trip.
- Britain is one country that is trying to crack down on executive cancellation penalties on package holidays.
- The Carnival Paradise will disembark passengers found smoking

9. Hotels

- Some hotels require 72 hours cancellation notice or the client must pay a penalty of one day's room cost.
- Most hotels have high charges for using in-room long distance service.
- Hilton, Hyatt, and Westin have early departure fees ranging from $25 to $50.

10. Restaurants

- Some now charge up to $50 per person for no show parties.

11. Retail Stores

- Circuit City and Best Buy are leading others in charging a 15 percent restocking fee on some items. A restocking fee is for putting a returned item back in inventory.

12. Trains

- Amtrak has a $20 penalty for a returned ticket, and charges the same fee for changing a ticket.

13. Universities

- Universities will give only a partial tuition refund if a student becomes ill after a course begins.

SOURCE: Eugene Fram and Michale McCarthy. "The True Price of Penalties," *Marketing Management*, Fall 1999, p. 51.

from customers not meeting their obligations. However, the perceived fairness of a penalty may affect some consumers willingness to patronize a business in the future.

One study found that most consumers (53 percent) had paid a price penalty in the past year. A "fair" penalty exists when consumers believe that they are reimbursing the seller for actual lost revenue and not simply making extra profit.[18]

Product Line Pricing

Product line pricing is setting prices for an entire line of products. Compared to setting the right price on a single product, product line pricing encompasses broader concerns. In product line pricing, the marketing manager tries to achieve maximum profits or other goals for the entire line rather than for a single component of the line.

Discuss product line pricing

product line pricing
Setting prices for an entire line of products.

joint costs
Costs that are shared in the manufacturing and marketing of several products in a product line.

Relationships Among Products

The manager must first determine the type of relationship that exists among the various products in the line:

- If items are *complementary,* an increase in the sale of one good causes an increase in demand for the complementary product, and vice versa. For example, the sale of ski poles depends on the demand for skis, making these two items complementary.
- Two products in a line can also be *substitutes* for each other. If buyers buy one item in the line, they are less likely to buy a second item in the line. For example, if someone goes to an automotive supply store and buys paste Turtle Wax for a car, it is very unlikely that he or she will buy liquid Turtle Wax in the near future.
- A *neutral* relationship can also exist between two products. In other words, demand for one of the products is unrelated to demand for the other. For instance, Ralston Purina sells chicken feed and Wheat Chex, but the sale of one of these products has no known impact on demand for the other.

Joint Costs

Joint costs are costs that are shared in the manufacturing and marketing of several products in a product line. These costs pose a unique problem in product pricing. In oil refining, for example, fuel oil, gasoline, kerosene, naphtha, paraffin, and lubricating oils are all derived from a common production process. Another example is the production of compact discs that combine photos and music.

The demand curve is influenced by the relationship between products. For example, the demand for bindings depends on the demand for skis. This kind of relationship is described as complementary.

Any assignment of joint costs must be somewhat subjective, because costs are actually shared. Suppose a company produces two products, X and Y, in a common production process, with joint costs allocated on a weight basis. Product X weighs one thousand pounds, and product Y weighs five hundred pounds. Thus, costs are allocated on the basis of $2 for X for every $1 for Y. Gross margins (sales less the cost of goods sold) might then be as follows:

	Product X	Product Y	Total
Sales	$20,000	$6,000	$26,000
Less: cost of goods sold	15,000	7,500	22,500
Gross margin	$ 5,000	($1,500)	$ 3,500

This statement reveals a loss of $1,500 on product Y. Is that important? Yes; any loss is important. However, the firm must realize that overall it earned a $3,500 profit on the two items in the line. Also, weight may not be the right way to allocate the joint costs. Instead, the firm might use other bases, including market value or quantity sold.

Pricing During Difficult Economic Times

Describe the role of pricing during periods of inflation and recession

Pricing is always an important aspect of marketing, but it is especially crucial in times of inflation and recession. The firm that does not adjust to economic trends may lose ground that it can never make up.

Inflation

When the economy is characterized by high inflation, special pricing tactics are often necessary. They can be subdivided into cost-oriented and demand-oriented tactics.

Cost-Oriented Tactics   One popular cost-oriented tactic is *culling products with a low profit margin* from the product line. However, this tactic may backfire for three reasons:

- A high volume of sales on an item with a low profit margin may still make the item highly profitable.
- Eliminating a product from a product line may reduce economies of scale, thereby lowering the margins on other items.
- Eliminating the product may affect the price–quality image of the entire line.

delayed-quotation pricing
A price tactic used for industrial installations and many accessory items, in which a firm price is not set until the item is either finished or delivered.

Another popular cost-oriented tactic is **delayed-quotation pricing**, which is used for industrial installations and many accessory items. Price is not set on the product until the item is either finished or delivered. Long production lead times have forced this policy on many firms during periods of inflation. Builders of nuclear power plants, ships, airports, and office towers sometimes use delayed-quotation tactics.

escalator pricing
A price tactic in which the final selling price reflects cost increases incurred between the time the order is placed and when delivery is made.

Escalator pricing is similar to delayed-quotation pricing in that the final selling price reflects cost increases incurred between the time an order is placed and when delivery is made. An escalator clause allows for price increases (usually across the board) based on the cost-of-living index or some other formula. As with any price increase, management's ability to implement such a policy is based on inelastic demand for the product. About a third of all industrial product manufacturers now use escalator clauses. However, many companies do not apply the clause in every sale. Often it is used only for extremely complex products that take a long time to produce or with new customers.

Any cost-oriented pricing policy that tries to maintain a fixed gross margin under all conditions can lead to a vicious circle. For example, a price increase will result in decreased demand, which in turn increases production costs (because of lost economies of scale). Increased production costs require a further price increase, leading to further diminished demand, and so on.

Demand-Oriented Tactics Demand-oriented pricing tactics use price to reflect changing patterns of demand caused by inflation or high interest rates. Cost changes are considered, of course, but mostly in the context of how increased prices will affect demand.

Price shading is the use of discounts by salespeople to increase demand for one or more products in a line. Often, shading becomes habitual and is done routinely without much forethought.[19] Ducommun, a metals producer, is among the major companies that have succeeded in eliminating the practice. Ducommun has told its salespeople, "We want no deviation from book price" unless authorized by management.

To make the demand for a good or service more inelastic and to create buyer dependency, a company can use several strategies:

- *Cultivate selected demand:* Marketing managers can target prosperous customers who will pay extra for convenience or service. Neiman Marcus, for example, stresses quality. As a result, the luxury retailer is more lenient with suppliers and their price increases than is Alexander's Stores, a discounter. In cultivating close relationships with affluent organizational customers, marketing managers should avoid putting themselves at the mercy of a dominant firm. They can more easily raise prices when an account is readily replaceable. Finally, in companies where engineers exert more influence than purchasing departments do, performance is favored over price. Often a preferred vendor's pricing range expands if other suppliers prove technically unsatisfactory.
- *Create unique offerings:* Marketing managers should study buyers' needs. If the seller can design distinctive goods or services uniquely fitting buyers' activities, equipment, and procedures, a mutually beneficial relationship will evolve. Buyers would incur high changeover costs in switching to another supplier. By satisfying targeted buyers in a superior way, marketing managers can make them dependent. Cereal manufacturers have skirted around passing on costs by marketing unique value-added or multi-ingredient cereals, increasing the perceived quality of cereals and allowing companies to raise prices. These cereals include General Mills' Basic 4, Clusters, and Oatmeal Crisp; Post's Banana Nut Crunch and Blueberry Morning; and Kellogg's Mueslix, Nutri-Grain, and Temptations.
- *Change the package design:* Another way companies pass on higher costs is to shrink product sizes but keep prices the same. Scott Paper Co. reduced the number of sheets in the smallest roll of Scott Clean paper towels from ninety-six to sixty and actually lowered the price by 10¢ a roll. The increases in costs for paper towels are tied to a 50 percent to 60 percent increase in the cost of pulp paper. The company also changed the names of the sizes to deemphasize the magnitude of the rolls. "We used to have three sizes: big, extra large, and megaroll," said Pete Judice, spokesperson for Scott. "We changed the names to single, double, and triple because they're easier [for the consumers] to relate to."[20]
- *Heighten buyer dependence:* Owens-Corning Fiberglas supplies an integrated insulation service (from feasibility studies to installation) that includes commercial and scientific training for distributors and seminars for end users. This practice freezes out competition and supports higher prices.

Recession

A recession is a period of reduced economic activity. Reduced demand for goods and services, along with higher rates of unemployment, is a common trait of a recession. Yet, astute marketers can often find opportunity during recessions. A recession is an excellent time to build market share, because competitors are struggling to make ends meet.

price shading
The use of discounts by salespeople to increase demand for one or more products in a line.

Two effective pricing tactics to hold or build market share during a recession are value pricing and bundling. *Value pricing,* discussed earlier in the chapter, stresses to customers that they are getting a good value for their money. Revlon's Charles of the Ritz, usually known for its pricey products, introduced the Express Bar during a recession. A collection of affordable cosmetics and skin treatment products, the Express Bar sold alongside regular Ritz products in department stores. Although lower priced products offer lower profit margins, Ritz found that increases in volume can offset slimmer margins. For example, the company found that consumers will buy two to three Express Bar lipsticks at a time. "The consumer is very conscious of how she spends her income and is looking for value and quality that she can find elsewhere in department stores," said Holly Mercer, vice president of marketing for Ritz.[21]

Bundling or *unbundling* can also stimulate demand during a recession. If features are added to a bundle, consumers may perceive the offering as having greater value. For example, suppose that Hyatt offers a "great escape" weekend for $119. The package includes two nights' lodging and a continental breakfast. Hyatt could add a massage and a dinner for two to create more value for this price. Conversely, companies can unbundle offerings and lower base prices to stimulate demand. A furniture store, for example, could start charging separately for design consultation, delivery, credit, setup, and hauling away old furniture.

Recessions are a good time for marketing managers to study the demand for individual items in a product line and the revenue they produce. Pruning unprofitable items can save resources to be better used elsewhere. Borden's, for example, found that it made about 3,200 sizes, brands, types, and flavors of snacks—but got 95 percent of its revenues from just half of them.

Prices often fall during a recession as competitors try desperately to maintain demand for their wares. Even if demand remains constant, falling prices mean lower profits or no profits. Falling prices, therefore, are a natural incentive to lower costs. During the last recession, companies implemented new technology to improve efficiency and then slashed payrolls. They also discovered that suppliers can be an excellent source of cost savings; the cost of purchased materials accounts for slightly more than half of most U.S. manufacturers' expenses. General Electric's appliance division told 300 key suppliers that they had to reduce prices 10 percent or risk losing GE's business. Allied Signal, Dow Chemical, United Airlines, General Motors, and Du Pont have made similar demands of their suppliers. Specific strategies that companies are using with suppliers include the following:

- *Renegotiating contracts:* Sending suppliers letters demanding price cuts of 5 percent or more; putting out for rebid the contracts of those that refuse to cut costs.
- *Offering help:* Dispatching teams of experts to suppliers' plants to help reorganize and suggest other productivity-boosting changes; working with suppliers to make parts simpler and cheaper to produce.
- *Keeping the pressure on:* To make sure that improvements continue, setting annual, across-the-board cost-reduction targets, often of 5 percent or more a year.
- *Paring down suppliers:* To improve economies of scale, slashing the overall number of suppliers, sometimes by up to 80 percent, and boosting purchases from those that remain.

Tough tactics like these help keep companies afloat during economic downturns.

When restaurants charge premium prices they can maximize their revenue if demand is inelastic. Also, if prices prove to be too high, they can simply lower them. It is easier to lower prices than raise them in a competitive marketplace. Premium prices do attract competition and may cause potential customers to dine elsewhere.

Restaurants can alter their base prices by using discounts, leader pricing, bundling, price lining, and two-part pricing. The type of discounts that could be offered are cash, cumulative quantity (frequent diner), and even seasonal discounts.

Use it Now!

Auctions will account for 29 percent of all e-commerce, or $129 billion by 2002.[22] Why not join the crowd? You must, however, avoid the "winner's curse"—that is, overestimating the value of an item and bidding too much. The best way to avoid this is to be informed. On eBay, bidders can study past auctions of similar items and also read feedback about sellers. Auction universe (**http://www.auctionuniverse.com**) offers content from niche magazines, such as *White's Guide to Collecting Figures*, to help customers decide what to bid.

For computer equipment, check out WebAuction (**http://www.webauction.com**). For musical instruments go to RockAuction (**http://www.rockauction.com**). For advice on how to sell at auction, try **http://www.auctionrover.com**. Auction news, reviews, message boards, and an appraisal center can be found at **http://www.auctionwatch.com**.

Want to try something different? Go to **http://www.klik-klok.com**, which is a Dutch auction. Modeled on Holland's famous flower markets, Dutch auctions are essentially the reverse of Yankee auctions: A set quantity of a certain item is available for a limited amount of time. On Klik-klok, for example, each auction lasts just two minutes, and there's an auction every three minutes. When the clock starts ticking, the item is available at its starting price. Then the price starts dropping—and keeps dropping by a few dollars every twenty seconds or so. Bidders try to hold out for the lowest price on the product that they want until just before all the items are bought by those willing to pay slightly more. The advantages of this format are obvious: The longer you play, the more prices go down instead of up—and you know immediately if your bid has "won."[23]

Summary

① **Describe the procedure for setting the right price.** Setting the right price on a product is a process with four major steps: (1) establishing pricing goals; (2) estimating demand, costs, and profits; (3) choosing a price policy to help determine a base price; and (4) fine-tuning the base price with pricing tactics.

A price strategy establishes a long-term pricing framework for a good or service. The three main types of price policies are price skimming, penetration pricing, and status quo pricing. A price-skimming policy charges a high introductory price, often followed by a gradual reduction. Penetration pricing offers a low introductory price to capture a large market share and attain economies of scale. Finally, status quo pricing strives to match competitors' prices.

② **Identify the legal and ethical constraints on pricing decisions.** Government regulation helps monitor four major areas of pricing: unfair trade practices, price fixing, predatory pricing, and price discrimination. Enacted in many states, unfair trade practice acts protect small businesses from large firms that operate efficiently on extremely thin profit margins; the acts prohibit charging below-cost prices. The Sherman Act and the Federal Trade Commission prohibit both price fixing—an agreement between two or more firms on a particular price—and predatory pricing—undercutting competitors with very low prices to drive

Key Terms

them out of business. Finally, the Robinson-Patman Act makes it illegal for firms to discriminate between two or more buyers in terms of price.

③ Explain how discounts, geographic pricing, and other special pricing tactics can be used to fine-tune the base price. Several techniques enable marketing managers to adjust prices within a general range in response to changes in competition, government regulation, consumer demand, and promotional and positioning goals. Techniques for fine-tuning a price can be divided into three main categories: discounts, allowances, rebates and value pricing; geographic pricing; and special pricing tactics.

The first type of tactic gives lower prices to those that pay promptly, order a large quantity, or perform some function for the manufacturer. Value-based pricing starts with the customer, considers the competition and costs, and then determines a price. Everyday low pricing, a form of value-based pricing, arose from trade loading. Trade loading is a manufacturer's temporary functional discount to induce wholesalers and retailers to buy more goods than can be sold in a reasonable length of time. Trade loading increases inventory expenses and channel expenses and lowers the manufacturer's profits. A tactic meant to overcome these problems is "everyday low pricing," or maintaining low prices over time while eliminating the discounts that result in trade loading. Other tactics in this category include seasonal discounts, promotion allowances, and rebates (cash refunds).

Geographic pricing tactics—such as FOB origin pricing, uniform delivered pricing, zone pricing, freight absorption pricing, and basing-point pricing—are ways of moderating the impact of shipping costs on distant customers.

A variety of special pricing tactics stimulate demand for certain products, increase store patronage, and offer more merchandise at specific prices.

More and more customers are paying price penalties, which is an extra fee for violating the terms of a purchase contract. The perceived fairness of a penalty may affect some consumers' willingness to patronize a business in the future.

④ Discuss product line pricing. Product line pricing maximizes profits for an entire product line. When setting product line prices, marketing managers determine what type of relationship exists among the products in the line: complementary, substitute, or neutral. Managers also consider joint (shared) costs among products in the same line.

⑤ Describe the role of pricing during periods of inflation and recession. Marketing managers employ cost-oriented and demand-oriented tactics during periods of economic inflation. Cost-oriented tactics consist of dropping products with a low profit margin, delayed-quotation pricing, and escalator pricing. Demand-oriented pricing methods include price shading and increasing demand through the cultivation of selected customers, unique offerings, changing the package size, and systems selling.

To stimulate demand during a recession, marketers use value pricing, bundling, and unbundling. Recessions are also a good time to prune unprofitable items from product lines. Managers strive to cut costs during recessions in order to maintain profits as revenues decline. Implementing new technology, cutting payrolls, and pressuring suppliers for reduced prices are common techniques used to cut costs.

Discussion and Writing Questions

1. A ma... desks, b... rer of office furniture decides to produce antique-style rolltop surge prote...atted for personal computers. The desks will have built-in ber of other fe... platform for raising or lowering the monitor, and a num- comparable prod... The quality, solid-oak desks will be priced far below and plan on a high v...e marketing manager says, "We'll charge a low price ...o reduce our risks." Comment.

2. Janet Oliver, owner of a midpriced dress shop notes, "My pricing objectives are simple: I just charge what my competitors' charge. I'm happy because I'm making money." React to Janet's statement.

3. Develop a price line strategy for each of these firms:
   a. a college bookstore
   b. a restaurant
   c. a video-rental firm

4. **WRITING** You are contemplating a price change for an established product sold by your firm. Write a memo analyzing the factors you need to consider in your decision.

5. Do you see everyday low prices as a solution to trade loading? Why are many manufacturers resisting EDLP?

6. Columnist Dave Barry jokes that federal law requires this message under the sticker price of new cars: "Warning to stupid people: Do not pay this amount." Discuss why the sticker price is generally higher than the actual selling price of a car. Tell how you think car dealers set the actual prices of the cars they sell.

7. Explain the difference between freight absorption pricing and uniform delivered pricing. When would it be appropriate to use each?

8. What is the difference between a price policy and a price tactic. Give an example.

9. **INFOTRAC COLLEGE EDITION** What kind of factors can push a respectable firm to enter a price fixing arrangement with a competitor? Using InfoTrac (**http://www.infotrac-college.com**), read about either the vitamin industry or the art auction industry price fixing scandals of 1999 and 2000. If there are more current scandals, read a selection of articles on a particular industry. Then compile a list of business practices and pricing issues that are present in the reports of each scandal. Is each scandal unique, or are there any overlapping characteristics? What conclusion can you draw about price fixing from the articles you read?

10. **TEAM** Divide into teams of four persons. Each team should choose one of the following topics: skimming, penetration pricing, status quo pricing, price fixing, EDLP, geographic pricing, adopting a single-price tactic, flexible pricing, or professional services pricing. Each team should then pick a retailer that it feels most closely follows the team's chosen pricing strategy. Go to the store and write down examples of the strategy. Interview the store manager and get his or her views on the advantages and disadvantages of the strategy. Each team should then make an oral report in class.

11. How is the "information age" changing the nature of pricing?

12. Have you ever paid a price penalty? How did it affect your attitude toward that company?

13. During a recession, what pricing strategies would you consider using to gain or maintain product-market share? Explain your answer.

14. **ON LINE** What pricing strategy does Microsoft seem to be using for the software offered via **http://www.microsoft.com/msdownload**.

15. **ON LINE** What pricing advantages does the Auto Connection (**http://www.autoconnection.com**) seem to offer compared to traditional auto dealers?

16. **ON LINE** Price a flight on Southwest Airlines (**http://www.iflyswa.com**) and price the same flight on American Airlines (**http://www.americanair.com**). Describe the kinds of price strategies ⌐ each company. ⌐lowing

17. **ON LINE** What kind of pricing strategies are being offered b⌐ four telecommunication competitors?

   http://www.att.com   **http://www.spri⌐**
   http://www.mci.com   **http://www.g⌐**

Application for Entrepreneurs

RoseAnn decided that time is, indeed, money. So she opened a Chinese buffet in Arlington, Texas. The new twist is that you pay by the minute. The restaurant, known as Rose's Chinese Buffet, is all-you-can-eat-by-the-minute.* The buffet table is piled with delectable seafood and steaming stir-fried dishes. Diners rush to their tables and wolf down spring rolls, fried noodles, fried rice, and other goodies. RoseAnn only allows the first thirty customers at lunch and dinner to pay by the minute. The rest must order from a traditional menu or pay the normal buffet price. By-the-minute lunch customers pay 30¢ a minute.

*Such restaurants do exist in Japan.

Questions

1. RoseAnn concedes that she only breaks even on her by-the-minute customers. Should she drop the concept?
2. What pricing tactics is she using?
3. Would such a restaurant be successful in your community?

Case

entrepreneurship

Next Step for NexTag

Founded in 1998 by entrepreneurs Purnendu Ojha (now CEO), Rafael Ortiz, and Frank Schmidt, NexTag.com's mission is to create a network of exchanges to trade products and services. Through the company's patent-pending Exchange software and Web site, NexTag is at the forefront of a dynamic pricing revolution. This dynamic pricing revolution was spurred by companies such as Priceline.com and eBay. However, NexTag claims to be leading the pricing revolution into new territory—where buyers *and* sellers negotiate prices and products in a unique web-based auction model.

How does NexTag work? A visitor to the site searches for a particular product. A search link pulls up a list of on-line stores that carry the product and shows the price (which includes shipping and handling) offered by each e-tailer. The visitor can accept any of the offered prices or can place a lower bid. Once a bid is

placed, an e-tailer can accept, reject, or counteroffer. The process allows the buyer to negotiate directly with multiple sellers. A counteroffer might be a new price (as in many traditional negotiations), or the seller might attempt to cross-sell its other products. For example, the seller might meet the buyer's price bid if the buyer will also purchase a complementary product (e.g., carrying case for the computer originally sought by the buyer).

How is NexTag.com different from a competitor such as Priceline.com? First, NexTag buyers can compare prices of multiple sellers. In most name-your-own-price processes, the buyer offers a particular price that is either accepted or rejected by a seller. Second, a buyer can negotiate directly and simultaneously with multiple sellers. Third, a buyer does not have to commit to making the purchase (e.g., giving a credit card number) prior to negotiating. (However, a user who consistently negotiates and does not purchase gets a bad reputation that can result in sellers eventually ignoring the user's bidding activities.) Fourth, sellers in the NexTag network can respond to buyers' requests within minutes due to the seller software provided by NexTag, which provides sellers with pricing guidance (i.e., how low to go on

Still Shaky? Here's a tip

Chapter 18 is a good place to revisit study tips from Chapters 5, 7, and 12 (pages 181, 240, and 419). Try to find additional examples for each pricing technique described in the chapter. Associate a pricing strategy with each of your personal belongings (furniture, clothing, toiletries, electronics, bike, books, car, etc.).

a bid) with input from inventory figures, wholesale cost data, and margin calculations. Fifth, buyers receive guidance by receiving a product's e-tail pricing history prior to making a bid or purchase decision.

Based in San Mateo, California, NexTag.com received $4 million in startup funding from Morgenthaler Ventures, a thirty-year-old technology investment firm. Initial funding allowed the company to begin operations on August 9, 1999. The company began its on-line service with computer hardware and software products. After raising an additional $10 million, the company added consumer electronics products, with a goal of nearly two million product offerings and dozens of e-tailers by 2000. NexTag plans to make money from transaction fees (a small percentage of each sale).

The notion of some form of auction bidding on the Internet appears to have been accepted by consumers. However, a key concern for NexTag.com is how far it can expand its product offering. That is, will consumers dicker over price for grocery products, CDs, books, and other generally low-ticket items? Ultimately, is the Priceline consumer different from the NexTag consumer?

Questions

1. How has NexTag.com captured the traditional steps in "setting the right price"?
2. What special pricing tactics are NexTag's suppliers practicing?
3. How does NexTag's supplier software create opportunities for cross-functional pricing interactions?

Bibliography

Charles Bermant. "E-Commerce Reviving the Art of Haggling." *The Oregonian*, March 27, 2000. On-line.

Chet Dembeck. "Online Sellers Compete for Buyers at NexTag.com." *E-Commerce Times*, August 9, 1999. On-line.

Janet Rae-Dupree and Diane Brady. "Let the Cyber Be in Control." *Business Week Online*, November 8, 1999. On-line.

Technologic Partners. "Private Profiles: NexTag." *ComputerLetter*, August 23, 1999. On-line.

http://www.nextag.com.

Case

video

World Gym: The Right Price

In the history of bodybuilding and the development of the modern gym, one name stands out—Joe Gold, the founder of World Gym. Joe never planned to expand beyond one location, but the popularity of the original gym captured the imagination of fitness enthusiasts around the country. When licensing began in 1981, the company goal was to make the World Gym name synonymous with quality nationwide. In 1989, the World Gym opened its doors in San Francisco, and pricing strategies were needed to build membership without compromising profitability. By the time the San Francisco location was opened, World Gym was a highly visible name in the fitness market, so initial membership pricing could capitalize on the strength of the entire World Gym network.

In order to stimulate demand quickly, the San Francisco owners adopted a penetration strategy. Fitness centers were in short supply in San Francisco at that time, and demand for a fitness facility ran high, so setting membership fees at a low price might have seemed on the surface to be counterintuitive. However, the city is geographically small, and it was estimated that the gym could draw residents from all over San Francisco, because the maximum travel time to the gym would be between eight and ten minutes.

What would entice residents to sign up was the uniqueness of the World Gym's facility—a cavernous space with state-of-the-art equipment to meet a variety of member needs and wants. From the experienced bodybuilder to the fitness buff to the overweight person, the clientele would be diverse and plentiful. The owners set a moderate membership price of $310 per year, which was lower than at competing gyms but set to attract 500 members the first year. So effective was this strategy that World Gym surpassed its first-year expectations and recruited 2,500 new members without suffering a rise in overhead costs.

Because their penetration pricing, supported by low overhead costs, discovered relatively free of competition Gym enjoyed a marketplace virtually free of competition for seven years. Additionally, the barriers for entry were very high. To open a gym in San Francisco were very high. To acquire, equipment costs were cisco were difficult, space was needed to be competitive. high, and it had started small but had expanded The World Gym 35,000 square feet, and its position as to a leader in fitness made its owners reevaluate their pricing. To take advantage of their market position they adopted a price-skimming strategy and began charging a high introductory price of $450 per year. Although this was a more than a 30 percent increase in the initial start-up membership offer, the price seemed justified because the target market perceived World Gym as having unique advantages, including programs for all fitness levels.

The owners of the gym, however, did not rest on their laurels. The price increase was accompanied by upgrades to facilities and programs designed to ensure that consumers got more value for their membership dollars. At the time of these changes, new demographic trends of the community were being reflected in the membership roster, where 75 percent of club members were 21 to 39 years old; 15 percent were 40 to 49; and 10 percent were 50 or over, with the fastest growing segment being the 50+ age group. These figures had specific implications for World Gym: it needed to offer a wide spectrum of services to meet the vastly different needs of the 21- and 71-year-olds. Coupled with shifting demographics was an overall increase in gym usage. The number of club members lifting free weights had increased by 49 percent, cardiovascular training boomed, treadmill use was up 46 percent, and stair climbing had grown by 144 percent. Faced with such success, World Gym initiated special events, massage sessions, nutrition counseling, tanning, discounts for students and senior citizens, and a line of gym clothing. Still, the price skimming strategy became an open invitation for competitors to enter the market.

Then market conditions changed. Two competitors, Gold's Gym and 24 Hour Fitness, opened up gyms within a mile from World Gym, and the market became more price sensitive. With other well-equipped gyms so close by, consumers did not need to consider services and convenience as heavily and could shop on price alone. Consumer demand became more elastic and responsive to price changes. These two factors,

price sensitivity and competitive pressure, caused World Gym's owners to rethink their pricing strategy.

To meet the competition and hold their ground, penetration pricing was once again adopted, and prices were lowered. Gold's Gym had a monthly fee of $24, which pushed World Gym to drop its monthly fee from $37. Despite competitive pricing, initially the World Gym lost customers to Gold's and 24 Hour Fitness, but World's owners still felt that with a roster of 8,000 members, an established reputation, and low overhead expenses, the gym could stay profitable. The new competitors could not say as much because they faced the disadvantage of high overhead costs. To stay ahead in a newly crowded market, World Gym owners continued to stress value, seeking to understand what customers wanted and what value was placed on those offerings. New fitness programs seemed to spring up in response to member demand so that when potential and actual customers compared World Gym to the competition, they found a World Gym membership offered more value. This perception of value for the money told the owners of World Gym that they had set the right price.

Questions

1. Using Exhibit 18.1, outline World Gym's steps for setting the right price.
2. Discuss the rationale for penetration pricing in this case.
3. Why did World Gym change to a price-skimming strategy?
4. How did World Gym respond to a more price-sensitive market?

Bibliography

Video by Learnet: *World Gym: A Case Study in Pricing Strategy*

World Gym Web site: **http://www.worldgym.com**

MARKETING MISCUES

IBM's Pricing Worked Too Well—for the Consumer, Not for the Company

When IBM began selling its Aptiva personal computers through retail stores in the 1990s, industry observers wondered if Big Blue was in the consumer business for the long term. They did not have to wait long to find out. In late 1999, the company stopped selling its Aptiva desktops in retail outlets. After fulfilling contractual commitments to OfficeMax, the desktop systems will only be available through IBM's company Web site, **http://www.ibm.com**. The bottom line—IBM was unable to price competitively and make money when selling the Aptiva through a middleman.

The growth potential for personal computers has been tremendous. In 1998, 43 percent of households in the United States owned a personal computer—a consumer market said to be both the fastest growing and changing segment of the computer industry. A key element of this fast-paced segment of the industry has been the downward spiral in prices to the end consumer.

As one of the leading developers and manufacturers of computer hardware, IBM's Consumer Division offers the Aptiva and ThinkPad i series of personal computers. The company won major design awards with its S Series Aptiva in 1996. In the constantly changing world of computer development where shelf life is very short, the company had begun to focus its efforts on the E Series Aptiva. Retail price points for the E Series were $999 to $1,599. For the first time ever, IBM was able to offer a high-speed personal computer for less than $1,000. By the fourth quarter of 1998, the E series offered a better price, feature for feature, than its competition. At that time, the company had introduced a $599 system. Such competitive pricing made the Aptiva very popular with end consumers. The Aptiva product line was sold through retailers such as OfficeMax, Comp-USA, Circuit City, and Best Buy—where consumer demand for the system was higher than available supply.

Unfortunately, IBM's wholesale price to retailers (which had to be low enough so retailers could offer a low price to its consumers) was not allowing the company to make money. Reportedly, IBM lost $1 billion in 1998 and $150 million in the second quarter of 1999 in the personal computer market. By the time IBM discounted its price to retailers, it was selling Aptiva computers at a loss.

The end result—IBM had to stop selling the Aptiva computers through retail stores. At the time of the company's exit from retail stores, 47 percent of the company's retail purchases were in the $600 price range. Such low-priced IBM computer systems were in big demand by consumers. But the company was losing money. IBM was not able to price the product at a wholesale price point that would enable both it and the retailer to make a profit.

Joining with other Web-based retailers, IBM is now selling the Aptiva via its company Internet site. With market demand still high in the home computer market, it is yet to be seen whether or not IBM can compete with Dell and Gateway when it comes to pricing computers over the Web.

Questions for Discussion

1. Why couldn't IBM price its computers competitively at the retail store level?
2. What is the role of the middleman in the pricing of personal computers?
3. Why do consumers buy personal computers over the Web when they can just go to the store to purchase them?

Bibliography

Sam Albert. "Is IBM Viable in the PC Consumer World?" *Midrange Systems*, February 9, 1998, p. 2.

Joel Smith. "No-Win Situation Forces IBM to Abandon Retail: Discount Manufacturers Cut Big Blue's Prices." *Detroit News*, October 18, 1999, p. B6.

Todd Wasserman. "IBM Scales Back on Most Retail Aptiva Activities." *Brandweek*, October 18, 1999, p. 5.

CRITICAL THINKING CASE

2000 Olympics—Price Tags for the Olympic Games

Ticket sales for the 2000 Olympic Games in Sydney, Australia, were supposed to be the third largest money-maker (behind television rights and corporate sponsorship) for the games. Surprisingly, Australians were reluctant to purchase tickets, and sales were not as expected. Critics cited the pricing of the tickets as the main deterrent to sales.

The Olympic Games in a Nutshell

The first Olympic Games were held in Olympia, Greece, in 776 B.C. Banned in A.D. 393 for being a pagan festival, the modern-day games were revived in the late 1800s. The first Olympic summer games were held in Athens in 1896. The first Winter Olympic Games were held in France in 1924. Once revived, the games were held every four years. However, in 1986, the summer and winter games began alternating every two years.

The International Olympic Committee (IOC), an umbrella organization that owns all rights to the Olympics, was founded in 1894. It is an international nongovernment, nonprofit organization, and it is credited with creating the Olympic Movement, an organization that consists of the IOC, the International Sports Federations, the National Olympic Committees, and the Organizing Committees for the Olympic Games (OCOG). The five Olympic rings in the Olympic symbol represent the five major regions of the world: Africa, the Americas, Asia, Europe, and Oceana.

The Sydney Olympics

Sydney, the oldest settlement in Australia, now boasts a population of over 3.5 million. Sydney is the ancestral home of the Daruk tribe and became famous as a penal colony in 1788. The harbor is the central focus of today's city, the Harbis made distinctive with landmarks such as Tower, and ridge, the Opera House, Centrepoint Represent ort Denison.

letes and 5,000 oo countries, more than 10,000 athgames, a two-week participated in the 2000 summer Sydney Organizing Co of events coordinated by the (SOCOG).

Unfortunately for SOCO for the Olympic Games games was below expectation orship for the scandal over the 2002 Salt Lake C tainted by the which members of the IOC accepted games (in for voting for Salt Lake City as the site change

games). Ticket sales were thus below expectations. Australians thought ticket prices were too high and that seat availability for Aussies was limited (as well as restricted to the worst seats).

Ticket Pricing

Ticket prices for the games ranged from A$8 for a preliminary event to almost A$1400. A$1 is equivalent to fifty-five cents U.S. Categories of seating ranged from "A," which were the best seats to "D," which were the budget (worst) seats. The highest priced tickets were for the opening and closing ceremonies. Around 82 percent of the 110,000 available opening ceremony tickets were in the "A" ticket category at the highest price of A$1382 each. Approximately 78 percent of the 110,000 closing ceremony tickets were also offered at this high price. The lowest-priced tickets (category "D") for the opening ceremony were A$105—yet, there were only 10,000 of these seats available. For the opening ceremony, that left only 9,000 seats in the "B" and "C" categories (at A$505 and A$985, respectively).

The SOCOG made approximately 50 percent of the 10 million game tickets available to the general public. However, the vast majority of these seats were in the "A" ticket category. For example, in the high-priced swimming events (racing and synchronized), 80 percent of the tickets were "A" tickets (at a price of A$140). The remaining 20 percent were broken down as follows: 8 percent "B" at A$95, 5 percent "C" at A$65, and 7 percent "D" at A$35. These cheaper seats, naturally, were far from the water (around 150 meters). Total ticket availability for racing and synchronized swimming was around 75,000 tickets. The cheapest event tickets were for archery (24,000 available tickets at A$19), baseball (133,000 tickets at A$19, A$15, and A$10), and handball (110,000 tickets at A$19).

Tickets were available by phone or mail, with payment via credit card, personal check, money order, or bank check. The plan was to follow a random selection process when demand exceeded supply. When supply was greater than or equal to demand, all orders would be filled.

Australians were angry that ticket prices were so high and that such a large number of tickets were designated as "A" tickets. Aussies felt that tickets were being offered to only the very rich—which meant a lot of non-Australians got to attend the games rather than a lot of Australians—a lot of Australians who bore the brunt of preparing and hosting the activity.

After winning the bid back in 1993 and pouring millions of dollars into development, did the Summer Games turn out to be an economic disaster for Sydney? Did the price of tickets (even to the wealthy) keep visitors away from the other Sydney attractions that were supposed to generate revenue for the city?

Questions

1. What were the economics of ticket pricing for the Sydney games?
2. Did Sydney poorly define its market segments?
3. What should Athens look at in pricing the 2004 games?

Bibliography

Rosanna DeLisle. "Australians Slow out of the Blocks for Olympics." *Foreign News*, July 18, 1999, p. 18.
Jeremy Eccles. "The World's Eyes Are on Oz." *Asiaweek Magazine*, January 21, 2000. On-line.
"What's the Deal?" *Washington Post*, March 26, 2000, p. E02.
http://www.olympic.org.
http://www.sydney2000.com.

MARKETING PLANNING ACTIVITIES

Pricing Decisions

The last part of the marketing mix to be described for the marketing plan is the price element. Be sure that

 your pricing plans match the needs and wants of the target market identified and described earlier and that they are compatible with the product, service, distribution,

and promotion issues discussed in the previous sections. Also, refer to Exhibit 2.8 for additional marketing plan subjects.

1. List possible pricing objectives for your chosen firm. How might adopting different pricing objectives change the behavior of the firm and its marketing plans?

Marketing*Builder* Exercises

- **Return on Investment** portion of the **Market Analysis** template
- **Break-Even Analysis** spreadsheet
- **Margin Structure** portion of the **Sales Plan** template

2. Pricing is an integral component of marketing strategy. Discuss how your firm's pricing can affect or be affected by competition, the economic environment, political regulations, product features, extra customer service, changes in distribution, or changes in promotion.

Marketing*Builder* Exercises

- **Pricing** portion of the **Sales Plan** template
- **Pricing** portion of the **Market Analysis** template

3. Is demand elastic or inelastic for your company's product or service? Why?
4. What are the costs that have to be covered in your chosen company?
5. What price policy should your firm use? Are there any legal implications of this choice?
6. List and describe the specific pricing tactics that your chosen company should use, including discounts, geographic pricing, and special prices.

E-MARKETING PLANNING ACTIVITIES

You began your strategic e-marketing plan by stating your business mission and objectives and detailing a SWOT analysis. In the second part of the plan you identified and described target market segments and identified sources of competitive intelligence and the need for further marketing research. Next, you began the process of defining the marketing mix, starting with the components of product, distribution, and promotion. Recall that you are either writing a strategic marketing plan for an existing bookstore retailer with a new on-line presence, a dot-com bookstore retailer, or an e-company of your own choosing.

For continued general assistance on business plans and marketing plans, visit **http://www.bplans.com** or **http://www.businessplans.org**. For electronic sources of information, search on the Electric Library at **http://www.elibrary.com** or the Internet Public Library at **http://www.ipl.org**. Another excellent source of information is the Sales and Marketing Executives Marketing Library at **http://www.sell.org**. You should also refer to Exhibit 2.8 for additional marketing plan checklist items (Part IV.B.4: Marketing Mix—Price).

The next stage of the strategic planning process—pricing—completes the elements of the marketing mix. Pricing is a special challenge to the e-marketer because prices can be quickly and easily compared on the Internet. Your goal should be to make pricing competitive and value-driven, as well as cover costs. Other features and benefits of your offering are likely to be more important than price.

Use the following exercises to guide you through the pricing part of your strategic marketing plan:

1. Gather information on tactics you decided on for the first parts of your marketing plan. What costs are associated with those decisions? Will you incur more or costsosts by selling on-line? Will your marketing ase or decrease? Why? Calculate the break-even point for selling your offering. Can you sell enough to cover your costs? To perform break-even analysis, go to **http://www.distributorworld.com/breakeven.cfm**.

2. What is the demand elasticity for your offering in an off-line world? Whatever the level, it is likely to be *more* elastic on-line. What tactics can you use to soften or reduce this on-line price sensitivity?

3. Will there be differences in on-line versus off-line pricing policies? Are these differences related to your cost structure in the on-line environment? Why? Are these differences legal?

4. Note how easy it is to compare prices on the Internet. Check out price comparison sites such as **http://www.pricescan.com**, **http://www.mysimon.com**, and **http://www.bizrate.com**. Given how products and prices are displayed, how can your offering show a differential advantage if there is a price difference? As prices reach parity on the Internet, how else will you differentiate your products or services?

5. What kinds of price discounts can your company offer? Should discounted prices be offered to on-line buyers that off-line buyers do not receive? Why might you charge your on-line customers less than your off-line customers?

6. How will you set geographic pricing policies? Will you appear as a nongeographic specific Internet provider and offer the same shipping costs to all, or will you have to charge more for longer distances? Will you market your product or services locally, regionally, or nationally? Just because you are on the Internet, does that mean you have to try to serve all markets? To check out how distances and even global transportation can affect your price, go to the United Parcel Rate Calculator at **http://www.ups.com/using/services/rave/rate.html** or **http://www.ltlrates.com**.

CROSS-FUNCTIONAL CONNECTIONS SOLUTIONS

Pricing to Satisfy Both Internal and External Demands

Questions

1. Should marketing play the lead role in coordinating the pricing decision? Explain why or why not.

   The marketing department is expected to be closest to the customer in terms of understanding consumer price elasticity. Additionally, marketing generally has the most current information on competitors' prices. However, it is the other business functions that focus on the cost component of pricing. Therefore, it is necessary to make the pricing process interactive in order to set the price ultimately at a level that will appeal to customers and make appropriate margins for the company.

2. How is activity-based costing more market oriented than traditional accounting methods?

   Traditional accounting methods do not make it easy to track marketing costs. Thus, the floor on price is determined by manufacturing's variable costs. Activity-based costing focuses upon *all* costs related to bringing a product to market, which will allow marketers to more accurately utilize cost as the floor in the pricing process for individual customers. For example, ABC would include travel time to visit a customer as a customer-related cost, which would be reflected in the pricing process for that particular customer.

3. What kinds of internal problems are caused by price promotions?

   The major impact of a price promotion is felt in the manufacturing department. The manufacturing group has to increase its level of production just prior to the price promotion in order to have enough product on hand for delivery to the customer (unless, of course, the price promotion is a means of reducing inventory) during the promotional period. The manufacturing department may have to schedule overtime workers in order to meet demand. Even if the actual price promotion period does not cause much disruption in the manufacturing process, the promotion may have longer-term ramifications. If a retailer purchases more of the product than can be sold during the promotional period, normal shipments to the retailer will be reduced until retailer inventory is back to normal levels. The manufacturing group often finds itself struggling to maintain stability in its production processes.

Suggested Readings

Michael Gering. "Activity Based Costing and the Customer." *Management Accounting,* April 1999, pp. 26–27.

Helen L. Richardson. "The New Shape of ABC." *Transportation & Distribution,* May 2000, pp. 111–116.

part 7

Technology-Driven Marketing

TECHNOLOGY'S ROLE IN FACILITATING INTERACTIONS BETWEEN THE COMPANY AND ITS CUSTOMERS AND AMONG INTERNAL FUNCTIONS

Businesses in the 21st century are expected to respond quickly to customer demands. Companies such as Charles Schwab, Priceline.com, Bank One, and Amazon.com have been able to meet consumers' demand for immediate service and fulfillment and, in doing so, have transformed industries. Schwab.com, Priceline.com, Wingspan.com (a Bank One internet initiative), and Amazon.com have the ability to interact personally with their customers in a virtual environment. In the financial world, Schwab.com made the corporation a full-service brokerage firm and Wingspan.com brought full–service banking to consumers. Priceline.com has changed the way consumers think about purchasing products, essentially bringing the pricing process into the consumer's home. Amazon.com was one of the first full-service retailers not associated with a brick–and–mortar location. Through information technology, companies such as these have been able to attract consumers. The successful interaction of all business functions, however, is what has kept customers returning to these companies as loyal and repeat users.

Understanding the marketplace and responding to its demands require technological linkages that were unheard of only a few decades ago. Advances in computer technology have already started to link marketing and its functional counterparts including the information technology, legal, financial, customer service, and research and development departments. All now have access to the same valuable market information. While there are great benefits to this easy networking, the actual process has not been without problems.

Internet marketing is leading to vast changes in the way all of a company's functional areas do business. One of the major points of contention within many organizations has been the necessary interaction between the mar-

keting and the information technology groups. Information technologists generally have backgrounds in computer science, mathematics, or engineering—areas not known for their interaction with the customer. However, these same information technologists may now be charged with developing the company's Web site, a major element of the firm's marketing communications program.

Traditionally, the marketing group has been in charge of developing the marketing communications program that reached the potential customer. The advent of corporate Web sites has dramatically changed most firms' marketing communication. In today's computer age, a company's Web site may be the customer's first and only contact with the company. What may have once been communicated in the form of a brochure or print ad is now on the consumer's computer screen instead.

Companies often refer to marketers as the site/content *strategists* and information technologists as the site/content *implementators*. Unfortunately, the separation into strategy and implementation has tended to exacerbate the conflict between marketing and information technology. The information technologists do not like "taking orders" from marketers about something that has always come under their purview (computers). Likewise, marketers fear that letting information technologists build the Web site will result in an overly complex, difficult-to-use site.

Not only must technologists and marketers work together in developing a company's web page, but the legal department also has to become intimately involved in the process. Domain registration (similar to trademarks and trade names), intellectual property rights, hidden language (called metatext), taxation, and privacy policies are all areas in which legal assistance is of utmost importance. The marketing and information technology departments have to develop appropriate material—material that will be interesting and easy to navigate. Having a lawyer who specializes in cyberlaw work in tandem with both marketing and information technology is extremely important.

Once a company's Web site is up and running—that is once marketing and information technology have gotten past their functional biases and the lawyers have reviewed legal issues—the necessary interactions between marketing and other business functions are highlighted. While the benefits of e-commerce can be substantial, considerable initial costs will be associated with doing business online. In addition to the start-up costs in developed Web pages, the firm's security expenses increase when involved in Internet marketing. As with many marketing initiatives, technology is treated by many companies as a cost center rather than as an investment. This tends to create tension between marketing/technologists and accountants.

Cisco Systems has been one of the front–runners in the link between marketing and technology. The California-based company is a global leader in electronic commerce. With a clear understanding of the importance of cross-functional interactions, Cisco emphasizes the importance of its human resources. In addition to its technological capabilities, Cisco personnel are well versed in customer service and customer satisfaction.

Not surprisingly, the Internet has worked wonders for customer service. Electronically fulfilling customer requests for technical support can dramatically improve customer satisfaction. Technicians are able to respond much more quickly to requests—bringing positive results to marketing in the form of satisfied customers and to engineering in the reduced number of engineers needed for technical product support. The decreased need for engineers in technical support means that they can devote more time to new product development.

Marketing directly to the consumer can pay off from manufacturing's viewpoint, too. Taking advantage of network capabilities and the use of personal digital assistants can lead to little or no inventory requirements. When a consumer places an order, the firm's suppliers receive electronic messages detailing the raw materials that will be needed to satisfy the customer's product demands. Raw materials can be shipped immediately to the manu-

facturing facility. The manufacturing facility will have received the order transmission at the same time as the suppliers, so it will be ready to begin production immediately upon receiving the necessary supplies. The manufacturer and the supplier are able to collaborate on scheduling production processes.

Internet marketing also allows customers to receive their orders more quickly. No longer does the customer's order have to work its way through various steps before finally reaching production. Rather, electronic order–taking can transmit the customer's request directly to the company's order fulfillment center drawing into focus the need for close relations with the logistics and transportation people.

Marketing via the Internet calls for necessary interaction between the marketing and the research and development departments—particularly as it relates to what engineers can do and what customers desire. Research and development may at times though reach beyond the consumer's wants and needs. A recent example involved the introduction of video datacasting, a technology that uses television airwaves to send Internet data. Video datacasting also allows consumers to watch television on their personal computers. In a recent trial, however, development engineers failed to recognize that consumers were unwilling to pay for having the television data receiving cards installed in their computer systems. Compaq Computer, the manufacturer of one such card, experienced mediocre consumer response to the product.

Technology is changing the way we market our products. It is expected as well, to have long-term implications for a company's organizational structure and management processes. Changes in the way consumers interact with companies will no doubt lead to even greater challenges regarding cross-functional coordination.

Questions for Discussion:

1. How has today's technology altered the role of marketing, both internally and externally?

2. What are some of the benefits of networking functional departments, customers, and suppliers?

3. Which functional areas are actively involved in making e-commerce a success? How?

Internet Marketing

Learning Objectives

1   Describe the impact of the Internet on business practice

2   Describe the current Internet marketing environment

3   Discuss on-line business strategies

4   Discuss Internet marketing objectives and strategies

Access chapter 19 at

http://lamb.swcollege.com

chapter 20

Learning Objectives

1 Define one-to-one marketing and discuss its dependence on database
technology

2 Discuss the forces that have
influenced the emergence
of one-to-one marketing

3 Compare the one-to-one
marketing communications
process with the traditional
mass marketing communi-
cations process

4 List eight common one-to-
one marketing applications

5 Discuss the basics of one-
to-one marketing database
technology

6 Describe one-to-one marketing using the Internet

7 Discuss privacy issues
related to one-to-one
marketing

One-to-One Marketing

Williams-Sonoma has emerged as the dominant home-specialty retailer and cataloger in the United States, mushrooming into a $1.1 billion home retailing giant. The catalog company has garnered much of its success by capitalizing on the booming home decor business as more and more consumers invest in their home surroundings. Its five distinct catalogs, *Williams-Sonoma's A Catalog for Cooks*, *Pottery Barn* home furnishings catalog, *Pottery Barn Kids* catalog for children's furnishings, *Hold Everything* organization products catalog and *Chambers* for upscale bed and bath products, now approach a combined circulation of 175 million a year. The company also operates over three hundred retail stores under the Williams-Sonoma, Pottery Barn, and Hold Everything banners.

But favorable consumer nesting trends are only half of Williams-Sonoma's success story. With a proprietary database containing more than nineteen million mail-order and retail households collected over the past 30 years, Williams-Sonoma's most important asset is the information it keeps on its upscale home-oriented customers. The company's extensive database allows it to know its customers on a one-to-one basis by providing a window into their past purchases from its retail stores, through its five mail-order catalogs, and from its Internet Web site.

The company's extensive in-house database contains transactional purchase behavior from each of its stores, catalogs, and Internet site, which can be accessed and analyzed to augment circulation and for cross-marketing between the different channels. The company also overlays its data on customers with outside information, such as demographics and lifestyle data, or information about purchases from other catalogs. Through sophisticated database analysis, the company can efficiently target individuals with offers to which they're likely to respond. Williams-Sonoma can accurately predict, for instance, which Pottery Barn customers are likely candidates to purchase from its Chambers catalog, if they will respond to e-mail solicitations, or be interested in a coupon to visit one of its retail stores.

Unlike other retailers who maintain separate databases for each channel, Williams-Sonoma's has merged its customer information from each catalog and retail channel into a single database. That is, information collected in its retail stores, from its catalog shoppers, and from its on-line commerce site are all merged into one fully-integrated repository of information. Industry observers note that Williams-Sonoma is the exception, rather than the rule. Synchronizing off-line and on-line databases, and even different catalog titles, is only now beginning to take hold among traditional retailers, many of whom are still trying to get caught up on the basic technological nuances of Internet commerce.

Having an integrated customer database is a boon for Williams-Sonoma's relationship-building efforts and gives the company an advantage over other retail and dot-com competitors who can't easily determine if a customer who buys on-line is the same one off-line. For instance, when a customer visits the company's Web site, Williams-Sonoma can readily identify what the customer has purchased in the past from either its stores, catalogs, or on-line and then quickly configure offers in real time that she might be interested in. E-mail campaigns alert its best customers when new inventory appears in stores nearest them and provides discount coupons for the products. Customers purchasing towels in one of its retail stores could be automatically sent a *Chambers* catalog filled with other bed and bath accessories or an e-mail message offering specials on bath products.

A seamless shopping experience is also helpful to Williams-Sonoma customers. Shoppers can order something on-line and then go to a retail store if it needs to be exchanged. Customers utilizing its wedding and gift registry are able to access the same registry information from either their personal computers, the company's call center, or their local Williams-Sonoma store. They can determine what items are on the bride's wish list, for example, verify availability, purchase the gift without duplication, and have the gift sent directly to the bride. When a gift is purchased from a bride's registry list, every store clerk, telephone customer service rep, and the on-line ordering system has the same information.[1]

What Is "One-to-One Marketing"?

Define one-to-one marketing and discuss its dependence on database technology

one-to-one marketing (customer relationship management)
An individualized marketing method that utilizes customer information to build long-term, personalized, and profitable relationships with each customer.

One-to-one marketing, like the personalized marketing efforts being initiated by Williams-Sonoma, represents a very revolutionary idea in the field of marketing today: communicate with customers on an individual, one-to-one basis. Contemporary marketers, from retailers to consumer goods manufacturers to business-to-business resellers, are being urged to look at their customers as individual entities rather than as mass markets.

Most businesses today follow the time-honored mass marketing rule of advertising and selling their products to the greatest number of people—that is, the goal is to increase market share by selling more goods to more people. However, selling more goods to *fewer* people through a one-to-one marketing philosophy is more efficient and more profitable. **One-to-one marketing**, sometimes called **customer relationship management (CRM)**, is an individualized marketing method that utilizes customer information to build long-term, personalized, and profitable relationships with each customer. One-to-one marketing focuses on *share of customer* rather than *share of market*. Whereas mass marketers develop a product and try to find customers for that product, one-to-one marketers develop a customer and try to find products for that customer.[2]

One-to-one marketing can easily be compared to strategic warfare and military weapons. During World War II, planes were deployed carrying hundreds of bombs to be dropped helter skelter with the hope that at least one would hit its intended target. Now fast-forward to contemporary warfare and Desert Storm, in which sophisticated laser-guided missiles were able to hit a specific target from hundreds of miles away.[3] Instead of scattering messages far and wide across the spectrum of mass media, one-to-one marketers are now honing in on ways to target each individual customer.

The Evolution of One-to-One Marketing

It may surprise many readers-especially those who grew up to the sound of advertising jingles on television and the sight of billboards dotting the landscape—that one-to-one marketing is not at all new. In fact, it is essentially a very old-fashioned idea. Before the Industrial Revolution, there was no mass advertising. Small businesses thrived and supported the community. Care of the customer flourished. Early small-town merchants remembered the products each customer purchased and made recommendations based on past purchases and lifestyles. Products could even be custom-produced or modified to fit the particular need of the customer.[4]

As time went by, mass production led to volume buying and mass media advertising. American businesses grew and prospered on the principle of "make and sell"—that is, companies manufactured large quantities of the same product, advertised it to the masses, and let the sheer numbers generate profitable sales.[5] As a result, marketers developed a different view of the customer. No longer unique, all customers were perceived as having the same needs and reachable through the same channels with the same message. As Henry Ford said it, "We'll give you any color you want, as long as it's black."[6]

Today, however, customers demand more choices in buying precisely what meets their needs and wants and expect individualized attention. Technology now makes it possible for companies to interact with these customers in new ways, by allowing companies to create databases that pull data from, and feed information to, those interactions. Companies are using technology to make it possible to tailor products, service, and communications to meet those expectations.[7]

As a result of one-to-one marketing and the benefits of technology, companies are increasingly shifting from a product-driven orientation to a customer-driven emphasis. Early visionaries of this change were Stan Rapp and Tom Collins, who cowrote the 1987 book *Maxi-Marketing*, which summarized the new direction emerging at the time:[8]

Every established norm in advertising and promotion is being transformed . . . We are living through a shift from selling virtually everyone the same thing a generation ago to fulfilling the individual needs and tastes of better-educated consumers by supplying them with customized products and services. The shift [is] from a "get a sale now at any cost" to building and managing customer databases to track the lifetime value of your relationship with each customer. As the cost of accumulating and accessing data drops, the ability to talk directly with prospects and customers, building one-to-one relationships with them, will grow.

As one-to-one marketing takes hold, it is no longer enough to understand customers and prospects by aggregate profiles. The one-to-one future requires that marketers understand their customers and collaborate with them, rather than use them as targets. The battle for customers will be won by marketers who understand how and why their customers *individually* buy their products—and who learn how to win them over, one customer at a time.[9]

One company that has embraced one-to-one marketing with much success is FedEx. The world's largest shipper recently transformed itself from a product-oriented marketer to a customer-oriented one-to-one marketer. By gathering information on customers and then segmenting them based on each individual customer's value to the company and service needs, FedEx can now target different customers with different messages based on what the company knows about them. For instance, if FedEx knows a certain customer only ships overnight letters but uses UPS to ship domestic boxes, then targeted messages are sent to this customer to educate him about FedEx's domestic services. Similarly, if the company learns that this customer uses another carrier to ship packages internationally, then FedEx can make sure the customer receives information about the company's international shipments. So far, FedEx's one-to-one approach has been successful; in its small-shipper segment, the company has realized an 8 to 1 return on its one-to-one marketing costs.[10]

Why One-to-One Marketing Needs Database Technology

How can marketers really communicate with their customers one at a time? How can huge corporations like FedEx or Williams-Sonoma communicate with each and every one of their thousands or millions of customers on such a personal level?

The answer lies in *database technology*. Fundamentally, one-to-one marketing is no more than the relationship cultivated by a salesperson with the customer. A successful salesperson builds a relationship over time, constantly thinks about what the customer needs and wants, and is mindful of the trends and patterns in the customer's purchase history. A good salesperson often knows what the customer needs even before the customer knows. The salesperson may also inform, educate, and instruct the customer about new products, technology, or applications in anticipation of the customer's future needs or requirements.

This kind of thoughtful attention is the basis of one-to-one marketing—but there's one major difference. For the successful salesperson, the process of one-to-one relationship building is intuitive. In one-to-one marketing using database technology, it is preplanned and consciously implemented. Database technology stores pertinent information about all of a company's customers and contacts and makes it readily available to the sales and marketing staff for assessing, analyzing, and anticipating customers' needs.[11]

Today's database technology allows marketers to do what the old-fashioned storekeepers of the 1800s did—get to know their customers on a personal, one-to-one basis. Whereas these early merchants may have had only fifty or one hundred customers at the most to keep track of, today's one-to-one marketers can track their customers as individuals through database technology, even if they number in the millions. In this age of increasing amounts of information, database technology allows marketers to sift through the millions of pieces of data to target the right customers, to develop the right communication based on these customers' needs, and to monitor the ongoing relationship, making adjustments in message strategy as needed. Database technology is the heart of one-to-one marketing.

Using database software, financial institutions can use customer information to provide personalized service for ATM users. Calling on data stored about a customer, an ATM can determine whether a customer has an individual retirement account at the bank and then flash a brief personalized message about a free Roth IRA deal that expires in two weeks, for instance. The ATM can remember that a customer likes to make withdrawals in $50 bills. Customers can even choose the background on the ATM's screen from a menu of designs that includes hockey team logos. Most customers enjoy the customized service. When ATM-maker NCR Corporation surveyed customers, about half said they wouldn't mind their bank using account information if it led to better services geared to their needs.[12]

Database Technology Investments Increase

One-to-one marketing using database technology is undoubtably on the rise. According to a recent database forecast survey, eight in ten companies have some sort of database. The investment in database technology is increasing, especially among health care, utilities, and insurance marketers. Health maintenance organizations are trying to solve customer retention and satisfaction problems and the utility companies, faced with an unregulated future, are trying to understand their customers for the first time. Insurance companies are looking to store "life events," such as marriage or childbirth, to serve as sales triggers.[13] Perhaps the most technologically advanced one-to-one databases are being developed by Internet marketers looking to create a more personalized, targeted experience for surfers visiting their sites. Using sophisticated data analysis techniques, Internet marketers can reconfigure their Web pages in real time to deliver offers customers are more likely to want.

The number of consumer names in many databases is astounding: American Express, 19 million names of prospective credit card holders; Mead Johnson, maker of Enfamil baby formula, 5 million names of expectant or new mothers; hotel operator Marriott International, 12 million names of frequent travelers; and catalog marketer Fingerhut, 65 million names of catalog shoppers.[14] The data some companies collect can take up huge amounts of computer memory. Wal-Mart's database, considered second in size only to the Pentagon, contains over a hundred terabytes (trillions of characters) of past customer transaction data. Wal-mart uses its massive database to help each of its store adapt its merchandising mix to local neighborhood preferences.[15]

Being able to target ad mailings is a tremendous advantage for marketers. This brochure, designed specifically for pregnant women and new mothers, was sent out by Franciscan Health Systems as part of their Family Education Programs.

Although developing databases for one-to-one marketing efforts can be expensive, the return on investment can be huge. KeyCorp, one of the largest financial services companies in the United States, realized a 364 percent return on investment from its one-to-one marketing efforts. KeyCorp collects data on its Web site where customers create a private profile, identifying their goals and interests. By knowing this information, KeyCorp was able to better respond to their financial needs, cross-selling additional products through direct mail, tellers, and the Internet.[16] Washington-based Franciscan Health Systems replaced its generic newsletters and mass mailings to its 37,000 female patients with a more targeted approach to get them to use its women's health services. The health provider segmented its database according to life stages, such as just having a baby or being over sixty-five, and sent information that matched corresponding needs. The initiative brought in more female patients for its services and generated $783 for every dollar spent, versus only $263 for earlier marketing efforts.[17]

Forces Influencing One-to-One Marketing

Several forces have helped shape this new one-to-one focus on customers. They include a more diverse society, more demanding and time-poor consumers, a decline in brand loyalty, the explosion of new media alternatives, and demand for marketing accountability.[18]

Discuss the forces that have influenced the emergence of one-to-one marketing

Increasing Diversity

In the 1950s and 1960s, Americans strove for the *Leave It to Beaver* and *Dick and Jane* ideal of the perfect lifestyle. The ideal family was Caucasian and lived in a comfortable suburban house, the father worked to support the family, and mom stayed home to keep a tidy house and raise the children. Life was simple. Dad came home from work at five o'clock, the family ate dinner together, and later gathered around the one television set to watch *The Ed Sullivan Show.* Although not everyone of that era lived this lifestyle, nearly everybody agreed that it was the ideal.

Today, less than 7 percent of households fit this profile. Modern families are split into many smaller segments, such as unmarried couples living together, fathers or mothers heading households alone, married couples without children, homosexual couples, singles living alone or with roommates, older "empty nesters," and many other permutations.

Even more important than the diversity of today's household, however, is the acceptance by society of that diversity. Today, people acknowledge and accept diversity, and our definition of what is acceptable has changed as the family has changed. No longer is being married to have children automatically thought better than being a single parent, or living in the suburbs better than living in the city, or being white better than being black or Hispanic or Asian.

More Demanding, Time-Poor Consumers

Consumers today are more strapped for time than any previous generation. While the continuing rise in the number of women in the workforce, the increase of working mothers, and the rise in single-parent households mostly headed by women are not new trends, women now constitute the majority of American workers for the first time. As a result, consumers have less and less time to spend on anything but the most pressing details of their lives. This has a profound impact on consumers' buying behavior. Consumers are becoming more demanding, more impatient, and much less likely to spend time agonizing over small purchases or driving across town to the mall. This is evident in the statistics that show over 128 million Americans—more than two-thirds of the population—order goods or services by phone, mail, or on-line each year. The growth of Internet commerce also attests to the decrease in time for Americans. In 1999, one in five Americans purchased something over the Internet, up from virtually no one just four years earlier.[19]

Decreasing Brand Loyalty

In a 1975 survey of male and female heads of households, over three-quarters agreed with the statement "I try to stick to well-known brand names." Ten years later, only a little over half agreed with the same statement. This trend has continued through the 1990s and into the new century. Consumers are now more likely to experiment with generics or switch back and forth between major brands in a category. They are also more likely to shop for discounts and, if presented with two comparable brands, consumers will likely choose based on price.

The decline in brand loyalty can be attributed in part to the excessive couponing, trade deals, and deep price promotions by manufacturers and retailers that have accustomed consumers to look for the best deal. Brand loyalty has also wavered due to the proliferation of brands available, with thousands more being introduced annually. With so many product choices, consumers often become confused about product differentiation or they lack the time to learn about each new brand. As a result, consumers often resort to basing their purchases on price.

The decrease in brand loyalty can also be attributed to the increasing power of many retailers today. Retailers are increasingly taking control of their relationships with brand marketers, dictating level and type of in-store promotions, placement of product, and price. These retailers are also more sophisticated at developing their own customer communications programs, including multicoupon direct mail and relationship-oriented marketing programs. As a result, consumers are building more of a relationship with a particular retailer than they are with a brand. For example, consumers may drive thirty or more miles to a Wal-Mart store to shop even though they can get the same brands at relatively the same prices in their own neighborhood.

Emergence of New Media Alternatives

Three decades ago, most Americans spent their evenings in front of their television set, watching network programming on NBC, CBS, or ABC. They were also more likely to read the newspaper and subscribe to a general news magazine such as *Life* or *Time*. Marketers reached consumers by blanketing mass media with image advertising.

Today's busy consumers are not at all likely to be found spending their evenings watching the latest sitcom on network television. Instead, they are probably surfing the hundreds of channels available through their direct satellite system, watching a rented movie, or visiting their favorite game or news site on the Internet. Newspapers and general-interest magazines have given way to an abundance of specialty publications that cater to a wide range of interests.

With the emergence of new and varied media alternatives, mass media advertising will never be the same. Marketers must increasingly divvy up their marketing dollars among the various media available, concentrating on those that will bring them the most bang for the buck. Although mass media advertising on network television or through general-interest magazines will continue to play an important role in communicating brand messages, it will never again be the dominant force it once was.

Demand for Accountability

The impact of mass media advertising on sales has always been difficult to measure. Generations of marketers have quoted John Wanamaker, the turn-of-the-century American merchant, saying, "I know half of my advertising is wasted. I just don't know which half." Historically, the results from a newspaper or television advertising expenditure could be measured only through future sales of the advertised offering, its increase in market share, or the increase in store traffic. Even sales promotional tactics, which provide more measurability than mass media efforts, have come under attack. For instance, coupons distributed through the freestanding inserts found in the Sunday paper are just as much a form of mass media advertising as a full-page image ad in the same paper, and therefore, largely unaccountable. Manufacturers today are under pressure to maintain growth and profits for stockholders. It is no longer acceptable to say that sales increased after an advertising campaign. Management now wants proof that monies spent on advertising and marketing will deliver results.

How Have These Trends Influenced One-to-One Marketing?

What are these forces telling marketers? How are they pushing forward the customer-focused philosophy of one-to-one marketing?

For starters, a more diverse society has ruled the one-size-fits-all marketing of yesteryear no longer fits. Consumers do not want to be treated like the masses. Instead they want to be treated as the individuals they are, with their own unique sets of needs and wants. By its personalized nature, one-to-one marketing can fulfill this desire.

Second, more direct and personal marketing efforts will continue to grow to meet the needs of consumers who no longer have the time to spend shopping and making purchase decisions. With the personal and targeted nature of one-to-one marketing, consumers can spend less time making purchase decisions and more time doing the things that are important.

Third, consumers will only be loyal to those companies and brands that have earned their loyalty and reinforced it at every purchase occasion. One-to-one marketing techniques focus on finding a firm's best customers, rewarding them for their loyalty, and thanking them for their business.

Fourth, mass media approaches will decline in importance as advances in market research and database technology allow marketers to collect detailed information on their customers, not just the approximation offered by demographics but the specific names and addresses. One-to-one marketing will increase in importance and offer marketers a more cost-effective avenue to reach customers. Finally, the demand for accountability will drive the growth of one-to-one marketing and justify its continued existence.

One-to-one marketing is a huge commitment and often a 180-degree turnaround for marketers who have spent the last half of the twentieth century thick in mass marketing efforts. Although mass marketing will probably always be part of the promotional mix, especially to create brand awareness or to remind consumers of a product, the advantages of one-to-one marketing cannot be ignored. As marketers begin the new millennium, the new commandment of marketing's future will ring loudly in every marketers' ears: "Know thy customer and communicate with him or her based on what you know."[20]

A Revised Marketing Communications Process

The traditional mass marketing communications process, introduced in Chapter 14, in which everyone receives the same message through the same channel, no longer holds true in a one-to-one marketing environment. Recall that the mass marketing communications process presented in Exhibit 14.2 depicts an advertiser or marketer sending a promotional message through some type of mass marketing channel, such as a television ad or an outdoor billboard, to the target audience. Noise from competing advertisements affects the encoding and decoding of the message. Feedback on the effectiveness of the communication comes through market research and changes in sales levels or market share.

Now, compare this process with Exhibit 20.1, which depicts marketing communications using one-to-one marketing and database technology. The revised

Compare the one-to-one marketing communications process with the traditional mass marketing communications process

Exhibit **20.1**

The One-to-One Marketing
Communications Process

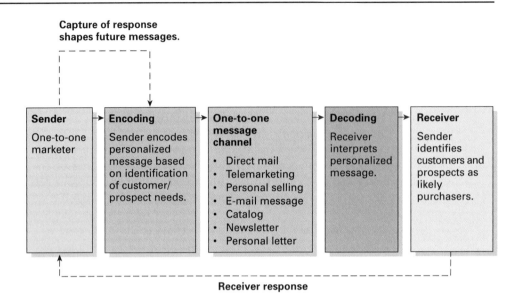

**Capture of response
shapes future messages.**

| **Sender**

One-to-one marketer | **Encoding**

Sender encodes personalized message based on identification of customer/prospect needs. | **One-to-one message channel**

• Direct mail
• Telemarketing
• Personal selling
• E-mail message
• Catalog
• Newsletter
• Personal letter | **Decoding**

Receiver interprets personalized message. | **Receiver**

Sender identifies customers and prospects as likely purchasers. |

Receiver response

one-to-one marketing communications process
A revised marketing communications process that depicts the individualized communication between the one-to-one marketer and the customer. The process is characterized by the use of personalized communication, the lack of interfering noise, and the ability to capture the response of the customer.

one-to-one marketing communications process flows as follows: (1) the one-to-one marketer, the *sender*, encodes individualized messages for customers and prospects identified from the database; (2) the message is then sent through a direct communications channel, such as direct mail, a salesperson, a telemarketer, or directly over the Internet; (3) the customer or prospect, the *receiver*, interprets the personalized message; (4) the customer or prospect responds to the communication in the form of a response, a purchase, or other communication; (5) the one-to-one marketer captures this response, feeding it back into the marketing database where it will help shape the next marketing communication.

Although the flow of the communications process is still basically the same, from marketer to customer, there are a few significant differences. First, the encoded message is *personalized* to the individual. Rather than a mass communication in which the same message is sent to a large group of potential respondents who may or may not be interested, a personalized, one-to-one communication is sent to relatively few individuals who are known to be interested. Novartis Seeds Inc., a Minneapolis-based agriculture business produces individually customized, full-color brochures for seven thousand farmers. Each piece features products selected by Novartis dealers specifically for the farmer based on information collected about the farm operation and the types of crops grown. Instead of the thirty-page catalog Novartis traditionally sends, these customers get a one-page brochure with only the five or six products they need, plus other complementary products dealers feel they should consider.[21]

Second, the channel used to send the message is a *direct* channel rather than a mass media channel. With mass media channels such as television or newspapers, marketers do not personally know the people with whom they are trying to communicate. With a direct one-to-one channel, the marketer has some information about each individual customer. Further, with mass media channels, the company is unable to respond immediately to customers' reactions to its message. Instead, they must wait to see whether people are reacting positively or negatively by conducting research or by monitoring sales and market share. With a direct one-to-one channel, marketers can capture individual customer response and use this information to shape future communications.

Third, notice that *noise*, or interference from competing advertisements, news articles, or other competing store displays, is not present in the one-to-one market-

Knowing and understanding his customers has helped Chris Zane implement a highly targeted relationship marketing strategy. His targeted child's bicycle mailing every March would not be possible without maintaining accurate records about customer purchases.

ing communications process. This is because the communication occurs directly from the marketer to the customer or prospect, with minimal interference from competing messages. Although there is no communications environment that is completely free of interfering noise—the dog may be barking, the children interrupting, or the telephone ringing—the one-to-one communications process comes as close as possible to being noise-free. With less interference, the receiver of the one-to-one marketing message is more likely to receive and interpret the communication correctly.

Last, in the one-to-one communications process the response of the individual can be captured, allowing the marketer to use the response to update the customer record, tailor the next marketing effort, and provide accountability for marketing dollars spent. Chris Zane, president of Zane's Cycles, in Branford, Connecticut, uses past responses from customers to tailor future marketing communications. Every March, Zane searches his database for customers who bought baby seats three years earlier. Knowing that they may wish to buy a child's bike soon, Zane sends these customers a postcard showcasing his inventory of children's bikes and offering a small discount on the purchase. About 60 percent of those who receive the postcard return to buy a bike.[22]

One-to-One Marketing Applications

As mentioned earlier, a marketing database is not an end in and of itself but rather a *tool* that helps marketers reach customers and prospects with one-to-one marketing communications. The information contained in marketing databases helps marketers know and understand their customers on an individual level. By analyzing and manipulating the information, marketers can identify sales opportunities and drive the communications process to address these opportunities. Several one-to-one applications for marketing databases are presented in Exhibit 20.2 and discussed in the text that follows.[23]

List eight common one-to-one marketing applications

Identifying the Best Customers

Smart marketers have found that not all customers are created equal; that is, a majority of sales will come from a minority of customers. When companies examine closely where their sales are coming from, most will find that the 80/20 rule applies: 20 percent of the customer base will provide 80 percent of sales. If a company could identify these customers and develop a relationship with them, chances are the company would enjoy enormous profitability. Thus, one of the most important values of a one-to-one marketing database is to track the 10 or 20 percent of customers who provide the majority of the sales. Casino operator Harrah's Entertainment, for instance, discovered that gamblers who spent between $100 and $499 a trip accounted for about 30 percent of its customer base but 80 percent of revenue and nearly 100 percent of profits. As a result, the company refocused its marketing

Exhibit 20.2

Eight Common One-to-One
Marketing Applications

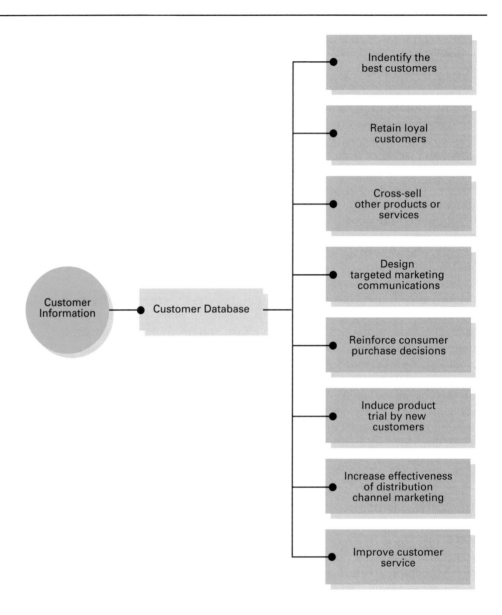

efforts on this group it calls "avid players."[24] Conversely, discount brokerage firm Charles Schwab determined who its most costly customers were and revised minimum balances required to justify free personal service. Now, those customers who are only comfortable talking to a company representative in a branch office may have to carry a certain balance, or pay for the service.[25] Similarly, FedEx imposed double-digit rate increases on some major shippers who it identified as generating lots of expensive residential shipments, in essence telling several they could take their business elsewhere.[26]

Retaining Loyal Customers

It follows, then, that if a company knows who its best customers are, it should make every effort to maintain and increase their loyalty to retain their business. One study concluded that if a company retains an additional 5 percent of its customers each year, profits will increase by at least 25 percent. What's more, improving customer retention by a mere 2 percent can decrease costs by as much as 10 percent.[27]

Loyalty programs reward loyal consumers for making multiple purchases with the objective of building long-term, mutually beneficial relationships between a company and its key customers. Loyalty programs take advantage of database technology built around the identification of a firm's best customers. Marriott Hotels, for instance, rewards its best customers with special perks not available to customers who stay less frequently. Travelers who spend more than seventy-five nights a year in any of Marriott's brand hotels—Marriott, Renaissance, Fairfield, Courtyard, Residence Inn, SpringHill Suites, or TownePlace Suites— receive reservation guarantees, welcome gifts like fruit baskets or mineral water in their rooms, room upgrades, free phone service, and access to concierge lounges.[28] SportsLine USA rewards its loyal customers just for visiting its Web site. Members of its loyalty program receive points for viewing pages that can be redeemed for sports merchandise, event tickets, or private e-mail messages from sports celebrities. The Internet site uses the information collected to understand the unique behavior and tendencies of the sports fans who visit its site.[29]

Although few sporting organizations take advantage of their large, loyal customer bases, executives at Santa Anita Park realized the value of creating a database to build a relationship with its loyal horse racing fans. Through the park's Thoroughbred Club, members get a card entitling them to a discounted admission price. The more customers visit, the cheaper the price becomes, dropping from $3 (the admission price for nonmembers is $4) to $1.75. Members' cards are scanned each time they enter the park. Santa Anita Park uses the collected attendance information to design promotions to boost attendance. A recent mailing to people in the database who had attended previous opening days but had not attended this year's promised attendees a racetrack calendar if they attended within two weeks. The promotion garnered a 25 percent response rate. The program also rewards frequent track visitors with prizes such as jackets and hats. Fifty percent of park guests are now members of the Thoroughbred Club and attendance has increased 10 percent, despite a national trend of declining attendance and betting at racetracks.[30]

Cross-Selling Other Products or Services

One-to-one marketing provides tremendous opportunities for cross-selling related products. A database allows marketers to match product profiles and consumer profiles to cross-sell customers other products that match their demographic, lifestyle, or behavioral characteristics. American Collegiate Marketing, a magazine subscription service targeted to students and educators, uses past customer purchase information gleaned from its database of millions of magazine subscribers to feature new magazines the customer may be interested in. Past purchase behavior may show that subscribers of *Sports Illustrated*, for instance, may also be interested in general news magazines such as *Time* or *Newsweek*. Similarly, the Internet music retailer CDNow develops profiles of music buyers who have purchased similar selections. When a buyer searches or purchases music titles that match a profile, he or she is then presented with titles that other buyers in the profile have bought.

Internet companies use product and customer profiling to reveal cross-sell opportunities while a customer is surfing their site. Past purchases, where a surfer goes on a site, and what site the surfer came from give clues to on-line marketers about the surfer's interests and what items to cross-sell. Cyberian Outpost (outpost.com), a computer-goods e-tailer adjusts the pages visitors see depending on what they click on at the site or what they purchased in the past. For instance, if a surfer always goes to computer game pages or has purchased simulation games in the past, Outpost will automatically put offers for other game titles on part of the screen. Depending on what a shopper puts in a shopping cart, Outpost will flash promotions for related materials—a leather case for someone who is buying a Palm Pilot, for example.[31]

Designing Targeted Marketing Communications

Using transaction and purchase data, a database allows marketers to track their customers' relationships to its products and services and modify its marketing message accordingly. For instance, a company may segment its customers as infrequent users, moderate users, and heavy users. It may then devise a segmented communications strategy based on which group the customer falls in. Marketing communications to infrequent users might encourage or stimulate a repeat purchase through a direct incentive such as a limited-time price discount to order again. Communications to moderate users may use fewer incentives and more reinforcement of past purchase decisions. Targeted communications to heavy users would be designed around loyalty and reinforcement of the purchase rather than price promotions.

Rite Aid Corporation's pharmacy division uses its database to create direct-to-patient targeted information in the form of informational pamphlets that also carry targeted advertising. A consumer filling a prescription for a diabetes medication, for example, will receive a pamphlet with different editorial and advertising than a consumer filling a prescription for a hypertension drug.[32] Dick's Supermarkets, an eight-store chain in Wisconsin, uses transaction data from its loyalty card program to personalize shopping lists it mails every two weeks to its nearly 30,000 members. The shopping lists contain timed offers based on past purchases. A consumer who bought Tide several weeks ago, for instance, may be offered a cents-off coupon to restock.[33]

Knowing other personal or demographic information besides past transaction data also allows marketers to tailor a message. For example, Marion Merrell Dow, maker of the drug Cardizem prescribed to patients with heart disease, developed a database of information about more than 440,000 Cardizem users. The company used information it collected to develop different messages and promotions based on specific concerns users had about their disease or factors in their life that could affect their health. To more than 90,000 Cardizem users who said they had difficulty remembering to take their second or third dose during the day, Marion Merrell Dow sent a personal letter and a gift: a pocket-sized, digital alarm clock pillbox to help them remember it was time to take the next pill. They also discovered that some 140,000+ customers were confused by conflicting reports on what was good or bad to eat for those with heart disease. So the drug maker sent these users a food shopping guide. To the more than one hundred thousand customers who told Dow they had difficulty dealing with the seemingly trivial stresses in their daily lives, they sent a book on coping with stress.[34]

Reinforcing Consumer Purchase Decisions

As you learned in Chapter 5, *cognitive dissonance* is the feeling consumers get when they recognize an inconsistency between their values and opinions and their behavior. In other words, they begin to doubt the soundness of their purchase decision. A database offers marketers an excellent opportunity to reach out to customers to reinforce the purchase decision. By thanking customers for their purchase and letting them know that they are important to the business, marketers can help cement a long-term and profitable relationship. Guests staying at the quaint Village Country Inn nestled in the Green Mountains of Vermont receive a hand-written thank-you note from the inn's proprietors within a week of their stay. The note thanks the guest for visiting and encourages them to return in the future. Updating customers periodically of the status of their order also reinforces purchase decisions. Minutes after customers order merchandise from Amazon.com's Web site, for example, they

One-to-one marketing offers unique opportunities for cross-selling. Outpost.com does this successfully by adjusting the pages that visitors see based on what they click on and what they have purchased in the past.

receive an e-mail acknowledging their order. Every few days thereafter, customers receive updates that allow them to track the shipment of the order, from ship date to receipt. Post-sale e-mails also afford the chance to provide more customer service or cross-sell another product or service. When customers make a purchase of digital storage equipment from Iomega Direct, the site automatically sends a confirmation e-mail. Then, once a week, Iomega sends a message to everyone who purchased in the previous week that provides links back to Iomega Direct's site, to a customer support site, and to a site where they can download Iomega software.[35]

Inducing Product Trial by New Customers

Although a significant portion of one-to-one marketing effort is expended on encouraging repeat purchases by a firm's best customers or market segments, a marketing database can also be used to identify new customers. Because a firm using a marketing database already has a profile of its best customers, it can easily find new customers that fit that profile.

One-to-one marketers generally use demographic and behavioral data overlaid on existing customer data to provide a detailed customer profile that is a powerful tool in evaluating lists of prospects. For instance, if a firm's best customers are thirty-five to fifty years of age, live in suburban areas, own luxury cars, like to eat at Thai restaurants, and enjoy mountain climbing, then the company can find prospects already in its database or customers who currently are identified as using a competitor's product who match this profile. FedEx analyzes transaction and demographic data in its database to create a profile of the 20 percent of its customers who are most valuable. FedEx then uses this profile to identify similar customers in its database who could be shipping with the company more frequently and shipping larger packages. Targeted marketing communications are then aimed specifically at these customers.[36]

Increase the Effectiveness of Distribution Channel Marketing

In Chapter 12 you learned that a *marketing channel* is a business structure consisting of interdependent organizations, such as wholesalers and retailers, that move a product from producer to ultimate consumers. Most marketers rely on heavily layered, indirect channels to move their products to the end user. Thus, marketers often lose touch with the customer as an individual since the relationship is really between the retailer and the consumer. Marketers in this predicament tend to view their customers as aggregate statistics because specific customer information is hard to gather.

With one-to-one marketing databases, manufacturers now have a tool to gain insight into who is buying their products. Instead of simply unloading product into the distribution channel and leaving marketing and relationship-building to dealers, auto manufacturers today are taking a more active role in learning about their customers. Car makers now keep in touch with owners and prospects, learning their life stages and hobbies, understanding their vehicle needs and developing relationships in the hopes that these consumers will reward them with their brand loyalty in the future. Car manufacturers then pass on the information they collect to their dealers so they can better understand their customers and tailor their dealerships to better meet customers needs. Mercedes-Benz USA, for instance, has developed a database of some 1.5 million consumers who have expressed an interest in the brand. The car manufacturer offers owners individual Web sites to communicate directly with Mercedes-Benz. Similarly, DaimlerChrysler sends new buyers a thank-you mailing with a free oil change and an invitation to communicate with the company by phone, mail, or the Web.[37]

Improving Customer Service

One-to-one marketing techniques are increasingly being used to improve the customer service experience for customers. Banks, for instance, use caller identification software to sort through in-coming calls. By matching telephone numbers to a customer profile, a call from a highly profitable customer might be routed to a special-operations group.[38] Capital One Financial Corporation, one of the top ten issuers of credit cards, discovered problems in connecting customers to the right person to answer their questions when they called the company. Customers waited on hold for long periods of time or were routed to someone untrained to help. Using sophisticated data analysis and redesigned processes, Capital One can now predict the nature of the call even before the phone is answered. By sifting through customer contact data, the company developed a system that correctly categorizes and routes up to 70 percent of calls automatically, resulting in less waiting for the customer and faster information. The company is also able to capitalize on cross-sell opportunities. By decreasing call time by a third, the firm freed up customer service representatives to spend more time selling. Now Capital One cross-sells other services when customers call in and are more receptive to marketing.[39]

The Basics of Marketing Database Technology

Discuss the basics of one-to-one marketing database technology

data-driven marketing
The process of gathering, maintaining, and analyzing information about customers and prospects to implement more efficient and effective marketing communications. Another term for one-to-one marketing.

database
A collection of data, especially one that can be accessed and manipulated by computer software.

marketing database
The compilation of names, addresses, and other pieces of pertinent information about individual customers and prospects that affects what and how marketers sell to them.

data warehouse
A very large, corporate-wide database in which the data are culled from a number of legacy systems, such as billing/accounting, order fulfillment, distribution, customer service, and marketing and sales, that are already in place within the organization.

In almost all cases, one-to-one marketing is characterized by the creation of a large computerized file of customers' and potential customers' profiles and purchase patterns used to direct marketing communications. One-to-one marketing using technology is commonly referred to as **data-driven marketing**. That is, by gathering, enhancing, and analyzing information about customers and prospects, marketers will be able to implement more efficient and effective marketing communications and perform precise marketing. With data, technology, and statistical techniques, one-to-one marketers communicate to individuals, not to mass market segments.[40]

At the very core of one-to-one marketing is, of course, a database. As defined by *Random House Webster's Dictionary*, a **database** is "a collection of data, especially one that can be accessed and manipulated by computer software."[41] More specifically, a **marketing database** is the compilation of names, addresses, and other pieces of pertinent information about individual customers and prospects that affects what and how marketers sell to them.

A database can store almost any kind of information about consumers. In its most basic form, database marketing relies on transactional processing systems that record the details of individual purchase transactions. For example, when consumers make a purchase on their credit cards, a database records the store name, the store location, the date of the purchase, and the purchase price, among other things. Over time this produces a transaction history for every customer. This basic transactional system provides critical information about purchasing patterns and preferences that are valuable in creating new products or sales offers. Transaction data can be further enhanced with additional information about individual customers such as age and income level, interests, or something that reflects their lifestyle or attitudes. Exhibit 20.3 comprises several different types of basic information that marketers could collect on their customers and prospects, divided by whether they are consumers or business-to-business customers.

In many cases, a database gives marketing decision-makers access to the vast amounts of customer information traditionally stored in separate computer systems throughout a company. Data kept for other purposes, such as financial data kept by the billing department or customer service problems kept by the service area, are merged together into a data warehouse to provide a complete picture of the customer. A **data warehouse** is essentially a very large, corporate-wide database, culled from a number of separate systems, such as billing/accounting, order

Exhibit **20.3**

Basic Consumer and
Business-to-Business Data

Consumer Data	Business-to-Business Data
• Name, address, telephone number, e-mail address	• Name, genderization (e.g., Mr./Mrs./Ms.), title of buyer, direct telephone number, e-mail address
• Demographic data: age, income, gender, ethnicity, household size, etc.	• Company name, address, and telephone number
• Lifestyle and leisure interests	• Company demographics: SIC code, number of employees, sales volume, number of branches, key contacts
• Financial characteristics such as credit history and rating	
• Recency, frequency, and monetary transaction history by date, dollar amount of purchase, and products purchased	• Recency, frequency, and monetary transaction history by date, dollar amount of purchase, and products purchased
• Source of order, inquiry, or referral	• Financial characteristics such as credit history and rating
• Promotional response data	• Predictive complementary product information (purchase behavior that indicates a propensity to purchase a complementary product)
	• Industry surveys
	• Assigned salesperson

fulfillment, distribution, customer service, and marketing and sales, already in place within the organization. Instead of the days, weeks, or months it traditionally took to create reports from data stored in different computer systems, a data warehouse allows today's managers the flexibility to answer questions in seconds. Marketing decision-makers can now ask a "what-if" question such as "What if we sent the last offer only to the top 20 percent of our customers instead of the top 50 percent?" When decision-makers can go from one question to the next in seconds rather than days or weeks, they ask not only more questions but better, and hopefully, the right questions.[42]

Marketers should remember, however, that having a marketing database is not a process in and of itself. Instead, the database is the *tool* used to achieve the full potential of one-to-one data-driven marketing. Any marketer can have a database of customer information. However, if the right data are not collected and effectively manipulated to provide answers and insights, or if the data are not properly maintained to ensure their integrity, then the marketer has not fully achieved one-to-one marketing.

Building a Marketing Database

Database marketing experts Rob Jackson and Paul Wang state in their book *Strategic Database Marketing*, "A database is only as powerful as the information it houses."[43] Data are the most important key building block for data-driven, one-to-one marketing. A company can have the most elaborate and expensive database system available and a staff of statistical professionals and marketing experts, but if the right data are not collected, then the other building blocks will never be used to their potential.

Many firms make it a point to gather customer information at the time of purchase at the same time transaction data are gathered. Toys "R" Us cashiers routinely ask for a phone number when the customer checks out. Walt Disney includes a postage-paid postcard in every video asking for customer information. Black & Decker includes product registration cards that can be returned with the purchase of every appliance. Marketers often provide an incentive in exchange for customer information. To build its database of loyal Doral smokers, R. J. Reynolds offers Doral smokers coupons, a quarterly magazine, and merchandise offers in exchange for answering survey questionnaires. Doral club members are also invited to the company's annual celebration held at its largest factory in North Carolina for a day of blackjack, country music performances, contests, and free cigarettes.[44]

Data gathering can be overt or covert. Members of frequent shopper clubs generally understand that the retailer is collecting information about their purchases in exchange for discounts or gifts. For instance, Virgin Entertainment offers free Internet appliances to customers who are willing to part with their personal information. The Internet devices allow users to surf the Internet and send e-mail in exchange for answering questions about shopping preferences, music, and entertainment interests, where and how customers generally get on-line, and how they spend their time once they get on the Web. In accepting the Internet appliances, customers give Virgin the right to track their movements on the Web and also agree to receive targeted advertising and e-mails from Virgin and other marketers.[45] The Ritz Carlton's data gathering, on the other hand, is generally invisible to consumers but can create a special relationship over time. The hotel keeps track of guest predilections and provides them with individualized service, right down to the question of whether they will want soft or firm pillows. The data gathering is very subtle—most guests don't even know their preferences are recorded in a database.[46]

Often, the beginning of a marketing database is right under the marketer's nose in the form of a response list. A **response list** includes the names and addresses of individuals at home or in the workplace who have responded to an offer of some kind either by mail, telephone, direct response television, product rebates, contests or sweepstakes, or billing inserts, to name a few.[47] Response lists tend to be most actionable, because past behavior is a strong predictor of future behavior. For instance, food products manufacturers often have the names of many people who responded to past recipe offers using their products. Not only are these people a good place to start a database, but these customers also have shown significant interest in their product and are therefore more prone to purchase.

Other firms can get a jump-start on building a customer database by purchasing a compiled list. A **compiled list** generally includes names and addresses gleaned from telephone directories or membership rosters. There are a great many compilations available, ranging from those owned by the large list companies such as American Business Lists, Database America, and Dun & Bradstreet for business-to-business data and Donnelley, Metromail, and R.L. Polk for consumer lists, to small groups or associations who are willing to sell their membership lists. Data compiled by large data-gathering companies are very accurate. American Business Lists, for instance, uses thousands of public sources, SEC records, 10-K reports, annual reports, trade journals, government publications, and newspapers to compile data on the nation's eleven million businesses. The company also utilizes a staff of hundreds of telemarketers to make over sixteen million phone calls a year to verify and compile additional information on every U.S. business.

Multinational companies building worldwide databases often face difficult problems when pulling together internal data about their customers. Differences in language, computer systems, and data collection methods can prove to be huge obstacles that must be overcome. For instance, when Inter-Continental Hotel & Resorts decided to develop a global customer database with the hopes of knowing its customers better, it discovered a world of new challenges. For starters, while hotel management could calculate how many total stays had occurred at its hotels, it could not determine how many guests it had altogether. Furthermore, with the exception of guests who were members of Inter-Continental's frequent-stay program, management had no way of aggregating multiple stays at

response list
A customer list that includes the names and addresses of individuals who have responded to an offer of some kind, such as by mail, telephone, direct response television, product rebates, contests or sweepstakes, or billing inserts.

compiled list
A customer list that was developed by gathering names and addresses from telephone directories and membership rosters, usually enhanced with information from public records, such as census data, auto registrations, birth announcements, business start-ups, or bankruptcies.

different properties into one comprehensive guest history. For example, if Jeanne Doe stayed at one of Inter-Continental's hotels in London, New York, Sydney, and Cairo, her value as a repeat customer could not be measured. Building a common database also required the conversion of more than forty currencies into U.S. dollars and keeping the conversion tables up to date. Further, language inconsistencies prevented guests from being properly matched in the database. When a guest from London stays at an Inter-Continental Hotel in Abidjan, Ivory Coast, his home address is often entered in French as Londres, Angleterre. His Stays in Europe and the United States, however, yield an English-language home address of London, England. The database development team, as a result, spent over three months adapting its match logic to encompass cultural and language influences to match guests correctly.[48]

Enhancing Customer Data

A customer database becomes even more useful to one-to-one marketers when it is *enhanced* to include more than simply a customer's or prospect's name, address, telephone number, and transaction history. **Database enhancement** is the overlay of information to customer or prospect records for the purpose of better describing or better determining the responsiveness of customers or prospects.[49] Types of enhancement data typically include demographic, lifestyle, or behavioral information about a customer.

There are three primary reasons to enhance a database with outside sources of information.[50] First, marketers use database enhancement to learn more about customers or prospects. By overlaying demographic, lifestyle, and behavioral data onto customer records, marketers can gain a valuable picture of customers by their relative value to the company. For instance, a marketer of athletic equipment would find it valuable to know which of its customers were considered its best customers using past transaction data. However, if that same marketer also knew that these customers have incomes over $50,000, enjoy outdoor recreation activities, especially biking and mountain climbing, and also are recent purchasers of mountain bikes, then the company would have a better understanding of who the customer really is.

Customer profiles allow marketers to distinguish different customer groupings by more than product purchases. For instances, direct marketer Spiegel's database contains the names of more than three million catalog shoppers who have purchased within the last eighteen months, each appended with credit data, demographic information, and dozens of other data points. Analysis of its data identified customer subgroups that Spiegel could better target through smaller specialty catalogs. Its On/View catalog, for example, is mailed to Spiegel's young career customers who prefer flowery, feminine clothing. Meanwhile, a subgroup of younger "post-feminist" shoppers culled from the On/View list now receives Spiegel Life, a catalog featuring relaxed natural fibers apparel.[51]

Second, database enhancement can increase the effectiveness of customer marketing programs. By learning more about the best and most profitable customers, marketers can understand how to maximize marketing communications and cross-selling opportunities. The same athletic equipment company, for example, now armed with a profile of its best customers, can tailor communications to these customers that now showcase its line of mountain bike gear, such as helmets, protective pads, and clothing.

Finally, by understanding the profiles of the best customers, marketers can find prospects who match that profile and increase the probability that they will respond to marketing communications. With data enhancement that adds demographic, lifestyle, and behavioral variables, the athletic equipment company can now prospect for new customers who look just like its best customers.

Compiled lists, mentioned earlier, are often enhanced with information gathered from public records, such as Census Bureau data, auto registrations, birth announcements, business start-ups, or bankruptcies.[52] Thus, compiled data can indicate several

database enhancement
The overlay of information to customer or prospect records for the purpose of better describing or better determining the responsiveness of customers or prospects.

key attributes about consumers that may suggest their financial status, demographics, buying preferences, lifestyle, or attitude patterns. Cox Direct, the cooperative mailer of both Carol Wright and Val-Pak coupons, launched its "See Them Grow" program targeted at parents of five- to eighteen-month-olds. "See Them Grow" is sent quarterly to a list of some 750,000 families with toddlers compiled from birth records. The mailing includes offers from Sears Portrait Studios, America Online, Gerber Life Insurance, and Grolier's Dr. Seuss & His Friends books.[53]

Another form of enhancement data is modeled data. **Modeled data** include information that has already been sorted into distinct groups or clusters of consumers or businesses based on census, household, or business-level data.[54] Several organizations specialize in collecting these types of data to develop models of consumer purchase behavior based on the theory of *geographic behavioral patterns*—that is, people who live near each other will have similar characteristics and will behave similarly. These systems have the added advantage of being able to work within geographic areas that are significantly smaller than a ZIP code, most often down to the ZIP+4 level. These companies have conducted a great amount of research analyzing demographics, psychographics, and sometimes response patterns to determine these geographic "pockets" of similar decision makers.[55]

The best known of these special database firms is Claritas, which created PRIZM (Potential Rating Index by ZIP Market). PRIZM is founded on the notion that "birds of a feather flock together." PRIZM breaks down the U.S. Census Bureau data by ZIP+4 codes and analyzes each code for social rank, mobility, ethnicity, family life cycle, and housing. The census data are supplemented with market research surveys and other statistics and with information from sixteen hundred municipal and regional agencies. ZIP+4 codes contain an average of six households.

PRIZM defines every micro-neighborhood in the United States in terms of sixty-two demographically and behaviorally distinct types, or "clusters." A sample of some of these clusters is shown in Exhibit 20.4. Claritas can analyze a company's customer database and then tell the firm into which PRIZM clusters a firm's customers fall. Club Med found that thirteen clusters accounted for over 80 percent of its membership. Also, persons in the "Urban Gold Coast" PRIZM cluster were seventeen times more likely to have been to a Club Med resort than the average American. PRIZM lifestyle analysis research reveals the types of products a consumer is more likely to purchase. According to PRIZM data, Elvis fans are more likely to purchase malt liquor, pickup trucks, white bread, Velveeta, menthol cigarettes, frozen dinners, and publications such as the *National Enquirer.*[56]

Marketers often have specific data enhancement elements on their wish list that cannot be collected via internal or external sources. Acquiring this information may involve a little creativity on the part of marketers to develop their own custom, primary source of enhancement data. Sources of **custom data** could include such things as customer surveys, customer participation programs, product registration, warranty cards, or loyalty marketing programs. Looking to capture more information about its customers' buying behavior, Shoebox Greetings, a division of Hallmark, recently gave away a free greeting card with the purchase of two simply for filling out a small questionnaire on the back of the coupon. The Shoebox coupon captured name, address, phone number, and birthday. It then asked these three questions:

1. About how many greeting cards (including boxed) has your household purchased in the last three months?
2. For the last ten cards you sent, how many were bought at a card/gift store?
3. On which holidays do you send cards?
   _____ Valentine's Day
   _____ Easter
   _____ Hanukkah
   _____ Christmas

Exhibit 20.4 Sample PRIZM Clusters

Nickname/ Description	Cluster Numbers	Percent of U.S. House-holds	Predom-inant Adult Age Range	Key Education Level	Predom-inant Employ-ment	Key Housing Type	Lifestyle Preferences
Suburban Elite (S1)							
Blue-Blood Estates Elite, super rich families *Socioeconomic rank: 1*	28	1.13	35–54	College grads	White collar	Single unit	New convertible car, business/finance magazines, full-service brokerage account
Money and Brains Sophisticated townhouse couples *Socioeconomic rank: 2*	8	0.91	45–64	College grads	White collar	Single unit	Tennis 10+ times a year, classical radio, $10,000+ in stock
Furs and Station Wagons Executive suburban families *Socioeconomic rank: 3*	5	3.78	35–54	College grads	White collar	Single unit	Own a CD player, all-news radio, 3+ stock transactions per year
Affluentials (S2)							
Pools and Patios Established empty nesters *Socioeconomic rank: 5*	7	3.32	45–64	College grads	White collar	Single unit	Foreign cruise, epicurean magazines, $5,000+ in mutual funds
Two More Rungs Mature couples with multi-ethnic roots *Socioeconomic rank: 6*	25	0.66	55–65+	College grads	White collar	Multi 10+	Broadway cast music, jazz radio, long-term CD
Young Influentials Upwardly mobile singles and couples *Socioeconomic rank: 7*	20	3.02	18–34	College grads	White collar	Multi 10+	New foreign car, science/technology magazines, American Express card
Greenbelt Families (S3)							
Young Suburbia Upscale young suburban families *Socioeconomic rank: 8*	24	6.25	25–44	College grads	White collar	Single unit	3-door/hatchback, news/talk radio, department store credit card
Blue-Chip Blues Upscale blue-collar families *Socioeconomic rank: 10*	30	6.25	25–44	High school grads	Blue/white mix	Single unit	Go fishing, watch headline news, interest checking
Urban Gentry (U1)							
Urban Gold Coast Elite urban singles and couples *Socioeconomic rank: 4*	21	0.44	25–65	College grads	White collar	High-rise	Go sailing, informa-tional TV, $10,000+ in stock
Bohemian Mix Bohemian urban singles *Socioeconomic rank: 11*	37	1.02	18–34	College grads	White collar	Multi 10+	Dance/rap music, watch MTV, educa-tional loan
Black Enterprise Upscale African-American families *Socioeconomic rank: 14*	31	0.69	35–54	Some college	White collar	Multi 2–9	Belong to health clubs, urban/contemporary radio, American Express card
New Beginnings Young mobile city singles *Socioeconomic rank: 15*	23	4.14	25–34	Some college	White collar	Multi 10+	Jog/run, AOR/ program radio, have first mortgage
Exurban Boom (T1)							
God's Country Executive exurban families *Socioeconomic rank: 9*	1	3.32	25–44	College grads	White collar	Single unit	Water ski, easy-listening radio, Keogh account
New Homesteaders Young middle-class families *Socioeconomic rank: 17*	17	4.78	18–34	Some college	Blue/white mix	Single unit	Ride motorcycles, MOR/nostalgia radio, veterans life insurance
Towns and Gowns College-town singles *Socioeconomic rank: 19*	12	1.57	18–34	College grads	White collar	Single unit	New-wave rock, learning channel, educational loan

SOURCE: Claritas, Inc., Arlington, VA, 1994.

With this inexpensive way of collecting custom information, Shoebox was able to determine the potential business that it might expect from the customer and how much of the business now goes to a competitor. In addition, the company captured religious affiliation and birthday, all in return for a buy-two-get-one-free coupon.[57]

Finding Answers by Analyzing Customer Data

One of the most important aspects of one-to-one marketing is not the names and addresses stored but its ability to go beyond creating mere mailing lists to manipulating the data to profile the best customers or segments of customers, analyze their lifetime value, and, ultimately, predict their purchasing behavior through statistical modeling. Database marketing expert James R. Rosenfield's recent comments on database marketing sum it up: "Marketers confuse a marketing database, which can simply be stored information about customers, with database marketing, which is a dynamic approach to managing customers. You can't do database marketing without modeling and profiling—that's what it's all about."[58]

The real value of one-to-one marketing, therefore, is not in the data. **VALUE** Actually, large quantities of data can remove value from one-to-one marketing by making the exercise confusing and complex. That is not to say that data are not necessary, only that to be valuable, data must be turned into marketing information in the form of customer profiles, scores, and predictions. The data must be transformed from operational bits and bytes into the information that marketers need for successful marketing communication.[59]

Common data analysis techniques for marketing databases include (1) customer segmentation, (2) recency-frequency-monetary analysis (RFM), (3) lifetime value analysis, (4) predictive modeling, and (5) data mining. Although other statistical and modeling techniques are available and widely used, these five types of data analysis are used quite often by one-to-one marketers. Most companies with customer databases should be able to conduct the first three data analysis techniques easily, given that transaction data and enhancement data are collected. Predictive modeling and data mining are more sophisticated techniques and generally require more data and expertise in statistical analysis. Predictive modeling provides an excellent means for marketers to ask "what if"questions, whereas data mining uses a variety of tools to uncover subtle patterns in consumer purchasing behavior.

Chris Childers, owner of the Macon Christian Bookstore in Macon, Georgia, uses the customer data in his computer to generate customer-specific mailings about new items in his store.
© 1995 Nation's Business/
T. Michael Keza

Customer Segmentation *Customer segmentation* is the process of breaking large groups of customers into smaller, more homogenous groups. One-to-one marketers use this analysis to paint a picture of what customers look like, in particular the best customers. By identifying a segment of customers in the database by any means, such as by survey, purchase data, response, or word of mouth, a firm then can find a way to compare the identified customer segment with the rest of its customers. These segmentations can be based on such characteristics as demographics, geographic location, previous purchase behavior, or psychographic variables. Some examples of these are shown in Exhibit 20.5. For instance, Hallmark Cards' Gold Crown Card loyalty program segments customers for targeted direct mail efforts. Quarterly mailings to members include a statement of points accumulated in the loyalty program, a coupon for merchandise based on the point level, and a brochure featuring seasonal cards and gift-related items. The company divides its huge database of sixteen million Gold Crown Card members into seven distinct segments based on past purchase information. The resulting

Exhibit **20.5**

Geographic	Demographic	Behavioral	Psychographic
• Country • Region • State • County • Metropolitan type (urban, suburban, rural, etc.) • Metropolitan statistical area • Census tract • Retail trading area • ZIP code • Telephone area code • Climate • Seasons	• Age • Gender • Height/weight • Marital status • Family size • Family life cycle • Ages of children • Race • Ethnicity • Nationality • Country of birth • First language • Religion • Education • Occupation • Industry • Income • Mobility • Dwelling type • Dwelling size • Autos registered	• Purchase occasion • Recent purchases • Benefits sought • User status (e.g., active or inactive) • Usage rate • Loyalty status (e.g., loyal users, frequent users, switchers, price buyers) • Readiness stage (i.e., is the customer ready to purchase now, in 12 months, in 24 months?) • Attitude toward the product • Charities contributed • Political affiliation	• Attitudes • Interests • Opinions • Activities • Lifestyle • Social class • Personality type • Conspicuous consumption (e.g., mean current auto value, home value)

segments portray the buying interests of their customers, such as "card fanatics" and "ornament fanatics." By segmenting its member base, Hallmark is able to get a better return on investment and bring the most targeted messages to its card consumers.[60] Refer back to Chapter 7 for more information about segmentation.

Recency–Frequency–Monetary Analysis (RFM)   Research has shown that customers who purchase most recently and more often and who spend more money are more likely to purchase again. **Recency–frequency–monetary analysis (RFM)** identifies those customers most likely to purchase again because they have bought most recently, bought most frequently, or spent a specified amount of money with the firm. With this data a firm can build a simple equation to identify the "best customers" by assigning a score to customer records in the database based on how often, how recently, and how much they have spent. These customers are then ranked to determine which customers rise to the top of the list and which ones fall to the bottom. This ranking provides the basis for maximizing profits because it enables the firm to use the information in its customer database to select those persons who have proved to be good sources of revenue. As an example of RFM analysis, refer to Exhibit 20.6, which depicts the breakdown of customers in categories that describe their value at a hypothetical company.

Many marketers take RFM analysis one step further by introducing *profitability* into the equation. For instance, a customer may float to the top of the RFM list when looking just at the monetary value of their purchases. However, if this customer only buys items on sale, then the profitability of this customer is less than for one that buys the same dollar amount in nonsale items. Charlotte, North Carolina–based First Union National Bank groups its customers into ten segments based on profitability. Top-ranking customers are routinely called on by First Union relationship managers who may educate them about a new product or just thank them for their business. Lower-ranking unprofitable customers, on the other hand, are encouraged to use lower-cost services like automated teller machines.[61]

**recency–frequency–
monetary analysis (RFM)**
A data manipulation technique
that determines the firm's best
customers by identifying those
customers who have purchased
most recently, most frequently,
and who have spent the most
money.

Exhibit 20.6 RFM Analysis: All Customers Are Not Created Equal

Best Customers N = 1,200 (10%)	Next-Best Customers N = 2,400 (20%)	Average Customers N = 3,600 (30%)	Poor Customers N = 4,800 (40%)
• High profit • Spent > $1,000 • Multiple purchases • Purchased in last six months • LTV: High • Total annual sales = $1,200,000	• Good profit • Spent approx. $500 • Multiple purchases • Purchased in last twelve months • LTV: Good • Total annual sales = $1,200,000	• Average profit • Spent $250 • One purchase • Purchased in last eighteen months • LTV: Average • Total annual sales = $900,000	• Low profit • Spent < $100 • One purchase • Purchased in last twenty-four months • LTV: Low • Total annual sales = $504,000

LTV = Lifetime value
N = Number of customers in category
Total annual sales = $3,804,000

Total number of customers: 12,000
Total number of orders per year: 20,000
Average order value: $190.20

SOURCE: Reprinted from *Desktop Database Marketing* by Jack Schmid and Alan Weber. © 1998. Used with permission of NTC/Contemporary Publishing Group, Inc.

lifetime value analysis (LTV)
A data manipulation technique that projects the future value of the customer over a period of years using the assumption that marketing to repeat customers is more profitable than marketing to first-time buyers.

Lifetime Value Analysis (LTV) Recency, frequency, and monetary data can also be used to create a lifetime value model on customers in the database. Whereas RFM looks at how valuable a customer is currently to a company, **lifetime value analysis (LTV)** projects the future value of the customer over a period of years. One of the basic assumptions in any lifetime value calculation is that marketing to repeat customers is more profitable than marketing to first-time buyers.[62] It costs more to find a new customer in terms of promotion and gaining trust than to sell more to a customer who is already loyal.

Customer lifetime value has a number of uses: (1) it shows marketers how much they can spend to *acquire* a new customer, (2) it provides a level of profitable spending to *retain* a customer, and (3) it provides a basis for targeting new customers who look like a company's most profitable customers.[63] Lifetime value analysis allows a marketer to identify its most valuable customers and profit from them over the long term by building relationships. Cadillac has calculated the lifetime value of its top customers at $332,000. Similarly, Pizza Hut figures its customers are worth $8,000 in bottom-line lifetime value.[64]

predictive modeling
A data manipulation technique in which marketers try to determine, based on some past set of occurrences, what the odds are that some other occurrence, such as a response or purchase, will take place in the future.

Predictive Modeling The ability to reasonably predict future customer behavior gives marketers a significant competitive advantage. Through **predictive modeling**, marketers try to determine, based on some past set of occurrences, what the odds are that some other occurrence, such as a response or purchase, will take place in the future. The occurrence a marketer is trying to predict through predictive modeling is described by the *dependent variable*, typically the likelihood of a response, making a sale, the amount of the sale, or all three. The *independent variables*, or predictor variables, are the things that affect the dependent variable. Past buying behavior, age, income, family size, or the neighborhood one lives in could all be independent variables that affect purchase behavior, the dependent variable.[65] Colorado-based Abacus Direct, for example, compiles data on consumers who have purchased merchandise from over a thousand catalogs circulated in the United States. The third-party data provider's database now contains over 2.9 billion consumer catalog transactions that can be manipulated to predict future purchasing behavior. Catalogers, like Williams-Sonoma, J. Peterman, and Bloomingdale's, use the data collected by Abacus to augment their own customer databases, predicting future purchases of current customers, as well as finding new prospects who are most likely to purchase from their catalogs.[66]

The sharp rise in paper costs and postal rates a few years ago forced many catalog companies to turn to predictive modeling techniques in an effort to better target catalog mailings. Catalog retailer Fingerhut Corporation, based in Minnetonka, Minnesota, uses more than three hundred predictive models to scour its six-terabyte database. One model predicts the likelihood of someone responding to a targeted electronics catalog, while another scores the chances of a customer returning merchandise. Predictive modeling allows Fingerhut to reduce the number of catalogs sent while increasing sales and profits. As a result, response rates to catalogs have increased while the company saves more than $3.5 million a year in decreased mailing costs.[67]

Data Mining   A relatively new and sophisticated modeling technique is data mining. **Data mining** is the automated discovery of "interesting," nonobvious patterns hidden in a database that have a high potential for contributing to the bottom line. The discovery process often involves sifting through massive quantities of data such as electronic point-of-sale transactions, inventory records, and on-line customer orders matched with demographics.[68] Data-mining software accesses the data in the database and offers analysis tools such as decision trees, cluster analysis, neural networks, and regression analysis. Data mining can create customer profiles; help determine the reason for customer loyalty; analyze the potential return for pricing, promotion, and direct mail strategies; and even help forecast sales.[69]

data mining
The process of using statistical analysis to detect relevant purchasing behavior patterns in a database.

Data-mining analysis assists researchers in discovering relationships between independent variables. For example, Farmers Group insurance company discovered through data mining that as long as a sports car wasn't the only vehicle in a household, the accident rate actually wasn't much greater than that of a regular car. Based on this information, Farmers changed its policy to allow sports cars to qualify for its lowest-priced insurance rates and, in the process, doubled its sports-car market. Similarly, Wal-Mart uses data mining to answer a number of questions, such as what commonly purchased items should be placed together on shelves and what soft drinks sell best in different areas of the country.[70] Camelot Music recently discovered after using data mining techniques that a large number of senior citizens were purchasing rap and alternative music. When they researched this finding more, they discovered these seniors were buying the music as gifts for their grandchildren. The company has since launched a direct marketing effort aimed at seniors, playing up the low prices of its offerings since it was also clear most of that target marked lived on a fixed income.[71]

Although data mining can detect behavior patterns, it can't always give a reason for the pattern. For example, researchers found through data mining that fathers often buy beer when buying diapers. Displaying beer closer to the diapers increased sales. Researchers surmised the beer to be an impulse purchase; fathers, who were asked to pick up diapers on their way home, looked up and noticed the beer display. Other less-understood correlations have appeared as the result of data mining. For instance, men who buy tweed jackets also tend to buy chocolate; and red bras outsell white bras only during the Christmas season in most lingerie shops, but in shops in resort communities, red bras are consistent best-sellers.[72]

Data mining techniques are also being used more commonly for nonmarketing applications. For example, credit card companies use data mining to detect fraudulent purchases, providing a valuable service to their customers. Data mining techniques are also transferring over to less commercial endeavors and into the world of medical research. Read about the controversial Icelandic project to develop a DNA database of its citizens in the "Global Perspectives" box.

MINING ICELAND'S GENETIC CODE

A controversial medical research project in Iceland is focusing international attention on the advantages, as well as the potential risks, of mining and refining personal data—efforts that are becoming increasingly common in the United States and around the world in commercial applications. Recently, Iceland became the first country in the world to sell the rights to its entire population of genetic code to a private research company with the ambitious goal of solving the genetic puzzles of several diseases. The company, deCODE Genetics, plans to collect and analyze DNA samples from the country's 270,000 residents and link this data to the detailed medical records that the government has kept on inhabitants for almost one hundred years. DeCODE, founded by a Harvard University-educated Icelandic scientist, hopes the data mining of Iceland's unique genome will one day lead the development of revolutionary new drugs.

The strikingly uniform DNA of Iceland's largely blue-eyed, blond-haired populace makes it an invaluable resource for studying human genetics, leading to fundamental insights into many diseases. Nearly all Icelanders are descended from the original founders, mostly Norse Vikings and Celtic seamen who first landed on Iceland about A.D. 870. Because of their remarkable homo-geneity, any disease-causing mutations in their DNA will standout as signposts during data mining. Iceland's comparatively simple set of genes makes genetic prospecting less daunting than attempting to track down faulty genes in more heterogeneous populations like that of the United States. Further, Iceland has a strong healthcare system with extensive medical and genealogical records that go back hundreds of years.

Not surprisingly, Iceland's DNA database project has many critics. Although the majority of Iceland's citizens support the plan, a vocal minority of opponents question the notion that anonymity can be protected with so much data being collected, even though names will be encrypted. Many worry that those with sensitive ailments, such as mental illness, risk being stigmatized, perhaps suffering job discrimination, if the data somehow ends up in the wrong hands. Additionally, in a country where some estimates say that about 10 percent of the population may have been born out of wedlock, long-held family secrets could leak out.

The deal that deCODE struck with Iceland's parliament is also controversial. While Icelanders would receive free any drugs developed through the project, profits from the research go to the compa-nies involved. The law authorizing the creation of the DNA database also grants deCODE Genetics a twelve-year monopoly on data marketing rights. Although deCODE's goal is limited to uncovering links between DNA and disease, it will be able to sell this information to other companies to develop new drugs based on its research. Critics fear this information may one day be made available not to just pharmaceutical companies developing drugs for incurable diseases, but to insurance companies, employers, and others who might want to get a closer look at an individual's makeup.[a]

Do you feel Iceland's DNA project is an invasion of privacy or a major advancement in medical research? Would your opinion be different if it was known that the results of mining the DNA of Iceland's citizens would lead to treatments for several incurable diseases like cancer, diabetes, or AIDS?

[a]John Greenwood, "In Reykjavik, Decoding Iceland's Genes," *National Post*, March 18, 2000, p. D1; John Schwartz, "For Sale in Iceland: A Nation's Genetic Code." *The Washington Post*, January 12, 1999. p. A1; Zina Moukheiber, "Genes for Sale: The Billion-Dollar Treasure Hunt for Human Genes Is On," *Forbes*, July 27, 1998, p. 203; Lara Weber, "DNA Project Raises Few Fears in Iceland," *Chicago Tribune*, February 21, 1999, p. 14.

One-to-One Marketing and the Internet

6

Describe one-to-one marketing using the Internet

ON LINE

Undoubtably, one of the most important trends in the field of one-to-one marketing is the emergence of one-to-one marketing over the Internet. While marketers have overwhelmingly adopted the Internet and World Wide Web as a new channel for promotions and commerce, many marketers are capitalizing on the Web's full set of interactive marketing capabilities. Internet companies are learning more about their customers and using this information to fine-tune their marketing efforts and build relationships with each customer on a more individual level.

One advantage of on-line one-to-one marketing is the ability to deliver personalized promotional messages to each customer visiting a company's Web site. Past customer transaction history, clickstream data, and survey responses are used to identify buying patterns and interests. Based on information known about the customer visiting its site, such as color and brand preferences, geographic location, and past customer transaction data, the marketer can develop a targeted and personalized on-line promotion or custom catalog. For example, Amazon.com creates a personalized experience each time the same customer visits its Web site. Customers are greeted by name and instantly provided with a customized Web page offering book, music, and video suggestions based on their past purchasing and viewing behavior. Similarly, American Airlines' Web site has the ability to build custom pages, creating the potential for each of the airline's 32 million frequent flyers to have a unique experience when visiting the site. After logging in on the site's home page, members of its frequent flyer program, AAdvantage, can create profiles based on home airport, preferred destination and destination types, such as family, beach or golf, hub airports, hotel and rental car choices, preferred class of services, and seating preferences. Each time a customer visits the site, they are greeted by name and the total number of accumulated frequent flyer miles. Based on their profile as well as past ticket purchase information, they are then shown relevant news, information, special offers, and travel packages as they page through the site.[73]

When used in conjunction with on-line ad-serving technology, one-to-one marketing has the power to make the Internet an effective and cost-efficient advertising vehicle. On-line database marketing helps advertisers improve their return on investment by reaching consumers with banner ads most likely to have an interest in their products or services. It also benefits consumers since they don't have to view ads that are of no interest to them.[74] Internet ad server specialists like DoubleClick, RealMedia, and MatchLogic are building huge databases filled with anonymous profiles about consumers' activity on the Web with the goal of delivering ads that will home in on a Web surfer's interests. By profiling Web visitors, marketers can send banner ads and messages to just those who are more likely to be interested instead of wasting money on sending advertisements to those who are not. So, someone surfing golf pages at sports sites would be a good candidate to receive on-line ads for golf resorts. MatchLogic reports that ads tailored to consumers' profiles get three to six times the response of other on-line ads.[75]

Increasingly, more and more companies are realizing that e-mail is the ideal one-to-one medium, capable of establishing and building enduring customer relationships with a highly targeted lists of prospects. This technique works much the same way as off-line one-to-one marketing campaigns: Companies build databases of e-mail addresses by enticing customers to register on a site in exchange for information or access to a special offer.[76] One-to-one e-mail campaigns are proving more effective than banner advertising on the Internet. Click-through rates for e-mail campaigns average 10 to 15 percent, compared to banner ad click rates that average around 1 percent, and traditional direct mail that averages between 0.5 and 2 percent.[77] Wine.com, for instance, allows wine aficionados to subscribe to its e-mail newsletter. The newsletter is sent to its thousands of subscribers every week touting product specials, links to its Web site, and commentary from the company's founder. In addition to collecting e-mail addresses, the site asks questions that help the company tailor unique messages and specials, such as how knowledgeable subscribers are about wine, how often they drink wine, whether they like reds or whites best, and how much they typically spend on a bottle. Wine.com can tag e-mail messages to determine not only how many bottles of wine were sold via an e-mail message, but also who bought them.[78]

Savvy marketers are increasingly leveraging the technology of the Internet to create effective one-to-one marketing campaigns. DoubleClick specializes in helping clients deliver highly-targeted ads to customers via the Internet.

One-to-one e-mail marketing should be strictly permission-based. That is, consumers should "opt-in" or give their permission to receive e-mail messages from a marketer. Palm Computing, the maker of the Palm Pilot, sends messages to some 400,000 customers who have opted-in through Palm's Web site or registration cards to receive e-mail. The personalized messages include the recipient's name and contain information relevant to the product and model they own and tips on using it better.[79] Similarly, software marketer Symantec Corporation sends its SmallBiz Newsletter to customers who have bought its ACT contact management software, Norton Utilities antivirus software, and PCAnywhere networking software. The monthly newsletter includes product offers, sweepstakes, surveys, and news on how to better use Symantec's small business tools. According to the software maker, more than 600 people join its opt-in e-mail newsletter list each month.[80]

Privacy Concerns with One-to-One Marketing

Discuss privacy issues related to one-to-one marketing

Before rushing out to invest in computer hardware and software to build a database, marketers should heed consumer reaction to the growing use of databases. One-to-one marketing concerns many Americans because of the potential for invasion of privacy, specifically the sheer volume of information that is aggregated in databases and the vulnerability of this information to unauthorized access and use. A fundamental aspect of one-to-one marketing is providing valuable services to customers based on knowledge of what customers really value. However, it is critical that marketers remember that these relationships should be built on trust. While database technology allows marketers to compile ever-richer information about their customers to build and manage relationships, if these customers feel their privacy is being violated, then the relationship becomes a liability.[81]

Most consumers are unaware of how personal information is collected, used, and distributed, and they are unaware of how technology helps in collecting personal data. The government actively sells huge amounts of personal information to list compilers. State motor vehicle bureaus sell names and addresses of individuals who get driver's licenses. Hospitals sell the names of women who just gave birth on their premises. Consumer credit databases, developed and maintained by large providers such as Equifax Marketing Services and TransUnion, are often used by credit card marketers to prescreen the targets for solicitations.

Further, there is widespread misunderstanding among consumers about existing privacy laws and regulations. Frustrated by their lack of control, consumers want more opportunities to determine how their personal information will be used. A recent study found that 45 percent of Americans strongly favor legislation that would regulate the use of consumer information, up from 23 percent in 1990.[82] However, only credit-related databases, such as those of Equifax and TRW, are regulated under the federal Fair Credit Reporting Act (FCRA). Non-credit-related databases, on the other hand, do not fall under the jurisdiction of the FCRA and for the most part they either escape state privacy legislation or are regulated by a patchwork quilt of law that provides very little protection of privacy. Changes to state laws to protect consumer privacy violated by non-credit-related databases could become reality in light of legal theories presented in a number of recent privacy cases. In the 1996 Virginia case, *Avrahami v. U.S. News & World Report, Inc.*, Avrahami claimed that U.S. News & World Report's sale of his name was for the purpose of trade, and therefore the sale violated his property interest in his name.[83]

The popularity of the Internet for direct marketing, consumer data collection, and as a repository of sensitive consumer data has also alarmed privacy-minded consumers. On-line users have complained of being "spammed," the Internet's equivalent of junk mail. Web surfers, including children who are using the Internet, are routinely asked to divulge personal information in order to access certain screens or purchase goods or services on-line. Internet users who once felt fairly anonymous in their use of the Web are now disturbed by the amount of information marketers collect on them as they visit various sites in cyberspace. America Online, for instance, keeps records on more than 21 million subscribers, including names, addresses, and credit-card numbers. The on-line service also tracks the movements of subscribers within AOL's proprietary service where users spend over 80 percent of their time, including chat rooms, e-mail, news services, and other content. AOL sells names and addresses of subscribers to direct mailers and also buys information about its members, such as the type of computer owned, from outside data suppliers. It then uses this information to target advertising when a subscriber comes on-line.[84]

 On-line privacy concerns were heightened recently when on-line advertising firm DoubleClick announced intentions of combining its anonymous clickstream data—information captured by placing small computer files called "cookies" on surfers' hard drives that track their travels through cyberspace, with off-line consumer databases that would provide them with names and addresses. By matching cookie data with information in traditional direct marketing databases, DoubleClick hoped to create a powerful repository of consumer information that could be used to precisely target individuals for marketing purposes. Consumers and privacy advocates, however, became anxious that DoubleClick's pioneering techniques could create enormous privacy breaches, triggering an investigation by the Federal Trade Commission.[85] Read more about this in the Marketing Miscues Case at the end of Part 7.

The case against DoubleClick is one of the latest examples of how the legal system is struggling to keep pace with technological changes. Because laws governing Internet privacy are nonexistent (the industry is largely self-regulated), consumers worry that sensitive information might become accessible over the Internet by those who may misuse the data, such as an employer or a divorce lawyer. While regulators have been debating future Internet privacy protection legislation, federal law to date is limited to the *Children's Online Privacy Protection Act of 1998* (COPPA), which bars sites from collecting personal information from children under thirteen without parental consent, and which went into effect in 2000.[86] Read more about COPPA in the "Ethics in Marketing" box.

As a result of the FTC's interest in Web privacy, many Internet companies have now adopted privacy policies and many are now giving Web users the ability to opt out of data collection in an effort to avert federal legislation.[87] The Direct Marketing Association has also published new guidelines for its member companies to help assure consumers that their privacy is being respected (see Exhibit 20.7 on page 31). But while an FTC study revealed that 90 percent of Web sites had posted privacy policies, only 20 percent met all the agency's proposed standards for privacy disclosure.[88]

While privacy policies for companies in the United States are largely voluntary and regulations on how personal data is collected and used are practically nonexistent, collecting data about consumers outside of the United States is a different matter. For database marketers venturing in new data territories, success requires careful navigation of foreign privacy laws. Under the European Union's *European Data Protection Directive*, for instance, any business that trades with a European organ-ization must comply with the EU's rules for handling information about individuals, or risk prosecution. This directive prohibits the export of personal data to countries not doing enough to protect privacy, in particular the United States.[89]

PROTECTING CHILDREN ON-LINE

Children's privacy on the Internet became a hot issue recently when it was discovered that nine out of ten Web sites aimed at children collected personal data about them, but only about 20 percent of those sites asked children to seek parental consent before supplying the information. In another study, researchers found that children and teens were willing to provide details about the family's buying habits, such as names of favorite stores and what kind of car the family drives, when enticed with a free gift on-line. The same study found that younger children were more willing to offer more sensitive details, such as financial information or whether their parents missed work often or drank alcohol.

In a highly publicized case, the Federal Trade Commission charged Boston money manager Liberty Financial with failing to protect the anonymity of children on its Young Investor Web site, where young Web surfers were persuaded to fill out a survey by offering them a chance to win prizes and a free newsletter. Liberty maintained that the personal information would be maintained anonymously. According to the complaint, however, the young investor site asked survey questions that were deemed too personal, such as weekly allowances, spending habits, part-time work history, plans for college, and family finances, including ownership of any mutual funds. Further, the FTC discovered that Liberty retained the names, addresses, and e-mails of those who participated in the Internet survey, even though the company stated that all personal information would be maintained anonymously.

As a result of this and other examples, legislators passed the Children's Online Privacy Protection Act, in an effort to protect children from unscrupulous data collection techniques by Internet businesses. The act, which went into effect in 2000, requires Web sites targeting children under thirteen to prominently disclose what personal information they collect from children, how it is used, and whether it is shared with third parties. The Web site must also obtain "verifiable parental consent" before collecting any personal data from children. Consent from parents can take the form of a physically signed note, a credit-card number, or an e-mail with a password.

While obtaining parental consent can be difficult in cyberspace, many Internet companies are developing their own methods of dealing with the law. Kid site SurfMonkey. com, for instance, set up an 800 number so that parents can confirm that their children have permission to log onto the Web site's chat rooms and bulletin boards. Alloy.com banned all children under thirteen from their chat rooms and other interactive areas. America Online deleted on-line profiles of members who identified themselves as under age thirteen. Lycos.com now requires children and their parents to establish a family account with a credit card before they can even log on.[a]

Enforcing laws in cyberspace will prove to be a challenge for the federal government. Children will undoubtably forge parental consent,

Alloy.com has an entire Parents' Resource Center designed to help parents monitor and set limits around their children's Internet usage. Although a resource for parents, this section ultimately protects the privacy of the children who surf the site.

lie about their age, and discover ways to get around the law to be able to visit their favorite chat room or Web site. As a parent, how would you encourage your children to abide by the law?

[a]Aaron Lucchetti, "FTC Shows Line Drawn for Internet Ads," *Wall Street Journal*, May 7, 1999, p. B2; John Simons, "New FTC Rules Aim to Protect Kid Web Privacy," *Wall Street Journal*, April 21, 1999, pp. B1, B4; Jennifer Gilbert and Ira Teinowitz, "Compliance Deadline Looms for Kids' Sites," *Advertising Age*, April 17, 2000, p. 54; Julia Angwin and Nick Wingfield, "New Children's Privacy Rules Pose Obstacles for Some Sites," *Wall Street Journal*, April 24, 2000, p. B8; Ted Bridis, "Teens Will Likely Disclose Family Data Over the Internet for a Free Gift Online," *Wall Street Journal*, May 17, 2000, p. B2.

Exhibit **20.7**

In October 1997, The Direct Marketing Association made a Privacy Promise to American consumers as a public assurance that by July 1, 1999, all members of the DMA will follow certain specific practices to protect consumer privacy. These practices were designed to have a major impact on those consumers who wish to receive fewer advertising solicitations. Specifically, members of the DMA must abide by the following four privacy protection practices.

1. Notify customers that their names may be rented, sold, or exchanged for marketing purposes so that they are aware of their ability to opt out of these information exchanges.
2. Honor customer opt-out requests not to have their contact information transferred to others for marketing purposes.
3. Accept and maintain consumer requests to be on an in-house suppress file to stop receiving solicitations.
4. Use the DMA Preference Service suppression files, which allows consumers who do not wish to receive unsolicited marketing offers by mail or telephone (and soon e-mail) to make a single request for name removal.

SOURCE: The Direct Marketing Association, **http://www.the-dma.org**.

More than fifty nations have, or are developing, privacy legislation. Europe has the strictest legislation regarding the collection and use of consumer data, and that legislation is what other countries look to when formulating their policies. Australia, for instance, recently introduced legislation that would require private companies to follow a set of guidelines regarding the collection, storage, use, and transfer of personal information about individuals. Common privacy rules include obtaining data fairly and lawfully, using it only for the original purpose specified, making sure it is accurate and up-to-date, and destroying data after the purpose for collection is completed. In the EU it is required that consumers be presented with an opt-out provision at the point of data collection.[90]

Looking Back

As you recall from the opening story, Williams-Sonoma, like many other marketers today, has embraced one-to-one marketing as an alternative to mass media marketing. Knowing customers on an individual basis with the help of database technology provides marketers with an efficient and effective means of providing customers with the individualized attention that they demand.

Williams-Sonoma uses its database of past customer transaction data to develop personalized service and promotional offers and to cross-sell other merchandise. Profiles of Williams-Sonoma's best customers also helps the company identify other potential customers who are more likely to purchase their upscale home furnishings.

Protect Your Privacy On-line

Many Internet surfers don't realize that on-line companies can track their movements on the Web through the use of "cookie" files. To help maintain your anonymity on the Web, refrain from answering on-line questionnaires, entering sweepstakes, or divulging information to Web sites that do not post a privacy policy. Also, check out each site's privacy policy to learn about what they do or might do with your personal information. It's also a good idea to periodically purge or clean out your cookie file on your hard drive. Keep only those cookie files for the sites you want to recognize you the next time you visit. To learn more about protecting your personal information as you surf, visit **http://www.junkbusters.com**. Become informed about your rights as a consumer by visiting the Direct Marketing Association at **http://www.the-dma.org**.

Summary

1 **Define one-to-one marketing and discuss its dependence on database technology.** One-to-one marketing, sometimes called customer relationship management, is an individualized marketing method that utilizes customer information to build long-term, personalized, and profitable relationships with each customer. Database technology makes it possible for companies to interact with customers on a personal, one-to-one basis. A database stores pertinent information about a company's customers and contacts and makes it readily available to the sales and marketing staff for assessing, analyzing, and anticipating customers' needs. Database technology allows marketers to sift through the millions of pieces of data to target the right customers, to develop the right communication based on these customer needs, and to monitor the ongoing relationship, making adjustments in message strategy as needed.

2 **Discuss the forces that have influenced the emergence of one-to-one marketing.** Forces that have helped shape one-to-one marketing include a more diverse society, more demanding and time-poor consumers, a decline in brand loyalty, the explosion of new media alternatives, changing channels of distribution, and demand for marketing accountability. Consumers no longer want to be treated like the masses. One-to-one marketing allows consumers to be treated as individuals with their own unique sets of needs and wants. Consumers today also have less time to spend shopping for the products they need. Through its targeted nature, one-to-one marketing can decrease the time consumers need to make purchase decisions. Further, consumers are less brand loyal than they were. One-to-one marketing techniques increase brand loyalty by focusing on finding a firm's best customers, rewarding them for their loyalty, and thanking them for their business. As mass-media approaches become less important, one-to-one marketing will increase in importance and offer marketers a more cost-effective avenue for reaching customers. Finally, the demand for marketing accountability will drive the growth of one-to-one marketing and justify its continued existence.

3 **Compare the one-to-one marketing communications process with the traditional mass marketing communications process.** The marketing communications process follows the flow of a marketing message from the marketer to the consumer. In the more traditional, mass-media version, an advertiser or marketer sends a promotional message through a mass marketing channel to its target audience. Noise from competing advertisements affects the encoding and decoding of the message. Feedback on the effectiveness of the communication comes through market research and changes in sales levels or market share. In the one-to-one marketing communications process, the flow is similar; however, the message encoded by the marketer is personalized, there is relatively little noise to affect encoding and decoding, and the marketer has the ability to capture the response from the consumer and feed this information back into the marketing database for future use.

④ List eight common one-to-one marketing applications. Common marketing applications of customer databases include (1) identifying the best customers, (2) retaining loyal customers, (3) cross-selling other products or services, (4) designing targeted marketing communications, (5) reinforcing consumer purchase decisions, (6) inducing product trial by new customers, (7) increasing the effectiveness of distribution channel marketing, and (8) improving customer service.

⑤ Discuss the basics of one-to-one marketing database technology. One-to-one marketing is characterized by the creation of a large computerized database of customers' and potential customers' profiles and purchase patterns used to direct marketing communications. A marketing database is the compilation of names, addresses, and other pieces of pertinent information about individual customers and prospects that affects what and how marketers sell to them. In its most basic form, database marketing relies on transactional processing systems that record the details of individual purchase transactions. These data can then be enhanced using external sources of modeled data or custom data. Marketers can analyze customer data using segmentation, recency–frequency–monetary analysis, lifetime value analysis, predictive modeling, or data mining techniques.

⑥ Describe one-to-one marketing using the Internet. Marketers have recently capitalized on the Internet's interactive capabilities as a one-to-one marketing tool. By collecting past customer transaction data and studying a user's movements on the Web, the on-line one-to-one marketer has the ability to create a personalized experience for each customer who visits its site. Additionally, banner advertising can be more efficiently targeted to just those Internet users who would be interested. An on-line marketer can also send personalized e-mail messages to those customers who give their permission.

⑦ Discuss privacy issues related to one-to-one marketing. One-to-one marketing concerns many Americans because of the potential for invasion of privacy, specifically the sheer volume of information that is aggregated in databases and the vulnerability of this information to unauthorized access and use. Most consumers are unaware of how personal information is collected, used, and distributed, and they are unaware of how technology helps in collecting personal data. Additionally, there is widespread misunderstanding among consumers about existing privacy laws and regulations. Frustrated by their lack of control, consumers want more opportunities to determine how their personal information will be used. The popularity of the Internet for direct marketing, consumer data collection, and as a repository of sensitive consumer data has also alarmed privacy-minded consumers.

Discussion and Writing Questions

1. Explain why one-to-one marketing today would not be possible without database technology.
2. Explain the differences between traditional mass media marketing communications and targeted one-to-one marketing communications. Why are these differences important to the success of one-to-one marketing?
3. List several local businesses that you feel would benefit form one-to-one marketing. Choose one business and develop a one-to-one marketing plan, outlining the one-to-one applications that could be utilized, identifying what data

Key Terms

compiled list   656
custom data   658
database   654
database enhancement   657
data-driven marketing   654
data mining   563
data warehouse   654
lifetime value analysis (LTV)
   662
marketing database   654
modeled data   658
one-to-one marketing
   (customer relationship
   management)   642
one-to-one marketing communications process   648
predictive modeling   662
recency–frequency–monetary
   analysis (RFM)   661
response list   656

should be collected about customers, and recommending data analysis methods. Also identify how the company could perform some of its one-to-one marketing using the Internet. Present your findings to the class.

4. Explain the statement "A database is only as powerful as the information it houses."

5. Define the two different types of database enhancement and give examples of each.

6. Assume that you are the manager of a local dry cleaning business. What types of information do you currently collect about your customers that you could use to develop one-to-one relationships with your customers? What factors would determine your best customers?

7. As the marketing manager of a local retailing chain, you have just analyzed your database of customers and determined that your best customers constitute 12 percent of your customer database and provide nearly 80 percent of your sales. Additionally, you have discovered that about 50 percent of the customers in your database have not purchased in over two years. What can you do with this knowledge?

8. Explain the concept of lifetime value. Why is this type of data manipulation so important to one-to-one marketers?

9. Visit the site developed by one-to-one marketing experts Don Peppers and Martha Rogers at **http://www.1to1.com** to read success stories of companies that have made one-to-one marketing strategies work for them. Select one of the articles at the "Publications" link (**http://www.1to1. com/publications/inside1to1**) and present a summary to the rest of the class.

10. The Data Warehousing Institute writes case studies of marketers who have adopted data warehousing solutions to provide their customers using enterprise-wide data. Go to the site's case study page, found under the "What Works?" link on **http://www.dw-institute.com**. Read three to five case studies and make a list of all of the one-to-one marketing issues discussed in the chapter which also appear in the articles. Are there any "hot" issues that recur in each article? What conclusions can you draw from your list?

11. Use InfoTrac to read how the Internet industry is taking privacy issues into its own hands. Request and read an article titled "Police Thyself" that appeared in the August 3, 1998 issue of *PC Week* magazine. Then conduct a key word search to find out current conversations about consumer privacy in general and on-line privacy in particular.

12. As marketing director for a regional chain of restaurants with a country gift shop theme, you have been assigned the task of developing a loyalty marketing program. Your boss has heard about a company called NetCentives. Visit the company's Web site at **http:// www.netcentives.com** and read about the various products and solutions. Write a brief memo describing what NetCentives can do for your company. Identify in your memo which of the eight common one-to-one marketing applications NetCentives can help you implement and how (see Exhibit 20.2). Also identify what tools NetCentives has to help you with your segmentation, RFM anaylsis, LTV analysis, and predictive modeling. If you decide NetCentives has insufficient programs or resources, indicate this in your memo and explain why.

Application for Entrepreneurs

Molly's Flowers is a small flower shop located in a medium-sized metropolitan area. The proprietor, Molly Edwards, has always measured the success of her business based on market share, which she estimates at roughly 10 percent. This is based on a report published by the local chamber of commerce that provides total flower sales from area flower shops in her city. This does not include flowers purchased at grocery stores.

Molly has used traditional mass-marketing approaches in an attempt to increase her market share, such as advertising heavily during holidays like Valentine's Day and Mother's Day and offering discounts during the low periods in between. These measures have increased sales, she believes, but she is not totally sure to what extent. Additionally, the ads cost money and the discounts eat into her profits. She knows that grocery stores cut into her business by offering lower prices on lower-quality flowers and arrangements, but she is not sure how to counter this because lowering her prices across the board would be devastating to her profits.

Molly knows that she has a number of customers who she sees order from her time and again, but she has never thought much about how to take advantage of this loyal customer base. Shuffling through a stack of flower orders on her desk from the past year, she begins to look closely at the information that she actually does collect about her customers. On each order form is the customer's name, address, telephone number, date of order, date flowers are to be delivered, type of flower arrangement requested, total price, to whom the flowers were sent, and what was to be printed on the card. Additionally, about nine out of ten orders were purchased over the phone with a credit card.

Questions

1. Suggest a one-to-one marketing plan in which Molly can use the customer information she collects to (1) identify her best customers, (2) increase sales from her best customers, and (3) reinforce their purchase decision.
2. Through credit card records, Molly can overlay data onto her customer database to provide more information about her customers. What additional enhancement data would you suggest she overlay?
3. What can Molly do to determine how much business her customers give to floral departments in grocery stores? With this information, what one-to-one marketing techniques could influence her customers to choose Molly's Flowers more often?

Case   entrepreneurship

The On-Line World of BabyCenter

When Matt Glickman was awaiting the arrival of his first child in 1996, he searched everywhere on the Internet for information on what he would need to take care of his new baby—everything from car seats to cribs. After discovering what was lacking and difficult to find on the Internet, Glickman left his marketing job with Intuit's personal finance software Quicken to start a Web site dedicated to new parents. With the help of Stanford business school classmate Mark Selcow, BabyCenter.com was born in November 1997.

Now one of the leading sites on the Internet for new and expectant parents, San Francisco–based BabyCenter.com is dedicated to helping parents and parents-to-be find the information, support, and products they need during pregnancy and for their infant or toddler. The easy-to-use site features original, high-quality content and practical advice from trusted medical sources as well as fellow parents. BabyCenter.com's editorial team consists of seasoned professionals who have worked at major magazines such as *Parenting*, *Parents*, and *Health*. Most importantly, though, they are moms and dads raising newborns, toddlers, and older children.

With the average new parent spending over $7,000 on their new baby in its first year of life, Glickman and Selcow knew that their site could also provide a valuable service to save new parents time as well as confusion on these first purchases. BabyCenter.com's personal shopping service provides guidance to overwhelmed parents and parents-to-be who face myriad choices in maternity clothes, baby clothes, nursery accessories, toys, and other baby essentials. For example, parents shopping for a new stroller can answer ten key questions regarding what features they want, including size, weight, color, and price range. After submitting their criteria, the BabyCenter Store immediately recommends strollers based on the customer's needs and interests.

BabyCenter also fosters a sense of community through bulletin boards and chat sessions that offer a support system for parents, letting them connect with other parents and medical professionals to help answer their questions and concerns. Medical advisors include a wide array of specialists: obstetricians, pediatricians, family practitioners, nutritionists and exercise physiologists, lactation consultants, nurse-midwives, family counselors, and sleep experts. Members also rate and provide feedback on items purchased from the BabyCenter Store. For instance, one parent wrote that while the baby outfit she had bought for her three-month-old son from the BabyCenter Store was adorable, after one wash it shrank and was too small to be worn again.

Information is key to building customer relationships at BabyCenter.com. The site cultivates one-to-one relationships with new parents through its on-line registration where parents enter their expected due date or the birth date of their child. Typically, sellers of baby products have to wait until prospective parents enroll in childbirth classes before getting this information. This usually happens when the mother is far along in her pregnancy and has often already made buying decisions about many of her baby's essentials. BabyCenter. com's advantage is that it attracts people learning about parenting, such as couples trying to get pregnant, or those who may have just found out they are expecting.

In return for information about their due date or child's birth date, members receive free, personalized e-mails written specifically for their stage of pregnancy or their baby's age. BabyCenter.com's "My Baby This Week" newsletter is sent weekly before the baby is born through the baby's first birthday, then monthly until age three. Inside, readers find information relevant to their pregnancy or growing baby. For example, a woman who is twenty-nine weeks pregnant might receive an e-mail message directing her to aim a flashlight at her expanding abdomen to see the baby turn toward the light, indicating the baby's eyesight is maturing. This may be followed by tips on exercise during the last trimester and products that a new parent might need, including links to the BabyCenter Store.

When members visit BabyCenter.com's Web site, they see an expanded version of the same information at "My BabyCenter." Suggestions include helpful books or articles to read and things to do at their particular stage of pregnancy or their baby's age. For instance, the same twenty-nine-week pregnant woman might see an article about taking one last vacation before the baby is born. Clicking on the word "vacation" brings the reader to an article about air travel during the last trimester.

BabyCenter.com's customer database has steadily grown as new parents learn about the site—there are now more than one million "unique visitors" to the site each month. The company sends more than five million e-mail newsletters monthly. Click-throughs from newsletters to the BabyCenter.com Web site are more than 25 percent. And BabyCenter.com's customers return an average of three times a month to shop or gather information.

Questions

1. Visit this company's Web site at **http://www. babycenter.com**. What information does BabyCenter collect on members at its Web site? How does it use this information to provide a personalized experience?
2. What advantages does BabyCenter realize from its e-mail marketing program?
3. How might BabyCenter use information on what members have purchased in the past or what information they were interested in to cross-sell other products and services?

Bibliography

BabyCenter: **http://www.BabyCenter.com**.

"Case Study: Web Site Develops Customized Content for New Parents, Providers." *Healthcare PR & Marketing News*, April 1999.

Renee M. Kruger. "Baby on Board," *Discount Merchandiser*, March 1999, p. 49.

Doug Levy. "Superstores Seek Online Customers: There's a New Group of Retailers Taking Aim at the Internet." *USA Today*, March 16, 1999, p. 3B.

Kris Oser. "Give Mama What She Craves: BabyCenter.com Fosters Loyalty with Customized E-Content." *1 to 1 Magazine*, September, 2000. On-line.

Elizabeth Owens. "Worth a Visit: Webby Awards Highlight Excellence." *Chicago Tribune*, May 25, 2000, p. 5.

Case

Toronto Blue Jays: One Fan at a Time

The Toronto Blue Jays score high marks with local baseball fans through their one-to-one marketing program, a customer-based, information-intensive method that focuses on one baseball lover at a time. By using database technology, the Jays can make a pitch to each fan and cultivate long-term relationships. The team's database is carefully planned to gather pertinent information about customers and contacts so the sales and marketing staff can analyze the data and use it to provide better customer service.

The need for one-to-one marketing results from today's more demanding and very busy sports enthusiasts. Baseball fans are more strapped for time now than in any previous generation. They demand better, faster service, are more impatient, and don't want to get stuck in line waiting to buy tickets. In today's ballgame, people prefer to order tickets and merchandise by phone, mail, or e-mail.

How do the Blue Jays create their database? A compilation of bits of key information about customers, the database stems from several sources: season ticket subscribers; group season ticket subscribers; single ticket holders who purchase by telephone or mail; and community programs such as "K for Kids," a fund-raiser with pledges phoned in. Tickets are sold at the Sky Dome, the Bullpen Souvenir Store, over the "SportLine," or toll free at 1-888-OKGOJAYS. Tickets are also available on-line at the Jays' Web site.

The Blue Jays' season ticket form asks for the name, address, phone number, zip or postal code, and e-mail address of each subscriber. This information is stored in a database along with seating options, which fall into several price ranges from preferred to general, and is regularly used by the sales staff in designing all sorts of marketing initiatives. The zip or postal code indicates a subscriber's neighborhood, which often pinpoints subculture, social class, income level, and lifestyle. This kind of geographic information can help direct further marketing effort. For example, if enough subscribers live in a zip code that has a large Asian community, the Blue Jays may consider advertising in Asian-language neighborhood publications. The database also helps identify fans who purchase high-end seats and who can then be rewarded with special perks.

A space for questions and comments on the ticket form provides additional information that helps the staff hone in on the right mix of products and services it needs to offer. If a person indicates that she or he is hard of hearing, the Jays can provide free of charge a hearing aid, called Phonic Ear, that amplifies sound levels and makes the game far more enjoyable. Amateur coaches, players, and parents of little leaguers seeking assistance in fundamental baseball skills can receive information about an inexpensive instructional video entitled "A Coaching Clinic."

The e-mail address on the subscription form allows the Jays to easily communicate with individual subscribers. By contacting subscribers one at a time rather than hitting the whole community with direct mail, the Jays reach those who live and breathe baseball, rather than waste valuable marketing dollars on those who don't. E-mail is also a fast way to give season ticket holders particulars about ordering postseason tickets over the Internet.

The season ticket form is not the only method the Jays use to collect crucial information. By asking for detailed information on the group ticket sales form, the staff can offer group benefits to a business or organization. With preferred group seating, promotional posters, and announcement of group names on the Jumbotron, the group sales staff really steps up to the plate to help businesses and organizations promote themselves by entertaining employees or members.

Database technology lets the Jays cross-sell their many products and services. Staff marketers match products to consumer profiles to cross-sell products that match demographic, lifestyle, or behavioral characteristics and further reach an already identified market. At the Blue Jays Baseball Camp, an intense, skill-oriented program for boys and girls ages eleven through nineteen, registration information including age is stored in the database. This gives the Jays the opportunity to mail the campers merchandise information about youth jackets, jerseys, and caps, or Blue Jays Kids Stuff—a youth batting glove, school kit, helmet bank, or MVP bear. While these items may be available at retail outlets around Toronto, the Jays' database has made it possible to explore selling through direct mail.

Still another way the Jays win with database marketing is in retaining loyal fans. By tracking season ticket holders, the Jays can give them special benefits, which can then boost ballpark attendance. Loyalty is strengthened by identifying long-standing fans who have generated the most revenue, creating different messages for new and long-term subscribers, and finding out exactly what the fans want.

Constructing this level of database only happens over time, but the investment has surely paid off for the Toronto Blue Jays. With one-to-one marketing, the Jays hit a home run with the fans every time.

Questions

1. Why do the Toronto Blue Jays use one-to-one marketing?

2. Why is one-to-one marketing timely?
3. What are the sources of the Toronto Blue Jays' database?
4. Describe some of the ways the Toronto Blue Jays use database technology.

Bibliography

Toronto Blue Jays Web site: **http://www.bluejays.ca**.

who wants to be a marketer?

click here!

Quiz yourself using this exciting marketing game where the questions on all topics start easy and get progressively harder. This is Marketing!

So you want to be a marketer?
Put your knowledge to the test.

http://lamb.swcollege.com

Closing 7

MARKETING MISCUES

DoubleClick's Consumer Tracking Capabilities Backfire

DoubleClick is a global Internet advertising company that delivers more than 5 billion on-line ads per month via its fourteen country networks. Through these sophisticated country networks, advertisers can reach computer users in over eighty countries with one ad purchase. These ads, which include sponsorships, pop-ups, and banners, can target users in any country in their native language. The company's yearly sales revenue was almost $200 million in 1999. However, this was only a small portion of industry on-line ad revenue of $3 billion in 1999—a market that is growing and expected to reach $12 billion by 2003.

DoubleClick, a 1995 entrepreneurial start-up based in New York, does not perform the creative aspects of advertising. Rather, the company sells and manages ads that appear on a network of around 1,500 Web sites that represent nearly 50 percent of all Web traffic. The company also provides the technology for tracking and customizing on-line ads, thereby allowing companies to tailor advertising for specific audiences (a service for which advertisers willingly pay a premium). Through the 1999 purchase of Abacus, a direct marketing company, DoubleClick garnered the power to cross-reference consumers' on-line habits with their names and addresses in databases at Abacus. This ability to link on-line habits with a person's identity ignited consumer outrage in early 2000.

Observing the buying habits of consumers is not a new phenomenon. Surveillance cameras view consumers as they shop, and credit card purchases make it easy for companies to understand consumers' buying practices. These buying practices can be linked easily to individual consumer identities, yet credit card companies do not sell this information to other companies to use in their advertising. Never before had an external organization been able to track computer activity on the Web and cross-reference (or associate) that activity with a person's name and address. The closest companies had come to being able to do this was if the computer user provided an e-mail address. Additionally, most retailers on the Web provided privacy information guaranteeing that personal information would not be sold to other companies. While tracking by software files called "cookies" allow for the monitoring of user movements on the Internet, user habits are not linked to a person's name and address. The potential for DoubleClick and Abacus to link specific individuals and their Internet habits (site visits, purchases) is enormous and could lead to DoubleClick having the most comprehensive consumer database in the world.

Consumers as well as consumer protection groups (such as the American Civil Liberties Union, the Center for Democracy and Technology, and the Electronic Privacy and Information Center) were outraged that DoubleClick would even think about invading the privacy of Internet users in this manner. The onslaught of lawsuits and accompanying negative publicity led to a decline in DoubleClick's stock value. Additionally, two business partners, Altavista and Kozmo, announced that they would either withdraw ads linked to DoubleClick or limit user information made available to the company.

Faced with such problems, DoubleClick halted its plan to link the capabilities of DoubleClick and Abacus. The company's CEO admitted the company had made a mistake and announced that it would not use its data mining capabilities until the Internet industry and the federal government had established guidelines to protect user privacy. Additionally, in an attempt to regain trust, the company created the DoubleClick Privacy Advisory Board and a new position of chief privacy officer. The company also began a national campaign to educate consumers about on-line privacy.

Questions for Discussion

1. Should companies be allowed to monitor consumer habits on the computer?
2. When buying behavior is tracked, should companies be allowed to sell the information to other companies who can then bombard consumers with on-line advertising and product offers?
3. How do you feel about your computer habits being tracked and, in essence, made public? How is this different from selling individual purchase information

that is accumulated at traditional brick-and-mortar outlets?

4. Do companies need to know who you are in order to provide you with a relevant on-line experience?

Bibliography

Mark Anstead. "Taking a Tough Line on Privacy." *Marketing*, April 13, 2000, p. 31.

Steven Cherry. "DoubleClick Recants on Privacy Issue." *IEEE Spectrum*, April, 2000, pp. 63–64.

Mark Fitgerald et al. "Triple Trouble for DoubleClick." *Editor & Publisher*, February 21, 2000, p. 3.

Loren Fox. "DoubleClick Climbs to the Top of the Ad World." *Upside*, February, 2000 pp. 58+.

Anita Hamilton. "Data Mining: DoubleClick's Double Take." *Time*, March 13, 2000, p. 95.

David E. Kalish. "Internet Ad Firm Yields to Critics Privacy." *The Orange Country Register*, March 3, 2000, p. C04.

http://www.doubleclick.com.

CRITICAL THINKING CASE

Staples.com: Reaping the Benefits of a Clicks-and-Bricks Strategy

Staples Inc., a $9 billion retailer of office supplies, furniture, and technology, is out to conquer the business-to-business market with its on-line business, Staples.com. At the core of Staples' e-business strategy is the technical interface that allows large corporate buyers to easily buy both products and services from various vendors. Such marketing alliances and partnerships could allow Staples.com to sell virtually everything to small business owners—from notepads to insurance—as part of the company's Business Solutions Center.

In late 1999, Staples Inc. named Kelly Mahoney as chief marketing officer at Staples.com, a new position within Staples. While the company is both a brick-and-mortar business and an on-line retailer, it is sending the signal that it recognizes that the two businesses are distinct by dividing the company into two core businesses—retail and delivery and the Staples.com Internet business. Mahoney must develop the marketing program that will allow the company to maintain its current customer base, while establishing itself as a premier dot.com company.

Staples is credited with inventing the office superstore concept. The largest operator of office superstores in the world, the company employs over 46,000 people in its more than 1,100 brick-and-mortar stores, its mail order direct marketing business, and its e-commerce business. Founded in the mid-1980s, the company has grown quickly from its single store in Brighton, Massachusetts. Headquartered in Framingham, Massachusetts, the company now has retail stores throughout the United States, Canada, the United Kingdom, and Germany.

Major Competitors

Until around the mid-1980s, the office product industry was dominated by independent specialty stores. However, three retailers—Staples, Office Depot, and OfficeMax—entered the market and revolutionized the industry. These retailers combined low overhead costs with high volume buying, bringing warehouse retailing to office products. Today they remain the top three office supply retailers.

Worldwide, the office supply retail market is expected to grow at 6 to 8 percent annually. The North American market, alone, is valued at about $200 billion. With annual sales of around $10 billion, Office Depot operates around 900 stores in the United States, Canada, France, and Japan. The number three office supply superstore, OfficeMax, has annual sales of around $5 billion. OfficeMax has around 950 stores in the United States and Puerto Rico, with joint ventures in Japan, Brazil, and Mexico.

Clicks and Bricks

The office supply superstores have entered the clicks-and-bricks domain with vigor. Web sites for the three major competitors are among the most heavily visited retail sites on the Net. The on-line market for office supplies is estimated to be around $100 million in 2000 and expected to reach $1.2 billion by 2003. Staples, Office Depot, and OfficeMax are building on their existing brand names/brand recognition to create a synergy between their brick-and-mortar stores and their on-line sites.

Other e-tailers in the office supply market include Works.com, Onvia.com, BizBuyer.com, and Officesupplies.com. Offerings of e-tail office suppliers vary from providing products on-line (e.g., Onvia) to linking buyers of products with sellers of products via bid solicitation from a database of vendors (e.g., BizBuyer).

E-commerce at Staples

Staples estimates that 70 percent of its on-line business is incremental sales, with its revenue estimated in late 1999 to be around $24 million. The dot-com business has become so successful that Staples Inc. now recognizes it as a distinctive core business. In late 1999, the company issued a tracking stock that reflected the value it places in its e-commerce efforts. By 2003, Staples hopes to achieve revenues of $1 billion on its dot-com endeavors.

Success in e-commerce has allowed Staples to expand beyond its office products in meeting the needs of its business-to-business customers. It is becoming an invaluable component of its customers' businesses by providing all aspects of services like high-speed Internet access, payroll management, financial services (e.g., 401(k) plans), and health insurance. Revenue-wise, Staples would receive commissions on services bought and sold. Staples expects to drive its dot-com business by establishing small business portals in which the company would not partner with existing service providers. Rather, Staples would serve as the technical interface between buyers and sellers.

Thus, the company will sell its current physical products both in the stores and on-line. It will then enhance its offerings and build on its brand recognition by becoming an on-line service provider. Mahoney and her team must formulate a business-to-business marketing strategy that allows Staples to build on a brand that is known for convenience.

Questions for Discussion

1. What is the difference between Staples' bricks-and-mortar stores and its dot-com business?
2. How will Staples.com allow the company to further penetrate the small business marketplace?
3. How do clicks-and-bricks companies differ from pure e-tailers?
4. What is Staples Inc. doing to establish a competitive edge in the office supplies industry?

Bibliography

John E. Frook. "Staples.com Takes on Office Depot." *Crain Communications, Inc.*, April 10, 2000, pp. 1+.

Robert D. Hof. "Clicks Don't Need Mortar." *Business Week E.BIZ*, June 5, 2000, p. EB 126.

Chris Reidy. "B2B, That is Staples' Quest." *Boston Globe*, February 18,2000, p. C3.

Ara C. Trembly and Susanne Sclafane. "Staples.com to Offer Insurance Online." *National Underwriter*, January 31, 2000, p. 27.

Mike Troy. "Office Supplies: Clicks-and-Mortar Dominates—for Now." *Discount Store News*, December 13, 1999, pp. 57+.

———. "Staples Maintains its Momentum." *Discount Store News*, November 8,1999, pp. 33+.

Lauren Wiley. "Staples.com Names Mahoney Marketing Chief." *Adweek*, November 22,1999, p. 2.

http://www.officedepot.com.
http://www.OfficeMax.com.
http://www.staples.com.

MARKETING PLANNING ACTIVITIES

Technology-Driven Marketing

 Technology will most likely play a key role in your marketing plan. Be sure to clearly identify the ways in which your company will leverage the capabilities of database technology and of the Internet in product, promotion, pricing, and distribution decisions. Also, refer to Exhibit 2.8 for additional marketing plan subjects.

1. Assume your company is or will be marketing its products and/or services over the Internet. How should your company enter this electronic marketplace? How will technology issues affect your firm?

Marketing*Builder* Exercises
- **Business Risk** portion of the **Market Analysis** template

- **Environmental Risk** portion of the **Market Analysis** template
- **Elements of Risk** table in the **Market Analysis** template

2. How will marketing over the Internet modify your target market segment(s)? Redefine the demographics, psychographics, geographics, economic factors, size, growth rate, trends, and any other applicable qualities of the target segment(s) you intend to reach through the Internet.

Marketing*Builder* Exercises
- **Market Segment** portion of the **Market Analysis** template
- **Customer Profile** portion of the **Market Analysis** template

3. What kinds of consumer or business product or service is your firm planning to market over the Internet? Identify ways that marketing over the Internet will change the basic design of your core product or service. How will modification of the product or service affect your costs? Identify any modification to your return policies that will need to be made to address new Internet customers.

4. Discuss the implications of adding the Internet as a channel to your already developed distribution network. How will this affect channel relationships? The final price offered to Internet customers? Any promotional efforts launched over the Internet?

Marketing*Builder* Exercises

- **Returns and Adjustments Policy** portion of the **Sales Plan** template
- **Distribution Channels** portion of the **Sales Plan** template
- **Product Launch Budget** portion of the **Marketing Budget** spreadsheet

- **Advertising Budget** portion of the **Marketing Budget** spreadsheet

5. Investigate the expansion of your marketing efforts to include a one-to-one database marketing program. How will you collect data? How will you use it? What effect will the creation of the database have on your diverse marketing methods (mailings, catalogs, e-mailings, coupon distribution, product sample distribution, and so on)?

Marketing*Builder* Exercises

- **Direct Mail** portion of the **Marketing Budget** spreadsheet
- **Direct Mail** Analysis spreadsheet
- Source Code Master List spreadsheet
- **Direct Response Mail, Direct Mail,** and **List Management** portions of the **Marketing Communications** template.

E-MARKETING PLANNING ACTIVITIES

You began your strategic e-marketing plan by stating your business mission and objectives and detailing a SWOT analysis. In the second part of the plan you identified and described target market segments and identified sources of CI and the need for further marketing research. Next, you defined aspects of the marketing mix, including product, distribution, promotion, and pricing tactics. Recall that you are either writing a strategic marketing plan for an existing bookstore retailer with a new on-line presence, a dot-com bookstore retailer, or an e-company of your own choosing.

Use the following exercises to guide you through the additional technology aspects of a strategic e-marketing plan:

1. How do your potential on-line customers compare with off-line customers? For customer profiles visit **http://www.cc.gatech.edu/gvu/user_surveys**. Other information about on-line users is at **http://www. survey.net**.

2. One of the most important aspects of having an e-marketing offering is to select the right Internet service provider (ISP). Different ISPs offer different prices and services. Checking up on e-commerce capabilities for secure on-line transactions will be particularly important. To find and compare ISPs and

Web hosts, go to **http://thelist.internet.com**. For a comprehensive list of Web design firms, go to **http://www.firmlist.com/main.shtml**.

3. Choosing a domain name that is easy to remember and spell, as well as one that uniquely identifies your firm, is an important challenge. Does your domain name have to be the same as your company name? To see if your desired domain name is already being used: **http://411direct.com/domainnamereg.htm**. Or check the "Who Is" area of **http://www. networksolutions.com**.

4. Web site development is a key tool to identify your offering, brand, and company. Development of a unique, secure, and user-friendly site will take time and money. Should you legally protect the contents of your site? Check out **http://www.benedict.com** to check on copyright issues for your Web site contents. Internet patent and trademark information is shown on **http://www.micropat.com**.

5. How can e-mail newsletters be a beneficial marketing tool? Should your company create and distribute one? If so, who will create the content and what will the content be?

6. Should your company participate in, monitor, or sponsor a mailing or on-line discussion list? One of the hottest topics in Internet marketing is how to

build a "sticky" on-line community at e-commerce sites—in other words, a community that keeps visitors at the site for a long time. Would your site benefit from having community resources? Why or why not? If so, what features would you add to build a community presence? How will you make it "sticky?" To search for lists in your company's area of interest, go to **http://www.liszt.com**.

7. With an eye toward database marketing, how should your company begin collecting data from on-line visitors and their transactions? How will this data be used? Write your on-line privacy policy. For more information about privacy policies, visit **http://www. privacyalliance.org** or **http://www.uscib.org/policy/ privmin.htm**.

The last and concluding part of a strategic marketing plan deals with implementation, evaluation, and control. A strategic plan is effective only when it is acted upon, so implementation guidelines should list specific action plans and a recommended time frame. Evaluation is needed to see if actual e-marketing activities are resulting in expected objectives. If not, control measures will need to take place.

For continued general assistance on business plans and marketing plans, visit **http://www.bplans.com** or **http://www.businessplans.org**. For electronic sources of information, search on the Electric Library at **http:// wwws.elibrary.com** or the Internet Public Library at **http://www.ipl.org**. Another excellent source of information is the Sales and Marketing Executives Marketing Library at **http://www.sell.org**. You should also refer to Exhibit 2.8 for additional marketing plan checklist items (Part V: Implementation, Evaluation, and Control).

Use the following exercises to conclude your strategic e-marketing plan with implementation, evaluation, and control:

1. Project management tools are the best way to set up your implementation, evaluation, and control program. Visit **http://www.allpm.com** or **http://www. bwebwide.com/folders/projects.htm** to learn about project planning, alternative software tools, and free project information. For a free timeline utility tool, visit **http://www.smartdraw.com**. Decide whether the marketing or operations department will manage the implementation and control of the plan.

2. Make sure performance standards are set for each area of the marketing plan. Comparing performance against objectives is why objectives must be stated in numerical terms. What will your objectives be in terms of traffic (hits), sales, page views, visits per customer, and length of average visit (in minutes)? Which measurement is most important? Why?

3. What is the financial impact of the plan if performance standards are met? How long can you last if they are not met? For on-line extensions of off-line businesses, how many resources should the off-line business put behind its on-line counterpart? Use financial spreadsheet software to set up a calendar-based pro-forma statement outlining expected sales and costs over the course of the e-marketing cycle.

4. Using additional spreadsheets, compare actual versus expected performance. Where actuals exceed expectations, what are the sources of success that should be further capitalized on? When actuals fail to meet expectations, what are the sources of problems and how can they be corrected? Are the sources directly related to doing business on-line?

5. What other marketing research is needed to assist in the evaluation and modification of your strategic e-marketing plan? Looking back over your now complete e-marketing plan, do marketing costs appear to be more or less intensive in the on-line business environment than in the traditional one?

CROSS-FUNCTIONAL CONNECTIONS SOLUTIONS

Technology's Role in Facilitating Interactions Between the Company and Its Customers and Among Internal Functions

Questions

1. How has today's technology altered the role of marketing both internally and externally?

Advertising and promoting products on the Internet have caused the marketing department, which in the past has been responsible for creating and developing the entire communications program for products/services, to share their marketing communications responsibilities with other functional groups within companies. Marketing has been forced to relinquish sole ownership of the creative process, due to its inability to design a Web site that echoes its vision for the communications program. Marketing must then work closely with information technology, a group that in turn translates the vision into a visual, interactive Web site. Traditionally, a product was marketed to a mass audience through brochures and/or print ads. Marketing departments created communications campaigns on a grand, informal scale to promote products. Due to the Internet, however, companies are marketing their products to consumers directly. Marketing must now develop, along with information technologists, Web sites (which may ultimately replace print ads and brochures) that clearly communicate the company as well as the products to the on-line user.

2. What are some of the benefits of networking functional departments, customers, and suppliers?

Very broadly, benefits include the following:

Facilitation of cross-functional communication: All functional groups have access to the same information, at the same time.

Speed of transaction: Customer orders can be sent electronically and simultaneously to all departments that will perform steps in processing the order, allowing all necessary groups to begin fulfilling tasks to get the order out the door (e.g., accounting can begin checking the firm's credit records, production can check stock for adequate levels, shipping can begin preparing to get the product to the customer).

Immediate delivery of component parts, materials, etc.: Suppliers become as aware of stock level as the customer, and they ship based on their reporting processes rather than waiting for the customer to place an order.

3. Which functional areas are actively involved in making e-commerce a success? How?

Marketing, information technology, legal, finance/accounting, and research and development are all functional areas that are involved in making e-commerce a success. Marketing and information technology partner to create a visual communication to the customer while lawyers, specialized in cyber law, analyze the site's legal logistics. Finance and accounting evaluate the costs of maintaining the site and determine its budget. Research and development continuously work on improving product offering. Together, these departments work to create a successful cyber experience.

Suggested Readings

Parry Aftab. "Master of the Domain." *Working Woman*, April 2000, p. 58.

Jerry Luftman and Tom Brier. "Achieving and Sustaining Business-IT Alignment." *California Management Review*, Fall 1999, pp. 109–122.

Careers in Marketing

One of the most important decisions in your life is deciding on your career. Not only will a career choice affect your income and lifestyle, but it also will have a major impact on your happiness and self-fulfillment. Probably the most difficult part of job hunting is deciding exactly what type of work you would like. Many students have had no working experience other than summer jobs, so they are not sure what career to pursue. Too often, college students and their parents rush toward occupational fields that seem to offer the highest monetary payoff or are currently "hot," instead of looking at the long run over a forty- to fifty-year working life.

In order to help you as you begin thinking about career goals and job hunting, the *Marketing* Web site contains an appendix titled "Careers in Marketing." Not only can it inform you about career opportunities in the marketing field, it also provides a wealth of information to help you at each stage of your job search:

- A self-assessment tool
- Career listings with compensation ranges
- Features-advantages-benefits model to help you determine job fit
- Resources for job prospecting
- How to write your résumé
- How to write a professional cover letter
- Self-preparedness test to determine readiness to interview
- Pre-interview checklist
- Tips to keep in mind while preparing for an interview
- More than seventy frequently asked job interview questions
- Questions to ask an interviewer
- How to conduct yourself during an interview
- How to handle objections raised by an interviewer
- Tips on following up after an interview
- How to write a letter accepting a job offer
- How to write a letter declining a job offer

Visit **http://lamb.swcollege.com** to find out how to market yourself to the marketing industry.

Getting Started

Getting started can be the toughest part of job hunting, especially if you are uncertain about what career you want to pursue. The careers appendix can help you in this initial stage with its self-assessment tool, career and compensation lists, features-advantages-benefits (FAB) matrix, and listing of resources for job prospecting.

A self-assessment tool can help you identify your personal needs, capabilities, characteristics, strengths, weaknesses, and desires. The on-line careers appendix includes a thirteen question assessment tool that can help you begin to analyze what is important to you in choosing the kind of work you will do and the kind of employer for whom you will work. There is also a complete listing of careers available in the marketing industry, with compensation figures for each. This information can help you determine what marketing fields interest you and meet your income needs. Using the FAB matrix, you can plot your abilities and skills against the employer's job requirements. Once you complete the model, you will have a better idea of what you have to sell a potential employer. If you have identified a career that suits you but are having trouble finding an employer that offers that particular career opportunity, the on-line careers appendix can help. It provides a list of resources that can be useful when prospecting for an employer. Information on where to locate and how to use the various resources is also included.

Are You Ready to Interview?

Once you have moved through the initial phase of your job search, the on-line careers appendix can still help you. It shows you how to write your résumé and cover letter so that you convey a positive and professional attitude. The information in the appendix can also help you determine how ready you are for a job interview. It provides you with a self-preparedness test, a pre-interview checklist, and a list of considerations to keep in mind when preparing for your interview.

Since interviewing can often be a source of nervousness and anxiety, the on-line careers appendix gives you tools you can use to feel calm and prepared during an interview. A list of over seventy frequently asked job interview questions is provided along with a list of questions for you to ask the interviewer. You can receive guidance on how to conduct yourself professionally during the interview and how to handle objections raised by the interviewer. You can also find tips on following up after the interview and on accepting or declining a job offer.

Go On-Line!

Many of the basic concepts of marketing introduced in this book can be used to help you get the career you want by marketing yourself. This complete on-line appendix, "Careers in Marketing," is designed to help you do just that, so visit **http://lamb.swcollege.com** to begin learning how to successfully market yourself to prospective employers!

glossary

A

accessory equipment Goods, such as portable tools and office equipment, that are less expensive and shorter-lived than major equipment.

adaptive channel Alternative channel initiated when a firm identifies critical but rare customer requirements that they do not have the capability to fulfill.

adopter A consumer who was happy enough with his or her trial experience with a product to use it again.

advertising Impersonal, one-way mass communication about a product or organization that is paid for by a marketer.

advertising appeal Reason for a person to buy a product.

advertising campaign Series of related advertisements focusing on a common theme, slogan, and set of advertising appeals.

advertising objective Specific communication task a campaign should accomplish for a specified target audience during a specified period.

advertising response function Phenomenon in which spending for advertising and sales promotion increases sales or market share up to a certain level but then produces diminishing returns.

advocacy advertising Form of advertising in which an organization expresses its views on controversial issues or responds to media attacks.

agents and brokers Wholesaling intermediaries who facilitate the sale of a product from producer to end user by representing retailers, wholesalers, or manufacturers and who do not take title to the product.

AIDA concept Model that outlines the process for achieving promotional goals in terms of stages of consumer involvement with the message; the acronym stands for Attention, Interest, Desire, and Action.

applied research Attempts to develop new or improved products.

aspirational reference group Group that someone would like to join.

assurance The knowledge and courtesy of employees and their ability to convey trust.

ATC. See **average total cost.**

atmosphere The overall impression conveyed by a store's physical layout, decor, and surroundings.

attitude Learned tendency to respond consistently toward a given object.

audience selectivity Ability of an advertising medium to reach a precisely defined market.

audit Form of observation research that features people examining and verifying the sale of a product.

augmented product A product or service developed when a company adds features not expected by the customer.

automatic vending The use of machines to offer goods for sale.

AVC. See **average variable cost.**

average total cost (ATC) Total costs divided by quantity of output.

average variable cost (AVC) Total variable cost divided by quantity of output.

B

baby boomers People born between 1946 and 1964.

bait pricing Price tactic that tries to get consumers into a store through false or misleading price advertising and then uses high-pressure selling to persuade consumers to buy more expensive merchandise.

base price The general price level at which the company expects to sell the good or service.

basic research Pure research that aims to confirm an existing theory or to learn more about a concept or phenomenon.

basing-point pricing Price tactic that charges freight from a given (basing) point, regardless of the city from which the goods are shipped.

BehaviorScan Scanner-based research program that tracks the purchases of three thousand households through store scanners.

belief Organized pattern of knowledge that an individual holds as true about his or her world.

benefit segmentation The process of grouping customers into market segments according to the benefits they seek from the product.

brainstorming Getting a group to think of unlimited ways to vary a product or solve a problem.

brand A name, term, symbol, design, or combination thereof that identifies a seller's products and differentiates them from competitors' products.

brand equity The value of company and brand names.

brand loyalty A consistent preference for one brand over all others.

brand mark The elements of a brand that cannot be spoken.

brand name That part of a brand that can be spoken, including letters, words, and numbers.

break-even analysis Method of determining what sales volume must be reached before total revenue equals total costs.

business analysis The second stage of the screening process, at which time preliminary figures for demand, cost, sales, and profitability are calculated.

business e-commerce Electronic transactions between companies.

business marketing The marketing of goods and services to individuals and organizations for purposes other than personal consumption.

business product (industrial product) Product used to manufacture other goods or services, to facilitate an organization's operations, or to resell to other customers.

business services Expense items that do not become part of a final product.

buyer Department head who selects the merchandise for his or her department and may also be responsible for promotion and personnel.

buyer for export Intermediary in the global market that assumes all ownership risks and sells globally for its own account.

buying center All those persons in an organization who become involved in the purchase decision.

C

cannibalization Situation that occurs when sales of a new product cut into sales of a firm's existing products.

cash cow In the portfolio matrix, a business unit that usually generates more cash than it needs to maintain its market share.

cash discount A price reduction offered to a consumer, an industrial user, or a marketing intermediary in return for prompt payment of a bill.

category killers Term often used to describe specialty discount stores because they so heavily dominate their narrow merchandise segment.

central-location telephone (CLT) facility A specially designed phone room used to conduct telephone interviewing.

chain stores Stores owned and operated as a group by a single organization.

channel Medium of communication-such as a voice, radio, or newspaper-for transmitting a message.

channel conflict Clash of goals and methods between distribution channel members.

channel control Situation that occurs when one marketing channel member intentionally affects another member's behavior.

channel leader (channel captain) Member of a marketing channel that exercises authority and power over the activities of other channel members.

channel members All parties in the marketing channel that negotiate with one another, buy and sell products, and facilitate the change of ownership between buyer and seller in the course of moving the product from the manufacturer into the hands of the final consumer.

channel partnering (channel cooperation) The joint effort of all channel members to create a supply chain that serves customers and creates a competitive advantage.

channel power Capacity of a particular marketing channel member to control or influence the behavior of other channel members.

CI audit A competitive intelligence audit of employees by their type of expertise, independent in-house databases, and marketing research studies available internally.

CI directory CI audit data entered into a database management file.

CIS. *See* **customer information system.**

CLT. *See* **central-location telephone facility.**

closed-ended question An interview question that asks the respondent to make a selection from a limited list of responses.

cobranding Placing two or more brand names on a product or its package.

code of ethics A guideline to help marketing managers and other employees make better decisions.

cognitive dissonance Inner tension that a consumer experiences after recognizing an inconsistency between behavior and values or opinions.

cold calling Form of lead generation in which the salesperson approaches potential buyers without prior knowledge of the prospects' needs or financial status.

commercialization The decision to market a product.

communication Process by which we exchange or share meanings through a common set of symbols.

comparative advertising Form of advertising that compares two or more specifically named or shown competing brands on one or more specific attributes.

competitive advantage The set of unique features of a company and its products that are perceived by the target market as significant and superior to the competition.

competitive advertising Form of advertising designed to influence demand for a specific brand.

competitive intelligence An intelligence system that helps managers assess their competition and their vendors in order to become more efficient and effective competitors.

compiled list A customer list that was developed by gathering names and addresses from telephone directories and membership rosters, usually enhanced with information from public records, such as census data, auto registrations, birth announcements, business start-ups, or bankruptcies.

component lifestyles Practice of choosing goods and services that meet one's diverse needs and interests rather than conforming to a single, traditional lifestyle.

component parts Either finished items ready for assembly or products that need very little processing before becoming part of some other product.

computer-assisted personal interviewing Interviewing method in which the interviewer reads the questions from a computer screen and enters the respondent's data directly into the computer.

computer-assisted self-interviewing Interviewing method in which a mall interviewer intercepts and directs willing respondents to a nearby computer where the respondent reads questions off the computer screen and directly keys his or her answers into the computer.

computer disk by mail survey Like a typical mail survey only the respondents receive and answer questions on a disk.

concentrated targeting strategy A strategy used to select one segment of a market or targeting marketing efforts.

concept of exchange Idea that people give up something to receive something they would rather have.

concept test Test to evaluate a new product idea, usually before any prototype has been created.

consumer behavior Processes a consumer uses to make purchase decisions as well as to use and dispose of purchased goods or services; also includes factors that influence purchase decisions and the use of products.

consumer decision-making process A five step process used by consumers when buying goods or services.

consumer e-commerce Electronic transactions between businesses and individuals that purchase for personal consumption.

consumer penalty An extra fee paid by the consumer for violating the terms of the purchase agreement.

consumer product Product bought to satisfy an individual's personal wants.

Consumer Product Safety Commission (CPSC) A federal agency established to protect the health and safety of consumers in and around their homes.

consumer sales promotion Sales promotion activities targeting the ultimate consumer.

continuous media schedule Media scheduling strategy, used for products in the latter stages of the product life cycle, in which advertising is run steadily throughout the advertising period.

contract manufacturing Private label manufacturing by a foreign company.

control The mechanisms for evaluating marketing results in light of the plan's goals and for correcting actions that do not help the organization reach those goals within budget guidelines.

convenience product A relatively inexpensive item that merits little shopping effort.

convenience sample A form of nonprobability sample using respondents who are convenient or readily accessible to the researcher, for example, employees, friends, or relatives.

convenience store A miniature supermarket, carrying only a limited line of high-turnover convenience goods.

cooperative advertising Arrangement in which the manufacturer and the retailer split the costs of advertising the manufacturer's brand.

core service The most basic benefit the consumer is buying.

corporate social responsibility Business's concern for society's welfare.

cost competitive advantage Being the low-cost competitor in an industry while maintaining satisfactory profit margins.

cost per contact The cost of reaching one member of the target market.

countertrade Form of trade in which all or part of the payment for goods or services is in the form of other goods or services.

coupon Certificate that entitles consumers to an immediate price reduction when they buy the product.

credence quality A characteristic that consumers may have difficulty assessing even after purchase because they do not have the necessary knowledge or experience.

crisis management Coordinated effort to handle the effects of unfavorable publicity or of another unexpected, unfavorable event.

cross-tabulation A method of analyzing data that lets the analyst look at the responses to one question in relation to the responses to one or more other questions.

culture Set of values, norms, attitudes, and other meaningful symbols that shape human behavior and the artifacts, or products, of that behavior as they are transmitted from one generation to the next.

cumulative quantity discount A deduction from list price that applies to the buyer's total purchases made during a specific period.

custom data Enhancement information acquired by the marketer, including customer surveys, customer participation programs, product registration, warranty cards, or loyalty marketing programs.

customer information system (CIS) A type of marketing database that is historical in nature and used primarily to record contact data, past purchase transactions, and response to marketing programs. These types of databases are the least sophisticated and least integrated into marketing strategy and decision support.

customer satisfaction The feeling that a product has met or exceeded the customer's expectations.

customer value The ratio of benefits to the sacrifice necessary to obtain those benefits.

D

database A collection of data, especially one that can be accessed and manipulated by computer software.

database enhancement The overlay of information to customer or prospect records for the purpose of better describing or better determining the responsiveness of customers or prospects.

database marketing The creation of a large computerized file of customers' and potential customers' profiles and purchase patterns.

data-driven marketing The process of gathering, maintaining, and analyzing information about customers and prospects to implement more efficient and effective marketing communications; another term for one-to-one marketing.

data mart A smaller database that logically groups information from the data warehouse pertaining to one area, such as for market segmentation or campaign management.

data mining The process of using statistical analysis to detect relevant purchasing behavior patterns in a database.

data warehouse A very large, corporate-wide database in which the data are culled from a number of legacy systems, such as billing/accounting, order fulfillment, distribution, customer service, and marketing and sales, that are already in place within the organization.

decision support system (DSS) An interactive, flexible computerized information system that enables managers to obtain and manipulate information as they are making decisions.

decline stage A long-run drop in sales.

decoding Interpretation of the language and symbols sent by the source through a channel.

delayed-quotation pricing Price tactic used for industrial installations and many accessory items, in which a firm price is not set until the item is either finished or delivered.

demand The quantity of a product that will be sold in the market at various prices for a specified period.

demographic segmentation Segmenting markets by age, gender, income, ethnic background, and family life cycle.

demography The study of people's vital statistics, such as their age, race and ethnicity, and location.

department store A store housing several departments under one roof.

derived demand The demand for business products.

development Stage in the product development process in which a prototype is developed and a marketing strategy is outlined.

differential advantage One or more unique aspects of an organization that cause target consumers to patronize that firm rather than competitors.

differential competitive advantage Advantage achieved when a firm provides something that is unique and valuable to buyers beyond simply offering a lower price than the competition offers.

diffusion The process by which the adoption of an innovation spreads.

direct channel Distribution channel in which producers sell directly to consumers.

direct foreign investment Active ownership of a foreign company or of overseas manufacturing or marketing facilities.

direct marketing (direct-response marketing) Techniques used to get consumers to make a purchase from their home, office, or other nonretail setting.

direct retailing The selling of products door-to-door, office-to-office, or at home parties by representatives.

discount store A retailer that competes on the basis of low prices, high turnover, and high volume.

discrepancy of assortment Lack of all the items a customer needs to receive full satisfaction from a product or products.

discrepancy of quantity Difference between the amount of product produced and the amount a customer wants to buy.

distribution resource planning (DRP) Inventory control system that manages the replenishment of goods from the manufacturer to the final consumer.

diversification A strategy of increasing sales by introducing new products into new markets.

dog In the portfolio matrix, a business unit that has low growth potential and a small market share.

DRP. *See* **distribution resource planning.**

drugstore A retail store that stocks pharmacy-related products and services as its main draw.

DSS. *See* **decision support system.**

dual distribution (multiple distribution) Use of two or more channels to distribute the same product to target markets.

dumping The sale of an exported product at a price lower than that charged for the same or a like product in the "home" market of the exporter.

E

EDI. *See* **electronic data interchange.**
EDLP. *See* **everyday low prices.**
80/20 principle Principle that holds that 20 percent of all customers generate 80 percent of the demand.

elastic demand Situation in which consumer demand is sensitive to changes in price.

elasticity of demand Consumers' responsiveness or sensitivity to changes in price.

electronic commerce (e-commerce) The process of selling goods and services on the Internet.

electronic data interchange (EDI) Information technology that replaces the paper documents that usually accompany business transactions, such as purchase orders and invoices, with electronic transmission of the needed information to reduce inventory levels, improve cash flow, streamline operations, and increase the speed and accuracy of information transmission.

electronic distribution Distribution technique that includes any kind of product or service that can be distributed electronically, whether over traditional forms such as fiber-optic cable or through satellite transmission of electronic signals.

empathy Caring, individualized attention to customers.

empowerment Delegation of authority to solve customers' problems—usually by the first person that the customer notifies regarding a problem.

encoding Conversion of the sender's ideas and thoughts into a message, usually in the form of words or signs.

environmental management When a company implements strategies that attempt to shape the external environment within which it operates.

environmental scanning Collection and interpretation of information about forces, events, and relationships in the external environment that may affect the future of the organization or the implementation of the marketing plan.

escalator pricing Price tactic in which the final selling price reflects cost increases incurred between the time the order is placed and when delivery is made.

ethics The moral principles or values that generally govern the conduct of an individual.

evaluation Gauging the extent to which the marketing objectives have been achieved during the specified time period.

everyday low prices (EDLP) Price tactic of permanently reducing prices 10 to 25 percent below the traditional levels while eliminating trade discounts that create trade loading.

evoked set (consideration set) Group of brands, resulting from an information search, from which a buyer can choose.

exchange The idea that people give up something to receive something they would rather have.

exclusive distribution Form of distribution that establishes one or a few dealers within a given area.

executive interviews A type of survey that involves interviewing businesspeople at their offices concerning industrial products or services.

experience curves Curves that show costs declining at a predictable rate as experience with a product increases.

experience quality A characteristic that can be assessed only after use.

experiment Method a researcher uses to gather primary data.

expert Someone with in-depth knowledge of a subject or activity.

export agent Intermediary who acts like a manufacturer's agent for the exporter. The export agent lives in the foreign market.

export broker Intermediary who plays the traditional broker's role by bringing buyer and seller together.

exporting Selling domestically produced products to buyers in another country.

express warranty A written guarantee.

extensive decision making Most complex type of consumer decision making, used when buying an unfamiliar, expensive product or an infrequently bought item; requires use of several criteria for evaluating options and much time for seeking information.

external information search Process of seeking information in the outside environment.

extranet A private network that uses Internet technology and a browser interface, also a network that links a company with its suppliers and customers.

F

factory outlet An off-price retailer that is owned and operated by a manufacturer.

family brand The marketing of several different products under the same brand name.

family life cycle (FLC) A series of stages determined by a combination of age, marital status, and the presence or absence of children.

Federal Trade Commission (FTC) A federal agency empowered to prevent persons or corporations from using unfair methods of competition in commerce.

feedback Receiver's response to a message.

field service firm A firm that specializes in interviewing respondents on a subcontracted basis.

fixed cost Cost that does not change as output is increased or decreased.

FLC. *See* **family life cycle.**

flexible pricing (variable pricing) Price tactic in which different customers pay different prices for essentially the same merchandise bought in equal quantities.

flighted media schedule Media scheduling strategy in which ads are run heavily every other month or every two weeks, to achieve a greater impact with an increased frequency and reach at those times.

FOB origin pricing Price tactic that requires the buyer to absorb the freight costs from the shipping point ("free on board").

focus group Seven to ten people who participate in a group discussion led by a moderator.

follow-up Final step of the selling process, in which the salesperson ensures that delivery schedules are met, that the goods or services perform as promised, and that the buyers' employees are properly trained to use the products.

Food and Drug Administration (FDA) A federal agency charged with enforcing regulations against selling and distributing adulterated, misbranded, or hazardous food and drug products.

four Ps Product, place, promotion, and price, which together make up the marketing mix.

frame error Error that occurs when a sample drawn from a population differs from the target population.

franchise The right to operate a business or to sell a product.

franchisee Individual or business that is granted the right to sell another party's product.

franchiser Originator of a trade name, product, methods of operation, and so on, that grants operating rights to another party to sell its product.

freight absorption pricing Price tactic in which the seller pays all or part of the actual freight charges and does not pass them on to the buyer.

frequency Number of times an individual is exposed to a given message during a specific period.

frequent buyer program A loyalty program in which loyal consumers are rewarded for making multiple purchases of a particular good or service.

full-line discounter A retailer that offers consumers very limited service and carries a broad assortment of well-known, nationally branded "hard goods."

fully industrialized society The fifth stage of economic development, a society that is an exporter of manufactured products, many of which are based on advanced technology.

functional discount (trade discount) Discount to wholesalers and retailers for performing channel functions.

G

gap model A model identifying five gaps that can cause problems in service delivery and influence customer evaluations of service quality.

General Agreement on Tariffs and Trade (GATT) Agreement that provided loopholes that enabled countries to avoid trade-barrier reduction agreements.

Generation X People born between the years 1965 and 1978.

Generation Y People born between the years 1979 and 1994.

generic product A no-frills, no-brand-name, low-cost product that is simply identified by its product category.

generic product name Name that identifies a product by class or type and that cannot be trademarked.

geodemographic segmentation Segmenting potential customers into neighborhood lifestyle categories.

geographic segmentation Segmenting markets by region of the country or world, market size, market density, or climate.

global marketing Marketing to target markets throughout the world.

global marketing standardization Production of uniform products that can be sold the same way all over the world.

global vision Recognizing and reacting to international marketing opportunities, being aware of threats from foreign competitors in all markets, and effectively using international distribution networks.

gross margin Amount of money the retailer makes as a percentage of sales after the cost of goods sold is subtracted.

group dynamics Interaction essential to the success of focus group research.

growth stage The second stage of the product life cycle when sales typically grow at an increasing rate, many competitors enter the market, large companies may start acquiring small pioneering firms, and profits are healthy.

H

heterogeneity Characteristic of services that makes them less standardized and uniform than goods.

horizontal conflict Channel conflict that occurs among channel members on the same level.

hypermarket Retail store that combines a supermarket and full-line discount store in a space ranging from 200,000 to 300,000 square feet.

I

ideal self-image The way an individual would like to be.

IMC. *See* **integrated marketing communications.**

implementation The process that turns marketing plans into action assignments and ensures that these assignments are executed in a way that accomplishes the plans' objectives.

implied warranty An unwritten guarantee that the good or service is fit for the purpose for which it was sold.

in-bound telephone surveys A new trend in telephone interviewing in which an information packet is sent to consumers, who are then asked to call a toll-free, interactive voice-mail system and answer questions.

independent retailers Retailers owned by a single person or partnership and not operated as part of a larger retail institution.

individual branding Using different brand names for different products.

industrial espionage An attempt to learn competitors' trade secrets by illegal or unethical or both means.

industrializing society The fourth stage of economic development when technology spreads from sectors of the economy that powered the takeoff to the rest of the nation.

inelastic demand Situation in which an increase or a decrease in price will not significantly affect demand for the product.

inflation A general rise in prices without a corresponding increase in wages, which results in decreased purchasing power.

infomercial Thirty-minute or longer advertisement that looks more like a TV talk show than a sales pitch.

informational labeling Labeling designed to help consumers make proper product selections and lower their cognitive dissonance after the purchase.

InfoScan A scanner-based sales-tracking service for the consumer packaged-goods industry.

innovation A product perceived as new by a potential adopter.

inseparability Characteristic of services that allows them to be produced and consumed simultaneously.

institutional advertising Form of advertising designed to enhance a company's image rather than promote a particular product.

intangibility Characteristic of services that cannot be touched, seen, tasted, heard, or felt in the same manner in which goods can be sensed.

integrated interviewing A new interviewing method in which a respondent is interviewed on the Internet.

integrated marketing communications (IMC) The method of carefully coordinating all promotional activities to produce a consistent, unified message that is customer focused.

intensive distribution Form of distribution aimed at having a product available in every outlet at which target customers might want to buy it.

internal information search Process of recalling past information stored in the memory.

internal marketing Treating employees as customers and developing systems and benefits that satisfy their needs.

Internet Worldwide telecommunications network allowing access to data, pictures, sound, and files throughout the world.

interpersonal communication Direct, fact-to-face communication between two or more people.

introductory stage The full-scale launch of a new product into the marketplace.

inventory control system Method of developing and maintaining an adequate assortment of products to meet customer demand.

involvement Amount of time and effort a buyer invests in the search, evaluation, and decision processes of consumer behavior.

J

JIT. *See* **just-in-time production.**

joint costs Costs that are shared in the manufacturing and marketing of several products in a product line.

joint demand The demand for two or more items used together in a final product.

joint venture A venture in which a domestic firm buys part of a foreign company or joins with a foreign company to create a new entity.

just-in-time production (JIT) Redefining and simplifying manufacturing by reducing inventory levels and delivering raw materials just when they are needed on the production line.

K

keiretsu A network of interlocking corporate affiliates.

keystoning Practice of marking up prices by 100 percent, or doubling the cost.

L

lead generation (prospecting) Identification of those firms and people most likely to buy the seller's offerings.

lead qualification Determination of a sales prospect's (1) recognized need, (2) buying power, and (3) receptivity and accessibility.

leader pricing (loss-leader pricing) A price tactic in which a product is sold near or even below cost in the hope that shoppers will buy other items once they are in the store.

learning Process that creates changes in behavior, immediate or expected, through experience and practice.

licensing The legal process whereby a licensor agrees to let another firm use its manufacturing process, trademarks, patents, trade secrets, or other proprietary knowledge.

lifestyle Mode of living as identified by a person's activities, interests, and opinions.

lifetime value analysis (LTV) A data manipulation technique that projects the future value of the customer over a period of years using the assumption that marketing to repeat customers is more profitable than marketing to first-time buyers.

limited decision making Type of decision making that requires a moderate amount of time for gathering information and deliberating about an unfamiliar brand in a familiar product category.

logistics The process of strategically managing the efficient flow and storage of raw materials, in-process inventory, and finished goods from point of origin to point of consumption.

logistics information system Information technology that integrates and links all of the logistics functions of the supply chain.

logistics service Interrelated activities performed by a member of the supply chain to ensure that the right product is in the right place at the right time.

loyalty marketing programs Promotional program designed to build long-term, mutually beneficial relationships between a company and its key customers.

LTV. *See* **lifetime value analysis.**

M

Maastricht Treaty Agreement among twelve countries of the European Community to pursue economic, monetary, and political union.

macrosegmentation Method of dividing business markets into segments based on general characteristics such as geographic location, customer type, customer size, and product use.

major equipment (installations) Capital goods such as large or expensive machines, mainframe computers, blast furnaces, generators, airplanes, and buildings.

mall intercept interview Survey research method that involves interviewing people in the common areas of shopping malls.

management decision problem Broad-based problem that requires marketing research in order for managers to take proper actions.

manufacturers' brand The brand name of a manufacturer.

marginal cost (MC) Change in total costs associated with a one-unit change in output.

marginal revenue (MR) The extra revenue associated with selling an extra unit of output or the change in total revenue with a one-unit change in output.

market People or organizations with needs or wants and the ability and willingness to buy.

market attractiveness/company strength matrix Tool for allocating resources among strategic business units on the basis of how attractive a market is and how well the firm is positioned to take advantage of opportunities in that market.

market development Attracting new customers to existing products.

marketing The process of planning and executing the conception, pricing, promotion, and distribution of ideas, goods, and services to create exchanges that satisfy individual and organizational goals.

marketing audit A thorough, systematic, periodic evaluation of the goals, strategies, structure, and performance of the marketing organization.

marketing channel (channel of distribution) Set of interdependent organizations that ease the transfer of ownership as products move from producer to business user or consumer.

marketing concept Idea that the social and economic justification for an organization's existence is the satisfaction of customer wants and needs while meeting organizational objectives.

marketing-controlled information source Product information source that originates with marketers promoting the product.

marketing database The compilation of names, addresses, and other pieces of pertinent information about individual customers and prospects that affects what and how marketers sell to them.

marketing information Everyday information about developments in the marketing environment that managers use to prepare and adjust marketing plans.

marketing intelligence Everyday information about developments in the marketing environment that managers use to prepare and adjust marketing plans.

marketing intelligence system (MIS) A type of marketing database that builds on the information captured in a customer information system by capturing a greater array of data than basic customer and transaction information through the overlay of information that provides insights into why the customer purchases and using this information to predict future response.

marketing mix A unique blend of product, distribution, promotion, and pricing strategies designed to produce mutually satisfying exchanges with a target market.

marketing myopia Business defined in terms of goods and services rather than in terms of the benefits that customers seek.

marketing objective A statement of what is to be accomplished through marketing activities.

marketing plan A written document that acts as a guidebook of marketing activities for the marketing manager.

marketing planning Designing activities relating to marketing objectives and the changing marketing environment.

marketing research The process of planning, collecting, and analyzing data relevant to a marketing decision.

marketing research objective Specific information needed to solve a market research problem; the objective should provide insightful, decision-making information.

marketing research problem Determining what information is needed and how that information can be obtained efficiently and effectively.

marketing strategy The activity of selecting and describing one or more target markets and developing and maintaining a marketing mix that will produce mutually satisfying exchanges with target markets.

market opportunity analysis The description and estimation of the size and sales potential of market segments that are of interest to the firm and the assessment of key competitors in these market segments.

market orientation Philosophy that assumes that a sale does not depend on an aggressive sales force but rather on a customer's decision to purchase a product.

market penetration A marketing strategy that tries to increase market share among existing customers.

market segment A subgroup of people or organizations sharing one or more characteristics that cause them to have similar product needs.

market segmentation The process of dividing a market into meaningful, relatively similar, and identifiable segments or groups.

market share A company's product sales as a percentage of total sales for that industry.

markup pricing Cost of buying the product from the producer plus amounts for profit and for expenses not otherwise accounted for.

Maslow's hierarchy of needs Method of classifying human needs and motivations into five categories in ascending order of importance: physiological, safety, social, esteem, and self-actualization.

mass communication Communication of a concept or message to a large audience.

mass customization (build-to-order) Production method whereby products are not made until an order is placed by the customer; also a strategy that uses technology to deliver customized services on a mass basis, with products being made according to customer specifications.

mass merchandising Retailing strategy using moderate to low prices on large quantities of merchandise and lower service to stimulate high turnover of products.

master brand A brand so dominant in consumers' minds that they think of it immediately when a product category, use situation, product attribute, or customer benefit is mentioned.

materials-handling system Method of moving inventory into, within, and out of the warehouse.

materials requirement planning (MRP) Inventory control system that manages the replenishment of raw materials, supplies, and components from the supplier to the manufacturer.

maturity stage A period during which sales increase at a decreasing rate.

MC. *See* **marginal cost.**

measurement error Error that occurs when there is a difference between the information desired by the researcher and the information provided by the measurement process.

media mix Combination of media to be used for a promotional campaign.

media planning The series of decisions advertisers make regarding the selection and use of media, allowing the marketer to optimally and cost-effectively communicate the message to the target audience.

media schedule Designation of the media, the specific publications or programs, and the insertion dates of advertising.

medium Channel used to convey a message to a target market.

merchant wholesaler Institution that buys goods from manufacturers and resells them to businesses, government agencies, and other wholesalers or retailers and that receives and takes title to goods, stores them in its own warehouses, and later ships them.

Mercosur The largest new trade agreement, which includes Brazil, Argentina, Uruguay, and Paraguay.

microsegmentation The process of dividing business markets into segments based on the characteristics of decision-making units within a macrosegment.

MIS. *See* **marketing intelligence system.**

mission statement The firm's long-term vision based on a careful analysis of benefits sought by present and potential customers and analysis of existing and anticipated environmental conditions.

modeled data Enhancement information that has already been sorted into distinct groups or clusters of consumers or businesses based on census, household, or business-level data.

modified rebuy Situation in which the purchaser wants some change in the original good or service.

morals The rules people develop as a result of cultural values and norms.

motive Driving force that causes a person to take action to satisfy specific needs.

MR. *See* **marginal review.**

MRP. *See* **materials requirement plan.**

multiculturalism A situation in which all major ethnic groups in an area—such as a city, county, or census tract—are roughly equally represented.

multinational corporation A company that is heavily engaged in international trade, beyond exporting and importing.

multiplier effect (accelerator principle) Phenomenon in which a small increase or decrease in consumer demand can produce a much larger change in demand for the facilities and equipment needed to make the consumer product.

multisegment targeting strategy A strategy that chooses two or more well-defined market segments and develops a distinct marketing mix for each.

mystery shoppers Researchers posing as customers who gather observational data about a store.

N

NAICS. *See* **North American Industry Classification System.**

need recognition Result of an imbalance between actual and desired states.

needs assessment Determination of the customer's specific needs and wants and the range of options a customer has for satisfying them.

negotiation Process of both the salesperson and the prospect offering special concessions in an attempt to arrive at a sales agreement.

networking Process of finding out about potential clients from friends, business contacts, coworkers, acquaintances, and fellow members in professional and civic organizations.

new buy A situation requiring the purchase of a product for the first time.

new product Product new to the world, the market, the producer, the seller, or some combination of these.

new-product committee An ad hoc group whose members manage the new-product development process.

new-product department A department that performs the same functions as a new-product committee but on a full-time basis.

new-product strategy Linking the new-product development process with the objectives of the marketing department, the business unit, and the corporation.

niche One segment of a market.

niche competitive advantage Advantage achieved when a firm seeks to target and effectively serve a small segment of the market.

noise Anything that interferes with, distorts, or slows down the transmission of information.

nonaspirational reference group Group with which an individual does not want to associate.

noncumulative quantity discount A deduction from list price that applies to a single order rather than to the total volume of orders placed during a certain period.

nonmarketing-controlled information source Product information source that is not associated with advertising or promotion.

nonprobability sample Any sample in which little or no attempt is made to get a representative cross section of the population.

nonprofit organization An organization that exists to achieve some goal other than the usual business goals of profit, market share, or return on investment.

nonprofit organization marketing The effort by nonprofit organizations to bring about mutually satisfying exchanges with target markets.

nonstore retailing Shopping without visiting a store.

norm Value or attitude deemed acceptable by a group.

North American Free Trade Agreement (NAFTA) An agreement between Canada, the United States, and Mexico that created the world's largest free-trade zone.

North American Industry Classification System (NAICS) A detailed numbering system developed by the United States, Canada, and Mexico to classify North American business establishments by their main production processes.

O

observation research Research method that relies on three types of observation: people watching people, people watching activity, and machines watching people.

odd–even pricing (psychological pricing) Price tactic that uses odd-numbered prices to connote bargains and even-numbered prices to imply quality.

OEM The acronym OEM stands for original equipment manufacturer. OEM's buy business goods that they incorporate into the products that they produce for eventual sale to other producers or to consumers.

off-price retailer Retailer that sells at prices 25 percent or more below traditional department store prices because it pays cash for its stock and usually doesn't ask for return privileges.

on-line retailing A type of shopping available to consumers with personal computers and access to the Internet.

one-to-one marketing (customer relationship management) An individual marketing method that utilizes customer information to build long-term, personalized, and profitable relationships with each customer.

one-to-one marketing communications process A revised marketing communications process that depicts the individualized communication between the one-to-one marketer and the customer. The process is characterized by the use of personalized communication, the lack of interfering noise, and the ability to capture the response of the customer.

open-ended question An interview question that encourages an answer phrased in the respondent's own words.

opinion leader Individual who influences the opinions of others.

optimizer Type of business customer that considers numerous suppliers, both familiar and unfamiliar, solicits bids, and studies all proposals carefully before selecting one.

order processing system System whereby orders are entered into the supply chain and filled.

outsourcing (contract logistics) Manufacturer's or supplier's use of an independent third party to manage an entire function of the logistics system, such as transportation, warehousing, or order processing.

P

penetration pricing Pricing policy whereby a firm charges a relatively low price for a product initially as a way to reach the mass market.

perception Process by which people select, organize, and interpret stimuli into a meaningful and coherent picture.

perceptual mapping A means of displaying or graphing, in two or more dimensions, the location of products, brands, or groups of products in customers' minds.

perishability Characteristic of services that prevents them from being stored, warehoused, or inventoried.

personality Way of organizing and grouping the consistencies of an individual's reactions to situations.

personalized economy Delivering goods and services at a good value on demand.

personal selling Planned presentation to one or more prospective buyers for the purpose of making a sale.

persuasive labeling Labeling that focuses on a promotional theme or logo with consumer information being secondary.

pioneering advertising Form of advertising designed to stimulate primary demand for a new product or product category.

planned obsolescence The practice of modifying products so those that have already been sold become obsolete before they actually need replacement.

planning The process of anticipating future events and determining strategies to achieve organizational objectives in the future.

point-of-purchase display Promotional display set up at the retailer's location to build traffic, advertise the product, or induce impulse buying.

portfolio matrix Tool for allocating resources among products or strategic business units on the basis of relative market share and market growth rate.

position The place a product, brand, or group of products occupies in consumers' minds relative to competing offerings.

positioning Developing a specific marketing mix to influence potential customers' overall perception of a brand, product line, or organization in general.

poverty of time Lack of time to do anything but work, commute to work, handle family situations, do housework, shop, sleep, and eat.

preapproach A process that describes the "homework" that must be done by the salesperson before he or she contacts the prospect.

predatory pricing The practice of charging a very low price for a product with the intent of driving competitors out of business or out of a market.

predictive modeling A data manipulation technique in which marketers try to determine, based on some past set of occurrences, what the odds are that some other occurrence, such as a response or purchase, will take place in the future.

preindustrial society A society in the second stage of economic development, involving economic and social change and the emergence of a middle class with an entrepreneurial spirit.

premium Extra item offered to the consumer, usually in exchange for some proof of purchase of the promoted product.

prestige pricing Charging a high price to help promote a high-quality image.

price That which is given up in an exchange to acquire a good or service.

price bundling Marketing two or more products in a single package for a special price.

price equilibrium Price at which demand and supply are equal.

price fixing An agreement between two or more firms on the price they will charge for a product.

price lining Practice of offering a product line with several items at specific price points.

price shading Use of discounts by salespeople to increase demand for one or more products in a line.

price skimming Pricing policy whereby a firm charges a high introductory price, often coupled with heavy promotion.

price strategy Basic, long-term pricing framework, which establishes the initial price for a product and the intended direction for price movements over the product life cycle.

primary data Information collected for the first time; can be used for solving the particular problem under investigation.

primary membership group Reference group with which people interact regularly in an informal, face-to-face manner, such as family, friends, or fellow employees.

private brand A brand name owned by a wholesaler or a retailer.

private-label brands Brands that are designed and developed using the retailer's name.

probability sample A sample in which every element in the population has a known statistical likelihood of being selected.

problem child (question mark) In the portfolio matrix, a business unit that shows rapid growth but poor profit margins.

processed materials Products used directly in manufacturing other products.

product Everything, both favorable and unfavorable, that a person receives in an exchange.

product advertising Form of advertising that touts the benefits of a specific good or service.

product category All brands that satisfy a particular type of need.

product development Marketing strategy that entails the creation of new products for present markets; process of converting applications for new technologies into marketable products.

product differentiation A positioning strategy that some firms use to distinguish their products from those of competitors.

product item A specific version of a product that can be designated as a distinct offering among an organization's products.

product life cycle A concept that provides a way to trace the stages of a product's acceptance, from its introduction (birth) to its decline (death).

product line A group of closely related product items.

product line depth The number of product items in a product line.

product line extension Adding additional products to an existing product line in order to compete more broadly in the industry.

product line pricing Setting prices for an entire line of products.

product mix All products an organization sells.

product mix width The number of product lines an organization offers.

product modification Changing one or more of a product's characteristics.

product offering The mix of products offered to the consumer by the retailer, also called the product assortment or merchandise mix.

production orientation A philosophy that focuses on the internal capabilities of the firm rather than on the desires and needs of the marketplace.

profit Revenue minus expenses.

profit maximization A method of setting prices that occurs when marginal revenue equals marginal cost.

promotion Communication by marketers that informs, persuades, and reminds potential buyers of a product in order to influence an opinion or elicit a response.

promotional allowance (trade allowance) Payment to a dealer for promoting the manufacturer's products.

promotional mix Combination of promotion tools—including advertising, public relations, personal selling, and sales promotion—used to reach the target market and fulfill the organization's overall goals.

promotional strategy Plan for the optimal use of the elements of promotion: advertising, public relations, personal selling, and sales promotion.

PSA. *See* **public service advertisement.**

psychographic segmentation Market segmentation on the basis of personality, motives, lifestyles, and geodemographics.

publicity Public information about a company, good, or service appearing in the mass media as a news item.

public relations Marketing function that evaluates public attitudes, identifies areas within the organization that the public may be interested in, and executes a program of action to earn public understanding and acceptance.

public service advertisement (PSA) Announcement that promotes a program of a federal, state, or local government or of a nonprofit organization.

pull strategy Marketing strategy that stimulates consumer demand to obtain product distribution.

pulsing media schedule Media scheduling strategy that uses continuous scheduling throughout the year coupled with a flighted schedule during the best sales periods.

push money Money offered to channel intermediaries to encourage them to "push" products—that is, to encourage other members of the channel to sell the products.

push strategy Marketing strategy that uses aggressive personal selling and trade advertising to convince a wholesaler or a retailer to carry and sell particular merchandise.

pyramid of corporate social responsibility A model that suggests corporate social responsibility is composed of economic, legal, ethical, and philanthropic responsibilities and that firm's economic performance supports the entire sturcture.

Q

quantity discount Price reduction offered to buyers buying in multiple units or above a specified dollar amount.

quota Statement of the individual salesperson's sales objectives, usually based on sales volume alone but sometimes including key accounts (those with greatest potential), new accounts, and specific products.

R

random error Error that occurs because the selected sample is an imperfect representation of the overall population.

random sample Sample arranged in such a way that every element of the population has an equal chance of being selected as part of the sample.

raw materials Unprocessed extractive or agricultural products, such as mineral ore, lumber, wheat, corn, fruits, vegetables, and fish.

reach Number of target consumers exposed to a commercial at least once during a specific period, usually four weeks.

real self-image The way an individual actually perceives himself or herself.

rebate Cash refund given for the purchase of a product during a specific period.

receiver Person who decodes a message.

recency–frequency–monetary analysis (RFM) A data manipulation technique that determines the firm's best customers by identifying those customers who have purchased most recently and most frequently and who have spent the most money.

recession A period of economic activity when income, production, and employment tend to fall—all of which reduce demand for goods and services.

reciprocity A practice in which business purchasers choose to buy from their own customers.

recruited Internet sample Sample in which respondents are prerecruited and, after qualifying to participate, are sent a questionnaire by e-mail or directed to a secure Web site to fill out a questionnaire.

reference group Group in society that influences an individual's purchasing behavior.

referral Recommendation to a salesperson from a customer or business associate.

relationship marketing The name of a strategy that entails forging long-term partnerships with customers.

relationship selling (consultative selling) Sales practice of building, maintaining, and enhancing interactions with customers in order to develop long-term satisfaction through mutually beneficial partnerships.

reliability The ability to perform a service dependably, accurately, and consistently.

repositioning Changing consumers' perceptions of a brand in relation to competing brands.

research design One that specifies which research questions must be answered, how and when the data will be gathered, and how the data will be analyzed.

response list A customer list that includes the names and addresses of individuals who have responded to an offer of some kind, such as by mail, telephone, direct response television, product rebates, contests or sweepstakes, or billing inserts.

responsiveness The ability to provide prompt service.

retailer Channel intermediary that sells mainly to consumers.

retailing All the activities directly related to the sale of goods and services to the ultimate consumer for personal, nonbusiness use.

retailing mix Combination of the six Ps—product, place, promotion, price, personnel, and presentation—to sell goods and services to the ultimate consumer.

return on investment (ROI) Net profit after taxes divided by total assets.

revenue The price charged to customers multiplied by the number of units sold.

RFP. *See* **recency–frequency–monetary analysis.**

ROI. *See* **return on investment.**

routine response behavior Type of decision making exhibited by consumers buying frequently purchased, low-cost goods and services; requires little search and decision time.

S

sales orientation Idea that people will buy more goods and services if aggressive sales techniques are used and that high sales result in high profits.

sales presentation Face-to-face explanation of the sales proposal to a prospective buyer.

sales process (sales cycle) The set of steps a salesperson goes through in a particular organization to sell a particular product or service.

sales promotion Marketing activities—other than personal selling, advertising, and public relations—that stimulate consumer buying and dealer effectiveness.

sales proposal A formal written document or professional presentation that outlines how the salesperson's product or service will meet or exceed the prospect's needs.

sample A subset of a population.

sampling Promotional program that allows the consumer the opportunity to try the product or service for free.

sampling error Error that occurs when a sample somehow does not represent the target population.

satisficer Type of business customer that places an order with the first familiar supplier to satisfy product and delivery requirements.

scaled-response question A closed-ended question designed to measure the intensity of a respondent's answer.

scanner-based research A system for gathering information from a single group of respondents by continuously monitoring the advertising, promotion, and pricing they are exposed to and the things they buy.

scrambled merchandising The tendency to offer a wide variety of nontraditional goods and services under one roof.

screened Internet sample Internet sample with quotas based on desired sample characteristics.

screening The first filter in the product development process that eliminates ideas that are inconsistent with the organization's new-product strategy or are obviously inappropriate for some other reason.

search quality A characteristic that can be easily assessed before purchase.

seasonal discount A price reduction for buying merchandise out of season.

seasonal media schedule Media scheduling strategy that runs advertising only during times of the year when the product is most likely to be used.

secondary data Data previously collected for any purpose other than the one at hand.

secondary membership group Reference group with which people associate less consistently and more for-

mally than a primary membership group, such as a club, professional group, or religious group.

segmentation bases (variables) Characteristics of individuals, groups, or organizations.

selective distortion Process whereby a consumer changes or distorts information that conflicts with his or her feelings or beliefs.

selective distribution Form of distribution achieved by screening dealers to eliminate all but a few in any single area.

selective exposure Process whereby a consumer notices certain stimuli and ignores other stimuli.

selective retention Process whereby a consumer remembers only that information that supports his or her personal beliefs.

self-concept How a consumer perceives himself or herself in terms of attitudes, perceptions, beliefs, and self-evaluations.

selling against the brand Stocking well-known branded items at high prices in order to sell store brands at discounted prices.

sender Originator of the message in the communication process.

service The result of applying human or mechanical efforts to people or objects.

service mark Trademark for a service.

shopping product Product that requires comparison shopping, because it is usually more expensive than a convenience product and found in fewer stores.

simulated (laboratory) market testing Presentation of advertising and other promotion materials for several products, including a test product, to members of the product's target market.

simultaneous product development A new team-oriented approach to new-product development.

single-price tactic Policy of offering all goods and services at the same price.

social class Group of people in a society who are considered nearly equal in status or community esteem, who regularly socialize among themselves both formally and informally, and who share behavioral norms.

socialization process Process by which cultural values and norms are passed down to children.

societal marketing orientation The idea that an organization exists not only to satisfy customer wants and needs and to meet organizational objectives but also to preserve or enhance individuals' and society's long-term best interests.

spatial discrepancy Difference between the location of the producer and the location of widely scattered markets.

specialty discount store Retail store that offers a nearly complete selection of single-line merchandise and uses self-service, discount prices, high volume, and high turnover.

specialty product A particular item that consumers search extensively for and are very reluctant to accept substitutes for.

specialty store Retail store specializing in a given type of merchandise.

star In the portfolio matrix, a business unit that is a fast-growing market leader.

status quo pricing Pricing objective that maintains existing prices or meets the competition's prices.

stimulus Any unit of input affecting one or more of the five senses: sight, smell, taste, touch, hearing.

stimulus discrimination Learned ability to differentiate among similar products.

stimulus generalization Form of learning that occurs when one response is extended to a second stimulus similar to the first.

stitching niches Strategy for multicultural marketing that combines ethnic, age, income, and lifestyle markets, on some common basis, to form a large market.

straight commission Method of compensation in which the salesperson is paid some percentage when a sale is made.

straight rebuy Buying situation in which the purchaser reorders the same goods or services without looking for new information or investigating other suppliers.

straight salary Method of compensation in which the salesperson receives a salary regardless of sales productivity.

strategic alliance (strategic partnership) A cooperative agreement between business firms.

strategic business unit (SBU) A subgroup of a single business or collection of related businesses within the larger organization.

strategic channel alliance Cooperative agreement between business firms to use the other's already established distribution channel.

strategic planning The managerial process of creating and maintaining a fit between the organization's objectives and resources and evolving market opportunities.

strategic window The limited period during which the "fit" between the key requirements of a market and the particular competencies of a firm are at an optimum.

subculture Homogeneous group of people who share elements of the overall culture as well as unique elements of their own group.

supercenter Retail store that combines groceries and general merchandise goods with a wide range of services.

supermarket A large, departmentalized, self-service retailer that specializes in food and nonfood items.

supplementary services A group of services that support or enhance the core service.

supplies Consumable items that do not become part of the final product.

supply The quantity of a product that will be offered to the market by a supplier at various prices for a specified period.

supply chain The connected chain of all of the business entities, both internal and external to the company, that perform or support the logistics function.

supply chain management Management system that coordinates and integrates all of the activities performed by supply chain members into a seamless process, from source to the point of consumption that results in enhanced customer and economic value.

supply chain team Entire group of individuals who orchestrate the movement of goods, services, and information from the source to the consumer.

survey research the most popular technique for gathering primary data in which a researcher interacts with people to obtain facts, opinions, and attitudes.

sustainable competitive advantage A differential advantage that cannot be copied by the competition.

SWOT analysis One that identifies internal strengths (S) and weaknesses (W) and also examines external opportunities (O) and threats (T).

T

takeoff economy The third stage of economic development that involves a period of transition from a developing to a developed nation.

tangibles The physical evidence of a service, including the physical facilities, tools, and equipment used to provide the service.

target market A group of people or organizations for which an organization designs, implements, and maintains a marketing mix intended to meet the needs of that group, resulting in mutually satisfying exchanges.

teamwork Collaborative efforts of people to accomplish common objectives.

telemarketing The use of the telephone to sell directly to consumers.

temporal discrepancy A situation that occurs when a product is produced but a customer is not ready to buy it.

test marketing The limited introduction of a product and a marketing program to determine the reactions of potential customers in a market situation.

trade allowance Price reduction offered by manufacturers to intermediaries, such as wholesalers and retailers.

trade loading Practice of temporarily lowering the price to induce wholesalers and retailers to buy more goods than can be sold in a reasonable time.

trademark The exclusive right to use a brand or part of a brand.

trade sales promotion Sales promotion activities targeted to a channel member, such as a wholesaler or retailer.

traditional society A society in the earliest stages of economic development, largely agricultural, with a social structure and value system that provide little opportunity for upward mobility.

two-part pricing Price tactic that charges two separate amounts to consume a single good or service.

U

UCC. *See* **Uniform Commercial Code filings**.

unbundling Reducing the bundle of services that comes with the basic product.

undifferentiated targeting strategy Marketing approach that views the market as one big market with no individual segments and thus requires a single marketing mix.

unfair trade practice acts Laws that prohibit wholesalers and retailers from selling below cost.

Uniform Commercial Code (UCC) filings Filings by banks with government agencies that identify goods that are leased or pledged as collateral.

uniform delivered pricing Price tactic in which the seller pays the actual freight charges and bills every purchaser an identical, flat freight charge.

Uniform Reference Locator (URL) Similar to a street address in that it identifies a unique location on the Web.

unique selling proposition Desirable, exclusive, and believable advertising appeal selected as the theme for a campaign.

unitary elasticity Situation in which total revenue remains the same when prices change.

universal product codes (UPCs) Series of thick and thin vertical lines (bar codes), readable by computerized optical scanners, that represent numbers used to track products.

universe The population from which a sample will be drawn.

unrestricted Internet sample One in which anyone with a computer and modem can fill out the questionnaire.

unsought product A product unknown to the potential buyer or a known product that the buyer does not actively seek.

UPCs. *See* **universal product codes.**

URL. *See* **Uniform Reference Locator.**

Uruguay Round An agreement to dramatically lower trade barriers worldwide.

usage-rate segmentation Dividing a market by the amount of product bought or consumed.

V

value Enduring belief that a specific mode of conduct is personally or socially preferable to another mode of conduct.

value-based pricing The price set at a level that seems to the customer to be a good price compared to the prices of other options.

value impressions Features of a product or service that signal value to the customer.

variable costs Costs that vary with changes in the level of output.

venture team A market-oriented group staffed by a small number of representatives from different disciplines.

vertical conflict Channel conflict that occurs between different levels in a marketing channel, most typically between the manufacturer and wholesaler or between the manufacturer and retailer.

W

want Recognition of an unfulfilled need and a product that will satisfy it.

warehouse membership clubs Limited-service merchant wholesalers that sell a limited selection of brand-name appliances, household items, and groceries on a cash-and-carry basis to members, usually small businesses and groups.

warranty Confirmation of the quality or performance of a good or service.

World Trade Organization (WTO) A new trade organization that replaces the old General Agreement on Trade and Tariffs (GATT).

World Wide Web (Web) Component of the Internet designed to simplify text and images.

WTO. *See* **World Trade Organization.**

Y

yield management systems (YMS) A technique for adjusting prices that uses complex mathematical software to profitably fill unused capacity by discounting early purchases, limiting early sales at these discounted prices, and overbooking capacity.

Z

zone pricing Modification of uniform delivered pricing that divides the United States (or the total market) into segments or zones and charges a flat freight rate to all customers in a given zone.

endnotes

CHAPTER 1

1. "Unit of One," edited by Lucy McCauley, *Fast Company,* March 2000, p. 94. Reprinted by permission of *Fast Company* ©2000.
2. "About Us," American Marketing Association [online]. Available http://www.ama.org/about/ama/markdef.asp. June 1, 2000.
3. Philip Kotler, *Marketing Management,* 10th ed. (Englewood Cliffs, NJ: Prentice-Hall, 2000), p. 11.
4. Scott Kirsner, "The Customer Experience," *Net Company,* pp. 12–33.
5. Laurie Freeman, "Keeping Em Happy," *Marketing News,* May 8, 2000, p. 21.
6. Rekha Balu, "Listen Up," *Fast Company,* May 2000, pp. 304–316.
7. McCauley, p. 93.
8. McCauley, p. 120.
9. J. W. Marriott and Kathi Ann Brown, *The Spirit to Serve: Marriott's Way* (New York: Harper Business, 1997), p. 5.
10. Balu, p. 312.
11. David W. Cravens, Charles W. Lamb, Jr., and Victoria Crittenden, *Strategic Marketing Management Cases* (New York: McGraw-Hill, 1999), p. 81.
12. Marcia Stepanek, "Using the Net For Brainstorming," *Business Week,* December 13, 1999, p. EB 55–59.
13. Cravens, Lamb, and Crittenden, p. 79.
14. Otis Port, "Customers Move into the Driver's Seat," *Business Week,* October 4, 1999, pp. 103–106.
15. Kirsner, p. 14.
16. Philip E. Hendrix, "Build It and They Will Come," *Marketing Management,* Winter 1999, pp. 31–35.
17. "Top 10 Things That Irked Holiday Shoppers," *Business Week,* February 7, 2000, p. EB12.
18. Leonard L. Berry, *Discovering the Soul of Service* (New York: Free Press, 1999), p. 147.
19. "Focus on the Customer," *Fortune,* September 7, 1998, p. 52.
20. Austen Mulinder, "Hear Today . . . or Gone Tomorrow? Winners Listen to Customers," *Retailing Issues Letter,* September 1999, p. 3.
21. Dana Jones, "Respondez-vous, b-to-b," *Marketing News,* May 22, 2000, pp. 1, 9, 10.
22. Nigel Piercy, *Tales From the Marketplace* (Oxford, England: Butterworth Heinemann, 1999), p. 22.
23. Robert Levering and Milton Moskowitz, "The 100 Best Companies to Work For," *Fortune,* January 10, 2000, pp. 81–110.
24. Berry, pp. 174–175.
25. Dave Carpenter, "Britannica Offers 32-Volume Encyclopedia Free on Internet," *Fort Worth Star-Telegram,* October 20, 1999, p. 7A.
26. Piercy, p. 22–24.
27. Kotler, p. 22.
28. Gina Imperato, "Get Your Career in Sight," *Fast Company,* March 2000, p. 326.

CHAPTER 2

1. Brad Stone, "Amazon's Pet Projects," *Newsweek,* June 21, 1999, p. 56.
2. Leslie Kaufman with Saul Hansell, "Holiday Lessons in Online Retailing," *New York Times,* January 2, 2000, p. C3.
3. Mara Reinstein and Steve McClellan, "Super Bowl Spots Don't Score," *Broadcasting & Cable,* February 7, 2000, p. 28.
4. Joel Enos, "Vying to Be the Top Dog," *Upside,* March 2000, pp. 160–165.
5. Charlie Fletcher, "Pets.com Publishes Print Magazine," *Catalog Age,* June 2000, p. 12.
6. Diane Rezendes Khirallah, "Pets.com Swallows Rival," *Informationweek,* June 19, 2000, p. 18.
7. Tary Knight, "The Relationship Between Entrepreneurial Orientation, Strategy, and Performance: An Empirical Investigation," in Barbara Stern, George Zinkhan, Peter Gordon, and Bert Kellerman, eds., *AMA Marketing Educators' Conference Proceedings* (Chicago: American Marketing Association, 1995), pp. 272–273.

8. Thor Valdmanis, "Nabisco Could Pick Buyer Today. Meeting Could Decide New Owner of Ritz Crackers, Oreos, LifeSavers," *USA Today,* June 23, 2000, p. 1B
9. "Wall Street Is Bracing For a Globalstar Bankruptcy, Wall Street Analysts Warn," *Satellite News;* June 19, 2000, p. 1
10. "Business Digest," *New York Times,* June 24, 2000, p. C1
11. Stephanie Thomson, "Homemade Frozen Goodness," *Advertising Age* , May 1, 2000, pp. 3, 73.
12. Levitt, Theodore, "Marketing Myopia," *Harvard Business Review,* September 1, 1975, pp. 1–14.
13. Saturn Corporation, *Face to Face with the Future* (Detroit: Saturn Corporation, 1994).
14. Anne Fisher, "The World's Most Admired Companies," *Fortune,* October 27, 1997, pp. 220–240.
15. Jennifer Merritt, "The Belle of the Golf Balls," *Business Week,* July 29, 1996, p. 6.
16. Scott Hensley, "New Race Heats Up to Turn Gene Information into Drug Discoveries," *Wall Street Journal,* June 26 2000, p. B1, B4.
17. Who Really Makes That Cute Little Beer?" *Wall Street Journal,* April 15, 1996, pp. A1, A8.
18. Stanley Slater and John Narver, "Improving Performance in the Market Oriented Business," in Barbara Stern, et al., ed., 1995 *American Marketing Association Educators' Conference Proceedings,* p. 367.
19. Carrie Shook, "The Art of Conspicuous Consumption," *Forbes,* June 1, 1988, pp. 73–76.
20. Jim Wilson, "Airbag Shield Foils Terrorists," *Popular Mechanics,* June 2000, p. 17.
21. Sandra I. Irwin, "Smart Armor Shield Deploys Like Air Bag to Stop Bullets," *National Defense,* May 2000, p. 23.

CHAPTER 3

1. Larry Greenberg, "Marketing the Great White North, Eh?" *Wall Street Journal,* April 21, 2000, p. B1.

2. From "The Emerging Culture" by Paul H. Ray, *American Demographics,* February 1997. Reprinted with permission from American Demographics magazine, © 1997 PRIMEDIA Intertec, Stamford, CT.

3. Leonard L. Berry, A. Parasuraman, and Valarie A. Zeithaml, "Improving Service Quality in America: Lessons Learned," *Academy of Management Executive* 8, No. 2, 1994, p. 36.

4. "No Place Like Home," *Wall Street Journal,* June 16, 1997, p. R4.

5. David Wolfe, "The Psychological Center of Gravity," *American Demographics,* April 1998, pp. 16–19.

6. James Steinberg, "The Millennial Mind Set," *American Demographics,* January 1999, pp. 60–64.

7. "Leisure Squeeze," *Roper Reports,* January 1999, p. 1.

8. Ibid.

9. "For Harried Workers in the Twenty-First Century, Six Trends to Watch," *Wall Street Journal,* December 29, 1999, p. B1.

10. "Latest Backlash Against Dual Earners Ignores Some Realities," *Wall Street Journal,* May 14, 1997, p. B1.

11. "Sorry, Boys—Donna Reed Is Still Dead," *American Demographics,* September 1995, pp. 13-14.

12. "Women-Owned Businesses Booming, But So Are Obstacles," *Associated Press Newswires,* April 11, 2000.

13. Gerry Myers, "Selling to Women," *American Demographics,* April 1996, pp. 36–42.

14. Ibid.

15. "Generation Y," *Business Week,* February 15, 1999, pp. 81–88.

16. Ibid.

17. "Where the Breakers Are," *American Demographics,* March 1999, pp. 50–51.

18. "Marketing to Generation X," *Advertising Age,* February 6, 1995, p. 27.

19. Susan Mitchell, "How to Talk to Young Adults," *American Demographics,* April 1993, pp. 50–54.

20. "Understanding Generation X," *Marketing Research,* Spring 1993, pp. 54–55.

21. "Hotels Target Generation X; Young Travelers Demand High-Tech Services, Amenities," *USA Today,* February 10, 2000, p. 1B.

22. "Harley-Davidson's New 'Buell Blast' Roars into 18–34 Year-Old Novice Market," *PR Newswire,* March 16, 2000.

23. "Survey Sheds Light on Typical Boomer," *Marketing News,* January 31, 1994, p. 2.

24. Cheryl Russell, "The Master Trend," *American Demographics,* October 1993, pp. 28–37.

25. Russell, pp. 28–37.

26. "Booming Business," *American Demographics,* December 1999, pp. 32–35.

27. Ruth Hamel, "Raging Against Aging," *American Demographics,* March 1990, pp. 42–45.

28. "American Maturity," *American Demographics,* March 1993, pp. 31–42.

29. "Boomers Come of Old Age," *Marketing News,* January 15, 1996, pp. 1, 6.

30. "Mature Market Often Misunderstood," *Marketing News,* August 28, 1995, p. 28.

31. Michael Major, "Promoting to the Mature Market," *Promo,* November 1990, p. 7.

32. "Bond Stronger with Age," *Advertising Age,* March 28, 1994, pp. 5–6.

33. Charles Schewe and Geoffrey Meredith, "Digging Deep to Delight the Mature Adult Customer," *Marketing Management,* Winter 1995, pp. 21–34.

34. "The Hottest Metros," *American Demographics,* April 1995, pp. 4–5.

35. "The Most Populous Metros," *American Demographics,* June 1997, p. 17.

36. William Frey, "The New White Flight," *American Demographics,* April 1994, pp. 40–47.

37. "Influx of Immigrants Benefits American Economy Overall," *Fort Worth Star-Telegram,* May 18, 1997, p. A18.

38. "Work Slowdown," *American Demographics,* March 1996, pp. 4–7.

39. www.census.gov (April 11, 2000).

40. Dunn, p. 40; "How to Sell Across Cultures," *American Demographics,* March 1994, pp. 56–58.

41. Jeffrey O. Zbar, "With Right Touch, Marketers Can Hit Multiple Cultures," *Advertising Age,* November 16, 1998, p. 24.

42. Jon Berry, "An Empire of Niches," *Superbrands: A Special Supplement to Adweek's Marketing Week,* Fall 1991, pp. 17–22.

43. "The Web Goes Multicultural," *Advertising Age,* November 29, 1999, pp. 51, 54.

44. Ibid.

45. Ibid.

46. www.census.gov (April 24, 2000).

47. U.S. Department of Commerce: Bureau of Economic Analysis (www.bea.gov), April 26, 2000.

48. "How Prosperity is Reshaping the American Economy," *Business Week,* February 14, 2000, pp. 101–110.

49. Ibid.

50. The American Airlines story is from Scott McCartney, "American Plays Hardball with a Start-Up Over All-First-Class Flights," *Wall Street Journal,* March 9, 2000, pp. B1, B4.

51. Jack Neff, "P&G and Unilever's Giant Headaches," *Advertising Age,* May 24, 1999, pp. 23–24.

52. Ibid.

53. Based on Edward Stevens, *Business Ethics* (New York: Paulist Press, 1979).

54. Anusorn Singhapakdi, Skott Vitell, and Kenneth Kraft, "Moral Intensity and Ethical Decisionmaking of Marketing Professionals," *Journal of Business Research* 36, March 1996, pp. 245–255; Ishmael Akaah and Edward Riordan, "Judgments of Marketing Professionals About Ethical Issues in Marketing Research: A Replication and Extension," *Journal of Marketing Research,* February 1989, pp. 112–120; see also Shelby Hunt, Lawrence Chonko, and James Wilcox, "Ethical Problems of Marketing Researchers," *Journal of Marketing Research,* August 1984, pp. 309–324; Kenneth Andrews, "Ethics in Practice," *Harvard Business Review,* September-October 1989, pp. 99–104; Thomas Dunfee, Craig Smith, and William T. Ross, Jr., "Social Contracts and Marketing Ethics," *Journal of Marketing,* July 1999, pp. 14–32; and Jay Handleman and Stephen Arnold, "The Role of Marketing Actions with a Social Dimension: Appeals to the Institutional Environment," *Journal of Marketing,* July 1999, pp. 33–48.

55. O. C. Ferrell, Debbie Thorne, and Linda Ferrell, "Legal Pressure for Ethical Compliance in Marketing," *Proceedings of the American Marketing Association,* Summer 1995, pp. 412–413.

56. This section adapted from Archie B. Carroll, "The Pyramid of Corporate Social Responsibility: Toward the Moral Management of Organizational Stakeholders," *Business Horizons,* July-August 1991, pp. 39–48; see also Kirk Davidson, "Marketers Must Accept Greater Responsibilities," *Marketing News,* February 2, 1998, p. 6.

57. Stephanie N. Mehta, "Black Entrepreneurs Benefit from Social Responsibility," *Wall Street Journal,* September 19, 1995, p. B1.

58. "Wrigley Ads to Focus on Minority Health," *Wall Street Journal,* June 4, 1997, p. B1.

59. "Business Ethics: Three Companies Show How Business Might Evolve Ethically in the Next Century," *PR Newswires,* November 16, 1999.

60. Ibid.

61. "The Best Corporate Reputations in America," *Wall Street Journal,* September 23, 1999, pp. B1, B20.

62. "The Promise of the New Economy Is at Risk," *Fast Company,* March 2000, pp. 166–167.

CHAPTER 4

1. Clifford Krauss, "Selling to Argentina," *New York Times,* December 5, 1999, p. BU7.

2. "Pillsbury Presses Flour Power in India," *Wall Street Journal,* May 5, 1999, pp. B1, B4.

3. "Potato Chips—To Go Global—Or So Pepsi Bets," *Wall Street Journal,* November 30, 1995, pp. B1, B10.

4. Statistics obtained from www.usatradeonline.gov, April 19, 2000.

5. Ibid.

6. Ibid.

7. Ibid.

8. Gene Koretz, "Awaiting the Export Surge," *Business Week*, March 2, 1998, p. 2.

9. "The Pros and Cons of Globalization," *Business Week,* April 24, 2000, p. 41.

10. "Anti-trade/Pro-Poverty," *Fortune,* January 10, 2000, p. 40.

11. Ibid.

12. "Pros and Cons," p. 41.

13. "Globalization: What Americans are Worried About," *Business Week,* April 24, 2000, p. 44.

14. Ibid.

15. Neil Jacoby, "The Multinational Corporation," *Center Magazine,* May 1970, p. 37.

16. "The Stateless Corporation," *Business Week,* May 14, 1990, pp. 98–105; see also Bruce Kogut, "What Makes a Company Global?" *Harvard Business Review,* January-February 1999, pp. 165–170; and Neil Bruce Holbert, "Worldwide Marketing Must Not Assume Imperialistic Air," *Marketing News,* February 14, 2000, p. 20.

17. Theodore Levitt, "The Globalization of Markets," *Harvard Business Review*, May-June 1983, pp. 92–102.

18. Saeed Samiee and Kendall Roth, "The Influence of Global Marketing Standardization on Performance," *Journal of Marketing,* April 1992, pp. 1–17; see also Aviv Shoham, "Global Marketing Standardization," *Journal of Global Marketing*, September 1995, pp. 91–119.

19. "For Peruvians, Fizzy Yello Drink Is the Real Thing," *International Herald Tribune,* December 27, 1995, p. 3.

20. Sherrie Zhan, "Marketing Across Cultures," *World Trade,* February 1999, pp. 80–82.

21. "Looking for Sincerity in Japan? It's a Wrap," *International Herald Tribune,* December 21, 1999, p. 2.

22. "Global Products Require Name-Finders," *Wall Street Journal,* April 11, 1996, p. B5.

23. Zahn, "Marketing," p. 80.

24. "Don't Be an Ugly-American Manager," *Fortune,* October 16, 1995, p. 225.

25. "Portrait of the World," *Marketing News,* August 28, 1995, pp. 20–21.

26. Zulia Hu and Mohsin Kahn, "Why Is China Growing So Fast?" *International Monetary Fund Staff Papers,* March 1997, pp. 103–131.

27. "Dell Cracks China," *Fortune,* June 21, 1999, pp. 120–125.

28. "Profiting from India's Strong Middle Class," *Marketing News,* October 7, 1996, p. 6.

29. "China Fosters Price-Fixing Cartels as Economy Crimps Firms' Profits," *Wall Street Journal,* December 3, 1999, p. A17.

30. "Enron's Plant in India Was Dead; This Month It Will Go On Stream," *Wall Street Journal,* February 5, 1999, pp. A1, A6.

31. "Clinton Moves to Impose Punitive Tariffs on Imports in Some Steel Industries," *Wall Street Journal,* February 14, 2000, p. A36.

32. www.wto.org, April 18, 2000.

33. "CD Piracy Flourishes in China, and West Supplies the Equipment," *Wall Street Journal,* April 24, 1997, pp. A1, A12.

34. "U.S., Canada, Mexico Announce New NAFTA Initiatives," *Dow Jones News Service,* April 26, 1999.

35. "The Real Winner: Canada Leads the Investment Race," *Business Week,* September 27, 1999, p. 34.

36. "Trade Debate," *Houston Chronicle,* April 19, 2000, p. 28.

37. "Latin Nations, Unsure of U.S. Motives, Make Their Own Trade Pacts," *Wall Street Journal,* January 9, 1996, pp. A1, A4; see also Masaaki Kotabe and Maria Cecilia Coutinho de Arruda, "South America's Free Trade Gambit," *Marketing Management,* Spring 1998, pp. 39–46.

38. "Road to Unification," *Sky,* June 1993, pp. 32–41.

39. "Here Comes the Euro," *Business Week,* April 27, 1998, pp. 90–113; and "Euro Wins Wide Acceptance Before Milestone Summit," April 30, 1998, pp. A12–A14.

40. Tony Horwitz, "Europe's Borders Fade, and People and Goods Can Move More Freely," *Wall Street Journal,* May 18, 1993, pp. A1, A10.

41. www.usatradeonline.gov.

42. "USA: Marvel Grants 4Kids License for Some of Its Brands," *Reuters English News Service,* April 20, 2000.

43. "Canada's MGI in Bundling Deal with Dell," *Reuters English News Service,* April 20, 2000.

44. "The Trade Gap Won't Be All That Bad," *Business Week,* March 30, 1998, p. 24.

45. "Mondavi Likes the Taste of Global Joint Ventures," *The Plain Dealer,* December 15, 1999, p. 3F.

46. PepsiCo Forms Big Venture in Latin America," *Wall Street Journal,* November 25, 1999, pp. A12, A13.
47. "AOL Launches New Assault in Europe by Building System of Local Alliances," *Wall Street Journal,* February 27, 1998, p. B11.
48. "Making Global Alliances Work," *Fortune,* December 17, 1990, pp. 121–123.
49. "P&G Squabbles with Vietnamese Partner," *Wall Street Journal,* February 27, 1998, p. A10.
50. "Overseas, The Price Is Right," *Business Week,* March 15, 1999, p. 8.
51. "Federal Express, UPS Battle for a Foothold in Asia," *Wall Street Journal,* January 22, 1997, pp. B1, B8.
52. "Old World, New Investment," *Business Week,* October 7, 1996, pp. 50–51.
53. "TI Teams Up in Asia," *Dallas Morning News,* February 4, 1996, p. H1.
54. "Herbal Remedies Aimed at East and West," *Wall Street Journal,* January 31, 2000, p. A26.
55. "Can TV Save the Planet," *American Demographics,* May 1996, pp. 43–47.
56. "Europe's Unity Undoes a U.S. Exporter," *Wall Street Journal,* April 1, 1996, p. B1.
57. "For Coke in India, Thums Up Is the Real Thing," *Wall Street Journal,* April 29, 1998, pp. B1, B2.
58. "A Simple Plan In a Complex World," *INC,* February 1999, p. 45.
59. "McD's Self-Defense Is Its French Connection," *Advertising Age,* September 13, 1999, p. 26.
60. "Kiddi Just Fine in the U.K., but Here It's Binky," *Marketing News,* August 28, 1995, p. 8.
61. "Why Countertrade Is Hot," *Fortune,* June 29, 1992, p. 25; Nathaniel Gilbert, "The Case for Countertrade," *Across the Board,* May 1992, pp. 43–45.
62. "Barter Grows As Trade Deals Hit Problems," *Financial Times,* September 17, 1999, p. 7.
63. "To All U.S. Managers Upset by Regulations: Try Germany or Japan," *Wall Street Journal,* December 14, 1995, p. A1.
64. "In the Unified Europe, Shipping Freight by Rail is a Journey into the Past," *Wall Street Journal,* March 29, 1999, p. A1, A8.

65. "In Japan, the Hub of E-Commerce Is a 7-Eleven," *Wall Street Journal,* November 1, 1999, pp. B1, B4.
66. "In Europe, Surfing a Web of Red Tape," *Wall Street Journal,* October 29, 1999, pp. B1, B4.
67. "E-Commerce Discovers Europe," *International Herald Tribune,* December 24, 1999, p. 15.
68. The steel market story is from Robert Guy Mathews, "Tariffs Impede Trade Via Web on a Global Scale," *Wall Street Journal,* April 17, 2000, pp. B1, B4.
69. Hal Lancaster, "Global Managers Need Boundless Sensitivity, Rugged Constitutions," *Wall Street Journal,* October 13, 1998, p. B1.

CHAPTER 5

1. Ellen Neuborne and Kathleen Kerwin, "Generation Y: Today's Teens—The Biggest Bulge Since Boomers—May Force Marketers to Toss Their Old Tricks," *Business Week,* February 15, 1999, p. 80; Laurie Freeman, "Fun with an Edge: Marketing to Gen Y," *Food & Beverage Marketing,* April 1999; Rachel McLauglin, "Targeting Teens," *Target Marketing,* January 2000, p. 84; Stacy Kravetz, "A Fad Flames Out, and Retailers Get Burned," *Wall Street Journal,* January 21, 1999, pp. B1, B10; Leigh Gallagher, "Rebound," *Forbes,* May 3, 1999, p. 60; Sally Beatty and Carol Hymowitz, "How MTV Stays Tuned in to Teens," *Wall Street Journal,* March 21, 2000, pp. B1, B4.
2. Stacy Kravetz, "Surprise! A Home Builder (Finally) Surveys Buyers," *Wall Street Journal,* February 11, 1998, pp. B1, B12.
3. Barbara Carton, "It's Niche! Twins, Triplets and Beyond," *Wall Street Journal,* February 2, 1999, pp. B1, B4.
4. Suzanne Bidlake, "P&G to Roll Laundry Tablet in Europe," *Advertising Age,* March 1, 1999, p. 18.
5. Nancy Ten Kate, "The Marketplace for Medicine," *American Demographics,* February 1998, p. 34.
6. Nancy Shepherdson, "New Kids on the Lot," *American Demographics,* January 2000.
7. Kate, "The Marketplace for Medicine," p. 34.

8. Ibid.
9. D. S. Sundaram and Michael D. Richard, "Perceived Risk and Information Acquisition Process of Computer Mail-Order Shoppers," in *1995 Southern Marketing Association Proceedings,* eds. Brian T. Engelland and Denise T. Smart (Houston: Southern Marketing Association), 1995, pp. 322–326.
10. Eric D. Bruce and Sam Fullerton, "Discount Pricing as a Mediator of the Consumer's Evoked Set," in *1995 Atlantic Marketing Association Proceedings,* eds. Donald L. Thompson and Cathy Owens Swift (Orlando: Atlantic Marketing Association), pp. 32–36.
11. F. Kelly Shruptrine, "Warranty Coverage: How Important in Purchasing an Automobile? In *1995 Southern Marketing Association Proceedings,* eds. Brian T. Engelland and Denise T. Smart (Houston: Southern Marketing Association), 1995, pp. 300–303.
12. Ronald Alsop, "The Best Corporation Reputations in America: Just as in Politics, Trust, Reliability Pay Off Over Time," *Wall Street Journal,* September 23, 1999, p. B1, B20; Ronald Alsop, "The Best Corporate Reputations in America: Johnson & Johnson (Think Babies!) Turns Up Tops," *Wall Street Journal,* September 23, 1999, p. B1, B6.
13. Don Umphrey, "Consumer Costs: A Determinant of Upgrading or Downgrading of Cable Service," *Journalism Quarterly,* Winter 1991, pp. 698–708.
14. Frederic M. Biddle, "After Years of Disdain, Korean Cars Rev Up Sales," *Wall Street Journal,* August 18, 1999, p. B1, B4.
15. Brandon Mitchener, "Mercedes Dealers Offer New Kind of Test Drive," *Wall Street Journal,* March 26, 1998, p. B8.
16. Stephanie Thompson, "Marketers Embrace Latest Health Claims," *Advertising Age,* February 28, 2000, pp. 20–22.
17. Ibid; see also John Urquhart, "A Health Food Hits Big Time," *Wall Street Journal,* August 3, 1999, pp. B1, B4.
18. Bill Stoneman, "Beyond Rocking the Ages: An Interview with J. Walker Smith," *American Demographics,* May 1998, pp. 44–49.

19. David B. Wolfe, "The Psychological Center of Gravity," *American Demographics*, April 1998, pp. 16–19.

20. Jennifer Harrison, "Advertising Joins the Journey of the Soul," *American Demographics*, June 1997.

21. Robert Levine, "The Pace of Life in 31 Countries," *American Demographics*, November 1997, pp. 20–29; Robert Levine, "Re-Learning to Tell Time," *American Demographics*, January 1998, pp. 20–25.

22. Jerry W. Thomas, "Finding Unspoken Reasons for Consumers' Choices," *Marketing News*, June 8, 1998, p. 10.

23. Miriam Jordan, "Pillsbury Presses Flour Power in India," *Wall Street Journal*, May 5, 1999, pp. B1, B4.

24. Joshua Harris Prager, "People with Disabilities Are Next Consumer Niche," *Wall Street Journal*, December 15, 1999, pp. B1, B6.

25. Ronald Alsop, "Cracking the Gay Market Code," *Wall Street Journal*, June 29, 1999, pp. B1, B4.

26. Jennifer Lach, "From Bland to Brand," *American Demographics*, March 1999.

27. Gary McWilliams, "Gateway Marketing Effort Has a Latin Pitch," *Wall Street Journal*, September 30, 1999, p. B10.

28. Rebecca Piirto Heath, "Life on Easy Street," *American Demographics*, April 1997.

29. Elia Kacapyr, "Are You Middle Class?" *American Demographics*, October 1996.

30. Rebecca Piirto Heath, "The New Working Class," *American Demographics*, January 1998, pp. 51–55.

31. Heath, "Life on Easy Street."

32. Michael J. Weiss, "A Tale of Two Cheeses," *American Demographics*, February 1998, pp. 16–17.

33. Grahame R. Dowling and Richard Staelin, "A Model of Perceived Risk and Intended Risk-Handling Activity," *Journal of Consumer Research*, June 1994, pp. 119–134.

34. Barbara Cooke, "Radar Fine-Tuned to 'Cool' Sets Some Teens Apart," *Chicago Tribune*, March 5, 2000, p. 1.

35. Norihiko Shirouzu, "Japan's High-School Girls Excel in Art of Setting Trends," *Wall Street Journal*, April 24, 1998, pp. B1, B6.

36. Ibid.

37. Nina Munk, "Peddling Cool: How Teens Buy," *Fortune*, April 13, 1998, pp. 28–30.

38. Hilary Stout, "Can Turkey Scaloppine Transform the Selling of a Typecast Bird?" *Wall Street, Journal*, September 10, 1999, p. B1.

39. Stephen E. Frank, "Tiger Woods Plays American Express," *Wall Street Journal*, May 20, 1997, pp. B1, B14.

40. "Chrysler, Johnson & Johnson Are New Product Marketers of the Year," *Marketing News*, May 8, 1995, pp. E2, E11.

41. James U. McNeal, "Tapping the Three Kids' Markets," *American Demographics*, April 1998, pp. 37–41.

42. Janice Rosenberg, "Tweens Mesh Latest Fads, Moms & Dads," *Advertising Age*, February 14, 2000, p. 40.

43. Nancy Shepherdson, "New Kids on the Lot," *American Demographics*, January 2000.

44. Matthew Klein, "He Shops, She Shops," *American Demographics*, March 1998, pp. 34–35.

45. Wendy Bounds and Rebecca Quick, "Men Who Shop: Retailers Target Male Shoppers as Santa's New Helpers; Gift-Wrapping Tips for Guys," *Wall Street Journal*, November 12, 1999, pp. W1, W4.

46. Diane Crispell, "Fruit of the Boom," *Marketing Tools*, April 1998.

47. Alison Stein Wellner, "Who's in the House?" *American Demographics*, January 2000.

48. Ibid.

49. Dana Milbank, "More Dads Raise Families Without Mom," *Wall Street Journal*, October 3, 1997, pp. B1, B2.

50. David Kiley, "Not Your Father's SUV," *American Demographics*, January 1999.

51. Jean Halliday, "Mitsubishi Kicks Off 2001 Campaigns," *Advertising Age*, March 13, 2000, pp. 20–21.

52. Nora J. Rifon and Molly Catherine Ziske, "Using Weight Loss Products: The Roles of Involvement, Self-Efficacy and Body Image," in *1995 AMA Educators' Proceedings*, eds. Barbara B. Stern and George M. Zinkhan (Chicago: American Marketing Association, 1995), pp. 90–98.

53. Jim Carlton, "Men Are on the Minds of Hair-Dye Makers," *Wall Street Journal*, January 17, 2000, p. B11; Michael J. Weiss, "Father's Day Special: Guys Who Dye," *American Demographics*, June 1999.

54. Cristina Merrill, "Mother's Work Is Never Done," *American Demographics*, September 1999.

55. William D. Wells and David Prensky, *Consumer Behavior* (New York: Wiley, 1996), p. 46.

56. Sarah Hall, "What Color Is Your Cart?" *Self*, September 1999, p. 150.

57. Judann Pollack, "Heinz Waxes Nostalgic Over Revived Glass bottle," *Advertising Age*, May 3, 1999, p. 17.

58. Joshua Rosenbaum, "Guitar Maker Looks for a New Key," *Wall Street Journal*, February 11, 1998, p. B1, B5.

59. Elizabeth J. Wilson, "Using the Dollarmetric Scale to Establish the Just Meaningful Difference in Price," in *1987 AMA Educators' Proceedings*, ed. Susan Douglas et al. (Chicago: American Marketing Association, 1987), p. 107.

60. Sunil Gupta and Lee G. Cooper, "The Discounting of Discounts and Promotion Thresholds," *Journal of Consumer Research*, December 1992, pp. 401–411.

61. Mark Stiving and Russell S. Winer, "An Empirical Analysis of Price Endings with Scanner Data," *Journal of Consumer Research*, June 1997, pp. 57–67; see also Robert M. Schindler and Patrick N. Kirby, "Patterns of Rightmost Digits Used in Advertised Price: Implications for Nine-Ending Effects," *Journal of Consumer Research*, September 1997, pp. 192–201.

62. Stacy Kravetz, "Dry Cleaners' New Wrinkle: Going Green," *Wall Street Journal*, June 3, 1998, pp. B1, B2.

63. Jennifer Lach, "Like, I Just Gotta Have It," *American Demographics*, February 1999.

64. "Asian Culture and the Global Consumer," *Financial Times*, September 21, 1998, p. 1.

65. Yumiko Ono, "Tiffany Glitters, Even in Gloomy Japan," *Wall Street Journal*, July 21, 1998, pp. B1, B18.

66. Gene Del Vecchio, "Keeping It Timeless, Trendy: From Barbie to Pez, 'Ever-Cool' Kids Brands Meet Both Needs," *Advertising Age*, March 23, 1998, p. 24.

67. Kate Fitzgerald, "The Marketing 100: Starbucks Ice Cream Shari Fujii," *Advertising Age*, June 29, 1998, p. s39.

68. Steven Lipin, Brian Coleman, and Jeremy Mark, "Pick a Card: Visa, American Express, and MasterCard Vie in Overseas Strategies," *Wall Street Journal*, February 15, 1994, pp. A1, A5.

69. Judann Pollack, "Egg Board Budgets $11 Mil for '98 Ads to Combat Cereal," *Advertising Age*, May 25, 1998, p. 10.

70. Tara Parker-Pope, "P&G Dresses Up Olestra in Farm Images," *Wall Street Journal*, February 11, 1998, p. B6.

71. Stephen E. Frank, "Got a Bank? Industry Launches TV Ads," *Wall Street Journal*, September 23, 1997, p. B8.

72. Gregory L. White, "Jeep's Challenge: Stay Rugged but Add Room for Golf Clubs," *Wall Street Journal*, August 26, 1998, pp. B1, B4.

73. Jack Neff, "James River Puts Muscle Behind Dixie Paper Brand," *Advertising Age*, June 16, 1997, p. 22.

74. Jean Halliday and Laura Petrecca, "Volvo Effort Extends Image Positioning," *Advertising Age*, March 30, 1998, p. 9; William J. Holstein, "Volvo Can't Play Safe: To Survive, the Swedish Auto Maker Needs to Be Fun, Too," *U.S. New & World Report*, July 27, 1998, pp. 40–41.

75. Miriam Jordan, "Debut of Rival Diet Colas in India Leaves a Bitter Taste," *Wall Street Journal*, July 21, 1999, pp. B1, B4.

CHAPTER 6

1. Norihiko Shirouzu, "GM Cracks Japan's Market with Its Wallet, Not Its Cars," *Wall Street Journal*, January 26, 2000, p. A17.

2. Robert L. Simison, Fara Warner, and Gregory L. White, "Big Three Car Makers Plan Net Exchange," *Wall Street Journal*, February 28, 2000, p. A3.

3. *Technology Forecast.* (Menlo Park, California: Price Waterhouse, 1997), p. 1.

4. "On-Ramp," *Marketing News*, April 26, 1999, pp. 1, 13.

5. George Anders, "Click and Buy," *Wall Street Journal Interactive Edition,* December 7, 1998, on-line.

6. John R. L. Rizza, "The Internet Gets Down to Business," *Entrepreneurial Edge Magazine,* Summer 1998, on-line.

7. Maryann Jones Thompson, "Spotlight: The Economic Impact of E-commerce," *The Industry Standard,* April 26, 1999, on-line.

8. Robert D. Hof, "The Click-Here Economy," *Business Week,* June 22, 1998, pp. 122–128.

9. "For B2B eCommerce: Today, North America. Tomorrow, The World!" *eMarketer,* February 22, 2000, on-line.

10. Tim Smart, "E-Sourcing: A Cheaper Way of Doing Business," *Business Week,* August 5, 1996, pp. 82–83.

11. Simison, Warner, and White, pp. A3, A16.

12. Fara Warner and Rick Brooks, "Ford Is Hiring UPS to Track Vehicles in Transit From Factories to Dealers," *Wall Street Journal Interactive Edition,* February 2, 2000, on-line.

13. Robert L. Rose, "For Whirlpool, Asia Is the New Frontier," *Wall Street Journal,* April 25, 1996, pp. B1, B4.

14. U. S. Census Bureau, "North American Industry Classification System (NAICS)—United States," www.census.gov/epcd/www/naics.html.

15. Ted Kemp, "Honeywell Targets Businesses with On-line Industrial Store," *DM News,* February 3, 1999, on-line.

16. James W. Taylor, *The Marketing Strategy & Planning Workbook* (South Nyack, NY: Wellington Press 2000), p. 9–9.

17. Shirouzu, p. A3.

18. Ibid.

CHAPTER 7

1. Teri Agins, "Claiborne Patches Together an Empire," *Wall Street Journal*, February 2, 2000, pp. B1, B4.

2. Rebecca Quick, "Ann Taylor Gets Its Groove Back," *Wall Street Journal*, February 16, 1999, pp. B1, B4.

3. Kipp Cheng, "Wee Web," *IQ*, May 3, 1999, pp. 16–20.

4. Becky Ebenkamp, "Tipping the Balance," *Upfront Markets*, May 10, 1999, pp. 4–6.

5. Ellen Neuborne and Kathleen Kerwin, "Generation Y," *Business Week*, February 15, 1999, pp. 81–88.

6. Fara Warner, "Volvo, Seeking Younger Buyers, Tries to Create a Sexier Image," *Wall Street Journal*, August 26, 1999, pp. B1, B4.

7. Matthew Grimm, "Media Circus," *Upfront Markets*, May 10, 1999, pp. 1–32.

8. "Marketers Reveal Industry Dos and Don'ts; Say Capitalize on Relationship Building," *Selling to Seniors*, November 1997, pp. 1–2.

9. Michael J. McCarthy, "A Design with Twists and Turns," *Wall Street Journal*, February 3, 2000, pp. B1, B4.

10. Joanne Cleaver, "Surfing for Seniors," *Marketing News*, July 19, 1999, pp. 1, 7.

11. Grimm.

12. "Rich Sutherland Goes for Golf Customers Others Fear to Serve," *The Front Lines* January 22, 1999.

13. Anne Faircloth, "Value Retailers Go Dollar for Dollar," *Fortune*, July 6, 1998, pp. 164–166.

14. Maricris G. Briones, "Coors Turns Up the Heat; Ethnic Drinkers More Key to Summer Sales," *Marketing News*, June 22, 1998, pp. 1, 15.

15. Lisa Skriloff and Dawn Cornitcher, "Multicultural Marketing: A Marketing Imperative," *Brandweek*, May 17, 1999, pp. 16–26.

16. "Minority Phone Users Make Different Demands," *Wall Street Journal* April 7, 1999, p. B1.

17. Skriloff and Cornitcher.

18. Roger O. Crockett, "Attention Must be Paid: The African American Web Community Is Swelling-and Underserved," *Business Week*, February 7, 2000, p. EB16.

19. Skriloff and Cornitcher.

20. Ibid.

21. Rick Wartzman, "A Push to Probe Buying Habits in Latino

Homes," *Wall Street Journal*, August 5, 1999, pp. B1, B4.

22. Dana James, "Lingua Franca: Human Touch Translates into Better Research of Hispanic Market," *Marketing News*, January 3, 2000, p. 17.

23. Marisa Taylor, "Bilingual Breakfast: New Cereal Brands are Aimed at U.S. Hispanic Market," *Fort Worth Star Telegram*, September 16, 1999, pp. C1.

24. Calmetta Y. Coleman, "Attention Shoppers: Target Makes a Play for Minority Group Sears had Cultivated," *Wall Street Journal*, April 12, 1999, pp, A1, A8.

25. Skriloff and Cornitcher.

26. Ibid.

27. Alex Taylor III, "Porsche Slices Up Its Buyers," *Fortune*, January 16, 1995, p. 24.

28. Karen Benezra, "The Fragging of the American Mind," *Superbrands*, June 15, 1998, pp. S12–19.

29. "Target TV Ads," *Marketing News*, March 2, 1998, p. 1.

30. Tamara Parker-Pope, "A New Front in Diaper Wars: Preventing Rash," *Wall Street Journal*, February 26, 1999, pp. B1, B4.

31. "Downsizing Megamarts: A Return to Mom-and-Pops?" *Firstlight*, March 2000, p. 22.

32. Jennifer Ordonez, "Cash Cows: Hamburger Joints Call Them 'Heavy Users'—But Not to Their Faces," *Wall Street Journal*, January 12, 2000, pp. A1, A10.

33. Much of the material in this section is based on Michael D. Hunt and Thomas W. Speh, *Business Marketing Management*, 6th ed. (Hinsdale, IL: Dryden Press, 1998), pp. 176–181.

34. Scott McCartney, "American Plays Hardball with a Start-up Over All-First-Class Flights," *Wall Street Journal*, March 9, 2000, pp. B1, B4.

35. Joshua Harris Prager, "People with Disabilities Are Next Consumer Niche," *Wall Street Journal*, December 15, 1999, pp. B1, B6.

36. Joshua Harris Prager, "Radio Host Is 'On a Roll' with Show for the Disabled," *Wall Street Journal*, February 25, 1999, pp. B1, B8.

37. Jim Salter, "Enterprise Seeking Airport Car Rentals," *Fort Worth Star Telegram*, October 15, 1999, pp. 2C.

38. Lisa Bannon, "Let's Play Makeover Barbie," *Wall Street Journal*, February 17, 2000, pp. B1, B4.

39. Jerry Useem, "Internet Defense Strategy: Cannibalize Yourself," *Fortune*, September 6, 1999, pp. 121–126.

40. Fara Warner and Gregory L. White, "Ford Bets on Safety, Not Style, for Comeback of Taurus," *Wall Street Journal*, March 30, 1999, pp. B1, B4.

41. "Can Levi's Be Cool Again?" *Business Week*, March 13, 2000, pp. 144, 148; see also Nina Munk, "How Levi's Trashed a Great American Brand," *Fortune*, April 12, 1999, p. 83.

42. Shelly Branch, "How Target Got Hot," *Fortune*, May 24, 1999, pp. 169–174.

43. "Brand Builders: Ingredient Branding," *Brandweek*, December 13, 1999, pp. 26–28.

44. Louise Kramer, "Mountain Dew Stays True to Its Brand Positioning," *Advertising Age*, May 18, 1998, p. 26.

45. Vanessa O'Connell, "What's Tasteless but Very Expensive?" *Wall Street Journal*, May 12, 1998, pp. B1, B8.

46. "Brand Builders"

47. Sally Beatty, "Recasting the Gun as Sports Equipment," *Wall Street Journal*, April 5, 1999, pp. B1, B4.

48. Ian Johnson, "Herbal Remedies Aimed at East and West," *Wall Street Journal*, January 31, 2000, p. A26.

CHAPTER 8

1. "How Sweet It Is—The 2000 David Ogilvy Research Awards," *American Demographics*, March 2000, p. S18.

2. "At Ford, E-Commerce Is Job 1," *Business Week*, February 22, 2000, pp. 74–78.

3. "Keebler Learns to Pay Attention to Research Right from the Start," *Marketing News*, March 11, 1996, p. 10.

4. "Why Some Customers Are More Equal Than Others," *Fortune*, September 19, 1994, pp. 215–224.

5. "Quality: How to Make It Pay," *Business Week*, August 8, 1994, pp. 54–59.

6. Kendra Parker, "Got Questions? All You Have to Do Is Ask," *American Demographics*, November 1999, pp. 36–39.

7. "Hey Kid, Buy This," *Business Week*, June 30, 1997, pp. 63–66.

8. Norihiko Shirouzu, "Japan's High-School Girls Excel in Art of Setting Trends," *Wall Street Journal*, April 24, 1998, pp. B1, B7.

9. John Vidmar, "Just Another Metamorphosis," *Marketing Research*, Spring 1996, pp. 16–18; Sharon Munger, "Premium Medium," *Marketing Research*, Spring 1996, pp. 10–12; and William Nicholls, "Highest Response," *Marketing Research*, Spring 1996, pp. 5–8.

10. Dana James, "The Future of Online Research," *Marketing News*, January 3, 2000, pp. 1, 11.

11. Chris Yalonis, "The Revolution in E-research," *CASRO Journal*, 1999, pp. 131–134.

12. Ibid.

13. Dana James, "Precision Decision," *Marketing News*, September 27, 1999, pp. 23–24.

14. This section was adapted from James Watt, "Using the Internet for Quantitative Survey Research," *Quirk's Marketing Research Review*, June/July 1997, pp. 67–71.

15. Carl McDaniel and Roger Gates, *Contemporary Marketing Research*, 5th ed. (Cincinnati: International Thomson Publishing, 2002).

16. Phone conversation between Kevin Bender, Information Resources, Inc., and Carl McDaniel on April 17, 2000.

17. "Competitor Intelligence Considered More Vital Now," *Marketing News*, October 9, 1995, p. 3.

18. Sheena Sharp, "New Techniques for Corporate Foresight," *Research Conference Report*, May 1998, pp. 7–8.

CHAPTER 9

1. Jennifer Ordonez, "Will Big Mac Find New Sizzle in Shoes, Videos?" *Wall Street Journal*, April 14, 2000, pp. B1, B4.

2. Mike Beirne, "Marriott Tiers Its Brands to Propel Chain Growth," *Brandweek*, November 22, 1999, p. 32.

3. Alec Klein, "Shutterbugs Ditch 35mm Gear for Digital Cameras, Computer Printouts," *Wall Street Journal Marketplace,* May 8, 2000, pp. B1, B6.

4. Gerry Khermouch, "Woodbridge Aims Higher," *Brandweek*, February 16, 1998, p. 14.

5. Stephanie Thompson, "Hostess Promises Great Taste Plus Nutrition with New Cereal Bar Line," *Brandweek*, March 9, 1998, p. 44.

6. Stephanie Thompson, "No-Mess Packs Aimed at Steak Sauce," *Brandweek*, August, 24 1998, p. 6.

7. Emily Nelson, "P&G Tries to Hide Wrinkles in Aging Beauty Fluid," *Wall Street Journal*, May 16, 2000, pp. B1, B4.

8. "Not the Flavor of the Month," *Business Week*, March 20, 2000, p. 322.

9. Sonia Reyes, "Minute Maid Juices Up Calcium-Fortified Line," *Brandweek*, March 13, 2000, p. 323.

10. Sean Mehegan, "Would She Buy Dandruff Shampoo?" *Brandweek*, January 26, 1998, p. 6.

11. Jonathan Welsh, "Black & Decker to Shed Some Lines and Focus on Tools," *Wall Street Journal*, January 28, 1998, p. B7.

12. Peter H. Farquhar et al., "Strategies for Leveraging Master Brands," *Marketing Research*, September 1992, pp. 32–43.

13. Bernhard Warner, "Digitizing Dinner," *Brandweek*, February 16, 1998, p. 38.

14. Lauren Gold and Michael Gold, "Change the Rules of Private-Label Packaging," *Marketing News*, November 22, 1999, pp. 20–21.

15. Peter Galuszka and Wendy Zellner, "Soap Opera at Wal-Mart," *Business Week*, August 16, 1999, p. 44.

16. Ellen Neuborne and Stephanie Anderson Forest, "Look Who's Picking Levi's Pocket," *Business Week*, September 8, 1997, pp. 68, 72.

17. Stephanie Thompson, "Brand Buddies," *Brandweek*, February 23, 1998, pp. 23–30.

18. Frederic M. Biddle, "American Express, Lexus in Co-Brand Pact," *Wall Street Journal*, February 9, 2000, p. B12.

19. Mike Beirne, "Co-branding a Hot Button for Candymakers," *Brandweek*, January 25, 1999, p. 10.

20. Stephanie Thompson, "The O's Have It," *Brandweek*, 30 March 1998, p. 1.

21. David D. Kirkpatrick, "No T-shirts! Landmark Buildings Trademark Images," *Wall Street Journal*, June 10, 1998, pp. B1, B12.

22. James Heckman, "Trademarks Protected Through New Cyber Act," *Marketing News*, January 3, 2000, p. 6.

23. Tammy Reiss, "Hey, It's Green—It Must Be Healthy," *Business Week*, July 13, 1998, p. 6.

24. Sonia Reyes, "Sunsweet Updates Look, Tells Families: 'Be Good'," *Brandweek*, February 7, 2000, p. 10.

25. Stephanie Thompson, "C&H Pours Forth Innovation in Sugar," *Brandweek*, March 23, 1998, p. 14. Reprinted with permission.

26. Gerry Khermouch, "Guinness Pours It on in Chicago," *Brandweek*, February 28, 2000, p. 18.

27. Hugh Pope, "Plying Ex-Soviet Asia with Pepsi, Barbie, and Barf," *Wall Street Journal*, May 6, 1998, pp. B1, B6.

CHAPTER 10

1. Jonathan Eig, "Behind the Tense Race to Create Dog Litter with the Right Stuff," *Wall Street Journal*, February 23, 2000. Reprinted by permission of the *Wall Street Journal*. ©2000 Dow Jones & Company, Inc. All Rights Reserved Worldwide.2000 Dow Jones & Company, Inc.

2. William C. Symonds, "Gillette's Edge," *Business Week*, January 19, 1998, p. 71.

3. "Number of New Products Sees Steady Rise Over Past Decade," *Marketing News*, March 29, 1999, p. 3.

4. Sonia Reyes, "Heinz Sets $29M for Entrée Line," *Brandweek*, February 7, 2000, p. 55.

5. Theresa Howard, "Cutty Sark 'Booze' Mixes with Babes, Bands in Brand Reinvention Effort," *Brandweek*, November 1, 1999, p. 14.

6. Stephen H. Wilstrom, "A Fax That Does It All," *Brandweek*, May 25, 1998, p. 18.

7. Marcia Stepanek, "Using the Net for Brainstorming," *Business Week*, December 13, 1999, p. EB 58.

8. Stepanek, p. EB 55.

9. Stepanek, p. EB 55.

10. Mark Maremont, "How Gillette Brought Its MACH3 to Market," *Wall Street Journal*, April 15, 1998, p. B1; James Heckman, "Razor Sharp: Adding Value, Making Noise with MACH3 Intro," *Marketing News*, April 29, 1999, pp. E4, E13.

11. Maremont, p. B1.

12. Stepanek, p. EB 55, 58.

13. Alex Taylor, III, "Kellogg Cranks Up Its Idea Machine," *Fortune*, July 5, 1999, pp. 181–182.

14. Gerry Khermouch, "A-B's New New Thing," *Brandweek*, February 14, 1999, p. 22–25.

15. Karen Benezra, "Contour Can Sales Drop," *Brandweek*, May 19, 1999, p. 2.

16. Maremont, p. B1.

17. Dennis D. Jorgensen, "Now, We Have a Brief Word from Our Sponsors," *Marketing News*, March 30, 1998, p. E4.

18. David W. Cravens, *Strategic Marketing*, 6e. (New York: Irwin McGraw-Hill, 2000), p. 235.

19. David Leonhardt, "It Was a Hit in Buenos Aires—So Why Not Boise?" *Business Week*, September 7, 1998, p. 56.

20. Leonhardt, p. 58.

21. Leonhardt, p. 58.

22. Eig, p. A1.

23. Eig, p. A1.

CHAPTER 11

1. Jathon Sapsford, "A Small Chain Grows by Borrowing Ideas from Burger Joints," *Wall Street Journal,* May 17, 2000, pp. A1, A10.

2. Valarie A. Zeithaml and Mary Jo Bitner, *Services Marketing* (New York: McGraw-Hill, 2000).

3. Christina Binkley, "From Orange Shag to Pin Stripes: Sheraton Gets a Makeover," *Wall Street Journal*, April 19, 2000, pp. B1, B10.

4. Richard Gibson, "Machine Takes Orders in Test by McDonald's" *Wall*

Street Journal, August 11, 1999, pp. B1, B4.

5. Zeithaml and Bitner.

6. Luey McCauley, ed., "Unit of One," *Fast Company,* March 6, 2000, p. 104.

7. Zeithaml and Bitner.

8. "Exceeding Customer Expectations," *Fortune,* March 6, 2000, p. S3.

9. Chad Rubel, "Managers Buy into Quality When They See It Works," *Marketing News,* March 25, 1996, p. 14.

10. David Kirkpatrick, "IBM: From Big Blue Dinosaur to E-Business Animal, *Fortune,* April 26, 1999, pp. 118–127.

11. Much of the material in this section is based on Christopher H. Lovelock, *Services Marketing* (Englewood Cliffs, NJ: Prentice-Hall, 1996), pp. 39–40.

12. Wendy Perrin, "Bells and Whistles," special business supplement 2000 to *Conde Nast Traveler,* pp. 21–22.

13. Ibid.

14. Susan Kuchinskas, "Organic: San Francisco," *IQnews,* February 14, 2000, p. 36.

15. Matt Murray, "On the Road with a Rolling Bank Branch," *Wall Street Journal,* November 6, 1997, pp. B1, B17.

16. Lovelock, pp. 238–240.

17. Much of the material in this section is based on Leonard L. Berry and A. Parasuraman, *Marketing Services* (New York: Free Press, 1991), pp. 132–150.

18. Jim McCann, "Building Relationships On-Line Is True Promise of Interactive Marketing," *Marketing News,* October 27, 1997, p. 10.

19. Sue Shellenberger, "To Win the Loyalty of Your Employees, Try a Softer Touch," *Wall Street Journal,* January 26, 2000, p. B1.

20. Berry and Parasuraman, pp. 151–152.

21. Kirstin Downey Grimsley, "At Your Service," *Fort Worth Star Telegram,* March 1, 2000, p. C1.

22. Ellen Graham, "Marriott's Bid to Patch the Child-Care Gap Gets a Reality Check," *Wall Street Journal,* February 2, 2000. P. B1.

23. Lisa Miller, "Religious Institutions Are Invoking Premiums to In-spire the Wealthy," *Wall Street Journal,* March 10, 1999, pp. A1, A6.

24. Steve Ditlea, "Click Here If You Care," *Brandweek,* May 4, 1998, pp. 58–60.

CHAPTER 12

1. Content and various press releases found on Webvan's Website at http://www.webvan.com; Connie Guglielmo, "Can Webvan Deliver?" *Interactive Week,* January 31, 2000; George Anders, "How Webvan Conquers E-Commerce's Last Mile," *Wall Street Journal,* December 15, 1999, pp. B1, B6; George Anders, "Co-Founder of Borders to Launch Online Megagrocer," *Wall Street Journal,* April 22, 1999, pp. B1, B4; Alice Z. Cuneo, "Peas Fill Up the Pod: E-Grocers Win With Customers, Lose on Wall Street," *Advertising Age,* April 3, 2000, pp. 52, 56; Joel Groover, "Harvesting the Web," *Shopping Center World,* November 30, 1999; Douglas A. Blackmon, "The Milkman Returns—With Much More," *Wall Street Journal,* December 15, 1999, pp. B1, B6.

2. "Dell Seizes No. 1 Market Position in U.S. Corporate Desktop PC Sales," September 10, 1997, Dell Computer Corporation press release, www.dell.com.

3. Douglas Blackmon, "Speed Limits: Overnight, Everything Changed for FedEx; Can It Reinvent Itself?" *Wall Street Journal,* November 4, 1999, pp. A1, A16.

4. Rhonda L. Rundle, "E-Commerce Coming to Health-Care Industry," *Wall Street Journal,* February 28, 2000, p. B4.

5. Gregory L. White, "E-ssembly Lines: How GM, Ford Think Web Can Make Splash on the Factory Floor," *Wall Street Journal,* December 3, 1999, pp. A1, A8; James Aaron Cooke, "The Dawn of Supply Chain Communities," *Logistics Management & Distribution Report,* February 2000.

6. Evan Ramstad, "Gateway Unit to Bolster Ties to PC Dealers," *Wall Street Journal,* April 20, 1998, p. B2; David Kirkpatrick, "New Home. New CEO. Gateway Is Moo and Improved," *Fortune,* December 20, 1999, pp. 44–46.

7. Gordon Fairclough, "Campbell's Recipe for Higher Profit: Reheat Soup Sales," *Wall Street Journal,* May 19, 1999, p. B6.

8. Jean Sherman Chatzky, "You've Got Groceries," *USA Weekend,* January 28, 2000, p. 4.

9. Vanessa O'Connell, "Starbucks, Kraft to Announce Pact for Selling Coffee," *Wall Street Journal,* September 28, 1998, p. B4.

10. "Fujitsu, Oracle Form Strategic Alliance in Asia," *Reuters,* August 21, 1997.

11. David Frederick Ross, *Competing Through Supply Chain Management: Creating Market-Winning Strategies Through Supply Chain Partnerships* (New York: Chapman & Hall, 1998), pp. 9–12.

12. Ibid.

13. Ibid.

14. Francis J. Quinn, "Supply-Chain Management Report: What's the Buzz?" *Logistics Management,* February 1997.

15. Benefits based on Francis J. Quinn, "The Payoff! Benefits of Improving Supply Chain Management," *Logistics Management,* December 1997, p. 37.

16. Francis J. Quinn, "Quantifying the Benefits of SCM," *Logistics Management & Distribution Report,* January 2000.

17. Francis J. Quinn, "The Payoff! Benefits of Improving Supply Chain Management," *Logistics Management,* December 1997, p. 37.

18. Shelly Branch, "P&G Buys Iams: Will Pet-Food Fight Follow?" *Wall Street Journal,* August 12, 1999, pp. B1, B4.

19. Evan Ramstad, "Inside Radio Shack's Surprising Turnaround," *Wall Street Journal,* June 8, 1999, pp. B1, B16.

20. G. Bruce Knecht, "Rack or Ruin: How Magazines Arrive on Shelves, and Why Some Soon May Not," *Wall Street Journal,* February 26, 1998, pp. A1, A6.

21. G. Bruce Knecht, "Independent Bookstores Are Suing Borders Group and Barnes & Noble," *Wall Street Journal,* March 19, 1998, p. B10.

22. Stephanie N. Mehta, "Cellular Carriers Bypass Dealers, Creating Static," *Wall Street Journal,* March 9, 1998, pp. B1, B10.

23. James R. Hagerty, "Ethan Allen's Revolutionary Path to Web," *Wall Street Journal*, July 29, 1999, p. B1.

24. David Frederick Ross, *Competing Through Supply Chain Management: Creating Market-Winning Strategies Through Supply Chain Partnerships* (New York: Chapman & Hall, 1998), pp. 60–61.

25. "Retailing: General," *Standard & Poor's Industry Surveys*, vol. 166, no. 6, sec. 1, February 5, 1998, p. 21.

26. Quinn, "Supply-Chain Management Report."

27. Francis Quinn, "Team Up for Supply-Chain Success," *Logistics Management*, October 1997, p. 39.

28. Toby B. Gooley, "On the Front Lines," *Logistics Management*, June 1997, p. 39.

29. Ibid.

30. Susan Avery, "Purchasing Forges New Supplier Relationships," *Purchasing*, June 5, 1998.

31. Erick Schonfeld, "The Customized, Digitized, Have-It-Your-Way Economy," *Fortune*, September 28, 1998, pp. 114–124.

32. Evan Ramstad, "PC Playing Field Tilts in Favor of Dell," *Wall Street Journal*, May 21, 1998, p. B8; Andrew Serwer, "Michael Dell Turns the PC World Inside Out," *Fortune*, September 8, 1997; Evan Ramstad, "Dell Takes Another Shot at Booming Home-PC Market," *Wall Street Journal*, December 16, 1997, p. B4.

33. Thomas A. Foster, "3PL's Serve Up Supply Chain Innovation," *Logistics Management & Distribution Report*, November 1999.

34. Robert Keehn, "Transforming the Grocery Industry," *Meeting the Challenge of Global Logistics*, Report Number 1207–98–CR (New York: Conference Board, 1998), pp. 25–27.

35. Ross, p. 232.

36. Ken Cottrill, "Reforging the Supply Chain," *Journal of Business Strategy*, November 19, 1997.

37. William Pesek, Jr., "Inventory Control Stabilizes Economy: Better Management Helps Companies Avoid Missteps," *Wall Street Journal*, August 29, 1997, p. B8B.

38. Rebecca Quick, "Behind Doors of a Warehouse: Heavy Lifting of E-Commerce," *Wall Street Journal*, September 3, 1999, pp. B1, B3.

39. Anna Wilde Mathews, "Cargo in Ships Offers Clues to What Will Go Under Tree," *Wall Street Journal*, August 6, 1997, p. B1.

40. Blackmon, pp. A1, A16.

41. Theodore P. Stank, Patricia J. Daugherty and Alexander E. Ellinger, "Pulling Customers Closer Through Logistics Service," *Business Horizons*, September 1998, p. 74.

42. Ibid.

43. James Aaron Cooke, "Warehousing: Great Expectations," *Logistics Management & Distribution Report*, Annual Report, July 1998.

44. "KPMG: Customer Service Increasingly Important in Supply Chain Management," *M2 PRESSWIRE*, September 28, 1998.

45. James Aaron Cooke, "Clicks and Mortar," *Logistics Management & Distribution Report*, January 31, 2000.

46. Anna Wilde Mathews, "New Gadgets Trace Truckers' Every Move," *Wall Street Journal*, July 14, 1997, pp. B1, B10.

47. James Aaron Cooke, "Making the Global Connection," *Logistics Management & Distribution Report*, June 1999.

48. Paul Gettings, "Top Three Trends in Logistics Today," *Industrial Distribution*, November 1997, p. S17.

49. Helen Atkinson, "Use of 3rd-Party Logistics Rising," *Journal of Commerce*, October 13, 1998, p. 16A.

50. "Ford Hands Off Vehicle Delivery to Third Party," *Logistics Management & Distribution Report*, March 2000.

51. Eryn Brown, "Costs Too High? Bring In the Logistics Experts," *Fortune*, November 10, 1997.

52. Raju Narisetti, "How IBM Turned Around Its Ailing PC Division," *Wall Street Journal*, March 12, 1998, pp. B1, B6.

53. Anna Wilde Mathews, "Logistics Firms Flourish Amid Trend in Outsourcing," *Wall Street Journal*, June 2, 1998, p. B4.

54. Don Clark, "Canceled Programs: Software Is Becoming an Online Service, Shaking Up an Industry," *Wall Street Journal*, July 21, 1999, pp. A1, A6.

55. George Anders, "Ebay, E-Stamp in Tie-Up to Market Online Postage," *Wall Street Journal*, January 12, 2000, p. B6.

56. Rhonda L. Rundle, "New Battlefield For E-Tickets: Home Printers," *Wall Street Journal*, February 17, 2000, pp. B1, B4; Bruce Orwall, "Six Theater Chains Will Join in Venture to Sell Movie Tickets Via Web, Phone," *Wall Street Journal*, March 3, 2000, p. B4.

57. Melinda Jensen Ligos, "Direct Sales: The Secret to Success in Japan," *Sales & Marketing Management*, February 1997, p. 14.

58. Robert Frank, "Video Pirates Rush Out 'Phantom Menace'," *Wall Street Journal*, May 28, 1999, pp. B1, B4.

59. Chris Adams, "Prescription-Drug Seizures from Abroad Surge," *Wall Street Journal*, January 11, 2000, p. B4.

60. Laurie P. Cohen, "CyberScripts: Drug Maker Protests Dispensing via Internet, but Practice Flourishes," *Wall Street Journal*, November 29, 1999, pp. A1, A16.

61. G. Bruce Knecht, "Pedaling Success: Bertelsmann Breaks Through a Great Wall with Its Book Clubs," *Wall Street Journal*, September 18, 1998, pp. A1, A6.

62. Charles Fleming, "Train Drain: In the Unified Europe, Shipping Freight by Rail Is a Journey into the Past," *Wall Street Journal*, March 29, 1999, pp. A1, A8.

63. Greg Steinmetz and Tara Parker-Pope, "All Over the Map," *Wall Street Journal*, September 26, 1996, pp. R4, R6.

64. Mara Lemos, "There's Awful Lot for Coffee in Brazil: As Its Price Climbs, Thieves Get Bolder," *Wall Street Journal*, September 22, 1997, p. B18E.

65. Richard Gibson, "Merchants Mull the Long and the Short of Lines," *Wall Street Journal*, September 3, 1998, pp. B1, B4.

66. Susan Carey, "The Web @ Work: Alaska Airlines," *Wall Street Journal*, December 20, 1999, p. B6.

67. Neal Templin, "Electronic Kiosks Check in Guests at More Hotels," *Wall Street Journal*, February 16, 1999, pp. B1, B4.

68. Clare Howard, "Bank Mobilizes to Better Serve Senior Citizens in Peoria, Ill., Area," *KRTBN Knight-Ridder Tribune Business News:*

Journal Star—Peoria, Ill., June 29, 1999.

69. Deborah Lohse, "Allstate Plans Direct Insurance Sales by Phone, Internet," *Wall Street Journal*, November 11, 1999, p. B12

70. Nancy Fonti, "Airlines Aim to Reroute Ticket Buyers to the Web," *Wall Street Journal*, April 19, 1999, p. B3A.

CHAPTER 13

1. Jay L. Johnson, "Switching Targets," *Discount Merchandiser*, August 1999, p. 29; Karen J. Sack, "Massive Retail Industry Propels U.S. Economy," *Standard & Poor's Industry Surveys*, November 25, 1999, p. 15; Calmetta Y. Coleman, "Target's Aim: 'Bring Fashion to Food' on a National Scale," *Wall Street Journal*, March 1, 2000, p. B4.; Laura Heller, "Target Opens FY on a High: New Stores in New Markets." *Discount Store News*, March 6, 2000, p. 7; Teri Agins, "Cheapskate Chic," *Wall Street Journal*, June 11, 1999, pp. W1, W14; Target press releases and information found at www.target.com

2. Karen J. Sack, "Massive Retail Industry Propels U.S. Economy," *Standard & Poor's Industry Surveys*, November 25, 1999, p. 5;

3. Ibid.

4. Hilary Stout, "Tiny Toy Stores Scramble for Ways to Lure Customers," *Wall Street Journal*, December 9, 1997, p. B2.

5. Leigh Gallagher, "Rebound," *Forbes*, May 3, 1999, p. 60.

6. Maureen C. Carini, "Retailing: Supermarkets and Drugstores," *Standard & Poor's Industry Surveys*, vol. 166, no. 14, sec. 1, April 2, 1998, pp. 12–13.

7. Joel A. Baglole, "Loblaw Supermarkets Add Fitness Clubs to Offerings," *Wall Street Journal*, December 27, 1999, p. B4.

8. Carini, p. 13.

9. Matt Nannery, "Pigging Out," *Chain Store Age*, July 1999, p. 77.

10. Carini, p. 14.

11. Emily Nelson, "Wal-Mart's 'Small-Marts' May Make It Biggest Grocer," *Wall Street Journal*, June 21, 1999. p. B4.

12. Carini, p. 12.

13. Ernest Beck and Emily Nelson, "Differences of Style: As Wal-Mart Invades Europe, Rivals Rush to Match Its Formula," *Wall Street Journal*, October 6, 1999, pp. A1, A6.

14. Emily Nelson, "Overhauling Its Web Site, Wal-Mart Will Push Toys and Electronics," *Wall Street Journal*, October 1, 1999, pp. B1, B4.

15. Carini, p. 15.

16. Tony Lisanti, "Extreme Segment, Extreme Growth," *Discount Store News*, July 26, 1999, p. 13.

17. Company press release, "Toys "R" Us Reports Fourth Quarter and 1999 Fiscal Year Results," March 8, 2000.

18. Robert J. Izmirlian, "Retailing: Specialty," *Standard & Poor's Industry Surveys*, vol. 166, no. 4, sec. 2, January 22, 1998, pp. 14–15.

19. Carini, p. 15.

20. "Outlet Malls: Do They Deliver the Goods?" *Consumer Reports*, August 1998, pp. 20–25.

21. "The Evolution of Outlets: From Simple to Showy," *Consumer Reports*, August 1998, pp. 24–25.

22. "Developers Bring Value Closer to Shoppers," *Chain Store Age*, September 1998, pp. 168–170.

23. Karen J. Sack, "Restaurants," *Standard & Poor's Industry Surveys*, vol. 166, no. 23, sec. 1, June 4, 1998, pp. 4, 7–8.

24. Sack, p. 8.

25. Sack, p. 11.

26. Ann Carrns, "Fill It Up and a Cheeseburger, Please: Gas Stations, Fast-Food Outlets Sharing Prime Space," *Wall Street Journal*, October 15, 1997, p. B18.

27. Eatzi's Market and Bakery Web site at http://www.eatzis.com.

28. Rodney Ho, "Vending Machines Make Change," *Wall Street Journal*, July 7, 1999, pp. B1, B4.

29. Ibid.

30. Nigel Powell, "PC Salesmen Go Door to Door," *The Times* (London), July 16, 1997, p. 6; "Reaching Out to Small-Town USA: Move Over Amway, PC Sales Firm Hand Technologies Adds Hi-Tech Touch," *South China Morning Post*, May 12, 1998, p. 8; Barbara Carton, "PCs Replace Lettuce Tubs at Sales Parties," *Wall Street Journal*, March 26, 1997, p. B1; "Hand Technologies: Background Information," *M2*

Presswire, May 2, 1997; Chad Kaydo, "Are PCs Like Tupperware? *Sales & Marketing Management*, June 1998, p. 20.

31. Wendy Bounds, "For Fashion Action, Look in Suburban Living Rooms," *Wall Street Journal*, November 24, 1997, pp. B1, B4.

32. Dennis Berman, "Is the Bell Tolling for Door-to-Door Selling? *Business Week*, November 1, 1999. pp. 58–60; Rachel Beck, "Amway Puts Direct Selling Model Online," *Marketing News*, March 29, 1999, p. 12.

33. Yumiko Ono, "On a Mission: Amway Grows Abroad, Sending 'Ambassadors' to Spread the Word," *Wall Street Journal*, May 14, 1997.

34. Calmetta Y. Coleman, "Mail Order Is Turning into Male Order," *Wall Street Journal*, March 25, 1996, p. B9A.

35. Dell Computers Web site, http://www.dell.com/us/en/gen/corporate.

36. Judann Pollack, "Food Marketers Develop Taste for Selling on QVC," *Advertising Age*, June 2, 1997, p. 20.

37. Karen J. Sack, "Consumer Spending Should Moderate in the Year Ahead," *Standard & Poor's Industry Survey*, November 25, 1999, p. 2.

38. Rebecca Quick, "Online-Retailing Revenue Is Expected to Total 2½ Times Last Year's Figure," *Wall Street Journal*, July 19, 1999, p. B5.

39. Douglas A. Blackmon, "The Milkman Returns—with Much More," *Wall Street Journal*, December 15, 1999, pp. B1, B6.

40. Calmetta Y. Coleman and Douglas A. Blackmon, "Retailers Strive for Shopping Synergy," *Wall Street Journal*, February 8, 2000, pp. B1, B6.

41. Kevin J. Delaney, "Where the E in E-Shopping Stands for 'Extreme'," *Wall Street Journal*, October 14, 1999, pp. B1, B17.

42. George Anders, "Yard Sale in Cyberspace," *Wall Street Journal*, April 1, 1999, pp. B1, B12.

43. Alexandra Peers and George Anders, "Web Auctions Get *Haute:* Sotheby's Deal Could Shake Art Market," *Wall Street Journal*, June 17, 1999, p. B1.

44. Gary McWilliams, "Dell to Launch Web Auction Site, Continuing Its Push into Retailing," *Wall Street Journal*, July 19, 1999, p. B6.

45. McDonald's Corporation, Inside the U.S. Franchising Fact Sheet, http://www.mcdonalds.com/corporate/franchise/inside/factsheet/factsheet.html.

46. Julie Bennett, "Inspired by America's Consumer Boom, Entrepreneurs Pursue New Markets," *Franchising: Focus on Retail*, special advertising section in *Wall Street Journal*, June 17, 1999, p. B18.

47. Richard Gibson, "Still-Golden Arches: McDonald's Problems in Kitchen Don't Dim the Lure of Franchises," *Wall Street Journal*, June 3, 1998, pp. A1, A6.

48. Julie Bennett, "Companies Go Abroad for Expanded Ownership Base, Greater Profits," *Franchising: Focus on Food*, special advertising section in *Wall Street Journal*, September 16, 1999, p. B14.

49. Emily Nelson and Alejandro Bodipo-Memba, "Gadzooks! Claire's Stores Moves in on a Rival," *Wall Street Journal*, September 17, 1998, pp. B1, B4.

50. Rebecca Quick, "Ann Taylor Gets Its Groove Back," *Wall Street Journal*, February 16, 1999, pp. B1, B4.

51. William F. Buckeley, "Ames to Please: Discounter Rebounds by Targeting Clientele Below the Wal-Mart Set," *Wall Street Journal*, January 11, 1999, pp. A1, A6.

52. George Anders, "Different Strokes: Amazon, Etoys Make Big, Opposing Bets; Which One Is Right?" *Wall Street Journal*, November 2, 1999, pp. A1, A14.

53. Eleena De Lisser, "Online Retailers Slice and Dice Niches Thinner Than Julienne Fries," *Wall Street Journal*, November 29, 1999, pp. B1, B6.

54. "An Exclusive Club," *Chain Store Age*, October 1998.

55. Jack Neff, "Wal-Mart Stores Go Private (Label)," *Advertising Age*, November 29, 1999, pp. 1, 34–38; Emily Nelson, "For Wal-Mart, A Soap War Looms Against Mighty P&G," *Wall Street Journal*, August 6, 1999, pp. B1, B3.

56. "Mining the Store," *Chain Store Age*, January 2000, p. 4A.

57. Rekha Balu, "Rural Kids Like Hip Clothes, Too, Hot Chain Discovers," *Wall Street Journal*, January 15, 1998, pp. B1, B10.

58. William M. Bulkeley, "Office-Supply Superstores Find Bounty in the Boonies," *Wall Street Journal*, September 1, 1998, pp. B1, B4.

59. "Updated Site-Selection Guide Covers All Bases," *Chain Store Age*, October 1998.

60. Joanne Gordon, "Saks Appeal: The Upscale Retailer's Main Street Stores Prove Size Doesn't Always Matter," *Chain Store Age*, May 1998, pp. 84–90.

61. Bill Levine, "The Store Stands Alone: For Some Retailers, Freestanding Sites Look Good from All Angles," *Chain Store Age*, April 1998, pp. 107–108.

62. "Growing Season: Iowa's Eastern Hub Gets Superregional Center," *Chain Store Age*, September 1998, pp. 159–160.

63. Calmetta Y. Coleman, "Making Malls (Gasp!) Convenient," *Wall Street Journal*, February 8, 2000, pp. B1, B4.

64. Anne Faircloth, "Value Retailers Go Dollar for Dollar," *Fortune*, 6 July 1998, pp. 164–166.

65. "Specialty Stores Dress Up with Fixtures," *Chain Store Age*, January 1998, pp. 86–87.

66. Evan Ramstad, "Best Buy Co. Is Stacking the Shelves to Add to Profits," *Wall Street Journal*, April 28, 1999, p. B4.

67. "Data Mining Is More Than Beer and Diapers," *Chain Store Age*, June 1998, pp. 64–68.

68. Emily Nelson, "Why Wal-Mart Sings, 'Yes, We Have Bananas!'," *Wall Street Journal*, October 6, 1998, pp. B1, B4.

69. Benjamin Todd, "Super Kmart Strives for Inner Peace," *Chain Store Age*, January 1998, p. 68.

70. Diane Welland, "Rhythm and Chews," *Cooking Light*, January/February 1997, p. 22.

71. Kate Murphy, "A Sales Pitch Right Under Your Nose," *New York Times*, September 13, 1998, p. 8.

72. "Playful Touches Dress Up the Box," *Chain Store Age*, June 1998, pp. 110–111.

73. "Repeat Business," *Chain Store Age*, October 1998.

74. Jennifer Gilbert, "Customer Service Crucial to Online Buiyers," *Advertising Age*, September 13, 1999, p. 52.

75. Karen J. Sack, "Mergers, Rivalry, and Price Sensitivity Will Continue," *Standard & Poor's Industry Surveys*, May 9, 1996, pp. R75–78.

76. "Global Retailing '97," Ernst & Young special report for *Chain Store Age*, December 1997, p. 4.

77. "Global Retailing '97," pp. 14–18.

78. "Global Retailing '97," p. 18.

79. "Sound Win for Virgin," *Chain Store Age*, February 1998, pp. 2RSOY–3RSOY.

80. Sack, "Retailing: General," p. 1.

81. Izmirlian, "Retailing: Specialty," p. 3.

82. Ibid.

83. Calmetta Y. Coleman, "Supermarkets Build Sales by Beguiling Shoppers' Kids," *Wall Street Journal*, January 19, 1998, pp. B1, B5.

84. Calmetta Y. Coleman, "Grocery List: Peas, Veal, Throat Culture," *Wall Street Journal*, May 20, 1998, pp. B1, B26.

85. Ahmed Taher, Thomas W. Leigh, and Warren A. French, "The Retail Patronage Experience and Customer Affection," *The Cutting Edge IV, Proceedings of the 1995 Symposium on Patronage Behavior and Retail Strategy*, ed. William R. Darden, American Marketing Association, May 1995, pp. 35–51.

86. Jack Neff, "Dawn of the Online Icebox," *Advertising Age*, March 15, 1999, p. 17.

87. This section based on "Customer Management," State of the Industry special report, *Chain Store Age*, August 1998, pp. 20A–23A.

88. "Camelot Reigns," *Chain Store Age*, October 1998.

CHAPTER 14

1. Jennifer Gilbert, "AOL's Marketing Builds Service into Powerhouse," *Advertising Age*, March 6, 2000, pp. s2, s16; "Warner Bros. Signs Sponsors to AOL-Themed Movie," www.adage.com, September 1998; Kate Maddox and Jeff Jensen, "Online Marketers Race for

Tie-Ins with 'You've Got Mail,'" www.adage.com, October 1998; Eric Strout, "America Online: They've Got Sales," *Sales & Marketing Management*, July 2000, p. 82.

2. Mark Maremont, "Gillette to Unveil Women's Version of Mach 3 Razor," *Wall Street Journal*, December 2, 1999, p. B14.

3. Don Evans, "Tom Brokaw: 'Secret Weapon'," *Advertising Age*, March 20, 2000, p. s14; Kyle Pope, "NBC Boosts Brokaw Book and Gets Boost Back," *Wall Street Journal*, January 25, 1999, p. B1, B4.

4. Stephanie Thompson, "Marketers Embrace Latest Health Claims," *Advertising Age*, February 28, 2000, pp. 20–22.

5. Ibid.

6. Stephanie Thompson, "New Milk Effort Promises Fame with Cap Game," *Advertising Age*, April 24, 2000, p. 34.

7. Kate Fitzgerald, "Freschetta's Tour Heats Up Awareness of Its Frozen Pizza," *Advertising Age*, February 21, 2000, p. 38.

8. Frank G Bingham, Jr., Charles J. Quigley, Jr., and Elaine M. Notarantonio, "The Use of Communication Style in a Buyer–Seller Dyad: Improving Buyer–Seller Relationships," *Proceedings: Association of Marketing Theory and Practice*, 1996 Annual Meeting, Hilton Head, South Carolina, March 1996, pp. 188–195.

9. Ibid.

10. Philip J Kitchen, "Marketing Communications Renaissance," *International Journal of Advertising*, vol. 12 (1993), pp. 367–386.

11. Kitchen, p 372.

12. AIDA concept based on the classic research of E. K. Strong, Jr., as theorized in *The Psychology of Selling and Advertising* (New York: McGraw-Hill, 1925) and "Theories of Selling," *Journal of Applied Psychology*, 9 (1925), pp. 75–86.

13. Thomas E Barry and Daniel J. Howard, "A Review and Critique of the Hierarchy of Effects in Advertising," *International Journal of Advertising*, vol. 9 (1990), pp. 121–135.

14. Kim Cleland, "The Marketing 100: Colgate Total, Jack Haber," *Advertising Age*, June 29, 1998, p. s44.

15. See Don E Schultz, Stanley I. Tannenbaum, and Robert F. Lauterborn, *Integrated Marketing Communications* (Lincolnwood, IL: NTC Business Books), 1993.

16. Jeff Jensen, "'Godzilla' Effort Looms Over '98 Movie Marketing," *Advertising Age*, May 4, 1998, p. 12; Jeff Jensen, "Monster-Size Outdoor Ads Presage Arrival of 'Godzilla,'" *Advertising Age*, April 6, 1998, p. 3.

17. Lynne Eagle, Philip Kitchen, Ken Hyde, Wilna Fourie, and Mani Padisetti, "Perceptions of Integrated Marketing Communications Among Marketers and Ad Agency Executives in New Zealand," *International Journal of Advertising*, February 1999.

CHAPTER 15

1. Bernard Weinraub, "New Potter Book Casts Its Spell, and Promotional Wizardry Helps," *New York Times*, July 3, 2000, p. 1; "Why Harry's Hot: With the Sweep of a Wand, 'Harry Potter and the Goblet of Fire,' the Fourth Book in J.K. Rowling's Magical Series, is the Fastest-Selling Title—of Any Kind—in History," *Newsweek*, July 17, 2000, p. 52; Daniel Fierman, "Wild About Harry," *Entertainment Weekly*, 21 July 2000, p. 34; Paul Gray, "Harry's Back Again," *Time*, July 17, 2000, p. 70; "For Potter Fans, Booksellers, a Christmas in July," *Wall Street Journal*, July 10, 2000, p. B10.

2. "Domestic Advertising Spending by Media," *Advertising Age*, September 25, 2000, p. 54.

3. US. Department of Commerce, Bureau of the Census, Statistical Abstract of the United States (Washington, DC: Government Printing Office, September 1995), p. 416.

4. "1999 Advertising-to-Sales Ratios for the 200 Largest Ad Spending Industries," *Advertising Age*, June 28, 1999, p. 58.

5. "Time Spent with Media," *Standard & Poor's Industry Surveys*, March 14, 1996, p. M1.

6. Joe Flint, "Commercial Clutter on TV Networks Rises to Record," *Wall Street Journal*, March 2, 2000, p. B18.

7. Amitava Chattaopadhyay and Kunal Basu, "Humor in Advertising: The Moderating Role of Prior Brand Evaluation," *Journal of Marketing Research*, November 1990, pp. 466–476.

8. Rajiv Grover and V. Srinivasan, "Evaluating the Multiple Effects of Retail Promotions on Brand Loyalty and Brand Switching Segments," *Journal of Marketing Research*, February 1992, pp. 76–89; see also S. P. Raj, "The Effects of Advertising on High and Low Loyalty Consumer Segments," *Journal of Consumer Research*, June 1982, pp. 77–89.

9. Mark Rechtin, "Honda Touts All Products in New Ads," *Advertising Age*, May 3, 1999, p. 17.

10. Michael Burgoon, Michael Pfau, and Thomas S. Birk, "An Inoculation Theory Explanation for the Effects of Corporate Issue/Advocacy Advertising Campaigns, *Communication Research*, August 1995, p. 485(21).

11. Richard B Schmitt, "Can Corporate Advertising Sway Juries?" *Wall Street Journal*, March 3, 1997, pp. B1, B3.

12. Gregory L. White, "Saturn Expands Brand in New Campaign," *Wall Street Journal*, June 28, 1999, p. B8; Dave Guilford, "Saturn Generates Big Hopes for Rejuvenation Via Midsize LS," *Advertising Age*, June 28, 1999, pp. 3, 64.

13. Louise Kramer, "As Sales Flatten, Top Pizza Chains Turn Up the Heat," *Advertising Age*, February 23, 1998, p. 4.

14. Louise Kramer, "Papa John's New Salvo Intensifies Pizza Battle," *Advertising Age*, September 27, 1999, p. 3.

15. "Judge Rules Papa Johns Must Stop Using Slogan," *Wall Street Journal*, January 4, 2000, p. B8.

16. Bruce Ingersoll, "FTC Orders Novartis Ads to Correct Claim," *Wall Street Journal*, May 28, 1999, p. B2; Ira Teinowitz, "Doan's Decision Worries Marketers: Novartis Will Appeal FTC Ruling Requiring $8 Mil in Corrective Ads," *Advertising Age*, May 1999, www.adage.com.

17. Jonathan Friedland, "P&G, Frito-Lay in Mexican-Ad Standoff," *Wall Street Journal*, March 19, 1999, p. B3.

18. Brandon Mitchener, "Border Crossings," *Wall Street Journal*, November 22, 1999, p. R41.

19. Alice Z. Cuneo, "Webvan Campaign Plays Upon Anti-Grocery Store Sentiment," *Advertising Age*, April 17, 2000, p. 58.

20. "The Best Awards: Outpost.com Humor Tough on School Band, Gerbils," *Advertising Age*, May 31, 1999, p. s6.

21. Mark Maremont, "How Gillette Brought Its MACH3 to Market," *Wall Street Journal*, April 15, 1998, pp. B1, B10; Susan Klahr, "Gillette Puts $300 Mil Behind Its Mach3 Shaver," *Advertising Age*, April 20, 1998, p. 6.

22. Mark Maremont, "Close vs Safe: Rivals Prepare to Market New Razors," Wall Street Journal, September 29, 1997, pp. B1, B6.

23. Klahr, p. 6.

24. Judann Pollack, "Pillsbury Puts Green Giant Back Out Front in New Ads," *Advertising Age*, August 9, 1999, p. 6.

25. Alice Z. Cuneo and Jack Neff, "Glad Resurrects Classic Tag for New Branding Campaign," *Advertising Age*, July 19, 1999, p. 8; Betsy McKay, "Coke to Open New Old-Bottle Campaign," *Wall Street Journal*, January 5, 2000, p. B8.

26. Marc G Weinberger, Harlan Spotts, Leland Campbell, and Amy L. Parsons, "The Use and Effect of Humor in Different Advertising Media," *Journal of Advertising Research*, May–June 1995, pp. 44–56.

27. "Best Awards," *Advertising Age*, May 29, 2000, p. s24; Hillary Chura, "The Marketing 100: Bud Light Andy Goeler," *Advertising Age*, June 26, 2000, p. s3.

28. Roger Thurow, "Shtick Ball: In Global Drive, Nike Finds Its Brash Ways Don't Always Pay Off," *Wall Street Journal*, May 5, 1997, pp. A1, A10.

29. Johnny K. Johansson, "The Sense of 'Nonsense': Japanese TV Advertising," *Journal of Advertising*, March 1994, pp. 17–26.

30. Russell Abratt and Deanna Cowan, "Client-Agency Perspectives of Information Needs for Media Planning," *Journal of Advertising Research*, November 1999, p. 37.

31. "Domestic Advertising Spending by Media," *Advertising Age*, September 25, 2000, p. s4.

32. "Radio: No Longer an Advertising Afterthought," *Standard & Poor's Industry Surveys*, July 20, 1995, p. M36; Rebecca Piirto, "Why Radio Thrives," *American Demographics*, May 1994, pp. 40–46.

33. Chuck Ross, "Study: Cable Wins in Ad Attentiveness," *Advertising Age*, May 17, 1999, p. 60.

34. Joe Mandese, "'Friends' Vaults into Top-Priced Syndie Spot," *Advertising Age*, January 18, 1999, p. s1–s2.

35. Joe Mandese, "Prime-Time Pricing Woes," *Advertising Age*, September 20, 1999, pp. 1, 12.

36. Joe Flint, "Super Bowl's Biggest Advertiser May Turn Out to Be ABC Itself," *Wall Street Journal*, January 24, 2000, p. B10.

37. Carol Krol, "Navy Infomercial Aims at Prospective Recruits," *Advertising Age*, May 31, 1999, p. 12.

38. Wayne Friedman, "Tae-Bo Marketer Adds Health Clubs, New Infomercials," *Advertising Age*, June 28, 1999, p. 12.

39. Barbara Martinez, "City Sight: Giant Ads Spring from Holes in the Ground," *Wall Street Journal*, 18 August 18, 1999, pp. B1, B10.

40. "Local Leads the Way," *Advertising Age*, April 19, 1999, p. 48; Outdoor Advertising Association of America.

41. Rhonda L. Rundle, "Outdoor Plans Billboard-Sized Purchase," *Wall Street Journal*, July 11, 1996, p. B6; Cyndee Miller, "Outdoor Gets a Makeover," *Marketing News*, April 10, 1995, p. 1, 26.

42. Jeffery D. Zbar, "Web Companies Fuel Outdoor Boom," *Advertising Age*, November 1, 1999, pp. 66–68.

43. Sally Goll Beatty, "Billboard Firms Ease into Smokeless Era," *Wall Street Journal*, October 30, 1997, p. B6.

44. Jennifer Gilbert, "'Really Booming' Net Grabs $3.6 Billion," www.adage.com, June 2000.

45. "Web Ads Are Said to Be Remembered as Often as TV Ads," *Wall Street Journal*, 26 May 26, 1999, p. B10.

46. Andrea Petersen, "Price of Internet Banner Ads Starts to Fall," *Wall Street Journal*, February 24, 1999.

47. Ann-Christine P. Diaz, "Consumers Less Likely to Trust Web Ads: MPA," *Advertising Age*, March 20, 2000, p. 34.

48. Kate Maddox, "Study: Broadband Ads More Effective Than Narrowband," *Advertising Age*, March 1, 1999, pp. s2, s8; Bradley Johnson, "Study: Rich-Media Ads May Overwhelm Consumers," *Advertising Age*, August 23, 1999, p. 17.

49. Eryn Brown, "The Silicon Valley Heart of Internet Advertising," *Fortune*, December 6, 1999, pp. 166–168.

50. Sarah Ellison, "On the Tables in the Cafes of France: Logo du Jour," *Wall Street Journal*, June 2, 2000, pp. B1, B4.

51. Karen Jacobs, "Elevator Maker to Add Commercial Touch," *Wall Street Journal*, December 7, 1999, p. B8; Terry McManus, "Advertisers Vie for the Eyes of Elevator Riders," *Advertising Age*, 21 February 21, 2000, p. 44.

52. Rodney Ho, "Baggage-Carousel Ad Business's Circuitous Launch," *Wall Street Journal*, February 15, 2000, p. B2.

53. Sara Teasdale, "Study Challenges Three-Plus Viewing Rule," *Business Marketing*, December 1995, p. 5; Hugh M. Cannon and Edward A. Riordan, "Effective Reach and Frequency: Does It Really Make Sense?" *Journal of Advertising Research*, March 1994, p. 19.

54. Cannon and Riordan, p. 19; Erwin Ephron, "A New Media-Mix Strategy: As Advertisers Eye Obvious Decline of TV, Agencies Expand Options," *Advertising Age*, February 28, 2000, p. s10.

55. Kate Lynch and Horst Stripp, "Examination of Qualitative Viewing Factors for Optimal Advertising Strategies," *Journal of Advertising Research*, May 1999, p. 7.

56. Sally Beatty, "Ogilvy's TV-Ad Study Stresses 'Holding Power' Instead of Ratings," *Wall Street Journal*, June 4, 1999, p. B2.

57. Chuck Ross, "Study Finds for Continuity vs. Flights," *Advertising Age*, April 19, 1999, p. 2.

58. Erwin Ephron, "Recency Planning: A New Media Approach," *Advertising Age*, July 1, 1999, p. 21.

59. Nicholas Maiese, "'Blair Witch' Casts Its Spell," *Advertising Age*, March 20, 2000, p. s8; Nancy Coltun Webster, "The Marketing 100: 'The Blair Witch Project' Amorette, Jones," *Advertising Age*, June 26, 2000, p. s22.

60. Tara Parker-Pope, "The Magnificent Seven: Marketers Fete Bare Bottoms, Open Mouths," *Wall Street Journal*, November 21, 1997, p. B1.

61. James R. Hagerty, "Krispy Kreme at a Krossroads," *Wall Street Journal*, February 24, 2000, pp. B1, B4.

62. Ibid., p. B1.

63. Sally Beatty, "For a Truck Maker, 18 Wheels of Product Placement," *Wall Street Journal*, October 29, 1999, pp. B1, B4.

64. Teri Agins, "The Art of 'Gilt by Association,'" *Wall Street Journal*, September 14, 1999, pp. B1, B26.

65. Kate Fitzgerald, "It's the Wheel Thing," *Advertising Age*, November 15, 1999, p. 30.

66. Laura Petrecca, "Defying Gravity: NBC, Petersen Connect with Cynical Teens via Sports Fest," *Advertising Age*, October 11, 1999, pp. 36–40.

67. Kate Fitzgerald, "Maui Comes to Mall," *Advertising Age*, February 7, 2000, pp. 30–32.

68. Fitzgerald, "It's the Wheel Thing," p. 32.

69. George Anders, "The Clout of the Online Critic," *Wall Street Journal*, June 28, 1999, p. B1.

70. Erin White, "'Chatting' a Singer Up the Pop Charts," *Wall Street Journal*, October 5, 1999, p. B1, B4.

71. Susan Carey, "Alaska Air Aims to Restore Credibility After Plane Crash," *Wall Street Journal*, April 28, 2000, p. B4.

72. Bruce Orwall and Nancy Keates, "Disney Ship's Maiden Voyage Delayed Again," Wall Street Journal, February 19, 1998, pp. B1, B8.

73. George Anders, "EBay to Refund Millions in Fees After Outage," *Wall Street Journal*, June 14, 1999, p. B8; George Anders, "EBay Scrambles to Repair Image After Big Crash," *Wall Street Journal*, June 15, 1999, pp. B1, B4.

CHAPTER 16

1. Andy Cohen, "Copy Cats," *Sales & Marketing Management*, August 2000, pp. 50–58.

2. "The 1997 Annual Report of the Promotion Industry," *PROMO Magazine*.

3. Lisa Phillips, "Your Savings Today," *American Demographics*, September 1999.

4. Kate Fitzgerald, "Instant-Reward Coupons Show Rebound," *Advertising Age,* May 12, 1997, p. 20.

5. Shelly Branch, "Crooner May Find New Audience in Barter Deal with Earth's Best," *Wall Street Journal*, January 25, 2000, p. B9.

6. William M Bulkeley, "Rebates' Secret Appeal to Manufacturers: Few Consumers Actually Redeem Them," *Wall Street Journal,* February 10, 1998, pp. B1, B2.

7. Mark Lacek, "Loyalty Marketing No Ad Budget Threat," *Advertising Age,* October 23, 1995, p. 20.

8. Ginger Conlon, "True Romance," *Sales & Marketing Management,* May 1996, pp. 85–90.

9. Judann Pollack, "Loyalty Program Takes RJR's Doral to No. 3," *Advertising Age*, August 30, 1999, p. 4.

10. Nancy Shepardson, "Holding All the Cards," *American Demographics*, February 2000.

11. Vincent Alonzo, "Money Isn't Everything," *Sales & Marketing Management*, April 2000, pp. 47–48.

12. "HGTV, Sears Join Forces for House Giveaway," *Advertising Age*, February 7, 2000, p. 30.

13. "Samples Have Ample Impact," *Sales & Marketing Management,* September 1997, p. 108.

14. Louise Kramer, "The Marketing 100: Dunkin' Donuts Eddie Binder," *Advertising Age,* 29 June 1998, p. s30.

15. Kate Fitzgerald, "Promotional Sprint," *Advertising Age*, May 3, 1999, pp. 30–32.

16. Kate Fitzgerald, "Venue Sampling Hot," *Advertising Age*, August 12, 1996, p. 19.

17. Matthew Martinez and Mercedes M. Cardona, "Study Shows POP Gaining Ground as Medium," *Advertising Age,* 24 November 1997, p. 43.

18. Rebecca Piirto Heath, "Pop Art," *Marketing Tools,* April 1997.

19. Erika Rasmusson, "Promotional Prowess," *Sales & Marketing Management*, July 2000, p. 112.

20. "The Most Popular—and Effective—Online Promotions," *Sales & Marketing Management*, July 2000, p. 110; Forrester Research Inc.

21. Dean Takahashi, "Sega Will Give Away Dreamcast Players to Lure Subscribers to the Web," *Wall Street Journal*, April 4, 2000, pp. B1, B4.

22. Debra Aho Williamson, "Program Rewards Frequent Visitors," *Advertising Age*, May 17, 1999, p. 50.

23. Yumiko Ono, "For Philip Morris, Every Store Is a Battlefield," *Wall Street Journal,* June 29, 1998, pp. B1, B6.

24. Frank G Bingham, Jr., Charles J. Quigley, Jr., and Elaine M. Notarantonio, "The Use of Communication Style in a Buyer–Seller Dyad: Improving Buyer–Seller Relationships," *Proceedings: Association of Marketing Theory and Practice,* 1996 Annual Meeting, Hilton Head, South Carolina, March 1996, pp. 188–195.

25. Marvin A. Jolson, "Broadening the Scope of Relationship Selling," *Journal of Personal Selling & Sales Management,* Fall 1997, p. 75; see also Donald W. Jackson, Jr., "Relationship Selling: The Personalization of Relationship Marketing," *Asia-Australia Marketing Journal,* August 1994, pp. 45–54.

26. Bingham, Quigley, and Notarantonio, pp. 188–195.

27. Geoffrey Brewer, "The Customer Stops Here," *Sales & Marketing Management,* March 1998, pp. 30–36.

28. Cohen, pp. 53–54.

29. Erika Rasmusson, "How to Manage Long-Term Leads," *Sales & Marketing Management,* January 1998, p. 77.

30. Roger Brooksbank, "The New Model of Personal Selling: Micromarketing," *Journal of Personal Selling & Sales Management,* Spring 1995, pp. 61–66; Donald W. Jackson, Jr., "Relationship Selling: The Personalization of Relationship Marketing," *Asia-Australia Marketing Journal,* August 1994, pp. 45–54.

31. "What's On Your Mind?" *Sales & Marketing Management*, October 1998, pp. 98–101.

32. Sarah Lorge, "The Best Way to Prospect," *Sales & Marketing Management,* January 1998, p. 80; Tricia Campbell, "What's a Referral Worth to You?" *Sales & Marketing Management,* September 1997, p. 103.

33. Lorge, p. 80.

34. Michele Marchetti, "Is Cold Calling Worth It?" *Sales & Marketing Management,* August 1997, p. 103.

35. "Leads Are a Terrible Thing to Waste," *Sales & Marketing Management,* August 1997, p. 108; Center for Strategic Communication.

36. Marvin A. Jolson and Thomas R. Wotruba, "Selling and Sales Management in Action: Prospecting: A New Look at This Old Challenge," *Journal of Personal Selling & Sales Management,* Fall 1992, pp. 59–66.

37. Robyn Griggs, "Give Us Leads! Give Us Leads!" *Sales & Marketing Management,* July 1997, pp. 67–72.

38. Robyn Griggs, "Qualifying Leads Online," *Sales & Marketing Management,* July 1997, p. 68.

39. Jolson, "Broadening the Scope of Relationship Selling," p. 75.

40. Adapted from Bob Kimball, *Successful Selling* (Chicago: American Marketing Association, 1994).

41. "Five Steps to Wrapping Up a Sales Call," *Sales & Marketing Management,* January 1998, p. 84.

42. Jolson, "Broadening the Scope of Relationship Selling," p. 75.

43. Geoffrey Brewer, "Dell's 'Expert' Advice for Customers," *Sales & Marketing Management,* April 1997, p. 77.

44. "How to Sound Like a Pro," *Sales & Marketing Management,* October 1997, p. 136.

45. Colleen Cooper, "Overcoming Last-Minute Objections," *Sales & Marketing Management,* March 1997, p. 32; Sarah Lorge, "How to Close the Deal," *Sales & Marketing Management,* April 1998, p. 84.

46. Cooper, p. 32.

47. Michele Marchetti, "Hey Buddy, Can You Spare $113.25?" *Sales & Marketing Management,* August 1997, pp. 69–77.

48. Sarah Lorge, "The Best Way to Negotiate," *Sales & Marketing Management,* March 1998, p. 92.

49. "Can Your Reps Sell Overseas?" *Sales & Marketing Management,* February 1998, p. 110.

50. "It's No Secret: Why Dell Gives Customers Insider Access to Prices and Products," *Sales & Marketing Management,* May 1998, p. 93.

51. "America's 25 Best Sales Forces: Best at Sales Process," *Sales & Marketing Management*, July 2000, p. 80.

52. "Reorganizing a Sales Force: How DoubleClick Aligns Its Salespeople with Its Customers," *Sales & Marketing Management*, March 2000, p. 90.

53. Erika Rasmusson, "The 10 Traits of Top Salespeople," *Sales & Marketing Management*, August 1999, pp. 34–37.

54. "America's 25 Best Sales Forces: Best at Sales Training," *Sales & Marketing Management*, July 2000, p. 68.

55. Ibid.

56. Arun Sharma, "Customer Satisfaction–Based Incentive Systems: Some Managerial and Saleperson Considerations," *Journal of Personal Selling & Sales Management,* April 1997, p. 61.

57. Andy Cohen, "America's Best Sales Forces: No. 4 General Electric," *Sales & Marketing Management,* October 1997, p. 57.

58. Vincent Alonzo, "Getting the Best Out of 'Em," *Sales & Marketing Management,* October 1997, pp. 34–38; "More Incentives on the Way," *Sales & Marketing Management,* December 1997, p. 96.

59. Erika Rasmusson, "The five Steps to Successful Sales Force Automation, *Sales & Marketing Management*, March 1999, pp. 34–40.

60. Brent Keltner, "Just Another Channel?" *Sales & Marketing Management*, January 2000, pp. 23–34

61. Ginger Conlon, "No Turning Back," *Sales & Marketing Management*, December 1999, pp. 50–55.

62. Keltner, pp. 23–34; Brent Keltner, "Harnessing the Internet's Potential," *Sales & Marketing Management*, February 2000, p. 29.

CHAPTER 17

1. Scott McCartney, "Airlines Find a Bag of High-Tech Tricks to Keep Income Aloft," *Wall Street Journal*, January 20, 2000, pp. A1, A6.

2. "Cost-Conscious Shoppers Seek Secondhand," *USA Today*, March 14, 1996, p. B1.

3. "Retailers Are Giving Profits Away," *American Demographics*, June 1994, p. 14.

4. "How IBM Turned Around Its Ailing PC Division," *Wall Street Journal*, March 12, 1998, pp. B1, B4.

5. Ramarao Desuaju and Steven Shugan, "Strategic Service Pricing and Yield Management," *Journal of Marketing*, January 1999, pp. 44–56.

6. "The Power of Smart Pricing," *Business Week*, April 10, 2000, pp. 160–164.

7. "Your Room Costs $250 . . . No! $200 . . . . No," *Wall Street Journal*, May 5, 1999, pp. B1, B16.

8. David Henderson, "What Are Price Wars Good For? Absolutely Nothing," *Fortune*, May 12, 1997, p. 156.

9. "Inflation's New Adversary," *Business Week*, October 4, 1999, p. 30.

10. "Good-Bye to Fixed Pricing?" *Business Week*, May 4, 1998, pp. 71–84.

11. Peter Elkind, "The Hype Is Big, Really Big at Priceline," *Fortune*, September 6, 1999, pp. 193–202.

12. "Name Your Price—For Everything?" *Business Week*, April 17, 2000, pp. 72–78.

13. "Going, Going, Gone . . . . . Sucker," *Business Week*, March 20, 2000, pp. 124–126.

14. "Online Auctions May Elicit Lower Prices for Shoppers than Online Catalogs," *Wall Street Journal*, September 23, 1999, p. A1.

15. "Going, Going, Gone," *Business Week*, April 5, 2000, p. 31.

16. "Stores' Demands Squeeze Apparel Companies," *Wall Street Journal*, July 15, 1997, pp. B1, B12; and Timothy Matanovich, Gary Lilien, and Arvind Rangaswamy, "Engineering the Price-Value Relationship," *Marketing Management*, Spring 1999, pp. 48–53.

17. Praveen Kopalle and Donald Lehmann, "The Effects of Advertised and Observed Quality on Expectations About New Product Quality," *Journal of Marketing Research*, August 1995, pp. 280–290; Akshay Rao and Kent Monroe, "The

Effect of Price, Brand Name, and Store Name on Buyers' Perceptions of Product Quality: An Integrative Review," *Journal of Marketing Research*, August 1989, pp. 351–357; Gerard Tellis and Gary Gaeth, "Best Value, Price-Seeking, and Price Aversion: The Impact of Information and Learning on Consumer Choices," *Journal of Marketing*, April 1990, pp. 34–35.

18. William Dodds, Kent Monroe, and Dhruv Grewal, "Effects of Price, Brand, and Store Information on Buyers' Product Evaluations," *Journal of Marketing Research*, August 1991, pp. 307–319; see also Akshay Rao and Wanda Sieben, "The Effect of Prior Knowledge on Price Acceptability and the Type of Information Examined," *Journal of Consumer Research*, September 1992, pp. 256–270; Ajay Kalra and Ronald Goldman, "The Impact of Advertising Positioning Strategies on Consumer Price Sensitivity," *Journal of Marketing Research*, May 1998, pp. 210–224.

19. Phillip Parker, "Sweet Lemons: Illusory Quality, Self-Deceivers, Advertising, and Price," *Journal of Marketing Research*, August 1995, pp. 291–307; Michael Etgar and Naresh Malhotra, "Determinants of Price Dependency: Personal and Perceptual Factors," *Journal of Consumer Research*, September 1981, pp. 217–222; Jeen-Su Lim and Richard Olshavsky, "Impacts of Consumers' Familiarity and Product Class on Price-Quality Inference and Product Evaluations," *Quarterly Journal of Business and Economics*, Summer 1988, pp. 130–141.

20. Donald Lichtenstein and Scott Burton, "The Relationship Between Perceived and Objective Price—Quality," *Journal of Marketing Research,* November 1989, pp. 429–443.

21. "Store-Brand Pricing Has to Be Just Right," *Wall Street Journal*, February 14, 1992, p. B1; see also George Cressman, Jr., "Snatching Defeat from the Jaws of Victory," *Marketing Management,* Summer 1997, pp. 9–19.

22. Dawar Niraj and Phillip Parker, "Marketing Universals: Consumers' Use of Brand Name, Price, Physical Appearance, and Retailer Reputation as Signals of Product Quality," *Journal of Marketing*, April 1994, pp. 81–95.

CHAPTER 18

1. "Entrée Economics," *Wall Street Journal-Weekend Journal*, March 10, 2000, pp. W1, W4.

2. "Building a Better Mousetrap Is No Claptrap," *Business Week*, February 1, 1999, p. 47.

3. "Take Me Out to the Ballgame, James," *Business Week*, March 13, 2000, p. 142.

4. Reed Holden and Thomas Nagle, "Kamikaze Pricing," *Marketing Management*, Summer 1998, pp. 31–39.

5. "Jury Convicts Ex-executives in ADM Case," *Wall Street Journal*, September 18, 1998, pp. A3, A4.

6. "Justice's Cartel Crackdown," *Business Week*, July 27, 1998, pp. 30–32.

7. For an excellent article on predatory pricing, see Joseph P. Guiltinan and Gregory T. Gundlack, "Aggressive and Predatory Pricing: A Framework for Analysis," *Journal of Marketing*, July 1966, pp. 87–102; see also "The Myth of Predatory Pricing—Exposed," *Fortune*, February 7, 2000, p. 49.

8. Patricia Sellers, "The Dumbest Marketing Ploy," *Fortune*, October 3, 1992, pp. 88–94. © 1992 Time Inc. All rights reserved.

9. "Eliminated Discounts on P&G Goods Annoy Many Who Sell Them," *Wall Street Journal*, August 11, 1992, pp. A1, A6.

10. Sellers, pp. 88–89.

11. "Ed Artzt's Elbow Grease Has P&G Shining," *Business Week*, October 10, 1994, pp. 84–86. For an excellent study on EDLP and its impact on retailers and manufacturers, see Stephen J. Hoch, Xavier Dreze, and Mary E. Purk, "EDLP, Hi-Lo, and Margin Arithmetic," *Journal of Marketing*, October 1994, pp 16–27.

12. Vicki Clift, "Loss Leaders Not Just for Retailers Anymore," *Marketing News*, February 1, 1999, p. 7.

13. Charles Quigley and Elaine Notarantonio, "An Exploratory Investigation of Perceptions of Odd and Even Pricing," in *Developments in Marketing Science*, ed. Victoria Crittenden (Miami: Academy of Marketing Science, 1992), pp. 306–309.

14. "Nine Cents of Separation," *American Demographics*, May 1998, p. 41.

15. "Three-for $3 and Other Numerical Pitches Work Magic in Stores," *Wall Street Journal*, March 12, 1998, p. A1; see also Herman Simon and Robert Dolan, "Price Customization," *Marketing Management*, Fall 1998, pp. 11–17; and Margaret Campbell, "Perceptions of Price Unfairness: Antecedents and Consequences," *Journal of Marketing Research*, May 1999, pp. 187–199.

16. Francis Mulhern and Robert Leone, "Implicit Price Bundling of Retail Products: A Multiproduct Approach to Maximizing Store Profitability," *Journal of Marketing*, October 1991, pp. 63–76; Dorothy Paun, "Product Bundling: A Normative Model Based on an Orientation Perspective," in *Developments in Marketing Science*, ed. Victoria Crittenden (Miami: Academy of Marketing Science, 1992), pp. 301–305; Manjit Yadav and Kent Monroe, "How Buyers Perceive Savings in a Bundle Price: An Examination of a Bundle's Transaction Value," *Journal of Marketing Research*, August 1993, pp. 350–358; R. Venkatesh and Vijay Mahajan, "A Probabilistic Approach to Pricing a Bundle of Services," *Journal of Marketing Research*, November 1993, pp. 509–521; Asim Ansari, S. Siddarth, and Charles Weinberg, "Pricing a Bundle of Products or Services: The Case of Nonprofits," *Journal of Marketing Research*, February 1996, pp. 86–93; and Francis Mulhern, Jerome Williams, and Robert Leone, "Those With More Buy Less," *American Demographics*, April 1999, pp. 18–20.

17. Vicki Morwitz, Eric Greenleaf, and Eric Johnson, "Divide and Prosper: Consumers' Reactions to Partitioned Prices," *Journal of Marketing Research*, November 1998, pp. 453–463.

18. This material on price penalties is from Eugene Fram and Michael McCarthy, "The True Price of Penalties," *Marketing Management*, Fall 1999, pp. 49–54.

19. "Ask and It Shall Be Discounted," *Business Week*, October 6, 1997, pp. 116–118.

20. "Marketers Try to Ease Sting of Price Increases," *Marketing News*, October 9, 1995, p. 5.

21. "Value Strategy to Battle Recession," *Advertising Age*, January 7, 1991, pp. 1, 44.

22. "Going, Going, Gone," *Business Week*, April 12, 1999, p. 30.

23. "What a Deal," *Fast Company*, November 1998, p. 298.

CHAPTER 19

Notes appear with the chapter on-line.

CHAPTER 20

1. Sharan Barnett and Frank Barnett, "Williams-Sonoma's Multi-Channel Marketing Leads to Niche Dominance," *Direct Marketing*, March 1999, p. 41; Dana James, "Synchronizing the Elements," *Marketing News*, February 14, 2000, p. 15; Thyra Porter, "Williams-Sonoma Web Registry Boosts Bridal Sales," *HFN: The Weekly Newspaper for the Home Furnishings Network*, May 15, 2000, p. 17; Eliza Gallo. "A Marriage of Convenience," *Gifts & Decorative Accessories*, October 1999, p. 37.

2. Don Peppers and Martha Rogers, *The One to One Future: Building Relationships One Customer at a Time* (New York: Currency/Doubleday, 1997).

3. Edward Nash, *Database Marketing: The Ultimate Marketing Tool* (New York: McGraw-Hill, 1993), p. xvii.

4. Rob Jackson and Paul Wang, *Strategic Database Marketing* (Lincolnwood, IL: NTC Business Books, 1997), p. 10.

5. Ernan Roman, *Integrated Direct Marketing* (Lincolnwood, IL: NTC Business Books, 1996), p. 1.

6. Jackson and Wang, p. 3.

7. Roman, p. 1.

8. Gerri Knilans, "Database Marketing: Fad, Fantasy or Reality?" *Direct Marketing*, May 1997, p. 48.

9. Jackson and Wang, p. 3.

10. Laura Loro, "Case Study: FedEx Mines Its Database to Drive New Sales," *Business Marketing*, March 1997, p. 4.

11. Paula Kephart, "Knowledge Is Power: One-to-One Database Marketing," *Marketing Tools*, October 1997, p. 32.

12. Matt Murray and Raju Narisetti, "Bank Mergers Hidden Engine: Technology," *Wall Street Journal*, April 23, 1998, pp. B1, B9.

13. Richard H. Levey, "What's Your Database IQ?" *Direct*, February 1998, p. 1.

14. Carol Krol, "Cayman Visits AmEx," *Advertising Age*, February 15, 1999, p. 18; Carol Krol, "Case Study: Mead Johnson Finds Winning Formula for Reaching Moms," *Advertising Age*, April 26, 1999, p. 25; Christina Binkley, "Marriott to Give Additional Perks to Frequent Guests," *Wall Street Journal*, April 25, 2000, p. B15; Jennifer Lach, "Data Mining Digs In," *American Demographics*, July 1999.

15. Todd Wasserman, Gerry Khermouch, Jeff Green, "Minding Everyone's Business," *Brandweek*, February 28, 2000, p. 32.

16. Don Peppers, "Banking on Strong Customer Relationships," *Inside 1to1*, March 16, 2000, http://www,.1to1.com/publications.

17. Ann Diver, "A Healthy Dose of ROI," *Inside 1to1*, April 27, 2000; http://www.1to1.com/publications.

18. This section based on Jackson and Wang, pp. 4–11; and Frederick Newell, *The New Rules of Marketing: How to Use One-to-One Relationship Marketing to Be the Leader in Your Industry* (New York: McGraw-Hill, 1997), pp. 10–32.

19. Direct Marketing Association press release "For National Consumer Protection Week February 14–20, 2000, More and More Americans are Experiencing the Benefits of Shopping Direct," www.the-dma.org; Direct Marketing Association, "Direct & Interactive Marketing Buying Practices Study," presented at the Direct Marketing Association's Annual Conference, October 1999, www.the-dma.org.

20. Jackson and Wang, p. 11.

21. Chad Kaydo, "Planting the Seeds of Marketing Success," *Sales & Marketing Management*, August 1998, p. 73.

22. Kaydo, p. 73.

23. This section based in part on Jackson and Wang, pp. 39–53.

24. Christina Binkley, "Lucky Numbers: A Casino Chain Finds a Lucrative Niche: The Small Spenders," *Wall Street Journal*, May 4, 2000, pp. A1, A10.

25. Julie Pitta, "Garbage In, Gold Out." *Forbes*, April 5, 1999, pp. 125–125.

26. David Bank, "Know Your Customer," *Wall Street Journal*, June 21, 1999, p. R18.

27. Ginger Conlon, "True Romance," *Sales & Marketing Management*, May 1996, pp. 85–90.

28. Christina Binkley, "Marriott to Give Additional Perks to Frequent Guests," *Wall Street Journal*, April 25, 2000, p. B15.

29. Debra Aho Williamson, "Program Rewards Frequent Visitors," *Advertising Age*, May 17, 1999, p. 50.

30. Erika Rasmusson, "This Database Is a Heavy Favorite," *Sales & Marketing Management*, June 1998, p. 73.

31. William M. Bulkeley, "We're Watching You," *Wall Street Journal*, November 22, 1999, pp. R32, R46.

32. Carol Krol, "Database Marketing Proves Rx Value," *Advertising Age*, March 15, 1999, p. s18.

33. Jennifer Lach, "Can We Talk?" *American Demographics*, March 1999.

34. Dick Shavers, "Outward Bound: Building a Dialogue with Consumers Makes Marketing Work Online," *Direct*, April 1997, p. 73.

35. Chad Kaydo, "As Good As It Gets," *Sales & Marketing Management*, March 2000, pp. 55–60.

36. Loro, p. 4.

37. Jean Halliday, "Carmakers Learn to Mine Databases," *Advertising Age*, April 17, 2000, p. s6; Michele Marchetti, "Shifting Gears," *Sales & Marketing Management*, December 1999, pp. 38–48.

38. David Bank, "Know Your Customer," *Wall Street Journal*, June 21, 1999, p. R18.

39. "Customer Relationship Management: A Senior Management Guide to Technology for Creating a Customer-Centric Business-Executive Summary," *PriceWaterhouseCoopers and the Direct Marketing association*, http://www.the-dma.org; Meryl Davids, "How to Avoid the 10 Biggest Mistakes in CRM," *Journal of Business Strategy*, November 1999, p. 22.

40. Jackson and Wang, p. 21.

41. *Random House Webster's Dictionary* (New York: Random House/Ballantine Books, 1993), p. 165.

42. Jack Schmid and Alan Weber, *Desktop Database Marketing* (Lincolnwood, IL: NTC Business Books, 1998), pp. 33–34.

43. Jackson and Wang, p. 83.

44. Gordon Fairclough, "Dancing, Blackjack and Free Smokes," *Wall Street Journal*, October 26, 1999, pp. B1, B6; Judann Pollack, "Loyalty Program Takes RJR's Doral to No. 3," *Advertising Age*, August 1999, http://www.adage.com.

45. Julia Angwin, "Virgin to Trade Web Use for Personal Data," *Wall Street Journal*, April 10, 2000, p. B16.

46. Rebecca Piirto Heath, "Loyalty for Sale: Everybody's Doing Frequency Marketing—but Only a Few Companies Are Doing It Well," *Marketing Tools*, July 1997, p. 40.

47. Denny Hatch, "The Business of Business Lists: A Look at This Incredibly, Unbelievably Complex World," *Target Marketing*, January 1997, p. 65.

48. Annette Kissinger, "You Say London, I Say Londres," *Marketing Tools*, May 1997.

49. Jackson and Wang, p. 86.

50. Jackson and Wang, pp. 86–87.

51. Diane Cyr, "Spiegel's Power Play," *Catalog Age*, April 30, 2000.

52. Hatch, p. 65.

53. Carol Krol, "Targeting Toddlers," *Advertising Age*, April 20, 1998, p. 29.

54. Jack Schmid and Alan Weber, *Desktop Database Marketing* (Lincolnwood, IL: NTC Business Books, 1998), pp. 33–34.

55. Roman, p. 33.

56. Jim Emerson, "Elvis Fans," *Direct,* June 1998, p. 103.

57. Peppers and Rogers, pp. 49–50.

58. James R. Rosenfield, "The Myth of Database Marketing," *Direct Marketing,* February 1998, p. 28.

59. David Cameron, "Do You Really Need a Data Warehouse?" *Direct Marketing,* June 1998, p. 43.

60. Carol Krol, "Case Study: Hallmark Uses Loyalty Effort for Segmenting Customers," *Advertising Age*, February 1, 1999, p. 36.

61. Michele Marchetti, "In Search of Profitable Revenues," *Sales & Marketing Management,* August 1998, p. 74.

62. Schmid and Weber, p. 132.

63. Newell, p. 82.

64. Heath, p. 40.

65. Schmid and Weber, *Desktop Database Marketing*, pp. 82–83.

66. "Alliance of Catalogers Creates Immense Database," *Direct Marketing*, March 1999, p. 41.

67. Jennifer Lach, "Data Mining Digs in," *American Demographics*, July 1999; Amanda Beeler, "Fingerhut Uses Optimization to Reduce Cascade of Catalogs," *Advertising Age*, June 5, 2000, p. 35.

68. Peter R. Peacock, "Data Mining in Marketing: Part 1: The Revolution Is upon Us, So Choose Your Weapons Carefully," *Marketing Management*, Winter 1998, pp. 9–18.

69. Skip Press, "Fool's Gold?" *Sales & Marketing Management,* June 1998, pp. 58–62.

70. Lisa Bransten, "Looking for Patterns," *Wall Street Journal*, June 21, 1999, pp. R16, R20.

71. Carol Krol, "Data Warehouse Generates Surprises, Leads for Camelot," *Advertising Age*, January 4, 1999, p. 20; Wasserman, Khermouch, and Green, p. 32.

72. Michael Jay Tucker, "Poppin' Fresh Dough," *Datamation,* May 1997, p. 50.

73. Amanda Beeler, "Customer Service Gets Boost from New Tech," *Advertising Age*, March 27, 2000, p. 44.

74. Don Peppers and Martha Rogers, "Opening the Door to Customers," *Sales & Marketing Management*, October 1998, pp. 22–29.

75. David J. Moore, "Database Marketing Holds Even More Promise Online," *Advertising Age*, March 1, 1999, p. s20.

76. Ira Teinowitz, "Consumers to Be Notified About Profiling," *Advertising Age*, November 15, 1999, p. 52.

77. Sarah Lorge, "Banner Ads vs. E-Mail Marketing," *Sales & Marketing Management*, August 1999, p. 15.

78. Kaydo, pp. 55–60; Debra Aho Williamson, "Virtual Vineyards Pumps Bottom Line with E-Mail," *Advertising Age*, April 19, 1999, p. 71.

79. Wine.com Web site at http://www.wine.com; Williamson, "Virtual Vineyards," p. 71.

80. Kaydo, pp. 56–57.

81. Jeffery D. Zbar, "Marketers Buoy Brands with E-Mail Newsletters," *Advertising Age*, October 25, 1999, p. 74.

82. Jim Costelli, "How to Handle Personal Information," *American Demographics,* March 1996, pp. 50–58.

83. Robert E. Thomas and Virginia G. Maurer, "Database Marketing Practice: Protecting Consumer Privacy," *Journal of Public Policy & Marketing*, Spring 1997, p. 147.

84. Frederick Newell, "Information Is Knowledge, Knowledge Is Power, and Power Can Be Frightening," *Direct Marketing*, April 2000, p. 59.

85. Nick Wingfield and Glenn R. Simpson, "With So Much Subscriber Data, AOL Walks a Cautious Line on Privacy," *Wall Street Journal*, March 15, 2000, pp. B1, B4.

86. Andrea Petersen, "A Privacy Firestorm at DoubleClick," *Wall Street Journal*, February 23, 2000, pp. B1, B4; Andrea Petersen and Jon G. Auerbach, "Online Ad Titans Bet Big in Race to Trace Consumers' Web Tracks," *Wall Street Journal*, November 8, 1999, pp. B1, B4.

87. Julia Angwin, Nick Wingfield, and Khanh T.L. Tran, "New Children's Privacy Rules Pose Obstacles for Some Sites," *Wall Street Journal*, April 24, 2000, p. B8.

88. Richard B. Schmitt, "Online Privacy: Alleged Abuses Shape New Law," *Wall Street Journal*, February 29, 2000, pp. B1, B4.

89. Ira Teinowitz, "FTC Policy Draft Provokes Debate About Web Privacy," *Advertising Age*, May 15, 2000, pp. 3, 84.

90. Erika Rasmusson, "The Perils of International Direct Mail," *Sales & Marketing Management*, April 2000, p. 107; E-Commerce III: Nations Fall Slowly in Line on Privacy-Protection Laws," *The Globe and Mail*, November 30, 1999, p E25; Mark Ward, "Connected: EU Deal with U.S. Over Privacy," *The Daily Telegraph*, March 23, 2000, p. 3; Beverley Head, "No Privacy, but at Least Some Control," *Business Review Weekly*, April 20, 2000, p. 44; Todd Wasserman, Gerry Khermouch, and Jeff Green, "Minding Everyone's Business," *Brandweek*, February 28, 2000, p. 32; "U.S., EU Make Safe Harbor Agreement, No Shelter for Financial Institutions," *Retail Delivery News*, March 29, 2000.

company index

subject index

A

Accelerator principle, 196
Accessibility, of market segment, 216
Accessory equipment, 199
Activity-based costing (ABC), 572
Ad creep, 516, 517. *See also* Advertising; Media
Ademiluyi, Mozella Perry, 72
Adopters, 331
  early, 330–331, 332, 333
  early majority, 331, 333
  innovators, 330, 332
  laggards, 331
  late majority, 331, 333
Adoption
  process, marketing implications of, 332–333
  rate of, for new products, 331–332
Advanced manufacturing systems (AMS), 376
Advertising, 487, 646–647
  advocacy, 504
  appeals
    to desire for love, 173
    developing and evaluating, 507–509
    to youthful looks, 169
  broadband, 516
  comparative, 505–506
  competitive, 505
  controlling false, 77, 506. *See also* Wheeler-Lea Act
  cooperative, 512
  cultural attitudes toward, 121
  defined, 475, 502
  economies, 299
  effects of, 502–504
    on consumers, 503–504
  expenditures, 502–503, 511, 512
    Internet, 515–516
    television, 514–515, 517, 520–521
  FTC regulation of Internet, 79–80
  global, 118, 509, 511, 524
  good, components of, 150
  institutional, 504
  lack of impact on industrial purchasing managers of, 209
  major types of, 504–506
  market share, 503
  media, 512–516
  message execution, 509–511
  objectives, 506–507
  outdoor, 515
  pioneering, 505
  product, 504, 505
  relation of social class to, 159. *See also* Social class
  relief of possible dissonance, through, 147
  repetitious, 174
  response of Generation Y to, 141
  status-conscious, for specialty products, 298
  use of, to promote business goods, 488
  using shock value, 170
  word-of-mouth, 241
Advertising campaigns
  AIDA model and, 507, 509
  defined, 506

developing advertising appeal in, 507–509
  evaluating, 511–512
  intrusive, 517
  objectives of, 506–507
Advertising response function, 503
Advocacy advertising, 504
African-Americans, 71, 73, 219
  Colby Care Nurses program for, 85
  events targeted toward, 233
  family farms, Ben & Jerry's use of, 93
  as largest minority group, 72, 220
  supermarket shopping habits of, 429
  technology-training program for, 364–365
  Wrigley health maintenance campaign for, 85
Age, 161
  bears for every, 183
  as factor in brand loyalty, 69
  impact of, on consumer behavior, 167
  -related tastes, 167
  in relation to car purchases, 144
  rising median, of Americans, 168
  segmentation, 218–219
Agents, as channel intermediaries, 382, 386
Aguilera, Christina, 525–526
AIDA concept, 486–487, 507, 546
  and promotional mix, 487–488
Akhtar, Rukhsana, 124
Alcoholics Anonymous (AA), 58
Alliances
  equity, 185
  strategic, 185, 189–190, 205
Alzheimer's, 40
Amae, 190
American Civil Liberties Union, 677
Anchor stores, 447–449
Anthony, Michael, 49
Anzt, Edward, 613, 615
Applied research, 75–76
Armani, Giorgio, 523–524
Asian-Americans, 71, 73, 429
  diversity of, 220–221
  events targeted toward, 233
  as fastest growing minority group, 72
  Wrigley health maintenance campaign for, 85
Aspirational reference groups, 160
Ater, Gwen, 267
Atmosphere, 449–451, 464
  in global market, 456
Attitudes, 175. *See also* Norms
  modifying, 176
  overcoming negative, 177
  unique, of Internet consumers, 182
Attributes
  advertising and brand, 504
  changing beliefs about, 175–176
  as positioning bases, 235
  product, 176, 507
Audience selectivity, 518
Augmented product, 38
Australian Federal Police, 131
Automatic identification systems (auto ID), 406–407
Average total cost (ATC), 586
Average variable cost (AVC), 586

Avrahani v. U.S. News & World Report, Inc., 666
Axelson, Per, 303

B

Baby boomers, 66, 67–69, 153, 218
  aging, 430
    interests of, 150
    products aimed at, 168
    Volvo's problem with, 176–177
  children of, 141. *See also* Generation Y
  individualism among, 68
  interest in health foods, of, 308
  targeting, 437
Bait pricing, 618
Baker, Beau, 596
Bar codes, 310. *See also* Universal product codes
  future uses of, 457–458
Barkley, Charles, 119
Barter. *See* Countertrade
Barton, Jim, 530
Base price, 612
Basic research, 75
Basing-point pricing, 615
Behavior
  business buying, 197, 200–203
  buyer, 46
  consumer, 161
  creating changes in, 173
  effect of sales promotion on, 536
  ethical, in business, 82–83
  postpurchase, 142, 146–147
  routine response, 147, 148
  shopping, 327
  unique, of Internet consumers, 182
BehaviorScan, 275
Beliefs, 175–176
Beller, Leslie, 364–365
Benchmarking, 138–139
Benefit segmentation, 224–225
Berg, Kevin, 229
Betty Ford Center, 59
Bexon, Robert, 229
Bezos, Jeff, 29
Bielinsky, Don, 210
Blacklow, Julie, 588
Blackshaw, Pete, 282
Bland, Donald C., 95
Bliss, Garrison, 588
Body image, 168
Bornstein, Rolf, 303
Boycotts, 106
Brabeck, Peter, 124
Brainstorming, 323
Brand
  becoming known as, 310
  defined, 301
  equity, 302
  family, 306
  master, 302
  preference, creating, 486
  price and, 597
  private-label, 423, 444–445
Brand equity, 302
Brand identity, 303. *See also* Brand image
  establishing global, 311
  strengthening, 310

Computers. *See also* PCs
  as giveaways, 541–542
  growth potential for, 631
  hand-held, 130
  in materials handling systems, 403
Concentrated targeting strategy,
  232–233
Concept test, 324
Conceptual learning, 173–174
Conflict, 2, 3
  among channel members, 395–396
  between marketing and manufactur-
    ing, 139
Conjoint analysis, 181
Consideration set. *See* Evoked set
Consultants, 323
Consultative selling. *See* Relationship
  selling
Consumer behavior, 142
  age, as factor of, 167
  family life-cycle stage, as factor of,
    167
  reference group infuence on, 161
  relationship between self-concept
    and, 168, 169
  relationship of learning to, 173
Consumer buying decisions
  continuum of, 147, 148
  factors influencing, 150–151
    cultural, 151–153
    individual, 164–169
    psychological, 169–177
    social, 160–164
Consumer e-commerce, 186. *See also*
  e-tailing
Consumer education, 524–525
Consumer goods, 186
  companies, 217
  promotion of, 488
Consumer involvement, 147–148
  factors determining level of, 149
  marketing implications of, 149–150
Consumer penalties, 619–621
Consumer privacy, 91–92
  regulation of Internet abuses of, 79–80
Consumer products, 292
  types of, 296–298
Consumer Product Safety Commission
  (CPSC), 77–78
Consumer Products Safety Act of 1972,
  325
Consumers, 645. *See also* Demand
  advertising invasion of, 517
  baby boomers, 67–69
  building profiles of, 56–57
  changing attitudes of target, 175
  and choice, importance of attributes
    in, 146
  constrained time budgets of, 64. *See
    also* Time
  consumption patterns of average, 68
  CPSC, to protect health and safety of,
    78
  decision-making process of, 142–143
  and decisions related to situation, 149
  effects of advertising on, 503–504
  emotional motives of, 221
  as environmentalists, 64
  family, 163
  FTC regulation of privacy, regarding,
    80
  Generation X, 66–67. *See also* Genera-
    tion X
  Generation Y, 67. *See also* Generation Y

high price and, 596–597
image-conscious, 173
interests of, 149
Internet development, driven by, 26
involved in production of services,
  345
need for understanding core values
  of, 153
older, 69–70
on-line, 182
perceived risk of, 144–145, 149. *See
  also* Risk
and previous experience, 149
product demand for, 195, 196
quality expectations of, 470
rewards for, 536
search process of, 145
social class and, 157–159
target, 62
targeted Internet messages to, 91
traits of affluent, 158
wants of, 143–144
Consumer sales promotion. *See* Sales
  promotion
Contests, 539
Continuous media schedule, 521
Continuous replenishment (CR), 401–402
Contract manufacturing, 113
Contracts
  in business marketing, 198
  purchasing, 203
Control, of marketing plan, 48
Convenience, in retail environment,
  456–458
Convenience products, 296
Convenience sample, 269
Convenience stores, 430
Conventional morality, 82–83
Conventions, 543
  generating leads through, 547
Cooperative advertising, 512
Cooper, Pashadow, 61
Core service, 349–350
Corporate silos, 2
Corporate social responsibility, 85–86
  pyramid of, 85, 86
Cosby, Bill, 163
Cost
  competitive advantage, 36–37
  determinant of price, 586–591
  differential advantages, 37–38
  effectiveness, 377
  estimating, 607
  fixed, 586
  introductory stage of product life cy-
    cle (PLC), 334
  leadership, 36–37
  -oriented tactics, 622
  per contact, 491
  per unit, 609
  product, 488–489
  reduction methods, 37–38
  variable, 586
Cost competitive advantage, 36–37
Cost differential advantages, 37–38
Costner, Kevin, 564
Cost per contact, 491, 518
  in magazine advertising, 512–513
Countertrade, 122–123
Coupons, 536, 537–538, 542, 646–647,
  656
Crawford, Cindy, 475
Creative friction, 293
Credence quality, 345

Credit, use of, 175
Crisis management, 523, 526
Cross-functional approaches, 2–3,
  138–139, 293
Cross-functional teams, 3, 138, 293, 325,
  376
Cross-tabulation, 271
Cruise, Tom, 566
Cultural creativity, 63
Culture, 82, 102–104
  defined, 152–153
  differences
    in global marketing, 95, 455, 456,
      482
    regarding branding and packaging,
      311–312
    regarding notion of time, 103
    understanding, 153, 155
  effect of, on marketing research, 117
  fusion, 156
  influence of
    on consumer decision making, 150,
      151
    on product preference, 102–104
Cumulative quantity discount, 612
Custom data, 658
Customer databases, 41, 437
Customer loyalty, 247–248, 293
  retaining, 650–651
Customer management, 458
Customer profiles, 224–225, 516, 550,
  657–658
Customer relationship marketing
  (CRM), 458, 642. *See also* One-to-
  one marketing
Customers, 15–16
  battle for, 643
  benefits sought by, 14–15
  business, 190–193, 197
    governments, 192
    producers, 190–191
    resellers, 191–192
  components of service evaluation by,
    346–347
  demands of, 405
  determination of product value by,
    613
  developing relationship with, 643
  and development of new products,
    322
  expectations of, 5, 405
  experience of, 11
  focus of, 2
  identifying best, 649–650
  lifetime value of, 662
  location of, segmenting by, 227
  loyalty of, 13, 247–248. *See also* Cus-
    tomer loyalty
  needs of, 550
  predicting future behavior of, 181
  pricing demands of large, 596
  as receivers, 480
  retention of, 464
    loyal, 650–651
  satisfying, 215
  size of, segmenting, 227
  and supply chain management,
    389–390
  type, segmenting by, 227
  understanding, 138
Customer satisfaction, 12, 13, 293, 413
  achieving, 376
  cross-functional planning, for, 377
  guarantee, 47

cultural differences, in global, 156
high-tech sector of, 74
need for professionals in growing, 110
personalized, 68
takeoff, 104
U.S.
dependence on retailing of, 424
immigrants, as benefit to, 70
impact of international business on, 97
Edgar, Christopher, 463
Efficiency, in retail environment, 456–458
Efficient consumer response (ECR), 401–402, 444
programs, 401
Eisenhower, Dwight D., 70
Eisner, Michael, 466
Elastic demand, 583, 584
Elasticity, of demand, 583–585
factors affecting, 584–585
Electronic bill presentment and payment (EBPP), 182
Electronic business (e-business). *See* e-commerce
Electronic commerce. *See* e-commerce
Electronic data interchange (EDI), 376, 401, 412, 444
Electronic distribution, 408
Electronic Privacy and Information Center, 677
Electronic retailing
on-line, 438–440
shop-at-home networks, 438
e-mail
advertising on, 475
alerts, 439, 641
customer uses of, 13
as one-to-one medium, 665–666
Empathy, of service, 346–347
Employees, 293
creation of new-product ideas by, 322
in retail stores, 450
and service quality, 346
Empowerment, 14
Encoding, 478–480
Endorsements, 163. *See also* Opinion leaders
celebrity, 353
Engels, Friedrich, 156
Entertainment, in retail environment, 455–456, 464
Environmentalism
consumers' advocacy of, 64
relation of, to packaging, 308
Environmental management, 63
Environmental Protection Agency, 173
Environmental scanning, 63
Equity, 133
Equity alliances, 185
e-retailers, failures of, 180–181, 182. *See also* e-commerce
Ericson, Dan, 303
Escalator pricing, 622
e-tailing, 438–440. *See also* Consumer e-commerce
Ethics
business, 82–83
checklist, 85
corporate codes of, 84
defined, 82
guidelines, 82

in marketing
children's privacy on the Internet, 668
digitally downloading music from Internet, 409
effect of price on vaccine usage, 617
gender-specific toy promotion, 166
guidelines regarding gifts and favors, 204
high-pressure sales tactics, 485
in-school product testing, 267
intrusive advertising, 517
marketers on campus, 81
nondisclosure of brand ownership, 328
preservationists protest expansion of drugstores, 448
protection for sweepstakes consumers, 540
questions about medical privacy on Web, 352
repackaging pills under different names, 309
selling water to world's poor, 124
an unusual medical consultancy, 588
use of customer data to encourage more frequent gambling, 10
purchasing, 203–204
and social responsibility, 85
Ethnic markets, 70–73
Ethnic segmentation, 219–221. *See also* Ethnic markets
European Central Bank, 108
European Commission, 108
European Community (EC), 106, 410
European Data Protection Directive, 667
European Monetary Union (EMU), 108
European Union (EU), 100, 108–110, 307, 667, 669
conflict of pricing in, 572–573
expansion of American retailers, through, 453
protectionist movement by, 109
Evaluation
of alternatives, 142, 146
criteria, for business buyers, 202
of marketing plan, 48
postpurchase, 147
Evaluators, in business buying center, 201
Everett, Bill, 315, 316
Everyday low pricing (EDLP), 449, 613, 615
Evoked set, 145
narrowing choices in, 146
Exchange, 6
Exchange control, 106
Exclusive distribution, 393–394
Exclusivity, 111
Executive interviews, 262
Experience quality, 345
Experiential learning, 173–174
Experiments, marketing research, 267–268
Export
agents, 112
brokers, 112
opportunities, 111
United States, 97
Export agents, 112
Export brokers, 112
Exporters, considerations for, 121

Exporting
federal resources for companies interested in, 114–115
Internet guide to small-business, 188
Express warranty, 312
Extensive decision making, 148–149. *See also* Decision making
External environment, 61
economic development, as major factor in, 104
effect of, on marketing mix, 117
factors in
competitive, 80–81
demographic, 66–70
economic, 74–75
political and legal, 76–80
social, 63–66
technological and resource, 75–76
global marketing problems, due to, 95, 101
growing ethnic markets in, 70–73
shortage of natural resources in, 111
understanding, 62–63
External stimuli, 143
Extranets, 187, 554
impact of, on pricing, 594
Extreme-value retailing, 431

F

Factory outlets, 426, 433
Fads, 141
teenage, 161
in Japan, 249
Family, 163–164
consumption, 218
Family brands, 306
Family life cycle, 167
segmentation, 221
Fanning, Shawn, 601
Farrel, Lawrence E., 248
Federal Trade Commission (FTC), 78–79, 505–506, 618, 667, 668
Federal Trade Commission Act, 76, 610, 611
Feedback, 481
Field of Dreams orientation. *See* Production orientation
Field service firm, 270–271
Firm mission, 14–15, 17, 135. *See also* Mission statement
First, Tom, 497
Fixed cost, 586
Fixtures, in retail stores, 450–451, 464
Flexible pricing, 616
Flighted media schedule, 521
Fluctuating demand, 196–197
Flynn, Robert E., 277
FOB factory, 615
FOB origin pricing, 615
FOB shipping point, 615
Focus groups, 262–264, 323
cyber, 263–264
benefits of, 264
Food and Drug Administration (FDA), 78, 80, 309, 310, 476
Ford, Harrison, 566
Ford, Henry, 16, 58, 231, 642
Forecasting, 138, 139
Foreign Corrupt Practices Act, 204
Foster, Jodie, 524
Frame error, 269
Franchisees, 440, 441, 442

Transportation, 403–404
   criteria for choosing, 404
   global considerations for, 411
   technology uses for, 405
Treaty on European Union. *See* Maastricht Treaty
Trialability, and new products, 332
Two-part pricing, 619

U

Ubiquity, 133
Unbundling, 619, 624. *See also* Price bundling
Underwriters Laboratories, 144
Undifferentiated targeting strategy, 230–231
Unethical practices, 83
Unfair trade practices, 610–611
Uniform Commercial Code, 312
Uniform Commercial Code Filings (UCC), 277
Uniform delivered pricing, 615
Unique selling proposition, 508–509
United Nations, 71, 110
Universal product codes (UPCs), 310
Universe, 268–269
Unsought products, 298
Upper class, 157
   interests of, 158. *See also* Social class
URL (Uniform Resource Locator), 252, 554
Uruguay Round, 107
   dumping law rewritten by, 122
Usage-rate segmentation, 225–226
U.S. armed forces, 566
U.S. Census Bureau, 157, 167, 657, 658
U.S. Customs Service, 411
U.S. Department of Agriculture, 428
U.S. Department of Commerce, 112, 122
Users, 236
   in business buying center, 201
U.S. Marines, 525
U.S. Navy, 514–515
U.S. Postal Service, 615

V

Value, 68
   customer, 10–11, 13, 47
      in supply chain management, 389
   impressions, 38
   perceived, 8
Value-based pricing, 613–615
Value impressions, 38
Value pricing, 624
Values, 151. *See also* Norms
   core American, 154
   defined, 153
Value system, 175
Variable cost, 586
Variable pricing, 616
Vasos, Michael, 609
Vending, automatic, 435
Vendor managed inventory (VMI), 401–402
Villa, Bob, 445
Viral marketing, 241, 282, 283. *See also* Word-of-mouth

Visual factors, in retail stores, 451–452, 464
Vogel, Mark, 91
Vorous, Brent, 340

W

Wainright, Julie, 29
Walker, Jay, 286
Wall Street, 134, 462
Walton, Sam, 456
Wanamaker, John, 646
Wang, Paul, 655
Wants, 143–144
   of customers, regarding new products, 322
   future, determining, 292
Warehouse membership clubs, 433
Warehousing, 406, 407
   global concerns for, 411
Warranties, 312
Warranty, 312
Web. *See also* e-commerce; Internet; Web sites; World Wide Web
   address, 252
   -based company stores, 49, 209
   design, consistent use of global context for, 129–130
   directories, 253, 254–255
   finding best price on, 177
   ordering groceries, on, 379
   price-comparison sites, 594
   privacy on, 91–92, 667
   search engines, 253, 254–255
   survey systems, 274
Web sites. *See also* e-commerce; Internet; World Wide Web
   cancer-related, 352
   catering to women, 350–351
   company, 26–27, 57, 129–130, 209, 304
   corporate, 186–187
      use of extranets on, 187
   customizing products on, 11
   e-business, 7. *See also* e-commerce; Internet
   European, 125
   Japanese, 125
   multicultural, 73
   need for informative, 12
   password-protected, 275, 554
   proliferation of, 24–25
   for promoting turkey consumption, 162, 163
   selling advertising on, 15
   selling services, 349
   for teenage girls, 463
   topographic maps, 315–316
   use of
      for career changes, 21
      by public relations professionals, 525–526
   using, for publicity, 522
   women's, 57
Web surfing, 25, 130
   advertising banners for, 515–516
   market research and, 247
   privacy issues related to, 667
   tracking, 91

Welch, Jack, 139
Wheeler-Lea Act, 77
Wholesalers, 199, 380, 386, 491. *See also* Industrial distributors
   exclusivity desires of, 394
   exertion of power by, 395
   in Japan, 410
   merchant, 382
   producers-versus, 396
   purchase of gray-market goods by, 593
   and trade loading, 613
   in United States, 192
Winter, Edward, 67
Wolf, Jaime, 605
Women
   2010 demographics for, 68
   as mothers, marketing strategies to reach, 169
   self-concept of, 169
   specialized Web sites for, 57
   as target market, 442
   Web sites aimed at, 350–351
   working, 65–66, 167, 436, 645
      fashions for, 213, 214–215
Woods, Tiger, 162–163, 166
Word-of-mouth. *See also* Viral marketing
   advertising, 241
   buzz, creating, 525–526
   communication, 332, 353, 354
   referrals, 283
Working class, 158. *See also* Social class
World Bank, 71, 97
World trade, 96. *See also* Global marketing
   advantages of, 98
   fear of, 97–98
   negatives related to, 98
World Trade Organization (WTO), 18, 71, 107
   dumping complaints and, 122
   protests during meeting of, 97, 98
World Wide Web, 65, 241, 558–559, 558–559. *See also* Internet; Web; Web sites
   advertising, 515–516
   mission statements displayed on, 34
Wu, Wendy, 18

X

Xylocaine, 303

Y

Yield management systems (YMS), 585–586
Ying, Qu, 524
Yonemura, Kanako, 249
You've Got Mail, 473

Z

Zane, Chris, 649
Zollo, Peter, 267
Zone pricing, 615

internet index

Campbell Soup	http://www.campbellsoup.com
Carpoint	http://carpoint.msn.com/home/New.asp
CarsDirect.com	http://www.carsdirect.com
CDNow	http://www.cdnow.com
Center for Science in the Public Interest	http://www.cspinet.org
Channel Seven	http://www.channelseven.com
Cheap Tickets, Inc.	http://www.cheaptickets.com
Chrysler	http://www.chryslercars.com
CIA World Factbook	http://www.cia.gov/cia/publications/factbook/index.html
Cincinnati Milacron	http://www.milacron.com
Cinergy	http://www.cinergy.com
CNET Shopper	http://www.cnet.com
Cobalt Group	http://www.cobaltgroup.com
Coca-Cola Company	http://www.cocacola.com
	http://www.surge.com
	http://www.thecolacompany.com
Colgate-Palmolive	http://www.colgate.com
Columbia House	http://www.columbiahouse.com
Commerce Bancorp	http://www.commerceonline.com
Commerce Business Daily	http://www.govcon.com
Compaq Computer Corporation	http://www.compaq.com
Consumer Product Safety Commission	http://www.cpsc.gov
Consumer Reports Online	http://www.consumerreports.org
Continental Airlines	http://www.continental.com
CoolSavings.com	http://www.coolsavings.com
The Copyright Websight	http://www.benedict.com
Covisint	http://www.covisint.com
Dale Carnegie	http://www.dale-carnegie.com/
Deaf World	http://www.deafworldweb.org
Delia's	http://www.delias.com
	http://www.contentsonline.com
Dell Computer	http://www.dell.com
Delta Airlines	http://www.delta-air.com
DigitalCars	http://www.digitalcars.com
Direct Marketing Association	http://www.the-dma.org
DirectLeads	http://www.directleads.com
Disney	http://www.disney.com
	http://www.disney.com/DisneyWorld/DisneyInstitute/ ProfessionalPrograms
Disney Store	http://www.disneystore.com
Distributor World	http://www.distributorworld.com/breakeven.cfm
DMusic	http://www.dmusic.com
Double Click, Inc.	http://www.doubleclick.com
	http://www.doubleclick.net
Dow Jones Publication Library	http://www.nrstg1p.djnr.com
Droog	http://www.droog.com
E*Trade	http://www.etrade.com
Eatzi's Market & Bakery	http://www.eatzis.com
eBay, Inc.	http://www.ebay.com
	http://www.ebay.com/community/aboutebay/overview/index.html
Egghead	http://www.egghead.com
Electric Library	http://wwws.elibrary.com
eMarketer	http://www.emarketer.com
Emotional intelligence test	http://www.utne.com/lens/bms/9bmseq.html
Encirq	http://encirq.com
Energy Marketplace	http://www.energymarketplace.com
Enterprise Rent-A-Car	http://www.enterprise.com
Entry Point	http://www.EntryPoint.com
Equal Exchange	http://www.equalexchange.com
Eslamboly & Barlavi	http://www.lawguru.com
E-Toys	http://www.etoys.com
EXE Technologies	http://www.exe.com
Exhibitor Magazine Group	http://www.exhibitornet.com
Export-Import Bank of the United States	http://www.exim.gov
Failure Mag.com	http://www.failuremag.com
Fair Market, Inc.	http://www.fairmarket.com
Fastsigns	http://www.fastsigns.com

Federal Communications Commission	http://www.fcc.gov
Federal Express	http://www.fedex.com
Federal Trade Commission (FTC)	http://www.ftc.gov
	http://www.advertisinglaw.com
	http://www.ftc.gov/index
Federation of International Trade Association	http://www.fita.org
Fingerhut	http://www.fingerhut.com
Food and Drug Administration	http://www.fda.gov
	http://www.fda.gov/hometext
Ford Motor Company	http://www.fordvehicles.com/showroom.asp
411 Direct	http://www.411direct.com/domainnamereg.htm
4Kids Entertainment	http://www.4kidsentertainmentinc.com
Fox Network	http://www.fox.com
Fragrance Net	http://www.fragrancenet.com
Franchise Handbook Online	http://www.franchise1.com
Free Samples.com	http://www.FreeSamples.com
Freebie Club	http://www.freebieclub.com
Freemarkets.com	http://www.freemarkets.com
Freight Tools, Ltd	http://www.ltlrates.com
Frontgate	http://www.frontgate.com
Fuld and Company	http://www.fuld.com/i3/index.html
Garden Escape	http://www2.garden.com
Gardenburger	http://www.gardenburger.com
GE Information Systems	http://www.geis.com
Genentech, Inc.	http://www.gene.com
General Social Survey	http://www.icpsr.umich.edu/gss
Georgia Tech College of Computing	http://www.cc.gatech.edu/gvu/user_surveys
GFI Entertainment	http://www.gfientertainment.com
GM	http://www.gm.com
Godiva	http://www.godiva.com
Good Housekeeping	http://www.goodhousekeeping.com
GoTo.com, Inc	http://www.goto.com
	http://www.auctionrover.com
GraingerAuction	http://www.specialbids.com
Grand Circle Travel	http://www.gct.com
Grateful Dead	http://www.dead.net
GTE	http://www.gte.com
Guerilla Marketing	http://www.gmarketing
gURL.com	http://www.gURL.com
GVU Semiannual Survey on Web Usage	http://www.cc.gatech.edu/gvu/user_surveys/
HandSpeak	http://www.handspeak.com
Hasbro, Inc. (Monopoly)	http://www.monopoly.com
Healthy Choice	http://www.healthychoice.com
Hewlett-Packard	http://www.hp.com/abouthp/environment
Hold Everything	http://www.holdeverything.com
Home Decorators	http://www.homedecorators.com
Home Office Association of America	http://www.hoaa.com
Honeywell's Industrial Store	http://www.industrialstore.honeywell.com\
Hotel Discounters	http://www.hoteldiscounters.com
Huffy Bicycle Company	http://www.huffybikes.com
I.C. Stars	http://www.icstars.org
I.C. Stars and William Blair & Company	http://www.iccapital.com
IBM	http://www.ibm.com
Illinois Institute of Technology	http://www.csep.iit.edu/codes/
Imagine Media	http://www.imaginemedia.com
Independent Bankers Association of America	http://www.ibaa.org
Infoseek Ultra	http://www.ultra.infoseek.com
InfoTrack	http://www.infotrac-college.com
Insight Express	http://www.insightexpress.com
Intellectual Property Owners Association	http://www.ipo.org
Inter-commerce Corporation	http://www.survey.net
Internal Revenue Service	http://www.irs.gov
International Career Employment Center	http://www.internationaljobs.org/
International Chambers of Commerce	http://www.worldchambers.com
International Computing Centre	http://www.unicc.org/untpdc/eto/abouteto.html
International Franchise Association	http://www.franchise.org
International Olympic Committee	http://www.olympic.org

International Sony Music Webs	http://www.sonymusic.be
International Trade Administration	http://www.ita.doc.gov
International, Ltd.	http://www.allpm.com
Internet Access for Promotional Products, Inc.	http://www.promotionalproducts.com
Internet Business Library	http://www.bschool.ukans.edu/intbuslib/virtual.htm
Internet Commerce Standards	http://www.gii.com/standard/index.html
Internet Public Library	http://www.ipl.org
Internet.com Corporation	http://www.cyberatlas.internet.com
Internet.com Corporation	http://www.thelist.internet.com
IRI	http://www.infores.com
Islandnet AMT Solutions Group, Inc.	http://www.islandnet.com/~deathnet/media_email.html
itools	http://www.iTools.com/research-it/research-it.html
Japan Information Network	http://www.jin.jcic.or.jp/statistics
JNCO	http://www.jnco.com
Junkbusters Corporation	http://www.junkbusters.com
Just for Feet	http://www.feet.com
Keebler	http://www.keebler.com
Keiretsu	http://www.keiretsu.com
Kellogg's	http://www.kelloggs.com
Kenneth Cole	http://www.kencole.com
Kinko's	http://www17.kinkos.com
Klik-Klok Productions	http://www.klik-klok.com
Koblas Currency Converter	http://bin.gnn.com/cgi-bin/gnn
Kraft General Foods, Maxwell House	http://www.kraftfoods.com/maxwellhouse/products.html
Kroger Company	http://www.kroger.com
L.L. Bean	http://www.llbean.com
	http://www.llbean.com/customerService/aboutLLBean/index.html
Labelle Management	http://www.labellemgt.com
Land's End	http://www.landsend.com
Levi Strauss & Co.	http://www.levi.com
Lillian Vernon	http://www.lillianvernon.com
Liz Claiborne	http://www.lizclaiborne.com
Loctite Corporation	http://www.loctite.com
Looksmart, Ltd	http://www.looksmart.com
	http://www.looksmart.com/aboutus/media
Lucky Brand Jeans	http://www.luckybrandjeans.com
Lycos, Inc.	http://www.lycos.com/press
Mall of America	http://www.mallofamerica.com
Malls of Canada International	http://www.canadamalls.com
Mark Lundholm	http://www.marklundholm.com
Marriott	http://www.marriott.com
Martha Stewart Living	http://www.marthastewart.com
Mary Kay Cosmetics	http://www.marykay.com
Matte Elsbernd	http://www.firmlist.com/main.shtml
Mattel, Scrabble	http://www.mattelscrabble.com
Maupintour	http://www.maupintour.com
McDonald's	http://www.mcdonalds.com
	http://www.mcdonalds.com/corporate/franchise/inside/factsheet/factsheet.html
MCI	http://www.mci.com
Mead Johnson Nutritional	http://www.meadjohnson.ca
Media Director	http://www.mediadirector.com
MediaFinder	http://www.mediafinder.com
Menlo Logistics	http://www.menlolog.com
Metabolife International, Inc.	http://www.metabolife.com
	http://www.metabolife.com/shop/ch_about.html
Metacrawler	http://www.metacrawler.com
MexPlaza	http://mexplaza.udg.mx
Micropotent	http://www.micropat.com
Microsoft	http://www.microsoft.com
Mission statement generator	http://umweb1.unitedmedia.com/comics/dilbert/career/bin/ms2.cgi
Monster.com	http://www.monster.com
Moody's Investors Services	http://www.moodys.com
Mopar Parts	http://www.moparcollection.com
Motorplace.com	http://www.motorplace.com
MSNBC	http://www.msnbc.com

Multilingual International Business Directory	http://m-link.com/menu.html
Mysimon	http://www.mysimon.com
Nabisco	http://www.nabisco.com
Nantucket Nectars	http://www.juiceguys.com
Napster	http://www.napster.com
National Association of Homebuilders	http://www.nahb.com
National Hot Dog and Sausage Council	http://www.hot-dog.org
National Pork Producers Council	http://www.nppc.org
National Retail Federation	http://www.stores.org
National Rifle Association	http://www.nra.org
National Shooting Sports Foundation	http://www.nssf.org
National Trade Data Bank (NTDB) STAT-USA	http://www.stat-usa.gov
National Turkey Federation	http://www.eatturkey.com
	http://www.turkeyfed.org
Netcentives, Inc	http://www.netcentives.com
NetTV	http://www.net-tv.net
Network Solutions	http://www.companyname.com
Netzmarkt cyber-mall	http://www.netzmarkt.de/neu/hinweise.htm
New York Times	http://www.nytimes.com
NexTag.com	http://www.nextag.com
North American Industry Classification System (NAICS)	http://www.census.gov/epcd/www/naics.html
Northpoint Group	http://www.northpoint.com
Office Depot	http://www.officedepot.com
Office Max	http://www.OfficeMax.com
Officesupplies.com	http://www.officesupplies.com
Omega	http://www.omega.ch
Oneida Limited	http://www.oneida.com
Online Privacy Alliance	http://www.privacyalliance.org
On-line transactions and privacy survey	http://www.hermes.bus.umich.edu/cgi-gin/spsurvey/questi.pl
Onvia.com	http://www.onvia.com
Open Market	http://www.openmarket.com
Oprah Winfrey	http://www.oprah.com
Owens Corning	http://www.owens-corning.com
Pacific Region Forum on Business and Management Communication	gopher://hoshi.cic.sfu.ca/11/dlam/business/forum
Palo Alto Software, Inc	http://www.bplans.com
The Paris Pages	http://www.paris.org
Pegasus Systems, Inc	http://www.travelweb.com
People for the Ethical Treatment of Animals (PETA)	http://www.peta-online.org
	http://www.milksucks.com
Peppers and Rogers Group	http://www.1to1.com/publications
PepsiCo	http://www.pepsico.com
Planetfeedback.com	http://www.planetfeedback.com
PlanetRx	http://www.planetrx.com
Polley Associates Real Estate Education	http://www.polley-edu.com/ethics.htm
Positioning Strategies	http://www.positioning.com
Pottery Barn	http://www.potterybarn.com
	http://www.potterybarnkids.com
Power Images	http://pwr.com/creative
Precision Machined Parts Association	http://www.pmpa.org
Press Release Distribution	http://www.press-release-writing.com
Priceline.com	http://www.priceline.com
Pricescan.com, Inc	http://www.pricescan.com
Primemedia Company	http://www.demographics.com
Procter & Gamble	http://www.pg.com
ProNet	http://www.pronett.com
Prudential Securities Investment Personality Quiz	http://www.prusec.com/quiz.htm
Quality Leads Management	http://www.quality.com
Quepasa.com	http://quepasa.com
Quixtar.com	http://www.quixtar.com
Radio Shack	http://www.radioshack.com
RadioGuide	http://www.radioguide.com
Ralston Purina	http://www.ralstonpurina.com
Rao Soft, Inc.	http://www.raosoft.com/raosoft
Razor USA	http://www.razorusa.com
RCA	http://www.rca.com

RCN Corporation	http://www.users.interport.net
Red Herring	http://www.redherring.com
Red Roof Inn	http://www.redroof.com
RockAuction	http://www.rockauction.com
Roots Canada, Ltd.	http://www.roots.com
Rossignol	http://www.rossignol.com
Rubbermaid	http://www.rubbermaid.com
Russian and East European Studies Business and Economic Resources	http://www.pitt.edu/~cjp/rsecon.html
Sales and Marketing Executives Marketing Library	http://www.sell.org
Sales and Marketing Management magazine	http://www.salesandmarketing.com/smmnew/resources/careers.asp
Saturn Corporation	http://www.saturn.com
Savoy Brands International	http://www.empresas-polar.com/polar
Scholastic Press	http://scholastic.com
Schwab	http://www.schwab.com
Sears, Roebuck	http://www.sears.com
Senco Products	http://www.senco.com
Sheraton	http://www.sheraton.com
ShopBest.com	http://www.shopbest.com
Showlearn.com	http://www.showlearn.com
Small Business by Quicken.com	http://www.cashfinder.com
Smart Draw	http://www.smartdraw.com
Smarter Living	http://www.smarterliving.com
Southwest Airlines	http://www.iflyswa.com
Sprint	http://www.sprint.com
Staples	http://www.staples.com
Star Alliance	http://www.star-alliance.com
Starbucks	http://www.starbucks.com
StarKist	http://www.starkist.com
Start Sampling, Inc.	http://www.StartSampling.com
Statistical Data Locators	http://www.ntu.edu.sg/library/stat/statdata.htm
Stat-USA	http://www.stat-usa.gov
Subway	http://www.subway.com
Sweepstakes Online	http://www.sweepstakesonline.com
Sydney Link.com	http://www.sydney2000.com
Sysco	http://www.sysco.com
Target Stores	http://www.target.com
Teen Research Unlimited, Inc.	http://www.teenresearch.com
3M	http://www.3m.com
TiVo	http://www.tivo.com
Tommy Hilfiger	http://www.tommy.com
Too Faced Cosmetics	http://www.toofaced.com
Topica, Inc.	http://www.liszt.com
Topozone	http://www.topozone.com
Toys 'R' Us	http://www.toysrus.com
Trade Compass	http://www.tradecompass.com
Trade Point Internet Incubator	http://www.wnicc.org/untpdc/training
Trade Show News Network	http://www.tsnn.com/sbs
Travelocity	http://www.travelocity.com
TSCentral	http://www.tscentral.com
Turnpike Corporation	http://www.emporium.turnpike.net/
Tylenol	http://www.tylenol.com
Unilever	http://www.unilever.com
United Parcel Rate Calculator	http://www.ups.com/using/services/rave/rate.html
United Parcel Service	http://www.ups.com
University of British Columbia Centre for Applied Ethics	http://www.ethics.ubc.ca
University of Texas, Advertising Dept.	http://www.advertising.utexas.edu/world
Upromote.com	http://www.upromote.com
USA Today	http://www.usatoday.com
U.S. Airforce	http://www.airforce.com
U.S. Army	http://www.goarmy.com
U.S. Census Bureau	http://www.census.gov
	http://www.tier2.census.gov/dbappweb.htm
U.S. Copyright Office	http://lcweb.loc.gov/copyright
U.S. Council for International Business	http://www.uscib.org
	http://www.uscib.org/policy/privmin.htm

U.S. Department of Agriculture	http://www.fas.usda.gov/info/agexporter/1997/shangsnk.html
U.S. Economic and Statistics Administration	http://www.esa.doc.gov
U.S. International Trade Administration	http://www.ita.doc.gov
U.S. Marines	http://www.marines.com
U.S. Navy	http://www.navy.com
U.S. Patent and Trademark Office	http://www.uspto.gov
U.S. Small Business Administration	http://www.sba.gov
	http://www.sbaonline.sba.gov/OIT
Values and Lifestyles (VALS) test	http://future.sri.com/vals/valshome.html
Vans	http://www.vans.com
Various on-line surveys on topics like politics and consumer trends	http://www.survey.net/
Various surveys	http://www.dssresearch.com/mainsite/surveys.htm
Varsity Group	http://www.varsity-group.com
Varsity Group, Inc.	http://www.varsitybooks.com
Verbind Inc.	http://www.verbind.com
Verio	http://www.webcom.com/impulse/prlist.html
Verisign Company	http://www.networksolutions.com
Verizon	http://bigbook.com
Vermont Teddy Bear Co. catalog	http://www.vtbear.com
Vertical Net	http://www.careermag.com
Virgin Connect	http://www.virginconnectme.com
Virtual Business Plaza (Czech Republic)	http://www.inet.cz
Virtual Vineyards	http://www.virtualvin.com
Volvo	http://www.volvocars.com
W. W. Grainger	http://www.grainger.com
Walgreens	http://www.walgreens.com
Wal-Mart	http://www.walmart.com
	http://walmartstores.com
	http://www.strategy-business.com/bestpractice/99403
Warehouse Location Simulation	http://www.orie.cornell.edu/~jackson/whsloc.html
Wave Net	http://www.wave.net/upg/immigration/sic_index.html
Web Wide Business Solutions	http://www.bwebwide.com/folders/projects.htm
WebAuction	http://www.webauction.com
WebMD	http://www.webmd.com
Webvan	http://www.webvan.com
Wendy's	http://www.wendys.com/the_ads/ads_frame.html
Western Union	http://www.westernunion.com
Wienerschnitzel	http://www.wienerschnitzel.com
Williams-Sonoma	http://www.williams-sonoma.com
Wine.com	http://www.wine.com/
Wm. Wrigley Jr. Company (Juicy Fruit)	http://www.juicyfruit.com
Women.com	http://www.women.com
Women's Wire	http://www.womenswire.com
Works.com	http://www.works.com
World Factbook	http://www.odci.gov/cia/publications
World Gym	http://www.worldgym.com
World Index of Chambers of Commerce & Industry	http://www1.usa1.com
Worldbank	http://www.worldbank.org
Xentis Corporation	http://www.nomina.net/
Yahoo!	http://www.yahoo.com
	http://www.yahoo.com/Regional/Countries
	http://www.yahoo.com/stores
	http://www.auctions.yahoo.com
	http://www.yahoo.com/info/advertising
Yankelovich MONITOR	http://www.yankelovich.com
Yellow Pages of Israel	http://www.gauss.technion.ac.il
YoungBiz	http://www.youngbiz.com
Zap!	http://www.Zapworld.com
Zapdata.com, Inc.	http://www.zapdata.com
Zero Junk Mail	http://www.zerojunkmail.com